ENCYCLOPEDIA OF GLOBAL CHANGE

ENCYCLOPEDIA OF

Global Change

Environmental Change and
Human Society

Andrew S. Goudie
EDITOR IN CHIEF

David J. Cuff
ASSOCIATE EDITOR

Volume 2

OXFORD
UNIVERSITY PRESS
2002

OXFORD
UNIVERSITY PRESS

Oxford   New York
Athens Auckland Bangkok Bogotá Buenos Aires Cape Town
Chennai Dar es Salaam Delhi Florence Hong Kong Istanbul Karachi
Kolkata Kuala Lumpur Madrid Melbourne Mexico City Mumbai
Nairobi Paris São Paulo Shanghai Singapore Taipei Tokyo Toronto Warsaw
and associated companies in
Berlin Ibadan

Copyright © 2002 by Oxford University Press, Inc.

Published by Oxford University Press, Inc.
198 Madison Avenue, New York, New York 10016
www.oup.com

Library of Congress Cataloging-in-Publication Data

Encyclopedia of global change : environmental change and human society /
Andrew S. Goudie, editor in chief.
p.   cm.
Includes bibliographical references and index.
ISBN 0-19-510825-6 (set) —
ISBN 0-19-514518-6 (v. 1) — ISBN 0-19-514519-4 (v. 2)
1. Global environmental change—Encyclopedias.
2. Nature—Effect of human beings on—Encyclopedias.
3. Global environmental change—Social aspects—Encyclopedias.
I. Goudie, Andrew.
GE149.E47   2000   363.7—dc21   00-058918

The photographs and line drawings used herein were supplied by contributors
to the work, members of the Editorial Board, major museums, and by commercial
photographic archives. The publisher has made every effort to ascertain that necessary
permissions to reprint materials have been secured. Sources of photographs and
line drawings are given in captions to illustrations where appropriate.

EDITORIAL AND PRODUCTION STAFF
Commissioning Editor: Sean Pidgeon
Project Editor: Norina Frabotta
Assistant Editor: Elizabeth Aldrich
Copyeditors: Sean Pidgeon, Larry Hamberlin, and Jane McGary
Proofreaders: Nancy Bernhaut, Sue Gilad, Gareth Ridout, and Rhoda Seidenberg
Indexer: Bonny McLaughlin
Book Designer: Joan Greenfield
Managing Editor: Matthew Giarratano
Publisher: Karen Casey

1 3 5 7 9 8 6 4 2
Printed in the United States of America
on acid-free paper

Abbreviations, Acronyms, and Symbols

AABW	Antarctic Bottom Water		CDIAC	Carbon Dioxide Information Analysis Center
ABRACOS	Anglo-Brazilian Climate Observation Study		CDM	clean development mechanism
AC	alternating current		CE	Common Era
AGCM	atmospheric general circulation model		CEOS	Committee on Earth Observation Satellites
AIDS	acquired immune deficiency syndrome		CEQ	(U.S.) Council on Environmental Quality
AIJ	activities implemented jointly		CERES	Clouds and the Earth's Radiant Energy System
AMIGO	America's Interhemisphere Geo-Biosphere Organization		CERLA	Comprehensive Environmental Response, Compensation, and Liability Act
AMIP	Atmospheric Model Intercomparison Project			
AMS	accelerator mass spectrometry		CET	central England temperature
ANC	acid-neutralizing capacity		CFC	chlorofluorocarbon
AOU	American Ornithologists' Union		CGIAR	Consultative Group on International Agricultural Research
APEC	Asia-Pacific Economic Cooperation			
AR	autoregressive		CGIS	Canada Geographic Information System
ASTER	Advanced Spaceborne Thermal Emission and Reflection Radiometer		CIA	cumulative impact assessment
			CIESIN	Center for International Earth Science Information Network
ATP	adenosine triphosphate			
ATSR	Along Track Scanning Radiometer		CIM	computer integrated manufacturing
AU	astronomical unit (1 AU = 1.496×10^8 kilometers)		CIMMYT	Centro Internacional de Mejoramiento de Maiz y Trigo (International Maize and Wheat Improvement Center)
AVHRR	(NOAA) Advanced Very High Resolution Radiometer			
			CIRAN	Centre for International Research and Advisory Networks
BAP	Bureau of Animal Population			
BASF	Badische Anilin- und Soda-Fabrik		CITES	Convention on International Trade in Endangered Species of Wild Fauna and Flora
BBSRC	(U.K.) Biotechnology and Biological Sciences Research Council			
BCA	benefit–cost analysis		CLIVAR	Climate Variability and Prediction Program
BCE	before the Common Era		CMS	Convention on the Conservation of Migratory Species of Wild Animals (or the Bonn Convention)
BCG	bacille Calmette-Guerin			
BLM	(U.S.) Bureau of Land Management			
BNC	base-neutralizing capacity		CN	condensation nuclei
BOREAS	Boreal Ecosystem-Atmosphere Study		CNRS	Centre National de la Recherche Scientific (France)
BP	before the present		CoCP	Council of Contracting Parties
Btu	British thermal unit		COM	cost of mitigation
CAD	computer-assisted design		COMECON	Communist Economic Community (or Council for Mutual Economic Assistance)
CBD	Convention on Biological Diversity			
CCAMLR	Convention on the Conservation of Antarctic Marine Living Resources		CoP	Conference of the Parties
			CoP1	First Conference of the Parties, Berlin, Germany, March–April 1995
CCGT	combined-cycle gas turbine		CoP3	Third Conference of the Parties, Kyoto, Japan, December 1997
CCN	cloud condensation nuclei			

CoP4	Fourth Conference of the Parties, Buenos Aires, Argentina, 2–13 November 1998
CPR	common-pool resource; contraceptive prevalence rate
CRED	Centre for Research on the Epidemiology of Disasters
CSD	(United Nations) Commission on Sustainable Development
CSERGE	Centre for Social and Economic Research on the Global Environment
DAAC	distributed active archive center
DARPA	(U.S.) Defense Advanced Research Projects Agency
DBMS	database management system
DDT	dichlorodiphenyltrichloroethane
DEM	digital elevation model
DGD	Decision Guidance Document
DHF	dengue hemorrhagic fever
DICE	dynamic integrated climate economy
DIF	Directory Interchange Format
DMS	dimethyl sulfide
DNA	deoxyribonucleic acid
DOC	dissolved organic carbon
DOD	(U.S.) Department of Defense
DSM	distributed shared memory
DSS	dengue shock syndrome
DU	Dobson unit
EA	environmental assessment
EBM	energy balance model
EC	European Community
ECC	electrochemical cell
ECE	(United Nations) Economic Commission for Europe
ECOSOC	(United Nations) Economic and Social Council
ED	electrodialysis
EDF	Environmental Defense Fund
EDR	electrodialysis reversal
EEA	environmental effects assessment
EEC	European Economic Community
EEZ	Exclusive Economic Zone
EIA	environmental impact assessment
EIS	environmental impact statement
EKC	environmental Kuznets curve
EM-DAT	Emergency Events Database: the OFDA/CRED International Disaster Database
ENMOD	Convention on the Prohibition of Military or Any Other Hostile Use of Environmental Modification Techniques
ENSO	El Niño–Southern Oscillation
EOS	(NASA) Earth Observing System

EOSDIS	EOS Data and Information System
EPA	(U.S.) Environmental Protection Agency
ERBE	(NASA) Earth Radiation Budget Experiment
ERS	(European) Earth Resources Satellite
ESA	Endangered Species Act
ESRC	(U.K.) Economic and Social Research Council
FAO	(United Nations) Food and Agriculture Organization
FCCC	(United Nations) Framework Convention on Climate Change
FFA	South Pacific Forum Fisheries Agency
FFT	fast Fourier transform
FGDC	U.S. Federal Geographic Data Committee
FIFE	First ISLSCP Field Experiment
FOE	Friends of the Earth
FoEI	Friends of the Earth International
FRG	Federal Republic of Germany
FRONTIERS	Forecasting Rain Optimised using New Techniques of Interactively Enhanced Radar and Satellite data
FS	(U.S.) Forest Service
FSU	former Soviet Union
FWS	(U.S.) Fish and Wildlife Service
G-7	Group of Seven (leading industrial nations)
GAC	Global Area Coverage
GARP	Global Atmospheric Research Program
GATS	General Agreement on Trade in Services
GATT	General Agreement on Tariffs and Trade
gC	grams of carbon
GCDIS	Global Change Data and Information System
GCM	general circulation model; global change model; global climate model
GCMD	Global Change Master Directory
GCOS	Global Climate Observing System
GDP	gross domestic product
GDR	German Democratic Republic (East Germany; now part of Germany)
GEC	global environmental change
GECHS	Global Environmental Change and Human Security
GEF	Global Environment Facility
GEWEX	Global Energy and Water Cycle Experiment
GFDL	Geophysical Fluid Dynamics Laboratory (NOAA)
GHG	greenhouse gas
GIS	Geographic Information Systems; Geographical Information Systems
GISS	Goddard Institute for Space Studies
GNP	gross national product

GONGO	governmental and nongovernmental organization
GPCP	Global Precipitation Climatology Project
GPS	Global Positioning System
GWP	global warming potential
HAP	hazardous air pollutants
HAPEX	Hydrological and Atmospheric Pilot Experiment
HCB	hexachlorobenzene
HCFC	hydrochlorofluorocarbon
HFC	hydrofluorocarbon
HIV	human immunodeficiency virus
HLW	high-level waste
HPLC	high-pressure liquid chromatography
IAA	International Association of Academies
IAEA	International Atomic Energy Agency
IAI	Inter-American Institute (for Global Change Research)
IARC	international agricultural research center
IARIW	International Association for Research in Income and Wealth
IAS	Institute for Advanced Study
IBAMA	Instituto Brasileiro do Meio Ambiente e dos Recursos Naturais Renováveis (Brazilian Institute of Environment and Renewable Natural Resources)
IBM	International Business Machines (Corporation)
ICAIR	International Centre for Antarctic Information and Research
ICAS	Interstate Council on the Aral Sea
ICBP	International Committee for Bird Protection (now BirdLife International)
ICCROM	International Centre for the Study of the Preservation and Restoration of Cultural Property
ICES	International Council for the Exploration of the Sea
ICESat	Ice, Cloud, and land Elevation Satellite
ICJ	International Court of Justice
ICOLD	International Commission on Large Dams
ICOMOS	International Council on Monuments and Sites
ICRW	International Convention for the Regulation of Whaling
ICSID	International Centre for Settlement of Investment Disputes
ICSU	International Council for Science (formerly the International Council of Scientific Unions)
ICZM	Integrated Coastal Zone Management
IDA	International Development Association

IDEAL	International Decade of the East African Lakes
IDGC	Institutional Dimensions of Global Change
IDN	(CEOS) International Directory Network
IDNDR	International Decade for Natural Disaster Reduction
IE	industrial ecology
IEA	International Energy Agency
IFAD	International Fund for Agricultural Development
IFAS	Interstate Fund for the Aral Sea
IFC	International Finance Corporation
IFOV	instantaneous field of view
IFPRI	International Food Policy Research Institute
IGBP	International Geosphere-Biosphere Programme
IGY	International Geophysical Year
IHDP	International Human Dimensions Programme on Global Environmental Change
IIASA	International Institute for Applied Systems Analysis
IISD	International Institute for Sustainable Development
ILW	intermediate-level waste
IM	industrial metabolism
IMF	International Monetary Fund
IMO	(United Nations) International Maritime Organization
IMS	Information Management System
INC5	Fifth Intergovernmental Negotiating Session for a Global POPs Treaty, Johannesburg, South Africa, 4–9 December 2000
INCD	Intergovernmental Negotiating Committee for the elaboration of an international convention to combat Desertification
INPA	Instituto Nacional de Pesquisas da Amazônia (National Institute for Research in the Amazon)
INPE	Instituto Nacional de Pesquisas Espaciais (Brazilian National Institute for Space Research)
INSEAD	European Institute of Business Administration
IPAT	I [environmental impact] = P [population] $\times$ A [affluence] $\times$ T [technology]; or FI = FP $\times$ FA $\times$ FT
IPCC	Intergovernmental Panel on Climate Change
IPF	Intergovernmental Panel on Forests
IPM	integrated pest management
IPP	independent power-producing
IPR	intellectual property rights
IR	infrared
IRC	International Research Council

ISCCP	International Satellite Cloud Climatology Project		MOBILHY	(HAPEX) Mode'lisation du Bilan Hydrique (France)
ISLSCP	International Satellite Land Surface Climatology Project		MODIS	Moderate Resolution Imaging Spectrometer
ISO	International Organization for Standardization		MoP	Meeting of Montreal Protocol Parties
ISSC	International Social Science Council		MOPITT	Measurement of Pollution in the Troposphere
IT	Industrial Transformation (IHDP); information technology		MORECS	U.K. Meteorological Office Rainfall and Evaporation Calculation System
ITCZ	intertropical convergence zone		MPP	massively parallel processor
ITO	International Trade Organisation		MSF	multistage flash
IUCN	International Union for the Conservation of Nature and Natural Resources (the World Conservation Union)		MSS	(Landsat) Multispectral Scanner
			MSY	maximum sustainable yield
			MTPE	Mission to Planet Earth (NASA)
IWC	International Whaling Commission		NADW	North Atlantic Deep Water
IWRB	International Waterfowl Research Bureau		NAFO	North Atlantic Fisheries Organization
IWRM	integrated water resources management		NAFTA	North American Free Trade Agreement
JERS-1	Japanese Earth Resource Satellite-1		NASA	(U.S.) National Aeronautics and Space Administration
JI	joint implementation			
K/T	Cretaceous-Tertiary		NASA ER-2	NASA high-altitude research aircraft
LAC	Local Area Coverage		NASDA	National Space Development Agency of Japan
LACIE	Large Area Crop Inventory Experiment			
Landsat	system of U.S. land-surface observation satellites		NAT	nitric acid trihydrate
			NATO	North Atlantic Treaty Organisation
LCA	life cycle analysis		NBII	(U.S.) National Biological Information Infrastructure
LDC	less developed countries; London Dumping Convention			
			NCB	National Coal Board
LEPA	low-energy precision application		NCDC	(U.S.) National Climate Data Center
LFG	landfill gas		NCP	(Montreal Protocol) Non-Compliance Procedure
LGM	last glacial maximum			
LIS	Lightning Imaging Sensor		NDVI	Normalized Difference Vegetation Index
LLN	Louvain-la-Neuve		NEP	net ecosystem production
LRTAP	(Convention on) Long-Range Transboundary Air Pollution		NEPA	National Environment Policy Act
			NERC	(U.K.) Natural Environment Research Council
LUCC	Land Use and Land Cover Change			
LULC	Land Use and Land Cover		NGO	nongovernmental organization
LWT	Lamb Weather Type		NHGRI	National Human Genomic Research Institute
MAB	(United Nations) Man and the Biosphere Programme		NIEO	new international economic order
			NMO	national member organization
MARC	Monitoring and Assessment Research Centre		NOAA	(U.S.) National Oceanic and Atmospheric Administration
MARPOL	negotiations of the International Convention for the Prevention of Pollution from Ships			
			NPP	net primary production; net primary productivity
MBIS	Mackenzie Basin Impact Study		NPS	(U.S.) National Park Service
MCA	multicriteria analysis		NSF	(U.S.) National Science Foundation
MDC	more developed countries		NWT	North West Territories (Canada)
MDR	multidrug resistance		OCMIP	Ocean Carbon-Cycle Model Intercomparison Project
ME	multieffect evaporation			
MIGA	Multilateral Investment Guarantee Agency		ODP	ozone depletion potential
MIS	marine isotope stages		OECD	Organisation for Economic Co-operation and Development
MM	Modified Mercalli intensity scale			
MNC	multinational corporation		OEM	original equipment manufacturers

OFDA	Office of U.S. Foreign Disaster Assistance
OGCM	ocean general circulation model
OGI	old growth index
OH	free radical hydroxyl
OIES	(UCAR) Office for Interdisciplinary Earth Studies
OPEC	Organization of the Petroleum Exporting Countries
OSL	optically stimulated luminescence
OTA	Office of Technology Assessment
PAGES	(IGBP) Past Global Changes
PAH	polyaromatic hydrocarbon
PAM	plant available moisture
PAN	plant available nutrients
PAT	population, affluence, and technology
PC	personal computer
PCB	polychlorinated biphenyl
PCE	perchloroethylene
PCH	polychlorinated hydrocarbon
PDMS	postdepositional modification stratigraphy
PET	polyethylene terephthalate; potential evapotranspiration
pH	hydrogen ion concentration
PIC	prior informed consent
PNA	Pacific North American
POC	particulate organic carbon
POP	persistent organic pollutant
ppb	parts per billion
ppbv	parts per billion by volume
ppm	parts per million
ppmv	parts per million by volume
ppt	parts per trillion
pptv	parts per trillion by volume
PR	Precipitation Radar
PRA	probabilistic risk assessment
PSC	polar stratospheric cloud
PURPA	Public Utility Regulatory Policies Act of 1978
PVC	poly(vinyl chloride)
PVP	parallel vector processor
QA/QC	quality assurance and quality control
QRA	quantitative risk assessment
quad	a unit of energy; one quad equals one quadrillion Btu
RAID	redundant array of independent devices
RC	one-dimensional radiative-convective model
RD	relative dating
RECLAIM	Regional Emissions Clean Air Incentives Market (Southern California)
REE	rare-earth element
RIS	reservoir-induced seismicity

RMP	(IWC) Revised Management Procedure
RMS	(IWC) Revised Management Scheme
RNA	ribonucleic acid
RO	reverse osmosis
ROEC	Reed Odorless Earth Closet
R-strategists	Short-lived organisms characterized by short generation times and the ability to produce and disperse offspring efficiently and abundantly (e.g., dandelions, cockroaches)
SAGE	Semi-Automatic Ground Environment (U.S. Air Force)
SAR	Second Assessment Report; (JERS-1) Synthetic Aperture Radar
SBI	Subsidiary Body for Implementation
SBSTA	Subsidiary Body for Scientific and Technological Advice
SBUV	Solar Backscatter Ultraviolet Instrument
SCAQMD	South Coast Air Quality Management District (California)
SCICEX	Scientific Ice Expeditions
SCOPAC	Standing Conference on Problems Associated with the Coastline
SCOPE	Scientific Committee on Problems of the Environment
SD	statistical dynamical (model)
SEA	strategic environmental assessment
SEEA	system of integrated environmental and economic accounts
SFS	sea floor spreading
SIA	social impact assessment
SMART	Save Money and Reduce Toxics
SNA	system of national accounting
SOHO	solar and heliosphoric observatory
SPM	Summaries for Policymakers; suspended particulate matter
SPOT HRV-XS	Systeme Pour l'Observation de la Terre (SPOT) High-Resolution Visible (HRV) Multispectral (XS)
SQHW	small quantities of hazardous waste
SSP	Second Sulfur Protocol (to the Convention on Long-Range Transboundary Air Pollution)
SSS	sea surface salinity
SST	sea surface temperature
SSURGO	Soil Survey Geographic Database
STAP	Scientific and Technical Advisory Panel (of the Global Environment Facility)
START	The global change SysTem for Analysis, Research and Training
STATSGO	State Soil Geographic Database
STP	sewage treatment plant
SVD	singular-value decomposition
SWDA	Solid Waste Disposal Act

SWE	snow water equivalent
TAR	(IPCC) Third Assessment Report
TCE	trichloroethylene
TCP	Technical Cooperation Programme
TEK	traditional ecological knowledge
TEL	tetraethyl lead
TFR	total fertility rate
TL	thermoluminescence
TM	(Landsat) Thematic Mapper
TMI	TRMM Microwave Imager
TOA	top of the atmosphere
TOC	total organic carbon
TOGA	Tropical Ocean and Global Atmosphere program
TOMS	Total Ozone Mapping Spectrometer
TRMM	Tropical Rainfall Measuring Mission
TSCA	(EPA) Toxic Substances Control Act
TSS	total suspended solids
TVA	Tennessee Valley Authority
UARS	Upper Atmosphere Research Satellite
UCAR	University Corporation for Atmospheric Research
UKMO	U.K. Meteorological Office
UN	United Nations
UNCED	United Nations Conference on Environment and Development
UNCLOS	United Nations Convention on the Law of the Sea
UNCOD	United Nations Conference on Desertification
UNDP	United Nations Development Programme
UNEP	United Nations Environment Programme
UNESCO	United Nations Educational, Scientific, and Cultural Organization
UNFPA	United Nations Population Fund (formerly United Nations Fund for Population Activities)
UNICEF	United Nations Children's Fund
UNIDO	United Nations Industrial Development Organization
UPS	United Parcel Service
URL	Uniform Resource Locator
USAID	U.S. Agency for International Development
USGCRP	U.S. Global Change Research Program
USGS	U.S. Geological Survey
UTH	upper tropospheric humidity
UTM	Universal Transverse Mercator
UV	ultraviolet (radiation)
UV-B	ultraviolet-B (radiation)

VC	vapor compression; Vienna Convention for the Protection of the Ozone Layer of 1985
VIP	ventilated improved pit
VIRS	Visible and Infrared Scanner
VOC	volatile organic compounds
WCED	World Commission on Environment and Development
WCP	World Climate Programme
WCRP	World Climate Research Programme
WHO	World Health Organization
WIPO	World Intellectual Property Organization
WMO	World Meteorological Organization
WOCE	World Ocean Circulation Experiment
WRAP	Waste Reduction Always Pays
WTO	World Trade Organization
WWF	World Wide Fund for Nature (formerly World Wildlife Fund)
WWW	World Weather Watch; World Wide Web
YD	Younger Dryas

Measures and Conversions

centimeter	0.39 inches
foot	12 inches (0.3048 meters)
gram	0.0353 ounces
inch	2.54 centimeters
kilogram	1,000 grams (2.2046 pounds)
kilometer	1,000 meters (3,280.8 feet or 0.62 miles)

Prefixes for International System of Units

yotta (Y)	10^{24}
zetta (Z)	10^{21}
exa (E)	10^{18}
peta (P)	10^{15}
tera (T)	10^{12}
giga (G)	10^{9}
mega (M)	10^{6}
kilo (k)	10^{3}
hecto (h)	10^{2}
deca (da)	10^{1}
deci (d)	10^{-1}
centi (c)	10^{-2}
milli (m)	10^{-3}
micro (μ)	10^{-6}
nano (n)	10^{-9}
pico (p)	10^{-12}
femto (f)	10^{-15}
atto (a)	10^{-18}
zepto (z)	10^{-21}
yocto (y)	10^{-24}

ENCYCLOPEDIA OF GLOBAL CHANGE

J

JOINT IMPLEMENTATION

In the context of a global climate change policy, the concept of joint implementation (JI) was discussed for the first time in September 1991, during the negotiations that preceded the establishment of a Framework Convention on Climate Change (FCCC). In the FCCC, which was signed by 154 nations at the United Nations Conference on Environment and Development (UNCED) in Rio de Janeiro (1992), JI was included in Article 4.2(a):

> developed country Parties and other Parties included in Annex I . . . may implement . . . policies and measures *jointly* with other Parties and may assist other Parties in contributing to the objective of the Convention. . . .

The idea is that since greenhouse gases (GHGs) are uniformly mixed gases, that is, one tonne of GHG emitted by party A does the same global damage as one tonne emitted by party B, it does not make a difference whether a particular GHG emission reduction takes place in the territory of party A or party B.

Although there were still many uncertainties surrounding the concept at the time, the JI concept essentially enables parties (countries that have ratified the FCCC) to fulfill a part of their greenhouse gas emission-reduction commitments through abatement action in the territory of another party (the JI host country). The rationale for such cooperation is that for parties with high marginal costs of abatement—for example, because of their already relatively high level of energy efficiency—it is cost-effective to invest in cheaper emission-reduction measures abroad than in expensive measures domestically. If the host countries also benefit from the same cooperation (for example, via financial compensation, technology transfer, or credit sharing), both parties can gain from JI. If, moreover, a larger cost-effectiveness of abatement through JI would enhance the acceptability of actual commitments, JI may also benefit the global economy and climate. Economic theory would suggest that, if the scale of application of JI were not restricted, JI cooperation would proceed to the point at which the marginal abatement costs for all parties are equal.

FCCC Negotiations and JI. The negotiations on the interpretation of the FCCC text, and therefore also on Article 4.2(a), continued after 1992, especially after 1994, when a sufficient number of ratifications had been registered for the FCCC to enter into force. JI attracted increasing attention but also turned out to be controversial. Opponents argued, for example, that JI would allow industrialized-country parties to postpone abatement action and the development of technology to save fossil fuel energy domestically, and would absorb the most attractive abatement opportunities in the host countries.

At the first Conference of the Parties to the FCCC (CoP1, Berlin, March–April 1995), the debate yielded a compromise: to develop the JI concept further during a pilot phase. To remove any sensitivities, it was decided that JI activities should be referred to as activities implemented jointly (AIJ) during this phase. Moreover, it was agreed that, during this phase, developed-country parties could not use AIJ to fulfill their obligations under the FCCC to stabilize their emissions of greenhouse gases by the year 2000. In other words, AIJ investments would earn no credit.

As of April 2000, 126 AIJ projects of various kinds had been reported to the FCCC secretariat. Thirty of the pilot projects will take place in Latin America, seventy-eight in central and eastern Europe, six in Africa, and twelve in Southeast Asia.

On 10 December 1997 in Kyoto (Japan) the Kyoto Protocol was adopted by CoP3. Under this Protocol, industrialized countries agreed to reduce the emissions of six greenhouse gases by at least 5 percent below the emission levels of 1990 in the first commitment period 2008–2012. Industrialized countries are allowed to achieve part of their GHG emission reduction commitments through cooperation with other countries via three flexibility mechanisms: GHG abatement project cooperation between industrialized countries (Article 6 of the Protocol); project cooperation between industrialized countries and developing countries under a multilateral regime called the Clean Development Mechanism (CDM, Article 12); and a system of international emissions trading (Article 17). The first two types of cooperation are based on the JI concept. In the following, both the Article 6 and the CDM project cooperation are referred to as JI.

Technical Issues. For a successful implementation of the JI concept under the Kyoto Protocol, the following technical issues need to be worked out.

Baseline determination. While developing the JI concept, a number of technical issues have been identified. To measure the GHG emission reduction through a JI investment, a reference scenario that indicates what the emissions would have amounted to in the absence of the investment must be developed: the baseline. This implies that projections must be made of factors, such as economic growth, (energy) price developments, and structural changes in the JI host country for the project lifetime, which may be quite long (in the case of forestry, for example). Such projections may not be easy, especially because of the counterfactual character of a project baseline (i.e., due to the JI project the situation that is described by the baseline will never exist). The FCCC negotiations focus on several approaches for baseline determination, varying from completely unstandardized and project-specific to standardized baselines based on category-wide information.

In order to ensure environmental integrity, baseline calculation should not overstate the emission reduction of a JI project since this would result in a transfer of too many credits from the host to the investor country. This is particularly relevant for projects implemented in countries without emission quota under the Kyoto Protocol (i.e., for CDM projects). In the case of Article 6 project cooperation, the environmental integrity is more likely to be safeguarded better as emission reduction credits from such projects are deducted from the emission budget of the host country (which is also an industrialized country with an emission reduction commitment). There is, therefore, an in-built checking mechanism in Article 6 of the Kyoto Protocol that is not present in the case of the CDM. [*See* Kyoto Protocol.]

JI project monitoring and verification. The GHG emission reductions achieved (or carbon sequestered) through a JI project have to be included in the national governments' reports to the FCCC. The Conference of the Parties will then decide on the quantity of credits to be issued. With respect to monitoring and verification of a JI project's performance, some experts suggest that project monitoring should be left to the project parties involved (either national or local governments, or private-sector parties); others suggest that this task should be delegated to independent experts (to prevent parties from cheating to inflate the credits' volume). Most experts agree that the verification of the reported GHG emission reduction (carbon sequestration) should be left to an international third-party auditing body.

Credit sharing. Once the JI project's abatement impact has been verified, one has to decide how the JI credits collected at the country level will be shared among the parties. During the pilot phase for JI (see above), this question has remained a theoretical one since crediting is not yet allowed, but it becomes a relevant issue under the Protocol. The discussion of this question is still in its infancy. It may well be that the credit-sharing issue will be left to negotiations between participants of individual JI projects (i.e., investors and host countries). It is also possible that some general guidelines will be agreed upon, such as distinguishing between categories of host countries according to the stringency of their emission-reduction commitments.

Sustainable development of CDM projects. An issue that is particularly relevant for the CDM is that, according to the Kyoto Protocol, one of the purposes of the CDM is to assist developing countries in achieving sustainable development. However, the Protocol does not define *sustainable development*. The question is whether it should be left to developing countries to define *sustainable development*, given countries' different priorities and circumstances, or whether the term should be defined by the CoP, for example, through a list of required project criteria. The risk of the first option is that some developing countries may opt for projects that, in their view, are sustainable, but which the international community considers not sustainable. An often-quoted example with respect to the latter is if nuclear energy would be carried out under the CDM. A risk of the second option is that it may conflict with developing countries' sovereignty.

JI in the Second Sulfur Protocol. In 1994 the Second Sulfur Protocol (SSP) to the 1979 Convention on Long-Range Transboundary Air Pollution was signed in Oslo. Article 2.7 of this Protocol (covering Europe and the economies in transition) enables parties to implement their obligations jointly. The cost-saving potential of JI in SSP, however, is considered rather limited (Foundation JIN, 1995). First, since sulfur is a nonuniformly mixed gas, third-party effects have to be taken into account (in the SSP these parties are therefore given an important say). Second, the parties' (differentiated) emission-reduction obligations under SSP were determined using a cost-minimization model, more or less equalizing the marginal sulfur dioxide abatement costs across the countries. Because of this, the cost-savings potential through sulfur dioxide trading—essentially equivalent to the JI concept discussed above—was largely undermined. To date, there is only limited experience with JI-like mechanisms that is directly applicable as a guide to how sulfur or greenhouse gas trading mechanisms should be (or will be) designed and operated.

[*See also* Convention on Long-Range Transboundary Air Pollution; Framework Convention on Climate Change; Global Warming; *and* Market Mechanisms.]

BIBLIOGRAPHY

Foundation JIN. "Progress Report on the Role of JI in Acidification Abatement." *Joint Implementation Quarterly* 1.0 (1995), 12.

Jepma, C. J., ed. *The Feasibility of Joint Implementation.* Dordrecht: Kluwer, 1995.

Jepma, C. J., and M. Munasinghe. *Climate Change Policy.* Cambridge: Cambridge University Press, 1997.

Jepma, C. J., and W. van der Gaast, eds. *On the Compatibility of the Flexible Instruments*. Dordrecht and London: Kluwer, 1999.

Kuik, O., P. Peters, and N. J. Schrijver, eds. *Joint Implementation to Curb Climate Change: Legal and Economic Aspects*. Dordrecht: Kluwer, 1994.

Lazarus, M., S. Kartha, M. Ruth, S. Bernow, and C. Dunmire. "Evaluation of Benchmarking as an Approach for Establishing Clean Development Mechanism Baselines." Tellus Institute, Stockholm Environment Institute, and Stratus Consulting, USA, 1999.

—CATRINUS J. JEPMA

K

KYOTO PROTOCOL

In 1992, at the Rio Conference on Environment and Development, governments created an institution for regulating global warming: the United Nations Framework Convention on Climate Change (FCCC). In 1995, the governments that had ratified the FCCC held their first Conference of the Parties (COP) in Berlin, where they adopted the Berlin Mandate, which declared that the FCCC was inadequate to contain the threat of global warming. The Berlin Mandate set COP-3, slated for December 1997 in Kyoto, as the deadline for adopting a new agreement with more stringent commitments. Governments established the Ad Hoc Group on the Berlin Mandate (AGBM) to manage the negotiations. During most of its lifetime, AGBM's deliberations were unfocused. With the threat of failure looming, national delegations hurriedly assembled an agreement late in 1997, which they finalized at Kyoto in a marathon ten-day negotiating session attended by ten thousand delegates and observers.

The Kyoto Protocol obliges industrialized nations—listed in Annex I of the FCCC—to cut their emissions on average by 5 percent below 1990 levels during the five-year "first budget period" of 2008–2012. The target is comprehensive, which means that it applies to all anthropogenic sources and sinks of all major greenhouse gases (Table 1). Through negotiation, the overall goal of a 5 percent cut was differentiated among the Annex I countries (see Table 2).

Developing countries (not listed in Annex I) successfully and adamantly resisted any formal controls on their future emissions, arguing that they must spend scarce resources on other more pressing problems such as alleviation of poverty and that the problem of global warming is principally due to emissions from industrialized nations. Some industrialized countries, led by the United States, are pushing developing countries to limit their future emissions at least voluntarily on the logic that greenhouse warming is a global problem caused by all nations and no solution to the problem can be effective without widespread participation. Indeed, total emissions from developing countries are growing rapidly and will overtake those of Annex I nations by approximately 2030; however, per capita emissions from virtually all developing countries will remain lower than those in nearly all industrialized nations for the foreseeable future.

Kyoto Protocol. TABLE 1. Gases Included in the Kyoto Protocol*

GAS	PERCENTAGE OF TOTAL GLOBAL WARMING IN 1990S	GWP	ANTHROPOGENIC SOURCES	ANTHROPOGENIC SINKS
Carbon dioxide (carbon dioxide)	70	1	Fossil fuels, cement, deforestation, and other land use changes	Afforestation and other land use changes
Methane (CH_4)	20	21	Rice paddies, domestic animals, fossil fuels, biomass burning, landfills	No direct sinks
Nitrous oxide (N_2O)	6	310	Nitrogen fertilizers, fossil fuels	None
Hydrofluorocarbons (e.g., CHF_3, CH_3CHF_2)	<1 (rising rapidly)	11,700 (CHF_3)	Replacements for ozone-depleting substances (e.g., refrigerants, solvents)	None
Perfluorocarbons (e.g., CF_4, C_2F_6)	<1 (rising rapidly)	6,500 (CF_4)	Byproduct of aluminum smelting, semiconductor production	None
Sulfur hexafluoride (SF_6)	<1 (rising rapidly)	23,900	Electrical equipment, magnesium smelting	None

*The table shows the six main gases included in the Kyoto Protocol. The percentage contribution to global warming is the percentage of the total increase (approximately 2.3 watts per square meter) over preindustrial ("natural") levels of greenhouse forcing in the 1990s. Global warming potentials (GWPs) are 100-year values adopted by the Intergovernmental Panel on Climate Change in 1995.

When the Kyoto Protocol was adopted after round-the-clock negotiations, most delegates were too exhausted to fully comprehend the implications of the agreement. Soon after the excitement of Kyoto, negotiators began to realize just how much had been left unresolved and how many decisions had been left for future meetings. Many of the advanced industrialized countries insisted that the Protocol contain various "flexibility measures," such as emissions trading, which could lower the cost of meeting the Protocol's emission targets. However, the practical complexity of making those measures workable meant that consensus could be achieved in Kyoto only by leaving nearly all of the critical details unresolved, such as what types of emission reduction projects would be eligible, who would determine whether claimed emission reductions were valid, and to what extent could a Party use these measures to reach its reduction target.

Between December 1997, when the Protocol was adopted, and the Fourth Meeting of the Conference of the Parties (COP-4) in November 1998, governments expended a considerable amount of time and effort assessing the Protocol's implications and the long list of matters that had to be resolved. The plan was to adopt a work plan at COP-4 that would fill in Kyoto's missing details along with a schedule of deadlines. Adopting the work plan should have been straightforward, but the effort became embroiled in conflict over an initiative, led by the United States, to urge developing countries to adopt voluntary commitments to limit their greenhouse gas emissions. Enraged, the developing countries refused to engage in substantive discussions on the mechanisms.

The result was a complex plan—the Buenos Aires Plan of Action (BAPA)—which contains six decisions for future work under the FCCC and the Kyoto Protocol. The BAPA was adopted to provide a clear indication of the Parties' intent to strengthen the implementation of the FCCC and to prepare for the Protocol's future entry into force, particularly as the decisions contain specific deadlines for carrying out the programs of work. Parties set the Sixth Conference of the Parties (COP-6), planned for late 2000, as the deadline for agreeing on the operational rules for the flexibility mechanisms. Meeting that timetable requires resolving disagreements on several difficult issues, including the criteria for determining whether a proposed CDM project activity contributes to the sustainable development of the developing country host, as required by the Protocol. Many countries raised concerns about whether carbon "sinks" projects or nuclear energy projects should be eligible for earning credit under the CDM. Emissions trading debates also became entangled in issues such as which party bears liability for credits that are transferred but later prove

Although the Kyoto Protocol targets are specific and stringent, the Protocol also includes several measures that will make it easier and less costly for Annex I countries to comply. First, because the target is comprehensive, it allows countries to focus controls on those sources and sinks for gases that are least costly to regulate. In practice, the most important advantage of this comprehensive approach is that it allows countries to offset emissions of carbon dioxide due to combustion of fossil fuels—the largest source of global warming—with carbon absorbed in biomass due to afforestation and other changes in land use. However, measurement of the growth of these carbon sinks is difficult; in Kyoto, negotiators deferred agreement on the detailed accounting rules needed to put this provision into practice.

Second, industrialized nations have flexibility to select favorable base years. Instead of 1990, several countries in the midst of transition from command economies have selected base years in the late 1980s when emissions were at their peak before economic collapse. In addition, the Kyoto Protocol allows any industrialized nation to select 1990 or 1995 as the base year for the synthetic gases—hydrofluorocarbons (HFCs), perfluorocarbons (PFCs), and sulfur hexafluoride (SF_6). Emissions of HFCs—replacements for gases phased out under the

Another critical debate centers on the Protocol's requirement that reductions achieved by Annex I Parties through use of the mechanisms must be "supplemental" to domestic actions. This requirement was intended to ensure that developed countries actually change their own national policies in order to lower emissions, rather than simply attempting to reach their targets solely through action in developing countries or buy purchasing windfall "hot air" emission permits from Russia and Ukraine. However, what constitutes "supplemental" actions was highly contentious; some countries called for particular limits on the use of the mechanisms, such as limiting the use of the mechanisms to 50 percent of a country's effort to achieve its Kyoto emission targets.

The BAPA also calls upon Parties to review the success of "Activities Implemented Jointly" (AIJ), a pilot phase for cooperative projects to lower emissions established in 1995. This review would examine issues such as the program's contribution to capacity building and institutional strengthening for the developing countries that hosted projects. Parties will also review the Convention's financial mechanism, which assists developing countries with actions such as the preparation of national climate change programs and strengthening their public awareness and education activities. They also set COP-6 as the deadline for agreeing on actions to implement FCCC Articles 4.8 and 4.9, which address the ecological effects of climate change, as well as the impacts of response measures on terms of trade, international capital flows and development efforts. Parties will also agree on the preparatory work necessary for the first meeting of the Parties to Kyoto Protocol and try to develop a "framework for meaningful and effective actions" for transferring environmentally sound technology to developing countries.

By COP-5 in November 1999, the process had acquired some momentum as governments began to demonstrate determination to meet the deadlines agreed in the BAPA. No substantive disagreements were settled at COP-5; however, some governments did adopt a self-imposed deadline of 2002 for the Protocol's entry into force. As of October 1999, eighty-four FCCC Parties had signed the Kyoto Protocol, but only sixteen had ratified it. And, for each question clarified at COP-5, many others were deferred or not raised at all, leaving a foreboding number of complicated issues to be resolved by COP-6 only one year later.

—CHAD W. CARPENTER

Montreal Protocol—were rising especially rapidly in the early 1990s. With higher base-year emissions, a given percentage cut can be achieved more easily.

Third, potentially the most important flexibility mechanism is the Protocol's provision for several types of emission trading. In principle, emission trading cuts the cost of complying with the Protocol by allowing nations and firms to trade the right to emit greenhouse gases—permits will be sold and abatement focused where regulation of sources and sinks is the least costly. Several industrialized countries are planning emission trading systems with Russia, which could allow them to purchase Russia's surplus emission rights at low cost. In Kyoto, Russia agreed to cap its emissions at 1990 levels in the first budget period; however, it is unlikely that, even with a modest recovery of the Russian economy,

emissions will reach even that level. The case illustrates the large value at stake when targets (and permits) are distributed. As controls on greenhouse gases tighten, the value of these permits will rise, making negotiations over permit allocations increasingly contentious. Moreover, no emission trading system of this scale and complexity has ever been attempted under international law. The Kyoto Protocol includes provisions for monitoring, accounting, enforcement, and other critical functions, but they have yet to be tested.

The Kyoto Protocol also includes two more limited forms of emission trading. One, known as *joint implementation* (JI), allows credits to be earned and traded on a project-by-project basis, which gives an incentive for cost-effective international emission control without necessarily confronting the difficulty of allocating per-

Kyoto Protocol. TABLE 2. Emission Targets for Annex I Countries*

KYOTO TARGET (PERCENT)	ANNEX I COUNTRY (OR REGIONAL ECONOMIC INTEGRATION ORGANIZATION)
−8	European Community
	Austria
	Belgium
	Denmark
	Finland
	France
	Germany
	Greece
	Ireland
	Italy
	Luxembourg
	Netherlands
	Portugal
	Spain
	Sweden
	United Kingdom
−8	Bulgaria
−8	Czech Republic
−8	Estonia
−8	Latvia
−8	Liechtenstein
−8	Lithuania
−8	Monaco
−8	Romania
−8	Slovakia
−8	Slovenia
−8	Switzerland
−7	United States
−6	Canada
−6	Hungary
−6	Japan
−6	Poland
−5	Croatia
0	New Zealand
0	Russian Federation
0	Ukraine
+1	Norway
+8	Australia
+10	Iceland

*The percentage change is from emission levels of 1990 (for all gases, weighted by GWP), with some provisions for flexibility discussed in the text. Parties may pool and reallocate their targets among their members; so far only the European Community has indicated that it will do so. Targets are listed in Annex B of the Protocol; that Annex includes the same list of countries as in Annex I of the FCCC, except that Turkey had objected to its listing in Annex I and thus was excluded from Annex B in Kyoto.

Kyoto Protocol. TABLE 3. Responsibility of Annex I Countries for Emissions of Carbon Dioxide in 1990*

ANNEX I PARTY	PERCENTAGE OF ANNEX I EMISSIONS
Iceland	0.0
Liechtenstein	0.0
Monaco	0.0
Luxembourg	0.1
Ireland	0.2
Latvia	0.2
New Zealand	0.2
Estonia	0.3
Norway	0.3
Portugal	0.3
Switzerland	0.3
Austria	0.4
Denmark	0.4
Finland	0.4
Slovakia	0.4
Sweden	0.4
Hungary	0.5
Bulgaria	0.6
Greece	0.6
Belgium	0.8
Czech Republic	1.2
Netherlands	1.2
Romania	1.2
Spain	1.9
Australia	2.1
France	2.7
Poland	3.0
Italy	3.1
Canada	3.3
United Kingdom	4.3
Germany	7.4
Japan	8.5
Russian Federation	17.4
United States	36.1

*Total Annex I emissions of carbon dioxide from industrial sources (fossil fuel combustion and cement production) in 1990 were 13.7 billion metric tons. Entry into force requires that countries representing at least 55 percent of these emissions ratify the accord.

SOURCE: Data based on the information from the thirty-four Annex I Parties that submitted their first national communications on or before 11 December 1997, as compiled by the Climate Change Secretariat.

mits and administering a full-blown emission trading system. [*See* Joint Implementation.] Through the JI mechanism, Annex I countries may make investments in other Annex I countries and earn credit if lower greenhouse gas emissions result. The other limited trading system is the Clean Development Mechanism (CDM), which allows Annex I nations to earn credits from investments in developing countries. However, implementing the CDM operation is more difficult than implementing the JI because the Protocol does not set limits for emissions from developing countries. Thus, for the CDM, it is especially important to determine the level of emissions that would have occurred without the investment so that proper credit is given for the difference between (lower) actual emissions and the baseline level that would have occurred otherwise. Technically and politically, this counterfactual calculation is extremely difficult to perform. Rules for operating and accounting under the CDM were left unresolved at Kyoto—in part, deferring the details explains why there was widespread agreement at Kyoto on the need for the CDM. Experience with JI-like emission offset programs in the United States shows that if the rules are too cumbersome, the system will fail to encourage such trading.

In addition to establishing new commitments, the Protocol is an integral part of the institutions established by the FCCC. Parties to the Protocol must be parties to the FCCC. The FCCC and the Kyoto Protocol will share the same secretariat, based in Bonn, Germany. The Protocol's supreme decision-making body—the Meeting of the Parties (MOP)—will meet at the same time as the FCCC's COP. The subsidiary bodies that serve the latter (for example, the Subsidiary Body for Implementation and the Subsidiary Body for Scientific and Technological Advice) will also serve the Protocol's MOP. The Kyoto Protocol also strengthens and clarifies the obligation, first codified in the FCCC, that each party report inventories of its emissions of greenhouse gases. Without extensive reporting and review of reports, it will be nearly impossible to verify whether parties have actually complied with the stringent obligations of the Protocol.

Entry into force of the Protocol requires ratification by fifty-five parties to the FCCC, representing 55 percent of the emissions of industrial carbon dioxide from Annex I countries in 1990 (see Table 3). For many industrialized nations, the Kyoto commitments will be costly to implement, and it may prove difficult to garner sufficient political support to assure that the treaty is binding under international law. If ratification falters, then the FCCC will remain in place as a backstop and as a framework for future efforts to slow global warming.

[*See also* Framework Convention on Climate Change; *and* Global Warming Potential.]

INTERNET RESOURCES

"Kyoto Protocol to the United Nations Framework Convention on Climate Change." FCCC/CP/L7/Add.1, 10 December 1997. http://www.unfccc.de/.

"Linkages." Reports on negotiations at Kyoto and beyond. http://www.iisd.ca/linkages/climate/climate.html/.

BIBLIOGRAPHY

Bartsch, U., and B. Muller. *Fossil Fuels in a Changing Climate: Impacts of the Kyoto Protocol and Developing Country Participation.* Oxford: Oxford University Press, 2000.

—DAVID G. VICTOR

L

LAKES

Lakes are diverse in shape, size, depth, and degree of openness, and so therefore is their response to environmental change. Closed lakes, which currently have no outlets, are particularly sensitive, but even the world's biggest lakes (Table 1) are not immune. The largest interior lakes, especially those that are salty, are often called *seas*. They have proved to be susceptible to human actions but are also good indicators of natural environmental changes.

Humans have a range of impacts on lake basins, which include eutrophication because of the addition of nutrients to their catchments, acidification because of acid precipitation or land use changes, contamination by chemical pollutants and heavy metals, explosive invasion by exotic introduced organisms, siltation because of land use and land cover changes, and changes in their water balance because of such processes as interbasin water transfers or changes in land use (Kira, 1998).

Anthropogenic Effects on Lake Levels. Changes in lake levels brought about by human activities have been known about for a long time. A lake basin for which there are particularly long records of change is the Valencia Basin in Venezuela (Böckh, 1973). It was the declining level of the waters in this lake that so struck the great German geographer Alexander von Humboldt in 1800. He recorded its level as being about 422 meters above sea level, whereas previous observations on its level, made by Antonio Manzano in 1727, had established it as being at 426 meters. The 1968 level was about 405 meters, representing a fall of no less that 21 meters in about 240 years. Humboldt believed that the cause of the declining level was the deforestation brought about by humans, and this has been supported by Böckh (1973), who points also to the abstraction of water for irrigation. This remarkable fall in level meant that the lake ceased to have an overflow into the River Orinoco. It has as a consequence become subject to a buildup in salinity and is now eight times more saline than it was two and a half centuries ago.

Even the world's largest lake, the Caspian Sea, has been modified by human activities. The most important change was the fall of 3 meters in its level between 1929 and the late 1970s (see Figure 1). This decline was undoubtedly partly the product of climatic change (Micklin, 1972). Nonetheless, human actions have contributed to this fall, particularly since the 1950s, because of reservoir formation, irrigation, municipal and industrial withdrawals, and agricultural practices.

In the 1970s, 1980s, and 1990s the Caspian has seen a restoration in its levels, caused by a decrease in the difference between evaporation and precipitation over its catchment. But for anthropogenic effects its level would have returned to pre-1930 levels (World Meteorological Organization, 1995, p. 124).

Perhaps the most severe change to a major inland sea is that taking place in the Aral Sea. Since 1960 the Aral Sea has lost more than 40 percent of its area and about 60 percent of its volume, and its level has fallen by more than fourteen meters (Kotylakov, 1991). This has lowered the artesian water table over a band 80–170 kilometers in width, has exposed 24,000 square kilometers of former lake bed to desiccation, and has created salty surfaces from which salts are deflated to be transported in dust storms, to the detriment of soil quality. The mineral content of what remains has increased almost threefold over the same period. It is probably the most dire ecological tragedy to have afflicted the Confederation of Independent States, and as with the Caspian's decline, much of the blame rests with excessive use of water that would otherwise replenish the sea. [*See* Aral Sea, Desiccation of the.]

Water abstraction from the Jordan River for irrigation purposes has caused a decline in the level of the Dead Sea at a rate of about 0.8 meters per year. The level dropped 20 meters during the twentieth century and may fall a further 100 to 150 meters over the next four hundred years (Yechieli et al., 1998). Under natural conditions, fresh water from the Jordan constantly fed the less salty layer of the sea, which occupied roughly the top 40 meters of the 320-meter-deep body of water. Because the amount of wa-

Lakes. TABLE 1. Major Lakes of the Continents

LAKE	CONTINENT	AREA (KM^2)
Victoria	Africa	63,000–69,000
Caspian	Europe	374,000–378,400
Aral	Asia	64,100
Superior	North America	82,100–83,300
Eyre	Australia	up to 40,000
South America	Maracaibo	13,000–14,3000

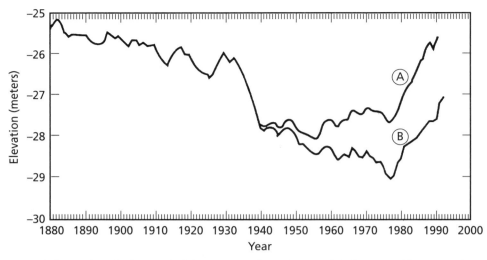

Lakes. Figure 1. Annual Fluctuations in the Level of the Caspian Sea, for the Period 1880–1993.

Curve A shows the changes in level that would have occurred but for anthropogenic influences, while curve B shows the actual observed levels. (Modified from World Meteorological Organization, 1995, Figure 15.3.)

ter entering the lake via the Jordan was more or less equal to the quantity lost by evaporation, the lake maintained its stable, stratified state, with less salty water resting on the waters of high salinity. With the recent human-induced diminution in Jordan discharge, however, the sea's upper layer has receded because of the intense levels of evaporation. Its salinity has approached that of the older and deeper waters. It has now been established that as a consequence the layered structure has collapsed, creating a situation where there is increased precipitation of salts. Moreover, now that circulating waters carry oxygen to the bottom, the characteristic hydrogen-sulfide smell has largely disappeared (Maugh, 1979).

Recent Climatic Changes and Lake Levels. Lake levels respond to changes in rainfall inputs and to the outputs of moisture by evaporation and transpiration, which are largely controlled by temperature. One of the most interesting examples of environmental change in the twentieth century has been the fluctuating level of lakes in the tropics. In particular, many equatorial lakes in Africa showed a dramatic increase in level in the early 1960s, which led to the flooding of port installations, deltaic farming land, and the like (Butzer, 1971). This rise contrasted sharply with the frequently low levels encountered in the previous decades.

The Great Salt Lake in Utah has an especially impressive record of fluctuating levels dating back to the middle of the nineteenth century. As Figure 2 shows, the lake rose from an elevation of about 4,200 feet in 1851 to a peak of around 4,210 feet (1,284 meters) in 1873. Thereafter it declined markedly, reaching the lowest recorded level in 1963. Since then it has risen from around 4,194 feet (1,279 meters) in elevation back to the sort of elevation achieved in the 1870s. There has thus been a total fluctuation of this great water body on the order of five meters over that time period (Stockton,

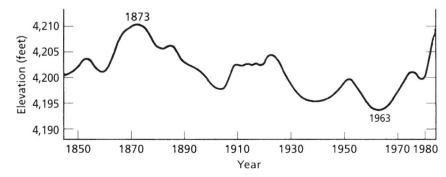

Lakes. Figure 2. The Changing Level of the Great Salt Lake, USA (1851–1984). (After Stockton, 1990.)

1990). The latest rise is a consequence of a run of very wet years since the mid-1970s.

Longer-Term Climatic Changes and Lake Levels. Lakes, like the oceans, can preserve a long record of sedimentation. Arid regions have more than their fair share of closed depressions, and these lake basins, as Gilbert (1890) and Russell (1885) noted over a century ago in the contexts of Lakes Bonneville and Lahontan, are rich depositories of paleoenvironmental information. Ancient shorelines demonstrate that at times what are now shrunken, salty relicts were once fine, large, freshwater bodies. In addition, lake basins, if they have not been deflated out, can provide a long sequence of information from the sediments that occur within them.

Since the late 1960s, at least two main developments have taken place in the study of tropical lake basins. The first of these has been the dating of former high stands of lake level using radiocarbon. The remarkable result of such work was the recognition that in low latitudes glacial and pluvial origins were not synchronous and that, if anything, the late glacial maximum could be equated with aridity and the early Holocene interglacial with humidity. This was pointed out for tropical Africa by Grove and Goudie (1971) and shortly thereafter by Butzer et al. (1972).

The second development, which builds upon the first, has been the construction of a global database of lake status that permits interregional comparisons to be made (Street and Grove, 1979). This work shows that while the midlatitude lakes of the American southwest may have been high at the time of the last glacial maximum, those of the tropics and monsoonal lands (e.g., West Africa, East Africa, southern Arabia, northwestern India, and tropical Australia) were low at that time and reached very high levels in the early Holocene (around eight thousand to nine thousand years ago).

Recently, such databases have been developed for more parts of the world (see, for example, Fang, 1991 on China). Their temporal resolution has also improved as more dates have become available, and this improvement has enabled some investigators to suggest correlations between tropical lake fluctuations and short-lived events such as the Younger Dryas of the Late Glacial (Gasse et al., 1990; Sirocko et al., 1996; Roberts et al., 1993). [*See* Younger Dryas.]

The Response of Lakes to Potential Global Warming. Just as lakes have responded to past climatic changes, so it is clear that they will respond to the temperature and precipitation changes that may result from global warming. An example of such responses is provided by models that have been developed for the Great Lakes of North America by Croley (1990) and Hartmann (1990). They suggest that for a doubling of carbon dioxide levels there may be a 23–51 percent reduction in net basin supplies of water to all the Great Lakes, and that as a result lake levels will fall at rates ranging from thirteen millimeters per decade (for Lake Superior) to ninety-three millimeters per decade (for Lake Ontario).

BIBLIOGRAPHY

Böckh, A. "Consequences of Uncontrolled Human Activities in the Valencia Lake Basin." In *The Careless Technology*, edited by M. T. Farvar and J. P. Milton, pp. 301–317. London: Tom Stacey, 1973.

Butzer, K. W. "Recent History of an Ethiopian Delta." *University of Chicago, Department of Geography, Research Paper* 136 (1971), 184.

Butzer, K. W., G. L. Isaac, J. L. Richardson, and C. Washbourne-Kamau. "Radiocarbon Dating of East African Lake Levels." *Science* 175 (1972), 1069–1075.

Croley, T. E. "Laurentian Great Lakes Double-CO_2 Climate Change Hydrological Impacts." *Climatic Change* 17 (1990), 27–47.

Fang, J. Q. "Lake Evolution during the Past 30,000 Years in China, and Its Implications for Environmental Change." *Quaternary Research* 36 (1991), 37–60.

Gasse, F., R. Tehet, A. Durand, E. Gilbert, and J. C. Fontes. "The Arid-Humid Transition in the Sahara and the Sahel during the Last Deglaciation. *Nature* 346 (1990), 141–146.

Gilbert, G. K. *Lake Bonneville*. U.S. Geological Survey Monograph 1, 1890.

Grove, A. T., and A. S. Goudie. "Late Quaternary Lake Levels in the Rift Valley of Southern Ethiopia and Elsewhere in Tropical Africa." *Nature* 234 (1971), 403–405.

Hartmann, H. C. "Climate Change Impacts on Laurentian Great Lakes Levels." *Climatic Change* 17 (1990), 49–67.

Kira, T. "Major Environmental Problems in World Lakes." In *Central Eurasian Water Crisis*, edited by I. Kobori and M. Glantz, pp. 13–21. Tokyo: United Nations University Press, 1998.

Kotlyakov, V. M. "The Aral Sea Basin: A Critical Environmental Zone." *Moscow Environment* 33.1 (1991), 4–9, 36–38.

Maugh, T. H. "The Dead Sea Is Alive and Well." *Science* 205 (1979), 178.

Micklin, P. P. "Dimensions of the Caspian Sea Problem." *Soviet Geography* 13 (1972), 589–603.

Roberts, N., M. Taieb, P. Barker, B. Damnati, M. Icole, and D. Williamson. "Timing of the Younger Dryas Event in East Africa from Lake-Level Changes." *Nature* 366 (1993), 146–148.

Russell, I. C. *Quaternary History of Lake Lahontan*. U.S. Geological Survey Monograph 11, 1885.

Sirocko, F., D. Garbe-Schönberg, A. McIntyre, and M. Molfino. "Teleconnections between the Subtropical Monsoons and High-Latitude Climates during the Last Deglaciation." *Science* 272 (1996), 526–529.

Stockton, E. W. "Climatic Variability on the Scale of Decades to Centuries." *Climatic Change* 16 (1990), 173–183.

Street, F. A., and A. T. Grove. "Global Maps of Lake-Level Fluctuations since 30,000 Years BP." *Quaternary Research* 12 (1979), 83–118.

World Meteorological Organization. *Climate System Review: Climate System Monitoring, June 1991–November 1993*. Geneva: World Meteorological Organization, 1995.

Yechieli, Y., I. Gavrieli, B. Berkowitz, and D. Ronen. "Will the Dead Sea Die?" *Geology* 26 (1998), 755–758.

—ANDREW S. GOUDIE

LAMB, HUBERT HORACE

Hubert Horace Lamb (1913–1997), arguably the greatest climatologist of his time, was born in Bedford, England, and read natural sciences and geography at Trinity College, Cambridge. His broad interests served him well when he came to develop his original ideas on climatic changes and the impact of climate on human societies. He joined the U.K. Meteorological Office in 1936. At the outbreak of World War II he was instructed to work on the meteorology of gas spraying, but refused. From 1940 to 1944 he was a research officer with the Irish Meteorological Service, where he showed great skill at forecasting while producing weather forecasts for the new transatlantic passenger flights.

In 1946, Lamb joined a whaling vessel to the Antarctic as expedition meteorologist. His observations of conditions in the Southern Ocean at this time led him to doubt the accepted viewpoint that climate was fundamentally unchanging. In 1950 Lamb published a classic paper on weather types and natural seasons in Britain. The Lamb Weather Type (LWT) classification that it described began a new era in climatological research. The LWTs have since been used to characterize atmospheric circulation changes in other geographical regions and have been applied in many areas, including air pollution forecasting. In 1963 Lamb was awarded a special merit promotion in the Meteorological Office. This gave him more freedom to pursue his research interests and resulted in his reconstructions of monthly atmospheric circulation over the North Atlantic and Europe back to the 1750s. This research confirmed his growing conviction of the reality of climate change and its significance to human time scales. He also started to make the first connections between sea surface temperatures and the atmospheric circulation. In 1970 he published a classic paper on the connection between volcanism and climate change. The estimate of the dust ejected into the atmosphere by historical eruptions became known as the *Lamb Dust Veil Index*. The author of more than one hundred scientific articles, Lamb's best-known other works are the masterly reference books published in two volumes as *Climate: Present, Past and Future* (Lamb, 1972, 1977).

In 1972 Lamb founded the Climatic Research Unit at the University of East Anglia. This was the first research center of its kind with a focus on research into climatology, in particular climate change, and on interdisciplinary and historical research into the climate of the past. He remained its director until 1978, when he became emeritus professor. Lamb's effect on climatological research and his inspiration to fellow climatologists is incalculable. His services to climatology are reflected in the many awards given to him. These include the L. G. Groves Memorial Prize (1960 and 1970); the Dar-

ton Prize of the Royal Meteorological Society (1963); the Murchison Award of the Royal Geographical Society (1974); the Vega Medal of the Royal Swedish Geographical Society (1984); and the Symons Memorial Medal of the Royal Meteorological Society (1987). In April 1997 he was honored by his colleagues at a celebration of the twenty-fifth anniversary of the founding of the Climatic Research Unit. His autobiography, *Through All the Changing Scenes of Life: A Meteorologist's Tale*, was completed just before he died in 1997.

[*See also* Climate Change.]

BIBLIOGRAPHY

Lamb, H. H. "Types and Spells of Weather around the Year in the British Isles: Annual Trends, Seasonal Structure of the Year, Singularities." *Quarterly Journal of the Royal Meteorological Society* 76 (1950), 393–438.
———. "The Early Medieval Warm Period and Its Sequel." *Palaeogeography, Palaeoclimatology, Palaeoecology* 1 (1965), 13–37.
———. *The Changing Climate*. London: Methuen, 1966.
———. "Volcanic Dust in the Atmosphere: With a Chronology and Assessment of Its Meteorological Significance." *Philosophical Transactions of the Royal Society, Series A* 266 (1970); 425–533.
———. *Climate: Present, Past and Future*, vol. 1, *Fundamentals and Climate Now*. London: Methuen, 1972.
———. *Climate: Present, Past and Future*, vol. 2, *Climate History and the Future*. London: Methuen, 1977.
———. *Climate, History and the Modern World*. London: Methuen, 1982.
———. *Historic Storms of the North Sea, British Isles, and Northwest Europe*. Cambridge: Cambridge University Press, 1991.
———. *Through All the Changing Scenes of Life: A Meteorologist's Tale*. East Harling, Norfolk, U.K.: Taverner Publications, 1997.
Lamb, H. H., and A. I. Johnson. "Climatic Variation and Observed Changes in the General Circulation," pts. I, II, and III. *Geografiska Annaler* 41 (1959), 94–134; 43 (1961), 363–400.
Ogilvie, A. E. J. "Lamb, Hubert Horace." In *Encyclopedia of Climate and Weather*, edited by S. H. Schneider, pp. 463–464. New York and Oxford: Oxford University Press, 1996.

—A. E. J. Ogilvie

LANDFILL. *See* Waste Management.

LAND RECLAMATION

Land reclamation is the improvement of land or its transformation from some inferior state to a better one. So defined, the term can describe the repair of land that was damaged or left inferior either by human action or by natural processes. It has been used in both senses, though the latter is the older one. Synonyms coined fairly recently and mostly used to denote the repair of areas damaged by human activity include land restoration, rehabilitation, and remediation. Older synonyms for reclamation denoting mostly the bettering of naturally poor or useless lands include land development, improvement, betterment, and beneficiation. Lands that invite reclamation are often described in such terms as badlands, disturbed lands, derelict lands, deserts, and wastelands. The single closest antonym to *land reclamation* is *land degradation*, though it is more often used to refer to human-induced damage to land than to its devaluation by such natural states or processes as aridity or permanent or seasonal inundation.

Classically, the term *land reclamation* referred chiefly to two activities: irrigation and wetland drainage. In the one case, it denoted the transformation to productive use of land that the natural climate had left too dry for ordinary farming. In the other, it denoted the creation of solid ground for cultivation or construction out of "swamp" or "overflowed" lands that had been left by nature in a useless state halfway between land and water, and often unsightly and disease- and vermin-ridden as well. The development and improvement of other lands that for one reason or another fell into the category of waste or unproductive ground—moorland, forest, scrub land—was also often described as land reclamation. So was land protection from periodic overflow through flood control works, and so was the fertilization with macro- or micronutrients of land previously ill-suited to productive use for farming or grazing. [*See* Irrigation.]

All of these transformations continue to be undertaken on a large scale around the world, though they are much less widely and generally than before seen as clear cases of land improvement by human intervention. As the side effects of irrigation, drainage, and similar interventions have become better understood, many people have come to regard as land degradation activities and outcomes that others still refer to as reclamation, development, or improvement. The terms have not changed in meaning, for they still refer to the bettering of land, but ideas of what constitutes "better" and "worse" have changed. The principal forms of reclamation in the older sense, irrigation and wetland drainage, are discussed under separate entries elsewhere in this volume. The focus of this entry is on the newer meaning of land reclamation, on the repair of lands damaged by human use.

Ideally, damage of this sort would be avoided by proper use instead of being repaired by efforts that are usually costly and imperfect. There are often perverse incentives built into tax systems, structures of property rights, and other social institutions that promote careless and destructive exploitation. Correcting them and developing more efficient techniques for land use offer much scope for preventing degradation at the outset. Yet from a practical point of view, it must be recognized that many activities for the foreseeable future will continue to degrade land, often quite severely. The returns

from doing so are often too large to be forgone. Developing tools and strategies for reclamation helps to ensure that change will not all be in the wrong direction and that some areas can be repaired or restored in compensation for those lost, disturbed, or impoverished in some way.

In the simplest sense, reclamation of this sort is and long has been ubiquitous in ordinary farming practice. When land depleted by cropping is fallowed for a season or longer, or when legumes are planted or fertilizers are applied to restore its fertility, one can say that it is being reclaimed. Other forms of agricultural impact are much more profound than the removal of nutrients through harvesting and require more elaborate interventions to restore the land affected by them. Soil salinization is a frequent unintended result of irrigation. It occurs when salts introduced in irrigation water or drawn up by it from the subsurface are left behind in the topsoil when the water evaporates. As salts accumulate, the land is rendered less productive and in extreme cases becomes entirely unfit for cultivation. Salinization is a serious problem in lands irrigated without proper precautionary measures. It has been a problem since antiquity in some regions. It may have been a driving force of large-scale land abandonment in Mesopotamia several millennia ago. Areas severely affected by salinization are currently most extensive in the Middle East, South and Central Asia, and western North America. The problem is better avoided by proper design at the outset than remedied by subsequent reclamation efforts. Technical measures to deal with some forms of it do exist, but they tend to be expensive and difficult to undertake. Chief among them are chemical treatment and flushing of the soil with water to remove excess salinity, but the fresh water required for the latter is likely to be scarce, and drainage works may have to be constructed at the same time to avoid waterlogging. The operation may also create problems of wastewater pollution downstream. Growing salt-tolerant plants for productive use or for ground cover is a less ambitious means of adapting or adjusting land use to a moderate degree of salinization.

Another form of land degradation associated chiefly with drylands is the syndrome commonly known as desertification. The single most widely accepted indicator of desertification is a decline in plant biomass. The chief immediate cause is generally seen as overgrazing of dryland vegetation, although much of what is ascribed to these factors may in some cases be the result instead of short- or medium-term fluctuations in climate. Technical measures for the reclamation of desertified land emphasize restoration of vegetation cover. Longer-term solutions proposed address the various underlying social factors that different analysts hold ultimately responsible for the problem. They range from growth in human and livestock populations to the pressure of political and economic forces. [*See* Desertification.]

Far more drastic alterations of land by human activity are the highly localized ones produced by surface mining of earth materials: the quarrying of stone, gravel, and sand and the strip mining of coal. These activities are often economically attractive if judged only by their immediate returns compared to those available from other uses of the land. They may, however, leave behind a disturbed or derelict landscape that is unsuited thereafter to many ordinary uses such as agriculture, forestry, or construction. Mining may physically disrupt, chemically alter, or completely remove soil; reconfigure the terrain of the site; alter or destroy the previous plant cover and the conditions necessary for spontaneous revegetation; and create a scarred and unsightly landscape. It may release chemical pollutants into local waters through runoff and sediment erosion into streams. In extreme cases, it may create a risk to nearby areas of landslides owing to slope failure of unstable accumulations of soil. Many of these problems are duplicated by those associated with the dumping of large amounts of waste: mine spoil itself, dredge spoil from navigation channels, and the large quantities of coal ash produced by electric power plants.

Efforts to reclaim lands thus disturbed usually focus on restoring a vegetation cover. The addition of topsoil, if it was removed, may be necessary as a first step. Treatment of the ground with nutrients to repair deficiencies or counteract contamination (liming against acidity, for example) may have to be undertaken. The area may need to be colonized with plant and tree species carefully selected for their tolerance of the specific physical and chemical conditions peculiar to its disturbed state. Successful revegetation lessens the problems of erosion, slope instability, and visual pollution, but the land may remain unsuitable for many uses.

Air pollution can have locally severe effects on nearby lands. Ore smelters release both toxic trace metals and acid precipitation that may kill vegetation over large surrounding expanses and leave the land bare and prone to erosion. Like mines, smelters often produce returns so much higher than those of agriculture that their activities are allowed to go on more or less unchecked despite the damage that they do to their surroundings. Apart from ending emissions, many of the same rehabilitative measures that can be taken to reclaim land disturbed by mining can also be applied. [*See* Mining.]

A still small but rapidly increasing share of the world's land surface is devoted to human construction—buildings, pavement, and the like. Such lands left derelict by abandonment themselves represent a small but rapidly growing share of lands judged to require reclamation. Vacant buildings, lots, and tracts and the larger phenomenon of central-city decay are problems in much of the developed world. They frequently occur in combination with a second and equally problematic process, that of rapid land development of the sprawl type on the metropolitan fringe that consumes open space and forest and agricultural land. Policy remedies against both problems include greenbelts and farmland preservation to stem sprawl and urban renewal programs and tax incentives for redevelopment of derelict central-city space. Chemical pollution is often a serious problem at derelict industrial sites, and measures for rehabilitating them include the removal and burial or incineration or the bioremediation *in situ* of the waste materials.

Wetland drainage, one of the two classic forms of land reclamation as the improvement of naturally inferior land, is still proceeding at a rapid rate worldwide and in most countries, despite many measures intended to slow it. Yet the term *land reclamation* can now be applied as well to a new form of change, wetland restoration or creation. Holland, for centuries the world's leader in drainage, in recent years has begun a policy of returning large areas to their previous state. In the 1980s, the U.S. government, announcing a policy looking toward "no net loss" of wetlands, gave a role to extensive efforts of this sort as a way to offset continued losses judged necessary for various activities. The benefits of creation and restoration include ones as direct and practical as streamflow and groundwater regulation and wildlife habitat; their success can also be measured by the degree to which they succeed in replicating the full range of natural wetland conditions.

Recent years have seen a rapid growth of interest in the related but broader topic of what is known as ecological restoration, or the attempt to recreate as far as possible the landscapes and ecosystems that existed in an area prior to significant human disturbance. Restoration projects undertaken by ecologists have been of great usefulness as scientific experiments in shedding light on the variety of factors that help to form ecosystems and the conditions needed for their maintenance. At the same time, they have made clearer some of the problems and paradoxes of restoration as a program of action. It is impossible to restore entirely any previous ecosystem, given all of the wider environmental changes necessarily impinging on it from outside. Species subsequently introduced to the area, for example, cannot be excluded from the restored landscape though they were no part of the original. Restoration projects have also underlined the necessity of choosing some point in the natural history of an area to restore, and thus the dominance of human choice and preference in the very act of attempting to restore nature. No piece of land has a single natural character or an inherent ecological identity; it always has a past consisting of many different ones.

Because different things may be desired of the land at any one time, land degradation and land reclamation alike are to a great extent in the eye of the beholder. The same projects of irrigation and wetland drainage can be and often are classified as both by different observers. It is not surprising, therefore, that many conflicts have arisen over land reclamation projects and proposals in the newer sense of the term. Restrictions on resident and user populations in national parks and preserves, meant to restore and protect the land and its biota, may hinder activities vital to residents and may in a sense degrade the land by making it less productive. The most ambitious ecological restoration project yet seriously discussed, that of converting much of the North American Great Plains to a "Buffalo Commons" closer to its preagricultural state has, not surprisingly, aroused the strongest antagonism in the region itself.

[See also Land Use, article on Land Use and Land Cover; Salinization; Wetlands; and World Bank, The.]

BIBLIOGRAPHY

Bradshaw, A. D., and M. J. Chadwick. *The Restoration of Land: The Ecology and Reclamation of Derelict and Degraded Land.* Berkeley: University of California Press, 1980. A classic treatment of the repair of disturbed and derelict land.

Harris, J. A., P. Birch, and J. Palmer. *Land Restoration and Reclamation: Principles and Practice.* Harlow, U.K.: Longman, 1996. An up-to-date technical text.

Jordan, W. R., III, M. E. Gilpin, and J. D. Aber, eds. *Restoration Ecology.* New York: Cambridge University Press, 1987. A classic survey of the chief issues in ecological restoration.

Urbanks, K. M., N. R. Webb, and P. J. Edmonds, eds. *Restoration Ecology and Sustainable Development.* Cambridge: Cambridge University Press, 1997. A fine recent collection addressing technical and social dimensions.

—WILLIAM B. MEYER

LAND SURFACE PROCESSES

The study of rates of land surface change has always been a central focus of geomorphologic research (Goudie, 1995). Geomorphologists, who study the nature and history of landform development and the operation of the processes of weathering, transport, erosion, and deposition, have for long asked a series of questions that require a knowledge of rates of change. How important are such factors as climate and tectonic setting as controls of geomorphologic processes? To what extent are humans influencing landform development? What is the potential useful life of a particular engineering structure? How much time is required for a particular landform assemblage to develop? What is the relative significance of different land-forming processes? And, how can environments be transformed by future global environmental changes? We shall consider here some of these issues in the context of certain key exogenic geomorphologic mechanisms: weathering, general fluvial denudation, mass movements on slopes, glacial activity, and coastal change.

Weathering is one of the most important geomorphologic processes. In general, two main types of weathering are recognized. Mechanical or physical weathering involves the breakdown of rock without any substantial degree of chemical change taking place in the minerals that make up the rock mass. It incorporates such processes as frost and salt weathering and may also be achieved by organic or biological means (e.g., root wedging). Chemical weathering, in which biological processes may play a major role, involves the decomposition of rock minerals through such processes as hydration, hydrolysis, oxidation and reduction, carbonation, and chelation. In most parts of the world, both types of weathering may operate together, though in differing proportions, and one may accelerate the other. For example, the physical disintegration of a rock will expose a greatly increased surface area to chemical attack.

Methods employed for the study of rates of weathering include analyses of soil and weathering profile development on landforms or monuments of known age, laboratory simulations, and direct monitoring using instrumentation (e.g., microerosion meters and rock tablets). On a global scale, the most important method of determining rates of weathering is to determine the amounts of dissolved material being transported in river water.

The Dissolved Load of Rivers. Analysis of river discharge and the concentration of dissolved material in such flow permits one both to establish rates of chemical denudation and to establish the relative efficiency of mechanical and chemical erosion.

On the global scale, a detailed analysis has been undertaken by Walling and Webb (1983), who built up a database for 490 rivers in which pollution was absent or limited. The authors admit that the database is not entirely representative of the global situation, as certain parts of the world (notably, regions of South America and Africa) are short on data. The mean load was found to be 38.8 metric tons per square kilometer per year ($t \ km^{-2} \ yr^{-1}$) and typically values lie in the range 5–100 $t \ km^{-2} \ yr^{-1}$. There were some values below 1.0 $t \ km^{-2} \ yr^{-1}$ (for small catchments in Alberta), while the highest value was for the River Iller in Germany (311 $t \ km^{-2} \ yr^{-1}$).

The data set also demonstrated a general influence of climate in that there was a positive relationship, albeit rather weak, between annual dissolved load (D) and mean annual runoff (Q), expressed by the following least-squares regression:

$$D = 3.3Q^{0.385} \ (r = 0.49).$$

The explanation for the positive trend may be that increasing moisture availability increases the rate of chemical weathering and solute evacuation. However, this is only part of the explanation. Many other factors control solute delivery, including temperature, seasonality, rock type, and vegetation. Of these, rock type may well be the most important, for the dissolved loads of rivers draining igneous rocks are, not surprisingly, lower than those found in areas of sedimentary rocks.

A third major finding arising from analysis of the database was that the dissolved load transport to the oceans on a global scale is considerably less than particulate transport. The ratio is about 3.6:1. Values of the ratio range from in excess of 100 to less than 0.5, and the particulate component exceeds the dissolved component in more than 60 percent of cases. Given that the chemical load may include a large precipitation input component, and given that large amounts of particulate sediment may not be delivered through the catchment and into the oceans, Walling and Webb (1983, p. 16) believe that mechanical erosion may be of considerably more importance in landscape development than is indicated by a simple comparison of particulate and dissolved loads. Indeed, they believe that the ratio of 3.6:1 may need to be increased "by an order of magnitude in order to produce a meaningful estimate of the relative important of mechanical and chemical erosion" (p. 17).

High rates of chemical denudation are invariably observed in high mountainous regions (Summerfield, 1991, p. 385). By contrast, minimal rates of chemical denudation are recorded in dry regions where runoff is low (Table 1). Rivers that drain largely semiarid regions, such as the Colorado, Orange, and Tigris–Euphrates, have low rates of solute transport in relation to total transport. This contrasts markedly with basins from humid and subarctic regions such as the Lena, Yenisei, Ob, and Dnieper, which have high rates of solute transport in relation to total transport. In the case of the St. Lawrence, the relatively high proportion carried by solute transport may be attributed to the large proportion of particulate sediment trapped in the Great Lakes.

Meybeck (1979; see Table 2) attempted to classify rates of chemical denudation according to climatic zonation. As can be seen, the highest rates occurred in pluvial temperate zones, many of which have very high rainfall amounts associated with high-relief conditions. Only slightly less important was the very humid tropical mountainous zone. But, surprisingly, the lowest rates occurred in dry environments (tundra and taiga, the seasonal tropics, and arid lands).

Meybeck (1987) has gone some way toward quantifying the lithological control on rates of denudation that was perceived by Walling and Webb to be one of the prime reasons for the weak relationship between climate and rate of denudation at the zonal scale. Drainage basins underlain by metamorphic and plutonic rocks tend to have lower values of chemical transport for a given runoff level than do volcanic rocks. The highest rates occur for sedimentary rocks. Meybeck also established a relative erosion rate normalized to granite weathering. The relative rates were as follows: granite, 1; gneiss and mica schist, 1; gabbro, 1.3; sandstone, 1.3; volcanics, 1.5; shales, 2.5; miscellaneous metamorphics (including serpentines, marbles, and amphibolites), 5; carbonates, 12; gypsum, 40; rock salt, 80.

General Fluvial Denudation. General rates of denudation by rivers can be obtained by a variety of techniques: measurements of material carried by streams; volumes of material deposited in lakes, reservoirs, and on continental shelves; apatite fission track dating; and the use of cosmogenic nuclides. The study of sediment loads in rivers has been most useful for assessing global and regional rates.

The most comprehensive recent attempt to relate sediment yield to climate was that of Walling and Kleo (1979). Using a large global database, they identified three zones in which rates may be especially high: the seasonal climatic zones of the Mediterranean type, monsoonal areas with large amounts of seasonal tropical rain, and semiarid areas (Figure 1).

A more recent attempt to produce a global map of suspended sediment yield is that made by Walling (1987), based on more than 1,500 measuring stations (Figure 2). The pattern relates to the sediment yields from intermediate-sized basins of around 10^4–10^5 square kilometers and is both generalized and complex. The high yields displayed for the Mediterranean area, southwestern United States and parts of East Africa may possibly be related to the presence of semiarid climatic conditions with seasonal rainfall and limited vegetation cover. On the other hand, the high sediment yields of the Pacific Rim may reflect the combined influence of high rainfall, tectonic instability, and high relief. Certainly, relief is a highly important control, with high, steep areas in the Himalayas, Andes, Alaska, and the Mediterranean lands producing high yields. Low rates are evident for much of the old shield areas of northern Eurasia and North America, with their low relief and resistant substrates, and for equatorial Africa and South America, which reflect the presence of subdued topography and the dense cover of rainforest vegetation.

In some parts of the world, suspended sediment yields can be extraordinarily high (Walling, 1987), exceeding 10,000 tons per square kilometer per year ($t\ km^{-2}\ a^{-1}$). The highest value comes from the Huangfuchuan River of China, a 3,199 square kilometer catchment with a mean annual yield of 53,000 $t\ km^{-2}\ a^{-1}$. This is a tributary of the Hwang Ho (Yellow) River and drains a gully region of loess. The reasons for such high values are probably highly varied and include the presence

Land Surface Processes. TABLE 1. Estimated Denudation Rate for the World's 35 Largest Drainage Basins Based on Solid and Solute Transport Rates

	DRAINAGE AREA (10^6 KM^2)	TOTAL DENUDATION (MM PER 1,000 YEARS)	CHEMICAL* DENUDATION (MM PER 1,000 YEARS)	CHEMICAL DENUDATION (AS % OF TOTAL)
Amazon	6.15	70	13	18
Zaire (Congo)	3.82	7	3	42
Mississippi	3.27	44	9	20
Nile	2.96	15	2	10
Paraná (La Plata)	2.83	19	5	28
Yenisei	2.58	9	7	80
Ob	2.50	7	5	70
Lena	2.43	11	9	81
Chiang Jiang (Yangtze)	1.94	133	37	28
Amur	1.85	13	3	22
Mackenzie	1.81	30	10	33
Volga	1.35	20	13	64
Niger	1.21	24	11	47
Zambezi	1.20	31	3	11
Nelson	1.15	—	—	—
Murray	1.06	13	2	18
St. Lawrence	1.03	13	12	89
Orange	1.02	58	3	5
Orinoco	0.99	91	13	14
Ganges	0.98	271	22	8
Indus	0.97	124	16	13
Tocantins	0.90	—	—	—
Chari	0.88	3	1	29
Yukon	0.84	37	10	28
Danube	0.81	47	16	35
Mekong	0.79	95	20	21
Hwang Ho (Yellow)	0.77	529	11	2
Shatt-el-Arab	0.75	104	11	11
Rio Grande	0.67	9	3	38
Columbia	0.67	29	13	46
Kolyma	0.64	5	2	31
Colorado	0.64	84	6	7
São Francisco	0.60	—	—	—
Brahmaputra	0.58	677	34	5
Dnieper	0.50	6	5	88

*Allowance made for nondenudational component of solute loads.

SOURCE: After Summerfield (1991, Table 15.6). Reprinted by permission of Pearson Education Limited.

of erodible stores of material (e.g. loess, glacial drift, volcanic ash), high relief and recent tectonic uplift, intense human pressures on the ground surface that have caused accelerated late Holocene erosion, and either a semiarid climate (with a limited vegetation cover) or highly erosive rainfall regimes dominated by tropical storms or very high annual totals.

Most of the data discussed so far have primarily involved suspended sediment loads. Comparative data on bedload transport fluxes under different climatic conditions are remarkably sparse. This applies not least to data for the world's arid zones where, because of infrequent and unpredictable floods, there is a paucity of reliable field data. A study by Laronne and Reid (1993) in

Land Surface Processes. TABLE 2. The Geographical Origins of Dissolved Loads to the Oceans and Variations of Chemical Erosion According to Morphoclimatic Region

| CLIMATIC REGION | AREA OF EXOREIC RUNOFF* | EXOREIC RUNOFF[†] | TRANSPORT OF SILICA | | TRANSPORT OF IONS | | CHEMICAL EROSION $(T\ KM^{-2}\ A^{-1})$ |
			DISSOLVED LEAD TO OCEANS $(10^6\ T\ A^{-1})$	%	DISSOLVED LEAD TO OCEANS $(10^6\ T\ A^{-1})$	%	
Tundra and taiga	20.0	10.7	15.0	3.9	466	13.1	14
Humid taiga	3.15	3.4	5.0	1.3	74	2.1	15.5
Very humid taiga	0.2	0.6	1.1	0.2	9	0.25	32
Pluvial temperate	4.5	15.3	45	11.8	540	15.4	80
Humid temperate	7.45	7.75	17.5	4.6	407	12.0	35
Temperate	6.7	3.35	9.4	2.5	301	8.8	28
Semiarid temperate	3.35	1.05	2.7	1.0	130	3.7	24
Seasonal tropical	13.25	5.85	31.1	8.2	119	3.4	6.4
Humid tropical	9.2	8.85	38.2	10.2	239	8.0	15.5
Very humid tropical (plains)	6.9	18.45	78.6	20.8	165	4.8	22
Very humid tropical (mountains)	7.95	24.05	130	34.4	908	25.6	67
Total of tropical zone	37.3	57.2	278	73.6	1431	41.8	—
Arid	17.2	0.65	3.9	1.0	3457	2.8	3
Pluvial regions of strong relief	12.65	40	176	47	1457	42	≈74

*Percentage of total land surface area.

[†]Percentage of total exoreic runoff quantity.

SOURCE: After Meybeck (1979).

the Negev Desert, Israel, based on monitoring of bedload movement in flash flood events, indicates just how crucial continuous monitoring of bedloading in such environments could be. Their data show that ephemeral desert rivers could be as much as 400 times more efficient at transporting coarse material than their perennial counterparts in humid zones. They argue that this may be because of the relative lack of bed armoring in desert streams. They suggest that the poor or nonexistent development of armored layers could be a function of the rapid rise and fall in water discharge that is characteristic of flash floods, the high rates of sediment transport, and the extended intervals of dormancy between flood events. These characteristics reduce the tendency toward the size-selective transport of clasts

and the winnowing of fines that are each thought to promote armoring in perennial channels.

Milliman (1990, 1991) has drawn attention to the particularly large amounts of sediment transported to the oceans from southeastern Asia and Oceania. These areas account for only about 15 percent of the land area draining into the oceans but contribute about 70 percent of the flux of suspended sediment. In contrast, rivers draining the Eurasian Arctic, a basin area similar in size to southern Asia and Oceania combined, contribute about two orders of magnitude less sediment.

Milliman and Syvitski (1992) believe that the sediment fluxes from small mountainous rivers, many of which discharge directly onto active continental margins, may well have been largely neglected in the past,

Land Surface Processes. FIGURE 1. Relationship between Mean Annual Sediment Yield and Mean Annual Precipitation. (After Walling and Kleo, 1979. With permission of IAHS Press.)

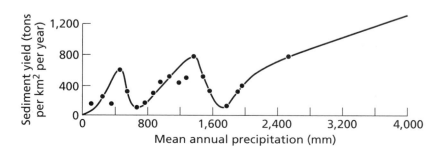

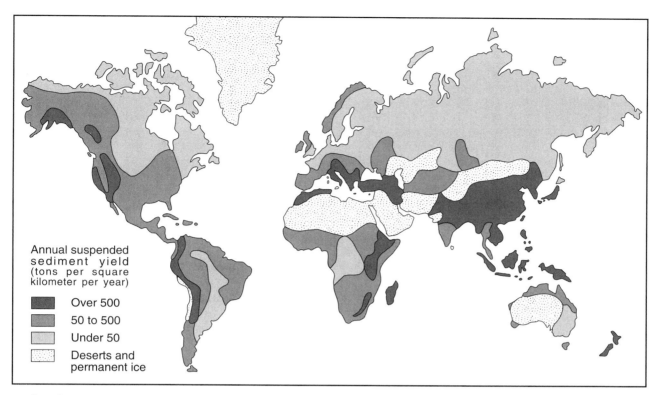

Land Surface Processes. Figure 2. A Global Map of the Pattern of Specific Suspended Sediment Yield Based on Data from over 1,500 Measuring Stations. (After Walling, 1987, Figure 4.4. Copyright John Wiley & Sons Limited. Reproduced with permission.)

but that their contribution of sediment to the oceans may be remarkably important. They point out, for example, that in North America the loads of the Sustitna, Cooper, Stekine, and Yukon collectively exceed that of the Mississippi. In Europe the Semani River of Albania discharges more than twice as much sediment as do the Garonne, Loire, Seine, Rhine, Weser, Elbe, Oder, and Vistula combined.

It is important, however, to stress that it is probably relative relief rather than elevation (altitude) per se that is the crucial control of rates of denudation. There need be no relationship between elevation and either mean slope gradient or local relief.

It has frequently been observed that sediment yield is scale dependent. Yields tend to be greater per unit area for small basins than for large, at least for basins up to 2,000 square kilometers in area. The basin area effect may largely disappear when very large basins are considered because the topographic controls tend to become less variable between basins at this scale. The inverse relationship is due to the following properties of smaller basins in relation to larger ones:

1. They commonly have steeper gradients, which encourage more rapid rates of erosion.

2. Small streams have a lack of flood plains, which gives less opportunity for sediment storage, resulting in a higher sediment delivery ratio.
3. Small basins are more prone to being blanketed by one high-intensity storm event, giving high maximum erosion rates per unit area.

However, the inverse relationship between sediment yield and basin area suggested above is by no means invariable. For example, Church and Slaymaker (1989) found a positive correlation between sediment and basin area in glaciated basins in British Columbia, Canada, at all spatial scales up to 30,000 square kilometers (see also Owens and Slaymaker, 1992). They explained this result in terms of secondary remobilization of Quaternary sediments along river valleys.

Glacial Denudation. Several methods have recently been used to measure amounts of glacial erosion. These have included the following:

1. The use of artificial marks on rock surfaces later scraped by advancing ice
2. The installation of plattens to measure abrasional loss
3. Measurements of the suspended, solutional, and bedload content of glacial meltwater streams and of the area of the respective glacial basins

4. The use of sediment cores from lake basins of known age that are fed by glacial meltwater

5. Reconstructions of pre- or interglacial land surfaces

6. Estimates of the volume of glacial drift in a given region and its comparison with the area of the source region of that drift.

The first four methods apply to present-day glacierized regions and the last two to regions of Pleistocene glaciation. It is by no means obvious that the two different time scales will lead to comparable results and that it is possible to use present-day rates of glacial denudation to infer what happened in the past. As Harbor and Warburton (1992, p. 751) have remarked, "During full-glacial times, . . . basins would have higher percentage glacier cover, but also far greater ice thickness, discharges, velocities, basal shear stresses and basal water pressures." Modern glaciers, the majority of which are decaying and retreating, are not necessarily satisfactory analogues for the vastly more active and substantial glaciers and icecaps of full glacial times.

There is also the problem of knowing how much of the debris transported by glaciers was originally glacially entrained. Much material falls onto glaciers as a result of nonglacial processes (e.g., rockfalls). In some high-relief, high-altitude areas, rates of denudation might be high in the absence of glaciation.

In 1968, Embleton and King tried to bring together most of the available information on rates of glacial erosion. They suggested, though with some caution given the paucity and sparseness of data, that erosion rates for active glaciers were 1,000 to 5,000 m^2 per km^2 per year and several times greater than for rivers. However, they drew an important distinction between the role of glaciers and the role of ice sheets on low-angle surfaces, suggesting that the latter would be relatively powerless.

When Andrews (1975) came to review the available data, he came to rather different conclusions than Embleton and King. Indeed, he believed that the view that the mean rate of erosion by active glaciers was in the range 1,000–5,000 millimeters per thousand years (mm $1,000$ a^{-1}) was probably wrong by a factor of between 2 and 10! He suggested that a more reasonable estimate was a rate of 50–1,000 mm $1,000$ a^{-1}, broadly the same as for normal fluvial catchments. He noted, moreover, that most of the data on rates determined from current meltwater streams are biased in favor of high mountain environments and are largely restricted to valley glaciers that are wet based. Such values, he argued (p. 122), "cannot be considered typical of values for the erosion of bedrock floors by a large ice sheet."

Eleven years later, Drewry (1986) again stressed the inadequacy of data on this important subject and presented some published data on erosion rates for selected glaciers based on the measurement of suspended sediment transport and suspended and bedload transport. The values range from 73 to 30,000 mm $1,000$ a^{-1} (with a mean of about 4,000 mm $1,000$ a^{-1}).

An example of the use of stratigraphic methods to determine long-term rates of glacial erosion is provided by the study of Bell and Laine (1985). They sought to estimate the degree of erosion achieved by the glaciation of the Laurentide region of North America through a study of sediment volumes determined through seismic studies and Deep Sea Drilling Project boreholes. They calculated that over a period of about three million years (the approximate duration of midlatitude glaciation in the late Cenozoic) somewhere between 120 and 200 meters (650 feet) of erosion would be required over the glaciated Canadian Shield to produce the observed volume of sediment. This is equivalent to a rate of between 40 and 67 mm $1,000$ a^{-1}. The region was not, of course, glaciated throughout the whole of the 3-million-year period, but even so these rates are less than most of the short-term rates determined from meltwater load studies. Plainly, however, great care needs to be exercised in using offshore sediment volumes because of the problems of determining the sediment source and because of potential problems caused by sea level changes.

Clearly, geographical location is an important control of the rate of glacial erosion. Some areas will have had characteristics that would limit the power of glacial erosion (e.g., resistant lithologies, low relief, frozen beds), but other areas would have suffered severe erosion (e.g., nonresistant lithologies, proximity to former fast ice streams, thawed beds).

Other Types of Exogenic Change. In addition to the major classes of denudational change discussed so far, it is also important to recognize the changes that may take place on slopes, on coasts, and by wind action. There is a great deal of information on rates of soil movement on slopes and on the operation of processes such as soil creep (Young and Saunders, 1986). Equally, there is a great deal of information on rates of coastal change, including cliff retreat. Sunamura (1992), using data from many parts of the world, found a general lithological control of the rates of cliff recession over periods that generally last from 10 to 100 years: 10^{-3} to 10^{-2} meters per year (m a^{-1}) for limestone; 10^{-2} m a^{-1} for flysch and shale; 10^{-1} to 1 m a^{-1} for Quaternary deposits; and 10 m a^{-1} for unconsolidated volcanic ejecta.

Rates of coastal erosion for the United States, including cliffed and noncliffed shorelines, have been plotted by Dolan and Kimball (1985). Retreat is dominant around much of the coastline. This is particularly true of the eastern seaboard, much of which is retreating at between 0.1 and 2.9 m a^{-1}. There are, however, a few local stretches (e.g., in Georgia and North Carolina) where accretion has been taking place. Conversely, there are a few small stretches where the rate of retreat lies between 3.0 and 5.0 m a^{-1}. The Gulf Coast also shows a dominance of retreat, most notably in the vicinity of the Mississippi delta and to the west of it. On the western coast of the United States, the rates of change appear to be markedly lower, which probably reflects the fact that it is in a very different tectonic and lithological situation from the eastern and southern coasts. Thus rates of retreat are nearly always less than 1 m a^{-1}. Some accretion has been taking place in southern California and also along the southern coast of Washington State, but even in these areas there are locations where cliff retreat is taking place at rates of up to 0.5 m a^{-1}.

Taking the United States as a whole and dividing it up on the basis of different shoreline types, Dolan and Kimball found that the pattern of rates was for the most part predictable. Coasts with fine-grained sediments, deltas, and mudflats that offer low levels of resistance to wave attack have the highest mean erosion rates (approximately 2.0 m a^{-1}). Most sandy beaches and barrier islands erode at slightly lower rates (roughly 0.8 m a^{-1}). By contrast, the rocky shorelines of the Atlantic coast show rates of accretion of as much as 1.0 m a^{-1}.

With respect to rates of denudation by wind, our data are surprisingly sparse. There is some information on rates of abrasion and land surface lowering by deflation, but studies of the amounts of material transported by dust storms suggest that it is an important agency of change in drylands underlain by susceptible materials. Global eolian (wind-borne) dust contributions to the atmosphere may reach 5,000 million metric tons per year (Schutz, 1980).

Conclusion. This discussion of rates of land surface process operation has essentially been concerned with long-term rates of change under predominantly natural conditions. However, natural rates have been greatly modified by human activities. [See Anthropogeomorphology; and Desertification.] Sediment yields have been transformed by land use and land cover changes, rates of weathering have been modified by such processes as acid deposition, mass movements on slopes have been generated by such actions as loading and undercutting, coasts have suffered from accelerated erosion because of sediment starvation created by engineering structures (e.g., dams), and wind erosion has been stimulated by vegetation removal and surface disturbance.

[See also Climate Impacts; Coastlines; Cryosphere; Earth History; Erosion; Glaciation; Natural Hazards; and Plate Tectonics.]

BIBLIOGRAPHY

Andrews, J. T. Glacial Systems—An Approach to Glaciers and Their Environments. North Scituate, 1975.

Bell, M., and E. P. Laine. "Erosion of the Laurentide Region of North America by Glacial and Glaciofluvial Processes." Quaternary Research 23 (1985), 154–174.

Church, M., and O. Slaymaker. "Disequilibrium of Holocene Sediment Yield in Glaciated British Columbia." Nature 337 (1989), 452–454.

Dolan, R., and S. Kimball. "Map of Coastal Erosion and Accretion." In National Atlas of the United States of America. Reston, Va.: Interior, Geological Survey, 1985.

Drewry, D. Glacial Geologic Processes. London: Edward Arnold, 1986.

Embleton, C., and C. A. M. King. Glacial and Periglacial Geomorphology. London: Edward Arnold, 1968.

Goudie, A. S. The Changing Earth: Rates of Geomorphological Processes. Oxford: Blackwell, 1995, p. 302. A general review of available information on a wide spectrum of geomorphologic processes.

Harbor, J., and J. Warburton. "Glaciation and Denudation Rates." Nature 356 (1992), 751.

Laronne, J. B., and I. Reid. "Very High Rates of Bedload Sediment Transport by Ephemeral Desert Rivers." Nature 336 (1993), 148–150.

Meybeck, M. "Concentrations des Eaux Fluviales en Éléments Majeurs et Apports en Solution aux Océans." Revue de Géologie Dynamique et de Géographie Physique 21 (1979), 215–246.

———. "Global Chemical Weathering of Surficial Rocks Estimated from River Dissolved Loads." American Journal of Science 287 (1987), 401–428.

Milliman, J. D. "Fluvial Sediment in Coastal Seas: Flux and Fate." Nature and Resources 26 (1990), 12–22.

———. "Flux and Fate of Fluvial Sediment and Water in Coastal Seas." In Oceanic Margin Processes in Coastal Change, edited by R. F. C. Mantouva, J.-M. Martin, and R. Wollest, Chichester, U.K., and New York: Wiley, 1991.

Milliman, J. D., and J. P. M. Syvitski. "Geomorphic/Tectonic Control of Sediment Discharge to the Ocean: The Importance of Small Mountainous Rivers." Journal of Geology 100 (1992), 525–544.

Owens, P., and O. Slaymaker. "Late Holocene Sediment Yields in Small Alpine and Subalpine Drainage Basins, British Columbia." IAHS Publication 209 (1992), 147–154.

Schutz, L. "Long-Range Transport of Desert Dust with Special Emphasis on the Sahara." Annals of the New York Academy of Sciences 338 (1980), 515–532.

Summerfield, M. A. Global Geomorphology: An Introduction to the Study of Landforms. Harlow: Longman Scientific and Technical, 1991.

Walling, D. E. "Rainfall, Runoff and Erosion of the Land: A Global View." In Energetics of the Physical Environment, edited by K. J. Gregory. Chichester, U.K., and New York: Wiley, 1997, pp. 89–117.

Walling, D. E., and A. H. A. Kleo. "Sediment Yields of Rivers in Areas of Low Precipitation: A Global View." International Association of Scientific Hydrology Publication 128 (1979), 479–493.

Walling, D. E., and B. W. Webb. "The Dissolved Loads of Rivers: A Global Overview." International Association of Scientific Hydrology Publication 141 (1983), 3–20.

Young, A., and I. Saunders. "Rates of Surface Processes and Denudation." In Hillslope Processes, edited by A. D. Abrahams. pp. 1–27. Boston: Allen and Unwin, 1986.

—ANDREW S. GOUDIE

LAND USE

[*This entry consists of two articles:* Land Use and Land Cover *and* Land Use Planning. *The first article covers the role of land use and land cover in global change and discusses its contributions to potential climate change, biodiversity, and sustainability over the past one hundred years and into the future. The second article defines the major issues linking global change (climate, biodiversity, and sustainability) to land planning.*]

Land Use and Land Cover

Change in land use and land cover is a central component in global environmental change. It significantly affects the structure and function of the biosphere through its impact on the state of terrestrial ecosystems and the flow of global biogeochemical cycles. Furthermore, land use and land cover change affects almost all "sustainability" issues, as well as biodiversity, disease vectors, potable water sources, and agricultural production. The central importance of land use and land cover changes stems from humankind's derivation of the majority of resources for its material existence and well-being from the surface of the Earth. Compounding this importance, the history of the human–Earth relationship is one of ever increasing pace, magnitude, and spatial reach of changes in the biosphere, including the land surface (Meyer and Turner, 1994).

Land cover refers to the biophysical condition of the terrestrial surface of the Earth. Forests, grasslands, wetlands, deserts, and settlements are broad categories of land cover. In contrast, *land use* refers to the human management of the biophysical condition for an intended purpose. This management may be direct and highly manipulative, as in farming, or obscured through decisions to preserve or not to develop, as in the case of biosphere reserves or perceived marginal lands left "underused." Cultivation, pastoralism and grazing, recreation, nature reserves, transportation infrastructure, and housing are broad categories of land use.

Management of land covers with the intent to increase resource extraction is ancient and probably began with the use of fire in the hunt of wildlife. Burning for this purpose may have contributed to worldwide Quaternary extinctions (Martin and Klein, 1984) and to the extension of grasslands and fire-dominated ecosystems in Africa, Australia, and elsewhere (Pyne, 1995). Large-scale use and cover changes, however, awaited the domestication of biota, also known as the "agricultural revolution." Evolving in its complexity and reach, the worldwide effects of this agrotechnological epoch were dramatic, if difficult to measure with precision. Between 1700 and 1980, as much as 1,162,000 hectares of

forest cover, 72,000 hectares of grassland (Richard, 1990), and an unestimated area of wetlands (Williams, 1990) had been converted to farmland throughout the world. These figures do not consider the apparently large land area devoted to shifting cultivation, cycling in and out of crop, bush and shrub, and forest covers, which may have been far more prevalent than previously believed in vast reaches of the tropics. Indeed, various regions of the world, especially in the Americas, are only today becoming as extensively utilized for cultivation as they were before the global expansion of European cultures and economies in the fifteenth century (Denevan, 1992; Turner and Butzer, 1992). Early livestock activities also had significant use and cover impact through the use of fire, as pastoralists sought to increase control over the forageable biomass for their herds. [*See* Biomass.]

European colonialism during the fifteenth to nineteenth centuries profoundly affected global land uses and covers, largely through the transoceanic transfer of flora, fauna, people, diseases, and technologies (Crosby, 1986). Crop species exchanges, especially between the Western and Eastern Hemispheres, forever changed dietary patterns and, with them, land use strategies and land covers. Foremost among these changes were the extensive spread of the plow and European livestock. The plow gave plants access to nutrients stored deep within soils and opened American grasslands to extensive cultivation. Introducing horses, cattle, and sheep, meanwhile, changed uses and cover across a wide range of environments. Ultimately, ranching and range animals encouraged ranchers to "Africanize" grasses throughout the American tropics.

The pace, magnitude, and spatial reach of land use and land cover change continued to escalate with the Industrial Revolution. As the industrial world stretched its reach, the global synergism between technological capacity, population, and affluence increased dramatically, as did the demand for food, fiber, and living space. The resulting changes in land use and land cover were key elements in promoting an even more dramatic population growth rate in the middle of the twentieth century. In the nineteenth century, massive land use and land cover changes took place in North America and Australia, where cultivation and livestock became the dominant land uses, forcing land cover. By the middle of the twentieth century, the major trends were toward increased intensification of use in the middle latitudes and semitropics, and more recently widespread deforestation of the tropics and Siberia (Richards, 1990). Intensification has been registered by the spread of irrigated cultivation (cautiously estimated at about 2.5 million square kilometers; L'vovich et al., 1990, p. 242), especially that of wet rice (a large source of methane), and the adoption of modern hybrid species and their demands for fertilizers, herbicides, and pesticides that affect various critical trace cycles (e.g., CH_4, NO_2; Dale, 1997), as well as tropospheric pollution (Chameides et al., 1994). And while the developed world undergoes forestation, especially in western Europe and northeastern North America, international agricultural and timber markets shift corporate production to lower-cost reigns in the tropics or Siberia. Even where command economies remain intact, such as China, significant changes in land use and land cover remain, owing to increasing stress on land resources. [See Food; and Food and Agriculture Organization.]

The current global state and condition of different land uses and covers is not well known, despite global observations from satellites and other remotely sensed imagery and international programs designated to gather such information. The Intergovernmental Panel on Climate Change (Leemans et al., 1996), for example, concludes that various aggregate land cover global data sets disagree by as much as 2.5 million hectares, a margin of error that increases significantly if the location of the different land use and covers is considered. Global ground-based inventories collected by international agencies rely on country-produced information, frequently inaccurate and politicized. Nevertheless, it seems that the pace of various land use and land cover changes globally continues to increase dramatically, with shifting emphasis in kind and location.

If the current trajectories of change continue well into the twenty-first century, as seems likely, then the following changes in land use and land cover seem especially important, independent of potential climate warming: (1) the expansion of urban and periurban (suburban) settlement, including roads and recreation spaces, everywhere but especially in Asia and frequently at the cost of prime agricultural lands; (2) increasing forest cover in the periurban developed world and decreasing agricultural uses of more marginal lands; (3) the loss of natural wetlands to settlement and agriculture and the growth of anthropogenic wetlands, especially in the developed world; (4) the intensification of land management in agriculture, from satellite- and computer-assisted farming to the spread of modern-input, wet rice cultivation; (5) significant timber extraction in tropical and Siberian forests; (6) large-scale tropical deforestation; (7) the expansion of mining and mineral extraction in frontier lands; (8) increasing livestock activities in developing regions; and (9) near-term stress on semiarid landscapes by impoverished peoples and by government-sponsored irrigation schemes. As the twenty-first century progresses, little if any land will remain unclaimed or under some form of management, even if set aside as reserves. [See Agriculture and Agricultural Land.]

The past and current trends in land use and land cover have significant implications for global environmental change. Use and cover, for example, serve as sources and sinks of trace gases (e.g., deforestation vs. forestation). In 1980, 1,500 petagrams (1 petagram equals 10^{15} grams) of carbon were estimated to be stored in the soil, along with another 560 petagrams stored in biomass (Houghton and Skole, 1990). Human uses (e.g., plowing, planting, deforesting) release this carbon to the atmosphere, while forestation takes it back. In the late twentieth century, approximately 50 percent of human-released CO_2 in the atmosphere was attributable to changes in land use and land cover. Industrial production and consumption now dominate carbon emissions, but land changes contribute as much as 30 percent (Houghton and Skole, 1990) and are the largest source of human-released methane (CH_4), the most potent "greenhouse gas." The condition of global land use and cover also affects the hydrologic cycle, especially through impacts on the Walker circulation (Henderson-Sellers and Gornitz, 1984). Finally, human uses of the land may usurp as much as 40 percent of the Earth's net primary productivity (Vitousek et al., 1990).

Impacts on the biochemical cycles of the biosphere are more than matched by those on landscape fragmentation and biotic diversity. The fragmentation of tropical forests into small patches may endanger their function, productivity, and diversity (e.g., Laurance et al., 1997). The fracturing of landscapes in general by complex sets of cropping, grazing, and settlement uses, especially in periurban areas, raises serious questions about species migration in the face of potential climate change (Root and Schneider, 1995). Also, the transformation of complex ecosystems, such as wetlands and tropical forests, into biotically simple if intensive cropping or grazing systems leads to soil degradation and loss and to increased fluvial sedimentation. For example, intensive land uses may lead to salinization, an important and difficult-to-reverse land degradation. These processes tend to decrease biotic diversity, either directly by anthropogenic changes in the vegetation or indirectly through the regeneration of vegetation. Habitat loss (land cover change) is estimated to lead to the annual loss of fourteen thousand to forty thousand species (Hughes, Daily, and Ehrlich, 1997), a rate labeled by some as "mass extinction" (Myers, 1997).

With the movement of the science and policy of global change toward the sustainability of the human–environment relationship, the prominence of changing land uses and covers increases (Vitousek, 1994). The sustainability principle implies maintaining an increasing human population at higher levels of material consumption with minimal impacts and drawdowns on the biosphere. These aims are largely carried out on land-based production systems within economic contexts that find difficulty in reconciling the often incongruent environmental impacts between individual actions and social benefits and between immediate and longer-term needs. As well, the ability to identify and measure what land use systems are sustainable or not is increasingly difficult because of "substitutability"—replacements for nature, land, labor, and capital. What is environmentally sustainable becomes intimately intertwined with what is economically viable.

These issues notwithstanding, changes in land use and cover involve not only "hot spots" of environmental degradation but also critical regions of human–environment relationships—those where the trajectory of change is toward environmental drawdowns linked to the decreasing material condition of the occupants (Kasperson, Kasperson, and Turner, 1995). The death of the Aral Sea is perhaps the most dramatic modern-day case of land use–driven human–environment collapse. Not only were the sea's area and volume reduced in the late twentieth century by 60 percent and 66 percent, respectively, but its once healthy fishing industry is also dead, symbolized by the decaying fishing fleet stranded in the sands that were once the lake's margin (Kotlyakov, 1991; Micklin, 1988). These impacts are directly related to the development of massive and poorly constructed irrigation systems on the two rivers that sustain the Aral Sea. The cropping systems were so mismanaged, and their efficiency in terms of water use and production so poor, that farming was sustainable only through state subsidies; moreover, their chemical inputs were so inappropriate that infant mortality rose, apparently from impacts on potable water. Yet these immediate land use causes belie others embedded more deeply within the fabric of the command economy that conceived and orchestrated the Aral Sea irrigation systems. These other causes included state needs for international stable currencies, unchecked state authority, distant production and management decisions, and rapid local population growth demanding employment opportunities. [See Aral Sea, Desiccation of the.]

The complexity of and synergisms in the causes of the Aral Sea critical region typify those of case-specific land use and land cover change everywhere. They tend to be lost, however, as the spatial and temporal scale of analysis enlarges. Over the long term and at large regional and global scales, the so-called PAT variables (population, affluence, and technology) venture to the statistical forefront (Meyer and Turner, 1992). The explanatory separation of the short term and local from the long term and global is foreboding because it strikes at the heart of different and contested ways of understanding. Those communities engaged in the "big" picture (i.e., the long-term global condition) that seek ways to model and project human–environment impacts typically find power in PAT and related variables. Other communities focus on more localized portrayals (e.g.,

recent regional changes), with narratives of the dynamics of changes revealing different kinds of variables, such as policy and institutions, complete with different causal implications. The two positions need not be as polarized as they have been in the past, and various integrations of them are under way in regionally scaled projects designed to elucidate their connections.

[See also Albedo; Biological Diversity; Biomes; Deforestation; Desertification; Ecosystems; Fire; Forestation; Human Impacts, article on Human Impacts on Biota; International Geosphere–Biosphere Programme; International Human Dimensions of Global Environmental Change Programme; Land Reclamation; Parks and Natural Preserves; Remote Sensing; Sustainable Development; United Nations Environment Programme; and Wilderness.]

BIBLIOGRAPHY

Chameides, W. L., P. S. Kasibhatla, J. Yienger, and H. Levy II. "Growth of Continental-Scale Metro-Agro-Plexes, Regional Ozone Pollution, and World Food Production." *Science* 264 (1994), 74–77.

Crosby, A. W. *Ecological Imperialism: The Biological Expansion of Europe 900–1900*. Cambridge: Cambridge University Press, 1986.

Dale, V. H. "The Relationship between Land-Use Change and Climate Change." *Ecological Applications* 7 (1997), 753–769.

Denevan, W. M. "The Pristine Myth: The Landscape of the Americas in 1492." *Annals Association of American Geographers* 82 (1992), 369–385.

Henderson-Sellers, A., and V. Gornitz. "Possible Climatic Impacts of Land Cover Transformations, with Particular Emphasis on Tropical Deforestation." *Climate Change* 6 (1984), 231–257.

Houghton, R. A., and D. L. Skole. "Carbon." In *The Earth as Transformed by Human Action: Global and Regional Changes in the Biosphere over the Past 300 Years*, edited by B. L. Turner, W. C. Clark, R. W. Kates, J. F. Richards, J. T. Mathews, and W. B. Meyer, pp. 393–408. Cambridge: Cambridge University Press, 1990.

Hughes, J. B., G. C. Daily, and P. C. Ehrlich. "Population Diversity: Its Extent and Extinction." *Science* 278 (1997), 689–692.

Kasperson, J. X., R. E. Kasperson, and B. L. Turner II. *Regions at Risk: Comparisons of Threatened Environments*. Tokyo: United Nations University Press, 1995.

Kotlyakov, V. M. "The Aral Sea Basin: A Critical Environmental Zone. *Environment* 33.1 (1991), 4–9, 36–38.

Laurance, W. F., S. G. Laurance, L. V. Ferreira, J. M. Rankin-de Merona, C. Gascon, and T. M. Lovejoy. "Biomass Collapse in Amazonian Forest Fragments." *Science* 278 (1997), 1117–1118.

Leemans, R., S. Agrawala, J. A. Edmonds, M. C. MacCracken, R. Moss, and P. S. Ramakrishnan. "Mitigation: Cross-Sectoral and Other Issues." In *Impacts Adaptation and Mitigation Options: Working Group 2 Contribution to IPCC Second Assessment Report*, edited by R. T. Watson, M. C. Zinyower, and R. H. Moss, pp. 799–819. Cambridge: Cambridge Univeristy Press, 1996.

L'vovich, M. I., G. F. White, A. V. Belyaev, J. Kindler, N. I. Koronkevic, T. R. Lee, and G. V. Voropaev. "Use and Transformation of Terrestrial Water Systems." In *The Earth as Transformed by Human Action: Global and Regional Changes in the Biosphere over the Past 300 Years*, edited by B. L. Turner

II, W. C. Clark, R. W. Kates, J. F. Richards, J. T. Mathews, and W. B. Meyer, pp. 236–252. Cambridge: Cambridge University Press, 1990.

Martin, P. S., and R. G. Klein, eds. *Quaternary Extinctions: A Prehistoric Revolution*. Tucson: University of Arizona Press, 1984.

Meyer, W. B., and B. L. Turner II. "Human Population Growth and Global Land-Use/Cover Change." *Annual Review of Ecology and Systematics* 23 (1992), 39–61.

———, eds. *Changes in Land Use and Land Cover: A Global Perspective*. Cambridge: Cambridge University Press, 1994.

Micklin, P. P. "Desiccation of the Aral Sea: A Water Management Disaster in the Soviet Union." *Science* 241 (1988), 1170–1176.

Myers, N. J. "Mass Extinction and Evolution." *Science* 278 (1997), 597–598.

Pyne, S. J. *World Fire: The Culture of Fire on Earth*. New York: Henry Holt and Company, 1995.

Richards, J. F. "Land Tranformation." In *The Earth as Transformed by Human Action: Global and Regional Changes in the Biosphere over the Past 300 Years*, edited by B. L. Turner II, W. C. Clark, R. W. Kates, J. F. Richards, J. T. Mathews, and W. B. Meyer, pp. 163–177. Cambridge: Cambridge University Press, 1990.

Root, T. L., and S. H. Schneider. "Ecology and Climate: Research Strategies and Implications." *Science* 269 (1995), 331–341.

Turner, B. L., II, and K. W. Butzer. "The Columbian Encounter and Land-Use Change." *Environment* 43 (1992), 16–20, 37–44.

Vitousek, P. M., P. R. Ehrlich, A. H. Ehrlich, and P. Matson. "Human Appropriation of the Products of Photosynthesis." *BioScience* 36 (1990), 368–373.

Williams, M., ed. *Wetlands: A Threatened Landscape*. Oxford and Cambridge, Mass.: Blackwell, 1990.

—B. L. TURNER II AND ERIC G. KEYS

Land Use Planning

Land use planning has received major attention within the global environmental change debate. The main reasons for this interest are the threats imposed by climate change, deforestation, desertification, and the loss of biodiversity in general (Meyer and Turner, 1994; Ostrom, 1990; Parry, 1990). Land use has a peculiar economic feature in that it has a derived nature. Production, consumption, investment, recreation, and human actions in general require the use of geographical space for their operation. Economic activities are projected on geographical space in various manifestations, such as housing, infrastructure, and agriculture, depending on the economic functions concerned. In a strict sense, however, space does not have an intrinsic value except as a capital asset.

Changes in land use are both a cause and an effect of global environmental changes. The spatial mapping of human activities has direct consequences for the environmental conditions of an area, since there are spatially distinct and conflicting land use possibilities (Frederick and Rosenberg, 1994; Walker, 1993). Land use choices also frame the development and the spatial pattern of economic activities, thus influencing the type

of medium- to long-term development, and the relationship between human activities and the environment. Furthermore, land use offers glaring examples of spatial environmental externalities. Externalities are costs accruing to an individual or group that are not included in the price of goods or services traded in the marketplace, for instance, air or water pollution caused by energy production, or landscape degradation caused by agriculture. A significant part of environmental externalities may be seen as distorted and unbalanced land use, biased in favor of specific activities that are incompatible with the environment.

Land use planning and management, as activities that seek the assessment of land potential and suitable land exploitation, become important analytical and policy issues in this context (Finco and Nijkamp, 1997). This also explains the relevance of the land use planning theme within the broader context of the sustainability debate (Turner et al., 1995).

Over the last centuries, a substantial and progressive transformation of natural areas into areas that support agricultural, urban, or industrial functions has been observed. Table 1 illustrates the extent of this transformation for the period 1850–1980. Apart from Europe, where both forests and grassland show a slight increase, the overall trend is toward a substantial loss of natural land in favor of cropland. The combined pressure of factors such as population growth, food production, wood production, and land tenure arrangements (Pearce, 1991) has influenced as much as 40 percent of the forests and grassland of some areas. This trend will continue in the future, as the demand for space and natural resources will probably continue to rise. Recent projections for the year 2010 (van Dieren, 1995) show that the progressive reduction of forested areas is expected to continue along the trend illustrated in Table 1. Irrigated land, cropland, rangeland, and pasture will in-

Land Use: Land Use Planning. TABLE 1. Changes in Percentage Land Cover in the Period 1850–1980

	FORESTS	GRASSLAND	CROPLAND
Tropical Africa	−20	+9	+288
Latin America	−19	−23	+677
North America	−3	−22	+309
China	−39	−3	+79
South Asia	−43	−1	+196
Southeast Asia	−7	−25	+670
Europe	+4	+8	−4
Former Soviet Union	−12	−1	+147
All	−15	−1	+179

SOURCE: World Resources Institute (1987). Adapted from Pearce (1991).

crease in absolute terms, but their availability per capita will decrease. Without countermeasures, this will necessarily lead to a further pressure on land, to an increasing environmental load, and to an impoverishment of the natural resources capital.

The negative effects of land use exploitation are manifested in soil erosion, loss of habitats, increased vulnerability of the soil, decrease in the carrying capacity of land, landscape modification, and loss of natural amenities. In addition, society increasingly registers natural and environmental catastrophes, such as floods, landslides, and droughts. These catastrophes are not the result of an increased frequency and intensity of extreme events, such as weather events, since there is no evidence that such events have increased globally in the past century. Clear evidence of these changes is available only at the regional scale for climatic variability, but some changes have been toward greater variability; some toward lower variability (Intergovernmental Panel on Climate Change, 1996, p. 173). Catastrophes are, to a large extent, the result of intensive occupation of areas that are intrinsically exposed to natural hazards (such as flood plains, coastal areas, and seismic areas), but also of the loss of natural protections (such as forest covers), or of the modification of natural systems dynamics (such as river diversions). The overall effect is an increase in the damage from natural events, which reach the level of disasters with increased frequency.

Although the negative effects of land use exploitation are clear, land uses and land use management are still rather poorly understood. According to the World Bank (1992):

> Degradation and destruction of environmental systems and natural resources are now assuming massive proportions in some developing countries, threatening continued, sustainable development. It is now generally recognised that economic development itself can be an important contributing factor to growing environmental problems in the absence of appropriate safeguards. A greatly improved understanding of the natural resource base and environment systems that support national economies is needed if patterns of development that are sustainable can be determined and recommended to governments.

There are multiple conflicting functions involved in space consumption, and there are many intricate linkages between economy, society, and the environment, in which land use and space act as the vehicles for transmitting externalities. Major gaps in our knowledge of the dynamic spatial context of externalities remain, in spite of the significant improvement achieved in understanding these externalities.

Economics, Land Use Planning, and Sustainability. The limited attention given to natural resources within economics has partly impeded understanding of land use planning and sustainable development. The productive capacity of the natural environment as a major source of welfare was recognized by the physiocrats (members of a school of political economists founded in the eighteenth century and characterized chiefly by a belief that land is the source of all wealth), but this position has been the exception rather than the rule in economic thinking. The main welfare generators in classical economics are capital and labor, in addition to land. Classical economics also assigns a minor role to government and institutions that frame actual decisions in the market.

Post–World War II neoclassical thinking does not view nature as such as the generator of welfare (such as income per capita) equivalent to labor, capital, technology, and land. The role of environmental capital and goods in traditional neoclassical economics is rather modest: ". . . there seemed no reason to accord land any special treatment that would suggest its role is quite distinct from that of the other factors. Land could safely be subsumed under broader aggregate of capital . . ." (Randall and Castle, 1985, p. 573).

The externalities and limits to growth have become a new focal point of economic research in the past few decades (with regard to both renewable and nonrenewable resources). In view of the long-term threats exerted by the (apparently) inevitable and persistent changes in local and global environmental conditions, the major policy challenge is to avoid a tragedy of the commons (Hardin, 1968). Against this background, land use and the spatial–environmental aspects of the economy deserve more attention from economists and science in general. [*See the vignette* Tragedy of the Commons *in the article on* Commons.]

Sustainable Land Use. Following the report of the Brundtland Commission (World Commission on Environment and Development, 1987), the meaning, consequences, and socioeconomic implications of sustainable development have been addressed in a wealth of research. The intensity and importance of the debate centered on the concept of sustainability (Redclift, 1993) illustrates the significance of land use to it (Turner, 1997). [*See* Brundtland Commission.]

Bryden (1994) distinguishes three major dimensions that characterize sustainable land use (see also Lier and Taylor, 1998). The husbandry dimension relates to the durability, exploitability, and continuity of natural resources over a long time horizon. The use of croprotation systems, the careful use of scarce natural resources, and the rehabilitation of degraded land can be seen as actions oriented toward the husbandry dimension. Keeping the amount and quality of the natural resources stock is at the core of this dimension. The interdependence dimension focuses on aspects such as fragmentation, segmentation, and relations between different types of land use. Traditional farming offers examples of interdependence, in which the farm and the surrounding natural areas achieve an equilibrium based on interaction and mutual system resilience. Maintaining the type and quality of the natural–human system interactions is at the basis of the interdependence dimension. The ethics dimension refers in particular to obligations toward future generations. Concepts such as option value, existence values, and the like can be interpreted in terms of the ethics dimension.

Land use planning has been traditionally concerned with the solution of a fundamental trade-off: conservation versus economic exploitation (Lier and Taylor, 1998). Conservation refers to the preservation of the natural resources stock (for example, water, soil, air) and of the biological stock (such as the genetic pool), but also the re-creation of lost land (for example, reforestation of fallow land) and the rehabilitation of degraded land (for example, cleanup of contaminated sites). The relationship between conservation and sustainability is rather straightforward. Conservation involves the prevention of disruptive developments and the retracing of past developments to make the environmental stock available for future generations. The economic dimension of land use management, in contrast, refers to the relationship between sustainability and a durable socioeconomic system.

Economic Growth and Environmental Policy. The conflict between conservation and development dominated most of twentieth-century thinking. Following the Brundtland report, a different view has emerged: conservation and development might be simultaneously attainable if sufficient economic resources are available. The green Kuznets curve (Heintz and Verbruggen, 1997; Stern, 1996; Stern et al., 1996; de Bruyn and Opschoor, 1994; Selden and Song, 1994) proposes an inverted U-shape relationship between environmental degradation and gross national product per capita (Figure 1). At very low income levels, economic activity is limited, implying a low environmental impact. As development

proceeds, the rate of resource use (land and natural resources) increases, together with waste generation. Above a certain income level, however, environmental degradation is expected to decrease because of the combined effect of such factors as structural changes toward information-intensive activities, higher environmental expenditures possible with higher wealth, better enforcement of environmental regulations, and consumer preferences toward environmentally oriented goods and services. According to Stern (1996, p. 1), "There are both proximate causes of the [green Kuznets curve] relationship—changes in economic structure or product mix, changes in technology, and changes in input mix—as well as underlying causes, such as environmental regulation, awareness, and education. These effects act to counteract or exaggerate the gross impact of economic growth or the scale effect."

Stern analyzed a wide range of studies that cover several indicators of environmental degradation, such as air quality, water quality, deforestation, waste production, and greenhouse gas emissions. These studies confirm the U-shape for some air pollutants (such as sulfur dioxide, nitrogen oxides, suspended particulate matter), but also show that some other sources of environmental pressure, such as waste production, increase with wealth. For some other indicators the evidence is at best mixed. For greenhouse gas emissions, for instance, the studies found either a very high turning point or an increase of emissions with wealth. The indications for deforestation are also ambiguous: some studies suggested the existence of a turning point, some found no significant relationship between deforestation and wealth, and some others concluded that economic growth will not prevent deforestation.

In general, the evidence collected so far does not support the conclusion that the green Kuznets curve applies to all types of environmental degradation (O'Neill et al., 1996). The inverted U-shape has been observed for environmental issues that have a direct, short-term relationship with human health and that can be associated with high costs of environmental degradation and remediation. This relationship is doubtful when the degradation is not reversible and when there is a feedback effect from environmental quality to economic growth. This may apply to such resources as ecosystems, forests, soil, and land cover.

The validity of an inverted U-shape relationship between income and environmental degradation would justify an emphasis on economic growth to reach a gross domestic product level commensurate with sustainability in the long term. The need for environmental policy and land use planning is thus questioned. However, the assumptions involved, and the uncertainty surrounding the validity of the green Kuznets curve, are such that, at least in the medium term, economic growth does not ap-

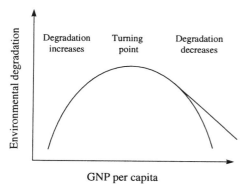

Land Use: Land Use Planning. FIGURE 1. The Green Kuznets Curve.

pear to be a substitute for environmental policy (Heintz and Verbruggen, 1997). In addition, as pointed out by Atkinson et al. (1997, p. 96), there is no evidence that this rise and fall of environmental degradation is the optimal development path, "in the sense that good policies could have increased overall welfare by flattening the Kuznets curve."

The green Kuznets curve does indicate, however, that environmental policy must be dynamic and evolve as societal and economic conditions change. The Dutch Committee for Long-Term Environmental Policy (1994) indicates five phases of the human–environment relationship: (1) environmental degradation as a side effect, (2) environmental degradation as a cost factor, (3) the environment as a boundary condition, (4) the environment as a policy-determining factor, and (5) the environment as an objective.

Land use planning emerges as an effective policy instrument especially in the fifth phase. It is an indirect means of addressing environmental objectives by focusing on the spatial distribution of human activities and natural resources. Land use is the result of a complex interplay among human and natural systems. By addressing them in their spatial dimension (in static terms, including spatial distribution, location and density, and dynamic terms, including attraction, pressure, and change), the issues of sustainability, environmental resilience, social equity, and economic competitiveness are ultimately addressed.

Spatial Concepts and Sustainability. Lier and Taylor (1998) consider three main spatial concepts as essential to land use design and management: integration and segregation, framework and dynamics, and ecological network concepts.

The concept of integration stresses the need for multiple coherent land uses, which implies different degrees of restrictions and expansion for different types of land use. While in the recent past, spatial segregation and functional parceling of the land have often been pursued for efficiency reasons, integration is based on the recognition of the importance of the links between multiple land uses. Examples are the attempts in certain areas to combine farming, recreation, and infrastructure development in such a way that the ecosystems can continue to function while also accommodating economic exploitation of the land (Nijkamp, 1997).

Different land uses show a different pace of change. Ecosystems and nature, in general, show a slow dynamics, while housing, recreation, and transport are highly dynamic. Different land use management approaches are therefore more or less appropriate depending on the dynamics of the systems considered. The framework concept aims at recognizing the dynamic features of the land and at applying stability measures for slow-dynamics sys-

tems, and flexible management schemes for highly dynamic ones.

The fragmentation of the landscape and the isolation of ever-smaller ecological areas may lead to situations in which the size and diversity of an ecological island is insufficient for the survival of plants and animals. Ecological networks aim at preventing this pattern by favoring the dispersion of species through an interconnected network of landscape elements, functional to the survival and spread of different species.

Trade-Offs in Sustainable Land Use Planning. Policies on sustainable development and land use planning have increasingly moved from a global level to a meso approach (areal level or a sector intervention). The introduction of the spatial dimension has also permitted the development of additional sustainability-management concepts, such as strong and weak sustainability (van Pelt, 1993; Pearce and Turner, 1990). Strong environmental sustainability would imply that in all areas an improvement of environmental quality conditions would take place. Weak sustainability refers to a situation in which an environmental degradation has to be accepted in some areas, provided that this is at least compensated for by improvements elsewhere. The substitution possibilities may be further widened if the concept of environmental sustainability is extended toward the broader concepts of sustainable development (which include the economic and social dimensions as well as the environmental dimension). Trade-offs between environmental, economic, and social conditions may thus be considered. Figure 2 illustrates these possibilities and can be used to identify the potential choice conflicts and trade-offs involved in land use management. Examples of critical choices are: (1) whether an environmental decay in a given area (for example, to allow industrial development) can be compensated by enhancing the environmental quality of another area (for example, reforestation of fallow land); (2) whether the benefits for a social group (such as citizens interested in the use of rural areas for recreation purposes) correspond to the interests of other groups (for example, farmers interested in simplifying landscape variability to increase production efficiency); or (3) whether the requirements placed on an economic sector (for example, transport) are compatible with other requirements (such as higher environmental quality).

This multifaceted feature attributes an integral economic value to land. Consequently, the question of whether some use of land leads to a sustainable outcome depends not only on external sustainability criteria of land use (for example, land degradation versus economic growth), but is also determined by internal sustainability criteria (for example, agriculture versus tourism). Some of these trade-offs are of a long-range

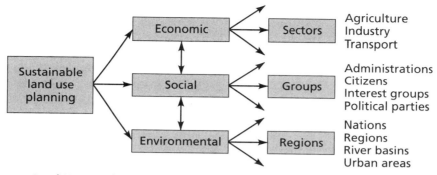

Land Use: Land Use Planning. FIGURE 2. Sustainable Land Use Planning.

nature and lead to intertemporal trade-offs, adding a temporal dimension to land use choices.

Methods for Sustainable Land Use Planning. The multifunctionality and complexity of land use is a source of much ambiguity in sustainable policy. There is no unidimensional denominator that can be used to assess and evaluate land use changes and policies. Consequently, land use planning requires an "intellectual family" of approaches (Kooten, 1993) that combine the experience and the strengths of many disciplines.

To develop an appropriate methodology for sustainable land use planning at the local or regional level, a set of scientific research methods and tools may be helpful. Examples are dynamic systems analysis, impact analysis, economic and social assessment, geographic information systems, scenario analysis, and multicriteria decision support.

Dynamic systems analysis (Nijkamp and Reggiani, 1993) seeks to analyze the driving forces and their interdependence in a multicomponent and dynamically complex system. This approach investigates the guiding principles of all subsystems that make up the whole, and examines the material basis on which these rules are based. It is then necessary to look at the causal linkages in comprehensive economic–environmental–human systems. Such a systems representation also forms the basis for an impact model, in which environmental and economic forces are put together in the framework of an open spatial land use system.

Impact analysis serves to assess and measure the relationships between developments and the effects on the environmental system and its subsystems' functions (Thérivel and Partidário, 1996; Wathern, 1988). The tools of impact analysis are widely used in environmental impact assessment and land use studies. They are applied at the strategic level, to assess the effects of policies, plans, and programs, and at the operational level, to assess the consequences of projects. Impact analysis can be applied at various spatial scales, such as at the na-

tional, regional, or local levels, and permits the use of several types of analytical method (for example, econometric and statistical models, simulation and scenario methods, goal-achievement methods). It should be noted that policy strategies regarding economic development and land use are often dynamic in nature and affect a system in successive and interlinked time intervals. Especially in land use studies, which are concerned with impacts that manifest themselves indirectly and in the long run, a dynamic approach to spatial impact analysis is necessary. Impact analysis must therefore be able to assess the impacts over time, and the synergetic and cumulative effects of successive development policies.

Economic assessment techniques, such as benefit-cost analysis (BCA; Brent, 1996), have long been applied to assess the economic rationale of public decisions. BCA requires a monetary valuation of the costs and benefits of a plan. It also uses a discount approach to compare costs and benefits that occur at different times. Several objections, from methodological and ethical perspectives, have been raised about the use of BCA for evaluating environmental and land use plans (Munda, 1995; Nijkamp, 1977): for example, the difficulties encountered in the assessment of the monetary value of nonmarket goods (such as environmental goods), and the issue of discounting future costs and benefits. However, BCA is well known and widely used. Its results can be very valuable if complemented by those of other approaches that focus on aspects other than the economic efficiency of a plan.

The social dimension of complex decisions is addressed in fields such as social impact assessment (SIA; Leistritz and Ekstrom, 1986), which offers tools for a systematic analysis of the social, economic, and cultural impacts of a development. The participatory dimension in these decisions can be addressed with the tools of stakeholder analysis (Burgoyne, 1994). This approach focuses on the relationship between multiple actors involved in a decision process, and includes analysis of the role of procedures, information flows, and behavioral effects. In the recent past, these approaches have been extended to land use management problems and spatial decisions, and integrated with information technology. Simulations can show how factors such as free markets versus government intervention, different levels of development, or specific government policies can alter the patterns of land use. The results of these studies will steer the adoption of policies designed to promote certain land uses.

Effective and accessible information systems are a precondition for strategic decision making. Digital and electronic technologies now offer sophisticated solutions for voice, data, and image transmission and processing. This trend has led to the design and use of Geographic Information Systems (GIS; Scholten and Stilwell, 1990). With a GIS, geographical units or objects are characterized by their geographical position and by a set of attributes (features, labels, or thematic compound). GIS offer a wide range of tools to collect, store, process, and visualize large amounts of spatial data in a coherent and efficient way. They are highly important for planning both on a global scale (such as monitoring of rainforest development) and on a local scale (for example, physical planning). Spatial information systems are also increasingly combined with pattern recognition, remote sensing, systems theory, topology, statistics, and finite-element analysis. These developments have changed the activity patterns and decision modes of spatial actors. In addition, concepts such as Collaborative Spatial Decision Support (Armstrong, 1994) have recently appeared. These approaches use the potentiality of information technology to increase the scope and effectiveness of group interaction in the search for solutions to complex spatial decision problems. They are an indication of a trend toward the integration of several disciplines to support land use planning activities. [See Geographic Information Systems.]

Scenario analysis is used to develop a set of hypothetical future images for a complex land use system. These images offer a rational frame of reference for evaluating development alternatives (Heijden, 1996). Scenario analysis may play an important role as a learning mechanism for decision makers or physical planners. By assessing all foreseeable and expectable scenarios, it may be possible to identify a policy strategy that fulfills the aim of an ecologically sustainable economic system in combination with land use. This idea is of utmost importance for the development of regional or local economic initiatives. Clearly, one has to recognize that a scenario analysis often leads to the construction of hypothetical spatial-development alternatives, which after empirical work may finally lead to the construction of feasible and desired choice alternatives.

Finally, the problem remains of evaluating the outcomes of alternatives and possibly to choose certain best alternatives based on a set of multiple criteria. A basic feature of land use choices is that the effects and the information concerning spatial decisions are multidimensional in nature. In addition, effects presented in the form of monetary units, physical units, or survey measurements must be comparable within a suitable methodology. To a large extent, multicriteria analysis (MCA; Beinat and Nijkamp, 1998; Beinat, 1997; Nijkamp et al., 1990) serves to meet these requirements, because it takes account of different and conflicting objectives in an applicable decision framework. MCA has evolved from a mechanism for the selection of the best alternative from a set of competing options to a set of decision-aid techniques that support the structuring of a decision problem, the exploration of the concerns of decision actors, the evaluation of alternatives under different perspectives, and the analysis of their robustness against uncertainty. MCA is also suitable for soft qualitative data. It forms an adequate tool for environmental policy analysis from global to local levels, and hence for land use policy.

Land use planning and the relationship between land use and sustainability are complex issues. The scientific basis and the methodological approaches available at present demonstrate the need for further research and for the development of more integrated and rigorous tools. However, the tools of rigorous assessment do not by themselves provide a complete means of achieving a more balanced and attractive state of the environment. The questions of what environmental conditions we want to achieve and what type of development we are willing to pursue in the future remain at the core of the land use debate.

[See also Agriculture and Agricultural Land; Economic Levels; Mass Consumption; Parks and Natural Preserves; Regulation; Urban Areas; Wilderness; and World Heritage Sites.]

BIBLIOGRAPHY

Armstrong, M. "Requirements for the Development of GIS-Based Group Decision Support Systems." *Journal of the American Society for Information Science* 45.9 (1994), 669–677.

Atkinson, G., R. Dubourg, K. Hamilton, M. Munasinghe, D. Pearce, and C. Young. *Measuring Sustainable Development.* Cheltenham, U.K.: Edward Elgar, 1997.

Beinat, E. *Value Functions for Environmental Management.* Dordrecht: Kluwer, 1997.

Beinat, E., and P. Nijkamp, eds. *Multicriteria Analysis for Land-Use Management.* Dordrecht: Kluwer, 1998.

Brent, R. J. *Applied Cost-Benefit Analysis.* Cheltenham, U.K.: Edward Elgar, 1996.

Bryden, J. M. "Some Preliminary Perspectives on Sustainable Rural Communities." In *Toward Sustainable Rural Communities,* edited by J. M. Bryden, pp. 41–50. Arkleton Trust and University of Guelph, 1994.

Burgoyne, J. G. "Stakeholder Analysis." In *Qualitative Methods in Organisational Research*, edited by C. Cassell and G. Symon. London: Sage, 1994.

Dieren, W. Van, ed. *Taking Nature into Account: A Report to the Club of Rome*. New York: Springer-Verlag, 1995.

Dutch Committee for Long-Term Environmental Policy. *The Environment: Toward a Sustainable Future*. Dordrecht: Kluwer, 1994.

Frederick, K. D., and N. J. Rosenberg, eds. *Assessing the Impacts of Climate Change on Natural Resource Systems*. Dordrecht: Kluwer, 1994.

Hardin, J. "The Tragedy of the Commons." *Science* 13 (1968), 1243–1248.

Heijden, K. Van Der. *Scenarios: The Art of Strategic Conversation*. Chichester, U.K.: Wiley, 1996.

Intergovernmental Panel on Climate Change. *Climate Change 1995: The Science of Climate Change*. Cambridge: Cambridge University Press, 1996.

Kooten, G. C. Van. *Land Resource Economics and Sustainable Development: Economic Policies and the Common Good*. Vancouver: UBC Press, 1993.

Leistritz, F. L., and B. L. Ekstrom. *Social Impact Assessment: An Annotated Bibliography*. New York: Garland, 1986.

Lier, H. N. Van, and P. D. Taylor. "Long Term Comprehensive Evaluation Strategies for Spatial Planning, Design and Management." In *Multicriteria Analysis for Land-Use Management*, edited by E. Beinat and P. Nijkamp, pp. 353–368. Dordrecht: Kluwer, 1998.

Meyer, W. B., and B. L. Turner, II, eds. *Changes in Land Use and Land Cover: A Global Perspective*. Cambridge: Cambridge University Press, 1994.

Munda, G. *Multicriteria Evaluations in a Fuzzy Environment*. Heidelberg: Physica-Verlag, 1995.

Nijkamp, P. *Theory and Application of Environmental Economics*. Amsterdam: North-Holland, 1977.

Nijkamp, P., and A. Reggiani, eds. *Non Linear Evolution of Spatial Economic Systems*. Berlin: Springer, 1993.

Nijkamp, P., P. Rietveld, and H. Voogd. *Multicriteria Evaluation in Physical Planning*. Amsterdam: North-Holland, 1990.

O'Neill, R. V., J. P. Kahn, J. R. Duncan, S. Alliot, R. Efroymson, H. Caldwell, and D. W. Jones. "Economic Growth and Sustainability: A New Challenge." *Ecological Applications* 6.2 (1996), 23–24.

Ostrom, E. *Governing the Commons*. Cambridge: Cambridge University Press, 1990.

Pearce, D. "Population Growth." In *Blueprint 2: Greening the World Economy*, edited by D. Pearce. London: Earthscan, 1991.

Pearce, D., and K. Turner. *Economics of Natural Resources and the Environment*. New York: Harvester Weatsheaf, 1990.

Randall, A., and E. N. Castle. "Land Resources and Land Markets." In *Handbook of Natural Resource and Energy Economics*, edited by A. V. Kneese and J. L. Sweeney. Amsterdam: North-Holland, 1985.

Scholten, H., and J. C. H. Stilwell, eds. *Geographical Information Systems and Urban and Regional Planning*. Dordrecht: Kluwer, 1990.

Selden, T. M., and D. Song. "Environmental Quality and Development: Is There a Kuznets Curve for Air Pollution Emissions?" *Journal of Environmental Economics and Management* 27 (1994), 147–162.

Stern, D. I. *Progress on the Environmental Kuznets Curve?* EEP Working Papers No. 9601. Canberra: Center for Resource and Environmental Studies, Australian National University, 1996.

Stern, D. I., M. S. Common, and E. B. Barbier. "Economic Growth and Environmental Degradation: The Environmental Kuznets Curve and Sustainable Development." *World Development* 24 (1996), 1151–1160.

Thérivel, R., and R. M. Partidário. *The Practice of Strategic Environmental Assessment*. London: Earthscan, 1996.

Turner, B. L., II. "The Sustainability Principle in Global Agendas: Implications for Understanding Land-Use/Cover Change." *Geographical Journal* 163.2 (1997), 133–140.

Turner, B. L., II, D. Skole, S. Sanderson, G. Fischer, L. Fresco, and R. Leemans. *Land-Use and Land-Cover Change*. IGBP Report No.35/HDP Report No. 7. Stockholm and Geneva: IGBP, 1995.

Wathern, P. *Environmental Impact Assessment*. London: Routledge, 1988.

World Bank. *World Development Report: Development and the Environment*. Washington, D.C.: World Bank, 1992.

World Commission on Environment and Development. *Our Common Future*. New York and Oxford: Oxford University Press, 1987.

World Resources Institute. *World Resources 1987*. New York: Basic Books, 1987.

—EURO BEINAT AND PETER NIJKAMP

LAW. *See* Environmental Law.

LAW OF THE SEA

The United Nations Convention on the Law of the Sea (1982) is currently in force and therefore has legal and political consequences for all states whether they have ratified the agreement or not. While it is a large document (containing 319 articles and nine annexes), and is sometimes referred to as the "constitution" of the ocean, it is not a comprehensive law of the sea. It deals with five major categories of human uses of the ocean: (1) extraction of living and nonliving resources, (2) marine highway, (3) arena for conflict, (4) dumping ground and sewer for human detritus, and (5) place to study.

Despite its many articles, the Convention is primarily a framework convention; its purpose is more to clarify jurisdiction (who has the right to make the rules) than to provide specific guiding rules on substantive questions. Its major policy thrust was to enclose or put under national jurisdiction about 36 percent (and perhaps more) of ocean space, via 200-mile Exclusive Economic Zones (EEZs). While this enclosure does solve some important jurisdictional problems, it also creates new difficulties for managing stocks of living resources that move across borders (called *transboundary stocks*), displaces traditional fishermen from waters now under another state's jurisdiction, and requires that ocean scientists gain the consent of coastal states before commencing research in the 200-mile EEZ (although such consent is not to be normally withheld). [*See* Fishing.] The Convention redefined the continental shelf, with elastic criteria that may not discourage further national attempts at enclosing ocean space.

The Convention resolved the delimitation of the territorial sea—the zone extending outward from the coast in which the coastal state has full sovereign rights minus a right of other states to innocent passage—at 12 nautical miles (considered a great success after three earlier failures in the twentieth century), and it established a new set of rights and duties for states exercising "transit passage" through straits used for international navigation. It created archipelagic states' rights—the claim of a state composed of many islands to bring under its jurisdiction (which may range from some degree of resource or transportation control to full sovereignty) the water areas within a line drawn on a map connecting the outermost points of the outermost islands—and also archipelagic sealanes for the assured passage of vessels from other states. Ocean pollution was also addressed as follows: first, all state parties promised to reduce and control ocean pollution, but these obligations did not include detailed implementation rules; and, second, port and coastal states were given new powers to deal with polluting vessels near their coasts, but were not allowed to make final disposition of cases brought against them. Much of the long conference was tied up by a more developed versus less developed nation quarrel over the creation of an agency to control exploitation of manganese nodules on the deep seabed. Although developing nations made many compromises in the Convention, and a Preparatory Commission wrote a supplemental agreement that converted the arrangements so that they are now based on capitalist principles, the United States still has not ratified the Convention. Finally, the Convention created an International Tribunal to help resolve legal disputes peacefully.

Recently, the negative effects of enclosure (uncontrolled high-seas fishing and the problem of transboundary stocks) have been addressed by a supplemental Convention on Straddling Stocks that requires states to manage living resources on a regional basis, and a Central Bering Sea Agreement that, by requiring all states fishing the region to be a member of a new regional organization, tries to limit access to formerly common property resources.

[See also London Convention of 1972; and Marine Pollution Convention.]

BIBLIOGRAPHY

Burke, W. The New Law of the Seas for Fisheries: UNCLOS 1982 and Beyond. New York and Oxford: Oxford University Press, 1994.
Friedheim, R. L. Negotiating the New Ocean Regime. Columbia: University of South Carolina Press, 1993.
Sanger, C. Ordering the Oceans. Toronto: University of Toronto Press, 1987.
Vidas, D., and Ostreng, W., eds. Order for the Oceans at the Turn of the Century. Hague: Kluwer International, 1999.
—ROBERT L. FRIEDHEIM

LEAD POISONING. See Pollution.

LEOPOLD, ALDO

Aldo Leopold (1887–1948) was an American conservationist, scientist, writer, and environmental philosopher. Over a professional career that spanned four decades, Leopold helped to shape the early American conservation movement through his fundamental contributions as a forester, wildlife biologist, activist, teacher, and prose stylist. His efforts to introduce concepts from the emerging science of ecology into land use practice and philosophy would, in the years following his death, make him an influential catalyst in the development of the modern environmental worldview.

After graduating from Yale University's Forest School in 1909, Leopold joined the U.S. Forest Service, where he became an innovative force in several fields, including forest and range management, soil conservation, recreation planning, game management, and wilderness protection. Disturbed by the impact of accelerated road-building on North America's remaining wild lands, he led efforts that in 1924 resulted in the designation of the nation's first wilderness area within the Gila National Forest in New Mexico. Leaving the Forest Service in 1928, Leopold devoted himself to the establishment of wildlife management as a distinct field. First as an independent field researcher (1928–1933), then as professor at the University of Wisconsin (1933–1948), Leopold endeavored to apply the insights of ecology (especially as defined by his friend and colleague Charles Elton) to the management of wildlife populations and habitats. His text Game Management (1933) was the first in the new field and remained in wide use for several decades. By the end of his life, his professional purview had expanded beyond the management of wildlife populations to encompass the larger-scale and longer-term impacts of human activities on the structure, composition, and functioning of natural communities and systems.

Through his many nontechnical writings, including editorials, committee reports, speeches, survey articles, and natural history essays, Leopold gave definition to an integrated approach to conservation, one that sought to combine elements of older utilitarian and preservationist traditions with contemporary ecological understanding. Framing his ideas within a historical critique of human environmental impacts, Leopold in 1939 described ecology as "a new fusion point for the natural sciences. . . . The emergence of ecology has placed the economic biologist in a peculiar dilemma: with one hand he points out the accumulated findings of his search for utility, in this or that species; with the other he lifts the veil from a biota so complex, so conditioned by interwoven cooperations and competitions, that no man can say where utility begins or ends." This "dilemma" led him to place greater emphasis on the protection and restoration of biological diversity and ecological processes in conservation planning.

In the final years of his life, Leopold compiled many of his natural history essays into a collection published posthumously as *A Sand County Almanac* (1949). This collection became, along with Rachel Carson's *Silent Spring* (1962), one of the basic texts in the environmental movement. [*See the biography of Carson.*] Its capstone essay, "The Land Ethic," remains especially influential as a foundational document in environmental ethics. In this essay, completed in the final year of his life, Leopold argues that the sphere of human ethical concern must expand to include "soils, waters, plants, and animals, or collectively: the land." Leopold's writings continue to inform other interdisciplinary fields as well, including environmental history, ecological economics, restoration ecology, sustainable agriculture, and conservation biology.

[*See also* Conservation; *and* Ethics.]

BIBLIOGRAPHY

Callicott, J. B., ed. *Companion to* A Sand County Almanac: *Interpretive and Critical Essays.* Madison: University of Wisconsin Press, 1987. An interdisciplinary collection of essays on Leopold's classic work.

Callicott, J. B., and S. Flader, eds. *The River of the Mother of God and Other Essays by Aldo Leopold.* Madison: University of Wisconsin Press, 1991. An excellent collection containing many of Leopold's important professional publications.

Flader, S. *Thinking Like a Mountain: Aldo Leopold and the Evolution of an Ecological Attitude toward Deer, Wolves, and Forest.* Columbia: University of Missouri Press, 1974; republished with a new preface, Madison: University of Wisconsin Press, 1994. The first book to explore Leopold's intellectual development, this is also a standard work in forest ecology and the history of forestry.

Meine, C. *Aldo Leopold: His Life and Work.* Madison: University of Wisconsin Press, 1988. A full-length biography that explores Leopold's experience in the context of the development of the American conservation movement.

—CURT D. MEINE

LIFE CYCLE ANALYSIS. *See* Industrial Ecology; *and* Waste Management.

LITTLE ICE AGE IN EUROPE

[*This case study explains the period known as the Little Ice Age in Europe and considers the physical and human consequences of the period's climatic conditions.*]

The Little Ice Age in Europe was a period, several centuries long within the last millennium, during which glaciers enlarged and their fronts oscillated about forward positions. The term refers to the behavior of glaciers, not the climatic circumstances causing them to expand. The Little Ice Age was not a time of prolonged, unbroken cold; in Europe, certain periods within it (such as 1530–1560 CE) were almost as benign as the twentieth century. European mean temperatures over the whole period varied by less than 2°C, although particularly cold years or clusters of years occurred from time to time. Very cold decades—the 1590s and 1690s, for example—saw prolonged snow cover, frozen rivers, and extensive sea ice around Iceland. The characteristics, meteorological causes, and physical and human consequences of this period, which was global in its impact, can be traced in the most detail in Europe. Here, the availability of historical data and concentrated field investigations have permitted the reconstruction of many glacier chronologies. Documentary information, ranging from ice cover around Iceland, sea surface temperatures, and the state of fisheries in the North Atlantic to the timing of the rye harvest in Finland and the incidence of drought in Crete, is unusually substantial (Figure 1). Deliberate monitoring of glacier behavior, initiated in Switzerland in 1880, and some exceptionally long series of meteorological measurements, including that reconstructed for central England (Manley, 1974), assist interpretation of earlier, more fragmentary information.

The Little Ice Age has commonly been seen as occurring during the last three hundred years, during which glaciers from Iceland and Scandinavia to the Pyrenees have advanced, in some cases across pastures or near high settlements. However, evidence is accumulating that these advances, culminating in the seventeenth and nineteenth centuries, were preceded by others of comparable magnitude, culminating in the fourteenth century (Holzhauser, 1995). The intervening period was not sufficiently long, and the effect of loss of ice volume over gain was not great enough, to cause withdrawal to positions held in the tenth to early thirteenth centuries. It is therefore logical to see the whole period from about the mid-thirteenth century to the start of recession in the late nineteenth and early twentieth centuries as one Little Ice Age. It was the most recent of several century-scale fluctuations to have affected Europe during the Holocene (the period extending from 10,000 BP to the present).

Glaciers enlarge when accumulation of snow and ice exceeds loss. The primary controls are temperature, especially in summer, and accumulation, especially in win-

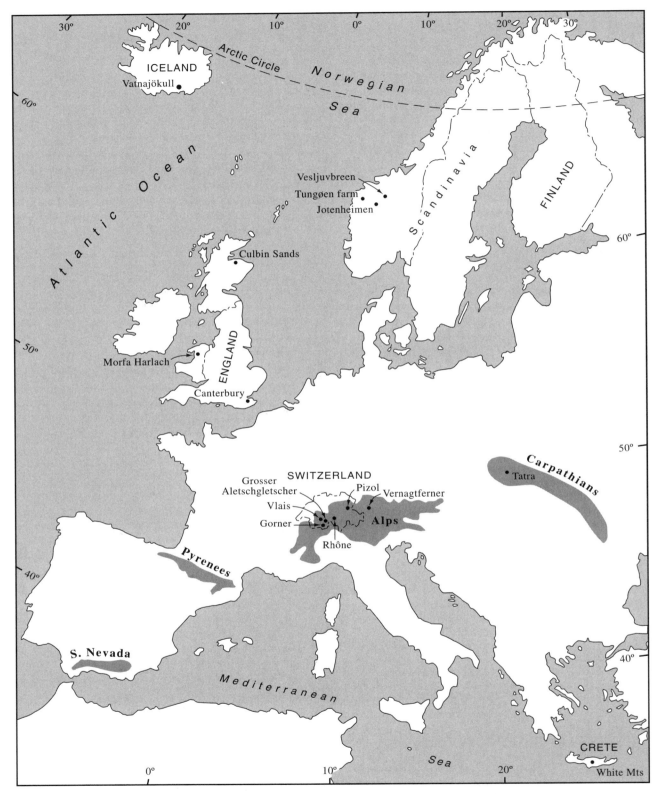

Little Ice Age in Europe. FIGURE 1. Sketch Map Showing Locations Mentioned in the Text.

ter. Temperatures were not low throughout the Little Ice Age; warmer and colder, wetter and drier decades followed each other. Advances occurred when volumes increased sufficiently for the lowest parts of glaciers adjacent to their fronts to be affected. Mapping and dating of moraines makes it possible to trace many past fluctuations in terminal position and extent. Moraines are accumulations of rock debris, formed alongside glacier tongues or around their fronts when they halt for a time, or advance pushing debris before them. It is because the three main culminations of the Little Ice Age were on a similar scale that the physical evidence from the earlier part of the Little Ice Age has only been recognized as long-concealed evidence has been exposed during ice recession (Grove, in press).

Information about glacial history in the Alps is outstandingly rich because of the wealth of documentary and pictorial evidence as well as persistent efforts made to date moraines and sedimentary sections (Holzhauser and Zumbühl, 1996). Because glaciers have frequently extended below treelines, wood, sometimes still *in situ*, is frequently found beneath or within moraines, simplifying problems of radiocarbon dating, and sometimes making absolute dating possible by allowing comparison with dendrochronological series. In Scandinavia, especially in the north, less documentary evidence is available, so that relatively greater reliance has to be placed on moraine dating using soil or plant samples and lake sediments of glacial origin. Lichenometric dating of moraines according to the sizes of lichens of species with known growth rates has been of assistance in disentangling Scandinavian glacial history, but has important limitations, particularly because it depends on the existence of dated surfaces for construction of growth curves over time. The glacial history of the Pyrenees is currently known only from the late eighteenth

century, and chronologies from elsewhere in southern and eastern Europe are even more fragmentary.

The most complete fluctuation history of any glacier in the world is that of the Grosser Aletschgletscher in the Swiss Valais, achieved by assembling data from absolutely dated tree stumps *in situ*, the heights and radiocarbon dates of numerous samples found in lateral positions above the glacier surface, and modern measurements (Figure 2). The Aletsch front moved as far forward in the fourteenth as in the seventeenth and nineteenth centuries (Holzhauser, 1984). Other large Swiss valley glaciers, including the Rhône and the Gorner, advanced to similar extents in the fourteenth century (Holzhauser and Zumbühl, 1996). Variations since the sixteenth century can be traced from contemporary documentary accounts, pictures, and measurements in even greater detail than their predecessors (Figure 3).

The history of the Grosser Aletsch can be taken as a model for the behavior of European glaciers, although the dates at which advances began and ended varied slightly from glacier to glacier. Within this general framework, exceptions and variations are caused by the sizes and response times of glaciers, particular locational and climatic influences, or abnormal flow characteristics. In Iceland, many glaciers did not reach their maximum extents until the late nineteenth century. The outlets of Jostedalsbreen, the largest icecap in continental Europe, did not expand so much in the fourteenth or sixteenth centuries as they did in the eighteenth, probably because of the time required for the ice mass to accumulate (Grove, 1988). The glaciers of western Scandinavia obtain more nourishment from westerly air streams than do those in the east, and so may advance, as in recent years, while those to the east are still dwindling in response to rising temperatures. Because of favorable combinations of altitude, relief, and aspect,

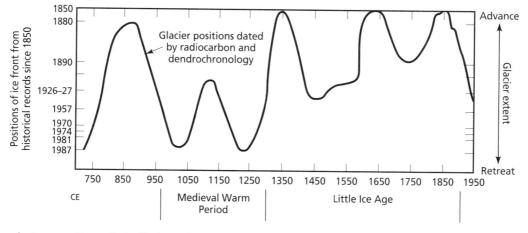

Little Ice Age in Europe. FIGURE 2. Oscillations of the Grosser Aletsch Glacier, Switzerland, Shown in Comparison with Positions Occupied by the Ice since 1850 CE. (After Holzhauser, 1984; from Grove, 1996. With permission of Routledge.)

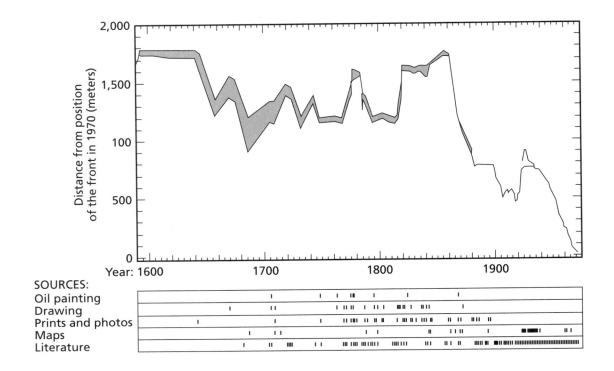

Little Ice Age in Europe. FIGURE 3. Frontal Positions of Lower Grindelwald, 1590–1970.

Note the minor fluctuations of the front during phases of glacier extension and during retreat. (From Grove, 1988, Figure 6.4. With permission of Routledge.)

small, high-altitude cirque glaciers such as Vesljuvbreen in Jotunheimen, southern Norway, or Pizol in the Swiss Alps (Figure 1) are immediately responsive to small-scale climatic variations. Advances of surging glaciers, such as the Vernagtfirner in Austria and several in Iceland, including many outlets of Vatnjökull, Europe's largest ice sheet, relate to instability associated with bed shape and temperature conditions rather than directly to climatic fluctuations. But the general pattern of Little Ice Age fluctuations has extended right across Europe, as might be expected from the coherence of measurements of frontal change and mass balance in the twentieth century (Grove 1988, Figure 6.7). Large valley glaciers typically lengthened by up to about 1 or 2 kilometers. A clear pattern emerges from the timing of advance, retreat, and stationary phases across all the monitored fronts of alpine glaciers in Europe, despite minor variations from glacier to glacier.

During the Little Ice Age centuries, zonal circulation, bringing moist, maritime air from the west, was frequently replaced by meridional circulation with blocking highs in northern and central Europe. All parts of the continent were affected by such low-index situa-

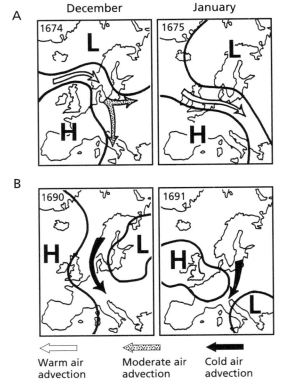

Little Ice Age in Europe. FIGURE 4. Circulation Patterns.

(A) in the winter of 1674–1675, when westerly winds were frequent; (B) in the winter of 1690–1691, when westerly winds were rare. (From Grove, in press. With permission of Routledge.)

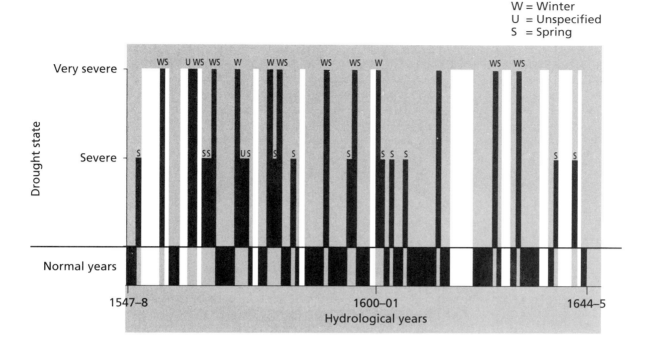

Little Ice Age in Europe. FIGURE 5. The Incidence of Droughts in Crete, 1547–1548 to 1644–1645.

White indicates years with no data. (From Grove, in press. With permission of Routledge.)

tions, with northerly or northeasterly flows of very cold, dry, Arctic, or polar continental air masses extending over large parts of Europe (Figure 4). The Mediterranean was not immune. In the eastern basin, outbursts of cold air from the north were associated with cyclone formation, bringing occasional bursts of torrential rain. Such conditions alternated with the invasion of warm, dry air from the south, causing long droughts even in winter and spring (Figure 5). In the western Mediterranean too, there were departures from mean twentieth-century values of temperature and precipitation lasting for decades or clusters of years, but not necessarily at the same time as in the east.

North Atlantic thermohaline circulation appears to have been disturbed, for when sea surface temperatures were periodically low and sea ice extensive, formation of the dense, saline North Atlantic Deep Water current was interrupted. This had long-distance effects on ocean circulation, reducing heat exchange between high and low latitudes. The large-scale alternation of pressure between the Azores region and the subpolar region east of Greenland, the North Atlantic Oscillation, was evidently involved in these switches from zonal to meridional circulation (Intergovernmental Panel on Climate Change, 1995, pp. 166–167). The extent to which century-scale climatic events such as the Little Ice Age are manifestations of periodic adjustments in the interaction between oceanic and atmospheric circulation (Grove, 1988, chap. 11), or responses of the global climatic system to external forcing caused by factors such as variations in geomagnetism or decreased solar input, remains to be clarified. A full explanation must involve the combined influence of several factors, including the part played by volcanic eruptions. [*See the vignette on* Thermohaline Circulation and the Cooling Effects of Warming *in the article on* Climate Change; *and the vignette on* The North Atlantic Oscillation *in the article on* Natural Climate Fluctuations.]

The ending of the Little Ice Age cannot be attributed simply to anthropogenic warming following the Industrial Revolution, in view of evidence of comparable warming in the Medieval Warm Period and a series of similar century-scale events, such as the Löbben, earlier in the Holocene (Grove, 1996). Just as Little Ice Age climate consisted of decadal and seasonal departures from longer-term means, it was itself but one of several fluctuations within the Holocene, each lasting several centuries. The Little Ice Age has to be seen as one of many natural climatic fluctuations on a scale that must be expected to continue to occur, modulating to some extent future warming induced by human activity (Wigley et al., 1990). Since evidence of its characteristics, especially in Europe, is more plentiful than that of any of its predecessors, its investigation here is especially well merited.

More details of Little Ice Age climatic characteristics,

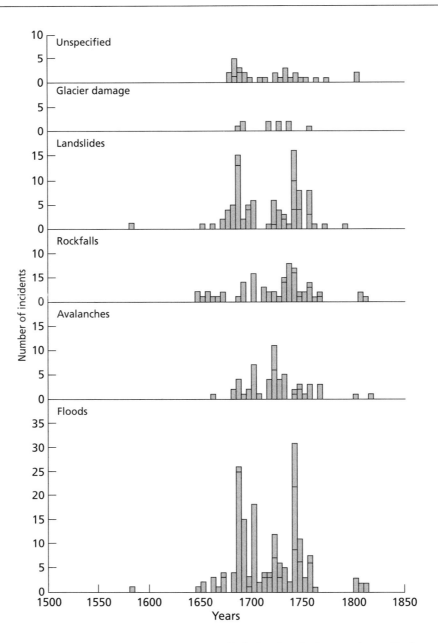

Little Ice Age in Europe. Figure 6. The Incidence of Mass Movements and Floods in Western Norway. (After Grove, 1988, Figure 12.2. With permission of Routledge.)

which are essential if its causes are to be identified, are emerging from the increasing sophistication of climatic reconstruction since it was developed by Lamb (1977). This approach now depends on the cross-dating of different types of proxy data, including information relating to stages in the development of plants, with descriptive evidence drawn from contemporary sources, making it possible to extend meteorological time series into the past (Pfister et al., 1996). The information assembled in the EURO-CLIMHIST database has already enabled past synoptic patterns and even monthly weather maps for Europe to be constructed for the Maunder Minimum period between 1645 and 1715, when sunspots were absent. Many aspects of this research are discussed in Frenzel et al. (1994).

The physical consequences of Little Ice Age climatic conditions affected highlands and lowlands as well as coastal areas. Snow cover was extended, and semipermanent snow appeared on midlatitude uplands, as in Scotland, and on high mountains in the Mediterranean, including the White Mountains of Crete. Snowlines fell; avalanches and mass movements increased greatly, as did floods (Figure 6), some caused by damming of main valleys by ice in tributary valleys. Periods of glacial advance were generally associated with increased flooding and sediment transport. Regime changes of proglacial streams and rivers led in the short term to both degradation and aggradation, according to the balance between meltwater load and stream competence. In the longer term, increased flooding and glacial erosion led to enhanced sedimentation rates and deposition of valley fills and deltas. Greater storminess caused flooding of low-lying coasts and the formation of belts of sand dunes, as at Morfa Harlech in northwest Wales (Lamb, 1977, p. 452; Lamb, 1982, p. 208).

Little Ice Age climatic fluctuations were sufficient to have biological consequences, ranging from shifts in treeline altitude to changes in fish distribution in response to displacement of water masses. The disappearance of cod (*Gadus morhua*) from the Norwegian

Sea area in the late seventeenth century, associated with the expansion of polar water, is attributable to the inability of cod kidneys to function in water below 2°C. The observation of northward extensions of the range of European birds during twentieth-century warming, such as the establishment of starlings (*Sternus vulgaris*) in Iceland after 1941, implies that more substantial changes in the distribution of birds and insects must have occurred during the most marked phases of the Little Ice Age.

The consequences for European populations ranged from ice advance on to farms and farmland (Figure 7), such as the obliteration in 1743 of Tungøen farm in Oldendalen, western Norway, the overwhelming of nine farms and extensive farmland by the Culbin Sands in Scotland around 1694 (Lamb, 1982), and the fourteenth-

Little Ice Age in Europe. Figure 7. The Mer de Glace in 1823.

Painted by Samuel Birmann (Au village des Prats Öffentliche Kunstsammlung Basel, Kupferstichkabinett, Inv. B1. 30.125). (From Grove, 1988, Plate 4.1. With permission of Routledge.)

century loss to the sea of over a thousand acres of farm-land belonging to Christ Church, Canterbury (England), together with many oxen, cattle, and sheep (Grove, 1996).

The human consequences of Little Ice Age climate were particularly marked in highland regions and areas near the limits of cultivation. When summer temperatures declined and growing seasons shortened, both grass and cereal crops suffered, and the upper limits of cultivation descended. The viability of upland farming decreased as the probability of harvest failure increased. If harvests failed in successive years, leading to consumption of seed corn, the results were disastrous. Failure of the grass crop limited the number of cattle overwintered, thus decreasing the quantity of manure, which was then essential for successful arable farming. Farm desertion was especially common in Iceland and Scandinavia, although it was not confined to such northern regions. In Iceland, migration out of the worst-affected north in the seventeenth century caused increased impoverishment in the south. A gradual decline in resource bases could increase sensitivity to other factors, including disease and unrelated economic problems, making the impact of a sequence of particularly hard years, such as occurred in the 1690s, much more serious. Crop failure was most dire in its effects if several staples were affected simultaneously, or if alternative supplies were unobtainable.

The human consequences of Little Ice Age climate were generally coincident with other social and economic factors from which they must be disentangled if they are to be assessed reliably. In the early fourteenth century the impact was enhanced, even in lowland regions in southern England, by the population growth encouraged by the rarity of harvest failures in the preceding Medieval Warm Period. Sequences of adverse weather in England between 1314 and 1322, coinciding with the rapid advance of the Swiss glaciers (Figure 1), had major economic and social effects, including famine, their severity varying from place to place and class to class (Grove, 1996). More resilient societies or those in prosperous regions, such as the Netherlands, were less affected.

BIBLIOGRAPHY

Bradley, R. S., and P. D. Jones. *Climate Since A.D. 1500*. London and New York: Routledge, 1992. The last half millenium is presented as a period of complex climatic anomalies by detailed studies of high-resolution data. Dismissal of the "Little Ice Age" as a useful term was based on the idea that it was a long period of unbroken cold.

Frenzel, B., C. Pfister, and B. Gläser, eds. *Climatic Trends and Anomalies in Europe 1675–1715*. ESF Project European Paleoclimate and Man 8. Paläoklimaforschung/Palaeoclimate Research 13. Stuttgart, Jena, and New York: Gustav Fischer Verlag, 1994.

Grove, J. M. *The Little Ice Age*. London and New York: Methuen, 1988. Presents the Little Ice Age as a global phenomenon, and includes chapters on its possible causes and consequences.
———. "The Century Timescale." In *Timescales and Environmental Change*, edited by T. S. Driver and G. P. Chapman, pp. 39–87. London and New York: Routledge, 1996. Places the Little Ice Age in its Quaternary and Holocene context and provides brief examples of the historical impact of climatic fluctuations.
———. *The Little Ice Age*. 2d ed. London and New York: Routledge, in press. This updates and extends the 1988 edition.
Holzhauser, H. "Zur Geschichte des Aletschgletscher und des Fieschergletscher." *Physische Geographie* 13 (1984), 1–448.
———. "Fluctuation of the Grosser Aletsch Glacier and the Gorner Glacier during the Last 2300 Years: New Results." *Paläoklimaforschung/Palaeoclimate Research* 24 (1997), 35–58.
Holzhauser, H., and H. J. Zumbühl. "To the History of the Lower Grindelwald Glacier During the Last 2800 Years—Paleosols, Fossil Wood and Pictorial Records—New Results." Translated by M. Joss, C. Bern, and T. Wachs. *Zeitschrift für Geomorphologie* 104 (1996), 95–127.
Intergovernmental Panel on Climate Change. *Climate Change 1995: The Science of Climatic Change*. Contribution of Working Group I to the Second Assessment Report of the Intergovernmental Panel on Climatic Change. Edited by J. T. Houghton, L. G. Meira Filho, B. A. Callander, N. Harris, A. Kattenberg, and K. Maskell. Cambridge: Cambridge University Press, 1995. The most recent scientific IPCC publication contains information on past climatic changes and includes data on influences such as the North Atlantic Oscillation.
Lamb, H. H. *Climate Present, Past and Future*, vol. 2. London: Methuen, 1977.
———. *Climate, History and the Modern World*. London and New York: Methuen, 1982. A good introduction for the nonspecialist; see especially Chapters 3, 8, 11, 12, and 13.
Manley, G. "Central England Temperatures: Monthly Mean 1659–1973." *Quarterly Journal of the Royal Meteorological Society* 100 (1974), 389–405. A classic paper, providing full details of the ways in which this, the longest European temperature series, was derived.
Pfister, C., G. Schwarz-Zanetti, and M. Wegman. "Winter Severity in Europe: The Fourteenth Century." *Climatic Change* 34.1 (1996), 91–108. A reconstruction of some of the European climatic conditions during the early part of the Little Ice Age.
Wigley, T. M. L., M. J. Ingram, and G. Farmer, eds. *Climate and History: Studies in Past Climates and their Impact on Man*. Cambridge: Cambridge University Press, 1981. One of the first works concerned with the interrelations between climate and history.
Wigley, T. M. L., M. J. Ingram, and P. M. Kelly. "Holocene Climatic Changes, 1414 Wiggles and Variations in Solar Irradiance." *Philosophical Transactions of the Royal Society of London* A330 1615 (1990), 547–660. Little Ice Age-type fluctuations must be expected to continue to influence future climate.

—JEAN M. GROVE

LONDON CONVENTION OF 1972

Dredged spoils, radioactive material, and a wide range of municipal and industrial waste have for decades been disposed of by dumping or incineration at sea. These options have been attractive partly for cost reasons and partly because land-based disposal may also cause severe environmental problems, among them groundwater contamination. Industrialized countries today tend to avoid dumping of hazardous and industrial waste, seeking instead to reduce waste production and resort to land-based treatment processes.

The basic principle of the Convention on the Prevention of Marine Pollution by Dumping of Wastes and Other Matter of 1972 (London Convention of 1972) is that sea disposal of toxic, persistent, and waste that accumulates in the food chain must be forbidden, except in cases where all other options are deemed more harmful. Dumping of high-level radioactive waste was prohibited already in 1972, whereas low- and medium-level waste was the subject of a 1983 voluntary moratorium. After years of scientific impact studies, gradually incorporating social and political aspects, the parties to the Convention finally banned dumping of all radioactive waste in 1993. They also prohibited sea-based incineration of sewage sludge and industrial waste and decided that dumping of the latter should be discontinued within three years; among the notable exemptions, however, are sewage sludge, dredged material, derelict vessels, and offshore platforms.

A range of international and nongovernmental organizations, including industrial and environmental groups, attend as observers at Consultative Meetings of the Parties, usually held every year. This provides an avenue for influence and also makes the deliberations more transparent. A black and gray list system is applied, in which substances on the former may not be dumped and the latter require special permits to be issued by governments and reported to the Secretariat, located with the International Maritime Organization. Pending entry into force, a 1996 Protocol will introduce a reverse listing, prohibiting all dumping unless explicitly permitted; the impact will be further enhanced by a strong statement of the precautionary principle. The Convention adopts legally binding provisions by a two-thirds majority, balanced by a reservation clause that allows parties to opt out of provisions. Implementation is speeded up by a tacit consent procedure, implying that provisions become binding on parties after a hundred days unless they file a reservation. In addition to flag-state enforcement, a coastal state may apply the Convention to its territorial waters, exclusive economic zone, and continental shelf.

An inability to recruit sufficiently wide participation, especially among developing coastal states, and a clearly inadequate compliance system are the main deficiencies of the regime. Obligations to lodge national reports on dumping and management activities are widely ignored, hence reducing actual transparency, and there is scant opportunity for the Secretariat or other parties to assess reports critically. Responding to a challenge from the United Nations Conference on Environment and Development held in Rio in 1992, the parties have elaborated an enhanced technical cooperation and assistance program to improve implementation in developing and transitional countries, but its financial basis is as yet unclear. On balance, the future effectiveness of the Convention will be determined less by further regulative advances than by stimulation of wider participation and implementation of existing provisions. This would require a stronger emphasis on programmatic activities—such as financing of projects, research, and monitoring—that can support the enhancement of administrative and physical waste management capacities where they are inadequate.

[See also Law of the Sea; Marine Pollution Convention; Ocean Disposal; and Precautionary Principle.]

BIBLIOGRAPHY

Birnie, P., and A. E. Boyle. International Law and the Environment. Oxford: Clarendon Press, 1992.

Coenen, R. "Dumping of Wastes at Sea: Adoption of the 1996 Protocol to the London Convention 1972." Review of European Community and International Law 6.1 (1997), 54–61.

International Maritime Organization. The London Dumping Convention: The First Decade and Beyond. London: International Maritime Organization, 1991.

Stokke, O. S. "Beyond Dumping? The Effectiveness of the London Convention." Yearbook of International Co-operation on Environment and Development 1998. London: Earthscan, 1998.

—OLAV SCHRAM STOKKE

M

MALARIA. *See* Disease.

MALNUTRITION. *See* Famine; *and* Food.

MALTHUS, THOMAS ROBERT

Thomas Robert Malthus (1766–1834) was an English social and demographic theorist. In his *Essay on the Principle of Population* (1798), Malthus depicted, in classic apocalyptic terms, the consequences of population outstripping the available food supply. He did not predict famine or universal resource scarcity, as commonly believed, but rather set forth the circumstances under which famine might occur.

Born in Sussex, England, and educated at Cambridge University, Malthus was both an ordained clergyman of the Church of England and a professor of economics at the East India College (Hertfordshire). His population essay, pamphlets on trade policy, and *Principles of Political Economy* (1820) are among the fundamental works of classical economics. The social-policy implications Malthus drew from his population theory made him a figure of controversy throughout his lifetime, and well beyond.

Malthus argued that population tends to increase at a geometric rate (1, 2, 4, 8, 16), while food supplies can only be increased at an arithmetic rate (1, 2, 3, 4, 5). Hence population tends to outstrip the means of subsistence. But humans do not blindly propagate up to the point of starvation. They are capable, unlike plants and animals, of foreseeing the consequences of their actions. Thus population is limited by prudential behavior—preventive checks that lower the birth rate—as well as by various positive checks, such as famine and disease, that raise the mortality rate. In Malthus's view, advancing societies come to rely less on the positive and more on the preventive checks. When population increases too rapidly, equilibrating forces come into play: expanded labor supply, lower real wages, postponed and less-frequent marriages, and higher mortality. This sets the stage for demographic recovery: higher wages, earlier marriages, lower mortality, and a rise in population. Malthus called these recurring cycles *oscillations*.

Considered one of the founders of demography, Malthus took a keen interest in historical and contemporary patterns of fertility, nuptiality, and mortality, not only in Britain but around the world. He considered his approach to social inquiry to be more empirical, and thus more sound, than that of his idealistic and utopian opponents. His understanding of British population dynamics in the eighteenth and early nineteenth centuries, while flawed in some respects, was based on the demographic data then available to him. The common assertion that he overlooked the possibilities of technological progress is not well supported by the content of his writings.

Malthus's influence has been wide and enduring. Both Charles Darwin and Alfred Russel Wallace cited the *Essay on Population* as a work that opened their minds to the idea of natural selection. In the twentieth century, renewed concern about excessive population growth, whether on economic, national security, quality of life, or environmental grounds, has rekindled interest in Malthus. Paul Ehrlich's widely read *Population Bomb* (1968) struck some as a kind of updated *Essay on Population*. Limits-to-growth-type models of global economic collapse are Malthusian in tone and inspiration, if not substance; and inquiries into the carrying capacity of the planet may be seen as raising some of the same questions that Malthus posed two centuries ago.

[*See also* Human Populations; *and* Population Dynamics.]

BIBLIOGRAPHY

Coleman, D., and R. Schofield, eds. *The State of Population Theory: Forward from Malthus.* New York: Basil Blackwell, 1986. Several essays take the measure of Malthus as a demographer.

Dupaquier, J., A. Fauve-Chamoux, and E. Grebenik, eds. *Malthus Past and Present.* London and New York: Academic Press, 1983. Wide-ranging essays on Malthus and his historical impact.

Hollander, S. *The Economics of Thomas Robert Malthus.* Toronto: University of Toronto Press, 1997. A comprehensive exposition of Malthus's economics.

James, P. *Population Malthus: His Life and Times.* London and Boston: Routledge and Kegan Paul, 1979. A fine and highly sympathetic biography.

—GEOFFREY GILBERT

MANGROVES

Mangroves are halophytic ("salt-tolerant") woody shrubs and trees that grow in the upper part of the intertidal zone on shores not exposed to strong wave action or tidal scour. More than seventy species have been identified. They form extensive communities bordering deltas, estuaries, inlets, tidal lagoons, and sheltered embayments, and are occasionally found behind beaches on coral islands.

Mangroves attain their greatest extent, diversity, and luxuriance on tropical coasts, where they can form forests several kilometers wide with trees up to 30 meters (100 feet) tall. A few species extend beyond the tropics, often associated with salt marshes, which occupy a similar intertidal zone, and replace them entirely on cooler coasts. The World Mangrove Atlas (1996) indicates that mangroves occupy a total of 181,000 square kilometers (km²), the largest stands being in Indonesia (42,550 km²), Brazil (13,400 km²), Australia (11,500 km²), and Nigeria (10,515 km²). The present latitudinal limits of mangroves on the Pacific coasts of the Americas are about 28° north latitude in the Gulf of California but only 3° 30′ south at Tumbes in Peru, where sea temperatures are lowered by the cold Peruvian current. On the Atlantic coast of the Americas they extend north to Florida and the Mississippi delta (Barataria Bay, 29° 20′ north) and south to Florianopolis in Brazil (27° 35′ south). In West Africa they extend north to the Senegal River (16° north) and south to Lobito in Angola (12° 20′ south). On the eastern coast of South Africa mangroves occur south to the Bashee River (32° 59′ south). They are found on the shores of the Red Sea north to near Hurghada, Gulf of Aqaba (28° north) and in western Australia south to Bunbury (33° 20′ south). In the western Pacific there are mangroves as far north as the Min Jiang (26° north) in China and on the Satsuma Peninsula in southern Kyushu, Japan (31° 37′ north). In the North Island of New Zealand mangroves extend south to Raglan Harbour on the western coast (37° 48′ S) and Ohiwa Harbour on the eastern coast (close to 38° S), while in Australia they reach their southernmost limit in Corner Inlet, Victoria (38° 55′ S).

Mangroves typically occupy muddy substrates and are structurally and physiologically adapted to survive in a marine tidal environment, although some species can also grow in fresh water. Adaptations include some species with networks of pneumatophores (snorkels that protrude vertically from the roots through the mud); others have prop-root systems. Mangroves are often arranged in clearly defined zones of a single species or group of species parallel to the coastline or the shores of an estuary, the zones being related to the depth and duration of tidal submergence. Some species (especially those with pneumatophores) influence patterns of sedimentation, intercepting and trapping mud and peat (the organic products of the mangrove ecosystem) to build up a depositional terrace, eventually to high tide level. As the terrace builds up, the mangrove zones migrate seaward, and other vegetation (such as rainforest) displaces them on the newly formed land as the high tide line advances. Such vegetation successions have occurred, for example, on the Amazon delta and in the Gulf of Papua. In Westernport Bay, Australia, cutting of mangroves was followed by dissection and degradation of the depositional terrace, but this terrace was rebuilt when the mangrove fringe revived.

To explain the existing global distribution of mangroves it is necessary to take account of several major climatic fluctuations and sea level oscillations that occurred during Quaternary times. Mangroves are closely related to existing intertidal levels, and must have migrated in response to rising and falling sea levels, subject to climatic and other constraints. They have thus survived large-scale global changes. About 20,000 BP, during a very cold phase of the Pleistocene, when sea level was at least 120 meters (400 feet) lower than it is now and the coastline lay close to the outer margins of the continental shelves, mangroves must have occupied sites on the lowered coastline where the sea was still sufficiently warm to permit their growth. It is possible, bearing in mind the occasional inland occurrence of mangroves (as near Broome in Western Australia) that have survived since Late Pleistocene phases of higher sea level, that some mangroves persisted in wetlands on the emerged continental shelf. [See Wetlands.]

Subsequently, between about 18,000 and 5,000 BP, there was a major worldwide sea level rise (the Late Quaternary or Flandrian marine transgression), in the course of which the coastline advanced across what is now the continental shelf up to its present position. Mangroves must have migrated with this sea level rise, occupying suitably sheltered sites and incorporating any mangrove outliers on the submerging shelf. Stratigraphic studies in northern Australia and southeastern Asia have shown that mangroves grew in accreting estuaries when sea level was rising between 7,000 and 5,500 BP, and that when the Late Quaternary marine transgression came to an end they spread out to embayments and other sheltered sites of muddy accretion along the coast. During the past five thousand years, sea level has been relatively stable, with minor oscillations in some places and a slow continuing rise in others, and mangroves have spread on sites where there has been continuing accretion of sediment (as on tropical deltas) or held their position where a peaty substrate has been maintained by the accumulation of their own organic products (as on the Florida coast). They may have disappeared from some sectors of coastline as the result of erosion, but during the past few centuries a relatively stable sea level and substantial sedimentary accretion has enabled mangroves to occupy extensive areas on tropical and warm temperate coastlines.

In terms of biological productivity, mangroves are among the richest of natural ecosystems, sustaining a varied flora and fauna, including fish, shellfish, reptiles, insects, and birds, and the world's mangrove forests have absorbed carbon from, and contributed oxygen to, the global atmosphere on a large scale, thereby contributing to global change. Mann (1982) estimated primary productivity (organic matter) in mangroves at up to 2,000 grams per square meter per year.

Mangrove communities have been modified extensively by human activities, especially during the last few decades. They have been destroyed in the course of land reclamation for agriculture, urban and industrial development, and port construction. In southeastern Asia there has been large-scale reclamation of mangrove areas for land development, particularly around Penang and Melaka in Malaysia and Jakarta and Surabaya in Indonesia. It is possible to manage mangrove forests on a sustained yield basis by careful extraction of timber and promotion of natural regeneration, but in many areas mangroves have been depleted by excessive cutting for timber and fuel wood, especially in Arabia and Africa. Elsewhere they have been cleared for the dredging of placer deposits, such as the tin that occurs beneath mangroves on the western coasts of Thailand and Malaysia, and generally they have failed to regenerate on the worked-over terrain. The most extensive clearance of mangroves in recent decades has been made for the establishment of aquaculture (fish and prawn ponds) and salt pans in such countries as Ecuador and Brazil, and especially in southeastern Asia. [See Fish Farming.] Mangroves have also been damaged or destroyed by pollution, especially oil spills near port areas, and by pesticides, as during the war in Vietnam. Globally, mangrove losses have already been substantial. Spalding (see bibliography) noted that in Thailand, for example, reclamation and aquaculture have reduced the mangrove area to less than half its natural extent, and similar reductions have occurred in the Philippines (60 percent), Vietnam (37 percent), and Malaysia (12 percent).

Where mangroves are still spreading, they show an unbroken rising canopy, the trees increasing in age and size landward; but where there has been erosion, there is a sharp margin in which the trunks of mature mangroves are exposed and undermined. Reduction of mangrove fringes by erosion has occurred where they are undercut by meandering river channels or where wave action has intensified on coasts on which previously there had been accretion and spreading mangroves. Once a protective mangrove fringe has been lost, low-lying hinterlands are exposed to erosion, and banks built to enclose reclaimed areas require strengthening and elaboration to solid sea walls. Mangroves are still spreading seaward on the fringes of growing deltas and alongside accreting estuaries, but elsewhere erosion has become prevalent, either because of diminishing sediment supply from the land (as where rivers have been dammed, or backing embankments have impeded runoff from reclaimed hinterlands) or where sea level is now rising, perhaps because of coastal land subsidence.

There is now a prospect of global warming and a worldwide sea level rise, the consequences of which are discussed by Bird (1993). Mangroves will respond to global warming by expanding their latitudinal range beyond the limits noted above, provided that suitable coastal habitats are available and that coastal currents enable seeds to reach them. Mangroves are likely to be spread northward along the northeastern coast of Florida, for example, and into Mauritania. Climatic changes that result in increased runoff and sedimentation from the land will also increase the available habitats and stimulate the expansion of mangrove areas if this is not prevented by other factors, such as human activities. However, the accompanying worldwide sea level rise is likely to prove damaging to mangroves, except where it is offset by tectonic uplift of coastal land, or at least compensated by accelerating intertidal accretion, most likely in estuarine and deltaic regions. Some possible responses are shown in Figure 1A. The response of mangroves to a rising sea level can already be seen on coasts that are subsiding, as in the Amazon delta, the Bight of Bangkok, the Adelaide region of South Australia, and northern New Guinea. [See Sea Level.]

It is possible that global warming and a rising sea level will result in the enrichment of intertidal areas with nutrients derived from erosion elsewhere, or enhanced runoff from the hinterland, thereby invigorating mangrove growth and producing sufficient peat to build up the substrate and match the sea level rise. Ellison and Stoddart (1991) decided that in the absence of sediment accretion, mangroves could maintain themselves on their accumulating peat while sea level was rising by up to 9 centimeters per century, but they would be impeded by a faster submergence, and collapse when sea level rise exceeded 12 centimeters per century. Mangroves that grow on coral reef islands, such as the Low Isles off northern Queensland, are unlikely to survive as sea level rise proceeds because rates of sediment accretion are very low.

In the absence of sustained accretion, coastal submergence by a rising sea level is likely to cause die-back and undercutting of the seaward mangroves. As larger waves arrive through deepening water, a cliff is cut in the intertidal mudflats, and this recedes through the mangroves, consuming the muddy terrace on which they grew (Figure 1B). Where such erosion is already in progress, as on the coast of West Johore in Malaysia, a rising sea level will accelerate it.

As submergence proceeds, mangrove zones will tend to migrate landward, invading a low-lying hinterland. In humid regions they will invade backing rainforest or formerly freshwater swamps, as on the Mamberano delta in Irian Jaya, while in drier areas they will colonize backing salt marsh and bare saline flats, as at Port Adelaide in South Australia. As this migration proceeds, it is likely

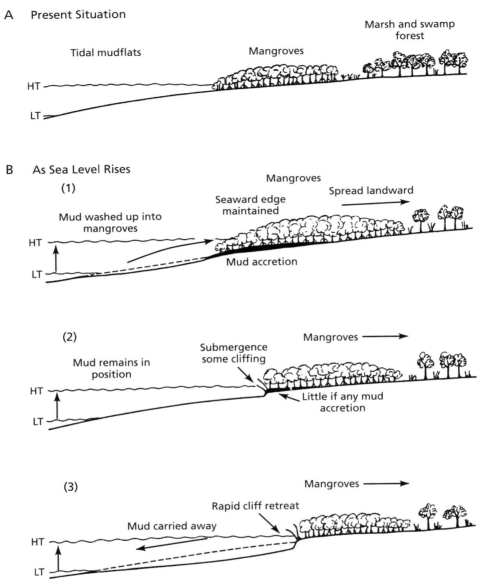

Mangroves. Figure 1. (A) Mangroves have spread forward on to tidal mudflats, and as the mud level is built up they are succeeded by other vegetation. (B) As sea level rises there are three possibilities: (1) that there will be sufficient mud accretion to maintain the seaward edge while the mangroves spread landward; (2) that in the absence of a sufficient sediment supply the seaward margin will become cliffed as the mangroves spread landward; and (3) that removal of mud will result in a deepening of nearshore waters and stronger wave action, causing rapid retreat of the seaward cliff as the mangroves spread landward. (After Bird, 1993. Reproduced with permission of John Wiley and Sons Limited.)

that some mangrove species will become more abundant and extensive, while others will diminish or even disappear.

In many places the landward migration of mangroves in response to a rising sea level will be prevented because the inner margin abuts a rising slope: the mangrove fringe will become narrower and eventually disappear. Where a bank has been built at the inner margin to protect reclaimed land or enclose ponds for aquaculture or pans for salt production, there will be a similar response: if the wall is maintained, the mangrove fringe will be reduced, and eventually destroyed as sea level rises.

Mangroves are important because they are biologically rich and productive, and play a significant role in sustaining estuarine and marine fish and crustaceans. As long as they persist, they protect low-lying hinterlands, intercept sediment and nutrients, and provide a habitat for associated plant and animal life. Mangrove areas yield timber, firewood, charcoal, and a variety of other products, especially for the use of people who live in or near them, and, in a world where marine inundation and dryland salting are increasing problems, they provide genetic stock from which halophytic trees and crops could be developed. Unfortunately, mangroves are still widely regarded as waste areas awaiting reclamation, particularly in southeastern Asia and Latin America, where governments are not yet implementing effective conservation programs.

The conservation of mangroves as sea level rises requires the raising of their substrates by artificial nourishment. On the subsiding coast of the Bight of Bangkok, Thailand, the mangrove fringe is diminishing, and in places has disappeared, but there has been vigorous growth and spread of mangroves in an intertidal area where mud dredged from the Chao Phraya River had been dumped. The implication is that mud could be deposited to renourish mangrove swamps in much the same way as sand has been placed to renourish beaches. Planting (or replanting) of mangroves has recently been attempted on eroded muddy shores in Bangladesh and Vietnam, and abandoned fishponds in Thailand.

BIBLIOGRAPHY

Bird, E. C. F. "Mangroves and Intertidal Morphology in Westernport Bay, Victoria." *Marine Geology* 69 (1986), 251–271. Discusses evidence for mangroves causing sediment accretion.
———. *Submerging Coasts*. Chichester, U.K.: Wiley, 1993.
Chapman, V. J. *Mangrove Vegetation*. Veduz: J. Cramer, 1976. A useful ecological study, a little out of date.
Ellison, J., and D. Stoddart. *Journal of Coastal Research* 7 (1991), 151–165.
International Society for Mangrove Ecosystems. *World Mangrove Atlas*. Okinawa: University of the Ryukus, 1996.
Kunstadter, P., S. Sabhasri, and E. C. F. Bird, eds. *Man in the Mangroves*. Tokyo: United Nations University, 1988. A collection of papers on aspects of mangrove utilization.
Mann, K. H. *Ecology of Coastal Waters: A Systems Approach*. Berkeley: University of California Press, 1982.
Robertson, A. I., and D. M. Alongi. *Tropical Mangrove Systems. Coastal and Estuarine Studies* 41 (1992). American Geophysical Union, Washington, D.C.
Spalding, M. http://www.brooktrout.gso.uri.edu/.
Woodroffe, C. D. "The Impact of Sea Level Rise on Mangrove Shorelines." *Progress in Physical Geography* 14 (1990), 483–520. An analysis including evidence of mangrove responses to past sea level changes.

—ERIC C. F. BIRD

MANUFACTURING

Manufacturing can be defined as the collection of activities and processes that transform raw materials into marketable products. These processes refine and add economic value to those components of raw materials—from agriculture, forestry, mining, or other extractive activities—that are physically embodied in the salable final product. At the same time, the components that are unwanted (wastes and contaminants) are separated and discarded. [*See* Industrial Ecology; *and* Industrial Metabolism.] From another perspective, the materials transformation and value-adding process can also be regarded as an information process, insofar as added value can be regarded as added information.

The manufacturing process can be divided conceptually into several stages (Figure 1). The first (primary) stage is concerned with the conversion of crude raw materials into finished materials suitable for use or further physical transformation. Processes involve physical separation and reaggregation and chemical conversion. Activities in this category include grain, oilseed, dairy, and meat processing; natural fibers separation (e.g., cotton ginning), carding, and spinning; lumber, wood products, and wood pulping; gas processing and petroleum refining; coking; electric power generation; inorganic and organic chemical and polymer production; beneficiation or concentration of metal ores; reduction, refining, and alloying of metals; and mineral calcination products (lime, cement, plaster). Primary materials also include products of high-temperature sintering or melting furnaces, such as ceramics, bricks, and glass.

Secondary processing is concerned with the physical transformation of primary materials into intermediate and final forms. Basic intermediate forms include products of spinning (thread, yarn, twine) and weaving (textiles) or knitting. They also include polymer films, paper and paperboard, metal foil, metal sheet and strip, metal wire and rod, metal stampings and forgings, metal castings, and machined products (e.g., screws and threaded components, gears). These intermediate forms can be further cut, laminated (e.g., plywood or composite packaging materials), plated, coated, printed, etched, or painted into finished components.

In the tertiary stage, final goods and structures are assembled from components and subassemblies by a variety of means including sewing (garments), cement and concrete (in structures), adhesives, welding, soldering, or by using mechanical fasteners (screws, nails, nuts and bolts, rivets, staples, snap fasteners, etc.). Needless to say, finished products may also be further combined and connected physically into "infrastructure" networks (such as the telephone, rail, or electric power networks) or linked by functional interactions into even larger systems such as water and sewer services and road or rail transport. The production of final goods, including networks and systems, is sometimes called tertiary activities.

Construction is not conceptually very different from manufacturing, although the construction sector is distinguished from manufacturing in government statistics.

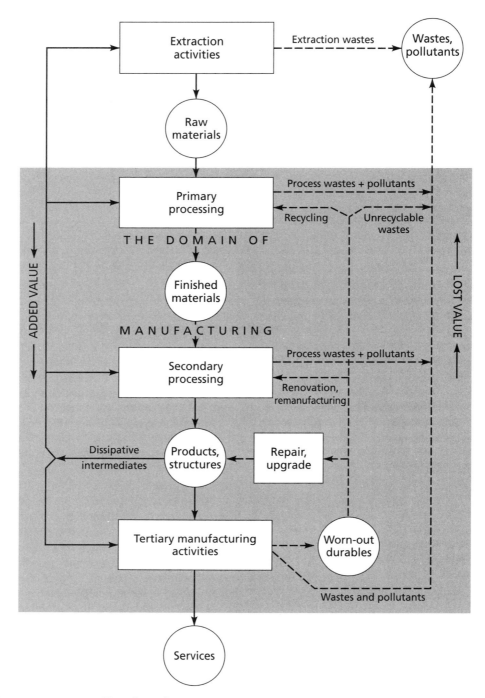

Manufacturing. Figure 1. Mass Flows in Manufacturing.

In practice, the distinction is based on mobility: the construction sector is essentially the manufacturing of immobile structures, on site, by craft methods, in contrast with (potentially) mobile machines, appliances, and other goods made in factories. The distinction is becoming increasingly less useful, however, as more and more subsystems of buildings—even concrete castings—are factory-made and "mobile homes" become increasingly common.

History. The first industrial revolution (c.1770–1830) is generally regarded as the period of adoption of steam power to replace water and horse power. At first, the motivation for using steam power was to replace horses for pumping water from coal (and other) mines, as they dug deeper. Later, steam engines gradually replaced horses and mules for hauling barges and carts to carry heavy goods (such as coal) between mine and city or factory. Railways could go where canals could not, and they were much faster. Still later, steam engines were adopted to drive power looms, air pumps for blast furnaces, boring machines, and other metalworking machine tools. This enabled textile mills, iron foundries, and other large-scale factories to locate near the ports and away from sources of water power, which was already scarce in eighteenth-century England. Finally, steam power and iron, together, created a new kind of ocean shipping.

It is important to note that the net effect of the introduction of steam power and its ramifications (e.g., railways, steamships) was to decrease the cost of energy (from coal) and of mechanical power, as delivered to both industrial and final consumers, especially in the growing cities [See Urban Areas.] This cost reduction trend, which began in the early eighteenth century, became quite rapid in the nineteenth. (In fact, the trend has continued ever since, although it has been driven by other technologies.) As consumer costs for energy and power fell, new applications emerged. Demand—both intermediate and final—for energy and for power-consuming goods and services increased, as did the substitution of machines in factories for human or animal muscles dispersed across the landscape. The latter process, in turn, generated increased demand for fossil fuels. Growing demand stimulated more technological innovation throughout the manufacturing chain as well as economies of scale. So the trend toward lower costs and increasing demand became a self-reinforcing (positive feedback) process.

The first industrial revolution began in Great Britain. By the late eighteenth century (in Britain, at least), the preindustrial period of craft guilds and cottage industry was beginning to be replaced by more centralized factories, beginning with cotton spinning. The first stage of mechanized manufacturing could be called the "English system." It applied power-driven machines to the old methods of production and added increased specialization and deskilling of labor. A more radical change, known as the "American system" (1850–1920), was pioneered initially in the arms industry of New England (Whitney, Colt, Remington) and subsequently exported back to England and around the world. The American system emphasized product standardization and interchangeability of parts, even when achieved at the expense of accuracy and precision of fit.

The second industrial revolution (1880–1930) was a variant of the first. Electric power and internal combustion engines—based on liquid fuels derived from newly available petroleum byproducts—were the two core technologies, although the new availability of low-cost carbon steel was also a factor. Electric power made it possible for centralized prime movers to deliver power to decentralized users, including individual machines within factories. Internal combustion engines made mechanical power truly mobile. This quickly led to self-propelled vehicles, both on and off the roads, eventually including practical heavier-than-air flying machines. It also resulted in the final displacement of horses and mules from the cities, the roads, and finally the farms.

Again, the net effect was to keep driving down the cost of energy and mechanical power, delivered at the point of use. This permitted the continuing substitution of machines for human and animal labor (not to mention agriculture and transportation). During the same period, manufacturing itself gradually overcame the difficulties of achieving standardization and interchangeability and became increasingly mechanized in response to the growing demand for standardized production-related machines such as metal-cutting machines, sewing machines, leather-stitching machines (for shoe manufacturing), harvesters, and so on. By the 1920s, electric motors and other electrical appliances, internal combustion engines, and automobiles were also being mass produced. Mass production of machines led to further cost reduction to users, which further stimulated demand and continued the self-reinforcing economic growth process.

The technological innovations of the second industrial revolution were multicentered. The internal combustion engine was invented in France (Lenoir, de Rochas) but most quickly developed and adapted to vehicles in Germany (Otto, Maybach, Daimler, Benz, and Diesel). Mass-production technology for metal products was pioneered by the New England arms industry, the sewing machine and bicycle industries, the farm machinery industries, and later by the U.S. auto industry (especially Ford). Germany and the United States were parallel innovators of the electrical equipment industry (Siemens, Edison, Tesla, Westinghouse).

The advent of mass production coincided with the heyday of "scientific management," developed and promoted by Frederick W. Taylor (c.1910) and adopted most enthusiastically by Henry Ford. This was, in some ways, the logical extension of the American system of manufacturing, mentioned earlier. It emphasized mechanical integration (assembly lines, transfer lines), hierarchical organizational structure, vertical integration, detailed cost accounting, and extreme division of labor. It required very detailed job descriptions and skill training, with remuneration based on output at each level.

The organizational innovation of Taylor and Ford, as applied to manufacturing, can be characterized as an attempt to overcome the inherent limitations of all hierarchical organizations: the tendency of independent parallel branches to compete rather than cooperate. The

Taylor-Ford solution to this growing problem was top-down centralized planning. (Taylor and Ford were, effectively, the spiritual godfathers of communist central planning). Only in recent decades has the Taylor-Ford hierarchical model for a manufacturing organization been challenged, mainly in Scandinavia and Japan. To date, however, the top-down model has been only slightly modified (e.g. by reducing the number of hierarchical levels and reducing the inflexibility of job descriptions); it has not been effectively replaced by anything radically new.

Future Trends in Manufacturing Technology. A third industrial revolution—or evolutionary change—seems to be in progress. There is no need to dispute terminology. The most important single feature of this change is that it is centered on the application of computers and information technology (IT) to manufacturing. [*See* Technology.] The first applications of IT were in the office, especially in the processing of enormous amounts of information required for the planning and coordination functions of a modern hierarchical multiproduct firm. Information technology (i.e., computers) has become a necessary tool of hierarchical centralized management.

After decades of anticipation, computers, robots and "smart sensors" are finally beginning to substitute for human eyes and hands on the factory floor. This is certainly true for simple repetitive tasks that do not require the active use of human intelligence, except to convert a flow of information from one form to another. Programmable machine tools, computer-aided design, and computer-aided process planning all offer major advantages in labor savings and information management.

Other key managerial innovations of recent decades were pioneered in Japan. Japanese-style "lean production" dates from around 1970. One was "total quality control," a formalized practical implementation of Frederick Deming's statistical quality control techniques, pioneered by Bell Laboratories and AT&T in the 1930s and 1940s. Another was a clever Toyota innovation that brought order into a chaotic parts delivery system. Toyota, like other Japanese auto manufacturers, was much less vertically integrated—hence more dependent on independent parts suppliers—than comparable U.S. firms. It was less able to rely on centralized computerized management of the system. At the same time, warehouse space was scarcer and more expensive in Japan than in the United States. To overcome these problems, Toyota invented an ingenious, decentralized, yet transparent manual control system known as *kan ban* that was easy to explain to workers. It did not require central computers. The system later became known as "just-in-time" delivery. It sharply reduced inventory costs for Toyota and incidentally revealed a major but neglected area of potential cost reduction for other manufacturers.

A third Japanese manufacturing innovation, also at Toyota, was "synchronous engineering." The objective was to cut the time from product design to initial production, which had become longer and longer as vehicles became more complex. The traditional sequential process started with the selection of a design from a set of competing prototype designs, followed by engineering design modifications and materials selection by the engineering staff to reduce manufacturing costs, followed by design of the manufacturing process itself, followed by construction of the manufacturing plant. By reexamining the sequence as a whole, it was realized that cutting the length of time from beginning to end of the sequence would offer greater gains than maximizing the savings that could be achieved by the engineering modifications. In effect, by carrying out detailed engineering analysis on several design variants in parallel, rather than in sequence, Toyota was able to bring out new designs faster than its competitors.

Another recent development has become known as "computer integrated manufacturing" (CIM). This is shorthand for functional integration of the entire design, engineering, and manufacturing chain with the help of computers. For example, much of the design and engineering process can be facilitated by computer simulation, which is a technology where the United States is ahead of Japan. The ability to collect and interpret real-time data about the manufacturing process, inventory, sales, purchases, and so forth can take "lean production" into a totally new dimension. CIM, while still far from full-scale implementation, can be regarded as the beginning of a new era. It marks a sharp break with the four decades (1950s through 1980s) during which computers consistently increased the speed and accuracy of a host of immediate applications but somehow failed to produce measurable increases in overall industrial productivity.

The era of CIM and IT is also on the verge of creating a new variant of the old engine of economic growth. Whereas the first and second industrial revolutions induced growth by driving down the cost of energy and mechanical power, the third industrial revolution will certainly obtain most of its efficiency gains and cost reductions from information technology. The rapidity of cost and price reductions for computers is already legendary, and this trend continues. Until fairly recently, the spectacular cost reductions were most visible in terms of creating consumer markets for personal computers. But behind the scenes a more fundamental process is also under way, namely, the pervasive application of computer and information technology to the entire manufacturing sector. Computers and software are now the main component of capital spending by industry, and this is no accident. Most future gains in labor productivity in manufacturing will be attributable, directly or indirectly, to this technology.

International Aspects. The original sequence of industrial development has been somewhat truncated by countries that began to industrialize in the nineteenth century or more recently. [See Industrialization.] The first country to embark on a deliberate "top-down" program of industrial development was Japan, with the so-called Meiji Revolution in the 1860s. Japan adopted some features of the earlier British model (mechanization of the textile sector, and the naval ship-building program) and some of the German (emphasis on heavy industry, especially steel and armaments manufacturing). Czarist Russia, also beginning in the 1860s, adopted a combination of German and American models, especially the emphasis on coal- and steel-based heavy industry, making possible the ambitious Trans-Siberian railway and the subsequent development of petroleum resources in Azerbaijan. Soviet development after the Russian Revolution was even more centralized, with special emphasis on mechanized agriculture in collective farms, heavy industry, and large-scale electric power. This centrally planned industrialization program was fairly successful through the 1930s. It became increasingly inefficient during the post–World War II years, however, as lack of competition inhibited innovation and manufacturing capacity was diverted from civil to military purposes.

The most successful economic and manufacturing development models of the last half century (since World War II) have been the countries of Southeast Asia, plus the outer fringe of Europe (including Israel). All of them bypassed railways (except for South Korea) and neglected heavy industry altogether. Israel was a special case, owing to injections of large numbers of educated immigrants, on the one hand, and large amounts of capital from Germany (as reparations) and America, on the other hand. Israel is the only recently developed country that is internationally competitive over a whole range of "high-tech" sectors.

Hong Kong, as a colony, always had unimpeded access to the British market, while Japan and South Korea were given easy access to the U.S. market in the 1950s (as a political consequence of the Korean War). All of the Southeast Asian countries adopted the Japanese model of export-driven growth, beginning with textiles, combined with protection for domestic industries. Thanks to falling international trade barriers and domestic political stability, Singapore, Malaysia, Indonesia, Thailand, and the Philippines have become offshore manufacturing and assembly "platforms" for multinational manufacturers centered in Japan or the United States, although Singapore is now mostly a regional entrepot and financial center. China is following this route to some extent, but mostly for offshore Chinese (especially Taiwanese) investors. All have made special efforts to attract high-tech industries, such as electronics, although only Korea now produces automobiles from domestic parts and steel, and only Taiwan produces internationally competitive electronic goods, though China is likely to do so soon.

The countries of Latin America, South Asia, the Middle East, and Africa (except South Africa) have a much less successful history. Virtually all of the Latin and postcolonial countries, as well as India and Pakistan, adopted protectionist import substitution policies and have kept them in place until some recent reforms. (Mexico became a partial exception, with its "Maquiladora" program of encouraging export-oriented international manufacturers to locate factories near the U.S. border.) In consequence, the smaller countries did not develop a significant manufacturing sector at all, while the larger ones became self-sufficient in some sectors but lagged so far behind in terms of technology that their protected manufacturers could not export to world markets. This situation may be changing, thanks to spreading economic liberalization. But change will be very slow, especially for the poorer countries, which have no large domestic markets to attract international investors.

The increasing importance of information technology and computer integration in manufacturing, noted in the previous section, has international implications. On the one hand, it is now possible to decentralize many information-related activities such as software development and large-scale database management. This has allowed firms in high-cost areas such as Europe to subcontract some computer-related operations to such places as Bangalore, India, where labor costs are much lower. On the other hand, the advent of CIM virtually eliminates the need for unskilled labor in manufacturing (except for a minor role in materials handling) and thus reduces the competitive advantage of countries, such as Indonesia, China, and India, with large numbers of rural villagers who are currently migrating to cities in search of manufacturing jobs.

Manufacturing and Wealth. The manufacturing process, taken as a whole, is a central element of wealth creation. In the first place, it is the direct source of consumer goods, which in turn produce consumer services that jointly contribute much of consumer welfare. In the second place, manufacturing also produces the so-called producer goods or physical capital stock that enables goods to be produced. The accumulation of physical capital increases the capacity of the manufacturing system to produce those goods.

The manufacturing and construction sectors taken together now account for less than one-third of total economic output and employment in the Organisation for Economic Co-operation and Development countries, and less than a quarter in the United States. Moreover, because labor productivity is growing more rapidly in manufacturing than in service sectors, the latter account for an ever-increasing share of both. But this should not be regarded as an indication that manufacturing is declining in importance. On the contrary, thanks to continuing efficiency gains and falling real prices of manufactured products (including capital goods), manufacturing remains the major engine of economic growth and generator of wealth.

An important distinction may be made between durable goods and consumables. Many consumables are in fact intermediates, while some so-called consumer goods (such as automobiles) are long-lived durables. Conceptually, a durable good provides a service to producers or consumers without itself being consumed. (Of course, it may become obsolescent or non-functional due to wear and tear.) A capital good is a durable good used by producers. An intermediate good, in contrast, is immediately converted into something else, either another material good or a waste. In one sense the distinction between durables and consumables is ultimately somewhat arbitrary, insofar as all material goods are ultimately "transformed" into nonmaterial services. But not all intermediates are converted into other goods. In practice, the difference between an intermediate good and a capital good is essentially a matter of reusability and useful lifetime. Material goods that are consumed or dissipated do not contribute directly to tangible real wealth, although they may be an integral part of the current production process.

Evidently the real value of tangible produced wealth—the ultimate source of most economic services—is strongly dependent on the real rate of depreciation of durable goods (not necessarily the rate determined by the tax authorities). It follows that reducing the real rate of depreciation of durable goods would increase the rate of accumulation of real tangible wealth and consequently the rate of economic growth. This fact, in turn, creates a strong incentive to conserve value added by renovation and remanufacturing of durable goods, which are the only material products that constitute real wealth (by generating immaterial services to final consumers). Financial wealth, in the long run, must correspond to real tangible (service-generating) wealth.

Manufacturing and the Environment. Other articles in this encyclopedia make the point that waste and pollution of the environment is an inevitable consequence of the extraction and processing of raw materials. [*See* Industrial Metabolism.] This is a straightforward implication of the conservation of mass and the materials balance principle. It follows that environmental protection can coexist with economic growth only if the use of raw materials per unit of economic value produced is sharply reduced. One approach, called "dematerialization," is usually associated with microminiaturization, as in the electronics industry. However, the large-scale uses

of materials (such as housing and transportation) are much less amenable to this approach.

Recycling is another commonly cited strategy. While not to be neglected, recycling is, however, only a special case of a more general approach: *conservation of value added to materials by manufacturing.* In brief, the strategy for conserving value added by manufacturing consists of two parts. The first is to eliminate, as far as possible, all dissipative consumptive uses of materials, whether intermediate or final. As pointed out previously, such materials are not embodied in durable goods and therefore do not contribute directly to the accumulation of real wealth, but they do contribute directly and immediately to environmental pollution loads. Examples of dissipative materials include fuels, lubricants, cleaning agents, coloring agents, bleaches, solvents, fertilizers, and biocides. Some of these may be difficult to eliminate in practice, of course, but finding non-material substitutes must be a high priority for the future.

The second part of the value-added conservation strategy can be termed the four *R*s, namely, reuse, repair/renovation, remanufacturing, and recycling, in that order of priority. The priority ordering reflects the potential for conserving value added. Reuse comes first because no investment is needed, in principle, although discovering new uses for old or obsolescent products may involve some effort. A good current example might be the use of older but still functional personal computers in schools for education and training purposes. Note that, under current conditions, manufacturers of new personal computers have relatively little incentive to promote this activity, since it may compete with sales of newer units. To change this, governments will have to change some of the rules of the game. One change that would encourage longer product life—hence more reuse—is the application of so-called take-back legislation, which would force manufacturers to take back their discarded products.

Repair/renovation is next in priority. Many small appliances and electronic products, as well as major components of larger appliances and systems, are designed to discourage repair, apparently to encourage replacement by newer items. The usual advice is for users to send the faulty unit back to the factory or simply discard it and buy another. This practice is generally defended on grounds of efficiency. Indeed, it is often true that, for mass-produced items, repair is not cost effective compared to replacement. It is also true, however, that most of these items could be more easily repairable if repair/renovation were not actively discouraged by design. Working parts are often hidden and inaccessible, or accessible only by means of specialized and costly tools. The days of replacing a burned-out tube or fuse are long gone. Yet it might very well be possible to facilitate many categories of repairs and upgrades, for instance, through design for disassembly, if manufacturers were motivated to do so. Again, take-back legislation might be one tool for government to encourage this.

Remanufacturing is only the third priority insofar as value recovery is concerned, but it has the greatest potential for growth. Remanufacturing can be regarded as repair/renovation that is carried out in a factory, making some use of large-scale production techniques. Some standard products such as truck or aircraft tires, gas turbines, and diesel engines have been remanufactured routinely for many years. Again, design for disassembly by original manufacturers must be more widely adopted by original equipment manufacturers (OEMs) to facilitate this shift. Take-back legislation would help to encourage this.

Currently, the remanufacturing industry is very small compared to original equipment manufacturing. Some remanufacturers are also OEMs, and these are among the largest. According to a recent survey, however, most remanufacturers are relatively small independent companies with less than U.S.$10 million in sales and one hundred employees. The average remanufacturer handles about ten products, so it can be seen that very few products are remanufactured on a large scale. (Toner cartridges and small "disposable" cameras are among the few exceptions.) It is also evident that independent remanufacturers are often in direct competition with OEMs, a situation that inhibits cooperation and increases costs.

The main problems of the remanufacturing industry at present are evidently related to small scale and lack of vertical integration with OEMs. Most remanufacturers cannot afford to use modern materials handling, cleaning, and processing technologies. Yet the number of successful and profitable firms engaged in remanufacturing, despite these drawbacks, suggests that the range of unexploited opportunities is large indeed. The opportunities for remanufacturing would be even greater with more direct feedback between remanufacturers and OEMs with regard to design problems and opportunities.

The fourth R is recycling of materials that cannot profitably be remanufactured. While recycling is not practiced nearly as would be desirable, there is not much to add on the subject here. It is worthwhile, however, to make one point: the major barrier to more efficient recycling is precisely the lack of remanufacturing. If remanufacturing were more prevalent, recycling would be also.

The reasons are obvious on reflection. In order to remanufacture a family of durable products, the obsolete or worn-out items must be collected, shipped to a central point, sorted, and tested. Then comes disassembly, cleaning, and various kinds of treatment. Some parts may be collected and shipped on to subcontractors for further treatment and so on. But obviously some leftover components and materials, especially packaging and wearing parts, are suitable only for recycling as materials. But having already been through a process of collection sorting and testing, these leftover materials are bound to be much more precisely characterized—and hence of higher value—than mixed scrap. It follows that there will be less waste sent to landfills and more recycling (either by means of remanufacturing or as materials) than would otherwise be the case.

Indeed, high-value metals such as stainless steel, copper, aluminum, and even chromium, gold, or platinum can be recovered from a sophisticated multistage recovery system. But such a system can rarely if ever be justified economically for purposes of materials recycling alone. It can be justified only if there is a potential for simultaneously recovering much higher-value subassemblies and components.

[See also Greening of Industry; and Pollution.]

BIBLIOGRAPHY

Ayres, R. U. *Computer Integrated Manufacturing*, vol. 1, *Revolution in Progress*. International Institute for Applied Systems Analysis CIM. London: Chapman and Hall, 1990.
Ayres, R. U., and D. Butcher. "The Flexible Factory Revisited." *American Scientist* (September–October 1993), 448–459.
Manufacturing Studies Board, Commission on Engineering and Technical Systems, and National Research Council. *Toward a New Era in U.S. Manufacturing: The Need for a National Vision*. Washington, D.C.: National Academy Press, 1986.
Schonberger, R. J. *World Class Manufacturing: The Next Decade. Building Power, Strength, and Value*. New York: Free Press, 1996.
Thierry, M. *Analysis of the Impact of Product Recovery Management of Manufacturing*. Rotterdam, Netherlands: Erasmus University, 1997.

—R. U. AYRES

MAPPING. *See* Geographic Information Systems; Information Management; *and* Remote Sensing.

MARGINAL SEAS

Marginal seas are semienclosed bodies of water open to the ocean. The Mediterranean and the Caribbean are marginal Atlantic seas, the South China Sea and the Sea of Japan are marginal to the Pacific, and the Red Sea and the Timor Sea to the Indian Ocean. Some are shallow, less than 200 meters deep, and are referred to as *shelf seas* (for example, Hudson Bay and the North Sea), while others are deep, connected to the ocean only at the surface and bounded at depth by submarine ridges (for example, the Yellow Sea and the Mediterranean). [See Mediterranean Sea; and North Sea.]

An important feature of all marginal seas is their proximity to the continental land masses, which influence their physical, chemical, and biological characteristics, and expose them in some cases to the effects of intensive human use. Land runoff, particularly via rivers, contributes nutrients, so that marginal seas with good vertical water mixing and exchange with the open ocean tend to be areas of high biological activity, with rich fisheries. [See Estuaries.]

Proximity to the land can, however, bring adverse effects. Coastal sites, particularly in estuaries, attract a buildup of commerce and industry, resulting in discharges of chemical wastes and oil, while rivers, sometimes draining extensive watersheds, provide a pathway that carries over nine billion metric tons of silt and wastes to coastal waters annually. Furthermore, the increasing migration of human populations to the edge of the sea, to take advantage of water transportation and the attractions of the marine environment, has resulted in the development of vast conurbations. These add additional stress, not least in the form of sewage, which, as well as containing industrial effluents and storm water runoff, is rich in nutrients and organic matter and carries pathogenic organisms that bring diseases to recreational users of the shore and to consumers of seafood. Thus marginal seas are much more polluted than the open oceans. Those that are regularly flushed by the ocean will be least at risk, but others that are relatively enclosed may suffer major degradation, and carry high concentrations of heavy metals, synthetic organic compounds (including industrial chemicals and pesticides), hydrocarbons, and radionuclides.

In addition to the direct inputs from land, there are two other sources of pollutants to marginal seas, shipping, and the atmosphere. Until the late 1980s, disposal from ships of wastes, particularly sewage sludge and chemicals, was a major global activity. However, dumping at sea has been largely phased out, and shipping inputs are now mainly from accidental spills and operational discharges. Pollution from the atmosphere, however, is continuous. Many contaminants from a wide range of sources, including industrial emissions and energy production, are carried in the air and deposited in the oceans, but the concentrations are low and the inputs diffuse, so that their importance in marginal seas is usually relatively small.

Eutrophication, the overenrichment of waters, has become a particular concern. A moderate addition of nutrients to the sea can have a fertilizing effect, raising the general level of productivity, but excessive inputs disturb the balance of growth and result in abnormal blooms of seaweeds on the shore and phytoplankton in the upper waters. When these plants die, their decay mediated by bacteria uses up oxygen, resulting in unfavorable conditions that can cause massive kills of fish and shellfish. The main sources of nutrients are sewage, agricultural runoff from heavy fertilizer use, and wastes from intensive livestock rearing and fish farming. If there is good mixing with the open sea, these inputs are quickly diluted and dispersed, but in more enclosed areas where the water is not regularly exchanged, the nutrients are able to build up to dangerous concentrations. In marginal seas of northern Europe, eutrophication occurs in the bays and inlets of the Baltic Sea and in the Southern Bight of the North Sea. Parts of the Mediterranean, particularly the Gulf of Lyons, the Lake of Tunis, and the Bay of Ismir, often show extreme effects, and in the northern Adriatic, heavy algal blooms seriously interfere with fisheries and tourism. In the Pacific, Tokyo Bay, Ise Bay, and parts of Seto Inland Sea are similarly affected and the important fish-farming industry in these areas is greatly disrupted. A special feature of some of these blooms is the increasing occurrence worldwide of toxic algae ("red tides"). Such blooms can kill other marine organisms, damage aquaculture, and cause illness and death to humans who eat contaminated shellfish. A longer-term concern is that eutrophication changes the nature of plankton populations, with knock-on effects throughout the whole food chain, resulting eventually in communities less suitable for commercial fish.

A significant pressure on marginal seas stems from the exploitation of nonliving resources, particularly oil and gas. Effects on the environment begin with the initial seismic surveys, which can break up fish shoals and disturb marine mammals, and continue through to production operations from which drill cuttings and a diversity of chemical effluents are discharged to the sea. However, these impacts are mainly restricted to the immediate vicinity of the installations. Much greater pressure on the environment arises from the exploitation of living resources. Fishing is a major activity in marginal seas, and in most is now so intensive that all commercial stocks are depleted. The ecological balance of the populations is upset, and physical changes can be detected on the seabed resulting from continuous trawling by heavy gear.

There is also extensive pressure from coastal development, which results in the widespread destruction of habitats by, for example, the drainage of wetlands for urban and industrial growth, the demands of tourism for hotels and marinas, and of aquaculture for shrimp ponds, constructed at the expense of mangrove forests.

[See also Coastlines; Ocean Chemistry; Ocean Disposal; and Ocean Life.]

BIBLIOGRAPHY

Anderson, D. M. "Red Tides." *Scientific American* (August 1994), 2–8. A useful review covering the main aspects of interest.
GESAMP (IMO/FAO/UNESCO/WMO/WHO/IAEA/UN/UNEP Joint Group of Experts on the Scientific Aspects of Marine Pollution). "The State of the Marine Environment." *UNEP Regional*

Seas Reports and Studies 115 (1990). An authoritative account of the condition of the oceans and the impacts of human activities; puts marginal seas into a wider context.

Jennings, S., and M. J. Kaiser. "The Effects of Fishing on Marine Ecosystems." *Advances in Marine Biology* (1998), in press. An excellent review of all aspects of the effects of fishing on the marine environment, with extensive references.

Newman, P. J., and A. R. Agg. *Environmental Protection of the North Sea.* London: Heinemann, 1988. A good coverage of the issues in one particular marginal sea.

Postma, H., and J. J. Zijlstra, eds. *Continental Shelves.* Amsterdam: Elsevier, 1988. Covers a number of marginal seas, giving useful descriptions.

Tolba, M. K., O. A. El-Kholy, E. El-Hinnawi, M. W. Holdgate, D. F. McMichael, and R. E. Munn, eds. *The World Environment 1972–1992.* London: Chapman and Hall, 1992. A comprehensive examination of the global environment, covering sea, air, and land, but with much on marginal seas.

—A. D. McIntyre

MARINE POLLUTION CONVENTION

Negotiations of the International Convention for the Prevention of Pollution from Ships in 1973 and its fully integrated protocol in 1978 (together known as MARPOL 73/78) constituted efforts to develop a comprehensive regime for ship-generated marine pollutants. Prompted in part by several dramatic oil tanker accidents, MARPOL built on several earlier intergovernmental treaties for marine pollution control, including the 1954 International Convention for Prevention of Pollution of the Sea by Oil (1954), the International Convention on Civil Liability for Oil Pollution Damage (1969), the International Convention Relating to Intervention on the High Seas in Cases of Oil Pollution Casualties (1969), the International Convention on the Establishment of an International Fund for Compensation for Oil Pollution Damage (1971), and the Convention on the Prevention of Marine Pollution by Dumping of Wastes and Other Matter (1972). Primarily concerned with nonaccidental pollution, MARPOL established five pollutant-specific annexes regulating oil, liquid chemicals, harmful packaged substances, sewage, and garbage discharged by ships. The United Nations International Maritime Organization (IMO) has since negotiated protocols and amendments to most of the above-mentioned agreements, as well as producing the International Convention on Oil Pollution Preparedness, Response and Co-operation (1990) and the International Convention on Liability and Compensation for Damage in Connection with the Carriage of Hazardous and Noxious Substances by Sea (1996). Recent negotiations under the auspices of IMO have sought to add regulations to MARPOL to address various ship-generated air pollutants (including sulfur dioxide, nitrogen oxides, and ozone-depleting substances).

Taken together, these conventions have produced a global regime composed of a vast network of regulations covering most intentional and accidental pollution of the ocean from ships. These conventions, *inter alia*, ban or limit the amounts and rates of discharge of various pollutants, establish financial liability for polluting accidents, require installation of equipment that precludes such discharges, and require the provision of shore facilities to receive various pollutants. Numerous regional agreements as well as many countries' domestic laws provide additional marine environmental protection by establishing further regulations regarding regional seas and land-based sources of marine pollution. National efforts to facilitate compliance with these regulations while detecting noncompliance have been bolstered by regional agreements in Europe, Latin America, the Asia–Pacific region, the Caribbean, the Mediterranean, the Indian Ocean, West and Central Africa, the Black Sea, and the Persian Gulf, which coordinate inport inspections and marine surveillance efforts. Ship-classification societies, insurance agencies, and shipbuilders have also played important roles in altering the institutional environment in ways that decrease the opportunities and incentives for shipowners to pollute the ocean.

As with many environmental problems, numerous obstacles prevent confident evaluation of the impact that these agreements have had on polluting behavior or on marine environmental quality. What evidence does exist suggests that the nations and ships of the world have become more conscientious in their treatment of the ocean, even though none of these pollutants has yet been eliminated from the marine environment. Both intentional discharges and accidental spills of oil appear to have decreased in size and frequency, and similar trends are evident for most of the other pollutants regulated under these agreements. At present, remaining obstacles to marine environmental protection appear to arise more from the absence of proper implementation and compliance than from the absence of appropriate regulations.

[*See also* Law of the Sea; London Convention of 1972; Ocean Disposal; *and* Petroleum Hydrocarbons in the Ocean.]

BIBLIOGRAPHY

Mankabady, S. *The International Maritime Organization.* London: Croom Helm, 1986. A good source for legal documentation on the IMO and the numerous conventions negotiated under its auspices.

M'Gonigle, R. M., and M. W. Zacher. *Pollution, Politics, and International Law: Tankers at Sea.* Berkeley: University of California Press, 1979. An excellent analysis of the history of international marine pollution regulation through the negotiation of MARPOL 73/78.

Mitchell, R. B. *Intentional Oil Pollution at Sea: Environmental Policy and Treaty Compliance.* Cambridge, Mass.: MIT Press, 1994. A detailed analysis of the effectiveness of efforts to implement and enforce international oil-pollution regulations.

Pritchard, S. Z. *Oil Pollution Control*. London: Croom Helm, 1987. A less analytic but more detailed history of marine pollution control than M'Gonigle and Zacher.

—RONALD B. MITCHELL

MARKET MECHANISMS

Although many environmental regulations over the past three decades have been effective in improving environmental quality, they have often done so at a relatively high cost to society. The unduly high cost stems from the reliance of regulators on direct regulations that provide little flexibility to firms in meeting environmental goals. This command and control approach often specifies a uniform level of pollution reduction that all firms must achieve, or a particular technology that must be installed. On the other hand, policies that create economic incentives for firms to reduce pollution, rather than a rigid mandate, provide firms with the flexibility to choose the most cost-effective method to achieve an environmental goal. Moreover, they encourage innovation by providing firms with an incentive to find or develop cleaner and less expensive technologies and production methods. Thus, policies that use market mechanisms such as environmental taxes or marketable permit schemes can meet an aggregate level of pollution reduction at lower overall costs.

Market-Based Approaches. Two major types of market-oriented policy that have been implemented are pollution charges and marketable-permit systems. A pollution charge system levies a fee or tax per unit of pollution. Under a charge system, firms face the same incentive to control at the margin, so that a firm will reduce its pollution up to the point at which the marginal cost of control just equals the tax. The result is that the total costs of pollution control are minimized compared with other allocations of the pollution-control burden across firms (Bohm and Russell, 1985). One problem with a charge system is that the regulators do not know in advance what level of cleanup will result from any given charge. Marketable-permit systems, on the other hand, can achieve the same cost-minimizing allocation of the pollution-control burden as a charge scheme in a way that avoids the problem of uncertain responses by firms (Hahn and Noll, 1982; Coase, 1960). A marketable-permit system typically limits pollution by establishing an overall level of permits and then allocating those permits to firms. Those that keep emission levels below the allotted level can sell or lease their surplus permits to other firms, or use them to offset excess emissions in other parts of their own facilities.

In addition to allowing greater levels of environmental protection for any given aggregate cost of control, market-oriented policies can provide powerful incentives for the development of new pollution-control technologies by the private sector. Because investments in pollution control can enhance profits under incentive-based systems, these policies can encourage firms to adopt new pollution-control technologies. The opportunity to profit creates incentives for firms to carry out research and development on cheaper and better pollution-abatement techniques.

In theory, the use of these mechanisms has the potential to achieve environmental objectives at the lowest cost. Many economic studies have projected substantial cost savings from replacing the traditional command-and-control regulations with more flexible incentive-based regulations. A review of *ex ante* empirical studies on cost savings from achieving least-cost air pollution control shows significant potential gains from incentive-based policies (Tietenberg, 1990). The ratio of costs from the traditional command-and-control approach to the least-cost policy for the eleven studies reviewed ranged from 1.07 to 22.00, with an average of 6.13. These *ex ante* simulations assume that incentive-based mechanisms achieve the optimal result. This is rarely the case in practice. Political obstacles frequently lead to markets that have high transaction costs and institutional barriers that reduce the potential for cost savings.

Market-Based Mechanisms in Practice. A broad array of incentive-based mechanisms have been used in the United States, but perhaps best known in terms of their potential for achieving cost savings are marketable permits, whose use has steadily increased over time. The primary application of this mechanism has been federal programs such as the Emissions Trading Program, the nationwide phasedown of lead in gasoline, the phaseout of some ozone-depleting chemicals, and the market in sulfur dioxide allowance trading for reducing acid rain. In addition, there are several programs at the regional level, such as Southern California's Regional Emissions Clean Air Incentives Market (RECLAIM), which allows polluters to trade emissions allowances to achieve air pollution goals.

The first U.S. experiment with marketable permits was the Emissions Trading Program implemented in 1974 to reduce the cost of meeting air pollution regulation. Hahn and Hester (1989b) produced the only comprehensive study of costs savings based on actual trades. They estimated that the program achieved savings on the order of U.S.\$1.4–19 billion over the first fourteen years. These savings come mainly from internal trading and, although substantial, do not represent the full extent of potential cost savings that could have been gained from external trading. The program generally failed to create an active market for emission-reduction credits, and did little to change the level of emissions. The program has not been widely used for several reasons. For example, the states that actually administer the Clean Air Act emissions-reduction requirements are not required to allow trading. The uncertainties about the future of the program made firms reluctant to participate. In addition, the high transaction costs of external trading have limited the interest in utilizing that option. The program did, however, allow for the environmental goals to be met at a lower cost.

The phasedown of lead in gasoline comes much closer to the economists' ideal for a smoothly functioning market. Two important features of this program helped the market to function properly. First, the amount of lead in gasoline could easily be monitored within the existing regulatory framework. Second, the program was established after the environmental goal was clearly defined. The U.S. Environmental Protection Agency (EPA) originally projected cost savings of U.S.$310 million to refiners from the banking provision of the program between 1985 and 1987 (Environmental Protection Agency, 1985). The actual cost savings may have been much higher than anticipated since the level of banking was higher than the EPA's expectations (Hahn, 1989).

Studies suggested that sizable cost savings could be achieved by using an incentive-based approach to curb the use of ozone-depleting chemicals. One study estimated that, between 1980 and 1990, a price-based incentive policy would save a total of U.S.$143 million over a command-and-control approach (General Accounting Office, 1982). The EPA implemented an allowance-trading program, and a tax on the ozone-depleting chemicals was later added. Although the primary purpose of the tax was to raise revenue, it may have been set high enough to have a significant incentive effect (Hahn, 1994). The actual cost savings from the two approaches, however, are unclear. [See Ozone.]

Studies projected savings on the order of U.S.$1 billion per year from the sulfur dioxide allowance-trading program to reduce acid rain (ICF Resources, Inc., 1992). The magnitude of actual cost savings achieved, however, is estimated to be significantly less. The prices of sulfur dioxide permits predicted in 1990 are significantly higher than the actual sulfur dioxide permit prices observed today. The discrepancy arises for a couple of reasons. First, early analyses did not include all provisions of the final bill, such as the distribution of 3.5 million extra bonus allowances. Second, much of the remaining difference between predicted and actual permit prices is due to railroad deregulation, and the resulting fall in the price of low-sulfur coal (Burtraw, 1996).

Although the absolute savings that were projected have not materialized, relative savings are in the range of what was predicted by *ex ante* studies—approximately 25–35 percent of costs absent trading (Carlson et al., 1998). Interestingly, Burtraw (1996) has found that the primary source of cost savings was not directly from trading across utilities, but rather from the flexibility in choosing abatement strategies within utilities, which is consistent with earlier predictions. Improvements in the trading program may therefore allow utilities to achieve further cost savings.

The RECLAIM program in Southern California has received much attention over the last few years. The program was expected to produce significant cost savings. The South Coast Air Quality Management District (SCAQMD) had estimated that the program would yield cost savings of U.S.$52 million in 1994 (Johnson and Pekelney, 1996). Although the potential savings are sizable, and a review of the trading activity to date suggests that significant cost savings have been achieved, there are no comprehensive studies that have assessed the actual savings.

As these examples show, the use of these mechanisms has increased over the years and the potential savings are substantial; however, a more detailed review of these applications suggests that their performance has varied widely (Hahn and Hester, 1989a). The variation in performance of these programs can be explained, in part, by differences in the underlying politics governing the choice and design of these programs. These political forces have led to policies that deviate from the economists' ideal.

Although the marketable-permit schemes reviewed here did not capture all potential cost savings, the programs generally improved environmental quality at a lower cost than alternatives under consideration. In contrast, the purpose of many environmental taxes and fees in the United States has been to raise revenue rather than reduce pollution. For example, the Superfund tax levied on crude oil, chemicals, and gross business profits is used to help finance cleanup. When fees have been levied directly on pollution, they have not been large enough to have significant impacts on behavior. Absent adequate incentives from fees, regulators have relied on command-and-control approaches to achieve desired levels of environmental protection.

Applications to Climate Change. A frequently discussed potential application of market mechanisms is a carbon tax or marketable permit scheme to help control global warming. As with other environmental problems addressed by a market approach, costs could be reduced substantially by using incentive-based instruments. Simulations based on the assumption that markets work efficiently suggest that potentially large savings might be achieved by moving to an international marketable-permit system if significant reductions were required. For example, if advanced industrial nations were required to stabilize emissions at 1990 levels by early in the twenty-first century, savings relative to the case with no trading with the rest of the world are in the range U.S.$0.5–3.0 trillion annually. These savings represent about 50 percent of the costs without trading.

The actual cost savings from economic approaches, however, are likely to fall far short of their theoretical potential. This is primarily because the design of economic approaches is intimately connected to politics. For example, in a marketable permit system, governments may initially be given the permits with no requirement to allocate these permits to private sector participants. If governments are central actors in trading, cost savings are likely to be lower because they have less of an incentive to minimize costs than do participants in the private sector. In addition, governments may need to play a central role in certain activities, such as the creation of carbon sinks on government land.

Government behavior could have a dramatic impact on the performance of the market, and hence the degree of cost savings achieved with a market. If a government is a major trader, private traders may fear that it will be more likely to change the trading rules to address short-term political concerns. In addition, even if a government stays on the sidelines, traders may fear that rule changes that diminish the value or security of property rights will occur, as was the case for emissions trading in the United States (Hahn and Hester, 1989b). A government can address this problem by clearly defining the nature of the property rights. Good examples include the market for phasing out lead in gasoline and the market for reducing sulfur dioxide in the United States.

If action is taken on global warming, market-based approaches have the potential to achieve reductions cost-effectively. But the degree to which cost savings are achieved depends critically on the design of such an approach. Economists are divided on the best approach to this problem; nevertheless, there is a consensus forming in the economics community that we need to focus on designing institutions that will help promote cooperation and achieve greenhouse gas reductions at a reasonable cost. Most of the existing literature on institution building suggests the need to focus on international institutions. Just as important, if not more so, is the need to develop adequate national institutions. Such institutions are crucial if novel market-based mechanisms are to be implemented effectively.

[See also Climate Change; Ecotaxation; Energy Policy; Joint Implementation; Public Policy; and Regulation.]

BIBLIOGRAPHY

Bohm, P., and C. S. Russell. "Comparative Analysis of Alternative Policy Instruments." In *Handbook of Natural Resource and Energy Economics*, vol. 1, edited by A. V. Kneese and J. L. Sweeney. Amsterdam: North-Holland, 1985.

Burtraw, D. "Cost Savings Sans Allowance Trades? Evaluating the SO$_2$ Emission Trading Program to Date." Discussion Paper 95-30-REV. Washington, D.C.: Resources for the Future, 1996.

Carlson, C., D. Burtraw, M. Cropper, and K. L. Palmer. "SO$_2$ Control by Electric Utilities: What Are the Gains from Trade?" Discussion Paper. Washington, D.C.: Resources for the Future, 1998.

Coase, R. H. "The Problem of Social Cost." *Journal of Law and Economics* 3 (1960), 1–44.

Environmental Protection Agency. "Costs and Benefits of Reducing Lead in Gasoline." Final Regulatory Impact Analysis III-2. Washington, D.C.: United States Environmental Protection Agency, 1985.

General Accounting Office. "A Market Approach to Air Pollution Control Could Reduce Compliance Costs Without Jeopardizing Clean Air Goals." PAD-82-15. Washington, D.C.: General Accounting Office, 1982.

Hahn, R. W. "Economic Prescriptions for Environmental Problems: How the Patient Followed the Doctor's Orders." *Journal of Economic Perspectives* 3 (1989), 95–114.

———. "United States Environmental Policy: Past, Present and Future." *Natural Resources Journal* 34 (Spring 1994), 305–348.

Hahn, R. W., and G. L. Hester. "Marketable Permits: Lessons for Theory and Practice." *Ecology Law Quarterly* 16 (1989a), 361–406.

———. "Where Did All the Markets Go? An Analysis of EPA's Emissions Trading Program." *Yale Journal of Regulation* 6 (1989b), 109–153.

Hahn, R. W., and R. Noll. "Designing a Market for Tradeable Permits." In *Reform of Environmental Regulation*, edited by W. Magat. Cambridge, Mass.: Ballinger, 1982.

ICF Resources, Inc. "Regulatory Impact Analysis of the Final Acid Rain Implementation Regulations." Washington, D.C.: United States Environmental Protection Agency, 1992.

Johnson, S. L., and D. M. Pekelney. "Economic Assessment of the Regional Clean Air Incentives Market: A New Emissions Trading Program for Los Angeles." *Land Economics* 72 (1996), 277–297.

Tietenberg, T. "Economic Instruments for Environmental Regulation." *Oxford Review of Economic Policy* 6 (1990), 17–33.

—ROBERT W. HAHN AND FUMIE YOKOTA

MARSH, GEORGE PERKINS

George Perkins Marsh (1802–1882), American conservationist, is best known for his pioneering insights in environmental conservation. A polymath, multilingual Vermonter, Marsh combined careers in law, farming, business, politics (United States Congressman 1843–1849), and diplomacy (American envoy to Turkey 1849–1853 and to Italy 1861–1882) with scholarly passions ranging from Old Icelandic and English linguistics to watershed analysis and irrigation.

Man and Nature (1864), subsequently subtitled *The Earth as Modified by Human Action*, was Marsh's single contribution to the field of conservation, whose components he began to develop in essays on forest economy, agricultural management, and fisheries resources in the 1840s and 1850s. Up to then, most human impacts on the globe were regarded as benign or, where deleterious, trivial and self-correcting. Marsh showed that human impact, because conscious and deliberate, long-term, and magnified by technology, was greater in magnitude than any other. The intended and above all the unintended consequences of human intervention deranged the normal stability of natural erosive and restorative processes, which otherwise alter the planet only at a slow geologic pace.

The essentially ecological insights of *Man and Nature* derived from close inspection of changes induced by settlement and deforestation in northern New England, along with wide reading, followed by personal observation, of the long-term devastation wrought by similar processes in Mediterranean and Alpine lands in Europe, North Africa, and the Middle East. The historically documented exhaustion, erosion, and desertification of Old World lands led Marsh to project a similar fate for the New World, unless restorative measures were undertaken to prevent further damage and as far as possible to repair the rapine already done by heedless or ignorant entrepreneurs.

Marsh's vivid depictions of past and present devastation, his graphic harbingers of an Earth as barren as the Moon, and his clearly reasoned practical remedies—afforestation, control of grazing, stream management, stabilization of sand dunes—rapidly made *Man and Nature* a bible among conservation-minded foresters and others in America and Europe, and as far afield as India, South Africa, and the Antipodes.

After a period of relative neglect, *Man and Nature* was rediscovered by geographers and planners in the 1920s and 1930s and served again to galvanize concern over human-induced misuse of natural resources. Celebrated in a 1955 Princeton symposium and again at Clark University in 1989, *Man and Nature* was republished in 1965 and remains in print to this day. A Marsh-Billings Rockefeller National Historical Park in Marsh's native Woodstock, Vermont, inaugurated in 1998, honors his pioneer insights, and aims to tell the story of conservation in America.

Although Marsh's specifics are long out of date, and environmental concerns unknown in his day now overshadow those with which he dealt, his basic insights into the complexity of relations among inorganic, organic, and human agencies remain valid, and his philosophy of restoration by judicious intervention is as relevant to our time as to his. No less enamored of nature than Henry David Thoreau and John Muir, Marsh was an early advocate of reserving wilderness areas for recreation and inspiration, and as laboratories of natural succession. But he never doubted that continued mastery and management of the earth was essential to civilization.

[*See also* Conservation; Environmental Movements; *and* Global Change, *article on* History of Global Change.]

BIBLIOGRAPHY

Lowenthal, D. "Awareness of Human Impacts: Changing Attitudes and Emphases." In *The Earth as Transformed by Human Ac-
tion*, edited by B. L. Turner II et al. New York: Cambridge University Press, 1990, pp. 121–135. Review of changes in views of environmental agency before, during, and after Marsh.

Marsh, G. P. *Man and Nature* (1864). Edited by D. Lowenthal. Cambridge: Harvard University Press, 1965. Marsh's canonical work, with significant revisions and additions from subsequent (1874, 1885) editions included in the notes.

———. *George Perkins Marsh: Prophet of Conservation*. Seattle: University of Washington Press, 2000.

Thomas Jr., W. L., ed. *Man's Role in Changing the Face of the Earth*. Chicago: University of Chicago Press, 1956. Results of a symposium organized by Carol Sauer, Marston Bates, and Lewis Mumford to honor Marsh and to assess the state of human impact on the planet ninety years on.

—DAVID LOWENTHAL

MASS CONSUMPTION

A major global social development of the twentieth century, mass consumption involves the spread of affluence and purchasing power within national populations, the rise of national markets and mass production of consumer goods and services, the advertising and purchase of a growing range of material goods by individuals, and the further spread of this pattern to a growing number of countries. In short, mass consumption involves the democratization of consumption, with an ever-larger percentage and number of people consuming at unprecedented levels. The temporal association between mass consumption and the globalization of environmental threats such as deforestation, loss of biodiversity, air and water pollution, and climate change prompts many scholars and practitioners to believe that mass consumption is a central driving force of environmental degradation globally.

One version of this mass consumption thesis holds that increased affluence leads inevitably to environmental degradation because of fundamental human needs and desires for material possessions, physical comfort, mobility, living space, and other amenities that are supplied by transforming materials and energy. [*See* IPAT.] In another variant, these desires are socioculturally induced and their environmental effects indirectly affected by advertising, competition for social status defined by material possessions, the portrayal of affluent North American lifestyles on television, and other social forces that spread a particularly resource-intensive style of consumption. A third version identifies structural features of modern life—suburbanization, the decline of mass transit, increased adult labor force participation, and so on—as essentially forcing the purchase of individualized commodities that burden the environment. Some analysts place ultimate responsibility on what Allan Schnaiberg (1981) calls a "treadmill of production": a capitalist economic system that compels firms to increase profits continually and therefore to expand production and sales. This system provides incentives for firms to create consumer needs through advertising and other means; it also gives capitalist economies and states incentives to develop foreign markets and thus expand consumption globally. Under any version of the thesis, a further spread of mass consumption will lead inevitably to further environmental degradation. However, the four variants offer different prescriptions for changing the trends: stop the growth of affluence; change cultural values; redevelop the social infrastructure; or alter economic systems.

In one country after another, the spread of affluence has been accompanied by widespread adoption of consumer technologies and practices, such as motorized travel and energy-intensive methods of heating and cooling living space that consume resources and cause pollution. Nevertheless, there are reasons to qualify or question the centrality of mass consumption as a cause of environmental degradation. First, much of the environmental impact of affluence is due to choices by producers, governments, and organizational consumers, not individual purchasers. The most extreme example was the former Soviet bloc, which gravely polluted the environment by mining and manufacturing without ever developing much mass consumption. The transition from state socialism may allow consumerism to blossom while the environment improves. Meanwhile, in the wealthiest countries, many environmental indicators have improved since about 1970, while consumerism has flourished. [See Air Quality; and Eastern Europe.]

A key issue in the consumption–environment debate concerns the potential to loosen the link between consumer spending (economic consumption) and energy and materials transformations (environmental consumption). A long-term trend in North America and western Europe has been toward dematerialization—a decrease in the ratio of materials and energy used and consequently of pollution produced to the amount of economic output. This has resulted in part from technological improvements in the efficiency of materials and energy conversion and from shifts toward lighter-weight and less polluting inputs to production processes (for example, from steel to aluminum, and from coal to oil to natural gas, decreasing pollutants per unit of delivered energy at each step). A related transformation claimed to be environmentally beneficial has been toward a service-based economy in which material goods make up a decreasing proportion of consumer expenditures. Some analysts claim that a value shift occurs among consumers who have achieved sufficient affluence to meet basic material needs, leading to increased desire for nonmaterial aspects of the good life and for environmentally protective public policies.

Whatever the causes of dematerialization and related trends, the ratio of environmental degradation to per capita income has decreased in countries that have achieved a fairly high level of affluence. The implications for the global environment depend on whether these trends can outpace the growth of population and economic consumption, on the income level at which the ratio begins to fall, and on whether it is possible to lower this level significantly. Although all these factors are uncertain, many analysts currently believe that reversal of environmental degradation within the next several decades will require that dematerialization and related trends proceed considerably faster than historical averages. This conclusion implies a need for new policy initiatives.

Many of the policy options for lowering the ratio of environmental to economic consumption focus on producers and distributors. They aim to encourage the development and use of environmentally beneficial technologies in mining, manufacturing, transportation, and commerce. These strategies, which indirectly lower the environmental impact of delivering consumer goods and services, sometimes have far greater impact than direct efforts to change consumer behavior.

Other initiatives target consumers directly, an approach requiring mass behavioral change. Focusing on consumerist values has had little or no demonstrable short-term effect on consumption, but is difficult to evaluate because the desired changes occur mainly on a generational time scale and because the links to behavior are indirect and mediated by many other factors. However, the rise of markets for organically grown produce suggests that shifts in consumerism may have proenvironmental potential. Many interventions try to change consumer behavior through exhortation, information, incentives, and other strategies focused on specific actions rather than on the broad phenomenon of mass consumption. These strategies address single factors that affect consumer behavior (for example, knowledge, attitudes, financial costs, convenience, social norms). Generally, each such strategy has only small effects in the short term, but combinations of them, such as incentives and information, can have large effects, especially when the goal is to promote adoption of environmentally beneficial technologies.

[See also Economic Levels; Environmental Economics; Human Populations; Industrialization; and Market Mechanisms.]

BIBLIOGRAPHY

Crocker, D. A., and T. Linden, eds. *Ethics of Consumption: The Good Life, Justice, and Global Stewardship.* Lanham, Md.: Rowman and Littlefield, 1998. Twenty-seven essays on the causes, nature, and effects of consumption, including discussions of environmental effects and debate on ethical norms about consumption.

Gardner, G. T., and P. C. Stern. *Environmental Problems and Human Behavior.* Needham Heights, Mass.: Allyn and Bacon,

1996. Reviews and analyzes the evidence on the causes of environmentally significant individual behavior and on the effectiveness of efforts to change it.

Goodwin, N. R., et al., eds. *The Consumer Society.* Washington, D.C.: Island Press, 1997. Summarizes over eighty works with critical viewpoints on consumption and consumerism from environmental, social, economic, and ethical standpoints.

The Liberation of the Environment. *Daedalus* 125.3 (Special Issue, Summer 1996). A good source of information on dematerialization trends with a generally optimistic viewpoint about the potential to reconcile economy and environment.

National Research Council. *Environmentally Significant Consumption: Research Directions*, edited by P. C. Stern, et al. Washington, D.C.: National Academy Press, 1997. Presents conceptual analysis and representative current research on technological, behavioral, and cultural factors that drive environmentally significant consumption.

Schnaiberg, A. *The Environment: From Surplus to Scarcity.* New York and Oxford: Oxford University Press, 1981.

—PAUL C. STERN

MEDICINES. *See* Biotechnology; Ethnobiology; Human Health; *and* Technology.

MEDIEVAL CLIMATIC OPTIMUM

[*This case study focuses on a controversial late Holocene period of possibly warmer conditions that occurred before the Little Ice Age.*]

The Holocene epoch (i.e., the past ten thousand years) has witnessed a whole series of climatic fluctuations at a range of scales. In the early to mid-Holocene there was a phase of prolonged relative warmth, often referred to as the "Climatic Optimum," and at other times there have been phases of relative cold, termed "neoglacials." One of these neoglacials was the so-called Little Ice Age, which occurred between the end of the Middle Ages and the later nineteenth century. Another climatic fluctuation that has been proposed is a period of warmth in early medieval or pre-Renaissance times. This has been called the "Medieval Climatic Optimum," "Medieval Warm Period," or "Little Climatic Optimum." [*See* Climate Change; *and* Natural Climate Fluctuations.]

Proponents of this idea, including Lamb (1966), would argue that from 750 to 1200–1300 CE there was a period of marked glacial retreat that on the whole appears to have been slightly more marked than was that of the twentieth century. The trees of this phase, which were eventually destroyed by the cold and the glacial advances from about 1200 CE onward, grew on sites where, in our own time, trees have not had time or the necessary conditions to grow again. In terms of a more precise date, the medieval documents suggested to Lamb that the most clement period of this optimum, with its mild winters and dry summers, was around 1080–1180. At this time the coast of Iceland was relatively unaffected by the ice, compared to conditions in later centuries, and settlements were established in what are now inhospitable parts of Greenland. It is also believed that the relative heat and dryness of the summers, which led to the drying up of some peat bogs, was responsible for the plagues of locusts that in this period spread at times over vast areas, occasionally reaching far to the north. For instance, during the autumn of 1195, they reached as far as Hungary and Austria. In northern Canada, west of Hudson Bay, fossil forest has been discovered up to one hundred kilometers north of the present forest limit, and four radiocarbon dates from different sites show that this forest was living about 870–1140. It is also interesting that the Camp Century ice core from Greenland has revealed to American and Danish workers that a cold wave is evident after about 1130–1160, but that for five centuries preceding this there was a phase of appreciable warmth. This has also been confirmed by an ice core at Crete, in central Greenland (Dansgaard et al., 1975).

One additional line of evidence that has been used to gain an appreciation of this phase is the presence of vineyards in various parts of Britain. The Domesday Book (1085) records thirty-eight vineyards in England besides those of the king. The wine was considered almost equal to the French wine in quality and quantity as far north as Gloucestershire and the Ledbury area of Herefordshire, the London Basin, the Medway Valley, and the Isle of Ely. Some vineyards even occurred as far north as York, and Lamb (1966) regards this as being indicative of summer temperatures 1°–2°C higher than today, a general freedom from May frosts, and mostly good Septembers. In China, at about the same time, lychees, sensitive trees that succumb at temperatures below −4°C, were an economic crop in the Szechuan Basin in western China, but today they are limited to the south of Nanling (Hsieh, 1976).

It has also been maintained that favorable conditions of the Little Optimum coincided with radical changes in the fortunes of agricultural peoples in various parts of what is now the United States. Considerable growth and development occurred from 700 to 1200 (Malde, 1964), whereas, shortly before the thirteenth century, a very rapid withdrawal of agricultural people took place as a result of cold, dry conditions (Woodbury, 1961). The response of the Anasazi people of Colorado to the medieval warm epoch is discussed by Grove (1996).

Some recent tree ring analyses for Fennoscandia by Briffa et al. (1990), however, have failed to find any unambiguous evidence for this warm phase, or for very extended runs of warm years. They conclude (p. 438) that their reconstruction "dispels any notion that summers in Fennoscandia were consistently warm throughout that period. Although the second half of the twelfth century was very warm, the first half was very cold. For most of the eleventh and thirteenth centuries, summers were near normal (relative to the mean for 1951–70)." They suggest that the significance of the Medieval Climatic Optimum has been overstated and that much of the historical evidence on which the concept was based was essentially sketchy.

Doubts of this sort were expressed during the early 1990s, and fundamental issues were addressed such as, Did the medieval warm period actually exist? Was it a global phenomenon? Was it continuous or discontinuous? And did it span the entire period identified by Lamb and others (Dean, 1994)? In a review of the evidence, Hughes and Diaz (1994, p. 109) came to a somewhat equivocal but probably very reasonable series of conclusions:

> For some areas of the globe (for example, Scandinavia, Chile, the Sierra Nevada in California, the Canadian Rockies and Tasmania), temperatures, particularly in summer, appear to have been higher during some parts of this period than those that were to prevail until the most recent decades of the twentieth century.
>
> These warmer regional episodes were not strongly synchronous. Evidence from other regions (for example, the Southeast United States, Southern Europe along the Mediterranean, and parts of South America) indicates that the climate during that time was little different to that of later times, or that warming, if it occurred, was recorded at a later time than had been assumed. Taken together, the available evidence does not support a *global* Medieval Warm period, although more support for such a phenomenon could be drawn from high-elevation records than from low-elevation records.

Similar doubts have been expressed by Oglivie and Farmer (1997), who reanalyzed much of the available documentary evidence. They argue that the period was one of climatic complexity and throw doubt on Lamb's basic scheme (p. 130):

> Interestingly, the century from 1260 to 1360, based on our improved historical data set, appears to have been one of relatively cold winters in England. Lamb's suggestion of a "Medieval Warm Period" is not supported by the documentary data, neither his nor ours. This is not necessarily a contradiction because his basis for a "Medieval Warm Period" is largely biological and phenological. Nevertheless, if such a "Medieval Warm Period" did exist, it was clearly less well-defined and climatologically more complex than has popularly been believed.

At the same time that the concept of a Medieval Climatic Optimum has come under closer scrutiny, so, too, the succeeding "Little Ice Age" is also being seen as having a less clear-cut character than previously thought. As Jones and Bradley (1995, pp. 659–660) wrote:

> The last 500 years was a period of complex climatic anomalies, the understanding of which is not well-served by the continued use of the term "Little Ice Age." . . . The period experienced both warm and cold episodes and these varied in importance geographically. There is no evidence for a world-wide synchronous and prolonged cold interval to which we can ascribe the term "Little Ice Age."

Plainly, the climatic fluctuations of the past millennium are still an area where there is a great deal of uncertainty. [*See* Little Ice Age in Europe.]

BIBLIOGRAPHY

Briffa, K. R., T. S. Bartholin, D. Eckstein, P. D. Jones, U. W. Karlén, F. H. Schweingruber, and P. Zetterberg. "A 1400-Year Tree-Ring Record of Summer Temperatures in Fennoscandia." *Nature* 346 (1990), 434–439.

Dansgaard, W., D. Rech, N. Ounderstrup, H. B. Clausen, and C. U. Hammer. "Climatic Changes, Norsemen and Modern Man." *Nature* 255 (1975), 24.

Dean, J. S. "The Medieval Warm Period on the Southern Colorado Plateau." *Climatic Change* 26 (1994), 225–241.

Grove, J. M. "The Century Time Scale." In *Time Scales and Environmental Change*, edited by T. S. Driver and G. P. Chapman, pp. 39–87. London: Routledge, 1996.

Hsieh, C.-M. "Chu K'O-Chen and China's Climatic Change." *Geographical Journal* 142 (1976), 248–256.

Hughes, M. K., and H. F. Diaz. "Was There a 'Medieval Warm Period,' and If So, Where and When?" *Climatic Change* 26 (1994), 109–142.

Jones, P. D., and Bradley, R. S. "Climatic Variations over the Last 500 Years." In *Climate since AD 1500*, edited by R. S. Bradley and P. D. Jones, pp. 649–665. London: Routledge, 1995.

Lamb, H. H. *The Changing Climate*. London: Methuen, 1966.

Malde, H. E. "Environment and Man in Arid America." *Science* 145 (1964), 123–129.

Oglivie, A., and G. Farmer. "Documenting the Medieval Climate." In *Climates of the British Isles: Present, Past and Future*, edited by M. Hulme and E. Barrows, pp. 112–133. London: Routledge, 1997.

Woodbury, R. B. "Climatic Changes and Prehistoric Agriculture in the Southwestern United States." *Annals, New York Academy of Sciences* 95 (1961), 705–709.

—ANDREW S. GOUDIE

MEDITERRANEAN ENVIRONMENTS

The impacts of global environmental changes on mediterranean environments are likely to be very marked. Five regions of the world have a mediterranean-type climate and these occur between approximately 30 and 40 degrees north and south of the equator, incorporating parts of the Mediterranean basin, California, central Chile, southwestern Africa, and southwestern and southern Australia (Figure 1). Their distinctive climatic conditions, which prevail over less than 1 percent of the Earth's surface, include a marked summer drought and cool moist winters, with mean annual precipitation varying from around 300 millimeters to more than 1,000 millimeters in the uplands. Strong rainfall seasonality is regarded as the key ecosystem determinant, with at least

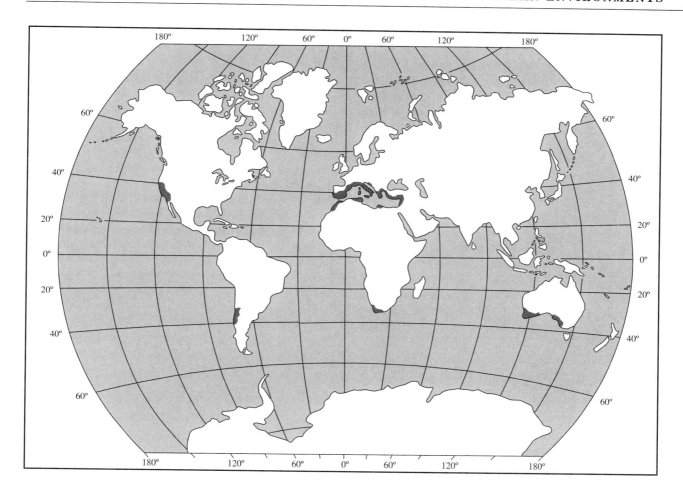

Mediterranean Environments. FIGURE 1. Distribution of Mediterranean Ecosystems and Representative Climatic Conditions. (After Archibold, 1995, p. 131, Figure 5.1. With permission of Kluwer Academic Publishers.)

65 percent falling within the winter months, although summer drought may be somewhat buffered in Chile, California, and the western coast of South Africa by the penetration of coastal fogs. The dry summer climate, which is a product of seasonal fluctuations in the position of the high-pressure zones centered on the tropical deserts at around 20° latitude, brings hot, dry conditions conducive to fire, especially in the late summer months.

Soils and geomorphology are distinctive in the mediterranean-type ecosystems. There is a characteristically high relief, although Australia and the eastern Mediterranean exhibit somewhat flatter landscapes. Soils are characteristically low in key plant nutrients, such as nitrogen and phosphorus; but the availability of potassium, calcium, and magnesium varies markedly from region to region. For example, soils of the south-ern African region of Mediterranean climate are especially low in calcium, while those of the Mediterranean basin itself often are derived from limestones and show high levels of calcium and other soluble cations. Generally, the soils of Australian and South Africa may be regarded as oligotrophic (nutrient-poor), those of Chile and the Mediterranean basin as largely eutropic (nutrient-rich), and those of California as intermediate.

Vegetation structural uniformity and vegetation "similarity complexes" between regions testify to the importance of seasonality of moisture availability and fire: all five regions are characterized by sclerophyllous (i.e., characterized by plants with hard, waxy, and drought-resistant leaves) shrublands known variously as *maquis* (Mediterranean basin), *chaparral* (California), *matorral* (Chile), *mallee* (Australia) and *fynbos* (South Africa). The woody shrubs are fire-resistant or fire-dependent, with evergreen leaves that are frequently broad, stiff, and sticky or waxy; an overstory of small trees is occasionally present, as is an understory of herbaceous annuals or perennials. The structural similarity between regions contrasts with their floristic distinctiveness, since constituent plant species differ markedly according to geography. For example, the Mediterranean basin

THE *FYNBOS* HOT SPOT

The southwestern cape of South Africa has a distinctive low heath type of vegetation called *fynbos*. It is particularly well developed on nutrient-poor, highly leached, acidic, sandstone-derived soils. It displays little or no development of woodland, is naturally subject to fire and drought, and has relatively low biomass per unit area. Its most striking characteristic is its extraordinary plant richness. There are some 8,500 plant species packed into what amounts, at least on a continental scale, to a very small geographical area (90,000 square kilometers). The level of endemism (68 percent of the species are native species) has rendered the flora sufficiently distinctive for it to be accorded the status of Floristic Kingdom, one of only six in the world.

The beautiful and diverse *fynbos*, typified by its many protea species, is, however, under threat. One of the biggest threats is posed by the introduction of alien plant species. The apparently vacant tree niche in the *fynbos* seems to have provided an opportunity for a number of aggressive introduced members of the genus *Acacia* from Australia to supplant *fynbos* over extensive areas. There are other threats as well, including the spread of cities, forestry, and agriculture. This area qualifies as one of the hottest of all hot spots both in terms of its diversity and the extreme threats on habitat.

BIBLIOGRAPHY

Cowling, R. M., ed. *The Ecology of* Fynbos: *Nutrients, Fire, and Diversity*. Cape Town: Oxford University Press, 1992.

is characterized by asteraceous (belonging to the Asteraceae, or daisy family of plants) woody shrubs with an overstory of varieties of oak, South African *fynbos* has almost unprecedented plant-species richness, particularly among the Ericaceae (heath), Proteaceae (protea), and Restionaceae (Cape reed) families, while the Australian mallee is typified by numerous *Eucalyptus* and *Banksia* elements. [*See the vignette* The *Fynbos* Hot Spot.]

Similarities among the five regions in respect of climate, geomorphology, pedology (soils), and ecological and evolutionary convergence are illustrated in their clustering into just three complexes (the Mediterranean basin, California/Chile, and Australia/South Africa) in Figure 2. To a large extent, the classification reflects the relative degree of evolutionary commonality, which in turn reflects geologic and climatic histories. The origins and development of the various mediterranean floral elements have been outlined by Raven (1973). In the Northern Hemisphere regions, about 40 percent of the species are endemic, being derived from ancestral groups which had a more continuous distribution in the early Tertiary or late Cretaceous. Since that time, the flora has been influenced by the transitional position of the mediterranean climate regions and the accession both of more temperate elements from the north and more tropical and xeric (i.e., drought-adapted) elements from the south. By comparison, the Southern Hemi-

sphere mediterranean floras are largely isolated from temperate elements and the tropical influence is much more substantial. The proportion of endemics is also relatively high, especially in the southwestern Cape, where almost 70 percent of all species are geographically restricted. In short, the evolutionary history of all the mediterranean climate regions is distinctive and they have evolved their flora and fauna in isolation from each other. Summer-dry climates appeared relatively recently, possibly as late as the Pleistocene, and prompted the strong degree of structural convergence that is evident.

Lessons of the Past: The Quaternary. Arguably the most important environmental changes to influence mediterranean-type ecosystems took place in the late Pleistocene and Holocene in response to large-scale fluctuations of climate associated with the advance and retreat of ice sheets and glaciers, and in response to the increasing impact of anthropogenic forces. Repeated Pleistocene glaciations, while they did not (with the exception of Chile) affect the five regions very directly, were accompanied by markedly reduced temperatures and lowered sea levels. The scale of Quaternary temperature change may be regarded as transitional in magnitude between the major oscillations of the temperate and polar latitudes and the attenuated changes of the tropics and subtropics. Quaternary environmental change has been the focus of considerable research effort in all five regions. The scenario of change is, per-

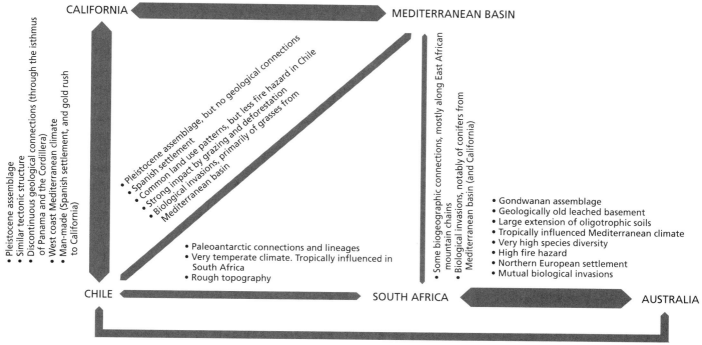

Mediterranean Environments. FIGURE 2. Similarities among the Five Regions of the World with a Mediterranean-Type Climate.

The main factors explaining the nature and degree of relationships are geologic, edaphic (i.e., relating to soil characteristics), and geomorphologic features, patterns of evolutionary convergence, phylogenetic commonalities, and type, and magnitude of human impact. The degree of similarity is proportional to the thickness of the connecting lines. (After di Castri, 1991. With permission of Cambridge University Press.)

haps, best illustrated by comparing and contrasting the situations that prevailed at the time of the last glacial maximum (LGM) with those of the mid-Holocene climatic optimum. [*See* Climate Change.]

Temperatures during the LGM were substantially cooler in all regions of mediterranean climate. In general, mean annual temperatures appear to have been lower—by as much as 9°C around 18,000 BP at appropriate latitudes. Across much of the Mediterranean basin of Europe, this produced a vegetation pattern dominated by the cold-tolerant shrub *Artemisia*, and it was only following the temperature amelioration after the Younger Dryas that significant woodland expansion took place around the Mediterranean. Unglaciated parts of central Chile, such as Isla de Chiloé, were occupied by so-called Megallanic moorland at this time, a kind of

vegetation that currently occupies the coast of Tierra del Fuego between 48° and 56° south latitude (Chiloé is at 42°); pollen evidence is thus indicative of mean temperatures cooler by 4°C. Palaeoenvironmental evidence for the LGM in the southwestern Cape of South Africa is scarce, but consistent with cooling of this order of magnitude. Precipitation conditions are rather more difficult to reconstruct, and vary strongly with geographical position. Thus the mean annual rainfall values of much of the Mediterranean basin around the LGM may have been marginally less than or approximately similar to those of today, whereas in Chile, southwestern California, and southwestern South Africa, considerably greater moisture availability may have prevailed, and this cannot all be accounted for by temperature depression alone. Still other mediterranean climate regions, such as southeastern Australia, may have been rather more arid than today at this time.

Climatic warming and sea level rise accompanied the onset of the Holocene in regions of mediterranean climate and, at such latitudes in the northern hemisphere, incident solar radiation was 7 percent higher in the summer months and correspondingly lower in the winter months compared with today. The resulting climatic and environmental patterns, however, were complex and remain difficult to elucidate. In at least two of the five mediterranean-type regions, South Africa and Chile, cooler conditions in the Holocene, with temperature departures of 1°–2°C, are concomitant with increases in precipitation. Conditions in the *fynbos* biome of the southwestern Cape of South Africa were probably somewhat warmer and drier by 5,000 BP, but parts of the Mediterranean basin remained cooler than the present day until rather later in the Holocene. Nevertheless, the cold and dry climates of the glacial period were ultimately replaced and trees, especially oaks, and shrubs typical of the maquis were abundant across much of the Mediterranean basin by about 6,000 BP. Warmer temperatures in Chile were also accompanied by drier climates, as they were in at least some parts of Australia with mediterranean climate. These mid-Holocene conditions cannot reliably provide an analogue for globally warmed mediterranean-type environments, however, in part because of the different forcing factors operating and in part because of uncertainties regarding their reconstruction.

Degree of Human Impact. In the Mediterranean basin in particular, human activity and significant anthropogenic impact on the environment have an extended history. Nevertheless, it is frequently difficult to distinguish between those environmental changes where direct human agency is involved and those where "natural" climate forcing is the predominant influence. Although climate change has not been irrelevant, much of the environmental history of the Mediterranean basin has been shaped by humans for at least the last five thousand years, and especially by those changes accompanying the spread of agriculture. This is illustrated by an analysis of valley fills in southern Europe. While the pattern of sedimentation and erosion may to some degree be determined by rainfall fluctuations, the importance of land use histories in the development of Mediterranean valleys has been conclusively demonstrated by van Andel and Runnels (1995). For example, at sites in southern France, charcoal and pollen evidence illustrates the absolute importance of people in determining the characteristic vegetation patterns of the region from about 6,000 BP. Deciduous oak woodland is shown to become degraded and replaced by evergreen oak, juniper, and pine as a result of the establishment of cultivation and livestock. In eastern Spain, it is pine forest

that is replaced by oak scrub following clearance. The Mediterranean basin, once 40 percent forested, has had its tree cover quite literally decimated by humans, such that forests now comprise just 4 percent of the area, and this clearance has been accompanied by accelerated erosion. Rates of fluvial erosion in various mediterranean climate regions suggest relatively low rates of contemporary sediment yield from catchments in the Mediterranean basin itself, a conclusion that points either to the efficacy of modern soil conservation methods or, alternatively, to the fact that vulnerable soils have already been removed by past accelerated erosion.

Elsewhere, human occupation of mediterranean-type landscapes may have had rather less impact, at least until the period of colonial occupation. This is certainly true of South Africa, where, despite the fact that southern Africa is the evolutionary home of modern humans, the impact of prehistoric cultures has been relatively limited by comparison with the Mediterranean basin. The influence of European settlers, however, has been very marked. For example, widespread changes in vegetation in the catchment of the Verlorenvlei River in the western Cape lowland *fynbos* occurred as a result of the colonial introduction of wheat and intensive grazing. A similar picture emerges from western Victoria, Australia, where no significant aboriginal impact on the landscape appears to have taken place, although marked changes in fire patterns, loss of tree cover and biodiversity, and increased soil erosion and salinity were all consequences of colonial settlement.

One of the most obvious recent human impacts on the mediterranean-type regions involves the introduction of alien plant and animal species, and their impacts appear to have been unusually severe. [*See* Exotic Species.] Indeed, mediterranean-type ecosystems are frequently occupied by introduced plant species to the extent that the native vegetation is almost entirely displaced from its habitat; the impacts of such invasions on biodiversity and other ecosystem properties, such as hydrology, have been very marked. Indeed, so intense is the overall effect of human utilization of these ecosystems that the term *desertification*, previously only associated with the desert margins, is used increasingly, especially in respect of the Mediterranean basin itself (Mairota et al., 1998). Even in the southwestern Cape, where the extent of soil erosion is relatively limited, the impact of other forms of degradation, in particular the spread of alien invasives, represents a major threat to the continued survival of its elevated plant species diversity. It is clear that the mediterranean-type ecosystems are subject to a high degree of anthropogenic disturbance. [*See* Desertification.]

The Future. The influence of natural climate variation and industrial, agricultural, demographic, social, and political change on the mediterranean-type ecosystems has been substantial, but what of the future? The complexity of the resulting environmental changes challenges the logic of prediction, although three recent publications address precisely this issue (Jeftic et al., 1992; Moreno and Oechel, 1995; Jeftic et al., 1996). Most of the scenarios are based on the implications of a global climate in which atmospheric carbon dioxide is approximately double its current concentration, although it has proved extremely difficult to translate this reliably to the regional scale.

For the Mediterranean basin, regional warming of some 1.2°–3.5°C by the late twenty-first century is predicted, a value slightly lower than the global mean temperature increase produced by the current general circulation models. The rate of warming is, nevertheless, up to seven times faster than during the past one hundred years, so the implications for the region are potentially enormous. Annual precipitation changes, even more difficult to predict, are relatively subtle, although marginal increases are predicted for the currently more temperate northern parts of the Mediterranean basin, with marginal decreases for the warmer and more arid southern parts. Furthermore, evapotranspiration is likely to increase substantially: simulation of the expected change in potential evapotranspiration in response to a 1°C increase in global mean temperature reveals that all localities in the European Mediterranean basin show an increase, while in some areas the values are double those of the present day (Palutikof et al., 1994).

Equivalent predictive research has been conducted in the other mediterranean climate regions. Only marginal mean annual precipitation increases are anticipated over the winter rainfall area of South Africa, although, along with the predicted temperature rise, elevated rainfall intensities resulting from an increased frequency of extreme events render such changes highly significant. Annual mean rainfall values over the mediterranean climate areas of South America are likely to be reduced under a scenario of doubled carbon dioxide concentration. Taken as a whole, the global warming scenarios for the five regions point to lower soil moisture availability and consequent ecological and agricultural problems.

Given the relatively small geographical area occupied by mediterranean-type systems, together with the fact that they are not significant carbon sinks or sources, the implications of global climate change for the five regions are relatively more important than the feedback effects that these systems have, or will have, on the climate system itself. The implications of predicted changes need to be considered in the context of the complex ecological interactions between climate, soil moisture regime, and fire that characterize the mediterranean-type ecosystems. Relatively small changes in climate and the subsequently induced changes in the fire regime can re-

sult in rapid shifts in pattern and process at landscape scales. Fire resilience is spatially variable in mediterranean shrub communities, although most are resistant to fire at return intervals of twenty to fifty years. Given the probable future increase in the degree of human disturbance, reduced soil moisture may increase fire frequencies and favor resprouting shrub species at the expense of reseeders, resulting in increased prevalence of resprouting shrubs, such as Protea nitida and fewer reseeding shrubs, such as most of the other proteas. Further impacts of global change will arise from the probable increased level of invasion by alien plant species, which may respond more positively to increased levels of ecological stress than the natural mediterranean communities. Any land use changes will have a significant impact on the runoff and soil erosion under mediterranean-type conditions. The highest values of sediment loss today occur under vines and wheat, so that any future increase in either form of land use is potentially problematic. Another side effect of global climate change, sea level rise, also has negative connotations, especially since a substantial proportion of the population lives within the coastal zone.

Any potential positive impacts emerging from the carbon dioxide fertilization effect appear to be relatively minor. There is limited response of *fynbos* shrubs to elevated carbon dioxide, although it is marginally better on plants grown on basic soils. For evergreen oaks, there may be a slightly improved degree of drought resistance and a statistically insignificant increase in root biomass among, for example, Californian ponderosa pines. Global change impacts, however, are largely negative.

Taken as a whole, climate changes of the future represent a real and serious threat to the mediterranean-type climate regions and their associated ecosystems, both natural and anthropogenic. Elevated mean annual temperature, reduced moisture availability, and increased fire frequency, coupled with increased intensity of land use, may prove conducive to accelerated land degradation and desertification in the mediterranean environments of the world. Global change is a severe global challenge for these systems.

[*See also* Biomes; *and* Fire.]

BIBLIOGRAPHY

Archibold, O. W. *Ecology of World Vegetation*. London: Chapman and Hall, 1995.

Brandt, C. J., and J. B. Thornes, eds. *Mediterranean Desertification and Land Use*. Chichester, U.K.: Wiley, 1996. A state-of-the art analysis of this important environmental problem.

Carrion, J. S., and M. Dupre. "Late Quaternary Vegetational History at Navarrés, Eastern Spain: A Two Core Approach." *New Phytologist* 134 (1996), 177–191.

di Castri, F. "An Ecological Overview of the Five Regions with a Mediterranean Climate." In *Biogeography of Mediterranean*

Invasions, edited by R. H. Groves and F. di Castri, pp 3–16. Cambridge: Cambridge University Press, 1991.

di Castri, F., and H. A. Mooney, eds. *Mediterranean Type Ecosystems*. Berlin: Springer, 1973. The first scientific account of the vegetation of the regions with a mediterranean-type climate.

Groves, R. H., and F. di Castri. *Biogeography of Mediterranean Invasions*. Cambridge: Cambridge University Press, 1991. A review of how plant and animal invasions have impacted upon mediterranean-type ecosystems.

Jeftic, L., S. Keckes, and J. C. Pernetta, eds. *Climatic Change and the Mediterranean*, vol. 2. London: Edward Arnold, 1996.

Jeftic, L., J. D. Milliman, and G. Sestini. *Climatic Change and the Mediterranean*. London: Edward Arnold, 1992. This volume and the previous reference present climate change scenarios and their implications for the Mediterranean basin.

Kruger, F. J., and R. C. Bigalke. "Fire in Fynbos." In *Ecological Effects of Fire in South African Ecosystems*, edited by P. de V. Booysen and N. M. Tainton, pp. 67–114. New York: Springer, 1984.

Mairota, P., J. B. Thornes, and N. Geeson. *Atlas of Mediterranean Environments*. Chichester, U.K.: Wiley, 1998. An illustrated guide to the Mediterranean basin, with a focus on desertification.

Moreno, J. M., and W. C. Oechel, eds. *Global Change and Mediterranean-Type Ecosystems*. Berlin: Springer, 1995. A collection of scientific papers dealing with the impacts of future climate change on various aspects of mediterranean-type system ecology.

Palutikof, J. P., C. M. Goodess, and X. Guo. "Climate Change, Potential Evapotranspiration and Moisture Availability in the Mediterranean Basin." *International Journal of Climatology* 14 (1994), 853–869. Technical work dealing with the climate of the Mediterranean basin under a scenario of doubled carbon dioxide.

Prentice, C., J. Guiot, and S. P. Harrison. "Mediterranean Vegetation, Lake Levels and Palaeoclimate at the Last Glacial Maximum." *Nature* 360 (1992), 658–660. Outlines the environmental conditions in the Mediterranean basin for 18,000 BP.

Raven, P. H. "The Evolution of Mediterranean Floras." In *Mediterranean Type Ecosystems*, edited by F. di Castri and H. A. Mooney, pp. 213–224. Berlin: Springer, 1973. A classic review of the development of mediterranean vegetation over time.

van Andel, T. H., and C. N. Runnels. "The Earliest Farmers in Europe." *Antiquity* 69 (1995), 481–500. Traces the history of agriculture in the Mediterranean basin.

Villagrán, C. "Glacial Climates and their Effects on the History of the Vegetation in Chile: A Synthesis Based on Palynological Evidence from Isla de Chiloé." *Review of Palaeobotany and Palynology* 65 (1990), 17–24.

—MICHAEL E. MEADOWS

MEDITERRANEAN SEA

[*This case study focuses on the present-day environmental state of the Mediterranean Sea and its coastal regions.*]

The Mediterranean is the sea with the longest and most persistent human impact. Since Neolithic times it served as food resource and waterway; in the Roman epoch the Mare Internum was the central part of the empire, with a major function for trading, exchange of goods, and people. Today—owing to the long settlement history of her bordering countries, the dense population along many of her European coasts, the high ship traffic, and the favorable climate for tourism—the ecological stress on the Mediterranean, and on its coasts in particular, is enormous. Therefore, a study of the Mediterranean's evolution, present state, and potential future is of high relevance.

The Natural Setting. With a surface area of 2.5 million square kilometers and a total water body of about 4 million cubic kilometers, the Mediterranean is the biggest marginal sea of the Earth. Its average depth is 1,475 meters; the maximum (5,015 meters) is reached west of Crete. Between Sicily and Africa a submarine ridge separates the western from the eastern basin. This semienclosed sea extends for less than 4,000 kilometers from the Strait of Gibraltar to the Dardanelles, but has 46,000 kilometers of beaches (46 percent) and rocky coasts (54 percent) if all gulfs, embayments, and islands are included. [*See* Marginal Seas.]

The Mediterranean Sea is a sensitive ecosystem: a low-productive, hyperthermal, oligotrophic, euhaline, highly polluted sea. Because of its latitudinal position in the subtropics with strong evaporation, and because no major rivers except for the Nile debouch from Africa, the water balance is negative and the salinity (3.7–3.9 percent) is higher than in the world oceans (3.5 percent). The average riverine input, which is rich in sediments and dissolved load, amounts to 15,000 cubic meters per second; 92 percent of it comes from the northern shores. With the Strait of Gibraltar being quite narrow, the natural exchange of water with the Atlantic Ocean is low; a total water exchange takes eighty to one hundred years (possibly even three hundred years; see United Nations Environment Programme [UNEP], 1996, p. v).

The Mediterranean Sea is an oligotrophic ecosystem; its biological productivity is among the lowest of the seas of the world. The Adriatic Sea's color is the proverbial blue because it is an ecological "desert"; the color results from the lack of nutrients and therefore organisms.

The present sea is one of the remnants of the ancient Tethys Ocean. Being part of the collision zone between the African and the Eurasian plates, the region faces considerable tectonic movements (subduction, uplift, subsidence, earthquakes) and orogenesis (the building up of mountain ranges and volcanism). The Mediterranean region is characterized by tectonic youth, steep relief, unconsolidated rocks, landslides and other mass movements, and a semiarid environment with high variability of rainfall, hot and dry summers, and mild and humid winters. It is vulnerable to natural hazards: earth- and seaquakes (major centers being the Aegean Sea and the Strait of Messina), tsunami waves, volcanism, torrential rains, catastrophic floodings, and severe droughts (Brückner, 1994).

Because of the ecological instability of the environment, even a slight change in one of the parameters may trigger big effects. The vulnerability of the ecosystem is amplified by the human impact, especially the clearing of the vegetation cover, sealing of the surface by roads and buildings, and construction of dams to channel the rivers. This impact has considerably increased the strong surface water runoff, with considerable load—sediment, pollutants, nutrients—being flushed into the sea. The underestimation of the power of torrential rivers has also led to man-made catastrophic events. Other effects are soil erosion and desertification. Many Mediterranean countries show all kinds of denudation and erosion features (gullies, landslides, piping), occasionally resulting in badland formation. Again, the coastal rivers and the littoral zone are loaded with sediments.

Both the present vegetation and land use in the Mediterranean areas of Europe strongly reflect human activities since Neolithic times. By Classical times, certain regions had already been extensively deforested and eroded. At the end of the Roman period, more than half of the Mediterranean forests had been devastated, and by the middle of the nineteenth century at least three-quarters of the Mediterranean forests had disappeared (Tomaselli, 1977, in Macklin et al., 1995, pp. 15–16). As a result of human impact, the Holocene climax vegetation—the evergreen-oak forest—had degenerated to maquis (scrub) or even garrigue (dry heath).

Looking Back in Order to Look Ahead. The reaction of the ecosystem—including especially the factors relief, sea level, and vegetation—to climate change can be deduced from the past. During the Last Glacial Maximum, about 18,000 years ago, sea level was 120–130 meters below its present stand. The northern Adriatic Sea was then dry land, large plains existed off the coast of Tunesia, several islands in the Aegean Sea were connected with the Anatolian mainland (e.g., Samos), and the atmosphere-ocean circulation had changed. The following Flandrian Transgression caused an enormous shift in the shoreline, drowned vast areas (especially those with a flat shelf), created deeply incised marine embayments (e.g., the Latmian Gulf in Western Turkey), and changed former peninsulas to islands. The maximum of this highstand—which probably reached the present level—was some 5,000–6,000 years ago. The following seaward shift in the shoreline is most noticeable in delta areas, such as those of the Ebro, Nile, Po, Rhone, and Büyük and Küçük Menderes. Human impact in the hinterland (devegetation with clearing of forests for agriculture, firewood, ship and house building, tanning, etc.) is probably the major reason for the enormous increase in erosion and accumulation rates.

Several geomorphological features are useful indicators of tectonic movements. The last interglacial marine terrace (ca. 125,000 years ago) has today a eustatically "normal" position at about 6 meters above present sea level. If it is missing, it has either been eroded or drowned, as is the case along the subsiding Adriatic coast of the former Yugoslavia; in southern Calabria this terrace is at an altitude of more than 160 meters above sea level, from which an average uplift rate of 1.30 meters per millennium can be calculated (Brückner and Radtke, 1990).

An excellent example for coastal changes due to tectonics is the island of Crete: uplifted bioerosion (notches) and bioconstruction (algal rims) features, indicating the former shoreline, prove that the destructive earthquake of 21 July 365 CE tilted the western part of the island, uplifting it for more than eight meters at the southwestern cape (Kelletat, 1996, Figure 1).

Coastal changes during the last centuries can be detected with historical documents (maps, literature), those during the last decades even with aerial photography. The delta regions have witnessed the greatest historical shifts in the shoreline. The delta fronts of Ebro and Po advanced five to seven kilometers per century in the Medieval and post-Medieval periods; Ostia Antica, the ancient harbor of Rome, is now many kilometers inland (Macklin et al., 1995, p. 19); the same is true for Ravenna (Sestini, 1992a). Another famous example is the Büyük Menderes (historically called Maeander or Maiandros) in Western Turkey: the ancient cities of Priene and Miletus lost their harbors owing to the strong silting up of the river. The same story can be told for the city of Ephesus. The major reason for the enormous delta progradation is the human impact: the clearing of the vegetation in the drainage basin (Brückner, 1997a, b, 1998).

Coastal neotectonics and altitudinal variability is well reflected in tide gauge records: at Thessaloniki, Port Said and Venice, sea level rise was greater (4.0 to 7.3 millimeters per year) than the global average (1–2 millimeters per year), whereas at Alexandria it was considerably less (−0.7 millimeters per year) for periods of the last one hundred years (Emery and Aubrey, 1991).

The presumed worldwide sea level rise of about thirty to fifty centimeters up to 2100 CE will considerably affect low-lying regions such as coastal wetlands and coastal cities; for example, dams will have to be erected for the city and industrial areas of Thessaloniki. In a very detailed case study, Hollis (1992) models the implications of a twenty-centimeter sea level rise on the coastal zone of northern Tunisia. Deltas may overcompensate the trend by their sediment load. Nowadays, however, several deltas (e.g., the Nile Delta) undergo marine erosion: the building of reservoirs and the extraction of water for irrigation purposes cause a deficit in sediment supply (Sestini, 1992b). [*See* Sea Level.]

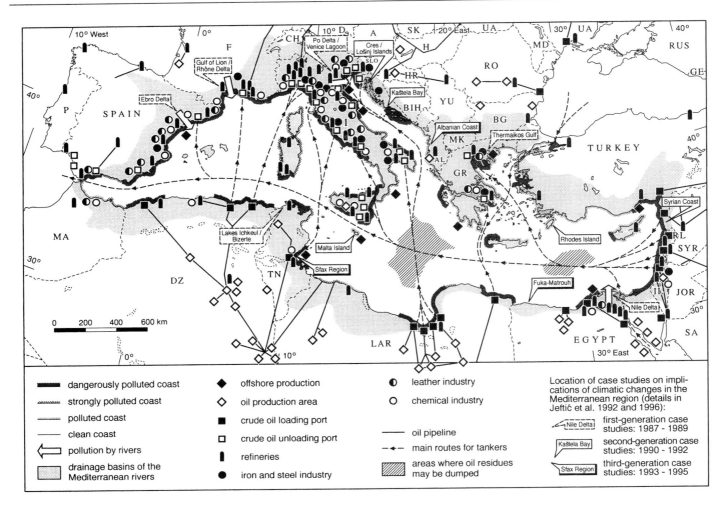

Mediterranean Sea. FIGURE 1. Pollution of the Mediterranean Sea and Its Coasts, with Location of Case Studies on Implications of Climatic Changes. (Modified from Klug, 1986, Abb. 2. Location of case studies according to Jeftić et al., 1996, p. 12.)

Generally, rainfall has decreased overall since the end of the last century owing to changes in the atmospheric pressure, the position of the Azores High, and sea surface temperature (Thornes, in Brandt and Thornes, 1996, p. 4). Decreasing precipitation will be a major challenge, especially for agriculture, the growing coastal population, and tourism.

Between 1900 and 1958 the temperature of the deep waters of the western Mediterranean had remained on the same level. Between 1959 and 1989, however, a warming of more than 0.1°C was measured; the salinity rose, too. Béthoux et al. (1990) interpret this as a consequence of the increased greenhouse effect. The temperatures in winter are higher, the wind patterns change, and the amount of precipitation decreases.

Based on a large databank of monthly temperature and precipitation records, Palutikof et al. (1996) pres-

ent seasonal scenarios of the changes in temperature, precipitation, and potential evaporation in response to a 1°C increase in global mean temperature. The largest area of warming is seen in autumn, the smallest in summer; the warming is greatest in the northeastern parts of the study area. Concerning precipitation changes in summer the data lack spatial coherence; in winter and spring the scenarios indicate higher precipitation in the north and lower in the south of the Mediterranean region.

Present-Day Environmental State of the Mediterranean Sea. The Mediterranean Sea is one of the world's biggest sewers. Her bordering countries discharge about 1.7×10^9 cubic meters of municipal waste water per year (about three-quarters without treatment) and about 66×10^9 cubic meters of industrial waste water per year. Half of the coastal population have no primary municipal sewage treatment. Add to this an annual load of 12 million metric tons of organic pollutants; 1.5 million metric tons oil; 1.1 million metric tons of nitrates; 360,000 metric tons of phosphates; 60,000 metric tons of detergents; 21,000 metric tons of zinc; 3,800 metric tons of lead; 2,400 metric tons of cadmium; 100 metric tons of mercury, and so on—besides the atmospheric input. If the latter is added, too, the figures are even much higher; for example, the zinc load sums up to 92,400 metric tons per year, the copper load to 29,000 metric tons per year (UNEP/FAO/WHO, 1996).

The pollution of the Mediterranean is six to thirty times higher than that of the open oceans (Klug, 1986). Apart from the general effect on the natural ecosystem, there is the danger that the pollutants enter the food chain and affect human health. [See Pollution.]

Reasons for the pollution of the Mediterranean include land-based pollution, dumping of liquid and solid waste from ships or airplanes, release of oil and oil mix by ship traffic or accidents, pollution due to the use and exploration of the sea floor and sea sediments, atmospheric pollution due to human or volcanic impacts, and thermic stress caused by the waste water of power plants—as well as the waste of the coastal population and the 150 million tourists during the summer season. Add to this the changes in the marine and littoral ecosystem caused by the human impact in the hinterland, such as increase in sediment load triggered by devegetation, decrease due to building of reservoirs, and change of the faunal assemblage because canals are built (e.g., Suez Canal).

The ecological stress comes from five major groups of pollutants:

- Oil: The annual oil pollution is 1.5 million metric tons
- Artificial organic chemicals (mostly polychlorinated hydrocarbons [PCHs]): The annual input through the River Ebro alone is 30 kilograms of hexachlorobenzene (HCB) (e.g., in plant-protective chemicals), 12 kilograms of polychlorinated biphenyls (PCBs), 8 kilograms of dichlorodiphenyltrichloroethane (DDT) (e.g., used as insecticides) (Cid Montañes, 1990)
- Metals, mostly heavy metals (see vignette)
- Waste waters: Of the untreated municipal waste water (e.g., 100 percent for Albania, 43 percent for Greece, 31 percent for Spain, 13 percent for France), the overwhelming majority goes into the rivers and the sea (UNEP, 1996, pp. 29–31). One effect is the addition of nutrients (phosphate and nitrate mainly in the form of excess fertilizers), which may lead to eutrophication and cause "red tides" (massive phytoplankton blooms). It can contaminate or kill fish and also affect tourism
- Solid wastes (e.g., plastic pellets): Of the over 2 million metric tons of solid wastes, more than 70 percent is disposed of by unspecified means, among others by being dumped near, at, or in the sea (UNEP, 1996, pp. 33–34)

Mediterranean Coasts under Stress. The present maritime and coastal ecosystems of the Mediterranean face the following risks: pollution (especially by oil

slicks), overfishing, mass tourism, industrial and communal wastewater input, heavy flooding, strong sediment input due to severe soil erosion in the adjacent land, and eutrophication due to strong input of nutrients. "Red tides" of algae, plagues of jellyfish, garbage, and tar balls on the beaches are obvious examples of marine or coastal pollution (see Figure 1; Kelletat and Zimmermann, 1978; Zimmermann and Kelletat, 1984; Klug, 1986).

Coastal population. In 1985 coastal population was about 133 million. The population densities of the Mediterranean countries were on the average three times higher in coastal zones than in noncoastal zones. And the trend is unbroken: the figure is expected to double by 2025 (UNEP, 1996, p. 29). Urbanization is intense around the major port cities. As a result of the high demand for residential and recreational facilities today some 70 percent of the coastal strip between Barcelona and Naples is occupied (UNEP, 1996, p. ii). The consequence is an enormous stress on land and water resources and an increasing demand for food, transportation, and recreation facilities; it also endangers biodiversity. After industry, urbanization is the main cause of atmospheric pollution; moreover, it changes the drainage and sedimentation patterns.

Tourism and recreation. Owing to the favorable climate, the Mediterranean is a magnet for tourism, especially during the hot and dry summer; then, however, the demand for drinking, washing, and shower water is high because the population of the seaside resorts and towns is increased several times. Each year the coastal residents are supplemented by 150 million tourists. By 2025, this figure is expected to rise to 340 million in addition to the still increasing domestic tourism. Already, France and Spain experience a doubling of their coastal population in the summer. Handling the solid and liquid waste and providing drinking water are by now an enormous task. During the summer season, several coastal areas have to cut off the freshwater supply for hours daily; others fight increased salination due to overexploitation of coastal aquifers for tourism or irrigation purposes. [See Tourism.]

Industry. Most industry is located mainly around the main port city conurbations. Italy, France, and Spain account for some 87 percent of industrial production in the Mediterranean basin. Industry is a major contributor to pollution, by direct emission or via the air-ocean pathway (UNEP, 1996, p. ii). Discharge of heated cooling water from energy production plants affects the biota near the emission centers.

Transportation systems. Some 200,000 vessels transit the Mediterranean annually, while about 2,000 ferry lines, 1,500 cargo vessels, and 2,000 commercial vessels operate in the Mediterranean regularly. The 305 ports face high risks due to shipping accidents, espe-

HEAVY METAL POLLUTION OF THE MEDITERRANEAN SEA: THE EXAMPLES OF MERCURY, ZINC, AND COPPER

Naturally, heavy metals are released through geological weathering and erosion and transported to the sea by rivers, surface runoff, and atmospheric deposition. Human impact, however, has changed the amount of heavy metals in natural ecosystems dramatically. In the context of the Mediterranean Sea, the major heavy metals are cadmium, mercury, lead, chromium, copper, and zinc.

It is estimated that 65 percent of the world's mercury resources are located in the Mediterranean basin (UNEP, 1996, p. 41). There is a debate on the specific danger of mercury, which may be extremely enriched in marine organisms and is very toxic. Bacci (1989) calculates the mercury budget of the Mediterranean as follows: Input via atmospheric deposition (150 metric tons [t] per year), Atlantic waters (50 t/year), rivers and direct inputs (32 t/year), and methylation (4 t/year). Output via volatilization (150 t/year), sedimentation (75 t/year), and fisheries (0.3 t/year). Stored in the Mediterranean water body are 3,700 metric tons; in fish and shellfish 104 t; in suspended solids 185 t; and in the bottom sediments 3,750 t. This annual input of 236 metric tons of mercury is not totally balanced by an output of 225 metric tons. UNEP (1996) quotes studies that figure 130 t/year from domestic and industrial sources as well as from rivers. In marine biota, mercury concentrations of more than seven parts per million (mg/kg, wet weight) were detected; however, the Mediterranean population in general was not at risk.

Anthropogenic sources for zinc and copper include mining, processing, industrial waste, sewage, sludges, and combustion. All inputs into the Mediterranean Sea—through the straits of Gibraltar and Dardanelles, by direct effluent discharges (domestic and industrial), by rivers, and by atmospheric input—sum up to 92,400 t/year for zinc and 29,000 t/year for copper (UNEP, 1996, pp. iii, 31). While the natural background of clean seawater is 1–5 micrograms per liter or even much less for zinc, it may reach up to 450 μg/l in polluted harbors. The copper concentrations vary from 0.2 to 50 μg/l. In marine biota, the highest concentrations were found in microplankton and in some mollusks (>100 μg/g for zinc and >20 μg/g (fresh weight) for copper).

Seafood is a major source of these heavy metals for humans. Whereas the lethal dose for humans is very seldomly reached, some marine life may already be endangered at lower doses. Therefore, the UNEP-MAP Technical Report (1996) recommends that for the protection of marine life the concentrations of total dissolved zinc and copper in sea water should not exceed 10 μg/l and 5 μg/l, respectively.

The "Protocol for the Protection of the Mediterranean Sea against pollution from land-based sources" (1980 LBS Protocol) lists twenty elements; all heavy metals are included.

—HELMUT BRÜCKNER

cially from oil, natural gas, and petroleum products (UNEP, 1996, p. iii).

Agriculture. The washing out of pollutants (pesticides, herbicides) and fertilizers either directly by surface runoff or indirectly by rivers has a significant negative impact on the coastal marine ecosystems and may cause eutrophication.

Fisheries. Overfishing—including dynamite fishing—is even a greater problem than pollution, since it endangers the natural regeneration of the marine ecosystems. In fact, both are a threat to the fishery resources, all the more because the shelves are the hatchery for many marine species. The capture fisheries remain at about 1.1

million metric tons per year (UNEP, 1996, p. iv). Mariculture—already supplying about 10 percent of the region's fish production—is a response to the demand for fish. However, a "foreign" guest to the Mediterranean, the alga *Caulerpa* sp., is killing major hydrobiological regions with extreme velocity.

Seafood and human health. The main risks to human health come from the consumption of sea food contaminated by heavy metals or certain bacteria, viruses, fungi, and phytoplankton toxins.

Global warming. Besides causing changes in the coastal wind field and in the air–sea interface, global warming will result in a thermal expansion and thereby a rise in sea level and a modification of circulation patterns. This will effect the ecosystems (e.g., faunal and floral distribution) and may cause coastal erosion (UNEP, 1996, p. vii). Many case studies on this subject are published in Jeftić et al. (1992, 1996).

Protection measures. The growing environmental pollution and the decrease in biodiversity have stirred efforts to establish protected areas to preserve endangered species. As of 1996, 123 specially protected areas were designated under the SPA Protocol of the UNEP, 47 of which having a marine component; among them are sand dunes (damaged by bathers and erosion); coastal lagoons, salt marshes, and wetlands (endangered by drainage and infillings); and the littoral zone (subject to waste disposal; UNEP, 1996, p. vii).

Based on information collected up to March 1995, the UNEP study of 1996 comes to the conclusion that the levels of the key pollutants in water, sediments, and organisms did not change since the previous study, concluding that there has been no obvious deterioration since 1990. The study notes the main factors of concern: pressure by tourism, waste disposal, sewage treatment, water supply, air pollution, soil erosion, coastal marine pollution, urbanization, and industrialization in coastal areas. Among the lesser but still important issues are deforestation; water resource contamination; pollution due to ports or in ports; algal bloom, jellyfish plagues, and other effects of eutrophication; and degradation of fisheries (UNEP, 1996, p. 112).

Future problems and risks for the Mediterranean Sea are exploitation and destruction of the natural marine resources; chemical pollution, which is normally limited to marine areas around river mouths and industrial complexes (except for long-living substances such as DDT and PCBs); physical pollution by floating oil and plastic garbage; and biological pollution triggered by waste waters, input of nutrients, and exotic organisms. Lagoons, embayments, and shallow coastal seas are especially endangered, in particular the coasts in the vicinities of Barcelona (Spain), Banyuls-sur-Mer (France), from the mouth of the Rhone up to Nizza, the Italian coast of the Adriatic Sea, the Gulf of Izmir (Turkey), the mouth of the Nile at Alexandria, and the coasts of Malta.

International Action to Cope with the Threats. The Mediterranean is one of the geographic areas covered by the Regional Seas Programme of the UNEP. It aims to analyze the potential implications of predicted climatic changes and to assist governments in avoiding or mitigating negative changes, or in adapting to them.

The major potential impacts and risks of the predicted climatic change have been identified for fourteen case studies (for locations see Figure 1). The results were published in two voluminous books (Jeftić et al., 1992, 1996) in which the fourth generation of case studies is also identified (Jeftić et al., 1996, pp. 3–7). Among others, the books contain examples of the effects of

higher temperatures on sea level rise and coastal erosion, and on fisheries, harbors, and beach tourism. The following conclusions are taken from Jeftić et al. (1992, 1996).

Protection and management of the natural resources is of major importance. Protection of the Mediterranean Sea must directly be done on a national level; examples include the reduction of the input of pollutants by building wastewater treatment plants and the reduction of the sediment load of the rivers by means of afforestation, especially in headwater areas and on steep slopes, and flood management through flood storage dams. Furthermore, this must be flanked by bi- and multilateral treaties. Several international organizations—apart from nongovernmental organizations—have the Mediterranean Sea on their agenda: the International Oceanographic Commission, United Nations Educational, Scientific, and Cultural Organization's (UNESCO's) Man and Biosphere Programme, the World Health Organization, the International Maritime Organization, and UNEP. In 1975, sixteen Mediterranean countries and the European Commission met in Barcelona under the auspices of UNEP and approved the Mediterranean Action Plan (MAP) under the UNEP's Oceans and Coastal Areas Programme and its component program for pollution monitoring and research in the Mediterranean Sea. In 1976 the Conference of Mediterranean States signed the Convention for the Protection of the Mediterranean Sea against Pollution, the so-called Barcelona Convention—a joint effort to prevent, abate, and combat pollution in the Mediterranean Sea (UNEP, 1997, pp. 7–8). Many technical reports have been issued under the umbrella of MAP and are distributed by the UNEP bureau in Athens.

The Action Plan for the Protection of the Marine Environment and the Sustainable Development of the Coastal Areas of the Mediterranean (MAP Phase II) was adopted in Barcelona 1995; it replaces the Mediterranean Action Plan of 1975. The protocols address pollution by dumping from ships, oil and other harmful substances, hazardous waste, pollution from land-based sources, and so on.

[*See also* United Nations Environment Programme.]

BIBLIOGRAPHY

Bacci, E. "Mercury in the Mediterranean." *Marine Pollution Bulletin* 20 (1989), 59–63.
Béthoux, J. P., B. Gentili, J. Raunet, and D. Tailliez. "Warming Trend in the Western Mediterranean Deep Water." *Nature* 347 (1990), 660–662.
Brandt, C. J., and J. B. Thornes, eds. *Mediterranean Desertification and Land Use.* New York: Wiley, 1996.
Brückner, H. "Das Mittelmeergebiet als Naturraum." In *Das Alte Rom*, edited by J. Martin, pp. 13–29. München: Bertelsmann, 1994.
———. "Coastal Changes in Western Turkey: Rapid Delta Progradation in Historical Times." In *Transformations and Evolution*

of the Mediterranean Coastline, Bulletin de l'Institut océanographique, Monaco, 18, edited by F. Briand and A. Maldonado, pp. 63–74. CIESM Science Series, vol. 3. Monaco: CIESM, 1997a.

———. "Geoarchäologische Forschungen in der Westtürkei: das Beispiel Ephesos." Passauer Schriften zur Geographie 15 (1997b), 39–51.

———. "Coastal Research and Geoarchaeology in the Mediterranean Region." In German Geographical Research on Coasts and Seas: The Past Ten Years, edited by D. Kelletat. Tübingen: Institute for Scientific Co-operation, 1998.

Brückner, H., and U. Radtke. "Küstenlinien: Indikatoren für Neotektonik und Eustasie." Geographische Rundschau 42 (1990), 654–661.

Cid Montañes, J. F. "Estimated Inputs of Organochlorines from the River Ebro into the Northwest Mediterranean." Marine Pollution Bulletin 21 (1990), 518–523.

Emery, K. O., and D. G. Aubrey. Sea Levels, Land Levels, and Tide Gauges. New York: Springer-Verlag, 1991.

Hollis, G. E. "Implications of Climatic Changes in the Mediterranean Basin: Garaet El Ichkeul and Lac de Bizerte, Tunisia." In Climatic Change and the Mediterranean: Environmental and Societal Impacts of Climatic Change and Sea-Level Rise in the Mediterranean Region, edited by Jeftić et al., pp. 602–665. London: Edward Arnold, 1992.

Jeftić, L., J. D. Milliman, and G. Sestini, eds. Climatic Change and the Mediterranean: Environmental and Societal Impacts of Climatic Change and Sea-Level Rise in the Mediterranean Region, vol. 1. London: Edward Arnold, 1992.

Jeftić, L., S. Kečkš, and J. C. Pernetta, eds. Climatic Change and the Mediterranean: Environmental and Societal Impacts of Climate Change and Sea-Level Rise in the Mediterranean Region, vol. 2. London: Edward Arnold, 1996.

Kelletat, D. "Perspectives in Coastal Geomorphology of Western Crete, Greece." Zeitschrift für Geomorphologie N. F., Suppl.-Bd. 102 (1996), 1–19.

Kelletat, D., and L. Zimmermann. "Die schleichende Ölpest am Beispiel der Küsten Kretas." Abhandlungen der Braunschweigischen Wissenschaftlichen Gesellschaft 29 (1978), 47–55.

Klug, H. "Meeres-und Küstenverschmutzung: Ursachen, Ausmaß, Konsequenzen." Geographische Rundschau 38 (1986), 646–652.

Macklin, M. G., J. Lewin, and J. C. Woodward. "Quaternary Fluvial Systems in the Mediterranean Basin." In Mediterranean Quaternary River Environments, edited by J. Lewin, M. G. Macklin, and J. C. Woodward, pp. 1–25. Rotterdam: Balkema, 1995.

Palutikof, J. P., M. Conte, J. C. Mendes, C. M. Goodess, and F. Espirito Santo. "Climate and Climatic Change." In Mediterranean Desertification and Land Use, edited by C. J. Brandt and J. B. Thornes, pp. 43–86. New York: Wiley, 1996.

Sestini, G. "Implications of Climatic Changes for the Po Delta and Venice Lagoon." In Climatic Change and the Mediterranean: Environmental and Societal Impacts of Climatic Change and Sea-Level Rise in the Mediterranean Region, edited by Jeftić et al., pp. 428–494. London: Edward Arnold, 1992a.

———. "Implications of Climatic Changes for the Nile Delta." In Climatic Change and the Mediterranean: Environmental and Societal Impacts of Climatic Change and Sea-Level Rise in the Mediterranean Region, edited by Jeftić et al., pp. 535–601. London: Edward Arnold, 1992b.

United Nations Environment Programme (UNEP). The State of the Marine and Coastal Environment in the Mediterranean Region. MAP Technical Reports Series, no. 100. Athens: UNEP, 1996.

———. The Mediterranean Action Plan: A Contribution to Sustainable Development in the Mediterranean Basin. Athens: UNEP, 1997.

United Nations Environment Programme (UNEP). Food and Agriculture Organization (FAO). World Health Organization (WHO). Assessment of the State of Pollution of the Mediterranean Sea by Zinc, Copper, and Their Compounds. MAP Technical Reports Series, no. 105. Athens: UNEP, 1996.

Zimmermann, L., and D. Kelletat. "Die schleichende Ölpest im Mittelmeer." Geoökodynamik 5 (1984), 77–98.

—Helmut Brückner

METALS

Metals are a broad group of chemical elements that are characterized by being opaque, lustrous, tough, ductile, malleable, fusible, and good conductors of heat and electricity. Although about half of all chemical elements possess some of these properties, those that we conventionally call "metals" exhibit two or more of these properties. Metal usage began in prehistoric times, but was restricted to the very small amounts that were found in the native, or free, state. Metals only came into prominence with the development of smelting between 5,500 and 3,000 BP, and large-scale employment in numerous applications only appeared after the Industrial Revolution. Today, metals constitute the backbone of the modern construction and transportation industries and provide for thousands of electronic and technological applications. Although many metals are used in their relatively pure forms, there also exist today thousands of alloys blended to provide special physical, chemical, or electrical properties.

Mining has always had a significant impact on the environment because it involves the excavation of ores, which leaves pits and tunnels; processing, which leaves waste (some of it acid generating); and smelting, which often releases sulfur and some metals. Until the onset of the Industrial Revolution, these impacts were relatively small and local, but have expanded in scope and number over the past 150 years. The combination of exhaustion of richer ores, higher costs, and stricter environmental regulations has led to a general trend of increased reliance of the industrialized nations upon developing nations for their metal needs.

Types of Metal and Mineral Sources. Metals may conveniently be classified on the basis of their natural concentrations in average rocks of the Earth's crust: (1) abundant metals are those occurring at 0.1 percent (one thousand parts per million) or more and (2) scarce metals are those occurring at lower concentrations. The scarce metals are then commonly subdivided into ferroalloy metals, base metals, precious metals, and special metals, as shown in Table 1. With the exception of gold, copper, and silver, which commonly occur in the native,

Metals. TABLE 1. Selected Important Metals and their Most Important Mineralogical Sources

	AVERAGE ABUNDANCE*	CRUSTAL MINERALS	MINIMUM ORE GRADE (%)
Abundant metals			
Iron	56,000	magnetite (Fe_3O_4), hematite (Fe_2O_3)	25
Aluminum	82,300	boehmite (AlOOH), diaspore (AlOOH)	40
Silicon	282,000	quartz (SiO_2)	100
Manganese	950	pyrolusite (MnO_2)	25
Titanium	5,700	rutile (TiO_2), ilmenite ($FeTiO_3$)	1.5
Magnesium	23,000	magnesite ($MgCO_3$), dolomite(($Ca,Mg)CO_3$), seawater and brines	—
Scarce metals			
Ferro-alloy Metals			
Chromium	100	chromite ($FeCr_2O_4$)	40
Nickel	75	pentlandite (($FeNi)_9S_8$)	1.0
Cobalt	25	pentlandite (($Fe,Ni,Co)_9S_8$)	0.2
Tungsten	1.5	scheelite $CaWO_4$	0.3
Molybdenum	1.5	molybdenite (MoS_2)	0.1
Vanadium	135	magnetite (($Fe,V)_3O_4$)	0.5
Base metals			
Copper	55	chalcopyrite ($CuFeS_2$), chalcocite (Cu_2S) bornite (Cu_5FeS_4)	0.5
Lead	12.5	galena (PbS)	2.5
Zinc	70	sphalerite (ZnS)	2.5
Tin	2	cassiterite (SnO_2)	0.5
Mercury	0.08	cinnabar (HgS), mercury (Hg)	0.1
Precious metals			
Gold[†]	0.004	gold (Au), electrum (Au,Ag)	0.0001
Silver[†]	0.07	electrum (Au, Ag), acanthite (Ag_2S) tetrahedrite (($Cu, Ag)_{12}Sb_4S_{13}$))	0.005
Platinum	0.005	ferroplatinum (Fe, Pt), sperrylite ($PtAs_2$) cooperite (($Pt, Pd)S$)	0.0002
Special metals			
Tantalum	2	tantalite (($Fe, Mn)Ta_2O_6$)	—
Arsenic[†]	1.8	arsenopyrite (FeAsS), realgar (AsS)	—
Germanium[†]	1.5	sphalerite (($Zn, Fe, Ge)S$)	—
Gallium[†]	15	sphalerite (($Zn, Fe, Ga)S$)	—
Cadmium[†]	0.2	sphalerite (($Zn, Fe, Cd)S$)	—
Beryllium	2.8	beryl ($Be_3Al_2Si_6O_{18}$)	—

*Abundance is given in parts per million; iron, for example, constitutes 5.6 percent of the average crust.

[†]Recovered largely as byproducts of the mining of other metals.

SOURCE: Data from Mason (1966).

or uncombined, form, the metals that we use are extracted from naturally occurring oxides and sulfides. Although there are many kinds of metal-bearing minerals (silicates, carbonates, sulfates, etc.), only those listed in Table 1 are economically mined, concentrated, and smelted for metals today.

History of Metal Usage. Metal usage by humans appears to have begun prior to 8,000 BP and perhaps as early as 11,000 BP, as evidenced by the presence of copper pins and trinkets found in Iran, Turkey, and Iraq. Gold objects have been found in graves dating from about 6,300 BP near the Bulgarian Black Sea port of Varna. These metals were no doubt the first used because they occurred as particles of nearly pure native

metals that could easily be shaped. By about 6,000 BP, the ability to smelt copper from copper-bearing ores, especially the bright green carbonate, malachite, had been developed. There is much speculation that this was an outgrowth of the discovery that baking of pottery decorated with brightly colored mineral paints in charcoal-fueled ovens resulted in some reduction of the malachite and the appearance of copper beads on the pots. The desirability of copper resulted in a rapid spread in the technology, so that copper mining and smelting was occurring throughout southern Europe by 5,000 BP and across northern Europe by 4,000 BP. Many copper ores also contain variable amounts of tin and zinc; hence the development of the first bronzes (copper and tin alloys)

THE HISTORY OF LEAD EMISSIONS

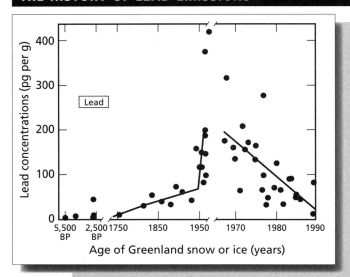

Lead Concentrations in Greenland Snow.

(After Boutron et al., 1991. Reprinted with permission from *Nature.* Copyright 1991. Macmillan Magazines Limited.)

Humans have used lead since prehistoric times, but it has been calculated that 85 percent of the total human output of lead has occurred since 1800 CE. The mining and subsequent processing and use of lead has caused it to be emitted into the atmosphere. In Roman times, global lead emissions were probably around 5,000–10,000 metric tons per year. Between 500 and 1500 CE, the emissions amounted to 500–1,500 metric tons per year. However, emissions rates climbed steadily in the nineteenth and twentieth centuries and peaked at 400,000 metric tons per year in the 1970s and 1980s. Large amounts of lead were emitted because of its use in automobile fuel. In recent years, because of changes in legislation and technology in many parts of the world, the figure has fallen to around 100,000 metric tons per year (Nriagu, 1998). The effects of these changes in emissions have been detected in the Greenland ice cores (see figure), where the lead content of dated ice appears to have risen markedly since the start of the Industrial Revolution and again after 1940, when widespread use of leaded gasoline began. They have declined 7.5 times since their peak in the 1970s (Boutron et al., 1991).

BIBLIOGRAPHY

Boutron, C. F., et al. "Decrease in Anthropogenic Lead, Cadmium and Zinc in Greenland Snow Since the Late 1960s." *Nature* 353 (1991), 153–156.
Nriagu, J. O. "Tales Told in Lead." *Science* 281 (1998), 1622–1623.

—ANDREW S. GOUDIE

and brasses (copper and zinc alloys) was probably an accidental byproduct of copper smelting. By 5,000 BP, it became clear that the alloys had properties of strength and durability greater than those of pure copper, and their preparation became intentional and widespread across the Middle East, southern Asia, and soon thereafter in the Far East. The oxides of lead and zinc could also be reduced relatively easily in charcoal fires; once recognized, the technology to produce lead and zinc also spread rapidly. Gold remained a metal of widespread but very limited use, because of its rarity and because it was only recovered from placer nuggets that had weathered out of original lode deposits.

Free iron is exceedingly rare in the Earth's crust, and it appears that the earliest discoveries of the metal were in meteorites found in desert and polar regions about 5,000 BP. The metal was so rare and so hard to work, relative to copper or gold, that its earliest uses were probably in amulets and ornaments. Recent discoveries reveal that Arctic peoples found meteoritic iron very valuable, and developed extensive trade networks to distribute it. The first uses of terrestrial iron are not well established, but the Hittites were producing iron-bladed knives by 4,500 BP. Iron smelting required a large tech-

nological step because normal wood or charcoal fires are not hot enough to melt iron. However, very hot charcoal fires might have been able to cause sufficient reduction of some iron oxides, common with copper minerals, to create a "bloom," or spongy iron mass, as is done by heating iron in a blacksmith's shop. Repeated pounding of the red-hot bloom will separate the waste oxides and impurities and ultimately produce a pure mass of iron that can be shaped as desired. The iron has never been melted but becomes pliable enough to be shaped easily into working weapons or tools. The next major step was the discovery that iron could actually be smelted to produce molten iron if there was a mechanism to preheat the air before it entered the chamber where the iron was reduced using charcoal. This was apparently recognized in several parts of the world, and iron was being produced in significant quantities by about 3,500 BP. The availability of iron ores, the spread of the technology, and the superior nature of iron in many applications soon led to its becoming the metal of choice.

The metals of the ancient world were relatively few, but they were sufficient for many human applications. Figure 1 illustrates that no additional metals were rec-

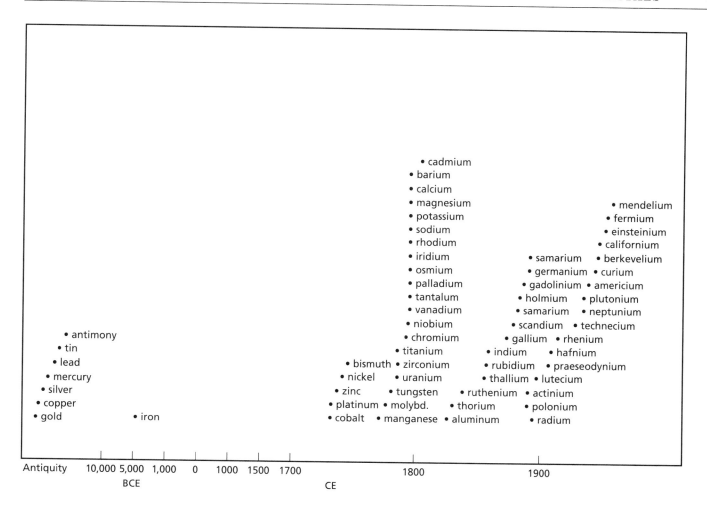

Metals. FIGURE 1. The Discovery of Metals through Time.

Prior to 1700, humans had only specifically identified eight metals. With the rise of modern chemistry came the discovery of most of the metals we know today.

ognized until the beginnings of the rise of modern chemistry in the eighteenth century. For the ancient world, gold, silver, and copper provided coinage, copper and tin provided weaponry and ornamentation, lead served for pipes, plates, and ceramic glazes, mercury served for pigments, and antimony served to alloy with tin and lead. Iron continued to rise in importance, filling both mundane and military needs. With the erosion of the Roman world, metal uses continued but there were few new technologies until the dawning of the Renaissance. With the birth of modern science, especially chemistry, there came a new pursuit of the nature of metals and the discovery of a host of new metals that had been in human hands but had gone unrecognized. World metal production was small and generally local until the dawn

of the Industrial Revolution, which is usually dated from the development of the first steam engine in 1698.

Production of Metals. The history of metals may extend back many millennia, but the production of more than 95 percent of nearly every metal has occurred in the past hundred years. Figure 2 shows world production of the most important base metals—copper, lead, and zinc—since 1700; Figure 3 shows the world production of gold and silver since 1700; and Figure 4 shows the world production of steel and aluminum since 1850. In each figure, it is apparent that production was relatively minor prior to 1900 and that there was a steady increase through the first half of the twentieth century. After the disruption of World War II, the production of these metals has accelerated rapidly. The one notable exception is lead which, because of the recognition of detrimental environmental and health effects, has begun to see a slight decline in usage in the past twenty years.

Although iron dominates world metal production and is used in countless applications, silicon and aluminum are perhaps the metals most symbolic of modern metal technology. Aluminum is highly visible in such forms as

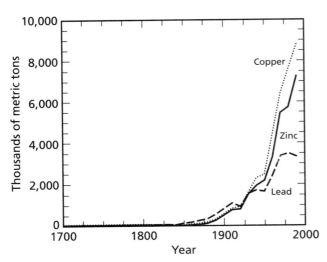

Metals. FIGURE 2. World Production of Copper, Lead, and Zinc since 1700.

Lead was the most important of the base metals until about 1920, when the demands of the electrical and construction industries made copper more necessary. The demand for lead has begun to decline because of environmental concerns, but the demand for copper and zinc is expected to continue to rise.

kitchen wrap, beverage cans, and aircraft bodies. In contrast, silicon, the most abundant metal, is highly used but nearly invisible because it is employed primarily in the refining of iron. In recent years, there has been a great

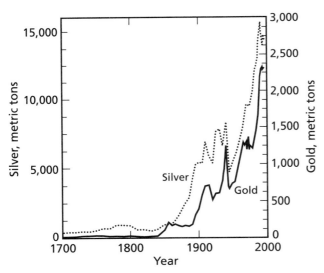

Metals. FIGURE 3. World Production of Silver and Gold since 1700.

Silver is about ten times more abundant than gold, and has long been produced in greater quantities. Gold production, which had been constant but very small, increased dramatically when gold was found in California in 1848. It then began rising again about the turn of the century and has now reached about 2,300 metric tons per year. The production of silver has paralleled that of gold and is now about 15,000 metric tons per year.

increase in the use of silicon in alloys and in electronic applications, especially semiconductor chips and photovoltaic solar cells. These applications will, no doubt, continue to increase in the near future but will continue to remain relatively invisible to the general public.

Early metal production, and some very minor modern production, has gone unrecorded, but the major production, as shown in Figures 2–4, is well documented and dwarfs any unrecorded data. Consequently, it is possible to estimate the total amounts of metals produced by humans through history. Table 2 lists the approximate total production of eleven major metals through 1995. These data reveal that iron and steel have accounted for more than 96 percent of all of the metals humans have ever produced. The 1995 world production data, given in Table 3, are very similar in proportion to the historic production figures.

On the basis of the trends in metal usage, both total quantities and per capita, and the projected rise in human population to 8.5 billion by 2050 and 11 billion by 2100, it is clear that metal demand will continue to rise for many years. The increased demands for all metals will require an increase in mining activities and may result in more environmental impacts from the mining and processing of the ores. There will also be increases in the use of energy to extract the metals, especially as the grade of many ores decreases.

Strategic metals. The term *strategic* has been applied to a variety of mineral resources, especially metals, and implies that the metals are ones for which the quantity required for essential civilian and military uses exceeds the reasonably secure domestic and foreign supplies. Today, most lists of strategic metals include chromium, cobalt, niobium, nickel, platinum, and tantalum, but titanium, manganese, aluminum, and up to ten others may also appear. The principal concerns in the past have been the availability of these metals for military purposes in wartime. With the ending of the Cold War, concerns have lessened but have not been completely forgotten, because these materials are still vital in a broad range of civilian applications. The U.S. government, like some others, holds significant quantities of these metals in the strategic stockpile in case supplies are disrupted.

Primary versus byproduct metals. The major metals are extracted from mines operated for their extraction as the primary products. In many mines, there are two or three primary metals recovered. Byproduct recovery of some metals is common when they are present in small but relatively easily recovered quantities. Such metals may occur as small amounts of their normal minerals (e.g., gold in copper ore) or as small amounts in solid solution in the structures of the primary metal-ore minerals (e.g., cadmium, germanium, gallium in sphalerite). Byproduct recovery of metals generally occurs because the removal of minor metals

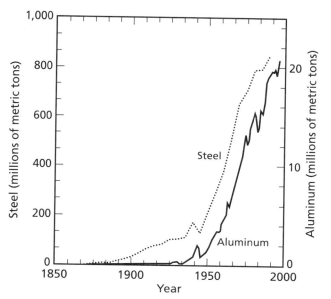

Metals. FIGURE 4. World Production of Steel and Aluminum.

World production of steel (and iron, which parallels the steel curve) began with the Industrial Revolution but saw its prominence grow in the early part of the twentieth century. The most dramatic rise has come since World War II, and production now approaches 800 million metric tons per year. The rise in the production of aluminum parallels that of steel, and has now exceeded 20 million metric tons per year.

mining, concentration, smelting, refining, and manufacturing. If the deposits are at or near the Earth's surface, mining is usually carried out by open-pit methods. This involves removal of any overlying noneconomic rock and then systematic mining downward to recover the ores. Mine shapes vary but are commonly large conical pits. Alternatively, if the ores are deeply buried, an underground mining system involving a shaft, tunnels, and water- and air-delivery systems must be constructed.

In general, open-pit mining will be conducted in preference to underground mining if possible because there are fewer infrastructure needs, it is safer, and it is easier to mine on a large scale. Indeed, many modern open-pit mines can remove 100,000 metric tons of rock per day. The large size and scale of such mines results in two major environmental impacts: a large hole where mining is conducted, and a large dump where waste rock and residue from ore processing is placed. The sides of the open pit must be maintained at safe and stable slopes; thus, as mining proceeds deeper, the surface opening of the pit must become ever wider. When the ore is exhausted or when the cost of widening the upper parts of the pit is no longer economic, mining ceases or must shift to underground methods.

Underground mining is much more expensive than open-pit mining because of the need to maintain the complex infrastructure and to leave sufficient material to support the overlying rock. Consequently, underground mines operate on much smaller scales, but are often able to be much more selective, mining as little waste rock and as much pure ore as possible. As a result, their actual environmental impact is often much smaller than that of open-pit mines; furthermore, in some mining operations, the waste is returned underground to refill the mined-out areas.

is necessary to refine the principal metal and because the minor metals can be recovered at little additional expense once the ores have been concentrated for recovery of the primary metal-bearing minerals.

Metal Mining and Processing. Metal recovery from ore deposits requires a complex series of steps involving

Metals. TABLE 2. Estimated Historical World Production of Eleven Important Metals through 1995

METAL	PRODUCTION (METRIC TONS)	PERCENTAGE OF TOTAL
Steel	29,891,000,000	55.1
Iron	22,276,000,000	41.1
Aluminum	504,000,000	0.93
Copper	360,000,000	0.66
Zinc	309,525,000	0.57
Lead	294,000,000	0.54
Chromium	104,040,000	0.19
Nickel	28,400,000	0.05
Tin	20,045,000	0.04
Silver	1,045,000	0.002
Gold	121,000	0.0002
Others	10,000,000	0.02
Total	53,798,176,000	

SOURCE: Data derived from the United States Bureau of Mines and from Schmitz (1979).

Metals. TABLE 3. World Metal Production in 1995

METAL	PRODUCTION (METRIC TONS)	PERCENTAGE OF TOTAL
Steel	752,000,000	55.7
Iron	554,000,000	41.0
Aluminum	19,890,000	1.5
Copper	10,000,000	0.74
Zinc	7,120,000	0.53
Lead	2,800,000	0.21
Chromium	2,370,000	0.18
Nickel	908,000	0.07
Tin	187,000	0.01
Silver	14,600	0.001
Gold	2,300	0.0002
Others	654,000	0.05
Total	1,349,945,900	

SOURCE: Data derived from the United States Bureau of Mines, and from Schmitz (1979).

Ore mineral concentration and recovery. Mining removes the bulk ore from the initial deposit and renders it available for processing. Even the richest ores commonly contain large percentages of waste materials. Thus, the principal iron ores mined today contain only about 50 percent iron oxides (equal to about 30–35 percent iron). Many of the world's principal lead or zinc ores contain only about 4–5 percent sphalerite or galena (or about 3 percent zinc or lead). The principal copper deposits contain less than 1 percent chalcopyrite, bornite, or chalcocite (about 0.5 percent copper). And the major gold ores being mined today in most parts of the world contain only about 0.0001 percent gold. Separation of the desired minerals from the useless ones usually requires a process of intense crushing and grinding followed by some sort of selective concentration. This final process is usually accomplished by using chemicals that preferentially cause certain minerals to stick to soap-like bubbles from which they are easily concentrated, or by selective dissolving of the metals with solvents.

The environmental impacts of the mine wastes are highly variable, with the greatest impacts arising from materials that contain significant amounts of pyrite. The pyrite, especially when finely ground, oxidizes readily and creates very acidic mine runoff, which has been responsible for the pollution of numerous sites and the destruction of much aquatic biota. In 1994, the U.S. Bureau of Mines estimated that there were more than 557,000 old mine sites in the United States with a total of more than 50 billion metric tons of mine waste and at least 280,000 acres of unreclaimed federal land affected by mining waste. Furthermore, metal mining in the United States processed more than 2.54 billion metric tons of ore and rock (2.49 billion metric tons from open-pit operations) in 1995, more than 90 percent of which was waste.

Approximately 45 percent (1.3 billion metric tons) of all the ore and rock handled in the United States in the mid-1990s was from gold mining (35 percent was from copper, 15 percent from iron). Twenty-five percent of the rock handled at gold mines (276 million metric tons) was primary ore, and approximately 90 percent of that was treated by cyanide solutions to recover the gold. The most common procedure is that in which the ore is crushed to 1–2 centimeters and piled on large plastic sheets. Dilute cyanide solutions are then sprayed on to the piles and allowed to percolate slowly down through the ore, dissolving as much as 90 percent of the gold. After the solutions are collected, the gold is recovered and the solutions neutralized or regenerated for additional use. Under ideal conditions, the cyanide-bearing solutions are kept in a closed system with zero discharge into the environment. Unfortunately, there have been a number of instances in which cyanide releases have contaminated rivers and lakes, sometime killing significant numbers of fish.

Smelting and refining. For metals to become useful products, they must be smelted (all metallic compounds separated from other nonuseful materials in the ore) and refined (each metal separated into its pure metallic form). In the past, these processes were major sources of air pollution because open burning or roasting was used to drive sulfur from the metallic minerals. Smelting and refining operations today generally recover most of the sulfur and process it into sulfuric acid.

Until the twentieth century, the recovery of metals from sulfide ores usually required the initial conversion of the metal sulfides into oxides by open roasting. Thus there was widespread pollution of the atmosphere by sulfur oxide gases, which are readily converted into acid rain and aerosols. The rapid increases in the use of copper, lead, and zinc, beginning in the late 1800s, resulted in many local environmental impacts. Although metal use in the Industrial Revolution is usually recognized as the cause of much of the rise in metal pollution, it has recently been recognized that the open roasting of lead ores for lead and silver by the Greeks and Romans spread not only acid rain, but also very large quantities of air-borne lead throughout Europe. [*See* Acid Rain and Acid Deposition; *and* Aerosols.]

Metal Resources, Reserves, and Grades. Metal resources are the concentrations of metals produced by a wide variety of geologic processes acting in the Earth's crust. The actual amounts of any metal concentrated into resources and the locations of all of these concentrations will never be known, but these are, of course, the targets of exploration. Those resources that are sufficiently high in grade, that lie close enough to the surface to mine, and that are in areas where extraction can be carried out economically, are defined as *reserves* and are commonly referred to as *ores*. In recent years, a somewhat broader term, *reserve base*, has been used

widely to include both presently minable deposits and those that are likely to become minable in the foreseeable future. The size of the reserves or reserve base of any metal is well defined, but varies every day as ores are mined away and as new deposits are deemed to be economic. Furthermore, increases in the market value of metals lead to increases in the quantity of reserves, but decreases in the market value lead to decreases in the quantity of reserves. [*See* Resources.]

The quantities of the abundant metals in the Earth's crust are very large, and even the most conservative estimates indicate that the mining of the reserves could go on for hundreds of years at present rates. In contrast, the quantities of reserves of the scarce metals, including most of the strategic metals, are much smaller, but would generally last for twenty to fifty years at present rates of production. Although the rates of production of most metals have continued to increase, the quantities of reserves of virtually all metals have remained constant or increased over the past twenty-five years (Figure 5). This indicates that the rates of discovery of new reserves have kept pace with the increasing production. Furthermore, the quantities of reserves are certainly conservative because (1) only a small portion of the Earth's crust has been explored, (2) changing technologies have improved the recovery of metals from lower-grade ores and thus converted some deposits that were

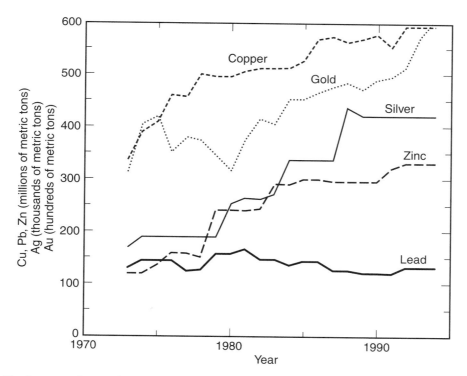

Metals. Figure 5. The Reserves of Several Metals.

With the exception of lead, where use is declining for environmental reasons, the reserves of all major metals have remained constant or have risen over the past twenty-five years. Note that the units on the vertical axis are different for different metals.

subeconomic into economic ones, and (3) companies have no incentive to drill out and define the full nature of many ore deposits if the ores are not to be mined in the next ten to twenty years.

Mining for metals has nearly always concentrated on the richest ores available, because they provide the greatest return in metal and profits. Such practices have, of course, reduced the availability of rich ores, leaving lower-grade ores to meet future needs. At the same time, there have been some innovations in technology that have permitted the efficient processing of lower-grade ores. Examples would include the use of cyanide leaching to extract gold, the application of flotation methods to concentrate very low-grade copper ores, and the use of iron ore pellet concentrates to increase the efficiency of iron smelting. Consequently, there has been a decline through the years in the average grade of some types of ore being mined and processed. Average gold ores have declined from about 0.4 ounces per ton in 1900 to 0.04 ounces per ton today; average copper ores have declined from about 4 percent in 1900 to about 0.5 percent today; average iron ores have declined from 50–60 percent iron to about 30 percent today. Many more complex ores are still being mined at similar grades as in the past, but from deeper mines or more remote locations as more accessible ores have been depleted.

Metal Recycling. The recycling of metals began with the earliest discoveries because the metals were rare and too valuable to be discarded. Although metals are much more accessible today, recycling continues to provide significant quantities of many metals for human use. While responding mainly to economic incentives, recycling also provides environmental benefits through energy savings, reduced mining impact, reduced quantities of waste, and reduced atmospheric emissions. The amount of recycling varies widely around the world, depending upon the degree of development and governmental policies. The United States is representative of many highly developed nations. Recycling in the United States in 1995 provided metal equivalent to approximately 35 percent of the iron and steel used, 60 percent of the lead, 25 percent of the aluminum, and 20 percent of the copper. The recycling of iron and steel scrap at 50 million metric tons per year in the United States dwarfs the quantities of all other metals. Lead is recycled very efficiently because most of it is used in automotive batteries, which are nearly always returned to the retail outlets from which they are purchased. The most visible metal recycling is that of aluminum cans, where approximately 65 percent of the 100 billion produced each year are now being recycled. In general, because of economic and environmental incentives, recycling is rising in both total amount and percentage of metal used.

[*See also* Air Quality; Energy; Industrialization; Mining; Nuclear Industry; Recycling; *and* Water Quality.]

BIBLIOGRAPHY

Aitchison, L. *A History of Metals*. New York: Interscience, 1960. A two-volume history detailing changes in technology of metal extraction and use to the mid-twentieth century.

Boyle, R. W. *The Geochemistry of Silver and its Deposits. Geological Survey of Canada Bulletin* 160 (1968). A detailed discussion of the occurrences of silver in the Earth's crust.

———. *Gold: History and Genesis of Deposits*. New York: Van Nostrand Reinhold, 1987. A collection of papers dealing with the nature of gold deposits, with some discussion of history.

Craddock, P. T. *Early Metal Mining and Production*. Washington, D.C.: Smithsonian Institution Press, 1995. A concise and well-referenced discussion of the development of mining and metal extraction.

Craig, J. R., D. J. Vaughan, and B. J. Skinner. *Resources of the Earth*. 2d ed. Upper Saddle River, N.J.: Prentice-Hall, 1996. A general review of Earth resources, with chapters on the occurrence and use of abundant and scarce metals.

Day, J., and R. F. Tylecote, eds. *The Industrial Revolution in Metals*. London: Institute of Metals, 1991. Six chapters discussing tin, lead, copper, zinc, iron, and steel and their parts in the Industrial Revolution.

Guilbert, J., and C. F. Park. *The Geology of Ore Deposits*. New York: Freeman, 1986. A discussion of the geology and processes involved in the formation of ore deposits of all types of metals.

Jastrom, R.W. *Silver: The Restless Metal*. New York: Wiley, 1981. A discussion of the history of silver, with emphasis on its economic impacts.

Maddin, R., ed. *The Beginning of the Use of Metals and Alloys*. Cambridge: MIT Press, 1988. A scholarly account of the earliest uses of metals and alloys.

Marx, J. *The Magic of Gold*. Garden City, N.Y.: Doubleday, 1978. An historical account of the uses of gold by humankind.

Mason, B. *Principles of Geochemistry*, New York: Wiley, 1966.

Nriagu, J. O. *Lead and Lead Poisoning in Antiquity*. New York: Wiley, 1983. A detailed discussion of the history of lead and its effects, with many data and extensive references.

Raymond, R. *Out of the Fiery Furnace*. University Park: Pennsylvania State University Press, 1984. Broad-based and very readable account of the way in which humans have used metals and subsequently been impacted by their presence.

Rickard, T. A. *Man and Metals*. New York: Arno Press, 1974. A discourse on the historical development of metals and their influences on humankind.

Schmitz, C. J. *World Non-Ferrous Metal Production and Prices 1700–1976*. London: Frank Cass and Company, 1979.

Tylecote, R. F. *A History of Metallurgy*. 2d ed. London: The Metals Society, 1992. Classic, in-depth history of the discovery and use of metals.

United States Bureau of Mines. *Annual Reports, Mineral Commodity Summaries*, and *Mineral Industry Surveys*. Washington, D.C.: United States Government Printing Office. Detail-rich reports on each metal, presenting data on production, trade, cost, and usage. (Publication of these reports was taken over by the United States Geological Survey in 1996.)

—JAMES R. CRAIG

METEORS. *See* Impacts by Extraterrestrial Bodies.

METHANE

Methane is a minor but very significant organic gas in the atmosphere. Consisting of a one-carbon, four-hydrogen bond (CH_4), it contributes the largest individual concentration from the several hundred that exist in the hydrocarbon family. An important component of the carbon cycle, methane is second only to carbon dioxide in contributing to the greenhouse effect. Current mixing ratios in the atmosphere indicate average concentrations of 1.72 parts per million by volume (ppmv) in the Northern Hemisphere and about 1.6 ppmv in the Southern Hemisphere. The difference is caused by the greater number of sources in the Northern Hemisphere.

Historical evaluation of methane concentrations from air bubbles in ice cores from Antarctica and Greenland indicates that, before 1900 CE, methane remained constant at close to 0.8 ppmv. After the Industrial Revolution, methane concentrations increased exponentially (see Figure 1), more than doubling in one hundred years. The increase in methane concentration strongly correlates with the increase in global population. The changes in atmospheric methane over the last century reflect human activities and a variety of sources. The total amount of methane presently in the atmosphere is about 3.5 billion metric tons of equivalent carbon. While this amount is a small percentage of that for carbon dioxide (750 billion metric tons), the impact of methane on climate change is still considered to be significant.

Table 1 presents the major sources and sinks of meth-

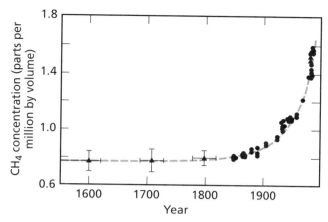

Methane. FIGURE 1. Trends in Atmospheric Methane Concentrations from 1600 to the Late 1980s.

The exponential increase after 1880 is strongly correlated with the increase in global population. Crosses indicate uncertainty in the old values. (After Turco, 1997, p. 375. With permission of Oxford University Press.)

ane. Natural sources, such as wetlands, oceans and lakes, and the activities of termites, provide about 25 percent of methane emissions to the atmosphere, mainly through decay processes. Agriculture and animal husbandry activities emit a further 32 percent, mainly through rice paddies (especially in Southeast Asia and China), bovines (cattle, sheep, and goats), and human beings. Methane escapes from rice paddies in a similar manner to wetlands, through decay, and also through fertilization processes. Bovine emissions are caused by inefficient digestion of fibrous grazing material, creat-

Methane. TABLE 1. Major Sources and Sinks of Methane*

SOURCES	RATE[†] (RANGE)	SINKS	RATE[†] (RANGE)
Methanogenesis		Reactions with hydroxyl radical	320 (260–380)
Natural wetlands	85 (75–150)		
Rice paddies	80 (45–130)	Atmospheric accumulation	35 (30–40)
Bovines	60 (45–75)		
Natural gas leakage	75 (60–90)	Soil uptake	20 (15–25)
Landfills/waste	60 (60–80)		
Biomass burning	40 (35–75)		
Termites	15 (5–75)		
Oceans and lakes	10 (5–15)		
Totals	425 (310–765)		375 (305–445)

*Numbers are approximate.

[†]Units are millions of metric tons of carbon equivalent per year.

SOURCE: From Turco (1997, p. 376). With permission of Oxford University Press.

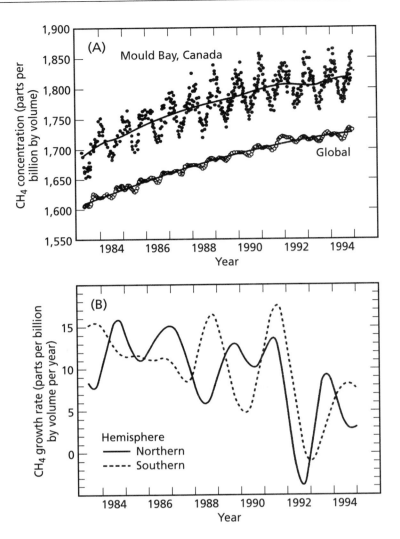

Methane. Figure 2.

(A) Recent trends in global average methane concentrations and
(B) variations in the annual growth rate, from 1982 to 1996.
(After Houghton et al., 1996, p. 87. With permission of the Inter-
governmental Panel on Climate Change.)

ing methane release from both the mouth and bowel
areas. Burning and leakage associated with fossil fuels
and deforestation adds another 27 percent to annual
methane emissions to the atmosphere. The natural gas
used for heating and cooking in homes is almost entirely
methane. Emissions from oil-fired and gas-fired power
stations and from oil wells fall in this category. The remainder comes from landfills and waste emissions, including mining activities.

There are three major sinks shown in Table 1. The
most important removal mechanism is reactions in the
troposphere and stratosphere with the hydroxyl radical
(OH). OH and the other radicals are fragments of molecules with lifetimes on the order of fractions of a sec-

ond. They are extremely important as triggers in atmospheric chemistry. Methane and OH react together to
form water and the methyl radical, CH_3. About 85 percent of methane loss is caused by this reaction. CH_3 is
unstable and reacts rapidly to form other compounds.
The methyl radical is a core component of peroxyacetyl
nitrate, an important component of photochemical
smog. A second, much smaller sink is methane interaction with and takeup by soil. The average lifetime of a
methane molecule in the atmosphere is on the order of
ten to twelve years.

About 35 million metric tons of carbon per year accumulates in the atmosphere, creating an annual average increase in concentration of about 0.6 percent.
Figure 2A presents a recent history of methane trends
(1982–1995). Figure 2(B) shows that the year-to-year
growth rate varies somewhat. In 1992, for example,
growth stopped in some parts of the globe. Suggested
causes include a decrease in biomass burning and a
decrease in the burning of fossil fuels across the globe,
enhanced exchange between the troposphere and

stratosphere associated with the Mount Pinatubo eruption, and lower emissions from wetlands. The growth rate returned to the usual level in the following year.

The source and sink totals in Table 1 do not match, creating a gap in the overall annual methane budget. The gap may be explained, however, by the uncertainties in the estimates, indicated by the ranges in Table 1. Future research will enhance the accuracy of the numbers and ensure a better understanding of the relationships between sources and sinks.

Methane is a greenhouse gas, and continuing annual increases in atmospheric concentrations add to the threat of anthropogenic impacts on the Earth's climate though artificial global warming. The International Panel on Climate Change classifies the global warming potential (impact according to a molecule-to-molecule comparison with carbon dioxide) for methane as ranging from fifty-six times higher over a twenty-year period to twenty-one times higher over a one-hundred-year period. Methane absorbs longwave radiation in wavelengths that are not saturated, for example around 7.7 micrometers. Increasing methane concentrations will be able to absorb in this wavelength band to maximum effect. Methane concentrations in the atmosphere are an order of magnitude lower than those of carbon dioxide, and the methane atmospheric lifetime is estimated to be at least five times lower than that of carbon dioxide. The impact of carbon dioxide on global warming remains about three times higher than that of methane.

The complex mix of sources listed in Table 1 indicates that control over methane emissions is a very difficult problem. There are, however, some potential benefits from waste methane. One example on a local or regional scale is to tap methane stored in solid waste facilities (dumps) for use as an energy source. Landfill gas (LFG), of which methane is a major component, is formed by decay of organic matter (anaerobic digestion), and with proper environmental management can be collected with minimal escape to the atmosphere. It is estimated that about 0.18 cubic meters of LFG is produced per kilogram of municipal solid waste, depending on the rate of decomposition of the organic matter and the age and fill rate of the facility. The LFG can be piped to an energy facility where it can be burned to generate heat or electricity. From a landfill generating 4 million cubic meters of LFG per year, if a 50 percent methane content is assumed, it is possible to generate about 5,000 megawatt hours of electricity. When methane is completely burned, it turns into carbon dioxide, but the equivalent emissions and greenhouse gas impacts are reduced considerably compared with releasing the methane into the atmosphere.

A second example is the relatively recent discovery of methane gas trapped in hydrates on the sea floor in various parts of the world. [See the vignette Methane Hydrates *in the article on* Fossil Fuels.] Methane hydrate is formed in ocean floor sediments under extreme pressure and low temperatures, where the water is compressed, leaving a solid gray mass similar to ice. It is estimated that about 160 cubic centimeters of methane at standard atmospheric conditions is contained in a compressed state in 1 cubic centimeter of methane hydrate. Estimates of the amount on the ocean floor indicate that there is enough energy potential to replace all the gas, oil, and coal reserves on land. However, methane hydrate is extremely unstable, and, once removed from its natural location, dissolves quickly, releasing methane to the atmosphere. There is a potential danger of a mass release of this greenhouse gas from the ocean floor to the atmosphere if major changes in ocean temperature and pressure occur. Much research is needed in the future if methane hydrate is to be used safely as a source of energy.

[See also Agriculture and Agricultural Land; Animal Husbandry; Atmospheric Chemistry; Biomass; Biomes; Climate Change; Deforestation; Fossil Fuels; Global Warming; Greenhouse Effect; Nitrogen Cycle; *and* Wetlands.]

BIBLIOGRAPHY

Environment Australia. *Waste Management Workbook: Methane Capture and Use.* Canberra, 1997.
Houghton, J., et al., eds. *Climate Change 1995: The Science of Climate Change.* United Nations Intergovernmental Panel on Climate Change. New York and Cambridge: Cambridge University Press, 1996.
Steele, L. P., et al. "The Global Distribution of Methane in the Troposphere." *Journal of Atmospheric Chemistry* 5 (1987), 125–171.
Turco, R. *Earth Under Siege.* New York and Oxford: Oxford University Press, 1997.

—HOWARD A. BRIDGMAN

MIDDLE EAST

[*This case study focuses on the major world region with the greatest actual and potential water deficiency and discusses management strategies for coping with resource geopolitics.*]

At all levels—from the international to the local—water management problems may merge into geopolitical issues. Geopolitics is the use of geography to illuminate politics and the concern of the subject is with the geographical setting in which political decisions are taken or conflict occurs. The provision of sufficient water may be affected by hydrological conditions or it may be influenced by geopolitical actions, such as the planned overabstraction of water by one party from a shared resource.

Water in the Middle East. In the Middle East, the focus of water management is upon the provision and distribution of a scarce resource to satisfy social, economic, and political needs. There has long been a preoccupation in this region with water and the security of access to it. Politically, the survival of states has depended upon water while, strategically, it has been a key element in military planning. It is germane that the word *rival* (derived from the Latin *rivus*, stream), originated from the concept of using the same stream.

The potential for resource geopolitics grows with the increasing scarcity of the resource. By any measure, the Middle East and, in particular, the core area of the Arabian Peninsula, Egypt, Jordan, Palestine, Syria, and Israel (Figures 1–3), is the major world region with the greatest actual and potential water deficiency. Water management problems are particularly acute, therefore, and political issues—actual and perceived—are never far below the surface.

Apart from the mountainous areas, annual precipitation totals range from well below 100 millimeters (four inches) in the deserts to 200 millimeters in the desert fringes, with maxima of approximately 500 millimeters. The lower the total, the less reliable the rainfall becomes. Despite these problems, until this century a basic balance was maintained between water, agriculture, and population.

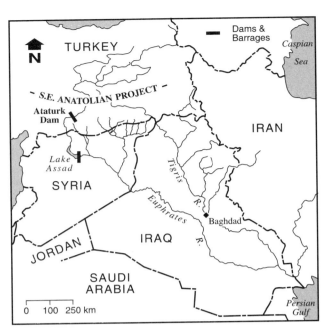

Middle East. FIGURE 2. Water Management along the Tigris–Euphrates.

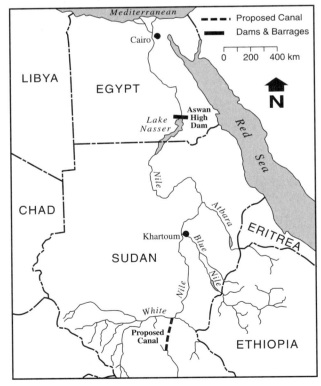

Middle East. FIGURE 1. Water Management along the Nile.

The situation has now been transformed. Perhaps the most important change has been in the extremely high rates of population growth in most Middle Eastern countries. As a result of modern medicine, infant mortality rates have been reduced and average life spans are increasing. If the present situation persists, the population of the Middle East will double within the next 25 years; and water supplies throughout most of the region are already under severe strain.

As a result of the increased rates of population growth and urban migration, there has been a marked increase in the size of the urban population, particularly in the oil-rich states. In several of the Middle Eastern countries, the urbanized proportion of the population already exceeds 75 percent. This change affects water demand: whereas a nomadic family may consume between 10 and 30 liters (2.5 to 7.5 gallons) per person per day, in the urban setting this figure is likely to rise to between 400 and 800 liters. Furthermore, urban growth has not only exerted a direct influence upon water use, but has increased pressure for industrialization and thereby generated further water demands. Another consequence of such expansion is pollution: urban growth has commonly exceeded the local capacity for the disposal of waste, and water supplies, both in the infrastructure and in the aquifers, have been put at risk.

A far greater concern than any of these, however, is agriculture. To satisfy the burgeoning requirement for food, vastly increased quantities of water are needed for irrigation, typically between 60 and 70 percent of na-

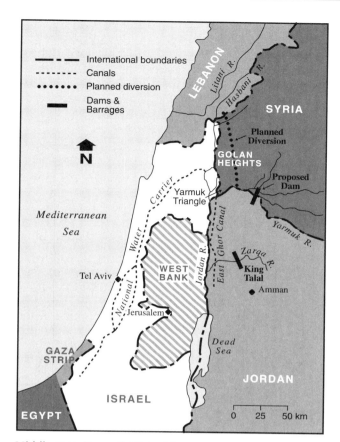

Middle East. FIGURE 3. Water Management along the Jordan.

tile as any on earth. Given its importance for so many facets of life, water is normally under governmental control. However, given its multiple functions, water is frequently a key concern of several government departments and, as a direct result of this, national water institutions tend to be weak and reactive. The fragmentation of responsibility and the heavy dependence on centralized administration have resulted in inefficiency of water management.

Management strategies need to take into account the many functions of water in maintaining health, habitats, the production of food, energy and industrial products, transport, and psychological well-being; and these needs must be prioritized. As water becomes scarcer, choices need to be made between incompatible demands. These include competition between upstream and downstream users and that between urban and rural users. Problems range from the international to the local, from that of an international drainage basin to that of a qanat (a small-scale irrigation system supplied by a subterranean channel from the nearest upland area).

A hydrological approach to water management would involve either an increase in water supply or a reduction in demand. The management of a national water system includes the development and coordination of all the sources on the supply side and the aggregation and prioritization of requirements on the demand side. Total demand can then be compared with total supply, for a particular time and budget, and a possible water balance computed. In the Middle East, the production of a water balance may necessitate the distribution of water to the various user sectors according to the national priorities.

Throughout the Middle East, storage typically takes the form of ground water in aquifers. However, in the three key international basins—the Nile, the Tigris–Euphrates, and the Jordan—there is surface water storage, and evaporation losses such as those from Lake Nasser and Lake Assad are extreme. The geology of aquifers is generally not well known unless they are relatively shallow; in particular, the relationship between inputs and outputs of water, especially in deep aquifers, is largely conjectural. The potential effectiveness of artificial recharge is therefore, in most cases, uncertain. [*See* Dams; *and* Ground Water.]

The two areas of research and development that have had the greatest impact upon water supply enhancement have been desalination and recycling. Desalination—the production of fresh water from brackish or sea water, principally by multistage flash or reverse osmosis processes—offers the only method of adding to the stock of fresh water but is, at present, relatively expensive. Costs are typically four to eight times those for urban water and as much as 20 times those for agricultural water. It is hardly surprising, therefore, that 60 percent of

tional water use, or near the upper possible limit. At the same time, the intensification of agriculture has frequently led to the excessive use of fertilizers and sprays—a further source of pollution for the aquifers. [*See* Irrigation.]

Hydrologists agree that when the available water supply falls below 1,000 cubic meters per person per year, the country is designated "water scarce" and there is a severe constraint on food production, economic development, and the protection of natural systems. The core area of the Middle East, as defined above, is already water scarce, while Israel and Jordan are said to suffer from absolute water scarcity. Water must therefore be considered a strategic resource and highly susceptible to resource geopolitics, or "hydropolitics." In areas of water scarcity, planning and policy making must take account of both hydrological and geopolitical considerations.

Management and Hydrology. Water management in the arid realm poses complex problems. Water is a finite, mobile, and vulnerable commodity, and the environmental conditions under which supplies need to be provided and distributed are, in the Middle East, as hos-

the installed capacity is located in the oil-rich Gulf Co-operation Council countries (Bahrain, Kuwait, Oman, Qatar, Saudi Arabia, and United Arab Emirates) of the Arabian Peninsula. Recycling of both domestic and industrial water is being implemented rapidly in the urban areas of the Middle East, but the impact on consumption patterns has been relatively negligible. [*See* Desalination.]

Opportunities for locating alternative sources within the Middle East are restricted. Most countries have already completed a detailed internal audit while, for the most part, neighboring countries are themselves water poor. There are, however, opportunities for interbasin transfers. The most spectacular example is provided by the Great Manmade River Project in Libya, intended to irrigate over 7,300 hectares (18,000 acres) at an annual cost of over U.S.$500 million. Water is transferred from deep aquifers, most notably Kufra in the southern Fezzan to the shores of the Gulf of Sidra. Since it appears almost certain that the aquifers are not recharged, the life of this project is limited. The most highly publicized proposal for international water transfer has been the Peace Pipeline, announced by Turkey in 1987, but, because of political difficulties, as yet not implemented. This is envisaged as carrying some 2.2 billion cubic meters of potable water from southeastern Turkey to the Arabian Peninsula littoral states of the Persian Gulf and Red Sea. More ingenious but still awaiting funding is Operation Medusa, in which water would be transferred by sea in huge bags from Turkey to the Turkish Republic of Northern Cyprus and possibly Israel. Another option for the enhancement of supply is cloud seeding, although the generally low relative humidity of the Middle East indicates that such a procedure is unlikely to be effective on a large scale. Furthermore, there are major potential geopolitical and legal issues at stake. Work on deep fractured rock aquifers, which dominate the major geologic watersheds, has produced significant water yields elsewhere, for example, in the United States and Botswana, and the Jordan basin appears to offer promise for this approach.

In the future, as a result of global warming, supply may be even more limited. Potential changes in runoff can be estimated using general circulation models, calibrated by historical data, for sub-basins. As yet, the results obtained from such models provide mixed signals. For the Nile, it can be shown that runoff demonstrates a high sensitivity to changes in precipitation, temperature, and potential evapotranspiration. However, forecasts of flow in the main channels depend very much upon the management of demand, flexibility in the allocation of water, and the policies of the various upstream riparian states. What seems indisputable is that there will be greater fluctuations in flow and therefore,

at least for limited periods of time, potential geopolitical problems will be exacerbated. These problems can only be reduced by detailed forward planning and the avoidance of last-minute crisis management.

Since the opportunities for increasing supplies in the Middle East are severely limited, attention has been paid to demand reduction. A number of procedures have been adopted, but the basis for the control of demand is increasingly seen as pricing. Throughout the region, water is either free or heavily subsidized, and hence there is little incentive to conserve supplies. In many countries there is virtually no monitoring of abstraction, and water law enforcement is negligible.

Apart from allocation and substitution, demand can also be curbed by conservation measures. These can be applied not only with regard to water use but also water transport in the infrastructure. Losses through leakage in urban water systems in the Middle East are conservatively estimated to range from 30 to 50 percent. Furthermore, there is little public appreciation of the value of water, and most education programs are in their infancy.

Water and Geopolitics. If, within one country, effective allocation between potential users is considered almost impossible, how much more difficult is apportionment between different states within the same catchment. Hydropolitics is not scale specific. Water abstraction from a well and a qanat that drain the same aquifer involves hydropolitical issues just as much as does competition between riparian states for water from the Jordan River. Furthermore, hydropolitical problems may arise with atmospheric water, ground water or even temporary flows. Because of their potentially wide-ranging implications, it is geopolitical issues arising in shared catchments that have dominated hydropolitical analysis. Rivers are considered international if their basins are shared by two or more states; and such basins accommodate over 40 percent of the world's population.

Research in conflict modeling has indicated several criteria against which the likelihood of conflict can be assessed, namely, disagreement over data, a marked asymmetry of power distribution, and clear ideological differences. These criteria are all fulfilled in the three key basins—the Nile, the Tigris–Euphrates, and the Jordan (Figures 1–3). In an alternative model, the potential for conflict or cooperation is considered to depend upon the relative geographical positions of the states, their degree of interest in water problems, and the power, essentially military, from internal or external sources that they can bring to bear to influence decisions. In all three basins, there is a high degree of interest in hydrological issues. Upstream states are in the best position to control flow, and Turkey and Ethiopia are particularly favored in this respect. However, there are marked differences in power within each basin, and Egypt, Turkey, and Israel are most obviously able to influence decisions. [*See* Security and Environment.]

Major drainage basins. A power asymmetry can be the immediate trigger for conflict in a noncooperative setting with an environmental imbalance. This description most closely matches the hydropolitical situation in the three Middle Eastern catchments. Cooperation within them is at best partial, and in all there are records of hostility. In the Tigris–Euphrates basin there is theoretically sufficient water, but there are obvious imbalances in abstraction and distribution. In the basin of the Nile there are already deficits. In the Jordan catchment there is a zero-sum situation and the riparian states have been defined as forming a "hydropolitical security complex." Water is therefore seen as a contributory factor in an environment that is already hostile. It is difficult to isolate water as the cause of conflict.

In the Nile Basin there have already been severe disagreements between Egypt and Sudan, and Ethiopia is in a delicate position since it controls the headwaters of the Blue Nile. The geopolitical focus in the Tigris–Euphrates catchment is the Ataturk Dam and the abstraction required for the Southeast Anatolian Project (Figure 2). The potential was clearly demonstrated on the 13 January 1990, when the diversion channel beneath the dam was closed and the flow of the Euphrates was effectively terminated for one month. Hydrologically, there were few concerns, but the geopolitical symbolism was immense.

In the Jordan River basin there are several hydropolitical foci, all related to the advantageous position of Israel (Figure 3). The Yarmuk Triangle allows Israel to influence the uptake of the East Ghor Canal, the major irrigation system of Jordan. Possession of the Golan Heights ensures control over the headwaters of the Jordan. The Israeli occupation of southern Lebanon offers the potential for using water from the Litani River. Most important, the occupation of the West Bank of the Jordan allows abstraction from aquifers previously inaccessible to Israel, and raises fundamental questions about a new state of Palestine and the concept of Israeli land for peace.

In situations of potential conflict, the objective of management must be to defuse the situation or, at worst, maintain the status quo. Politically, this may be achieved through a variety of approaches from cooperative development to military action. Current thinking on cooperation is more broadly based, with a focus upon "rational water," the concept that water is a unifying rather than a divisive issue.

When negotiation fails, there can be recourse to international law but, in the case of water, the question of sovereignty is still not agreed. There are in fact four major traditional alternative principles concerning the sovereignty of states over water resources. Upstream states are supported by the principle of absolute territorial sovereignty and downstream states by the principle of absolute territorial integrity. The other principles are less extreme, the principle of community and the principle of equitable utilization or limited territorial sovereignty. According to the latter, a state may use international waters insofar as this does not interfere with their utilization by coriparians. From this principle, the International Law Association developed the Helsinki Rules. More recently, there have been further developments, particularly the 32 Articles on the subject produced in 1992 by the United Nations International Law Commission.

To date, the most effective form of persuasion has been financial. Since major water projects are well beyond the means of most countries, international funding is necessary, and is most frequently sought from the World Bank, which has been able to develop a policy of refusing support when there are clearly conflicting viewpoints about a project. [*See* World Bank, The.]

BIBLIOGRAPHY

Agnew, C. and E. W. Anderson. *Water Resources* in the *Arid Realm*. London: Routledge, 1992. A comprehensive coverage of arid zone hydrology, including management and geopolitics.

Allan, J. A., and Mallat Chibli, eds. *Water* in the *Middle East: Legal, Political* and *Commercial Implications*. London: Tauris Academic Studies, 1995. A collection of essays with important contributions on the commercial aspects of water.

Beaumont, P. *Drylands*. London: Routledge, 1989. A systematic and regional survey with several Middle Eastern examples.

Hillel, D. *Rivers Out of Eden*. New York: Oxford University Press, 1994. A broadly based, elegantly written overview with some excellent detailed examples.

Kliot, N. *Water Resources and Conflict in the Middle East*. London: Routledge, 1994. The definitive book on the detailed hydrology of the three key drainage basins.

Lowi, M. R. *Water and Power*. Cambridge: Cambridge University Press, 1993. The most up-to-date discussion on political thinking with regard to water resources.

Naff, T., and R. Matson, eds. *Water in the Middle East—Conflict or Co-Operation*. Boulder: Westview, 1984. The book that set the scene for hydropolitcal considerations in the Middle East.

Newson, M. *Land, Water and Development*. London: Routledge, 1992. A comprehensive guide to river basin management with a few Middle Eastern examples.

Ohlsson, L., ed. *Hydropolitics*. London: Zed Books, 1995. The most detailed current consideration of the subject; uses predominantly Middle Eastern examples.

Serageldin, I. *Towards Sustainable Management of Water Resources*. Washington, D.C.: World Bank, 1995. A key guide to sustainable management of water.

Starr, J. and D. C. S. Stoll. *US Foreign Policy on Water Resources in the Middle East*. Washington, D.C.: Center for Strategic and International Studies, 1987. This volume raised many of the key issues in Middle Eastern hydropolitics.

United Nations Register of International Rivers. Oxford: Pergamon, 1978. The definitive inventory of shared drainage basins.

—Ewan W. Anderson

MIGRATIONS

Migration encompasses all forms of human spatial mobility, ranging from local exchanges of partners for marriage to transcontinental movements associated with job transfers or settlement. Movements within countries and those across national boundaries, as well as voluntary and forced movements, all fall within the ambit of the study of human migration. Within such a vast and complex topic we can identify three broad divisions:

1. Population redistribution, which covers internal movements and, most importantly, rural-to-urban migration
2. International movement, which encompasses emigration and immigration and issues as diverse as the brain drain and labor migration
3. Forced movements of political refugees and also, increasingly, those in flight from environmental hazards or induced environmental change.

These three broad flows, by bringing peoples of very different backgrounds together and concentrating populations in particular locations, are among the most powerful forces of global change.

The three divisions certainly do not constitute mutually exclusive subject areas; there are close interrelationships among them. For example, the issue of the loss of talent, or brain drain, can be as relevant at the local village level as at the national level, and the flows of wealth from destinations to origins in the form of remittances can apply equally to internal and international migrations. There are also important, if as yet poorly understood, linkages between internal and international migrations. For example, the arrival of immigrants may increase competition for jobs and may be a factor in pushing native populations out of certain areas, and the arrival of rural migrants in cities may be an important precursor for their later movement overseas. Nevertheless, because the study of internal and international migrations involves the use of very different data sets and analytic techniques, the two have become institutionalized as virtually separate branches of the topic. Both, however, deal with what is considered to be a voluntary move, which apparently separates them from the forced movements of refugees. Thus, movements that are seen not to be the result of individual choice fall into a separate analytic and policy category from individual moves. However, as recent experience has demonstrated, the difference between an economic migrant and a refugee can depend as much on *Realpolitik*, and how a refugee or migrant is defined, as on the factors behind the move.

In addition, in the context of voluntary migration, much has been shown to have been controlled by institutional factors such as company transfers, labor contracts, availability of housing, and so on, rather than by individual decision; hence, clear, logical divisions between forced and free migrations become difficult to sustain. Thus, despite intuitive differences among the three broad divisions, it is becoming increasingly important that they be examined within some type of unified framework and the interrelations among them specified.

Current Trends. Major changes have occurred in the pattern of global migration in recent history, and we can identify four main sets of factors that have brought these changes about. First, the expansion of free-market economic activities, initially within Europe and then overseas, particularly from the 1960s, created nuclei that drew in the rural populations to metropolitan areas through the creation of national, and later international, divisions of labor in a process that has come to be known as *globalization.* [*See* Global Economy.] Second, the spread of more open, stable forms of government has allowed the international division of labor to function more effectively. Third, the decline in fertility to levels below replacement level in the most developed parts of the world has created tight local labor markets. The resulting response of entrepreneurs has been to export labor-intensive industries, to import labor, or to move up from labor-based to knowledge-based industrialization, or some combination of all of these. Fourth, developments in the technology of transportation have allowed mass transfers of population over long distances at great speed, the result of the mass production of the Boeing 747 and subsequent generations of widebodied aircraft.

In 1800, only about 12 percent of Europe's population and around 5 percent of the population of the United States lived in towns and cities. By 1950, these proportions had risen to 51 and 57 percent respectively, and by 1990 had reached 73 and 75 percent. In 1990, fully 45 percent of the world's population was classified as urban, representing 2.4 billion people; and more people are being added every year to the world's urban population than to the rural population. Migration is but one component of urban growth, the others being natural increase and reclassification. However, migration has been a major factor in bringing about the increase in the proportion of urban population worldwide and in the concentration of populations in the largest cities yet seen in human history, with all their attendant environmental and infrastructural problems. The number of megacities, defined by the United Nations as cities with a population in excess of eight million, has increased from eleven in 1970 to roughly twenty-five in the year 2000, with nineteen of these in the developing world. [*See* Urban Areas.]

As the world has become more urban, so too has the global system of migration been transformed. International migration from the nineteenth to the mid-twentieth century was dominated by movements out of Europe westward across the Atlantic toward the Americas, or eastward across Eurasia to Siberia and Central Asia. There were other significant movements out of southern China and out of India, but these too tended to be controlled by European (primarily British) or American interests, rather than being independent systems in their own right. As fertility declined in Europe from the 1960s, and as Europe experienced the post–World War II economic boom, it became a continent of net immigration rather than of net emigration. The migration to the main settler societies of Australia, Canada, New Zealand, and the United States, on the other hand, shifted from streams dominated by people of European origins to those dominated by people of Asian and Latin American origins. The reasons for these changes were not solely demographic, of course; in the case of the settler societies, the triumph of liberal democratic systems of government at the end of World War II had made the maintenance of racist immigration policies that excluded the entry of non-Europeans an anathema. These discriminatory laws were finally swept away in the reform of immigration policies of Canada (1962), the United States (1965), Australia (1973), and New Zealand (1978), although the full impact of the reforms was not felt for several years after their implementation.

The shift from an essentially Atlantic-centered international migration system to one centered around the Pacific has been accompanied by the emergence of regional systems of movement: from South and Southeast Asian countries to the oil-rich countries of the Gulf States after the rise in oil revenues from 1973; to Southeast and East Asia as Japan and the "tiger" economies of South Korea, Taiwan, Hong Kong, Singapore, Malaysia and even Thailand have evolved from labor-surplus to labor-deficit over the last 25 years; and there are smaller, though no less significant, nuclei of regional attraction in southern Africa, Israel, northern Venezuela, and central Argentina. More people are moving in more different ways than ever before even if, on a per capita basis, international movements from Asian and Latin American countries today do not yet rival those from Europe during the great migration of the late nineteenth and early twentieth centuries. The United Nations has estimated that, during the last half of the 1980s, somewhere between 750 million and one billion people migrated. We are indeed in an age of migration, even if the vast majority moved within their countries of origin. Only a minority have moved from the poorest countries of the "south," which lie primarily in Africa, to the rich countries of the "north." [See Economic Levels.]

Issues and Consequences. The modern migrant flows are made up of many different types of mover: those going for long-term or more permanent settlement, short-term laborers, students, the highly skilled, and professionals. These can be more clearly differentiated in international movements, although they are also found in internal flows. The illegal migrant, or the migrant who moves outside the official procedures, is unique to international migration and to those countries such as China, where internal movements are still tightly controlled (in theory if not in practice). These migrant types are purely a convenient way of subdividing complex flows for analysis and are not necessarily immutable or exclusive categories. Nevertheless, they can be used to highlight significant issues and consequences of the current migration streams.

If there is one universal characteristic of migration, it is that the majority of movers are young adults and that they tend, initially at least, to be better educated and more innovative than the average for the population from which they come. The loss of these people, even on a temporary basis, has been seen as negative for their places of origin and has given substance to the idea of a "brain drain." It is difficult, however, to draw any hard-and-fast generalizations. The emigration of up to 30 percent of the highly skilled workforce from sub-Saharan Africa, and the loss of hundreds of thousands of scientific personnel from the Russian public service after 1989, almost certainly had a negative impact on subsequent developments in these areas. Yet thousands of students left the "tiger" economies of eastern Asia as these areas were embarking upon their period of rapid economic growth, and it is difficult to imagine them growing even faster if the students had stayed at home. When increasing numbers did return later to participate in the new prosperity, they played important leadership roles in industry and government and appear to have been a catalyst in recent trends to more open forms of government in these areas. Hence, whether there are indeed brain drains, in contrast to brain gains through the return of highly skilled migrants, or negative or positive impacts of migration, will depend largely upon other contextual factors.

The loss of personnel, skilled or otherwise, has to be balanced against the gains in funds sent back home by the migrants in the form of remittances. Notoriously difficult to measure accurately, these have almost certainly emerged as second only to oil in terms of value in international trade, and accounted for at least U.S.$71.1 billion in 1990. Countries such as Pakistan, the Philippines, and Egypt, as well as traditional sources for the supply of labor to Europe such as Portugal, have come to depend upon remittances from overseas workers as one of their most significant sources of foreign exchange and a resource of fundamental importance to national development. These countries have come to regard their populations as major resources to exploit in international labor markets. The use of these monies at both local and national levels has been the subject of controversy, the implication being that they increase dependency and undermine countries' programs of self-sustaining development. The balance of the evidence, however, indicates that migrants tend to use the proceeds prudently and that the net effects are positive rather than negative.

Return migration need not imply a definitive move back to the home area. One of the characteristics of both modern internal and international migration systems is the significance of circulation: the constant movement back and forward between origins and destinations. In international migration, facilitated by developments in modern technologies of communication and transportation, this phenomenon has led to the "astronaut" and "parachute kids" syndromes. In the former, a family moves to a settler society but the principal breadwinner, usually the husband, returns to the origin to continue his profession or business and commutes across the Pacific at regular intervals. In the latter, both parents return to the origin to maintain their careers, leaving the children in Los Angeles, Vancouver, or Sydney in the care of a relative or older sibling. This pattern has been prominent among the new Asian migrant streams, particularly the Chinese. While these patterns generate specific social concerns as the result of split families, giving a new dimension to the concept of extended family, a more general concern has emerged of nationality and loyalty to the state. Dual and multiple nationalities are becoming more common, with resultant security concerns.

The global migration system is riven by contradictions. Developed countries need labor to enhance the declining growth of their indigenous labor forces. Yet the increasingly diverse backgrounds from which the labor is being drawn are leading to a transformation in the ethnic composition of destination countries and raising sensitive questions about national identity. The importation of temporary workers might seem to be a solution, but experience has shown that there is nothing so permanent as a temporary worker, and those entering on short-term visas use that status to obtain permanent residence, with all the ensuing rights to apply for the admission of family members. Developing countries, on the other hand, are concerned about the loss of scarce manpower or about the new ways of life and ideas to which their sons and daughters will be exposed when they are overseas, but they have come to depend upon the remittances sent back by these same migrants. Where the linkages within the migrant communities, encompassing both origins and destinations, are seen to be stronger than linkages across wider na-

tional communities in either origin or destination, the migration is seen to erode the very integrity of the nation-state, the political linchpin of the present world. These diasporic, transnational communities are an important element in the redefinition of the global community in the post–Cold War period.

While the transnational mixing of cultures since the 1960s has been most intense in the traditional settler societies, and also in Europe, it has affected the once homogeneous societies of Japan, Korea, and Taiwan. At the other end of the development spectrum, however, the migration pressures are very different. Whereas, in the most developed areas, there is a reassertion of the polyethnic norm in the least developed countries the pressures are to create homogeneous units and expulsion; ethnic cleansing and forced migration are common. United Nations estimates indicated thirteen million refugees in the world in 1996, up from fewer than two million in 1965, but down from the eighteen million of 1993. These are concentrated in sub-Saharan Africa and in western and central Asia, often in countries where the state has ceased to exist as a functional unit and rival ethnic groups struggle for dominance. It is in these poorer areas, too, that the impact of natural and human environmental damage is greatest.

Policies clearly must vary depending upon the needs of the country. In the 1990s, however, developed countries appear to be converging toward a greater degree of control, tightening entry and raising immigrant acceptance criteria. Paradoxically, at the same time, increasing numbers are moving as undocumented and illegal migrants. While still representing a minority of total migrants, illegal movers are significant because of their linkages with organized crime, which channel them into sweatshops at destination areas—thus maintaining outdated industrial labor-intensive technologies. The trafficking of human beings, linked to prostitution and pedophile rings, is proving a challenge to states in the new age of global movements.

Just as the international migration systems have changed significantly over the last decades, so too have the ways of looking at, and conceptualizing, human movements. Initially, migration was seen as a relatively simple economic response to variable opportunities available both nationally and internationally. Migrants moved to places where they could best maximize their return, and they moved on the basis of an individual decision on how to act. However, later research has highlighted the significance of institutional constraints and family linkages in the process of movement, with migration thus conceptualized as a group rather than an individual phenomenon. The significance of structural, macro-level economic and political factors, while well taken, does tend to downplay the fact that migration flows are made up of individuals, each with their own hopes and aspirations. The most recent approaches tend to focus on the experience of migration, of exile and of identity. Thus, the trend has been from rigorous and objective, if fairly simple, economic models of migration toward much more complex, if subjective, approaches that highlight the significance of macro-level political and social factors as well as the individual experience of movement.

It is the appreciation of global forces impacting upon migration that has become apparent: for example, the significance of transnational corporations and the new international division of labor in drawing unskilled labor into factories in locations spread around the world, and in moving the highly skilled from country to country. The incorporation of women into these labor forces has a significant effect, not just in reducing fertility, but on the whole status and position of women in what were once conservative, male-dominated societies. Migration, so often associated with the exploitation of female labor, can also be a powerful catalyst for an improvement in the status of women. Migration can also be a harbinger of disaster through the transfer of infections, not simply of the more dramatic viruses such as acquired immune deficiency syndrome (AIDS), but through the diffusion of significantly greater, traditional killers such as malaria. Among the global forces being built into the increasingly complex picture of migration are those associated with environmental change. Migration, through the concentration of populations in cities, is a major factor contributing to urban and industrial effluent and emissions, and the movement of peoples into tropical forests and the clearance of these forests through burning contribute to increased carbon dioxide in the atmosphere. As contributors to global warming, these in turn may lead to a rise in sea level, which might be on the order of one meter by 2100: this would force hundreds of thousands to move in Bangladesh, China, and Egypt, as well as in the island world of the Pacific. While this scenario is largely speculation, what is abundantly clear is that the increasing migrations that are already being observed at both ends of the development spectrum will transform societies of origin, as well as societies of destination, to create a very different world.

[See also Global Change, article on Human Dimensions of Global Change; and Human Populations.]

BIBLIOGRAPHY

UNITED NATIONS PUBLICATIONS

The Population Division of the Department of Economic and Social Affairs of the United Nations Secretariat produces valuable source materials and timely basic analysis. For the topic of migration, four recent publications are directly relevant.

International Migration Policies 1995. ST/ESA/SER.A/154. New York, 1995. A useful, concise presentation of the key issues in the form of a wall chart.

International Migration Policies. ST/ESA/SER.A/161. New York, 1997. The most comprehensive review of migration policies to date.

Population Distribution and Migration. ST/ESA/SER.R/133. New York, 1995. A useful collection of essays on all aspects of migration, including urbanization and internal movements.

World Population Monitoring 1997. International Migration and Development. ST/ESA/SER.A/169. New York, 1998. A broad assessment of all the leading issues in international migration.

GENERAL WORKS

Castles, S., and M. J. Miller. *The Age of Migration: International Population Movements in the Modern World.* 2d ed. Basingstoke, U.K.: Macmillan, 1998. A useful introduction to the main issues in international migration.

Cohen, R. *Global Diasporas: An Introduction.* London: UCL Press, 1997. An analysis of the evolution of transnational communities.

———, ed. *The Cambridge Survey of World Migration.* Cambridge: Cambridge University Press, 1995. A massive review of international migration consisting of a series of short, high-quality essays based on regions rather than topics.

Cornelius, W. A., et al., eds. *Controlling Immigration: A Global Perspective.* Stanford: Stanford University Press, 1994. A useful analysis of the migration policies of the developed countries, with critical commentaries.

McNeill, W. H. *Poly-ethnicity and National Unity in World History.* Toronto: University of Toronto Press, 1986. A short, perceptive examination of the mixing of cultures in world history.

Skeldon, R. *Population Mobility in Developing Countries: A Reinterpretation.* London: Belhaven, 1990. A comparative analysis of the evolution of internal migration in developing countries.

———. *Migration and Development: A Global Perspective.* London: Longman, 1997. A comprehensive attempt to consider, within a unified framework, internal and international migration, and movements in developed and developing countries.

Stalker, P. *The Work of Strangers: A Survey of International Labour Migration.* Geneva: International Labour Office, 1994. A well-constructed empirical assessment of international labor migration.

United Nations High Commissioner for Refugees. *The State of the World's Refugees: A Humanitarian Agenda.* Oxford: Oxford University Press, 1997. An insightful overview of the global refugee situation.

Weiner, M. *The Global Migration Crisis: Challenge to States and to Human Rights.* New York: HarperCollins, 1995. An introduction to security issues and to international relations and migration.

—RONALD SKELDON

MILANKOVITCH, MILUTIN

Milutin Milankovitch (1879–1958) was a Serbian mathematician who specialized in astronomy and geophysics. He was born in Dalj, Slavonia (part of Austro-Hungary until 1919, then part of Yugoslavia, and now in Croatia). He completed his secondary school in Osijek, 15 kilometers from Dalj. He graduated as a doctor of technical sciences on 17 December 1904 from the Technical High School of Vienna. Shortly afterward, he was employed as chief engineer to some large construction companies specializing in reinforced concrete. He worked on complex projects and introduced new methods of construction, which were patented. He wrote numerous papers relating to engineering mechanics, but was attracted quite rapidly by fundamental research. On 1 October 1909, he was elected professor at the University of Belgrade, where he lectured on rational mechanics, theoretical physics, and celestial mechanics until his retirement forty-six years later. He was a member of the Serbian Academy of Sciences, the Yugoslav Academy of Sciences and Arts, the German Academy of Naturalists Leopoldine Halle, and the Italian Institute of Paleontology. In November 1954, fifty years after receiving his original diploma, he received the Golden Doctor's diploma from the Technical High School of Vienna.

At the 1984 symposium on Milankovitch and Climate, Vasko Milankovitch remarked that his father "Milutin Milankovitch was barely tall and of fine frame. He had brown eyes, which were always alert and quietly smiling. His finely-cut lips had a barely noticeable twist giving a faint mocking expression to his face. He was not the bespectacled-professor type of scientist, for he admired and enjoyed nature and loved all things aesthetically harmonious and maintained a constant interest in history, literature, painting, and sculpture. Of all the arts, music was his favorite and opera his first love. But he enjoyed also a glass of wine with his meals and would later relax with a favorite cigar."

Milutin Milankovitch was a contemporary of Alfred Wegener (1880–1930), with whom he became acquainted through Vladimir Köppen (1846–1940), Wegener's father-in-law. Roughly between 1915 and 1940, Milankovitch put the astronomical theory of the Pleistocene ice ages on a firm mathematical basis. His first book, written in French, dates from 1920, but his massive Special Publication of the Royal Serbian Academy of Sciences, entitled *Kanon der Erdbestrahlung*, was published in German in 1941 and was translated into English in 1969.

Milankovitch's main contribution was to explore in great detail the solar irradiance at different latitudes and seasons, to compute its long-term variations from the orbital parameters, and to relate them in turn to climate. His theoretical investigation provided the basis for the core of his argument that "under those astronomical conditions in which the heat budget around the summer solstice falls below average, so will summer melt [fall below average], with uncompensated glacial advance being the result." The essential product of the Milankovitch theory is therefore his curve demonstrating how the intensity of summer sunlight has varied over the past 600,000 years. This curve was used to identify the European ice ages reconstructed by Albrecht Penck and Eduard Brückner, from which he concluded that these geologic data constituted a verification of his theory.

Until the 1960s, the Milankovitch theory was disputed as a result of discussions based on fragmentary geologic records and because the climate was considered too resilient to react to such small changes as observed in the summer insolation by Milankovitch. In the late 1960s, a systematic approach and the use of modern techniques led to major discoveries that progressively supported the astronomical theory of Milankovitch.

In 1976, Hays et al. demonstrated from the spectral analysis of climate-sensitive indicators obtained from selected deep-sea records that the astronomical frequencies corresponding to precession, obliquity, and eccentricity are significantly superimposed upon a general red-noise spectrum. Moreover, the geologic observation of the bipartition of the precessional peak was confirmed by Berger's independent astronomical computations (1977), and was one of the first most delicate and impressive of all tests of the Milankovitch theory.

Although a number of scientists questioned the correctness of his theory after World War II, Milankovitch seemed little disturbed by the different opinions, believing firmly that his theory was correct. Modern evidence now shows that he was right, strongly supporting his essential concept: namely, that orbital variations exert a significant influence on climate.

Milutin Milankovitch wrote some seventy books and papers, including some on popular astronomy. He was involved in the reform of the Julian calendar, became a writer, and wrote his memoirs (Milankovitch, 1950, 1952, 1957) "not because I thought I was such an important person, but because I have lived in an historically interesting and turbulent period, and I described these events as a trustworthy witness. My work spanning some 30 years has been closely connected with the work of other scientists who have used my results in their respective fields. The mutual collaboration has been documented with more than 600 letters and 100 publications. Therefore, these memoirs are, for a good part, the history of a branch of the sciences called 'Astronomical Theory of Climatic Changes.'" These memoirs formed the basis of the biography written on Milankovitch by his son Vasko Milankovitch (1995).

[*See also* Climate Change; Earth Motions; *and* Natural Climate Fluctuations.]

BIBLIOGRAPHY

Berger, A. "Support for the Astronomical Theory of Climatic Change." *Nature* 268 (1977), 44–45.
———. "Milankovitch Theory and Climate." *Review of Geophysics* 26.4 (1988), 624–657.
Berger, A., et al., eds. *Milankovitch and Climate: Understanding the Response to Orbital Forcing.* Dordrecht: Reidel, 1984.
Hays, J. D., et al. "Variations in the Earth's Orbit: Pacemaker of the Ice Ages. *Science* 194 (1976), 1121–1132.
Imbrie, J., and K. P. Imbrie. *Ice Ages, Solving the Mystery.* Hillside, N.J.: Enslow, 1979.
Milankovitch, M. *Théorie Mathématique des Phénomènes Ther-

miques Produits par la Radiation Solaire. Paris: Académie Yougoslave des Sciences et des Arts de Zagreb, Gauthier-Villars, 1920.

————. *Kanon der Erdbestrahlung und seine Anwendung auf das Eiszeitenproblem.* "Canon of Insolation and the Ice Age Problem," Royal Serbian Academy, Special Publication 132, section of Mathematical and Natural Sciences, vol. 33. Belgrade, 1941. English translation by Israel Program. Published for the U.S. Department of Commerce and the National Science Foundation, Washington, D.C., 1969, and by Zavod za Udzbenike i nastavna Sredstva in cooperation with Muzej nauke i technike Srpske akademije nauka i umetnosti, Beograd, 1998.

————. *Memoirs, Professional Experience and Knowledge,* vol. 1, *1879–1909,* vol. 2, *1909–1944,* vol. 3, *After 1944.* Belgrade: Serbian Academy of Sciences, section of Mathematical and Natural Sciences, 1950, (1979), 1952, 1957.

————. *Milutin Milanković 1879–1958, from his Autobiography with Comments by his Son, Vasko, and a Preface by André Berger,* p. 181. Katlenburg–Lindau, Germany: European Geophysical Society, 1995.

Penck A., and E. Brückner. *Die Alpen im Eiszeitalter.* Leipzig: Tauchnitz, 1909.

—A. BERGER

MINING

Life as we know it today requires mined products such as precious metals, nonferrous metals, iron and ferroalloy metals, radioactive metals, minor metals, fuels, ceramic clays, building materials, metallurgical and refractory materials, industrial and manufacturing materials, chemical materials, abrasive minerals, fertilizer minerals, and gemstones. All human endeavors—farming, construction, transportation, communication, space exploration, and so on—consume the products of mining. Annually, about 5 billion metric tons of coal is mined and used by the countries of the world. In recent years, the annual growth of world coal production has averaged about 2 percent, although it is much higher in countries such as China and India. Worldwide, a billion metric tons of iron ore is mined per year. The amount of new mineral materials required annually for each U.S. citizen is about 20,000 kilograms, making a total of over 5 billion metric tons per year for the entire U.S. population. Half of this amount is fuel materials—coal, oil, and natural gas. The annual production of stone, sand, and gravel in the United States is over 2 billion metric tons and is growing.

Given that the Earth is currently the only viable source of these metals, minerals, and materials, their economic extraction, processing, and utilization will continue to be an essential, productive human activity for the foreseeable future, as it has been in the past. However, the mining industry of the future will be characterized by an intense search for top-quality deposits, greater exploitation of poorer ores, significant competition from substitutes, and accelerating progress toward development of environmentally friendly ("green") technologies. [*See* Greening of Industry.]

History of Mining. Over the course of human history, minerals have been used as a symbol of wealth, a measure of military prowess, a basis for trade, a tool for political gain, a means for exerting economic pressure, and a catalyst for industrial and economic development. Their importance is further acknowledged by reference to particular eras of human development in terms of the mineral or metal whose use began in that period. The markers are named the old stone age (500,000 BP), the new stone age (8,000 BCE), the copper age (5,000 BCE), the bronze age (3,000 BCE), the iron age (1,400 BCE), the coal age (1,600 CE), the petroleum age (1,850 CE), and the uranium age (1,950 CE). It is widely accepted that mining is one of the earliest human activities, although when exactly mining began is not known. The stone for the paleolithic man's tools may not have come from mining, but mining of ocherous hematite (blood stone) for use in funeral and other purposes took place around fifty thousand years ago in the Bomvu Ridge of Southern Africa (now in Swaziland). Gold in streambeds came to the attention of humans in 6,000 BCE. Early knowledge of gold mining and gold smithing is evident from the importance it attained in ceremonial functions from around 3,000 BCE. The copper and bronze ages brought metals and alloys into use to make a wide assortment of tools, weapons, and other products. That all ancient civilizations—including the Mesopotamian, Egyptian, Indian, Chinese, Greek, Roman, Spanish, Portuguese, and Inca—developed techniques for mining and using minerals and metals is evident from the artifacts of the relevant periods.

In more recent times, the Industrial Revolution was powered by the coal and iron ore resources of the participating nations. The gold rushes of the 1800s led to the settlement of California, Alaska, Western Australia, and the Canadian Klondike. Mining of stone, sand, and gravel for construction is one of the most widely dispersed industrial activities in most countries. The remarkable ability of humans to use the gifts of nature to make new materials to enhance the quality of life has continued to this day.

Importance of the Mining Industry. As one of the primary industries (the other two being agriculture and forestry), mining provides raw materials that are essential inputs to the secondary industries for manufacturing value-added products demanded by society. Tertiary industries provide the communities with essential services such as infrastructure, transportation, banking, education, and recreation (Gregory, 1980). The continued success of a thriving economy depends on the uninterrupted flow of materials and services to and from these three levels of industry.

No country is completely self-sufficient in all its

mineral needs. Most countries import and export some minerals. As a country becomes industrially more mature, more of the demand for mineral resources may have to be supplied by imports. Some developing countries are saddled with shortages of food, housing, and education, leaving little or no time for a planned search, categorization, and exploitation of mineral riches. Consequently, involvement by large, foreign companies has been an established practice. Unfortunately, the changing political and economic environment of a country and conflicting objectives of investing companies versus governments can cause drastic disruption of mineral supplies.

In highly developed economies, the mining industry's direct contribution to employment earnings and taxes is relatively small. In the United States in 1995, it was U.S.$50 billion, whereas the indirect effects are over ten times the direct effect. The total contribution to the U.S. gross domestic product (GDP) is only 9 percent. In developing countries, however, mining activities, in addition to high direct contributions to GDP, can attract land, capital, and labor, all essential for industrialization and economic development. The possession of rich mineral resources and their exploitation alone does not ensure strong and stable economic growth. The potential of the mineral revenues to serve the larger goals of the country's development programs and to contribute to the evolution of the other sectors of the economy must be planned and implemented. An undeveloped deposit, on the other hand, contributes very little—directly or indirectly—to a country's economy, and may even lose all potential value as a result of technological advancements (Vogely, 1985).

Scope of Mining Activities. A schematic diagram of the scope of mining activities, from finding a mineral deposit through exploration and mining to processing and marketing the final product, is shown in Figure 1. The stages of mining include prospecting, exploration, development, extraction, beneficiation (product improvement processes), decommissioning, and rehabilitation of mined lands.

Minerals occur in diverse environments. Gold and gemstones are found in streambeds. They also occur in veins thousands of meters deep. Beach sands contain valuable minerals, as do sands in shallow and deep ocean beds. Minerals are found as consolidated and unconsolidated deposits in ocean floors and in solution in marine waters. Coal is widely distributed throughout the world in both surface and underground deposits. Salt occurs as evaporites, laminar beds, and huge domes. Porphyry deposits containing copper are massive and low grade, often 4–8 kilometers across and containing less than 1 percent copper. As a consequence, exploration and extraction methods for mineral deposits are diverse. [*See* Metals.]

The processing of the mined ore can vary from a fairly simple operation to a series of complex operations. It may involve only crushing and sizing, as is usually the case with stone that is mined for use as a construction aggregate. For metalliferous ores (metal-bearing mineral deposits), the processes involved include concentration, smelting, and refining before the metal is ready for casting. It is common practice to site the mill or the concentrator near the mine to produce the concentrate from the mined ore. Smelters are placed in locations where energy is abundant, and comparatively less expensive than at the mine site. In some cases, such as coal mining, where conditions are favorable, the mining, processing, and utilization facilities are sited next to each other, leading to mine mouth power plants. In other cases, transport of mined products over thousands of kilometers and across the oceans cannot be avoided.

A mine is a major industrial activity requiring extensive planning and development regarding health and safety, environmental control, power, communication, maintenance, workforce, administration, housing, township, and so forth. In the mine itself, major support operations that must be properly planned for the smooth and safe functioning of the production operations include the following: transport of miners and materials in and out of the mine; ventilation for the supply of fresh air to the miners and for the control of gases, dusts, heat, and humidity; ground control in the face area to prevent roof and side falls; protection of surface and permanent features; pumping and drainage of water; disposal of waste from development or tailings from the surface plant; and control of erosion, sediments, and other pollution agents.

In all countries, there is usually a small-scale mining sector that is an important component of the local and rural economy. The small-scale mines are generally less capital intensive, have lower levels of mechanization, recover resources that otherwise would be lost, and generally do not employ technically qualified personnel. Further, while mining operations may look alike, the site-specific features of geography, geology, mineralogy, and terrain have a controlling influence, making each operation a unique entity requiring its own detailed consideration in planning and design.

Types of Mining. The processes of extracting ore from the ground can be grouped into three broad categories: surface mining, underground mining, and nonentry mining. In surface mining, the soil and strata above the deposit are removed, exposing the ore body for its removal. In underground mining, the deposit is first accessed by suitable openings from the surface, and a network of openings is driven in the surrounding rocks and the deposit for the installation of service facilities for the transport of miners, materials, ventilating air, water, and so on, and for the subsequent extraction of the de-

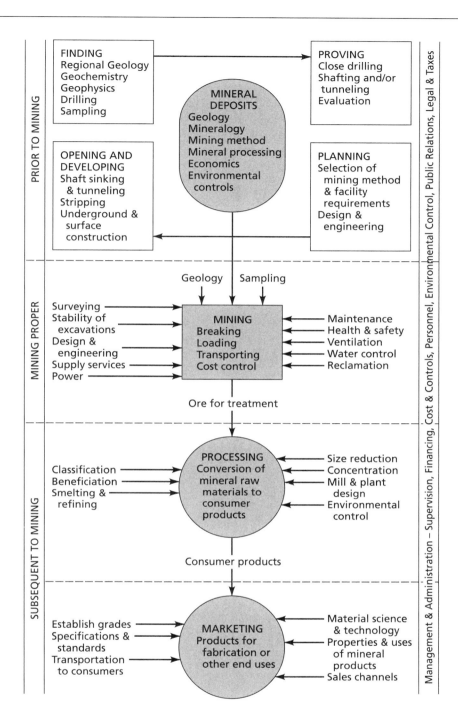

Mining. FIGURE 1. Scope of Mining Activities. (After Beall, 1973, with permission of the Society for Mining, Metallurgy, and Exploration, Inc.)

posit itself. In nonentry mining, the deposit is accessed from a suitable opening on the surface but the extraction process does not require the miners to go underground (Hartman, 1992; Husturlid, 1982; Kennedy, 1990).

Surface mining is superior to underground mining in terms of ore body recovery, ore quality control, operational flexibility, safety, productivity, and cost. However, when the removal cost of the soil and strata above the deposit becomes prohibitively high, it is common practice to switch over to underground mining of the deposit. Surface mining methods can be broadly classified into four subcategories: open-pit mining, quarrying, stripping, and placer mining. Tremendous technological developments in earth-moving equipment have enabled surface mining of deposits that, a few years ago, would have been uneconomical to mine by either surface or underground methods. In the United States, nearly all clays, stone, sand, and gravel, over 90 percent of the metallic ores, and over 60 percent of the coal, are surface mined.

In underground mining, extensive development of the ore body is required to create blocks of ore that are either not extracted, or partially or fully extracted, according to the mining plan. Underground mining methods have been categorized into three classes based on the manner in which the stability of openings and the systematic control of the strata above the deposit are maintained for the duration of mining: unsupported, supported, and caving methods.

Special health and safety considerations in underground mining include the problems of toxic, noxious, and explosive atmospheres caused by gases and dust. Design of stable structures in the strata and their support, lighting of the workings, and control of noise in confined spaces are some problems unique to underground mining.

Nonentry mining is widely practiced for the extraction of oil, natural gas, and coal bed methane. Underground gasification of coal and oil shale deposits and *in situ* retorting (distillation of volatile materials in a vessel called a retort) of oil shale have also found application in the recovery of oil and combustible gas. Some nonentry mining methods are really adaptations of underground mining methods to remove portions of the deposit that are easily accessible from the surface. In the nonentry mining methods, *in situ* solution mining of deposits is a primary method of production, whereby the valuable minerals are recovered by either dissolving, melting, leaching or slurrying the minerals in place, and transporting the resulting product to the surface for further processing. The important factors for the success of this type of mining are the ease of access, the solubility of the minerals, the permeability of the ore body, the flow of the fluids, and the recovery and reuse of the reagents. This approach has been used to recover salt, potash, trona, sulfur, uranium, and copper.

Ocean mining refers to mining in the marine environment. The technology for the recovery of dissolved minerals in sea water is well advanced. While offshore drilling for oil and gas has been remarkably successful, mining of the solid mineral deposits, even in shallow waters, is not common. Ocean mining faces formidable political and legal obstacles in addition to tremendous technological challenges for mining in deep waters (Hartman, 1987).

There are numerous variations in each type of mining, each one most effective for a particular combination of the types of strata above and below the mineral deposit, and the thickness, depth, inclination, extent, and type of mineral deposit. The difficulty of extraction increases tremendously with increases in depth and inclination. Great difficulties are presented by very thin or very thick deposits, and also by steep topography.

Decisions on whether an ore body will be mined or not, and the mining method to be practiced, depend on many technological, economic, and social factors. Often the technological factors constrain the mining engineer to a particular extraction technique, while the economic and social factors determine whether the ore body can be mined at all.

Environmental Impacts of Mining. The impacts of mining on the environment may be felt on-site (internal to the mine) and off-site (external to the mine) on varying time scales, from the near term to long into the future. The impacts are physical, affecting the land, water, air, wildlife, and vegetation, and economic, affecting the supply and demand of minerals/metal commodities, revenues, tax base, employment, and so on. The impacts have health and safety implications for individuals and communities. Environmental impacts also arise from operations upstream to mining (prospecting, exploration, development, etc.) and from those downstream to mining (processing, transport, concentration, smelting, refining, etc.; Down and Stocks, 1977). The effect of mining operations commences from the exploration stage and continues until after the mine has been closed and rehabilitated. In between, the lifetime of a mine is quite variable—from a few years to several decades.

Advances in mining technology have enabled mining of lower-grade materials, planning of larger-scale operations, and recovery of more of the ore body from the ground. At the same time, concern for the environment has grown, for a number of reasons including the general increase in environmental consciousness, the increase in the volume of wastes, the appearance of hazardous materials, worries about climate change and global warming, and concern for the quality of life and the ability to sustain the present trend in growth and development.

Abandoned mine sites of the past are a constant reminder that mining without control results in serious blights and hazards to the public, contaminates air and water resources, adversely affects land values, creates public nuisances, and generally interferes with community development. The scars of mining from the distant past reveal that the altered environment is not repaired by nature alone in a reasonable time or to a desirable state. The solid, liquid, and gaseous residuals move through different paths into the larger environment. The altered physical, chemical, and biological systems take time to stabilize, and may never do so.

All types of mining affect, at least temporarily, the land, water, and air quality in an area. Surface, underground, and nonentry mining have several common and several different environmental impacts. The major environmental impacts from mining operations on air, water, and land resources are summarized in Figure 2.

				Pre-mining Development	Surface Mining	Underground Mining	No-Entry Mining	Ocean Mining	Process Waste	Post Mining	Abandoned Land
AIR QUALITY	Noise	Blasting/Explosives		•	•						
		Equipment		•	•		•		•		
	Particulates (Dust)	Produced in Operations		•	•				•		
		Produced from Waste			•				•	•	•
	Air Blast/Outbursts				•	•					
	Emissions	Explosives									
		Equipment			•		•				
		Formation		•	•	•			•		•
		Fires			•	•	•		•		•
		Waste			•	•			•	•	•
WATER	Surface Water	Water Quality	Solids Dissolved		•	•	•		•	•	•
			Solids Suspended	•	•	•	•	•	•	•	•
			pH		•	•	•		•	•	•
			Toxic Elements		•	•	•	•	•	•	•
		Water Quantity	Operationally Related Consumed		•	•			•		
			Operationally Related Produced						•		
			Changes to Natural Distribution	•	•	•	•		•	•	•
	Ground Water	Water Quality	Solids Dissolved		•	•	•		•	•	•
			Solids Suspended					•			
			pH		•	•	•	•	•	•	•
			Toxic Elements		•	•	•		•	•	•
		Water Quantity	Operationally Related Consumed								
			Operationally Related Produced								
			Changes to Natural Distribution	•	•	•				•	•
LAND	Land Use and Productivity	Surface Stability	Subsidence			•	•			•	•
			Slope Stability	•	•				•	•	•
		Supportive Capacity	Habitat	•	•	•	•	•	•	•	•
			Agricultural	•	•	•	•		•	•	•
		Land Form		•	•	•	•		•	•	•
	Aesthetics			•	•	•		•	•	•	•
SOCIAL CULTURAL	Historical (Archeological)			•	•	•					
	Infrastructure			•						•	
	Public Safety				•	•	•		•	•	•
	Public Perceptions			•	•	•	•		•		•

Mining. FIGURE 2. Major Environmental Impacts of Mining. (Modified from Kaas, 1977, personal communication.)

These impacts are not mutually exclusive, because air pollution may eventually lead to water pollution, and both combined can render the land uninhabitable. Among the often-cited undesirable, long-term environmental effects of mining are disruption of the hydrologic cycle, contributions to loss of biological diversity, to deforestation, and to desertification, loss of industrial activity, and poor future development potential.

Factors influencing the extent of environmental impacts are both natural and cultural. Among the important natural factors are geographic and geologic location, the characteristics of the minerals being mined, topography, and climate. Cultural factors include the method of mining, the scale of operation, and the existing and planned land uses. Mining and processing of gold and silver ores are associated with cyanide and mercury. Pyrites and sulfide ores are sources of sulfur dioxide and sulfuric acid. High concentrations of salts are associated with the mining of sodium and potassium ores. Uranium mining presents unique problems of tailings management for the containment of radionuclides. Higher concentrations of heavy metals (aluminum, iron, manganese, lead, nickel, etc.) are likely to occur in the mining and processing of metallic ores. Mining of asbestos, silica sands, and mica presents challenging health, safety, and environmental problems. The impact of ground movements from underground caving methods requires detailed consideration in environmental planning. Deep open pits present numerous challenges for safe decommissioning. Stone, sand, and gravel operations near urban areas present different opportunities for reclamation and land use planning compared with mining operations in remote places where the climate is harsh and the soil not very fertile. Environmental concerns arising from mining, and planning for adequate attention to these concerns, are clearly site specific.

Effects on air. Mining, by itself, may not be a major contributor to the air pollution problem. However, downstream processes such as burning of oil and coal and roasting and smelting of metalliferous ores are major contributors to atmospheric emissions. Furthermore, there are many areas in which mining and related operations do emit particulate and gaseous substances to the atmosphere. Improper sealing of outcrops, abandoned strip mines, and near-surface underground mines have contributed to spontaneous combustion and serious mine fires in active and inactive mining areas. Burning and nonburning waste banks left over from abandoned mining operations spread toxic and noxious gases that pollute the air and threaten health. Float dust arising from haul roads, screens in preparation plants, blasting in surface mines, and mine exhaust from underground mines are also sources of air pollution.

In general, recognition of the air pollution problem has been increasing rapidly and air quality criteria have been established not only for suspended particulates, but also for sulfur dioxide, sulfates, fluorides, nitrogen oxides, hydrogen sulfide, carbon monoxide, and other relevant substances. These, in turn, have affected the markets for coal and other fossil fuels and for the processing and smelting of sulfide and other metallic ores. Well-proven and effective technology is readily available to remove particulates and gaseous contaminants before atmospheric discharge, and most current operations incorporate advanced emissions control technology. [*See* Acid Rain and Acid Deposition.]

Effects on water. Wherever mining has been practiced, mining engineers have been confronted with water. In some cases, metric tons of water have to be pumped for every metric ton of ore mined as a result of normal inflow into the mine through permeable rock beds and geologic disturbances. In underground mining, as minerals and fuels are removed, the roof and overlying strata cave in to fill the void. Breakage of the overlying strata affects normal drainage patterns. In surface mining, waterways are diverted to permit mining without flooding the pit. Even then, seepage and rain water have to be pumped out to keep the pit dry. Abandoned mines, with little or no drainage control, are a continuous source of water. Water pollution potential arises from the solubility of the minerals in the ore body and the associated strata. The water can be acidic and contain large amounts of sulfates and dissolved iron, or it can be alkaline. Significant factors affecting the quality and quantity of the drainage include the chemical composition of rocks in and around the ore body, their access to air, the water infiltration rate, the bacterial inhabitants of the mine, and the processes of chemical, electrochemical, and biochemical oxidation and biochemically catalyzed reactions.

Fine solid particles from mining sites and preparation plants can be carried to neighboring streams and waterways. Plant spillages, truck haulage routes, conveyor transfer points, and rail loading areas are some common sources contributing to the carry-off. Silting and sedimentation of waterways are also caused by hydraulic mining and dredging operations. Abandoned mill tailings and waste banks, including coal refuse piles, spoil banks, and other waste dumps in mining areas, contain significant amounts of dissolved minerals. If not properly constructed and stabilized, these can be chronic sources of stream pollution, and may result in a total absence of flora and fauna along the stream route. The fitness of water for potable and industrial use can be severely restricted by the undesirable pH levels, ionic content, and suspended solids. Streams and sites affected by water pollution are also aesthetically undesirable. [*See* Water Quality.]

Most of the water pollution problems have sound engineering solutions. The many techniques to abate mine drainage include at-source control by prevention or reduction of the formation of acid mine drainage; dispersion or dilution of pollutants; treatment of polluted waters; and permanent containment or isolation of polluted waters. In underground mining, in-mine entry sealing and drainage diversion can constrain the movement of air and water, reducing the volume of air and the contact time for the reactions. Air (or inert gas) sealing and water sealing of underground mines have been tried. Bacteria have been used for various types of control, some to reduce acid mine drainage constituents (e.g., iron and sulfates), and some to fight against the acid-forming bacteria. In surface mining, several strategies have been tried at various times: extraction of all the minerals and burial of toxic products, grading of earth, construction of water ditches, revegetation of ground disturbed by excavations, water impoundments, channeling and drainage diversion, and regulated pumping and discharges (volume, rate, time, and location) from settling tanks. Water inundations from sealed-off areas and overflow or bursting of water dams on the surface have occurred in the past, with extensive loss of lives and property. Before such a method is selected, the design of these structures must be properly evaluated because, with the passage of time, the strength of the structures may be drastically reduced. Attempts have also been made to place polluted water into the subsurface through deep well injection.

Where prevention is not possible, treatment of polluted water to meet sanitary standards is necessary. Neutralization, flash distillation, reverse osmosis, ion exchange, and desulfating are some of the many methods developed to treat polluted water. The process of chemically counteracting the polluting effects (i.e., neutralization) is at present the most common. Today, carefully designed mine and plant layouts significantly reduce uncontrolled discharges and minimize the water pollution problem. Closed water circuits, covered material transport, silo storage, proper catchment areas and drains, settling ponds, and treatment plants all greatly aid the control of water pollution.

Effects on land. Mining as a land use is often in competition with uses of land for soil and water, living space, recreation, and industry. Mineral exploration, development, extraction, and processing all have different impacts and conflict with these uses, at least in the short term. Land damage from underground mining has been due mainly to ground movement and surface subsidence. Property damage can be extensive. The effect on ground and surface waters can be substantial and difficult to quantify. In shallow mines, the broken strata may provide for air and water circulation to the workings, which can result in mine fires and drainage.

Land disturbances from surface mining are mainly due to the destruction of surface topographies and soil conditions that existed before mining commenced. After mining, the potential productivity of the soil for plant growth can be greatly reduced. Soils that are churned up by these operations can be chemically active and toxic, thereby becoming a source for water pollution. Improperly abandoned surface mines have been used as dumping grounds for waste and refuse. In addition to becoming potential fire hazards, these sites present a safety hazard in inhabited neighborhoods.

A much larger area may also be affected by the preparation and processing of plant wastes, particularly where low-grade ores are being processed. Often these wastes have unique disposal problems associated with them. If the waste is suspended in a colloidal form, much ground will be required to create settling ponds before the water can be discharged or recirculated. Because of the comminution process (baking a substance into finer sizes) in the preparation plant, some mineral wastes are very fine and can easily be carried away by wind and rain.

While abandoned mining areas of the past continue to be major polluters of the air, water, and land resources of a region, in recent years, with suitable planning, a more productive land use has been achieved on mined lands. In fact, the planning of reclamation and postmining uses of land is required by law in several countries. Safe closure of underground and surface mines and proper rehabilitation of all affected sites (waste piles, buildings, plants, etc.) have become extremely important. In the United States, mining reclamation and land-use plans have to be approved not only by federal, state, and local agencies, but also by special-interest groups and the general public who are concerned with preserving or enhancing the long-term use of the land. Rehabilitation of surface-mined land is being accomplished through the systematic application of reclamation technology, which is an orderly approach to grading, soil handling and stabilization, revegetation, and hydraulic control, all necessary for returning surface-mined land to productive use (Figure 3). Spoil banks that can be revegetated present minor problems and have great potential for development. Various reclamation programs that are being actively pursued include restoring the ground for agricultural and livestock farming, reforestation, recreation, and housing and industrial sites. The possibilities for development under these conditions are limited only by cost-benefit considerations. There are, however, marginal and problem spoils (acid, toxic, etc.) that require special attention and additional planning.

The environmental impacts at the mine site and their solutions reveal clearly that mining modifies the existing physical environment and the preexisting distributions of metals, minerals, and energy. The effects of

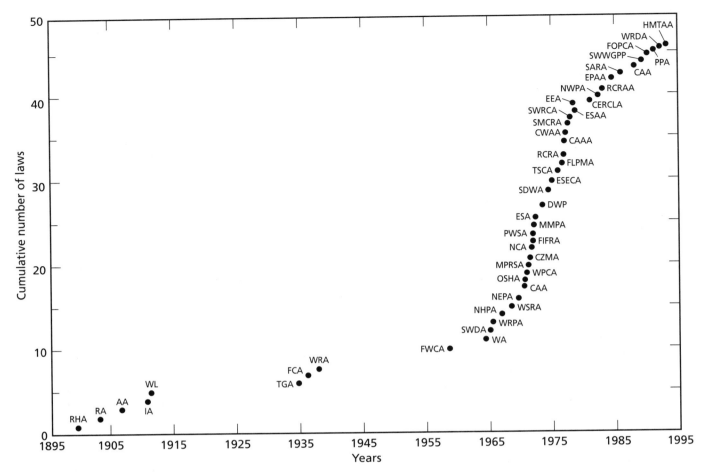

Mining. Figure 3. U.S. Laws on Environmental Protection.
Growth in the number of environmental laws in the United States. Starting in the late 1960s, a mix of standard-setting, right-to-know, and product licensing laws has created a complex maze of legislation addressing the environmental issues associated with air, land, water, energy, wildlife, antiques, and scenic human resources. The standard-setting legislations are, for example, CAA (1970), WPCA (1972), SDWA (1974), RCRA (1976), and OSHA (1970). The right-to-know legislation includes NEPA (1969) and CERCLA (1980). Among the product licensing legislation are TCSA (1976) and FIFRA (1972). Several legislations have been amended, often repeatedly (e.g., CAA 1970, 1977 to 1990), to enhance the comprehensiveness of the legislative mandates.

these alterations on the stability of regional ecosystems are not well understood.

The Mining Industry Today. In the last two decades, record achievements in health, safety, and productivity have characterized every segment of the mining industry. In the United States, innovative applications of high technology are widespread. In the coal mining sector, the remote and automatic control of highly productive longwall machines is becoming standard in underground mining; in the industrial stone segment, the industry has moved from its traditional composition of individual operations to large vertically integrated conglomerates; and in the metal mining sector, impressive achievements have been made in the mining and processing of low-grade ores. Similarly, *in situ* mining and heap leaching processes have revitalized an industry that was faced with a declining demand

and severe competition. Huge productivity gains in the surface mining of coal and metallic and nonmetallic deposits have been spurred by more effective application of technological advancements in mining, processing, monitoring, and control equipment. New tools and technologies for exploration and mining have enhanced understanding of geology, the physics of processes, mine design requirements, mine production, and environmental issues. Significant advances in real-time monitoring and telemetry tools and analytical techniques, coupled with greatly increased computational power, are allowing real-time control of mining operations.

As a result of these spectacular technological advances, the knowledge gap that existed between the exploration, production, and management phases of a mineral deposit has been greatly narrowed, and the costs of production have declined. Yet increasing efficiency in all end-use sectors has resulted in a moderation of prices and increasing competition among suppliers, calling for even greater efficiencies in exploration and production.

On the environmental front, almost all mining operations are conducted under several environmental laws that are either specific to the mining industry or applied to all industrial activities. In the United States, there has been a tremendous growth in the number of laws that have been passed at the national level (Figure 4). In addition, several U.S. states have enacted their own laws to address state-specific requirements. All of these laws address a fairly comprehensive list of issues with regard to the environment (air, water, land, wildlife, toxic substances, resource recovery, health, safety, etc.) and have led to the creation of new agencies and detailed regulations. Under these laws and regulations, detailed plans are required on assessment and control of air, water, and land effects before permission is granted to start mining. The scope of the plans extends across premining,

A

B

Mining. FIGURE 4. An Abandoned Surface Mine Site.

(A) showing the exposed highwall, coal seam, and water accumulation and (B) the same site after it was reclaimed with sealing the outcrops, grading, top soiling, and seeding. In addition to being more aesthetically pleasing, this reclaimed site offers the potential for development of several land uses.

mining, postmining, beneficiation, and utilization activities. The mining industry has already devoted many resources and much effort to this end. There is little doubt that mining operations in some countries today are much more environmentally friendly than ever before. The disparity in environmental laws and regulations of different countries is a cause for concern, however, because severe local problems may develop in countries where inadequately controlled activities take place. Moreover, some environmental effects may have global impacts.

The Future Mining Industry. The future promises a world in which the search for top-quality mineral resources, the competition from international producers, and the pressures of substitution and environmental conservation are likely to be more intense than ever before. Issues of improved health and safety, increased environmental conservation, and enhanced quality of life will continue to demand more attention from the mineral industry. At the societal level, fundamental questions are being raised about the assumptions and consequences of growth, and these have stimulated intellectual discussions on the role of science, technology, and society. All this has altered in a fundamental way the acceptance of industrial growth as a necessity for national economic well-being. While it is widely recognized that societal aspirations cannot be satisfied without the mining industry continuing to provide the basic needs of energy and materials, the issues of global warming, acid rain, solid waste disposal, and deteriorating hydrologic resources will require increased efforts to:

1. Enhance resource characterization techniques for *in situ* resources and for various stages of resource exploitation to improve understanding of heterogeneities, thus reducing the high risk of operations
2. Improve resource conservation and recovery through novel resource exploitation schemes
3. Develop advanced technological systems to encompass multiple resource utilization and wasteless mineral extraction technologies
4. Advance health and safety and productivity of mineral engineering activities through innovative applications of monitoring and control technology
5. Assess and abate the potentially negative environmental impacts of mineral-related activities on the ecosystem.

Surface and underground extraction and the associated surface processing of minerals will continue to be the principal focus in the mineral industries. However, it will be increasingly necessary to synchronize industrial development with natural ecosystems and to integrate the activities of the energy and mineral sectors with geologic, biological, ecological, cultural, and socioeconomic considerations. The applications of the

new concepts of industrial metabolism and industrial ecology need to be explored and developed.

Even without human activities, the environment is ever changing. However, mining is a drastic and dramatic source of change. The mining industry's efforts in environmental management have progressed through the stages of pollution control to understanding the environment and its conservation. The larger issues of ecosystem stability and the role of the mineral industry in ecosystem management are important to address. More knowledge is needed on the effects of mining on ecosystem properties such as energy flow, climate, food webs, structure, diversity, biogeochemical cycles, and life-sustaining capacity (Ripley et al., 1996). Questions on cause-and-effect relationships, the safe upper limit for pollutant growth curves, and the transformations and transmutations in the environment must be addressed through research and development. Until the full impact of mining on the ecological balance is understood, it is only prudent that mining in the future be conducted in a manner that reduces the potential for drastic imbalances by minimizing its impacts on the local environment.

[*See also* Fossil Fuels; Industrialization; Land Reclamation; Land Use, *article on* Land Use and Land Cover; Nuclear Hazards; Nuclear Industry; *and* Recycling.]

BIBLIOGRAPHY

American Geological Institute. *Dictionary of Mining, Mineral and Related Terms*. Alexandria, Va.: American Geological Institute, 1997.
Beall, J. V. "Mining's Place and Contribution." In *SME Mining Engineering Handbook*, vol. 1., sect. 1, New York: Society of Mining Engineers of AIME, 1973, pp. 2–13.
Down, C. G., and J. Stocks. *Environmental Impact of Mining*. New York: Wiley, 1977.
Gregory, C. E. *A Concise History of Mining*. New York: Pergamon, 1980.
Hartman, H. L. *Introductory Mining Engineering*. New York: Wiley, 1987.
———. *SME Mining Engineering Handbook*, vols. 1 and 2. Littleton, Colo.: Society for Mining, Metallurgy and Exploration, Inc., 1992.
Husturlid, W. A. *Underground Mining Methods Handbook*. New York: Society of Mining Engineers of AIME, 1982.
Kennedy, B. A. *Surface Mining*. Littleton, Colo.: Society for Mining, Metallurgy and Exploration, Inc., 1990.
Ripley, E. A., et al. *Environmental Effects of Mining*. Delray Beach, Fla.: St. Lucie Press, 1996.
Vogely, W. A. *Economics of the Mineral Industries*. 4th ed. New York: American Institute of Mining, Metallurgical and Petroleum Engineers, 1985.

—Raja V. Ramani

MODELING OF NATURAL SYSTEMS

The Earth's natural system encompasses the totality of the atmosphere, hydrosphere, biosphere, and geosphere and their interactions. Thus it spans very many variables, time scales, and spatial scales. One definition of the "Earth system" might be all of the statistics of the natural state determined over an agreed time interval (seasons, decades, or longer), computed for the globe or for all identified regions that together comprise the whole system. This definition is broad, but it does serve to emphasize that higher-order statistics, such as variance (variability), can often be as useful in characterizing the system state as the mean (average). The definition also permits further description of change as the difference between two system states, and an anomaly as the difference between a current state and the mean state. The variations of the system arise from interactions between different parts of the system and from external forcings.

Modeling of this complex and multifaceted natural system is challenging and stimulating. Researchers apply many different types of modeling techniques, including laboratory, analog, and numerical models. Laboratory models are scaled-down constructed models such as the laboratory flasks used to contain gaseous mixtures like those of the Earth's Archean atmosphere. By discharging electric currents through these mixtures in the laboratory, scientists have manufactured complex organic molecules that are the precursors of life. A particularly famous laboratory model on a much larger scale is Biosphere 2 (Figure 1). [See the vignette Biosphere 2.]

Analogue models are naturally occurring locations or times (or both) that appear to be similar to the system being studied. For example, the effect of a positive feedback can be simply illustrated by employing the analogy of self-image and alcohol. Someone slightly prone to drinking alone can become depressed by their increased alcohol intake and so drink more and rapidly become enmeshed in a detrimental positive-feedback effect. An analogue model of a different kind can be used to illustrate negative feedback. As a community grows, there is a tendency for immigration to occur, but the additional influx of industry, cars, and people is often detrimental to the environment, so that it may be balanced, or even exceeded, by an outflux of wealthier inhabitants, with a possibly detrimental impact on the economy. The search for analogues can be rewarding, but it is important not to push any analogy beyond its limits.

Numerical models are computer-based methods of solving equations or reaching logical solutions based on agreed representations of information and processes. Computer modeling offers one means of answering questions requiring predictions. Although there have been great advances made in such modeling over the past thirty to forty years, even the most sophisticated numerical models are still far removed in complexity from the full Earth system (see Figure 2). Modeling in such a widely ranging subject is a formidable task, and

it requires cooperation between many disciplines if reliable conclusions are to be drawn.

The importance of all types of models in understanding the complex interactions between various components of the Earth's natural system cannot be overestimated. Numerical models are only one, apparently sophisticated, method of study. They are not necessarily the best tools, and analogue and laboratory models are often used in conjunction with, or sometimes even to the exclusion of, numerical models. The literature contains many fascinating examples of very simple models being used to demonstrate failures in much more complex systems. Observational evidence is critically important for validation of all model types.

Desertification provides a good example. This is a problem that affects millions of people worldwide. The sparse vegetation natural to arid and semiarid areas can easily be removed as a result of relatively minor changes in the climate, or by direct influence of human activity such as overgrazing or poor agricultural practices. Removal of vegetation and exposure of bare soil decreases soil water storage because of increased runoff and increased albedo. Less moisture available at the surface means decreased latent heat flux, leading to an increase in surface temperature. On the other hand, the increased albedo produces a net radiative loss. In numerical model calculations the latter effect appears to dominate and the radiation deficit causes large-scale atmospheric subsidence. In this descending air, cloud and precipitation formation is impossible, and desert aridity increases. Observational evidence of this phenomenon has been obtained from semiarid locations in the southwestern United States and in Western Australia, where fences separating landowners and hence agriculture practice represented the locus of differing vegetation types and densities. This laboratory model (an actual representation of the process somewhat smaller than reality) generates results in good agreement with the numerical model simulations. [See Desertification.]

The Earth system is a dynamic system in transient balance. This concept, which is vitally important in natural system modeling, can be visualized using an analogue model of mammal movement. In the heart of New York City, Central Park experiences very little small-mammal flow but a sizable human influx each morning and an equally large outflux in the evening. Over periods greater than a few days, Manhattan has an (approximate) human and other-mammal balance, while over periods of a few hours there are large negative and positive fluxes of people but a negligible flux of, for example, squirrels. If the city authorities decided to flood Central Park to turn it into a permanent lake, the fluxes of people and other mammals would alter considerably, and the net flux budget would change in this part of the New York subsystem.

BIOSPHERE 2

Biosphere 2 Center.

(The whole Earth system is "Biosphere 1.") In the first two operations of Biosphere 2 between 1991 and 1994, people (termed "biospherians") as well as plants and animals were sealed inside. (Photograph courtesy of Karen Silva and Columbia University Biosphere 2 Center, Oracle, Arizona.)

Probably the largest laboratory model ever built is the Biosphere 2 complex in Arizona. Biosphere 2 is named to remind those who visit it that it is a representation of biosphere 1—the Earth! It is an enormous building enclosing over 1.25 hectares (3.1 acres) of land and standing 28 meters (91 feet) tall at its highest point. There are over thirty-eight hundred species living in Biosphere 2, but most are insects and plants. The ocean, which is 8 meters deep, cannot offer much room for large species, even though it contains millions of liters of salt water.

When Biosphere 2 was first constructed, it was used as a way of studying how people might manage to live in confined environments such as may exist in future space colonies on the Moon or Mars. The first experiment was between 1991 and 1993, during which eight "biospherians" were sealed inside the dome. They had their own quarters, a farm, and other natural environments to tend and monitor. However, this laboratory experiment produced some unexpected results—especially for the first biospherians. Soon after the miniature world was sealed up, computer monitors showed that the oxygen levels in the atmosphere were dropping rapidly. By January 1993, the oxygen level in the biospherians' air was only 14 percent, compared with the outside level of 21 percent. For the scientists inside Biosphere 2 it was like living on a mountain about a kilometer higher than the Matterhorn. They were all exhausted and also very thin because the farm was not able to produce as much food as had been expected. Many of the species in this biospheric laboratory fared even worse than the people. Most insects went extinct, and, of the twenty-five vertebrates released in the dome at the beginning, only six survived the first experiment. A few species prospered, however, including cockroaches, "crazy" ants, katydids, and morning glory vines. Today, Biosphere 2 is an environmental and ecological research laboratory operated by Columbia University. Students and professors study there, but no one is sealed inside.

—ANDREW S. GOUDIE

Fluxes are thus seen to be vectors (they are the movement of some quantity from one place to another, and the direction of flow is important) and net fluxes differ considerably as a function of the time interval considered. Also, different budgets, the result of the net fluxes, are established when the imposed disturbance changes. The most important fluxes in the Earth's system are fluxes of radiant (solar and heat) energy, fluxes of water, and fluxes of mass (matter), especially carbon, nitrogen, and oxygen.

The Earth's natural system is also clearly extremely heterogeneous. There are many subsystems that interact with one another to produce feedback effects—which occur when a portion of the output from the action of a system is added to the input and subsequently alters the output. The result of such a loop system can either be an amplification of the process or a dampening, and such feedbacks are labeled positive and negative, respectively. Positive feedbacks enhance a perturbation, whereas negative feedbacks oppose it.

For example, if some external or internal perturbation acts to decrease the global surface temperature, then the formation of additional areas of snow and ice is likely. These cryospheric elements are bright and white, reflecting almost the entire solar radiation incident upon them. Their albedo (ratio of reflected to incident radiation) is therefore high. The surface albedo increases, and probably the planetary albedo (the re-

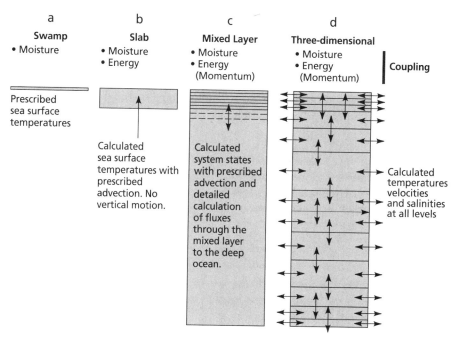

Modeling of Natural Systems. FIGURE 2. Schematic Illustration of the Level of Complexity and Coupling Associated with Various Types of Ocean Model.

(a) Swamp ocean with only moisture coupling, (b) slab of ocean with moisture and energy coupling, (c) diffusive mixed-layer model with energy and moisture (and some momentum) coupling, (d) full three-dimensional ocean model with momentum, moisture, and energy coupling and full three-dimensional interactions in the water column. (After McGuffie and Henderson-Sellers, 1996. Reproduced with permission of John Wiley and Sons.)

flectivity of the whole atmosphere plus surface system as seen from outside the planet) as well. Thus a greater amount of solar radiation is reflected away from the planet and temperatures decrease further. A further increase in snow and ice results from this decreased temperature, and the process continues. This positive-feedback mechanism is known as the ice albedo feedback mechanism. Of course, this mechanism is also positive if the initial perturbation causes an increase in global surface temperatures. With higher temperatures, the areas of snow and ice are likely to be reduced, thus reducing the albedo and leading to further enhancement of temperatures. The existence of clouds over regions of snow and ice can greatly modulate the shortwave feedbacks associated with the cryosphere. The presence of a snow or ice surface also affects the temperature structure of the atmosphere, introducing feedbacks associated with longwave radiation. [See Albedo.]

Evaluation of Earth system models can produce a range of outcomes, which have been grouped as follows: (1) predictions that are unreasonable; (2) predictions that are so reasonable as to be already known; (3) predictions that are unexpected, but can be readily understood and accepted; and (4) predictions that, while reasonable, identify novel outcomes that challenge current theories. Normal practice in model development would screen out all developments producing unrea-

sonable results, and there is little benefit in detailed examination of results that are totally reasonable and well known. Thus model evaluations tend to try to focus on results in categories (3) and (4): new predictions that are consistent with theory and those that challenge existing ideas.

The uptake and release of carbon dioxide at the land and ocean surfaces controls its atmospheric concentration. The magnitude and extent of terrestrial and oceanic sources and sinks of carbon dioxide must be fully understood if predictions are to be made of the future levels of atmospheric carbon dioxide and hence of the future climate, crop viability, and so on. Two recent projects were designed to evaluate the performance of ocean carbon simulation and of terrestrial vegetation exchanges of carbon dioxide with the atmosphere.

The Vegetation/Ecotype Modeling and Analysis Project has the goal of intercomparing the performance of vegetation model simulations. These models simulate the influence of the physical environment on (1) the availability of plant functional types (i.e., which plants can grow and reproduce), (2) competition for resources, and (3) the emergent equilibrium vegetation cover. Associated models, termed terrestrial biogeochemistry models, have been used to simulate the flow of carbon and mineral nutrients within vegetation, surface litter, and soil organic matter pools. These models have also been used to examine the global patterns of net primary production, carbon storage, and mineral uptake, and their sensitivity to climate change.

Oceanic uptake and release of carbon dioxide completes the global carbon system. Ocean–atmosphere carbon exchanges occur both as a result of the degree of solubility and as a function of the ocean biology. The Ocean Carbon-Cycle Model Intercomparison Project (OCMIP) is evaluating the capability of models to predict both anthropogenic and natural carbon dioxide exchange by comparison with observations of radiocarbon data, with determinations of the extent and type of ocean biology derived from satellite observations of ocean color. It is expected that results from OCMIP will be a valuable resource for the further development of the three-dimensional ocean components of Global Climate Models.

The natural variability of the ocean circulation is an important factor for climate and other components of the Earth system. The ocean circulation varies on glacial time scales, when the circulation is known to change markedly, and on interannual time scales, where the El Niño–Southern Oscillation phenomenon is important. El Niño events were first identified by fishermen who noticed the lack of anchovies off the Peruvian coast. These fish were responding to the change in ocean upwelling, itself indicative of atmospheric and oceanic changes across the tropical equatorial Pacific. [See El Niño–Southern Oscillation.] In this case, observations of a societal impact prompted the development of complex numerical models. This is one future for Earth system modeling.

Recently, simple integrated assessment models have been used to include economic considerations in numerical model calculations relating to anthropogenic gas emissions and their significance in terms of the global mean temperature and sea level changes. These new Earth system models are a response to Article 3 of the Framework Convention on Climate Change, which states that "policies and measures to deal with climate change should be cost-effective so as to ensure global benefits at the lowest possible cost." This requires that, if two greenhouse gas emission futures are indistinguishable in terms of their environmental implications, then the emission future with the lower mitigation (i.e., emissions reduction) costs will be preferred. Other economic constraints include that the implied emissions should not change too abruptly and that the resulting emissions trajectories initially track a business-as-usual path: an idealization of the assumption that the initial departure from the business-as-usual path would be slow, for economic and developmental reasons that include (1) the further into the future the economic burden lies, the smaller the present resource base required to undertake it; (2) time is therefore needed to reopti-

mize the capital stock; and (3) the availability of substitutes is likely to improve and their costs to reduce over time. Thus an integrated assessment model adds an additional constraint to those more commonly seen in numerical model evaluations of greenhouse impacts and policy outcomes.

[See also Atmosphere Dynamics; Climate Models; Future Studies; Global Warming; Greenhouse Effect; Ocean–Atmosphere Coupling; Ocean Dynamics; and Ozone.]

INTERNET RESOURCE

BIOSPHERE 2
More information can be obtained from http://www.bio2.edu/.

BIBLIOGRAPHY

Dickinson, R. E. "Climate Sensitivity." In *Issues in Atmospheric and Oceanic Modelling. Part A. Climate Dynamics*, edited by S. Manabe, vol. 28, *Advances in Geophysics*, pp. 99–129. New York, 1985. This is one of the earliest detailed discussions of climate sensitivity.

Global Atmospheric Research Programme (GARP). *The Physical Basis of Climate and Climate Modelling*. GARP Publication Series No. 16. Geneva: WMO/ICSU, 1975. A landmark description of the climate system.

Houghton, J. T., ed. *The Global Climate*. Cambridge: Cambridge University Press, 1984. A full and comprehensive textbook on the global climate.

Houghton, J. T., G. J. Jenkins, and J. J. Ephraums. *Climate Change: The IPCC Scientific Assessment*. Cambridge: Cambridge University Press, 1990. The first IPCC science report describing greenhouse warming.

Houghton, J. T., L. G. Mera Filho, B. A. Callander, N. Harris, A. Kattenberg, and K. Maskell, eds. *Climate Change 1995: The Science of Climate Change Contribution of Working Group I of the Intergovernmental Panel on Climate Change*. Cambridge: Cambridge University Press, 1996. The second IPCC science report identifying the human contribution to greenhouse warming.

Howe, W., and A. Henderson-Sellers, eds. *Assessing Climate Change: Results from the Model Evaluation Consortium for Climate Assessment*. London: Gordon and Breach, 1997. A detailed description of the first industry-funded climate modeling of greenhouse warming and its impact.

McGuffie, K., and A. Henderson-Sellers. *A Climate Modelling Primer*, 2d ed. Chichester, U.K.: Wiley, 1997.

Peixoto, J. P., and A. H. Oort. *Physics of Climate*. New York: American Institute of Physics, 1992. A classic observationally based analysis and description of the climate system.

Schlesinger, M. E., ed. *Physically Based Modelling of Climate and Climatic Change: Parts 1 and 2*. NATO ASI Series C, No. 243. Dordrecht: Kluwer, 1988. A multiauthored graduate-level text on climate modeling.

Trenberth, K. E. *Coupled Climate System Modelling*. Cambridge: Cambridge University Press, 1992.

—A. HENDERSON-SELLERS

MODELS. See Climate Models; Future Studies; Modeling of Natural Systems; Scenarios; and Weather Forecasting.

MONSOONS. *See* Atmosphere Dynamics; *and* Ocean–Atmosphere Coupling.

MONTREAL PROTOCOL

International cooperation in the protection of the stratospheric ozone layer has been taking place for almost twenty years. From 1977 to 1997, concerns about the threat to the ozone layer helped to develop one of the most sophisticated international environmental regimes, comprising a complex system of interrelated institutions. Its evolution has been a remarkable success story, not only in dealing with the substance of the problem, but also in providing a model for regime building that serves as a guide for the negotiation of other environmental instruments. The development of the ozone regime between 1985 and 1997 has been a laboratory in which many important elements were developed, and subsequently adapted to the needs of other global negotiation processes.

From the Vienna Convention for the Protection of the Ozone Layer of 1985 (VC), which contains few or no concrete obligations for parties other than that they cooperate on research into and monitoring of the problem, the regime evolved to the Montreal Protocol on Substances that Deplete the Ozone Layer of 1987. Through various amendments and adjustments (London, 1990; Copenhagen, 1992; Vienna, 1995; San José, 1996; and Montreal, 1997), the Montreal Protocol has established a regime that:

1. Contains binding obligations for the complete elimination of an environmental problem based on industrial processes, not by elimination of the underlying functions, but by complete substitution
2. Is based on the principle of common but differentiated responsibilities between industrialized- and developing-country parties, at a time before that concept became recognized as a legal principle
3. Includes a two-level flexible system for the further development of the regime
4. Creates a clear link between the responsibilities of parties or groups of parties to implement their obligations under the regime and the provision of financial and technical support by other parties
5. Includes the Multilateral Fund as a specific financial mechanism created to provide financial support for the solution of a global environmental problem, separately from regional or local environmental issues, recognizing the global responsibility for the solution to that problem
6. Operates a system for the monitoring, control, and resolution of questions regarding the implementation of the obligations, beyond the traditional system for dispute settlement.

The ozone regime now enjoys almost universal participation. As of 13 June 1997, 165 states were parties to the Vienna Convention, 162 were parties to the Montreal Protocol in its original form, and 114 and sixty-six states were parties to the London and Copenhagen Amendments, respectively. The original Framework Convention was little more than an agreement on cooperation in research and monitoring. The assumption was that, in the implementation of the Convention, the scientific and technical understanding of the environmental issue would be developed further, and the ground for negotiations on concrete obligations would in this way be prepared. The international community was, however, ready to start negotiations on a more concrete Protocol containing binding obligations for the reduction and elimination of hazardous substances immediately after the adoption of the Convention. This readiness was certainly also brought about by industrial research that demonstrated the probable availability of substances that could be used as substitutes for the offending chemicals. It was not foreseen at that time that some of these substitutes would in turn become part of the environmental problem. The negotiations were concluded in September 1987, before the Vienna Convention had even entered into force. The Vienna Convention and the Montreal Protocol in fact entered into force shortly after one another (22 September 1988 and 1 January 1989, respectively).

The Protocol of 1987 already contained most elements that were to characterize the instrument:

1. Binding control measures for ozone-depleting substances (chlorofluorocarbons and halons), although no phase-out was agreed at that time
2. The possibility of using an "adjustment procedure" (Article 2.9 of the Protocol) to tighten the control measures included in the Protocol, simply by decision of the Meeting of the Parties, without ratification by state parties
3. Control of trade in substances with nonparties (Article 4 of the Protocol)
4. A provision for a grace period for developing countries (Article 5 of the Protocol), linked to certain objective conditions
5. An enabling provision for the establishment of a Non-Compliance Procedure (Article 8 of the Protocol).

Two important elements were still missing, however, and were added via the London Amendment of 1990. First, an extension of the grace provisions for developing countries (Article 5), in particular the establishment of a clear link between the provision of financial and technical assistance by industrialized countries and the implementation of the commitments of parties that are listed as developing-country parties (Article 5.5 of the Protocol, as amended in London); and second, establishment of a financial mechanism, the Multilateral Fund, specific to the Protocol (Article 10 of the Protocol, as amended in London).

In the years between 1990 and 1997, the ozone regime was greatly expanded and refined. New substances (carbon tetrachloride, methylchloroform, hydrochlorofluorocarbons, methyl bromide, etc.) were added to the list of controlled substances, and phase-out dates were agreed for most of those substances. A complex system of reporting (Article 7), data gathering (Articles 6 and 9), scientific, technical, and economic assessment, special exemptions from the control measures ("essential uses" and "critical uses", Articles 2A–H), and compliance monitoring and supervision (Article 8) have been put in place. The innovative Non-Compliance Procedure was applied for the first time to several parties (the Russian Federation, Belarus, Ukraine, Poland, and Bulgaria) in 1995. It can be said that with the ninth Meeting of the Parties held in Montreal in September 1997, the expansive period of the Montreal Protocol had come to an end, as phase-out plans for all the controlled substances are now adopted both for developed and developing countries. The ozone regime has become a mature regime, and the focus of its future work will be on implementation—as demonstrated by the increasing concentration on matters such as illegal trade in ozone-depleting substances. The next years will show whether the implementation successes achieved in the industrialized countries can be repeated in the transitional economies and in the developing world.

[*See also* Multilateral Fund; *and* Ozone.]

BIBLIOGRAPHY

Benedick, R. E. *Ozone Diplomacy: New Directions in Safeguarding the Planet.* Cambridge: Harvard University Press, 1998.
Lang, W., ed. *Sustainable Development and International Law.* London: Graham and Trotman, 1995.
————. "The Ozone Treaties and Their Influence on the Building of International Environmental Regimes." *Österreichische Außenpolitische Dokumentation* Special Issue (Vienna), 1996.
United Nations Environment Programme. *Handbook for the International Treaties for the Protection of the Ozone Layer.* 4th ed. Nairobi, 1996.

—HUGO-MARIA SCHALLY

MOUNTAINS

Mountains occupy nearly one-fourth of the land surface of the Earth. Their importance in relation to global change derives particularly from their role in influencing regional and global climates, particularly through the interception of atmospheric moisture. Since most of the world's major rivers rise in mountain regions, changes in mountain climates, and especially in runoff, will affect a large proportion of the global population. In addition, mountains are core areas of global biodiversity, and the origin of many of the world's food crops. In many regions, this global heritage is significantly endangered by changes in land use driven by a range of economic and political pressures. Climate change may further exacerbate these processes.

Although mountains can be identified immediately by anyone who visits or flies over them, there is no uniform definition of mountains; they are best defined as regions of accentuated relief (that is, with steep slopes) and altitude. Mere altitude is not a defining characteristic; many mountains start at sea level and, while mountains are the highest features of all of the continents, there are also many high-altitude areas that are not steep; for instance, the Tibetan (Xi-zang) Plateau, the South American Altiplano, and the high plains and plateaus of North America and Africa. Nevertheless, it is worth noting that 27 percent of the Earth's land surface is above 1,000 meters, and 11 percent is above 2,000 meters.

Created by tectonic forces, mountains are dynamic environments whose relief is determined by glacial and fluvial action, mass movement, and weathering. Although the mountains originating in the Caledonian and Hercynian/Appalachian orogenies (mountain-building periods) are now largely characterized by rounded relief, those that began their development during the Alpine orogeny, starting during the Tertiary (from 65 million years ago), are still growing. These include the Alps, the Himalayas, the Rocky Mountains, and the Andes: long mountain systems originating in the collision of continental plates. Other mountains are of volcanic origin, particularly around the Pacific Rim. The world's highest mountain, from base to summit, is not Mount Everest (known locally as *Sagarmatha* or *Qomolangma*), but Mauna Loa, the highest peak of Hawaii, a volcano rising from the bed of the Pacific Ocean.

Glaciers, Geomorphology, and Climate. During the Pleistocene (from about 1,800,000 to 11,000 years ago), many of the world's mountains were far more glaciated than at present, and those that were not glaciated experienced far cooler climates. Many ranges in temperate and high latitudes were largely ice-covered, with only the highest peaks extending above ice sheets and glaciers. In the postglacial period, starting approximately ten thousand years ago, the higher parts of these mountains have been successively exposed and subjected to a variety of geomorphic processes. The long, steep slopes of mountain regions promote rapid movement under gravity, not only of water and snow, but also of rocks and soil. While some processes are very rapid—floods, avalanches, rockslides, rockfalls, debris flows, lava and ash flows—gradual processes, such as soil erosion, can also endanger mountain people and affect water quality. Soil erosion derives not only from the steepness of slopes, but also from human mismanagement, often combined with other dynamic processes such as heavy rainfall, strong winds, and changes in temperature. [*See* Erosion.]

The vestiges of glaciation are shown by moraines (accumulations of material transported by ice), where these have not been removed by subsequent denudation. In the postglacial period, the world's glaciers have not retreated uniformly. There have also been periods of advance, notably during the Little Ice Age from the fourteenth to the eighteenth century CE. However, in recent decades, most glaciers have been retreating. This appears to be linked to atmospheric warming, which has been measured in a number of subtropical and tropical mountain regions. Only along the margins of continents, such as Scandinavia and the Pacific Northwest of North America, have glaciers advanced in response to increased winter precipitation. If recent trends continue, most glaciers will continue to retreat—for example, the ice mass in the Alps in 2025 could be only 25 percent of that in 1850—and the catastrophic release of large volumes of water from ice-dammed lakes could become more frequent. In addition, the melting of permafrost and residual ice in rock glaciers will lead to surface subsidence and, possibly, large debris flows. [*See* Glaciation; *and* Little Ice Age in Europe.]

Records of mountain climates are limited in length and representativeness even in the regions with the best measurement networks (the Alps, parts of the Carpathians), not least because most recording stations are in valleys, which are not representative of regional climates. Outside Europe and North America, information on current mountain climates is very limited. In addition, our understanding of many processes of mountain meteorology and the altitudinal variability of climates is poor. Given this lack of knowledge, projection of future mountain climates is highly uncertain; especially because the computer models typically used to predict future climates have too coarse a resolution to depict mountains. However, the recent application of statistical approaches and regional models provides the first step toward understanding of likely future mountain climates.

Hydrology. For the people and ecosystems of mountain regions, and also the vast number of people downstream who depend on mountain water, changes in the hydrologic regime are of particular concern. However, existing computer models suggest quite a wide range of likely future trends—in both magnitude and direction—in precipitation and evaporation. Two key predictions, with reasonable agreement between models, are that winter precipitation in higher latitudes is likely to increase, as is annual precipitation in the Asian monsoon region. Nevertheless, the models provide little information concerning changes in the proportion of precipitation falling as snow, and especially the likely increases in the intensity and frequency of extreme events, which may be even more critical.

At least in the short term, the wasting of glaciers leads to increased runoff. However, the result over the long term, as the supply dwindles, is decreased runoff, as is already apparent in the Alps and the Pamirs. Even before climate change becomes a factor, the quality and quantity of water supplies in many mountain regions are already limiting factors, especially in winter. Semiarid and arid regions are likely to be particularly sensitive to climate change, especially where irrigated agriculture is a basis for local economies. Overall, climate change is likely to increase the uncertainty of water supplies for mountain people, and there will be great need for adaptation and flexibility in both the infrastructure and the institutions used to manage and allocate water supplies. These challenges will often be heightened by demands for storing and releasing water to provide increased supplies of hydroelectricity in response to the policy imperative of decreasing the combustion of carbon-based fuels.

Agriculture and Forestry. In principle, global warming could have positive impacts for mountain farmers and foresters, as higher temperatures permit crops to be grown at higher altitudes, and increasing levels of carbon dioxide lead to increased agricultural and forest production. However, to grow at higher altitudes, crops and trees also require appropriate soil conditions. These may often not be available, either because the soils have unsuitable physical or chemical characteristics, or because of their deterioration as a result of human activities such as leaching following the removal of trees—to create pasture, fodder, and fuelwood—below the current anthropogenic timberline, which is 400 meters below its climatic optimum (maximum altitude under current climate) in parts of the Alps. Soil characteristics are likely to change rather gradually in response to climate changes. Other factors that may limit the ability of domesticated plants to become established and thrive at higher altitudes include increased competition from other species (such as weeds, diseases, pests), lack of obligate species (species biologically essential for survival; for example, pollinators), and changes in the frequency and timing of extreme events (particularly frosts) and cloud cover. Nevertheless, the great variety of crop varieties developed by generations of mountain farmers and adapted to a wide range of microclimates may provide a vital resource for ensuring food security. This is more likely to be endangered in regions in which native crops have been largely or entirely displaced by varieties that only give high yields under restricted climate conditions, often with high inputs of fertilizer.

Similarly, it is not possible to make unequivocal predictions concerning the likely impacts of climate change on mountain forests. These provide the primary fuel source to most mountain people and are also important for providing fodder and shade for grazing animals, as well as diverse societal benefits such as protection from landslides and floods and places for recreation. While increasing levels of carbon dioxide may promote increased growth of mountain trees, this may not all be directed to the most valued parts of trees and, as with crop species, may be offset by increased competition and predation. The frequency of fires may well increase in many regions; a problem likely to be exacerbated in many parts of Europe and North America by the high fuel loading resulting from decades of fire suppression and decreasing harvests. [*See* Fire.] Consequently, forest management strategies will have to be increasingly flexible, considering not only the diverse functions of forests but also the likely environmental changes. In addition, as with crops, there is a clear need to maintain genotypes adapted to a wide variety of conditions.

Mountain Ecosystems. Natural and seminatural mountain ecosystems will also be affected by climatic changes. As with domesticated species, the natural vegetation of most mountains can be classified into altitudinal zones. There are many classifications, depending primarily on latitude and altitude; the European colline-montane-alpine-nival model has been widely applied. The highest two of these zones are characterized by a lack of trees; in the nival zone, only species that are particularly adapted to the prevailing harsh conditions can survive. While such classifications are useful for summarizing ecological knowledge, larger mountain systems cannot easily be described by a simple vertical zonation, since the limits of the zones depend on factors including latitude, orientation (such as south versus north), the position of massifs within a group of ranges, and exposure to prevailing winds (for example, windward/oceanic versus leeward/continental).

Mountain ecosystems are of global importance as core areas of biological diversity, especially in the tropics, but also in the subtropics. In the temperate zone, mountains are typically centers of biodiversity, not only because many species have been extirpated in adjacent lowlands, but also because many mountains provide the last habitats for relic species from the last ice age, and the complexity and diversity of ecological niches provides particular opportunities for the evolution of species and subspecies. Many of the mountain areas with the greatest biological and landscape diversity have been recognized by their designation as protected areas (national parks, nature reserves, etc.), often with additional international status awarded by United Nations Educational, Scientific, and Cultural Organization (UNESCO): thirty-nine natural World Heritage Sites and 141 Biosphere Reserves are in mountain regions. Protected areas are not only valuable for protecting endemic and threatened species, but also as test cases for sustainable development in collaboration with local people, for recreation and tourism, and for monitoring of environmental changes. [*See* Conservation.]

The diversity of species, with many strategies for survival, means that mountain plant and animal communities are resilient. At the same time, they are also fragile because they require long periods of time to recover when damaged or stressed beyond a certain point, or when key species or soils are removed. In a period of global warming, the optimum habitat for most species is likely to move upslope. This presents particular challenges for the conservation of mountain species, as the area available for a particular species or ecosystem will generally decrease with altitude; changes in vegetation zones are usually not symmetrical along altitudinal gradients; and, at the tops of mountains, the coolest habitats may disappear. These constraints on the ability of wild species to adapt and respond to global warming may be ameliorated or exacerbated by human actions. For example, while migration corridors could be established and kept open by appropriate land-use practices and policies, the expansion of agriculture to higher altitudes could decrease possibilities for dispersal. In addition, management strategies must recognize that each species responds individualistically to changes in climate, so that animal and plant communities tend to disassemble. Consequently, while it is possible to surmise the potential distribution of broad ecoclimatic zones, many of today's plant and animal communities may no longer exist in the future.

Anthropogenic Changes. The prospect of changes in natural and seminatural ecosystems, resulting from climate change, must be evaluated in the appropriate context. In many mountain regions, direct anthropogenic causes of change are, and are likely to continue to be, as great a threat to biological diversity. In tropical and subtropical mountains, the introduction of exotic species has already greatly changed the species composition of many plant and animal communities, often leading to species extinction, especially on islands. With growing demographic and economic pressures, clearing for agriculture and logging for timber threaten mountain forests; the rate of deforestation in tropical upland forests is 1.1 percent per year, greater than in any other forest biome. In addition, fire and overgrazing endanger grasslands such as the *páramo* of the Andes.

Overgrazing is also of particular concern in arid and semiarid mountains, where the genetic diversity of native ungulates (hoofed mammals) is being lost through hybridization with domesticated stock. In temperate mountains, large-scale logging, fire, and the fragmentation of habitats are all direct threats to biological and landscape diversity. To these may be added the changes in, and loss of, habitats through air pollution and soil acidification in regions downwind from major industrial areas. For some decades at least, the forces of global change that drive changes in land use and cover in the mountains of Europe are likely to derive at least as much from government policies and market forces as from global climate change. The demise of communist regimes has already led to significant changes in the mountains of central and eastern Europe, with substantial increases in grazing pressure, logging, and hunting linked to the renewed ownership of private resources.

Tourism. The biological and landscape diversity of mountain regions is one of the prerequisites for an economic sector of growing and, in some cases, overwhelming importance in these regions: tourism, the world's largest industry. Tourism is already a major agent of environmental change in mountains around the world, both directly (for example, through the construction of infrastructure, disturbance of plant and animal species, production of artificial snow) and indirectly (that is, through changes in land use related to the availability of employment in the tourist sector, demands for products, land prices). Equally, climate change is likely to affect mountain tourism both directly (such as through changes in the amounts and timing of snowfall and in the timing of good weather) and indirectly (for example, through changes in landscapes and in patterns of demand for specific activities, concern about the health risks of ultraviolet radiation at high altitudes). Finally, rises in fuel prices resulting from the likely taxes on the consumption of fossil fuels would affect mountain tourism disproportionately, since the costs of access to mountain regions tend to be a relatively high proportion of total costs. Increasingly, policies for the development of mountain regions will have to consider the complex interactions between all sectors of local, regional, and global economies and the uncertainty of the future environment. [*See* Tourism.]

[*See also* Earth History; *and* Plate Tectonics.]

BIBLIOGRAPHY

Barry, R. G. *Mountain Weather and Climate.* 2d ed. London: Routledge, 1992. The most detailed review of the subject.
Beniston, M. *Environmental Change in Mountains and Uplands.* London: Edward Arnold, 2000.
———, ed. *Mountain Environments in Changing Climates.* London: Routledge, 1994. The proceedings of the first conference on the topic.
Beniston, M., and D. G. Fox. "Impacts of Climate Change on Mountain Regions." In *Impacts, Adaptations and Mitigation of Climate Change: Scientific-Technical Analyses,* edited by R. T. Watsonet et al., pp. 191–213. Cambridge: Cambridge University Press, 1996. The state-of-the-art review for the Intergovernmental Panel on Climate Change.
Gerrard, A. J. *Mountain Environments: An Examination of the*
Physical Geography of Mountains. London: Belhaven, 1990. A good overview of the subject.
Messerli, B., and J. D. Ives, eds. *Mountains of the World: A Global Priority.* New York and Carnforth, U.K.: Parthenon, 1997. An excellent overview of mountain issues, organized thematically.

—MARTIN F. PRICE

MOUNT PINATUBO

[*This case study highlights the causes and consequences of atmospheric changes produced by the great 1991 volcanic eruption of Mount Pinatubo.*]

Mount Pinatubo, on the island of Luzon in the Philippines, produced the second largest volcanic eruption of the twentieth century in June 1991. Eruption columns of ash and gas reached in excess of 35 kilometers altitude and injected about 17 megatons (1 megaton = 10^{12} grams) of sulfur dioxide gas into the stratosphere, about twice the amount produced by the 1982 eruption of El Chichón, Mexico. The sulfur dioxide formed a layer of sulfate aerosols about 28 megatons in mass, the largest perturbation to the stratospheric aerosol layer since the eruption of Krakatau (Indonesia) in 1883. Pinatubo's aerosol cloud spread rapidly around the Earth in about three weeks and attained global coverage one year after the eruption. It had a far-reaching impact on Earth's radiation budget, affecting atmospheric chemistry, surface and atmospheric temperatures, and regional weather patterns. The cloud caused a dramatic decrease in the net amount of radiation reaching the Earth's surface. Observed cooling in the Northern Hemisphere was up to 0.5°–0.6°C, equivalent to a hemisphere-wide reduction in net radiation of 4 watts per square meter and a cooling of 0.4°C over large parts of the Earth in 1992–1993. Environmentally important atmospheric effects such as an increase in ultraviolet radiation at the surface and global depletion of the ozone layer in the early 1990s can also be attributed to the presence of the Pinatubo aerosol cloud. Midlatitude ozone concentrations reached their lowest levels on record during 1992–1993, the Southern Hemisphere ozone hole increased in 1992 to an unprecedented size, and ozone depletion rates were observed to be faster than ever before recorded. [*See* Ozone.]

The Eruption and Aerosol Cloud. After ten weeks of precursory activity, Mount Pinatubo (15°07′ north latitude, 120°20′ east longitude) erupted on June 12–15, 1991, producing the largest stratospheric sulfur dioxide cloud ever observed by modern instruments. By far the greatest volume of ejecta (greater than 90 percent), the highest eruption columns, and the longest duration of stratospheric injection occurred during eight hours of more-or-less continuous high-output activity from about 1340 to about 2230 (local time) on June 15. A dense magma volume of 5–7 cubic kilometers was ejected, of which the sulfur dioxide gas was a very small mass fraction (about 0.1–0.2 percent).

During the eight-hour climax of the eruption, a huge eruption cloud of ash and gas at an altitude of 20–35 kilometers grew to more than 1,100 kilometers in diameter, covering an area of 300,000 square kilometers in the stratosphere (Figure 1). Ash fell downwind over the China Sea, and as far away as Vietnam and Singapore, as well as on Luzon. An area of about 500 square kilometers around the volcano was devastated and covered by new pyroclastic flow deposits up to 200 meters thick.

The main ash cloud was transported southwest by the prevailing winds in the middle stratosphere to the upper troposphere, typical of tropical circulation at that time of year in the easterly phase of the quasibiennial oscillation (QBO). The QBO is an alternation from easterly to westerly winds in the equatorial stratosphere at about 20 kilometer altitude that has an average period of twenty-seven months (Figure 2). Transport of the volcanic cloud was tracked on weather satellite images until June 17, after which sufficient ash fell out to make the plume hard to define, leaving mainly the gaseous component dominated by water and sulfur dioxide. After this, the spreading could be defined by the sulfur dioxide cloud, which was tracked and measured by the Total Ozone Mapping Spectrometer satellite at 20 ($\pm$6) megatons of sulfur dioxide.

As well as sulfur dioxide, carbon dioxide, water, and a small amount of chlorine were released into the stratosphere. Some of the water may have been important in early formation of aerosols. Although 3 megatons of chlorine was erupted and was potentially available for subsequent participation in ozone-destroying reactions, observations by airborne infrared Fourier transform spectrometry of the stratospheric cloud three weeks after the June 15 eruption showed little increase in hydrochloric acid (HCl) above stratospheric background. Erupted chlorine, as HCl, is highly soluble in water and is very efficiently scavenged by water droplets in the eruption column and rapidly returned to the surface of the Earth as precipitation. Much of the chlorine may have thus been removed from the atmosphere during or shortly after eruption.

The Pinatubo eruption was much larger in terms of magma volume than the other notable volcanic events of the past century that have caused widespread atmospheric perturbations, such as Agung (Bali, Indonesia, 1963) and El Chichón (1982). However, magma volume erupted and amount of sulfur dioxide released are not always proportional to each other. The small El Chichón eruption yielded just less than half the amount of sulfur dioxide released by Pinatubo and generated just less than half the amount of aerosols, but the magma volume erupted was an order of magnitude smaller than at Pinatubo.

The early summer date of the eruption and the tropical location of Pinatubo resulted in global coverage by the aerosol cloud, producing a widespread impact. The

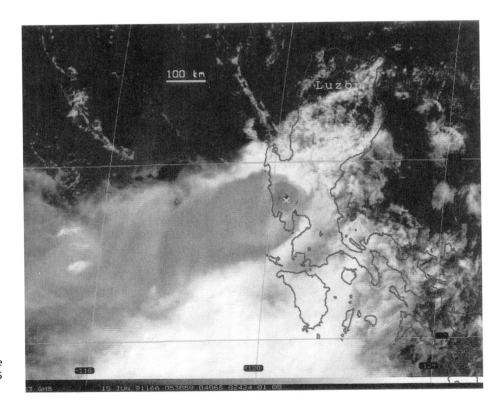

Mount Pinatubo. FIGURE 1. Japanese GMS Visible Wavelength Satellite Image of Top of Giant Umbrella Cloud Developing above Eruption Column of Mount Pinatubo on 15 June 1991. (After Self et al., 1996.)

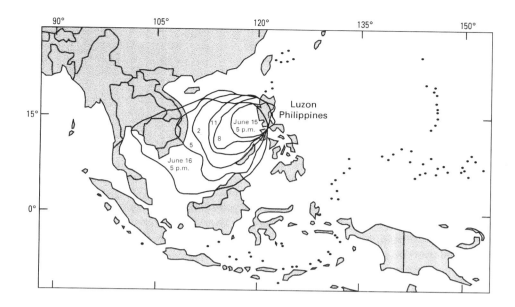

Mount Pinatubo. FIGURE 2. Spreading of Pinatubo Eruption Cloud as Derived from Japanese GMS Satellite Images at the Given Times (Philippine Local Time).

cloud that enveloped the Earth from the end of June 1991 to late 1993 was the largest since the rather larger-volume Krakatau eruption in late August 1883, which also produced an aerosol veil of global extent. In fact, the approximately 30-megaton Pinatubo stratospheric aerosol cloud may not have been significantly smaller than Krakatau's, variously estimated at between 30 and 50 megatons.

Formation of Stratospheric Aerosols. The high-altitude Pinatubo sulfur dioxide cloud began to spread rapidly and to oxidize, forming stratospheric sulfuric acid aerosols. Approximately half of the sulfur dioxide had been converted to sulfuric acid aerosol by about twenty-eight days after the eruption, and after two months 28 megatons of new aerosol was generated. These newly formed aerosol droplets grew to larger sizes by condensation of sulfuric acid and water vapor and by the coagulation process, leading to optical depth spectra that peaked at midvisible (greater than 500 nanometers) or longer wavelengths, starting about two months after the eruption. Optical depth, $\tau(\lambda)$, is a measure of the amount of solar radiation at a given wavelength (λ) that penetrates the atmosphere, providing an estimate of the amount of solid and liquid material suspended in the atmosphere. It is defined as the natural logarithm of the ratio of incident to transmitted direct beam radiation of wavelength λ, assuming vertical incidence. Over 90 percent of the particles collected from the volcanic clouds were composed of water and sulfuric acid in solution. Numerical modeling has reproduced

the observed microstructure and optical properties of the Pinatubo aerosols during the period of the formation and growth in the stratosphere.

Data from the U.S. National Oceanic and Atmospheric Administration (NOAA)-11 polar orbiting satellite revealed that the Pinatubo aerosol cloud encircled the entire Earth in twenty-one days, and had spread to 30° north latitude and 10° south latitude within the same period. The cloud resided mainly between 17 and 27 kilometers altitude. By mid-August 1991, the aerosol cloud covered 42 percent of the Earth's surface and the maximum mean optical depth at mid-visible wavelengths was 0.3, compared to a nonvolcanic background level of ~0.03.

After the first two to three months, the aerosol cloud slowly dispersed toward the polar regions for the next eight months. One reason why the bulk of the aerosol cloud was slow to penetrate to northern latitudes, thereby increasing the lifetime of the dense aerosol over tropical latitudes, was because it was located in the middle stratosphere above the zone affected by the quasibiennial oscillatory easterly shear that transports tropical aerosols polewards. By one year after the eruption, measurements of optical depth from satellite-borne instruments showed that the aerosol cloud had covered almost the entire globe. At this point, the concentration of aerosols decreased exponentially, again reaching background levels after about four years. [*See* Aerosols.]

Impact on Stratospheric Chemistry and Ozone. Sulfate aerosols in the stratosphere can catalyze heterogeneous reactions that affect global ozone abundance. These heterogeneous processes occurring on the surface of sulfate particles can convert stable chlorine reservoirs (such as HCl and $ClONO_2$) into photochemically active chlorine species (Cl_2, $ClNO_2$, $HOCl$) that destroy ozone. Increases in aerosol surface area after the

Pinatubo eruption had a considerable effect on global ozone. For example, reduced ozone concentrations with peak decreases as large as 20 percent at 16–25 kilometers in altitude were found in the tropical stratosphere as soon as September 1991. Up to a 6 percent reduction in equatorial total ozone was observed by satellite measurements by early 1992. At the time of maximum aerosol development, up to a 20 percent depletion in ozone was measured over Colorado and Hawaii, and midlatitude ozone abundance reached its lowest level on record during 1992–1993.

Startling decreases in ozone abundance and in rates of ozone destruction were also observed over Antarctica in 1991 and 1992. This ozone decrease may have been due in part to the presence of Pinatubo aerosols, but also to extra aerosols caused by the Mount Hudson eruption in Chile during August 1991. A sharp decrease in ozone at 9–11 kilometers in altitude (approximately at the tropopause) in the austral spring of 1991 was noted at the time of arrival of the Pinatubo and Mount Hudson aerosols. The Southern Hemisphere ozone hole increased in 1992 to an unprecedented 27 million square kilometers in size, and depletion rates were recorded to be faster than ever before. In late 1992, weather patterns caused a shift in the polar vortex, and warm ozone-rich tropical air entered the antarctic atmosphere to partially halt the ozone depletion. Ozone depletion after the Pinatubo eruption also caused an enhancement in the amount of biologically destructive ultraviolet (UV) radiation that reached the Earth's surface, and increases in UV were measured, especially in southern latitudes.

Effects on Temperature, Weather, and Climate. Radiative forcing of the climate system by stratospheric aerosols depends on the geographic distribution, altitude, size distribution, and optical depth of the aerosols. The optically dense Pinatubo aerosol cloud caused marked changes in the amount of radiation reaching the Earth's surface. These changes, in turn, affected weather and climate for up to four years after the eruption.

As observed after several eruptions, including Agung in 1963 and El Chichón in 1982, stratospheric warming and lower tropospheric and surface cooling were noticed after the Pinatubo eruption. Warming of up to 2°–3°C in the lower stratosphere at heights of 16–24 kilometers (equivalent to a pressure of 30–100 millibars) occurred within four to five months of the eruption between the equator and 20° north latitude, and was also later noticed in middle-northern latitudes. The distribution of warming closely mirrored the dispersal pattern of the aerosol cloud, strongly suggesting that the temperature increase was due to absorption of incoming solar radiation by the aerosols. The warming was more intense in southern temperate to polar latitudes, perhaps because of the presence of additional aerosols

from the Mount Hudson eruption. Since the peak of stratospheric warming in late 1991, temperatures in the 18- to 24-kilometer region cooled considerably, passing the average in early 1993. Stratospheric temperatures in late 1993 were the coldest ever recorded and may have been related to ozone destruction in the lower stratosphere. Stratospheric temperatures also plummeted and stayed cooler than average for seven years after the El Chichón eruption.

Several experiments measured the radiative climate forcing of the Pinatubo aerosols. The U.S. National Aeronautics and Space Administration (NASA) Earth Radiation Budget Experiment provided the first unambiguous direct measurement of large-scale climate forcing by an eruption, an average radiative cooling of 2.7 watts per square meter by August 1991. Direct solar beam reductions of 25–30 percent were measured at widely distributed surface stations, while satellite measurements suggested that the globally averaged net radiation at the top of the troposphere may have decreased by about 2.5 watts per square meter in late 1991. These values translated into a global cooling of at least 0.5°–0.7°C, as seen in the global and Northern Hemisphere temperature records.

A net cooling effect of approximately 0.3°C was estimated as a result of the El Chichón aerosol cloud, but the overall potential cooling caused by El Chichón was moderated by warming associated with the El Niño–Southern Oscillation. Pinatubo's cloud had a much larger radiative influence in the Southern Hemisphere than El Chichón's and caused about 1.7 times the global radiative forcing of the 1982 eruption. Warmer-than-average winters and cooler-than-average summers over continental Northern Hemisphere areas have been documented and modeled after several eruptions, including Pinatubo, and this appears to be part of the normal climatic response in the Northern Hemisphere after volcanic aerosol events.

Climate models appear to have predicted the Pinatubo-related cooling with a reasonable degree of accuracy. The interest in Pinatubo's atmospheric effects was both as a natural experiment and as a climatic perturbation. It allowed researchers to examine the changes in surface temperature and circulation that a large volcanic aerosol event can bring about—and it also offered validation of climate models. With a three-dimensional global circulation model, atmospheric scientists were able to predict the global cooling in 1991–1993 and then check their results against real surface temperature trends (Figure 3). Using a forcing in the model equivalent to a global mean optical depth of about 0.15, based on conditions appropriate for the Pinatubo aerosol cloud, a model radiative forcing at the tropopause of −4 watts per square meter was obtained. The maximum average cooling of up to 0.6°C by late

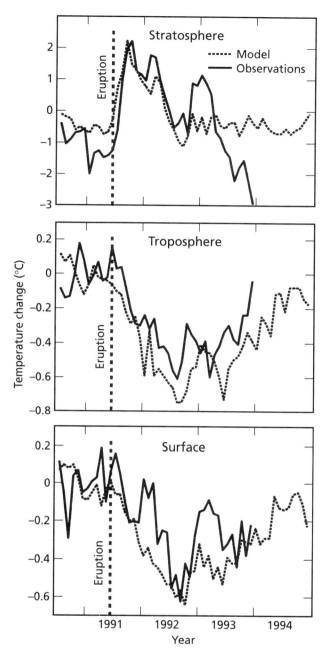

Mount Pinatubo. Figure 3. Observed and modeled monthly temperature change of the stratosphere, troposphere, and surface after the Mount Pinatubo eruption. Stratospheric observations are 30 millibar zonal mean temperature at 10° south latitude; model results are 10–70 millibar layer at 8–16° south latitude. Other results are essentially global, with observed surface temperature derived from a network of meteorological stations. The base period for tropospheric temperatures is 1978–1992, while troposphere and surface are referenced to the twelve months preceding the Pinatubo eruption, the latter marked by a vertical dashed line. (After Hansen et al., 1993.)

1992 over high-latitude land masses was in good agreement with the modeled cooling.

The superimposition of Pinatubo's aerosol-induced climatic effects on long- and short-term variable trends, such as El Niño–South Oscillation and greenhouse warming, led to speculation about the cooling effects on the current, late-twentieth-century warming trend. Global temperature trends show a gradual, unsteady rise from the mid-1970s to the present, perhaps due to forcing by greenhouse gases, and this rise led to record high temperatures in the early to mid-1990s. However, cooling after the Pinatubo eruption offset the warming trend considerably, such that cooler-than-normal conditions dominated the Northern Hemisphere. The Pinatubo climate forcing was stronger than the opposite-warming effects of either the El Niño event or anthropogenic greenhouse gases in the period from 1991 to 1993. [*See* Natural Climate Fluctuations.]

The Pinatubo aerosol cloud was, like that of El Chichón, coincident with sudden warming due to an El Niño event, but this warming event was not nearly as strong as in the El Chichón case. El Niño may have provided a warming of about 0.2°C, partially offsetting the Pinatubo-induced cooling in the tropics. Although there have been suggestions that the Pinatubo eruption triggered the 1991–1993 El Niño event, modeling suggests a coincidence rather than a cause-and-effect relationship between eruptions and El Niño.

The predicted and observed climatic cooling resulted in noticeable changes in the local climate and weather. For example, in 1992, the United States had its third coldest and third wettest summer in seventy-seven years. Floods along the Mississippi River in the summer of 1993 and drought in the Sahel area of Africa may be attributable to climatic shifts caused by the Pinatubo aerosols. Aerosol-induced cooling related to Pinatubo manifested itself globally in changing regional climate and weather patterns until about mid-1995.

[*See also* Global Warming; *and* Volcanoes.]

BIBLIOGRAPHY

Bhartia, P. K., et al. "Effect of Mount Pinatubo Aerosols on Total Ozone Measurements from Backscatter Ultraviolet (BUV) Experiments." *Journal of Geophysical Research* 98 (1993), 18547–18554.

Bluth, G. J. S., et al. "Global Tracking of the SO_2 Clouds from the June 1991 Mount Pinatubo Eruptions." *Geophysical Research Letters* 19 (1992), 151–154.

Brasseur, G. "Ozone Depletion: Volcanic Aerosols Implicated." *Nature* 359 (1992), 275–276.

Deshler, T., et al. "Volcanic Aerosol and Ozone Depletion within the Antarctic Polar Vortex during the Austral Spring of 1991." *Geophysical Research Letters* 19 (1992), 1819–1822.

Hansen, J., et al. "Potential Climate Impact of the Mount Pinatubo Eruption." *Geophysical Research Letters* 19 (1992), 215–218.

———. "How Sensitive Is the World's Climate?" *National Geographic Research and Exploration* 9 (1993), 143–158.

————. "Global Surface Air Temperature in 1995: Return to Pre-Pinatubo Level." *Geophysical Research Letters* 23 (1996), 1665–1668.

Hofmann, D. J., et al. "Ozone Loss in the Lower Stratosphere over the United States in 1992–1993: Evidence for Heterogeneous Chemistry of the Pinatubo Aerosol." *Geophysical Research Letters* 21 (1994a), 65–68.

————. "Record Low Ozone at the South Pole in the Spring of 1993: Evidence for Heterogeneous Chemistry of the Pinatubo Aerosol." *Geophysical Research Letters* 21 (1994b), 421–424.

McCormick, M. P., et al. "Atmospheric Effects of the Mt. Pinatubo Eruption." *Nature* 373 (1994), 399–404.

Minnis, P., et al. "Radiative Climate Forcing by the Mount Pinatubo Eruption." *Science* 259 (1993), 1411–1415.

Prather, M. "Catastrophic Loss of Stratospheric Ozone in Dense Volcanic Clouds." *Journal of Geophysical Research* 97 (1992), 10187–10191.

Self, S., et al. "The Atmospheric Impact of the Mount Pinatubo Eruption." In *Fire and Mud: Eruptions and Lahars of Mount Pinatubo, Philippines*, edited by C. G. Newhall and R. S. Punongbayan, pp. 1089–1115. Quezon City, Philippines and Seattle: Philippine Institute of Volcanology and Seismology and University of Washington Press, 1996.

Solomon, S., et al. "Increased Chlorine Dioxide over Antarctica Caused by Volcanic Aerosols from Mount Pinatubo." *Nature* 363 (1993), 245–248.

Tabazadeh, A., and R. P. Turco. "Stratospheric Chlorine Injection by Volcanic Eruptions: Hydrogen Chloride Scavenging and Implications for Ozone." *Science* 20 (1993), 1082–1086.

Trepte, C., et al. "The Poleward Dispersal of Mount Pinatubo Aerosol." *Journal of Geophysical Research* 98 (1993), 18563–18573.

Vogelmann, A. M., et al. "Enhancements in Biologically Effective Ultraviolet Radiation Following Volcanic Eruptions." *Nature* 359 (1992), 47–49.

—STEPHEN SELF

MULTILATERAL FUND

The Multilateral Fund, established in 1990, provides funding and technical assistance to developing countries to meet their obligations under the Montreal Protocol on Substances the Deplete the Ozone Layer. It is the first funding mechanism to be included in a global environmental agreement, and is widely regarded as setting a precedent for funding transfers between developed and developing countries for environmental protection. It also represented an instance in which developing countries were able to gain leverage in international negotiations because of the importance of their involvement in the process of environmental protection. They would not participate in the ozone layer protection process until they were guaranteed assistance and decision-making power. [*See* Ozone.]

After vague promises in the 1987 Montreal Protocol that developing countries would be given financial and technical assistance to meet their obligations failed to convince most countries to join, the parties negotiated a provision for a funding mechanism as part of the 1990 London Amendments to the Protocol. Under Article 5, developing countries whose annual consumption of controlled substances is below 0.3 kilograms per capita are eligible for financial assistance. Funding is contributed by those developed countries with an initial annual consumption of ozone-depleting substances of more than 0.3 kilograms per capita, based on the United Nations scale of assessments. Developed countries may provide part of their contribution to the fund through bilateral programs.

The Fund has an independent secretariat based in Montreal. Decisions on funding allocation are made by an Executive Committee composed of seven Article 5 countries and seven non-Article 5 countries, each elected for three-year terms. Decisions are made by consensus when possible and otherwise by a two-thirds majority vote that must comprise a majority of both developed and developing countries.

Four agencies—the United Nations Environment Programme, the United Nations Development Programme, the United Nations Industrial Development Organization, and the World Bank—implement projects in Article 5 countries. Recipients first undertake a Country Study in which they determine their use of ozone-depleting substances and create a strategy for phaseout. The implementing agencies propose specific projects for strengthening of institutions, technical assistance, demonstration, and investment. Funding is based on incremental costs; those costs of shifting to non-ozone-depleting substances and processes that do not give any direct return for the expenditure.

By the middle of 1997, the Multilateral Fund had allocated upwards of U.S.$1 billion for more than one thousand activities. China has received the most funding, followed by India and Argentina. When currently approved projects have been implemented, at least 84,000 metric tons of ozone-depleting substances in Article 5 countries will have been phased out, accounting for more than 40 percent of their consumption of these substances.

Difficulties the Multilateral Fund has faced include slowness of project implementation, lateness in contribution of funds by developed countries, and disagreement over how to calculate incremental costs. The Secretariat and Executive Committee have made progress in addressing these problems, and have focused on increasing the cost-effectiveness of projects and increasing the speed of phaseout activities.

[*See also* Montreal Protocol.]

BIBLIOGRAPHY

Bowser, R. "History of the Montreal Protocol's Ozone Fund." *International Environmental Reporter* (November 21, 1991).

DeSombre, E. R., and J. Kauffman. "The Montreal Protocol Multilateral Fund: Partial Success Story." In *Institutions for Environmental Aid*, edited by R. O. Keohane and M. A. Levy. Cambridge: MIT Press, 1996.

United States General Accounting Office. *International Environ-*

ment: Operations of the Montreal Protocol Multilateral Fund. GAO/T-RCED-97–218, July 30, 1997. United States GAO Documents are available free of charge from the GAO. This report consists of testimony to Congress on the activities of the Fund, and contains data about contributions and expenditures that are otherwise difficult to find.

—Elizabeth R. DeSombre

MULTINATIONAL ENTERPRISES

In the half-century following the end of World War II, most of the world's large business firms outside the socialist world underwent a metamorphosis in structure that transformed them from national entities to multinational enterprises. In the beginning of that half-century, a few hundred large firms, engaged largely in oil production, mining, and manufacturing and headquartered mainly in the United States and Europe, had already displayed some of the characteristics of a multinational enterprise by acquiring subsidiaries outside their home base. By the close of the century, thousands of large firms had acquired a network of producing subsidiaries and affiliates located in foreign countries and usually organized as corporations under the respective laws of those countries. In most cases, notwithstanding that they had been created under the laws of a number of different countries, the parent and its subsidiaries shared a common strategy and drew on a common pool of technology, management, and capital to achieve their goals. Networks of that kind, operating under such names as Toyota, Siemens, IBM, and Coca-Cola, are referred to variously as multinational enterprises, multinational corporations, and transnational corporations. (The focus here is on commercial enterprises, although other enterprises, such as nonprofit public interest groups, increasingly display similar multinational characteristics.)

Nevertheless, the definition of a multinational enterprise remains imprecise in a number of respects. How is one to classify an enterprise, for example, whose foreign activities are insignificant compared with its activities at home? Or an enterprise that conducts its foreign activities through contracts or franchises rather than through affiliates in which it holds an ownership interest? Or one that shares the ownership of a subsidiary with another enterprise? Because of such uncertainties, estimates of the number and scope of multinational enterprises vary widely. Using U.S. criteria for the classification of such enterprises, one would place their aggregate global number in the neighborhood of ten thousand; but some countries, using criteria of their own, report much higher numbers. The United Nations (1997, p. 6), basing its figures on country reports, records global totals of 44,508 parent firms and 276,659 foreign affiliates; but many of the numbers so reported are so high as to appear *prima facie* implausible.

Like other data purporting to measure the activities

of multinational enterprises, data on the aggregate investments of the multinational enterprises in their foreign subsidiaries are subject to considerable margins of error. But such enterprises are so highly concentrated in size that a few enterprises account for most of the global activity. Indeed, among U.S.-based multinationals, the five hundred enterprises with the largest foreign holdings were reported as accounting for 95 percent of the total foreign holdings of all U.S. firms (Dunning, 1992).

The advanced industrialized nations have been especially prominent as both home country and host country for the units of multinational enterprises. The estimates of the United Nations place about three-quarters of all such investments within the advanced industrialized countries. It is not surprising, therefore, that the parents and subsidiaries of multinational enterprises occupy a dominant position in the national economies of such countries. The 3,400 firms that are identified in U.S. data as parents of an international network, for instance, accounted for about 60 percent of the country's industrial output during the 1990s, while foreign-owned subsidiaries in the United States, coming mainly from Europe and Japan, contributed more than 10 percent to such U.S. output. All told, these member units of multinational networks were responsible for over 80 percent of the merchandise exports of the United States.

Practically all estimates of the activities of multinationals in the global economy showed signs of rapid increase during the 1980s and 1990s. Foreign-owned subsidiaries were increasing in number and were taking on more of the functions previously reserved largely to their parents, such as exporting and research. During the later 1980s and the first years of the 1990s, according to United Nations estimates, the sales of these subsidiaries grew much more rapidly than did the world's foreign trade, and far exceeded such foreign trade in total (United Nations, 1995, p. 37).

Nevertheless, possibly as a result of the increasing importance of the foreign subsidiaries in multinational networks, the place of parent firms engaged in manufacturing in their home economies may have peaked or even declined in the 1990s. Indeed, in the United States—the only country providing the relevant data—parent firms had begun to lose their relative position in the national economy even earlier. But, at the same time, the subsidiaries of foreign parents engaged in manufacturing in the United States were expanding their relative positions in the U.S. economy, offsetting the decline in the position of the U.S. parents (see Table 1).

By the 1990s, in spite of their limited number, the parents and subsidiaries making up the world's multinational enterprises had come to account for a major part of the world's output of goods and services, as well as a major part of the international flow of goods, services, capital, and technology. For the world as a whole, back-of-the-envelope extrapolations of the incomplete data

Multinational Enterprises. TABLE 1. Shares (Percentages) Contributed to United States Gross Product in Manufacturing

YEAR	U.S.-BASED PARENT FIRMS	FOREIGN-OWNED SUBSIDIARIES IN THE UNITED STATES	TOTAL
1977	68.8	3.4	72.2
1982	65.7	7.4	73.1
1989	61.1	11.3	72.4
1994	57.6	13.2	70.8

SOURCES: Various publications of the U.S. Department of Commerce.

suggest that, in the 1990s, multinational enterprises accounted for about half of the world's international trade in goods and only a little less of the world's total merchandise output. The figures for multinational enterprises in services such as banking, telecommunications, and retail trade would be much lower; but there were signs that multinational enterprises were enlarging their role in these activities as well.

The Developing World. Although North America, Europe, and Japan dominate as both the home and host countries for multinational enterprises, such enterprises have had profound effects on the rest of the world as well. Their impact has been particularly strong because developing nations and those that were once part of the Soviet empire have drawn heavily on the technology and expertise of multinational enterprises to support their industrialization policies. To be sure, some firms in these countries have matured to the point at which they have created their own multinational networks; the United Nations (1997) reports fifty multinational enterprises with headquarters in developing countries, most of them with enterprise assets of several billion dollars. The extent to which countries in Africa, Latin America, and Asia have relied on multinationals for their industrialization programs has varied enormously from one country to the next. While Singapore has reported that 70 percent of its manufacturing output was in the hands of foreign-owned firms, Thailand has reported a comparable figure of only 15 percent and Taiwan a figure of 10 percent (Vernon, 1998, Tables 1–6). Figures for Latin American countries, when reported, have usually fallen between these extremes. [See Economic Levels.]

In spite of such differences, leaders in practically every country in the developing world have at times linked the problems created by the industrialization process with the presence of the multinational enterprise, including environmental degradation, congestion, urbanization, rootlessness, and crime. The propensity to make that connection has varied from one country to the next, depending in part on the history of the country's relationships with such enterprises.

One factor in the linkage between environmental degradation and multinational enterprises is the technical character of the principal industries involved, which commonly require advanced technologies and high capital investments. These requirements often discourage local investors and create opportunities for multinational enterprises. A United Nations study of foreign direct investment classifies the production of chemicals, pulp and paper, petroleum and coal products, and metals as pollution intensive. These industries, according to the study, have typically accounted for one-quarter to two-thirds of the investments of multinationals in foreign countries (United Nations, 1992).

On the whole, however, academic studies find little evidence of a tendency of multinationals in these industries to seek out production locations in an effort to escape strict antipollution regulations (see, for example, Markusen, 1997). Investments of multinational enterprises in the pollutant-prone industries have been primarily in other advanced industrialized countries, and they have not shown any undue clustering in developing countries. Occasionally, some egregious cases of pollution have been detected. But the United Nations study concludes, "The general impression is that, because of their visibility, resources, and access to clean 'off-the-shelf' technology, large TNCs (multinational enterprises) may have better records than local firms, that they may be more interested in environmental protection than their local joint-venture partners and that small- and medium-size firms, whether foreign or local, have the worst record." (United Nations, 1992, p. 234). The experience of eastern Germany and other remnants of the Soviet empire with the destructive practices of state-owned enterprises has also tended to cast multinational enterprises in the pollution-prone industries in a more favorable light.

[See also Chemical Industry; Fossil Fuels; Global Economy; Manufacturing; Metals; Mining; Policy Analysis; Technology; and Trade and Environment.]

BIBLIOGRAPHY

Dunning, J. H. *Multinational Enterprises and the Global Economy.* Wokingham, U.K.: Addison Wesley, 1992, pp. 14–53. A statistical overview of the place of multinational enterprises in the global economy.

Markusen, J. R. "Costly Pollution Abatement, Competitiveness and Plant Location Decisions." *Resource and Energy Economics* 19.4 (November 1997), 299–320.

United Nations. *World Investment Report 1992.* Geneva, 1992, pp. 232, 234. Summarizes a series of studies conducted by public and private agencies.

———. *World Investment Report 1995.* Geneva, 1995, p. 37.

———. *World Investment Report 1997.* Geneva, 1997, pp. 32–33.

Vernon, R. *In the Hurricane's Eye: The Troubled Prospects of Multinational Enterprises.* Cambridge: Harvard University Press, 1998.

—RAYMOND VERNON

N

NATIONAL PARKS. *See* Wilderness.

NATURAL CLIMATE FLUCTUATIONS

The climate varies naturally on all time scales, from a few weeks to millions of years [*See* Climate Change.] Some of these fluctuations are caused by factors outside the climate system, such as volcanic eruptions, variations in the Earth's orbit around the sun, or even, on the longest time scales, tectonic variations in the positions of the continents. Others are generated internally by interactions within and between the various components of the climate system, including the atmosphere, oceans, biosphere, and cryosphere.

Most of the variability on time scales up to a century in any climate record can generally be attributed to a process so simple that it is debatable whether it should be referred to as a fluctuation in the climate at all. This is the effect of "accumulated weather noise" (Hasselmann, 1976). To understand how it works, and why it is questionable whether it should be referred to as a source of climate variability, we first have to go back to the definition of *climate* itself. *Climate* is often loosely defined as the average weather for a particular time of year. What is often misunderstood is that "average," in this definition, has a very specific meaning. It does not mean the average over a particular year, or even the average over a number of successive years. It means an average taken over all possible years with the same governing "boundary conditions" (factors that control the climate, including large-scale patterns of ocean circulation, ice extent, and solar parameters).

A more precise definition of *climate*, therefore, is the "expected" weather, along with its expected variability, for a given set of boundary conditions. Suppose we had a perfect climate model and perfect knowledge of the boundary conditions and were able to perform an infinitely large ensemble of simulations of a particular year. Each member of the ensemble would be different from every other, owing to the unpredictable and chaotic nature of weather, but they would also have much in common. This common component, the ensemble average, is the expected weather for these particular boundary conditions. This, together with the way in which individual members vary about the ensemble average, defines the climate. A useful analogy is to think of the individual simulations, or "possible weathers," as pieces of string that are all tangled up in a ball. Each piece of string is different from every other, but they all lie in the same ball. The climate defines the position and shape of that ball.

The important implication of this more rigorous definition of *climate* is that the average weather in a particular month or season can be very different from one year to the next without implying any change in the climate. These essentially unpredictable fluctuations in the weather affect the ocean: strong winds, for example, mix surface waters with cooler waters below, reducing sea surface temperatures. When the winds die, ocean temperatures do not recover immediately: the influence of the strongest winter storms is detectable in the thermal structure of the midlatitude oceans for a year or more (Frankignoul, 1985). Sea surface temperatures therefore vary like a system with a significant inertia (set by the heat capacity of the near-surface ocean) that is subjected to a continuous series of unpredictable shocks (heating and cooling due to weather events). In such a system, low-frequency fluctuations tend to be larger than high-frequency ones, leading to the term *red noise*, since low frequencies dominate red light. If there is only a single inertial time scale, two parameters are enough to describe this kind of red-noise behavior. One sets the average size of the heating and cooling perturbations, the other sets the time scale over which temperature fluctuations dissipate. Together, these determine the overall level of variability and the extent to which variability is concentrated toward low frequencies.

Fluctuations in sea surface temperature in turn feed back onto the atmosphere by heating or cooling the air above them, making this a remarkably accurate description of seasonal to centennial variability in a whole range of climate indicators. For example, the central England temperature (CET) series is one of the longest climate records available based primarily on instrumental observations, extending back almost to the invention of the thermometer. The dotted line in the upper panel of Figure 1 shows annual mean temperatures from the CET series after subtracting the 335-year average, and the solid line shows a ten-year running average. Large fluctuations are visible on decadal and interdecadal time scales, and a naive analyst might be tempted to seek mechanistic explanations of these fluctuations in terms of external influences or internally generated oscillations. Similar fluctuations are, however, equally visible in the output of a simple, two-parameter red-noise model (lower panel of Figure 1) that, by construction, supports no real trends or oscillations. If we compare

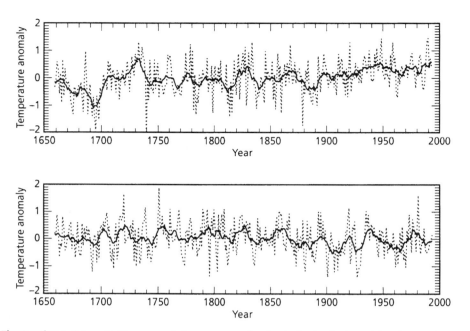

Natural Climate Fluctuations. FIGURE 1. Upper panel: time series of annual-mean near-surface air temperatures in central England from 1658 to 1993, based primarily on instrumental observations augmented with diary reports in the earliest decades. Solid line: ten-year running average. Lower panel: sample output of a simple "red-noise" model and ten-point running average. Notice how "decadal" and "interdecadal" fluctuations feature in both series, indicating the danger of interpreting any such fluctuation in terms of oscillations.

the power spectrum of the CET series (Figure 2, solid line) with the range of spectra we would expect from red noise, the agreement is remarkably good over a wide range of time scales. The gray band in Figure 2 shows the 95 percent range for the noise spectra. On time scales less than a century, the CET series remains within this interval over more than 95 percent of frequencies, indicating it could have been generated by just such a red-noise process.

Red-noise variability involves no change in the factors governing the expected weather; given our more rigorous definition, it probably should not be referred to as a climate fluctuation at all. Many of the climate trends and oscillations that have been reported in the literature on the basis of analyses of climate records have turned out, on closer inspection, to be equally explicable as red noise (Burroughs, 1992). Because red noise is exactly what we should expect from a system with a large heat capacity subjected to essentially random heating and cooling by the weather, this represents the simplest logical explanation of any climate variable. It must, therefore, be considered before any more complex theories involving internal or externally generated oscillations are entertained.

The remainder of this entry catalogs some of the aspects of climate variability that depart from this simple model. The climate is a complex system, so it is not surprising that it does occasionally deviate from a simple,

two-parameter noise process. What is often remarkable, however, is how small these departures are. Even on the time scales associated with the various oscillations detailed below, the red-noise "background" variability (which would be there even if the oscillation were absent) is often stronger than any variability due to the oscillation. This has important practical implications: one

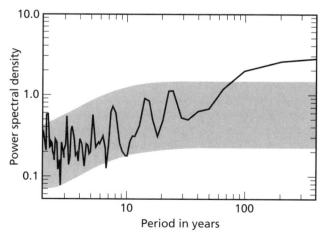

Natural Climate Fluctuations. FIGURE 2. Power spectrum of central England temperature (CET) series (solid line) compared with the 95 percent range of spectra expected from the simple red-noise model (gray band). On interannual to century time scales, the CET series is remarkably consistent with this simple model.

of the key reasons for interest in climate oscillations is that they raise the prospect of medium-range climate prediction. If an oscillation is genuine and persistent, we may be able to predict its evolution over one or two cycles in the future. Any such prediction will, however, be practically useless if the predictable signal is dominated by unpredictable noise.

The catalog, which is by no means complete, is arranged roughly in order of ascending time scale, beginning with one year. A number of subannual time-scale oscillations have been reported, the most prominent being the forty- to sixty-day period Madden-Julian oscillation in tropical circulation and convection. These, however, are generally accepted as being generated internally by the atmosphere and so, by our definition, should be regarded as examples of weather variability rather than climate fluctuations. We have focused on fluctuations that have some sort of preferred time scale associated with them, but these are by no means the only sources of climate variability. Random events such as large volcanic eruptions and asteroid impacts can have a significant impact on climate, but these are normally considered in terms of probabilities rather than specific time scales.

The Annual Cycle. The annual march of the seasons is the strongest cyclic component of almost any climate variable and is generally thought of as a component of the climate itself rather than a climate oscillation. Because, however, there is more energy in the climate system at the period of the annual cycle than at any other time scale out to hundreds of millions of years, no other mode of climate variability can be understood without it. The wintertime storm season in midlatitudes and the explosive development of the tropical monsoons act effectively to "erase the memory" of all but a few components of the climate system every year. Information can be carried over from one year to the next in only a few, relatively simple, forms, such as the heat content of the upper ocean over a large area. Subtle details of the state of the climate system during the previous year are wiped out, limiting the number of mechanisms available to drive internal climate oscillations on interannual time scales. This partly explains why the low-frequency spectra of so many climate variables are relatively uninteresting and why year-to-year climate prediction continues to prove so elusive.

While the length of the year may seem the least controversial aspect of the climate system, it is in fact more complicated than it seems. The average length of the annual cycle is determined by the time from solstice to solstice, when the axis of the Earth's rotation tilts toward the Sun, which is the familiar 365.25 days. The Earth, however, is in an elliptical orbit that is processing slowly under the gravitational influence of Jupiter, so the timing of *perihelion* (the point of closest approach to the Sun) advances by a fraction of a day every year. While the tilt in the Earth's axis determines how solar energy is distributed over the planet, it is the distance from the Sun that determines the total energy incident at the top of the atmosphere. Controversial evidence suggests that some aspects of the climate system may temporarily follow the perihelion year for up to several centuries, leading the timing of midwinter and midsummer to drift around by a week or two (Thomson, 1995). What is less controversial is that the 22,000-year cycle over which the solstice and perihelion years move in and out of phase with each other plays a significant role in the Pleistocene ice-age cycles (Berger, 1980).

The Stratospheric Quasi-Biennial Oscillation (QBO). The main manifestation of the stratospheric QBO is a 2- to 2.5-year oscillation in the equatorial jet in the lower stratosphere (Angell, 1988). The QBO is by far the most regular internally generated oscillation in the climate system. Strictly speaking, however, it is an internal atmospheric phenomenon and thus should perhaps be regarded as a feature of stratospheric weather rather than as a climate oscillation. Winds at high altitudes (between twenty-three and thirty kilometers) near the equator below alternately eastward and westward, reversing approximately every twenty-seven months. The QBO is caused by atmospheric waves, primarily originating from energetic convection events in the troposphere, propagating up into the stratosphere. As these waves dissipate, they deposit their energy in a different form and at different altitudes according to the strength and direction of the equatorial stratospheric winds. Thus at a given altitude, the upgoing wave energy acts alternately to reinforce these equatorial winds or, at another point in the quasi-biennial cycle, to reverse them.

The influence of the QBO permeates the entire stratosphere. One practical consequence is that it affects the dynamics of the stratospheric polar vortex and thus the springtime distribution of stratospheric ozone (Baldwin and Dunkerton, 1998). The QBO is thus essential to understanding and interpreting ozone trends and ozone-depletion mechanisms. The influence of the QBO on the surface and lower troposphere is less clear. Most current atmospheric general circulation models do not have enough resolution in the equatorial stratosphere to display a QBO, but this does not appear to preclude an otherwise reasonable simulation of present-day climate or seriously impair their use in weather prediction. It is generally accepted that the stratospheric QBO is unrelated to biennial variability in the Asian monsoon and El Niño–Southern Oscillation (ENSO). [*See* El Niño–Southern Oscillation.]

Biennial Variability in the Asian Monsoon. There is some tentative evidence of a weak two-year cycle (almost certainly generated internally by the climate system) in the strength of the Asian monsoon. This is the large-scale weather system that brings a season of heavy rain once per year to the Indian subcontinent and Far Eastern countries and (at a different time of year) to northeastern Australia. The two-year cycle is a slight bias toward a relatively weak monsoon following a relatively strong one and vice versa (Lau and Yang, 1996). The origin of this effect remains unclear. Two components of the climate system, both of which have been related to the strength of the monsoon, might provide the necessary year-on-year "memory." One is the depth and extent of Eurasian wintertime snow cover, whose influence might persist from one year to the next through its residual impact on soil moisture conditions. The other is the subsurface temperature structure of the tropical oceans (Meehl, 1997), possibly related to the ENSO phenomenon. Biennial variability in the Asian monsoon appears to be unrelated to the stratospheric QBO. Convincing evidence of a clear physical mechanism underlying any two-year cycle in the monsoon remains elusive, part of the reason probably being the extreme weakness of the signal: random or chaotic fluctuations in monsoon strength far outweigh any biennial cycle.

The El Niño–Southern Oscillation Phenomenon. After the annual cycle, ENSO is probably the most energetic, and certainly the best known, mode of climate variability. The recent exceptionally strong El Niño events in 1982–1983 and 1997–1998 both caused substantial climatic anomalies, socioeconomic disruption, and ecological devastation worldwide. ENSO is an internally generated fluctuation of the climate system that arises out of interactions between the tropical oceans and tropical atmosphere (Philander, 1990). In a normal year, winds blow from east to west (easterly) along the equator in the tropical Pacific, feeding into a region of intense convection over Indonesia (the wettest area of the world) and providing part of the "Walker circulation." This, by a process known as "Ekman transport," displaces surface waters in the eastern Pacific northward and southward away from the equator, drawing up and exposing colder water beneath them. The resulting "equatorial cold tongue" extends from the South American coast up to two-thirds of the way to the Date Line.

Equatorial sea surface temperatures (SSTs) in a normal year are therefore up to 8°C colder in the eastern Pacific than in the west. Since relatively high SSTs in the western Pacific are part of the reason convection occurs over Indonesia in the first place, these normal conditions are self-reinforcing. Convection drives an atmospheric circulation, which creates an east-west equatorial SST gradient, which in turn reinforces the conditions responsible for that convection. A self-reinforcing system, however, can also reinforce its own ter-

mination, which is what happens during an El Niño event.

Every three to ten years, through a sequence of events that is still not completely understood, the normal east-west SST gradient along the equator is suppressed, drawing the center of atmospheric convection out into the mid-Pacific and often creating drought conditions in Australia and Indonesia. The usual equatorial easterly winds become much weaker and may even reverse, reducing the strength of the cold tongue and allowing warmer waters to spread even further across the Pacific (Bjerknes, 1972). The first obvious manifestation of an El Niño event is often the appearance of unusually warm waters off the coast of Peru, typically around late December—hence the name El Niño, or the Christ Child. These signals appear at the eastern side of the basin, but their origin can often be traced back to wind "bursts" (lasting up to ten days) in the far western Pacific. These wind bursts induce subsurface "Kelvin waves" that propagate slowly along the equator, taking about two months to traverse the Pacific basin and altering the temperature conditions in the east when they arrive.

Although wreaking havoc in the fishing industry, these warmer waters bring rain to many Peruvian desert regions that are completely dry under normal conditions. Eastern Pacific SSTs, which normally rise by about 5°C during the September to March period, instead rise by up to double that amount. Abnormally warm conditions persist for the remainder of that calendar year, typically returning to normal early in the following year. In exceptional cases, such as the "extended" events in the 1940s and early 1990s, El Niño conditions can persist over two or more seasonal cycles.

The dynamics of these subsurface waves and their interactions with the atmosphere are relatively well understood. Thus, through a combination of computer models and intensive monitoring of subsurface temperatures across the entire equatorial Pacific, it is now possible to predict the evolution of an El Niño event several months ahead once it is under way. Reliable year-on-year prediction of the occurrence of an El Niño remains elusive, because it is still not clear what sets the preferred recurrence time. A simple hypothesis is that the "reservoir" of warm water in the western Pacific takes time to "recharge" after an El Niño event. Every year, therefore, there is a chance that the passage the annual cycle will trigger an El Niño, but the probability of its doing so tends to increase the longer the time interval from the previous event. This idea was first suggested by Wyrtki in 1985 and remains as good an explanation as any of the observed record of tropical Pacific variability. Many more-complicated mechanisms have been suggested since, often involving multiple reflections of subsurface waves on either side of the Pacific basin, to explain ENSO-like oscillations in coupled ocean-atmosphere models (e.g., Neelin et al., 1998).

The standard indicator of the current state of ENSO is the Southern Oscillation Index (SOI), based on the difference in sea level pressure between Tahiti (in the eastern Pacific) and Darwin (in the west). [*See the biography of Walker.*] A high positive SOI means that surface pressures are relatively high in the eastern Pacific, forcing easterly winds along the equator, which are associated with low eastern Pacific surface temperatures. A strong negative SOI implies the reverse (El Niño) conditions.

The power spectrum of the SOI is shown in Figure 3, along with the expected spectrum from a red-noise process. The SOI emerges from the red-noise range at periods around two and five years, which has led to speculation about possible multiple frequencies in ENSO (Rasmusson et al., 1990). The simplest explanation of the two-year "component" of ENSO (which appears to be related to biennial monsoon variability) is, however, that El Niño events typically last about a year, which introduces power at two years into any ENSO-related spectrum. Notice, in conclusion, how small the departures from red noise are, despite this being the strongest known example of an internally generated climate oscillation.

Decadal and Interdecadal Variability in Midlatitudes. Large-scale oceanic and atmospheric variability in the midlatitudes is generally more complicated and chaotic than in the tropics. Together with the "memory-erasing" effect of the annual cycle, this acts against any predictable or periodic interannual to interdecadal variability. Almost all midlatitude climate indicators therefore conform closely to the simple red-noise spectrum

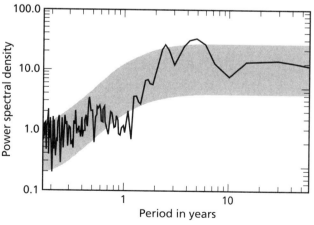

Natural Climate Fluctuations. Figure 3. Power spectrum of quarterly Southern Oscillation Index (SOI) compared with the range of spectra expected from the simple red noise model. Small departures above the noise range occur at two- and five-year periods, indicating the approximate time scales of the El Niño phenomenon.

that we would expect if random fluctuations in the atmosphere are driving more sluggish changes in the ocean (Frankignoul, 1985).

The absence of any preferred time scale does not necessarily mean these midlatitude regions are completely unpredictable. Signals may persist in the thermocline region of the ocean (immediately below the surface wind-mixed layer), being transported by ocean currents and subsurface waves. Thus conditions in one region may provide information about conditions elsewhere several years later, without either region being particularly predictable on its own.

There are a few regions outside the tropical Pacific where the ocean displays a weak preference for a particular time scale, the most prominent being the subtropical *gyres*. These are basin-scale patterns of clockwise flow generated by the prevailing winds, spanning both the Atlantic and Pacific basins between latitudes 20°N and 45°N. Through a combination of subsurface waves (primarily westward-propagating *Rossby waves*) and ocean currents, temperature signals typically take ten to twenty years to circulate around the Atlantic subtropical gyre and about twenty to forty years to circulate around the larger gyre in the Pacific (Latif and Barnett, 1994). This introduces a weak kind of "resonance" into the system on these periods, leading to small departures from the simple red-noise spectrum.

Whether this ten- to twenty-year (Atlantic) and twenty- to forty-year (Pacific) variability has any significant influence on the atmosphere remains controversial. Decadal and interdecadal variability is evident in such atmospheric indicators as the North Atlantic Oscillation (NAO) and, less prominently, in the Pacific North America (PNA) pattern. Simply because the atmosphere is very unlikely to have a strong enough memory on its own to sustain a decadal oscillation, interactions with the ocean provide the most plausible explanation. The PNA pattern, which is associated with weather conditions across Canada and the United States, is strongly influenced by ENSO, although there is some evidence that it may also react to interdecadal variability in the North Pacific. The NAO is linked to the orientation and strength of the belt of westerly winds across the North Atlantic. The high NAO index values that prevailed from the late 1980s to the mid-1990s, for example, implied warm, wet winters in northern Europe and drier conditions around the Mediterranean. The influence of ENSO on the NAO is somewhat weaker, and decadal oceanic variability in the North Atlantic may have contributed to these long-lived NAO fluctuations.

Various, more complex mechanisms for interdecadal variability have also been put forward involving, for example, interactions between sea ice, the arctic and subpolar oceanic gyres, oceanic convection, meteorological conditions in the far North Atlantic, and so on (Deser

THE NORTH ATLANTIC OSCILLATION

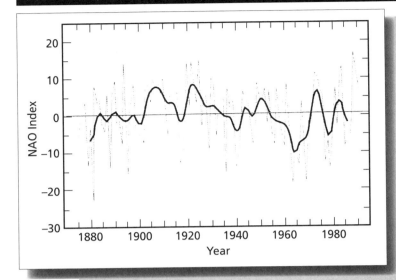

Time series of the winter index of the North Atlantic Oscillation (NAO; light line), obtained by subtracting the mean pressure departure in Iceland from that over the Azores. The year on the x-axis denotes the end of the winter season. The binomially filtered index values (bold line) represent low-frequency variations in the NAO. (Reprinted with permission from Hurrell, 1995. Copyright 1995 American Association for the Advancement of Science.)

The North Atlantic Oscillation (NAO), first named and described by Sir Gilbert Walker in the 1920s, is the alternation of atmospheric mass between the subpolar and subtropical portions of the North Atlantic. It is characterized by variations in the regional sea level pressure gradient, sea surface temperatures, and the midlatitude westerly winds.

The positive mode of the NAO is where the Azores subtropical high is anomalously strong, while the Icelandic low is simultaneously very deep. The Atlantic westerlies are then abnormally strong, and warm surface ocean water and mild air masses advect northeastward across the Atlantic toward Europe and the Atlantic Arctic. Western Greenland and Labrador are unusually cold, and large amounts of sea ice may be transported southward from Davis Strait.

In the negative mode of the NAO, the two pressure centers are both anomalously weak. The Icelandic low is displaced to the southwest, near Newfoundland, while atmospheric blocking patterns occur in the flow aloft and polar anticyclones push southward over the eastern Atlantic and Europe. The winters of this mode are comparatively mild in Greenland, but they are unusually severe in northern and western Europe (e.g., the winters of 1941–1944, 1962–1963, and 1968–1969). It has been argued that the negative model of the NAO is a good analogue to the atmospheric circulation that prevailed during both the European Little Ice Age, from about 1450–1850, and the last ice-age glacial maximum at around eighteen thousand years ago. The winter index of the NAO varies on an approximately biennial basis when one considers a run of years, but it also shows some variability from decade to decade.

BIBLIOGRAPHY

Hurrell, J. W. "Decadal Trends in the North Atlantic Oscillation: Regional Temperatures and Precipitation." *Science* 269 (1995), 676–679.

—ANDREW S. GOUDIE

and Blackmon, 1993). Most of the evidence for these mechanisms is, however, based on climate models. Largely because of the shortness of the available records, there is little compelling evidence for their operating in the real world.

Unlike the tropical ENSO signal, in which atmospheric conditions are completely different from normal during an El Niño year, any decadal signal in midlatitudes is much weaker than the unpredictable year-to-year fluctuations. Storms may be slightly more probable in a particular year relative to five years previously, but it might take several decades to tease any signal out of the noise. Even a weak signal can, however, have important practical consequences. Insurance companies typically compute storm damage premiums based on the historical record of storm frequency and intensity. A systematic tendency toward more frequent, more powerful storms over a five- to ten-year period could have a serious impact on the insurance marker.

Solar-Induced Variability in the Middle and Upper Atmosphere. The total power output of the Sun varies slightly (by less than 0.1 percent) over an eleven-year cycle associated with sunspot activity. Larger variations occur at ultraviolet wavelengths and in the strength of the *solar wind* (flux of energetic particles from the Sun). Since solar ultraviolet radiation is responsible for generating ozone in the stratosphere, this eleven-year cycle has a significant influence on stratospheric ozone (Labitzke and van Loon, 1997). This, in turn, has an impact on stratospheric climate and possibly on that of the upper troposphere as well (Haigh, 1996). The solar wind has a clear influence on the ionosphere (above the stratosphere), but any evidence for an influence further down remains controversial.

Despite considerable effort over the years, there is relatively little evidence that the eleven-year solar cycle has a significant influence on surface climate: correlations have often been reported that turned out to be coincidental and short-lived. This is unsurprising: the amplitude of the cycle is so weak that any influence is likely to be almost completely dominated by internal climate variability. The picture is further complicated by the fact that the recent record of volcanic eruptions happens to display some (purely coincidental) coherence with the solar cycle. Moreover, there may be internal oscillations in the climate system with periods near eleven years. For example, a pattern of Atlantic sea surface temperatures that has been associated with the sunspot cycle also matches that expected from an internal mode of decadal variability. Determining conclusively which explanation is correct from only a few decades of continuous observations is likely to be virtually impossible, and detailed modeling is hampered by the fact that direct observations of solar output have been available only since 1978.

Centennial Variability in the Thermohaline Circulation. Much of the climate of the deep oceans is characterized by a slow overturning "conveyor belt" known as the *thermohaline circulation* (THC). Cold, saline (and therefore relatively dense) water sinks down from the surface in a few regions in the North Atlantic and near Antarctica. This water spreads out through the ocean depths, eventually returning to the surface as far away as the North Pacific. Individual water masses can take hundreds of years to pass around the THC, introducing a mechanism for very slow internal climate oscillations, possibly coupled to moisture transport in the atmosphere, that have been reported in several climate-modeling studies (Weaver et al., 1993). As is the case with decadal variability, the difficulty of modeling key processes accurately makes it unclear how model-derived mechanisms of THC variability relate to the real world. While the surface temperature record is relatively short, observations of the ocean depths are even more sparse. [*See* Ocean Dynamics.]

There is evidence from marine sediment and ice core samples that sufficiently strong changes at the surface can "shut down" the THC relatively rapidly, with dramatic consequences for the global climate. One coupled model study suggested that, without the THC and the heat it transports into the North Atlantic, the Arctic ice-cap would extend south of Iceland (Manabe and Stouffer, 1988). There is strong circumstantial evidence that just such an event occurred as the climate was emerging from the last ice age about eleven thousand years ago. For reasons that remain unclear, the THC appears to have shut down within the space of a few decades, plunging Europe and North American back into ice-age conditions for several centuries (Broecker et al., 1985). The possibility that anthropogenic climate change might trigger such a shutdown in the THC remains speculation, although our present level of understanding of the THC makes it difficult to rule it out. The record seems to suggest that the present-day THC is rather more stable than it was during the last ice age, when several such large and rapid climate oscillations occurred.

Centennial Variability in Solar Forcing. Indirect evidence and observations of Sun-like stars suggest that the power output of the Sun could vary on century time scales by much more than the eleven-year solar cycle. Solar output appears to have been significantly lower than at present during the so-called Maunder minimum around the seventeenth century, when summer temperatures across the Northern Hemisphere were over half a degree colder than typical of the twentieth century. This period is sometimes referred to as the "Little Ice Age," although it is unclear how global the cold conditions really were (Bradley and Jones, 1993). [*See* Little Ice Age in Europe.] Milder conditions appear to have prevailed a few centuries earlier, which may have been a period of enhanced solar activity. These century-scale fluctuations in solar forcing are the main confounding issue in the interpretation of twentieth-century warming trends as a response to anthropogenic greenhouse gases. In terms of energy input into the climate system, solar forcing is estimated to have increased by at most 1.4 watts per square meter (W/m^2) since the Maunder minimum. Forcing due to anthropogenic greenhouse gas emissions since 1850 is over 2.5 W/m^2 and projected to exceed 4 W/m^2 before the middle of the twenty-first century. Solar forcing may therefore have contributed to the recent warming trend, but it is unlikely to be responsible for all, or even most, of it.

The Pleistocene Ice Age Cycles. We have already mentioned that the alignment of the Earth's axis of rotation with respect to its orbit about the Sun varies periodically with the dominant time scales being 22,000 and 41,000 years. [*See* Earth Motions.] The shape of the orbit itself varies over about 100,000 years. These so-called Milankovitch cycles are generally believed to be responsible for the periodic onset and decay of Northern Hemisphere ice sheets that have characterized the

HEINRICH EVENTS

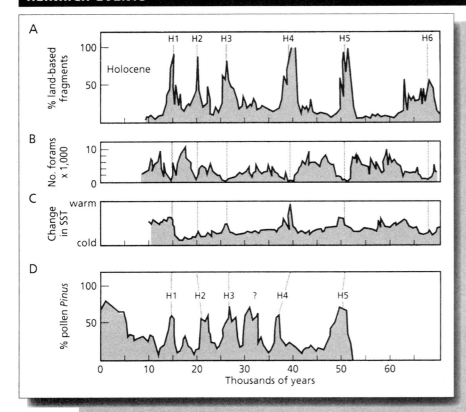

Record of Henirich ice rafting events (H1–H6) in the North Atlantic: (A) ice-rafted sediment derived from land sources; (B) number of foraminifera; (C) change in sea surface temperature (SST); (D) Pollen record of *Pinus* from Florida. (After Bryant, 1997, Figure 5.3. With permission of Cambridge University Press.)

In the 1980s, the German paleoceanographer Hartmut Heinrich (Heinrich, 1988) extracted samples at regular increments from northeastern Atlantic sediment cores that had been retrieved by drilling into the ocean floor. He analyzed his samples and determined their lithic content and their content of planktonic foraminifera fragments. He found that the relative numbers of lithics (sand, stones, and so forth) and foraminifera fluctuated in a surprising manner and that the transitions between lithic dominated (light-colored) and foraminifera-dominated (dark-colored) sediments were unexpectedly abrupt. These phases with sudden increases in the amount of lithics have subsequently been termed *Heinrich events* (Broecker et al., 1992). The key features of sediment delivery among Heinrich events are the presence of icebergs, meltwater plumes, and massive gravity flows called *turbidites*. These processes, which are associated with cold events (stadials), produce sediments with a high lithic content, whereas the foraminifera-rich non-Heinrich sediments were deposited during warmer (interstadial) periods.

The lithic sediments of Heinrich events, which contain iceberg-rafted detritus, have a high carbonate content that is probably derived from the source region of Paleozoic limestones and dolomites in eastern Canada and possibly northwestern Greenland (Bond et al., 1992). This suggested that the lithic sediments of the Heinrich events were carved by the Hudson Strait ice stream, which drained a large fraction of the former Laurentide ice sheet. Rapid fluctuation in this ice stream not only produced the sudden Heinrich events (of which there have been six over sixty thousand years), but also led to the creation of plumes of extremely fresh glacial meltwater. These flowed into the normally salty North Atlantic and so would have affected the thermohaline circulation in the North Atlantic. This in turn could cause abrupt climatic changes far afield.

BIBLIOGRAPHY

Bond, G., H. Heinrich, W. S. Broecker, L. Labeyrie, J. McManus, J. T. Andrews, S. Huon, R. Jantschik, S. Clasen, C. Simet, K. Tedesco, M. Class, G. Bonani, and S. Ivy. "Evidence for Massive Discharges of Icebergs into the Glacial North Atlantic." *Nature* 360 (1992), 245–249.

Broecker, W. S., G. Bond, M. Klas, E. Clarke, and J. McManus. "Origin of the North Atlantic's Heinrich Events." *Climate Dynamics* 6 (1992), 265–273.

Bryant, E. *Climate Process and Change.* Cambridge: Cambridge University Press, 1997.

Heinrich, H. "Origin and Consequences of Cyclic Ice Rafting in the Northeast Atlantic Ocean during the Past 130,000 Years." *Quaternary Research* 29 (1988), 143–152.

—ANDREW S. GOUDIE

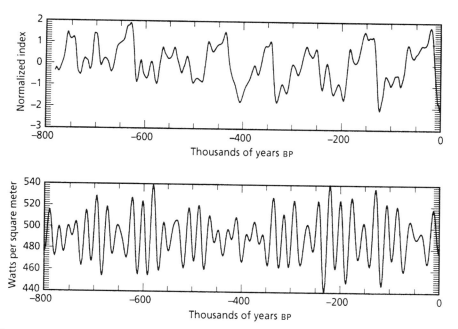

Natural Climate Fluctuations. FIGURE 4. Upper panel: global ice volume inferred from oxygen isotope ratios in marine sediment core samples (Data from SPECMAP.) Lower panel: June insolation rate at 60°N inferred from orbital parameters, assuming no change in the power output of the sun. (Data provided by Andre Berger to the National Geophysical Data Centre.)

climate of the Pleistocene (the past 2 million years; Kutzbach, 1992). [*See the biography of Milankovitch.*] The two shorter periods are evident throughout the Pleistocene, while for some reason the 100,000-year cycle appears important only over the past 700,000 years. The upper panel in Figure 4 shows how global ice volume has evolved over this period, while the lower panel shows how orbital changes affect the amount of solar energy reaching the Northern Hemisphere in summer (ignoring solar variability). This "Northern Hemisphere Insolation" index is thought to be the critical parameter: ice sheets cannot grow in the Southern Hemisphere because Antarctica is entirely surrounded by ocean. Notice how ice sheets tend to grow slowly and decay relatively rapidly, often (but by no means always) following periods of maximum Northern Hemisphere insolation. Establishing the relative timing of ice-sheet collapse and insolation changes is complicated by the difficulty of accurate dating of marine sediment samples.

According to Milankovitch theory, the current interglacial period, or Holocene, is due to terminate with another ice age at some point over the next couple of thousand years, although anthropogenic changes in climate may have rendered that prediction irrelevant. Climatic changes due to Milankovitch forcing appear to have been amplified by changes in greenhouse gas levels. Atmospheric carbon dioxide levels, inferred from air bubbles trapped in ice-core samples, have varied considerably over the past 100,000 years: under glacial conditions, the oceans absorb more carbon dioxide,

reducing atmospheric levels, which further contributes to the cooling—a positive feedback effect. [*See also* Glaciation.]

BIBLIOGRAPHY

Angell, J. K. "Variations and Trends in Tropospheric and Stratospheric Global Temperatures." *Journal of Climate* 1 (1988), 1296–1313.

Baldwin, M. P., and T. J. Dunkerton. "Quasi-Biennial Modulation of the Southern Hemisphere Stratospheric Polar Vortex." *Geophysical Research Letters* 25 (1998), 3343–3346.

Berger, A. "The Milankovitch Astronomical Theory of Paleoclimates: A Modern Review." *Vistas in Astronomy* 24 (1980), 103–122.

Bjerknes, J. "Large-Scale Atmospheric Response to the 1964–65 Pacific Equatorial Warming." *Journal of Physical Oceanography* 2 (1972), 212–217.

Bradley, R. S., and P. D. Jones. "'Little Ice Age' Summer Temperatures: Their Nature and Relevance to Recent Global Warming Trends." *The Holocene* 3 (1993), 367–376.

Broecker, W. S., D. Peteet, and D. Rind. "Does the Ocean-Atmosphere System Have More Than One Stable Mode of Operation?" *Nature* 315 (1985), 21–26.

Burroughs, W. J. *Weather Cycles: Real or Imaginary?* Cambridge: Cambridge University Press, 1992.

Deser, C., and M. L. Blackmon. "Surface Climate Variations over the North Atlantic Ocean during Winter: 1900–1989." *Journal of Climate* 6 (1993), 1743–1753.

Frankignoul, C. "Sea Surface Temperature Anomalies, Planetary Waves, and Air-Sea Feedback in the Middle Latitudes." *Reviews in Geophysics* 23 (1985), 357–390.

Haigh, J. D. "The Impact of Solar Variability on Climate." *Science* 272 (1996), 981–984.

DANSGAARD-OESCHGER CYCLES

The fine-resolution climate record provided by the deep ice-core record from the poles has indicated the rapid and frequent "flickering" of climate during a glacial-interglacial cycle. The oxygen isotopic study of the cores for the last glacial shows twenty-four intervals of relatively high and low $\delta^{18}O$ (oxygen isotope values). Variations are of the order of four to six per thousand, which implies a temperature change of 7–8°C. The intervals of less negative $\delta^{18}O$ values, representing warmer interglacials, lasted between five hundred and two thousand years. An important element of this pattern of change is the abruptness of the shift (within a few decades) from cold to warm temperatures at the onset of these interstadials (warmer intervals). In contrast, the initial part of the return of colder stadial conditions is more gradual. There is thus a characteristic saw-tooth form of very rapid warming to interstadials followed by slower cooling to the next stadial. This is termed a *Dansgaard-Oeschger cycle,* named after the pioneers of ice core drilling.

BIBLIOGRAPHY

Bond, G., et al. "Correlations between Climatic Records from North Atlantic Sediments and Greenland Ice." *Nature* 365 (1993), 143–147.

—ANDREW S. GOUDIE

Hasselmann, K. "Stochastic Climate Models. I. Theory." *Tellus* 28 (1976), 473–485.

Kutzbach, J. E. "Modeling Large Climatic Changes of the Past." In *Climate System Modeling*, edited by K. E. Trenberth, pp. 669–688. Cambridge: Cambridge University Press, 1992.

Labitzke, K., and H. van Loon. "Total Ozone and the 11-Year Sunspot Cycle." *Journal of Atmospheric and Solar-Terrestrial Physics* 59 (1997), 9–19.

Latif, M., and T. P. Barnett. "Causes of Decadal Climate Variability over the North Pacific/North American Sector." *Science* 266 (1994), 634–637.

Lau, K. M., and S. Yang. "The Asian Monsoon and Predictability of the Tropical Ocean-Atmosphere System." *Quarterly Journal of the Royal Meteorological Society* 122 (1996), 945–957.

Manabe, S., and R. J. Stouffer. "Two Stable Equilibria of a Coupled Ocean-Atmosphere Model." *Journal of Climate* 7 (1988), 5–23.

Meehl, G. A. "The South Asian Monsoon and the Tropospheric Biennial Oscillation." *Journal of Climate* 10 (1997), 1921–1943.

Neelin, J. D., D. S. Battisti, A. C. Hirst, F.-F. Jin, Y. Wakata, T. Yamagata, and S. E. Zebiak. "ENSO Theory." *Journal of Geophysical Research* 103 (1998), 14261–14290.

Philander, S. G. *El Niño, La Niña, and the Southern Oscillation.* New York: Academic Press, 1990.

Rasmusson, E. M., X. Wang, and C. F. Ropelewski. "The Biennial Component of ENSO Variability." *Journal of Marine Systems* 1 (1990), 71–96.

Sutton, R. T., and M. R. Allen. "Decadal Predictability of North Atlantic Sea Surface Temperature and Climate." *Nature* 388 (1997), 563–567.

Thomson, D. J. "The Seasons, Global Temperature and Precession." *Science* 268 (1995), 59–68.

Weaver, A. J., J. Marotzke, P. F. Cummins, and E. S. Sarachik. "Stability and Variability of the Thermohaline Circulation." *Journal of Physical Oceanography* 23 (1993), 39–60.

Wyrtki, K. "Water Displacements in the Pacific and the Genesis of El Niño Cycles." *Journal of Geophysical Research* 90 (1985), 7129–7132.

—MYLES R. ALLEN

NATURAL GAS. *See* Fossil Fuels; *and* Methane.

NATURAL HAZARDS

Natural hazards are created by environmental processes that pose a danger to people and what they value. The most severe hazards are a potential threat to human life and economic development. Typically, natural hazards result from concentrated releases of energy or materials from the Earth–atmosphere system that have a rapid onset and short duration, although there are notable exceptions, such as drought. Many natural hazards arise from extreme geophysical events of tectonic origin, such as earthquakes or volcanic eruptions, but atmospherically created events (climatic variations, storms and floods) are the most frequently occurring group of natural hazards worldwide. [*See* Extreme Events.] Other natural hazards, such as disease epidemics or plant and animal invasions, are primarily dependent on biological processes. In some cases, it is difficult to make a distinction between natural processes and processes modified by anthropogenic activity. For example, a landslide may be generated by a combination of heavy rainfall or unwise land use practices, such as the deforestation of a slope. When long-term episodes of either human-induced environmental pollution or land degradation occur, complex hazards that endure for decades may result. For example, the burning of fossil fuels leads to global warming, which, in turn, produces sea level rise and greater risks from coastal flooding. [See Drought; and Earthquakes.]

Natural hazards embrace a wide range of interactions between people and their environment. Many events are seen as hazardous because they impose stresses on human society that, under more normal environmental conditions or in alternative locations, would be perceived as natural resources. A river in spate that unexpectedly floods an urbanized flood plain rather than providing the expected water supply would be an example. However, such spates are necessary to maintain high biological diversity in the river and its adjacent flood plain. To this extent, entirely "natural" hazards have never existed. A landslide in a remote, unpopulated region may be of interest to geomorphologists but would not constitute a natural hazard because there is no interaction with humans.

As the world becomes increasingly settled and transformed by humans, the hazard potential grows. Most commentators now agree that natural hazards are really quasi-natural or hybrid events reflecting diverse interactions between environmental, technological, and social processes. The term *na-tech hazard* has been used to describe the combination of environmental and technological processes when, for example, an earthquake results in urban fires after the rupturing of gas pipelines.

The importance attached to natural hazards by victims, policy makers, and governments tends to mirror the perceived scale of the negative socioeconomic impacts on communities and nations. Some natural hazards have only a minor—or nuisance—value, as when snowfalls temporarily disrupt road and rail communications. On the other hand, when either the number of people killed and injured or the direct economic losses are sufficiently large to prompt widespread reporting through the international media, the event is usually termed a *disaster*. Unfortunately, a direct link between the physical scale of the relevant environmental processes and the socioeconomic significance of the resulting disaster is often lacking. Many natural hazards can be scaled according to measurable scientific criteria that may suggest the likely extent of loss, such as their predictability, intensity, rate of onset, and duration. But an earthquake of the same Richter scale intensity will have widely different consequences for mortality and property loss according to local cultural factors such as the density of population, the level of earthquake preparedness in the community, the time of day

the earthquake occurs, and the types of building materials and methods near the epicenter.

There are further complications, because no general agreement exists on the minimum level of loss that has to occur before a disaster is officially declared. Once again, absolute measures such as the number of people killed or the cost of direct damage do not always reflect the real significance of the event. While the death of twenty people accompanied by economic costs of U.S.$1 million may be catastrophic for a small, remote fishing community, the same losses may hardly touch the functioning of a large industrial city. The Centre for Research on the Epidemiology of Disasters (CRED) at the University of Louvain, Belgium has standardized an international hazards database called EM-DAT that can be used to identify the relative significance of disasters for each country: number of deaths per event—at least one hundred; direct damage—at least 1 percent of national gross national product; adversely affected people—at least 1 percent of national population.

The field of natural hazards is conceptually and empirically diverse. Throughout the history of both theory and practice, there has been a progressive trend away from an emphasis on extreme geophysical events and a policy response aimed at the physical controls of hazards toward a more multidisciplinary view that recognizes hazards as an intrinsic part of the social fabric and recommends stronger elements of human responsibility and avoidance at the personal level.

Initially, natural hazards were seen as isolated and random events in an acts of God paradigm. Since these events were thought to be controlled by some higher being external to society, this led to a fatalistic attitude on the part of victims and the absence of positive management responses. This view is still retained by a few traditional cultures in the modern world. Eventually some environmental processes, mainly those dependent on the passage of the seasons, such as annual floods, became better understood, and primitive flood control dams were first constructed in the Middle East four thousand years ago. This was the start of the engineering paradigm that continued to interpret natural hazards as unscheduled geophysical events disrupting the normal order of society. Because the problem was now perceived to originate in nature, it was logical to believe that the control and prediction of natural events, through the application of science and technology, would provide a solution. Flood defense has always been at the forefront of this response, as illustrated by the creation of the Army Corps of Engineers in the United States as early as 1799, dedicated to the construction of large-scale flood control projects.

The engineering paradigm soon became the dominant hazard perspective throughout the developed world. It has been much favored by government bodies wishing to confront hazards in a visible way. Environmental monitoring, scientific explanation, and managerial control are the hallmarks of this strategy, which has led to widespread defensive structures as varied as river dams, levees, coastal barriers, avalanche sheds, and antiseismic building construction. Advances in communications technology have also been adopted—often very successfully—to mitigate natural hazards. For example, the advent of the telephone, computers, satellites, radar, and telemetry has transformed weather forecasting in the twentieth century. On the other hand, some important natural hazards such as earthquakes, volcanic eruptions, and drought have proved resistant to scientific forecasting and control.

A major shift occurred around the middle of the twentieth century when American geographers promoted what became known as the *behavioral paradigm*. This view still emphasized extreme geophysical events as a disruption of normal life, but also recognized the contributing role played by the victims. For example, in the developed countries, ill-informed human behavior was thought to include poor hazard perception, which allowed further settlement in unsafe areas such as flood plains and seashores. In the developing countries, human actions such as deforestation and overgrazing increased the hazard potential. Proponents of the behavioral paradigm argued that "technical fix" solutions alone were inappropriate for hazard mitigation and that a broader mix of options designed to modify human behavior, such as financial measures and land use controls, should be adopted. In turn this led to a greater study of the perception of extreme events and the choice of hazard mitigation adjustments by both individual and corporate decision makers.

In the mid-1970s, the emergence of the *structural paradigm* provided a more radical and political interpretation. It was pointed out that the emphasis on the choice of mitigation strategies ignored the structural constraints imposed on people by historical, cultural, and institutional forces that transcend local decision making. For example, in the developed countries, national governments, regional authorities, and financial bodies—rather than individuals—control many land use decisions, while in the developing countries, the legacy of colonialism and economic underdevelopment precludes many hazard adjustments possible in richer nations. Workers with field experience in developing countries also questioned the largely Western assumption that extreme geophysical events disrupted normal life. They argued that, in these countries, hazards occupy an integral—rather than an exceptional—place in human livelihoods that are often permanently fragile. For the poorest people, therefore, extreme natural events are merely triggers that expose deep political, so-

cial, and economic problems. The structural paradigm thus forges a link between hazard impact and human vulnerability created by disadvantage, and its advocates envisage solutions based on the redistribution of wealth and power in society rather than the application of science.

This political–economic view of hazards has been expressed most powerfully in relation to developing countries in which large-scale global processes associated with the expansion of global capitalism lead to the blight of underdevelopment. Other constructs illuminate different aspects of human vulnerability. For example, sociologists in the United States have extended the concept into the developed countries with surveys of household-scale social inequalities, such as poverty, gender, age, ethnicity, and language and literacy issues following events such as Hurricane Andrew (1992) and the Northridge earthquake (1994). Other researchers have explored human vulnerability to natural hazards in the historical context of the colonial legacy and the spatial context of the geographical region.

The 1990s International Decade for Natural Disaster Reduction (IDNDR) is the most determined attempt yet made to mitigate hazards, mainly by assisting developing countries to assess hazard potential and deploy relevant early-warning schemes and hazard-resistant structures. The IDNDR was established by the United Nations to address two problems: the apparent increasing frequency of natural hazards worldwide, and the unacceptable burden of loss in the developing countries. Time series of natural hazards are available from the 1960s, but are difficult to interpret because of environmental and social changes over recent decades, including new technology, population growth, and more comprehensive disaster reporting by the news media. Nevertheless, some trends do exist. According to the CRED database, the number of disasters claiming at least one hundred lives has more than doubled from the late 1960s to the early 1990s, while the number of people affected adversely has grown from less than fifty million per year to around 250 million per year. Economic losses also tend to increase. Even after allowing for price inflation (indexed to 1990 U.S. dollars), average annual flood losses in the United States rose from some U.S.\$100 million in 1925 to about U.S.\$4 billion in 1995. Disaster losses are not evenly spread throughout the world. For example, it is believed that over 90 percent of hazard-related deaths occur among the two-thirds of the world population that lives in the developing countries. Although some three-quarters of all the direct economic damage is confined to the developed countries, the relative effect—expressed as a proportion of gross national product—is many times more severe in the poorest countries.

Few of the recorded increases in hazard impact can

be attributed entirely to natural processes. For example, no evidence exists for a greater frequency of earthquakes or volcanic eruptions. On the other hand, there is a growing awareness that human activity is changing atmospheric processes and that such effects may well create increased human vulnerability in the future. Much atmospheric pollution is now intercontinental, or even global, in scale. As a consequence, climatic hazards as varied as acid deposition (leading to the corrosion of buildings and the contamination of water supply systems) and the depletion of stratospheric ozone (leading to greater human exposure to harmful ultraviolet-B wavelengths and the risk of skin cancer) have already been documented. The most publicized threat is that of global climate change due to increased concentrations of radiatively active gases in the atmosphere. Global warming is likely to lead to sea level rise and increased danger from hurricane winds and storm surges along coasts, while also leading to a more energetic hydrologic cycle with prospects for more damaging floods and droughts.

Pressure on natural resources due to population increase, economic development, and modernization is raising basic questions about the ability of the Earth to sustain future growth. Environmental degradation and the further invasion of unsafe zones have many implications for natural hazards in the future. For example, one concern relates to the rise of megacities. There are already about three hundred cities with populations in excess of one million in the world, and eighteen megacities containing over ten million people. Many of these cities have expanded with little regard for the biophysical environment, and are located on low-lying shorelines, river flood plains, and unstable slopes or in topography that accentuates any risk from air, ground, or water pollution. These very large cities are under threat because they contain unprecedented concentrations of people who are dependent on commercial, industrial, and transportation infrastructures vulnerable to hazard. Many of the fundamental support services are under capacity, especially in the developing countries, and there are few resources available for hazard reduction.

On the other hand, the threat from natural hazards is declining in some areas. In practice, many authenticated decreases in hazard impact are due to improved forecasting and warning procedures and the ability to construct better hazard-resistant structures. For example, the increasing efficiency with which communities in the United States can be evacuated from low-lying coastlines has reduced the number of hurricane deaths per decade from over eight thousand in 1900–1909 to around 250 in 1980–1989. In Bangladesh, specially built cyclone refuges provide limited safety from severe storms. Rapid deployment teams, with skills as varied as disaster medicine and the restoration of electricity supplies, are now stationed around the world, poised to maximize the life-saving opportunities of the first few golden hours following a disaster. [See Coastlines.]

In the postindustrial age, natural hazards and their effective mitigation are the focus of considerable debate. Science and technology will continue to make vital contributions toward a safer world, as envisaged by the IDNDR. However, the prime need is not necessarily for more science, but for a better deployment of the science that already exists. For example, there is a growing awareness of the adverse side effects of some classic environmental engineering schemes, such as river dams and coastal defenses, that interfere with sediment supplies and related ecological processes. Other schemes are criticized for being economically unrealistic, especially in the less developed parts of the world. Increasingly, natural hazards are seen as an indicator of unsustainable growth and as obstacles to future economic well-being, even in wealthy countries. For example, the Kobe earthquake of 1995 killed over six thousand people in Japan, injured thirty-five thousand, and rendered a further 300,000 homeless, with national economic losses estimated at U.S.$100 billion.

Since natural hazards can never be completely eliminated, a new *living-with-hazards paradigm* is likely to emerge. This is based on the fact that economic development and modernization will not, in themselves, mitigate natural hazards. Indeed, such trends may well erode traditional lifestyles and indigenous hazard responses. Future hazard-reducing technologies will have to be more sensitive to the ecological, financial, and social framework in which they operate. For example, this means encouraging "softer, environmentally friendly" engineering defenses in the context of coastal zone and river basin management plans, together with more self-reliant responses from people at risk. Such responses will need to be supported by better risk communication, practical first-aid training, more help for strengthening weak dwellings and, where necessary, assistance for a managed retreat of people and property from the most hazardous areas.

[See also Insurance; Risk; and Sea Level.]

BIBLIOGRAPHY

Alexander, D. *Natural Disasters.* London: UCL Press, 1993. A wide-ranging introduction to the subject with an emphasis on natural processes.

Blaikie, P., et al. *At Risk: Natural Hazards, People's Vulnerability and Disasters.* London and New York: Routledge, 1994. A thought-provoking and innovative statement of human vulnerability in the developing countries.

Bolin, R., and L. Stanford. *The Northridge Earthquake: Vulnerability and Disaster.* London and New York: Routledge, 1998. Explores the role of community vulnerability to hazard in one of the wealthiest parts of the world.

Bryant, E. A. *Natural Hazards.* Cambridge: Cambridge University

Press, 1991. A geophysical interpretation of hazards firmly in the tradition of the engineering paradigm.

Burton, I., et al. *The Environment as Hazard.* 2d ed. New York and London: Guilford Press, 1993. An update of the behavioral perspective by the pioneers of the human-ecology view of hazards.

Gross, E. M. "The Hurricane Dilemma in the United States." *Episodes* 14 (1991), 36–45. A good illustration of how the impact of a specific hazard can be evaluated.

Hewitt, K. *Regions of Risk: A Geographical Introduction to Disasters.* Harlow, U.K.: Longman, 1997. A fresh and critical appraisal of the geography of natural hazards and other risks.

————., ed. *Interpretations of Calamity.* Boston and London: Allen and Unwin, 1983. Seminal case studies that marked the arrival of the structural perspective on hazards.

Mitchell, J. K., ed. *Crucibles of Hazard: Megacities and Disasters in Transition.* Tokyo: United Nations University Press, 1999. Authoritative case studies on the growing threat of natural hazards to the largest cities in the world.

Peacock, W. G., et al., eds. *Hurricane Andrew: Ethnicity, Gender and the Sociology of Disasters.* London and New York: Routledge, 1997. Presents a sociopolitical interpretation of natural hazard impact, with a focus on the city of Miami.

Pielke, R., and R. Pielke. *Storms.* 2 vols. London: Routledge, 2000.

Sapir, D. G., and C. Misson. "The Development of a Database on Disasters." *Disasters* 16 (1992), 74–80. A good description of the strengths and weaknesses of the CRED database.

Smith, K. *Environmental Hazards: Assessing Risk and Reducing Disaster.* 3d ed. London and New York: Routledge, 2000. A comprehensive and accessible introduction to the theoretical study and practical mitigation of hazards.

Smith, K., and R. C. Ward. *Floods: Physical Processes and Human Impacts.* Chichester, U.K.: Wiley, 1998. Illustrates differing perspectives on, and human responses to, the most common of all natural hazards.

White, G. F., and J. E. Haas. *Assessment of Research on Natural Hazards.* Cambridge, Mass. and London: MIT Press, 1975. Reviews the classic geophysical and sociological systems material at the core of the behavioral approach.

—KEITH SMITH

NICHOLSON, MAX

Max (Edward) Nicholson (1904–), British ornithologist, ecologist, and environmentalist, was born in Ireland and has had a long and distinguished career. Interested in birds since the age of seven, he has played an important part in ornithological bodies in the United Kingdom, together with many other natural history organizations. He left school at an early age, soon after World War I, and earned a living as a natural history writer. He subsequently returned to university, taking a degree at Oxford, where he was a member of Hertford College. While there, he was instrumental in setting up the Oxford Bird Census, which was the forerunner of both the British Trust for Ornithology and the Edward Grey Institute of Field Ornithology of the University of Oxford.

He was also a founding member of the Oxford University Exploration Club, and participated in the first two of its many important expeditions—to Greenland and British Guiana (as it then was)—thus helping to set a trend whereby some hundreds of university students now participate annually in such expeditions and gain great experience from them. Before going to Oxford, he published his first book, *Birds in England.*

After World War II, he became Secretary of the Office of the Lord President of the Council (Herbert Morrison), who was the Deputy Prime Minister and also Minister for Science. He served on the Advisory Council for Scientific Policy from 1948 to 1964. In 1952 he moved from there to become Director-General of the newly founded Nature Conservancy (which later became the Nature Conservancy Council and the Institute for Terrestrial Ecology; the former is now split into three bodies: Scottish Natural Heritage, Countryside Council for Wales, and English Nature). He built up this body throughout its formative years, leaving it only when it was well established, in 1966. He then set up Land Use Consultants, probably the first environmental consultancy. He was involved in the setting up or expansion of many United Kingdom and international conservation bodies, including the Royal Society for the Protection of Birds, the Society for the Promotion of Nature Reserves (now the Royal Society for Nature Conservation), the Wildfowl Trust (now the Wildfowl and Wetlands Trust), Earthwatch Europe, the World Wildlife Fund, and the Ecological Parks Trust (now the Trust for Urban Ecology). Most recently, he was Founder and Chairman of the New Renaissance Group.

Nicholson's books include *Birds in England* (1926), *Birds and Men* (1951), *Britain's Nature Reserves* (1958), *The System* (1967), *The Environmental Revolution: A Guide for the New Masters of the World* (1970), *The Big Change: After the Environmental Revolution* (1973), *The New Environmental Age* (1987), and *Bird-Watching in London: A Historical Perspective* (1995). He was a cofounder of "West Palearctic Birds Ltd," which produced *The Birds of the Western Palearctic,* vols. I–IX (1978–1994); he was an editor and wrote all the habitat sections of this work.

His awards include: Companion of the Order of the Bath (1948), Commander of the Royal Victorian Order (1971), Honorary L.L.D., Aberdeen University (1964), Honorary D.L., Birmingham University (1983), Geoffroy St. Hilaire Gold Medal, Société National de Protection de la Nature de France (1956), John C. Phillips Medallist, International Union for Conservation of Nature and Natural Resources (1963), Europa Preis für Landespflage (1972), and Commandeur of Golden Ark, the Netherlands (1973).

[*See also* Environmental Movements.]

BIBLIOGRAPHY

Nicholson, M. *Birds in England.* London: Chapman and Hall, 1926.
———. *Birds and Men.* London: Collins, 1951.
———. *Britain's Nature Reserves.* 1958.
———. *The System: The Misgovernment of Modern Britain.* New York: McGraw-Hill, 1967.
———. *The Environmental Revolution: A Guide for the New Masters of the World.* New York: McGraw-Hill, 1970.
———. *The Big Change: After the Environmental Revolution.* New York: McGraw-Hill, 1973.
———. *The New Environmental Age.* New York and Cambridge: Cambridge University Press, 1987.

—CHRISTOPHER PERRINS

NITROGEN CYCLE

The availability of nitrogen (N) often determines the rate of plant growth on land and in the sea. Nitrogen is an integral part of enzymes, which mediate all life's biochemical reactions, including photosynthesis. Changes in the availability of N are likely to have controlled the size and activity of the biosphere through geologic time.

A large number of biochemical transformations of nitrogen are possible, since nitrogen is found at valence states ranging from -4 (in NO_4^+) to $+5$ (in NO_3^-). Microbes convert nitrogen between these different forms and use the energy released by the movement of electrons to fuel their life processes. Collectively, these microbial reactions drive the global cycle of nitrogen (Figure 1).

The most abundant form of nitrogen on Earth, N_2, is the least reactive species. Nitrogen fixation converts atmospheric N_2 to one of the forms of "fixed" (or "odd") nitrogen that can be used by biota (e.g., NH_4^+ and NO_3^-). Nitrogen-fixing species are most abundant in nitrogen-poor habitats, where their activity increases the availability of nitrogen for the biosphere. At the same time, denitrifying bacteria return N_2 to the atmosphere, lowering the overall stock of nitrogen available for life on Earth. The balance between nitrogen fixation and denitrification through geologic time has determined the nitrogen available to biota and the global nitrogen cycle.

The atmosphere contains about 3.9×10^{21} grams of nitrogen (Figure 1). Relatively small amounts of nitrogen are found in land plants (3.5×10^{15} grams) and soil organic matter (95×10^{15} grams). The nitrogen in the

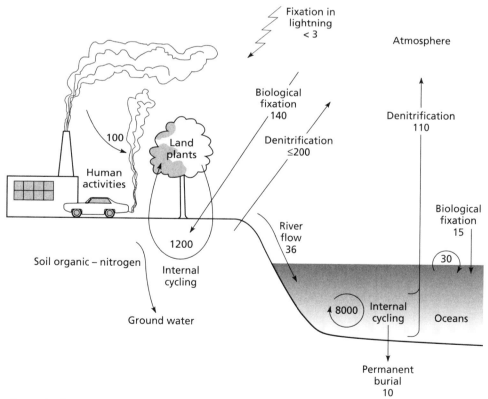

Nitrogen Cycle. FIGURE 1. The Global Nitrogen Cycle, Showing Annual Flux in Units of 10^{12} Grams of Nitrogen per Year. (From Schlesinger, 1997. With permission of Academic Press.)

atmosphere is not available to most organisms because the great strength of the triple bond in N_2 makes this molecule practically inert. All nitrogen that is available to biota was originally derived from nitrogen fixation, either by lightning or by free-living and symbiotic microbes. The rate of nitrogen fixation by lightning, which produces momentary conditions of high pressure and temperature allowing N_2 and O_2 to combine, is poorly known but relatively small. Most recent, global estimates are less than 3×10^{12} grams of nitrogen per year.

A widely cited estimate of biological nitrogen fixation in soils is 140×10^{12} grams of nitrogen per year. This is equivalent to about 10 kilograms of nitrogen per year for each hectare of the Earth's land surface. This flux is not, however, distributed uniformly among natural ecosystems; the greatest values are often found in areas of disturbed or successional vegetation. Each year about 40×10^{12} grams of nitrogen are added to agricultural fields as a result of the cultivation of nitrogen-fixing crops (e.g., soybeans). In any case, in the modern world, nitrogen fixation by soil bacteria dwarfs lightning as the source of fixed nitrogen on land. Taking all forms of nitrogen fixation as the only source, the mean residence time of nitrogen in the terrestrial biosphere is about seven hundred years (i.e., pool/input).

Assuming a global estimate of terrestrial net primary production of 60×10^{15} grams of carbon per year and a mean carbon to nitrogen ratio of fifty in plant tissues, the nitrogen requirement of land plants is about $1,200 \times 10^{12}$ grams per year. Thus nitrogen fixation supplies only about 12 percent of the nitrogen that is assimilated by land plants each year. The remaining nitrogen is derived from internal recycling and by the decomposition of dead materials in the soil. When the turnover in the soil is calculated with respect to the input of dead plant materials, the mean residence time of nitrogen in the soil is greater than one hundred years.

Humans have a dramatic impact on the global nitrogen cycle. In addition to planting nitrogen-fixing species for crops, humans produce nitrogen fertilizers through the Haber process, that is,

$$3CH_4 + 6H_2O \rightarrow 3CO_2 + 12H_2$$

$$4N_2 + 12H_2 \rightarrow 8NH_3,$$

in which natural gas is burned to produce hydrogen, which is combined with N_2 to form ammonia under conditions of high temperature and pressure. Today's fertilizer production supplies more than 80×10^{12} grams of nitrogen per year to agricultural ecosystems worldwide.

Every year fossil fuel combustion releases about 20×10^{12} grams of nitrogen as NO_x. Some of this is derived from the organic nitrogen contained in fuels, but it is best regarded as a source of new, fixed nitrogen for the biosphere because in the absence of human activi-

ties, this nitrogen would remain inaccessible in the Earth's crust. A small portion of this NO_x undergoes long-distance transport in the troposphere, accounting for the rising levels of NO_3^- deposited in Greenland snow (Figure 2). The presence of NO_x in the lower atmosphere allows the formation of ozone (O_3), a major air pollutant and health hazard downwind of industry. Owing to the short residence time of NO_x in the atmosphere, most of this nitrogen is deposited by precipitation over land, where it enters biogeochemical cycles. Forest ecosystems downwind of major population centers now receive enormous nitrogen inputs that may be related to their decline.

In total, about 240×10^{12} of grams of newly fixed nitrogen is delivered from the atmosphere to the Earth's land surface each year—40 percent by natural and 60 percent by human-derived sources. In the absence of processes removing nitrogen, a very large pool of nitrogen would be found on land in a relatively short time. Each year rivers carry at least 36×10^{12} grams of nitrogen from land to the sea. Globally, humans may account for as much as half of the present-day transport of nitrogen in rivers. Human additions of fixed nitrogen to the land have also resulted in marked increases in the nitrogen content of ground waters, especially in many agricultural areas. The global loss of nitrogen to ground waters may approach 11×10^{12} grams per year. Despite these large transports, riverflow and ground water cannot account for all of the nitrogen that is deposited on land. The remaining nitrogen is assumed to be lost by denitrification in wet soils, wetlands, and forest fires.

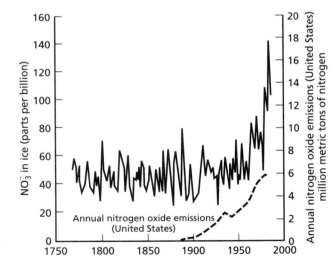

Nitrogen Cycle. FIGURE 2. The Two-Hundred-Year Record of Nitrate in Layers of the Greenland Ice Pack and the Annual Production of Nitric Oxides by Fossil Fuel Combustion in the United States. (Modified from Mayewski, 1990. Reprinted with permission from *Nature*. Copyright 1990 Macmillan Magazines Limited.)

NITRATES IN RIVERS AND ICE CORES

Human activities such as the use of synthetic fertilizers and the burning of fossil fuels have changed the amounts of nitrates present in soils, rivers, and the atmosphere. This can now be identified at the global scale through the study of river water and ice core chemistry. In 1991, Peierls et al. demonstrated that the quantity of nitrates in world rivers now appears to be closely correlated to human population density. Using published data for forty-two major world rivers, they found a highly significant correlation between annual nitrate concentration and human population density in their catchments that explained 76 percent of the variation in nitrate concentration for these rivers. They maintained that "human activity clearly dominates nitrate export from the land."

In 1990, Mayewski et al. studied the nitrate concentration in the upper layers of an ice core retrieved from the Greenland Ice Sheet. They found that nitrate levels were relatively stable and at a low level until around 1900 but that they have climbed since then, and are now about 2.5 times their natural background levels.

BIBLIOGRAPHY

Peierls, B. L., et al. "Human Influences on River Nitrogen." *Nature* 350 (1991), 386.

—ANDREW S. GOUDIE

Estimates of global denitrification in terrestrial ecosystems range from 13 to 233×10^{12} grams of nitrogen per year. At least half of the denitrification on land occurs in wetlands. If nitrogen-fixation and denitrification were once in balance, then a terrestrial denitrification rate of at least 70×10^{12} grams of nitrogen per year was most likely in the preindustrial world (i.e., fixation minus riverflow). Most of the loss occurs as N_2, but a small fraction is lost as N_2O, which contributes significantly to the global budget of this gas. The current rise in atmospheric N_2O indicates that the overall loss of N_2 from denitrification may have increased by as much as 90×10^{12} grams of nitrogen per year, helping to balance the present-day nitrogen budget on land.

During fire, the nitrogen in plant tissues is volatilized as NH_3, NO_x, and N_2—the latter constituting a form of pyrodenitrification. About 30 percent of the nitrogen in fuel is converted to N_2, and globally, biomass burning may return as much as 50×10^{12} grams of nitrogen per year to the atmosphere as N_2. To the extent that the rate of biomass burning has increased in recent years, this form of denitrification may have increased as well.

Each year, the world's oceans receive about 36×10^{12} grams of nitrogen per year in dissolved forms in rivers, at least 15×10^{12} grams of nitrogen per year from biological nitrogen fixation, and about 30×10^{12} grams of nitrogen in precipitation. Note that while the flux in rivers is a small component of the terrestrial cycle, it contributes about 40 percent of the total nitrogen delivered annually to the sea. The riverflux of nitrogen assumes its greatest importance in coastal seas and estuaries, whereas nitrogen deposited from the atmo-

sphere is most important over the open oceans. Despite these inputs, at any time, the pool of inorganic nitrogen in the surface ocean is very small. Most of the net primary production in the sea is supported by nitrogen recycling in the sea. The deep ocean contains a large pool of inorganic nitrogen (570×10^{15} grams of nitrogen) derived from the decomposition of sinking organic materials. Permanent burial of organic nitrogen in sediments is small, so most of the nitrogen input to the oceans must be returned to the atmosphere as N_2 by denitrification. Important areas of denitrification are found in the anaerobic deep waters of the eastern tropical Pacific Ocean and the Arabian Sea. Globally, marine denitrification may account for the yearly return of more than 110×10^{12} grams of nitrogen to the atmosphere as N_2.

With respect to nitrogen fixation, the mean residence time of atmospheric nitrogen is about 20 million years. This is much shorter than the history of life on Earth, and it speaks strongly for the importance of denitrification in returning N_2 to the atmosphere over geologic time. Denitrification closes the global biogeochemical cycle of nitrogen, but it also means that nitrogen remains in short supply for the biosphere. In the absence of denitrification, most nitrogen on Earth would be found as NO_3^- in seawater, and the oceans would be quite acidic.

Human activities have now disrupted steady-state conditions in the nitrogen cycle. Humans have greatly accelerated the natural rate of nitrogen fixation; the current production of nitrogen fertilizers is increasing at an exponential rate. Elevated levels of nitrogen added to the environment reduce the number of species that can persist in many plant communities, rivers, and coastal seawaters. Enrichments of nitrogen in terrestrial ecosystems, stimulating the rates of nitrification and denitrification, are likely to account for the rapid rise in the atmospheric content of N_2O, which is a greenhouse gas and a cause of ozone destruction in the stratosphere.

[*See also* Acid Rain and Acid Deposition; Agriculture and Agricultural Land; Biological Productivity; Biosphere; Deforestation; Nitrous Oxide; *and* Water Quality.]

BIBLIOGRAPHY

Galloway, J. N., W. H. Schlesinger, H. Levy, A. Michels, and J. L. Schnoor. "Nitrogen Fixation: Anthropogenic Enhancement-Environmental Response." *Global Biogeochemical Cycles* 9 (1995), 235–252.

Mayewski, P. A., W. B. Lyons, M. J. Spencer, M. S. Twickler, C. F. Buck, and S. Whitlow. "An Ice Core Record of Atmospheric Response to Anthropogenic Sulphate and Nitrate." *Nature* 346 (1990), 554–556.

Schlesinger, W. H. *Biogeochemistry: An Analysis of Global Change.* San Diego: Academic Press, 1997.

Vitousek, P. M., J. D. Aber, R. W. Howarth, G. E. Likens, P. A. Matson, D. W. Schindler, W. H. Schlesinger, and D. G. Tilman. "Human Alteration of the Global Nitrogen Cycle." *Ecological Applications* 7 (1997), 730–737.

—WILLIAM H. SCHLESINGER

NITROUS OXIDE

A natural biogenic and anthropogenic atmospheric trace gas, nitrous oxide (N_2O) is active as a modulator of the Earth's protective stratospheric ozone layer and as a greenhouse gas. A comparatively unreactive atmospheric gas, it represents an intermediate oxidation state in the biological nitrogen cycle. Its presence in the atmosphere was discovered in 1939 from its effect on the solar spectrum. Its mean global tropospheric abundance in January 2000 was 314 parts per billion (ppb, expressed on a molecular basis in dry air), which is increasing at about 0.7 ppb per year, presumably because of anthropogenic activity, and its mean interhemispheric gradient is about 2 ppb, with the Northern Hemisphere being higher. Model calculations and measurements of air trapped in polar ice cores fix the preindustrial abundance of tropospheric nitrous oxide at about 275 ppb. Precise atmospheric measurements of tropospheric nitrous oxide carried out since the middle 1970s show that its abundance has increased continuously over this period, although there have been variations in the rate of increase and in the interhemispheric gradient that have not been explained.

The principal natural source of nitrous oxide is as a byproduct of bacterial denitrification and nitrification processes, mainly in soils but also in the oceans and in other natural waters. Its principal anthropogenic sources are the enhancement of these bacterial processes through agricultural activity and the use of anthropogenic fertilizers, releases of organic wastes, changes in land use, and, to a lesser degree, industrial activity and some forms of combustion. Its principal natural sink takes place through gradual upward mixing into the stratosphere, where it is destroyed primarily by dissociation by solar ultraviolet radiation, and, to a lesser degree, by reaction with electronically excited atomic oxygen atoms. Because the ultraviolet radiation required to initiate these destruction processes is absorbed by the stratospheric ozone layer, tropospheric destruction of nitrous oxide is minor and occurs primarily through uptake on some land and water surfaces. The lifetime of tropospheric nitrous oxide is thus believed to be about 120 years, based primarily on modeling calculations of its stratospheric destruction rate.

The preindustrial atmospheric nitrous oxide abundance and lifetime fix the preindustrial total natural source at about 17 teragrams (1 teragram = 10^{18} grams) of nitrous oxide per year (about 11 teragrams of nitrogen in nitrous oxide per year). Of this total, about one-third is believed to come from the oceans by air–sea gas exchange, based on global measurements of nitrous oxide in surface oceans and models of the gas exchange rate, and the remaining two-thirds is believed to be of terrestrial origin. Because of the latitudinal distribution of tropospheric nitrous oxide, tropical sources are believed to dominate the terrestrial budget. The mean rate of increase in atmospheric abundance over the past two decades fixes the mean total anthropogenic source strength at about one-third of the total natural sources, about 6 teragrams per year (about 4 teragrams of nitrogen in nitrous oxide per year), or about the same magnitude as the global oceans. Attempts to reconcile the detailed global budget of nitrous oxide by equating the sum of specific identified sources with the sum of specific identified sinks have been only partially successful, and the errors are large enough that the existence of significant unidentified sources and sinks cannot be ruled out.

When nitrous oxide is destroyed in the stratosphere, approximately 95 percent of its nitrogen forms unreactive nitrogen gas, but about 5 percent forms nitric oxide (NO) and nitrogen dioxide (NO_2) that together act in a catalytic cycle to convert ozone (O_3) to molecular oxygen (O_2). In 1970, P. J. Crutzen showed that this catalytic process serves to regulate the abundance of stratospheric ozone in the natural atmosphere. [*See* Ozone.] Similarly, the anthropogenic production of nitrous oxide can reduce the abundance of stratospheric ozone below natural levels, with model calculations showing a mean reduction in ozone abundance of about 1 percent for every 10 percent increase in nitrous oxide abundance. However, in the presence of elevated levels of stratospheric chlorine due to anthropogenic chloro-fluorocarbons, the effects can be far more complex because of the formation of compounds such as chlorine nitrate ($ClNO_3$) that have the effect of temporarily sequestering reactive chlorine and nitrogen species from reaction with ozone. Although nitrous oxide is an ozone-depleting substance, its production has not been regulated by the Montreal Protocol. [*See* Montreal Protocol.]

Nitrous oxide is also an effective greenhouse gas. Based on model calculations using current atmospheric composition, nitrous oxide is about three hundred times as effective per added molecule or per added unit mass as carbon dioxide in warming the Earth's surface. This is primarily because the lower abundance of nitrous oxide in the atmosphere makes its infrared absorption spectrum less saturated than is the case for carbon dioxide. The net warming effect of increases of nitrous oxide since preindustrial times is estimated to be about one tenth that of carbon dioxide increases over the same period. Because of the long lifetime of atmospheric nitrous oxide, these effects are expected to continue to be significant well into the next century. Nitrous oxide is among the greenhouse gases that are to be regulated under the Kyoto Protocol. [*See* Kyoto Protocol.]

[*See also* Atmosphere Dynamics; Atmosphere Structure and Evolution; Atmospheric Chemistry; Biomes; Biosphere; Climate Change; Deforestation; Global Warming; Greenhouse Effect; Land Surface Processes; Nitrogen Cycle; Ocean Chemistry; Ocean Dynamics; *and* Water Vapor.]

BIBLIOGRAPHY

Crutzen, P. J. "The Influence of Nitrogen Oxides on the Atmospheric Ozone Content." *Quarterly Journal of the Royal Meteorological Society* 96 (1970), 320–325. Pioneering work on the catalytic role of nitrous oxide in modulating the ozone layer, recognized by the awarding of the 1995 Nobel Prize in Chemistry.

Graedel, T. E., and P. J. Crutzen. *Atmospheric Change: An Earth System Perspective.* New York: Freeman, 1993. A basic text on the chemistry of the changing atmosphere.

Intergovernmental Panel on Climate Change. *Climate Change 1995: The Science of Climate Change,* edited by J. T. Houghton et al. Cambridge: Cambridge University Press, 1996. An overview for scientists and policy makers on the state of research on greenhouse gases and their impact on climate change.

Wayne, R. P. *Chemistry of Atmospheres.* 2d ed. New York and Oxford: Oxford University Press, 1991. A general textbook on the principles of atmospheric chemistry.

Weiss, R. F. "The Temporal and Spatial Distribution of Tropospheric Nitrous Oxide." *Journal of Geophysical Research* 86 (1981): 7185–7195. The discovery that global tropospheric nitrous oxide is increasing.

World Meteorological Organization. "Scientific Assessment of Ozone Depletion: 1998." WMO Report No. 44. Geneva, 1999. An overview of the state of research on atmospheric ozone chemistry for scientists and for policy makers.

—RAY F. WEISS

NOISE POLLUTION. *See* Pollution.

NONGOVERNMENTAL ORGANIZATIONS

Nongovernmental organizations (NGOs) play critical roles in the management of global change. Despite their importance, however, it has been difficult to categorize the types of NGOs and identify exactly the many ways in which they operate, because NGOs have been defined principally by what they are not—they are not formal entities of the state. But what they are is a complex array of actors who adopt a wide array of goals and strategies.

So long as the state has not had complete control over economic and social life, various types of NGOs have been influential. Inside countries, political parties and religious organizations have long had influence on public and private life. Many of these have also operated across borders to form multinational enterprises, such as Socialist International or the Catholic Church. In addition, commercial firms have long organized into associations to pursue their common interests. Using a broad definition of NGO, the firm itself is a form of nongovernmental organization.

Although the phenomenon of NGOs is as old as society, several factors have elevated their importance in recent decades. One is the increased number of narrow and broad interests—with the progress of science, culture, and society, we are aware today of many new concerns that simply were not knowable in the past. Another factor is the increased ease of identifying and organizing around common interests, even when those interests are highly dispersed. As Mancur Olson identified in 1965 (Olson, 1965), concentrated special interests tend to be well organized and to pursue their causes in the political system. But diffuse interests are more difficult to mobilize because each member gains only a small amount from collective action—no individual has a sufficiently strong interest to take on the task of organizing the group. With greater ability to communicate information at lower cost—for example, through television, specialized publications produced with desktop publishing, lower-cost travel, and mass mailings by post and the Internet—it is easier for entrepreneurs to identify and organize people and organizations with common interests. Because NGOs often form networks and alliances based around common ideas, these effects typically compound. Thus the number of NGOs and awareness of their influence have grown exponentially. These effects, because they include transnational links, are one manifestation of the phenomenon often labeled *globalization.*

NGOs take many different forms; Table 1 shows a typology based on the goals and types of issue that they pursue. The most general classification typically used

Nongovernmental Organizations. TABLE 1. Goals, Funding, Strategy, and Tactics of NGOs

TYPE OF NGO	GOALS	FUNDING SOURCES	STRATEGY AND TACTICS
Public interest, such as environmental, human rights, development (e.g., Greenpeace, Amnesty International, Pugwash, Friends of the Earth)	Promote "public interest"	Dues and donations; grants from foundations and like-minded governments; in-kind contributions	Exposure of offending actions and other means of increasing transparency of behavior; mobilizing consumers; lobbying; provide community atmosphere
Commercial associations (e.g., Chemical Manufacturers Association, Global Crop Protection Federation, Global Climate Coalition)	Promote common profit interest	Dues and donations	Lobbying; research; education of members
Scientific and analytic associations (e.g., American Geophysical Union, International Council of Scientific Unions, Pugwash)	Promote science and scientific research; promote use of "independent" analysis	Grants from governments; dues from individuals and organizations; in-kind contributions	Provide forum and platform for experts; provide coordinated and consensus research plans (thus making fundraising easier); provide consensus expert views on complex topics
Spiritual associations (e.g., World Council of Churches)	Promote spirituality and spiritual organizations	Dues (tithing); assessments on member organizations; in-kind contributions	Represent God or other spiritual authority; provide community
Political parties	Get elected	Donations; government contributions; in-kind contributions	Campaigns to mobilize public interest generally and for particular candidates

for a NGO is based on goals—public interest, commercial, scientific, and so on. Over the last decade, public interest groups have attracted the most attention from practitioners and scholars who have observed the rising power of NGOs as organizers and promoters of mass public movements. However, the phenomenon is hardly new. Since the 1960s, many analysts have speculated that transnational networks of corporations—some formally organized—had eclipsed the power of the state. And even earlier during European colonialization, entities that were part state and part nonstate—quasi-nongovernmental organizations (QUANGOs), such as the Dutch East Indies corporation—dominated or supplanted local governance.

The broad groups shown in Table 1 are often further subdivided according to the issue that they pursue—for example, environmental NGOs (ENGOs), human rights groups, and so on. The goals and issues of an NGO partially determine the resources that are available to be tapped by the group. In turn, goals, issues, and funding affect tactics and strategy. For example, as Bonner (1993) shows, groups that depend on dues from broad memberships must select issues (for example, the ban on trade in elephant ivory) and tactics (campaigns based on salient images) that appeal to the broad nature of the resources that they tap. Thus Table 1 associates funding,

tactics, and strategy with the different types of NGOs. Note that the table is intended only to indicate tendencies, since there are many exceptions and complications.

Fundamentally, the many different types of NGO all face similar challenges and tasks. Typically an NGO is formed, or an existing NGO takes on an issue, because it is inefficient for individual interests to act alone. The NGO exists to provide a collective benefit to its supporters. When the benefits of NGOs are commonly available, they often face the problem of free riders. Thus NGOs often attempt to restrict their benefits to supporters, for example by providing informative newsletters and magazines only to dues-paying members. Often NGOs exist in highly competitive environments, with many strategies for survival and growth. Some groups are highly specialized—they pursue one issue, with one source of funding and a single set of tactics. Other groups generalize, often building up their reputation with a small number of issues and trading on their brand to expand. The environmental group Greenpeace, for example, earned its reputation with protests against whaling and nuclear testing in the 1960s and 1970s; since then, Greenpeace has grown into a multinational nongovernmental enterprise active on most major environmental issues. In Europe, green political parties have gained power by specializing on issues (the environment) that attract voters and forming alliances with other parties to form governing parliamentary majorities.

When NGOs act in public forums, such as through lobbying, all typically claim that they are acting in the public interest. Terminology that is widely used to classify and discuss NGOs, such as in Table 1, may be somewhat biased—fundamentally, all interest groups act for some segment of the public. Identifying the true public interest in that collection of views is a perennial challenge of democratic political systems.

The density of NGOs is greatest in pluralistic democracies, notably the United States. Those societies favor the creation of private special interests. In some cases they reward successful NGO directly, such as by awarding court fees and damages in citizen suits brought by NGOs. Governments in these countries often fund NGO activities, both inside their own borders and in other countries that advance the government's policies. Examples include direct funding and political support for human rights and dissident groups in countries that have been deemed oppressive or otherwise contrary to the interests of the supporting country's interests. Government support of NGOs, working inside other countries, is an extension of power politics by other means. The rising number and influence of NGOs is both cause and consequence of spreading democratic principles of government, such as the freedom of speech, the right of association, and the protection of broad human rights.

Indeed, the line between government and nongovernment is increasingly blurred. Traditionally, NGOs were seen as instruments for giving a voice to interests— for example, an NGO would identify issues, expose injustices, or lobby for action by government. But NGOs also play an important, perhaps growing, role by implementing policy. For example, debt-for-nature swaps—in which public debt is bought and extinguished at a discount price in exchange for governmental promises to protect environmental assets such as rainforests—were conceived and mainly implemented by NGOs such as Conservation International.

Often partnerships between public (government) and private (NGO) bodies are most effective, especially for the complicated task of implementing public policies. For example, the Global Environment Facility (GEF) of the United Nations Development Programme, the United Nations Environment Programme, and the World Bank includes a program for small grants conceived by NGOs. Moreover, the standard practice for implementing projects—whether or not the project is initiated by NGOs—entails the active participation of local public interest groups to shape the design and carry out the elements of the project. These experiences are relatively recent—extensive public participation in World Bank projects has been commonplace only since the 1980s. Over the long run, this approach probably empowers NGOs, which may lead to a further weakening of governmental monopoly on power, further blurring the line between government and nongovernment actors.

NGOs raise many important issues with respect to how society organizes itself. Many celebrate the rising influence of NGOs as a sign of a new form of stakeholder democracy. The logical extension of that argument holds that not only should a wide array of NGOs influence public policy decisions, but NGOs should also implement those decisions, perhaps funded by tax revenues transferred from the state. The function of the state, itself, may change—from the single central actor in political life to a switchboard. However, it is hardly clear that NGOs are eclipsing the state or that they are always democratic. Indeed, the rising importance of NGOs also raises many challenges for democracy. Nongovernmental actors can often perform governmental functions more efficiently; but this blurring of government and nongovernment, public and private, leads many to fear that critical functions of government are being captured by special interests. Moreover, not all interests are equally well organized and heard, as Mancur Olson correctly argued; minority and diffuse interests may be especially trampled by stakeholder democracy.

Truly balanced NGO participation is not easy to achieve or guarantee. Much of the policy debate over how to promote the creation and participation of NGO has focused on rights of participation, such as access to policy debates, access to information, and the right to be heard. Those factors are important, but access often does not translate into influence, and often the opening of a decision-making forum to outsiders merely results in the shifting of decision making to other, closed forums.

[See also Basel Convention; Chemical Industry; Convention on International Trade in Endangered Species; Environmental Movements; Friends of the Earth; Global Environment Facility; Greenpeace; International Institute for Applied Systems Analysis; and World Conservation Union, The.]

BIBLIOGRAPHY

Bonner, R. *At the Hand of Man: Peril and Hope for Africa's Wildlife*. New York: Knopf, 1993.

Charnovitz, S. "Two Centuries of Participation: NGO and International Governance." *Michigan Journal of International Law* 18 (1996), 183–286.

Finger, M., and T. Princen. *Environmental NGO in World Politics: Linking the Local and the Global*. New York: Routledge, 1994.

Olson, M. *The Logic of Collective Action*. Cambridge: Harvard University Press, 1965.

United Nations Center for Human Settlements (HABITAT). *An Urbanizing World: Global Report on Human Settlements*. New York and Oxford: Oxford University Press, 1996.

Victor, D. G., et al., eds. *The Implementation and Effectiveness of International Environmental Commitments: Theory and Practice*. Cambridge: MIT Press, 1998.

Weale, A. *The New Politics of Pollution.* Manchester, U.K.: Manchester University Press, 1992.

Wirth, D. "Reexamining Decision-Making Processes in International Environmental Law." *Iowa Law Review* 79 (1994), 769–802.

World Bank. *The World Bank Participation Sourcebook.* Washington, D.C., 1996.

—DAVID G. VICTOR

NONRENEWABLE RESOURCES. *See* Resources.

NORTH SEA

[*This case study focuses on natural and anthropogenic changes in the North Sea and on the international actions being taken to regulate waste inputs in this area.*]

The total area of the North Sea is 575,000 square kilometers. The southern end is constricted at the Straits of Dover, but there is no geographical northern boundary, although for practical purposes it can be regarded as a line from Shetland to the Norwegian coast near Bergen. The southern and eastern parts are shallow, with depths mostly less than 50 meters. The northern part is 45–120 meters deep, with deeper water off the Norwegian coast. It is not a homogeneous body of water, and a number of areas can be distinguished between which water exchange is relatively slow (Figure 1). Flushing time in these areas varies between 46 and 333 days, although surface water to a depth of 10 meters is exchanged more rapidly. Overall there is an excess of precipitation over evaporation but, in winter, the lee effect of the British Isles produces a net water loss by evaporation in the western and southwestern parts of the North Sea. During summer, all parts of the North Sea receive an excess of water by precipitation and, with surface water becoming less saline, stratification of warm, less dense water over the deeper water (i.e., a thermocline) is encouraged. [*See* Marginal Seas.]

The North Sea is used as intensively and for as great a variety of purposes as any sea area in the world. The Straits of Dover and the southern North Sea are among the most heavily trafficked sea lanes in the world; gravel and sand for the construction industry are dredged in a number of areas; and gas and oil are extracted in the central and northern North Sea. It contains highly productive fisheries, which are exploited intensively. It provides wintering grounds for dense flocks of seabirds and shorebirds from northern Europe and Siberia and, particularly on its northern coasts, supports large breeding colonies of seabirds and seals.

A largely urban and industrialized population of

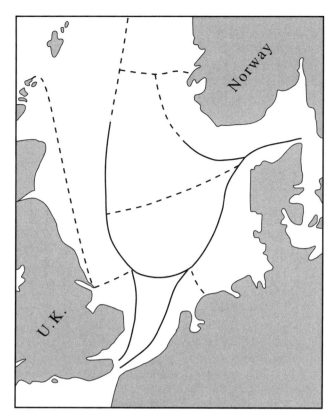

North Sea. FIGURE 1. Relatively Isolated Areas within the North Sea.

Broken lines indicate partial separation of water bodies. (Adapted from Korringa, 1968 and Clark, 1997. *Marine Pollution*, Figure 9.1.)

thirty-one million lives around the North Sea and its estuaries, and to these is added an influx of summer visitors, particularly to the sandy beaches. The North Sea receives the wastes from this population, together with those carried in by a number of major rivers draining much of central Europe—the Rhine, Elbe, Weser, Scheldt, and Ems—as well as the Thames, Trent, Tees, Tyne, Forth, and Tay from Britain. There is also a substantial input of wastes from atmospheric deposition derived from a wide area of Europe.

Natural Change. The southern half of the English North Sea coast sinks at the rate of about 1 millimeter per year. One 60-kilometer stretch of coast in East Anglia has receded by 1–6 meters per year for the last thousand years, losing an average of 1 million cubic meters of cliff per year; a number of medieval villages and towns are now submerged and are several kilometers off the present shoreline (Barnes, 1977). Erosion continues on these coasts and, if predictions of a rise in sea level as a consequence of global warming are fulfilled, the rate will increase.

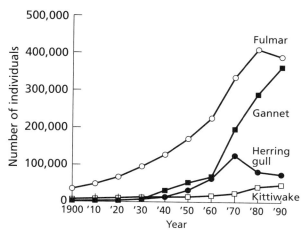

North Sea. FIGURE 2. Trends in Seabird Populations Breeding on North Sea Coasts. (After Oslo and Paris Commissions, 1993.)

Seabirds. About ten million seabirds are present in the North Sea, and four million birds of twenty-eight species breed on northern coasts. In addition, large numbers of waders and seaduck feed on mud and sand flats, particularly those bordering the southern North Sea; six to twelve million birds of more than fifty species use the Wadden Sea. Many birds leave in autumn but are replaced by visitors from northern and western waters.

Throughout the twentieth century, there has been a steady increase in seabird populations (Figure 2). The fulmar *Fulmarus glacialis* first bred on the North Sea coast in 1878, but by 1990 had become the second most abundant species. Breeding colonies of many species on British coasts, representing more than 80 percent of the North Sea breeding populations, doubled in size between 1969–1970 and 1985–1987; skuas increased by 150–220 percent (Lloyd et al., 1991). A few species declined in numbers during this period. In other areas, such as the Wadden Sea, the majority of population changes have also been increases (International Council for the Exploration of the Sea, 1995).

The reasons for these population changes are uncertain. The northward recession of subarctic species, principally guillemot (murre) *Uria aalge* and puffin *Fratercula arctica*, on both sides of the Atlantic during this century, with the depletion or disappearance of breeding colonies at the southern fringe of their geographical range in the English Channel and on the coast of Maine and increases in more northerly populations, is probably related to climatic change and is correlated with the northward extension of the range of temperate flora and fauna. However, much of the increase in seabird populations in the North Sea is attributed by ornithologists to the increased availability of food pro-

vided by the offal and unwanted fish discarded as a result of the expansion of the fishing effort in the North Sea.

Seals. Two species of seal breed on North Sea coasts: the gray seal *Halichoerus grypus* (of which 40 percent of the world population breeds on northern North Sea coasts) and the common or harbor seal *Phoca vitulina*. Both species have increased in numbers in this century (Figure 3). Numbers of common seals were drastically reduced by epidemic disease in 1988, but have since recovered in most areas.

The reasons for this increase are unknown. The cessation of seal hunting after the early years of the twentieth century may have been a contributory factor, but Baltic populations of ringed seal *Phusa hispida*, also no longer hunted, have declined steadily, it is thought because of contamination with chlorinated hydrocarbon pollutants, but North Sea seals are equally contaminated without suffering in this way (Clark, 1997). The feeding habits of seals do not suggest that fishing discards have increased their food supply.

Anthropogenic Changes. Reclamation of land from the sea in the Netherlands began in the twelfth century, and Dutch experts assisted in the drainage of coastal wetlands in East Anglia in England from the sixteenth to the early nineteenth century. Since 1919, the Zuider Zee and Delta Plan have been in progress in the Netherlands to isolate the Zuider Zee and Rhine–Meuse estuary from the North Sea and convert the impounded

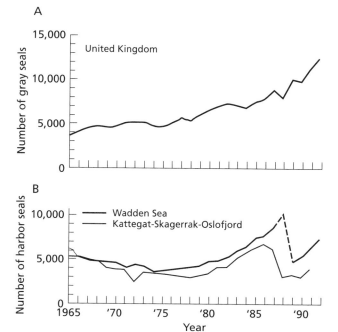

North Sea. FIGURE 3. Trends in Seal Populations.

(A) Estimated gray seal pup production on U.K. North Sea coasts. (B) Numbers of harbor seals in the North Sea (excluding Scotland and Norway). (After Oslo and Paris Commissions, 1993.)

areas to agricultural land. Almost a quarter of the land in the Netherlands has been reclaimed from the sea or coastal lakes and marshes (Barnes, 1977). [*See* Land Reclamation.]

Immigrant species. Thirty alien species have established themselves in the North Sea (Eno et al., 1997). The oyster *Crassostrea gigas* and clams *Mya arenaria* and *Mercenaria mercenaria* were deliberately introduced from North America for commercial purposes, and self-sustaining populations now exist on a number of North Sea coasts. *Mya* is thought to have been introduced from the American coast in the sixteenth or seventeenth century, but there is evidence that the Vikings transported this species from America to Europe as early as 1245. A number of oyster pests were introduced accidentally, probably with imported oysters: they include the American oyster drill *Urosalpinx cinerea*, the slipper limpet *Crepidula fornicata*, the ascidian *Styela clava*, and the alga *Sargassum muticum*. Four other algae, although not pests, are also thought to have been introduced on imported oysters.

Most accidental introductions have been from spores or larvae carried in ships' ballast water or from fouling organisms on ships' hulls. These include five species of planktonic diatom, two species of algae, the cordgrass *Spartina* (although, once this became established, it was planted extensively to stabilize mud flats), two hydroids, three polychaetes, a copepod, a barnacle, and two crabs. The small gastropod *Potamogyrus antipodarum* was accidentally carried to England from Australia in drinking water barrels, probably in 1859. It is a freshwater species and is now the commonest freshwater gastropod in Britain; however, it can also live in estuaries and saline lagoons, and by about 1900 had reached the European mainland, where it is now widespread. The American jack knife clam *Ensis americanus* was first reported from the German Bight in 1978, and has spread widely since then; it was probably introduced as larvae in ballast water. [*See* Exotic Species.]

Eutrophication. In recent years there has been growing concern about eutrophication (overenrichment of waters) in the North Sea. There have been various alarm signals, chiefly in continental coastal waters. Between 1962 and 1985, the phytoplankton biomass at Heligoland in the German Bight increased fourfold, and the plankton community structure changed. This was correlated with an increase in plant nutrient levels. A further sign of eutrophication was the deoxygenation of bottom waters accompanied by the disappearance of fish and death of the benthic fauna that was observed in the German Bight in three consecutive years in the early 1980s. In 1988, an unprecedented bloom of the flagellate *Chrysochromulina polylepis* spread from Danish waters around southern Norway, causing great damage to salmon farms.

The areas most seriously affected by eutrophication are the German Bight and Danish coastal waters. These are shallow and often develop a thermocline in summer. The outflow from the rivers Rhine and Elbe moves northward up the coast of Denmark and does not mix appreciably with the central part of the North Sea. This water carries a large burden of plant nutrients derived from agricultural runoff, and variations in phytoplankton biomass are correlated with the flow rates of these rivers.

Measures to reduce the input of nutrients were introduced after the 1985 North Sea Conference. At that time, 103,000 metric tons per year of phosphorus and 1.5 million metric tons per year of nitrogen entered the North Sea from river inputs, atmospheric fallout, direct discharges, and the dumping of sewage sludge. By 1995, phosphorus inputs had been halved by all North Sea states except France (which had a 25 percent reduction). Nitrogen inputs had been reduced by 25 percent, failing to achieve the objective of a 50 percent reduction. Discharges of untreated sewage from coastal towns had been reduced to a very low level or eliminated altogether in most countries, although 14 percent of sewage discharges from France, and 50 percent from Belgium, are still untreated. Sewage sludge dumping at sea ceased altogether by 1998. Intensive animal farming in Denmark and Holland has had to be limited because of the problems of disposing of the large amount of waste generated (Oslo and Paris Commissions, 1993).

Conservative pollutants. Conservative pollutants (chlorinated hydrocarbons and metals) are not subject to bacterial degradation and are therefore essentially permanent additions to the sea. Since the 1970s, there has been a concerted effort to reduce the input of such substances to the North Sea. Organochlorine pesticides have been withdrawn from use, and an effort to destroy all existing polychlorinated biphenyls (PCBs) by high-temperature incineration is in progress. The use of mercury and mercurial compounds has been severely reduced or discontinued. Sediments of industrialized estuaries contain the legacy of more than one hundred years of uncontrolled discharges. Formerly, dredgings were discharged at sea, making a substantial contribution of metals from contaminated estuarine sediments. Remedial measures have included dumping the highly contaminated dredgings from the Thames estuary on marshes bordering the estuary, capping them with soil, and turning the area into pasture; dredgings from Rotterdam and Hamburg harbors are now dumped on artificial islands instead of at sea. There is now strict regulation of permitted discharges from outfalls and dumping at sea.

Attention has been focused particularly on the bioaccumulating metals mercury and cadmium that may enter the human food chain or reach top predators such as seals. Concentrations in fish are generally low: in the range 0.03–0.22 milligrams per kilogram for mercury and 0.02–0.66 milligrams per kilogram for cadmium. The higher values are recorded in fish from the Southern Bight and the German Bight, including the Thames, Humber, and Ems estuaries. Concentrations of cadmium in the livers of seals from the east coast of England are 0.104–1.0 milligrams per kilogram, and, in the kidneys of Scottish seals, 0.04–4.0 milligrams per kilogram wet weight, both figures well below the concentration of 13–15 milligrams per kilogram considered hazardous. Contamination by other metals can be detected in most parts of the North Sea, but concentrations are generally not sufficient to cause concern.

Although dichlorodiphenyltrichloroethane (DDT) has long been withdrawn from use, and a downward trend in contamination levels can be detected, high levels of it still occur at several places and there are clear concentration gradients off the estuaries of the Thames, western Scheldt, Weser, and Elbe. There is thus a continuing input, presumably derived from runoff from agricultural land. PCB contamination of mussels and fish has similarly shown a downward trend, although high concentrations can still be found in fish from the western Scheldt estuary, the Thames estuary, and those parts of the Waddensee influenced by the rivers Ems, Weser, and Elbe.

Oil pollution. The Straits of Dover are too shallow to allow the passage of a fully laden Very Large Crude Carrier, so the North Sea has been spared catastrophic oil spills, although it has had its share of tanker accidents. The largest oil spill followed the 1977 blowout in the Ekofisk oilfield in the Norwegian sector of the North Sea, when 20,000–30,000 metric tons of crude oil were discharged, but dissipated without detectable effect.

Chronic small-scale oil pollution from general shipping is probably more significant than shipping accidents and oil spills. The North Sea has been designated a "Special Area" by the Oslo and Paris Commissions, and it is illegal for ships to discharge oily ballast and bilge water, but these practices continue and are responsible for the large number of small oil slicks that are reported.

The principal casualties of oil spills are seabirds and, because of the great concentrations of birds, even small oilslicks can cause disproportionate numbers of casualties. Regular counts of dead oiled birds found on North Sea coasts during the last twenty to thirty years have shown a steady reduction in the number of casualties (Camehuysen, 1997). The greatest number of casualties is in winter, when the prevailing westerly winds drift both the floating oil and the birds toward the continental coast, where 70–80 percent of dead birds on the beaches have been oiled (Bourne, 1976). Despite these continuing losses, seabird populations in the North Sea have increased steadily, as discussed above.

Fisheries. Since the resumption of fishing after World War II, the North Sea has been subjected to great fishing pressure. The fishing is monitored and regulated, and catch quotas are agreed upon each year, depending on the strength of recruitment to the fish stocks, but these quotas are often exceeded, and the intensity of fishing pressure has been responsible for a serious decline of some fish stocks. In the 1960s, mackerel *Scomber scombrus* became severely depleted, and the spawning stock has remained low ever since. In the late 1970s, the North Sea herring (*Clupea harengus*) fishery collapsed and was closed for five years. In the early 1990s, haddock *Melanogrammus aeglefinus* and cod *Gadus morhua* stocks were at their lowest for thirty years, creating concern about the future of these fisheries also. [*See* Fisheries.]

The fishery is wasteful because of the large number of unwanted species or undersized fish that are discarded. Trawlers in the western and northwestern North Sea discard 52 percent of their catch; in the eastern North Sea, seine fishing discards 55 percent; in the southern North Sea, beam trawlers discard 56 percent of the catch.

An important development increasing the pressure on fish stocks has been the introduction of "industrial" fishing of small fish for the production of oil and fish meal. Denmark even has an electricity-generating station fueled by fish oil. Before the 1970s, herring and mackerel formed the basis of this industry, but depletion of these fish stocks resulted in Norway pout *Trisopterus esmarkii* and sprats *Sprattus sprattus* being used in their place (Norway pout had not formerly been fished). With the decline of these stocks, they were replaced by sand eels *Ammodytes* after 1985, which now represent two-thirds of the catch for fish meal.

Modern fishing techniques also result in damage to the benthic fauna. Beam trawls and otter boards may remove the top 10 centimeters of substratum and the fauna that it contains, and evidence suggests that recovery from this damage is slow.

Although the strength of recruitment varies from year to year, the practices of the fishing industry have a dominant influence on the size of exploitable fish stocks in the North Sea. Against this background, it is difficult to detect any effects that pollution may have on the fishery. An exception is the incidence of fish diseases, such as epidermal papillomas on flatfish, in some areas where the bottom sediments remain contaminated by conservative pollutants.

International Action. Atmospheric and riverborne inputs account for a considerable fraction of the wastes entering the North Sea, and these are derived from much of western and central Europe, not simply from the population of the coastal zone. The river Elbe carries water from the Czech Republic and Germany into the North Sea, the Rhine receives inputs from Switzerland, France, Germany, Luxembourg, and Holland, while the Scheldt rises in Belgium but flows to the North Sea through Holland. While it is within the power of individual states to improve the quality of some of their waters, in many cases, particularly in areas influenced by the outflow from continental rivers, only international action can achieve any improvement.

In 1974, under an international convention, the Oslo Commission was established to regulate discharges and dumping from ships into the North Sea. The comparable Paris Commission was set up a little later to regulate direct discharges from land. In addition, since most North Sea states are members of the European Union, the European Commission has some power to regulate waste inputs.

The International Council for the Exploration of the Seas includes representatives of all the countries fishing the North Sea, and for almost a hundred years has been responsible for evaluating fish stocks and recommending annual fishing limits. For the last twenty-five years it has also had an important role in arranging monitoring programs and collecting information about pollution levels and impacts.

Since 1984, environment ministers of the North Sea states have met at intervals to discuss the extent and source of the more important wastes reaching the sea and have agreed upon phased reductions of inputs, particularly those affecting the most vulnerable areas in the eastern North Sea.

[See also Greenpeace.]

BIBLIOGRAPHY

Barnes, R. S. K., ed. *The Coastline*. London and New York: Wiley, 1977.

Bourne, W. R. P. "Seabirds and Pollution." In *Marine Pollution*, edited by R. Johnston, pp. 122–140. London and New York: Academic Press, 1976.

Clark, R. B. *Marine Pollution*. 4th ed. New York and Oxford: Oxford University Press, 1997.

Eno, N. C., et al. *Non-Native Species in British Waters: A Review and Directory*. Peterborough, U.K.: Joint Nature Conservation Committee, 1997.

International Council for the Exploration of the Sea. "Report of the Study Group on Ecosystem Effects of Fishing Activities." ICES Cooperative Research Report No. 200. Copenhagen, 1995.

Korringa, P. "Biological Consequences of Marine Pollution with Special Reference to North Sea Fisheries." *Helgolander wissenschaftlichen Meeresuntersuchengun* 17 (1968), 127–140.

Lloyd, C., et al. The *Status of Seabirds in Britain and Ireland*. London: Poyser, 1991.

Oslo and Paris Commissions. *North Sea Quality Status Report, 1993*. London, 1993.

van den Bos, D. J. "Environmental Protection Strategies for Organic Chemicals." In *Environmental Protection of the North Sea*, edited by P. J. Newman and A. R. Agg, pp. 122–140. Oxford: Heinemann, 1988.

—ROBERT B. CLARK

NUCLEAR ACCIDENT AND NOTIFICATION CONVENTIONS

Following the nuclear accident at Chernobyl, Ukraine, in 1986, treaties were negotiated under the auspices of the International Atomic Energy Agency (IAEA) on emergency notification and assistance. They were intended to address the widely perceived failure of the Soviet Union to provide adequate information to neighboring states, and delays in the provision of assistance from outside the Soviet Union.

The 1986 IAEA Convention on Assistance in the Case of a Nuclear Accident or Radiological Emergency was modeled on existing IAEA guidelines and bilateral and other regional arrangements. It is intended to "facilitate prompt assistance in the event of a nuclear accident or radiological emergency to minimize its consequences and to protect life, property and the environment from the effects of radioactive releases" (Article 1(1)). The Convention applies whether or not the accident occurred within the requesting state's territory or jurisdiction, and requires requesting states to specify the assistance they require and to provide any necessary information (Articles 2(3) and (4)). Once a state has received a request for information, it must promptly decide and notify the requesting state whether it is in a position to render the assistance requested and the scope and terms of assistance it might provide, and to notify the IAEA of experts, equipment, and material that could be made available. The IAEA responsibilities include making appropriate resources available for emergency purposes, transmitting information about resources, and, if requested, coordinating available assistance at the national level (Articles 3, 4, 6, 7, 8, and 10). The Convention includes administrative provisions on the direction and control of assistance, competent national authorities, reimbursement of costs, and confidentiality of information. The Convention does not yet appear to have been invoked in an accident. [See Nuclear Hazards.]

The 1986 IAEA Convention on Early Notification of a Nuclear Accident, which supplemented existing bilateral and other treaties, was also modeled on earlier IAEA guidelines. The Convention has been followed by numerous bilateral and regional arrangements. Its adoption occurred in the context of the question of whether a state must warn all other states that are or might be affected by a nuclear accident causing transboundary radioactive harm. This was described as "the main legal issue involved in the Chernobyl nuclear disaster," and the failure by the Soviet Union to inform other states led to the Convention. It incorporates many of the recommendations of the 1985 guidelines and applies in the event of any "accident involving facilities or activities of a state Party or of persons or legal entities under its jurisdiction or control" (Article 1(i)). In the event of such an accident, state parties must notify those states that are or may be physically affected with details of the accident (Article 2). They must also promptly provide the states and the IAEA with such available information as is relevant to minimization of the radiological consequences in those states. This includes the cause and foreseeable development of the accident, the general characteristics of the radioactive release (including its nature, form, quantity, composition, and effective weight), current and future meteorological and hydrological conditions, protective measures planned or taken, and the predicted behavior over time of the release (Article 5(1)). Such information is to be supplemented at "appropriate intervals" by the provision of relevant information, including the foreseeable or actual termination of the emergency situation. States should also respond promptly to requests for further information or consultations sought by an affected state (Article 6). The Convention is the first multilateral agreement to provide detailed rules on the provision of information in emergency situations, including a role for the national authorities of state parties (Article 7) and the IAEA, as well as a binding dispute settlement mechanism.

[*See also* Chernobyl; *and* International Atomic Energy Agency.]

BIBLIOGRAPHY

Adede, A. *The IAEA Notification and Assistance Conventions in Case of a Nuclear Accident.* Leiden: Martinus Nijhoff, 1987.
Sands, P. *Chernobyl: Law and Communication.* Cambridge: Grotius, 1988.
———. *Principles of International Environmental Law*, vol. 1. Manchester, U.K.: Manchester University Press, 1995.

—Philippe J. Sands

NUCLEAR ENERGY.

See Chernobyl; Electrical Power Generation; Energy; Hazardous Waste; Human Health; Insurance; International Atomic Energy Agency; Nuclear Accident and Notification Conventions; Nuclear Industry; Risk; *and* Security and Environment.

NUCLEAR HAZARDS

There is no doubt that all things nuclear are hazardous and dangerous, albeit to varying degrees. However, the mere existence of nuclear hazards does not mean that there are measurable and attributable harmful effects. Many nuclear hazards will fortunately never translate into a consequence that will impact on people and property, but there is always a risk that they could do so. As a result, much debate focuses on the acceptability of these risks and who has the legal or moral right to ac-

cept these risks on behalf of others. Another difficulty is that people's perceptions of the risks associated with various types of nuclear hazard vary and can be modified and perhaps even manipulated by education and propaganda, so that people's beliefs often bear virtually no relationship to the scale or extent of the consequences that could result if a potential hazard were to translate into a real catastrophe. Attitudes toward nuclear hazards are also strongly affected by knowledge (what is hazardous reflects scientific development), by decisions about what is deemed to be acceptable (a function of standards of living), by state secrecy (what we are told), and by fearfulness (based on emotion rather than science).

Nuclear Roulette. Nuclear power promises virtually unlimited low-pollution power supplies for at least the next ten thousand years, nuclear medicine offers various life-saving technologies, and nuclear weapons have brought the longest period of peace between the major powers since the Industrial Revolution. Yet these technologies could also lead to unimaginable disaster. Nuclear accidents have the potential to affect the lives of billions. The high-level atomic wastes created by the arms race and commercial nuclear power programs must be stored safely, virtually forever. A disaster at a major high-level radioactive waste storage facility could require the evacuation of enormous areas, and a major nuclear war could end civilized life. Yet for over thirty years of cold war there was a general acceptance by the developed countries of an explicit military strategy of Mutually Assured Destruction. It now seems genuinely "mad" to have actually gambled with the Earth in this manner, yet this doctrine kept the peace because no one pressed the button. But what right did the North Atlantic Treaty Organisation (NATO) and Russia have to gamble with the life of the entire planet? How long before other nuclear powers start their own mad games on our behalf? Nuclear medicine seems more innocent, but it can also cause harm as well as heal. Every dose of extra radiation, no matter how small, can be harmful to health.

Nuclear Management. It is essential that nuclear hazards be properly managed. Long-lived radioactive wastes accumulate. What starts as a small problem grows incrementally into a large one. Short-term contingency solutions are seldom adequate, as various waste accidents in Russia, the United States, and the United Kingdom have demonstrated. Safety standards and acceptable practices also change over time; for example, sea disposal and the U.K. practice of "dilute and disperse" are no longer acceptable. If one is going to store or dispose of long-lived nuclear waste, then the containment structure has to be designed to last across appropriate, often geologic, time scales. Yet it is also now too late for the world to decide against the nuclear option. If a nuclear power station is closed, the resulting radioactive monument has to be managed for hundreds of years because the technology to demolish it and reclaim the site does not exist. Some nuclear facilities will have to be maintained for the foreseeable future. The Dounreay Facility in the United Kingdom is to be closed, but over a fifty-year period, and even that assumes many billions of dollars are available to perform the decommissioning in a safe manner; so it will probably never happen. The collapse of the Soviet Union as a military power has increased global concern about nuclear management and the safe control of our existing stockpiles of nuclear weapons.

A common difficulty is that the nuclear hazard management systems needed to guard nuclear weaponry against theft or accident, to regulate civilian uses, and to safeguard wastes have to be practically perfect. Yet humans are unable to guarantee anything to 100 percent levels of safety forever. Safety is also a relative concept that depends on the current state of knowledge of harm, on the ability to afford and run the best available technologies, on the absence of overriding state-related factors (such as security aspects), and on comparisons with other sources of harm judged to be similar in magnitude. It is not sufficient to argue that nuclear hazards are not unique because there are several other planet-threatening sources of possible mass destruction that we apparently accept happily or tolerate. The classic bad example is to equate cigarette smoking with the risks of nuclear accidents. An equally inappropriate comparison could be made between, say, predicted accident frequency at major reactors and the theoretical occurrence of large natural disasters, asteroid strikes, biological weaponry of mass destruction, or killer viruses unleashed by terrorists.

Types of Nuclear Hazard. A catalog of nuclear hazards would include the following contributions from the nuclear fuel cycle, nuclear weapons, medical uses, and storage:

- Uranium mining, processing, and waste heaps
- Nuclear power station sites
- Decommissioned nuclear reactors
- Reprocessing and enrichment facilities
- Radioactive waste storage and disposal sites
- Emissions into atmosphere and water from normal, unusual, and secret activities
- Transport of radioactive materials by road, sea, and air
- Manufacture and ultimate safe disposal of medical and consumer products
- Medical imagery using radiation
- Nuclear weapons: manufacture, accidental or intentional detonation, lost weapons and missing components, and sunken atomic-powered submarines
- Nuclear weapons testing: above and below ground

- Nuclear power sources on satellites that partially burn up on or survive reentry

Attitudes to Nuclear Hazards. There are at least five different viewpoints that condition views about the degree of hazard. First, there are nuclear industry scientists, with their calculated and balanced risk assessments, which, because they are followers of a logical positivist science, they genuinely believe until shown to be wrong. Second, there are military, political, and religious leaders who, under extreme circumstance of external threat, will accept virtually any risk, provided it is kept secret. Third, there are members of the public, and some politicians, who expect that the expert nuclear scientists are correct in their risk assessments, and who interpret a scientific risk estimate of, say, 0.0001 percent as zero, meaning that 100 percent safety is guaranteed. Fourth, there are environmental or community groups who worry about the "real" risks, the hidden secrets, the consequences of limited and imperfect scientific knowledge, and corporate and government complacency. Finally, there are adamant foes of nuclear power who are not constrained by fact or logic or science but are fueled by emotion, intuition, and fear about the potential damage that nuclear hazards could entail.

Principal Nuclear Risks. While there are many possible sources of nuclear hazard, not all hazards are equal. The microcuries of americium in domestic smoke detectors are not thought to matter, provided that the material is disposed of safely. Two major areas are of greatest concern: hazards associated with commercial nuclear power programs, and hazards associated with the production, storage, and potential use of nuclear weapons.

Nuclear power has the potential of offering virtually unlimited, clean, carbon-dioxide-free power generation almost indefinitely, but only if one tolerates the environmental risks of the nuclear fuel cycle, if major reactor accidents can be avoided, and if economic and social barriers can be overcome. The nuclear fuel cycle starts with uranium mining. Uranium is shipped to an enrichment plant, and fuel is produced, which is then molded into fuel rods and used to generate electricity. After a few years in a reactor, the spent radioactive fuel is either stored or reprocessed to separate out the plutonium and the unused uranium, both of which can be reused in reactors. The plutonium can be used to fuel fast reactors that will in turn breed more plutonium, thereby permitting more fast reactors to be built. At each step in this process, high- and intermediate-level radioactive wastes are produced, and need to be stored in an environmentally inaccessible form for extremely long periods. Plutonium needs to be guarded constantly to ensure zero diversion into weapons manufacture. The emissions from fuel production and reprocessing operations

NUCLEAR WASTE: SURFACE STORAGE OR DEEP DISPOSAL?

There is considerable controversy as to the best means of the disposing of nuclear long-lived intermediate-level wastes (ILW) and high-level wastes (HLW). On the one hand, some advocate on-site storage (i.e., at the nuclear facility), where no long-distance transport is required, where monitoring is relatively simple, and where one does not have the technical uncertainties that are attached to deep underground disposal. Others advocate deep disposal in underground caverns, on the grounds that this does not expose workers and the local community to the risk of radioactivity, it is safe from terrorist attack, theft, or some accident (e.g., a plane crash), it concentrates the waste at a few (usually remote) locations, and it provides a long-term solution. It is argued that deep disposal in stable geologic formations with a series of containment measures will prevent escape of radionuclides over the periods of time that it will take for them to decay to harmless levels. Against this, however, it has been argued that over the time scales involved (ten thousand to one million years), climatic and geologic stability is unlikely. To find geologically suitable conditions in areas that are politically acceptable seems to be a well-nigh insuperable problem in many countries.

BIBLIOGRAPHY

Blowers, A., and D. Lowry. "The Politics of Radioactive Waste Disposal." In *Energy, Resources and Environment*, edited by J. Blunden and A. Reddish. London: Hodder and Stoughton and Open University, 1996.

need to be minimized because they contribute to both local and global radiation levels. Accidents are to be avoided at all costs. The limitless potential supply of nuclear electricity depends on reprocessing all spent fuel, but the consequences of a global plutonium economy require a degree of control, management, and discipline that hitherto has never existed in human history.

The principal unknowns relate to the storage of high-level waste and safe reactor operation. There are currently no satisfactory high-level waste disposal facilities. The surface storage of highly concentrated wastes constitutes a major hazard, the significance of which is directly related to the associated management systems and the absence of military or terrorist attack. The safety of power reactors is only partially an engineering problem. The Windscale, Three Mile Island, and Chernobyl accidents were considered impossible events until they happened. The cause in all three cases was a combination of human and technical error. Replacing humans with computers does little to provide 100 percent assurance of safety when the latter is a reflection of both tangible and intangible factors such as software bugs, maintenance quality, financial resources, and staff morale. Another nuclear hazard with unknown probability or consequence is a terrorist attack on a power station. The empirical *a priori* risk probability estimate of this happening is zero because it has not yet occurred anywhere in the world. However, common sense suggests that nuclear power stations are strategically im-

portant terrorist and military targets, that they can be severely damaged from a distance, and that the probabilities of such events will vary regionally, but in the aggregate may be very high.

Another, more worrisome risk is that of an intentional exchange of weapons. The breakup of the Soviet Union has increased the risk of weapons being diverted, sold, or stolen. The number of states with nuclear weapons capabilities is also increasing. Confirmed new entrants to the nuclear weapons club (such as India and Pakistan) join other countries that are thought to have nuclear weapons or the ability to build them, such as North Korea, Iran, South Africa, Israel, Brazil, and perhaps Iraq. Finally, the prospect of nuclear terrorism as a crime is increasing as it becomes easier to buy the necessary weapons on the black market.

The problem is that a major nuclear accident or explosion, fire, or weapon use anywhere in the world affects people's perceptions of nuclear hazards everywhere. The no-nuclear option for the world has expired and, as a result, we have now entered a far more dangerous era.

Over the next hundred years there may be a major expansion of commercial nuclear power generation (even if there is a decline in the short to medium term) and a major proliferation of atomic and hydrogen nuclear weapons. The former may be necessary to reduce carbon dioxide emissions as global energy demands increase; the latter may be deemed necessary to ensure the security of nations. At the same time, advances in molecular biology seems likely to provide a basis for a better scientific understanding of the risks of low-level radiation and lead to a further lowering of current safety standards. Better science may permit the construction of suitably safe atomic waste depositories, but, until we can be certain, it would be better to build repositories from which material can be retrieved. The future prospects for hazards associated with nuclear weapons proliferation are frankly grim.

[*See also* Chernobyl; Electrical Power Generation; Energy; Hazardous Waste; Human Health; Insurance; International Atomic Energy Agency; Nuclear Accident and Notification Conventions; Nuclear Industry; Nuclear Winter; Risk; *and* Security and Environment.]

BIBLIOGRAPHY

Hodgson, P. E. *Nuclear Power, Energy and the Environment.* London: Imperial College Press, 1999.
Mounfield, P. R. *World Nuclear Power.* London: Routledge, 1991.
Openshaw, S. *Nuclear Power Siting and Safety.* London: Routledge, 1986.
Openshaw, S., S. Carver, and J. Fernie. *Britain's Nuclear Waste: Siting and Safety.* London and New York: Behaven Press, 1989.

—STAN OPENSHAW

NUCLEAR INDUSTRY

The nuclear industry exploits the nuclear fuel cycle (Figure 1) in two major ways: through the manufacture of nuclear weapons, and through the production of electricity.

Historically, weapons manufacture came first. In the United States, a pilot plant to produce plutonium was built at Oak Ridge, Tennessee in 1943, and was soon followed by three full-size plutonium production reactors at the Hanford Engineering Works, Washington State. Their product was used in the first successful detonation of a nuclear weapon on 16 July 1945.

With the end of World War II, nuclear weapons continued to be amassed, particularly by the United States and the Soviet Union, but reactor technology was turned increasingly to civilian use. Heat is one of the two main products of a nuclear reaction; the other is radiation. It is the heat that is used in the production of electricity. When that heat is held at a low level, reactors are useful for plutonium production but become less capable of producing steam to drive turbines. The close connection is clear, though: once a nation has a nuclear power plant, it is well on the way to being able to produce nuclear weapons.

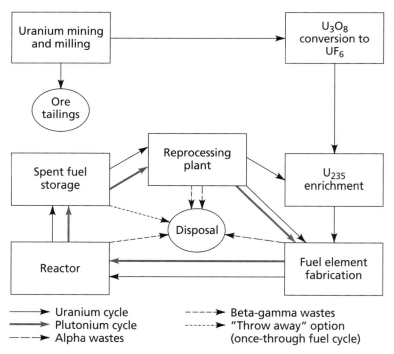

Nuclear Industry. FIGURE 1. The Nuclear Fuel Cycle.

The diagram shows the main stages in the nuclear fuel cycle and the main radioactive waste streams that require disposal. Variants of the cycle are (1) the "once-through" cycle, in which plutonium is left in the spent fuel elements that are not reprocessed and which become the main radioactive waste stream; (2) the reprocessing cycle, in which plutonium is stored pending development of fast reactors; (3) thermal recycling, in which plutonium has some value as replacement fuel burned in thermal reactors, at most 16 percent of the uranium fuel charge; and (4) the fast reactor cycle. (After Mounfield, 1991.)

The Nuclear Fuel Cycle. This widely used term embraces all major phases in the production of heat and radiation by means of nuclear reactors. The front end of the cycle includes uranium mining and milling, conversion of ore concentrate to the standards required for nuclear fuel, fuel enrichment (where required), the manufacture and assembly of fuel elements, and their delivery to reactor sites. The reactor phase includes the storage of fresh fuel at power reactor sites, the burn-up of the fuel in reactors, and the short-term storage of spent fuel after removal from the reactor core. The back end of the fuel cycle begins with the transport of the used fuel away from reactor storage ponds and with the disposal of wastes from reprocessing or long-term storage of the spent fuel. The sequence of back-end events depends upon national and power company policies. In the reprocessing cycle, used fuel assemblies are taken to reprocessing plants such as Sellafield in the United Kingdom and Cap de la Hague in France, where unused uranium and plutonium are separated out for further use. In the once-through fuel cycle, spent fuel is stored following appropriate treatment.

In 1996 there were 447 reactors worldwide producing 17 percent of the world's electricity; thirty-nine others were under construction. Table 1 shows the distribution of reactors country by country. It is clear that at the global level there are four major geographical groupings: (1) the United States and Canada; (2) western Europe; (3) Russia and Belarus, Ukraine, Armenia, Kazakhstan, and certain east European states; (4) East Asia, especially Japan.

Estimates by the International Atomic Energy Agency (IAEA) indicate that the world's nuclear generating capacity will peak in the year 2011 and then begin a steady decline, to produce approximately 12 percent of the electricity generated in 2015. In short, given the long lead times needed to build a nuclear power plant, often over ten years, those under construction and projected are insufficient to maintain existing capacity as existing plants reach the end of their operating lives. The IAEA surmises that, between 2020 and 2030, seventy-five reactors are likely to close in North America, with a loss of 64,000 megawatts, while 108 reactors may be shut down in western Europe, accounting for about 92,000 megawatts of installed capacity. In the third group, fifty will be shut down, losing 42,500 megawatts. Only Asia is expected to show a net increase. There may be some imprecision in these figures because much attention is being given to extending the lives of some existing plants by means of a variety of technical fixes— much of the nuclear engineering industry is now engaged in what is wryly termed *nuclear gerontology*—but a large reduction is inevitable. In the post-Chernobyl era, public acceptance of nuclear power has been difficult to maintain and, in a significant number of regions, other fuels such as natural gas have proved to be cheaper alternatives for electricity generation.

Nuclear Proliferation. The production of nuclear weapons and the generation of electricity by nuclear power plants both contribute to the accumulation of quantities of plutonium and highly enriched uranium. Although it is technically easier to engineer an explosive nuclear device with uranium-235, the simplest route for plutonium production is the reprocessing of spent nuclear fuel to separate its plutonium-239 content. Only 10 kilograms of plutonium-239 are required to trigger a powerful nuclear weapon. Thus controlling the spread of the means by which plutonium is produced and accounting for that in existence at any time, down to very small quantities, have become major preoccupations for those involved in regulating the industry.

The main international agency concerned with regulation is the IAEA, which came into existence in 1957 as part of U.S. President Dwight D. Eisenhower's Atoms for Peace plan. The IAEA was given two tasks: to help United Nations countries acquire nuclear skills in electricity production, health care, agricultural development, and industry, and to prevent the proliferation of nuclear weapons through the diversion of nuclear materials to military use by nonnuclear powers. The arrival of the Nuclear Non-Proliferation Treaty (NPT) in 1970, with 186 signatories by 1997, emphasized the second role: signatories without nuclear weapons have been obliged to allow regular IAEA scrutiny of their civil nuclear programs. The five recognized nuclear weapons states are France, Russia, the United States, the United Kingdom, and China, but three others—India, Pakistan, and Israel—either have nuclear weapons or the means to make them, and have not signed the NPT.

In the period 1985–1995, three events in particular emphasized the importance of the IAEA: the Chernobyl nuclear power plant accident in 1986, the discovery of a clandestine nuclear weapons program in Iraq in 1991, and the breakup of the Soviet Union into independent states. The IAEA failed to detect the Iraqi bomb program because until 1991 it relied upon an inadequate system of accounting for nuclear materials. It now uses an array of verification techniques including challenge inspections, space satellite imagery, and modern forms of environmental monitoring involving analysis of air, water, and soil samples by laser mass spectrometry. But careful accounting is still required. Since the breakup of the Soviet Union, police across the world, but especially in Europe, have been intercepting scores of smugglers unlawfully carrying small quantities of stolen material.

In 1970 the NPT was granted a lifetime of twenty-five years by the signatories. In May 1995 the 178 countries then party to the treaty agreed to extend it indefinitely, and confirmed that the treaty involved a commitment to disarmament by the nuclear weapons states. Table 2 in-

Nuclear Industry. TABLE 1. Nuclear Power Reactors in Operation and under Construction as of June 1997

COUNTRY	In Operation		NUCLEAR PERCENTAGE OF TOTAL ELECTRICITY GENERATION (DEC. 1996)	Under Construction	
	RATING (MWE)	UNITS		UNITS	RATING (MWE)
United States	100,579	110	22		
France	59,948	57	77	3	4,355
Japan	42,335	53	33	2	2,111
Germany	22,282	20	30		
Russian Fedn.	19,843	29	13	4	3,375
Canada	14,902	21	16		
Ukraine	13,765	16	44	5	4,750
UK	12,928	35	26		
Sweden	10,040	12	52		
South Korea	9,770	12	36	4	3,220
Spain	7,207	9	32		
Belgium	5,712	7	57		
Taiwan	4,884	6	29		
Bulgaria	3,538	6	42		
Switzerland	3,078	5	45		
Lithuania	2,370	2	83		
Finland	2,335	4	28		
China	2,167	3	1	1	
South Africa	1,842	2	6		
Hungary	1,729	4	41		
India	1,695	10	2	4	808
Czech Rep.	1,648	4	20	2	1,824
Slovakia	1,632	4	45	4	1,552
Mexico	1,308	2	5		
Argentina	935	2	2	1	692
Romania	650	1	1	1	650
Slovenia	632	1	38		
Brazil	626	1	1	1	1,245
Netherlands	504	2	5		
Armenia	376	1	37		
Pakistan	125	1	1	1	300
Kazakhstan	70	1	>1		
Iran				2	2,146
World	351,475	443	17	35	27,028

SOURCE: From *IAEA Bulletin* 39.2 (June 1997, p. 37).

dicates a total of 2,075.23 metric tons of plutonium and highly enriched uranium accumulated in nine countries by 1995. Less than 400 metric tons are required to sustain nuclear arsenals at their reduced levels, so around 1,675 metric tons are counted as excess. To this total the principal reprocessing countries, Britain, France, and Russia, add around 7–8 metric tons of plutonium each year from reprocessing of spent fuel.

Radioactive Waste. Each phase of the nuclear fuel cycle produces radioactive waste in the form of gases, liquids, sludges, and solids, which, because of their inherent toxicity, must either be treated to remove most of the contaminants or diluted to a point where they reach permitted levels, prior to controlled release to the environment: wastes incapable of being so handled must be stored. Uncontrolled releases of radioactive conta-

Nuclear Industry. TABLE 2. Estimated "Surplus" Military Plutonium and Highly Enriched Uranium Stocks in 1995

COUNTRY	WEAPONS-GRADE PLUTONIUM (METRIC TONS)	HIGHLY ENRICHED URANIUM (METRIC TONS)
Russia	130	1,050
United States	85	645
France	5	24
China	4	20
UK	3.1	8
Israel	0.4	
India	0.3	
North Korea	0.03	
Pakistan		0.4
Total	327.83	1,747.4

SOURCE: From Albright et al. (1996).

minants have occurred in accidents at nuclear reactors, reprocessing plants, and storage facilities, and have sometimes caused severe environmental damage. The worst to date occurred at Chernobyl in Ukraine on 26 April 1986. [See Chernobyl.]

The general characteristics of radioactive waste relevant to waste disposal are summarized in Table 3: they are qualitative and vary between countries. Such waste is categorized, too, according to the volume produced, the amount of activity it contains, and its form—whether liquid, solid, or gaseous.

High-volume, low-activity solid wastes arise in mining and uranium ore processing at the front end of the fuel cycle, from reactor operations, and from plant decommissioning. Generally speaking, low-activity wastes contain radionuclides with short half-lives and are short-lived.

Most of the world's annual total of mined uranium—around 34,000 metric tons in 1995—is mined in Canada (32 percent), southern Africa (21 percent), the former Soviet Union (18 percent), Australia (11 percent), and the United States (7 percent). In the early days, uranium mining was conducted without much knowledge of any possible adverse environmental effects from mine waste dumped on the surface and subject to wind, rain, and runoff. Indeed, such waste was sometimes used as building aggregate, with adverse consequences later for residents (such as those at Grand Junction, Colorado and Canonsburg, Pennsylvania). In normal reactor operation, low-activity solid waste is produced in the form of discarded protective clothing, paper, and equipment originating from the active area of the plant. Commonly, this type of waste is buried in designated shallow trenches and much of it is almost free of contamination.

The disposal of low-activity liquid waste from nuclear power plants and fuel reprocessing factories depends upon the siting of the works. Those with a coastal location, or on the bank of a large river or lake, remove sufficient radionuclides from liquid waste by distillation or floc precipitation (when particles—in this case radioactive—are so small that they would pass through a filter, they can be brought together into a sediment that can then be removed from the liquid waste stream) to produce effluents of "acceptable" purity prior to discharge into the adjacent water body. In the past, some inland nuclear fuel reprocessing plants in the United States and Russia have discharged wastes into seepage ponds.

Medium-volume, medium-activity wastes are produced by reactor operation and fuel reprocessing; such wastes include ion-exchange resins, sludges, and precipitates, and may include some plutonium-contaminated material (PCM). The liquid waste may be concentrated by evaporation and then stored for a number of years or treated by floc precipitation.

Solid low-volume high-activity waste comprises fuel element cladding and solidified material from reprocessing. At present, the common practice is to store cladding waste pending a satisfactory means of ultimate disposal. High-activity liquid waste is produced entirely in fuel reprocessing operations. It is stored in double-walled tanks, a practice that may work for tens of years but not for longer, or as vitrified borosilicate glass.

At Hanford the storage of quantities of liquid waste in single-walled tanks has justifiably given rise to harsh criticism by concerned scientists and environmentalists. The disposal of high-activity wastes presents problems because of their potential as biological hazards. Not only

Nuclear Industry. TABLE 3. General Characteristics of Radioactive Waste Categories Relevant to Waste Disposal*

WASTE CATEGORY	IMPORTANT CHARACTERISTICS
I. High level long lived	High β–γ Significant α High radiotoxicity High heat output
II. Intermediate level long lived	Intermediate β–γ Significant α Intermediate toxicity Low heat output
III. Low level long lived	Low β–γ Significant α Low–intermediate radiotoxicity Insignificant heat output
IV. Intermediate level short lived	Intermediate β–γ Insignificant α Intermediate radiotoxicity Low heat output
V. Low level short lived	Low β–γ Significant α Low radiotoxicity Insignificant heat output

*Note that "insignificant" indicates that the characteristics can generally be ignored for disposal purposes. An alpha emitter (α) is a radionuclide that emits alpha particles. An alpha particle consists of two protons and two neutrons and has a net charge of +2. Alpha emission is a high linear energy transfer radiation. A beta emitter (β) is a radionuclide that emits beta particles, which have a mass and charge equal to an electron (−1). Beta emission is a low linear energy transfer radiation. Gamma rays (γ) are photons emitted from the nucleus of a radionuclide during radioactive decay.

SOURCE: From Mounfield (1991, p. 333).

are they highly active, but they also contain some very long-lived activity (for example, americum-241, with a half-life of 458 years; plutonium-239, with a half-life of twenty-four thousand years, and others even longer). There is also a need to dissipate heat caused by radioactive decay.

Such waste has to be stored in isolation from the Earth's biosphere and remote from the human environment—but where, and for how long? The half-lives of many of the elements in highly active wastes come close to geologic time scales. In the relevant technical literature, however, the notion of storage of high-level waste for around a thousand years is increasingly common, and there is general agreement that the technology to build stores successfully is available. There is less agreement as to whether they should be deep underground, benefiting from barriers to water ingress provided by a suitable geologic environment, or on the surface, where they may be more easily monitored. And there is no agreement at all regarding where they should be. The result of these uncertainties is that a carefully engi-

neered long-term storage facility for high-level radioactive waste exists nowhere in the world, despite the fact that the nuclear industry has existed for half a century and each year is producing steadily increasing inventories of such waste. In the United States, the WIPP (Waste Isolation Pilot Plant), 650 meters (2,150 feet) underground in the salt fields of New Mexico, may become such a store, but in country after country, including the United States, public acceptance of facilities to store even intermediate-level waste has proved difficult to obtain. No community wants a radioactive waste store in its backyard, and the nuclear industry meanwhile has to entrust high-level waste to interim storage facilities. [See Nuclear Hazards.]

The status of radioactive waste storage in the territory of the former Soviet Union is a cause for concern. Russia, Belarus, Kazakhstan, Ukraine, and Armenia all have nuclear industries that are chronically short of money and in disarray to a greater or lesser degree. Responsible press reports indicate that Russia does not have an accurate inventory of its nuclear waste and does not know where all of it is. A "best guess" is that in 1996 there were approximately 610 million cubic meters of solid waste, of different activity levels, much of it poorly stored on open ground or at radiochemical establishments. Meanwhile, thousands of nuclear weapons are being decommissioned and metric tons of plutonium and weapons-grade uranium added to existing stocks. There is a chronic shortage of facilities for the interim storage of spent nuclear fuel, and the explosion of a tank at Tomsk containing a solution of uranium and plutonium in April 1993 indicated incompetent disposal. From the 1950s to 1994 the former Soviet Union injected half of the liquid radioactive waste that it produced into the ground at three sites, widely dispersed but all close to big rivers. One was at Dimitrovgrad near the River Volga, flowing into the Caspian Sea, the second was at Tomsk, near the River Ob, flowing into the Arctic Ocean, and the third was at Krasnoyarsk on the Yenisey River, also flowing to the Arctic. The material was injected under layers of shale and clay, it is not retrievable, and the best hope is that it will stay underground away from aquifers for long enough to be reasonably safe. The scandal of rusting nuclear submarines in harbors around Murmansk is widely acknowledged. There are about a hundred such vessels, well out of use, but even by November 1996 the nuclear fuel had been removed from less than a quarter of them. The Russian navy suffers an acute shortage of storage facilities for old reactor cores and fuel assemblies. In the past it has "solved" the problem by dumping the reactors at sea, some of them still containing their spent fuel. It has been reported that, between 1966 and 1991, eighteen reactors were dumped in the Barents and Kara Seas, six of them still containing fuel, together with thirteen thousand containers of solid radioactive waste. Eight such vessels lie in shallow water in Abrosimova Bay in Novaya Zemlya.

The waste disposal situation in the territories of the former Soviet Union constitutes one of the most serious current environmental and security policy challenges faced anywhere in the world. The United States has tried to help. In November 1994, 600 kilograms of highly enriched uranium was moved from the Ust-Kamenagorsk storage facility in Kazakhstan to the United States after Kazakhstan advised Washington that it could not guarantee the safety and security of the stockpile. This material was sufficient to produce more than twenty nuclear bombs. But radioactive waste disposal arrangements in the United States itself are far from ideal. There is no final depository for high-level waste. The United States Department of Energy (DOE) in 1983 was granted fourteen years to achieve the safe disposal of high-level waste, its efforts funded by a tax on the consumption of electricity produced by nuclear power plants. In February 1997 the agency admitted that it would not be able to complete development of a suitable permanent site until the year 2010, and even a temporary site would not be ready until 2001. Meanwhile, there are big decommissioning problems such as those posed by the 1,300 square kilometer (500 square mile) Hanford site on the Columbia River. This contains a former plutonium production center and an energy and weapons research complex. In 1996 there were 177 underground tanks of high-level waste; five buildings where plutonium was extracted, 2,100 metric tons of irradiated fuel in store, and the remains of nuclear reactors built over half a century earlier. In May 1997 an explosion occurred at the plutonium processing section in a storage tank in which chemicals had been poorly stored. A toxic plume was released, and plutonium-contaminated water ejected outside the plant.

The United States has decided to dispose of its surplus weapons plutonium by burning it in power plants and by vitrification combined with burial. Around 33 metric tons of metallic plutonium is to be burned and 17 metric tons immobilized in a glass or ceramic matrix. One part of plutonium mixed with twenty parts of natural uranium oxide makes a mixed oxide fuel (MOX) that has been used for some years in Europe to fuel reactors. It is more expensive than uranium oxide fuel, but afterwards the spent fuel can be treated like any other high-level radioactive waste.

Fast Breeder Reactors. The main argument in favor of fast breeder reactors has always been that the world's supply of uranium at economic prices is limited and that such reactors can be designed and built to produce more fuel than they use, in the form of plutonium. Thus they have been attractive to nations short of fossil fuels, such as France and Japan, but Russia, too, has valued them highly. The United States has a long-standing policy of opposing the technology, which has never been part of Canada's program either. The United Kingdom's prototype fast breeder reactor at Dounreay, in the far north of Scotland, was closed as a government policy decision in 1994, effectively ending forty years of research and development. France's 1,300 megawatt Superphenix, built at Creys-Malville, south of Lyons, as the world's largest fast breeder reactor and subject to a four-year shutdown in 1990, was revived in August 1994, but as a center for research into the burning of plutonium and nuclear waste.

Breeders are expensive to build and offer siting and technological problems. In Japan, fast breeder development is focused on the Monju reactor located near the coastal town of Tsuruga, 320 kilometers west of Tokyo. It was commissioned in August 1995, ten years after its inception. It is a large installation, rated at 280 megawatts, but in 1995 it suffered leakage of around 3 metric tons of liquid sodium. After this, the fast reactor program in Japan, already subject to severe criticism as expensive and unnecessary at a time of falling uranium prices, became subject to the same opprobrium and unpopularity faced by the rest of the nuclear program.

In the former Soviet Union a fast reactor, the BN600, has operated at Beloyarsk since 1981 with a claimed availability level of 80 percent. A larger unit, the BN800, is destined for a site at Chelyabinsk in the southern Urals and, intriguingly, is reputed to have been designed to produce no more plutonium than is burned. In the West, however, such reactor technology has lost favor because of its expense in the face of falling fuel prices and rising plutonium stocks.

Current Status in the United States and Canada. Table 1 shows that there are no nuclear power plants under construction in the United States. Four units, Bellefonte 1 and 2, Watts Bar 2, and Perry 2 have been granted construction licenses but are indefinitely deferred. Nuclear power in the United States, for a variety of reasons, is perceived at present as an option that power utilities cannot afford. Major suppliers such as Westinghouse and General Electric have kept their reactor research and design teams intact but have downsized elsewhere and turned much of their expertise to nuclear gerontology. Canada's prime exponent of nuclear power, Ontario Hydro, operates nineteen nuclear power stations, which provide 90 percent of the country's nuclear energy. In August 1997 an independent report by the Nuclear Performance Advisory Group, a private U.S. nuclear industry consultant, found that the utility did not have the management competence to operate all its stations safely. By March 1998 the company will have shut down seven of the operating nuclear power stations, as most of the senior management are replaced and its 8,400 employees retrained.

Western Europe. In France, three new nuclear units were under construction in 1997. There were none under construction in Germany, the United Kingdom, Sweden, Spain, Belgium, or any other country in the region. Retrenchment has been the theme in the nuclear construction industry, with serious attempts made in 1996 to merge the Anglo-French company GEC Alsthom with the French state-controlled nuclear construction company Framatome.

Former Soviet Union and Eastern Europe. In July 1995 a U.S. report identified ten nuclear reactors posing a "serious safety risk" because of design flaws and lax safety procedures in Slovakia (Bohunice), Lithuania (Ignalia), Russia (Kola), Bulgaria (Koztodny), and Ukraine (Chernobyl). In March 1997 an international expert report judged Lithuania's two 1500 megawatt reactors at the Ignalia facility to be unsafe. These are the largest Chernobyl-style RBMK reactors ever built. They have no reactor core containment of the sort that is customary in Western and Japanese nuclear power plants. Many of the early Soviet-built reactors are based on that at Obninsk, southwest of Moscow, the world's first nuclear power station built specifically to provide electricity, commissioned in 1954 and still in operation as a research facility. These are the RBMK reactors, all designed without containment and all suffering leaks of water and steam from badly designed joints in complex circuitry that raises steam to drive the turbines. At Chernobyl, reactor 3 has been entombed in concrete since the accident in 1986 and reactor 2 was damaged by fire in 1991, but the two remaining reactors are still in operation. For safety reasons, the European Union wants to see all the Chernobyl units closed down permanently. In the Ukraine, since 1990 five new reactors have been under sporadic construction at three sites—Zaporizhzhya, Rivne, and Khmel'nyts'kyy—but the Ukraine's nuclear industry has lacked funds for their completion. Protracted negotiations with the West have been based on a deal balancing the finance for these units against the complete shutdown of all reactors at Chernobyl, and early in 2000 the United States made funds available to achieve this shutdown. The chronic financial state of the Russian industry, too, has been freely acknowledged by Gosatomnadzor, the country's regulatory body, and in the report of the Yoblokov Commission, published in Moscow in 1993. There is wide acceptance of an urgent need to raise safety standards and modernize all phases of the nuclear fuel cycle, but there is very little money to accomplish the task, and most of the available scientific and technological expertise is Russian—a fact often resented by the other republics.

East Asia. Japan has seen nuclear power as a logical solution for an industrial country lacking significant fossil fuel resources. The government has called for fifteen new plants by 2010 to provide 22,000 megawatts of new generating capacity. Because of the atom bombs dropped on Hiroshima and Nagasaki, however, public opinion in Japan has always been anxious about the country's nuclear industry and, after Chernobyl, a number of accidents at nuclear facilities within Japan itself have stiffened public opposition. They have included the Monju incident, leakage of tritium from an advanced thermal reactor at Fugen, 330 kilometers west of Tokyo, and a fire at the nuclear reprocessing plant at Takaimura, 115 kilometers northeast of Tokyo, which caused thirty-seven workers to be exposed to low-level radiation. Public resistance at the sites proposed for new power stations has made it difficult for the power companies to proceed with projects. For example, the Kyushu Electric Power Company, which operates in the southern island of Kyushu, announced in 1996 the cessation of its plans to build a nuclear power station at Miyazaki because of strong local resistance. Such opposition has caused the nuclear industry to falter, and equipment suppliers such as Mitsubishi, Hitachi, and Toshiba have been forced to scale down and restructure their nuclear plant divisions. They are looking, too, for orders elsewhere in East Asia, where China, Indonesia, Malaysia, the Philippines, Thailand, and South Korea are expecting to increase significantly their commitment to nuclear power.

In 1940 it would have been impossible to find anything other than one or two scientific laboratories that could have been described as a nuclear industry: it is a field of human endeavor created in a mere half century. There is no doubt, however, that the effort has been expensive. The cleanup operation at nuclear industrial sites in the United States alone will take the best part of a century and has created a financial liability second in size only to the federal deficit.

The future is uncertain, too. When electricity is generated by nuclear power, the levels of carbon dioxide released, thought to contribute significantly to the greenhouse effect, are only 4 percent of those produced by coal-generated electricity and 8 percent of those produced by burning of natural gas (the figures include mining of the fuels, construction of the plant, and its running). As old nuclear power plants are decommissioned and the task of dismantling them undertaken, new ones are being built, but they will not be sufficient to replace more than a fraction of the capacity that will be lost by 2030. Since the Chernobyl disaster of 1986, only two big industrial countries, France and Japan, have retained a policy of expanding nuclear capacity. Many others have imposed moratoria or outright bans on new nuclear plants. Costs, too, have worked against the nuclear option. The long lead times needed to build nuclear stations may strengthen the case for preserving viable nuclear programs in anticipation of possible fuel shortages sometime into the next century, but for this to happen the problem of safe disposal of nuclear waste will have to be solved. The basic question is whether there is any way of guaranteeing that high-level waste can be stored safely for at least a thousand years. Meanwhile, opportunities for growth in the industry over the short term seem to lie in the developing countries of East Asia rather than in the West.

[*See also* Electrical Power Generation; Energy; Human Health; Risk; *and* Security and Environment.]

INTERNET RESOURCE

International Atomic Energy Agency. *Power Reactor Information System (PRIS)*. Online database containing information on reactor status. BITNET/INTERNET to ID:NES@IAEA.1.IAEA. OR.AT.

BIBLIOGRAPHY

Albright, D., et al. *Plutonium and Highly Enriched Uranium*. New York and Oxford: Oxford University Press, 1996.
Egorov, N. N., V. M. Novikov, F. L. Parker, and U. K. Popov. *The Radiation Legacy of the Soviet Nuclear Complex*. London: Earthscan, 1999.
IAEA Bulletin 39.2 (June 1997), 37.
Mounfield, P. R. *World Nuclear Power*. London and New York: Routledge, 1991.
Spector, L. S., with M. G. McDonough and E. Medeiros. *Tracking Nuclear Proliferation*. Washington, D.C.: Carnegie Endowment for International Peace, 1995.
United States Energy Information Administration. *International Energy Outlook*. Washington, D.C., 1997.
Uranium Institute. *Global Nuclear Fuel Market: Supply and Demand 1995–2015*. London, 1996.

—PETER R. MOUNFIELD

NUCLEAR WINTER

Nuclear winter is a term associated with a constellation of physical and chemical effects associated with the wholesale detonation of nuclear weapons. Aside from the extensive direct destruction and intense radioactive fallout accompanying hostile nuclear explosions, it has been postulated that accompanying changes in the atmosphere and climate might prove to be worse. Massive emissions of smoke and dust would lead to unprecedented pollution of the troposphere, strong attenuation of sunlight, deep surface cooling in continental areas—up to 10°–20°C in the northern midlatitudes—heating and stabilization of the atmosphere, sharply reduced rainfall in some regions, accelerated interhemispheric transport of nuclear debris, and global stratospheric ozone depletion.

Our knowledge of these potential widespread environmental impacts of a nuclear war has advanced considerably since the earliest work on this subject (e.g., Crutzen and Birks, 1982; Turco et al., 1983; NRC, 1985; Pittock et al., 1986). The basic mechanisms that occur

in nuclear winter have been studied, and modified, through increasingly sophisticated theoretical and experimental analyses. The magnitude of predicted land temperature perturbations has decreased from original estimates, as values of key physical parameters have been refined over time. Meanwhile, the severity of other effects—such as potential ozone depletion and exposure to radioactivity—have been projected to be greater. While the most recent forecasts of a nuclear winter are not as dire as first thought, they nevertheless point to enormous global human casualties—very likely greater than those from the direct effects of the nuclear detonations, owing in large part to disruptions in food production and distribution, and the destruction of health facilities and services (Harwell and Hutchinson, 1985; Solomon and Marston, 1986). Significant uncertainties will always remain in such analyses, and these forecasts should be considered as qualitative or indicative.

The demise of the Soviet Union as a superpower has reduced concerns about global nuclear warfare. Nevertheless, thousands of nuclear weapons remain under active command and control and so continue to pose a threat. Moreover, new nations are achieving "nuclear" capability, most recently India and Pakistan. Thus, none of the dangers associated with existing nuclear arsenals—either from the viewpoint of national security or of nuclear winter—have been resolved. Indeed, to avoid the possibility of nuclear winter, it has been suggested that close to total disarmament is needed (Sagan and Turco, 1990). In this regard, it is debatable whether the realization of nuclear winter has stimulated a fundamental reevaluation of strategic policy and doctrine or played a role in the recent movement toward nuclear arms reductions, although their coincidence is apparent.

Effects comparable to nuclear winter have been associated with historical volcanic explosions ("volcanic winter") and large meteor impacts on the Earth ("meteorite winter"), both of which inject large quantities of particles into the upper atmosphere. For example, following the eruption of the Indonesian volcano Tambora in 1815, the weather in the Northern Hemisphere was highly unusual and is remembered as the "year without a summer" (Stommel and Stommel, 1979). Farmers in the northeastern United States had difficulty growing crops because sporadic frosts occurred throughout the spring; in the sparsely settled western United States, the unseasonable weather was recorded as frost damage to tree rings among the hearty bristlecone pines of that region. Across Europe—recovering from the Napoleonic wars—crops failed under stressful climatic conditions. Anecdotal evidence from China testifies to strange weather and poor agricultural output there as well. [*See* Volcanoes.] These events are thought to reflect the impacts of a mild nuclear winter. In another related phenomena, the smoke palls from forest fires and other large fires (such as those in Kuwait during the Persian Gulf War of 1991) have been shown to cool land surfaces rather quickly, and often deeply, by tens of degrees Celsius. In the case of nuclear detonations (and the resultant firestorms in urban locales), such cooling could be exacerbated owing to the larger amount and extent of the smoke clouds and their greater height of injection.

The widespread effects described above are largely related to the microscopic particles—so-called aerosols—that are generated by nuclear detonations and fires. Airborne smoke and dust particles scatter and absorb solar radiation and absorb and emit heat radiation. The overall energy budget of the underlying surface is thus altered, in some instances resulting in an "antigreenhouse" effect accompanied by temperature drops. The magnitude of the aerosol-induced cooling is determined by the spatial distribution and radiative properties of the particles. Smoke, especially sooty smoke, has optical constants most likely to produce cooling. Soot is the black carbonaceous byproduct of combustion and is one of the most efficient light-absorbing materials in nature. [See Aerosols.]

Field experiments and numerical simulations focusing on the behavior of large fires suggest that sooty smoke from nuclear-ignited city fires (like those brought about in Hiroshima and Nagasaki by the first atomic bombs) can be directly lofted into the upper atmosphere, where the smoke will have a relatively long residence time. Moreover, other experiments have shown that soot clouds exposed to direct sunlight warm and rise further into the atmosphere—an effect referred to as "self-lofting." This process, in turn, may enhance the geographic dispersion and residence time of the soot. Consequently, surface cooling beneath a large soot cloud may be deeper and longer-lasting. Other experiments indicate that precipitation, which is normally very efficient at removing most types of particles from the atmosphere, might be less efficient at washing out soot. This helps the soot to remain suspended for a longer time.

Continental land masses would cool much more rapidly than the oceans under nuclear winter conditions. Surface temperatures in coastal regions and on smaller land areas, however, would be moderated by the advection of heat through the atmosphere from neighboring oceans. Nevertheless, in the deep interiors of continents, such as in North America and Euro-Asia, land temperatures could drop rapidly and deeply.

Agriculture is essential to the survival of human civilization as we know it (some estimates place the fraction of the human population supported by agriculture as opposed to natural ecosystems at 99 percent; Harwell and Hutchinson, 1985). Accordingly, agricultural performance in response to nuclear winter climatic (and socio-economic) perturbations has been a focus of investigation (ibid.). Most domestic crops have semitropical origins and are vulnerable to even modest temperature decreases of several degrees on average during the growing season. Hence, nuclear winter forecasts pointing to month-long temperature drops of 5°–10°C represent a clear danger to agriculture—and therefore to much of the human population. Another profound climatic alteration that appears consistently in nuclear winter predictions is the failure of the Asian monsoons, which would have strong implications for agriculture over much of the southern range of that continent.

Many of the basic physical concepts and processes associated with nuclear winter have been successfully incorporated into modern climate models. Particularly important has been the recognition—heightened by nuclear winter studies—of the importance of aerosols in the global climate system and their role in modifying atmospheric radiation and chemistry.

[See also Atmosphere Structure and Evolution; Climate Change; Extreme Events; and Fire.]

BIBLIOGRAPHY

Crutzen, P. J., and J. W. Birks. "Twilight at Noon: The Atmosphere after a Nuclear War." *Ambio* 11 (1982), 114–125.

Harwell, M. A., and T. C. Hutchinson. *Environmental Consequences of Nuclear War.* vol. 2. *Ecological and Agricultural Effects.* SCOPE-28. Chichester, U.K.: Wiley, 1985.

National Research Council (NRC). "The Effects on the Atmosphere of a Major Nuclear Exchange." Washington, D.C.: National Academy Press, 1985.

Pittock, A. B., T. P. Ackerman, P. J. Crutzen, M. C. MacCracken, C. S. Shapiro, and R. P. Turco. *Environmental Consequences of Nuclear War.* vol. 1. *Physical and Atmospheric Effects.* SCOPE-28. Chichester, U.K.: Wiley, 1989.

Robock, A. "Enhancement of Surface Cooling due to Forest Fire Smoke." *Science* 242 (1988), 911–913.

Sagan, C., and R. P. Turco. *A Path Where No Man Thought: Nuclear Winter and the End of the Arms Race.* New York: Random House, 1990.

Solomon, F., and R. Q. Marston, eds. *The Medical Implications of Nuclear War.* Washington, D.C.: Institute of Medicine and National Academy of Sciences, National Academy Press, 1986.

Stommel, H., and E. Stommel. "The Year without a Summer." *Scientific American* 240.6 (1979), 176–186.

Turco, R. P., O. B. Toon, T. P. Ackerman, J. B. Pollack, and C. Sagan. "Nuclear Winter: Global Consequences of Multiple Nuclear Explosions." *Science* 222, (1983), 1283–1297.

———. "Climate and Smoke: An Appraisal of Nuclear Winter." *Science* 247 (1990), 166–176.

World Health Organization (WHO). "Effects of Nuclear War on Health and Health Services." Geneva: WHO, 1988.

—RICHARD P. TURCO

NUTRITION. *See* Agriculture and Agricultural Land; Disease; Economic Levels; Famine; Food; Nongovernmental Organizations; Risk; *and* World Health Organization.

O

OCEAN–ATMOSPHERE COUPLING

[This article provides a technical treatment of the subject intended for readers at an advanced level. For lower-level discussions of climate models, see Climate Models.]

The atmosphere and ocean form a complex nonlinear system coupled through the exchange of properties across the sea surface. The exchanges of interest here are those directly affecting the system's dynamics and thermodynamics; namely, the surface fluxes of heat, momentum, and fresh water. The coupling arises because these fluxes both depend on and influence the states of the atmosphere and of the ocean. There are important climatic consequences of this coupling. The extreme example is that both geophysical fluids are heated in the tropics and release this heat at higher latitudes. Without this poleward heat transport, high latitudes would be much colder and the tropics warmer. The surface heat flux is a balance between four processes: solar and infrared (longwave) radiation, and sensible and latent fluxes. The coupling is very effective at moderating atmospheric temperature fluctuations by keeping the air temperature from getting too far away from the sea surface temperature.

The exchange of momentum from atmosphere to ocean is the principal driver of the ocean's wind-driven circulation and a major drag on atmospheric motions. Some direct consequences of this process are the structure of the atmospheric and oceanic boundary layers, the ocean surface wavefield, and the transfers of both mean and turbulent kinetic energy. Indirect effects on the ocean are the ocean gyre circulations, including western boundary currents such as the Gulf Stream and the Kurishio, the equatorial current structure, and the Antarctic Circumpolar Current.

The ocean is essentially an infinite source of water. However, to play its role in the global hydrological cycle this water needs to be delivered to the atmosphere through the interfacial process of evaporation. Although about 90 percent of the evaporated moisture precipitates directly back to the ocean, the remainder is the ultimate source of terrestrial fresh water. Evaporation also extracts latent heat from the ocean, making the sea surface colder, saltier, and more dense, and combines with other heat flux processes, mixing, and precipitation to drive the ocean's thermohaline circulation. This circulation and the wind-driven circulation combine to produce the ocean's poleward heat transport. Along the equatorial Pacific Ocean, the wind driving and heat flux combine to produce El Niño years of anomalous ocean heating with widespread climate impacts.

Our ability to model and predict the Earth's climate therefore depends critically on the treatment of these air–sea exchanges. To have confidence in modeled variability and predictability in either geophysical fluid, a realistic mean state is required. However, the mean state of atmospheric and oceanic models is very sensitive to the wind forcing (or drag) and surface heat and moisture boundary conditions.

Sea Surface Fluxes. The most straightforward surface exchanges are the radiative heat fluxes. The two components are the solar and the longwave. The former is transferred through the atmosphere and all but a small fraction (the sea surface albedo, approximately 7 percent), is absorbed by the upper ocean where it is the dominant diurnal forcing.

The ocean surface is very nearly a black-body radiator (emissivity $\varepsilon \approx 1$) of longwave radiation. Hence this component of the surface heat flux is well modeled as

$$LW_{up} = \varepsilon \, \sigma \, SST^4,$$

where σ is the Stefan–Boltzmann constant and SST is the sea surface temperature. However, the downward longwave flux emitted by the overlying atmosphere is a complicated function of atmospheric temperature, humidity, and cloud properties. Reflection of this flux from the surface can be accounted for by setting $\varepsilon = 1$. Although empirical relationships for the downward longwave flux appear to be accurate to within about 15 watts per square meter in clear skies, they are much less reliable in cloudy conditions. However, the total radiation flux is much less sensitive, because often the presence of more cloud decreases solar radiation by about the same amount as it increases longwave radiation.

The turbulent fluxes of momentum, sensible heat, and latent heat (evaporation) are so called because the vertical transfer to the air–sea interface is accomplished by turbulent eddies in the planetary boundary layers of the atmosphere and ocean. However, the actual interfacial exchange is governed by molecular diffusion and small-scale pressure fluctuations in a very thin viscous sublayer that is a millimeter or less thick. These processes are relatively well understood compared with surface-renewal theory, which attempts to describe how much flux the boundary-layer eddies can supply to the sublayer.

The turbulent transport itself occurs over a wide range of spatial scales, from millimeters to kilometers. It is computationally impossible for a model to represent this entire range. One class of models, Large Eddy Simulation, attempts to capture the most important of these motions over a small domain (order 1 kilometer). The idea is that the smaller scales can be very well parameterized because they are better understood theoretically and that the model solutions will be relatively insensitive to the parameterization because the most important scales are resolved.

Climate models are required to span global scales, so the smallest resolved scales are of the order of 100 kilometers. Hence the entire turbulent and viscous transport must be parameterized in terms of resolved model properties. Fortunately, observations and Large Eddy Simulations indicate that this may be successful. Time and/or space averages of turbulent fluxes can be related to the average wind speed W, the air temperature T_a, the air humidity q_a, and the SST. In practice, twenty minutes to an hour of averaging is required to obtain a reliable flux measurement. The result is the familiar bulk formulas:

$$\tau_x = \rho_a \, C_D \, W \, U$$

$$\tau_y = \rho_a \, C_D \, W \, V$$

$$H_S = \rho_a \, c_p \, C_H \, W \, (T_a - SST)$$

$$H_L = \Lambda \, E = \rho_a \, \Lambda \, C_E \, W \, (q_a - SSQ).$$

Here the zonal wind component and momentum flux are U and τ_x, the meridional wind component and momentum flux are V and τ_y, the sensible heat flux is H_S, the latent heat flux is H_L, and the evaporation is E. The wind here should be taken relative to the ocean surface currents, but usually it is not. Also, $\rho_a = 1.2 \text{ kg m}^{-3}$ and $c_p = 1{,}004 \text{ J kg}^{-1} \text{ K}^{-1}$ are the air's density and specific heat, respectively, $\Lambda = 2.5 \times 10^6 \text{ J kg}^{-1}$ is the latent heat of vaporization, and the sea surface humidity, SSQ, is a function of SST. The much larger value of Λ compared with c_p means that the latent heat flux usually dominates the sensible.

There are numerous formulations for the transfer coefficients C_D, C_H, and C_E, some strictly empirical and others based at least in part on surface-renewal theory. The coefficients depend on the reference height of T_a, q_a, and W, and on the atmospheric stability, which itself is a function of these atmospheric properties, the reference height, and SST. Theoretically, C_H and C_E depend on the square root of C_D. In addition, the drag coefficient C_D is known to be a function of wind speed and surface-wave parameters. Incorporating the latter is an active area of research that would allow accurate, hourly surface fluxes provided all the necessary wave information is available. In the usual case of few or no wave data, the accuracy of bulk fluxes decreases with wind–wave variability but increases with averaging. Accuracies commensurate with direct flux measurements require as much as a three-day average in highly variable midlatitude conditions, but often less than twelve hours in the more steady tropics. The respective spatial averages are the 1,000-kilometer scale of midlatitude storms and order 100 kilometers in the trade winds.

General Circulation Models. An examination of the bulk formulas reveals that, if surface currents are neglected, the only ocean parameter is SST. Therefore, specification of SST as an atmospheric bottom-boundary condition allows complete specification of the surface fluxes through the LW_{up} and bulk formulas. This is the standard way of forcing an atmospheric general circulation model (AGCM). A notable example is the Atmospheric Model Intercomparison Project (AMIP), where ten years (1979–1988) of satellite-based SST fields were used as bottom-boundary conditions for fifteen different AGCMs. However, as noted by Gleckler et al. (1995), when models are forced in this way, the circulation can be reasonable even though the radiation fluxes into the ocean are very poor. They also show that the implied oceanic heat transport at 45° south latitude was equatorward in most of the AMIP AGCMs, rather than poleward as it must be to transport the equatorial heat toward Antarctica.

There is an analog method of forcing an ocean general circulation model (OGCM), known as restoring boundary conditions. Everywhere, the downward net surface heat and freshwater fluxes are, respectively,

$$Q_{net} = R_Q(SST_s - SST_m)$$

and

$$F_{net} = -R_F(SSS_s - SSS_m),$$

where SST_m and SSS_m are the model's evolving sea surface temperature and salinity. These model properties are restored toward specified temperature and salinity fields, SST_s and SSS_s, at rates given by the restoring coefficients R_Q and R_F, respectively. The restoring time scales range from days to months. Often, SST_s and R_Q vary with time and space and are designed to give the observed surface heat flux when SST_m equals observed SST. Observations are usually used for SSS_s and often for SST_s. Such a formulation precludes the possibility of a correct flux coincident with correct surface values, except in the rare locations of zero observed flux. There are two other serious objections to restoring boundary conditions. First, there are two components of the true freshwater flux, evaporation and precipitation, and neither can be written in restoring form and neither depends on SSS. Second, heat and freshwater fluxes are linked through the evaporation in reality, but not when restoring boundary conditions are used.

Alternatively, flux boundary conditions can be employed by specifying the net momentum, heat, and fresh-water fluxes everywhere over an OGCM domain. This is the usual mode of applying the momentum boundary conditions. However, with heat flux forcing, model SSTs have been found to evolve far from the observed SST used to compute the fluxes with bulk formulas. This physical inconsistency is due to the lack of air–sea feedbacks, which can be overcome by bulk forcing where the evolving model SST is used in bulk formulas. Ocean-variability studies have employed mixed tracer boundary conditions, where the surface temperature is restored but the freshwater flux is specified. However, this flux is usually diagnosed from an OGCM integration with restoring in salinity.

An AGCM can be uncoupled by specifying the ocean state, say OCE_s. In AMIP experiments, OCE_s is just observed SST. In this mode it reaches equilibrium after some tens of years. If this state is denoted as ATM_e, then an atmospheric surface flux is $F_A (ATM_e, OCE_s)$. A necessary but insufficient condition for equilibrium is zero heat and moisture fluxes globally averaged over an annual cycle. Similarly, an OGCM can be uncoupled by specifying the atmospheric state, say ATM_s. It takes several thousand years for the deep ocean to reach an equilibrium state, OCE_e, because of slow diffusive processes. At that point an incoming surface flux is $F_O (ATM_s, OCE_e)$, and again the global average over an annual cycle of the heat and moisture fluxes must be zero. In general, $F_A(ATM_e, OCE_s)$ and $F_O(ATM_s, OCE_e)$ are not equal, which becomes problematic when the two component models are coupled.

Coupled Ocean–Atmosphere Climate Models. In fully coupled models the only prescribed forcing is the value of the incoming solar flux at the top of the atmosphere, which in equilibrium is balanced by the fraction (the planetary albedo, approximately 30 percent) reflected and the outgoing longwave radiation emitted by the Earth. Radiative transfer equations transport the solar radiation through the atmosphere, where about 25 percent of the incoming radiation is absorbed. However, in the "anomalous absorption" controversy, one side claims that these equations absorb too little in cloudy conditions, and the other side disagrees. The resolution of this issue is very important to future coupled models because, unlike AMIP AGCMs, the solar heating of the atmosphere and the ocean surface does influence coupled-model circulation.

The radiative transfer equations also compute the downwelling longwave radiation incident on the ocean surface. The model atmosphere also produces the precipitation. The bulk formulas and the above LW_{up} expression give the remaining components of the surface momentum, heat, and moisture exchange. The resulting nonlinear, coupled system may have multiple equilibrium states. Such behavior has also been found in idealized

ocean–atmosphere coupled models. Unfortunately, most fully coupled models have not been integrated long enough to reach equilibrium.

Fully coupled models are usually initialized with equilibrium states ATM_e and OCE_e of uncoupled components. When coupled, both the atmosphere and ocean tend to evolve to different states ATM_c and OCE_c. At any time there is a coupled flux $F_C(ATM_c, OCE_c)$, and there is conservation, but there are nonzero global averages over annual cycle, and no equilibrium results. There is always a short (order ten years) transient response, and early experience was that this was followed by a slow "climate drift" throughout the coupled integration (order one hundred years) that made interpretation of numerical experiments difficult. In most nonlinear systems, variability and sensitivity depend on the mean state. Hence the large differences that developed between ATM_c and ATM_s and between OCE_c and OCE_s raised doubts about the representativeness of the coupled climate model's variability and sensitivity.

The most common solution to this climate drift problem is to employ "flux correction." In this approach, conservation is deliberately violated by making fluxes seen by the atmosphere different from those seen by the ocean for the purpose of maintaining desired coupled climate states. It guarantees that ATM_c and OCE_c will be very close to ATM_e and OCE_e. Sausen et al. (1988) detailed a sophisticated flux-correction scheme designed to eliminate the drift caused by small model errors without affecting other aspects of the coupled-model dynamics. Experiments utilizing the scheme are akin to anomaly response experiments, where the atmosphere and ocean are coupled only by flux anomalies relative to ATM_e and OCE_e. Before coupling, equilibrium solutions of the uncoupled models are used to compute the reference fluxes $F_R(ATM_e, OCE_e)$. Then flux corrections to the atmosphere and to the ocean are calculated, respectively, as

$$\Delta F_A = F_A(ATM_e, OCE_s) - F_R(ATM_e, OCE_e)$$

and

$$\Delta F_O = F_O(ATM_s, OCE_e) - F_R(ATM_e, OCE_e).$$

These corrections are added to the computed flux, $F_C(ATM_c, OCE_c)$. In general they can be applied to all fluxes and to the ocean and atmosphere, but often only the ocean heat and salt fluxes are corrected. "Soft" flux correction is applied to keep desired annual mean states, whereas "hard" flux correction keeps desired seasonal cycles as well. On a global average over an annual cycle, fluxes $F_C - F_R$ are conserved, and in equilibrium the necessary condition of zero net flux implies $F_C = F_R$ for heat and fresh water. Thus the coupled ocean–atmosphere equilibrium state is constrained to give computed fluxes that agree with fluxes from uncoupled equilibrium states. Other disconcerting characteristics are that the corrections can be several times larger than the computed fluxes, that they produce spurious northward heat transports, and that slow climate drift may still occur.

It has always been recognized that the proper approach would be to reduce model errors to the point where the climate drift is acceptable. Recent coupled-model integrations without flux corrections may have reached this stage. These are described in the June 1998 special issue of the *Journal of Climate*. Following an initial transient adjustment of order ten years, the remainder of a three-hundred-year integration displays no statistical trend in surface temperature, either globally or hemispherically averaged. The absence of climate drift in the *SST* and the lower atmosphere means that the surface fluxes are also drift free, although they display significant variability over a wide range of time scales. The coupled atmosphere is very nearly in equilibrium, with a numerical and top-of-atmosphere loss of heat balanced by an area average gain of 0.35 watts per square meter across the air–sea interface. In the ocean, this flux is seen as a steady cooling of the deep ocean, which also becomes saltier at the expense of an upper-ocean freshening. In the absence of river runoff, fresh water is conserved by imposing zero net ocean surface flux. The imperfections of this coupled model may be acceptable for some applications and not for others. However, for many of the problems the source has been identified and solutions are being implemented.

The requirements put forward for eliminating climate drift in coupled models are state-of-the-art component models, which in uncoupled mode produce compatible poleward heat transport and a careful spin-up to avoid positive-feedback problems. It would seem that meticulous attention to flux conservation is necessary. Since the component ocean and atmosphere models of a coupled system tend to operate on different horizontal grids, conservation of fluxes from one grid to the other is not straightforward. For example, suppose average *SST* from a finer ocean grid is seen by a coarser atmospheric grid as $\langle SST \rangle$, where $\langle \ \rangle$ denotes an average over the ocean grid underlying a single atmospheric grid point. Then longwave flux from the former is $\varepsilon\sigma\langle SST^4\rangle$, but the flux seen by the latter is $\varepsilon\sigma\langle SST\rangle^4$, so conservation is violated. Inevitably, there are marginal seas, such as the Black, Red, Caspian, and Baltic, that are treated neither as active ocean nor as part of the land surface. Nevertheless, their surface fluxes must be properly formulated. The use of simple restoring boundary conditions in heat and fresh water, for example, can result in marginal seas becoming infinite sources or sinks of heat and fresh water. Conservation issues are further complicated by the sea ice component of coupled models, but these are beyond the scope of this article.

[*See also* Atmosphere Dynamics; Climate Change; El Niño–Southern Oscillation; Hydrologic Cycle; Ocean Dynamics; *and* Surprise.]

BIBLIOGRAPHY

Barnier, B., L. Siefridt, and P. Marchesiello. "Surface Thermal Boundary Condition for a Global Ocean Circulation Model from a Three-Year Climatology of ECMWF Analyses." *Journal of Marine Research* 6 (1995), 363–380.

Clayson, C. A., C. W. Fairall, and J. A. Curry. "Evaluation of Turbulent Fluxes at the Ocean Surface Using Surface Renewal Theory." *Journal of Geophysical Research* 101 (1996), 28503–28513.

Cubash, U., K. Hasselmann, H. Hock, E. Maier-Reimer, U. Mikolajewiez, B. D. Santer, and R. Sausen. "Time-Dependent Greenhouse Warming Computations with a Coupled Ocean–Atmosphere Model." *Climate Dynamics* 8 (1992), 55–69.

Gleckler, P. J., D. A. Randall, G. Boer, R. Coleman, M. Dix, V. Galin, M. Hefland, J. Kiehl, A. Kitch, M. Lau, X-Z. Liang, V. Lykossov, B. McAvaney, K. Miyakoda, S. Planton, and W. Stern. "Cloud Radiative Effects on Implied Oceanic Energy Transports as Simulated by Atmospheric General Circulation Models." *Geophysical Research Letters* 22 (1995), 791–794.

Large, W. G., G. Danabasoglu, S. C. Doney, and J. C. McWilliams. "Sensitivity to Surface Forcing and Boundary Layer Mixing in a Global Ocean Model: Annual Mean Climatology." *Journal of Physical Oceanography* 27 (1997), 2418–2447.

Manabe, S., K. Bryan, and M. J. Spelman. "A Global Ocean–Atmosphere Climate Model with Seasonal Variations for Future Studies of Climate Variability." *Dynamics of Atmospheres and Oceans* 3 (1979), 393–426.

Manabe, S., and R. J. Stouffer. "Century-Scale Effects of Increased Atmospheric CO_2 on the Ocean–Atmosphere System." *Nature* 364 (1993), 216.

Meehl, G. A., G. J. Boer, C. Covey, M. Latif, and R. Stouffer. "Analyzing and Intercomparing Global Coupled Atmosphere–Ocean–Sea Ice Climate Models." *Eos* 78 (1997), 445–451.

Murphy, J. M. "Transient Response of the Hadley Centre Coupled Ocean–Atmosphere Model to Increasing Carbon Dioxide. Part I: Control Climate and Flux Correction." *Journal of Climate* 8 (1995), 36–56.

Randall, D. A., ed. *Journal of Climate* 2 (June 1988 special issue).

Saravanan, R., and J. C. McWilliams. "Multiple Equilibria, Natural Variability, and Climate Transitions in an Idealized Ocean–Atmosphere Model." *Journal of Climate* 8 (1995), 2296–2323.

Sausen, R., K. Barthel, and K. Hasselmann. "Coupled Ocean–Atmosphere Models with Flux Corrections." *Climate Dynamics* 2 (1988), 154–163.

Trenberth, K. E., ed. *Climate System Modeling*. Cambridge: Cambridge University Press, 1992.

Washington, W. M., and C. L. Parkinson. *An Introduction to Three-Dimensional Climate Modeling*. New York and Oxford: University Science Books and Oxford University Press, 1986.

—W. G. LARGE

OCEAN CHEMISTRY

Water is such an important component of life on Earth that it is often used as a tracer in searches for extraterrestrial life. Not only is it the most plentiful substance on the surface of this planet, but its many unusual chemical and physical properties set it apart from most other liquids as well. The source of the great abundance of water on the Earth remains an unresolved issue, although there are at least two plausible explanations. The more popular theory suggests that a small fraction of the water that was present in the primeval mantle rose to the surface as vapor and condensed out as the young Earth cooled some 4 billion years ago. A recent alternative theory proposes that 30-ton balls of ice ("small water comets"), which have been observed entering the Earth's atmosphere at the rate of 20 per minute, would be capable of producing the present amount of water over the Earth's lifetime.

The present disposition of water on the Earth's surface and its cycling through the atmosphere, lithosphere, and cryosphere are discussed in an independent article. [See Hydrologic Cycle.]

Evolution of Sea Water. About 3.5 percent (by mass) of sea water consists of solutes (Table 1), most of which come from sources on the land and are deposited in the ocean through river discharge. Chlorine, sulfur, and carbon, for example, are produced mainly by volcanic activity, while sodium, magnesium, calcium, and potassium derive from the weathering of igneous rocks such as feldspars. Water discharged from rivers has a very different composition from that of sea water. How the present composition of sea water evolved is not fully understood, but it clearly involved a large number of complex inorganic and organic reactions taking place over a long period of time in a huge vessel well mixed by winds and currents. Differing solubilities and reactivities led to some components of the river discharge being concentrated and others precipitating out and being deposited as sediments. The present composition, which is remarkably uniform geographically with

Ocean Chemistry. TABLE 1. Constituents, Abundance, and Residence Times of Sea Water and River Discharge

SUBSTANCE	CHEMICAL FORMULA	Sea Water CONCENTRATION (%)*	Sea Water RESIDENCE TIME[†] (YR)	RIVER DISCHARGE CONCENTRATION (%)
Water	H_2O	965	3,000	
Major Constituents				
Chloride	Cl^-	18.980	∞	0.0083
Sodium	Na^+	10.556	260,000,000	0.0072
Sulfate	SO_4^{-2}	2.649	11,000,000	0.0115
Magnesium	Mg^{+2}	1.272	45,000,000	0.0037
Calcium	Ca^{+2}	0.404	8,000,000	0.0147
Potassium	K^+	0.390	11,000,000	0.0014
Bicarbonate	HCO_3^-	0.105		0.0530
Bromide	Br^-	0.065		
Boric acid	H_3BO_3	0.026		
Strontium	Sr^{+2}	0.0078	19,000,000	
Fluoride	F^-	0.0013		
Minor Constituents[‡]				
Silicon	Si	0.003	10,000	0.0049
Lithium	Li	0.00018	19,000,000	
Rubidium	Rb	0.00012	270,000	
Iodine	I	0.00006		
Iron	Fe	0.00001	140	
Aluminum	Al	0.00001	100	
Molybdenum	Mo	0.00001	500,000	
Barium	Ba	0.00001	84,000	
Arsenic	As	0.000004		
Uranium	U	0.0000033		
Nitrogen	N_2	0.01–0.02		
Oxygen	O_2	0.0001–0.010		
Carbon dioxide	CO_2	0.0004–0.004	5–10	
Nitrate	NO_3	0.000005–0.002		
Phosphate	PO_4	0.000001–0.00005		
Organic carbon	C	0.0003–0.002		

*Parts per thousand by mass (or grams per kilogram).

[†]Average time an atom of the substance spends in the ocean (= total content ÷ outflow).

[‡]Typical concentrations of these mostly nonconservative constituents.

regard to the major constituents, represents a balance between inputs from rivers, atmosphere, and hydrothermal vents and outputs to ocean sediments. Evidence from marine sedimentary rocks indicates that this salinity has not changed for at least 1.5 billion years. The atmospheric inputs derive mainly from volcanic gases, many of which become condensation nuclei and fall out in precipitation. Hydrothermal vents (discovered in the 1970s) and their associated biota circulate a volume of water estimated to be about 0.5 percent of river discharge, to which they add helium, calcium, manganese, hydrogen, and carbon dioxide (CO_2) while removing substances such as magnesium and sulfate.

In summary, sea water composition represents a balance between material *gains* from:

- The weathering of continental rocks, which is enhanced by precipitation acidity, and transport by rivers
- Volcanic emissions to the atmosphere of chlorine, carbon, and sulfur compounds and subsequent fallout in precipitation
- Hydrothermal releases of calcium, potassium, and other metals from the oceanic crust

and material *losses* through:

- Biological processes (such as shell-forming organisms) that precipitate out calcium carbonate ($CaCO_3$), opaline silica (SiO_2), and pyrite (FeS_2) and deposit them as sediment
- Precipitation of sodium chloride ($NaCl$) and calcium sulfate ($CaSO_4$) in restricted basins because of evaporation (i.e., evaporite deposits)
- The formation of new minerals in sediments on the ocean floor
- Adsorption of ions on very fine clay particles
- Pore-water burial and sea spray
- Removal of magnesium and sulfate through reaction between cold sea water and hot, newly formed volcanic rocks

Conservative Constituents. Four ions (chloride, sodium, sulfate, and magnesium) make up over 97 percent of the total salt content of sea water, and the eleven major components (Table 1) comprise 99.99 percent. The relative concentrations of these eleven is remarkably constant in time and in space, as well as with depth. This constancy was first documented in 1884 by W. Dittmar following analysis of the large number of samples collected from the Northern Hemisphere oceans during the H.M.S. *Challenger* expedition of 1872–1876. These constituents are generally termed *conservative* because of their constant relative concentrations, which is attributable to the great quantities present, their long replacement times and nonreactive nature, and the efficient mixing of the ocean. A number of minor compo-

nents should also be classified as conservative because of their homogeneous distribution: cesium, lithium, molybdenum, rubidium, uranium, and vanadium, and dissolved nitrogen and the noble gases.

Nonconservative Constituents. In contrast to the major components described above, many substances in sea water do show significant variations from place to place and over time, owing mainly to biological activity, high turnover rates, or association with localized sources or sinks. These constituents are termed *nonconservative* and may be grouped into:

- Nutrient types, such as silica, phosphate, and nitrate, as well as barium, cadmium, germanium, nickel, and zinc. These tend to be reduced in surface waters owing to biological uptake and enriched in deeper waters by regeneration from sediments.
- Scavenger types, such as aluminum, bismuth, cerium, cobalt, lead, manganese, and thorium, which are highly reactive in sea water and are scavenged by particulate matter settling out by gravity. They have extremely low concentrations and residence times in the range of one hundred to one thousand years. They are found in higher concentrations in surface waters and, because of their terrestrial sources, to a greater extent in the Atlantic than in the Pacific.
- Redox-controlled types, such as arsenic, chromium, iodine, selenium, tellurium, and plutonium, which exist in sea water in more than one oxidation state. Unstable reduced species of these elements, formed biologically, tend to be oxidized to their higher-valency state in the open ocean.

Salinity. Salinity is defined as the mass fraction of total dissolved material in water when all carbonate is converted to oxide, all bromine and iodine replaced by chlorine, and all organic material completely oxidized. Because of the constancy of the relative concentrations of the major components, it is necessary to measure the concentration of only one in order to determine the overall salinity. This has traditionally been done using a chemical determination of the most abundant chloride ion (by titration) and calculating salinity from an equation such as:

$$salinity = 1.80655 \times chlorinity$$

Nowadays, salinity is more usually measured with an electrical conductance instrument called a salinometer.

Variations of salinity in the surface mixed layer of the ocean (100–500 meters in depth) are due to water gains (from precipitation or runoff from land) and water losses to the atmosphere (due to evaporation). Salinity tends to be low where freshwater input exceeds evaporation and high where the opposite is the case. Globally, the salinity of surface waters varies from 3.4 to 3.7 percent (average is just under 3.5 percent), although

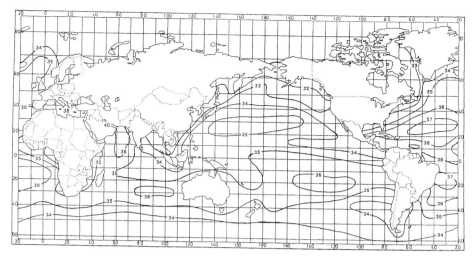

Ocean Chemistry. FIGURE 1. Salinity of Oceanic Surface Waters during Northern Hemisphere Summer (parts per thousand by mass).

much lower values are found near river mouths and somewhat higher values in the subtropics (Figure 1). High evaporation and low precipitation contribute to values between 4.0 and 4.2 percent in the Red Sea, while the reverse can produce levels below 1.0 percent off Finland. At a particular location, salinity (and other properties) is quite uniform in the surface mixed layer, below which it often varies considerably before becoming relatively constant in the deep ocean. This transition layer, the halocline, may exhibit a salinity increase or decrease with depth (Figure 2). In the lower midlatitudes and tropics, salinity tends to be higher near the surface dropping sharply through the halocline, while in more northerly waters salinity increases from 3.3–3.4 percent at the surface to 3.4–3.5 percent at depth. Near the poles, seasonal freezing and thawing affect surface salinity. When ice freezes, most of the salt is left behind; the salinity of the remaining water thus rises, dropping back when the ice melts again. Although salinity varies slightly with depth in the deep ocean, there is relatively little variation with time and geographical location. Local pockets of very saline water (as high as 25 percent) have been found at depth in locations such as the Red Sea that are cut off from the main ocean circulation.

The presence of dissolved salts affects many of the properties of water. Sea water is more viscous and is less likely to produce foam (which may, however, form locally due to additives such as kelp exudates); salinity lowers the vapor pressure and increases the osmotic pressure; and its density is about 3 percent greater and its freezing point about 2°C lower than fresh water.

Dissolved Gases. All of the atmospheric gases dissolve in the ocean, which tends to be saturated with respect to each, at all depths. They are not present in the same ratios as in the atmosphere, however, because of their vastly different solubilities in sea water. The least reactive, nitrogen and the noble gases, are conservative constituents, whose concentrations are controlled mainly by water temperature, salinity, and pressure; higher values of the first two factors and lower values of the last tend to lower gas solubilities.

Both oxygen and carbon dioxide are nonconservative constituents owing to their heavy involvement in biological processes. Photosynthesis uses sunlight to convert carbon dioxide and water to carbohydrate and molecular oxygen; respiration and decomposition oxi-

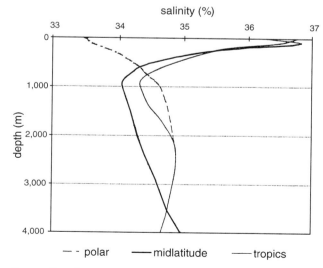

Ocean Chemistry. FIGURE 2. Salinity Profile Examples for the Major Oceans.

dize the carbohydrate, releasing chemical energy, carbon dioxide, and water as byproducts. Oxygen concentration tends to be high near the surface because of dissolution of atmospheric oxygen as well as plant photosynthesis in the photic zone; it diminishes below the surface to a depth of about 1,000 meters, rebounding to a value near 5 milliliters per liter at great depth. The reason for the increase at depth is not clear, but it may be related to the lower temperature and to transport by deep ocean currents from the poles (the "ocean conveyor belt"), where concentrations are higher owing to the greater solubility in cold water.

Carbon dioxide dissolves readily in sea water, where it reacts with the water to form carbonic acid (H_2CO_3), which in turn dissociates to form hydrogen (H^+), bicarbonate (HCO_3^-), and carbonate (CO_3^{--}) ions. These reactions are shown in the following equations:

$$CO_2 + H_2O \rightleftarrows H_2CO_3$$

$$H_2CO_3 \rightleftarrows HCO_3^- + H^+ \rightleftarrows CO_3^{--} + 2H^+$$

Bicarbonate is the most abundant carbon dioxide species as well as one of the major constituents in sea water (Table 1). The net result of these carbonate-cycle reactions is to produce a pH for sea water that is slightly alkaline (about 8.1), in comparison with the neutrality of pure water (7.0). The carbonate and bicarbonate give up hydrogen ions freely in sea water, creating a buffer against changes in acidity and helping to maintain a constant chemical environment for marine organisms. When acid is added to the water, the reaction in the second equation above moves to the left, creating more bicarbonate and returning the pH to near what it was. Photosynthesis and respiration, which deplete and augment carbon dioxide concentration respectively, thus have little effect on pH. [See Carbon Cycle.]

Nutrients and Organic Matter. Living organisms make up only 0.1 percent of the total mass of organic material in the ocean, the remainder being nonliving dissolved (95 percent) or particulate (5 percent) organic material. Dissolved organic material is most abundant in near-surface waters and has a turnover time of many thousands of years. Its main sources are the decomposition of dead plants and animals and secretions from living plants. Dissolved organic substances enter the food chain mainly through consumption by bacteria. It is estimated that there are 10^{10} metric tons of particulates in the ocean; that is, their concentration is about 0.0000007 percent. The rain of particles from the surface to the sea floor provides food for benthic organisms and is the source of ocean sediments, and their partial decay and remineralization, as they descend, controls the balances of oxygen, nutrients, and other trace constituents in the deep ocean.

Human Influences. Although the Earth's oceans appear to have existed in their present state for over 1.5 billion years, there is some concern about how long they will continue to do so under the assault of human changes to the environment. The assumption that the land and sea have infinite capacities to absorb wastes has resulted in indiscriminate dumping of a wide variety of materials on land and in waterways, which has increased dramatically since the beginning of the Industrial Revolution. The list includes sewage, mining and petroleum industry wastes, fertilizer runoff, herbicides and pesticides, industrial process wastes, discarded packaging and fishing gear, urban refuse, and heat. Most of these wastes, or their breakdown products, end up in the ocean. Nitrogen pollution of coastal waters, mainly due to runoff from agricultural fertilizers, has produced anoxic zones uninhabitable by many species.

While this type of pollution may have serious effects on a local or regional scale and may make the water unsuitable for many plants and animals, it does not pose as great a threat to the ocean as do increasing greenhouse gases in the atmosphere. [See Global Warming; and Greenhouse Effect.] A consensus of climate modelers have predicted that rising concentrations of these gases will produce an increase in the Earth's surface temperature of several degrees Celsius during the next century; recent climatic data appear to confirm that this is happening.

Oceanic impacts are expected from the higher carbon dioxide concentration per se, as well as from higher temperature. Of the approximately 6 billion metric tons of carbon released annually by human activities, half is accounted for in the atmosphere, and the remainder is believed to go to the ocean (2 billion tons) and to terrestrial plants (1 billion tons). This large flux to the oceans can enhance biological productivity, change species composition of the phytoplankton communities, and affect ocean pH, surface salinity, and the carbonate cycle. A possible scenario would be for the increased carbon dioxide to lower pH sufficiently to dissolve calcium carbonate, causing the demise of coral reefs and shellfish such as oysters, mussels, and foraminifera. This scenario may, however, overestimate future carbon dioxide production and underestimate the pH-buffering capacity of the ocean.

Rising surface temperature will warm surface waters, forming a stable layer that resists vertical mixing. If this occurs in the polar regions, it may shut down the ocean conveyor belt, which transfers an immense amount of heat around the planet. [See Ocean Dynamics; and Ocean Structure and Development.] A similar effect would be produced by a large increase in freshwater runoff into the Arctic Ocean (through precipitation increase and ice melt); some evidence of this has been discovered recently in the Labrador Sea. If the conveyor belt does not shut down, the huge thermal buffering capacity of the ocean should be sufficient to slow down greenhouse warming by fifty years or so, allowing time for mitigative action to be taken. If, however, the deep ocean warms up very much, ocean bottom gas hydrates may begin to decompose and release their gases (principally methane) to the atmosphere, adding to the greenhouse effect. The average temperature of the global oceans has been found to have warmed 0.06°C between the mid-1950s and the mid-1990s, representing an increase in heat content of 2×10^{23} joules. There is also recent evidence of warming of the flow of Atlantic water into the Arctic Ocean, and of the destruction of coral reefs, which may be early signs of the greenhouse effect; it is, however, too soon to confirm this.

The ocean is the "sleeping giant" of carbon dioxide control. It contains twenty times as much carbon in solution as there is in all terrestrial plants, animals, and soil. Although only the broad outline of the global carbon cycle is known at present, there is good reason to believe that the ocean's controlling role that has served the Earth so well over billions of years will be able to handle the changes expected during the next few centuries.

BIBLIOGRAPHY

Berner, E. K., and R. A. Berner. *The Global Water Cycle: Geochemistry and Environment.* Englewood Cliffs, N.J.: Prentice-Hall, 1987.

Crompton, T. R. *Analysis of Sea Water.* London: Butterworths, 1989.

Drever, J. I. *The Geochemistry of Natural Waters.* 2d ed. Englewood Cliffs, N.J.: Prentice-Hall, 1988.

Gross, M. G. *Oceanography: A View of the Earth.* 6th ed. Englewood Cliffs, N.J.: Prentice-Hall, 1993.

Ingmanson, D. E., and W. J. Wallace. *Oceanography: An Introduction.* 4th ed. Belmont, Calif.: Wadsworth, 1989.

Ittekkot, V., P. Schäfer, S. Honjo, and P. J. Depetris. *Particle Flux in the Ocean,* SCOPE Report 57. Chichester, U.K.: Wiley, 1996.

Levitus, S., J. I. Antonov, T. P. Boyer, and C. Stephens. "Warming of the World Ocean." *Science* 287 (2000), 2225–2229.

Li, Y. N. "Distribution Patterns of the Elements in the Ocean: A Synthesis." *Geochimica Cosmochimica Acta* 55 (1991), 3223–3240.

Miller, D. H. *Water at the Surface of the Earth: An Introduction to Ecosystem Hydrodynamics.* New York: Academic Press, 1977.

Millero, F. J. *Chemical Oceanography.* 2d ed. Boca Raton, Fla.: CRC Press, 1996.

Quinby-Hunt, M. S., and K. K. Turekian. "Distribution of Elements in Sea Water." *EOS: Transactions of the American Geophysical Union* 64 (1983), 130–131.

United Nations Educational, Scientific, and Cultural Organization (UNESCO). *World Water Balance and Water Resources of the Earth.* Studies and Reports in Hydrology No. 25. Paris: UNESCO, 1978.

Van der Leeden, F., ed. *Water Resources of the World: Selected Statistics.* Port Washington, N.Y.: Water Information Center, 1975.

—EARLE A. RIPLEY

OCEAN DISPOSAL

Pollutants are substances introduced into the environment by human activities that have a deleterious effect on living resources, human health, quality and use of the environment, or other amenities (Clark, 1992). They are introduced or disposed of into the ocean from point sources and nonpoint sources. Point sources are deliberate discharges from outfalls and ocean dumping. Oil drilling platforms, more than one thousand of which are in use or abandoned worldwide (GESAMP, 1990), are also point sources of a variety of pollutants. Nonpoint sources include runoff from land surfaces (streets, parking lots, agricultural lands, lawns, and so forth), seepage through aquifers, and wet and dry atmospheric deposition. Rivers entering coastal waters usually contain pollutants from both point and nonpoint sources. [*See* Marginal Seas.]

Point Sources. Sewage treatment plant (STP) effluent—the primary product of sewage treatment—is usually discharged through outfalls to the marine environment. Industrial waste can be treated on-site and discharged through an outfall or discharged to a municipal STP for treatment and discharge. Storm water is diverted primarily from paved areas and eventually discharged through stormwater outfalls, gullies, and ditches. In many coastal cities, storm water is combined with domestic sewage for treatment in a sewage treatment plant. During dry weather or low-flow conditions, sewage is treated and discharged as sewage effluent; but, during a significant rainfall, the combined sewage and stormwater flow may exceed the capacity of the STP, and some fraction of the total flow may be discharged, untreated, through a combined sewer outfall.

Ocean dumping is the intentional release, for the sole purpose of disposal, of waste materials into the sea from a vessel. Sewage sludge (the solid, semisolid, and liquid residue from sewage treatment), dredge material (sediments removed from navigational channels and harbors as they are constructed or maintained), industrial wastes, low-level radioactive wastes, construction debris, and garbage have all been ocean dumped—usually at specifically designated sites. In the United States, low-level radioactive wastes and garbage have not been ocean dumped for decades. The Soviet Union is the only country thought to have dumped high-level nuclear wastes in the ocean. Dumping of sewage sludge and industrial waste was banned by the United States in the early 1990s, leaving dredge material as the only waste that may legally be ocean dumped.

Nonpoint Sources. Pollution in coastal waters from nonpoint sources is ubiquitous, and the sources are elusive. Runoff not channeled through an outfall is considered to come from a nonpoint source. It may come from city streets and other hardened surfaces, suburban lawns, golf courses, agricultural activities, construction sites, landfills, septic systems, and cesspools. There are many nonpoint sources of pollution discharging directly into coastal waters. Commercial shipping and recreational boating and their support facilities, shipyards, mooring facilities, and marinas are sources of a spectrum of contaminants including oil and grease, metals from antifouling paints, and sewage. The atmosphere quickly disperses pollutants such as automobile exhaust, stack gases, and sprays used in pesticide control and agriculture. Many of these fall out onto the ocean surface through dry and wet deposition.

Accidental Releases. Unintentional releases of polluting materials can reach the ocean even through well-regulated and well-managed facilities. Treatment plant breakdowns and malfunction of processing facilities occasionally occur, releasing excessive quantities of permitted discharges and perhaps substances prohibited from legal discharge. There are also dramatic accidental discharges such as oil spills from supertankers. Devastating as these are, oil spills are responsible for only a small fraction of the total amount of oil reaching the ocean from anthropogenic activities (Clark, 1992).

Pollutants of Concern. Pollutants that are discharged into the marine environment from various sources reflect the very nature of society. [*See* Pollution.] Among these are particulate material, microorganisms (including pathogens), trace elements such as metals (cadmium, mercury, silver, copper, chromium, iron), synthetic organic compounds (for example, dichlorodiphenyltrichloroethane [DDT], polychlorinated biphenyls or PCBs), petroleum-related compounds, and radionuclides. These pollutants are introduced primarily to harbors, particularly those with industrial facilities. They are also introduced along populated stretches of the coastal zone. Because most of the industrialized world is in the Northern Hemisphere, many of the world's polluted harbors are located there. However, many harbors in the developing world are also badly polluted because they may lack regulations to restrict polluting materials from entering waterways, and they may not have facilities to treat polluted waste streams before they enter the marine environment. Today, because of the availability of cheap labor and also because of inadequate regulation, some industries are relocating from developed nations to developing nations. The primary pollution concerns in the developing world are of sewage contamination and perhaps sedimentation from poor agricultural practices. In the future, pollution in

these harbors may rival the worst of the developed world.

As of the early 1990s, the United Nations estimated the percentage contribution of all pollutants entering the world's oceans as follows (GESAMP, 1990): offshore production, 1 percent; maritime transportation, 12 percent; dumping, 10 percent; runoff and land-based discharges, 44 percent; atmosphere, 33 percent.

Impacts of Pollution. The impacts of disposal on the oceans and their biota depend upon the physical and chemical nature of the disposed material and also upon the location of disposal. Some locations may be dispersive, others may tend to accumulate wastes. Some chemical constituents may dissolve, others may have an affinity for particles and tend eventually to settle with the particles to the sea floor. Because the oceans are interconnected, disposed material may be transported globally. Synthetic organic chemicals that do not readily degrade (such as many pesticides) are a particular concern in this regard.

Ecosystem impacts experienced by organisms could include smothering, toxicity, carcinogenicity, and reproductive failure. Some pollutants, such as synthetic organics, can be bioconcentrated and passed up the food web. Excess nutrients can lead to eutrophication in coastal waters.

Discharged contaminants can also impact humans. Pathogens as well as toxic and potentially carcinogenic materials can reach people through consumption of seafood. Direct contact via swimming in contaminated waters can lead to gastroenteritis and possibly other illnesses as well.

The United Nations (GESAMP, 1990) determined that the most important threats to the marine environment are nutrient contamination; microbial contamination in seafood; debris; synthetic organic compounds in sediment; oil; trace contaminants such as cadmium, lead, and mercury; and radioactive contamination.

Reducing and Regulating Marine Disposal. There is a considerable body of legislation in the United States that encourages reduction of wastes entering the marine environment, requires treatment of those that do, and restricts the concentration of pollutants in waste streams approved for disposal. Among these are the Marine Protection, Research and Sanctuaries Act, the Federal Water Pollution Control Act, and the Ocean Dumping Ban Act. The latter put an end to ocean dumping of all materials except some dredge material.

Internationally, the most significant mechanism for reducing and controlling marine disposal is the Convention on the Prevention of Marine Pollution by Dumping of Wastes and Other Matter. Also known as the London Dumping Convention, it requires member states (more than ninety) to adhere to minimal standards for ocean disposal of wastes seaward of signatories' territorial seas. It prohibits dumping of a number of black-listed substances (such as organohalogen compounds, mercury and cadmium and their compounds), permits others to be dumped with special care, and encourages members to develop individual protocols and regional agreements to improve the quality of marine waters (Office of Technology Assessment, 1987; GESAMP, 1990). Important regional environmental conventions include the Oslo Convention, the Paris Convention, the Barcelona Convention, the Helsinki Convention, and the Bonn Agreement. The United Nations Environment Programme has also established the Regional Seas Programme, which encourages pollution control and protection of living marine resources. Currently, there are ten such regional-seas programs, including the Mediterranean, the Caribbean, and the Red Sea.

[*See also* Atmosphere Dynamics; El Niño–Southern Oscillation; Natural Climate Fluctuations; Ocean–Atmosphere Coupling; Ocean Structure and Development; *and* Sea Level.]

BIBLIOGRAPHY

Clark, R. B. *Marine Pollution*. 3d ed. Oxford: Clarendon Press, 1992. A clear introductory text, broadly covering pollution sources and effects with useful examples.

GESAMP (Joint Group of Experts on Scientific Aspects of Marine Pollution). *The State of the Marine Environment*. UNEP Regional Seas Reports and Studies No. 115. Nairobi, 1990. Provides a general status of the health of the marine environment, as compiled by some of the world's leading scientists in marine pollution, and ranks marine pollution sources and problems; easy to read.

Office of Technology Assessment. *Wastes in the Marine Environment*. Washington, D.C., 1987. A comprehensive overview of marine pollution in the United States, with some excellent examples; includes descriptions of pertinent laws and agency responsibilities.

Swanson, R. L. "A History of Ocean Dumping." *MSRC Bulletin*. Stony Brook, N.Y.: Marine Sciences Research Center, The University at Stony Brook, 2000. An up-to-date discussion of ocean dumping primarily in the United States.

—ROBERT LAWRENCE SWANSON

OCEAN DYNAMICS

Ocean waters flow over a continuum of spatial and temporal scales. Waves and small-scale processes with scales of meters and seconds coexist in an ocean basin with circulation features that have scales of thousands of kilometers and millennia. A fundamental challenge to physical oceanographers is an understanding of how flow at one scale affects and interacts with flow at another. For a study of the modern ocean's climate and its evolution, the interest is on flow within and between basins, with a time scale of years to tens of years. Flow at these scales of space and time is referred to as the *large-scale circulation*. The large-scale circulation transports heat, water, and other properties of importance to the global climate.

Forces and Accelerations. The large-scale ocean circulation principally results from the persistent action of wind on the sea surface and from the exchange of heat and moisture across the sea surface. A determination of the flow resulting from these forces comes from the application of Newton's second law to this fluid system. Newton's second law states that the acceleration of the fluid must equal the sum of the forces applied to the fluid per unit mass. The primary forces that drive the large-scale ocean flow are the gravitational, frictional, and pressure gradient forces. The major effects of the gravitational force on the large-scale flow field are that the flow principally lies on surfaces of constant density and that the vertical force balance is essentially hydrostatic, with pressure increasing with depth owing to the weight of the overlying water. Movement along density surfaces requires no gravitational work, and in general the surfaces of constant density, termed *isopycnals*, are quasi-horizontal surfaces. This constraint creates a welcome simplification for ocean dynamicists because the fundamentally three-dimensional flow field can be locally approximated as layers of flow with the circulation lying mainly in the horizontal plane. Pressure gradient forces in the ocean are created by changes in the sea surface elevation from one locale to the next, and by horizontal gradients of density within the ocean. Measurement or estimation of those height and density gradients are often used to diagnose the horizontal flow. The forces that ultimately establish the pressure gradients derive from the action of wind on the sea surface, which causes convergence or divergence of the surface waters, and from air–sea exchanges of heat and fresh water, which create density differences through the alteration of oceanic temperature, salinity, or both. Frictional forcing is important at the ocean surface, where the winds shear the sea surface, creating a vertical transfer of momentum from the atmosphere into the upper ocean.

Understanding how the combination of gravitational, pressure gradient, and frictional forces create flow in the ocean's basins is complicated by the rotation of our planet on its axis. Newton's second law applies to an inertial, nonrotating coordinate system. While the effect of our planet's rotation is not evident in the course of our daily movements, the much larger temporal and spatial scales of ocean flow are profoundly affected by rotation. In a determination of fluid motion on a rotating planet, the total velocity is the sum of the local velocity of the fluid relative to a point fixed on the Earth and the velocity of that fixed point, created by the spin of the Earth on its axis. The total acceleration of this fluid becomes the sum of three terms: a local acceleration, a Coriolis acceleration, and a centrifugal acceleration. In the description of the ocean flow field, our interest is in the movement of the flow relative to a fixed point on Earth—the rotating reference frame in which we live. Thus, Newton's second law is written such that the Coriolis and centrifugal accelerations are expressed as forces (called pseudo-forces) on the right-hand side of the equation, leaving the local acceleration as the only acceleration recognized in the rotating frame. Because a fluid's centrifugal force, directed toward the Earth's rotational axis, is a function only of its latitudinal position, it is combined with the gravitational force to produce what is known as *effective gravity*. The Coriolis force is negligible in the vertical force balance, yet it is a dominant term in the horizontal force balance. The magnitude of the Coriolis force depends not only on the latitudinal position of the fluid but also on the fluid velocity. Ocean flow that is initially accelerated by spatial pressure differences from a high pressure area to a low pressure area is deflected to the right, looking downstream, in the Northern Hemisphere (a counterclockwise rotating system) and to the left, looking downstream, in the Southern Hemisphere (a clockwise rotating system) by the Coriolis force. After some transient conditions, an equilibrium is established whereby ocean flow moves across the pressure gradient, rather than along it, as would be the case in a nonrotating system. Thus, in a rotating system, water does not flow "downhill," destroying the pressure difference; rather, it flows across the hill, and pressure differences are maintained. (This is the oceanic equivalent of the relation between winds and pressure contours used in interpreting weather maps.) The combined action of the Coriolis force and the horizontal pressure gradient force creates a steady-state balance known as *geostrophic flow*, which relates the pressure gradient to the horizontal velocity. Large-scale horizontal oceanic flows, like the large-scale atmospheric winds, are primarily geostrophic. The vertical force balance for the large-scale circulation is hydrostatic, where the vertical pressure gradient is in equilibrium with the effective gravitational force. Thus, a description of oceanic circulation requires a knowledge of the three-dimensional distribution of pressure in the ocean.

Thermohaline Circulation. Large-scale ocean circulation is often described in two main categories: the wind-driven and thermohaline circulations. While this division is valid in terms of forcing mechanisms, it is important to keep in mind that these circulations coexist, separable neither geographically nor dynamically. The ocean, unlike the atmosphere, is forced from its upper boundary. All inputs of momentum, heat, and fresh wa-

ter occur at the upper surface. The restriction of these inputs to the surface creates an ocean where the full range of temperatures and salinities appears at the sea surface. This feature is key to the concept of a thermohaline circulation. Because the ocean is differentially heated, surface temperatures generally decrease from the tropics to the poles. In addition to receiving a relatively small amount of radiative heating, the waters at high latitudes also lose a tremendous amount of heat to the atmosphere via sensible or latent heat exchanges. The strong cooling of the high-latitude waters causes the density of the surface waters to increase to the point where they are denser than the waters below, and thus they sink. These heavy waters, being denser than any water at lower latitudes, flow equatorward beneath lighter waters, establishing the vertical stratification of the mid- and low-latitude waters. Evidence for these deep, cold equatorward flows first came in 1751, when the first temperature of the deep ocean was recorded. Henry Ellis, a British sea captain, discovered that water at depth in the tropics is quite cold, much colder, in fact, than the tropical surface waters and overlying air. Count Rumford in 1800 used these measurements to deduce that the cold water must have originated at the poles and that, in order to conserve mass, there must be an accompanying poleward flow of warm water at the surface. Thus, approximately 250 years ago, the concept of an ocean overturning cell, or an ocean conveyor belt, was born.

Today, numerous measurements have confirmed the existence of such meridional overturning cells, although oceanographers now recognize the three-dimensionality and geographic complexity of this buoyancy-driven flow. If there were no continents on Earth, the convection cells in the ocean would be symmetric about the equator, with waters sinking at each pole and rising near the equator, similar in geometry to the Hadley circulation of the tropical atmosphere. However, the deep-water convection sites in our global ocean are few and isolated, shaped by the continents' disruption of the ocean circulation. The majority of the world's deep water is formed in the northern North Atlantic, specifically in the Norwegian/Greenland Sea and in the Labrador basin. A smaller amount of deep water is formed in the Weddell Sea and other sites around Antarctica. A simplified schematic of the global pattern of exchange established by these convective flows is shown in Figure 1. These schematics are called "conveyor belts" and are intended to illustrate the principal pathways by which the ocean exchanges heat with the atmosphere. This system of meridional overturning cells constitutes the thermohaline circulation for the global ocean. Net warm-to-cold-water conversion occurs in the northern North Atlantic, while cold-to-warm-water conversion occurs in the subtropical Indian and Pacific Oceans. Of note is the warm

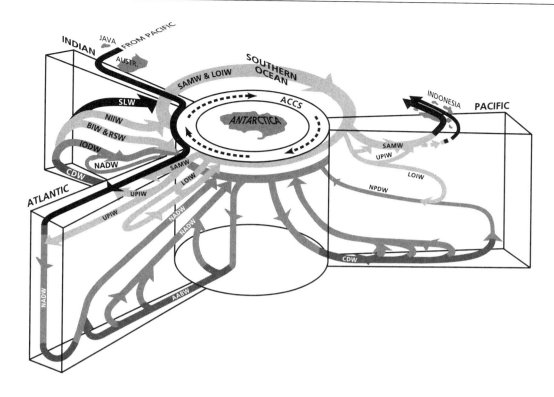

SLW	Surface Layer Water
SAMW	Subantarctic Mode Water
RSW	Red Sea Water
AABW	Antarctic Bottom Water
NPDW	North Pacific Deep Water
ACCS	Antarctic Circumpolar Current System
CDW	Circumpolar Deep Water
NADW	North Atlantic Deep Water

UPIW	Upper Intermediate Water, $26.8 \leq \sigma_\theta \leq 27.2$
LOIW	Lower Intermediate Water, $27.2 \leq \sigma_\theta \leq 27.5$
IODW	Indian Ocean Deep Water
BIW	Banda Intermediate Water
NIIW	Northwest Indian Intermediate Water

Ocean Dynamics. FIGURE 1. A Simplified Schematic of the Global "Conveyor Belt," Which Shows the Upper, Intermediate, Deep, and Bottom Water Pathways.

The acronyms are used to designate the various water masses involved in the thermohaline circulation. (Reproduced with permission from Schmitz, 1996b.)

surface current that wends its way through each of the basins to terminate in the northern North Atlantic, where it supplies water for the formation of deep water. While the schematic shows principal pathways of the conveyor belt system, it intentionally suppresses the existence of major oceanic recirculation gyres. In detail, the conveyor belt system could be more aptly described as a set of linked baggage carousels, for the parcels of water moving along the conveyor belt get shunted into these gyres and spend considerable time recirculating rather than directly moving along the conveyor belt. Many of these gyres are part of the wind-driven circulation, which is discussed in the next section.

Wind-Driven Currents. According to Newton's law of viscosity, when a shear stress is applied to a fluid, a velocity shear results. In a nonrotating system, the ac-

tion of wind over the surface of the ocean would result in a current moving in the direction of the wind, with the magnitude of this current decreasing as depth increases because of frictional losses. On our rotating planet, the Coriolis force modifies the direct response of the ocean water to the wind forcing. The interplay of the wind stress, the interfacial drag, and the Coriolis force produces surface currents that move 45° to the right (or left) of the wind in the Northern (or Southern) Hemisphere. As the surface water moves, it sets into motion the water beneath, which will, because of the combination of interfacial drag and Coriolis forces, move to the right (or left) of the surface flow in the Northern (or Southern) Hemisphere. Shifts in the force balance continue with depth, causing the current to veer to the right (or left, depending on the hemisphere) as depth increases. This action results in a flow pattern known as the Ekman spiral, named after the Scandinavian oceanographer who in 1902 described the ocean response to wind forcing. The depth of this spiral is typically 50–200 meters; thus, the wind directly sets in motion only a small fraction of the water column.

The depth-integrated mass transport created by the Ekman flow, known as the Ekman transport, is at 90° to the right (or left) of the wind in the Northern (or Southern) Hemisphere. For example, a westerly wind in the Northern Hemisphere would produce a southward Ekman transport. Given the alternating pattern of easterlies and westerlies established by the large-scale atmospheric circulation in each hemisphere, the direction of the Ekman transport will also change with latitude. For example, north of 30°N the westerlies will produce a southward Ekman transport, while south of 30°N the easterly trade winds will create a northward transport of the surface waters. Thus, at approximately 30°N there will be a convergence of the surface waters, while to the south in the tropics and to the north in the subpolar seas there will be a divergence of the surface waters. In turn, these convergences and divergences of the surface waters create, respectively, uplifted and depressed sea surface height, such that high and low pressures result in the ocean beneath the Ekman layer. These differences in sea surface height and pressure result in a westward geostrophic flow to the south of 30°N and an eastward geostrophic flow to the north. Because boundaries in each ocean basin block the zonal currents, meridional currents result. This combination of meridional and zonal flows constitute the wind-driven gyres, which are referred to as Sverdrup flows. These basin scale gyres are characterized by a distinct asymmetry owing to the influence of our rotating planet: intensified, narrow boundary currents exist on the western boundary of each ocean gyre, while relatively broad and slow flow marks the eastern edge of the ocean gyres. Without coastal boundaries, all ocean currents would move completely around the Earth, like the atmospheric winds. The sole example of such unblocked oceanic flow is the Antarctic Circumpolar Current, located between 50° and 60°S.

The pattern of alternating easterlies and westerlies produces high pressure centers in each of the five subtropical basins and low pressure centers in each of the three identifiable subpolar gyres. The resultant geostrophic flow is anticyclonic for the subtropical gyres (clockwise in the Northern Hemisphere and counterclockwise in the Southern Hemisphere) and cyclonic for the subpolar gyres (counterclockwise in the Northern Hemisphere and clockwise in the Southern Hemisphere). These gyres are shown in the schematic of the surface circulation in Figure 2. In addition to the subtropical and subpolar gyres, the tropics also have identifiable gyres, driven by the winds in the equatorial belt. Because of the seasonal shifting of the intertropical convergence zone, these gyres are highly variable relative to the subtropical and subpolar gyres. The pressure gradients that create these surface gyres extend to the deep ocean as well. Deep pressure gradients drive geostrophic flow at depth. This deep geostrophic flow, however, may vary considerably from the surface flow, both in intensity and pattern, because of interior density differences that alter the pressure gradient established by the near-surface convergences and divergences.

Intergyre and interbasin exchange are also highlighted in Figure 2. This exchange represents the upper limb of the thermohaline circulation, described in the previous section. Thus, the surface circulation is comprised of gyres, primarily wind-driven, which recirculate waters within a basin, and throughflows from one gyre to another, driven by the thermohaline circulation.

The high and low pressure centers in each of the gyres are responsible not only for driving the horizontal geostrophic flows that define the limbs of each of these gyres, but also for establishing an important vertical motion. High pressure centers, or areas of convergence, are sites where water is downwelled to maintain continuity of mass: the convergent Ekman transports are "pumped" downward into the ocean interior. Likewise, low pressure centers, or areas of surface divergence, are areas of upwelling, with the divergent Ekman layer transport drawn upward from the ocean interior. Upwelling sites are quite important to the local biological productivity of the area, since upwelling brings a fresh supply of nutrients to the euphotic zone. Conversely, downwelling resists the upward mixing of nutrients from the deeper levels. Thus, downwelling regions are characterized as biological deserts. Each of the subtropical gyres in the ocean are high pressure systems and thus downwelling sites, while the low pressure of the subpolar gyres create upwelling conditions that lead to high concentrations of phytoplankton and zooplankton.

Global Heat Budgets. The global climate system is driven by a gross radiative imbalance at the top of the atmosphere between the tropics and the poles (Figure 3A). The tropics absorb more shortwave solar radiative energy than is returned to space by longwave terrestrial radiation, leading to an energy surplus. The situation is reversed for the poles, leading to an energy deficit. At the equator the surplus is roughly 100 watts per square meter (W/m^2), while at the poles the deficit is similarly about 100 W/m^2. The 38° latitude in both hemispheres approximately separates the zone of net radiative heating from high-latitude caps of net radiative cooling. These local radiative imbalances would steadily warm the tropics and cool the poles if it were not for a poleward flow of heat in both the atmosphere and ocean

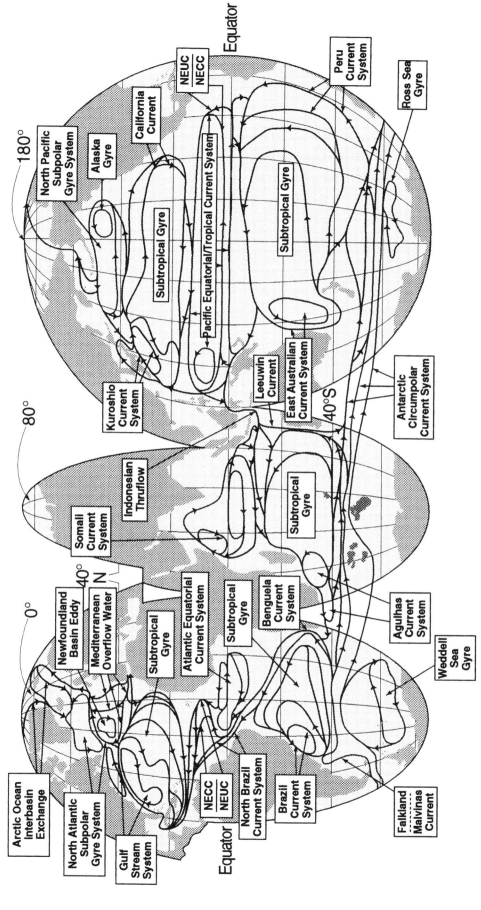

Ocean Dynamics. Figure 2. A Schematic of the Global Surface Circulation, with an Identification of Major Ocean Gyres and Currents. (Reproduced with permission from Schmitz, 1996b.)

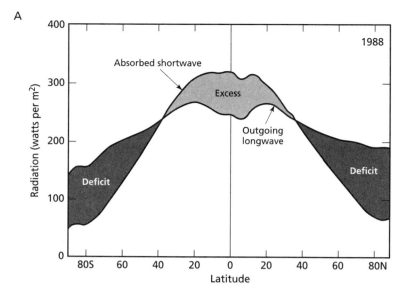

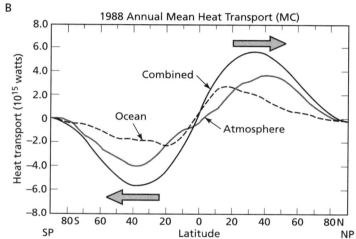

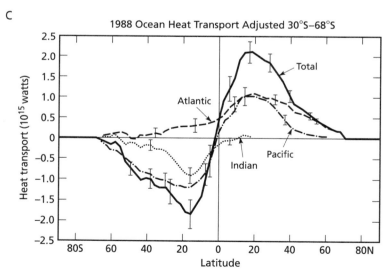

Ocean Dynamics. FIGURE 3. (A) The absorbed shortwave (incoming) radiation and the longwave (outgoing) radiation at the top of the atmosphere as a function of latitude. The difference in these curves illustrates the radiative excess at low latitudes and the radiative deficit at high latitudes. (B) The total mean northward transport of heat required by the differential heating of the globe, the atmospheric contribution to this total, and the oceanic contribution to this total. (C) The mean northward transport of heat in each ocean basin and in total. (After Trenberth and Solomon, 1994. Reproduced with permission from Springer-Verlag.)

(Figure 3B). This poleward heat transport exists because there are temperature differences between poleward and equatorward flows, as explained further in the next section. Consistent with the divide between latitudes of energy surplus and those of energy deficit, the combined oceanic and atmospheric meridional heat transport curve in Figure 3B has a maximum near 38°; equatorward of 38° the heat flux increases poleward as radiative heating in these latitudes adds to the "burden" of heat which is transported poleward. Poleward of 38°, the flux decreases with increasing latitude as radiative cooling at each latitude removes some of the heat being transported poleward. The transition between where the ocean is gaining heat and where it is losing heat is marked by the peak in its meridional heat transport curve, at approximately 20° in both hemispheres. The ocean absorbs heat principally in the tropics, by means of radiative heating and heat gain from the atmosphere, and then advects the heat to higher latitudes, where it is released back to the atmosphere, primarily through latent heat fluxes but also through sensible heat fluxes. The peak in the meridional heat transport curve for the atmosphere (Figure 3B) occurs at approximately 38°. Equatorward of this latitude the atmosphere is gaining a surplus of solar heat. From 20° and 38° the atmosphere is also gaining heat from the ocean. Poleward of 38° there is a net radiative cooling of the atmosphere, yet the atmosphere maintains its warmth by the heat released from the ocean waters.

There are interesting differences in the oceanic heat transport among the five midlatitude oceanic basins, as shown in Figure 3C. Four of the five individual curves exhibit the same structure as the overall oceanic heat transport curve in Figure 3B, with heat transports declining poleward from about 15°–20° latitude. Such decline indicates a heating of the overlying atmosphere in each of these basins. The South Atlantic is anomalous in that its oceanic heat transport is equatorward rather than poleward, delivering approximately 0.5 PW (1 PW [petawatt] = 1×10^{15} joules per second) across the equator to the North Atlantic. As a result, the relatively narrow North Atlantic transports as much heat northward as the much wider North Pacific at 25°N, and more than twice the heat that the North Pacific transports at 50°N. The northward oceanic heat transport throughout the length of the Atlantic is a manifestation of the strength of the global thermohaline circulation. As discussed above, the majority of the world's deep water is formed in the high latitudes of the Atlantic. The cold, deep waters spreading southward throughout the Atlantic and the compensating warm surface return flow create the strong northward heat transport. As such, the thermohaline circulation causes the largest oceanic heating of the atmosphere to occur in the subtropical and subpolar/polar regime of the North Atlantic, as

shown in Figure 4A, where the annual average net heat exchange (the sum of the latent and sensible heat fluxes with the net radiative fluxes) across the North Atlantic sea surface is shown. Only in the tropics and eastern subtropics does the North Atlantic show an annual receipt of heat from the atmosphere. This heat gain is relatively weak compared to the intense oceanic heating of the atmosphere in the western subtropics and the subpolar basin. The heating of the atmosphere extends over the subpolar region and much of the subtropics well south of 40°N in the North Atlantic. The strongest oceanic heating of the atmosphere is aligned with the path of the Gulf Stream, which conveys the bulk of the warm waters in the upper limb of the oceanic conveyor belt. The contribution from the latent heat flux is generally larger than that from the sensible heat flux; for example, the >200 W/m² maximum oceanic heating of the atmosphere that occurs over the Gulf Stream comes about as the sum of latent (>240 W/m²) and sensible heating (>60 W/m²), and by a net radiative cooling term at the sea surface of about 100 W/m².

The annual range of net air–sea heat exchange is large, as exemplified by the annual variation across the North Atlantic (Figure 4B). This seasonality is one of the difficulties in constructing oceanic and atmospheric heat budgets. For example, the North Atlantic's average oceanic heating of the atmosphere is 17 W/m² per year. This average results from a seasonal cycle with a January atmospheric heating of 126 W/m² and a July atmospheric cooling of 85 W/m². Over the Gulf Stream, where the annual average oceanic heating of the atmosphere exceeds 200 W/m², the December value rises to more than 500 W/m², while in July the ocean there absorbs heat at a rate of about 50 W/m². Assessing the annual average air–sea exchange requires accurate measurements throughout the year because that average is small compared to the seasonal oscillation of terms. Assessing climate change signals on interannual, decadel, and longer time scales is even more difficult than the task of determining the mean climate. The difficulty stems from the fact that the accuracy of air–sea heat exchange estimates is not sufficient for tightly constraining the estimated annual average state, and thus it is difficult to discern if variability is due to longer-term climatic change or whether it is within the envelope of the mean climatic conditions. In the North Atlantic the accuracy suffers in part because winter oceanic data coverage is not as thorough as the summer coverage. In the other ocean basins the accuracy is even worse because of the poor observation density throughout the seasons.

Mechanisms of Exchange. The motions of the ocean associated with the meridional heat transport can be decomposed into three circulation configurations, which are described below: meridional overturning, standing eddies, and transient eddies. In all three cases

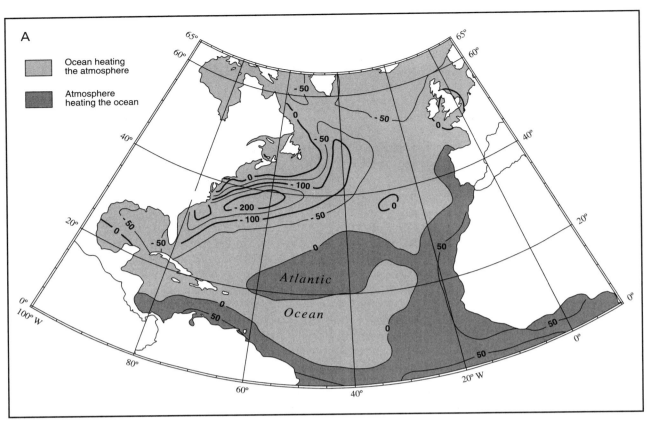

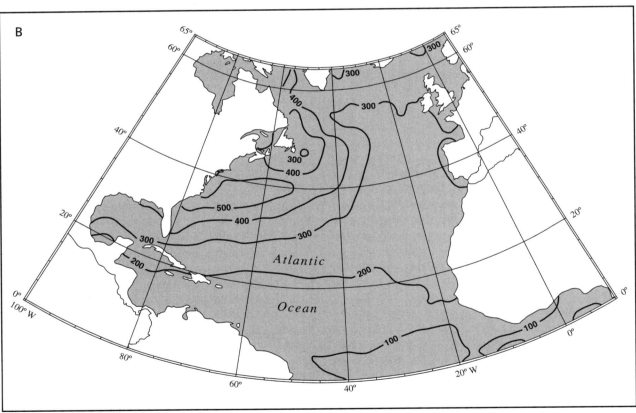

Ocean Dynamics. FIGURE 4. (A) Net air–sea heat exchange (W/m²) for the North Atlantic, annually averaged. Negative values denote oceanic heating of the atmosphere. (B) The difference, in W/m², between the largest and smallest monthly averaged net air–sea heat exchange for the North Atlantic. (After Isemer and Hasse, 1987. With permission of Springer-Verlag. Copyright 1987.)

there is flow moving poleward and flow moving equatorward, yet no net transport of mass results. Because there is a temperature difference between the opposing flows, however, a net heat transport, proportional to the temperature difference between the limbs, results. In addition to heat, the meridional transport of fresh water, carbon, and other physical, chemical, and biological quantities results from the same mechanism.

Meridional overturning circulations involve two or more vertical layers with opposing flows and different temperatures. These are circulation cells in the meridional plane, most easily revealed by a zonal integration of the velocity field. The Hadley circulation, dominant in the tropics, is an example of a meridional overturning circulation in the atmosphere. In the ocean, the global thermohaline circulation (Figure 1) comprises a linked system of such meridional overturning circulations. When cold water at one depth is transported equatorward and relatively warmer water at a shallower depth is transported poleward, a net heat transport results. This configuration of meridional overturning cells plays a large role in the ocean's contribution to meridional heat transport.

Standing eddies and meanders involve laterally opposing flows that create a poleward heat transport when warm water or air in one region flows poleward and cold water or air in another region, but in the same depth range, flows equatorward. The Icelandic and Aleutian low pressure centers and the Siberian and Canadian high pressure centers are examples of standing eddies in the atmosphere. Each of the basin-scale gyres shown in Figure 2 is an oceanic standing eddy. A subtropical gyre is a permanent anticyclonic circulation system where the poleward-flowing western boundary current is often warmer than the recirculating equatorward flow of water in the gyre interior. Such a temperature difference yields a meridional heat transport. Many of the regions of strong warming of the atmosphere by the ocean lie over these subtropical western boundary currents, reflecting the intense advection of heat by these strong narrow currents. A subpolar gyre is a cyclonic circulation with an equatorward-flowing western boundary current and poleward flow in the gyre interior, with the latter the warmer limb if poleward heat transport is to result, as it does, for example, in the subpolar North Atlantic. However, the oceanic heating of the atmosphere overlying the interior of the subpolar gyre is not as intense as the heating associated with a subtropical western boundary current because the poleward heat flux is not as strong. The weaker poleward heat flux principally results from a weak poleward flow in the interior.

Transient eddies also involve opposing flows, yet in this case the flow varies in time and not in space. At a particular locale, if at one point in time warm water is carried poleward and at another time cold water is carried equatorward, then over time a net poleward heat transfer is achieved. To a large degree, midlatitude weather involves transient atmospheric eddies, such as the cyclones or anticylones spawned by the unstable Jet Stream. Gulf Stream rings are an example of transient eddies in the ocean. A meandering Gulf Stream alternately pinches off a counterclockwise eddy to its south and a clockwise one to its north. The former has a column of cold subpolar water trapped in its center, which is eventually mixed into the subtropical gyre, while the latter has a core of warm subtropical water trapped in its center, which is subsequently mixed into the subpolar gyre. The exchange results in a cooled subtropical gyre and a warmed subpolar gyre, and thus a poleward transport of heat. In the ocean the transient eddies are relatively ineffectual in meridional heat transport compared to oceanic meridional overturning and standing eddy circulations. This is a distinct contrast to the situation in the atmosphere where transient eddies play a dominant role in the midlatitude meridional heat transport, especially in the Southern Hemisphere. It is important to note here that the mathematical decomposition into standing and transient eddies is arbitrary as to a selected time scale. For example, the interannual or interdecadel shifts of the strengths and positions of atmospheric pressure centers are a very low-frequency form of transient eddy activity.

Global Pattern of Air–Sea Heat Exchange. Two maps of air–sea heat exchange are shown in Figure 5. The top panel is an estimate of the air–sea heat exchange based on observations of sea surface temperature, surface air temperature, humidity, wind speed, and cloudiness. To produce estimates of air–sea heat flux from these measurements, it is necessary to use empirical relationships and parameterizations. In the Northern Hemisphere the data coverage is deemed adequate, and the knowledge of the parameterizations is good enough for this computation, but in the Southern Hemisphere the results are suspect, particularly south of 40°S. It is known from oceanic measurements that cold intermediate and deep waters are produced southward of 40°S, which requires oceanic cooling by the atmosphere, yet the estimated fluxes (Figure 5A) show heat being added to the ocean over a large portion of the region. This sort of problem causes the total estimated heat exchange for the world ocean to depart from zero. Based on the air–sea heat fluxes in Figure 5A, the estimated global average exchange is an oceanic heating rate of 50 W/m^2. In reality, that rate should be essentially zero, since measurements of the world's oceans do not show secular heat content changes. [*See* Ocean–Atmosphere Coupling.]

The bottom panel of Figure 5 shows the results of a numerical simulation of the ocean–atmosphere–land climate system. While such simulations are at a very early

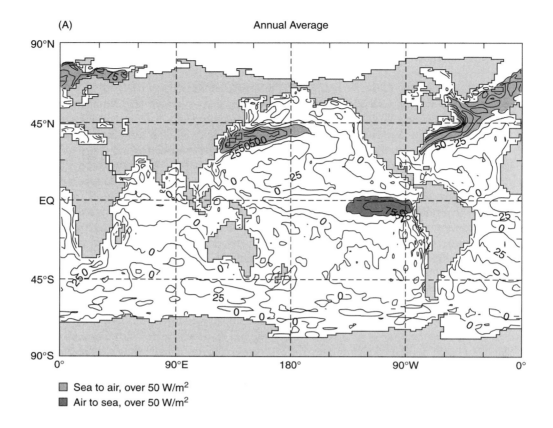

(A)   Annual Average

Sea to air, over 50 W/m²
Air to sea, over 50 W/m²

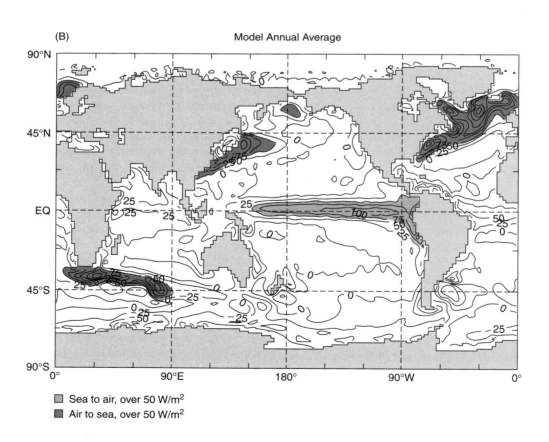

(B)   Model Annual Average

Sea to air, over 50 W/m²
Air to sea, over 50 W/m²

stage of development, they do represent, by construction, a dynamically consistent representation of the climate system. Thus, these model-simulated fluxes when globally averaged over time show no net heat gain or loss for the ocean. This simulation shows a belt of oceanic heating of the atmosphere along the coast of Antarctica, where deepwater formation is observed, and a second belt of oceanic heating spiraling southward from southern Africa to Drake passage south of South America. This belt is where Subantarctic Mode Water and Antarctic Intermediate Water are formed in the "real" ocean in the Antarctic Circumpolar Current. Our discussion of the global pattern of air–sea heat exchange takes advantage of both the fluxes derived from measurements (Figure 5A) and the model-simulated fluxes (Figure 5B). We will rely particularly on the latter field for the latitudes south of 40°S, where, as mentioned above, the estimated fields are of questionable accuracy.

Globally, the sites for strong ocean and atmosphere heat exchange, as seen in Figure 5, are a function of the upper ocean circulation (Figure 2). The regions of most intense oceanic heating of the atmosphere are associated with the two regions of strongest poleward flow by western boundary currents: the Gulf Stream and the Kuroshio, both located in the Northern Hemisphere. These strong advective pathways create large air–sea contrasts and the largest air–sea heat and moisture fluxes to the overlying atmosphere. Over the three subtropical western boundary currents in the Southern Hemisphere, the East Australian Current, the Agulhus Current, and the Brazil Current, comparatively weak oceanic heating of the atmosphere is found, only slightly exceeding the background mid- to high-latitude heating. The air–sea contrasts over the Gulf Stream and Kuroshio are enhanced over those found in the Southern Hemisphere's western boundary currents because the westerlies off of North America and northern Asia bring cold, dry, continental subarctic and arctic air directly over these warm currents. Because winds from Africa, Australia, and South America are not as strong, cold, and dry, the Southern Hemisphere's subtropical western boundary currents only weakly heat the atmosphere relative to the Kuroshio and the Gulf Stream.

The Antarctic Circumpolar Current is a massive current system but does not have a strong poleward component. Cold and dry antarctic air is brought northward across the antarctic zone to the warmer parts of the Antarctic Circumpolar Current by northerly winds on the trailing side of transient cyclones moving along the westerlies. The cold antarctic air coming north is continuously heated by the antarctic waters before arriving over the main eastward flow of the Antarctic Circumpolar Current. Because of this, the air–sea contrast is reduced over the Antarctic Circumpolar Current, and the fluxes attained are not as great as what would result from direct contact of the antarctic air with the current's waters.

The subpolar North Atlantic and the Southern Ocean have appreciable warming of the atmosphere above them, but not much heating occurs above the subpolar North Pacific. This appears to reflect the lack of significant northward branching of the warm waters of the Kuroshio Current from the subtropical gyre into the subpolar North Pacific (Figure 2), compared to the major injection of Gulf Stream warm waters into the eastern subpolar gyre in the North Atlantic via the thermohaline circulation. The tropical belts of each basin are sites of oceanic cooling of the atmosphere, particularly in the eastern tropical Pacific; interannual variability in this area occurs in the El Niño phenomenon. [*See* El Niño–Southern Oscillation.]

Global Freshwater Budget and the Freshwater Cycle. The large amplitude of the latent heat flux at midlatitudes (>240 W/m^2 on annual average and >500 W/m^2 in the winter over the Gulf Stream) underscores the importance of evaporation at the sea surface in the oceanic heating of the overlying atmosphere. This moisture exchange is also central to the atmospheric moisture budget. Unlike the situation for heat, there is essentially no net gain or loss of moisture at the top of the atmosphere; the moisture budget for the Earth is closed internally. On the whole, the oceans provide moisture to the atmosphere because of an excess of evaporation over precipitation of about 1.3 Sv (1 Sverdrup = 1 Sv = 10^6 m^3/s); the land gains 1.3 Sv of moisture from the atmosphere via an excess of precipitation over evaporation. That amount of moisture is carried by runoff from land to ocean, closing the system and maintaining a quasi-steady state. [*See* Hydrologic Cycle.]

The compensating exchanges between the ocean, atmosphere, and land are not locally achieved; rather, they involve the meridional movement of water, principally in the ocean and atmosphere, since the meridional transport of water by rivers is rather small. The zonally integrated meridional transport of fresh water in the ocean and atmosphere is shown in Figure 6. (This figure is analogous to the meridional heat transport curve in Figure 3A.) The regimes of moisture exchange between ocean and atmosphere are deduced from the change of sign in the slopes of the curves. The atmo-

Ocean Dynamics. FIGURE 5. Net Air–Sea Heat Exchange (W/m^2) for the Global Ocean.

(A) Annually averaged and based on observed surface climatological fields. (B) Annually averaged and derived from the NCAR Climate System Model. (Reproduced with permission from Doney et al., 1998.)

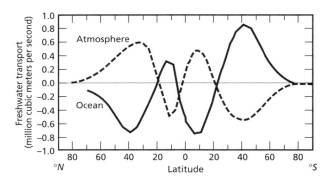

Ocean Dynamics. FIGURE 6. Meridional Transport ($\times 10^6$ m³/s) of Fresh Water as a Function of Latitude, Zonally Averaged, for the Ocean (solid curve) and the Atmosphere (dashed curve).

The meridional transport by rivers on land is very small. (Reproduced with permission from Schmitt and Wijffels, 1993.)

the tropical regime, between latitudes of about 40° and about 10°–15°. In the tropics around the equator, the atmosphere supplies moisture to the ocean. The atmosphere thus gains moisture from the ocean at midlatitudes and returns moisture to the ocean in the low latitudes and high latitudes. This exchange differs from the pattern of heat exchange, where the atmosphere gains heat from the ocean at high latitudes and loses heat at low latitudes (Figure 3B). A comparison of Figure 3B with Figure 6 shows that in the 20°–40° latitude belt, where the ocean heats the atmosphere, it is also providing moisture to the atmosphere. North of 40°N the ocean continues to heat the atmosphere but is freshened by the moisture from the atmosphere. For comparison to the annual average net heat exchange, Figure 7 shows the annual average evaporation minus precipitation for the North Atlantic. The evaporation estimate follows from the estimation of latent heat flux and involves the measurement of wind speed, humidity, and sea surface temperature from ships. The measurement of precipitation at sea is problematic, and its errors dominate the uncertainty in the global moisture budget. The distribution in Figure 7 gives some sense of the geography underlying the zonal averages of Figure 6. The signature

sphere provides moisture (excess precipitation) to the ocean poleward of about 40° latitude in the subpolar/polar regime, and gains moisture (excess evaporation) from the ocean in the subtropical regime and in part of

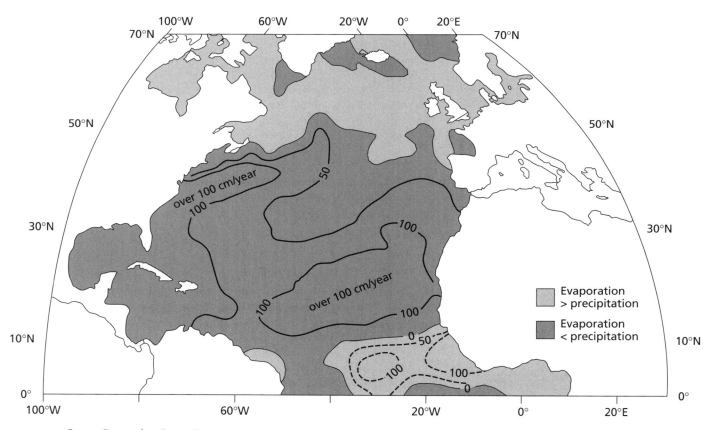

Ocean Dynamics. FIGURE 7. Net Air–Sea Freshwater Exchange (cm/year), Annually Averaged, Calculated as the Difference between Evaporation and Precipitation. (Reproduced with permission from Schmitt et al., 1989.)

of the very large evaporative heat exchange over the Gulf Stream is evident. Another center of strong moisture exchange is found beneath the trade winds, sharply truncated to the south by the large precipitation of the intertropical convergence zone.

[*See also* Atmosphere Dynamics; Natural Climate Fluctuations; Ocean Structure and Development; *and* Sea Level.]

BIBLIOGRAPHY

Bryden, H. L. "Ocean Heat Transport across 24°N Latitude." In *Interactions between Global Climate Subsystems: The Legacy of Hann*, edited by G. A. McBean and M. Hantel. *Geophysical Monographs* 75 (1993), 65–75.

Doney, S. C., W. G. Large, and F. O. Bryan. "Surface Ocean Fluxes and Water-Mass Transformation Rates in the Coupled NCAR Climate System Model." *Journal of Climate* 11 (1998), 1422–1443.

Isemer, J.-H., and L. Hasse. *The Bunker Climate Atlas of the North Atlantic Ocean.* vol. 2. *Air–Sea Interactions.* New York: Springer-Verlag, 1987.

Open University Oceanography Course Team. *Ocean Circulation.* Milton Keynes, U.K.: Open University; Oxford: Butterworth-Heinemann, 1989.

Persson, A. "How Do We Understand the Coriolis Force?" *Bulletin of the American Meteorological Society* 79.7 (1998), 1373–1385.

Schmitt, R., P. S. Bogden, C. E. Dorman. "Evaporation Minus Precipitation and Density Fluxes for the North Atlantic." *Journal of Physical Oceanography* 19 (1989), 1208–1221.

Schmitt, R. W., and S. E. Wijffels. "The Role of the Oceans in the Global Water Cycle." In *Interactions between Global Climate Subsystems: The Legacy of Hann*, edited by G. A. McBean and M. Hantel. *Geophysical Monographs* 75 (1993), 77–92.

Schmitz, W. J., Jr. *On the World Ocean Circulation.* vol. 1. *Some Global Features: North Atlantic Circulation.* Woods Hole Oceanographic Institution Technical Report, WHOI-96-03, 1996a.

———. *On the World Ocean Circulation.* vol. 2. *The Pacific and Indian Oceans: A Global Update.* Woods Hole Oceanographic Institution Technical Report, WHOI-96-08, 1996b.

Trenberth, K. E., and A. Solomon. "The Global Heat Balance: Heat Transports in the Atmosphere and Ocean." *Climate Dynamics* 10 (1994), 107–134.

—MICHAEL S. MCCARTNEY AND M. SUSAN LOZIER

OCEAN LIFE

Between the seashore and the deep ocean there exists an enormous diversity of marine life. This diversity stems from the wide variety of marine habitats found in the world's oceans and the biological plasticity that allows marine organisms to adapt to them.

The intertidal zone is that area of the shoreline that lies between the depth of maximum high tide and minimum low tide. Organisms that live in the intertidal zone are adapted to withstand the drying effects of the Sun and wind for at least part of each day, the duration depending upon the tidal cycle. Encrusting plants and animals are the most common inhabitants of rocky intertidal regions, although more mobile creatures, such as crabs, snails, limpets, and chitons, are also common. Frequently, there is a high degree of vertical zonation, with different organisms living at different levels among the rocks. In areas without a hard substrate, a wide variety of burrowing organisms such as clams, worms, and crustaceans are frequently present in large numbers within the intertidal zone.

The continental shelves contain the most productive oceanic areas. Where the continental shelf has a shallow slope, such as off the coast of Maine, waters are often enriched in nutrients because of their shallow depth and proximity to the shore. These high-nutrient concentrations allow for the luxuriant growth of phytoplankton, single-celled plants that form the base of much of the oceanic food web. This high phytoplankton productivity provides a rich source of food for small animal grazers (zooplankton) such as small shrimplike crustaceans called *copepods*, which are in turn eaten by larger predators such as jellyfish, comb jellies, and small fish. Some of the most productive fisheries on Earth lie on continental shelves, such as on the Georges Bank off the east coast of Maine and on the Grand Banks of Newfoundland. Unfortunately, overfishing has reduced the stocks of commercially valuable cod and haddock in these regions to very low levels, necessitating a temporary ban on fishing until the populations rebound. [*See* Fishing.]

Coral reefs are also found on shallow continental shelves, albeit in tropical regions only. Coral reef systems are among the most productive and biologically diverse ecosystems on Earth, rivaled only by the tropical rainforests on land. The high species diversity of coral reefs is due to the environmental stability and structural complexity of this ecosystem. Tropical, shallow water systems where coral reefs thrive are characterized by their nearly constant conditions of temperature, salinity, day length, sunlight, and wave activity. In general, only the occasional storm disturbs the environmental constancy of the coral reef, allowing a great number of organisms to adapt to life there. The structural complexity of the corals themselves provides a wide variety of ecological niches for other organisms to inhabit, increasing the species richness of this system. The high productivity of the coral reef is due to the tight symbiotic relationship between the living coral (a relative of the jellyfish) and a small, single-celled brown alga called zooxanthellae. The zooxanthellae live within the tissues of the coral polyps (the individual flower-shaped structures), where they carry out photosynthesis. In doing so, some of the carbohydrates they produce are transferred to the coral, providing a ready food source. In turn, some of the nitrogenous waste material produced by the coral is used by the zooxanthellae for the production of amino acids and proteins. Consequently, despite often low concentrations of nutrients and particulate material in the water column, both coral and zooxanthellae are able to grow and reproduce at rapid rates. [*See* Reefs.]

Many continental shelves are much steeper and narrower than those found off the coast of northeastern North America. For example, off the western coast of both North America and South America, the continental shelves can be very narrow, with very deep waters relatively close to shore. In these regions, the sources of nutrients that support phytoplankton are far removed from surface waters where light is plentiful, and so, for most of the year, phytoplankton productivity is low. However, under the right conditions, a unique mechanism develops that is capable of bringing large amounts of nutrients from deep waters to the surface where phytoplankton can grow. During the spring, southward-flowing winds along the coasts of Washington, Oregon, and California tend to push the surface water along with them, forming the California current. However, soon thereafter the spin of the Earth initiates the Coriolis force that causes this southward-flowing water to make a sharp turn to the right (in the Northern Hemisphere; in the Southern Hemisphere the Coriolis force moves fluid to the left) and move offshore. As the waters near the coast move offshore, they are replaced by high-nutrient waters "upwelled" from deep below the surface. If this coastal upwelling persists, highly productive blooms of phytoplankton, which can support enormous quantities of fish, develop in these regions. In fact, the upwelling system off the coast of Peru once supported the largest anchovy fishery on Earth, before overfishing reduced anchovy stocks to extremely low levels.

Unlike the continental shelf regions, the open-ocean (pelagic) realm of the oceans is relatively unproductive because of the lack of a ready supply of nutrients. Nutrients that are often in short supply include nitrate, phosphate, silicic acid, and trace metals such as iron. Once nutrients in surface waters of the major central ocean basins become depleted, there are no efficient ways to replenish them. Consequently, phytoplankton growth remains low for most of the year. Exceptions exist in regions where adjacent ocean currents are moving in opposite directions, such as along the equatorial Pacific current system, or in regions where there is a great deal of turbulent motion, such as near the spinning eddies associated with the Gulf Stream current. Under these conditions, nutrients may be brought to the surface, allowing localized phytoplankton blooms to develop.

Some of the most poorly understood, and consequently most interesting, marine communities are those that survive at the ocean floor near hydrothermal vents and oil seeps. Both hydrogen sulfide and oil represent an energy source that is readily utilized by bacteria.

These bacteria form the basis of a complex benthic food web that includes filter feeding worms and mussels, predatory crustaceans, and fishes. Although currently of no significant economic value, these deep-ocean communities are useful for studying evolutionary processes as well as the biochemical adaptations that allow them to survive under such extreme conditions of light, temperature, and pressure.

[*See also* Biogeochemical Cycles; Biomass; Biomes; Driftnet Convention; Human Impacts, *article on* Human Impacts on Biota; Law of the Sea; *and the vignette on* Life at Oil Seeps *in the article on* Petroleum Hydrocarbons in the Ocean.]

BIBLIOGRAPHY

Backus, R. H., and D. W. Bourne. *Georges Bank*. Cambridge: MIT Press, 1987.
Carefoot, T. W. *Pacific Seashores*. Seattle: University of Washington Press, 1979.
Chantraine, P. *The Last Cod-Fish: Life and Death of the Newfoundland Way of Life (Food for Thought)*. Robert Davies Publishers, 1993.
Gage, J. D. *Deep-Sea Biology: A Natural History of Organisms at the Deep-Sea Floor*. Cambridge and New York: Cambridge University Press, 1993.
Martin, J. H., et al. "The Case for Iron." *Limnology and Oceanography* 36 (1991), 1793–1802.
Pauly, D. *Peruvian Upwelling Ecosystem: Dynamics and Interactions*. New York: International Specialized Book Service, 1989.
Raffaelli, D. G., et al. *Intertidal Ecology*. New York: Chapman and Hall, 1996.
Ricketts, E. F., and J. W. Hedgepeth. *Between Pacific Tides*. Stanford: Stanford University Press, 1986.

—KEVIN R. ARRIGO

OCEAN SEDIMENTS. *See* Climate Change, *article on* Climate Change Detection; *and* Climate Reconstruction.

OCEAN STRUCTURE AND DEVELOPMENT

The water in the oceans was delivered to the Earth by the "late veneer" accretion of cometary ices, and oceans have existed in some form since the very early history of the Earth. The chemistry of the ocean is controlled by the removal mechanisms of solutes from sea water, so that sea water does not resemble simply concentrated river water. Communication between the atmosphere and the deep sea is regulated by the thousand-year turnover time of the ocean circulation.

The Origin of Oceans on Earth. The oceans consist of molecules and elements that geochemists regard as "light" or "volatile": "light" because these are elements of low atomic weight (hydrogen, carbon, nitrogen, oxygen), and "volatile" because these elements are among the last to condense from a gas of solar composition. The elements that constituted the early solar system were dominantly hydrogen (about 89 percent) and helium (about 9 percent), with smaller amounts (about 2 percent) of oxygen, carbon, nitrogen, neon, magnesium, silicon, iron, nickel, and sulfur, as well as trace amounts of the remainder of the periodic table. In the solar nebula from which the planets formed, hydrogen was present mainly as H_2 gas, while oxygen, carbon, and nitrogen were present as carbon monoxide (CO) and nitrogen (N_2) at high temperature (e.g., 400–1,500 K), reacting to form water vapor (H_2O), methane (CH_4), and ammonia (NH_3) as the nebula cooled (e.g., <400 K). Subsequently, at temperatures of about 150 K, these condensed to their respective ices, the basic constituents of comets and the Jovian planets (Jupiter, Saturn, Uranus, and Neptune). The Earth and the other terrestrial planets (Mercury, Venus, and Mars), consisting principally of rock (magnesium and silicon oxides) and metal (iron and nickel), were accreted at temperatures too high to accumulate these ices (except by later cometary contributions) and therefore have about a thousand times less hydrogen, carbon, and nitrogen than the solar system average composition.

Volatile depletion. In the solar nebula, a small proportion of the gaseous inventory of light elements were held in hydrous silicate minerals (silicate minerals with bound hydroxyl groups, e.g., clays), carbonates (e.g., $CaCO_3$), and even complex organic polymers. Such minerals are observed in certain classes of meteorites, the carbonaceous chondrites, derived from the asteroid belt between the orbits of Mars and Jupiter. Orbital perturbations of the asteroids and comets by the larger planets (principally Jupiter) resulted in the clearing of the asteroid belt (only about 0.1 percent of the original mass of the asteroid belt remains) with some of these volatile-rich bodies impacting the early terrestrial planets—witness the presence of heavily cratered terrain on Mercury and the Moon. This process is widely believed to have contributed a "late veneer" of volatile-rich material from the cooler regions of the solar system, providing the constituents of the present oceans and atmosphere on Earth. Support for this hypothesis comes from a curious source: the abundances of the platinum group elements, a rare class of noble metals that includes iridium, platinum, and gold. The affinity of these elements for metallic iron has sequestered these elements into the Earth's core, 3,000 kilometers beneath the surface rocks of the Earth's crust and upper mantle. If the mantle were in chemical equilibrium with the core, these metallic elements would reside in the core, and concentrations in the mantle would be orders of magnitude lower than what is observed. Meteorite bombardment by primitive bodies, objects that were too small to melt and form cores of their own (a process commonplace in the larger asteroid as evidenced by iron meteorites), imparts a distinct chemical signature to the Earth's upper mantle in the form of elevated abundances of iridium, platinum, and gold. As much as 1 percent of the Earth's mass may have accreted after the end of core formation, an amount sufficient to supply the observed inventory of volatiles to the planet. (Incidentally, this is also the main source of elements that have played such a crucial role in coinage and technology since ancient times.)

Fast degassing. Once accreted, volatile materials such as water tended to separate from the solid phase to accumulate in an atmosphere and oceans, a process termed *outgassing*. Marine sedimentary rocks have been found in the earliest geological record, 3.8 billion years ago, implying the existence of liquid water on Earth since that time. During the intense bombardment in the period 4.4–3.9 billion years ago, the oceans may have been partially or wholly vaporized as a steam atmosphere. Such an atmosphere has an essentially transient character: formed by very large impacts, it recondenses on time scales of hundreds or thousands of years, short compared to the frequency of vaporizing impacts, a few per hundred million years. Thus, the oceans have been a steady feature of the Earth's surface since the earliest record available. [*See* Earth History.]

Mantle outgassing continues today; volcanic gases include "juvenile" water and other gases that are only now degassing from the mantle and reaching the atmosphere. This raises the possibility that the oceans once were smaller than they are today and are slowly increasing their volume with time as the mantle degasses. Geochemists believe that most of the degassing occurred early in Earth's history, based on the present-day degassing rates and the atmospheric inventories of noble gases such as argon and krypton. Noble gases are handy for this purpose because they are chemically unreactive; once they reach the atmosphere, they accumulate there. If the degassing of the mantle were slow compared to the lifetime of the Earth, then the present-day degassing rate of noble gases multiplied by the age of the Earth would about equal the atmospheric inventory. If, on the other hand, degassing occurred quickly at the beginning of Earth's history and has since tapered off, the present-day degassing rate would be inadequate to account for the atmospheric inventory within the age of the Earth. This second case is the one that is borne out by measurements, implying that volatile elements probably separated quickly from the mantle to form the atmosphere and oceans.

Water partitioning into mantle? Water is more complicated than noble gases in that it is reactive. Igneous rocks, created at ocean spreading centers, react with water beneath the oceans to create hydrated rocks.

These water-bearing rocks are carried to subduction zones and returned to the mantle. Much of the subducted water returns quickly to the surface through arc volcanoes, but the mantle is so large that it could hide a lot of water. Measurements of the water content of anhydrous mantle minerals indicate that an ocean's worth of water or more could easily reside in the mantle today. This raises the possibility that water, unlike the noble gases, might be continuing to accumulate in the oceans. Alternatively, if water is more stable in the cooler mantle of today than it was in the hotter mantle of the early Earth, then we could be slowly losing sea water by subduction into the mantle. Shallow marine sedimentary deposits are found throughout the geologic record, implying that sea level has always been close to the elevation of the continental crust. If we knew that the mean area and elevation of the continents have remained constant through time, then we could say that ocean volume has remained similarly constant. However, continental volume may be evolving; it could be, for example, that continental elevation itself follows sea level, because continents are ground down ("weathered") by exposure to the atmosphere, but do not weather if they are submerged. In summary, we do not really know whether the oceans have maintained their present volume throughout geologic time or continue to grow.

The History of Sea Water Composition. For some elements, the chemistry of the oceans is determined simply by the availability of those elements on Earth. Notable examples are sodium and chloride, which compose common table salt and the main ingredients of sea salt. Occasionally, some sea salt is removed from the oceans in evaporite deposits, which form when some corner of the ocean becomes isolated from the main basin and evaporates. Extensive evaporite deposits are found, for example, under the Mediterranean Sea.

For other elements such as calcium and silicon, the concentration in sea water is determined by the rates at which these elements are supplied to the ocean in river waters and the rate at which they are removed from the oceans. Calcium is much more abundant in river waters than is sodium, but because calcium is removed from sea water by biological precipitation of calcium carbonate ($CaCO_3$), which forms limestone, the concentration of calcium is much lower in sea water than it is in river water. One cannot manufacture sea water by simply concentrating the salts in river water.

We can estimate the chemistry of the past oceans by examining the minerals deposited in evaporite sequences. When water is evaporated from a salt solution, the concentration of the salts remaining behind in the brine increases until eventually the solution becomes unstable with respect to some solid phase. When sea water evaporates, the first solid mineral to form is calcium carbonate, followed in sequence by a calcium sulfate (gypsum-anhydrite) and sodium chloride (halite). If the chemistry of the ocean long ago were significantly different than it is today, say, a factor of ten higher or lower in some of the constituents of sea salt, then the sequence of evaporite minerals would be altered. The observed sequence in evaporite deposits tells us that this has not happened, implying that the major chemistry of the oceans has remained fairly stable for the past 700 million years or so.

The Geometry of the Oceans Today. The oceans comprise 71 percent of the surface of the Earth and have an average depth of 3,800 meters. Although some component of elevated continental crust is submerged by sea water, most of the oceans overlie oceanic crust; 80 percent of the area of the oceans is between 3,000 and 6,000 meters deep. Dividing the inventory of water in the ocean (1,370 million cubic kilometers) by the average rate of evaporation from the oceans (361,000 cubic kilometers per year) gives us a residence time of water in the oceans of about four thousand years. Only a small fraction of evaporated water reaches land and returns to the oceans via river runoff; the average water molecule can expect to make this trip every thirty thousand years. Thirty-one percent of the total river discharge can be accounted for by the twenty largest rivers in the world; the Amazon, the largest, accounts for 11 percent of the global river discharge.

Perhaps more relevant to human concerns about global change due to rising carbon dioxide is the circulation rate of the oceans. Near the sea surface, ocean currents are driven by friction from winds. In contrast, the deep ocean is driven primarily by variations in the density of sea water. Sea water becomes denser when it cools or gets saltier by evaporation. The densest water in today's ocean is cold, coming from the North Atlantic Ocean and the Southern Ocean around Antarctica. In these locations, dense water is created by heat loss to the cold atmosphere and sinks to the deep sea. Throughout the rest of the ocean, mixing with warmer surface waters gradually erodes this pool of cold, deep water. We can trace the circulation time of the deep oceans using a variety of natural and anthropogenic tracers, such as natural and bomb-produced carbon-14, freons, and bomb-produced tritium. The overturning time of the deep sea is roughly one thousand years. This time scale determines the time scale for ocean uptake of fossil fuel carbon dioxide and tells us something about the thermal inertia of the deep sea. [See Ocean Dynamics.]

Above the deep waters of the ocean, at depths of 200–1,000 meters or so, are found the density-stratified waters of the thermocline. Water within the thermocline flows along surfaces of constant seawater density, with a characteristic replenishment time of ten to one hundred years. The waters of the sea surface flow chaotically in eddies that are typically 10–100 kilometers in size, but they also participate in ocean basin-scale circulation cells called *gyres*. Because of the rotation of the Earth, the western boundary currents of the gyres concentrate into intense flows such as the Gulf Stream in the North Atlantic and the Kuroshio in the North Pacific. The circulation time scale of the gyres is on the order of ten years.

The atmospheric imprint enters the deep ocean primarily in the North Atlantic, as salty subtropical surface water delivered by the extension of the Gulf Stream cools and sinks in the Norwegian, Greenland, and Labrador Seas. North Atlantic Deep Water (as it is called) carries oxygen into the deep sea, and presumably fossil fuel carbon dioxide as well. Within a few hundred years, North Atlantic Deep Water reaches the Southern Ocean around Antarctica, where a strong circumpolar current carries it quickly around the globe. This circumpolar water mass outcrops at the sea surface around Antarctica, where it cools further and forms Antarctic Bottom Water. The presence of sea ice prevents much oxygen or fossil fuel carbon dioxide from entering the ocean at the Antarctic outcrop. Antarctic Bottom Water feeds slowly into the deep Pacific and Indian Ocean basins. The oldest (most isolated) waters of the deep ocean are found in the intermediate depths of the Pacific and Indian Oceans, where carbon-14 dating indicates an age of approximately fifteen hundred years since the last significant atmospheric exposure. In addition to low carbon-14 and oxygen concentrations, old subsurface water is marked by high concentrations of dissolved nutrients (fertilizers) such as nitrate and phosphate, which derive from decomposition of sinking organic matter. When deep water finds it way back to the sea surface, such as in the equatorial Pacific and in high latitudes, the exposure of nutrient-rich waters to sunlight stimulates phytoplankton (plant) growth and abundant populations of herbivorous zooplankton and fish.

[*See also* Hydrologic Cycle; Ocean Chemistry; Sea Level; *and the vignette on* Thermohaline Circulation and the Cooling Effects of Warming *in the article on* Climate Change.]

BIBLIOGRAPHY

Broecker, W. S., and T. H. Peng. *Tracers in the Sea.* Palisades, N.Y.: Eldigio Press, 1982.
Holland, H. D. *The Chemistry of the Atmosphere and Oceans.* New York: Wiley, 1978.
———. *The Chemical Evolution of the Atmosphere and Oceans.* Princeton, N.J.: Princeton University Press, 1984.
Righter, K., and R. Canup. *Origin of the Earth and Moon.* Tucson: University of Arizona Press, 2000.

—DAVID ARCHER AND MUNIR HUMAYUN

OGALLALA AQUIFER, DEPLETION AND RESTORATION OF THE

[*This case study focuses on the history of this crucial supply of ground water and on the increasing risk and consequences of its depletion.*]

The Ogallala Aquifer, the dominant geologic formation in a series of formations known as the High Plains Regional Aquifer, is a vast ancient repository of ground water underlying the central third of the United States, from southern South Dakota to the southern high plains of Texas, an area of roughly 450,660 square kilometers (174,000 square miles; see Figure 1). The Ogallala supplies roughly 30 percent of all irrigation water pumped from groundwater sources in the United States, providing the water for about 20 percent of all irrigated farmland (Kromm and White, 1992b). The Ogallala is frequently referred to as the "lifeblood of the plains"; 95 percent of the water pumped from it is used for irrigation. However, it is generally agreed that the practical lifetime of the aquifer is nearing depletion, and fundamental change is approaching for the people of the high plains. [*See* Irrigation.]

Formed approximately 10 million years ago in the late Miocene and early Pliocene, the aquifer formation is made up of ancient alluvial deposits: mixed sequences of clay, sand, silt, and gravel dropped by ancient streams flowing from the eastern face of the then-forming Rocky Mountains. Underlain by impermeable Permian to Cretaceous Age shales, and overlain by a layer of low-porosity lime/clay material known as *caliche*, the aquifer is essentially a contained unit in which only those areas with sufficient saturated thickness can sustain irrigation (Bittinger and Green, 1980; Cronin, 1969). The total usable amount of water stored in the aquifer is estimated at about 4.01 trillion cubic meters (3.25 billion acre feet; Kromm and White, 1992b). The saturated thickness of the aquifer, that stratum of the aquifer from which water is extractable, has great spatial variation. Some areas, such as the central plains region of Nebraska and northwestern Kansas, overlay saturated thicknesses in excess of 113 meters (340 feet), whereas 30 meters or less underlies other areas in the more depleted and depletable southern high plains. Saturated thickness is significant because it provides a measure of the extent of water available for irrigation and other uses. The heaviest withdrawals have occurred in areas of relatively thin saturated thicknesses with relatively shallow depths to water, leading to significant problems of groundwater mining and depletion.

Social History. The southern high plains was one of the last regions in the contiguous United States to be settled. The absence of appreciable surface water out-

A

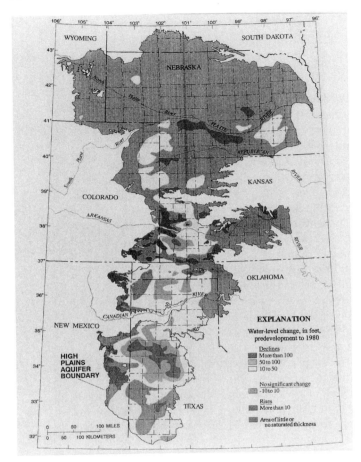

B

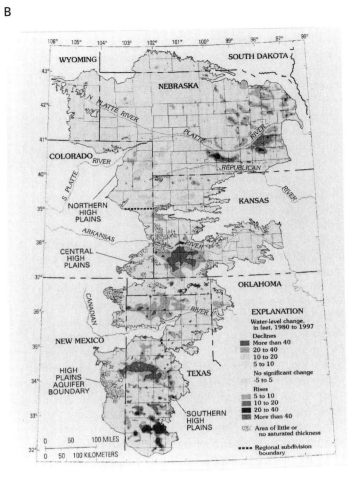

Ogallala Aquifer, Depletion and Restoration of the.
FIGURE 1. (A) Water Level Change to 1980. (B) Water Level Change 1980–1987. (C) Saturated Thickness. (Photos courtesy of the U.S. Geological Survey.)

weighed the benefits of the endlessly level land, with no timber to clear or rocks to haul. The region's eastern boundary is also aligned along the edge of the 550-millimeter (20-inch) isohyet (line of equal precipitation), long recognized as the margin of nonirrigated agriculture. Moreover, the climate of the high plains was and is highly variable, with a marked tendency to drought, interrupted by occasions of normal rainfall and, rarely, greater than usual amounts (Bowden, 1977).

The closing of the frontier, the decline of the cattle culture, and the growing realization of the existence of the vast underground water reserves eventually led to the permanent settlement of the region. By the start of the twentieth century, individual agricultural homesteads were succeeding, and small settlements were growing. The primary forces driving this development were the unusually agreeable climatic conditions (as reconstructed from dendrochronologic data; see Lawson and Stockton, 1981), and the use of windmill-powered pumping rigs tapping the upper fringes of the Ogallala (Webb, 1931). Withdrawals probably did not have significant impacts on water levels during the first decade or so of the twentieth century, but pumping rigs

were soon adapted from automobile engines, and deeper reaches of the formation were tapped in the late 1920s and early 1930s (Green, 1992).

However, market demands and overextended capital investment soon became victims of the generalized economic depression of the early 1930s (Worster, 1979). The farmers of the plains, being commodity based, believed themselves immune to the eastern economic crisis, but it soon became clear that commodities producers would be the hardest hit in the collapse of national and international trading markets (White, 1991). Combined with unrelenting drought settling over the region in the mid-1930s, the high plains region was soon engulfed in the legendary era of erosion, dryness, and displacement known as the "Dust Bowl" (Worster, 1979). [*See* Dust Storms.]

The chief lesson learned from the environmental and

C

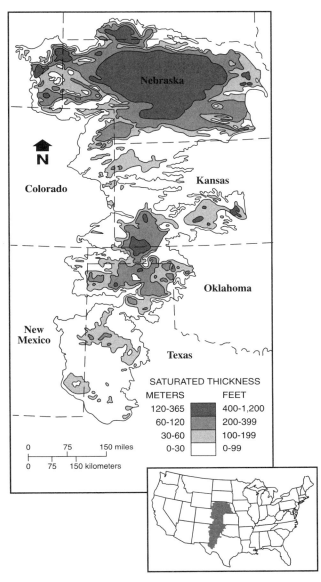

SATURATED THICKNESS

METERS	FEET
120-365	400-1,200
60-120	200-399
30-60	100-199
0-30	0-99

FIGURE 1. Continued

water from ever-greater depths (Green, 1992). Ground water was extracted at accelerating rates throughout the 1950s, in areas with both large and small saturated thickness. The discovery of a seemingly unlimited supply of ground water and equally limitless, and cheap, energy sources fueled an era of unmatched agricultural expansion on the high plains.

The measurement of withdrawal rates is problematic, largely because it was not until 1988 that the United States Geological Survey (USGS) began a comprehensive ground water monitoring program, taking water-level readings at over seven thousand wells located throughout the Ogallala, chiefly in response to dramatic declines in water levels—particularly in Nebraska and Texas. Observations of water level declines from 1940 to 1980 revealed an average area weighted decline of roughly 3 meters, or 10 feet (McGuire and Sharpe, 1997). (For measurement purposes, the USGS uses 1940 as a baseline year, prior to the post–World War II large-scale exploitation of the Ogallala.) From 1980 to 1997, the overall average area-weighted decline was measured at slightly less than 0.8 meters (2.7 feet), with localized changes varying from drops of 2.25 meters (7.4 feet) to rises of 0.9 meters (3.0 feet). However, one must look at the increase in irrigated area to gain a sense of the increase in pumping. By one count, there were some 8,350 irrigation wells in use on the high plains in 1948; less than a decade later, there were five times as many wells—over 42,000 (Bowden, 1977). By yet another measure, more than 2.2 million hectares (5.5 million acres) were being irrigated on the high plains by the mid-1960s. At the peak of extraction, around 1978, 5.3 million hectares (13 million acres) were being irrigated. By the late 1980s, however, irrigated land area had declined by as much as 20 percent, presumably in reaction to increasing costs and increasing depths to water (Kromm and White, 1992b).

Rates of decline had slowed considerably by 1997 compared with the earlier era of massive withdrawals. The energy shocks of the early and late 1970s ultimately led to prohibitively high fuel prices for pumping works (government price controls dampened the impact of the 1973 oil embargo crisis, but, by the end of the 1970s and the advent of the Reagan era of deregulation, energy prices began to rise rapidly in response to market demands; Rees, 1985). The result was a dramatic slowing in pumping rates, which did increase again somewhat in the early 1980s when international grain deals and federal agricultural price support/surplus programs boosted farm production on the high plains (Hansen, 1991). The practical solution to recurrent drought was typically to pump more ground water, when energy costs were once again under control.

The overall stabilization of withdrawal rates, however, has been attributed to several factors: expansion

economic devastation was the imperative of a dependable and generous supply of water (Brooks and Emel, 1995). The outbreak of World War II reinvigorated markets for overproduced grains and fiber from the region, and this, together with a shift away from drought, slowly lifted the high plains out of despair. However, it was the technological and industrial boom precipitated by the end of World War II, together with federal agricultural support programs created in response to the Dust Bowl, that provided the real answer to the vagaries of markets and climate that were becoming ominously familiar.

Sophisticated pumping technology combined with powerful drilling engines soon enabled farmers to tap

of irrigation withdrawals shifted somewhat from areas of rapid decline (the southern high plains) to areas of much slower decline (the northern high plains); conservation and efficiency measures for irrigation equipment have reduced total amounts withdrawn; and land use practices have been refined to limit water loss from the field (Dugan and Sharpe, 1995; McGuire and Sharpe, 1997). Market and other economic considerations have worked to force more intensively irrigated land out of production (McGuire and Sharpe, 1997). Moreover, the extreme spatial variability of access to the water has resulted in localized areas of practical depletion. Some of the most actively mined areas are those that originally had the least depth to water, for example, a region known as the Shallow Water Belt in the southern high plains, and were thus the most vulnerable areas. This is also an area with perhaps the most intensive investment in irrigation and the most to lose from its collapse.

These stabilizing trends were reversed locally by severe drought on the southern high plains, starting in 1992 and ending in 1996. Annual depletion rates increased to over 2.5 times the annual rate of the previous five years in this region of the aquifer, to offset the devastating effects of the drought. (Some parts of the southern high plains received less than half of typical rainfall amounts for three to five consecutive seasons; *The Cross Section*, July 1996.)

Impacts and Responses. The effects of a changing economic climate will probably have far greater impacts on the future life and health of the Ogallala Aquifer than any technological or conservation measures could. Clearly, what water can be withdrawn will be. With the exception of a very few surface streams, the Ogallala Aquifer is virtually unrelated to any surface water systems. Thus, the environmental costs of effectively depleting the aquifer (a monumental task to the extent that it can be done) can only be truly read on the land's surface. Intensively irrigated lands and extensively cultivated drylands have dominated the landscape in the past and continue to do so in the present. With the likely retirement of increasing amounts of farmland in some parts of the aquifer's region, other impacts will inevitably follow. Already in the southern high plains, deserted townscapes mark unused intersections of abandoned farm-to-market roads.

Without federal price support or maintenance programs, farmers will be far more vulnerable to physical impacts of drought or improvident weather shifts, as well as changing demands for grain, cotton, and beef in international markets. The Ogallala has been mined for nearly a century, and, in parts of the aquifer, will be mined for decades to come. The infrastructure necessary to take advantage of the water is slowly dismantling across the southern high plains, was never really present in the northern high plains, and is probably sta-

ble in those areas of the central high plains where depths to water are shallow and saturated thickness substantial. The 184 counties that comprise the Ogallala region have, moreover, a relatively stable population. The widespread crises that have periodically defined life in the region have led to much intraregion migration, but, aside from the massive emigration of the late 1930s, little out-migration has occurred (Kromm and White, 1992a). Home to roughly 2.2 million people in the 1980 census, population actually increased by some 4 percent in the period 1980–1990.

Irrigated acreage on the high plains represents 65 percent of all irrigated land in the United States. Significant percentages of U.S. grain production and finished cattle and 15 percent of U.S. cotton production (the largest concentration of total cotton production in the world—3.5 percent—is on the southern high plains; see *The Cross Section*, 1995) are supported by Ogallala water. At some point, however, the limits of efficiency will be reached and the rising costs of pumping irrigation water from greater depths will outstrip prices for farm products. By some estimates, prices per unit of grain are on a par with prices in the 1950s, whereas costs for producing that same unit have increased a hundredfold (Brooks and Emel, 1995).

Several responses have been generated in the southern high plains as a direct consequence of the depletion risk and to put off the apparently inevitable imbalance of inputs. One recurring response is precipitation enhancement: a four-year program initiated in the spring of 1997 operates under the auspices of the local groundwater management district (High Plains Underground Water Conservation District #1; *The Cross Section*, June 1997). In addition, tapping of deeper fossil water aquifers is widely debated; however, attendant issues of streamflow interference and poor water quality must be addressed (*The Cross Section*, 1996). Numerous artificial recharge programs have been attempted with quite limited success—overall recharge rates hover around the 2.5 centimeter (1 inch) per year rate.

Another response has been the search for more water. In the optimistic 1960s and 1970s, massive water importation plans involving the transport of billions of liters of water across vast distances were devised to support irrigation agriculture on the high plains. The Texas Water Plan involved the building of pipelines to bring water across thousands of kilometers and up significant elevation from the Mississippi River to the high plains. The North American Water and Power Alliance project proposed a network of pipelines and canals to bring water diverted from rivers flowing into the Bering Sea to the western United States, the high plains, and Mexico (Bittinger and Green, 1980). With prohibitive delivered costs for the water and extraordinary expenditures of energy, these plans were eventually shelved.

On a more realistic level, improved conservation practices and innovations in irrigation technology are being developed and disseminated by university research groups and agricultural extension services. Groundwater management districts play a significant role in prolonging the life of the Ogallala. As conservation and improved efficiency of operation grow in importance, the agencies that convey the latest information and techniques to their constituents will be even more crucial to the maintenance of agricultural production.

Conclusion. In his survey of the high plains completed in 1898–1899, Willard D. Johnson described vast underground reserves of fresh water throughout the region (Johnson 1900/1901). He also warned of the balance that must be struck to avoid exhausting the supply: withdrawals must be matched by recharge to maintain the resource. At the time, Johnson's admonitions were ignored, and instead rumors abounded of vast underground rivers flowing endlessly to the sea and of blind trout found in wells. Today, the precise nature of the Ogallala is well understood and its limits fully appreciated.

A century after Johnson's prescient report, as a result of massive effort and expenditures by farmers, irrigators, and governments, this major source of fresh water on the globe is becoming significantly depleted. But what is the real environmental cost of exhausting this water? Streamflows and land surfaces are largely unaffected, and no plant or animal species are directly dependent on the Ogallala as a water source. Does the importance then lie with the decrease in agricultural production? In areas of depletion, it does. For example, on the southern high plains, cropland retirement exemplifies the decline in agricultural production; when irrigators can no longer afford to irrigate, they also cannot afford to convert to dryland farming. Climatically, this region cannot reliably support large-scale dry farming. But one can reasonably argue that in the central high plains the practical depletion of the aquifer is at least many decades off. Can such a distant horizon be the equivalent of an endless supply of water? Or can the outcome of the changing scenario of the southern high plains be considered an object lesson for coping with the inevitability of depletion?

Here the importance of the case study is obvious: lives and livelihoods, and significant contributions to the world's agricultural production and the U.S. economy, are at risk as the depth to water, and hence the costs of getting that water, increase. Groundwater mining issues are of increasing importance globally as many urban and agricultural areas come to recognize the limits of the underground water supply, frequently compounded by water quality problems and more direct environmental repercussions than those experienced on the high plains.

[*See also* Ground Water.]

BIBLIOGRAPHY

Bittinger, M., and E. Green. *You Never Miss the Water Til . . . (The Ogallala Story)*. Littleton, Colo.: Water Resources Publications, 1980.

Bowden, C. *Killing the Hidden Waters: The Slow Destruction of Water Resources in the American Southwest*. Austin: University of Texas Press, 1977.

Brooks, E., and J. Emel. "The *Llano Estacado* of the American Southern High Plains." In *Regions at Risk*, edited by J. X. Kasperson et al. Tokyo: United Nations University Press, 1995, pp. 255–303.

Cronin, J. G. *Groundwater in the Ogallala Formation in the Southern High Plains of Texas and New Mexico*. Hydrologic Investigations Atlas HA-330. Washington, D.C.: United States Geological Survey, 1969.

Daniel, T. "Texas High Plains Enjoys Distinction as a Leading Cotton Producing Region." *The Cross Section* 41.11 (November 1995), 3–4.

"Drought Conditions Prompt Consideration of Water from Deeper Aquifers." *The Cross Section* 42.5 (May 1996), 1–3.

"Drought Relief Information Meetings Scheduled for West Texas Cities." *The Cross Section* 42.7 (July 1996), 1.

Dugan, J., and J. Sharpe. *Water-Level Changes in the High Plains Aquifer, Predevelopment to 1994*. USGS Fact Sheet FS-215–95. Washington, D.C., 1995.

Green, D. "A History of Irrigation Technology." In *Groundwater Exploitation in the High Plains*, edited by D. E. Kromm and S. E. White. Lawrence: University Press of Kansas, 1992, pp. 28–43.

Hansen, J. *Gaining Access: Congress and the Farm Lobby 1919–1981*. Chicago: University of Chicago Press, 1991.

Johnson, W. D. *The High Plains and Their Utilization*. 22d Annual Report of the United States Geological Survey. Washington, D.C.: Government Printing Office, 1900/1901.

Kromm, D. E., and S. E. White. "Groundwater Problems." In *Groundwater Exploitation in the High Plains*, edited by D. E. Kromm and S. E. White. Lawrence: University Press of Kansas, 1992a, pp. 44–63.

———. "The High Plains Ogallala Region." In *Groundwater Exploitation in the High Plains*, edited by D. E. Kromm and S. E. White. Lawrence: University Press of Kansas, 1992b, pp. 1–27.

Lawson, M. P., and C. W. Stockton. "Desert Myth and Climatic Reality." *Annals of the Association of American Geographers* 71 (1981), 527–535.

McGuire, V., and J. Sharpe. *Water-Level Changes in the High Plains Aquifer, 1980 to 1995*. USGS Water-Resources Investigations Report 97–4081. Washington, D.C., 1997.

Moseley, L. "Economic Impacts of Aquifer Depletion Discussed at Water Plan Meeting." *The Cross Section* 44.1 (January 1998), 3–4.

Rees, J. *Natural Resources: Allocation, Economics and Policy*. London: Methuen, 1985.

"Water Precipitation Enhancement Program Now in Operation." *The Cross Section* 43.6 (June 1997), 1.

Webb, W. P. *The Great Plains*. Boston: Ginn and Co., 1931.

White, R. *"It's Your Misfortune and None of My Own": A New History of the American West*. Norman: University of Oklahoma Press, 1991.

Worster, D. *Dust Bowl: The Southern Plains in the 1930s*. New York and Oxford: Oxford University Press, 1979.

—ELIZABETH A. BROOKS

OIL SEEPS. *See* Ocean Life.

OIL SPILLS. *See* Petroleum Hydrocarbons in the Ocean.

ORIGIN OF LIFE

Terrestrial biological processes, encompassing all of life as we know it, have their origin in events that occurred in an epoch 4.5 to 3.8 billion years ago, a period to the end of which can be dated the earliest relics of stromatolite-forming microbial communities found in the fossil record. Scientific theories of the origin of life seek to explain the transition that apparently occurred before this time from widely dispersed, disordered chemical processes to encapsulated, ordered complexes of biochemical processes incorporating genetic inheritance, as are envisaged to have constituted the earliest "living" cell-like structures. Various scientific and non-scientific explanations of the existence of organisms are based not only on different definitions of what constitutes life, but also on different philosophical notions of causation. Within the Western intellectual tradition from which modern science largely arose, the attempts of the atomists to give a mechanistic, materialistic account of animal life arising from heat, by undergoing some sort of fermentation, were repudiated by Socrates in favor of a theory of causation that gave primacy to intelligent agency. Deistic interpretations of this point of view have found recent expression in the doctrine of creationism, which has influenced sectors of dominantly Christian cultures in the twentieth century. Diverse tribal societies with ancient traditions prefer naturalistic, sometimes theistic, accounts of life's origin based on the agency of some cosmic generative principle, of which the precept *whakapapa* ("genealogy" or "layering") espoused by the New Zealand Maori is perhaps the most comprehensive in its scope of application.

Scientific speculation concerning the origin of life has been strongly influenced by developments in the fundamental theories of physics and chemistry and their interpretation. Newton's establishment of universal laws, apparently capable of describing the physical mechanism of all observable natural change, effected the banishment of Aristotle's idea of teleology, or intrinsic purpose, from the Western conception of nature, and paved the way for the elaboration of Charles Darwin's theory of evolution. Microscopic cells were identified as integral living structures, and Louis Pasteur's experiments refuted the continual spontaneous generation of the simplest forms of life. Pasteur also showed, by studying fermentation, that life could exist in the absence of oxygen. Investigations into the chemical com-position and transformations of simple materials, and the demonstration that physiological and other biological processes involved many of the same substances and effects as nonbiological processes, demanded that any explanation of the phenomena of life be consistent with what was known about the mechanisms and energetics of change in the inorganic world. Notwithstanding Friedrich Wöhler's synthesis in 1828 of the organic compound urea from inorganic ammonia and cyanic acid, various forms of nineteenth-century vitalism signified different points at which scientists from diverse disciplines marked the limits of their ability to account for what happened in organisms in terms of known physicochemical processes and ascribed causation to a nonmaterial *élan vital*. In the twentieth century, rapid advances in biochemistry and methods of molecular structural analysis, culminating in the Watson–Crick double-helical model of the structure of deoxyribonucleic acid (DNA), the genetic material, pushed vitalism beyond the range of scientific respectability and paved the way for the modern era of molecular biology and the philosophy of reductionism, which ascribes all causation in biology ultimately to microscopic physical phenomena. It thus became necessary to explain how the molecular components of cells could be spontaneously synthesized and assembled into stable structures capable of autonomous reproduction. Theorizing about the origin of life then became focused on the chemistry of the early terrestrial environment.

Modern theories of chemical evolution were anticipated by Darwin when he conceived "in some warm little pond with all sorts of ammonia and phosphoric salts—light, heat, electricity &c. present, that a protein compound was chemically formed, ready to undergo still more complex changes" (letter dated 1 February 1871). However, the first detailed speculations on the spontaneous emergence of living matter, the "protoplasm" observed inside cells, under conditions that might have existed on the early Earth, were not made for another sixty years. In the 1920s, both I. A. Oparin and J. B. S. Haldane (see Bernal, 1967) sought, in terms of already known chemical phenomena, to account for the appearance of what they took to be the most basic cellular processes. An important aspect of this approach was the acceptance that vital processes and materials are in principle no different from those known in the inorganic world, except perhaps in terms of their level of complexity, implying the existence of forms intermediate between simple molecules and fully functioning cells. The role of enzymes as catalysts of elementary reactions was clearly recognized, raising the question of whether the characteristic chemical components of living systems could have been synthesized from their simpler elements in the early terrestrial environment without the help of catalysts. E. C. C. Baly had already shown that, in the absence of oxygen, sugars could be formed from water, carbon dioxide, and ammonia by using ultraviolet light and, in 1953, by using an electric spark, Stanley Miller achieved the synthesis of some amino acids, building blocks of more complex proteins, from vapors of water, ammonia, methane, and hydrogen, said to represent the primitive terrestrial atmosphere. Whereas the molecules produced in the experiments of Baly and Miller are racemic mixtures of the D- and L-sugars or amino acids, biological systems contain only one of these mirror-image forms and rely on the presence of the chosen form for maintenance of biochemical functions. An excess of L-amino acids, the biological form, has been found in the meteorite that fell near Murchison, Australia, in 1969. It is generally agreed that the selection that resulted in only one of the optical forms of sugars and amino acids occurring in organisms was a symmetry-breaking process that took place early in the development of the complex chemistry of terrestrial life. Although the cause of this selection remains obscure, the observed emanation from some stellar environments of circularly polarized light has been suggested as providing a mechanism for the partial destruction of one optical form of sugars and amino acids in interstellar space and tilting the balance in favor of the other form.

Uncertainties concerning the composition of the early Earth's atmosphere, the extent of volcanic gassing, the magnitude of the inbound flux of interstellar matter, and the duration of bombardment by objects large enough to cause vaporization of the oceans have confounded attempts to define the source and modes of transformation of carbonaceous compounds likely to have been involved in prebiotic chemistry. A large variety of simple organic compounds have been detected in interstellar space. Interplanetary dust contains organic matter that can undergo a wide variety of transformations as the dust aggregates, eventually to form comets. Comets themselves contain ices of water, ammonia, and methane. Comets and smaller bodies may have served as the primary source of organic matter and water on the early Earth, rather than, or in addition to, formation from atmospheric components. Carbonaceous chondrites, such as the Murchison meteorite, contain a suite of organic compounds ranging from amino acids and carboxylic acids through aromatic hydrocarbons to complex polymers. However, in spite of all the uncertainties, there is general scientific agreement that the early terrestrial environment supported a rich organic chemistry from which life could have evolved. It has been suggested that the first replicating entities were inorganic minerals, and that life originated in the chemistry of hydrated silicates (clays) such as form the structural matrix of much interplanetary dust, but in any case it is necessary to postulate an abundance of or-

ganic compounds to account for the eventual transition to living cells. There is some evidence, as well as speculation, that specific structures in montmorillonite clays, which absorb aliphatic as well as amino acids, are able to replicate when swelled by water. [See Atmosphere Structure and Evolution.]

Since about 1970, much theoretical research into the origin of life has focused on describing the most elementary of possible systems of molecular replicators. Elucidation of the mode of replication of genetic material and the role this process plays in biological inheritance was an obvious stimulus for this research and corresponding experimental studies. Many systems consisting of small nucleic acids or similar compounds capable of catalyzing their own synthesis out of simpler constituents have been devised and studied and, in 1996, a similar system consisting of small protein molecules (peptides) was created. These systems are considered to shed light on the origin of life, not so much on account of the fact that the molecules of the types involved are found in biological systems or are similar to such molecules, but because they demonstrate the existence of inherently propagative chemical processes. Even if the oceans of early Earth were full of organic compounds reacting with one another, the emergence of living systems demands the existence of molecular components that somehow give rise to their own synthesis, either by direct replication or through more general processes of regeneration or autocatalysis. One school of thought, championed by Harold J. Morowitz (1992), holds that the most elementary metabolic reaction pathways and cycles, now catalyzed in cells by enzymes, began in a sustained and connected manner on the early Earth without the aid of protein or other catalysts and led to the selective accumulation of the very organic molecules that are now fundamental to all biochemical processes and are the modular constituents from which more complex macromolecular species, such as proteins, nucleic acids, and complex lipids, are made up.

Whatever chemical reactions can be hypothesized to have occurred or become sustained in an oceanic primordial soup, the evolution of living cells requires that biochemical functionality become integrated and compartmentalized. This aspect of the problem of life's origin was central to Oparin's analysis of coacervates consisting of microscopic "droplets" of organic matter in an aqueous environment. The concentration and accelerated synthesis of selected organic molecules could be demonstrated in coacervates. Similar phenomena were demonstrated by Sidney Fox (1988) in microspheres that self-assemble from proteinoid material synthesized from more simple components in laboratory conditions resembling terrestrial hydrothermal environments. Some of the components of biological membranes can be formed by photochemical oxidation from compounds like those found in carbonaceous meteorites. It is now known that microscopic vesicles or micelles can reproduce by catalyzing the formation of the lipid molecules of which their membranes are made up. Vesicles of this sort are demonstrably reproducing entities, and the formation of their molecular components is autocatalytic. The membrane components are usually synthesized inside the vesicle from substrates that diffuse in from the external environment, although in particular cases the chemical synthesis occurs within the vesicle membrane. In more complicated systems, resembling biological cellular membranes more closely, enzymes that catalyze the formation of membrane components are incorporated into the membranes themselves.

Some chemical reactions that are central to cellular metabolism, including the concatenation of amino acids needed to make proteins, have been demonstrated to occur at appreciable uncatalyzed rates at the high temperatures and pressures and in the presence of minerals that occur in the region of deep-ocean volcanic vents (smokers), where hyperthermophilic bacteria are still to be found, suggesting that life could have originated in an extreme hydrothermal environment. Bacterial phylogeny corroborates this hypothesis. The shortest and deepest branches closest to the common root of the reconstructed bacterial phylogenetic tree, based on analysis of ribosomal ribonucleic acid (RNA) from present-day organisms, are all occupied by hyperthermophiles—bacteria that live at high temperatures, up to 113°C. The alternative possibility, that the ability to live at high temperatures is an adaptation that occurred after the appearance of the first cells in a cooler environment, is more consistent with other reconstructed phylogenetic tress as well as with what is known about the instability of vital organic compounds such as ribose and cytosine, but especially RNA, at high temperatures. Microorganisms have adapted to life in extreme environments of temperature and pressure, utilizing virtually every available energy source, deep in the Earth's crust, in fractured igneous rocks like granite and basalt, as well as in sedimentary rocks. Thermophilic bacteria have been found living as deep as 3.5 kilometers in a South African gold mine. The existence of these organisms could indicate that life first originated before the last evaporation of the oceans, survived in the Earth's crust, and reemerged later as the dominant cause of global change on the planet's surface. Microzones of water in perennial antarctic lake ice have also been found to be a habitat for complex microbial communities.

The discovery of microorganisms living in extreme environments has forced a reexamination of the range of locations within the solar system, and farther afield in the cosmos, where life could have evolved, at least to the stage of microorganisms, and survived in some form or another. The planet Mars has long been in contention as the most likely alternative environment close to Earth that may have been able to support life at some stage in cosmic history. Moons of Jupiter, Europa in particular, have likewise been mooted as having had environments suitable for the origin of life. Ice is the dominant form of water on the surface of both Mars and Europa. A meteorite found in Antarctica in 1984, and believed to have fallen there 13,000 years ago, has been identified as coming from deep within the Martian subsurface and is presumed to have been ejected into space by an impact event 15 million years ago. The age of the rock itself is estimated at 4.5 billion years, but there is evidence that water penetrated fractures in it between 4.0 and 3.6 billion years ago, when it is widely believed that the surface of Mars was much warmer and wetter than it is now. The fractures have been found to contain organic matter (endogenous polycyclic aromatic hydrocarbons), minerals (carbonate globules, magnetite, and pyrrhotite) and structures (ovoid and tubular deposits) reminiscent of fossilized remnants of the tiniest microorganisms, nanobacteria, found in ancient Earth limestone, leading to the suggestion that life existed on Mars during the epoch in which it appeared on Earth.

Claims that life on Earth had a remote origin are demanding serious scientific scrutiny. A modern version of Michael Faraday's *panspermia* hypothesis, that the seeds of life pervade the cosmos, has been espoused by Fred Hoyle and Chandra Wickramasinghe (1978). These scientists trace the essential biochemical requirements of life to the dense interstellar clouds of gas called "molecular clouds" and describe the arrival of this material on Earth in cometlike bodies as an "infection." Such ideas are consistent with the supposition that life exists at many cosmic locations. Francis Crick (1981) has revived the notion that life evolved elsewhere in the cosmos to the level of advanced civilizations billions of years ago, that intelligent organisms identified the Earth's surface as a suitable environment for supporting life and deliberately infected it with microorganisms. The panspermia hypothesis leaves unanswered any questions of scientific principle concerning life's origin; it simply relocates the problem.

Although Darwin's theory of evolution and the principle of natural selection still underpin all scientific thinking about the biology of global change and its history, Darwin's theory elucidates the origin of neither the organisms on which natural selection acts nor the processes of genetic inheritance, now understood in terms of the replication of nucleic acids. However, in the 1970s, Darwin's conception of the survival of the fittest was applied with great effect to the problem of molecular replication and the accumulation of genetic information in prebiotic systems. The Eigen–Schuster genetic stability criterion specifies the selective fitness that a molecular replicator must have in order to maintain a given quantity of genetic information when mutations occur at a constant rate. This theory established the concept of the "quasispecies," a coexisting population of closely related molecular mutants, as the entity whose evolution must be accounted for, and it has been instrumental in elucidating the evolution of viruses such as human immunodeficiency virus (HIV), whose rate of mutation is such that significant divergence between strains can be observed on a time scale of decades or even years. It was also hypothesized that the first self-organized molecular systems were made up of genetic replicators (presumably nucleic acid molecules) and enzymes (presumably protein molecules) arranged in a closed loop of mutually promoting chemical reactions, in which an enzyme synthesized by using genetic information in one replicator catalyzed the replication of the next gene in a "hypercyclic" pattern. By focusing attention on the relationship between the definition of life and ideas about the structural organization of dynamic chemical systems, the theory of the hypercycle helped to frame analysis of the origin of life within a new context, but it did not explain the origin of genetic coding, that is, how processes for utilizing genetic information to construct the phenotype of catalysts in the system apparently coevolved with the genetic replicators.

In 1983, Thomas R. Cech and Sidney Altman independently discovered that, as well as serving as genetic replicators, some RNA molecules called ribozymes could act as chemical catalysts, even able to transform themselves or others like them. This coincidence of information-carrying capacity and autologous catalytic functional capability within a single class of molecules gave rise to a new postulate, that of the "RNA World." This was a hypothetical epoch in which self-sustaining catalytic networks of RNA molecules were established in the primordial soup and, through processes of metabolism, replication, mutation, and natural selection, gave rise to ever-increasing levels of replicative accuracy, information-carrying capacity, and functional complexity, perhaps within competing protocell compartments. The main attraction of the hypothetical RNA World is that it appears to solve a difficult theoretical problem by obviating the need for proteins and the establishment of genetic coding prior to the evolutionary development of specific catalytic functions. Corroboration for the hypothesis is provided solely by the existence of ribozymes, strengthened by the discovery of particular RNA fragments derived from ribosomes and involved centrally in the complex mechanisms of catalysis needed for cellular protein synthesis.

The theory of the quasispecies has been elaborated further to describe, at least in the case of RNA sequences, how changes in molecular structure, prototypical phenotypic features, correlate with changes in nucleotide sequence, representing genetic information. The theory leads to the expectation that the biological evolution of both genotypes and phenotypes is likely to be characterized as a process of "punctuated equilibrium," variable-length periods of relative stasis or "neutral drift" punctuated by bursts of rapid change. Such a mode of evolutionary change, for which there is considerable evidence in phylogeny from both the fossil record and contemporary genetic relationships, is typical of systems whose dynamic behavior is poised in a "critical" state between regimes of order and disorder. Per Bak (1997) postulates that being in such a state is a generic feature of biological systems at all scales, ranging from the dynamics of biochemical processes to the evolutionary history of the biosphere, and that "self-organized criticality" is a unifying principle that explains the emergence of complex entities and behavior, such as organisms, in systems consisting of large numbers of much simpler components, such as organic molecules or biological macromolecules.

There is disagreement among scientists about whether it is meaningful to talk of general biological principles that might have the same sort of status as physical principles such as those of quantum mechanics, relativity, or thermodynamics. If such natural principles exist for biology, then knowledge of them would certainly enlighten inquiry into the origin of life. Much effort has therefore been invested by theoreticians in attempting to enunciate principles of biological self-organization. While Manfred Eigen (1992) is satisfied that Darwin's principle of natural selection is adequate to explain the progressive increase in the complexity of biological systems from the advent of the hypothetical first molecular replicator to the appearance of mammals like humans, Stuart A. Kauffman (1993) believes that genetic reproduction, variation, and selection are but one aspect of more general phenomena of self-organization that manifest themselves at the molecular level in the origin of life. Kauffman emphasizes the role of interrelated functionalities in maintaining the integrity of molecular biological systems and suggests that the integration of distinct catalytic processes into closed networks preceded the evolution of any means for molecular replication such as is needed by systems such as terrestrial organisms that store information in nucleic acid genes. It is irrelevant whether the original catalysts were protein enzymes capable of synthesizing further proteins or RNA ribozymes capable of synthesizing further RNA molecules; closure of the catalytic network is what counts for the origin of a living system. According to this view, life should be expected to originate whenever a certain threshold of molecular and catalytic diversity is reached in a chemically active system, and the phenomena of life can probably be found all over the cosmos in one form or another.

Whether or not the views of Eigen or Kauffman concerning the fundamental principles of biological organization are essentially correct, the origin of genetic coding is thought by some scientists to represent the crux of the problem that the origin of life poses, and it is a field for almost unlimited speculation. Based on the premise that life cannot be said to exist until there is a primitive organism capable of reproducing itself through replication of its genetic material by means of processes that are maintained under at least some degree of molecular genetic control, the existence of genetic coding poses a variation of the problem usually expressed as the dilemma "What came first, the chicken or the egg?" In the case of molecular biology and genetic coding, the problem concerns the simultaneous need for not only functional catalysts of adequate specificity to maintain the system's genetic information through cycles of error-prone replication, but also a quantity of the genetic information sufficient to maintain the encoding of catalysts with the degree of specificity required for their proper functioning. These simultaneous requirements constrain the pattern of relationships between the structures and functional properties of molecules participating in coding processes. Although cellular proteins and nucleic acids fulfill the specified constraints and make genetic coding possible, it is not known whether there are other chemical species with capacity for similar cooperative functional versatility. Consequently, it is not known whether genetic information storage, replication, and translation, which underpin terrestrial molecular biology and evolution, could have different realizations elsewhere in the cosmos or if life uniquely requires molecules closely akin to nucleic acids and proteins.

Through a number of early evolutionary transitions, entities capable of independent replication appear to have become dependent parts of a larger replicating whole, the origin of genetic coding and translation being a central example of this phenomenon. It is not known whether nucleic acids or proteins were the first replicating entities, or whether vesicle formation and reproduction preceded or followed the origin of coding or even polymer replication. However, definite answers to these questions will not of themselves explain the origin of the cooperative maintenance of different specific sequences and classes of polymers, especially nucleic acids and proteins, involved in cellular processes. Competition for metabolic resources could be expected to result in predominance of the most rapidly autonomously replicating entity, not a cooperative network of

mutually sustaining species and processes. Much current theoretical research into the origin of life seeks to address this central problem. It is largely irrelevant where the boundary marking the beginning of "life" is placed. In some discussions, computer programs are given the capacity to create life, albeit an "artificial life" consisting of replicating and mutating populations of interacting symbolic strings. By means of simulation, it is hoped to elucidate the mechanisms and circumstances that give rise to complex modes of replication and coexistence between diverse elementary entities, be they molecules or digitally encoded representations of them.

The origin of life remains a matter of scientific dispute, particularly between parties with differing views of how "life" should be defined. The question even raises the philosophical problem of what constitutes an explanation in science. Some who reject the prevailing materialistic reductionism of molecular biology and evolutionary theory maintain that no mechanistic description of the biological processes can ever be adequate, but that yet-to-be-elucidated holistic concepts of the constitution of organisms and yet-to-be-developed ideas of causation and intentional agency will eventually lead to more satisfactory theories of life and its origin on Earth. Evidence of this trend of thought can be found in the revival of the notion of the Earth as a superorganism, sustaining inherent life. [See Gaia Hypothesis.] Many adherents to the Gaia hypothesis, which postulates that the phenomenon of life as a whole has regulated terrestrial planetary conditions to maximize its chances of development and survival, emphasize the symbiotic relationships that exist between entities at all levels in biological systems and look for essential features of life that cannot be located in the identity of individual organisms such as can be described as the product and target of natural selection. No final resolution of the controversy over the origin of life is in sight.

[See also Biogeochemical Cycles; Biological Diversity; Earth History; and Evolution of Life.]

BIBLIOGRAPHY

RECENT WORKS

Bak, P. How Nature Works. New York and Oxford: Oxford University Press, 1997. An overview of how the idea of self-organized criticality illuminates our understanding of diverse phenomena.

Crick, F. Life Itself: Its Origin and Nature. New York: Simon and Schuster, 1981. A relatively modern exposition of panspermia by a prominent molecular biologist.

Eigen, M., with R. Winkler-Oswatitsch. Steps Towards Life. Translated from the German by Paul Woolley. New York and Oxford: Oxford University Press, 1992. An introduction to theories and methods of analysis of the replication of genetic information.

Fleischaker, G. R., et al., eds. Production of Supramolecular Structures: From Synthetic Structures to Models of Minimal Living Systems. London: Kluwer, 1994. Proceedings of a 1993 scientific meeting. Articles express a wide spectrum of contemporary technical opinion about complex processes of chemical reproduction.

Fox, S. *The Emergence of Life.* New York: Basic Books, 1988. A scientific outsider defends his unpopular view of the primacy of proteins over nucleic acids.

Greenberg J. M., et al., eds. *The Chemistry of Life's Origins.* London: Kluwer, 1993. Proceedings of a 1991 scientific meeting. Contains technical articles covering contemporary knowledge and views of chemical evolution.

Kauffman, S. A. *The Origins of Order: Self-Organization and Selection in Evolution.* New York and Oxford: Oxford University Press, 1993. A comprehensive technical account of biological phenomena in terms of complexity theory.

———. *At Home in the Universe: The Search for Laws of Self-Organization and Complexity.* New York and Oxford: Oxford University Press, 1995. Gives a popular interpretation of the ideas contained in *The Origins of Order.*

Maynard Smith, J., and E. Szathmáry. *The Major Transitions in Evolution.* Oxford: Freeman, 1995. Chapters discuss the main stages of evolution, including molecular replication and the origin of the genetic code, from the perspective of contemporary biological theory.

Morowitz, H. J. *Beginnings of Cellular Life: Metabolism Recapitulates Biogenesis.* New Haven, Conn.: Yale University Press, 1992. A simple, clear discussion of how elementary chemical processes might have combined progressively to give rise to complex networks inside cells.

Orgel, L. E. "The Origin of Life on the Earth." *Scientific American* 271 (October 1994), 52–61. A nontechnical account, with special emphasis on the idea of the "RNA World." There are related articles in the same issue of the journal.

Space Studies Board, United States National Research Council. *The Search for Life's Origins: Progress and Future Directions in Planetary Biology and Chemical Evolution.* Washington, D.C.: National Academy Press, 1990. Space scientists' perspectives on life in the cosmos and the relevance of space exploration to our understanding of biological origins.

OLDER SOURCES

Bernal, J. D. *The Origin of Life.* London: Weidenfeld and Nicolson, 1967. An excellent source on the history and foundation of modern theories about life's origins. Includes reprints of the original works of I. A. Oparin and J. B. S. Haldane.

Calvin, M. *Chemical Evolution.* New York and Oxford: Oxford University Press, 1969. A comprehensive account of the natural occurrence, production, and behavior of the molecular constituents of biological systems.

Fox, S. W., ed. *The Origins of Prebiological Systems and of Their Molecular Matrices.* New York: Academic Press, 1965. Proceedings, including lively discussions among prominent scientists, from a 1963 conference at which the major scientific and philosophical questions concerning the chemical origins of life and biological phenomena were addressed.

Hoyle, F., and C. Wickramasinghe. *Lifecloud.* London: Dent, 1978. An analysis and defense of the hypothesis that life originates in space, probably on comets.

Miller, S., and L. E. Orgel. *The Origins of Life on the Earth.* Upper Saddle River, N.J.: Prentice-Hall, 1974. A detailed compendium of the processes, particularly chemical processes, needed for the terrestrial origin of life.

—PETER R. WILLS

OVERFISHING. *See* Fishing; *and* Food.

OVERGRAZING. *See* Agriculture and Agricultural Land; *and* Desertification.

OXYGEN CYCLE

Molecular oxygen (O_2) is the second most abundant gas in the Earth's atmosphere, in sharp contrast to its near absence from the atmospheres of other planets in the solar system. The principal source of O_2 on Earth is oxygenic photosynthesis. In this process, organisms use light energy to synthesize organic compounds from water (H_2O), carbon dioxide (CO_2), and inorganic nutrients. The electrons needed to reduce the carbon atoms in CO_2 are obtained by splitting H_2O molecules, thereby releasing free O_2 as a byproduct. Oxygenic photosynthetic organisms include green plants, algae, and cyanobacteria. These organisms are the main producers of biomass on today's Earth. Hence, their activity couples the global biogeochemical cycle of O_2 to those of organic carbon and nutrients.

Light can also be used to produce organic matter via anoxygenic photosynthesis, a process carried out by anaerobic microorganisms, for example, green and purple sulfur bacteria, that live in environments lacking free O_2. These organisms use reduced inorganic compounds, such as hydrogen sulfide, thiosulfate, and molecular hydrogen (H_2), as electron donors (reductants) for organic synthesis, but the oxidation of these compounds does not produce O_2. At the present time, anoxygenic photosynthesis is a minor contributor to global primary production. Under the anaerobic conditions prevailing on the early Earth, however, anoxygenic photosynthesis was probably an important process converting sunlight into biomass.

Oxygenic photosynthesis took over as the major photosynthetic pathway somewhere between 3.8 and 2.2 billion years ago. This led to a more efficient use of the available solar energy, as well as to the buildup of free O_2 in the atmosphere–hydrosphere system. Photosynthetically produced O_2 did not accumulate immediately, however, because the presence of many reduced chemical species, such as ferrous iron and hydrogen sulfide, rapidly removed any free O_2. This situation remained until the production of O_2 began to outpace the resupply of reduced chemicals by volcanic degassing and hydrothermal activity. The appearance of a fully oxygenated atmosphere may have occurred relatively late in Earth's history, around 2 billion years ago, although this is still a matter of debate. Whatever the exact timing, the accumulation of free oxygen at the Earth's surface fundamentally changed the course of biological evolution and the functioning of biogeochemical cycles. [*See* Atmosphere Structure and Evolution; *and* Evolution of Life.]

As O_2 became available, aerobic respiration emerged as the favored pathway for the mineralization of organic matter. Compared with other potential electron acceptors (oxidants), O_2 yields more energy per unit of organic carbon oxidized, thereby conferring a competitive advantage to aerobic organisms. As a result, in today's global environment, more than 90 percent of all organic matter is decomposed via aerobic respiration.

The oxygenation of the atmosphere also resulted in the formation of ozone (O_3), which absorbs harmful solar ultraviolet radiation. [*See* Ozone.] Shielded by atmospheric ozone, and taking advantage of efficient aerobic biochemical pathways, more sophisticated life forms were able to evolve. Symbiotic associations between the early primitive cells (prokaryotes) led to the appearance of eukaryotic cells (cells containing a nucleus and specialized organelles), which assembled into larger units and, through differentiation, gave rise to multicellular organisms.

The radiation of eukaryotes points to a sustained presence of free O_2 in the Earth's atmosphere over the past 1.8 billion years. More stringent constraints on the level of atmospheric O_2 can be deduced for the final 500 million years, the time span during which animals and higher plants evolved and spread quickly on land. To maintain viable conditions for these organisms, the concentration (or partial pressure) of atmospheric O_2 must have stayed within fairly narrow bounds, probably between 0.1 and 0.4 atmospheres (the present level is 0.21 atmospheres). As discussed below, such a stable O_2 level implies the existence of one or more feedback mechanisms that help balance the production and consumption of O_2 in the global biogeochemical system.

When new biomass is produced from inorganic constituents (primary production) during photosynthesis, O_2 molecules are released as a result of the transfer of electrons from H_2O to CO_2. Most of the organic matter synthesized during primary production is rapidly decomposed (oxidized) by aerobic respiration, thereby consuming almost all of the photosynthetically produced O_2. A very small fraction of the organic matter fixed during primary production is preserved, however, through burial of residual organic carbon and its reduced mineral equivalent, pyrite (FeS_2), in ocean sediments. Pyrite forms as the result of reaction between ferric iron (Fe^{3+})–containing minerals and hydrogen sulfide (H_2S) produced during the anaerobic decomposition of organic matter by bacteria that use sulfate as an electron acceptor. Because burial of organic matter and pyrite removes photosynthetically fixed electrons from the atmosphere–hydrosphere system, it leaves behind a small excess of O_2 molecules. In any given year, this ex-

cess in O_2 production has little effect on the total mass of free oxygen present at the Earth's surface but, over geologic time scales (greater than ten thousand years), the sedimentary burial of organic matter and pyrite acts as the main net source of O_2 to the atmosphere–hydrosphere system (Figure 1).

The organic matter and pyrite stored in marine sediments are recycled through the global sedimentary cycle, driven by tectonic processes. After undergoing variable degrees of chemical and physical transformation in the Earth's interior, the constituents of ocean sediments are ultimately returned to the Earth's surface. The buried organic matter and pyrite, or the products of their transformation at depth, are then exposed to chemical weathering, and the electrons they carry are transferred back to O_2 molecules. The consumption of O_2 that results from the oxidative weathering of recycled sedimentary rocks represents the main net sink in the global biogeochemical cycle of O_2 (Figure 1).

To keep the level of O_2 at the Earth's surface within a fairly narrow range, as inferred for the past 500 million years, the long-term rates of production and consumption of O_2 must track each other closely. This is not a trivial task because of the relatively short residence time of O_2 in the atmosphere–hydrosphere system, on the order of several millions of years. (The residence time is estimated by dividing the total mass of free O_2 by the rate at which it is being consumed via oxidative weathering, or the rate at which it is produced by sedimentary burial of organic matter and pyrite.) Therefore, if an imbalance between production and consumption were maintained for a time span exceeding a few million years, it would significantly alter the abundance of free O_2 on Earth. The likelihood of this happening is illustrated by the following thought experiment.

Suppose primary production in the oceans were to increase, causing greater amounts of organic matter and pyrite to be buried in ocean sediments. The corresponding faster production of O_2 would create an imbalance between the production and consumption of O_2. The rate of removal of O_2 by oxidative weathering would ultimately realign itself with the higher O_2 production rate. However, it would do so only after a long lag time, because it takes on average 400 million years before the organic matter and pyrite buried in marine sediments are exposed again on land. The imbalance between the source and sink of O_2 would persist for a period longer than the residence time of O_2 in the atmosphere–hydrosphere system. The same would be true if a change in the intensity of oxidative weathering on land were to disturb the balance between production and consumption of O_2.

The available geologic records show that biological productivity in the oceans and weathering on land have varied significantly during Earth's history. It is therefore

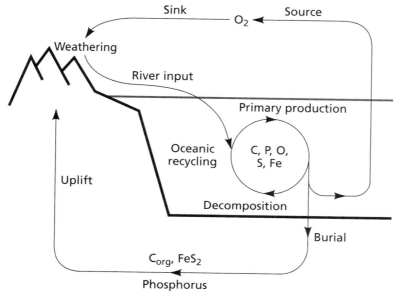

Oxygen Cycle. FIGURE 1. Schematic Representation of Major Processes and Chemical Actors Involved in Regulating the Level of O_2 at the Earth's Surface, on Geologic Time Scales.

The O_2-dependent oceanic recycling of nutrient phosphorus links the biologically driven source of O_2 (primary production) to its tectonically driven sink (weathering). See text for detailed discussion.

difficult to explain the relative stability of atmospheric O_2 in the Earth's surface environment without some mechanism that allows the O_2 cycle to quickly counteract any imbalance between production and consumption. A possible mechanism derives from the coupling of the biogeochemical cycles of O_2 and phosphorus.

Because it is required in the synthesis of key cellular constituents, such as nucleic acids and phospholipids, phosphorus is an essential nutrient for the biosphere. On geologic time scales, the availability of phosphorus controls the rate at which photosynthetic organisms in ocean surface waters are able to produce new biomass. Marine productivity is therefore a function of the rate at which bioavailable phosphorus is delivered by rivers, as well as the efficiency with which it is recycled within the oceans (Figure 1). A more efficient oceanic recycling of phosphorus accelerates the supply of phosphorus to the sea surface and, therefore, enhances primary production.

When the oceans are fully oxygenated, aerobic bacteria and ferric oxyhydroxide minerals are abundant at the sea floor. The former actively bioaccumulate phosphorus in their tissues, while the latter have a high capacity to bind dissolved phosphate chemically. Under these conditions, bioavailable phosphorus is removed from the water column and buried in sediments. When anaerobic waters fill the bottom of the oceans, phosphorus is not as easily removed from the water column, because aerobic bacteria and ferric oxyhydroxides are absent from the underlying sediments. Hence an inverse relationship exists between the availability of phospho-

rus in the oceans and water column oxygenation. This relationship produces a negative feedback that stabilizes the level of O_2 on Earth.

The feedback alters the rate of O_2 production in response to changes in the oxygen content of the atmosphere–hydrosphere system. Consider, for instance, a situation where consumption of O_2 exceeds its production. The O_2 level begins to drop. All other things being equal, this decreases the oxygenation of ocean waters, rendering sediments less efficient at removing bioavailable phosphorus from the water column. The greater availability of phosphorus in the oceans stimulates biological productivity and, therefore, increases the burial of organic matter and pyrite. The resulting enhancement of the rate of O_2 production then counters the initial decrease in O_2 level. The feedback also works in the opposite direction, should the O_2 level suddenly begin to rise. Mass balance calculations show that the feedback system is highly effective because of the fast responses of ocean oxygenation, phosphorus recycling, and sedimentary burial to variations in the O_2 level of the atmosphere–hydrosphere system.

The phosphorus-mediated link between marine biological productivity and the abundance of O_2 at the Earth's surface couples the cycles of oxygen, phosphorus, carbon, iron, and sulfur (Figure 1). Such coupling is widespread among biogeochemical cycles and is often characterized by the existence of negative feedback loops. The latter play an essential role in regulating and stabilizing the chemical state and climate of the Earth's global environment.

[*See also* Biogeochemical Cycles; Biosphere; Carbon Cycle; Earth History; *and* Phosphorus Cycle.]

BIBLIOGRAPHY

Berner, R. A., and D. E. Canfield. "A New Model for Atmospheric Oxygen over Phanerozoic Time." *American Journal of Science* 289 (1989), 333–361.

Canfield, D. E., and A. Teske. "Late Proterozoic Rise in Atmospheric Oxygen Concentration Inferred from Phylogenetic and Sulfur-Isotope Studies." *Nature* 382 (1996), 127–132.

Holland, H. D. *The Chemical Evolution of the Atmosphere and Oceans*. Princeton, N.J.: Princeton University Press, 1984.

Schlesinger, W. H. *Biogeochemistry: An Analysis of Global Change*. 2d ed. San Diego: Academic Press, 1997.

Schopf, J. W., and C. Klein, eds. *The Proterozoic Biosphere: A Multidisciplinary Study*. Cambridge: Cambridge University Press, 1992.

Van Cappellen, P., and E. D. Ingall. "Redox Stabilization of the Atmosphere and Oceans by Phosphorus-Limited Marine Productivity." *Science* 271 (1996), 493–496.

—PHILIPPE VAN CAPPELLEN

OZONE

Ozone, a molecule made of three oxygen atoms (chemical formula O_3), is an exceedingly rare constituent of the Earth's atmosphere. Ninety percent of the ozone content of the atmosphere lies in a layer between 10 and 50 kilometers altitude, in a region called the *stratosphere*. The altitude distribution of this stratospheric ozone layer exhibits a maximum ozone concentration between 20 and 27 kilometers, which corresponds to absolute values on the order of $2.5–5.1 \times 10^{12}$ molecules per cubic centimeter, or relative values of 4–8 parts per million, corresponding to four to eight molecules of ozone for one million air molecules. The remaining 10 percent of the ozone content lies in the lower region of the atmosphere, known as the *troposphere*, which extends from the Earth's surface up to 10–12 kilometers. Ozone is continuously formed at altitudes above 30 kilometers from the photodissociation of molecular oxygen by solar radiation. The ozone balance in the stratosphere is maintained by destruction of ozone through catalytic cycles that involve nitrogen, hydrogen, chlorine, and bromine species. The chemistry of the stratosphere, with respect to the production and catalytic destruction of ozone, is thus a highly complex system, involving a very large number of elementary chemical reactions.

Ozone plays a major role in the Earth's atmosphere because it absorbs solar radiation at wavelengths shorter than 300 nanometers that is not absorbed by molecular nitrogen or molecular oxygen, the two main constituents of the atmosphere. It thus preserves the Earth's surface from damaging high-energy ultraviolet-B (UV-B) radiation. Indeed, if ozone were not present in the stratosphere, this energetic radiation emitted from the Sun would reach the surface and destroy molecules such as deoxyribonucleic acid (DNA) and proteins that constitute the living material of the biosphere. Life on Earth is thus directly dependent on the existence of the ozone layer. In addition, the absorption of UV radiation by ozone between 10 and 50 kilometers creates a heat source and thus a positive temperature gradient in the stratosphere. This temperature gradient enhances the stability of the atmosphere, by reducing the intensity of the vertical transport as compared to the troposphere.

In contrast to its beneficial role in the stratosphere, ozone in the troposphere interacts directly with living matter, with potential detrimental effects on ecosystems and human health. These effects arise from ozone's properties as a powerful oxidant, even at the low concentrations that are currently observed in the free troposphere, which range from 20 to 50 parts per billion. The harmful effects of ozone on forest growth and crop production have been clearly demonstrated, while, at the higher concentration levels observed in polluted areas (where relative concentrations can reach hundreds of parts per billion), ozone can directly affect human health. Also, ozone in the troposphere is a greenhouse gas with an efficiency on a per molecule basis in the atmosphere twelve hundred times larger than that of carbon dioxide, the main contributor to the greenhouse effect. Ozone is thus responsible, directly and indirectly through chemical processes that affect other greenhouse gases such as methane, for about 20 percent of the increase in the greenhouse effect observed since the beginning of the twentieth century. [*See* Greenhouse Effect.]

Scientific evidence gathered by continuous atmospheric observation over more than three decades shows that the vertical distribution of ozone is strongly perturbed by human activities. Since the early 1970s, the increase of chlorine and bromine compounds in the stratosphere, linked to the continuous increase in anthropogenic production of chlorofluorocarbons (CFCs) and halons, has led to a decrease in the thickness of the ozone layer. CFCs and halons are destroyed by solar radiation once they have reached the stratosphere through vertical diffusion. They then liberate chlorine and bromine atoms, which further enhance the efficiency of ozone-destroying catalytic cycles. The most recent evaluation of the long-term evolution of the ozone layer shows negative trends in the total ozone content, with the largest deficits observed in the high latitudes of both hemispheres in winter. In the higher-latitude regions of the Southern Hemisphere, the springtime ozone deficit is now a permanent feature of the antarctic stratosphere, and a direct link has been established between anthropogenic chlorine and the large decrease in the ozone concentration, up to 90 percent, observed between 15 and 20 kilometers. Similar decreases have appeared since 1995 in the arctic winter stratosphere, where record low temperatures (relative to the average values recorded over the last 20 years) have been observed. These measurements constitute additional observational evidence of the destructive effects of CFCs and halons on the stratospheric ozone layer. They are also a clear indication of the fragility of the ozone balance in the atmosphere, and of the nonlinearities that can occur in complex chemical and dynamic systems.

In the troposphere, the background ozone concentration, relative to the concentration observed at the Earth's surface during the last decades of the nineteenth century in nonpolluted areas, has increased threefold in the Northern Hemisphere and twofold in the Southern Hemisphere. These changes, together with increased frequency of ozone pollution episodes in large urban areas, can be related unambiguously to increased emissions of nitrogen oxides and hydrocarbons. Since the lifetime of ozone molecules in the lower atmosphere ranges from a few days to a few weeks, this additional ozone is not transferred to the stratosphere. If one also considers that the regions in which ozone increases in the troposphere (mainly the middle latitudes of the Northern Hemisphere) are geographically distinct from those regions in which ozone decreases rapidly in the stratosphere, one can see that the two human-induced perturbations to the vertical distribution of atmospheric ozone do not compensate for each other.

To quantify the detrimental effects on atmospheric ozone linked to emissions from industry, transport, and agriculture, one should first quantify the natural balance of ozone in the stratosphere and the troposphere. Although the chemistry of these two atmospheric regions is very different, ozone always originates from one single process, the recombination reaction of atomic oxygen in its fundamental state $O(^3P)$ with molecular oxygen in the presence of a third body M, which is required to carry away the energy released in the reaction:

$$O(^3P) + O_2 + M \longrightarrow O_3 + M. \qquad (1)$$

The variation with altitude in the chemical processes governing the concentration of ozone relates first to the origin of the oxygen atoms required for reaction (1) to occur, and second to the chemical and photochemical reactions involving other minor constituents of the atmosphere that also affect the ozone balance.

Ozone in the "Natural" Stratosphere. In the stratosphere, the net production of oxygen atom results almost exclusively from the photodissociation of molecular oxygen at UV wavelengths shorter than 242 nanometers:

$$O_2 + h\nu(\lambda < 242nm) \longrightarrow O + O. \qquad (2)$$

This photodissociation process, which is the source of odd oxygen (i.e., O and O_3) in the stratosphere, has a rather long time constant (defined as the time delay required to reduce the molecular oxygen concentration by a factor of 1/e), varying from 10^9 seconds at 60 kilometers to 10^{11} seconds (over 100 years) at 40 kilometers. Ozone is in turn photodissociated by UV and visible solar radiation throughout the atmosphere:

$$O_3 + h\nu(\lambda < 1200nm) \longrightarrow O + O_2. \qquad (3)$$

Reactions (1) and (3) are very fast and serve only to partition the odd oxygen species between O and O_3. The net chemical budget of the cycle (1) + (3) is zero, although it provides the main energy source of the stratosphere by converting solar radiation into heat. Ozone is thus responsible, through this dissociation–recombination cycle (which occurs in less than 100 seconds throughout the stratosphere), for the positive temperature gradient observed from the tropopause to the stratopause.

Until the early 1960s, the chemical loss of the odd oxygen species was attributed to a reaction proposed by Chapman (1930):

$$O(^3P) + O_3 \longrightarrow O_2 + O_2. \qquad (4)$$

However, this reaction could only account for about 20 percent of the odd oxygen loss in the stratosphere. It turns out that ozone is predominantly removed through catalytic cycles involving homogeneous gas phase reactions of active free radical species originating from hydrogen (HO_x), nitrogen (NO_x), chlorine (ClO_x), and bromine (BrO_x) species.

The quantification of the catalytic cycles that govern the behavior of the stratospheric ozone layer is dependent on a detailed understanding of the chemical reactions that form, interconvert, and remove the chemically active components of each family of species (Wayne, 1985). These chemical interactions can be thought of as global cycles starting from source species diffusing slowly from the surface through the troposphere, before reaching the stratosphere after three to five years. This time constant implies that only long-lived species in the troposphere can constitute sources of chemically active species in the stratosphere. The sources of hydrogen compounds are water vapor (H_2O), with an average mixing ratio at the tropopause of 4–5 parts per million (ppm), methane (CH_4, 1.8 ppm), and molecular hydrogen (H_2, 0.5 ppm). The source of nitrogen species is nitrous oxide (N_2O, 0.3 ppm). The main source of chlorine compounds at the surface is in the form of inorganic chlorine (Cl_2, HCl, NaCl) emitted by the oceans and volcanic plumes. However, these compounds are water soluble and have a very short lifetime in the lower troposphere; they are washed out by precipitation in only a few days. Hence they do not constitute a significant stratospheric source. The only known natural source of chlorine for the stratosphere is methylchloride (CH_3Cl), produced by microorganisms in the ocean, with an atmospheric lifetime of eighteen months.

From these source species, radicals—which have a high chemical reactivity—are formed by photodissociation and oxidation processes that take place only in the stratosphere, induced by the enhanced solar UV radiation present at this altitude. The most active radicals are the hydroxyl (OH), nitrogen (NO), chlorine (ClO), and bromine (BrO) monoxides. The ozone-destroying catalytic cycles then take the general form:

$$X + O_3 \longrightarrow XO + O_2 \tag{5}$$

$$XO + O \longrightarrow X + O_2 \tag{6}$$

$$O + O_3 \longrightarrow O_2 + O_2. \tag{4}$$

where X = OH, NO, ClO, BrO. Cycles (5) and (6) are equivalent to the single reaction (4). The relative importance of each "family" of constituents for the ozone budget in the stratosphere is dependent on the altitude range. Nitrogen species control the ozone content at altitudes below 45 kilometers, and hydrogen species above. The maximum effect of the gas phase chlorine and bromine cycles is expected at 40 kilometers. However, under natural conditions, this effect only contributes a small percentage of the total ozone destruction.

The spatial repartition of ozone is further controlled by dynamic processes that result in a poleward transport from the production regions in the tropics, where the solar insolation is a maximum, to the polar regions; here, ozone accumulates, mainly because of the low levels of insolation and thus of active chemistry. These continuous dynamic movements lead in turn to fluctuations in the ozone content on various temporal and spatial scales. These variations are of the order of tens of percent, and correspond to day-to-day, seasonal, and interannual variability in the total ozone content and ozone vertical distribution in the atmosphere. The thickness of the ozone layer thus varies between 220 Dobson units (DU) in the tropical regions to more than 450 DU at high latitudes (100 DU corresponds to a thickness of the ozone layer of 0.1 centimeters when compressed to the surface pressure and temperature).

The Perturbed Stratosphere. Perturbation of the ozone balance in the stratosphere occurs because of increased emission of source species at the surface. Chlorine species play a dominant role, and the main source of stratospheric chlorine is anthropogenic—the result of emissions of stable organic chlorine as CFCs or chlorinated hydrocarbons. The most significant species are $CFCl_3$ (CFC-11), CF_2Cl_2 (CFC-12), carbon tetrachloride (CCl_4), and methylchloroform (CH_3CCl_3). The total chlorine level in the stratosphere has increased from 0.6 parts per billion in the 1950s, a value that can be considered as the background level, to 3.8 parts per billion

in 1997. Anthropogenic brominated hydrocarbons, known as halons, also reach the stratosphere. The present total abundance of bromine in the stratosphere is, however, much lower than that of chlorine, reaching 15 parts per trillion in 1997.

These increased levels of chlorine and bromine lead to an additional ozone destruction at 40 kilometers, where the chlorine-controlled destruction cycles are the most efficient. Based on a simple consideration of CFC and halon emissions, the estimated decrease in the thickness of the ozone layer resulting from these gas phase processes should have been limited to 1–2 percent per decade over the period 1975–1995. But much larger effects identified in the mid-1980s completely changed our understanding of ozone chemistry in the presence of high chlorine levels in the stratosphere.

The seasonal ozone depletion that occurs over Antarctica during the Southern Hemisphere spring was discovered by Farman et al. (1985). This phenomenon, which has recurred every spring since the early 1980s, when total chlorine in the stratosphere reached a threshold value of about 2 parts per billion, was completely unexpected and could not be accounted for by chemical models that incorporated only gas phase chemistry. This was the first recorded evidence of a large change in ozone climatology. It corresponded to a change in the seasonal cycle of column ozone, as the spring minimum of 270 DU, observed since the late 1950s at various stations in Antarctica, suddenly deepened to reach values as low as 100 DU during October. Ozone is completely depleted at altitudes from 15 to 20 kilometers. As a result of several coordinated campaigns conducted in the Antarctic since 1987, a clear picture has now emerged of the combination of dynamic, radiative, and chemical processes that are responsible for the antarctic ozone depletion.

The dynamic processes in the antarctic winter stratosphere are dominated by strong westerly zonal winds—the polar vortex—surrounding a region of very cold air at latitudes higher than 65° south. These winds are generated by the large temperature gradient between the midlatitude regions and the polar night areas, where very low temperatures, below −83°C, are reached as a result of radiative equilibrium in the absence of solar light. The Southern Hemisphere vortex is very stable because of the circular symmetry observed in the energy forcing occurring in the troposphere, which is dominated by regions of low pressure in the 50°–60° south latitude belt. In the very cold area over the antarctic continent, polar stratospheric clouds can be formed at altitudes between 15 and 20 kilometers as a result of the condensation of either nitric acid trihydrate (HNO_3, $3H_2O$) at −83°C, or of water vapor itself when the temperature drops below −88°C. Polar stratospheric clouds play two distinct roles in the processes that lead to ozone depletion. First, pro-

THE NORMAL LATITUDINAL AND SEASONAL PATTERN OF OZONE

Total Ozone (Average 1957–1975) Showing Seasons and Latitudes of Greatest Normal Concentration.

Values over 340 Dobson units are shaded. (After London and Angell, in Morris and Barras, 1978. Copyright American Society for Testing and Materials. Reprinted with permission.)

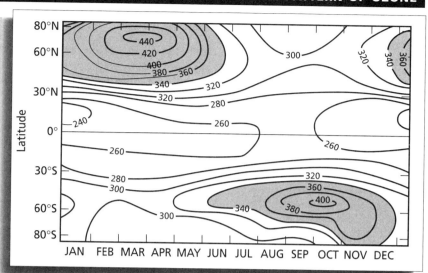

The graph, which resembles a map, shows how the normal ozone content of the stratosphere varies with latitude and with the seasons. Because of transport poleward from equatorial regions, ozone concentration is highest in high latitudes; it is stored there during the polar night and then appears strongly in the spring months (February–May in the Northern Hemisphere, October–November in the Southern Hemispheres). In connection with current concern about the ozone layer and its interception of harmful ultraviolet radiation, two points are worth noting:

1. It is the springtime maxima of ozone concentration (in which values of 400 Dobson units are normal) that are disrupted by ozone holes, as sunlight returns after the polar night and drives chemical reactions in which chlorine and bromine pollutants rapidly destroy ozone.
2. Labeled isolines show that, year round, under normal conditions, the lowest concentrations of ozone (and the least protection from ultraviolet radiation at the Earth's surface) are in lower latitudes, not at the poles.

BIBLIOGRAPHY

Morris, A. L., and R. C. Barras, eds. *Air Quality Meteorology and Atmospheric Ozone.* Philadelphia: American Society for Testing and Materials, 1978.

—DAVID J. CUFF

vide sites for heterogeneous chemical reactions, which convert inactive chlorine compounds into ozone-destroying radicals. Second, they remove nitric acid by sedimentation, and thus, indirectly, active nitrogen species (NO_x), which are then no longer available to buffer the active chlorine being released. In midlatitude regions where gas phase chemistry dominates, only 3 percent of the total chlorine is in the form of chemically active chlorine, Cl or ClO. The remaining species are either the CFC sources or reservoir species such as hydrogen chloride (HCl) and chlorine nitrate ($ClONO_2$), which do not destroy ozone. In contrast, in the polar stratosphere, the conversion of chlorine and nitrogen reservoirs into active chlorine on the surface of the polar stratospheric clouds occurs through the following mechanisms, which

have been identified in laboratory studies of ice–gas reactions:

$$ClONO_2 + HCl \xrightarrow{\text{surface}} Cl_2 + HNO_3 \qquad (7)$$

$$ClONO_2 + H_2O \xrightarrow{\text{surface}} HOCl + HNO_3 \qquad (8)$$

$$N_2O_5 + HCl \xrightarrow{\text{surface}} HNO_3 + ClNO_2 \qquad (9)$$

$$N_2O_5 + H_2O \xrightarrow{\text{surface}} 2HNO_3. \qquad (10)$$

Reactions (9) and (10) also provide a removal channel for nitrogen species. All of these heterogeneous chemical reactions result in the accumulation of active chlorine into the polar vortex, which then represents almost 50 percent of the total chlorine content. When solar light returns to the antarctic stratosphere in early spring, photochemical reactions are initiated. The new chlorine reservoirs, such as molecular chlorine (Cl_2), are photodissociated rapidly enough to produce chlorine atoms:

$$Cl_2 + h\nu(visible\ light) \longrightarrow Cl + Cl. \qquad (11)$$

Chlorine atoms then react with ozone via reaction (5) to produce ClO, which accumulates very rapidly because of the inhibition of the nitrogen interactions that results from the denitrification of the polar stratosphere. But the oxygen atom required to initiate reaction (6) is not present because the low elevation angles of the sun in the polar spring stratosphere do not provide the appropriate UV wavelengths for molecular oxygen photodissociation. The classical cycle of reactions (5) and (6) therefore does not take place, and ozone destruction occurs through a more complex catalytic cycle involving the formation of the dimer of chlorine monoxide (Cl_2O_2), further photodissociated by solar light:

$$ClO + ClO + M \longrightarrow Cl_2O_2 + M \qquad (12)$$

$$Cl_2O_2 + h\nu \xrightarrow{visible} 2Cl + O_2 \qquad (13)$$

$$2(Cl + O_3 \longrightarrow ClO + O_2) \qquad (14)$$

$$2O_3 \longrightarrow 3O_2. \qquad (15)$$

This catalytic cycle is the major cause of ozone loss in the antarctic polar stratosphere, which can occur at a rate of more than 1 percent per day. It is complemented by an alternative cycle involving a coupling between chlorine and bromine species:

$$ClO + BrO \longrightarrow Cl + Br + O_2 \qquad (16)$$

$$Br + O_3 \longrightarrow BrO + O_2 \qquad (17)$$

$$Cl + O_3 \longrightarrow ClO + O_2 \qquad (14)$$

$$2O_3 \longrightarrow 3O_2. \qquad (15)$$

All experiments performed since 1987 have demonstrated that such mechanisms, which involve a strong coupling between dynamic processes (i.e., the polar vortex) and complex heterogeneous chemistry, are the only possible explanation for the large ozone depletion observed during the Southern Hemisphere springtime. These mechanisms therefore link, in a direct cause-and-effect relationship, anthropogenic chlorine (which represents 90 percent of the chlorine reservoir in the stratosphere) and ozone depletion.

In the Arctic, the dynamic conditions are different since the polar vortex is less stable because of a continuously varying tropospheric forcing related to the alternation of continents and oceans that characterizes the midlatitude regions of the Northern Hemisphere. Air is continuously mixed during winter between the colder polar regions and the warmer midlatitude regions, resulting in average temperatures about 15°–20°C higher than those observed in the antarctic stratosphere. Until the early 1990s, the early breakdown of the vortex and the subsequent warming that occurs in the polar strato-

sphere prevented the occurrence of large depletions similar to those observed over Antarctica. Nevertheless, heterogeneous processes similar to those occurring over Antarctica are also taking place at the surface of polar stratospheric clouds in the Arctic, resulting in high levels of active chlorine in January and February. Since 1994, lower temperatures have been observed in the arctic stratosphere, and these have led to increased ozone depletion during the spring. Observations from several field experiments confirm that large ozone losses, reaching about 25 percent by the end of March, are now occurring in the northern high latitudes on surface areas similar to those observed in Antarctica.

Stratospheric Ozone Depletion and Changes in Surface Ultraviolet Radiation. Until the 1980s, measurements of the ozone content of the atmosphere were mainly performed using ground-based instruments. These instruments (such as the Dobson spectrophotometer, designed for ozone measurements in the 1920s) use spectrometric techniques, in which the absorption of direct or diffuse solar radiation is measured in the wavelength regions in which ozone absorbs. Until the 1950s, there were fewer than twenty regularly operating measurement stations, most of which were located in the Northern Hemisphere. An international network of stations was first implemented by the International Ozone Commission and the World Meteorological Organization during the International Geophysical Year in 1957–1958 and then expanded to more than one hundred stations, which now operate almost continuously. In addition, new instrumentation based on the same spectrometric techniques, such as the Brewer spectrophotometer and the filter ozonemeter, were implemented in the 1970s to complement this network. Since 1978, satellite instruments such as the Total Ozone Mapping Spectrometer (TOMS) and the Solar Backscatter Ultraviolet Instrument (SBUV) have provided daily global coverage of the Earth's total ozone content by measuring the solar irradiance and radiance backscattered by the atmosphere at several wavelengths in the UV absorption bands of ozone.

Total ozone content. The measurements provided over the last three decades by these ground-based and space-borne systems constitute the experimental basis from which trends in the ozone total content have been determined (World Meteorological Organization, 1990a, 1992, 1994, 1998). Statistical models are used to fit the measured values, adjusting for the seasonal variation in mean ozone values, for solar cycle effects, and even for the nuclear tests performed in the atmosphere in the early 1960s. The fit is made for each month and each location or spatial area (latitude bands, longitude dependence) using a "hockey stick" approximation with a baseline level prior to December 1969 and a linear trend afterward. It is thus important to note that the trends determined from these fitting procedures correspond to linear averages over the full period for which the fit is performed.

Trends in total ozone content have recently been updated through early 1998 (World Meteorological Organization, 1998). The following major features are apparent. Whereas no trends are observed in the equatorial regions, in any season, from 20° south latitude to 20° north latitude, large and statistically significant trends are observed in both hemispheres at middle and high latitudes. In the Northern Hemisphere, the trends are approximately −3 to −6 percent per decade in the winter and spring, and are limited to about −1 to −3 percent per decade during summer and fall. For the Southern Hemisphere high latitudes, very large negative trends are observed in winter, up to −6 percent per decade, and especially in springtime, when this value reaches −10 percent per decade because of the influence of the antarctic ozone hole. The Southern Hemisphere polar regions show average trends of −22 percent per decade. In the summer, the trends are smaller although still significant, between −2 and −5 percent per decade. More detailed analyses also show that the trends have accelerated over the last decade (World Meteorological Organization, 1994, 1998).

Ozone vertical distribution. The determination of trends in the ozone vertical distribution is of paramount importance for understanding the origin of the evolution of the ozone layer and the main processes responsible for it. However, because of the scarcity of relevant data, this problem is more difficult to handle than the study of ozone integrated content. The Dobson spectrophotometer can be used to obtain information on the vertical distribution of ozone, using the Umkehr method (Götz, 1931). The determination of vertical ozone profiles requires an inversion of the measured radiances, which are usually given in terms of the mean ozone partial pressure in layers about 5 kilometers thick. However, a careful analysis of the algorithms shows that the vertical resolution is actually on the order of 11–14 kilometers and that the data are accurate enough for trend detection only from 20 to 43 kilometers altitude (World Meteorological Organization, 1990b). The determination of trends via the Umkehr technique is further affected by instrument drifts, by changes in calibration, and by stratospheric aerosols. Although Umkehr observations date back to the 1930s, regular measurements were only started following the International Geophysical Year in 1957. Only ten stations currently have a sufficient number of observations over a sufficient period to allow the study of trends. These stations cover the latitude range from 24° to 53° north and are thus not representative for global trends.

Balloon-borne ozonesondes are also flown regularly at several stations with standard meteorological radiosondes. In particular, a considerable quantity of data on ozone vertical distribution up to 30 kilometers has been obtained with the Brewer ozonesonde and the more recently developed electrochemical cells (ECC) ozonesonde. However, there are again only a few stations for which measurements have been made over a sufficiently long period with appropriate temporal sampling.

The only global record of ozone vertical distribution has been obtained from satellite observations. The instruments SAGE and SAGE II, launched by the U.S. National Aeronautics and Space Administration (NASA) in 1979 and 1984, respectively, are multiwavelength radiometers that use the solar occultation technique to monitor the ozone vertical distribution. These instruments measure the attenuation of solar radiation by ozone in the Chappuis absorption band at 600 nanometers, as the Sun sets or rises relative to the spacecraft. Such measurements are self-calibrating in that only relative radiance measurements are required to determine the transmission and thus the ozone concentration. A limitation of this technique is the relatively small quantity of data available for global estimates, since only two vertical profiles are obtained for each orbit and this results in an undersampling of the natural variability of ozone.

The most recent analysis of the trends in vertical ozone distribution (World Meteorological Organization, 1998), based primarily on the SAGE/SAGE II and ozonesonde data, shows negative trends at all altitudes between 10 and 65 kilometers. Two maxima in the altitude distribution of the trends are observed, namely, −7.5 percent per decade at 15 kilometers and at 40 kilometers. The first is the signature of the heterogeneous processes leading to chlorine and bromine activation that affect the ozone vertical distribution in the lower stratosphere. The second relates to homogeneous gas phase chlorine and bromine catalytic cycles. Because the greatest abundance of ozone is found at lower altitudes, the most detrimental effects are observed in the lower stratosphere. One should also note that this picture is consistent with the trends evaluated for the total ozone content.

Despite the difficulty of determining trends from instruments that have not all been specifically designed for that purpose, there is some evidence from both ground-based and satellite measurements that large variations have occurred in the ozone concentration in the lower and upper stratosphere over the last few decades. These downward trends, which cannot be explained by natural causes such as the solar cycle, are much larger than the values predicted from our present knowledge of the chlorine catalytic cycles, for both gas phase and heterogeneous chemistry. In contrast to the Southern Hemisphere, where the antarctic ozone hole has been related directly to the presence of anthropogenic chlorine in the stratosphere, no such direct cause-and-effect link has yet been established between the Northern Hemisphere ozone depletion and the emission of halocarbons into the atmosphere. Although mechanisms involving chlorine and bromine from anthropogenic sources appear to be largely responsible for the measured ozone losses, the main difficulty resides in quantifying the relative importance of the various processes that are presently thought to be acting in the stratosphere. These include local heterogeneous chemistry acting on the surface of sulfate particles, transport of ozone-depleted air masses from the polar regions toward the middle latitudes, and transport of chemically perturbed polar air with high levels of reactive chlorine and low levels of nitrogen species toward the midlatitude regions.

The June 1991 eruption of the Mount Pinatubo volcano in the Philippines, which released a very large quantity of sulfate particles directly into the stratosphere, has provided an opportunity to test some of these hypotheses. From observations made in the years following this large perturbation, it is known that heterogeneous reactions can also occur on the surface of such sulfate aerosols, especially in the cold stratosphere. Evidence that the stratospheric ozone layer has been strongly perturbed by this eruption as a result of the high level of anthropogenic chlorine in the stratosphere, which in turn induces chlorine-catalyzed ozone destruction, is provided by the low values of ozone total content obtained from ground-based and satellite measurements in 1992 and 1993. The 1993 values are about 15 percent lower than the lowest values recorded over the decade 1980–1990.

Ultraviolet Radiation at the Surface. In the absence of other interfering absorbers or scatterers of UV radiation such as clouds or pollution, decreases in stratospheric ozone content lead to an increase in surface UV-B radiation (280–315 nanometers). This inverse relationship has been established firmly in both theory and measurements. It is confirmed by several experiments conducted in Antarctica over the last decade. These are quite large effects; for example, in ozone hole conditions, the UV-B intensity at the Palmer station in Antarctica in late October is more intense than that observed in San Diego at any time throughout the year. However, such observations are currently restricted to areas in which large ozone depletions (more than 60 percent) have been observed. In other areas, UV-B increases are more difficult to detect because they are complicated by changes in cloudiness or by local pollution, as well as by the difficulty of keeping the detection instruments in precisely stable observation conditions over long periods. Prior to the late 1980s, instruments with the necessary accuracy and stability were not available. Hence the record of ground-based measurements is not long enough for the reliable determination of decadal changes in UV fluxes. However, as the effects of altitude, aerosols, and geographic differences have become better understood, estimates have been made from satellite observation using the TOMS instrument; these show increases in UV-B fluxes at latitudes poleward of 35°, in agreement with the observed ozone decreases. As a result of such observations, public interest in UV exposure has been addressed in many countries by the establishment of a standardized UV index to provide daily information about the intensity of UV radiation based on ozone measurements and weather forecasting.

Tropospheric Ozone. Until the 1970s, photochemical production of ozone in the troposphere was considered to be important only in highly polluted areas. This ozone buildup in urban smog was known to be due to oxidation of methane, carbon monoxide, and volatile organic compounds (VOCs) in the presence of nitrogen oxides and solar radiation. Early studies demonstrated that *in situ* photochemical production of ozone from the same precursors, nitrogen oxides and VOCs, could also occur in remote areas, induced by both natural and artificial sources. This additional production of ozone is likely to have changed the oxidation efficiency of the atmosphere during the past century.

To assess this perturbation to tropospheric ozone distribution, the mechanisms of formation and loss of ozone must be quantified. The basic processes have been known since the late 1960s, but, because of the complexity of the formation and loss of ozone in the lower atmosphere and the fact that ozone buildup depends strongly on the behavior of numerous chemical species with quite low relative abundances, there are large uncertainties in predicting the future evolution of the troposphere. The origin of the oxygen atoms required to produce ozone through reaction (1) differs between the stratospheric and tropospheric processes. Because solar radiation reaching the Earth's surface no longer contains the shorter wavelengths necessary to photodissociate molecular oxygen (these wavelengths are blocked completely by the stratosphere), the oxygen atoms are produced by the photodissociation of nitrogen dioxide, which occurs at longer wavelengths in the visible part of the solar spectrum:

$$NO_2 + h\nu(\lambda < 400nm) \longrightarrow NO + O. \qquad (18)$$

Ozone is then formed by rapid recombination with molecular oxygen:

$$O(^3P) + O_2 + M \longrightarrow O_3 + M. \qquad (1)$$

However, nitrogen monoxide (NO) reacts very rapidly with ozone:

$$NO + O_3 \longrightarrow NO_2 + O_2 \tag{19}$$

so that a steady-state equilibrium is reached, in which ozone cannot accumulate. For this accumulation to occur, one requires a chemical process by which NO is converted into NO_2 without consuming ozone. This is provided by reactions of NO with organic peroxyradicals that originate through the atmospheric degradation of methane, carbon monoxide, and organic compounds. A key species in this degradation chain is the hydroxyl radical OH, which is produced by a two-step process involving ozone and water vapor:

$$O_3 + h\nu(\lambda < 310\text{nm}) \longrightarrow O(^1D) + O_2 \tag{20}$$

$$O(^1D) + H_2O \longrightarrow 2OH, \tag{21}$$

where $O(^1D)$ is an electronically excited state of atomic oxygen with a very high chemical reactivity, which allows a fast reaction with water vapor to occur. Although water vapor is rather abundant in the lower atmosphere, this process only leads to absolute concentrations of the OH radical in the range 10^5–10^6 molecules per cubic centimeter, or relative values of 10^{-13}–10^{-14}. When OH radicals and nitrogen oxides are present in the troposphere, the oxidation chain of hydrocarbons leads to ozone production as illustrated by the following sequence written, as an example, for an alkane of chemical formula RCH_3:

$$OH + RCH_3 \longrightarrow RCH_2 + H_2O$$

$$RCH_2 + O_2 \longrightarrow RCH_2O_2$$

$$RCH_2O_2 + NO \longrightarrow RCH_2O + NO_2$$

$$RCH_2O + O_2 \longrightarrow RCHO + HO_2$$

$$HO_2 + NO \longrightarrow OH + NO_2$$

$$2(NO_2 + h\nu(\lambda < 400\text{nm}) \longrightarrow NO + O)$$

$$2(O(^3P) + O_2 + M \longrightarrow O_3 + M)$$

$$RCH_3 + 4O_2 \xrightarrow{h\nu} RCHO + 2O_3 + H_2O$$

This cycle leads to the production of ozone molecules, with a possibility for further oxidation of the RCHO molecule. These oxidation steps for an alkane have their analogues for other hydrocarbons, including methane, and for CO oxidation. But in all cases the reactions depend on the switch between peroxyradicals RO_2 (represented in this case by the hydroperoxyradical HO_2) and oxyradicals RO (represented by the hydroxyradical OH) in an interaction with NO to form NO_2. This process becomes dominant as soon as the nitrogen oxide relative concentration reaches a threshold of 10–20 parts per trillion. If the NO concentration is lower, then RO_2 reacts with ozone, leading to ozone destruction. This threshold is very low, so that it is reached in most geographical areas of the troposphere, except in remote locations over the oceans.

Oxides of nitrogen are thus a central element of the oxidation scheme because they affect the switching reaction and are the only source of ozone and thus of OH radicals. Natural sources of nitrogen oxides include microbial activity in the soils, oxidation of biogenic ammonia, and lightning discharges in the atmosphere. The other ozone precursors—methane, carbon monoxide, and VOCs—also have natural sources, mainly linked to biogenic processes and further oxidation processes in the atmosphere. In particular, VOCs in the form of terpenes and isoprenes are found over regions with high densities of trees such as pines or citrus fruit. Anthropogenic sources have been superposed over time on these natural sources, which not only affect densely populated areas but also remote sites. In 1995, these anthropogenic sources dominated the global emissions of methane, accounting for 63 percent of the total sources (World Meteorological Organization, 1998), carbon monoxide (65 percent), and nitrogen oxides (75 percent). They are linked to industry (fossil fuel burning, combustion processes, natural gas emissions), agriculture (soil fertilization, rice paddies, cattle), and transport (terrestrial, aviation). For hydrocarbons and VOCs, although the anthropogenic sources dominate in polluted areas (industry and transport through combustion processes), natural sources linked to biogenic emissions are still predominant on the global scale, accounting for 80 percent of the total emissions.

The global budget of tropospheric ozone is thus influenced by ozone produced directly by photochemical processes in urban and industrialized regions and transported downwind, as well as *in situ* production such as that resulting from biomass burning in the tropical belt. Almost 80 percent of the present tropospheric ozone content is thought to be of photochemical origin, whereas the downward transport from the stratosphere only accounts for 20 percent of the global budget. An average yearly increase in tropospheric ozone content of 0.5–2 percent in the temperate Northern Hemisphere is one of the many indications that the photochemistry of the troposphere is changing, with potential consequences for plant life, human health, and climate change.

Clear evidence has emerged over the last two decades that the distribution of ozone in the atmosphere, both in the stratosphere and the troposphere, is directly affected by human activities. In such conditions, two types of response to this global environmental problem can be considered, namely, cure and prevention. Considering the huge volume of the Earth's atmosphere and the magnitude of the changes occurring in ozone content, in particular the ozone depletion in the stratosphere, possible cures for the problem have proved to be far too expensive, impractical, and potentially damaging to the global environment. The alternative is to apply the precautionary principle as reflected in the internationally agreed Montreal Protocol (1987) and its further amendments made in London (1990), Copenhagen (1992), Vienna (1995), and Montreal (1997). These agreements call for a total elimination of the production and use of CFCs and other ozone-damaging substances. In addition, regulatory measures proposed or adopted in many developed countries to reduce emissions of ozone precursors in the troposphere, especially nitrogen oxides, are also part of the effort to reduce the impact of human activities on the global environment.

[See also Air Quality; Atmosphere Structure and Evolution; Atmospheric Chemistry; Chemical Industry; Chlorofluorocarbons; Climate Impacts; Greenhouse Effect; Human Health; Montreal Protocol; Oxygen Cycle; and Pollution.]

BIBLIOGRAPHY

Brasseur, G., and S. Solomon. *Aeronomy of the Middle Atmosphere*. Dordrecht: Reidel, 1984.

Chapman, S. "A Theory of the Upper Atmospheric Ozone Layer." *Memoirs of the Royal Meteorological Society* 3 (1930), 103.

Farman, J. C., B. G. Gardiner, and J. D. Shanklin. "Large Losses of Total Ozone in Antarctica Reveal Seasonal ClO_x/NO_x Interaction." *Nature* 315 (1985), 207.

Götz, F. W. P. "Zum Strahlungs Klima des Spitzbergen Sommers." *Gerlands Beitrage zur Geophysik* 31 (1931), 119–154.

Solomon, S. "The Mystery of the Antarctic Ozone Hole." *Reviews of Geophysics* 26 (1988), 131–151.

Wayne, R. P. *Chemistry of the Atmosphere*. Oxford: Clarendon Press, 1985.

World Meteorological Organization. "International Ozone Assessment: 1989." World Meteorological Organization Global Ozone and Monitoring Network, Report 20. Washington, D.C., 1990a.

———. "Report of the International Ozone Trends Panel: 1988." World Meteorological Organization Global Ozone and Monitoring Network, Report 18. Washington, D.C., 1990b.

———. "International Ozone Assessment: 1991." World Meteorological Organization Global Ozone and Monitoring Network, Report 22. Washington, D.C., 1992.

———. "International Ozone Assessment: 1994." World Meteorological Organization Global Ozone and Monitoring Network, Report 37. Washington, D.C., 1994.

———. "International Ozone Assessment: 1998." World Meteorological Organization Global Ozone and Monitoring Network, Report 44. Washington, D.C, 1999.

—GÉRARD J. MÉGIE

OZONE HOLE. *See* Antarctica; Atmospheric Chemistry; Chlorofluorocarbons; *and* Ozone.

P

PALEOCLIMATE

The climate of the world has been ever changing. It is invariable only in its variability. It has changed repeatedly and substantially throughout geologic time and both before and during the presence of humans on the face of the Earth. Changes have ranged from the essentially minor fluctuations within the period of instrumental record (with durations in the case of events like the Sahel drought since the mid-1960s, on the order of a decade or decades) to those of the most significant geologic periods, with durations of many millions of years. For example, over the last billion years there have been at least six major ice ages, when great icecaps have enveloped substantial parts of the Earth's surface. Such extensive phases of ice-age activity appear to have been separated by millions of years of relative warmth, when icecaps and glaciers have been largely absent. This variability is illustrated in Table 1 and in Figure 1. General reviews of climatic change are provided by Goudie (1992), Crowley and North (1991), and Williams et al. (1998), while Bradley (1985) and Lowe and Walker (1997) provide good surveys of the techniques used to date and reconstruct past environments. [See Climate Reconstruction.]

The Evidence for Past Climatic Changes. The types of evidence that can be used to reconstruct past climatic conditions are diverse and can be divided into five main classes (Table 2). First is the evidence that can be derived from ice cores drilled through ice sheets. This has been particularly useful for understanding climates over that last few hundreds of thousands of years. [See the vignette on The Vostok, Antarctica, Ice Core.] Second is geologic evidence derived from the study of sediments and associated landforms. This evidence can be subdivided into that derived from the oceans and that derived from the land. For example, coral reefs, sand dunes, and glacial hills all have clear climatic implications. Third is the biological evidence provided by the remains of organisms, many of which can provide a clear signal of environmental conditions. Past vegetation cover, for example, can be estimated by pollen analysis (palynology). Fourth is historical evidence for the last few thousands of years, while fifth is archaeological evidence. Extensive archaeological remains in the dead heart of the Sahara, for instance, may indicate moist climatic phases.

Climatic Changes in the Geologic Record. The long-term history of climate is progressively more difficult to decipher the further back one goes in time and the level of resolution deteriorates. Nonetheless, Crow-

Paleoclimate. TABLE 1. Orders of Climatic Variation

TIME SCALE UNIT	DURATION (YEARS)	TYPICAL PHENOMENA	PRINCIPAL BASES OF EVIDENCE
1. Minor fluctuations within the instrumental record	10	Minor fluctuations that give the impression of operating over intervals on the order of 25–100 years, with somewhat irregular length and amplitude	Instrumental; behavior of glaciers; records of riverflow and lake levels; noninstrumental diaries: crop yields, tree rings
2. Postglacial and historic	10^2	Variations over intervals on the order of 250–1,000 years	Earlier records of extremes: fossil tree rings; archaeological finds; lake levels; varves and lake sediments; oceanic core samples; pollen analysis
3. Glacial	10^4	The phases within an ice age, e.g., the duration of the last glacial was about 9×10^3 years	Fauna and flora characteristics of interglacial deposits; pollen analysis; variation in height of snow line and extent of frozen ground; oceanic core samples
4. Minor geologic	10^6	Duration of ice ages as a whole, periods of evolution of species	Geologic evidence: character of deposits; fossil fauna and flora
5. Major geologic	10^8	Intervals between ice ages	Geologic evidence: character of deposits; fossil fauna and flora

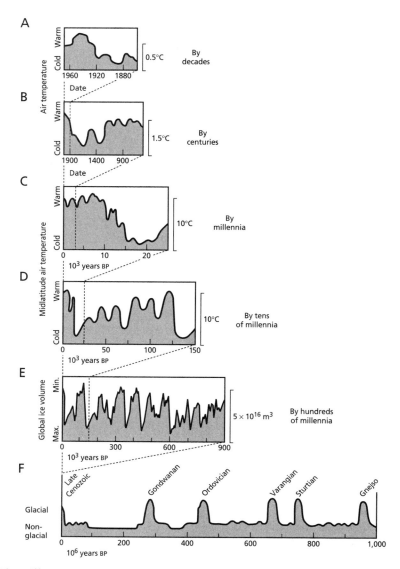

Paleoclimate. Figure 1. The Different Scales of Climatic Change.

(A) Changes in the five-year average surface temperatures over the region of 0°–80°N. (B) Winter severity index for eastern Europe. (C) Generalized Northern Hemisphere air temperature trends, based on fluctuations in alpine glaciers, changes in tree lines, marginal fluctuations in continental glaciers, and shifts in vegeta-
tion patterns recorded in pollen spectra. (D) Generalized Northern Hemisphere air temperature trends, based on midlatitude sea surface temperature, pollen records, and worldwide sea level records. (E) Fluctuations in global ice volume recorded by changes in isotopic composition of fossil plankton in a deep-sea core. (F) The occurrence of ice ages in geologic time. (After Goudie, 1992. With permission of Oxford University Press.)

ley and North (1991) have suggested the following major tendencies since the Earth came into being 4.6 billion years ago:

1. From 4.6 to about 2.5 billion years ago (i.e., Azoic and early Precambrian times), Earth was probably ice free, despite a substantially lower solar luminosity. An enhanced greenhouse effect may account for this paradox and may have compensated for the decreased insolation receipt.
2. At around 2.5 billion years ago, atmospheric temper-

atures appear to have dipped, producing the first glaciation.
3. Between then and 900 million years ago (i.e., during the heart of the Precambrian), Earth was again largely ice free.
4. From 900 to 600 million years ago (i.e., from the late Precambrian into the Cambrian period), at least three major phases of glaciation occurred; virtually all regions of the Earth that contain Precambrian rocks show evidence for glaciation during this time. Glaciation appears to have penetrated into low latitudes.

Paleoclimate. TABLE 2. Principal Sources of Proxy Data for Paleoclimatic Reconstructions

(1) Glaciological (Ice Cores)
    (a) oxygen isotopes
    (b) physical properties (e.g., ice fabric)
    (c) trace element and microparticle concentrations
(2) Geologic
    (A) Marine (ocean sediment cores)
        (i) Organic sediments (planktonic and benthic fossils)
            (a) oxygen isotopic composition
            (b) faunal and floral abundance
            (c) morphological variations
        (ii) Inorganic sediments
            (a) Mineralogical composition and surface texture
            (b) Accumulation rates and distribution of terrestrial dust and ice-rafted debris
            (c) Geochemistry
    (B) Terrestrial
        (a) glacial deposits and features of glacial erosion
        (b) periglacial features
        (c) glacio-eustatic features (shorelines)
        (d) eolian deposits (loess and sand dunes)
        (e) lacustrine deposits and erosional features (lacustrine sediments and shorelines)
        (f) speleothems (age and stable isotope composition)
(3) Biological
    (a) tree rings (width, density, stable isotope composition)
    (b) pollen (type, relative abundance or absolute concentration)
    (c) plant macrofossils (age and distribution)
    (d) insects (type and assemblage abundance)
    (e) modern population distribution (refuges and relict populations of plants and animals)
(4) Historical
    (a) written records of environmental indicators (parameteorological phenomena)
    (b) phenological records
(5) Archaeological
    (a) stone tools
    (b) pottery, coins, metal objects

SOURCE: Bradley, 1985 (Table 1.1), with modifications.

5. From 600 to 100 million years ago (virtually all of the Paleozoic and Mesozoic eras), climates were generally milder but punctuated by two major phases of ice growth. In the Ordovician period (500–435 million years ago), for example, there was extensive glaciation of what is now the Sahara Desert.

6. From 100 to 50 million years ago, in the heart of the Cretaceous period, a mild nonglacial climate prevailed. There is, for example, a considerable amount of evidence for warmer temperatures in high latitudes during the mid-Cretaceous, when dinosaurs of presumed warm-weather affinity ranged north of the Arctic Circle. Relative warmth continued into the early Cenozoic era (Paleocene and Eocene epochs, 65–37 million years ago), and plant fossils reflect such conditions in the high latitudes of both the Northern and Southern Hemispheres. A rich tropical flora from the London Clay (Eocene) indicate that tropical conditions extended to about 45°N paleolatitude.

7. In the late Cenozoic a climatic decline started that in due course led to the ice ages of the Plio-Pleistocene (some 5 million to 10,000 years ago).

The Cenozoic Climate Decline. During the Tertiary period, which started at the end of the Cretaceous about 65 million years ago, Earth's climate underwent one of the longer duration changes—the so-called Cenozoic climate decline (Figure 2). Temperatures showed a general tendency, though not steady or uninterrupted, to fall in many parts of the world. At the end of the Eocene (36 million years ago) there was a climatic shift so that in the Oligocene the climate of western Europe may have been more comparable to that of a region like the southeastern United States.

The warmth of the first half of the Tertiary (the Paleocene) in Britain had both local and global causes. At a local scale, Britain was 10°–12° farther south than today. At a global scale, the oceans and continents had a very different form, affecting the patterns of ocean currents and monsoon circulations, but there may have been much more elevated atmospheric carbon dioxide conditions (creating a greenhouse effect) and a marked reduction in the angle of tilt of the Earth's axis, which would have affected incoming solar radiation.

By Pliocene times (5.5 million years ago), the degree of cooling was such that a more temperate flora was present in the North Atlantic region, and at 2.4 million years ago glaciers started to develop in midlatitude areas and many of the world's deserts came into being.

The Quaternary. In the Quaternary period (beginning 1.8 million years ago), the gradual and uneven progression toward cooler conditions that had characterized the Earth during the Tertiary gave way to extraordinary climatic instability. Temperatures oscillated wildly from values similar to, or slightly higher than, today in interglacials to levels that were sufficiently cold to treble the volume of ice sheets on land during the glacials. Not only was the degree of change remarkable but so also, according to evidence from the sedimentary record retrieved from deep-sea cores, was the frequency of change. In all, there have been about seventeen glacial/interglacial cycles in the last 1.6 million years. The cycles tend to be characterized by a gradual buildup of ice volume (over a period of ca. 90,000 years), followed by a dramatic "termination" in only about 8,000 years. Furthermore, over the 3 or so million years dur-

THE VOSTOK, ANTARCTICA, ICE CORE

In January 1998 the Vostok project yielded the deepest ice core ever recovered, reaching a depth of 3,623 meters. This has allowed the extension of the ice record of atmospheric composition and climate to the past four glacial-interglacial cycles, a period of 420,000 years. Among the results from the analysis of this core are:

1. Present-day atmospheric burdens of carbon dioxide and methane seem to have been unprecedented over the past 420,000 years.
2. There is a strong correlation between atmospheric greenhouse gas concentrations and antarctic temperature.
3. There is a strong imprint of two orbital characteristics—obliquity and precession—in most of the climate time series.
4. For all four climate cycles, there is the same "sawtooth" sequence of a warm interglacial, followed by increasingly colder interstadial events, and ending with a rapid return toward the following interglacial.
5. The dust record preserved in the ice confirms that continental aridity, dust mobilization, and transport are more prevalent during glacial climates.
6. The Holocene, which has already lasted 11,000 years, is by far the largest stable warm period recorded in Antarctica during the past 420,000 years.

BIBLIOGRAPHY

Petit, J. R., et al. "Climate and Atmospheric History of the Past 420,000 Years from the Vostok Ice Core, Antarctica." *Nature* 399 (1999), 49–436.

—ANDREW S. GOUDIE

ing which humans have inhabited the Earth, conditions such as those we experience today have been relatively short-lived and atypical of the Quaternary on the whole (Bowen, 1978). Figure 3 illustrates the changes that have taken place over the last 850,000 years. [*See* Climate Change.]

The last glacial cycle reached its peak about 18,000 years ago, with ice sheets extending over Scandinavia to the northern German plain, over all but the south of Britain, and over North America to 39°N (Figure 4). To the south of the Scandinavian ice sheet was a tundra steppe underlain by permafrost, and forest was relatively sparse to the north of the Mediterranean.

Ice covered nearly one-third of the land area of the Earth, but the additional ice-covered area in the last glacial was almost all in the Northern Hemisphere, with no more than about 3 percent in the Southern Hemisphere. Nonetheless, substantial ice cover developed over Patagonia and New Zealand. The thickness of the now-vanished ice sheets may have exceeded 4 kilometers, with typical depths of 2–3 kilometers. The total ice-covered area at a typical glacial maximum was 40 million square kilometers. [*See* Glaciation.]

Highly important changes also took place in the state of the oceans. During the present interglacial conditions of the Holocene, the Atlantic is at least seasonally ice-free as far north as 78°N in the Norwegian Sea. This condition reflects the advection of warm water into this region by the Gulf Stream. During the last glacial maximum, however, the oceanic polar front probably lay at about 45°N, and north of this the ocean was mainly covered by sea ice during the winter.

The degree of temperature change that occurred over land was particularly great in the vicinity of the great ice sheets. The presence of permafrost in southern Britain suggests a temperature depression on the order of 15°C. Midlatitude areas probably witnessed a lesser decline—perhaps 5°–8°C was the norm—though in areas subject to maritime air masses, temperatures were more likely to have been reduced by 4°–5°C.

The transfer of large volumes of water from the oceans to the icecaps caused a global fall in sea levels. The degree of this worldwide (or eustatic) change at the time of glacial maxima is the cause of some debate but may have been of the order of 120–150 meters. [*See* Sea Level.]

In addition to their global effect, the ice sheets had a more localized effect on sea levels through the process of glacio-isostasy. They depressed the Earth's crust beneath them and caused some upward displacement in a surrounding peripheral prebulge. When the ice load was removed upon deglaciation, the reverse process occurred, and in North America parts of Laurentia have "popped up" by more than 300 meters during the Holocene.

The cold glacials had a multitude of impacts on the

A

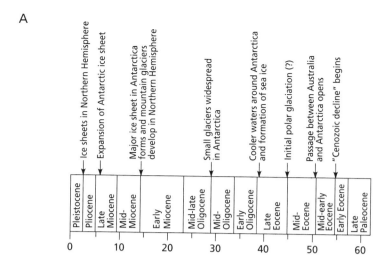

B

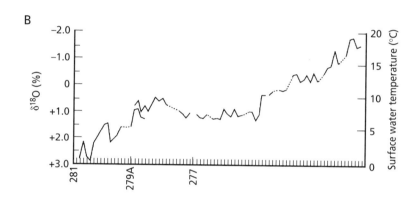

C

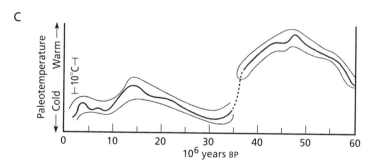

Paleoclimate. FIGURE 2. The Cenozoic Climate Decline.

(A) A generalized outline of significant events in the Cenozoic climate decline. (B) Oxygen isotopic data and paleotemperature indicated for planktonic foraminifera at three subantarctic sites (277, 279A, and 281). (C) Temperature changes calculated from oxygen source values of shells in the North Sea. (After Goudie, 1992. With permission of Oxford University Press.)

landscape. The ice sheets produced characteristic landform assemblages with cirques, arêtes, U-shaped valleys, *roches moutonnées*, and other forms. They also transformed drainage patterns, as the lacustrine landscapes of the Laurentian Shield and Scandinavia testify. Elsewhere, they deposited boulder clay and outwash gravels, some as sheets and some as distinctive land-

forms. Beyond the glacial limit fine particles blown from outwash plains settled to produce belts of loess in such areas as central Europe, Tajikistan, China, New Zealand, and the Mississippi Valley. [*See* Dust Storms.]

Areas equatorward of the great icecaps were not unaffected by the great cooling. The cyclone-bearing westerlies brought rain to what are now the arid lands of the

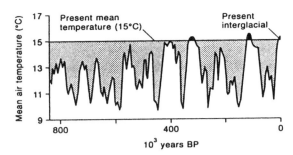

Paleoclimate. FIGURE 3. Temperature of the Earth for the last 850,000 years, as inferred from ice volume derived by oxygen isotope measurements from ice cores. (After Gates, 1993. With permission of Sinauer Associates.)

southwestern United States, transforming the current Great Salt Lake into a freshwater body—Lake Bonneville—the size of present-day Lake Michigan. Conversely, because the oceans were cooler, the tropical circulation was weaker, causing the Sahara, the Thar, and the Australian Deserts, with their associated dune fields, to expand. Large tracts of what is now savanna were transformed into sand sea, and the great rainforests of Amazonia and the Congo Basin were fragmented.

Stadials and Interstadials. Each glacial cycle had some complexity of form, with phases of intense glacial activity and advance, called *stadials*, being separated by periods of slightly greater warmth, called *interstadials*, when glacial retreat occurred. During the last glacial cy-

cle there were various interstadials, including a particularly marked one during the period 50,000–23,000 years BP, and some rather shorter ones nearer the beginning of the cycle.

Short, warm phases have been identified in ice-core records. Between 115,000 and 14,000 years ago, twenty-four of these have been recognized and have been called Dansgaard–Oeschger events. The nature and causes of such abrupt climatic fluctuations within glacials have been discussed by Adams et al. (1999).

The most extreme stadial of the last glaciation occurred about 20,000–18,000 years BP (the Last Glacial Maximum), and in Britain is known as the Dimlington stadial. Shortly thereafter, glaciers began to retreat only to advance briefly in the Younger Dryas stadial, about 12,000 years ago. [*See* Climate Change, *article on* Abrupt Climate Change.]

Some of the cold snaps during the glacials have been identified in the ocean cores through the evidence of iceberg-rafted debris. These have been termed Heinrich events (Andrews, 1998). At least seven *Heinrich events* occurred between 66,000 and 12,000 years ago.

Interglacials. In general terms, the Quaternary interglacials, though short-lived, appear to have been essentially similar in their climate, fauna, flora, and landforms to the Holocene interglacial in which we live today. One of the most important characteristics was that they witnessed the rapid retreat and decay of the great ice sheets and saw the replacements of tundra conditions by forest over the now temperate lands of the Northern Hemisphere. At their peak they may have been

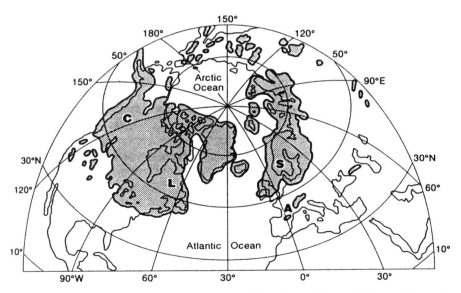

Paleoclimate. FIGURE 4. The possible maximum extent of glaciation in the Pleistocene in the Northern Hemisphere. C = Cordilleran ice; L = Laurentide ice; S = Scandinavian ice; and A = Alpine ice. (After Goudie, 1992. With permission of Oxford University Press.)

a degree or two warmer than now. In recent years considerable information on conditions in the last interglacial (the Eemian) has been obtained from ice cores extracted from polar icecaps. In particular, their stable isotopic composition provides a means of calculating past atmospheric temperatures. The Greenland Ice Core Project (GRIP) managed to drill through 3,029 meters of ice under the summit of the Greenland ice sheet, and the core dates back to around 250,000 years ago. During the Eemian there may have been some very rapid, indeed abrupt, climate changes (GRIP, 1993).

The general sequence of vegetational development during an interglacial has been described for northwest Europe by Birks (1986). The first, or *cryocratic* phase, represents cold glacial conditions, with sparse assemblages of pioneer plants growing on base-rich skeletal mineral soils under dry, continental conditions. In the second, or *protocratic* phase, there is the onset of interglacial conditions. Rising temperatures allow the base-loving, shade-intolerant herbs, shrubs, and trees to migrate and expand quickly to form widespread species-rich grasslands, scrub, and open woodlands, which grow on unleached, fertile soils with a still low humus content. In the third, or *mesocratic* phase, temperate deciduous forest and fertile, brown-earth soils develop under warm conditions, allowing the expansion of shade-giving forest genera such as *Quercus*, *Ulmus*, *Fraxinus*, and *Corylus*, followed by slower immigrants such as *Fagus* and *Carpinus*. In the fourth and last retrogressive phases, the *telocratic* phase, soil deterioration and climatic decline lead to the development of open conifer-dominated woods, ericaceous heaths, and bogs growing on less fertile humus-rich podzols and peats.

The Transition from Late Glacial Times. The maximum of the last glacial, as we have already seen, occurred at around 18,000 years BP. Studies of the oxygen isotope composition of deep-sea core sediments suggest that deglaciation started at around 15,000–14,500 years BP in the North Atlantic and at 16,500–13,000 years BP in the Southern Ocean (Bard et al., 1990). The years between the maximum and the beginning of the Holocene are usually termed the *Late Glacial*, and they were marked by various minor stadials and interstadials.

The character, identification, and correlation of the Late Glacial interstadials is a matter still in need of clarification (Anderson, 1997). The classic threefold division into two cold zones (I and III) separated by a milder instadial (II) emanates from a type section at Allerød, north of Copenhagen, where an organic lake mud was exposed between an upper and lower clay, both of which contained pollen of *Dryas octopetula*, a plant tolerant of severely cold climates. The lake muds contained a cool temperate flora including some tree birches, and

the milder stage that they represented was called the Allerød interstadial. The interstadial itself, and the following Younger Dryas temperature reversal, are sometimes called the Allerød oscillation. The dating of the Younger Dryas used to be to between 11,000 and 10,000 years BP but now is thought to have started at around 12,700 years BP and to have lasted for 1,300 years. The Younger Dryas stadial was a time when glaciers readvanced in Scotland—the so-called Loch Lomond Readvance—and it may have been caused by a rapid cooling of the ocean caused by the breaking up of large ice shelves from the Arctic (Ruddiman and McIntyre, 1981), or by a sudden influx of meltwater from the Laurentide ice sheet into the Atlantic via the St. Lawrence system, causing salinity changes in the ocean. These in turn affected the seawater density and currents and thus the climate (Broecker and Denton, 1989). [*See* Younger Dryas.]

The Holocene. The ending of the Late Glacial period was not the end of substantial environmental change. Indeed, as the Holocene progressed, the impact of climatic change was augmented as a cause of environmental fluctuation by the increasing role of humans (Roberts, 1998).

The warming in postglacial times set off the successive return of species of trees with different tolerances of cold and different powers of colonization to lands that had been under ice or dominated by open tundra (Birks, 1990). If we consider Europe, pollen analysis suggests that at 12,000 years BP *Pinus* (pine) was mainly in southern and eastern parts, but by 6,000 years BP it was abundant in northern, central, and Mediterranean Europe but absent from much of the western European lowlands. *Quercus* (oak) spread northward from southern Europe and reached its maximum range limits by 6,000 years BP, as did *Ulmus* (elm), *Corylus* (hazel), and *Tilia* (lime).

For comparison, Bernado and Webb (1977) have produced a summary of vegetational changes in the northeast of North America. As Figure 5 shows, there have been major changes in the relative importance of spruce, pine, oak, and herb pollen (characteristic of temperate grasslands). The largest changes occurred in the early Holocene, between 11,000 and 7,000 years BP. Especially notable was the decline of the spruce between 11,000 and 8,000 years BP as it gradually moved northward. Another important feature of the area's Holocene vegetational history has been the fluctuating position of the boundary between prairie and forest. The signs of prairie development in the western portion of the Midwest are visible in the pollen record over 11,000 years ago, as the vast region formerly occupied by the Late Glacial boreal forest began to shrink. The largest eastward shift of the prairie took place between 10,000 and 9,000 years BP, and it reached its maximum eastward ex-

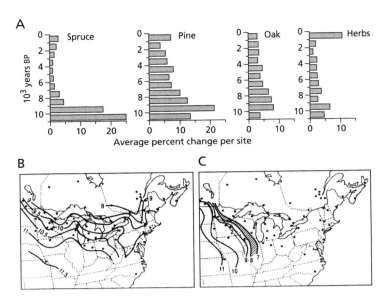

Paleoclimate. Figure 5. Holocene Vegetation Change in Eastern North America.

(A) Graph depicting the average percentage change per site, between each 1,000-year level from 11,000 BP to the present, for spruce, pine, oak, and herb pollen. The figure shows important shifts in the amount of change these major pollen groups underwent during the Holocene. Values were obtained by summing the total changes (regardless of signs) seen from all mapped sites and then dividing by the number of sites. (B) Isochrones plotting the time, in thousands of years BP, when spruce pollen declined to below 15 percent. (C) Isochrones in thousands of years BP, illustrating the movements of the prairie-forest ecotone. The position of the prairie border is based on ispoll maps for herb pollen. Shaded areas show the region over which the prairie retreated after reaching its maximum postglacial extent at 7,000 BP. (After Bernado and Webb, 1977. With permission of Academic Press.)

tent 8,000 years BP. The rate at which plants were able to migrate in response to Holocene warming in the eastern part of North America ranges from 100 meters per year for chestnut to 400 meters per year for jack and red pines (Gates, 1993).

Some portions of the Holocene may have been slightly warmer than the present, and terms like *climatic optimum* have been used to denote the existence of a possible phase of mid-Holocene warmth, when conditions may have been 1°–2°C warmer than now. There may also have been a medieval warm period between 750 and 1300 CE. [*See* Medieval Climatic Optimum.] There have also been times that have been rather colder than today, however, as is made evident by phases of glacial readvance (neoglaciation) in alpine valleys. The latest of these was "Little Ice Age," which peaked around 1700 CE and ended toward the end of the nineteenth century (Grove, 1988). [*See* Little Ice Age in Europe.]

Fluctuations of climate also occurred in lower latitudes, and of especial importance for vegetation and human activities was the early to mid-Holocene pluvial, which transformed the Sahara (Ritchie et al., 1985). The hyperarid belt more or less disappeared for one or two millennia before 7,000 years BP. The northern limit of the Sahel shifted about 1,000 kilometers to the north between 18,000 and 6,000 years BP, and about 600 kilometers to the south between 6,000 years BP and the present. [*See* Holocene in the Sahara.]

Conclusions. The history of the Earth demonstrates that climates have been highly subject to variation through time at a range of temporal scales. The precision and resolution of paleoclimatic reconstruction becomes greater as the present is approached. The causes of these changes are extremely complex and include changes in output of radiation from the Sun; changes in the altitude, extent, and configurations of the continents and oceans in response to plate tectonic activity; changes in the nature of the Earth's orbit with respect to the Sun; and changes in the gas and aerosol content of the atmosphere. Our ability to explain particular climatic changes becomes increasingly speculative as we go back in time. Given the degree, frequency, and (in some cases) the abruptness of changes, it is certain that they have played a major role in the evolution and extinction of organisms and that, latterly, they have impinged on human affairs. For example, the transition from Pleistocene glacial to Holocene interglacial may have been a stimulus for domestication and may have contributed to the demise of some of the Earth's megafauna around 11,000 years ago.

[*See also* Albedo; Atmosphere Structure and Evolution; Biosphere; Carbon Dioxide; Earth History; Earth

Motions; Evolution of Life; Ocean Dynamics; Plate Tectonics; Sun; *and* System Dynamics.]

BIBLIOGRAPHY

Adams, J., M. Maslin, and E. Thomas. "Sudden Climate Transition during the Quaternary." *Progress in Physical Geography* 23 (1999), 1–36.

Anderson, D. "Younger Dryas Research and Its Implications for Understanding Abrupt Climatic Change." *Progress in Physical Geography* 21 (1997), 230–249.

Andrews, J. T. "Abrupt Changes (Heinrich Events) in Late Quaternary North Atlantic Environments." *Journal of Quaternary Science* 13 (1998), 3–16.

Bard, E., L. D. Labergrue, J. J. Pichon, M. Labracherie, M. Arnold, J. Duprat, J. Moyes, and J. C. Duplessy. "The Last Deglaciation in the Southern and Northern Hemispheres." In *Geological History of the Polar Oceans: Arctic versus Antarctic*, edited by V. Bleil and J. Thiede, 405–415. Dordrecht: Kluwer, 1990.

Bernado, J. C., and T. Webb. "Changing Patterns in the Holocene Pollen Record of Northeastern North America: A Mapped Summary." *Quaternary Research* 8 (1977), 64–96.

Birks, H. J. B. "Quaternary Biotic Changes in Terrestrial and Lacustrine Environments, with Particular Reference to Northwest Europe." In *Handbook of Holocene Paleoecology and Paleohydrology*, edited by B. E. Bergland, 3–65. Chichester, U.K.: Wiley, 1986.

———. "Changes in Vegetation and Climate during the Holocene in Europe." In *Landscape-Ecological Impact of Climatic Change*, edited by M. M. Boer and R. S. de Groot, pp. 133–158. Amsterdam, 1990.

Bowen, D. Q. *Quaternary Geology.* Oxford: Pergamon Press, 1978.

Bradley, R. S. *Quaternary Paleoclimatology.* Boston: Allen and Unwin, 1985.

Broecker, W. S., and G. H. Denton. "The Role of the Ocean–Atmospheric Reorganizations in Glacial Cycles." *Geochimice et cosmochimice acta* 53 (1989), 2465–2501.

Cronin, T. M. *Principles of Paleoclimatology.* New York: Columbia University Press, 1999.

Crowley, T. J., and G. R. North. *Paleoclimatology.* New York: Oxford University Press, 1991.

Gates, D. M. *Climate Change and Its Biological Consequences.* Sunderland, Mass.: Sinauer, 1993.

Goudie, A. *Environmental Change.* 3d ed. Oxford: Oxford University Press, 1992.

GRIP (Greenland Ice-Core Project) Members. "Climate Instability during the Last Interglacial Recorded in the GRIP Ice Core." *Nature* 364 (1993), 203–207.

Grove, J. M. *The Little Ice Age.* London and New York: Methuen, 1988.

Lowe, J. J., and M. J. C. Walker. *Reconstructing Quaternary Environments.* 2d ed. Harlow, U.K.: Longmans, 1997.

Ritchie, J. C., C. H. Gyles, and C. V. Haynes. "Sediment and Pollen Evidence for an Early to Mid-Holocene Humid Period in the Eastern Sahara." *Nature* 314 (1985), 352–355.

Roberts, N. *The Holocene.* 2d ed. Oxford: Blackwell, 1998.

Ruddiman, W. F., and A. McIntyre. "The North Atlantic Ocean during the Last Deglaciation." *Paleogeography, Paleoclimatology, Paleoecology* 35 (1981), 145–214.

Williams, M. A. J., D. Dunkerly, P. De Dekker, P. Kershaw, and J. Chappell. *Quaternary Environments.* 2d ed. London: Arnold, 1998.

Wilson, R. C. L., S. A. Drury, and J. L. Chapman. *The Great Ice Age:* *Climate Change and Life.* London: Routledge; New York: Open University, 2000.

—Andrew S. Goudie

PALEOMAGNETISM. *See* Dating Methods; *and* Plate Tectonics.

PALYNOLOGY. *See* Climate Change, *article on* Climate Change Detection; *and* Climate Reconstruction.

PARKS AND NATURAL PRESERVES

[*This entry consists of two articles*, Historical Overview *and* Ecological Value. *The first article reviews the history and roles of parks and their significance in conservation of biological diversity. The second article explains the distinction between parks and preserves.*]

Historical Overview

Parks and preserves are social and cultural institutions as well as natural entities. The word *park* derives from Old French and Middle English—*parc* meant an enclosure for hunting—and the original parks were the hunting preserves of Persian royalty in Asia Minor between 550 and 350 BCE. Another antecedent was the landscaped garden estate of eighteenth-century England—a privatized space dominated by a pastoral idea of nature. A further influence on modern versions, the city park, is rooted in the ancient Greek *agora*, a place of public relaxation and shaded recreation.

Public access to exclusive parklands in western Europe, part of a response to industrialization and urbanization and also a function of democratization, began with the opening of London's royal parks in the eighteenth century. Victoria Park in London's East End was the first park of any kind specifically acquired and designed for public use (1842). But Birkenhead Park near Liverpool, established soon after, is better known because, with its informal style, it inspired the world's most famous example: New York City's Central Park (1861). North America's urban park movement was related to the "rural" cemetery phenomenon. From the 1830s, urbanites frequented cemeteries on city outskirts to stroll and picnic. The prototype was Mount Auburn, near Boston, and by the 1970s, cemeteries constituted 35 percent of the open space within Greater Boston. These enclosures also functioned as de facto wildlife sanctuaries; a 1974 study located ninety-five species of bird and twenty species of mammal.

National Parks. The national park, however, dominates current conceptions. It is one of ten major categories of nature conservation recognized by the International Union for Conservation of Nature and Natural Resources (IUCN) in 1978 (protected area category number 2). The IUCN definition stresses the national park's ecological role, referring to preservation "in a natural state" of "representative samples of physiographic regions, biotic communities and . . . species in danger of extinction to provide ecological stability," and envisaged parks being established in ecosystems "not materially altered by human exploitation and occupation." Yet the conservation of ecological diversity is a relatively recent (largely post-1960s) objective. Moreover, though over a hundred countries now boast national parks, many fall far short of IUCN ideals.

The chunk of the royal forest of Fontainebleau near Paris assigned as a nature reserve and public recreational area in 1853 (complete with marked hiking trails) was an additional precursor, but the term *national park* was first employed in the proclamation of Royal National Park near Sydney, Australia (1879). Both Canada and New Zealand had reserved national parks before the actual words were first used in the United States (1899). These technicalities aside, the national park as idea and institution is rightly associated with the United States, many nations being inspired directly by U.S. example. The first national park in all but name was Yellowstone (1872), which differed from previous parks by virtue of its wilder scenery and larger size, the greater measure of public access envisaged, and its ownership by the national government.

The pioneering wave of parks served as surrogates for "Old World" cultural heritage, sources of national pride, and outlets for a desire for contact with nature in its more rugged guises. Early parks encompassed lands that possessed what later generations would recognize as wilderness value and biodiversity. But their main aim was to protect "monumentalist" scenery from private acquisition or exploitation by extractive industries in the form of "pleasuring ground(s) for the benefit and enjoyment of the people" (to quote the Yellowstone Park Act). Economic development was by no means proscribed, but roads and resort facilities were privileged over logging and mining. During the 1960s, African national parks became particularly vital components of national economies. By 1968, Murchison Falls generated 70 percent of Uganda's tourist revenue.

Before the 1930s, the only serious contenders for park status beyond Africa (where wildlife spectacle was more often the *raison d'être*) were dramatic topographies—often alpine. Florida's Everglades National Park (authorized in 1934) marked a sharp departure: biological splendor was placed before scenic feast. Yet Everglades also involved incomplete ecosystem protection;

park flora and fauna remained affected by drainage and other agricultural policies beyond. Political and economic requirements usually dictated boundaries, bestowing "island" status. Some African parks and preserves resorted to elephant culling in the late 1970s and early 1980s to deal with overpopulation in confined spaces. Wildlife in Kenya's Amboseli National Park (1947) migrates seasonally onto the lands of Maasai pastoralists.

The birthplace of Europe's first national parks in the early 1900s was northern Scandinavia. This was the continent's last region largely devoid of agriculture, however, and it was hard to replicate similar parks elsewhere in Europe. According to IUCN specifications regarding ownership, environmental conditions, degree of protection, and range of permissible activities, the nine national parks designated in England and Wales during the 1950s are neither national nor parks. These patches of high moorland and mountain, which deviate radically from the central principle of public ownership, encompass not only towns, roads, farms, reservoirs, and quarries but even a nuclear power plant and live artillery ranges, catering to more powerful constituencies than conservationists and recreationists (not least the military). The IUCN classifies them as "Protected Landscapes."

Game Preserves and Other Protective Units. The distinction between nature preserves (IUCN protected area category 1) and national parks, often blurred, has been clearest in the former Soviet Union. *Zapovedniki* (meaning "forbidden areas"), were identified in the 1920s specifically to protect rare plants and animals, and use was restricted to ecological study (a major innovation). *Zapovedniki* served as specimens of healthy environments to guide land usages elsewhere. Soviet national parks—sites for outdoor amusement—were installed in the 1960s in response to public pressure for recreational access to *zapovedniki*.

Wildlife preservation was a concern in some national parks during the formative years, and the roles of wildlife preserve and national park have overlapped. Italy's first national park, Gran Paradiso (established in 1922), hitherto a royal hunting reserve, aimed to protect alpine ibex. But wildlife refuges were essentially game reserves, spaces where production of economically valuable species or those prized by sports hunters was maximized regardless of cost to predators. Late-nineteenth-century sportsmen in North America and sub-Saharan Africa spearheaded efforts to secure their sport's future by protecting birds and mammals they hoped would spill over into hunting areas. These reserves and refuges were generally smaller than parks (perhaps limited to a few acres covering breeding grounds) and not intended for recreation.

Parks and preserves usually occupied emptied rather

than empty spaces. Medieval Europe's peasantry raged against hunting reserves that annulled their standard activities. Central Park displaced the shacks and piggeries of Irish immigrants, while national parks such as Glacier and Yosemite were carved out of the domain of American Indians. From Italy's Abruzzo National Park (established in 1923) to Amboseli, locals have perceived them as colonial impositions catering to outside interests, resenting the loss of opportunities to graze livestock, cut timber, and hunt. The tensions characterizing relations with locals were exemplified by the controversy in India over the creation of tiger reserves that excluded all human use and occupation. Project Tiger (launched 1973) was highly effective; India's tigers increased from 1,827 in 1972 to 3,015 in 1979. But the project also displaced forty villages, affecting six thousand people and their livestock. Villagers denounced it as a collaboration between discredited local elites and international wildlife conservationists that condemned them to perpetual underdevelopment. Resentment was inflamed by a spate of killings by tigers in the late 1970s and early 1980s (conversion of grassland to sugar-cane fields south of Dudhwa National Park impinged on tiger habitat).

Parks and preserves have become increasingly sensitive to the interests of indigenes. In the late 1970s, Aborigines in Australia's Northern Territory leased their lands to create Kakadu National Park, which incorporated their customary subsistence pursuits. The mission statements of the ten Alaskan parks, preserves, and monuments designated in 1980 refer to the protection of both natural values and traditional cultures by allowing gathering, fishing, and hunting to continue. Native hostility gives way to a new appreciation of parks and preserves as a valuable means to protect the natural resources that constitute their lifeblood.

Conflicts between Use and Conservation. Conflicts have also stemmed from the parks' equivocal dual mandate of preservation and public access. The challenge faced by early managers in the developed world, that of providing adequate facilities to persuade people to visit in numbers sufficient to ensure their viability, has been supplanted by that of guaranteeing the survival of treasures in danger of being "loved to death." Though the 1972–1982 period saw unprecedented expansion (new units boosted the protected area by over 80 percent), the "use versus preservation" dilemma intensified. In the 1970s, twenty-five thousand people climbed Japan's Mount Fujiyama daily, and permits and quotas for rafting through Grand Canyon were introduced. Unregulated rock climbing in the German-Luxembourg Nature Park (established in 1965) nearly wiped out a rare fern, and a surfeit of canoeists threatened its freshwater pearl mussel. Whereas rangers in Africa might risk their lives to protect endangered species such as the white rhinoceros from poachers, their counterparts in the United States formulate plans to ban private vehicles, replacing them with free, nonpolluting electric minibuses.

[*See also* Biological Diversity; Biomes; Carrying Capacity; Wilderness; *and* World Heritage Sites.]

BIBLIOGRAPHY

Anderson, D., and R. Grove, eds. *Conservation in Africa: People, Policies and Practice.* Cambridge: Cambridge University Press, 1987. Part 2 (pp. 103–186) contains essays analyzing relations between wildlife, parks, and pastoralists in Ethiopia, Kenya, and Tanzania in a historical context.

Beinart, W., and P. Coates. "Nature Reserves and National Parks." Chapter 5 in *Environment and History: The Taming of Nature in the USA and South Africa.* London: Routledge, 1995. A concise, properly integrated comparative history of parks and reserves in the United States and South Africa.

Carruthers, J. *The Kruger National Park: A Social and Political History.* Pietermaritzburg, South Africa: University of Natal Press, 1995. This examination of South Africa's premier national park (established in 1926) situates its story within the wider currents of South African history, paying particular attention to relations with local peoples.

Federation of Nature and National Parks of Europe (FNNPE). *Loving Them to Death? Sustainable Tourism in Europe's Nature and National Parks.* Grafenau, Germany: FNNPE, 1993. A watchdog body's report on visitation pressures and proposed solutions.

MacEwen, A., and M. MacEwen. *National Parks: Conservation or Cosmetics?* London: Allen and Unwin, 1982. Part 1 discusses the origins of parks in England and Wales. The rest of the book is a vigorous indictment of their inadequacies. *Greenprints for the Countryside? The Story of Britain's National Parks* (London: Allen and Unwin, 1987) is a popularized and updated version focusing on developments since 1981.

Machlis, G. E., and D. L. Tichnell. *The State of the World's Parks: An International Assessment for Resource Management, Policy, and Research.* Boulder, Colo.: Westview Press, 1985. The first systematic treatment of the various threats facing parks in the early 1980s, based on data from 135 parks in over fifty countries.

McNeely, J. A., and K. R. Miller, eds. *National Parks, Conservation, and Development: The Role of Protected Areas in Sustaining Society.* Washington, D.C.: Smithsonian Institution Press, 1984. Edited by members of the Commission on National Parks and Protected Areas, International Union for Conservation of Nature and Natural Resources (IUCN), these are the proceedings of the Third World Congress on National Parks, Bali, Indonesia, 1982. The second world congress (held in Grand Teton/Yellowstone National Parks, 1972) also resulted in a useful publication: H. Elliott, ed., *Second World Conference on National Parks* (Morges, Switzerland: IUCN, 1974).

Nash, R. "The Confusing Birth of National Parks." *The Michigan Quarterly Review* 16 (1977), 216–226. Examines Australian claims and seeks to explain why the term *national park* was not attached to Yellowstone in 1872.

———. "International Concepts of Wilderness Preservation." Chapter 3 in Hendee, J. C., et al. *Wilderness Management,* edited by J. C. Hendee et al. Washington, D.C.: U.S. Department of Agriculture, Forest Service, 1978. A survey of attitudes to wilderness and wilderness area management from Japan to East Africa that contains considerable insight into national parks and their historical backgrounds.

Nelson, J. G., R. F. Needham, and D. L. Mann, eds. *International Experience with National Parks and Related Reserves*. Waterloo, Ontario: University of Waterloo, Department of Geography, 1978. Containing individual papers on a range of countries and types of protected unit (from Israel to Iran) and a wealth of figures and tables, this is the first comparative study of the purposes, effects, and management of nature reserves, past, present, and future.

Runte, A. *National Parks: The American Experience*. 2d ed. Lincoln: University of Nebraska Press, 1987. Still the most authoritative history of U.S. parks from the standpoint of cultural and intellectual history. For an insider's critique of the U.S. Park Service's ecological policies, see Richard Sellars, *Preserving Nature in the National Parks: A History*. New Haven: Yale University Press, 1997.

Waycott, A. *National Parks of Western Europe*. Southampton, U.K.: Inklon, 1983. A popular guide to eighty-four parks in fifteen countries that contains snippets of useful historical information.

—PETER COATES

Ecological Value

Today in parks and preserves we expect to continue our traditional uses of: harvesting timber and using nature's products (for example, bark and seeds); hunting game animals and grazing domesticated animals, which may be indigenous or introduced species; researching, studying, and photographing plants and animals in a "living museum"; hiking as individuals or conducting tour groups led by amateur or professional guides; and continuing our lives without visiting an area, but content in the knowledge that it is there for others to enjoy and for the benefit of future generations. However, all of these uses are dependent on maintaining viable ecological functions of parks and preserves and ensuring that biological diversity is protected. We also need to understand the dynamics of natural systems and the influence of human-induced environmental change.

The Ecological Function of Parks and Preserves. Parks and preserves provide important ecological functions that make them an indispensable element in the conservation of global biodiversity. First, parks and preserves play significant roles in maintaining those ecological processes that depend on natural ecosystems, such as purifying water and air by natural ecological processes. In addition, the natural functioning of nutrient cycles and energy flows is facilitated by parks and preserves. Some of these products may also move outside the protected area and benefit the surrounding landscape, for example, the movement of a wildlife population or the flow of rivers through catchments. The role of protected areas in maintaining ecological processes is crucial since it is almost impossible to study ecological relationships within ecosystems that are un-

der constant stress from human activities in areas beyond the boundaries of parks and preserves.

Second, parks and preserves help to preserve species diversity and genetic variations within species. Protected areas therefore play an important part in preserving representative samples of plant and animal populations. This role is especially important when considering global change, since genetically poor species are highly vulnerable to environmental changes. Hence parks and preserves help prevent irreversible damage to natural ecosystems.

Third, parks and preserves provide benchmarks by which the impact of humans on the environment can be better understood and compared. Natural or near-natural parks and preserves provide ecological baselines for measuring change both within parks and in nearby areas.

Finally, protected areas maintain the productive processes of ecosystems and safeguard habitats critical for the sustainable use of species. Thus the natural productive processes in parks and preserves can be used as models for developing sustainable utilization strategies outside park boundaries.

Our expectations of activities and opportunities in parks, however, are changing as technology changes. For example, the use of four-wheel-drive vehicles has increased the ability to intrude into previously inaccessible landscapes, with resultant effects such as weed and pest introduction, erosion of tracks, and petrochemical pollution of waterways. Now we have the capacity to "tread more lightly" by using helicopters to reach remote places, even though there are new adverse effects (such as noise). The development of new technology often means that traditional approaches to calculating carrying capacity of areas need to be rethought.

Other changes are occurring because indigenous people want recognition of the need to link their identity to place and history. They also want to be partners in managing parks and preserves or species of importance to their traditional ways of life.

Business is becoming increasingly involved in management of protected areas—concessions to provide transport, food, and accommodation; revenue-generating activities along with operational services such as management of water supply, sewerage, and road/path systems. Sponsorship of places and species for protection or research is also important to cash-strapped government management systems.

Effects of Human Activities. Some activities have local or regional effects on the environment: for example, individual lakes polluted by boating activity, poor management of facilities, and overharvesting of local species. However, environmental effects on national parks and preserves are becoming increasingly global in nature as the Earth's landscapes are extensively transformed, including systemic changes in water, vegetation, soil, atmosphere, and energy and material flows. Collectively, these changes are referred to as *global change*. [*See* Global Change.] Global change should not be equated with climate change, since the former encompasses both changes in climate and large-scale changes in land use associated with industrialization, urbanization, and large-scale agriculture. Major landscape changes and transformations have associated environmental consequences, which are discussed in terms of their effects on the world's biomes (see Table 1). [*See* Biomes.]

Global change presents enormous challenges to the conservation of parks and preserves and to the protection of biodiversity generally. While we are already observing the effects of landscape change on parks and preserves, the impacts of climatic change on these protected areas are generally only predictions (for example, the prediction that a 1°C change in temperature is equivalent to a 2° change in latitude in the midlatitudes). As more land is exploited and suffers land use change due to population pressure, parks and preserves are becoming increasingly insular, semi-isolated "habitat islands" in a sea of human-dominated or human-altered landscapes. This trend is expected to intensify as global population increases. Possible impacts on parks and preserves from the insularization process include elimination of potential sources of immigrant species, a reduction in immigrant species by conversion of natural landscapes between habitat patches and preserves, and the removal of vital resources outside reserve boundaries upon which species depend for survival. The insularization process may also create a situation in which much of the world's terrestrial biota is confined to national parks and preserves.

Predictions from scientists investigating the implications of climate change for species survival suggest that the resulting changes in habitats from climate change would cause the ranges of many species to shift outside the boundaries of parks and refuges now established to protect them. For instance, climatic changes in the drier critical Mediterranean regions in southern Europe, the

Parks and Natural Preserves: Ecological Value. TABLE 1. Effects of Global Change

GLOBAL PROCESS	ENVIRONMENTAL EFFECTS	AREAS/SPECIES MOST AT RISK
Global warming	• Latitudinal biome shift • Altitudinal biome shift • Sea level rise • Increased sea surface temperatures • Precipitation changes	• Tundra and wet coastal tundra • Alpine areas, needle forests, coastal wetlands • Low islands, lowland wetlands, estuarine areas, coral reefs • Coral reefs, cold waters • Lakes, wetlands, estuarine areas
Ozone depletion	• Changes in ultraviolet radiation	• Semi-arid regions
Industrialization	• Acid rain discharges • Discharge of toxic emissions/particulates • Distortions to nitrogen cycle • Eutrophication of wetlands and lakes • Disposal of waste	• Northern America • Northern Europe • North America, Japan, Europe, Australia, Southeast Asia
Urbanization	• Vehicle emissions • Reduction in local water tables • Local temperature • Increased demand for landfill areas • Increase in transport space (roads, airports, container yards)	• Forests and natural areas • Flooding of lakes, wetlands, estuarine, and instream areas • Natural areas within and nearby
Agricultural industry	• Mono-cropping, double-cropping • Poisoning of air, water, and soil from pesticides/herbicides/weedicides • Hydrological cycle disrupted • Nitrogen cycle disrupted • Die back in forests • Eutrophication of freshwater bodies • Increased demand for water	• Rangelands, plains, coastal plains • Lakes, wetlands, rivers; poisoning of birds of prey, seabirds, and carnivores • Semi-arid areas, lowlands, plains • Europe, North America, Canada • Temperate and semi-arid lowlands
Deforestation	• Increased runoff • Increased sediment production • Loss of natural habitat • Decrease in biodiversity	• Tropical forests of Central and South America • Dry forests of South Asia, Africa, and Pacific Islands

Levant, and North Africa could accelerate the desertification process, causing a rapid shift of the subdeserts and desert biomes far into the Mediterranean region of Israel and elsewhere. A. P. Dobson (1996) points out that climatic changes may already be apparent in the Everglades National Park in Florida, where the park loses 25 square kilometers of area for every 30 centimeters of mean sea level rise. As a result, endangered marshland species of the park are being trapped between the rising sea and the large human settlements located inland.

It is certain that species and ecosystems contained within protected areas will be affected by climate change (for example, since many protected areas are now "islands" of habitat to which species are closely adapted, climate change could cause extinctions among reserve species without being compensated by immigrating "new" species). It is also unrealistic to expect boundaries of existing protected areas to change very much because they are usually surrounded by more intensive human land uses that limit changes.

Conserving Biodiversity in Parks and Preserves. The protection of habitats is considered the best approach to protecting species and thus conserving global biodiversity. Most nations have established legal means for protecting habitats that are important for conserving biodiversity, and these protected areas include national parks and preserves. The growth in the number and area of formally protected areas during the past thirty years has been considerable, although the rate of growth has slowed significantly since 1980. J. A. McNeely and J. Harrison (1994) have compiled a detailed inventory of formally protected areas for the World Conservation Union (IUCN) and classified them in terms of international criteria.

The extent of protection varies greatly from one region to another: from 2.8 percent of land area in North Africa and the Middle East to 12.6 percent in North America. Although these percentages are regional generalizations and therefore conceal variations within a region, there are significant gaps in the extent of protected areas and in the protection of global biodiversity. For instance, in *Global Biodiversity Assessment* (Heywood and Watson, 1996), several authors estimate that the total worldwide extent of protected areas needs to be increased by at least three times if global biodiversity is to be managed over the long term in an environmentally sound way.

Furthermore, efforts by the IUCN to establish a global protected-area system that would ensure adequate representation of the full range of biome types have shown that particular attention should be paid to further development of protected areas in temperate grassland regions and in the major lake systems. Studies of the extent of parks and preserves in South America and East Africa have shown that the area of land set aside to protect biodiversity is only a small fraction of the total area of natural habitat (including tropical forests, savannas, and wetlands) that is being converted to agriculture or harvested for timber. Furthermore, most of the parks and preserves in these continents are only around 10–30 square kilometers in size, and some of the largest parks and preserves in those areas are located in desert or mountain areas that contain unique collections of species but at very low densities. Dobson believes that only 3.5 percent of those parks and preserves and only 5–10 percent of national parks in tropical areas may be large enough to maintain their present level of biodiversity. Such statistics highlight the need for more national parks and preserves of sufficient size throughout the world for the protection of global biodiversity. [*See* Biological Diversity.]

Much of the current research has concentrated on terrestrial biodiversity, despite the fact that 71 percent of the Earth's surface and much of its biodiversity is found in oceans, coastal waters, and estuaries. About 60 percent of the human population lives within 60 kilometers of the coast, and much of the oceans' productive coastal margin has been strongly affected by human exploitation (for example, many marine fisheries are unsustainable because of overexploitation). The critical need to conserve and sustainably use marine and coastal biological resources was recognized by IUCN, the United Nations Environment Programme, and the World Wildlife Fund (World Conservation Union, 1991). All of the marine regions have inadequate representation of biogeographic variation and detailed levels of biodiversity. For instance, in the Mediterranean region, where only 6 percent of the coastline is protected, some of the most crucial ecosystems—the seagrass meadows and the wetlands—urgently require protection (McNeely and Harrison, 1994).

However, the setting aside of parks and preserves, both terrestrial and marine, does not necessarily protect biodiversity. Many parks and wilderness areas are bordered by other public lands, which are open to consumptive development activities, or by unregulated private lands. Since this trend is expected to intensify, parks and preserves will succeed only to the extent that the areas themselves are managed effectively, and to the extent that the management of the surrounding landscape is compatible with the objectives of the protected areas. This will require an integrated approach to the management of parks and preserves in which protected areas become part of larger regional schemes to ensure biological and social sustainability.

Integrated management would provide for the successful protection of marine biodiversity. Often, coastal environmental and resource policies and management approaches have concentrated on specific activities and resources or the environment generally, and they have therefore failed to reflect the linkages between all issues.

AGRICULTURAL LANDSCAPE
Existing Patches and Corridors

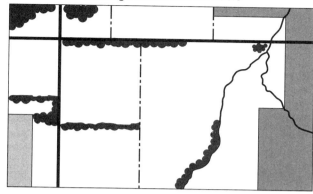

Proposed Patches and Corridors

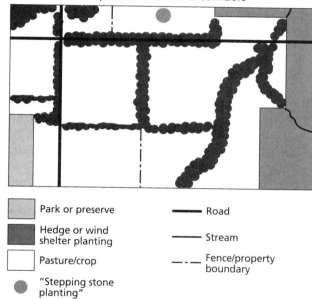

Park or preserve   Road

Hedge or wind
shelter planting   Stream

Pasture/crop   Fence/property
                                    boundary
"Stepping stone
planting"

Parks and Natural Preserves: Ecological Value. FIGURE 1.
Making Connections: Integrated Landscape Management.

Integrated management aims to address the conflicting uses and interrelationships between physical processes and human activities, and to promote linkages and cooperation between coastal activities among different domains. This approach will therefore facilitate the sustainable use of coastal and marine resources while providing for the protection of marine biodiversity.

In recognition of the issues associated with global change, other approaches for the integrated management of biodiversity have been offered that require protected areas to be managed not as isolated systems, but as part of the whole landscape. The ecosystem management approach, for example, requires park and preserve managers to shift away from setting aside special

sites toward the creation of interconnected systems linking various types of conservation areas along protected corridors. The integrated management of protected areas and their surrounding landscapes is crucial because the ecological health of a park depends on the natural processes in its surroundings near and far.

Integrated Approaches to Landscape Management. Examples of integrated systems include the "Multiple Use Modules" suggested by R. F. Noss and A. Y. Cooperrider (1994), in which a graduation of buffer zones around reserves can insulate natural areas from external influences, and "greenways" consisting of landscape linkages designed to connect open spaces form protected corridors that may follow natural or man-made terrain features and embrace ecological, cultural, and recreational amenities where possible. The application of the greenway concept is shown in the European Ecological Network, in which national networks of ecologically important areas are being built throughout Europe so that the individual protected areas are strengthened and connected. All approaches require consideration of landscape connections at various scales, as demonstrated in Figure 1.

In Australia, subnational governments are adopting the bioregion as the unit of management in planning. The basis of the bioregion is one whole or several nested ecosystems that are identified by the community and government and managed via a collaborative planning process. The key criteria of success are the extent to which the planning and management process increases the capacity of people living in the bioregion to identify ecological priorities, the effects of people's activities, and the technical, financial, and management ability to deal with the issues. Essential components of Australia's *National Strategy for the Conservation of Australia's Biological Diversity* (Commonwealth of Australia, 1996) are to increase the representativeness of terrestrial and marine protected areas and to integrate, within the next ten years, management plans for protected areas with plans for resource management in surrounding landscapes.

[*See also* Carrying Capacity; Wilderness; *and* World Heritage Sites.]

BIBLIOGRAPHY

Commonwealth of Australia. *National Strategy for the Conservation of Australia's Biological Diversity.* Canberra, 1996.

Dearden, P., and R. Rollins, eds. *Parks and Protected Areas in Canada: Planning and Management.* Toronto: Oxford University Press, 1993. A collection of articles presenting issues concerned with protected-area management.

Dobson, A. P. *Conservation and Biodiversity.* New York: Scientific American Library, 1996.

Greening Australia Ltd. *Local Greening Plans: A Guide for Vegetation and Biodiversity Management.* Canberra, 1995. Demonstrates how practical local outcomes can be achieved in biodiversity management using cooperative methods, existing data, and available resources.

Heywood, V. H., and R. T. Watson, eds. *Global Biodiversity Assessment*. Cambridge: Cambridge University Press, 1996.

Lewis, C. *Managing Conflicts in Protected Areas*. Gland, Switzerland: IUCN, 1996. A useful resource for people who play a role in resolving conflicts in protected-area management, including examples of comanagement with indigenous peoples and nongovernmental organizations.

Long, F. J., and B. A. Arnold. *The Power of Environmental Partnerships*. Orlando: Dryden Press, 1995. An essential guide to establishing and maintaining successful partnerships between government, business, and nongovernmental organizations to achieve positive ecological outcomes in national parks and surrounding lands.

McNeely, J. A., and J. Harrison, eds. *Protecting Nature: Regional Reviews of Protected Areas*. Gland, Switzerland: IUCN, 1994.

Meyer, W. B., and B. L. Turner, II, eds. *Changes in Land Use and Land Cover: A Global Perspective*. Cambridge: Cambridge University Press, 1994. A key collection of essays examining land transformation over the long term, and presenting information about data modeling and analysis of global change and its consequences.

Noss, R. F. "Landscape Connectivity: Different Functions at Different Scales." In *Landscape Linkages and Biodiversity: Defenders of Wildlife*, edited by W. E. Hudson, pp. 27–38. Washington, D.C.: Island Press, 1991. A useful analysis of the spatiotemporal scales of conservation problems and issues related to the establishment of regional corridors.

Noss, R. F., and A. Y. Cooperrider. *Saving Nature's Legacy: Protecting and Restoring Biodiversity*. Washington, D.C.: Island Press, 1994.

Noss, R. F., and J. M. Scott. "Ecosystem Protection and Restoration: The Core of Ecosystem Management." In *Ecosystem Management*, edited by M. S. Boyce and A. Heney, pp. 239–264. New Haven: Yale University Press, 1997. A useful critique of piecemeal environmental management and a guide to approaches for ecosystem management to conserve ecosystems and ecological integrity.

Organisation for Economic Co-operation and Development. *Investing in Biological Diversity*, Proceedings of the OECD International Conference on Incentive Measures for the Conservation and Sustainable Use of Biological Diversity, Cairns, Australia, 25–28 March 1996. Paris: OECD, 1997. A collection of papers outlining methodologies for setting conservation priorities, estimating biodiversity costs and benefits, and providing information about experiences and concerns regarding the appropriate mix of incentives and strategies for supporting biodiversity incentives in non-OECD nations.

Solbrig, O. T., et al., eds. *Biodiversity and Global Change*. Wallingford, U.K.: CAB International, 1994. A major collection of essays about all types of biodiversity and issues of identifying and protecting terrestrial and marine biodiversity. Emphasis is placed on the transformation of natural landscapes, subsequent losses of habitats and fauna, and analysis of the long-term implications of global change.

World Conservation Union. *Caring for the Earth Strategy*. Gland, Switzerland: IUCN/UNEP/WWF Report, 1991.

—JOHANNA ROSIER AND RICHARD G. HEERDEGEN

PERFLUOROCARBONS. *See* Chemical Industry; Framework Convention on Climate Change; Global Warming; Greenhouse Effect; *and* Kyoto Protocol.

PERMAFROST

Permafrost is a contraction for "permanently frozen ground" and is most conveniently defined as earth material whose temperature is perennially below 0°C whether or not it contains ice (Muller, 1947). As a temperature condition, its distribution depends exclusively on the local heat balance in cold regions. The widely discussed models for contemporary greenhouse warming generally predict that changes will be accentuated in these cold regions (Houghton et al., 1996) and that they could significantly alter the temperature and distribution of permafrost (Chapin et al., 1992, Chapter 2). This expectation has led to a growing interest in the nature of permafrost and the dynamics of associated landscapes, the subject of this article. The definition of *permafrost* formally includes soil and rock beneath glaciers, but glaciers themselves are generally considered separately. [*See* Cryosphere.]

Permafrost is important primarily because its "ground water" generally occurs as ice, often in massive segregated forms. (Important exceptions result from freezing-point depression by hydrostatic and capillary forces and dissolved solids.) Environmental impacts of permafrost and its growth and deterioration are largely manifestations of the dramatic contrast in strength and heat-transfer properties accompanying the change of water to and from ice. The frozen condition generally inhibits organic decay and renders permafrost impermeable to water flow, resistant to the penetration of plant roots, and subject both to brittle fracture under seasonally induced thermal stress and to mechanical failure and flowage when thawed by natural processes or disturbed by human activity. In combination, these characteristics and their changes can have major impacts on (1) the nature of the land surface and the environments for biological communities, (2) the development of infrastructure and the economics of land use and resource extraction, and (3) the exchange of heat, moisture, and gases between the solid Earth and the atmosphere.

A knowledge of the factors controlling the geothermal regime and their time scales is fundamental to an understanding of the unique geomorphic and ecological processes that control the overlying landscape, and for the successful design of engineering structures such as roadways, heated buildings, and pipelines in permafrost terrains. Fortunately, much of this understanding can be obtained from simple heat conduction models that, unlike in other geologic materials, can be applied to within a meter or so of the surface in the absence of heat transfer by moving ground water. Because summer surface temperatures are generally above 0°C, permafrost is generally overlain by a thin (typically 20 centimeters to 2 meters) "active layer" that thaws annually. Within the active layer, the thermal regime is much more complex than in permafrost.

Distribution of Permafrost. The mean annual temperature of air near the ground is known to vary systematically with latitude, altitude, and global climatic patterns. Because the mean ground surface temperature roughly follows the air temperature, the depth and distribution of permafrost follows a similar systematic pattern, as shown in Figure 1. In the zone mapped as "continuous," permafrost is commonly colder and

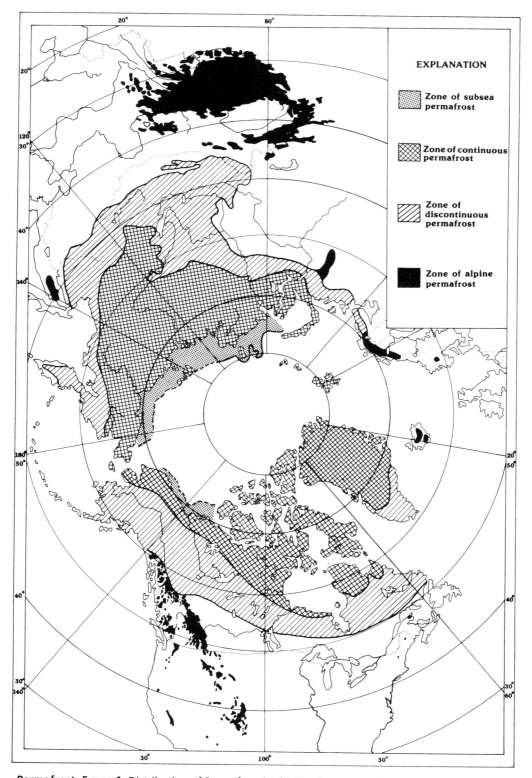

Permafrost. FIGURE 1. Distribution of Permafrost in the Northern Hemisphere. (After Péwé, 1983.)

deeper, and it underlies all but the most anomalous local surface areas, such as deep lakes. At the boundary between the "continuous" and "discontinuous" zones, mean annual air temperatures are typically in the range from −6°C to −9°C. Permafrost-free areas in regions of deep snow accumulation, good drainage, south-facing slopes, or otherwise favorable heat balance grow to dominance southward across the "discontinuous" zone. "Alpine permafrost" is a high-altitude subset of "discontinuous permafrost." The exact positions of the zone boundaries are not well defined because of extreme local variability, inadequate observational data, and difficulties with definition of these intergradational units. Nevertheless, maps such as that in Figure 1 provide a useful perspective, showing that roughly one-fourth of the land area in the Northern Hemisphere lies in permafrost zones, a figure valid as well in the Southern Hemisphere, where almost all the permafrost is in Antarctica. The maps also provide a necessary starting point for assessing the role of permafrost in global change scenarios (e.g., Anasimov et al., 1997).

Temperatures in Permafrost. If a secular change in surface conditions causes the mean annual ground surface temperature to drop below 0°C, the depth of freezing in winter will (with some simplification) exceed the depth of thawing in summer, and a layer of permafrost will grow downward from the base of the seasonal frost. It will thicken progressively with the passage of each succeeding winter. Under a stabilized surface temperature, the lower limit of permafrost ultimately approaches an equilibrium depth (Figure 2A) at which the temperature increase toward the Earth's warm interior

(generally 1°C for every 25–50 meters of depth) just offsets the subfreezing value of the mean surface temperature.

The transitional thermal conditions during the growth or deterioration of permafrost in response to a changing surface regime are illustrated schematically in Figure 3. These surface temperature changes can be brought about in permafrost terrains by changes in climate, surface drainage, or vegetation; by the shifting of shorelines of oceans, lakes, or rivers; or by engineering modifications of the surface. An appreciation of the time required for these processes is provided by a rule of thumb for heat conduction in which t is time in years after a rapid change (D°C) in surface temperature and x is the depth in meters at which we are interested in the effect.

$$t \text{ years} = (x \text{ meters})^2 / n$$

where:

$n = 250$ gives time at which temperature change at x is first detectable (5 percent D)

$n = 25$ gives time at which change at x is half the surface change (50 percent D)

$n = 1$ gives time at which change at x approaches full surface value (90 percent D)

(For a *gradual* linear increase in surface temperature to $D°$ at time t, the corresponding values of n are 135, 10, and 1/4. We have assumed a thermal diffusivity of 10^{-6} m²/sec.) Thus a rapid 2°C surface change (D) would not be significant (<0.1°C) at 100 meters (x) for about 40 years and at 500 meters for about 1,000 years ($n = 250$). Warming of 1°C would occur at 100 meters only

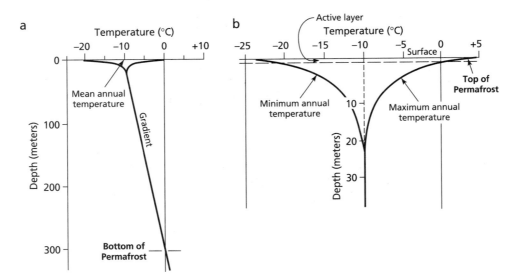

Permafrost. Figure 2. Relationships between temperature and depth showing how the lower limit (a) and upper limit (b) of permafrost are established. Shown for ground surface temperature with seasonal amplitude of 15°C, mean T_0, of −10°C, and geothermal gradient of 1°C per 30 meters.

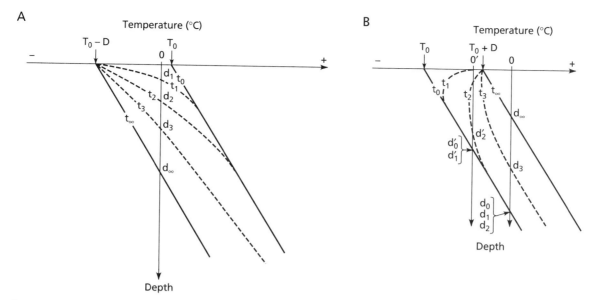

Permafrost. Figure 3. (A) Mean annual temperature at successive times (t_0, t_1 . . . t_∞) after a *decrease* in mean ground surface temperature from T_0 to T_0–D. The initial temperatures are represented by curve t_0. At time t_1, permafrost extends to depth d_1; at t_2, it extends to d_2, etc. The equilibrium curve t_∞ is parallel to the initial curve t_0. (B) Mean annual ground temperature at successive times (t_0, t_1 . . .) after an *increase* in mean ground surface temperature from T_0 to T_0 + D. If the final temperature is below 0°C (the case in which 0°C lies at point 0), the base of permafrost rises successively from d_0 to d_∞. If the final temperature is above 0°C (i.e., 0°C lies at point 0') the permafrost degrades first from the top (curve t_1), then from both top and bottom (curve t_2), and finally vanishes (curves t_3 and t_∞).

after about 400 years, and at 500 meters after 10,000 years ($n = 25$). The full effect ($n = 1$) is not approached at 100 meters for 10,000 years, and at 500 meters for 250,000 years, during which time several other events will no doubt have occurred ($n = 1$). Application of simple heat conduction rules of this sort—refined as necessary for inhomogeneity or phase change in ice-rich media—can be used to predict subsurface effects of future surface changes (the "forward problem"), or to learn about past surface changes by measuring their lingering subsurface effects on today's permafrost temperatures (the "inverse problem").

As an example of the latter, many temperature profiles from abandoned oil wells in the Alaskan Arctic (Figure 4B) are like curves t_1 and t_2 referred to the unprimed zero in Figure 3B, indicating a recent locally variable warming (D) of a few degrees when the curves are extended to the surface. The stippled areas represent the heat accumulated by the Earth during the warming process—it has penetrated to depths of about 100 meters. Comparison with the calculated detectable depth for a sudden ("step") or gradual ("linear") warming (marginal arrows, Figure 4B) reveals without further analysis that the warming event must have occurred over much of the last century; otherwise, it could not have penetrated so deeply. (Near-surface measurements, deleted from Figure 3, detail the still superficial

impact of gravel pads emplaced during the last decade for drilling.) Additionally, the profiles show that the extra heat flux entering the Earth's surface during this warming was on the order of the Earth's deep heat flow (10^{-1} W/m^2), as it nullifies the geothermal gradient. This disturbance is two orders of magnitude less than the net surface radiation, and it would not be detectable from surface flux measurements in spite of its conspicuous subsurface signal. Easily observed permafrost anomalies of this sort preserve a record of ecologically significant surface changes that have occurred on regional and local scales, largely unknown from sparse arctic climatological data.

As a second illustrative example, we consider the geothermal effect of a sudden increase of surface temperature by 10°C for typical arctic coastal conditions illustrated for Barrow and Prudhoe Bay, Alaska, by curves labeled "0 years" in Figure 5. (Curvature in the upper 100 meters from the twentieth-century warming seen in Figure 4B is omitted). This temperature change is larger than predictions of climate models, but it is an accurate representation of the "climate change" that occurs where arctic seas override the land, a process that must have occurred over millions of square kilometers on the arctic continental shelf as it was inundated by rising sea level following the last glaciation. Transgression continues today at rates exceeding a meter per year along

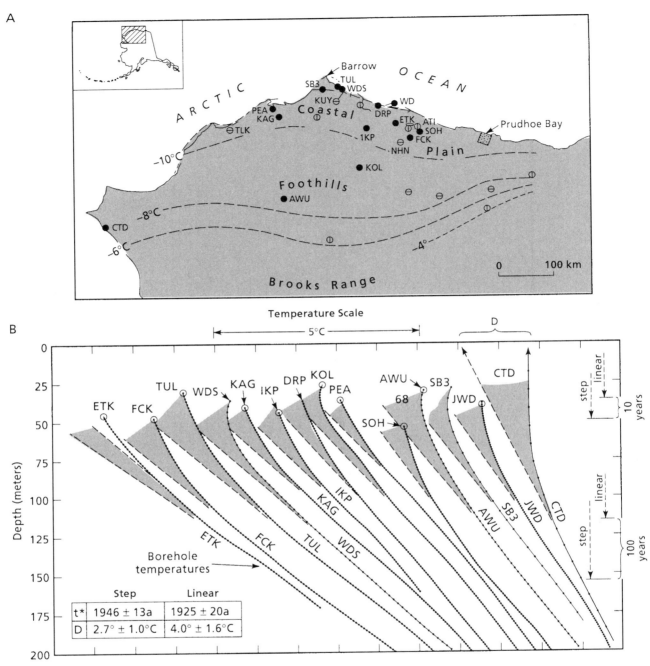

Permafrost. FIGURE 4. Evidence for twentieth-century warming from permafrost temperatures in abandoned Alaskan oil wells. (A) dashed contours show long-term mean surface temperature (T_0, Figure 3B), and solid circles show sites for the temperature curves shown in (B). The shaded region for each curve is the recent warming anomaly. The insert in part B summarizes the statistics for starting date (t*) and total warming (D) for best-fitting step and linear models. The arrows in the right-hand margin show calculated depth of detectable warming for a step or linear event starting ten or one hundred years ago. (After Lachenbruch and Marshall, 1986.)

much of the arctic coastline. The difference in behavior of the two models illustrates the important role of high ice content in the coarse-grained permafrost at Prudhoe Bay. First, it increases the thermal conductivity by about 50 percent, causing a comparable decrease in thermal gradient and increase in permafrost thickness from 400 meters at Barrow to 600 meters at Prudhoe Bay. Second, the latent heat required to melt the ice at Prudhoe

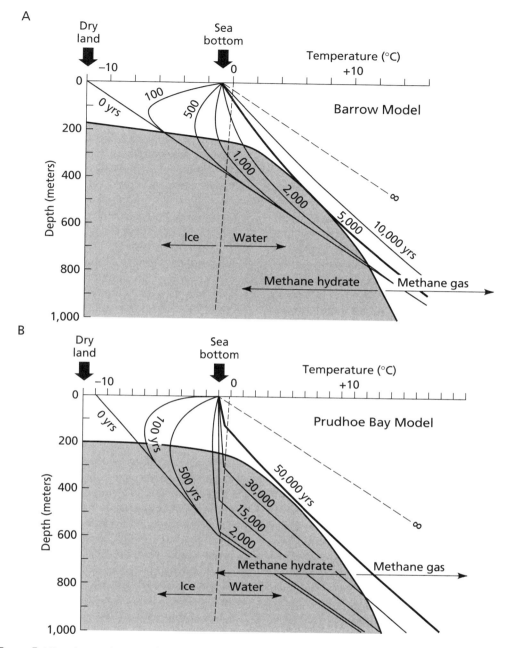

Permafrost. Figure 5. Warming and Decay of Permafrost and Methane Hydrate after Inundation beneath an Advancing Arctic Ocean Shoreline.

Land with geotherm typical of Barrow, Alaska (A), or Prudhoe Bay, Alaska (B), is submerged by the relatively warm sea with mean annual bottom temperature of −1°C. Numbers on temperature curves denote calculated time in years since inundation. Complete destabilization of methane hydrate (where temperature curves no longer intersect the shaded stability field) takes ten times longer at Prudhoe Bay (fifty thousand years compared to five thousand years at Barrow) because of the extra heat required to melt its high ice content permafrost. (After Lachenbruch, United States Geological Survey Open-File Report 94-694.)

Bay greatly retards warming. Geotherms at Barrow are as anticipated from the equation displayed earlier—offshore permafrost, if present there, would be very thin a few millennia after inundation. For Prudhoe Bay, however, offshore permafrost would still be thicker fifteen thousand years after inundation than it is onshore at Barrow today. Variations in ice content or the occurrence of brines would cause offshore permafrost to be variable between these extremes. In either case, offshore permafrost in just a millennium becomes "warm" and vulnerable to lateral discontinuity, like other permafrost with surface temperatures near 0°C found in the "discontinuous zone" at lower latitudes (Figure 1). Understanding these controls on the distribution and characteristics of offshore permafrost is important to the interpretation of exploratory seismic surveys and to problems of drilling, production, and transportation of potentially large oil reserves on the arctic continental shelf. This offshore permafrost also contains a lingering, partially recoverable temperature record of the history of postglacial shoreline transgression.

Shown also in Figure 5 is the stability field for methane hydrate, a crystalline combination of methane and water that is stable under conditions of low temperature and high pressure found on the continents only in regions of cold permafrost (or beneath continental ice sheets). Although the amount of carbon sequestered in this form is speculative, Gordon MacDonald (1990) gives a plausible estimate of 400×10^{15} grams of carbon, comparable to the more widely discussed carbon pool (up to 455×10^{15} grams of carbon, according to Oechel et al., 1993) in near-surface permafrost and active layer soils. Both are more than half the closely watched carbon currently stored in the atmosphere as carbon dioxide (750×10^{15} grams of carbon and growing). A widely expressed concern is that predicted greenhouse warming might destabilize large quantities of these hydrates, releasing the greenhouse gas methane and thereby enhancing the global warming with positive feedback. In this connection the foregoing example illustrates (1) that present-day climate change should not cause such a release for millennia, and (2) that present-day contributions to atmospheric methane from destabilized hydrate are more likely to be found on the arctic continental shelf, where permafrost warming started with inundation thousands of years ago. Preliminary measurements by Kvenvolden (1993) have not revealed anomalously high methane emissions on the continental shelf north of Alaska. [*See* Methane.]

The greatest local departures from the systematic patterns of permafrost distribution established by climate are those caused by local regions where the surface temperature is anomalous, the most important being bodies of water. As in the foregoing one-dimensional examples, simple heat conduction models permit useful estimates of thermal effects at depth as shown in Figure 6A—if the feature is old, the effect on permafrost temperature is the anomalous surface temperature weighted by the solid angle the feature subtends at the point of interest. Figure 6B shows the effect of a typical distribution of such features on permafrost. Fresh bodies of water that do not freeze to bottom (commonly, lakes deeper than about 2 meters) have positive mean bottom temperatures—the underlying thawed material occupies a closed basin or a chimney through permafrost depending on

whether the lake diameter is small or large relative to undisturbed permafrost thickness. These considerations are useful in the search for water supplies in continuous permafrost areas. If the steady-state theory represented by Figure 6A does not fit the temperature observations, it can be taken as evidence that the surface features are not in thermal equilibrium, and a transient theory can sometimes be applied to study their history.

Some Surface Manifestations. Not surprisingly, the most conspicuous environmental processes in permafrost terrains involve water and its thermal and mechanical changes in the transition to and from ice—water is generally abundant at the surface in spite of the usual aridity of polar climates because of the low evaporation rates and impermeability of permafrost. When water freezes in ice-rich permafrost (as in the formation of ice wedges or pingos), the surface is differentially uplifted; when ice-rich permafrost thaws (as from interannual variation in summer thaw depth), the surface generally settles differentially. In the extreme called *thermokarst*, it causes thaw lakes (as in Figure 6), or thaw pits, retreating scarps, and mudflows. [*See the vignette on* Thermokarst *in the article on* Tundra.]

An important terrain feature illustrating both the aggradational and degradational processes results from the percolation in summer of surface water into recurring thermal contraction cracks that form in winter when permafrost is cold and brittle (Figure 7). The resulting polygonal network of vertical ice wedges (Figure 8) infuses large masses of ice into permafrost, causing both a general surface uplift and local relief that controls drainage and consequently the local distribution of ponds, wet and dry habitats, plant assemblages, and heat balance. Efficient heat transfer by runoff water, causing melting and differential settlement ("thermal erosion"), often establishes the surface drainage in a reticulate pattern of troughs underlain by selectively thawed ice wedges, thereby controlling the geometry of drainage networks. One result is the common tundra beaded stream, with thaw pools ("beads") above ice-wedge intersections, joined by ice-wedge-floored channels often too deep to ford but narrow enough to step across.

Drainage channels working headward by thermal erosion of ice wedges (or sometimes retreating coastal or river bluffs) commonly intersect deep thaw lakes (see Figure 6), which then drain rapidly, causing the surface temperature to return to cold background values. Ice expansion during the subsequent refreezing of the thawed lake basin sediments may ultimately cause a pingo (Mackay, 1979)—a mound in the refrozen lake bed analogous to the bump on a refrozen ice cube. Pingos, with heights up to tens of meters, are a conspicuous topographic feature over large areas of arctic lowlands. A historical record of the lake draining is preserved in

A

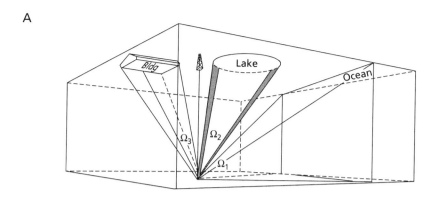

B

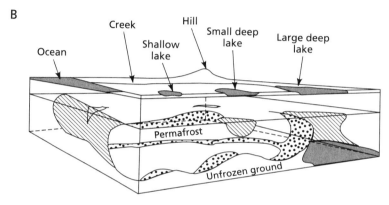

Permafrost. Figure 6. (A) Representation of the solid angle, Ω, which determines at any point the steady-state disturbances caused by thermally anomalous surface features. (B) Schematic representation of permafrost distribution, showing the collective effect of thermally anomalous surface features (A) in a region of continuous permafrost where the mean temperature of the ocean bottom is greater than 0°C. (After Gold and Lachenbruch, 1973.)

a new generation of ice-wedge polygons and anomalously warm permafrost beneath the old lake.

The process of pingo formation, like that for ice wedges, produces massive ice deposits at depth; other massive forms include segregated ice formed *in situ* during soil freezing and buried surface ice from glaciers, rivers, lakes, and snow. The distribution of these important deposits has recently been mapped for the Northern Hemisphere (Brown et al., 1997). They have the potential to cause abrupt differential surface settlement when thawed by either natural processes or human activities. This can cause disruption to landscapes by thermokarst or severe damage to engineering structures such as heated buildings, pipelines, roadways, and airfields that destroy the insulating value of the surface vegetation and peat, and in some cases introduce a heat source of their own.

An additional conspicuous feature of many permafrost terrains is the mobility of the active layer owing to its commonly saturated summer condition and the low resistance to its mass flow offered by the underlying smooth frozen permafrost surface. Mass movement of sediment under gravity is conspicuously absent at depth because of the relative immobility of permafrost.

The Active Layer. In permafrost terrains, the portion of the ground that has the greatest influence on surface processes is the very portion that is *not* permafrost, namely, the active layer (Figures 2 and 7). The permafrost, of course, imparts to the active layer its important characteristics: a base generally at subfreezing temperature, impermeable to moisture, and impenetrable to roots. Hence under typical conditions the active layer is the principle growth medium for surface plant communities and the reservoir for their water and nutrient supply, the locus of most terrestrial hydrologic activity, and a boundary layer across which heat, moisture, particulates, and gases are exchanged between the solid Earth and atmospheric systems. The thickness of the ac-

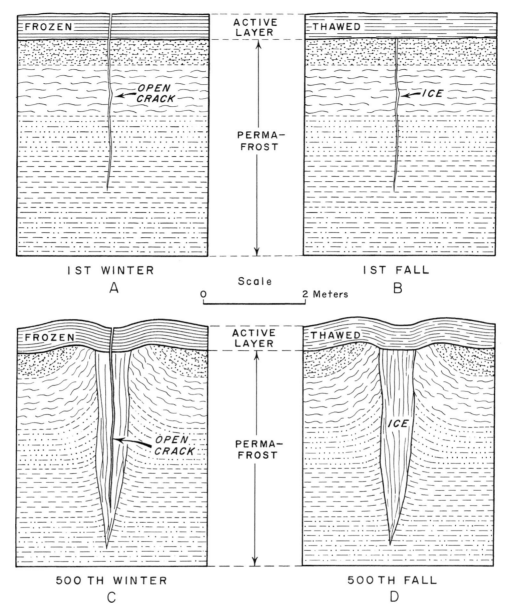

Permafrost. Figure 7. Schematic Representation of the Evolution of an Ice Wedge.

(A) Thermal contraction causes horizontal tension that exceeds strength of the cold embrittled surficial sediments, causing vertical tension cracks that form a surface network resembling giant mud cracks. (B) Spring meltwater freezes in cracks before it can be closed by summer reexpansion of permafrost. (C) Seasonal cracks reappear at old sites, which are zones of weakness, to form ice wedges. (D) Permafrost sediments displaced by a growing ice wedge often form ridges peripheral to the trough above the ice wedge. (After Lachenbruch, 1962.)

tive layer and the distribution and motion of its soil water can influence the thermal and chemical balance, including the rates of biogeochemical reactions, the productivity of living systems, the decomposition of organic matter, the generation or uptake of the greenhouse gases carbon dioxide and methane, and other characteristics of the active layer that influence (and are influenced by) the distribution of plant communities.

To understand the relation between permafrost and climate, it is necessary to understand the relation between temperatures routinely measured above the ground (T_{air}, Figure 9) and the temperature at the bottom of the active layer (T_{pf}, Figure 9), the boundary condition for the wealth of thermal information we obtain from the application of heat conduction theory to permafrost. Because of complex nonlinear heat transfer

Permafrost. Figure 8. Ice-Wedge Polygons on the Arctic Coastal Plain.

Wedges are delineated by peripheral ridges (Figure 7D), and troughs are accentuated by thermal erosion. (Photo courtesy of George Gryc.)

processes in the active layer and overlying snow, the mean annual temperatures in the air near the ground (T_{air}), at the ground surface (T_{gs}), and at the bottom of the active layer (T_{pf}) will have differing values in the

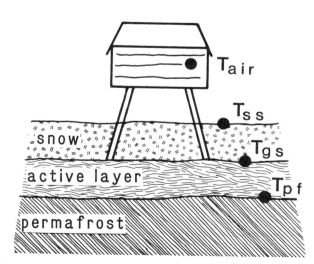

Permafrost. Figure 9. Measurement sites for the different annual mean temperatures: T_{pf} at the upper surface of permafrost; T_{gs} at the ground surface; T_{ss} at the solid surface of the snow pack when it is present and ground surface when it is not; and T_{air} in a standard observatory thermometer shelter. (After Lachenbruch and Marshall, 1962.)

same year. Two of the most important causes of these differences are probably (1) the snow effect, which insulates the ground selectively in winter, retarding the penetration of the winter cold wave, and (2) a change in the active layer from a good conductor when it is frozen in winter to a poorer one inhibiting downward flow of heat when it is thawed in summer (ice is four times as thermally conductive as water). The snow effect generally causes mean ground surface temperature to exceed mean air temperature ($T_{gs} > T_{air}$) by 1°–7°C, depending on the thickness, timing, and properties of the snow cover and, more subtly, on characteristics of material beneath the snow and the annual range of temperature (Lachenbruch, 1959)—if a climate becomes more continental with no other change, the snow effect will cause the mean ground temperature to increase. The seasonal contrast in active layer conductivity typically causes a temperature offset opposite to the snow effect ($T_{pf} < T_{gs}$) of 1°–2°C in wet materials, decreasing as moisture content and seasonal range decrease. Although much remains to be learned about the complex snow–active layer system, we generally expect the mean annual air temperature to be several degrees colder than the mean annual upper permafrost boundary temperature, T_{pf}, which in turn may be a degree or so colder than the mean annual ground surface temperature T_{gs}. At the margins of discontinuous permafrost stable in today's climate, the mean ground surface temperature can be slightly above 0°C in wet materials, but the mean air temperature is generally substantially below 0°C.

The time history of temperature at the top of permafrost (T_{pf}) is the quantity that is estimated in so-called climatic reconstructions from borehole temperature measurements (e.g., Figure 4). However, understanding the full range of implications of changing T_{pf} requires a knowledge of the complex interactions in the snow–

active layer system. Past changes in T_{pf} may be a direct response to changing climate parameters (such as air temperature or snowfall), or to modifications of the active layer due to changing geomorphic conditions, drainage patterns, forest fire, or the heat and water balance of a changing plant cover. In any case, past changes in T_{pf} reconstructed from present-day borehole temperatures are a unique source of information on century-scale changes in past environmental factors (including but not limited to climate) that are controlling the dynamics of changing ecosystems.

Concerns over the implications of contemporary warming in permafrost terrains are essentially concerns over the response of the active layer system, which controls the surface processes and the top of permafrost with virtually no thermal time delay; significant changes at the bottom of permafrost will generally lag any climate forcing by centuries or millennia (see the equation displayed earlier). There are two distinct classes of change to consider: (1) those that change the state of the active layer, principally its thickness, leaving the underlying permafrost intact, and (2) those that cause the seasonal thaw to exceed the depth of refreeze, thereby creating a growing permanently thawed zone or *talik* and depleting underlying permafrost.

In the first case, warming is usually expected to thicken the active layer, although it need not if the "warming" involves a decreased annual temperature range, a thickening organic mat, or increased wetness—the heat needed to vaporize 5 millimeters of extra water or melt 4 centimeters of extra ice is sufficient to warm 30 centimeters of dry soil by 20°C. Improved modeling to accommodate such factors in predicting active layer thickness (e.g., Romanovsky and Osterkamp, 1997) is limited by the availability of the physical data needed for extensive parameterization and by uncertainties in the changing thermal role to be played by future plant communities. An increment of permafrost transferred to the active layer would contribute to settlement of the surface if it were ice rich and its organic material, removed from deep freeze, could contribute to the efflux of carbon dioxide or methane, depending largely on soil wetness and other hydrologic conditions and on a still uncertain complex of biogeochemical feedbacks (see, for example, part 3 of Reynolds and Tenhunen, 1996; Weller et al., 1995).

In the second case—increasing surface temperatures cause summer thawing too deep to refreeze in winter—permafrost becomes an unstable relict of an extinct climate, and the landscape crosses an environmental threshold. The fate of this relict permafrost is sensitive to flowage of water (or sometimes mud) in the taliks. With little or no flowage, inefficient conductive heat transfer prevails, as described in the earlier equation and in Figure 5 (see also Lunardini, 1996; Osterkamp, 1983);

even relatively shallow permafrost can then persist unstably for centuries, and deep ice-rich permafrost for tens of eons. If water percolates into the talik, however, it can transfer summer heat into the ground efficiently, causing complex thermal and hydrologic regimes in marginal permafrost that can cause it to deteriorate rapidly. If the permafrost is ice rich, the resulting thermokarst can cause severe disruption of forests, tundra, human settlements, and other ecosystems, and nutrients and organic carbon released from permafrost can become more available to the surface systems. Unlike the slow thinning of continuous permafrost by heat conduction, the rapid loss of warm, discontinuous permafrost by the hydrologically influenced growth of taliks is a process that is not well known in detail. Near the southern margins of discontinuous permafrost, the North–South change of mean annual air temperature (and, on average, probably T_{pf} as well) generally ranges from 50 to 200 kilometers per degree Celsius. Thus in some regions, such as central Canada and Siberia, climatic warming of a few degrees can subject large areas of marginal, discontinuous permafrost to decay. This process, together with effects of a changing active layer in colder permafrost, will be responsible for the major prompt (one- to fifty-year) impacts on the dynamics of permafrost terrains subjected to a warming climate.

[*See also* Global Warming; Greenhouse Effect; *and* Tundra.]

BIBLIOGRAPHY

Anasimov, O. A., and F. E. Nelson. "Permafrost Zonation and Climate Change in the Northern Hemisphere: Results from Transient General Circulation Models." *Climatic Change* 35 (1997), 241–258.

Britton, M. E. "Vegetation of the Arctic Tundra." In *Arctic Biology: Oregon State Colloquium.* Eighteenth Annual Biology Colloquium, pp. 26–61. Corvallis: Oregon State College, 1957. A broad overview of tundra vegetation types in relation to thaw lakes, ice-wedge polygons, and other features of the permafrost landscape in northern Alaska.

Brown, J., O. J. Ferrians, Jr., J. A. Heginbottom, and E. S. Melnikov. *Circum-Arctic Map of Permafrost and Ground-Ice Conditions.* U.S. Geological Survey Map CP-45, scale 1:10,000,000, 1997. A comprehensive international effort to summarize the distribution and character of permafrost and ground ice in the Northern Hemisphere.

Brown, J., P. C. Miller, L. L. Tieszen, and F. L. Bunnell, eds. *An Arctic Ecosystem: The Coastal Tundra at Barrow, Alaska.* Stroudsburg, Pa.: Dowden, Hutchinson, and Ross, 1980. An integrated group of basic studies covering biotic and abiotic aspects of an ecosystem dominated by continuous permafrost.

Chapin, F. S., III, R. L. Jefferies, J. F. Reynolds, G. R. Shaver, and J. Svoboda, eds. *Arctic Ecosystems in a Changing Climate: An Ecophysiological Perspective.* San Diego: Academic Press, 1992. Timely, readable papers on the interactive role of plant physiology in the dynamics of changing ecosystems, largely in permafrost terrain.

French, H. M. *The Periglacial Environment.* 2d ed. London: Longman, 1996. An intermediate-level college text and useful up-to-date source for geomorphic processes and landforms in cold regions.

Gold, L. W., and A. H. Lachenbruch. "Thermal Conditions in Permafrost: A Review of North American Literature." In *Permafrost: Second International Conference*, pp. 3–23. Washington, D.C.: National Academy of Sciences, 1973.

Harris, S. A. *The Permafrost Environment*. Totowa, N.J.: Barnes and Noble Books, 1986. A nonmathematical summary of the permafrost environment and problems it poses for human use and economic development.

Houghton, J. T., L. G. Miera Filho, B. A. Callander, N. Harris, A. Kattenberg, and K. Maskell, eds. *Climate Change 1995*. Cambridge: Cambridge University Press, 1996.

International Conference on Permafrost. *Permafrost: Proceedings*. 7 vols. to date. Washington, D.C.: National Academy of Sciences; Wushan: South China University of Technology Press, 1963–. The best overall source for all aspects of permafrost science and engineering, with easily accessible review papers, short topical reports, and bibliographies.

Kvenvolden, K. A., M. D. Lilley, T. D. Lorenson, P. W. Barnes, and E. McLaughlin. "The Beaufort Sea Continental Shelf as a Seasonal Source of Atmospheric Methane." *Geophysical Research Letters* 20 (1993), 2459–2462.

Lachenbruch, A. H. "Periodic Heat Flow in a Stratified Medium with Application to Permafrost Problems." *U.S. Geological Survey Bulletin* 1083-A (1959), 36.

———. *Mechanics of Thermal Contraction Cracks and Ice-Wedge Polygons in Permafrost*. Special Paper 70. Washington, D.C.: Geological Society of America, 1962.

Lachenbruch, A. H., and B. V. Marshall. "Changing Climate: Geothermal Evidence from Permafrost in the Alaskan Arctic." *Science* 234 (1986), 689–696.

Lunardini, V. J. *Heat Transfer in Cold Climates*. New York: Van Nostrand Reinhold, 1981. A rigorous, systematic presentation of thermal fundamentals applied to engineering practice in permafrost and related problems of cold regions.

———. "Climatic Warming and the Degradation of Permafrost." *Permafrost and Periglacial Processes* 7 (1996), 311–320.

MacDonald, G. J. "Role of Methane Clathrates in Past and Future Climates." *Climatic Change* 16 (1990), 247–281.

Mackay, J. R. "Pingos of the Tuktoyaktuk Peninsula Area, Northwest Territories." *Géographie Physique et Quarternaire* 33 (1979), 3–61.

Muller, S. W. *Permafrost, or Permanently Frozen Ground, and Related Problems*. Ann Arbor, Mich.: Edwards, 1947. The seminal first book on permafrost in the English language, prepared by a Stanford University paleontologist from the relatively advanced Russian literature.

Oechel, W. C., S. J. Hastings, G. Vourlitis, M. Jenkins, G. Riechers, and N. Grulke. "Recent Change of Arctic Tundra Ecosystems from a Net Carbon Dioxide Sink to a Source." *Nature* 361 (1993), 520–523.

Osterkamp, T. E. "Response of Alaskan Permafrost to Climate." In *Final Proceedings of the Fourth International Conference on Permafrost*, pp. 145-152. Washington, D.C.: National Academy of Science Press, 1983.

Péwé, T. L. "Alpine Permafrost in the Contiguous United States: A Review." *Arctic and Alpine Research* 15 (1983), 145–156.

Reynolds, J. F., and J. F. Tenhunen, eds. *Landscape Function and Disturbance in Arctic Tundra*. Ecological Studies 120. Berlin: Springer, 1996. A multidisciplinary collection of comprehensive studies at a research site in continuous permafrost emphasizing linkages controlling ecosystem changes in disturbed regions.

Romanovsky, V. E., and T. E. Osterkamp. "Thawing of the Active Layer on the Coastal Plain of the Alaskan Arctic. *Permafrost and Periglacial Processes* 8 (1997), 1–22.

Washburn, A. L. *Geocryology: A Survey of Periglacial Processes and Environments*. New York: Wiley, 1980. A very readable and authoritative reference for permafrost and related high-latitude and periglacial geomorphic processes.

Weller, G., F. S. Chapen, K. R. Everett, J. E. Hobbie, D. Cane, W. C. Oechel, C. L. Ping, W. S. Reeburgh, D. Walker, and J. Walsh. "The Arctic Flux Study: A Regional View of Trace Gas Release." *Journal of Biogeography* 22 (1995), 365–374.

—ARTHUR H. LACHENBRUCH

PESTICIDES. *See* Chemical Industry; Pest Management; *and* Water Quality.

PEST MANAGEMENT

Organisms are considered to be pests when they cause problems in crops or livestock, compete with humans for food and fiber, or otherwise cause economic or other problems for humans. The range of pests is wide, including insects, nematodes, mites, plant pathogens, vertebrate pests, and weeds. Their distribution and economic effects depend on a wide range of factors that include changes in farming patterns and in agroclimatic and ecological conditions. Pests have coexisted with humans from the beginning of civilization. Whenever humans engage in agriculture, pest problems always emerge, particularly weeds, to the extent that in the tropics most of the cultural practices associated with crop production are directly or indirectly related to the control of weeds; hence the statement that "every field always has a weed problem."

Pest management principles and objectives should aim at manipulating the pests and their environment in such a way as to maintain populations below levels that cause economic crop losses, thereby protecting crops from pest damage and/or destruction. Pest management requires the designing of cropping systems or the development of productive farming systems that minimize farmers' economic, health, and environmental risks by using a combination of control practices such as host plant resistance, high-quality seeds, crop rotation, field sanitation, sound farming practices, and judicious use of pesticides (herbicides, insecticides, nematocides, etc.) at critical periods during the cropping period. Pest management takes into consideration the agroecosystem, the interaction of weather with farming practices, and the population dynamics of coexisting organisms (including humans and their environment) to avoid altering the delicate balance of the ecosystem.

Crop Losses. Estimates of crop losses vary widely by location and by year, but in general about one-third of potential global agricultural production in the form of food, fiber, and feed in developing countries is estimated to be destroyed annually by over twenty thousand pest species. Total annual losses are estimated to be about U.S.$300 billion. Estimates of yield loss range between 30 and 40 percent on the average. Crop losses are generally much higher in many tropical and subtropical countries; total losses are not uncommon in such countries because of a climate favorable to the proliferation and growth of pests, limited resources for crop protection programs, and the continuing intensification of agricultural production to meet food demands and income needs.

Use of Agrochemicals. The need for rapid increases in agricultural productivity to meet the food demands of growing human populations has caused agricultural scientists to develop higher-yielding crop varieties. Many such crop varieties are grown intensively in vast areas in monocultures with complementary yield-enhancing inputs such as fertilizers and irrigation. Pest attack under such conditions can be damaging, especially if new pests have emerged for which resistant crop varieties are not yet available. However, host plant resistance to insects and diseases in particular should always be the first line of defense in pest management, and the idea that traditional varieties have more resistance to pests than modern varieties is mostly not true. Farmers in the past have used mixtures of crops or crop varieties to try to buffer the effects of pest attack.

Pesticides are used in pest management as one of a group of potential practices to keep pest populations below levels that would cause damage. Pesticides can also help to protect the crops from total loss or damage due to pests. Agrochemicals are used not only in agriculture but also for residential purposes to control pests. Pesticide use has unfortunately resulted in a number of problems that are sometimes associated with their inappropriate use. Such problems can include toxicity to nontarget organisms, including humans and animals; problems of residue on crops or environmental contaminants; the buildup of pest resistance to pesticides; and the need for frequent subsequent applications.

Pesticide use in agriculture increased after World War II, as agriculture became more intensive and crop yield improvement continued apace. Also, a wide array of chemicals became available in most Western countries, offering immediate, cheap, and reliable protection against pests. Most of these chemicals are petroleum based and were affected when oil prices began to rise in the early 1970s. Also, the potential environmental costs of chemical pest control began to be recognized,

and public awareness of the economic, health, and environmental risks of pesticides increased. Policy and decision makers in a number of countries are thus faced with growing public environmental concerns along with rising concern about higher costs of pest protection in highly specialized farming operations in developed countries.

Today, it is not only environmentalists who are concerned about pesticide availability and use. Farmers are increasingly worried that in the future many inputs on which they depend may not be available, or may not be as effective or as affordable as in the past. Farmers are therefore searching for farming systems and related practices that are more sustainable, yet productive and profitable, through intensive management of available internal resources.

Recent and Future Strategies. Pesticides are often a necessary means of protecting crops and ornamental plants from complete loss or damage by pests, and their proper use can be a low-risk practice. Nevertheless, there are still risks in pesticide usage, including increasing resistance of some pests to certain pesticides and environmental contamination or damage to nontarget species. For these reasons, farmers and scientists are seeking more effective ways to combat pests in production systems. Integrated pest management (IPM) was developed as a way to combat pests by using a combination of tried-and-tested as well as new technologies in a rational, integrated way. Practices used include (1) varietal resistance; (2) new-generation pesticides, sometimes biodegradable, with short life spans in the field; (3) sex attractants (substances that attract males or females of the target pests to traps, baiting stations, or other control systems); (4) juvenile hormones that interfere with pest maturation; and (5) modifications of cropping patterns and practices. IPM is knowledge and management intensive, and involves training of extension workers and farmers in target areas to help them in its implementation. Key areas of training include recognition of pests in the field, identification of beneficial and harmful organisms, determination of when proper treatment thresholds have been attained, and setting of harmful and beneficial pests against each other to the point of restoring an ecological balance.

Diversified farming and multiple cropping systems traditionally adopt crop rotations to control pests, conserve moisture, and maintain adequate productivity. The adoption of integrated cropping and livestock systems has often resulted in lower feed costs, recycling of waste, and stabilized farm incomes. In turn, such systems can lead to a more stable environment that allows the density and variety of beneficial parasites and predators alike to increase.

Hopes for success in the future seems to lie in finding ways of combining sound management practices with emerging tools and technologies, such as biotechnology and microcomputers, along with traditional knowledge of farmers that can contribute to IPM. An example of such traditional knowledge is the Neem tree (*Azadirachta indica*), which from African and Asian experience is known to have pest-control properties derived from natural plant products. Some such plants are used in their natural forms at the village level by limited resource farmers.

Biotechnology has much to offer in pest management. It has already produced diagnostic tools for identifying and managing pests in crops, and genetic engineering shows great potential for new approaches to pest management. For example, scientists recently discovered the gene that causes the *Bacillus thuringiensis* (B.t.) fungus to produce a protein that is active against certain pests. The scientists inserted this gene into cotton to enable the plant to produce the protein on its own, but without changing the plant's composition. Such transformed cotton is then able to repel or kill budworms because of the B.t. protein, thus eliminating the need for pesticides. Also, new, less hazardous chemicals can be sprayed in fields prior to planting of crops to kill the weeds, without affecting the crop later on. This eliminates the need to plow and in turn minimizes soil erosion.

[*See also* Agriculture and Agricultural Land; Biotechnology, Chemical Industry; *and* Prior Informed Consent for Trade in Hazardous Chemicals and Pesticides.]

BIBLIOGRAPHY

Graing, M., and S. Ahmed. *Handbook of Plants with Pest-Control Properties*. New York: Wiley, 1987.
Hahn, S. K., and F. E. Caveness. *Integrated Pest Management for Tropical Root and Tuber Crops*. Proceedings of the Workshop on Global Status and Prospects for Integrated Pest Management of Root and Tuber Crops in the Tropics. Ibadan, Nigeria: IITA, 1987.
Haney, P. B., et al. *Reducing Insecticide Use and Energy Costs in Citrus Pest Management*. Davis: University of California, 1997.
Magretta, J. "Growth through Global Sustainability: An Interview with Monsanto's CEO, Robert B. Shapiro." *Harvard Business Review* (January–February 1997).
Waage, J. *Making IPM Work: Developing Country Experience and Prospects*. International Institute of Biological Control. Wallingford, U.K.: CAB International, 1989.
Wiebers, U.-C. *Integrated Pest Management and Pesticide Regulation in Developing Asia*. Washington, D.C.: The World Bank, 1993.
Yudelman, M., et al. *Pest Management: The Expected Trends and Impact on Agricultural and Natural Resources to 2000*. Washington, D.C.: International Food Policy Research Institute, 1998.

—DONALD L. PLUCKNETT AND
ROBERT B. KAGBO

PETROLEUM HYDROCARBONS IN THE OCEAN

Hydrocarbons are formed by the alteration of deeply buried organic material under extreme heat and pressure. Once formed, hydrocarbons tend to migrate upward until they are either trapped in porous sedimentary rock or escape by seepage or erosion through faults that extend to the surface. Our civilization currently depends on extracting and burning the oil and gas that is trapped in reservoir rocks, most of which (such as ancient deltas or reefs) are ancient marine features. A large fraction of global oil and gas reserves is thus associated with oceanic systems. The continental margins of many present-day ocean basins contain significant hydrocarbon reserves: of the 3 billion tons of total proven reserves, approximately one-third is under the ocean. [*See* Marginal Seas.]

Sources, Processes, and Quantities of Hydrocarbon Input to the Oceans. Many processes contribute to the total input of hydrocarbons to the oceans. Natural release of oil and gas into the ocean through seepage has been under way at least since the Miocene epoch (23 million years BP) and probably much longer. Tectonic processes such as earthquakes or movement of salt layers promote faulting of the upper sediment column and lead to increased seepage. Reservoirs that empty through seepage may be simultaneously refilling because of ongoing hydrocarbon generation, contributing to an ongoing cycle. Human use of hydrocarbon fuels during the twentieth and twenty-first centuries has accelerated at a rate that is completely out of scale with natural processes. [*See* Energy and Human Activity.] In a single day, humanity burns from ten to one hundred times more oil and gas than is generated over an entire year. Our combustion of hydrocarbon fuels has greatly increased the input of carbon dioxide to the atmosphere and ocean. Transport and handling processes necessary for a civilization based on hydrocarbons also results in significant accidental releases into the ocean. Human population growth and industrial development have been most intense along coastal regions. [*See* Coastlines.] Consequently, industrial and municipal waste and non-point-source runoff contribute a very large fraction of the petroleum hydrocarbons that reach the ocean.

Industrial extraction of hydrocarbons began on land and did not move offshore until the early 1950s. The first offshore platform was built off the coast of Louisiana in 1947. Increasingly, production has moved offshore in regions such as the Gulf of Mexico and the North Sea. Most recently, technological advances have made production possible at ocean depths of 1,000 meters or more. Overall, there has been little spillage from platforms compared to the amounts spilled in transport accidents.

Hydrocarbons enter the oceans at two rates. These can be generalized as sudden releases, which are concentrated in space and time, and slow, continuous seepage from points dispersed over a large region. Releases to the ocean from human and natural sources can occur at both rates. Tanker spills are examples of sudden, concentrated releases—although the amount released is a vanishingly small fraction of the total amount transported by sea. Between 1974 and 1992 there were an average of thirty-seven spills of greater than 40 tons (10,000 gallons) for every billion tons transported by sea. The amount of oil spilled from vessels per year appears to have peaked at the end of the 1970s with a maximum of approximately 800,000 to 1,000,000 metric tons (Figure 1). Improved vessel design and more stringent regulation have contributed to the decline. Historically, the greatest loss of oil at sea from vessels undoubtedly occurred during World War II, when upward of forty-five hundred vessels were sunk, releasing their entire fuel supplies and cargoes into the ocean. Waste and runoff constitute slow and continuous releases. The total quantities are more difficult to ascertain but probably exceed the amount released by spills. Natural seeps are another form of slow and continuous release but can contribute very large amounts of oil over time. An individual seep in the Gulf of Mexico will release on the order of 100 liters per day, and there are, conservatively, fifty to one hundred active seeps in this region, so the amount released on an annual basis would constitute a significant spill. There is also good evidence that natural seeps can release oil at much higher rates if triggered by earthquakes or other geologic phenomena.

The most comprehensive efforts to quantify the total amount of oil from natural and human sources released per year in the oceans were conducted in the 1980s and summarized in the National Research Council volume *Oil in the Ocean*. The estimates obtained were between 1.7 and 8.8 million metric tons per year, with a best estimate of 3.2 million metric tons per year. Partitioning this amount among the sources described above produces the graph in Figure 2.

Fate. Over geologic time, hydrocarbons are intermediate products that will eventually be remineralized to carbon dioxide and water. The natural pathways to this fate include the following:

- Continued burial and gradual combustion due to geothermal heating at depth
- Upward migration and microbially mediated mineralization uppermost in the sediment column

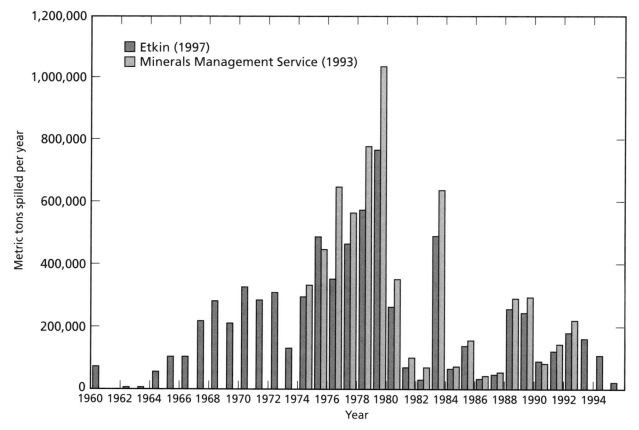

Petroleum Hydrocarbons in the Ocean. FIGURE 1. Oil Spills from Vessels per Year. (After Etkin, 1997.)

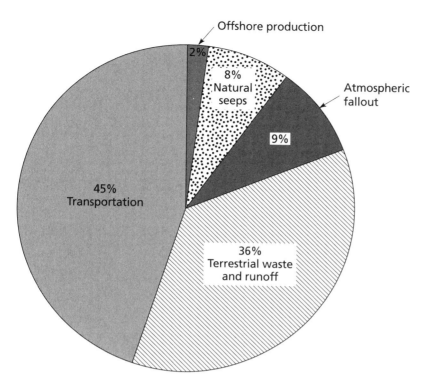

Offshore production

2%

8% Natural seeps

Atmospheric fallout

9%

45% Transportation

36% Terrestrial waste and runoff

Petroleum Hydrocarbons in the Ocean.
FIGURE 2. Relative Magnitude of Petroleum Hydrocarbon Inputs to the Oceans.

Assumes a global total of 3.2 × 10⁶ metric tons per year. (Modified after Kvenvolden and Harbaugh, 1983.)

- Seepage or erosion leading to dissolution and dispersion in the ocean and atmosphere

Gas and oil entering the ocean from natural seeps migrate along fault planes that penetrate reservoirs, then diffuse through unconsolidated sediments approaching the sea floor. Formation of gas hydrate, layers of biota, and carbonate rock entrap hydrocarbons in upper sediments, where they are rapidly altered by free-living bacteria that utilize the lighter carbons in the oil and gas. The remaining residues become tarry and heavy compared with most unaltered product. What does escape the sea floor drifts toward the surface in tight plumes that may drift laterally with midocean currents and surface as much as 10 kilometers from the source. At the surface, the oil which is still liquid spreads into a thin (less than 1 micrometer), almost invisible film or slick that continues to drift with wind and current until it finally dissipates. Tar balls from natural seeps may be colonized by barnacles and other pelagic fauna.

Oil entering the ocean from a tanker spill is usually delivered to the water surface unaltered and in a layer that may be tens of centimeters thick at the source. Once in the water, spilled oil is also rapidly altered by a variety of weathering processes. Volatile fractions evaporate rapidly, depending on water temperature, with the results that most spilled crudes remain inflammable only for a matter of hours. The oil layer thins rapidly as it disperses from the source. Moderate wave action generates a gooey mixture of oil and water known as mousse. Extreme sea states may dissipate large quantities of oil by mixing it vertically so that it becomes partially or completely dissolved in the water.

Detection. Visibility of an oil layer floating on water depends on its signature in visible and ultraviolet or infrared wavelengths and, indirectly, on the physical effect it has on surface water. In thickness from 4 micrometers to 1 centimeter—the magnitude that might result from a shipping accident—fresh oil forms an obvious covering, reddish brown to tan in color. With exposure, the volatile fraction of the oil rapidly evaporates, leaving a waxy residue that makes a foamy emulsion with sea water and tends to coagulate into gooey tar balls and floating mats. In thickness of 1–4 micrometers, an oil layer refracts incident light to form the rainbow sheen familiar from curbside puddles. Oil-coated water tends to be slightly cooler than unoiled water and produces a thermal signature in the infrared wavelengths. At its thinnest—from less than .01 to 1 micrometer—floating oil layers may be only a few tens of molecules thick, but the polar bonds between hydrocarbons are sufficient to create a surprisingly durable film at the interface between air and water. This surface-active or "surfactant" layer suppresses the fine-scale surface ripples caused by wind, which in turn increases the intensity of specular reflection off the water and gives a patch of floating oil its "slick" appearance.

Biological Effects. Marine plants and animals take up hydrocarbons from the water or from eating contaminated foods. [See Ocean Life.] Most, with the ex-

LIFE AT OIL SEEPS

Although oil spills from tankers are a threat to wildlife in the oceans and on shorelines, natural seeps of oil and gas on the ocean floor are far more gradual and appear beneficial to certain forms of life.

In 1984 researchers from Texas A&M University, hoping to study how chronic exposure to oil affects marine life (to aid in assessing accidental spills at the surface), trawled above known seeps roughly 80 miles off the Louisiana shore in the Gulf of Mexico. They expected to find a few sick specimens, but instead they hoisted a net loaded with mussels and tube worms.

They had discovered a community of ocean life supported by methane and hydrogen sulfide, existing without direct connection to photosynthesis, and possibly covering hundreds of square miles where seeps are known to occur. The mussels seem to prefer pools of dense brine, whereas tube worms favor hills on the ocean floor. These communities are analogous to tube worm communities at hydrothermal vents (Lutz and Haymon, 1994). In those occurrences, nutrient chemicals are borne by hot waters that circulate deep into igneous rock of the ocean floor.

Oil and gas production typically leads to some leakage into the environment. Ironically, however, if oil companies active in the Gulf of Mexico tap the reservoirs that now feed natural seeps, they may reduce pressure in the reservoir rock and thereby slow or stop the seepage of oil and gas. This will benefit some ocean life but not the mussels and tube worms.

BIBLIOGRAPHY

Lutz, R. A., and R. M. Haymon. "Rebirth of a Deep Sea Vent." *National Geographic* 186.5, (1994), 115–126.
MacDonald, I. R. "Natural Oil Spills." *Scientific American* (November 1998), 57–61.
MacDonald, I. R., and C. F. Fisher. "Life without Light." *National Geographic* 190.4 (1996), 86–97.

—DAVID J. CUFF

ception of certain bivalve species, are able to metabolize petroleum and clear their tissues by returning waste products to the water. Sublethal effects of chronic exposure to petroleum hydrocarbons have been documented in estuaries and in the vicinity of oil production platforms. Such effects include altered feeding behaviors, lowered reproductive rates, and possible increased tumors and mutagenicity. Sublethal effects are of particular concern where exposure occurs in larval stages, which may encounter petroleum hydrocarbons in nursery areas with a subsequent impact on adult populations. Important coastal plants, such as mangroves, suffer significant interference with respiratory function and increased mortality as a result of chronic exposure. Less is documented regarding impacts on algae and plankton.

The adhesive, hydrophobic properties of petroleum are a primary cause of mortality under acute exposures. Oil tends to coat respiratory or sensory tissues, and the volatile fractions are major irritants. Seabirds and marine mammals suffer additional injury because oiled fur or feathers lose the ability to provide thermal insulation.

Because many marine organisms depend on special breeding, nesting, or nursery habitats, a localized spill can have a devastating effect on a widespread population of marine animals.

In marked contrast to lethal or sublethal effects noted above, specialized ecosystems in deep-sea habitat achieve high rates of productivity and high biomass by harnessing hydrocarbon seepage as a microbial foodstock. As noted, hydrocarbons in sea floor sediment are oxidized by free-living bacteria at rates that generate high levels of hydrogen sulfide—just as would occur in an organically enriched salt marsh. In the deep sea, however, species of tube worms and clams have evolved a symbiotic relationship with bacteria that in turn reoxidize the hydrogen sulfide, with oxygen supplied by the host, and use the energy to fix new carbon. A group of mussels has a different symbiont living in its gills that is able to utilize methane directly. These tube worms, mussels, and clams settle in dense colonies around active seeps. Their presence attracts fish and invertebrates that are common elsewhere in the deep sea but occur with uncommon abundance around seeps.

Gas Hydrates. Although the most commonly recognized marine hydrocarbon reserves are oil and gas reservoirs, there is now good evidence to show that the most abundant marine hydrocarbons are layers of gas hydrate. Gas hydrate is an icelike solid that forms under extreme pressures when molecules of methane are trapped in a regular lattice of water molecules. The material remains a solid at temperatures as high as $7°$–$8°C$. Globally, methane incorporated in this form may comprise some 100,000 gigatons of organic carbon, which would be more than all the known oil, gas, coal, and living organic matter combined. [See Methane.] Hydrate layers are common around the lower edges of the continental slope worldwide. Generally, they are buried by several hundred meters of sediment but are found at or on the sea floor in some regions. The long-term fate of gas hydrate deposits is not well understood, but they should be considered rather unstable in a geologic context. In their shallow occurrence, gas hydrates can form and dissociate quite dynamically under the influence of fluctuating water temperatures. They can, in fact, act like check valves, alternately stemming and releasing oil seepage to the water column.

Summary. Petroleum hydrocarbons are a minor component of the natural marine ecosystem. Under natural circumstances, the environment copes with chronic release of oil and gas with little ill effect and with marked increased productivity under deep-sea conditions. Recent industrial development has greatly accelerated the rate at which oil enters the ocean. Most significantly, it has increased the dosage rate, whereby large quantities of oil are released in concentrated areas. This can overwhelm available mechanisms for response, with acute toxic effects in local areas. As a component of global change, release of hydrocarbons to the ocean pales in comparison to burning hydrocarbons as fuel. However, possible perturbation of the carbon cycle through destabilizing marine deposits of gas hydrate should not be overlooked when assessing possible outcomes of changing climate.

[See also Energy; Fossil Fuels; and Marine Pollution Convention.]

BIBLIOGRAPHY

Etkin, D. S. Oil Spills from Vessels, 1960–1995. Oil Spill Intelligence Report, Cutter Information Corporation. Minerals Management Service Worldwide Tanker Spill Database, 1997.
Kvenvolden, K. A., and J. W. Harbaugh, 1983. "Reassessment of the Rates at Which Oil from Natural Sources Enters the Marine Environment." Marine Environmental Research 10 (1983), 223–243.
National Research Council. Oil in the Sea: Inputs, Fates, and Effects. Washington, D.C.: National Academy Press, 1985.

—IAN R. MACDONALD

PHOSPHORUS CYCLE

The global phosphorus cycle has four major components: (1) tectonic uplift and exposure of phosphorus-bearing rocks to the forces of weathering; (2) physical erosion and chemical weathering of rocks, producing soils and providing dissolved and particulate phosphorus to rivers; (3) riverine transport of phosphorus to lakes and the ocean; and (4) sedimentation of phosphorus associated with organic and mineral matter that is buried in aquatic sediments (Figure 1). The cycle begins anew with uplift of sediments into the weathering regime.

Phosphorus is an essential nutrient for all life forms. It is a key player in fundamental biochemical reactions involving genetic material (deoxyribonucleic acid [DNA], ribonucleic acid [RNA]) and energy transfer (adenosine triphosphate [ATP]), and in structural support of organisms provided by membranes (phospholipids) and bone (the biomineral hydroxyapatite). Photosynthetic organisms utilize phosphorus, carbon, and other essential nutrients to build their tissues, using energy from the Sun. Biological productivity is contingent upon the availability of phosphorus to these organisms, which constitute the base of the food chain in both terrestrial and aquatic ecosystems.

Phosphorus locked up in bedrock, soils, and sediments is not directly available to organisms. Conversion of unavailable forms to dissolved phosphate, which can be directly assimilated, occurs through geochemical and biochemical reactions at various stages in the global phosphorus cycle. In environments with adequate phosphorus, production of biomass results in the deposition of organic matter in soil and sediments, where it acts as a source of fuel and nutrients to microbial communities. Microbial activity in soils and sediments, in turn, strongly influences the concentration and chemical form of phosphorus incorporated into the geologic record. Estimates of the mass of important phosphorus reservoirs are given in Table 1.

Terrestrial Phosphorus Cycle. In terrestrial systems, phosphorus resides in three pools: bedrock, soil, and living organisms (biomass). Weathering of continental bedrock is the principal source of phosphorus to the soils that support continental vegetation; atmospheric deposition is relatively unimportant. Phosphorus is weathered from bedrock by the dissolution of phosphorus-bearing minerals such as apatite $(Ca_{10}(PO_4)_6(OH,F,Cl)_2)$, the most abundant primary phosphorus mineral in crustal rocks. Weathering reactions are driven by the exposure of minerals to acids mainly derived from microbial activity. Phosphate solubilized during weathering is available for uptake by terrestrial plants and is returned to the soil by the decay of dead plant material.

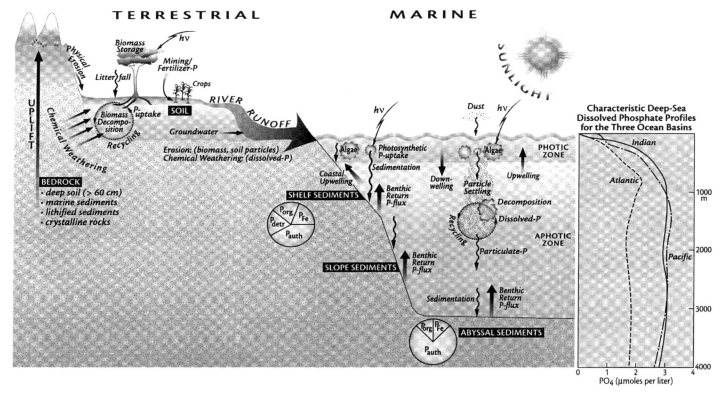

Phosphorus Cycle. FIGURE 1. The Global Phosphorus Cycle.
Cartoon illustrating the major reservoirs and fluxes of phosphorus described in the text. The oceanic photic zone, idealized in the cartoon, is typically thinner in coastal environments due to turbidity from continental terrigenous input, and deepens as the water column clarifies with distance away from the continental margins. The distribution of phosphorus among different chemical/mineral forms in marine sediments is given in the pie diagrams, where the abbreviations used are organic phosphorus (P_{org}), iron-bound phosphorus (P_{Fe}), detrital apatite (P_{detr}), and authigenic/biogenic apatite (P_{auth}). The vertical water column distributions of phosphate typically observed in the three ocean basins are shown in the panel to the right of the global phosphorus cycle cartoon, and are from Sverdrup et al., 1942. With permission of Prentice-Hall.

Low phosphate concentrations are found in soil pore solutions as a result of phosphorus sorption by various soil constituents, particularly ferric iron and aluminum oxyhydroxides. Sorption is considered the most important process controlling the terrestrial bioavailability of phosphorus. Plants have different physiological strategies for obtaining phosphorus despite low soil solution concentrations, including increasing root volume and surface area, the secretion by plant roots or associated fungi of chelating compounds that solubilize phosphorus bound with ferric iron and calcium, and the release of enzymes or acids in the root vicinity to solubilize phosphate. Plants also minimize phosphorus loss by resorbing much of their phosphorus prior to litterfall, and by efficient recycling of phosphorus from fallen litter. In extremely unfertile soils (e.g., in tropical rainforests), phosphorus recycling is so efficient that topsoil contains virtually no phosphorus; it is all tied up in biomass.

Systematic changes in the total amount and chemical form of phosphorus occur during soil development. In initial stages, phosphorus is present mainly as primary minerals such as apatite. In midstage soils, the reservoir of primary apatite is diminished; less soluble secondary minerals and organic phosphorus make up an increasing fraction of soil phosphorus. In highly weathered soils, phosphorus is partitioned mainly between refractory minerals and organic phosphorus. At this latest stage of soil development, atmospheric phosphorus deposition can take on disproportionate importance as a source of bioavailable phosphorus.

Transport of Phosphorus from Continents to the Ocean. Phosphorus is transferred from the continental to the oceanic reservoir primarily by rivers. Deposition via atmospheric dust is a minor flux. Groundwater seepage to the coastal ocean is a potentially important but undocumented flux.

Riverine phosphorus derives from weathered continental rocks and soils. Dissolved phosphorus in rivers occurs in both inorganic and organic forms. The scant data on dissolved organic phosphorus suggests that it

Phosphorus Cycle. TABLE 1. Major Reservoirs Active in the Global Phosphorus Cycle*

RESERVOIR NO.	RESERVOIR DESCRIPTION	RESERVOIR SIZE (MOLES $\times 10^{12}$)	REFERENCE
1	Sediments (crustal rocks and soil >60 cm deep and marine sediments)	0.27×10^8–1.3×10^8	Richey (1985) / Lerman et al. (1975); Jahnke (1992); Mackenzie et al. (1993)
2	Land ($\approx$ total soil < 60 cm deep: organic + inorganic)	3,100–6,450	Richey (1985) / Lerman et al. (1975); Jahnke (1992); Mackenzie et al. (1993)
3	Land biota	83.9–96.8	Richey (1985) / Lerman et al. (1975); Jahnke (1992); Mackenzie et al. (1993)
4	Surface ocean (total dissolved phosphorus)	87.4	Lerman et al. (1975); Jahnke (1992)
5	Deep sea (total dissolved phosphorus)	2,810	Lerman et al. (1975); Jahnke (1992)
6	Oceanic biota	1.61–4.45	Richey (1985) / Lerman et al. (1975); Jahnke (1992); Mackenzie et al. (1993)
7	Minable phosphorus	323–645	Lerman et al. (1975); Jahnke (1992) / Richey (1983); Mackenzie et al. (1993)
8	Atmospheric phosphorus	0.0009	Richey (1983); Jahnke (1992); Mackenzie et al. (1993)

*Because these reservoir sizes are difficult to quantify, different opinions exist on the quantity of phosphorus they contain. The ranges reported represent the maximum and minimum estimates found in a survey of the literature cited. References cited before the "/" refer to the lowest estimate; those after the "/" refer to the highest estimate. Methods of calculation, underlying assumptions, and sources of error are given in the references cited.

may account for 50 percent or more of dissolved riverine phosphorus. By most estimates, over 90 percent of the phosphorus delivered by rivers to the ocean is in particulate form. The chemical form of phosphorus associated with riverine particles is variable and depends on drainage basin geology and topographic relief, and on climatically controlled factors such as runoff. Available data suggest that approximately 20–40 percent of phosphorus in suspended particulate matter is organic. The majority of inorganic phosphorus is found in ferric oxyhydroxides and apatite, but aluminum oxyhydroxides and clays may also be significant carriers of the element.

The fate of phosphorus entering the ocean via rivers is variable. Some phosphorus is deposited in estuarine and coastal sediments by the coagulation of humic-iron complexes and by biological uptake and sedimentation of biogenic matter. A portion of suspended and sedimented phosphorus is released into the water column by various biogeochemical reactions, including desorption from freshwater particles entering high ionic strength marine waters, release of phosphorus from decaying organic matter, and dissolution of phosphorus-containing minerals. Estimates of the flux of dissolved phosphorus entering the ocean must take into account the amount of particulate phosphorus released to solution when rivers enter the ocean.

The Marine Phosphorus Cycle. Phosphorus in its simplest form, dissolved orthophosphate, is taken up by photosynthetic organisms (phytoplankton) at the base of the marine food web. When this pool of phosphorus is exhausted, organisms may utilize more complex forms by converting them to orthophosphate by means of enzymatic and microbiological reactions. In the open ocean, most phosphorus contained in biogenic particles is recycled within the upper water column. Efficient stripping of phosphate from surface waters by photosynthesis, combined with a buildup of phosphate at depth, where it is released by the decay of biogenic particles, results in the classic oceanic dissolved-nutrient profile (Figure 1). The progressive accumulation of respiration-derived phosphate at depth along the global deepwater circulation trajectory results in higher phosphate concentrations in the deep Pacific Ocean at the end of the trajectory, than in the North Atlantic, where deep water is initially formed by the sinking of cold surface waters in polar regions (Figure 1). [*See* Ocean Chemistry.]

The sole means of phosphorus removal from the oceans is by burial in marine sediments. The phosphorus flux to shelf and slope sediments is by most estimates larger than the phosphorus flux to the deep sea for several reasons. Coastal waters receive continentally derived nutrients via rivers, which stimulate high rates of primary productivity relative to the open ocean. The resulting higher flux of organic matter to sediments is accompanied by a larger terrigenous flux and higher sedimentation rates. Because of the shorter water column in coastal waters, less decay of organic matter occurs prior to deposition. These factors combine to enhance the retention of sedimentary phosphorus. During high sea level stands, the sedimentary phosphorus reservoir on continental margins expands, increasing the phosphorus removal flux and therefore shortening the oceanic element's residence time.

Terrigenous-dominated shelf and slope (hemipelagic) sediments and abyssal (pelagic) sediments have distinct phosphorus distributions. All are dominated by authigenic calcium-phosphate compounds (mostly apatite), but this reservoir is more important in pelagic sediments. Phosphorus is also found bound with ferric iron (mostly oxyhydroxides) and in organic forms in both environments, although detrital apatite is important only in hemipelagic sediments. Certain coastal environments characterized by extremely high, upwelling-driven biological productivity and low terrigenous input are enriched in authigenic apatite; these are protophosphorite deposits. A unique process contributing to the loss of phosphorus from sea water in pelagic environments is sorptive removal of phosphate onto ferric oxyhydroxides created in midocean ridge hydrothermal systems.

Solubilization of particulate phosphorus by microbial activity in sediments causes dissolved phosphate to accumulate in sediment pore waters, promoting the release of phosphate to bottom waters. The combined flux from coastal and abyssal sediments to sea water is estimated to exceed the total riverine phosphorus flux to the ocean. Reprecipitation of pore water phosphorus in secondary minerals in sediments can also occur, effectively reducing the return flux of phosphate to overlying sea water. The balance between these two processes impacts the marine phosphorus cycle by affecting the amount of phosphorus available for primary productivity in oceanic surface waters.

Phosphorus as a Limiting Nutrient. In terrestrial soils and in the surface waters of lakes and the ocean the concentration of dissolved orthophosphate is typically low. When bioavailable phosphorus is exhausted prior to more abundant nutrients, it limits biological productivity. Phosphorus limitation in lakes is widely accepted, and terrestrial soils are often phosphorus-limited. In the oceans, however, phosphorus limitation is the subject of controversy and debate.

The prevailing wisdom often favors nitrogen as the limiting nutrient in the oceans. Limitation by phosphorus can also occur in marine systems, however, sometimes shifting seasonally from nitrogen to phosphorus limitation in concert with changes in environmental features such as upwelling and river runoff. Whereas an abundant reservoir of nitrogen (gaseous N_2) in the atmosphere can be rendered bioavailable by nitrogen-fixing organisms, phosphorus supply to the ocean is limited to that weathered off the continents and delivered by rivers. Because continental weathering controls phosphorus supply to the oceans, phosphorus limitation is more likely than nitrogen limitation on geological time scales.

Human Impacts on the Global Phosphorus Cycle. The mining of phosphate rock (mostly from phosphorite deposits, ancient marine sediments enriched in phosphorus) for use as agricultural fertilizer increased dramatically in the latter half of the twentieth century. In addition to fertilizer use, deforestation, increased cultivation, and urban and industrial waste disposal all have enhanced phosphorus transport from terrestrial to aquatic systems, often with deleterious results. For example, elevated phosphorus concentrations in rivers resulting from these activities have resulted in eutrophication in some lakes and coastal areas, stimulating nuisance algal blooms and promoting hypoxic or anoxic conditions harmful or lethal to natural populations.

Increased erosion due to forest clear cutting and widespread cultivation has increased riverine suspended-matter concentrations, and the riverine flux of particulate phosphorus has increased as a result. Dams, in contrast, decrease sediment loads in rivers and therefore diminish phosphorus flux to the sea. The overall effect has been a large increase in riverine phosphorus flux to the oceans as a result of human activities.

Links to Other Biogeochemical Cycles. The biogeochemical cycles of phosphorus and carbon are linked through photosynthetic uptake and release during respiration. During times of elevated marine biological productivity, enhanced uptake of carbon dioxide by photosynthetic organisms results in increased carbon dioxide invasion from the atmosphere to oceanic surface waters, which persists until the supply of the least abundant nutrient is exhausted. On geologic time scales, phosphorus is likely to function as the limiting nutrient and thus play a role in the regulation of atmospheric carbon dioxide by limiting its drawdown by marine photosynthetic activity. This connection between nutrients and atmospheric carbon dioxide may have played a role in triggering or enhancing the global cooling that resulted in glacial episodes in the geologic past. [*See* Biogeochemical Cycles.]

The phosphorus and oxygen cycles are linked through the chemistry of iron. Unstable at the Earth's surface in the presence of oxygen, reduced iron oxidizes to form ferric iron oxyhydroxides, which are extremely efficient scavengers of dissolved phosphate. The resupply of phosphate to surface waters, where it can fertilize biological productivity, is reduced when oceanic bottom waters are well oxygenated and ferric oxyhydroxides are present. During times in Earth's history when oxygen was not abundant in the atmosphere (Precambrian), and when expanses of the deep ocean were anoxic (e.g., Cretaceous), there may have been much higher concentrations of dissolved phosphate in the deep sea owing to the diminished importance of sequestering with ferric oxyhydroxides. This iron-phosphorus-oxygen coupling produces a negative feedback that may have kept atmospheric O_2 within the narrow range of concentrations required to sustain aerobic life throughout the Phanerozoic. Thus, it is in the oceans that the role of phosphorus as a limiting nutrient has the greatest repercussions for the global carbon and oxygen cycles.

[*See also* Carbon Cycle; Earth History; Mining; Oxygen Cycle; *and* Soils.]

BIBLIOGRAPHY

Chadwick, O. A., L. A. Derry, P. M. Vitousek, B. J. Huebert, and L. O. Hedin. "Changing Sources of Nutrients during Four Million Years of Ecosystem Development." *Nature* 397 (1999), 491–497.

Colman, A. S., and H. D. Holland. "The Global Diagenetic Flux of Phosphorus from Marine Sediments to the Oceans: Redox Sensitivity and the Control of Atmospheric Oxygen Levels." In *Marine Authigenesis: From Global to Microbial*, edited by C. R. Glenn, L. Prevot-Lucas, and J. Lucas, pp. 53–75. Society of Economic Paleontologists and Mineralogists Special Publication No. 66, 2000.

Delaney, M. L. "Phosphorus Accumulation in Marine Sediments and the Oceanic Phosphorus Cycle. *Global Biogeochemical Cycles* 12.4 (1998), 563–572.

Duce, R. A., et al. "The Atmospheric Input of Trace Species to the World Ocean." *Global Biogeochemical Cycles* 5 (1991), 193–259.

Jahnke, R. A. "The Phosphorus Cycle." In *Global Geochemical Cycles*, edited by S. S. Butcher, R. J. Charlson, G. H. Orians, and G. V. Wolff, pp. 301–315. San Diego: Academic Press, 1992.

Karl, D. M. "A Sea of Change: Biogeochemical Variability in the North Pacific Subtropical Gyre." *Ecosystems* 2 (1999), 181–214.

Lerman, A., F. T. Mackenzie, and R. M. Garrels. "Modeling of Geochemical Cycles: Phosphorus as an Example." *Geological Society of America Memoir* 142 (1975), 205–217.

Mackenzie, F. T., L. M. Ver, C. Sabine, M. Lane, and A. Lerman. "C, N, P, S Global Biogeochemical Cycles and Modeling of Global Change." In *Interactions of C, N, P, and S Biogeochemical Cycles and Global Change*, NATO ASI ser. 1, vol. 4, edited by R. Wollast, F. T. Mackenzie, and L. Chou, pp. 1–61. Berlin: Springer-Verlag, 1993.

Meybeck, M. "Carbon, Nitrogen, and Phosphorus Transport by World Rivers." *American Journal of Science* 282.4 (1982), 401–450.

Petsch, S. T., and R. A. Berner. "Coupling the Geochemical Cycles of C, P, Fe, and S: The Effect on Atmospheric O_2 and the Isotopic Records of Carbon and Sulfur." *American Journal of Science* 298 (1998), 246–262.

Richey, J. E. "The Phosphorus Cycle." In *The Major Biogeochemical Cycles and Their Interactions*, SCOPE 21, edited by B. Bolin, and R. B. Cook, pp. 51–56. Chichester, U.K.: Wiley, 1983.

Ruttenberg, K. C. "Reassessment of the Oceanic Residence Time of Phosphorus." *Chemical Geology* 107 (1993), 405–409.

Ruttenberg, K. C., and R. A. Berner. "Authigenic Apatite Formation and Burial in Sediments from Non-upwelling, Continental Margin Environments." *Geochimica et Cosmochimica Acta* 57.5 (1993), 991–1007.

Sverdup, H. V., M. W. Johnson, and R. H. Fleming. *The Oceans, Their Physics, Chemistry and General Biology.* New York: Prentice-Hall, 1942.

Tiessen, H., ed. *Phosphorus in the Global Environment: Transfers, Cycles and Management.* SCOPE 54. Chichester, U.K.: Wiley, 1995.

Tyrell, T. "The Relative Influences of Nitrogen and Phosphorus on Oceanic Productivity." *Nature* 400 (1999), 525–531.

Walker, T. W., and J. K. Syers. "The Fate of Phosphorus during Pedogenesis." *Geoderma* 15 (1976), 1–19.

—K. C. RUTTENBERG

PHOTOVOLTAICS. *See* Electrical Power Generation.

PINCHOT, GIFFORD

Gifford Pinchot (1865–1946), founder of the American Forest Service, was born in Simsbury, Connecticut, and was a major player in the progressive conservation movement at the turn of the century. A graduate of Yale University, Pinchot studied forestry in Europe and returned to the United States in 1890, determined to apply scientific management techniques to the forests of his native land. Appalled by the devastation created by timber companies cutting over vast acreage for the most valuable wood and destroying other growth, he became convinced that private ownership of forest land was not conducive to wise use of natural resources.

In 1898, Pinchot was appointed head of the Forestry Division in the Department of Agriculture and set out to wrest control over the national forest preserves from the Department of Interior's General Land Office, whose primary function was to transfer title to private owners. A fellow outdoorsman and big-game hunter, Pinchot became a confidant of President Theodore Roosevelt, who helped convince Congress to transfer control over the forest preserves to the renamed Forest Service in 1905.

Pinchot agreed with the purpose of the American Forestry Association, which had urged Congress in 1891 to keep some of the public domain out of private ownership. As a utilitarian, he differed with many conservationists who wanted to prevent development of these public lands. Pinchot advocated development of all resources in the national forests, including harvesting of timber, grazing of sheep and cattle, and development of hydropower and power sites, as long as it was done in a manner that ensured a continuous lumber supply for a growing nation and protected the watersheds for future use. Hence he split with preservationists such as John Muir over locking up natural resources in national parks. Their most public dispute occurred over developing the Hetch Hetchy Valley into a reservoir for San Francisco's water supply, which Pinchot supported.

A skilled administrator, Pinchot organized the Forest Service around a professional ethos of "wise use" designed to obtain maximum economic utility for the public from the forest reserves. At a time when most bureaucrats were political appointees, he recruited his rangers from professional forestry schools, including Yale's, founded in 1900 with an endowment from his father, James Pinchot. He emphasized the importance of the rangers' maintaining independent judgments about how to manage forests and insisted that timber companies and ranchers who used these resources pay fair market value for them.

Conservation sentiment waned after the election of William Howard Taft in 1908. Although Pinchot remained chief forester, James Garfield, Roosevelt's secretary of the interior and a friend of Pinchot's, was replaced by Richard Ballinger, who advocated selling coal lands in Alaska to private developers. Pinchot, who wanted to lease the lands and maintain public control, clashed openly with Ballinger and President Taft over this issue and was fired in January 1910. He later served two terms as governor of Pennsylvania and remained active in the conservation movement and the Society of American Foresters until his death in 1946.

[See also Prior Informed Consent for Trade in Hazardous Chemicals and Pesticides.]

BIBLIOGRAPHY

Culhane, P. Public Lands Politics. Baltimore: Johns Hopkins University Press, 1981.
Hays, S. P. Conservation and the Gospel of Efficiency. Cambridge: Harvard University Press, 1959.
Klyza, C. M. Who Controls Public Lands? Chapel Hill: University of North Carolina Press, 1996.
Pinchot, G. Breaking New Ground. New York: Harcourt, Brace, 1947.

—LETTIE MCSPADDEN

PLANETARY ATMOSPHERES

The Earth's atmosphere is just one of a series of atmospheres we can observe in the solar system. The comparative study of these atmospheres is increasing our understanding of the Earth's atmosphere and of the types of circulation it may have experienced during its geologic past. This article focuses on the circulation of planetary atmospheres, a crucial influence on climatic conditions at a planet's surface. The most important factors determining an atmospheric circulation include the strength and distribution of heat sources and sinks, the rotation rate of the planet, and the nature of the planet's surface. Other factors, such as the chemical composition of the atmosphere and its total mass, are less important.

For the purpose of characterizing their atmospheric motions, the planets may be classified as terrestrial planets and gas giant planets. Terrestrial planets are relatively small, rocky bodies with more tenuous atmospheres overlying a much denser surface. Earth, Mars, and Venus are the terrestrial planets with significant atmospheres; Titan, the largest satellite of Saturn, counts as a terrestrial planet for the purposes of this discussion. Gas giants are much larger bodies that lie farther from the Sun and are composed mainly of light elements such as hydrogen and helium. They are fluid throughout most of their bulk and have no rigid surface. The gas giant planets are Jupiter, Saturn, Uranus, and Neptune. [See Planets.]

Heat Sources. The generation of the energy associated with the motion of a planet's atmosphere requires that the heating take place at a lower level than the cooling. [See Atmosphere Dynamics.] Basic thermodynamic principles imply that heat energy is converted into mechanical energy of motion as circulating parcels of gas are heated at high pressure and cooled at lower pressure. If the heating were at higher levels than the cooling, the atmosphere would remain motionless (a result sometimes called "Sandstrom's theorem"). The Earth's oceans are both heated and cooled near their surface. The existence of a deep thermohaline circulation in the oceans implies that some heat must be mixed downward in certain regions in order to drive the circulation.

All the gases that make up atmospheres in the solar system are relatively transparent to the short-wavelength radiation emitted by the Sun. This radiation can penetrate to relatively deep levels in the atmosphere before it is absorbed to heat the air. In contrast, atmospheres in the solar system are relatively opaque to the longer-wavelength, infrared radiation emitted by a planet. This opacity is due mainly to complex molecules, made up of three atoms or more; it means that the emitting layers, from which radiation is emitted by the atmosphere to space, are relatively high in the atmosphere.

The atmospheres of Earth and Mars share a common pattern of heat sources and sinks, with heating at low levels concentrated in the tropics, and cooling at upper levels that is strongest toward the polar regions; the atmospheric circulation transports heat both upward and poleward. The circulation associated with this configuration consists of an axially symmetric Hadley cell (see Figure 1) in the tropics and unsteady baroclinic waves in the midlatitudes, especially in the winter hemisphere.

In the case of Mars, two further complications modify the atmospheric circulation. The first is associated with seasonal changes in the heating patterns. Because of its axial tilt and thin, transparent atmosphere, the Martian surface experiences extreme seasonal temperature variations. In midwinter, the polar regions receive

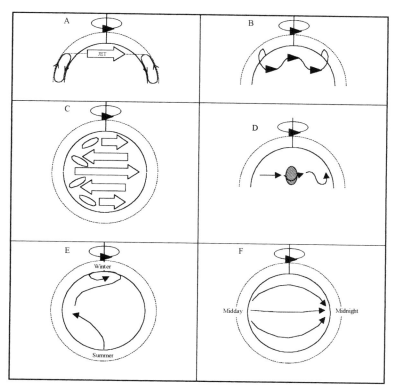

Planetary Atmospheres. Figure 1.

Examples of (A) Hadley circulations, with slow, axially symmetric overturning circulations. Examples include Earth (tropics), Mars (summer hemisphere), Venus, and Titan. (B) Sloping convection, with unstable wavelike disturbances that transport heat upward and poleward. Examples include Earth (midlatitudes) and Mars (winter). (C) Geostrophic turbulence, where a random field of small-scale eddies eventually drives a series of parallel easterly and westerly jets. Examples include Jupiter, Saturn, and Neptune. (D)

Orographically excited Rossby waves, with a wake of stationary waves disturbing places remote from the mountains. Examples include Earth (especially the Northern Hemisphere in winter) and Mars. (E) Condensation flow, where condensation at the winter pole and evaporation at the summer pole drives an interhemispheric circulation. Mars exhibits this type of flow. (F) Thermal tides, where heating at the subsolar point and cooling of the night hemisphere lead to a large-scale circulation. Examples include Venus and possibly Titan.

no sunlight and become so cold that the carbon dioxide that makes up most of the tenuous atmosphere condenses onto the surface as a dense frost. At the strongly heated summer pole, this frost evaporates back into the atmosphere. As a result, an important part of the Martian global circulation is the "condensation flow" from the warm summer pole to the cold winter pole.

The second factor is the large dust storms that develop in some years near the spring pole of Mars. So much dust can be raised off the ground that the lower atmosphere becomes opaque to sunlight, and the absorbing level moves off the ground into the upper troposphere. In these conditions, the nature of the atmospheric weather systems is completely changed; they become more regular and more extensive, with weaker heat transport. Similar circulation changes might occur if the Earth's atmosphere were to become heavily laden with particulate matter—for instance, after a nuclear war; this possibly has happened after impacts of comets or large asteroids on the Earth's surface. The resulting

climate changes are thought to have played an important role in various mass extinction events in the Earth's history, especially the mass extinction at the end of the Cretaceous period.

The gas giant planets Jupiter, Saturn, and Neptune receive much less heat from the Sun than do the inner planets. Measurements of the infrared radiation they emit to space reveal that they radiate considerably more heat than they receive. The difference is accounted for by internal heat sources that receive their energy from slow gravitational collapse. In the case of Jupiter, a shrinkage of its radius of about 1 millimeter each century would account for the extra heat. For Neptune and Saturn, it has been suggested that the energy is released by continuing differentiation within the planets, as denser elements migrate toward the core and lighter ones float upward. The presence of an internal heat source means that heating of the lower atmosphere takes place nearly uniformly at all latitudes, so that the temperature difference between the equator and the pole on these planets is very small. The atmospheric circulation is required to transport heat upward but not over great distances in the poleward direction.

Uranus is an exception: although in size, mass, and composition it is very similar to Neptune, it has no measurable internal heat source. The reasons for this difference are not understood. Observations show that the circulation of Uranus's atmosphere is much weaker than that observed on the other gas giants.

Rotation Rate. The rate at which a planet rotates is a crucial constraint on its atmospheric dynamics. Rapid rotation inhibits vertical motion and limits the extent of poleward motion. The giant planets rotate extremely rapidly relative to their size, and the flows in their atmospheres are characterized by several parallel zonal jets, with characteristic contrasting zones and bands in the clouds associated with these jets. Some insight into these jets has been gained from theories of "geostrophic" or "two-dimensional" turbulence, discussed below.

Earth and Mars have more moderate rotation rates. Overturning Hadley cells dominate the circulation at low latitudes, where the effects of rotation are slight. In middle and high latitudes, the character of the flow is more constrained by rotation, with Rossby waves and sloping convection dominating the heat transporting motions (Figure 1).

Venus, in contrast, is an example of a very slowly rotating planet, with overturning motions extending from the equator to the pole. It also has a cloud-filled atmosphere in which much of the incident solar radiation is absorbed at high levels, about 60 kilometers above the surface. The atmosphere of Venus at the cloud-top levels is observed to rotate much more rapidly than the solid planet. No completely satisfactory explanation of this "superrotation" has yet been proposed, but it is thought to arise when the thermal tide, excited by the maximum of heating on the sunlit side of the planet, transfers momentum to the mean winds. Titan is also a slowly rotating body with a dense, cloudy atmosphere. Little is known about the circulation of its atmosphere, but, like that of Venus, it appears to be superrotating.

Nature of the Surface. The friction that ultimately restrains the winds in the atmosphere is also a crucial factor. Mars, with its rough mountainous surface, has greater surface friction than Earth, where two-thirds of the surface is covered by relatively smooth ocean. In contrast to the terrestrial planets, the giant planets have no solid surface that can support stress, and they are therefore characterized by very low levels of frictional dissipation. These low levels provide a strong constraint on the nature of the atmospheric circulations that can develop on these planets.

The solid surfaces of the terrestrial planets all have regions of high mountains, and these mountains can have an important influence on the climate of the surface. Clearly, mountains have a strong local influence on temperature and winds. On Earth, these effects are well known: nearly all aspects of the climate of even modest mountain regions differ sharply from conditions in the neighboring lowland regions. For our purposes, however, more important are the circumstances in which mountains can disturb the atmosphere at places remote from the mountains themselves. Such disturbances are generally the result of a wake of Rossby waves formed as air flows over the mountains. Such mountain wakes are important for Earth's atmosphere. Rossby waves generated by the Rocky Mountain ranges mean, for example, that the winter climate of New York is much colder than that of Rome, even though they lie at similar latitudes. Rossby wave wakes are also an important feature of Martian meteorology.

Geostrophic Turbulence. The vast giant planets are characterized by the wide range of scales of their atmospheric motions, from the scale of the planet itself, through the smaller scales of the individual zones and bands (associated with easterly and westerly jets in the atmosphere), down to the small scales of individual spots and waves observed within the individual bands.

The observed jet structure is thought to arise from a balance between turbulent mixing and Rossby wave propagation. Turbulence tends to wrap up structures in the flow, generating very small-scale features. Rossby waves enable eddy activity to be propagated to remote parts of the atmosphere and opposes the wrapping effects of turbulence. Balancing these two effects leads to a realistic estimate of the intensity and horizontal scale of the zonal jets observed on Jupiter and Saturn. Similar reasoning also clarifies the scale and intensity of currents observed in the Earth's oceans.

A Synthesis. The considerations of the previous sections suggest that observed planetary circulations can be categorized into certain basic classes or forms. Each class may be present in different atmospheres with different intensities and with different horizontal and vertical scales. Figure 1 summarizes six of the most important circulation types and suggests examples of where they may be observed.

To summarize, Venus is dominated by global-scale type I Hadley circulations, with a thermal tide, type VI, generating a super-rotation. Similar factors are probably active on Titan. Earth and Mars exhibit type I Hadley circulations in their tropics and in the summer midlatitudes of Mars, and type II sloping convection in the midlatitudes. Type V condensation flows are important on Mars. Type IV Rossby wave wakes are important in the winter hemispheres of both Earth and Mars. The gas giant planets are best thought of as the result of type III geostrophic turbulence. Some regard the spots and waves observed in gas giant bands and zones as manifestations of type II sloping convection associated with the jets.

BIBLIOGRAPHY

Beatty, J. K., and A. Chaikin, eds. *The New Solar System*. Cambridge: Cambridge University Press, 1990. See especially chapters 8 and 11.

James, I. N. *Introduction to Circulating Atmospheres*. Cambridge: Cambridge University Press, 1995. See especially chapter 10.

—I. N. JAMES

PLANETS

Our solar system consists of nine planets, the Sun, and numerous smaller bodies, including asteroids, comets, and moons. In order of increasing distance from the Sun, the planets are Mercury, Venus, Earth, Mars, Jupiter, Saturn, Uranus, Neptune, and Pluto. The four innermost planets are often referred to as *terrestrial* planets because, like Earth, they are composed primarily of rock-forming materials such as iron and silicate minerals. The outer planets (except for Pluto) are "gas giant" planets that contain large amounts of ice-forming compounds such as water, methane, and ammonia. Jupiter and Saturn contain large amounts of hydrogen and helium as well, presumably because they formed quickly enough to capture these gases from the solar nebula before it dispersed. Pluto is a small, icy body that is more like a moon than a planet.

Of the four terrestrial planets, only Venus, Earth, and Mars have atmospheres, so this article focuses on these bodies. A list of basic physical properties of these planets is given in Table 1. In terms of mass, Venus is close to Earth, whereas Mars is about ten times smaller. However, Venus and Mars are both very different from Earth with respect to surface temperature, surface pressure, and atmospheric composition. Venus has a dense, extremely hot atmosphere and Mars has a thin, cold atmosphere. The atmospheres of Venus and Mars consist primarily of carbon dioxide, whereas Earth's atmosphere is dominated by nitrogen and oxygen.

Why are the atmospheres and climates of Venus and Mars so different from those of Earth? As one might expect, a large part of the difference stems from their different orbital radii. Venus, being closer to the Sun, receives 1.91 times as much solar radiation as does Earth. Mars, being farther away, receives only 0.43 times Earth's radiation flux. These differences in the amount of sunlight received cause corresponding differences in the planets' surface temperatures. However, this factor by itself cannot explain the large variation that we observe. Venus has a very high albedo (about 0.8), which means that it only absorbs about 20 percent of the sunlight incident upon it. (The albedo is high because of scattering by the dense carbon dioxide atmosphere and by the planet-encircling sulfuric acid clouds.) By comparison, Earth's albedo is only about 0.3. Thus, Earth actually absorbs almost twice as much solar radiation as does Venus. [*See* Albedo.]

The surface temperature of Venus is so high because of the greenhouse effect of its atmosphere. Carbon dioxide is a good absorber and emitter of infrared radiation; hence, it retards the outward flux of infrared radiation from Venus's surface. Other trace gases in the Venusian atmosphere, especially sulfur dioxide, water vapor, and carbon monoxide, also absorb outgoing infrared radiation, as do the sulfuric acid clouds. The result is a greenhouse effect of over 500°C. By comparison, Earth's greenhouse effect is 33°C, and that of Mars is only about 6°C. Mars actually has about fifty times as much carbon

Planets. TABLE 1. Key Planetary Characteristics

	VENUS	EARTH	MARS
Mean orbital radius (AU)*	0.723	1	1.524
Orbital period (Earth years)	0.615	1	1.881
Rotation period (Earth days)	243	1	1.03
Mass (Earth masses)[†]	0.815	1	0.107
Mean surface temperature (K)	730	288	218
Mean surface pressure (Atm)	93	1	0.007
Albedo	0.8	0.3	0.21
Primary atmospheric constituents	CO_2 (96%) N_2 (3.5%)	N_2 (78%) O_2 (21%) Ar (0.9%)	CO_2 (95%) N_2 (2.7%) Ar (1.6%)

*1 AU = 1 astronomical unit = 1.496×10^8 kilometers.

[†]1 Earth mass = 5.976×10^{24} kilograms.

dioxide in a vertical column of atmosphere as does Earth. The reason that Mars's greenhouse effect is so small is that its cold atmosphere has very little water vapor in it. Water vapor is an even better infrared absorber than is carbon dioxide, so its low abundance in the Martian atmosphere allows that planet to radiate energy to space very efficiently. [*See* Greenhouse Effect.]

Although Venus and Mars are quite different from Earth today, both planets are thought to have been more Earth-like in the past. For Venus, the evidence comes from hydrogen isotopes: the deuterium/hydrogen (D/H) ratio in Venus's atmosphere is about 150 times that in Earth's oceans. The most likely explanation is that Venus had significantly more water in the past but lost it as a result of photodissociation by solar ultraviolet radiation followed by escape of hydrogen to space. The lighter hydrogen isotope (H) escaped more rapidly than the heavier isotope (D), causing the atmospheric D/H ratio to increase with time.

The process by which Venus lost its water is sometimes referred to as a *runaway greenhouse*. But it may not have involved a true runaway, in which all the water was present as steam. Early in solar system history, the solar flux is thought to have been approximately 30 percent lower than today. As a result, Venus may actually have had liquid water on its surface at one time. Water vapor was very abundant in Venus's lower atmosphere, however. The latent heat released when this water vapor condensed to form clouds caused the tropospheric cold trap—the cold region at the top of the convective layer—to move to a very high altitude. The stratosphere became moist, and this in turn allowed photodissociation and hydrogen escape to proceed very rapidly. Once Venus lost its water, carbon dioxide could no longer combine with surface minerals to form carbonates, so that volcanic carbon dioxide accumulated to form the dense atmosphere that we see today. Sulfur gases (which dissolve in rainwater on Earth) could also not be removed, so sulfur dioxide and its photolysis byproduct, sulfuric acid, also became abundant.

Mars also appears to have had liquid water on its surface in the past. The more heavily cratered parts of the Martian surface exhibit numerous channels that were formed by a flowing liquid—almost certainly water. We know from the lunar record that most of the cratering in the inner solar system happened during the first 700 million years of its history, so we infer that Mars was much warmer and wetter during that time than it is today.

Why was Mars warm in the past, and what caused it to cool down over time? The first question is still something of a mystery. It has been shown that gaseous carbon dioxide and water vapor could not have kept Mars's surface temperature above the freezing point in the past, when solar luminosity was low. Either additional greenhouse gases must have been present or the surface was kept warm by the radiative effect of carbon dioxide ice clouds. Recent calculations indicate that such clouds can indeed strongly warm the surface by backscattering outgoing infrared radiation. In this respect, they differ from water vapor clouds, which absorb infrared radiation and reradiate it in both the upward and downward directions.

Why Mars cooled off with time is somewhat better understood. Because Mars is much smaller than Earth, it lost its internal heat much more quickly. This caused volcanism to decrease, preventing Mars from recycling carbon dioxide back into its atmosphere. Carbon dioxide was adsorbed into the regolith (the Martian soil) and may also have formed deposits of carbonate rock. On Earth, such carbonate rocks are reconverted into carbon dioxide when plate tectonics pushes them deep into the crust. This may have happened on early Mars as well, but the recycling process shut down once Mars became volcanically inactive. Mars's atmosphere grew colder and thinner with time and eventually approached its present state. [*See* Plate Tectonics.]

Studies of the climate evolution of Mars and Venus allow us to estimate the width of the liquid water habitable zone (HZ) around the Sun. Because all known organisms require liquid water during at least part of their life cycle, the presence of liquid water on a planet's surface is considered fundamental to planetary habitability. In our own solar system, Earth has evidently remained within the HZ through most of its history. Evidence for liquid water and for life both date back about 4 billion years. Venus is clearly inside the inner edge of the HZ (and, hence, is not habitable), whereas Mars appears to be just within the outer edge of the HZ. A larger planet at Mars's distance, which had plate tectonics and was able to recycle carbon dioxide back into its atmosphere, might very well be habitable.

In the future, observational studies of other planetary systems may put these ideas to the test. Astronomers have now found planets around at least thirty main-sequence (normal, hydrogen-burning) stars. Those identified so far are all giant planets like Jupiter, but astronomers hope to find Earth-sized planets within the next fifteen to twenty years. Consideration of our own solar system implies that the chance of finding an extrasolar planet within the HZ around its star is at least 50 percent, and possibly higher if carbon dioxide clouds are as strongly warming as has been suggested. Thus it seems likely that many other potentially habitable planets exist elsewhere in the galaxy. The question then will become: Are any of these planets actually inhabited?

[*See also* Atmosphere Structure and Evolution; Biosphere; Earth Motions; Earth Structure and Development; *and* Sun.]

BIBLIOGRAPHY

GENERAL REFERENCE

Beatty, J. K., and A. Chaikin. *The New Solar System.* 3rd ed. New York and Cambridge: Cambridge University Press, 1990. A good general reference on planets and the solar system.

CLIMATE EVOLUTION OF VENUS

Gurwell, M. "Evolution of Deuterium on Venus." *Nature* 378 (1995), 22–23.

Kasting, J. F. "Runaway and Moist Greenhouse Atmospheres and the Evolution of Earth and Venus." *Icarus* 74 (1988), 472–494.

CLIMATE EVOLUTION OF MARS

Forget, F., and R. T. Pierrehumbert. "Warming Early Mars with Carbon Dioxide Clouds that Scatter Infrared Radiation." *Science* 278 (1997), 1273–1276.

Kasting, J. F. "Carbon Dioxide Condensation and the Climate of Early Mars." *Icarus* 94 (1991), 1–13.

CLIMATE EVOLUTION OF EARTH

Kasting, J. F., O. B. Toon, and J. B. Pollack. "How Climate Evolved on the Terrestrial Planets." *Scientific American* 256 (1988), 90–97.

Sagan, C., and G. Mullen. "Earth and Mars: Evolution of Atmospheres and Surface Temperatures." *Science* 177 (1972), 52–56.

Walker, J. C. G., P. B. Hays, and J. F. Kasting. "A Negative Feedback Mechanism for the Long-Term Stabilization of Earth's Surface Temperature." *Journal of Geophysical Research* 86 (1981), 9776–9782.

HABITABLE ZONES AND PLANETS AROUND OTHER STARS

Angel, J. R. P., and N. J. Woolf. "Searching for Life on Other Planets." *Scientific American* 274 (April 1996), 60–66.

Kasting, J. F., D. P. Whitmire, and R. T. Reynolds. "Habitable Zones around Main Sequence Stars." *Icarus* 101 (1993), 108–128.

—JAMES F. KASTING

PLASTICS. *See* Recycling.

PLATE TECTONICS

[This article provides a technical treatment of the subject intended for readers at an advanced level.]

Plate tectonics is a metatheory of Earth behavior that encompasses both continental drift and sea floor spreading (SFS). It was advanced in the late 1960s as a means of describing the motions of the continents observed using paleomagnetic directions and those seen in the oceanic portions of the plates through observations of earthquakes and sea floor magnetic anomalies. [*See* Earthquakes.]

Although there had been ideas about continental drift since before the nineteenth century, the first serious proponent of this hypothesis was Alfred Wegener, in 1912 (Wegener, 1966). [*See the biography of Wegener.*] He used a wide variety of data to suggest mobility of the continents. Although many of his ideas have been proven correct, he was wrong in one major area, speed of motion, because his speeds were more than a factor of ten larger than those now known to exist. Early supporters of his ideas were du Toit (1937) and Holmes (1944). The field advanced greatly when paleomagnetic data became available. [*See the vignette on* Paleomagnetic Evidence of Crustal Movement.*]

Sea Floor Spreading. Hess (1962) is credited with the first detailed description of SFS. He based his ideas on paleomagnetic results; mantle convection currents as suggested by Holmes; the sparse sediment cover of the ocean basins, suggesting that they were much younger than the continents; the high heat flow over the oceanic ridges; the frequency of seamounts (undersea volcanic edifices) in the ocean basins; and the uniform thickness of the oceanic crust. His ideas about the latter, in which he proposed an oceanic crust made largely of serpentinized peridotite, with uniform thickness caused by the depth to the 500°C isotherm, above which serpentinite does not form have been superseded. The uniform thickness is now thought to arise from melting following passive uplift and depressurization of undifferentiated mantle caused by extension (McKenzie and Bickle, 1988).

The hypothesis of Fred Vine and Drummond Matthews in 1963 was advanced to explain the magnetic anomalies seen near small topographic features and close to the ocean ridges, where zones of normal and reversed magnetization alternate symmetrically on each side of the ridge crest. Vine and Matthews proposed a magnetized layer of thickness between 8 and 14 kilometers. Later, Vine and Wilson (1965) and Vine (1966) expanded this hypothesis to define a more rigorous SFS theory that called for SFS at the ridge crests and magnetization of the rock so produced by the Earth's magnetic field. Reversals of the field leave their mark on the rocks, somewhat akin to a gigantic tape recorder, which can then be "played back" by ships towing magnetometers. Note also that other people were thinking about SFS: for example, Schmalz (1961) and Morley (unpublished paper, 1963; published in 1981). Emiliani (1981) has a very useful history of the events leading up to the beginning of the Deep Sea Drilling Project, which is continuing more than thirty years later in the guise of the Ocean Drilling Program. One of the major tasks of DSDP was to test the hypothesis of SFS.

The theory of SFS was developed to explain the lineated magnetic anomalies seen on either side of the ridge crest. The spacing of these magnetic anomalies close to the ridge crest was shown to be in the same ratio as the dates of reversals of the Earth's magnetic field during the past few million years, thus proving that the ocean floor was acting as a "tape recorder" for the field,

PALEOMAGNETIC EVIDENCE OF CRUSTAL MOVEMENT

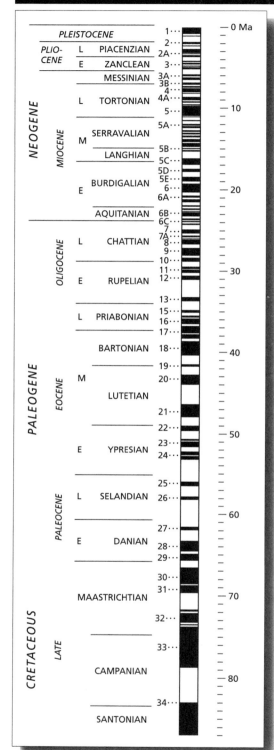

Geomagnetic Polarity Time Scale. (After Cande and Kent, 1992, pp. 13, 935. Copyright by the American Geophysical Union.)

When an iron-rich igneous rock, such as basalt, solidifies from lava, magnetic particles in the lava align with the magnetic field of that location on the Earth in a way that is consistent with the polarity of the field at that time in Earth history.

Location is expressed in two ways in the magnetic texture of a rock. First is the compass direction of alignment toward a magnetic pole: if the rock's magnetic texture does not align with the direction of today's magnetic field in that location, this indicates some movement of the continent since the rock was formed. Second is the vertical dip of the alignment. Near a magnetic pole, the rock particles will align with a force field that plunges steeply into the Earth; whereas, near the equator, the field lines run parallel to the Earth's surface: if an ancient basalt in a midlatitude location shows horizontal magnetic alignment, then the rock and its host continent have probably drifted poleward. These two aspects of paleomagnetism provide vital evidence for the movement of continents, but they do not suggest a mechanism for that movement.

It is the polarity of the magnetic field at the time of imprint that provides evidence to clinch the idea of plate movement and sea floor spreading. In certain periods, the Earth's magnetic field has been normal (as today), while in other periods it has been reversed, with north polarity at the south magnetic pole. Before the reversal occurs, the intensity of the Earth's magnetic field declines; then it strengthens again as the new polarity is adopted. Study of hundreds of volcanic rocks of various ages has revealed a series of normal versus reversed periods extending back to 85 million years ago (see graph). When, in the 1960s, magnetic surveys of the Atlantic sea floor showed normal versus reversed rocks in a striped pattern symmetrical about the mid-Atlantic Ridge, it became apparent that outlying pairs of stripes, matching in polarity, were older, while innermost matching pairs were formed most recently. Sea floor spreading and the repeated birth of new ocean floor at the ridge were demonstrated.

BIBLIOGRAPHY

Monastersky, R. "Earth's Heart Beats with a Magnetic Rhythm." *Science News* (20 November 1993), 327.

—DAVID J. CUFF

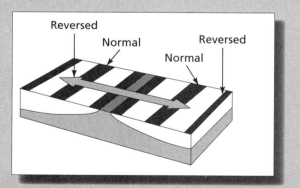

The Ocean Floor, Showing Polarity Stripes Schematically.

moving at a rate of 10–100 kilometers per million years—which is well suited for recording reversals, which happen randomly at a current rate of about five every million years. In many cases, this results in magnetic anomalies that are symmetrical about the ridge crest, the best example being shown by Pitman and Heirtzler (1966). Other phenomena explained by the theory of SFS include the pattern of heat flow observed in well-sedimented portions of the oceanic crust, the long-wavelength portion of ocean basin bathymetry, the pattern of earthquakes seen on the midocean ridges and transform faults, and the increase in sediment thickness and basal sediment age away from the ridge crests. The theory of SFS has proved to be very powerful. It has allowed the history of magnetic field reversals to be documented in considerable detail for most of the Neozoic (younger than 180 million years). Although the direct dating of reversals from continental rocks can only be done for the past 10 million years, it is occasionally possible to obtain dates from oceanic crustal rocks that can be identified with specific reversals of the field, or from basal sediments through the biostratigraphic time scale. The reversal history has shown that the rate of reversals has changed considerably in the past, with periods of several tens of millions of years when no reversals occurred. In contrast, today the average rate of reversals is about five every million years.

The original attempt to date the reversal time scale using magnetic anomalies is found in Heirtzler et al. (1968). The most recent time scale of reversals for the late Cretaceous and Cenozoic is by Cande and Kent (1992, 1995). This time scale has benefited from the accurate dating of lavas that were erupted during specific reversal events, and also from the application of astrochronology, which is the dating of sediments by the use of precessional, obliquity, or ellipticity signals. A Mesozoic time scale was presented by Gradstein et al. (1994) and tabulated by Opdyke and Channell (1996).

Once the reversal time scale was developed, scientists were able to date most parts of the oceanic crust with considerable confidence, because it was usually possible to determine which set of reversals was recorded in the oceanic crust under consideration. An example of this is the map showing the age of the oceanic crust (Müller et al., 1997). Areas of oceanic crust formed during a long period of no reversals (120–83 million years ago) during the Cretaceous (140–65 million years ago) cannot be dated accurately, however. This important period in Earth history is known as the Cretaceous quiet zone and has never been satisfactorily explained. [See Earth History.] Because of the ability to date oceanic crust, it is possible to reconstruct the positions of the continents fairly accurately for the Neozoic. This is done by essentially unspreading the oceanic crust sequentially. Knowledge of the positions of the subduction zones then allows the continents to be placed on the globe in their correct relative positions. However, their absolute position (i.e., their paleolatitude) is not defined by this process. To put the continents in their correct paleogeographic location, further information is needed. Three approaches have been suggested: paleomagnetism, hot-spot locations, and paleolatitude measurements.

Measurements of paleolatitude, such as the locations of desert formations, can frequently be useful but often lack the accuracy of the other two methods. One method that appeared to give good results was the location of the equatorial band of high sedimentation in the Pacific, caused by high productivity resulting from equatorial upwelling. This band of rapid sedimentation could be seen in sediments of different ages and appeared to show a northward motion of the Pacific plate similar to what was expected from hot-spot and paleomagnetic observations. However, the fact that the present-day band of high sedimentation is displaced from the equator indicates that this method has systematic errors that cannot at the moment be compensated for. So we are left with paleomagnetism and hot spots.

Hot spots are linear manifestations of volcanic activity that are caused by the lithosphere moving over a mantle plume, the source of the hot-spot volcanism. The best example of a hot-spot trace is the Hawaii–Emperor seamount chain. Hot-spot traces can certainly give some idea of absolute plate motions but also suffer from systematic errors. One piece of dogma that has crept into the literature, and which has recently come under more criticism, is that hot spots remain fixed with respect to each other. This cannot be true if the whole mantle is convecting, as scientists now believe. Whole-mantle convection (with or without layering) is necessary to remove the heat generated within the core as a consequence of processes required to produce the Earth's magnetic field. With all of the mantle convecting, there can be no region in which the source of hot spots can be sought that is not in some form of motion. Proponents of the fixed-hot-spot hypothesis claim that the origin of hot spots is in a portion of the mantle that is moving very slowly, and so the hypothesis is not absolutely correct but practically useful.

Tarduno and Cottrell (1997) have recently shown that, during the Cretaceous and early Tertiary, there was considerable relative hot-spot motion of more than 30 centimeters per year. At other times, they suggest, hot-spot motion may have been smaller. However, 30 centimeters per year is equivalent to 30° of arc in 10 million years, and so will give erroneous paleoclimatic information if neglected.

Plate Tectonics. Plate tectonics supposes that the Earth is divided up into a small number of—roughly a dozen—plates. The plates are generally considered to be about 100 kilometers thick (equivalent to the lithosphere) resting on the more mobile asthenosphere. Within each plate there is little or no deformation, although plates can change their shape by addition (SFS) or subtraction (subduction) at their edges. Figure 1 shows the current boundaries of the plates (Duxbury and Duxbury, 1997). Plate boundaries can be narrow or wide and diffuse (Robaudo and Harrison, 1993a; Gordon, 1998).

Plates move with respect to each other, and there are three types of interaction at plate edges. Where plates move away from each other, the normal boundary is a midoceanic ridge related to SFS, such as the mid-Atlantic Ridge or the East Pacific Rise. This is marked by high heat flow and elevated topography. In some cases, extensional boundaries (two plates moving away from each other) occur in continental regions, in which case the boundary may be marked by rift valleys, as in East Africa. Rift valleys also occur in most slow-spreading midoceanic ridges. Ridges are marked by earthquake activity, which is normally quite shallow, and can often be shown to be caused by normal faulting, signifying extension. The oceanic crust formed at ridge crests is made of tholeiitic basalt and gabbro.

When two oceanic plates move toward each other or collide, the result is subduction, in which one plate plunges beneath the other. In contrast to the normally symmetric spreading, subduction is asymmetrical. Subduction zones are marked by many large earthquakes (the largest on Earth), some of which can be as deep as 650 kilometers. Deep earthquakes only occur in these places because in other places the material at these depths is too plastic to store elastic energy. In contrast, a subducting plate can retain its cool temperature acquired at the surface of the Earth for a long time, reflecting the low thermal diffusivity of silicates. One example out of many surrounding the Pacific plate is the Mariana Trench: at 11,000 meters, the deepest known depression of the surface of the Earth. Volcanic activity is high and leads to the creation of island arcs in these locations. The volcanoes are mainly andesitic (an extrusive rock formed of intermediate plagioclase feldspar, pyroxene, and sometimes biotite, hornblende, and potassium (K) feldspar) in composition. [*See* Volcanoes.]

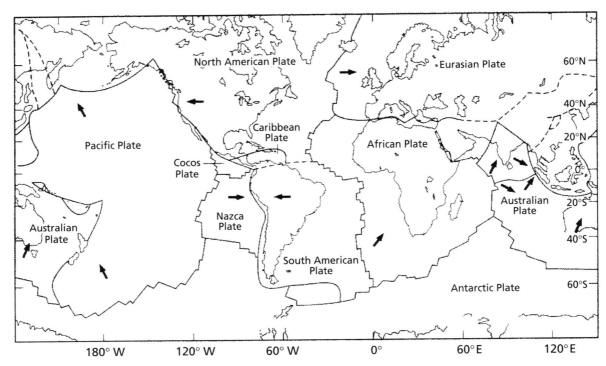

Plate Tectonics. Figure 1. Lithospheric Plates in Existence Today.

Between the African and Australian plates are the Arabian and Indian plates. There is a small plate to the west of North America and north of 40° north latitude called the Juan de Fuca plate. The Philippine plate is split up by the edges of the map. The jagged pattern of the midoceanic ridges is caused by alternating ridge crests (usually perpendicular to the relative plate motion) and transform faults (parallel to relative plate motion). The East African Rift Valley (not shown) is sometimes considered as a plate boundary separating the Nubian plate (to the west) from the Somalian plate (to the east). The black arrows show the directions of motion of the plates. Note that the North American plate stretches all the way to Siberia and is thought to run down to the Lena River delta and then across to Kamchatka. The plate boundaries are marked by earthquakes, but only the subducting boundaries have intermediate and deep earthquakes. (After Duxbury and Duxbury, 1997. With permission of McGraw-Hill.)

When an oceanic and a continental plate collide, the oceanic plate usually subducts (e.g., the Nazca plate beneath South America), but in rare cases the continental plate subducts, as is apparently happening in Taiwan today. Andesitic volcanic activity in these areas is high and produces mountains such as the Cascades in western North America and the Andes in South America. There is much seismic activity, with epicenters varying in depth from shallow to very deep.

When two continental plates collide, the result is continental collision and mountain building, because of the difficulty in subducting continental crustal material. The major example today is the collision of India with Asia, resulting in the Tibetan plateau and the Himalayas. Some elevated areas in South America (the Altiplano and Puna plateaus of Bolivia and Argentina) are caused by continental shortening and collision (Norabuena et al., 1998). Seismic activity is high in these regions and is often spread over a wide area.

The third type of plate boundary occurs when plates move past each other, conserving area. These are known as transform faults. The discovery of transform faults by Wilson (1965) was a key observation that persuaded people of the merits of SFS as an explanatory hypothesis. Also important was the observation that earthquakes that occurred between offsets of the ridge crest had slip vectors (showing directions of first motion) that were in the opposite direction to the offset, as predicted by Wilson's hypothesis, and that there were almost no earthquakes on the fracture zone continuations of the offsets outside of the ridge crests. Transform faults mostly occur at ridge offsets (ridge–ridge transform

faults), where they are marked by elongated topographic features (ridges and valleys) running parallel to the direction of relative motion. A good example is the Romanche fracture zone on the equator in the Atlantic. The San Andreas fault is a transform fault separating two continental areas. One end connects to the oceanic spreading center in the Gulf of California, and the other end connects to a trench–transform–transform triple junction (McKenzie and Morgan, 1969), where it meets the transform fault running westward along the Mendocino escarpment to the Gorda Ridge and the subduction zone running northward that is responsible for the Cascade volcanoes. Figure 2 illustrates some of the basic processes in plate tectonics and the three types of plate boundary.

Instantaneous plate motions. McKenzie and Parker (1967) showed that earthquake slip vectors taken from plate boundaries around the Pacific Ocean agreed with the plate tectonic theory of Earth behavior. They also confirmed that transform fault azimuths agreed with the directions seen in slip vectors. But they did not use any information about spreading rates in their model. Morgan (1968) was the first person to use both directional and rate information to determine some present-day plate motions. By analysis of two types of information, it is possible to calculate the current velocities of the major plates of the Earth. The two types of information pertain to relative plate motion direction and relative plate speed.

Plate speeds are measured by determining the distance between magnetic anomalies straddling the mid-oceanic ridges. The anomaly caused by the same reversal

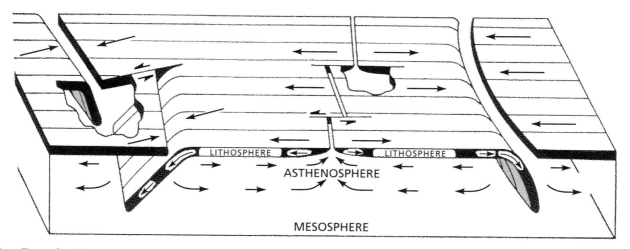

Plate Tectonics. Figure 2. Plate Tectonic Processes.

The more rigid lithosphere is 100–150 kilometers thick and is underlain by the more plastic asthenosphere. In the middle of the diagram there are sections of ridge crest joined by ridge–ridge transform faults. To the left there are two sections of trench, in which subduction goes in opposite directions, joined by a trench–

trench transform fault. To the right there is a simple trench with subduction all in one direction. The three types of plate boundary are all marked by earthquakes, but ridges and transform faults do not have any deep earthquakes. Volcanoes are common on the nonsubducting side of consuming plate boundaries. (After Isacks et al., 1968. Copyright by the American Geophysical Union.)

pattern on each side of the ridge crest is used to remove any error due to asymmetrical SFS, where one limb of the spreading center grows at a different rate than the other.

Plate directions are measured either by transform azimuths (directions of lineation of transform faults) or earthquake slip vectors. The end result is a model in which the relative motions of eleven plates are described. These eleven plates are the Pacific, Nazca, Cocos, North America, South America, Caribbean, Antarctica, Africa, Eurasia, Arabia, and Australia plates. In addition, DeMets et al. (1990) used information from other sources to describe the motions of two additional plates (Philippine and Juan de Fuca).

Finite plate motions. Bullard et al. (1963) introduced the idea of rotating portions of the Earth's crust on the surface of the Earth, using Euler poles, to match up the shape of the continental boundaries on either side of the Atlantic. Their jigsaw puzzle fit is shown in Figure 3. In contrast to the instantaneous rotations dis-

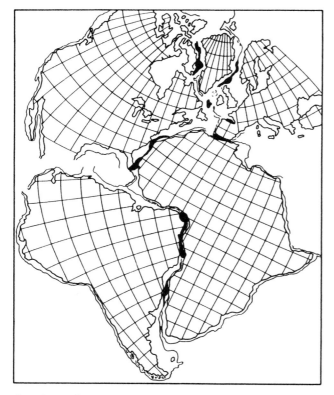

Plate Tectonics. Figure 3. The fit of the continents around the Atlantic Ocean proposed by Bullard et al. (1965) and shown by Van der Voo (1990) to be the best fit available.

The dark areas show overlap or underlap. Spain has been rotated to close the Bay of Biscay. Iceland has been neglected because it has been formed since the opening of the North Atlantic. Central America has also been neglected. The fit was done to the continental slope, not the shoreline. (After Bullard et al., 1965. With permission of the Royal Society.)

cussed in the previous section, finite rotations have to be used for this type of operation. Finite plate motions are much more complex to deal with than instantaneous plate motions because they cannot easily be combined. Graphical and arithmetic methods of dealing with the addition of finite rotations are given by Le Pichon et al. (1973) and Cox and Hart (1986).

Other Phenomena Influenced by Plate Tectonics. Plate tectonics can have a large influence on continental freeboard (the amount that the continents are exposed above sea level). Many phenomena affect the continental freeboard through time, but the one with the largest effect is the variation of the rate of oceanic crustal production with time (Harrison, 1988). Because of the topography of the ocean ridges, more rapid production of oceanic crust results in the ridges taking up more space in the ocean basins, causing the water to be displaced upward, thereby reducing continental freeboard.

Another important sea level effect produced by plate tectonics is caused by the formation and breakup of supercontinents. [*See* Sea Level.] During the formation of supercontinents, the rate of continental collision is much larger than the average. This collision causes continents to thicken at their edges, they occupy less area, and their average elevation increases. The ocean basins become larger in area and the water level falls. Supercontinents therefore have a larger freeboard than do continents during times of dispersal (Harrison, 1994).

Plate tectonic processes produce volcanic activity both at the ridge crests and at the subduction zones. Since SFS rates are known to vary, it might be expected that this variation could cause a change in atmospheric composition and hence influence climate through greenhouse gases. This phenomenon only seems to have been studied for carbon dioxide. Berner (1994) has produced a model (GEOCARB II) of atmospheric carbon dioxide in which carbon dioxide is released at subduction zones when calcium (Ca) and magnesium (Mg) carbonates in sediments are converted to silicates at high temperatures. To get at the subduction rates, Berner inverts sea level curves to arrive at SFS rates, and correctly assumes that subduction rates mimic spreading rates. However, the effect on the carbon dioxide content of the atmosphere is small compared with some of the other causes of carbon dioxide variation. Berner also looked at other effects, such as that of continental relief on weathering rates. This is also affected by SFS rates, although not as directly as subduction rates. Berner uses the strontium isotope (Sr-87/Sr-86) ratio in sea water as a mountain-building proxy. This effect produces significant variations in atmospheric carbon dioxide, especially in the Neozoic, and so will have an influence on climate through the greenhouse effect.

The carbon dioxide released at the subduction zones

is essentially a recycling of atmospheric and crustal carbon dioxide, but volcanic activity at ridge crests and hot spots brings up mantle volatiles that could have an effect on climate. Estimates of carbon dioxide outgassing are between 40 and 400 teragrams per year (Arthur et al., 1985). For a more recent estimate, if we use the geometric average CO_2/He-3 ratio of 7.11×10^9 from Sedwick et al. (1994) and the He-3 mantle flux of 4 per square centimeter per second from Craig and Lupton (1981), we get a flux of 335 teragrams per year, or 7.61 teramoles per year. In the GEOCARB II model of Berner (1994), the seven rates of carbon exchange between the various reservoirs vary between 1.3 and 20 teramoles per year, indicating that a flux of 7.61 teramoles per year is as important as several of the other fluxes. A flux of 7.61 teramoles per year will produce all of the current carbon in the reservoirs in about 800 million years. Therefore, over Phanerozoic time, this source of carbon dioxide must be considered in the model, as well as a long-term sink such as removal into the mantle at subduction zones. The addition of this factor to GEOCARB II could make this model much more susceptible to changes in plate tectonics, such as SFS rates, and thereby indicate the effect of plate tectonics on global change.

The flow of hydrothermal fluids through the ocean crust is known to have a significant effect on ocean chemistry, so that the rate of crustal production could change ocean chemistry through time. Elderfield and Schultz (1996) review the data pertaining to fluxes of elements into the ocean from hydrothermal circulation and from the dissolved load in rivers. Since the latter is only weakly dependent on plate tectonic processes (its main control is precipitation, not elevation), it is assumed that if the hydrothermal source is weaker than the river source, not much change could take place in composition as a result of changing rates of SFS. It turns out that only six substances (rubidium, cesium, manganese, lithium, and iron from high-temperature hydrothermal vents, and SO_4 from low-temperature off-axis flow) have higher hydrothermal fluxes than river fluxes. Of these, iron and manganese have essentially zero concentration in sea water, indicating that they are rapidly removed from it. For the rest, the ratio of total substance in sea water to yearly flux will give a residence time measured in years. If this is very long, then it will be difficult to change the concentration in the ocean except over an equivalent length of time, if the hydrothermal flux changes. However, all of the substances have short residence times (cesium, 0.931 years; rubidium, 1.85 years; lithium, 2.925 years; and SO_4, 4.725 years), indicating that their concentrations can change as a result of plate tectonic processes. A more complex model by Hardie (1996) suggests that much larger changes should occur in calcium, magnesium, and potassium as a result

of variations in oceanic crustal production rates during the Phanerozoic. Stanley and Hardie (1998) have postulated that these changes in magnesium and calcium have affected the types of reef-building and sediment-producing organisms during the Phanerozoic. Hydrothermal circulation of water through oceanic crust removes magnesium and adds calcium to the water. During times of rapid SFS (Cretaceous and Ordovician to Devonian), the circulation of water through the oceanic crust produces an ocean with high calcium and low magnesium concentrations, whereas, at other times (early Cambrian, Pennsylvanian to Triassic, and today), lower SFS rates have produced oceans with higher magnesium and lower calcium concentrations. High Ca/Mg ratios and high calcium concentrations favor the growth of reefs by calcitic taxa, whereas low Ca/Mg ratios and low calcium concentrations favor aragonitic and high-magnesium calcite organisms, such as is happening today and also occurred during the existence of the supercontinent Pangea (end of the Paleozoic to the Jurassic).

Hay (1996) has discussed many ways in which plate tectonics can influence climate. For example, models suggest that the effect of an opening in Central America will have a major influence on ocean currents in the Atlantic and Pacific Oceans. If the Drake Passage (between Cape Horn and the South Shetland Islands) is closed at the same time, a condition that probably existed between the mid-Cretaceous and the Oligocene, the amount of Antarctic Bottom Water (AABW) produced is likely to have been more than three times its present value. The enhanced upwelling of AABW in the northern Atlantic reduces the salinity and prevents the formation of North Atlantic Deep Water. Such changes in ocean circulation could have profound effects on global climate. It is well known that the closing of the straits of Gibraltar in the Messinian resulted in the formation of evaporite deposits in the Mediterranean and must have had a large influence on local climate.

Vertical tectonic events can also have large climatic results. The best known is the formation of the Tibetan plateau and the Himalayas. The high Tibetan plateau is responsible for the development of the monsoonal circulation, which does not occur in models without a plateau at least 2.5 kilometers high, half the current elevation of the Tibetan plateau (Hay, 1996). The specific effect of the elevation of the Andes (roughly 25–30 million years ago) does not seem to have been studied, however.

Over a longer time scale, plate tectonics can cause more profound changes in the way the Earth works. Heat-producing radioactive elements were more active earlier in Earth history, the time constant for these changes being about 3.5 billion years. Since SFS is the main method whereby Earth loses radiogenically produced heat, it follows that SFS must have been much more active during the Archean than today. Concomitant with more rapid SFS will be increased rates of mountain building because of continental collision and subduction. To balance the larger rates of mountain building, increased mechanical erosion is necessary, and this can only be achieved over the long term by increasing the freeboard of the continents (Harrison, 1994), because mechanical erosion is highly dependent on elevation. The rate of change in freeboard with time is about 136 meters per billion years.

Conclusions. Plate tectonics has a profound effect on many geologic and geophysical phenomena over time scales of tens to hundreds of millions of years. Of most significance are changes in sea level or continental freeboard as a function of spreading rates and continental collision rates. Also important are oceanographic and climatic effects produced by horizontal tectonics, such as the opening and closing of oceanic gateways, and vertical tectonics produced by continental collisions or subduction volcanism. The effect on climate, through greenhouse mechanisms, of variable volatile production associated with plate tectonic volcanic activity at the ridge crests has scarcely been explored, but profound changes in climate could be effected.

[*See also* Earth Structure and Development; Land Surface Processes; *and* Natural Hazards.]

BIBLIOGRAPHY

Arthur, M. A., et al. Variations in the Global Carbon Cycle during the Cretaceous Related to Climate, Volcanism, and Changes in Atmospheric Carbon Dioxide." In *The Carbon Cycle and Atmospheric Carbon Dioxide: Natural Variations Archean to Present*, edited by E. T. Sundquist and W. S. Broecker. Washington, D.C.: American Geophysical Union, 1985.

Berner, R. A. "GEOCARB II: A Revised Model of Atmospheric Carbon Dioxide over Phanerozoic Time." *American Journal of Science* 294 (1994), 56–91.

Bullard, E. C., et al. "The Fit of the Continents around the Atlantic." *Philosophical Transactions of the Royal Society* 258A (1965), 41–51. A historic paper showing that the jigsaw fit of the continents around the Atlantic is very good.

Cande, S. C., and D. V. Kent. "A New Geomagnetic Polarity Time Scale for the Late Cretaceous and Cenozoic." *Journal of Geophysical Research* 97 (1992), 13917–13951. The latest compilation of the geomagnetic reversal time scale for the past 80 million years; a slight revision is presented in Cande and Kent, 1995.

———. "Revised Calibration of the Geomagnetic Polarity Timescale for the Late Cretaceous and Cenozoic." *Journal of Geophysical Research* 100 (1995), 6093–6095.

Cox, A., and R. B. Hart. *Plate Tectonics*. Palo Alto, Calif.: Blackwell, 1986.

Craig, H., and J. E. Lupton. "Helium-3 and Mantle Volatiles in the Ocean and the Oceanic Crust." In *The Sea*, vol. 7, *The Oceanic Lithosphere*, edited by C. Emiliani, pp. 391–428. New York: Wiley, 1981.

DeMets, C., et al. "Current Plate Motions." *Geophysical Journal International* 101 (1990), 425–478. A very detailed description of the current relative motions of the plates.

Du Toit, A. L. *Our Wandering Continents*. Edinburgh: Oliver and Boyd, 1937.

Duxbury, A. C., and A. B. Duxbury. *An Introduction to the World's Oceans*. 5th ed. Dubuque, Iowa: W. C. Brown, 1997.

Elderfield, H., and A. Schultz. "Mid-Ocean Ridge Hydrothermal Fluxes and the Chemical Composition of the Ocean." *Annual Review of Earth and Planetary Science* 24 (1996), 191–224.

Emiliani, C. "A New Global Geology." In *The Sea*, vol. 7, *The Oceanic Lithosphere*, edited by C. Emiliani, pp. 1687–1723. New York: Wiley, 1981. Interesting historical facts about the Deep Sea Drilling Project.

Gordon, R. G. "The Plate Tectonic Approximation: Plate Rigidity, Diffuse Plate Boundaries, and Global Plate Reconstructions." *Annual Review of Earth and Planetary Science* 26 (1998), 615–642.

Gradstein, F. M., et al. "A Mesozoic Time Scale." *Journal of Geophysical Research* 99 (1994), 24051–24074.

Hardie, L. A. "Secular Variation in Seawater Chemistry: An Explanation for the Coupled Secular Variation in the Mineralogies of Marine Limestones and Potash Evaporites over the Past 600 M. Y." *Geology* 24 (1996), 279–283.

Harrison, C. G. A. "Eustasy and Epeirogeny of Continents on Time Scales between About 1 and 100 M. Y." *Paleoceanography* 3 (1988), 671–684.

———. "Rates of Continental Erosion and Mountain Building." *Geologisches Rundschau* 83 (1994), 431–447.

Hay, W. W. "Tectonics and Climate." *Geologisches Rundschau* 85 (1996), 409–437.

Heirtzler, J. R., et al. "Marine Magnetic Anomalies, Geomagnetic Field Reversals and Motions of the Ocean Floor and Continents." *Journal of Geophysical Research* 73 (1968), 2119–2136. The first reversal time scale derived from marine magnetic anomalies.

Hess, H. H. "History of Ocean Basins." In *Petrologic Studies: A Volume in Honor of A. F. Buddington*, edited by A. E. J. Engel, et al., pp. 599–620. Boulder: Geological Society of America, 1962. A classic early description of sea floor spreading.

Holmes, A. *Principles of Physical Geology*. Sunbury-on-Thames: Nelson, 1944. This textbook has some discussion of sea floor spreading.

Isacks, B., et al. "Seismology and the New Global Tectonics." *Journal of Geophysical Research* 73 (1968), 5855–5899.

Le Pichon, X., et al. *Plate Tectonics*. Amsterdam: Elsevier, 1973.

McKenzie, D., and M. J. Bickle. "The Volume and Composition of Melt Generated by Extension of the Lithosphere." *Journal of Petrology* 29 (1988), 625–679.

McKenzie, D. P., and W. J. Morgan. "Evolution of Triple Junctions." *Nature* 224 (1969), 125–133.

McKenzie, D., and R. L. Parker. "The North Pacific: An Example of Tectonics on a Sphere." *Nature* 216 (1967), 1276–1280. One of the first papers on plate tectonics.

Morgan, W. J. "Rises, Trenches, Great Faults and Crustal Blocks." *Journal of Geophysical Research* 73 (1968), 1959–1982.

Morley, L. W. "An Explanation of Magnetic Banding on Ocean Basins." In *The Sea*, vol. 7, *The Oceanic Lithosphere*, edited by C. Emiliani, pp. 1717–1719. New York: Wiley, 1981.

Müller, D., et al. "Digital Isochrons of the World's Ocean Floor." *Journal of Geophysical Research* 102 (1997), 3211–3214.

Norabuena, E., et al. "Space Geodetic Observations of Nazca-South

America Convergence across the Central Andes." *Science* 279 (1998), 358–362.

Opdyke, N., and J. E. T. Channell. *Magnetic Stratigraphy*. San Diego: Academic Press, 1996.

Pitman, W. C., and J. R. Heirtzler. "Magnetic Anomalies over the Pacific–Antarctic Ridge." *Science* 154 (1966), 1164–1171.

Robaudo, S., and C. G. A. Harrison. "Measurements of Strain at Plate Boundaries Using Space Based Geodetic Techniques." *Geophysical Research Letters* 20 (1993), 1811–1814.

Schmalz, R. F. "A Case for Convection." *Mineral Industries* 30.5 (1961), 8.

Sedwick, P. N., et al. "Carbon Dioxide and Helium in Hydrothermal Fluids from Loihi Seamount Hawaii USA: Temporal Variability and Implications for the Release of Mantle Volatiles." *Geochimica et Cosmochimica Acta* 58 (1994), 1219–1227.

Siever, R. "The Dynamic Earth." *Scientific American* 249.3 (1983), 46–65.

Stanley, S. M., and L. A. Hardie. "Secular Oscillations in the Carbonate Mineralogy of Reef-Building and Sediment-Producing Organisms Driven by Tectonically Forced Shifts in Seawater Chemistry." *Paleogeography, Paleoclimatology, Paleoecology* 144 (1998), 3–19.

Tarduno, J. A., and R. D. Cottrell. "Paleomagnetic Evidence for Motion of the Hawaiian Hotspot during Formation of the Emperor Seamounts." *Earth and Planetary Science Letters* 53 (1997), 171–180.

Van Der Voo, R. "Phanerozoic Paleomagnetic Poles from Europe and North America and Comparisons with Continental Reconstructions." *Reviews of Geophysics* 28 (1990), 167–206.

Vine, F. J. "Spreading of the Ocean Floor: New Evidence." *Science* 154 (1966), 1405–1415. The keystone paper of sea floor spreading.

Vine, F. J., and J. T. Wilson. "Magnetic Anomalies over a Young Oceanic Ridge off Vancouver Island." *Science* 50 (1965), 485–489.

Wegener, A. The Origin of Continents and Oceans. Translated from *Die Entstehung der Kontinente und Ozeane* (1929) by John Biram. New York: Dover, 1966.

Wilson, J. T. "A New Class of Faults and Their Bearing upon Continental Drift." *Nature* 207 (1965), 343–347. The basic description of transform faults, which were vital in understanding ridge crests and sea floor spreading.

—CHRISTOPHER G. A. HARRISON

PLUTONIUM. *See* Nuclear Hazards; *and* Nuclear Industry.

POLICY ANALYSIS

Policy analysis is the use of methods from the physical, biological, and social sciences, philosophy, mathematics, and the humanities to predict and evaluate the consequences of alternative policies. Policy analysis is intended to help answer the question "What should we do?" by organizing and structuring complex problems and using analysis to provide insights in support of making decisions. It intends to help those who make decisions to understand the implications of those decisions, especially the trade-offs that may be involved in choosing one course of action over another. While the field of policy analysis has emphasized public policy—choices made by governments—the logic of policy analysis can be applied to private decisions made by firms, nongovernmental organizations, or even individuals. In fact, many policy analysis tools may see wider application in the private sector than in the public sector.

Any policy analysis is comparative in that it attempts to weigh various alternative courses of action. A starting point is usually the "no change in policy" scenario that serves as a baseline for comparison with other policies. Because it usually is employed to understand the consequences of policies not yet adopted, policy analysis must provide information about what may happen in the future.

The tools developed to help understand the implications of alternative decisions can be sorted into two general categories. *Descriptive*, or positive, tools attempt to depict the future under alternative policies but offer no basis for judging which alternative is preferable. *Prescriptive*, or normative, tools include methods for assigning values or weights to the multiple impacts of a policy and thus are intended to suggest which alternatives are to be preferred. Both descriptive and prescriptive tools face special challenges when applied to global change. Most methods of policy analysis were developed to deal with relatively small or marginal changes in biophysical and social systems over time frames of a few years or a decade and within a single society or culture. But global change involves the possibility of radical, nonmarginal changes, with some processes working on time scales of multiple decades or centuries. And every policy to address global change has, by definition, global implications and thus affects individuals with diverse cultures, circumstances, and values.

Descriptive Analysis. Most policies, especially policies intended to respond to global change, have multiple effects on physical, biological, and socioeconomic systems. In order to make sound choices, all substantial consequences of a policy choice must be considered, including both the changes the policy is designed to bring about and those that may occur unintentionally. Two general strategies used to conduct descriptive policy analysis are evaluation research and policy modeling.

Evaluation research uses the historical record to understand the impacts of previous changes similar to the policies now under consideration. In some cases, we have experience with previous policies that can be analyzed as a guide to what might happen with similar policies in the future. In other cases, history has provided "natural experiments" that look like proposed policy changes. For example, the global oil price shocks of the 1970s provide clues as to how energy or carbon taxes intended to reduce greenhouse gas emissions might affect the global economy. Sometimes a policy is implemented using an experimental design that allows direct evaluation of its effects. But usually the need to evaluate policy impacts is not built into the design of a policy, so that statistical tools have to disentangle the effects of the policy from other causes of change. The two principle challenges to evaluation research are the difficulty in finding historical cases that match current policy proposals and in differentiating the effects of a policy from other ongoing changes.

Policy modeling uses mathematical or sometimes verbal models to anticipate what may happen. There are many causes and consequences of global change, and policies intended to deal with them may have multiple effects. This complexity has encouraged the development of integrated assessment models that incorporate key aspects of physical, biological, and socioeconomic systems in a single model or linked set of models. The goal is to understand the complex interactions among these systems and their components and thus provide better insight about what might happen under alternative policies.

Because policy analysis requires the analysis of possible future events, it always involves dealing with uncertainty. In some analyses, this is done in a very formal way, by estimating the probabilities of various outcomes. For example, an analysis might report that "there is a 95 percent probability that an energy tax as proposed will reduce carbon emissions by at least 10 percent." In other cases, uncertainty is handled simply by noting the assumptions made in the analysis and the limits of available data and methods. A substantial body of research describes methods for assessing uncertainty and incorporating information about uncertainty into analyses.

Prescriptive Analysis. Descriptive analysis stops short of suggesting what policy should be adopted. Policies attempting to address problems as complex as those posed by global change will usually have many impacts. For example, an energy tax might reduce greenhouse gas emissions but might also advantage some industries and regions, disadvantage others, and slow overall economic growth. A decision maker must weigh these outcomes against each other. Prescriptive, or normative, policy analysis provides tools that aid in making such trade-offs.

Cost-effectiveness. The simplest and least controversial method of prescriptive analysis is that based on cost-effectiveness. Cost-effectiveness analysis searches among policy alternatives for the one that will achieve the most of a desired goal for the funds expended or that meets a specified objective at the lowest cost. For example, a descriptive analysis might identify sites that

provide habitat to endangered species but are threatened with development. If there is not enough budget to purchase all sites, some sites must be selected and others left unprotected. A naive approach would be to begin with the site with the most species threatened. A cost-effectiveness analysis might divide the number of species saved by the costs of purchasing the site, then rank sites according to where the most species can be saved for the amount of money expended. By starting with the site that saves the most species per expenditure and continuing down the list until funds are exhausted, far more species can be protected than if the cost-effectiveness analysis were ignored.

Cost-effectiveness analysis does not provide clear guidance when a proposed policy has more than one impact and analyses of separate impacts do not lead to the same ordering. It may be that whereas some sites lead to the protection of many species, other sites lead to the protection of only a few species, but these are quite distinct in their evolutionary history, perhaps having no close kin in existence. Or it may be that the agency planning to purchase sites also has a mandate to provide recreation. A simple cost-effectiveness analysis that only counts the number of species protected is assuming that all threatened species are equal, whatever their evolutionary history, and that recreation does not matter. A cost-effectiveness analysis based on evolutionary lineages or recreation potential might lead to a different set of priorities.

Benefit-cost analysis. Multiple impacts of a policy raises the central problem of normative policy analysis—how to make trade-offs across the impacts. The most commonly used and best-developed approach is benefit-cost analysis (BCA). BCA is based on the utilitarian philosophy developed by Jeremy Bentham and John Stuart Mill and elaborated in welfare economics. The approach holds that a good decision is one that provides the greatest good to the greatest number of people. An analyst should search for a policy that is "Pareto optimal"—a policy that makes as many people as much better off as possible without making anyone worse off, or a policy that improves the lot of some enough that they can compensate those who are made worse off. This idea is implemented in BCA by identifying all the benefits and costs associated with a proposed policy, quantifying and summing each benefit and cost in monetary terms, and calculating the difference. The policy with the highest net benefit after costs are taken into account is the best policy.

In BCA, assigning a monetary value to each impact solves the problem of comparing multiple impacts. BCA is often criticized for considering only monetary values, but the logic would apply no matter what units are used for comparison as long as all impacts can be translated into a single measure. The advantages of using monetary units are twofold. First, in market-based societies there is a great deal of information available about prices, thus easing the analytical task. Second, the theory of welfare economics suggests that in competitive markets that have reached an equilibrium, prices reflect social values; using prices to make trade-offs in BCA is thus using social values that happen to be expressed in monetary units.

The criticisms of BCA include those that accept the basic utilitarian logic but note weaknesses in implementation, and those that reject the utilitarian logic. The first set of criticisms centers on the use of prices in real markets as social values, discounting the future, ignoring the distribution of costs and benefits, picking a boundary for the analysis, and finding a value for goods and services not priced in the market. The second set of criticisms includes arguments that ethical considerations must include a consideration of rights, duties, and procedural rules as well as (or instead of) utility calculations, and arguments that social rationality must be based on discussion, not market exchanges.

The theory of welfare economics that argues for using prices as reflections of social values relies on a number of assumptions about the behavior of markets. If the markets generating the prices used in BCA do not match the theoretical ideal, then the prices will not be accurate reflections of social value. Real markets for energy, land, and many other goods and services include taxes and subsidies and exclude many environmental costs, with the result that prices provide inaccurate measures of social value and thus distort a BCA based on those prices. An active research literature tries to assess the extent to which prices are distorted by subsidies, taxes, and other market imperfections and to make appropriate corrections.

In a typical BCA, it is assumed that a benefit or cost that will occur in the future is worth less than the same benefit or cost that occurs now. The usual practice is to discount future benefits and costs. This is done by applying a discount rate that is rather like running compound interest on a savings account backward. Since global change involves events that may be decades in the future, discounting has a substantial effect on BCA of such policies. For example, if the discount rate is 2 percent, a benefit worth U.S.$1 million occurring fifty years in the future would have a present value of only about U.S.$364,000. If the benefit occurred a century in the future, its present value would be U.S.$132,000. If the discount rate is 5 percent, the present value of a U.S.$1 million benefit fifty years in the future would be only about U.S.$77,000 and a benefit one hundred years off would have a present value of about U.S.$5,900. It is difficult for discounted future benefits to outweigh present costs in such an analysis, yet many global change policy proposals call for current costs to provide future

benefits (or to avoid future costs). Some researchers have argued that it is inappropriate to apply discounting in environmental policy analysis, and there is a lively debate on this issue.

BCA usually ignores the distribution of benefits and costs. A dollar of costs visited on a billionaire counts the same as a dollar of costs visited on someone who has an income of U.S.$100 per year. BCA could give different weights to benefits and costs depending on who would receive the benefits and who would bear the costs. Such weights might be based on "normalizing" benefits and costs in terms of equivalent purchasing power or time required to earn a given amount of income. But no generally accepted mechanism has been developed for deciding what those weights should be, so distributional or equity issues are ignored in most BCAs.

To conduct a BCA, the analyst must select a boundary for the analysis. In theory, it is possible to do a BCA for the entire planet, but most policies are made at the national level, and so most BCAs are conducted at that level as well. The BCA counts only benefits and costs that accrue within the geographic and other boundaries used for the analysis; benefits and costs elsewhere in the world are thus ignored. But the policy with the most favorable BCA when analyzed with one set of boundaries may not be the best policy when a different set is considered.

Finally, the use of prices as a measure of value cannot assign values to goods and services that are not exchanged in the market. This is a serious problem for the analysis of environmental policies, since many of the benefits of such policies are not market goods. It is possible to estimate with reasonable accuracy the costs of new technology to improve energy efficiency and reduce greenhouse gas emissions or the costs of land purchased to hold as a biodiversity reserve. But it is much harder to find the price of changes in climate or biodiversity. The biosphere, and the ecosystems within it, provides a diversity of goods and services to humanity. These are called ecosystem services. Researchers are just beginning to identify them, to understand how ecosystems generate them, and to estimate how much value they have for human societies. Most researchers would argue that market prices do not adequately capture the value of ecosystem services. In addition, some researchers have noted that many people value the existence of other species and of wilderness areas even when no use is made of them. Again, most researchers would argue that prices don't provide an accurate guide to these existence values.

A great deal of research is in progress to improve our understanding of ecosystem services and existence values and to develop methods for assigning value to them. One of the most actively debated techniques for assessing existence values is the *contingent valuation method*. Contingent valuation uses survey methods to ask people what they would be willing to pay for an increase (or to prevent a decrease) in environmental quality, or what they would be willing to accept in exchange for a decrease in quality. The responses are in monetary units that can then be used in a BCA. Because survey respondents are not required to make the payments they propose, critics have argued that the responses are not realistic estimates of value. A large and rapidly growing literature debates the contingent valuation approach and offers improvements on it.

The problems of distorted prices, discounting, distributional effects, scope of analysis, and the valuation of nonmarket goods and services are all debated within the utilitarian paradigm. But other criticisms reject the entire approach or argue that the use of BCA is too limited when applied to global change and other environmental policies. These criticisms are based on different approaches to what constitutes a good decision.

Other approaches. It is common to hear BCA (and economics in general) criticized because "there are some things you can't put a price on." But utilitarians note that the real issue is placing a value on everything, and prices are just a mechanism to assign values. A deeper critique of welfare economics argues that prices are not a reasonable way to measure social values because prices are determined in markets that give disproportionate power to the wealthy ("one dollar, one vote") and that emphasize decisions based on competition and self-interest rather than on cooperation and altruism. From this position, the use of market prices privileges some kinds of concerns over others.

There are alternatives to monetizing all impacts of a proposed policy. One is to draw on multiobjective decision methods. These are mathematical and procedural tools that assume that a proposed course of action has multiple goals. In the case of a program to set aside natural areas, there might be three goals: providing habitat for endangered species, increasing recreational opportunities, and sequestering carbon through increased vegetation. The problem faced by the decision maker is deciding which sites to purchase as preserves given a limited budget and many candidate areas. In a BCA, the ability of each potential site to achieve each goal would be translated into monetary units, as would any costs associated with purchasing and maintaining the site. Then the site with the highest benefit-to-cost ratio should be the highest priority for purchase. A multiobjective approach would acknowledge the difficulty of translating all policy goals into monetary units and attempt to find good choices keeping all goals in mind at once. In some cases, it is possible to use mathematical tools to find a mix of decisions (a set of sites) that will do better than any other choice on all the goals. In most

cases, however, it is necessary to find weights that represent the trade-offs between various policy goals. For example, some function must be found to compare tons of carbon sequestered, days of recreation, and number of species protected. In BCA this trade-off is done with prices. In multiobjective methods, a structured group process involving experts and interested parties is sometimes used. In such cases, there is a strong link between multiobjective methods and the deliberative processes described below.

Another alternative to BCA is to find a measure of value other than market prices. There have been a number of suggestions for such a metric. One approach is to adjust existing economic data to better account for environmental impacts. These efforts include estimates of an "environmentally adjusted gross domestic product." The conventional gross domestic product can be thought of as the sum of all economic transactions that occur within a nation. The adjusted product subtracts environmental damage and consumption of nonrenewable resources from the conventional product. Those studying the adjusted gross domestic product suggest that, by ignoring environmental costs, we overestimate how well off we are economically.

Some researchers have moved away from economic accounts altogether and suggest completely different metrics for assessing the value of alternative policies. These include efforts to translate all impacts into land areas based on the amount of land required to support a good or service, or into total tons of materials required to produce the good or service, or the amount of energy consumed in producing the good or service. Research on these approaches is still in its early stages.

Cost-effectiveness analysis and BCA follow from the utilitarian tradition in philosophy. Other philosophical traditions also have implications for policy analysis, especially in emphasizing equity issues rather than efficiency, which is the focus of the utilitarian vision. An approach based on the arguments of the philosopher Immanuel Kant argues that the utilitarian benefit-cost logic is appropriate for some kinds of decisions, but it must always be limited by strict rules that take precedence over any benefit-cost calculation. For example, we should not allow other humans to be enslaved or murdered, no matter what a benefit-cost calculation might indicate. In considering policy to address global change, the Kantian approach suggests that we need to develop appropriate rules and apply BCA or cost-effectiveness analysis only within the constraints of the rules. Such rules might take the form of minimum standards for the protection of habitat or endangered species or maximum amounts of climate change to be tolerated. Then the policy choice is within the set of all policies believed to achieve those goals—policies that do not meet these standards are precluded. Many nations have endangered species laws that implement such rules—actions that would drive an endangered species to extinction are forbidden no matter what other benefits might accrue from those actions.

The philosopher John Rawls argued that a good decision is one that improves the condition of the most disadvantaged members of society. This is sometimes expressed in terms of a "veil of ignorance": we should make decisions as if we did not know what position in society we will occupy when the policy is implemented. This is like the rule of letting one person cut the cake and another person pick who gets which piece. The Rawlsian approach has not been much developed around global change policy except as a call for attention to the effects of policies on the least affluent nations and people.

The deliberative approach that draws on the discursive ethics proposed by the sociologist Jürgen Habermas also emphasizes process. This view argues that proper decisions can be made only through the process of free and unconstrained discussion among all parties who will be affected by the decisions. In environmental policy this has been implemented in the form of "analytic deliberation." Analytic deliberation is a structured group process in which interested parties are able to discuss their concerns. The process draws on the best available policy analyses and is sometimes used to suggest new questions for analysis. The deliberation is structured with rules that take advantage of the benefits of group discussion while minimizing the problems that can occur in traditional committee meetings and public hearings. The goal of deliberation is to have interested parties reach a consensus on as many issues as possible, to clarify the nature of disagreements, and to identify topics where further policy analysis might resolve disputes. The process often builds trust among those who are concerned about a policy, even when they disagree, and can focus research efforts on issues that are consequential to conflicts about a policy. Because analytic deliberation is a new approach, it is not nearly as well developed as BCA, and several key issues, such as how to ensure representative participation and how to structure an effective group process, are still subject to research and experimentation.

Implementation and the Policy System. Formal policy analysis of the sort described above is only one input into the decision-making process. Given the limitations of all policy analysis methods, most researchers feel this is appropriate. The decision maker should weigh the strengths and weaknesses of analysis rather than simply adopting the policy that looks best in a particular analysis. Policy analysis should guide decisions but not be a substitute for judgment.

Policy analysis takes place in a policy system. For global change policies, this system includes government agencies (including sometimes international agencies), nongovernmental organizations, private firms and the industry associations that represent them, labor unions, law and consulting firms, and researchers at universities and research centers. Each of these groups may offer its own policy analyses based on assumptions that seem appropriate to its members. Ideally, the debate between alternative analyses should hone understanding of a proposed policy. But in examining such debates, it is important to remember that the system is not balanced. Governments and private firms have far more analytic resources than environmental and other public interest nongovernmental organizations. Further, the historical development of science and technology has emphasized knowledge useful for producing goods and services over knowledge useful for understanding the impacts of the production and consumption process. An awareness of this imbalance has led some commentators to call for more investment in public-interest science to balance the large investment in analyses by private interests.

Policy analysis must make assumptions about how a policy will be implemented. The political and administrative process will make changes that cause the policy as implemented to deviate from the policy as analyzed, and thus the impacts of what is actually done will almost certainly deviate to some degree from the impacts predicted by analysis. This is one important merit of evaluation research: it provides guidance as to the impacts of policies as they are implemented rather than policies as proposed.

Even the most extensive policy analyses are uncertain and must incorporate assumptions that will not seem reasonable to everyone. Further, global change is so multidimensional and nonlinear that we cannot expect to forecast with great accuracy all or even most consequences of our actions. These limitations on our knowledge have led many researchers to call for adaptive management or policy experimentation. They suggest that we view each policy implemented as an experiment and carefully monitor the results as they unfold over time, using the new information that results to adjust the policy in an adaptive fashion. A corollary of this approach is that policies should avoid irrevocable changes because no subsequent modification is possible.

[*See also* Economic Levels; Energy Policy; Integrated Assessment; Multinational Enterprises; Nongovernmental Organizations; Population Policy; Public Policy; *and* United Nations.]

BIBLIOGRAPHY

CONVENTIONAL WELFARE ECONOMICS
Freeman, A. M., III. *The Measurement of Environmental and Resource Values: Theory and Methods.* Washington, D.C.: Resources for the Future, 1993. The standard comprehensive text

on environmental economics in the utilitarian tradition, including a detailed discussion of benefit-cost analysis.

Mitchell, R. C., and R. T. Carson. *Using Surveys to Value Public Goods: The Contingent Valuation Method*. Washington, D.C.: Resources for the Future, 1989. The comprehensive standard text on the contingent valuation method.

Nordhaus, W. D. *Economic and Policy Issues in Climate Change*. Washington, D.C.: Resources for the Future, 1998. A collection of essays on utilitarian policy analysis applied to climate change.

COMPARISONS OF POLICY ANALYSIS METHODS

Dietz, T. "'What Should We Do?' Human Ecology and Collective Decision Making." *Human Ecology Review* 1 (1994), 301–309. Contrasts policy analysis based on welfare economics with deliberative approaches.

Freeman, D. M. *Choice against Chance: Constructing a Policy-Assessing Sociology for Social Development*. Niwot: University Press of Colorado, 1992. An accessible comparison of the philosophical bases of policy analysis.

Jaeger, C. *Taming the Dragon: Transforming Economic Institutions in the Face of Global Change*. New York: Gordon and Breach, 1994. Presents important proposals to supplement conventional economic analysis.

Jaeger, C., O. Renn, E. A. Rosa, and T. Webler. *Risk, Uncertainty and Rational Action*. London: Earthscan, 2000. A comprehensive theoretical overview of risk in environmental policy.

Morgan, M. G., M. Kandlikar, J. Risbey, and H. Dowlatabadi. "Why Conventional Tools for Policy Analysis Are Often Inadequate for Problems of Global Change." *Climatic Change* 41 (1999), 271–281. An assessment of the strengths and weaknesses of policy analysis methods applied to climate change.

U.S. National Research Council. *Perspectives on Biodiversity: Valuing Its Role in an Everchanging World*. Washington, D.C.: National Academy Press, 1999. Compares methods and philosophical underpinnings of policy analysis in the context of biodiversity.

ALTERNATIVE METHODS OF VALUATION

Costanza, R., ed. *Ecological Economics*. New York: Columbia University Press, 1991. A collection of important papers on alternatives to traditional economic approaches to environmental policy.

Daily, G. C. ed. *Nature's Services: Societal Dependence on Natural Ecosystems*. Washington, D.C.: Island Press, 1997. A pioneering collection of studies of the value of ecosystem services, including lucid essays on the theory of valuation.

Martinez Alier, J., and K. Schluepmann. *Ecological Economics: Energy, Environment and Society*. Oxford: Blackwell, 1990. A careful examination of new approaches to valuation.

DELIBERATIVE APPROACHES, ADAPTIVE MANAGEMENT, AND THE POLICY SYSTEM

Dietz, T., and P. C. Stern. "Science, Values and Biodiversity." *BioScience* 48 (1998), 441–444. Describes the advantages of deliberative policy analysis in biodiversity conflicts.

Gunderson, L. H., C. S. Holling, and S. S. Light, eds. *Barriers and Bridges to the Renewal of Ecosystems and Institutions*. New York: Columbia University Press, 1995. A collection of important essays on adaptive management.

Renn, O., T. Webler, and P. Wiedemann, eds. *Fairness and Competence in Citizen Participation: Evaluating Models for Environmental Discourse*. Dordrecht: Kluwer, 1995. Important theoretical essays and case studies on the use of deliberative methods.

Schnaiberg, A., and K. A. Gould. *Environment and Society: The Enduring Conflict*. 2d ed. Caldwell, N.J.: Blackburn Press, 2000. An accessible analysis of the environmental policy system, including discussion of biases in policy analysis.

Stern, P. C., and H. Fineberg, eds. *Understanding Risk: Informing Decisions in a Democratic Society*. Washington, D.C.: National Academy Press, 1996. A comprehensive analysis of risk analysis and the use of deliberative methods.

—THOMAS DIETZ

POLLUTION

In its broadest sense, *pollution* can be defined as any impact on the natural environment that is created by anthropogenic (that is, human) sources. Pollution is an extremely complex problem and can potentially influence all aspects of the environment. Its impact is normally assessed in a negative sense, by level of damage: to human health, to quality of life, to the well-being of other planetary organisms, and to aesthetics and impacts on inanimate structures. In this discussion, pollution associated with four major global features is considered: the atmosphere, water, soil, and the ocean.

Sources of pollution are many and varied. At the broadest level, they can be divided into two categories. Point source pollution occurs from identifiable specific locations, such as a chimney attached to a factory, a sewage discharge pipe into a river, a damaged oil tanker on the ocean, or an accident at a nuclear power station. Nonpoint pollution sources include the mix of individual sources from an area or region. Examples include smog over cities and polluted river water entering the ocean. In both cases, the term *emission* is used to define the release of pollutants to the environment.

Air Pollution. Pollution emitted to the atmosphere has the potential to create respiratory health problems, to damage vegetation and buildings, and to cause aesthetic unpleasantness. Air pollutants consist of gases and particulate matter (or aerosols) and can be divided into three categories of scale: global, national and/or regional, and local/regional. [*See* Air Pollution.]

Air pollutants influencing the global environment are gases that contribute to greenhouse warming and stratospheric ozone depletion. The major gases involved are carbon dioxide, methane, chlorofluorocarbons (CFCs), and nitrous oxide. With the exception of CFCs, all of these gases occur naturally in the atmosphere. As Table 1 shows, all have been increasing steadily in concentration since the Industrial Revolution. The increase in methane is directly linked to the increase in global population. The increase in carbon dioxide is created by increased burning of fossil fuels. Extra nitrous oxide is created mainly through use of agricultural fertilizers. CFCs are artificial compounds created for refrigeration,

Pollution. Table 1. Characteristics of Major Gases that Cause Greenhouse Warming

CHARACTERISTIC	CARBON DIOXIDE	METHANE	NITROUS OXIDE	CFCs*
Pre-1850 concentration	280 ppmv[†]	700 ppbv[†]	275 ppbv	0
1992 concentration	355 ppmv	1714 ppbv	311 ppbv	503 pptv[†]
1980s rate of change	1.5 ppmv per year 0.4 percent per year	13 ppbv per year 0.8 percent per year	0.8 ppbv per year 0.25 percent per year	20 pptv per year 4 percent per year
Residence time (years)	50–200[‡]	12–17	120	85–400

*Represents at least five chlorofluorocarbons (CFCs); most prevalent are CFC-11 and CFC-12.

[†]ppbv = parts per billion (of air) by volume; ppmv = parts per million by volume; pptv = parts per trillion by volume.

[‡]Unclear because of incomplete knowledge of the carbon cycle.

SOURCE: Intergovernmental Panel on Climate Change (1994, p. 25).

aerosol spray cans, and foam mattresses. [*See* Aerosols; Air Quality; Carbon Dioxide; *and* Nitrous Oxide.]

Greenhouse warming is a natural phenomenon caused by the absorption by the above-mentioned gases of long-wavelength radiation emitted from the Earth's surface, keeping the average global surface temperature at about 15°C. The increase in gas concentrations resulting from anthropogenic activities is likely to create extra absorption and warming. The question is, How much? Carbon dioxide is the major greenhouse gas in this group, but the other gases have the potential to sharply increase warming because their molecular absorption is more efficient. Potential impacts include raised sea levels, changing atmospheric circulation patterns, some melting of glaciers, and increased frequency of extreme weather. Impacts will vary around the globe. [*See* Global Warming; *and* Greenhouse Effect.]

CFCs also create problems in the stratospheric ozone layer, which protects organisms on the Earth's surface from potentially fatal ultraviolet radiation. After entering the stratosphere from the troposphere, the chlorine in the CFCs is released by ultraviolet activity and then reacts to destroy the ozone. In springtime over Antarctica, satellite and ground-based measurements have shown an ozone loss of over 95 percent in some layers of the stratosphere. There is evidence of loss over the Arctic as well. If the flux of ultraviolet radiation at the Earth's surface increases, there will be an increased incidence of melanoma skin cancers, cataract problems in eyes, and possible reproductive and other biological problems throughout the food chain. [*See* Chlorofluorocarbons.]

On a national or regional scale, air pollutants are transported from point and area sources over many thousands of kilometers. In the Arctic, pollutants from point sources in Europe and Siberia move across the north polar region to Alaska and northern Canada during March and April each year as arctic haze. In eastern North America, northern Europe, and parts of China, the interaction of pollutants with clouds during transport

leads to major acidity problems in rain and fog. While representative acidity in clean rainwater is between pH 5.0 and 5.6, polluted rain has a pH of 3.5–4.5, indicating that the rainwater is 50 to 150 times more acidic. This increased acidity is caused by chemical reactions between the acid gases sulfur dioxide and nitrogen oxides, which are emitted from tall chimneys associated with industry and power stations. Acid rain and acid deposition can cause fish kills in lakes, create damage to vegetation, and cause soil quality problems through leaching of toxic metals into the ecosystem. [*See* Acid Rain and Acid Deposition.]

On the local/regional scale, the most important air pollution problems originate from the extensive use of automobiles and trucks in cities. Extensive emissions of hydrocarbons and nitrogen oxides into a stable urban atmosphere, with the addition of strong sunlight, create photochemical smog in the summertime. The major pollutant in photochemical smog is ozone, which in high concentrations can cause burning eyes and respiratory problems in sensitive people, as well as damage to vegetation. Photochemical smog has been the major pollution problem in cities such as Los Angeles and Athens for decades. As large cities have expanded in developing countries, photochemical smog has become uncontrollable. As shown in Table 2, air pollution levels in cities such as Mexico City, Bangkok, São Paulo, and Jakarta are among the worst in the world.

Water Pollution. Clean water is essential for human life. Pollution of water supplies by human populations causes disease, illness, and sometimes death. Water-based sanitation is the main method by which human sewage is removed as waste. In developed countries, legal requirements for proper sewage removal and disposal require local councils and water authorities to invest heavily in treatment infrastructure to avoid water pollution and ensure public safety and health. The greatest concern is bacteria, such as streptococci, and viruses, but excess nutrients and other water quality concerns require a range of monitoring and testing

Pollution. TABLE 2. Examples of Air Pollution Problems in Megacities (More than Ten Million Population) of the World*

MEGACITY	SO$_2$	SPM	Pb	CO	NO$_2$	O$_3$
Bangkok, Thailand	*	‡	†	*	*	*
Beijing, China	*	‡	*	*	*	†
Cairo, Egypt	*	‡	‡	†	*	*
Jakarta, Indonesia	*	‡	†	†	*	†
Los Angeles, U.S.A.	*	†	*	†	†	‡
Manila, Philippines	*	‡	†	*	*	*
Mexico City, Mexico	‡	‡	†	‡	†	‡
Moscow, Russia	*	†	*	†	†	*
New York, U.S.A.	*	*	*	†	*	†
Sao Paulo, Brazil	*	†	*	†	†	‡
Seoul, Korea	‡	‡	*	*	*	*
Shanghai, China	†	‡	*	*	*	*

*Low pollution or data not available.

†WHO health guidelines exceeded by up to a factor of two (moderate).

‡WHO health guidelines exceeded by at least a factor of two (serious).

SO$_2$ = sulfur dioxide; SPM = suspended particulate matter; Pb = lead; CO = carbon monoxide; NO$_2$ = nitrogen dioxide; O$_3$ = ozone.

SOURCE: Modified from World Health Organization and United Nations Environment Programme (1992).

methodologies, as shown in Table 3. Treated sewage is often discharged into oceans by coastal cities, or into rivers and lakes by inland cities. Other, more controversial methods include the drying of sewage to form sewage sludge for use as a fertilizer, or spraying on forests or pastures to enhance growth. Unfortunately, untreated sewage may also be discharged, especially during storm water flows, but also from leaking or poorly maintained septic systems and pipes, through accidental release from pump-out systems, or through system breakdowns. In many developing countries, sewage control systems do not exist, and sewage is discharged untreated into open drains, streams, and rivers, making the water unusable for any other purpose.

Near industrial locations, water quality can be threatened by the discharge of undesirable chemicals into rivers and oceans. In particular, heavy metals such as lead, copper, cadmium, zinc, and mercury are extremely hazardous. Heavy metals may accumulate in bottom sludge in riverbeds and lakes, to be rereleased, perhaps many years later, as a result of some disturbance. Metals can also enter the food chain. Uncontrolled mercury discharges into Minimata Bay in Japan were transferred into shellfish and fish, which, when eaten by the local population, caused birth defects in children. Oil and fuel spillage from boats and ships using waterways can also create a pollution hazard, damaging local wildlife populations and interfering with normal life cycles.

Other forms of water pollution include increased temperatures in lakes caused by thermal discharges from powers stations and industries, and increased salinity from a range of activities, including liquid discharges from coal, metal, and mineral mining. Runoff from agricultural practices such as fertilization and application of pesticides adds excess nutrients and poisons to rivers, lakes, and streams. Under hot, dry conditions, one consequence is the development of large areas of blue-green algae, which is extremely toxic to animals and humans and makes the water undrinkable without treatment. [See Water; and Water Quality.]

Most human populations create excess litter or trash, which often pollutes waterways attached to population centers. Trash accumulates because the discharge of unwanted materials is not controlled. These materials consist predominantly of plastic and paper, with bottles and cans as important secondary components. Especially in stormwater situations, where runoff removes much of the ground trash into drains, streams, and rivers, such pollution is a major aesthetic problem and a potential health hazard.

Nuclear hazards can result from accidental spillage or discharge from nuclear power plants, or, in a worst-case scenario, from a nuclear explosion. Pollutants include a range of radioactive elements and compounds, including daughter elements of uranium, plutonium, cesium, and iodine. Radioactive materials are injurious to human health, can contaminate large areas for decades or centuries (depending on the half-life of decay of the

Pollution. TABLE 3. Water Quality Parameters Measured in a Stormwater Sampling Program

PARAMETER	UNITS*	ABBREVIATION
General		
Alkalinity (as $CaCO_3$)	mg/l	Alk
Biological oxygen demand	mg/l	BOD5
Chloride ion	mg/l	Cl
Chloride (free)	mg/l	FCL
Chlorine (total)	mg/l	TCL
Color	Color units	Color
Conductivity	mS/m	Cond
Dissolved oxygen	mg/l	DO
Hardness (as $CaCO_3$)	mg/l	Hard
PH		PH
Suspended solids	mg/l	SS
Turbidity	NTU	Turb
Biological		
Fecal coliforms	Per 100 ml	FC
Total coliforms	Per 100 ml	TC
Fecal streptococci	Per 100 ml	FS
Nutrients		
Ammonia-nitrogen	mg/l	Amm-N
Oxidized nitrogen	mg/l	NOX-N
Kjeldahl nitrogen	mg/l	TKN-N
Total phosphorus	mg/l	TP

*mg/l = milligrams per liter; mS/m = millisiemens per meter; NTU = nephelometric turbidity unit.
SOURCE: Bridgman et al. (1995, p. 89).

radioactive element), and can create abnormalities in humans and other animals, which can be transferred from generation to generation. The most famous nuclear accident in recent history occurred at Chernobyl in the former Soviet Union in April 1986. The accident was caused by human error. Fortunately, nuclear accidents are extremely rare, but the older nuclear reactors such as that at Chernobyl are still hazardous because of obsolete and decaying equipment. Modern nuclear power stations have a range of protection devices designed to prevent discharges in case of accident. [*See* Chernobyl; *and* Nuclear Hazards.]

Soil Pollution. Apart from possible problems created by acid rain and nuclear accidents, pollution of the soil tends to be local in scale and is caused mainly by industrial and manufacturing activities, agriculture, and solid waste disposal. The improper disposal of hazardous chemicals and poisons can result in leakage and contamination of ground water and may interfere with the normal structure and life cycle of the soil. Such contamination can create major health hazards many years after the industrial or disposal activity has ceased. Housing developments have been built on old industrial sites, only to have liquid and solid contaminated material seep out of the ground, affecting health and aesthetics alike. For example, the famous Love Canal incident in New York State in 1976 brought hazardous chemicals close to families when a new housing development was built on the site of a chemical dump, which subsequently caused major environmental and health problems.

In their efforts to control insects and other pests that affect agricultural production, farmers have used a variety of organic and inorganic poisons. The potential impacts of these on the environment first gained international recognition in the 1960s through Rachel Carson's book *Silent Spring* (1962). The major focus of this work was on the role of pesticides, especially dichlorodiphenyltrichloroethane (DDT), in compromising the reproduction of songbirds. Carson also discussed how transport of pesticides through ground and surface water spread destructive impacts well away from the original point of use. She also showed that DDT and other similar pesticides were not removed from the environment after use, but remained a threat decades later. Most modern pesticides are more acceptable, breaking down rapidly after use. However, there is a tendency for pesticides to be overused by the farming community, to the potential long-term detriment of the environment. [*See* Chemical Industry; *and the biography of Carson.*]

Solid waste disposal, especially associated with the massive populations in cities, can also be a major source of soil pollution. In the past, solid waste was simply dumped into open pits on the landscape, allowing leaching of toxins by rainfall into ground water or adjacent waterways. The breakdown of organic refuse can produce undesirable gases such as methane, which can cause explosions if not properly controlled. Such dumps still exist in many developing countries. In cities such as Manila in the Philippines, people live on the dump by scavenging waste material discarded by others.

A modern, well-maintained solid waste management facility will provide extensive controls to minimize pollution to waterways and the soil. Waste pits may be lined with impermeable plastic or rubber to prevent leaching. Excess water after rain events is captured in holding ponds where pollutants are allowed to settle to the bottom, to be removed later. Solid waste dumped at the facility is covered daily with soil and gravel to minimize the spread of vermin and other pests. Most solid waste can be recycled, including green waste (to garden mulch), paper, cans, bottles, and certain types of plastic. Methane gas buildup is monitored, and the gas may be tapped as an energy source for home and office heating. [*See* Waste Management.]

Ocean Pollution. Apart from potential coastal problems associated with polluted river and sewage discharges, the main cause of pollution to oceans is oil, through deliberate or accidental discharge and oil well leaks and blowouts. Other important sources include ocean disposal of solid waste and contaminated material. The impact of oil on the ocean environment can be catastrophic, depending strongly on the length of time for which the contamination is present. The most spectacular and well-publicized discharges of oil to the oceans occur when supertankers suffer accidents during transit. Examples include the *Torrey Canyon* off the coast of Cornwall, United Kingdom, in 1967, the *Exxon Valdez* in Alaska in 1989 (discharge 41,600 metric tons), and the *Braer* in the Shetland Islands off the northern coast of Scotland in 1992 (discharge 85,000 metric tons). Estimates suggest that about 6 million metric tons of oil are spilled into the ocean in any one year, the majority from undetected sources such as the flushing of oil tanks with sea water, which may discharge millions of gallons of oil into the open ocean. Small discharges of oil can be dispersed by natural ocean processes. Since oil floats on the surface, large discharges may cause long-term damage to the surface environment by destroying elements of the ocean food chain, especially plankton, fish, and birds. Living organisms coated with oil are unlikely to survive. Oil is a continuing threat to a range of highly sensitive ocean environments, including coral reefs, coastal wetlands, and fish-spawning areas. [*See* Petroleum Hydrocarbons in the Ocean.]

Ocean disposal has been used for urban garbage and hazardous waste from large cities such as New York, Seoul, and Tokyo. While such disposal is now regulated by the London Dumping Convention (1972), the corrosion of existing storage containers allows slow leakages, causing an unknown amount of continuous contamination of the ocean. [*See* Ocean Disposal.]

Policy Regulation Issues. Pollution and problems on a global scale are extremely difficult to control, especially for the ocean and the atmosphere. International agreements may be signed, but monitoring to ensure adherence is almost impossible. There have been a few successes. The Montreal Protocol, signed in 1987 and followed by subsequent updates in London (1990), Copenhagen (1992), Vienna (1995), and Montreal (1997), recognized CFCs as the major cause of stratospheric ozone depletion and constituted an international agreement to phase out production and use. On national, regional, and local scales, regulation of pollution very much depends on political will and the recognition that pollution control is as essential as economic development. The Pollyanna–Cassandra debate focuses on whether continuing expansion of the global economy and consumerism is possible (Pollyanna) or whether the whole structure will come apart in an economic and environmental calamity (Cassandra). If Pollyanna continues uncontrolled, a continuing negative impact on the environment through increased pollution is inevitable. With a proper balance between economic development and pollution control and reasonable control over consumption, the disasters predicted by Cassandra should not come to pass. [*See* Catastrophist–Cornucopian Debate.] A focus on the practices of sustainability, incorporating the precautionary principle (according to which, economic development should not proceed without full consideration of the environmental consequences), is essential. Most countries have control legislation designed to minimize pollution to air, water, and soil. Enforcement and community cooperation are essential if these controls are to be effective.

BIBLIOGRAPHY

Aplin, G., P. Mitchell, H. Cleugh, A. Pitman, and D. Rich. *Global Environmental Crises—An Australian Perspective.* Melbourne: Oxford University Press, 1995. A useful introduction to a wide range of pollution issues.

Bridgman, H. A., R. Warner, and J. Dodson. *Urban Biophysical Environments.* Melbourne: Oxford University Press, 1995. Focuses on pollution and environmental problems in cities.

Elsom, D. *Atmospheric Pollution: A Global Problem.* 2d ed. Oxford: Blackwell, 1997. An excellent review of air pollution and its problems.

Intergovernmental Panel on Climate Change. *Climate Change 1994: Radiative Forcing of Climate Change.* Cambridge: Cambridge University Press, 1994. A definitive discussion of anthropogenic impacts on the global climate.

Mannion, A. M., and S. R. Bowlby, eds. *Environmental Issues in the 1990s.* New York: Wiley, 1992. A series of chapters on pollution and environmental problems from a global perspective.

O'Riordan, T., ed. *Environmental Science for Environmental Management.* London: Longman, 1995. An excellent overview of a range of global pollution problems.

Seager, J. *The State of the Environment Atlas.* London: Penguin, 1995. A brief but nicely packaged overview of global environmental problems with very interesting maps.

World Health Organization and United Nations Environment Programme. *Urban Air Pollution in Megacities of the World.* Oxford: Blackwell, 1992. The definitive evidence on air pollution in the world's twenty largest cities.

World Resources Institute. *World Resources 1994–95.* New York: Oxford University Press, 1994. An excellent overview of the state of the world environment.

—HOWARD A. BRIDGMAN

POLLYANNA–CASSANDRA DEBATE. *See* Catastrophist–Cornucopian Debate.

POPULAR CULTURE

The idea of global change lies deep in the collective imagination of the Western tradition. Drawing on widespread antecedent accounts of worldwide flooding—the Sumerian epic of Gilgamesh, the Greek story of Pyrrha and Deucalion (although indeed many peoples have told such tales)—the story is told in the biblical Genesis of the Noachian God who floods the Earth in repentance for his creation: "And the flood was forty days upon the Earth . . . and the high hills that were under the whole heaven were covered . . . every living substance was destroyed which was upon the face of the ground, both man and cattle, and the creeping things, and the fowl of the heavens." In the eschatological account of Saint John that concludes the New Testament is unfurled another vision of global change: "The first angel sounded, and there followed hail and fire mingled with blood . . . and the third part of the trees were burnt up . . . and a third part of the creatures which were in the sea, and had life, died . . . and many men died of the waters because they were made bitter," and so on through a lengthy catalog of further environmental disasters.

These two accounts, and the extensive cataclysmic, apocalyptic, and millenarian literatures that they structure, provide the framework within which the contemporary imagination unfolds its understanding of the reality, threat, and promise of global change. The essential elements are an apocalyptic conflict between good and evil, a retributive cataclysm, and a new world as cleansed and innocent as at the first creation.

These clear visions of a decadent world destroyed by its creator in repentance or anger, which enabled Westerners to understand and deal with flood, drought, plague, and other regionwide catastrophes for centuries, were complicated by the development in nineteenth-century Europe of a vision of the world undone by the scientific progress and the technological hubris of its inhabitants. The cornerstone of this literature was Mary Shelley's *Frankenstein* (1818), but it was her *The Last Man* (1826) that sketched the devastated landscape of urban ruins reverting to nature, with its dwindling band of survivors (in this case from the plague), that has become the touchstone of contemporary visions of global change.

The human agency of such transformations was anticipated, as was so much else, by Jules Verne in the series of novels that he wrote between 1879 and his death in 1905. Less popular than his earlier travelogues, they picked up the dark apocalyptic vision of his first, but only recently published, novel, the Orwellian *Paris in the Twentieth Century* (1863 [1997]). *Propeller Island* (1895) predicted the devastation of the indigenous populations of Polynesia; *The Ice Sphinx* (1897) foresaw the extinction of whales, and *The Village in the Treetops* (1901) that of elephants, by overhunting; and *The Will of an Eccentric* (1899) anticipated the realities of oil pollution. In *The Purchase of the North Pole* (1889), sequel to the popular *From the Earth to the Moon* (1865), the protagonists propose to exploit the mineral wealth of the pole by using a giant cannon to change the tilt of the Earth and melt the icecap, inadvertently releasing a flood of precisely Noachian proportions.

Other writers in this prophetic vein pursued similarly dystopian visions, notably, Ignatius Donnelly, whose *Caesar's Column: A Story of the Twentieth Century* (1891) anticipated the auto-destruction of New York in 1988 (the survivors set up camp in Uganda); and H. G. Wells in *The Time Machine* (1895) and *The Invisible Man* (1897). If few couched the environmental consequences of industrialization, urbanization, and globalization in terms so global as Verne, writers of many persuasions—Charles Dickens, Thomas Hardy, Mark Twain, Oswald Spengler, Jack London, Joseph Conrad—observed environmental change, albeit local, in terms no less bleak. In their work, the sun shone only on childhood or the vanishing countryside, while cities became increasingly sites of fog, gloom, anonymity, alienation, destitution, repression, and oppression, approximating in Hardy, for example, the urban whore of the *Apocalypse of St. John*.

It nevertheless remained possible to mount counter-futures of equally compelling power, in Wells's utopian writing, for instance, that looked forward to the promises of technology and socialism, and especially on the radio and in the movies; but, after World War I, the Great Depression, and World War II, these became more and more difficult to sustain. The didactic classics of Aldous Huxley (*Brave New World*, 1932), George Orwell (*Nineteen Eighty-Four*, 1949), and Anthony Burgess (*A Clockwork Orange*, 1962) capture the increasingly apocalyptic tone. Images of brighter futures survived for a while in off-planet fantasies (*Amazing Stories*, whose publisher is responsible for the term *science fiction*, appeared in 1926) and superhero comics (*Superman* debuted in 1938); or were absorbed into historical or ahistorical fantasy. Yet even here the tone darkened.

J. R. R. Tolkien's *The Hobbit* (1937) is a sunny tale about the destruction of a dragon by the least of a little people. His *Lord of the Rings* (1954–1955), recently voted by a broad British readership one of the ten most significant books of the century, concludes its Manichaean conflict with the end of the world as it had been known. The often optimistic images of future metropolises that had ushered in the century, toga-clad men and women navigating sleek vehicles along highways swooping among gleaming spires, gradually gave way to the overcrowded, dirty, violent, nightmare conurbations of John Carpenter's *Escape from New York* (1981), Ridley Scott's widely influential *Blade Runner* (1982), William Gibson's *Neuromancer* (1984), and Terry Gilliam's *Brazil* (1985).

Decisive in this process of revision was the bombing of Hiroshima and Nagasaki. These local catastrophes were immediately and everywhere read as harbingers of a nuclear Armaggedon, of global change at the hands of man on a scale and of a completeness heretofore the exclusive province of the gods. As the Americans locked themselves into a cold-war struggle with the Soviet Union, they began to dig fallout shelters, practice air raid drills, and otherwise indulge the delusional fantasy of Civil Defense: that is, to construct a nationwide underground Ark. In coping with the imminence of catastrophic global change and "the possible suicide of the human race," the popular imagination mobilized both its most ancient biblical resources and those variants matured during the nineteenth and twentieth centuries, to develop powerful images of blast wastelands and primitivist survival fantasies, not infrequently in the form of "radiation romances" reworking the story of Adam and Eve in a world cleansed by cataclysm.

Unlike the delayed (with the exception of John Hersey's 1946 *Hiroshima*) and ultimately sublimated response of elite writers, the popular response was immediate, florid, and enduring, and initially evolved within the increasingly broad domain of science fiction. Important examples include Bernard Wolfe's *Limbo* (1952), John Wyndham's *The Chrysalids* (1955), and Pat Frank's *Alas, Babylon* and Walter Miller's influential *A Canticle for Leibowitz* (both of 1959). Films such as *Five* (1951), *Them!* (1954) with its radiation-mutated ants attacking Los Angeles, *The World, the Flesh and the Devil* (1959), *The Day the Earth Caught Fire* (1961), in which U.S.–Soviet atomic testing causes global warming by tilting the Earth's axis, *A Boy and His Dog* (1975), about survival communities below the Earth's surface, along with midbrow responses such as *On the Beach* (1959) and *Dr. Strangelove* (1964), typify the range. J. G. Ballard generalized the threat in a series of novels in the early 1960s in which he successively flooded (*The Drowned World*), sandblasted (*The Wind from Nowhere*), baked (*The Drought*), and petrified (*The Crystal World*) the Earth.

The tone changed in 1979 when, twelve days after the release of *The China Syndrome*, a film about the meltdown of a reactor, a nuclear accident occurred at Three Mile Island, Pennsylvania. Work heretofore read as satire or fantasy began to be read as dramatized reality. *The Day After*, 1983's made-for-television movie about nuclear holocaust, was seen by an immense audience that took it as a kind of documentary of the future; while *Silkwood* (1983), about the radiation pollution associated with weapons production, was viewed as investigative reporting.

The growing environmental self-consciousness that began to appear in films like these resulted from the emergence in the 1960s of the environmental movement. Frequently dated to the appearance in 1962 of Rachel Carson's *Silent Spring*, it was perhaps as much a product of new attitudes toward nature owing more to Walt Disney than to John Muir and Henry David Thoreau. The fact that *Bambi* (1942) was the largest grossing film of the 1940s encouraged Disney to think about films involving live as well as animated animals. He launched his True-Life Adventure Series with *Seal Island* (1948), which not only played to large audiences and won an Academy Award, but had a far greater return on investment than expensive animation. Films like *The Living Desert* (1953), *The Vanishing Prairie* (1954), *Secrets of Life* (1956), *The White Wilderness* (1958), and *Islands of the Sea* (1960), among others, exerted a profound influence on popular attitudes toward nature; were recycled in Disney's theme parks and on Disney's hugely popular television show; and paved the way for an increasingly popular genre of television nature shows that has included *Nature*, *Wild Kingdom*, *Wild America*, *Untamed World*, *Animal Safari*, *National Geographic Explorer*, and the Jacques Cousteau series. Carson's *Silent Spring* detonated in a public that had come to care for nature, at least Disney's version of it, in a way never before true, a public that folded the threat from pesticides into the looming threat of nuclear Armaggedon to produce a radically generalized concern for the future of nature as well as mankind. During the 1960s it even became a subject for popular song, culminating in Marvin Gaye's socially conscious theme album, *What's Going On* (1971), whose "Mercy, Mercy Me (The Ecology)" remains the most frequently played song about the changing environment. In it, Gaye laments that times have changed and wonders where the once-blue skies have gone. His catalog of environmental damage includes poisoned wind, waste oil in the oceans, mercury-contaminated fish, underground and atmospheric radiation, die-offs of birds and animals, and an overpopulated Earth. Gaye poses the ultimate question about the changing world: How much abuse can it stand? Topical as it was, the echoes of Saint John's *Apocalypse* in this work of a preacher's son were hard to miss.

Yet ecology largely proved an intractable subject for popular art, especially popular narrative art. Despite sporadic efforts like Ernest Callenbach's *Ecotopia* (1975), and at the very time that phrases like "ozone depletion" and "global warming" were seeping into popular consciousness via the news media, the theme languished, essentially because the kinds of incremental change involved were difficult to work through inside the apocalyptic framework that the popular imagination of the West had always used to deal with global change. Inaugurated in 1970, Earth Day went uncelebrated in the Reagan–Thatcher 1980s. Films like *The Road Warrior* (1981) and *Mad Max: Beyond Thunderdome* (1985) reverted to the post-Hiroshima blast wasteland survival fantasies, updated with a post-punk sensibility and a novel concern for resource depletion brought into popular consciousness by the oil crisis of the early 1970s, although in the post–*China Syndrome* era even these carried a less fantastic and more prophetic weight.

Indeed, they seemed to prophesy the world of the late 1980s. Environmental crises dominated the news in 1988. Medical waste washed onto the beaches of the northeastern United States, huge numbers of Atlantic seals died of unknown causes, the worst drought in years set the West ablaze—a third of Yellowstone National Park burned, the photos were everywhere—and George Bush "drowned" Michael Dukakis's bid for the presidency in the polluted waters of Boston Harbor. When in March of the following year the *Exxon Valdez* spilled 10 million gallons of crude oil into Alaska's Prince William Sound, and later that year it was concluded that changing environments, principally rainforest devastation, were the main cause of the acquired immune deficiency syndrome (AIDS), Ebola, and Marburg infections, the popular imagination was seized by the reality and imminence of catastrophic global change. When Earth Day was revived in 1990, 200 million people around the world turned out to celebrate it. Marketers responded to the air of crises and unprecedented display of public concern by pouring billions of dollars into "environmentally friendly" products, packaging, and advertising; and Hollywood, in 1990 alone, announced no fewer than fourteen major projects with ecological themes.

All of this did raise the level of popular awareness of the importance of "the environment," but did nothing to change the framework within which it was conceptualized. Among the proposals from Hollywood were a CBS television series, *E.A.R.T.H. Force*, recycling the cold-war *A-Team* as eco-warriors; an enviro-action film from Sylvester Stallone in which his action-hero, Rambo, would battle Earth exploiters instead of communists; and *Captain Planet and the Planeteers*, a cartoon series from Ted Turner featuring a caped enviro-crusading superhero. The lack of fit between the systemic, global, polycausal, and often invisible incremental change characteristics of global warming or species loss and the time-worn apocalyptic, cataclysmic, and millenarian framework into which it has by default been crammed has had the consequence of trivializing and sentimentalizing its causes, principally by isolating them to the explicitly criminal behavior of a heinous few: no more than supplanting cold-war villains and drug dealers with environmental criminals. "We'll be seeing more and more James Bond– or *Lethal Weapon*–type films in which criminals are doing antienvironmental things," is how one Hollywood producer put it.

Although the cataclysm in Kevin Costner's *Waterworld* (1995) was an unexplained, global warming–induced Noachian flood—breathlessly animated in the film's opening minutes—the film otherwise reverted to the bomb-inspired blastland fantasies of *A Boy and His Dog* or the later *Road Warrior*, played out on water instead of on land (although admittedly with a new sensitivity to micro-issues of resource use); as *Medicine Man* (1992), in which Sean Connery scours the rainforest for a cancer cure, reverted to the "radiation romances" of *Five* or *On the Beach*. But far more typical of environmental films was *Naked Gun 2½* (also 1992), perhaps the most profitable environmental film ever made, in which the hapless Lieutenant Drebin defeats an unholy alliance of oil, coal, and nuclear lobbies (S.P.I.L.L., S.M.O.K.E., and K.A.B.O.O.M., respectively) to make the world safe for solar energy; and Steven Seagal's *On Deadly Ground* (1994), an old-fashioned western in which grazing or water rights have been supplanted by the environmental consequences of oil extraction. The documentary trailer that concluded the film, in which Seagal laid the problem at the door of oil consumers, only underscored the inability of the film itself to describe, much less work through, the problem. In comic books and the omnipresent television cartoons, the now-pervasive issue has been even further reduced to the classical megalomania of evil criminals, business tycoons, or politicians with conventional world-takeover plans, now armed with powerful antienvironment weapons; or the threat has been displaced to that of children equipped with uncontrollable psychokinetic powers capable, as in Katushiro Otomo's *Akira* (1985–1995), of cataclysmic environmental change. The best of these—Frank Miller's and Dave Gibbons's *Give Me Liberty* (1990), for example—are more subtle in their analysis than anything film or television have had to offer, but remain shackled by the dramatic imperatives of the apocalyptic model to portray global change in moral terms—black and white, all or nothing—lodging causation in a single, more or less evil individual or cabal, and the solution in more or less heroic others, thus relieving the rest of us, as in almost all popular art, of complicity in, or responsibility for, the state of the world.

[*See also* Global Change, *article on* Human Dimensions of Global Change.]

BIBLIOGRAPHY

Berger, J. *After the End: Representations of Post-Apocalypse.* Minneapolis: University of Minnesota Press, 1999.

Boyer, P. *When Time Shall Be No More: Prophecy Belief in Modern American Culture.* Cambridge: Harvard University Press, 1992.

Bull, M. *Apocalypse Theory and the Ends of the World.* Oxford: Blackwell, 1995.

Cohn, N. R. C. *The Pursuit of the Millennium.* Fair Lawn, N.J.: Essential Books, 1957.

Davidson, J. W. *The Logic of the Millennial Thought.* New Haven: Yale University Press, 1977.

Dellamora, R., ed. *Postmodern Apocalypse: Theory and Cultural Practice at the End.* Philadelphia: University of Pennsylvania Press, 1995.

Hellholm, D., ed. *Apocalypticism in the Mediterranean World and the Near East.* Proceedings of the International Colloquium on Apocalypticism, Uppsala, 12–17 August 1979. Tübingen: Mohr, 1983.

Kumar, K. *Utopia and Anti-Utopia in Modern Times.* Oxford: Blackwell, 1987.

Paley, M. D. *Apocalypse and Millennium in English Romantic Poetry.* Oxford: Clarendon Press and New York: Oxford University Press, 1999.

—DENIS WOOD

POPULATION DYNAMICS

The science of population dynamics treats the change in numbers of individuals in a population. The changes in numbers are often important to human welfare and environmental management. We may wish to achieve population growth for harvested populations and endangered populations; we may wish to achieve population declines for pest populations or agents of infectious disease; we may wish to limit population fluctuations that might affect an ecological balance; and we may be concerned to predict human population numbers as a guide to social and economic planning.

The analysis of change in population numbers may operate at the level of the simple count of numbers, but it is often informative to decompose the change in numbers into effects owing respectively to birth and death rates for different age classes of individuals. The decomposition may reveal which age classes are the most promising targets for intervention, and this in turn may suggest the types of environmental management most likely to achieve the desired result.

The extrapolation of population sizes into the future, and the relation between the overall population growth rate and the component rates, are inherently mathematical issues. The estimation of population numbers and birth and death rates from limited data involves substantial statistical challenges. Understanding how environmental conditions affect the component birth and death rates encompasses much of the science of ecology.

Mathematics of Change in Population Numbers. If the instantaneous average per capita birth rate among individuals in a population is b offspring per individual per unit time, and the instantaneous average per capita death rate is μ deaths per individual per unit time, then the instantaneous per capita rate of change in numbers of individuals in the population is

$$r = b - \mu \tag{1}$$

individuals per individual per unit time. The instantaneous rate of change in numbers of individuals in the total population then is rN, where N is the current number of individuals.

If these per capita birth and death rates, b and μ, remain constant, then the population will grow exactly exponentially, so that

$$N_t = N_0 e^{rt} \tag{2}$$

where N_t is the population size after an elapsed time t, N_0 is the initial population size, and e is the base of the natural logarithms (roughly 2.7).

Exponential growth, like compound interest, is a self-accelerating process: the rate of growth of the total population itself grows exponentially with time. Thus, when conditions allow approximate constancy of the per capita birth and death rates, and the birth rate is larger than the death rate (so that r is positive), the population in time will grow explosively. And, for similar constancy, with the death rate larger than the birth rate, the population decline will be exponential, and the population will decline steadily to extinction.

This potential for exponential growth or decline gives the dynamics of populations a capability for extreme volatility. At times, this potential is expressed in actuality, when we see epidemics, outbreaks of pest species, and population crashes. Much of the time, however, many natural populations are relatively stable, with their numbers varying within a limited range. So the constancy of conditions that fosters the dynamics of exponential growth is more the exception than the rule.

Generally, the highly volatile dynamics are perceived as undesirable from the standpoint of human welfare, so we are motivated to learn to recognize, to predict, and perhaps to control the determining circumstances. Also, there is the intellectual challenge of wanting to understand how some populations in nature achieve comparative stability, contrary to the dynamics predicted by our most elementary model of population growth.

Population Composition. One factor that can cause departures from constancy of per capita birth and death rates in a population is population composition—age structure and sex ratio. If, for example, a population is composed mostly of individuals of prime reproductive age, then for a time the birth rates in the population will be abnormally high; but, as this parental generation ages, and as its offspring (which are initially too young to reproduce themselves) come to make up a larger fraction of the population, the per capita birth rates will decline for a while.

The effects of population composition can routinely make enough of a difference in predicting the details of population growth rates that these effects need to be taken into account in assessing human population growth or in assessing the dynamics of harvested renewable resources, where modest differences in rates can have substantial economic or public health impacts. But the effects of population composition on population dynamics do not make the difference between stability and instability of the sort that concerns us in the bigger ecological picture.

In fact, if the birth and death rates of each age class are constant over time (but not age), then, regardless of the initial composition, the effects of age composition in temporarily increasing or decreasing the rate of population growth will be cyclic, with a cycle time approximately of the same duration as the population's generation time, but with the magnitude of the departure from constant growth rate diminishing in each successive generation. The age composition of such a population will eventually become constant, at which time the per capita birth and death rates, averaged over the entire population, will become constant, and then the population grows exponentially in accordance with equation (2). The equation linking the age-specific birth and death rates with the eventual exponential population growth rate that this population will display, if those rates continue to hold, is

$$\int_0^\infty e^{-(rx + \int_0^x \mu_y dy)} b_x dx = 1 \qquad (3)$$

where x designates age, b_x is the birth rate to individuals age x, and μ_x is the death rate of individuals age x. The mathematics of dealing with this forbidding-looking equation, and the practicalities of obtaining estimates of the age-specific birth and death rates from real data, are treated in the discipline of mathematical demography.

Biology of Change in Population Numbers. The crucial terms appearing in the mathematical formulas for population dynamics are biological characteristics of individuals in the population. At best, these properties conform approximately to the assumptions of the mathematical model, in which case the dynamics of the real population will approximate the dynamics we deduce from the mathematics. With respect to the key assumption of constancy of the per capita age-specific birth and death rates, the biological reality may depart

very greatly from the simple assumptions, and then the dynamics of the population may be vastly different from the dynamics deduced from the simple model. Indeed, the differences can even be qualitative, such as stable versus unstable. It is therefore up to us to examine the plausibility of the assumptions of our mathematical models, judging them against what we know about biological mechanisms. [*See* Modeling of Natural Systems.]

Even when we know that a model is seriously unrealistic, we may still be able to draw worthwhile conclusions from investigating the mathematical behavior of the model, provided we keep the conclusions in proper perspective. For example, we might construct a series of simplified models, where each model captures the essence of one particular mechanism while ignoring other mechanisms. Then we could use this series of models to learn the dynamic consequences of each mechanism, which might not be nearly as understandable in a more complicated model in which all the mechanisms were operating simultaneously.

Equation (2) has revealed the dramatic dynamic consequences of constant per capita birth and death rates. Next we need to consider the reasonableness of the assumption of such constancy, the circumstances under which it might apply, the types of departure from constancy that we might expect to result from different biological mechanisms, and the kinds of dynamics that result from each major pattern of departure from constancy.

Constant Conditions. The per capita birth and death rates reflect how favorable are the conditions that individuals in the population experience. This will be a function of factors such as nutritional status as influenced by food supply per capita, availability of shelter, incidence of disease, rates of predation, and the physiological tolerance of the species to the prevailing physical characteristics (such as temperature and moisture) of the environment that the population occupies.

To an extent, these factors can vary under their own dynamics, because the natural world, as we know it, is variable. But many of these factors will also be correlated with the size of the population, since they respond causally to the level of crowding in the population. As the population becomes more crowded, some resources will be in short supply, predators may be attracted to the concentration of prey, disease transmission may be more rapid, and some individuals of the population may be forced into less-preferred habitat. In this light, constant per capita birth and death rates appear quite unlikely over any period of time long enough for the population to grow or decline appreciably.

Constant conditions as experienced by each individual. Approximate constancy of birth and death rates is plausible in a stable environment for a limited period of time if, during that time, the population is so sparse that crowding effects are negligible and the population growth is limited only by basic physiological constraints on an individual's maximum rate of growth from birth to maturity and on an individual's maximum rate of producing offspring. It is implausible that individuals in a population should indefinitely experience constant conditions, even approximately, both because of background variation in the environment and because the exponential population growth or decline that occurs under constant conditions must eventually lead to enough change in population size that changes in the level of crowding *will* begin to have a substantial effect on the per capita birth and death rates.

Human populations. On a global scale, the human population over the past few centuries seems to have escaped the iron law that crowding will eventually terminate an episode of exponential population growth. The explanation for this apparent exception is that continuing progress in technology during this period, especially in agriculture and medicine, has compensated for the effects of numerical density, so that the effective biological crowding of humans has not changed substantially, even though the total human population has grown, and is continuing to grow, at a rate that in some respects is alarming.

Beneath the surface of this appearance, in aggregate, of constant effective human crowding allowing ongoing exponential population growth, there are many local and temporal inconstancies, many complicated details of social, biological, ecological, and economic processes, and unanswered questions about eventual limits to human knowledge and feasible technology. Our science does not have an adequate basis for predicting how far into the future the advances in technology will keep pace with the escalating growth of human population. Likewise, there is not an adequate basis for predicting whether the eventual end of this phase of approximately exponential growth in human population will be a gradual deceleration of growth until approximate population constancy is achieved, or whether there will be a catastrophic crash of some sort. Our inability to predict these outcomes with any certainty is not necessarily comforting.

Constant resource supply. If we imagine that the background environmental conditions for a population are constant, and the critical resources are in constant supply, then this constant total resource base will be divided among a varying number of individuals as the numbers of individuals change. If we imagine that the per capita birth and death rates change in proportion to the resources available per individual, with birth rates decreasing as population increases, and death rates increasing as population increases, we can readily construct a model in which the instantaneous per capita

population growth rate, r, declines smoothly as the number of individuals in the population increases. This is a simple form of density-dependent population dynamics.

Such a model will exhibit very stable dynamics. For example, a population initiated at small numbers will initially grow exponentially, and then the growth rate will slow as crowding effects exert themselves in the larger population; and finally the population will cease to grow when the crowding just reaches the level where the birth rate (which has been declining as population increases) just balances the death rate (which has been increasing as population increases). If a population is initiated at larger numbers than this equilibrium level, the death rate will exceed the birth rate, so that the population will decline, and the rate of decline will diminish as the population approaches the equilibrium level (from above); and the population will cease declining when it reaches the same equilibrium level where birth rates equal death rates.

Carrying capacity. The dynamics described above, for a single population whose individuals share a constant (constant total, *not* constant per capita) resource supply, reveal an equilibrium population level to which the population will return, under its own dynamics, regardless of whether the population is temporarily displaced to larger or smaller numbers. This equilibrium population level is conventionally called the *carrying capacity* of this environment for this species. [*See* Carrying Capacity.]

Discussions of human population growth sometimes attempt to estimate the carrying capacity of the entire Earth for human beings, in an attempt to estimate the global population size at which the growth of the human population will cease. It must be understood that human carrying capacity in the context of those discussions is a moving target, since it depends on technology and culture.

Density-Dependent Growth in a Random Environment. If we imagine a population whose individuals share a resource supply that varies randomly over time, the variation in resource supply results effectively in a random variation in the carrying capacity of that environment for that population. At any moment, the population may be above or below the carrying capacity, and for the moment the population numbers will change in the direction that approaches the current carrying capacity. But the carrying capacity itself changes, randomly, so the effect is an appearance of the population numbers "chasing" after the fluctuating carrying capacity.

If, over time, the average carrying capacity is large relative to the range of variation in carrying capacity, the variation of population numbers will also be bounded by the "envelope" of the random carrying capacity. But if the fluctuations in carrying capacity are too wide, the variations in carrying capacity may occasionally carry the population to very low numbers. At very low numbers, additional chance factors begin to influence the population dynamics.

Population extinction. Recall that the per capita birth and death rates with which we began this discussion of population dynamics are averages over all the individuals in the population. When the number of individuals is large, differences between individuals will tend to cancel out in the average. But when numbers are small, the chance differences between individuals can dominate the dynamics of the population, as "luck of the draw" determines individual birth events and death events. For this reason, chance mechanisms operating in small populations can cause chance extinction following a run of bad luck.

Thus, on a particular time scale, there are two categories of population extinction. Chance extinction is driven primarily by the frequency with which random environmental variation brings the population to sufficiently low numbers that chance mechanisms operating on individuals can result in a string of deaths outstripping births until the last individual is dead. Deterministic extinction occurs when constant conditions (relative to the chosen time scale) are so unfavorable for the population that it declines approximately exponentially to extinction.

The forces of expanding human populations and land use changes are gradually driving many populations of many species to smaller and smaller numbers. This is resulting in an era of abnormally high extinction rates, which has motivated concerns for the preservation of biodiversity. The trends causing the persistent declines of these populations are deterministic, in the sense described above. In attempts to prevent some extinctions, protected reserves may be set aside for remnant populations. In designing and managing such reserves, it is important to allow a sufficient margin of safety to protect the small remnant population from chance extinction. The branch of population dynamics called *population viability analysis* deals with the prediction of extinction probabilities as a function of population size, environmental conditions, and conservation policies.

Other Populations. Far from being an inanimate and constant source of a flux of resources, the environment that real biological populations occupy includes other biological populations. The dynamics of these other populations, as they interact with the target population of interest, will dynamically revise the conditions defining the favorability of the environment for the target population and will dynamically revise the numerical value of the carrying capacity. Thus we need to understand the principal kinds of mechanism underlying the biological interactions among populations, and the

implications of each interaction for the resulting dynamic stability and for the maintenance of biodiversity.

Competition. In the simplest model of two-species competition in an otherwise constant environment, individuals of both species compete in the consumption of the common resource, which is presumed to be in constant supply. This is an extension to two species of the model of population growth with a constant carrying capacity. Contrary to the stability manifested by the one-species version of this model, the two-species version tends to instability, because whichever species is most efficient at competing for the common resource tends to crowd out, and eliminate, the other (at which point the continuing dynamics are those of a one-species model, which is stable).

These unstable dynamics of systems of populations of two competitors are commonly encountered in real biological populations in simplified experimental laboratory conditions. But this degree of instability is obviously not characteristic of the dynamics of populations in natural communities of species.

In the simple two-species models, a stable equilibrium in which both species persist requires that each species depress its own growth, through self-crowding effects, more strongly than its growth is depressed by the competitive crowding effect of the other population. Ecologically, this implies that each species must be in some sense a "specialist," so that the supply or availability of some aspect of the environment that is uniquely important to that species is more important than the supply of the common resource. This interpretation of the mathematical modeling result has given rise to the concept of an ecological niche.

According to niche theory, each species in an ecologically stable system plays a uniquely specialized role, and this specialization is at the heart of the dynamic stability of natural ecological systems, at least from the perspective of the persistence of the species in question. Whether the persistence of the species is instrumental to the stability of much of the rest of the system is less clear, but at least *some* other species will depend on this species' persistence for its own stability.

Predator and prey. The second major mode of interaction between populations is one population using the other as a "resource," as occurs in interactions between predator and prey or between parasite (or pathogen) and host. As with the simplest models of competition, the simplest models of predator–prey interaction tend to instability. The instability in the predator–prey models expresses itself as a tendency toward population cycles. The basic force behind the cycles is predator population buildup in the presence of ample prey, causing reduction of the prey population until the scarcity of prey leads to a decline in the predator population, which in turn allows the prey population to recover, and the cycle repeats. These cycles are dynamically similar to the "boom and bust" cycles of economic theory.

The predator–prey cycles, in the most elementary form of the models, can become so extreme that the predator exterminates the prey, or the predator itself becomes extinct when it has driven the prey to such sparseness that the predator cannot find enough prey to sustain itself. These extremely unstable dynamics are commonly encountered in actual predator–prey systems in simplified laboratory conditions, but obviously they are not characteristic of dynamics in natural communities of species.

As with the analysis of the dynamics of competition models, the stabilization of predator–prey dynamics seems to hinge on mechanisms whereby the predator population, or the prey population, or both, are to some degree self-limited in their dynamics.

The Whole and the Sum of Its Parts. While the stability of natural populations is far from absolute, there is no question that natural communities exhibit a greater degree of stability than would be predicted from the simplest models of population dynamics and two-species interaction. Natural communities also exhibit a greater degree of stability than is usually seen in attempts to maintain multispecies systems in a simple laboratory setting. In this sense, real natural communities are not just haphazard assemblages of species. Somehow or other, the species have to "fit" together, in part through mutual compatibility of their respective specializations. Thus we see that the dynamics of stable natural communities cannot be explained satisfactorily in terms of the most elementary dynamic models of their component species populations, or elementary dynamic models of pairwise interactions. The key to the system's relative dynamic stability seems to derive from particular properties that make each species different, and possibly also from a history of trial-and-error, or evolutionary, adjustment of species composition and species properties.

Niche theory, which was motivated at first by the discovery of the stabilizing effect of ecological specialization in competition models, seems to draw additional credibility from the discovery of the stabilizing effect of similar sorts of ecological specialization in predator–prey models. The theory leads to an image of ecological systems as intricately tuned mechanisms in which each species plays a functional, and possibly unique, role in the aggregate dynamics. This, in turn, suggests the possibility that a stable ecological system could be vulnerable to destabilization if some of its component species populations are eliminated, or if some new species that was not originally part of this system invades from the outside, or if physical conditions change

in a way that disrupts the basis for some of the dynamic balance between species by eliminating one or more of the "specialties."

This theorizing is behind the popular metaphors representing the global ecological system as a ship that might sink for the loss (or addition) of one rivet in the wrong place. The magnitude of ecologically significant global change, and the ongoing loss of biodiversity of at least some types of species, raises reasonable concerns about wholesale ecological collapse associated with mass extinctions. It is possible to construct multispecies computer models that display these sorts of catastrophic dynamics. But ecological reality is far too complicated, and these multispecies models themselves are too complicated, for us to be certain, before the fact, that any one such model is a dynamically accurate portrayal of reality.

Much important debate in environmental policy revolves around the prudent courses of action that should be recommended, given this uncertainty: Should socially and economically costly programs of intervention be undertaken as a precaution, or is it reasonable to allow an experiment with the ecology of an entire planet to proceed as in a science-fiction movie?

[*See also* Biological Productivity; Growth, Limits to; Human Populations; Migrations; Urban Areas; *and the biography of Malthus.*]

BIBLIOGRAPHY

Cohen, J. E. *How Many People Can the Earth Support?* New York: Norton, 1995.

Emlen, J. M. *Ecology: An Evolutionary Approach.* Reading, Mass.: Addison-Wesley, 1973.

———. "The Demography of Chance Extinction." In *Viable Populations for Conservation,* edited by M. E. Soule, pp. 11–34. Cambridge: Cambridge University Press, 1987.

Goodman, D. "Optimal Life Histories, Optimal Notation, and the Value of Reproductive Value." *American Naturalist* 119 (1982), 803–823.

Keyfitz, N. *Applied Mathematical Demography.* 2d ed. New York: Springer, 1985.

Yodzis, P. *Introduction to Theoretical Ecology.* Cambridge: Cambridge University Press, 1989.

—DANIEL GOODMAN

POPULATION POLICY

Population policies are sets of principles, strategies, programs, and spending plans devised by governments—and sometimes by intergovernmental, nongovernmental, and private organizations—chiefly to influence the course of human population growth and distribution. In the sciences, the term *population* denotes the aggregate of specified organisms in a habitat or area; this article limits the term to the number of human beings on the planet and in nations. In a few cases, population policies aim either to enlarge family size in order to accelerate population growth (for example, Romania during the era of Nicolae Ceausescu), or to restrict family size in order to brake population growth (for example, China in the 1980s and 1990s). More often, population policies guide the funding or distribution of contraceptive information and supplies as well as the overall care of reproductive and sexual well-being. This branch of public health, called *reproductive health*, is strongly associated with population outcomes. People who use these services, however, rarely have a direct interest in such outcomes. Their interest is rather to avoid or delay pregnancy, plan families, have healthy babies, and maintain health through their reproductive lives. Reproductive-health providers share these objectives for their clients. *Population policy* nonetheless remains the overarching term that most often covers the dissemination, expansion, and improvement of these reproductive health services worldwide. This seeming paradox serves as a useful reminder that a set of policies and programs that directly benefits individuals and couples also has the side benefit of slowing population growth. To the extent that population dynamics influence natural resources and the natural environment, population policies also indirectly slow human-induced environmental change. This article deals primarily with these linkages and the evolution of policies related to them.

Population policies could, in theory, go beyond reproductive health programs, but in practice they rarely do. The education of girls through secondary school and the economic empowerment of women also contribute to slower rates of population growth, but governments tend not to associate these two objectives with population trends, and so they still lie largely outside the realm of population policy. Laws and regulations that influence migration within and among nations could also qualify as population policies, but these typically are driven not by demographic ends but by economic, cultural, political, and other social considerations. In 1998, the Sierra Club, a major U.S. environmental organization, polled its membership on whether the organization should advocate for more restrictive immigration policies in order to slow U.S. population growth; the members opposed the idea by a modest margin.

Policy makers and analysts in some industrialized countries have expressed concern about falling, or "sub-replacement" birth rates (that is, birth rates too low to replace parental generations) among their populations. The populations of Japan and most European countries have national fertility rates significantly below the replacement level of a fraction more than two births per woman. (The national fertility rate is the number of children born to the average woman, assuming current national birth patterns are sustained through her lifetime.) These trends have undoubtedly fueled political support

for policies favoring parents in France and some other European nations. In 2000, the United Nations (UN) Population Division issued a report on developed-country population trends which argued that some nations should consider increasing immigration to maintain population size and, possibly, current ratios of workers to retirees. Few if any governments, however, have instituted policies expressly aimed at increasing fertility or in drawing immigrants for demographic purposes. Although factors other than family planning and reproductive health are infrequently addressed in population policies, they may well be in the future; the rest of this article, however, addresses population policies related to those two areas.

It is important to distinguish the population policies of the world's relatively wealthy and industrialized, or developed, countries from those of the less wealthy, less industrialized, developing countries. Most developed countries have modest or even negative population growth, and none of their governments has chosen to institute policies to influence domestic population growth. Population policy, in the context of these nations, means their direct funding or technical assistance to developing countries to expand the reach of family planning and related services. In contrast, most of the world's developing nations have national policies related to domestic population growth and the need for services to help couples and women space or limit births. Hence, there are two broad types of population policies: those involving foreign aid in developed countries and those involving domestic population policy and provision of reproductive-health services in developing ones. [*See* Economic Levels.]

Population History and Current Trends. From the standpoint of demographics, the millennium now ending could scarcely have differed more dramatically from the one that preceded it. From the year 1 to 1000 CE, world population was essentially stable, with any increases eventually balanced by equal decreases. By demographers' best estimates, the first millennium began with 300 million people on the planet and ended with about the same number. As the second millennium closes, there are twenty times more people on the planet, and no way to be certain when or at what number population growth will end.

Demographic trends today are contradictory. Human numbers are still rising at a pace that would lead to 12 billion people by the middle of the new century, if that pace fails to slow. In much of the world, per capita income and natural resource consumption are increasing even more rapidly. Many analysts fear the twenty-first century will witness growing scarcities of key natural resources that may lead to conflicts and increases in death rates. At the same time, however, population growth rates are declining significantly. This has led to concerns that populations will become progressively older and may even begin to decrease in the twenty-first century if this trend continues.

It helps to understand that current demographic patterns vary considerably among regions and levels of economic development. It also pays to consider the long view and to be wary of demographic prediction. We can examine ranges of likely outcomes, but we cannot know the future. The spread of most likely outcomes calculated by UN demographers suggests that the century will end with between 5 and 16 billion people, but we cannot be sure even of this. Projections of population change are neither forecasts nor estimates. Rather, they are straightforward calculations based on current population trends and assumptions about future rates of births, deaths, and migration.

Current population projections assume continued declines in both birth and death rates, but neither of these trends may continue for long without major new investments in education and health care—especially in reproductive health programs that encourage lower birth rates through family planning and prolong life by dampening transmission of the human immunodeficiency virus/acquired immune deficiency syndrome (HIV/AIDS) virus. Whatever happens to world population tomorrow depends critically on what governments and individuals decide to do today.

At the opening of the new millennium, there are more than 6 billion human beings, almost four times as many as in 1900. Life expectancy has soared, especially in regard to the survival of infants and children, which was the dominant factor in the population growth of the 1900s. Settlements and farm fields dominate much of the six habitable continents, and human beings are almost as likely to live in a city or suburb as in a village. On average, each person is or will become a parent to 2.5 children, and world population grows by about 1.3 percent annually. The planet is home to roughly 78 million more people each year, 215,000 more each day, 9,000 more each hour.

All but 3 percent of this growth occurs in developing countries, yet many industrialized countries—especially the United States—also contribute to world population growth. The average age of human beings is rising as birth rates decline and life expectancy increases, yet a billion of the planet's inhabitants are between fifteen and twenty-four years old, and in many countries school construction barely keeps pace with the need for new classrooms.

It is increasingly a demographically uneven world, mirroring to some extent the economically skewed world in which one-fifth of the population, mostly in industrialized countries, earns the vast bulk of monetary income. Life expectancy continues to rise in much of the world, but over the past quarter century it fell in

eighteen countries, most of them overwhelmed by the HIV/AIDS pandemic in sub-Saharan Africa. In Europe and Japan, sub-replacement fertility sets the stage for current or future population declines. In the United States, Canada, and Australia, fertility rates are closer to replacement level; high proportions of young people and net immigration combine to produce average population growth around 1 percent annually in these countries. In Latin America and in Asia—the continent on which most human beings live—fertility rates have fallen by half in little more than a generation. Population growth rates in these regions resemble that of the world as a whole.

In most of Africa and in the Middle East, the transition to later childbirth and smaller families has not yet advanced very far. Family size still averages five or six children, and population projections envision a doubling or even a tripling of population in some countries, many of which are already critically short of cropland, forests, and renewable fresh water. Population growth rates tend to exceed 2.6 percent, twice the global rate, in many countries where governments have the fewest resources for critically needed education and health care.

Population and Environmental Change. These relationships between changing population size and the natural resources on which human well-being depends contribute to policy makers' concerns about population growth. It may be that human resources are the most important resources for development and prosperity, yet history and current experience demonstrate that this is most true when natural resources are abundant, cheap, and accessible to all. Supplies of most critical natural resources are diminishing or degrading as more human beings use them with greater intensity. The finite resources must be shared among more people, and this can begin a sequence of competing claims and rising anxieties that challenge governments and other institutions. The long debate over the impact of population growth on the environment is gradually converging on general agreement that contemporary population growth is among a handful of factors that strongly influence the sustainability of natural resource use. The relationship is never simple, and a population never acts alone in causing such environmental problems as water scarcity and global warming; however, its influence cannot be severed from such direct causes as overdrawn aquifers and rising greenhouse gas emissions.

Consumption patterns also influence relationships between population and natural resources. The average individual in the United States or another industrialized country consumes a volume of natural resources dozens of times larger than the amount consumed in many developing countries. If every one of the world's 6 billion inhabitants consumed as much paper and petroleum as does each of the United States' 277 million inhabitants, the damage to forests, soils, air, and climate would be catastrophic. The logical place to begin to transform this simple equation is within the wealthy countries that promulgate the high-consumption, high-waste model of happiness and prosperity. No wealthy countries have begun to contemplate even the concept of "consumption policy," however.

The role of population growth is also impossible to sever from the management of human affairs by governments and other legal, social, and economic institutions. Analysts of population–environment interactions often consider how much of a particular natural resource is available—in the sense of simply "being there"—to each person in a country. Also important is how much of a resource people are actually extracting from the Earth, processing, using, and disposing. But mediating the flow of natural resources between the Earth and human beings are the social regulating valves known as institutions. These may be governments and their policies and programs, or they may be rules of law, economic markets, and such legal principles as the right to hold and dispose of property.

The development of these social structures and processes plays a critical role in the management and conservation of natural resources worldwide. Institutions may or may not work well. Acknowledging disparities in institutional development is essential to understanding the effects of population change; indeed, population change itself plays important roles in institutional development. One linkage may connect population growth, scarcity of essential natural resources, and the weakening of vulnerable institutions.

How do institutions, population growth, economic growth, and the environment interact? Some economists suggest that poorly developed institutions and high fertility reinforce each other in a cycle of social and economic stagnation. Such a vicious cycle could explain why high fertility is frequently associated with low levels of institutional development. It may also help us understand how declines in fertility can stimulate institutional and economic development and be stimulated themselves by that development.

Evolution of Population Policy. Should governments act to influence population growth? That question first emerged in the nineteenth century, after the English economist and clergyman Thomas Robert Malthus hypothesized that population growth without adequate individual or collective restraint always tends to outstrip the natural resources on which human beings depend. Malthus continually reworked his 1798 *Essay on Population.* His final essay, published posthumously in 1830, suggested (far more optimistically than his more famous initial essay) both that human beings could adapt under many conditions to growing population and that the right social policies might even slow

the increase of human numbers. His writing engendered philosophical debate that continues to this day, and he may be considered the author of the concept of population policy. [*See the biography of Malthus.*]

As a staunch opponent of contraception, however, Malthus in no sense can be considered a pioneer of contemporary population policy, which rests on the foundation of contraceptive availability and use. The true pioneers were a handful of mid-twentieth-century social scientists and policy analysts who argued that couples would have fewer children if governments subsidized or otherwise supported the distribution of safe and effective contraceptives, including sterilization for those who wanted no more children.

As early as 1951, India began such a program in an effort to stem the rapid rise of its postindependence population. A half century later, despite some success at helping to lower national fertility from roughly 6 children per woman to 3.4 in the late 1990s, India's government continues to experiment in an effort to expand the reach of its population program. In July 2000, for example, Prime Minister Atal Bihari Vajpayee proposed a public–private fund dramatically to increase spending on family planning throughout the country, which now has more than a billion people.

In instituting a population program so early, India set a precedent that few other developing countries followed until the 1960s. In developed countries, a number of demographers and government officials argued, beginning in the 1950s and early 1960s, that the post–World War II efforts to stimulate economic development in the former colonies of European powers should include assistance with family-planning services. The reasoning was chiefly that such assistance would slow the increase of population resulting from dramatic declines in infant and child mortality after the war's end. By 1965, the United States had instituted such a foreign assistance program through its Agency for International Development (USAID). By 1969, the United Nations Population Fund (formerly United Nations Fund for Population Activities; UNFPA) was accepting contributions from many developed nations for the purpose of helping to disseminate family-planning assistance worldwide. (This agency was later renamed the United Nations Population Fund but still carries its original acronym.)

From the beginning, population policies were controversial, and though the nature of the controversy has changed, it has never disappeared. Dozens of developing countries asked USAID and UNFPA to help with national family-planning programs in the late 1960s and early 1970s. (Eventually, the World Bank became a major lender for family-planning programs in developing countries.) Yet in 1974, when the world's nations gathered under UN auspices in Bucharest for the World Population Conference, most delegations from developing nations repudiated the concept of population policies and population assistance. "Development is the best contraceptive" was the slogan that dominated the conference, signaling the still-popular view in developing-country intellectual circles that poverty, not population, is the root issue to be addressed, and that family planning is less important than prosperity in lowering birth rates. The idea of population policies based on family planning lost more luster after an overzealous Indian population program, based on assigning family-planning workers quotas for sterilization procedures and other types of contraceptive acceptance, contributed to the 1977 fall of Prime Minister Indira Gandhi's government.

By the next decade's population conference, however, the simplistic view that wealthy countries wanted to foist "population control" on unwilling developing countries was no longer tenable. Almost all developing-country governments had promulgated population policies and family-planning programs by the time of the 1984 International Conference on Population in Mexico City. Developing-country delegations agreed that family-planning programs were crucial to their economic and social development, and most asked for more assistance from industrialized "donor-country" governments to help pay for these programs and expand their reach. But now a new element came into play. Under President Ronald Reagan, the U.S. government—long the world's leader in providing population assistance—tempered its involvement by declaring that population growth was a "neutral factor" in economic development. Reagan promulgated a presidential order requiring that no U.S. foreign aid money go to nongovernmental organizations (NGOs) that provided abortion services or counseling. Since many of the NGOs providing contraceptive assistance in developing countries also used their own funds for abortion-related services, this prohibition reduced the effectiveness of U.S. population assistance until President William Clinton reversed the doctrine, as one of his first presidential acts, in 1993.

In the 1980s, China emerged as a special case in the evolution of population policies. During the long reign of Mao Zedong, the prevailing communist government view of China's population (which included, then as now, about one in five of the planet's human beings) was that there could never be too many Chinese. Contraception was available only to a favored few, and fertility averaged more than five children per woman. After Mao's death in 1976, however, China's new leaders considered with alarm the challenge the country faced in feeding and housing its rapidly growing population. They instituted a population policy based largely on expanding the availability of contraceptive services. The policy also encouraged late marriage, avoiding childbirth before age twenty and after age forty, and greater employment of women in collective farms and state fac-

tories. The result was a precipitous decline in fertility, to roughly three children per woman.

By the early 1980s, however, China's leaders feared that this population policy was insufficient to lead to a manageable population maximum in the twenty-first century and sustainable economic growth. They altered the policy to stress that most Chinese couples should have no more than a single child, and they granted local authorities relatively free rein to enforce this one-child policy. The result was a far less impressive decline in fertility—and numerous reports of coercion, including forced abortion. By the late 1990s, the central government of China was insisting it was working to eliminate such excesses. China's experience offers a forceful illustration of the extremes to which a highly demographically focused population policy can go.

Cairo and the New Paradigm of Population Policy. The 1990s were a period of optimism related to population policy. Demographic researchers were beginning to converge on several key findings that have since come to guide that policy internationally. One was that fertility rates were falling significantly worldwide, and that the thirty-year international movement to expand access to a range of contraceptive services could take major credit for this trend. Another was that popular acceptance and continued use of family planning were more likely when service providers focused on the overall reproductive-health needs of their clients, rather than on government fertility preferences and demographic goals. These findings began to shape a new approach to population that is based less on numbers and more on the reality of people's lives—especially the lives of women—and the need to encourage access to health care, education, and economic opportunities.

In 1994, delegations from almost every government converged in Cairo for the third United Nations decadal population meeting, this time called the International Conference on Population and Development. The world was spending roughly U.S.$4 billion on family-planning services in the developing world, up from just U.S.$50 million a year in 1965. These figures include money contributed by donor countries, the developing countries themselves, and consumers in developing countries. Two years earlier, delegates to the Earth Summit in Rio de Janeiro had agreed that demographic trends were an important element in global environmental change, but they had failed to recommend concrete steps to build on that linkage. At the same time, many social scientists and an increasingly influential community of NGOs representing women were insisting that women had the right make their own decisions about reproduction and sexuality without outside interference, regardless of governmental interest in population trends. In the United States and elsewhere, several private foundations were directing substantial resources to raising public and policy makers' awareness about the potential for slowing global population growth through support for international family planning.

These independent and even contradictory strands of thinking converged in Cairo. There, despite opposition from the delegations of some countries (and the Vatican, which enjoys the status of a national government at such UN conferences), the world's nations worked out a historic agreement on population and development that is likely to guide international population policies for some time to come. The strategies endorsed in Cairo were designed to attract popular and government support, regardless of whether population growth proves to be a decisive factor in environmental change and human well-being or a mere footnote to history. Population policies and programs consistent with this agreement are primarily grounded not in demographic objectives, but rather in the development of each person's capacity to decide for herself or himself how many children to have, and when. In Cairo, the governments of 179 nations agreed to allocate U.S.$17 billion annually to assure universal access to basic reproductive health services by the year 2015. Five years later, in 1999, the same governments renewed this pledge and specified the importance of including young people among those who deserve such access to reproductive health services. Except for some developing-country governments, however, most have failed to live up to their commitments. Population-program spending in 1997 amounted to about U.S.$10 billion, but only around $2 billion of this came from donor nations. The U.S. government, torn internally over the side issue of abortion, was now contributing less than it did in 1995. In 1999, a conservative-dominated U.S. Congress forced President Clinton to accept statutory restrictions on U.S. population assistance that were similar to those President Reagan imposed administratively in 1984. Such developments cast some doubt on whether sufficient funding will emerge for the kind of widespread reproductive health services that would enable the world to follow the path suggested by the "median variant" UN population projection, which would bring world population to 8.9 billion people in 2050.

The primary objective of reproductive-health providers is not to alter global demographic trends, but to improve the lives of individuals directly. Access to good reproductive health care, decent schools, and opportunities to earn a living can mean the difference between happiness and misery—or even between life and death—for women and their children. But an important side benefit of addressing these individual needs is that population growth will slow and eventually end, not because of more deaths, but through fewer births. At what level and in what decade population growth halts, and what kinds of societies will witness this peak, will depend very much on how seriously governments and other social institutions take the commitments agreed to in Cairo in 1994.

[*See also* Belief Systems; Catastrophist–Cornucopian Debate; Ethics; Human Populations; IPAT; Population Dynamics; *and* Religion.]

BIBLIOGRAPHY

Ahlburg, D. A., et al. *The Impact of Population Growth on Well-Being in Developing Countries.* Berlin: Springer, 1996. Essays by experts in demographics, economics, and other social sciences on linkages between population dynamics and aspects of human well-being.

Ashford, L. S. *New Perspectives on Population: Lessons from Cairo.* Washington, D.C.: Population Reference Bureau, 1995. Analysis and commentary on the Program of Action agreed to by the nations participating in the 1994 International Conference on Population and Development.

Bongaarts, J. "Population Policy Options in the Developing World." *Science* 263 (1994), 771–776. Consideration of the role of population policy in fertility decline and population change in developing countries, including an influential analysis of the role of maternal age of childbearing on population trends.

Bongaarts, J., et al. "The Demographic Impact of Family Planning Programs." *Studies in Family Planning* 21.6 (1991), 299–310. Quantifies the impact of international family-planning efforts on world population dynamics, calculating that the global total in 1991 would have been at least 400 million higher without the programs (in 1999, Bongaarts revised the number to 700 million for that year).

Casterline, J. B., and S. W. Sinding. *Unmet Need for Family Planning in Developing Countries and Implications for Population Policy.* Population Council Policy Research Division Working Paper no. 135. New York: Population Council, 2000. A discussion of the meaning of the term *unmet need* for family planning (referring to the unrealized intentions of many women to delay or otherwise limit pregnancy), with a defense of its importance as a concept in population policy.

Cincotta, R. P., and R. Engelman. *Economics and Rapid Change: The Influence of Population Growth.* Washington, D.C.: Population Action International, 1997. Summarizes and expands upon existing literature on the impact of population growth on economic growth in developing countries, with special consideration of the link to the environment and the role of institutions in demographic, economic, and environmental change.

Cohen, J. E. *How Many People Can the Earth Support?* New York: Norton, 1995. A comprehensive overview of the work of those who have pondered the question the title poses, from before Malthus to the present.

Conly, S. R., and S. de Silva. *Paying Their Fair Share? Donor Countries and International Population Assistance.* Washington, D.C.: Population Action International, 1999. An overview of industrialized-country financial assistance for developing-country population programs, and a country-by-country graded assessment of donor performance in the mid-1990s.

Donaldson, P. J. *Nature against Us: The United States and the World Population Crisis, 1965–1980.* Chapel Hill: University of North Carolina Press, 1990. A historical review of the early development of U.S. population policy and its role in shaping international population.

Engelman, R., et al. *People in the Balance: Population and Natural Resources at the Turn of the Millennium.* Washington, D.C.: Population Action International, 2000. A comprehensive updating of data on population and natural resources, with an original essay on global population trends and population policy.

Kelley, A. C., and R. M. Schmidt. *Population and Income Change: Recent Evidence.* World Bank Discussion Paper no. 249. Washington, D.C.: World Bank, 1994. An examination of the accumulated research of the last few decades of the twentieth century on the influence of population dynamics on economic growth.

Malthus, T. R. *On the Principle of Population.* 2 vols. New York: Dutton, 1993. A modern edition, including Malthus's first and last versions of his essay on population.

Mazur, L., ed. *Beyond the Numbers: A Reader on Population, Consumption, and the Environment.* Washington, D.C.: Island Press, 1995. More than three dozen essays on the link between population and the environment, and its implications for population policy.

Moffett, G. D. *Critical Masses: The Global Population Challenge.* New York: Viking, 1994. A consideration of the hazards of population growth and the benefits of policies addressing it.

Piotrow, P. T. *World Population: The Present and Future Crisis.* New York: Foreign Policy Association, 1980. A dated but still useful overview of the beginnings of international population assistance. Its foreword was authored by then-congressman George P. Bush, who as president later refused to support international assistance to slow rapid population growth.

Robey, B., et al. "Fertility Decline in Developing Countries." *Scientific American* 269.6 (1993), 60–67. An examination of the reasons why human fertility has declined in recent decades in developing countries, including a consideration of the role of family-planning programs and population policy in this decline.

United Nations Department of Economic and Social Affairs, Population Division. *World Population Prospects.* Vol. 1, *Comprehensive Tables;* Vol. 2, *The Sex and Age Distribution of the World Population.* New York: United Nations, 1999. Definitive estimates of past and current population in the world, its regions, and each of its nations, along with various projections of future population change to the year 2050. The UN population estimates and projections, published every two years, are those most commonly used in scientific and policy work related to population trends.

—ROBERT ENGELMAN

POVERTY. *See* Brundtland Commission; Catastrophist–Cornucopian Debate; Economic Levels; Famine; Food; Human Health; Human Populations; IPAT; Migrations; Nongovernmental Organizations; Risk; United Nations Conference on Environment and Development; *and* World Bank, The.

PRECAUTIONARY PRINCIPLE

The precautionary principle is a legal and policy principle addressing the problem of scientific uncertainty in environmental decision making. Although numerous formulations have been advanced, the core idea is expressed in a familiar adage: better safe than sorry. The principle has implications for both the timing and substance of environmental measures: (1) states should anticipate and respond to potential environmental harms, rather than only known or proven harms; and (2) environmental risks should be managed with a margin of error in case they are more serious than originally expected.

The importance of precaution is recognized in many national environmental laws—for example, the 1970 U.S. Clean Air Act, which requires regulators to apply an "ample margin of safety" in setting emissions limits for hazardous pollutants—and is reflected in international actions such as the 1982 moratorium on commercial whaling. However, as an explicit precept, the precautionary principle originated in Germany and made its way into international environmental law in the mid-1980s. The principle has been included in numerous policy declarations, as well as in most recent environmental treaties, including the Climate Change and Biological Diversity Conventions. [*See* Biological Diversity; *and* Climate Change.] The most widely cited international formulation is Principle 15 of the 1992 Rio Declaration on Environment and Development, which states:

> In order to protect the environment, the precautionary approach shall be widely applied by States according to their capabilities. Where there are threats of serious or irreversible damage, lack of full scientific certainty shall not be used as a reason for postponing cost-effective measures to prevent environmental degradation.

The precautionary principle's applicability is a function of both the severity and the evidence of environmental risk. Most formulations of the principle address these issues only in somewhat general terms. Typically, application of the principle is limited to risks of serious or irreversible harm. With regard to evidence, lack of full scientific certainty is not an excuse for delay. Instead, precautionary action only depends on prima facie grounds for concern. Some formulations assert more specifically that precautionary action is warranted when there is (1) knowledge that an effluent is persistent, toxic, and liable to accumulate in the environment, even though no environmental harm has yet been proved; or (2) knowledge of an environmental harm, even though the causal link with an activity is only suspected, not proved.

Like other international environmental principles such as sustainable development and intergenerational equity, the precautionary principle does not dictate particular environmental measures; instead, it serves as a general orientation or guide. Different formulations frame the principle in more or less absolutist terms. The Rio Declaration incorporates the notion of benefit-cost balancing, but some treaty formulations are oblivious to cost. At a minimum, the precautionary principle would appear to entail environmental impact assessment. Beyond that, a precautionary approach may involve clean production techniques, best available technology, or a reversal of the burden of proof. An example of the latter is the reverse listing procedure of the 1996 Protocol to the London (Dumping) Convention, which forbids the dumping of wastes at sea unless a material is specifically determined to be safe. [*See* Rio Declaration.]

Outside the context of treaty law, the legal status of the precautionary principle is controversial. Although the principle has been included in many international agreements and policy declarations, as well as in European Union law and some national statutes and court decisions, scholars disagree about whether the principle has attained the status of customary international law, given the variety of formulations and the lack of consistent national practice.

[*See also* Environmental Law; London Convention of 1972; *and* Straddling and Migratory Stocks Agreement.]

BIBLIOGRAPHY

Bodansky, D. "Scientific Uncertainty and the Precautionary Principle." *Environment* 33.7 (1991), 4–5, 43–44. A critical appraisal of the precautionary principle's ambiguities and difficulties of application.

Cross, F. B. "Paradoxical Perils of the Precautionary Principle." *Washington and Lee Law Review* 53 (1996), 851–925. Criticism of the precautionary principle as a simplistic rhetorical device that may increase rather than decrease overall environmental risk.

Freestone, D., and E. Hey, eds. *The Precautionary Principle and International Law*. London: Kluwer, 1996. An excellent collection of essays focusing on how to put the precautionary principle into practice.

Hickey, J. E., Jr., and V. R. Walker. "Refining the Precautionary Principle in International Environmental Law." *Virginia Law Review* 14 (1995), 423–454.

O'Riordan, T., and J. Cameron, eds. *Interpreting the Precautionary Principle*. London: Cameron and May, 1994. A multidisciplinary collection of essays on scientific, policy, and legal aspects of the precautionary principle.

—DANIEL M. BODANSKY

PREDICTION. *See* Climate Models; Modeling of Natural Systems; *and* Weather Forecasting.

PRESERVATION. *See* Conservation; *and* Environmental Movements.

PRIOR INFORMED CONSENT FOR TRADE IN HAZARDOUS CHEMICALS AND PESTICIDES

In 1989, the Food and Agriculture Organization (FAO) and the United Nations Environment Programme (UNEP) both established voluntary systems to require that exporters obtain the prior informed consent (PIC) of importing nations before shipping hazardous chemicals or pesticides. Ever since the growth of the environmental movement in the late 1960s and 1970s, industrialized countries have had increasingly stringent rules to control the use of hazardous substances within their borders. But an increasing quantity of these substances were exported to developing countries, where environmental rules were incomplete or the administrative capacity to enforce them was poor. PIC was created to address that problem by shifting some of the responsibility for regulating trade from importers to the exporters who had higher administrative capacity.

FAO's PIC system was created by revising the FAO *Code of Conduct on the Distribution and Use of Pesticides*, which had been in place since 1985. The UNEP system was created by amending the 1987 *London Guidelines*. Neither instrument is legally binding. Both require nearly identical procedures, and thus the two systems were merged at the end of 1989; UNEP and the FAO jointly provide the secretariat functions for PIC.

The prior consent procedures apply only to chemicals and pesticides on the "PIC list." Any "control action" to ban, severely restrict, or withdraw a chemical or pesticide from the market for health or environmental reasons makes a substance eligible for inclusion on the list. In addition, pesticide formulations that are particularly hazardous under particular conditions of use—for example, in hot, steamy fields where it is impractical to wear heavy rubber protective clothing—are eligible.

For each substance included in PIC, an expert prepares a Decision Guidance Document (DGD) that summarizes the known hazards, antidotes, and so on. A joint FAO/UNEP expert group sets priorities for the preparation of DGDs, reviews drafts, and makes other operational decisions. The secretariat sends final DGDs to all countries that participate in PIC and allows them to make informed decisions about whether (and under what conditions) to allow future imports. Those decisions are, in turn, transmitted by the secretariat to all participating countries. Thereafter, exporters are expected to obey the wishes of importers.

By the end of 1997, thirty-eight industrial chemicals or pesticides were on the PIC list or soon to be added, and 143 governments participated in the PIC system. There have been no known violations. Industry associations have promoted compliance by their members because chemical and pesticide producers feared that, if PIC failed, more onerous regulation would result. PIC's effectiveness is also partially due to public-interest groups that monitored compliance and proposed new substances (especially pesticides) for inclusion in PIC. In addition, several international organizations—including the FAO and the United Nations Institute for Training and Research—conducted training programs that helped to build competence for implementing PIC in developing countries.

Although the voluntary PIC system has been quite effective, governments agreed in 1998 to a binding PIC Convention that will employ similar procedures as under the voluntary PIC system. After fifty countries ratify it, that legally binding convention will enter into force.

[*See also* Chemical Industry; Food and Agriculture Organization; Pest Management; *and* United Nations Environment Programme.]

BIBLIOGRAPHY

Victor, D. G. "'Learning by Doing' in the Nonbinding International Regime to Manage Trade in Hazardous Chemicals and Pesticides." In *The Implementation and Effectiveness of International Environmental Commitments: Theory and Practice*, edited by D. G. Victor et al., chap. 6. Cambridge: MIT Press, 1998.

—DAVID G. VICTOR

PRODUCTIVITY. *See* Agriculture and Agricultural Land; *and* Growth, Limits to.

PUBLIC POLICY

[*This entry focuses on U.S. policy.*]

Global environmental problems, such as global climate change and the accelerating extinction of many biological species, must eventually be recognized internationally if they are to be effectively treated. While most policy makers agree with this generalization, all nation-states jealously guard their sovereignty and their right to make their own public policies independent of international opinion. Hence, while international agreements have been reached on such issues as the thinning of the ozone layer in the Earth's stratosphere, implementation of these policies depends on individual sovereign states' national policies. Until an effective means of enforcing international agreements is found, the fate of the biosphere will depend on the policies of individual nation states.

Environmental policy is divided into two major categories: conservation of natural resources and control of pollutants that affect the health of the human species. In the twentieth century, the United States led in the development of both types of environmental policy. While the first European settlers of the Western Hemisphere initially squandered natural resources from forests to watersheds, by the late nineteenth century such naturalists as John Muir, concerned about future generations' resource needs, pressed for the conservation of resources for a growing population. At President Theodore Roosevelt's urging, Congress established the first U.S.

national park, Yellowstone, in 1872, and thus began an effort to preserve part of the nation's most scenic natural heritage, a dramatic change of policy from that of Europe.

Americans were less concerned with conserving renewable resources, which seemed boundless in the nineteenth century. The United States followed slowly the lead made by European states whose natural resources had been dramatically depleted over centuries of use. During the Theodore Roosevelt administration Gifford Pinchot, who had studied forestry techniques in Europe, created the Forestry Division in the Department of Interior (later moved to the Department of Agriculture as the Forest Service) to develop a policy of sustained yield designed to harvest timber from our national forests at a rate that could be replaced by new growth. [*See the biography of Pinchot.*]

The Public Land Office, whose *raison d'être* had been to sell off public landholdings as fast as possibly, was replaced with the Bureau of Land Management in the Department of the Interior to manage other public lands. After deep plowing techniques had created Dust Bowl conditions in the prairies, during the New Deal of the 1930s, the Soil Conservation Service was started in the Department of Agriculture to convince farmers and ranchers to conserve their richest resource—the land itself. Using the carrot of shared funding, the federal government coaxed state and local government agencies to participate in a joint effort to restore some of the lands that had been devastated in the early years of U.S. history.

Only in the latter half of the twentieth century did the federal government became substantially involved with preserving public health through reducing human contact with biological and chemical contaminants. Many local public health officials had worked for decades to avoid polluting their clean water sources, as when Chicago engineered the Chicago River to flow backward from Lake Michigan and avoid polluting the city's supply of drinking water. In the late twentieth century, the federal government also became involved in water, air, and land pollution, in that order.

The framers of the U.S. Constitution deliberately designed the process of public policy making in the United States to be slow and complex in order to avoid inadequately considered change. In 1789 the former colonies were cautious of placing too much power into the hands of any one government institution. Hence they parceled out authority carefully, preserving some prerogatives for each branch: legislative, executive, and judicial, to check one another's assumption of power. In addition, the central government's powers were constrained by the autonomy of state and local governments. This division of authority was the only politically possible way at that time to bring all thirteen of the colonies recently in rebellion against the English king into one federated nation.

In environmental policy making in the twentieth century, these institutional checks and balances remain extremely important. Natural resource conservation laws were designed primarily to conserve public lands owned by the federal government. The later pollution-control laws were carefully drafted to allow for state and local control of many aspects of the laws. The U.S. Environmental Protection Agency (EPA) was not established until 1970, and then by executive order rather than by legislated act. The EPA has authority to set ambient standards for clean air throughout the nation, but it must depend on the states to devise individual state implementation plans to bring about this elusive goal. While the EPA prescribes the best available technology for water treatment plants, states are empowered to issue national pollutant discharge permits specifying how much of each pollutant may be emptied into a given waterway by each industrial or municipal treatment plant.

Agenda Setting and Policy Formation. Normally, the U.S. political system formulates policy in an incremental fashion. The federal government entered the issue of water pollution after World War II by offering local governments partial funding for municipal sewage treatment plants. In the following years, from 1948 to 1990, the water pollution law was amended numerous times, first by urging states to set ambient water standards for all their waterways, and eventually by empowering the federal government to set standards for effluents discharged by every major industry's treatment plants as well as municipal sewage plants.

Before gradual increases in authority can be made to a program, the issue must be accepted as a legitimate concern of the federal government. Americans tend to be wary of increasing governmental power, and this reluctance to extend social welfare policy has been reinforced in recent decades by politicians who run for election on platforms that tend to deny the legitimacy of government programs. Before environmental issues could become legitimate concerns of federal officials, they had to work their way onto the national public agenda.

Natural scientists such as John Muir argued for years that preserving part of our natural heritage was worthy of official consideration by national policy makers. Most elected officials resisted this idea until President Theodore Roosevelt, propelled by his own policy preferences, joined enthusiastically into the movement for environmental conservation. Other politicians, influenced by the "back to nature" movement exemplified in the works of Ralph Waldo Emerson and Henry David Thoreau, were convinced that their careers would flourish if they supported the new national parks. [*See the biography of Thoreau.*]

Similarly in the 1960s the writings of such natural scientists as Rachel Carson introduced the public to the idea that government should take an active role in controlling the widespread use of dangerous chemicals such as dichlorodiphenyltrichloroethane (DDT). The accelerating decline in numbers of many native species drew the attention of many natural scientists who banded together to pressure policy makers to acknowledge the need for a new kind of policy. Their writings were given wide publicity by the mass media and encouraged organized groups such as the Sierra Club, which had been formed as part of the push for the national park law. These organizations proliferated during the 1960s and 1970s and lobbied elected officials throughout the nation to put all types of conservation and pollution-control issues on their agendas. [*See the biography of Carson.*]

Once a new issue obtains a place on the national political agenda, most politicians who rely on popular support to retain their jobs will formulate their own positions on the issue. Other groups who believe that they will be disadvantaged by any new public policy will defend the status quo equally vigorously. It is especially difficult to initiate control over behavior that has traditionally been condoned or even rewarded by society. Thus the chemical industry argued against the ban on DDT, and the auto industry denied the possibility of devising technology to control carbon monoxide emissions. It was only after years of debate in Congress and the press that Congress gained the courage to create technology forcing legislation to reduce air pollutants for mobile sources. Opportunities for such radical changes in public policy are rare. They occur only when there is a convergence of public interest in a problem and sympathetic policy makers who see the opportunity to enhance their own political standing by embracing the new issue.

It takes time for industry to accept the concept that air and water resources into which it has been discharging its wastes for centuries are not common sinks but rather valuable resources owned by the community and regulated by the government. Nevertheless, public-interest groups' demands that government at all levels accept a new agenda item are occasionally met. Elected and appointed decision makers within local, state, and national governmental institutions give legitimacy by creating new policies that formerly were considered unacceptable by the majority of the population.

Although this is not uniformly true, demands for policy changes often are introduced into the national legislature. Congressional representatives with ties to the interests involved may introduce bills to initiate new or amend preexisting policies. Alternatively, the administration in power may introduce a proposal for change. Actors in the political system who start such initiatives can be White House staff, political appointees heading executive departments, or other executive officials. Often career bureaucrats who have long harbored their own ideas about how a problem can be solved will seize the opportunity of new or renewed public interest in a policy problem to suggest their own solutions to it.

After a bill has been formally introduced to Congress, the party leaders there assign the bill to standing committees they consider to have jurisdiction over the subject matter. In most controversial policy areas, there may be considerable competition among committee chairs about the distribution of authority over the issue. Natural resource development, public health, and commercial committees may all vie for control over any environmental bill. Authorizing committees may hold extensive hearings, during which members of the policy network testify about what they believe to be the best policy. Included in these networks are stakeholders on all sides of the issue, administration spokespersons, and policy experts, including academics, who have become recognized as authorities in the field.

Such policy networks may reach a mutually acceptable compromise among themselves; if they do not, any proposal will likely languish in committee. After the members of the committee or subcommittee modify the bill to their satisfaction, often reflecting changes made to appease important stakeholders, a floor debate follows. In this phase of the policy process, individual members of Congress try to convince their colleagues to accept amendments to the bill that will advance the interests of their major supporters.

After both Senate and House have passed versions of the same bill, a joint committee is appointed by the majority and minority leaders of both houses to reconcile the two versions of the bill. It is at this stage that concessions to the targets of regulations to extend the time allowed for compliance are often made. These changes must be taken back to each chamber, and the same wording must be passed by both houses before the new law can be presented to the president for signature. If he disagrees with the policy or believes that the administration's needs have not been sufficiently considered, he may veto the bill. Then it is up to party leaders in Congress to determine whether they can repass the same bill with a two-thirds majority in both houses in order to override the president's veto.

Policy Implementation. Once Congress has generated a new law, or more likely passed amendments to an old one, it remains for the executive branch to make these goals a reality. More steps must be taken by both Congress and other actors before there is any apparent effect from the policy. After authorizing national legislation has been passed, it is also necessary for the Congress to make budget allocations that will enable the

agencies assigned to carry out the new mandates to hire personnel and begin their operations. Without human and fiscal resources, the policy would remain a symbol of concern but hardly a national policy.

During the passage of a law, Congress must assign responsibility for its implementation to a specified part of the executive branch. Authorizing legislation may create a new government bureau, as in the case of the Soil Conservation Service, established within the Department of Agriculture in 1935 to convince farmers to use soil conservation techniques. Alternatively, it may give power to enforce a new policy to a previously existing agency, as when the Soil Conservation Service in 1985 was also authorized to restrict the right of farmers to drain wetlands and convert them to cropland. Congress may also choose to create a new agency separate from any cabinet department to carry out the new policy. For example, the EPA was established in 1970 out of parts of earlier government organizations to enforce the ambitious clean air and water laws passed in the early part of the 1970s.

Because of the federal nature of our government, responsibility for the enforcement of most environmental policies is shared among levels of government. State legislatures use procedures similar to those used by Congress to pass laws at the state level authorizing state agencies to participate in enforcement. City councils may also create legislation that is binding only in their jurisdictions. For example, the 1935 Soil Conservation and Domestic Allotment Act authorized states to set up county conservation districts to achieve the goals set by Congress. Before such districts could be created, however, state legislatures had to give authority to state departments to set them up.

Environmental protection legislation varies widely in the kinds of instruments given to agencies to achieve compliance. There are great contrasts in the culture of administrative agencies. Both the Department of Interior's Land Management Bureau and the Forest Service in the Department of Agriculture receive requests from would-be private users of publicly held land. These public managers must determine how much timber can be cut at any one time, how many cattle can feed on a specified area in the grasslands, and how fast and under what conditions minerals can be extracted from the Earth without depleting our resources. Thus employees of the Bureau of Land Management and Department of Agriculture often come to regard themselves as providing services to individual citizens and corporations, not acting as a guardian of the nation's natural resources.

In many cases, public-interest organizations such as the Sierra Club, Audubon Society, and Natural Resources Defense Council have come to regard members of the bureaucracy as spokespersons for industry, labeling the Bureau of Land Management, for example, as the Bureau of Livestock and Mining. Individuals employed in those administrative cultures regard their role as one of providing services and help to farmers and ranchers. Both are accustomed to distributing benefits to their clients, and not to forcing them against their will to comply with a law. Thus when they are called upon to tighten regulations, to insist that wetlands be preserved or highly erodible soil not be plowed, they may be less enthusiastic about the new role than they were about handing out benefits to their old friends.

Farmers were initially offered the carrot of government subsidies to participate in soil conservation policy. By the time clean air and water acts were passed, however, Congress believed that more forceful methods would be needed to achieve compliance. Therefore, it gave the EPA authority for setting specific effluent and emission levels for certain pollutants and issuing permits to individual dischargers. In such a new field of regulation, permits would be meaningless unless provisions were also made for agency personnel to monitor the effectiveness of new treatment plants and issue administrative orders or initiate court cases if the dischargers did not conform to the terms of their permits. The EPA thus had to put a significant amount of its resources into bringing lawsuits to the federal courts to achieve compliance. Employees of the EPA consequently tend to think of themselves as guardians of public health. They regard their regular customers (industry dumping wastes into the public sinks) as their natural opponents and are not averse to taking an adversarial posture when dealing with them.

In recent years there has been an attempt in government agencies to reform both extreme models and to get each to learn something from each other's technique. Both kinds of bureaucratic culture are finding it difficult to make the transition to a more neutral stance regarding their clienteles. Various reforms have been instituted, the latest under the concept of "reinventing government." The Reagan administration ordered all regulatory agencies to justify new regulations with cost-benefit analyses that proved that industry's costs to clean up would be more than compensated by improvement in public health or some other public benefit of the regulation. Economic methods have been created to motivate plant managers to find new tools for pollution control and especially for its prevention. One example is allowing industry to buy and sell its pollution allowances rather than following the more traditional command-and-control system of permits and fines. This, it is hoped, will motivate industrial engineers to seek less costly ways of producing fewer pollutants rather than treating them after production.

Inducing change in the opposite direction has been less successful. U.S. Department of Agriculture employees have been instructed to withhold agricultural subsidies from farmers who will not comply with soil conservation methods or persist in filling wetlands. However, it is more difficult to change an entrenched benefits-providing bureaucracy to a regulatory one than it is to accomplish the reverse.

Policy Adjustment. If any agency is less than zealous in enforcing public policy, one can expect little effect from it. Most stakeholders in various policies, therefore, are careful to continue to scrutinize enforcement and evaluate its influence long after the legislation has been written. The General Accounting Office is used by Congress to study how well the responsible agencies are administering laws. In addition, the same committees that wrote the original law may hold oversight hearings to determine how well their mandates are being carried out. The executive branch conducts its own evaluations of policy through the responsible agency or, more likely, by contracting out studies to independent research foundations or universities.

When government is divided between the two major parties, there can be considerable difference of opinion among evaluators about how well the laws are being administered. Stakeholders in a policy will also monitor the effectiveness of policies they helped shape after they have been enforced for a time. Some members of the policy network will be happier than others with the outcomes, but no one will be completely satisfied. Those who are least happy with the policy—and there are always dissatisfied groups—will try to change it. Thus policy making never ends. Those stakeholders who feel they have lost the most in the legislative process will attempt to make their weight felt in administrative hearings about the regulations set to implement the laws. If they do not succeed there, they will then turn to the courts.

Many environmental laws, including the clean air and water acts, provide authority for private citizens to sue in federal court in order to have the policies enforced if the agencies do not perform adequately. Understandably, the actors who have taken most advantage of these private attorney general clauses have been environmental groups attempting to get the laws actively enforced. In addition, industries and trade associations have attacked the laws, arguing that they are so harsh as to interfere with the economic health of the country. Often, these arguments are couched in constitutional terms. For example, property owners argue that all types of land use control laws, from local zoning laws to the enforcement of the Endangered Species Act, take their property without due process of law. Thus the courts, like the other branches of government, have come to be intimately involved in all kinds of environmental policy. Although they are usually regarded as enforcers or implementers of policy, by interpreting what the laws means, they are also clearly involved in formation and reformation particularly. [*See* Environmental Law.]

Just which part of the policy network uses the courts will depend on how much success each group believes its attempts to influence the legislature and executive have had. An organization that feels most disadvantaged before Congress or in the department where the policy is enforced is the most likely to turn to the judiciary as their last best chance to get the policy modified. Their decision to do so is likely to hinge on the organizations' best estimate of the personal values of the judges who make the decisions. These judgments in turn may be partially determined by the political affiliation of the president who appointed the judges. This is the reason that so many lobbying groups actively participate in the nomination and confirmation process for the federal judiciary.

Whether a group believes an agency is on its side or the opposition's will often depend on the political party that controls the executive branch at the time. In recent years the White House and Congress have seldom been in the same political party's control at the same time. Party control of the various branches of government changes over time. It is expected, therefore, that various stakeholders' use of agency, courts, and Congress will all depend on their estimation of that branch of government's sympathy for their cause at any time. Everything in politics is relative, however. All policy outputs are judged according to the group's expectations of success in other institutional forums.

Only one generalization regarding policy making can be made with confidence: the policy cycle is never finished. No matter what the policy, some of the stakeholders will challenge it in the future by lobbying the agencies to change their regulations or rulings, by suing in court to alter its impact, and finally by taking the issue once more to Congress for further amendment. The strategy they select will depend on the politicians who occupy various institutions at the time. When they will act depends on the urgency that they perceive and the importance of other policy issues competing for the attention of the policy system.

[*See also* Energy Policy; Market Mechanisms; Policy Analysis; Population Policy; *and* Regulation.]

BIBLIOGRAPHY

Peters, B. *American Public Policy: Promise and Performance.* 3d ed. Chatham, N.J.: Chatham House, 1999.

Ringquist, E. *Environmental Protection at the State Level.* Armonk, N.Y.: M. E. Sharpe, 1993.

Rosenbaum, W. *Environmental Politics and Policy.* 3d ed. Washington, D.C.: Congressional Quarterly Press, 1995.

Smith, Z. *The Environmental Paradox.* 3d ed. Upper Saddle River, N.J.: Prentice-Hall, 2000.

Vig, N. J., and M. E. Kraft, eds. *Environmental Policy: New Directions for the Twenty-first Century.* Washington, D.C.: Congressional Quarterly Press, 2000.

Wenner, L. *One Environment under Law.* Pacific Palisades, Calif.: Goodyear Publishing, 1976.

—Lettie McSpadden

R

RADIOCARBON DATING. *See* Dating Methods.

RAILROADS. *See* Transportation.

RAINFORESTS. *See* Deforestation; *and* Forests.

RAMSAR CONVENTION

The Ramsar Convention (in full, the Convention on Wetlands of International Importance Especially as Waterfowl Habitat) seeks to conserve waterfowl by preserving their wetland habitat. It does so by obliging its parties to establish at least one Ramsar site that they must conserve.

The Convention is one of a group of 1970s treaties focused on wildlife preservation that includes the Convention on International Trade in Endangered Species of Wild Fauna and Flora (CITES) and the Convention on the Conservation of Migratory Species of Wild Animals (or the Bonn Convention; CMS). All three had their origins in increasing popular concern about declining populations of wild fauna.

The treaties' popular origins are reflected in the fact that all were originally demanded by nongovernmental organizations (NGOs). CITES and the CMS were first called for by the International Union for the Conservation of Nature and Natural Resources (the World Conservation Union; IUCN), and the Ramsar Convention originated in 1962 with a call for a treaty on wetlands from the International Committee for Bird Protection (now BirdLife International; ICBP), the International Waterfowl Research Bureau (IWRB), and the IUCN.

After a very long gestation period the agreement (drawn up mainly by the IWRB and the Dutch government), was signed by eighteen countries in Ramsar, Iran, in January 1971. The first meeting of the parties was not held until 1980, however, five years after the agreement came into force. The treaty requires each member to nominate, monitor, and protect at least one wetland site within its borders. It also makes provisions for financial assistance to help states protect wetlands.

For some time it looked as though the Convention might founder because of lack of financial resources. The costs of the first Conference of Contracting Parties (CoCP) and most other running costs were borne almost entirely by the IUCN and the IWRB. Indeed, the Convention was deficient in several financial and administrative aspects. Eventually, in 1987, a Standing Committee was established together with a small secretariat (the Ramsar Bureau) at IUCN headquarters, linked to a small technical and scientific group at the IWRB. A funding mechanism was also set up.

Since 1987, the Convention has become far more effective. Membership has grown considerably to over eighty. There are now more than six hundred Ramsar Sites worldwide, covering more than 40 million hectares. The Convention has also developed more muscle.

Although the CoCP cannot force parties to nominate wetlands as Ramsar Sites, it does publish "Recommendations" in which it expresses concern about parties' wetlands. In 1990 the CoCP made recommendations for nominating sites in Germany, Greece, Hungary, Jordan, Poland, Spain, the United States, and Yugoslavia, as well as praising some states for making nominations.

The Convention also obliges the parties to promote the "wise use" of wetlands, by which the negotiators meant, in modern parlance, sustainable use. Strongly linked to the wise-use issue has been monitoring. In 1990 the Convention adopted a "Monitoring Procedure," together with the Montreux Record, which is a published list of Ramsar Sites in which adverse changes in ecological character are either occurring, or are likely to occur.

The Monitoring Procedure is presented as an assistance process rather than a noncompliance procedure. If the Bureau finds that a site is changing, it asks the party concerned for more information and proposes application of the Monitoring Procedure. The Bureau is required periodically to review progress on the conservation status of sites that come to its attention (publishing them in the Montreux Record). In spite of its intrusiveness (teams of experts sometimes visit sites for long periods), the Procedure has gained almost universal acceptance. It has been applied to countries as diverse as Austria, Bolivia, Greece, Iran, Pakistan, Romania, Russia, Trinidad and Tobago, the United Kingdom, Uruguay, the Ukraine, and Vietnam.

[*See also* Wetlands.]

BIBLIOGRAPHY

Davis, T. J., ed. *Towards the Wise Use of Wetlands.* Gland, Switzerland: Ramsar Convention Bureau, 1993.
———. *The Ramsar Convention Manual: A Guide to the Convention on Wetlands of International Importance Especially as Waterfowl Habitat.* Gland, Switzerland: Ramsar Convention Bureau, 1994.

Jones, T. *A Directory of Wetlands of International Importance.* Gland, Switzerland: Ramsar Convention Bureau, 1993.

Matthews, G. V. T. *The Ramsar Convention on Wetlands.* Gland, Switzerland: Ramsar Convention Bureau, 1993.

—JOHN LANCHBERY

RANGELANDS. *See* Grasslands.

RECLAMATION. *See* Land Reclamation.

RECYCLING

Over the last two decades recycling has grown in popularity in the United States. This may be attributed to public awareness of environmental issues, public interest in conserving natural resources, and the landfill crisis of the 1980s (Vining, Linn, and Burdge, 1992; Levenson, 1993). This article provides an overview of recycling of municipal solid waste (MSW). It begins by explaining the basic concept of recycling along with the environmental and economic reasons for the practice. The article reviews the history of recycling and compares its status in the United States to selected industrialized countries. It then discusses issues that impede recycling, as well as policy and other measures to increase recycling in the next century. The article concludes by summarizing recycling policy options in terms of sustainability.

Basic Concept. The U.S. Environmental Protection Agency classifies "reduce," "reuse," "recycle," and "recover" as four options (Figures 1 and 2) for managing solid waste in its Integrated Solid Waste Management Hierarchy (U.S. EPA, 1989). "Reduce" means lessening the quantity and toxicity of materials and energy discarded over the life cycle of products (Figure 2). "Reuse" means using the discarded product or resource with minimal processing. A used car is an example of reuse. "Recycle" means to obtain new products after dismantling and reprocessing old ones. This includes composting, in which organic discards are decomposed into soil conditioner. "Recover" generally refers to energy. It means obtaining energy from the combustion of discarded products. Strictly speaking, recycling is only one option in the EPA's waste management hierarchy. This article considers recycling in a broad way, however, as a set of options for conserving and recovering materials and energy. Therefore, we include options such as reuse and recover as forms of recycling as well.

Recycling is attractive because it can conserve materials, possibly consume less energy, and may be less costly than production from virgin materials. Recycling conserves materials by using discarded products as feedstock for manufacturing. If the discarded products

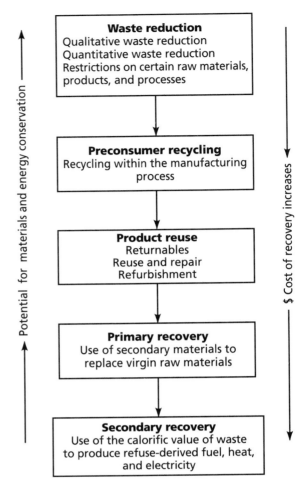

Recycling. FIGURE 1. The Hierarchy of Solid Waste Management Options. (Adapted from Gandy, 1993. With permission of John Wiley and Sons.)

can be collected, transported, and reprocessed with less energy and at lower cost than it takes to extract, preprocess, transport, and manufacture from virgin materials, then recycling can save energy and be efficient. Similarly, if recycling can be achieved with lower quantities and toxicity of secondary wastes (waste heat, gaseous emissions, and liquid discharges) than production from virgin materials, then it is also desirable because of lower health and environmental risk.

Recycling and source reduction are also attractive from a thermodynamics standpoint. Entropy is a measure of the lost thermodynamic potential to do useful work. The manufacture of products increases total entropy in the universe. Barton (1979) showed that increases in entropy are lower when energy and materials are recycled earlier in the product life cycle (Figures 3 and 4).

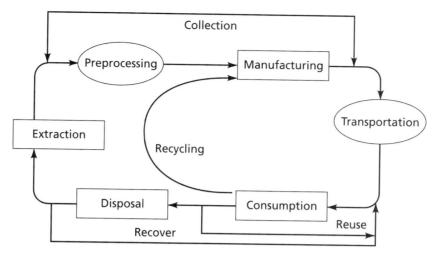

Recycling. Figure 2. The Product Lifecycle.

Recycling's environmental benefits include materials and possibly energy conservation. They also include reduced human health risk and avoided environmental impacts of waste incineration and landfilling (Louis and McMichael, 1998; Vining, 1992), such as reduced greenhouse gas emissions (U.S. EPA, 1998a). Economic benefits include the dollar value of recycled materials and products, the avoided cost of extracting virgin materials, the avoided cost of disposal, the value of extended landfill and incinerator capacity, and any net gains to gross domestic product produced from recycling activities (Louis and McMichael, 1998; U.S. EPA, 1998b).

History of Recycling. Recycling is as old as waste generation itself. In preindustrial times, food waste was fed to animals, human and animal waste were applied to the land, and metal objects were melted and recast into new products (Louis, 1996; Melosi, 1981). Human

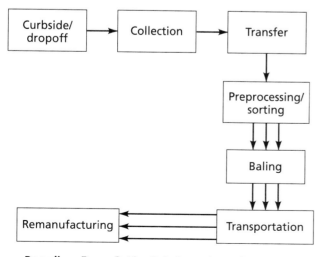

Recycling. Figure 3. The Unit Operations of Recycling.

settlements in cities led to organized waste collection. Groups of waste pickers recycled cloth, glass, wood, and metal. Waste pickers still recover materials at the curb in many cities. In some developing countries, they operate at open dumps.

In the United States, recycling as a matter of public policy is rooted in the environmental movement of the 1960s. The Solid Waste Disposal Act (SWDA) of 1965 initiated modern federal legislation focused on solid waste. The SWDA was amended by the Resources Recovery Act (RRA) of 1970. This later act shifted the national solid waste management focus away from disposal toward recycling, including energy recovery from waste incineration. Since 1976, through the Resource Conservation and Recovery Act (RCRA), the federal EPA has been responsible for promulgating regulations and setting guidelines for the practice of solid waste management (Louis, 1996). [*See* Waste Management.] States subsequently enact their own equal or more stringent regulations, which are implemented at the operational level by local governments.

Current Practices and Programs of Recycling. Figure 5 summarizes the national trends in MSW management from 1960 to 1996. It shows that 27 percent of the nation's MSW stream (by weight) was recycled in 1996, up from 6.4 percent in 1960. Figures 6 and 7, respectively, show the composition of MSW generation in 1996 and the quantity of different materials recovered in that same year (U.S. EPA, 1998d). These statistics do not include waste reduction accomplished through source reduction, reuse, or energy recovery.

The EPA first proposed the goal of recycling 25 percent of the nation's solid waste stream in 1988. This, along with the integrated solid waste management hierarchy of 1989 (U.S. EPA, 1989) are two of the most notable federal recycling guidelines that influence re-

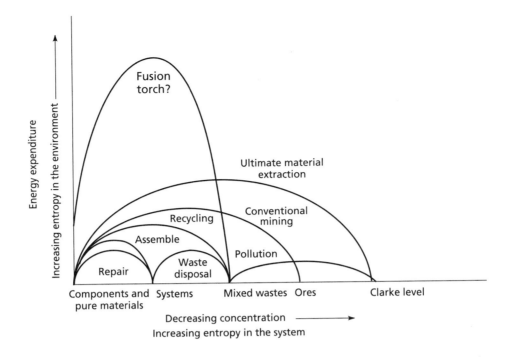

Recycling. FIGURE 4. The Thermodynamics of Recycling. (Adapted from Barton, 1979. With permission of John Wiley and Sons.)

cycling policies in the states. In addition, the federal government provides grants for state solid waste management plans, as well as financial and technical support for recycling through a variety of programs, such as the EPA's "Jobs through Recycling" program (U.S. EPA, 1997c).

All states except Alaska, Colorado, and Montana had enacted recycling laws or disposal bans by December 1995. Table 1 summarizes the types of state recycling laws and disposal bans at that date. Table 2 shows that the majority of state recycling laws have target recycling rates and dates. It also shows the six main types of state programs that promote and support recycling: tax incentives, grants, loans, recycling zones, economic development initiatives, and recycling market development councils or task forces (Louis and McMichael, 1998).

Table 3 compares the recycling rates of selected industrialized countries. In these countries, recycling is an element of national environmental policy. For example, Germany's Green Dot program and Ordinance on the Avoidance of Packaging Waste requires that manufacturers and distributors take full responsibility for the packaging of the products that they produce and sell respectively (Bernhardt, 1992; U.S. EPA, 1991).

Recycling is also growing in the industrial sector. In September 1996 the International Organization for Standardization (ISO) formally published ISO 14000, the environmental management system family of standards. ISO 14000 provides firms with a coherent framework for efficiently managing and improving waste minimization, pollution prevention, and recycling and reuse activities (Johnson, 1997). The standards promote sound environmental management as good business. Many firms worldwide have adopted the standards.

Issues That Impede Recycling. Today, the U.S. average recycling rate is an unprecedented 27 percent. Achieving higher rates is becoming more difficult. The EPA reports that recycling and composting increased by 4 percent from 1995 to 1996, much less than the 10.8 percent average annual growth over the previous five years (Douglass, 1998; U.S. EPA, 1998d). This may reflect a decreasing marginal rate of recycling due to increasing marginal costs, as curbside and voluntary drop-off programs approach their maximum participation rates. Moreover, several other factors impede recycling.

Environmental issues. Some recent studies question whether recycling is always environmentally beneficial. These questions arise from life-cycle analyses of the environmental impacts of the processes associated with recycling compared to production from virgin materials. One key factor in this debate is the collection and transportation of recyclables, which contributes to air pollution (Leach et al., 1997; Louis and McMichael, 1998).

Economic issues. In general, collection costs are the dominant share of recycling program costs and tend to outweigh revenues. Even after subtracting recycling

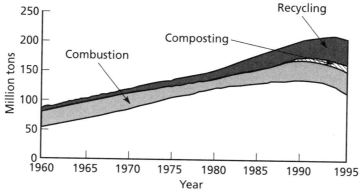

Recycling. FIGURE 5. Municipal Solid Waste Management in the United States (1960–1996).

revenues from the cost of collection and processing, recycling still has the highest dollar cost per unit of all the available waste management options (Louis, 1996; Louis and McMichael, 1998). This unfavorable comparison is compounded by weak and unstable markets for many recycled materials (Gandy, 1993). The "Iron Law of Recycling" (Hendrickson et al., 1995) states that recycling is worthy only if the collection cost plus sorting cost minus the proceeds from selling the material is less than the collection and disposal cost of MSW.

The exclusion of social and environmental costs makes recycling look economically less attractive than disposal. However, one life-cycle assessment that includes environmental costs has shown recycling to be environmentally superior to incineration and landfilling under the general conditions assumed in the analysis (Denison, 1996).

Organizational issues. Recycling is popular with the public (BioCycle 1989–1996) but is not yet part of the ethos of manufacturing. There is currently no for-

mal industrial infrastructure for product takeback (U.S. EPA, 1997c) or for incorporating postconsumer recycled content into new products. The absence of manufacturing buy-in to the value of recycling at all stages of the product life cycle stifles the innovation needed to make recycling competitive with production from virgin stock.

Behavioral issues. The growth of curbside recycling programs in the 1980s and 1990s may be taken as evidence of strong public support for recycling. Policy makers can capitalize on this to advance market-based approaches that move recycling merely from the curbside to the inside of manufacturing facilities. They may also be able to use incentive policies to extend the popularity of recycling programs to high-rise residential areas where per capita waste generation rates are high but recycling rates are relatively low.

Other technical issues. Currently, small levels of contamination quickly make recycled materials uncompetitive with virgin stock (Grayson, 1984). Specifica-

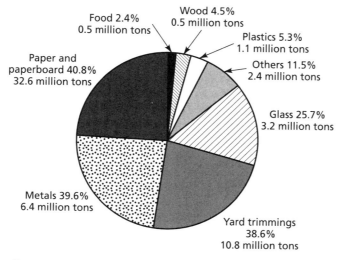

Recycling. FIGURE 6. Materials Generated in Municipal Solid Waste by Weight, 1996. (After U.S. EPA, 1998d.)

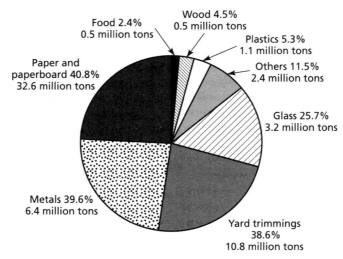

Recycling. FIGURE 7. Materials Recovered from Municipal Solid Waste by Weight, 1996. (After U.S. EPA, 1998d.)

tions of materials composition and product form must be upgraded to accommodate recycling.

Improving the Efficiency of Recycling. Before committing to increased recycling, we must compare the marginal costs and benefits of this action. It may be possible to achieve higher rates of recycling. Without major technological changes, however, the marginal cost of recycling will increase as it becomes more costly to add new programs in areas of low participation. Furthermore, marginal benefits will decrease as new health and environmental gains are added to an expanding base of previous benefits. The optimal level of recycling occurs when society's marginal benefit from recycling equals its marginal cost. For a given marginal benefit curve, the optimal level of recycling for a society depends on the position of its marginal cost curve for recycling (Figure 8). Given this caveat, we consider four approaches that may lead to higher recycling rates: (1) the adoption of a systems approach to evaluating recycling, (2) a shift to market-based approaches, (3) the engraving of green design into the ethos of manufacturing, and (4) expanding commodity markets for recyclables.

Systems approach. A systems approach enhances the EPA's integrated solid waste management hierarchy by the complementary use of a variety of waste management technologies and practices to handle municipal solid waste efficiently or cost effectively. The approach frees municipalities from rigid mandates that set targets for recycling with no consideration of their opportunity costs. Mandates require priority allocation of resources to meet preset goals, at the expense of more efficient investments in waste management systems as a whole. Thus, while 25 percent of a 1,000-ton-per-day waste stream might meet state recycling mandates for a municipality, 20 percent of an 800-ton-per-day waste

stream would be better if the municipality could devote its resources to reducing waste generation by 20 percent. Furthermore, a systems approach also facilitates coordinated program planning so that aggressive recycling programs are not at conflict with Waste-to-Energy (WTE) for recycled material (Louis, 1996).

Market-based approaches. The popularity of recycling programs is measured by the number of curbside collection programs, and their effectiveness by the quantity of material collected for recycling. These measures do not capture the amount of collected material that constitutes recycled content in consumer products (postconsumer recycled content). In reality, these existing measures of recycling popularity and effectiveness do little more than assess progress toward achieving preset schedules and target recycling rates (Table 2).

Market-based approaches create incentives for recycling by each decision maker. Three different market approaches are full-cost pricing, user fees, and deposit refunds. Full-cost pricing (U.S. EPA, 1995, 1997a, 1998c) charges the full economic and social cost for materials and energy. Under this scheme there would be no advantage to the use of virgin materials instead of recyclables. The external costs, presently excluded from the price of virgin stock, would be included. This could result in higher prices that would make their way up the chain to consumers. Competition would then spur manufacturers to find lower-cost alternatives, including recycling.

Full-cost pricing is still largely theoretical and not available as an operative policy option. However, environmental taxes reflect the full-cost pricing approach and are in use. They impose a premium on materials, processes, or practices that society deems nonconserv-

Recycling. TABLE 1. State Recycling Laws and Disposal Bans, 1995

STATE	RECYCLING LAW*	DISPOSAL BANS†	STATE	RECYCLING LAW*	DISPOSAL BANS†
AL	Recycling plans	ad	MT	—	—
AK	—	—	NE	—	abcdef
AZ	Opportunity to recycle	ab	NV	Recycling plans	d
AR	Opportunity to recycle	abc	NH	Recycling plans	acf
CA	Recycling plans	abde	NJ	Source separation	acf
CO	—	—	NM	Recycling plans	ad
CT	Source separation	ce	NY	Source separation	ab
DE	Opportunity to recycle	b	NC	Opportunity to recycle	abcdef
D.C.	Source separation	—	ND	—	ade
FL	Opportunity to recycle	abcdef	OH	Recycling plans	abc
GA	Opportunity to recycle	abc	OK	Recycling plans	b
HI	Recycling plans	abcef	OR	Opportunity to recycle	abdef
ID	—	ab	PA	Source separation	ac
IL	Recycling plans	abce	RI	Source separation	a
IN	Recycling plans	abc	SC	Opportunity to recycle	abcde
IA	Recycling plans	abcdf	SD	Recycling plans	abcdef
KS	—	ab	TN	Recycling plans	abd
KY	Recycling plans	sb	TX	Recycling plans	abd
LA	—	abe	UT	—	ab
ME	Source separation	a	VT	Recycling plans	abdef
MD	Recycling plans	bc	VA	Recycling plans	a
MA	Recycling plans	abcef	WA	Opportunity to recycle	ad
MI	Recycling plans	acd	WV	Source separation	abc
MN	Opportunity to recycle	abcdef	WI	Opportunity to recycle	abcdef
MS	—	a	WY	—	a
MO	Recycling plans	abcdef			

*Recycling plans = local government must prepare a recycling plan; opportunity to recycle = local government must offer an opportunity to recycle via curbside collection or drop-off center or by recovery from mixed MSW; source separation = local government must mandate the separation of one or more components of the MSW stream.

†a = vehicle batteries; b = tires; c = yard waste; d = motor oil; e = white goods; f = other (includes portable batteries, scrap automobiles, glass and metal containers, antifreeze, newsprint, and cardboard).

SOURCE: From Louis and McMichael (1998). With permission of John Wiley and Sons.

ative of resources or otherwise environmentally undesirable. For example, a premium on virgin pulp might shift paper manufacturing to higher percentages of post-consumer recycled content. Ideally, in this example, environmental taxes would accompany the removal of subsidies on virgin materials. However, each of these decisions is associated with a complex chain of costs and benefits. Thus, rather than a blanket approach, decisions about environmental taxes are best made on a case-by-case basis. [*See* Market Mechanisms.]

User fees associate the cost of waste management directly with the product (U.S. EPA, 1997b). Thus, instead of paying for MSW collection in general taxes, consumers would pay a fee for the amount of MSW they generate and set out for disposal. No charge (or a significantly lesser charge) would apply to materials set out for recycling. Thus consumers would be given a fee-based signal to increase their recycling rate and reduce their rate of waste disposal.

Deposit refund systems, especially on beverage containers, are common around the world. The deposit usually takes the form of a tax on the container, which is wholly or partially refunded when the container is handed in to a recycling depot. Deposit refund systems can also be imposed on intermediate inputs to reduce transaction costs to consumers (Palmer et al., 1997). The deposit refund systems may get rid of the incentive for illegal disposal using the user fees approach.

Green design. Green design refers to the design of products and processes that consume less material and energy resources, produce less harmful environmental impacts, and have lower life-cycle costs than traditional

Recycling. TABLE 2. State Recycling Goals, Achievement, Budget Allocations, and Programs (1995–1996)

STATE	RECYCLING GOAL (%)	TARGET DATE	1995 RATE (%)	1995 RECYCLED (MILLION TONS)	1995–1996 BUDGET ($ MILLION)	TONS RECOVERED PER BUDGET $	PROGRAMS*
AL	25	None	15	0.81	0.27	3.00	bf
AK	10	1996	6	0.03	0.10	0.30	n/a
AZ	None	None	10	0.45	1.20	0.38	abef
AR	40	2000	25	0.54	0.33	1.63	af
CA	50	2000	25	11.00	38.80	0.28	abcd
CO	50	2000	18	0.54	1.20	0.45	ace
CT	40	2000	23	0.70	2.40	0.29	f
DE	None	None	33	0.40	2.10	0.19	ae
D.C.	45	1994	15	0.04	0.30	0.13	n/a
FL	30	1995	40	9.72	25.00	0.39	aef
GA	25	1996	n/a	n/a	n/a	n/a	f
HI	50	2000	20	0.40	2.40	0.17	b
ID	25	1995	n/a	n/a	n/a	n/a	n/a
IL	25	1996	27	3.84	12.70	0.30	abcd
IN	50	2001	19	1.10	4.40	0.25	ace
IA	50	2000	28	0.89	0.19	4.66	ab
KS	None	None	8	0.28	1.50	0.19	ae
KY	25	1997	15	0.55	0.15	3.66	aef
LA	25	1992	6	0.29	n/a	n/a	ae
ME	50	1998	33	0.43	0.26	1.64	a
MD	20	1994	27	1.43	0.26	5.49	abcef
MA	46	2000	31	2.19	5.20	0.42	c
MI	25	2005	25	3.38	14.00	0.24	bce
MN	35,[†] 50[‡]	1996	44	2.11	22.00	0.10	abcf
MS	25	1996	12	0.29	0.50	0.58	bef
MO	40	1998	18	1.35	3.80	0.36	bef
MT	25	1996	6	0.04	0.05	0.88	a
NE	50	2002	19	0.32	4.00	0.08	n/a
NV	25	1994	12	0.31	0.23	1.34	a
NH	40	2000	12	0.13	0.225	0.56	bc
NJ	50	1995	42	3.57	1.80	1.98	abc
NM	50	2000	12	0.24	0.23	1.03	a
NY	50	1997	32	8.16	n/a	n/a	bce
NC	40	2001	30	3.00	1.10	2.73	aef
ND	40	2000	22	0.11	0.06	1.83	a
OH	25,[†] 50[‡]	2000	34	8.26	3.50	2.36	bef
OK	None	None	12	0.30	0.28	1.07	a
OR	50	2000	32	1.10	2.50	0.44	abcf
PA	25	1997	17	1.53	36.00	0.04	bcef
RI	70	None	24	0.26	1.20	0.22	n/a
SC	30	1997	16	1.11	5.40	0.21	f
SD	50	2001	30	0.25	n/a	n/a	n/a
TN	25	1995	10	n/a	2.60	n/a	f
TX	40	1994	14	3.09	9.50	0.32	adef
UT	None	None	18	0.53	0.02	26.33	n/a
VT	40	2000	35	0.21	n/a	n/a	bc
VA	25	1997	33	2.85	1.40	2.04	af
WA	50	1995	38	2.69	1.70	1.58	be
WV	30	2010	13	0.26	2.30	0.11	a
WI	None	None	28	1.52	47.50	0.03	abcf
WY	None	None	4	0.02	0.04	0.53	e

*a = tax incentive; b = grants; c = loans; d = zones; e = economic development (state agency involved in recycling market development); f = market development councils; n/a = not available.

[†]rural. [‡]urban.

SOURCE: From Louis and McMichael (1998). With permission of John Wiley and Sons.

Recycling. TABLE 3. **Recycling of Municipal Waste by Major Countries**

COUNTRY	WASTE RECYCLED IN 1995 (%)
United Kingdom	2
France	3
Italy	3
Canada	11
Spain	13
Germany	16
Netherlands	16
Sweden	16
Japan	20
Switzerland	22
United States	23

SOURCE: *WARMER Bulletin* (February 1995).

manufacturing. Green design requires that manufacturers design and make products that are easy to return, disassemble, and recycle. Green design may also increase the attractiveness of a product to environmentally concerned consumers. Product life-cycle analysis is a useful tool in this approach (Curran, 1996). In some applications, green design can provide an option for profitable, sustainable manufacturing through cost reductions from built-in waste minimization and recycling over the product life cycle. [*See* Greening of Industry.]

Expanding commodity markets for recyclables.
Commodity markets for recyclables could be expanded by using the Internet as a clearinghouse for recycling markets and information. Employing the Internet could transform recycled materials into internationally traded production commodities and help to stabilize their often capricious prices. Several commodity exchanges already exist for recycled materials. Some on the Internet include Recycler's Exchange (1999) and Recycler's World (1999).

Conclusions. Recycling has grown in popularity because the public perceives it as the right thing to do. It can result in the conservation of natural resources and reduce the environmental impacts of production from virgin materials and excessive waste disposal. To the extent that recycling maintains society's marginal output with lower marginal inputs of energy and materials, it is thermodynamically more efficient than production from virgin materials and represents a lower-entropy option. Without innovations in technology or other improvements in recycling efficiency, increased rates of recycling can be achieved only at increased marginal cost. Thus, policy makers must weigh the marginal benefits against the marginal costs of policies to promote increased recycling.

Sustained growth of recycling depends on policies that integrate it into the ethos of manufacturing practice. Policy makers can capitalize on strong public support for recycling to create market-based incentives for innovations to make recycling technically and economically competitive with production from virgin materials. These policies should begin with a shift away from command-and-control recycling policies to the use of market-based approaches. These approaches rely on full-cost pricing through the use of environmental taxes, user fees, or deposit refunds to reflect the full costs of production, disposal, and recycling. They make it economically desirable for all users to seek the lowest-cost alternatives for production and consumption. Recycling can compete as an attractive candidate in this search for alternatives.

Finally, sustainability implies the development of present society without compromising the capability of future generations to develop. One means of doing this is to conserve natural resources and reverse generations of environmental degradation. Recycling can facilitate both of these goals and help to assure a sustainable legacy for future generations.

[*See also* Energy; Industrial Ecology; Industrial Metabolism; Manufacturing; *and* Metals.]

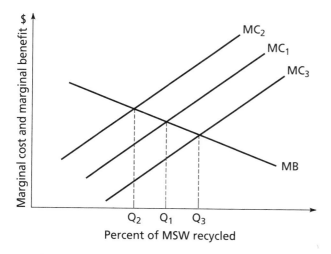

Recycling. FIGURE 8. Selecting the Desired Recycling Rate. (After Louis and McMichael, 1998. With permission of John Wiley and Sons.)

BIBLIOGRAPHY

Arthur D. Little, Inc. *Recycling State-of-the-Art for Scrapped Automobiles: Final Report to the American Iron and Steel Institute.* Cambridge, Mass.: Arthur D. Little, Inc., 1992.

Barton, A. *Resource Recovery and Recycling.* New York: Wiley, 1979.

Bernhardt, K. "Germany's New Packaging Laws: The Green Dot Arrives." *Business America* 1134 (1992), 36–37.

BioCycle. *The State of Garbage in America.* Annual reports. 1989–1996.

Carson, R. *Silent Spring.* Boston: Houghton Mifflin, 1962.

Curlee, T. R. *The Economic Feasibility of Recycling: A Case Study of Plastic Waste.* New York: Praeger, 1986.

Curran, M. A. *Environmental Life-Cycle Assessment.* New York: McGraw-Hill, 1996.

Denison, R. "Environmental Life-Cycle Comparisons of Recycling, Landfilling, and Incineration: A Review of Recent Studies." *Annual Reviews of Energy and the Environment* 21 (1996), 191–237.

Douglass, C. *Government's Hand in the Recycling Market: A New Decade.* Policy Study no. 148. St. Louis: Washington University, Center for the Study of American Business, 1998.

EducateUSA. http://educateusa.com/index1.html. 1998.

Gandy, M. *Recycling and Waste: An Exploration of Contemporary Environmental Policy.* Aldershot, Gant, U.K.: Avebury Studies in Green Research, 1993.

———. *Recycling and the Politics of Urban Waste.* New York: St. Martin's Press, 1994.

Goetsch, D. L., and S. B. Davis. *Understanding and Implementing ISO9000 and ISO Standards.* Upper Saddle River, N.J.: Prentice-Hall, 1998.

Grayson, M. *Recycling, Fuel, and Resource Recovery: Economic and Environmental Factors.* Encyclopedia Reprint Series. New York: Wiley, 1984.

Hendrickson, C., L. Lave, and F. McMichael. "Reconsider Recycling." *Chemtech* (1995), 56–60.

Heumann, J., E. Striano, and K. Egan. "Ready to Leave the Nest?" *Waste Age,* August 1996, 35–47.

Johnson, P. *ISO 14000: The Business Manager's Complete Guide to Environmental Management.* New York: Wiley, 1997.

Kimball, D. *Recycling in America: A Reference Handbook.* Santa Barbara, Calif.: ABC-CLIO, 1992.

Leach, M., A. Bauen, and N. Lucas. "A Systems Approach to Materials Flow in Sustainable Cities: A Case Study of Paper." *Journal of Environmental Planning and Management* 40.6 (November 1997), 705.

Levenson, H. "Municipal Solid Waste Reduction and Recycling: Implications for Federal Policymakers." *Resources, Conservation, and Recycling* 8.1–2 (1993), 21–37.

Louis, G. E. "Regional Integrated Municipal Solid Waste Management in the Northeastern United States." Ph.D. diss., Carnegie-Mellon University, 1996.

Louis, G., and F. C. McMichael. "Recycling Municipal Solid Waste." In *Encyclopedia of Environmental Analysis and Remediation,* edited by Robert A. Meyers. New York: Wiley, 1998.

McCarthy, J. E. *Solid Waste Issues in the 105th Congress: Updated May 14, 1998.* Report no. 97006. Washington, D.C.: Congressional Research Service, 1998.

Melosi, M. *Garbage in the Cities: Refuse Reform and the Environment, 1880–1980.* College Station: Texas A&M University Press, 1981.

Miller, C. "Recycling in the States: 1994 Update." *Waste Age* (March 1995), 92–98.

Palmer, K., H. Sigman, and M. Walls. "The Cost of Reducing Municipal Solid Waste," *Journal of Environmental Economics and Management* 33.2 (1997), 128–150.

The Recycler's Exchange. http://www.recycle.net/recycle/RNet/RE_fp.html. 1999.

The Recycler's World. http://www.recycle.net/. 1999.

Steuteville, R. "The State of Garbage in America." 2 parts. *BioCycle* (April 1996), 55–61; (May 1996), 35–41.

U.S. EPA. *The Solid Waste Dilemma: An Agenda for Action.* EPA/530-SW-89-019. Washington, D.C.: GPO, 1989.

———. *Variable Rates in Solid Waste: Handbook for Solid Waste Officials,* EPA/530-SW-90-084. Washington, D.C.: GPO, 1990.

———. http://www.epa.gov:80/opptintr/environmental-labeling/docs/greendot.pdf. 1991.

———. *Full Cost Accounting Resource Guide.* EPA530-R-95-077. Washington, D.C.: GPO, 1996.

———. *Full Cost Accounting for Municipal Solid Waste Management: A Handbook.* EPA530-R-95-041. Washington, D.C.: GPO, 1997a. http://www.epa.gov/epaoswer/non-hw/muncpl/fullcost/docs/epadocs.htm#fcahandbook.

———. *Pay-As-You-Throw Success Stories.* EPA530-F-97-007. Washington, D.C.: GPO, 1997b. http://www.epa.gov/epaoswer/non-hw/payt/success.htm.

———. *Extended Product Responsibility: A New Principle for Product-Oriented Pollution Prevention.* EPA530-R-97-009. Washington, D.C.: GPO, 1997c. http://www.epa.gov/epaoswer/non-hw/reduce/epr/epr.htm.

———. *Characterization of Municipal Solid Waste in the United States: 1996 Update.* EPA/530-R-97-015. Washington, D.C.: GPO, 1997d.

———. *Jobs through Recycling Program.* EPA530-F-98-001. Washington, D.C.: GPO, 1997e.

———. *Greenhouse Gas Emissions from Management of Selected Materials in Municipal Solid Waste.* EPA530-R-98-013. Washington, D.C.: GPO, 1998a.

———. *Puzzled about Recycling's Value? Look Beyond the Bin.* EPA530-K-98-008. Washington, D.C.: 1998b.

———. *Questions and Answers about Full Cost Accounting.* EPA530-F-98-003. Washington, D.C.: GPO, 1998c.

———. *Characterization of Municipal Solid Waste in the United States: 1997 Update.* EPA530-R-98-007. Washington, D.C.: GPO, 1998d.

———. *Guide for Industrial Waste Management.* EPA530-R-99-001. Washington, D.C.: GPO, 1999.

Vining, J., N. Linn, and R. Burdge. "Why Recycle? A Comparison of Recycling Motivations in Four Communities." *Environment Management* 16.6 (1992), 785–797.

—JHIH-SHYANG SHIH, GARRICK E. LOUIS,
AND KAREN PALMER

REEFS

Reefs are accumulations of carbonate that derive largely from the skeletal materials of various marine organisms. The principal reef-building organisms are algae and corals. Algal reefs can develop in most oceans, but corals are restricted to those in which temperatures remain in the range 18°–36°C (optimally, 26°–28°C) and in which salinity is 3.3–3.6 percent. In terms of size and importance in global change studies, coral reefs significantly outweigh other types of reef, and are thus the focus of this entry.

Living coral reefs occupy over 600,000 square kilometers of the Earth's surface, confined mostly to tropical oceans. Exceptions occur when warm water is continuously moved into higher latitudes; examples include the northwestern Hawaiian islands, Lord Howe Island in the southwestern Pacific, the Ryukyu Islands of Japan, and Bermuda in the western Atlantic.

Reefs are most simply classified into fringing reefs, barrier reefs, and atoll reefs (Figure 1). Fringing reefs tend to be young and surficial, rising from comparatively shallow depths on the submerged flanks of the land. Barrier reefs rise from greater depths and, since they rise almost vertically, they break the ocean surface at some distance from the coast. Atoll (or ring) reefs rise upward from a submerged edifice, typically a sunken volcanic island.

In 1842, Charles Darwin was the first to recognize that fringing reefs could develop into barrier reefs, which could develop into atolls by the progressive subsidence of a reef-fringed volcanic island (Figure 1). This Subsidence Theory of Atoll Formation attracted a lot of criticism initially, most of which it withstood, particularly when atoll reef drilling confirmed that such reefs rose from submerged volcanic foundations. Yet to insist (as Darwin did not) that every atoll must have once been a barrier reef and that every barrier reef must have once been a fringing reef has proved unhelpful, especially

in tectonically active parts of the coral seas in the Caribbean and southwestern Pacific.

Islands exist on reefs in many places. These may be surficial and transient (cays), often created and removed in successive storm events, or they may be more enduring (*motu*) as the result of having developed beachrock or other armor. In places where slight emergence has taken place, reef islands will be even more enduring, a good example being the low emerged reef Aldabra in the western Indian Ocean.

Although coral reefs have existed since the Ordovician (500–440 million years ago), most of those living in the world today have foundations of Neogene age (25–1.8 million years ago). These reefs have proved to be sensitive recorders of many environmental changes and have thus been the object of studies by many global change researchers.

A good example of this is the use of reefs as accurate recorders of tectonic changes. Most ancient mid-ocean atolls, such as those in the northwestern Pacific, have been subsiding very slowly for several million years. In response to this subsidence, the veneer of liv-

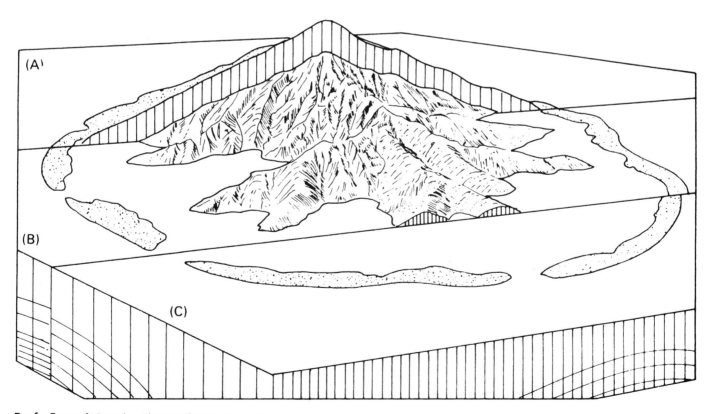

Reefs. FIGURE 1. Darwin's Theory of Atoll Formation.

Through submergence, a volcanic island with a fringing reef (A) may become an island with an embayed coast and a barrier reef (B), and finally an atoll reef (C). (After Nunn, 1994.)

ing reef that caps the edifice of dead reef below has been growing slowly upward. Hence dated cores through the reef can provide information about the long-term subsidence rate.

Knowledge of subsidence rates can also help in understanding past sea level changes. Solution unconformities found within reef cores represent times when sea level fell below the reef surface, which was exposed and eventually lowered by subaerial (rainwater) solution. By measuring the depths of unconformities of particular ages, it has been possible to determine precise levels of former low stands of global sea level relative to the present.

The comparatively rapid recurrence of sea level oscillations during the later Neogene (Quaternary) caused the frequent exposure of reef surfaces during times of low sea level, approximately coincident with glacial maxima. At such times, the regions within which coral reefs were able to grow shrank markedly. As temperatures warmed once again and sea level began rising, the surfaces of the reefs became gradually flooded and corals once more became established. [See Sea Level.]

There has been considerable debate about the relationship between such periods of sea level rise and the shape of modern atolls. When an atoll reef has been exposed during a Neogene sea level low, subaerial solution has caused it to develop a characteristic rim-and-basin morphology in its highest parts. When flooded by rising sea level, most reef growth has taken place along the rim rather than in the basin. Thus the form of most modern atolls reflects the form of the most recent rim to have developed on its submerged reef foundation (Figure 2).

In some places, a combination of uplift and sea level fall has caused the emergence of a reef edifice. Most high limestone islands in the world are emerged reefs, yet only a few of these appear to be authentic "elevated atolls," despite their characteristic rim-and-basin form. On account of their often remote, midocean locations, emerged reefs have often been a focus for seabird colonization, which has led to the development of phosphate rock on islands such as Christmas Island in the Indian Ocean and Nauru and Banaba (Ocean Island) in the Pacific.

Corals, the principal warm-water reef-builders today, are sensitive to changes in water temperature, salinity, and turbidity. While clearly resilient in the long term, many coral reef ecosystems have been adversely affected by human and nonhuman activities in the recent past.

Through land use changes, typically logging, on nearby land areas, uncommonly high amounts of sediment have been released onto proximal reefs. This has increased turbidity to such an extent that insufficient light penetrates to the reef surface for photosynthesis to take place, so that the corals and their dependent or-

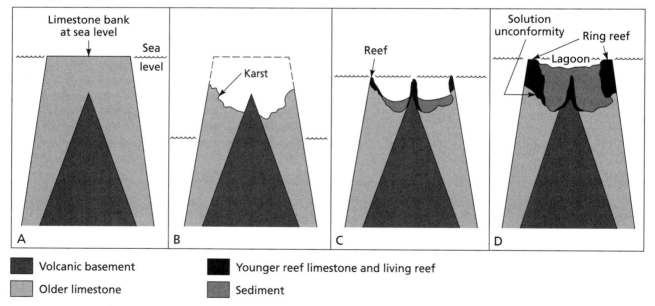

Reefs. Figure 2. Atoll Formation Following a Fall and Rise in Sea Level.

(A) A limestone bank exists at a relatively high (interglacial) sea level. (B) Sea level falls (during the subsequent glacial period) and subaerial erosion causes the exposed limestone bank to develop a saucer shape. (C) Sea level begins to rise (during the early post-glacial period), reef is established and begins growing upward (as sea level continues rising) on the highest parts of the island. (D) As sea level continues rising (to its interglacial maximum), upward reef growth continues around the periphery but is gradually stifled by sediment accumulation in the center of the drowned "saucer"; an atoll develops. (After Nunn, 1994.)

CORAL BLEACHING

Increased sea surface temperatures resulting from global warming could have dele-terious consequences for corals, which are near their thermal maximum of tolerance, and increased temperatures in recent years have been identified as one potential or actual cause of a phenomenon called *coral bleaching*. This involves the loss of symbiotic zooxanthellae or a decrease in the photosynthetic pigmentation in these zooxanthellae. This in turn has an adverse effect on the coral host since these photo-synthetic symbionts typically supply about two-thirds of the coral's nutrients and also facilitate calcification. Those corals thus stressed by a rise in temperature or by various types of pollution, might well find it more difficult to cope with rapidly rising sea levels than would healthy corals. Moreover, it is possible that increased ultraviolet radiation due to ozone depletion could aggravate bleaching and mortality caused by global warming. Various studies have addressed the issue of coral bleaching (e.g., Brown, 1990), and some have demonstrated an increasing incidence of bleaching events during the warm years of the 1980s and 1990s (e.g., Glynn, 1996).

Indeed, Goreau and Hayes (1994) have produced maps of global coral bleaching episodes between 1983 and 1991 and have related them to maps of sea surface temperatures over that period. They find that areas of severe bleaching are related to what they describe as ocean "hot spots" where marked positive temperature anomalies exist. They argue that coral reefs are ecosystems that may be uniquely prone to the effects of global warming:

> If global warming continues, almost all ecosystems can be replaced by migration of species from lower latitude, except for the warmest ecosystems. These have no source of immigrants already adapted to warmer conditions. Their species must evolve new environmental toler-ances if their descendants are to survive, a much slower process than migrations.

A more recent survey of the future of the world's coral reefs (Hoegh-Guldberg, 1999), based on modeling changes in sea surface temperatures using various global climate models, is even more pessimistic, concluding that "bleaching events are projected to increase in frequency until they become yearly events by 2050 in most oceans" (p. 15). Noting that previous bleaching events (since 1979) have been triggered by unseasonably high temperatures associated with El Niño events, the author goes on to note that "in 20–40 years from now, bleaching is projected to be triggered by seasonal changes in water temperature and will no longer depend on El Niño events to push corals over the limit" (p. 15).

BIBLIOGRAPHY

Brown, B. E. "Coral Bleaching." *Coral Reefs* 8 (1990), 153–232.
Glynn, P. "Coral Reef Bleaching: Facts, Hypotheses and Implications." *Global Change Biology* 2 (1996), 495–510.
Goreau, T. J., and R. L. Hayes. "Coral Bleaching and Ocean 'Hot Spots.'" *Ambio* 23 (1994), 176–180.

—Andrew S. Goudie

ganisms die and the reef surface becomes barren. Clear-ance of mangrove forests along many tropical coasts has also contributed to reef death, largely by releasing large amounts of sediment, formerly held together by the root systems of the mangroves, onto nearby reefs. Human demands on reef ecosystems have often led to their overexploitation (particularly where subsistence de-mands have been replaced by commercial ones), phys-ical damage (from trampling, anchors, and dynamite) and chemical pollution (from fish poison and industrial and domestic waste).

Coral mining is another destructive practice on many coral reefs that is increasingly contributing to their degradation. On island nations that have no other source of hard rock for construction, reefs are routinely blasted or excavated by hand. Increasing demand for reef fish has also led to the overexploitation of reefs in many countries.

Nonhuman causes of reef stress are also common. They include predation by occasionally massive numbers of crown-of-thorns starfish (*Acanthaster planci*). Storms often cause significant structural damage to reefs, and may occasionally cover them with detritus brought up their faces from depth. Reefs can generally recover from structural damage; the reefs off Florida recovered within seven years of the passage of a hurricane packing 200-kilometer-per-hour winds. Indeed, it has been suggested that periodic storms are necessary for the purposes of rejuvenation and extension of reefs. Conversely, many reef flats appear to have been denuded beyond recovery as the result of storm damage. The increasing frequency of such storms in some places over the last few decades implies that the normal recovery of reefs, following such events, may increasingly be inhibited.

Although the El Niño–Southern Oscillation has affected the Earth for most of the Holocene, in common with many other effects, its impacts on reefs have been understood only recently. One major effect is the prolonged low sea levels, which may cause reef surfaces to be exposed for several weeks. These cause the living veneer of reefs to be exposed for so long that it dies. El Niño also involves temperature changes, which must be distinguished in their cause from those associated with global warming, although the effect is the same (Table 1).

The effects of severe storms or widespread coral death associated with El Niño, for example, may be to allow the initiation of other processes that may complete the degradation of a particular reef. Bioerosion on eastern Pacific reefs that experienced widespread coral death in the 1982–1983 El Niño now exceeds carbonate buildup, a process that will convert the reef framework into sediment if it continues. [*See* El Niño–Southern Oscillation.]

As the Earth's surface has warmed in recent decades, so too has the uppermost ocean. Temperature rise in some places has increased stress on coral reefs to the point where coral bleaching has occurred. This phenomenon is essentially a response to a high level of stress (to which temperature rise is but one contributor) and involves the corals expelling the symbiotic algae (zooxanthellae) within them and dying as a consequence. Since the algae give most corals their color, this process involves a bleaching that is easily recognizable.

Should Earth surface temperatures increase as predicted, reefs throughout the world are likely to experience increases in stress that may prove fatal in some cases. Yet even if Earth surface temperatures do not rise as much as predicted, increases in stress will still occur on many reefs. To understand why, it is necessary to appreciate that many reefs are located in places where economic growth takes precedence over environmental conservation. In much of the developing world, at both the national and the individual level, reef protection is sometimes perceived as a preoccupation of the developed world to which only lip service need be paid.

As much as 85 percent of the sediment entering the ocean comes off land in the tropical western Pacific, where the greatest diversity of coral reef ecosystems also occurs. The threats to coral reef diversity in this region—particularly in the Philippines, Indonesia, and Papua New Guinea—are manifest, and they are spread-

Reefs. TABLE 1. Incidences of Reef Death Associated with the 1982–1983 El Niño

REGION	PHENOMENON	SUGGESTED CAUSE
Bahamas	Bleaching of corals *Diploria* to depths of 5–8 meters	Unclear
Florida	Bleaching and death of some corals, gorgonians, and *Millepora* to depths of 14 meters	Exposure and overheating
Caribbean reefs	Bleaching and death of some corals and other anthozoans (twenty-five species in total)	Overheating
Caribbean reefs	Mass mortality of urchins and asteroids	Unclear
Eastern Pacific	Bleaching and death of 60–90 percent of corals	Overheating
Tokelau (central Pacific)	Bleaching and death of corals in shallows	Long exposure and overheating
Great Barrier Reef, near Cairns, Australia	Bleaching and death of corals down to 15 meters depth	Exposure and overheating
Okinawa, Japan	Bleaching and death of corals and actinians to 10 meters depth	Overheating
Indonesia	Bleaching and death of corals and actinians to 10 meters depth	Unclear

SOURCE: Adapted from Sorokin (1995).

ing. The Solomon Islands, for example, are a large group of reef-fringed tropical islands with one of the highest population densities in the Pacific, where most of the people live on the coasts and depend on coral reefs for their daily sustenance. In 1997, the Australian government withdrew certain aid from the Solomon Islands on the grounds that if deforestation continued at its present rate, there would be no forests left within fifteen years. In addition to depriving people of their terrestrial resources, the effects on nearby reef systems of terrestrial sediment released from the land as a result of logging would lead to their degradation.

Coral reefs are also tourist attractions. More than three million tourists visit one of Hawaii's reefs each year. The effect of such pressure has been understood and legislated for in a few countries, but many of the countries in the Caribbean and the South Pacific have little opportunity for foreign income generation besides tourism, so are very reluctant to impose constraints that they fear may drive tourists away.

Future temperature rise is predicted to be accompanied by sea level rise. Although predictions of the magnitude of this rise have been downgraded considerably in recent years, it still seems likely that sea level will rise perhaps 30 centimeters in the next fifty years or so. The effects of this rise on reef ecosystems have been discussed by a few authors (Hoegh-Guldberg, 1999). Some believe that reefs will be able to grow upward at the same rate as sea level rises and thus maintain reeffringed shorelines much as they are now. This view has encouraged complacency among many government planners and bodes ill for the future of many reefs. An alternative view recognizes that, although reef surfaces grew upward during the Holocene sea level rise at rates far in excess of that needed in the next fifty years to keep pace with predicted sea level rise, they may not do so. One reason is that sources of stress (see above) exist today that did not exist thousands of years ago. The other reason is that modern reefs have not had to grow upward for several millennia. Thus the types of coral that are critical for upward reef growth are rarer today and there will need to be a significant change in species composition on many reefs before they will be in the optimum state to respond to sea level rise. How long this change will take is unclear, particularly in reef ecosystems that are already stressed for other reasons.

Increasing degradation of coral reefs in the future will greatly impact the biodiversity of the oceans, both directly through reef species loss and indirectly through the loss in many places of a habitat that is essential to the life cycle of various other organisms. For example, fisheries dependent on coral reefs total about 9 million metric tons per year, around one-tenth of total marine fisheries.

About half the calcium entering the ocean every year gets into a coral reef, at least temporarily. Since calcium combines with carbon dioxide in this process, it has been calculated that around 700 billion kilograms of carbon is sunk into coral reefs annually. The importance of conserving the reefs is thus emphasized, given that degradation will release massive amounts of carbon dioxide, which might then be transferred to the Earth's atmosphere—where it could plausibly exacerbate the effects of global warming.

Any realistic evaluation of the future of the world's coral reefs must at present be pessimistic. Stress levels on many modern reefs are at unprecedented levels, and the most authoritative predictions of the future suggest that the principal sources of stress—direct human impact, temperature rise, and sea level rise—are likely to increase, at least over the next hundred years or so. Increased awareness of the fragility of the world's living reefs, especially among people who interact with them on a daily basis, is probably the best long-term hope for their conservation.

[*See also* Coastal Protection and Management; *and* Marginal Seas.]

BIBLIOGRAPHY

Birkeland, C., ed. *Life and Death of Coral Reefs.* New York: Chapman and Hall, 1997. A first-rate compilation on the workings of coral reefs and the concerns about their future.

Brown, B. E., and J. C. Ogden. "Coral Bleaching." *Scientific American* 268 (1992), 64–70. A concise review of the main occurrences of coral bleaching.

Carpenter, R. A., and J. E. Maragos. *How to Assess Environmental Impacts on Tropical Islands and Coastal Areas.* Honolulu: East-West Center, 1989. A practical guide that incorporates many examples of poor practice and illustrates realistic solutions.

Darwin, C. *The Structure and Distribution of Coral Reefs.* London: London, Smith, Elder & Co., 1874. The first systematic scientific observations of coral reefs and the classic statement of subsidence theory, still largely valid in its essentials.

Davis, W. M. *The Coral Reef Problem.* Washington, D.C.: American Geographical Society, 1928. An exhaustive account of reef genesis, adhering uncritically to subsidence theory. Although many of the conclusions have since been invalidated (particularly as the complexity of Neogene sea level changes has become apparent), this remains a reference classic for many reefs.

Guilcher, A. *Coral Reef Geomorphology.* New York: Wiley, 1988. A geographically well-balanced and systematic account of reefs and the various forms they assume.

Hoegh-Guldberg, O. *Climate Change, Coral Bleaching and the Future of the World's Coral Reefs.* Amsterdam: Greenpeace International, 1999.

Hopley, D. *The Geomorphology of the Great Barrier Reef: Quaternary Development of Coral Reefs.* New York: Wiley, 1982. A thorough description of the world's largest living reef system, with good summaries of ideas about Neogene reef genesis and development.

Nunn, P. D. *Oceanic Islands.* Oxford and Cambridge, Mass.: Blackwell, 1994. Includes a chapter on coral reefs and islands, with examples worldwide.

―――. *Keimami sa vakila na liga ni Kalou (Feeling the Hand of God): Human and Nonhuman Impacts on Pacific Island Environments.* 3d ed. Suva, Fiji: University of the South Pacific, 1997. Includes a discussion of the various causes of reef damage and degradation in the Pacific Islands.

Raloff, J. "Sea Sickness: Marine Epidemiology Comes of Age." *Science News* (January 30, 1999), 72–74.

Smith, S. V. "Coral-Reef Area and the Contributions of Reefs to Processes and Resources in the World's Oceans." *Nature* 273 (1978), 225–226. An unsurpassed set of statistics about reefs.

Sorokin, Y. I. *Coral Reef Ecology.* Berlin: Springer, 1995.

Wiens, H. J. *Atoll Environment and Ecology.* New Haven: Yale University Press, 1962. A comprehensive account of the subject.

—PATRICK D. NUNN

REFUGES. *See* Wilderness.

REGIONAL ASSESSMENT

Regional assessment is the process of making synthesized, integrated interdisciplinary research available to assist public and private decision making in response to global environmental change at regional levels of spatial resolution. Regional assessment differs from integrated assessment at the global scale by focusing at continental, national, subnational, river basin, or local scales. It brings a systems approach that analyzes the contributions of regions to global change and, in turn, traces regional impacts and potentials for adaptation to change and mitigation of adverse activities. In the context of climate change, regional assessment includes, on the one hand, local contributions to greenhouse gases and, on the other hand, downscaling from general circulation models to local climate change, tracing the consequences of that change, suggesting the resulting impacts on society, and specifying possible responses.

Human effects on environment and environmental change impacts on society do not occur in a vacuum. Thus regional assessment examines the interactions of these factors with other dimensions of the region—such as impacts of economic globalization, development of local policy in the context of national and international policy, land use change, and population dynamics. The results of integrated assessment at the regional level are meant to inform local policy and adaptation and to elucidate the ways in which global processes play out at scales of activity in which humans live and work.

The Rationale for Regional Assessment. Regional assessments are imperative from the viewpoints of policy makers and stakeholders, as well as those of the scientific community. The 1995 report of the Intergovernmental Panel on Climate Change (IPCC; Bruce et al., 1996) clearly recognized the importance of regional variations in contributions to and impacts of climate change. This report documented problems of global-scale analysis across regions with vastly different economic systems and levels of development, noting that net economic effects of changing climate range from adverse in one region to positive in another. Global integrated assessment models bring together interdisciplinary research, but do not effectively capture the reality of transitional and developing economies or processes occurring at regional scales. There are important regional differences in vulnerability to climate change and to risks inherent in delaying responses to climate change. Potential low-cost and cost-effective approaches to mitigation and adaptation also vary regionally. Thus national and international organizations have called for and sponsor climate change research at a regional scale. For example, the 1997 report of the United States Global Change Research Program differed from its predecessors in calling explicitly for regional assessments, listing regional-scale estimates of the timing and magnitude of climate change and regional analyses of environmental and socioeconomic factors, in the context of other stresses, among "Key Research Challenges for the Next Decade."

Why should policy makers and stakeholders want regional assessments? Human activities vary in their vulnerability to climate change. Whereas industry and energy production may be less sensitive to climate change, agriculture, forestry, water resources, recreation, and health may be more sensitive. All of these sectors have great regional differentiation. Regions differ in their dependence upon specific economic activities and interaction with other regions. Some important elements of concern to policy makers and stakeholders include the following:

- regional and national security
- judging the relative importance of climate change in the face of other challenges
- understanding, anticipating, and exploiting regionally unique opportunities to meet the exigencies of national and international commitments
- selecting regionally appropriate mitigation and adaptation strategies
- judging when and where actions must be taken in the face of limited social, technological, and economic choices
- determining socially and spatially marginal areas and differential impacts on them that might occur
- addressing local issues of mitigation and adaptation inequity
- helping to resolve the different viewpoints of scientists, policy makers, and lay persons

Why are regional assessments imperative from a scientific viewpoint? Scientists researching human dimensions of climate change argue strongly for the importance of regional assessments. The spatial variability of changing weather and climate patterns important at the regional scale is not captured in global climate models, and, similarly, the temporal as well as spatial variability of hydrological processes may be obscured by the use of low-resolution global approaches. Regional assessments are consistent with the use of environmental and social-science models developed for higher-resolution phenomena, providing the proper scale for matching social and environmental data and interactions. Moreover, a regional scale is more appropriate for process (versus statistical) modeling. In addition, aggregation or averaging of nonlinear social and environmental relationships is more sound at a regional scale. Social and amenity values as expressions of local culture and society are captured only at a regional or local level. There have been increasing calls for a cyclical regional–global modeling approach in which regional and global models would interact. Such a strategy would allow testing of the regional components of the global assessment, provide bounds for the regional model, and create an opportunity for the synergistic advancement of assessment methods and knowledge.

Examples of Regional Assessment. According to the IPCC report (Bruce, 1996), several global integrated assessment models have some degree of regional specificity. These include FUND (Vrije Universiteit Amsterdam), ICAM-2 (Carnegie-Mellon University), IMAGE 2.0 (RIVM, Netherlands), MARIA (Science University of Tokyo), MERGE (Stanford and Yale Universities, Electric Power Research Institute), MiniCAM and ProCAM (Pacific Northwest Laboratory, EPRI, University Consortium for Atmospheric Research), MIT (Massachusetts Institute of Technology), PAGE (Cambridge University and Environmental Resources Management), PEF (U.S. Environmental Protection Agency, Decision Focus Inc.), RICE (Yale University and MIT), and SLICE (University of California, Santa Barbara). However, global approaches with regional disaggregation have characteristically inadequate treatment of land use change, population, and economic development outside the western, industrialized economies.

Schmandt and Clarkson (1992) emphasized the importance of a regional approach to both control and mitigation of greenhouse gases and adaptive strategies. The 1993 Hanford Symposium on Health and the Environment (Ghan, 1996) similarly argued for a regional approach. Although the contributions in these volumes were not integrated assessments at the regional level, they pointed the way for the critical role of the regional perspective. Rayner and Malone (1998b) include an admonition to "take a regional and local approach to climate policymaking and implementation." Parry et al. (1995) addressed the economic impacts of climate change on the United Kingdom. In the United States, a series of regional climate change workshops in 1997–

1998 initiated regional assessments in that nation. National and regional assessments of climate change are increasing in number, emphasizing the importance of the regional dimension.

A number of specific regional assessments have been undertaken, including the early Missouri–Iowa–Nebraska–Kansas (MINK) study (Rosenberg, 1993) and the Mackenzie River Basin Impacts Study (Cohen, 1997). Other examples include the Susquehanna Basin Integrated Regional Assessment, the CLIMPACTS integrated assessment in New Zealand, and AIM, the Asian Pacific Integrated Model, at increasing spatial scales, as well as START (Global Change SysTem for Analysis, Research, and Training) regional initiatives representing increasingly larger areas.

Challenges in Regional Assessment. Key concepts for regional assessment are integration in place, interdependencies between places, and interdependencies among scales. Examples of integration in place include society–environment dynamics (e.g., land use change) as well as the distinctiveness of individual places—both elements important in understanding the impact of global change in specific places. Interdependency between places is similarly a core concept of global change in specific regions: external events affect driving forces and consequences within the region. Finally, interdependency among scales helps to elucidate processes otherwise obscured by analysis at the wrong scale or by incorrect attribution of causal effects. Thus "critical questions for science in understanding global change include (1) clarifying the scale(s) at which change should be observed and analyzed and (2) tracing linkages between processes that operate at macro- and microscales" (National Academy of Sciences, 1997).

How does one define a region? "Formal regions" are defined by commonalities of some phenomenon or phenomena—soil types, climate, biomes, transitional and developing countries, and island nations are examples. Such regions need not be spatially contiguous. Examples of noncontiguous regional assessments include the developing and transitional economies included in the U.S. Department of Energy Country Studies Program of greenhouse gas emissions and mitigation and the AMIGO (America's Interhemisphere Geo-Biosphere Organization) focus on cross-equatorial matched zones such as temperate forests and riverine ecosystems. The "functional" or "nodal" region, in contrast, refers to places tied together by interaction such as hydrological systems, trade, communication, or other human interaction: the idea of spatial contiguity is implicit. Both formal and functional regions can also be seen from a hierarchical perspective, with regions of more local extent being part of more general regions at a wider geographical scale. In general language, there is considerable ambiguity in the scale and nature of "region." Some

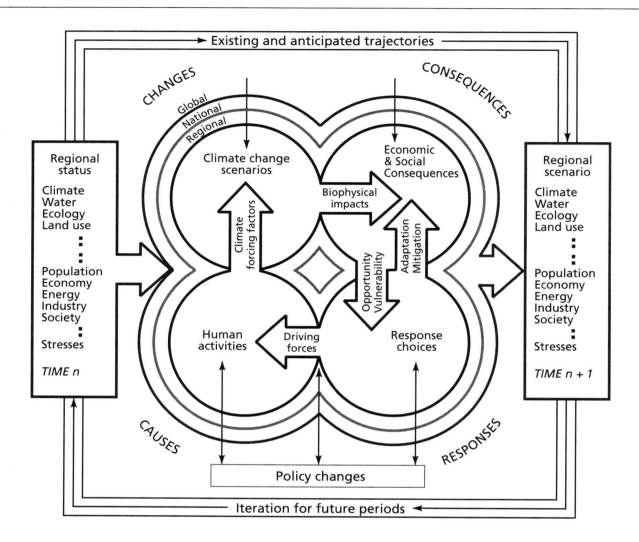

Regional Assessment. Figure 1. A Framework for Integrated Regional Assessment of Global Climate Change. (After Knight et al., 1999.)

regions are officially recognized with accepted nomenclature and definite boundaries (a river basin, a political jurisdiction); others are vernacular, informal, or indefinite. In scale, regions could extend from a neighborhood of a few city blocks or a mountain valley to multicountry domains (such as sub-Saharan Africa). For START or the Inter-American Institute, a region consists of a multicountry grouping based on geographical contiguity (e.g., the Mediterranean basin). Global change studies also focus on subnational entities (e.g., Texas), nations (e.g., the Netherlands), or river basins (e.g., the Nile).

For regional assessment, an overlapping spatial scale extends from individual places, at scales of perhaps 10^1–10^4 square kilometers, to less than the global scale (10^8 square kilometers). "Localities" encompass 10^3–10^5

square kilometers, focusing on the equivalent of the equatorial degree square (10^4 square kilometers) as used in some global change studies. "Regions" and "Basins" might focus on areas of 10^4–10^7 square kilometers; "Countries" range upward to 10^6 square kilometers; and multicountry "Domains" (such as those used in START) range from 10^6 to 10^7 square kilometers, a level consistent with the regionalization used in some global models. Within the scale of analysis are embedded varying degrees of spatial and temporal resolution, with a subregional resolution appropriate to the topic of analysis (perhaps 1–4 square kilometers) and a temporal resolution appropriate to the phenomena being modeled (perhaps days to a year, although as fine as hours in some climate modeling and as coarse as decades in some scenario creation).

Regional assessment includes elements and strategies of integrated assessment in general. Issues specific to regional assessment involve both research and implementation. One of the most difficult challenges to the regional assessment of climate change is the development of climate scenarios at a suitable scale and resolution. Thus climate downscaling by process modeling or statistical approaches is important; some assessments have instead used historical climate as an analogy (MINK: Rosenberg, 1993). Regional assessments can be quantitative (involving regional assessment models), qualitative, or, most frequently, a combination. Other relevant issues include establishment of dialogue among scientists, stakeholders, and decision makers as the assessment proceeds; the range of decision choices considered; establishment of boundary conditions with assessments at wider spatial scales; reconciliation of data of different spatial and temporal resolutions; selection of an integrated or modular format; specification of end-to-end versus integrated models; choice between an inventory and an issue orientation; decision to use a model or models (and choice of model components); assessment and communication of uncertainty; and selection of integration strategies (most often economic in nature, but potentially ecological, social, or geographic). There are areas of scientific understanding that would seem to be relevant for regional assessment beyond model components drawn from disciplinary areas. These include the long tradition of human-environment studies in geography and anthropology; environmental perception and behavior in psychology and geography; interdisciplinary natural-hazards studies; environmental and social impact analysis; political economy; spatial change and diffusion; and postmodern criticism of resource knowledge and management. The ties between these traditions and the regional assessment of global change remain largely unexploited.

There is currently no well-developed prototype for regional assessment. The ESCAPE (Evaluation of Strategies to Address Climate Change by Adapting to and Preventing Emissions) model for Europe provides one analytical framework; AIM and CLIMPACTS are also helpful contributions toward a common approach. A framework for integrated regional assessment of global climate change has been proposed by researchers at the Center for Integrated Regional Assessment at the Pennsylvania State University (Figure 1; Knight et al., 1999). In this framework, the analysis of changes in regional characteristics and environmental stresses resulting from climate change is a circular process in which climate change is used to predict ecological and physical impacts. Evaluation of the potential economic and social consequences of these impacts, in turn, helps to define both opportunities and vulnerabilities to climate change. Similarly, consequences for society and response choices delineate opportunities for adaptation to these impacts and for mitigation of regional contributions to global change. Response choices at a local level, interacting with policy changes at wider scales, in turn, alter the driving forces of human activities that contribute to climate

forcing, such as greenhouse gas emissions and land use change. Important in the framework is the recognition that regions (at whatever scale) interact across space through hierarchical processes (regional, national, global) and contiguity processes (with adjoining regions). These linkages between one region and others at a similar level of resolution, and up and down hierarchies of regions, are important to understand; otherwise, important changes outside the region may not be traced to consequences inside, and generalization at one level may hide significant detail and impacts at another.

Regional assessment is an emerging field of research, drawing on the traditions both of integrated assessment in general and of the more recent integrated assessment of climate change at the global scale. The future of this approach to understanding global climatic change is most likely to evolve through a multiplicity of activities at various scales in different places. The opportunity to compare approaches, to develop and elaborate frameworks, and to synthesize across geographical locations and spatial scales lies ahead, providing a tantalizing inducement for the participation of scientists and policy makers alike.

[*See also* Climate Change; Climate Impacts; Global Change, *article on* Human Dimensions of Global Change; Human Impacts, *article on* Human Impacts on Earth; *and* Integrated Assessment.]

BIBLIOGRAPHY

Blaikie, P. M. "Post-Modernism and Global Environmental Change." *Global Environmental Change* 6.2 (1996), 81–85.
Bruce, J. P., H. Lee, and E. F. Haites, eds. *Climate Change 1995: Economic and Social Dimensions of Climate Change.* Cambridge: Cambridge University Press, 1996. This consensus volume from Working Group III of the IPCC summarizes many issues relevant at regional as well as global level.
Chen, R. S., E. Boulding, and S. H. Schneider, eds. *Social Science Research and Climate Change: An Interdisciplinary Appraisal.* Dordrecht: Reidel, 1983. Insightful contributions to human dimensions of global change.
Cohen, S. J., ed. *Mackenzie Basin Impact Study (MBIS) Final Report.* Downsview, Ont.: Atmospheric Environment Service, Environment Canada, 1997. The summary volume of an important regional assessment.
Easterling, W. E. "Why Regional Studies are Needed in the Development of Full-Scale Integrated Assessment Modeling of Global Change Processes." *Global Environmental Change* 7.4 (1997), 337–356. Discusses the importance of the regional dimension for research on global change.
Fuchs, R. J. "START: The Road from Bellagio." *Global Environmental Change* 5.5 (1995), 397–404. The origins of the START organization.
Ghan, S. J., et al., eds. *Regional Impacts of Global Climate Change: Assessing Change and Response at the Scales that Matter.* Columbus, Ohio: Battelle Press, 1996. Illustrates the importance of regional-scale analysis.
Knight, C. G., et al. "The CIRA Framework for Integrated Regional Assessment." In *Progress Report, March 1, 1999,* pp. 45–48.

University Park: Center for Integrated Regional Assessment, Pennsylvania State University, 1999. One possible protocol for integrated regional assessment.

Miller, R. B., and H. K. Jacobson. "Research on the Human Components of Global Change." *Global Environmental Change* 2.3 (1992), 170–182. This article elaborates social processes included in global change studies.

National Academy of Sciences. *Rediscovering Geography: New Relevance for Science and Society.* Washington, D.C.: National Academy Press, 1997, p. 99.

North, G. R., J. Schmandt, and J. Clarkson, eds. *The Impact of Global Warming on Texas.* Austin: University of Texas Press, 1995. An example of a state-level assessment of global change.

Parry, M., and R. Duncan, eds. *The Economic Implications of Climate Change in Britain.* London: Earthscan, 1995.

Parson, E. A. "Integrated Assessment and Environmental Policy Making: In Pursuit of Usefulness." *Energy Policy* 23.4/5 (1995), 463–475.

Rayner, S., and E. L. Malone, eds. *Human Choice and Climate Change.* Columbus, Ohio: Battelle Press, 1998a. A four-volume collaboration examining the interactions among society, technology, and policy related to climate change.

Rayner, S., and E. L. Malone. *Ten Suggestions for Policy Makers.* A booklet summarizing *Human Choice and Climate Change.* Columbus, Ohio: Battelle Press, 1998b.

Rosenberg, N. J., ed. *Towards an Integrated Impact Assessment of Climate Change: The MINK Study.* Boston: Kluwer, 1993. The summary volume of a now-classic study.

Rotmans, J., and H. Dowlatabadi. "Integrated Assessment Modeling." In *Human Choices and Climate Change, Tools for Policy Analysis,* edited by S. Rayner and E. L. Malone, pp. 291–377. Columbus, Ohio: Battelle Press, 1998.

Schmandt, J., and J. Clarkson. *The Regions and Global Warming.* New York: Oxford University Press, 1992.

Subcommittee on Global Change Research, Committee on Environment and Natural Resources, National Science and Technology Council. *Our Changing Planet, the FY 1998 United States Global Change Research Program.* Washington, D.C.: U.S. Global Change Research Program, 1997.

Yarnal, B. "Integrated Regional Assessment and Climate Change Impacts in River Basins." *Climate Research* 11.1 (1998), 65–74. Review of the rationale and progress of regional assessment at the river basin scale.

—C. GREGORY KNIGHT

REGULATION

Regulations are frequently necessary to achieve a desired level of environmental protection, but they need to be designed carefully. Moreover, they need to be designed in full recognition that they often have unintended or perverse consequences. For example, the imposition of stringent new pollution-control standards for electric utilities may have made pollution worse by encouraging existing high-emitting sources of electricity to stay open longer. The important point to remember is that the potential for remedying market failure through government intervention must be weighed carefully against the potential for government failure.

An important justification for regulation is that unrestrained competition may fail to yield a socially efficient outcome. In the case of pollution, for example, if producers are not required to account for the costs of environmental degradation imposed on others, this could lead to excessive levels of pollution. The problem is particularly acute where environmental costs are spread over a large population, but the benefits of polluting are concentrated with a few producers. One approach to addressing this problem is through direct regulation—whereby the government specifies a level of pollution a firm must achieve and sometimes specifies the technology that must be used. An example of such command-and-control regulation is the requirement that zero-emitting vehicles be sold.

As concerns over the quality of the air we breathe and the water we drink have grown, various laws have been passed to improve the state of the environment. The main instruments in efforts by the United States to curb pollution are major federal laws enacted by Congress. The implementation of these laws is left to the executive agencies, which pass rules that the private sector and state and local governments are required to follow. Those rules are compiled in the *Code of Federal Regulation.* The primary administrator of environmental laws is the Environmental Protection Agency (EPA), which is charged with implementing mandates to improve environmental quality. The Department of the Interior and the Department of Agriculture also play important roles by administering regulations to implement the Endangered Species Act and the conservation provisions of the Farm Bill. In some cases, the specifics of implementing the laws are left to the states. In addition, some states, most notably California, often pass regulations that are more stringent than the federal government's. The courts also play a role in the regulatory process by forcing agencies to comply with statutory deadlines and imposing major penalties if they are not met.

When the EPA was formed in 1970, it was given the task of administering existing environmental statutes such as the Federal Insecticide, Fungicide, and Rodenticide Act, the Water Pollution Control Act (Clean Water Act), and the Air Pollution Control Act (Clean Air Act). The authority of the EPA has increased considerably since its inception through the addition of new environmental statutes as well as amendments to existing laws. There are now at least ten major U.S. federal laws that address environmental quality administered by the EPA. Some of those laws are media specific—aimed, for example, at improving air or water quality. Others cover the use of specific chemicals such as pesticides or toxic pollutants. The largest in terms of the estimated cost of recent regulations is the Clean Air Act, second is the Resource Conservation and Recovery Act, and third is the Safe Drinking Water Act (Hahn, 1998).

Over the last three decades, as the number of environmental laws and the resulting regulations have increased, the total annual cost of those mandates has increased considerably. Figure 1 shows that annual costs of environmental regulation have increased steadily both in absolute value and relative to the gross domestic product. Indeed, according to the first comprehensive government report on the benefits and costs of federal regulation produced by the Office of Management and Budget, the direct costs of federally mandated environmental quality regulations is now approximately U.S.$150 billion in 1996 dollars (Office of Management and Budget, 1997). This is more than half of total federal government spending on all domestic discretionary programs. Estimates of direct and indirect costs using general equilibrium economic modeling suggest that the costs are substantially higher (Hazilla and Kopp, 1990; Jorgenson and Wilcoxen, 1990). The benefits from those laws are less certain. Some estimates suggest that aggregate benefits are approximately equal to costs (Freeman, 1990; Hahn and Hird, 1991; Office of Management and Budget, 1997); others suggest that they substantially exceed costs (Environmental Protection Agency, 1997). [See Environmental Law.]

The aggregate analysis of benefits and costs masks some important information on individual regulations. It appears that many environmental regulations would not pass a standard benefit-cost test, even when the government's own estimates are used. For example, from 1980 to 1995, more than two-thirds of the federal government's environmental quality regulations fail a strict benefit-cost test (Hahn, 1998). As the EPA attempts to regulate even smaller risks in the future, there is a real danger that a larger fraction of rules could fail such a test. At the same time, there is reason to believe that more flexible regulations could save substantial amounts of money while reducing health risks. For example, one study found that a reallocation of mandated expenditures toward those regulations with the highest payoff to society could save as many as sixty thousand more lives a year at no additional cost (Tengs and Graham, 1996).

One reason for the relatively high level of inefficient environmental regulation is that many of the laws prohibit the balancing of economic benefits and costs (Crandall et al., 1997; Fraas, 1991; Portney, 1990). There have, however, been some recent attempts by Congress to place a greater emphasis on the balancing of benefits and costs. For example, under the Unfunded Mandates Reform Act of 1995, executive-branch agencies must prepare benefit-cost analyses for major rules. In addition, under the 1996 Safe Drinking Water Act Amendments, the EPA Administrator is required to publish a finding of whether the benefits of a maximum contaminant level standard justify the costs. Some scholars suggest that all major regulations, including environmental regulations, be required to pass a broadly defined benefit-cost test (Crandall et al., 1997). Others express more skepticism about the extent to which benefit-cost analysis should be relied upon in developing regulatory policy (for example, see Lave, 1996).

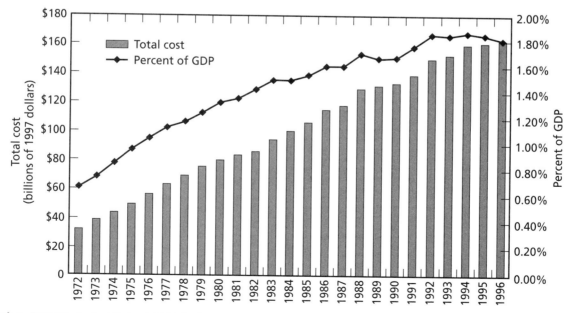

Regulation. FIGURE 1. Cost of Federal (U.S.) Environmental Regulation. (After Council of Economic Advisors, 1998; Environmental Protection Agency, 1990; and Office of Management and Budget, 1996.)

Another significant problem with environmental regulation is that current laws are overly prescriptive. The EPA has traditionally used a command-and-control approach to set uniform technology-based or performance-based standards. Both statutes and regulations frequently specify a preferred technology or set of technologies for achieving a given policy goal. For example, scrubbers were effectively required for some power plants as part of a compromise reached under the 1977 Clean Air Act Amendments (Ackerman and Hassler, 1981). Uniform performance standards are slightly more flexible, allowing a regulated entity to choose its own method for achieving a particular emission limit. While these approaches have been fairly successful in meeting some environmental goals, they are unduly costly because they do not take into account differences in pollution-control costs across firms.

Economists have long recommended more flexible approaches, such as an emissions tax or a marketable permit scheme that could achieve the same or similar environmental results at much lower cost (for example, see Bohm and Russell, 1985; Tietenberg, 1985). These market-based approaches create economic incentives that encourage firms to find cleaner and less expensive technologies to meet the environmental goal. For example, a firm that faces a tax on its air pollution has an incentive to reduce its emissions up to the point at which the cost of abatement is equal to the tax. By ensuring that each firm controls its emissions at the same marginal cost, the result is a cost-effective allocation of the overall burden of achieving the aggregate emissions-reduction goal. Many factors, such as the rising cost of environmental regulation and the increased importance of productivity and competitiveness in an increasingly global economy, have led to wider political support for market-based approaches (Hahn and Stavins, 1991). In recent years, tradable-permit schemes and taxes have been used to implement programs such as the phaseout of ozone-depleting chemicals and the reduction of sulfur dioxide emissions. [See Market Mechanisms.]

In general, economists agree that market-based mechanisms can help meet specified environmental goals cost-effectively. In addition, the use of economic analysis in balancing the costs and benefits of regulations can help ensure that environmental goals are set at desirable levels. But there is also widespread agreement that the practical application of these tools needs to be studied carefully to see how they can be designed and implemented most effectively.

The problem of selecting the right mix of regulatory instruments is formidable. In general, the appropriate regulatory tool will vary with the nature of the problem. If, for example, pollution results in local "hot spots," direct regulation may be the most effective tool. In con-

trast, for problems covering a broad area with a large number of sources, taxes or tradable permits may be more appropriate. The regulator will want to consider a number of factors in designing and implementing a policy, including economic efficiency, equity, transparency, and ease of administration.

[See also Joint Implementation; and Public Policy.]

BIBLIOGRAPHY

Ackerman, B. A., and W. T. Hassler. *Clean Coal/Dirty Air: Or How the Clean Air Act became a Multibillion-Dollar Bail-Out for High-Sulfur Coal Producers and What Should be Done About It.* New Haven: Yale University Press, 1981.

Bohm, P., and C. Russell. "Comparative Analysis of Alternative Policy Instruments." In *Handbook of Natural Resource and Energy Economics*, vol. 1, edited by A. V. Kneese and J. L. Sweeney. Amsterdam: North-Holland, 1985.

Council of Economic Advisers. "Economic Report of the President." Washington, D.C.: U.S. Government Printing Office, 1998.

Crandall, R. W., C. DeMuth, R. W. Hahn, R. E. Litan, P. S. Nivola, and P. R. Portney. "An Agenda for Reforming Federal Regulation." Washington, D.C.: AEI Press and Brookings Institution Press, 1997.

Environmental Protection Agency. *Environmental Investments: Cost of a Clean Environment.* EPA-230–11–90–083. Washington, D.C, 1990.

———. "The Benefits and Costs of the Clean Air Act: 1970 to 1990." Washington, D.C., 1997.

Fraas, A. G. "The Role of Economic Analysis in Shaping Environmental Policy." *Law and Contemporary Problems* 54 (1991), 113–125.

Freeman, A. M. "Water Pollution Policy." In *Public Policies for Environmental Protection*, edited by P. R. Portney. Washington, D.C.: Resources for the Future, 1990.

Hahn, R. W. "United States Environmental Policy: Past, Present and Future." *Natural Resources Journal* 34 (Spring 1994), 305–348.

———. "Regulatory Reform: Assessing the Government's Numbers." In *Reviving Regulatory Reform: A Global Perspective*, edited by R. W. Hahn. New York: Cambridge University Press and AEI Press, 1998.

Hahn, R. W., and J. A. Hird. "The Costs and Benefits of Regulation: Review and Synthesis." *Yale Journal on Regulation* 8 (Winter 1991), 233–278.

Hahn, R. W., and R. N. Stavins. "Incentive Based Environmental Regulation: A New Era from an Old Idea?" *Ecology Law Quarterly* 18 (1991), 1–42.

Hazilla, M., and R. J. Kopp. "The Social Cost of Environmental Quality Regulations: A General Equilibrium Analysis." *Journal of Political Economy* 98 (1990), 853–873.

Jorgenson, D. W., and P. J. Wilcoxen. "Environmental Regulation and U.S. Economic Growth." *Rand Journal of Economics* 21 (1990), 314–340.

Lave, L. B. "Benefit–Cost Analysis: Do the Benefits Exceed the Costs?" In *Risks, Costs, and Lives Saved: Getting Better Results from Regulation*, edited by R. W. Hahn. New York: Oxford University Press and AEI Press, 1996.

Office of Management and Budget. "More Benefits, Fewer Burdens." Washington, D.C., 1996.

———. "Report to Congress on the Costs and Benefits of Federal Regulation." Washington, D.C., 1997.

Portney, P. ed. *Public Policies for Environmental Protection.* Washington, D.C.: Resources for the Future, 1990.

Tengs, Tammy O., and John D. Graham. "The Opportunity Costs of Haphazard Social Investments in Life-Saving?" In *Risks, Costs, and Lives Saved: Getting Better Results from Regulation,* edited by R.W. Hahn. New York: Oxford University Press and AEI Press, 1996.

Tietenberg, T. *Emissions Trading: An Exercise in Reforming Pollution Policy.* Washington, D.C.: Resources for the Future, 1985.

—ROBERT W. HAHN AND FUMIE YOKOTA

RELIGION

The vast majority of humans identify with one or another of the world religions. The *International Bulletin of Missionary Research,* which provides estimates of world religious identifications, lists only 225 million atheists and 886 million nonreligious among the globe's six billion inhabitants. While there are great gaps between nominal identification and active practice among those listed, the major religions influence cultures far beyond the immediate sphere of committed members.

Reckoning nominal identification, one-third of humanity is Christian, with 2 billion followers, while Islam is growing rapidly, having attracted one-seventh of the global population at midcentury, and moving toward one-fifth, or 1.15 billion people, near the century's end. The third example of what are often called the *Abrahamaic, Jerusalemaic,* or *Peoples of the Book* communities, Judaism, is comparatively small—numbering about fifteen million—but is influential far beyond its numbers. Meanwhile, faiths classified as "Eastern" attract hundreds of millions: 806 million are listed as Hindu, 328 million are Buddhist, while Sikhs claim 20 million. The New-Religionist and Tribal Religionist movements, which are harder to classify, number 125 million and 100 million, respectively.

Adherence and participation in the various religions mean vastly different things in different cultures, but the numbers of estimated adherents themselves suggest how vital it is for those who think of population, development, and environmental responsibilities to make religion an important consideration.

What Religions Signify. Religion in these contexts does not mean only dogma or doctrine (many religions around the world have no formal versions of these), attendance at sanctuaries for sacred rites, or membership in congregations that can be numbered in yearbooks or encyclopedias. Religion instead deals first with what theologian Paul Tillich called people's "ultimate concern." Normally, people form communities that reinforce such concern. They prefer mythic language and symbolic forms to pragmatic expression, and enhance these with rites and ceremonies that relate to the passages of life, the seasons of the year, or presumed historic events at the root of such religions. Most imply or specify what might be called a *metaphysical backdrop,* which would mean a claim that, behind the ordinary visible human scene, a cosmic drama is occurring. All of this also calls for prescribed or encouraged behavioral forms.

Religious Implications. This picture of religion suggests why so many people relate to natural and anthropogenic change through religion, and why topics such as population, development, and the environment cannot be exhausted by resort only to political, scientific, or practical agendas.

Population, for example, alludes to the intimate and vital processes relating to love and marriage, birth and death, themes in which all religions specialize as humans try to make sense of an often mysterious world and their part in it. Development implies concern for the resources of the Earth and their cultivation, distribution, and stewardship. The myths and symbols, rites and ceremonies of the various faiths relate to precisely these themes. And environmental responsibility is integral to most religious proclamations and commandments.

However otherworldly some faiths may be, they survive also because they address the ordinary daily lives of people who are dependent upon resources of water, air, and earth. If what might be called "merely secular forces and impulses" address these zones of concern, they will meet resistance from religious leaders or be ignored by many informed and obedient followers. If, however, they tap into the religious impetuses, they will also be advanced by religious forces.

Thus Judaism and Christianity, on the first page of their sacred scriptures in the book of Genesis, hear of divine commands to the storied first human pair. These commands are ambiguous or can be interpreted in ways that may either enhance or be destructive of care. "Be fruitful and multiply, and fill the Earth and subdue it; and have dominion over . . . every living thing that moves upon the Earth." Though long cherished as a divine charter for parental responsibility in an underpopulated world and a call to vocational creativity in the natural environment, in recent decades—especially after an influential essay by critic Lynn White (1967)—this passage has been seen as a destructive agent. Under its influence, it was said, humans interpreted global life far too anthropocentrically and rendered nature exploitable by believers who thought they had a sacred charter for misusing and overusing environmental resources to the point of despoiling and depleting them.

When religious beliefs and practices are monitored or disciplined by effective religious authority, they acquire special power. A modern dictator, Joseph Stalin, is said to have sneered at formal churchly authority with a disdainful question, "How many divisions has the pope?" The pope, as head of the 992-million-member Catholic Church, did not need military divisions to wield power at the 1994 Cairo Conference on Population and Development. In tandem with spokespersons for some schools of Islamic thought, particularly those often classified as "fundamentalist," the Vatican, Catholicism's headquarters and a state that has a voice in the United Nations, attracted headlines and redirected the agenda for days. Its actions were in opposition to most methods of birth control and family planning that are advocated by the non-Catholic, non-Muslim-fundamentalist majorities. So long as the Vatican opposes what is often called "artificial means of birth control," it is difficult for the United Nations or private sources to be effective in population planning, especially in poorer regions of the world. It might be noted that in nations such as the United States, the vast majority of Catholic women, when polled, make clear that they do not follow Catholic strictures against birth control, but that does not lessen the energy or do much to limit the influence of Catholic authority on the global scene.

At the same time, Pope John Paul II, traveling around the world proclaiming a familiar theme of his papacy, *dignitatis humanae* ("of human dignity"), argues that the needs of expanding populations can be met if nations develop policies that make the best use of the resources of the Earth and enlarge their potential and production.

Religious Diversity. When religious leadership convenes to address development and environmentalism, authorities who cannot agree on God—who God is, whether God is, how one transacts with the sacred, and who determines truth about relations to the sacred—tend to concur that religions are chartered to support human dignity. Critics see most religion to be focused on otherworldliness and thus irresponsible about the global environment. It was true that many religions, by encouraging asceticism as religious discipline or offering hope to the hopelessly poor in this life (by promising compensation and reward in the life to come), devalued earthly concerns. So it was that many spiritual agencies were late to address the dangers of exploitation in the world of nature and human endeavor.

As movements encouraging sustainable development and global environmental responsibility have spread in the last third of the twentieth century, however, many religious leaders have explored anew their scriptures and tenets and have begun to accent underemphasized and overlooked themes. In the world of Western religion, often characterized as too devoted to human dominion over the nonhuman scene, this new exploration has encouraged the uncovering of scriptural and tradi-

tional devotion to the beauties of creation as gifts of the divine.

In an age of increasingly rapid communication and efficient use of media, populations have become aware of environmental attitudes of religions that had once seemed remote and had been regarded merely as competitors to their own cherished and exclusive faiths. So Westerners were taught by others to listen to and to respect as sacred the voices of earth, sky, and stream and to live in harmony with the rhythms of the year and the cycles of nature. Meanwhile, Western gospels of efficiency and productivity, many of them religiously informed, spread worldwide. As technological medicine led to increased population and the importation of exploitative practices to places where nature had not previously been regarded as a resource to be despoiled by humans, new problems arose. As an illustration, Native American attitudes to tribe, nature, and spirit, long dismissed as superstition by Christian and secular Americans, came to be regarded as offering valuable lessons far beyond the reservations in which American Indians had been segregated.

On Balance. At the end of the twentieth century, any balance sheet on which religious influence is to be appraised would reveal drastic changes and developments. Forces that have conventionally been labeled *secularizing* have increased in strength. There has been an increase in the influence of industry, technology, and commerce. Encroaching ideological forces—such as Communist materialism in the former Soviet Union and China, or post-Enlightenment thought prevailing in European and American universities—have increased their hold on human imagination and practice. Religion, then, has been expected progressively to dwindle, if not to disappear. If religion was to survive, it was often foreseen that only smaller defensive movements, of the sort that remained in the totalitarian world, or compromising and genteel versions in the free world, would endure. Instead, by all reckonings, religion has prospered, and its burgeoning versions are often those that make intense demands, possess strong holds on emotions, and are expressed in hard-line versions with which political forces have had to reckon.

While these versions of religions have often blocked a full range of approaches to population, development, and environmental issues, concurrently there has spread on the global scene both an awareness of religions that urge the celebration of the environment and concern for the nonhuman world, just as they promote population planning and sustainable development as pleasing to God or congruent with the sacred, and an awareness of the fragility of the environment and human responsibility to prosper and share intelligent use of resources.

[*See also* Belief Systems; Human Populations; *and* Population Policy.]

BIBLIOGRAPHY

Kurtz, L. *Gods in the Global Village: The World's Religions in Sociological Perspective.* Thousand Oaks, Calif.: Pine Forge Press, 1995.

White, Jr., L. "The Historical Roots of Our Ecologic Crisis." *Science* 155 (1967), 1203–1207.

—MARTIN E. MARTY

REMOTE SENSING

Remote sensing involves the collection of information about the Earth—the land surface, oceans, and atmosphere—from a distance, using instruments that measure electromagnetic radiation. Although aircraft are still widely used as platforms for these instruments, it is now more common for them to be mounted on satellites in Earth orbit. The main benefit of observing the Earth from orbital vantage points is that we can collect global-scale information, since almost the entire surface of the Earth can be monitored at regular intervals using a consistent methodology. The data yielded by satellite monitoring programs provide a powerful tool for assessing changes in the global environment.

Remote Sensing Systems. Remote sensing developed from the military application of aerial photographs for surveillance purposes. Aerial surveys use cameras fixed to look vertically down at the surface, and the exposures are timed to ensure at least a 60 percent overlap, so that every point on the surface appears on at least two photographs. Because the overlapping photographs are taken from slightly different vantage points (the aircraft has moved forward between the two exposures), parallax (relative displacement of objects in the two photographs depending on how far away they are from the camera) can be exploited to take three-dimensional measurements from the photographs, provided that the photograph scale, flying height, and focal length of the camera are known. The derivation of three-dimensional measurements from remotely sensed data is known as *stereo photogrammetry*. Although largely superseded nowadays by digital processing of satellite images for global monitoring, the many libraries of aerial photographs in existence provide unique palimpsests that are invaluable for extending temporal change analyses back before the satellite age.

Early manned space missions of the 1960s, such as the American Apollo missions, demonstrated the potential of orbital photography as a data source for environmental monitoring. Despite the acquisition of many thousands of photographs, the manned vehicle launches were too irregular, infrequent, and limited in spatial coverage to provide a global database of environmental information. The need for a constant source of remotely sensed data to build up a time series of images of the Earth taken with a uniform methodology led to the development of unmanned satellite remote sensing missions.

The initial civilian impetus behind this came from the requirement for meteorological data, and this is still the form of remote sensing that receives the widest audience. Here the requirement is for frequent collection of images to enable dynamic atmospheric features (such as depressions) to be tracked so that their movements and behavior can be predicted. For this, the satellite must remain above the same point on the Earth's surface, so that it may continually scan the area beneath. This requires the satellite to travel at the same speed as the Earth is rotating below, and is achieved in the so-called geostationary orbits, nearly 36,000 kilometers above the surface on the equatorial plane. A ring of these geostationary satellites is now in continuous Earth orbit; each scans the entire Earth disk (between one-third and one-quarter of the surface); and together they provide global data, mostly updated every thirty minutes or so, albeit at low spatial resolutions (typically 2.5–5 kilometers at the point immediately beneath the satellite).

The need for data at higher spatial resolutions necessitates lower Earth orbits, usually at less than 1,000 kilometers altitude. Because the satellite will be able to see only a small part of the Earth at these altitudes, it is necessary for it to fly in a roughly north–south direction so that, given the rotation of the Earth beneath it, a global coverage is achieved over time. It usually takes about two weeks for the entire Earth to be overflown in this way, before the satellite returns to look down at the same area again (this is known as the *repeat frequency*). The orbits are chosen to ensure that the Sun will always be the same distance above the horizon every time a particular area is overflown by the satellite, thereby simplifying comparison of images taken on different dates. Satellites that use this orbital configuration are known as Sun-synchronous polar orbiters, although they do not, as a rule, go right over the poles, but approach to within 8° or so.

A variety of instruments are carried on both geostationary and polar orbiting missions to collect information about the Earth's surface and atmosphere. Use of photographic film is limited to manned missions, such as space shuttle flights, since film must be returned to Earth for processing. Unmanned missions of long duration must use radio communications to download their observations to ground receiving stations, and so data must be captured electronically. The most common approach is to use radiometers, instruments that measure the amount of radiation upwelling through the atmosphere. By fixing a mirror to scan across the direction of flight, and using the forward motion of the spacecraft, a two-dimensional array of measurements of radiation can be made (this is called a *scanning radiometer;* see

Figure 1A). An alternative approach dispenses with the scanning mirror and uses instead a line of detectors (this is called a *multilinear array*; see Figure 1B). Each instantaneous measurement of upwelling radiation corresponds to an area of the Earth's surface known as a pixel. By splitting the upwelling radiation into its different wavelength components (Figure 2), simultaneous measurements can be made of different types of radiation coming from each pixel. Typically, these systems sample radiation in the visible, near and shortwave in-

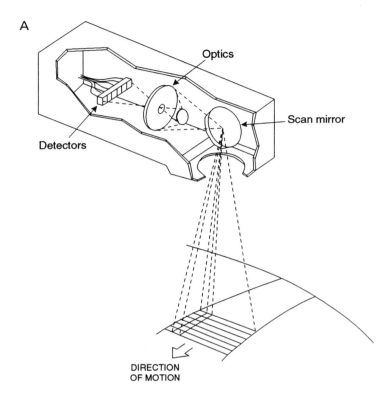

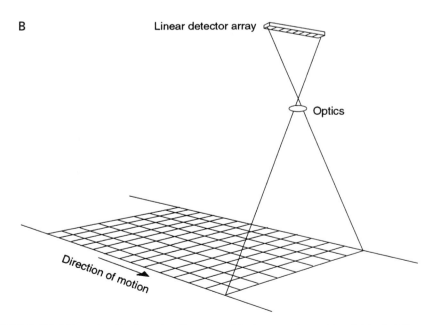

Remote Sensing. FIGURE 1. (A) A Scanning Radiometer. The mirror scans across the track of the orbiting satellite to build up a two-dimensional image. (B) A Multilinear Array. The line of detectors samples a strip of data, building up a two-dimensional image as the satellite advances.

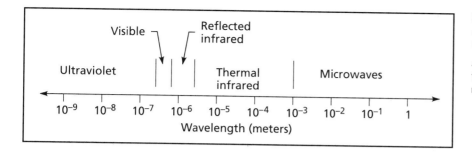

Remote Sensing. Figure 2. The Part of the Electromagnetic Spectrum Used in Remote Sensing.

A package of detectors that are sensitive to different wavelength ranges can be mounted on satellites.

frared (the range of wavelengths produced by the Sun), and thermal infrared (emitted by the Earth as it warms by absorption of solar radiation) regions of the electromagnetic spectrum. This simultaneous measurement of several wavelength channels of radiation forms the basis of multispectral remote sensing. The systems are referred to as *passive*, in the sense that they merely measure ambient radiation (either solar radiation reflected by the Earth or thermal radiation emitted from the Earth).

The utility of multispectral systems for Earth observation arises because the amount of energy absorbed or reflected at different wavelengths can be interpreted to yield information about the target being observed. Figure 3 shows the reflectance characteristics of soil, vegetation, and water in the visible to shortwave infrared region of the spectrum. The vegetation spectral reflectance curve shows strong absorption of photosynthetically active radiation around 0.4 and 0.6 micrometer, which corresponds to visible blue and visible red light; the small peak in between at 0.5 micrometer (visible green) gives healthy vegetation its characteristic green color, but the higher-magnitude reflectance peak at 1.0 micrometer results from strong reflectance in the near infrared due to scattering by the leaf cell structure. These changes in absorption and reflectance with wave-

length yield a characteristic spectral signature for vegetation, which enables it to be readily distinguished from water and soil using measurements from multispectral remote sensing instruments. Many land cover types have characteristic spectral signatures and can easily be mapped by multispectral systems. Even subtle differences between different types of vegetation can be discriminated with modern systems, but confusion can occur between targets with similar spectral signatures. Similar signatures can also be defined at longer thermal wavelengths for many surface cover types, but in this case they result in wavelength-dependent variations in radiation emitted from the Earth. The extraction of information from remotely sensed data, such as the identity and composition of the target, is achieved by computer image processing, using algorithms designed to handle the digital data yielded by remote sensing instruments.

A growing number of satellite missions are making use of active systems that provide their own source of radiation. Most commonly, an antenna is used to irradiate the Earth with longer-wavelength microwave radiation; these systems are known by the acronym radar (radio detection and ranging). Imaging of the Earth by radar is completely different from the passive techniques discussed above, and different sorts of computer algorithm are needed to process the data. Radar systems point an antenna at the surface below, to one side of the ground track of the satellite (Figure 4), a configuration that gives radar images a characteristic side-lit appearance. A pulse of microwave energy is transmitted to the Earth, and the antenna waits to receive the signal that is scattered back from the surface. Objects nearer the antenna (near range) will yield returns sooner than objects farther away (far range). This means that the returning signal can be spatially referenced relative to the position of the antenna. By the time the antenna is ready to produce its next pulse, the spacecraft will have moved on, so that the next pulse irradiates an adjacent strip of ground. Although the pulse tends to spread out as it goes away from the antenna (yielding a lower spatial resolution of the return as one moves further along range), it is possible by measuring the Doppler shift of objects in the returning signal to process the data in

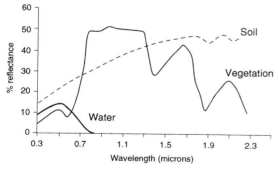

Remote Sensing. Figure 3. The Reflectance Characteristics of Soil, Vegetation, and Water in the Visible to Shortwave Infrared Region of the Electromagnetic Spectrum.

Detectors can sample sections of this wavelength range, allowing multispectral analysis of surface reflectance.

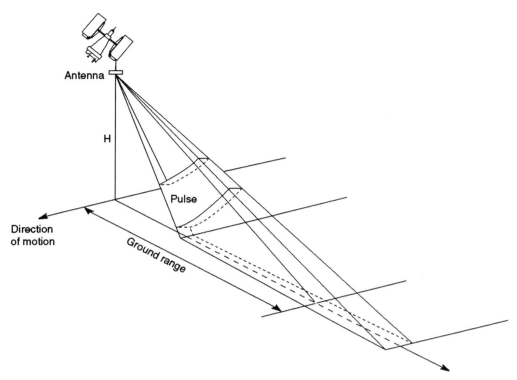

Remote Sensing. FIGURE 4. Principles of a Radar (Active Microwave) Remote Sensing System.

A pulse of microwave radiation is transmitted to the surface, to one side of the subsatellite track. The antenna then measures the amount of this pulse backscattered from targets along the range. Because of the forward motion of the satellite, the next pulse will collect information about the adjacent strip, so building up a two-dimensional image.

such a way that an apparent narrow strip is maintained along the full range. The principle is that objects in the path of the advancing radar swath will appear to be approaching the antenna (phase shifting the microwave pulse toward higher frequencies), switching to a phase shift toward lower frequencies after the target has been overflown and appears to be receding from the antenna. This phase shift can be resolved by modern orbital radar systems and incorporated into the processing to yield spatial resolutions of 12–15 meters or so. This is known as the "synthetic aperture" technique and the instruments are known by the acronym SAR (Synthetic Aperture Radar). The intensity of the returning signal is controlled by the nature of the surface being observed. Surfaces oriented toward the antenna will appear bright since they scatter more incident radiation back in that direction, while surfaces facing away from the antenna will scatter more radiation in the opposite direction, and so will appear darker in the image. At much smaller scales, rougher surfaces will scatter back more energy than smoother surfaces, and moister surfaces will scatter back more radiation than dry surfaces. Another important aspect of radar is that the longer wavelengths involved are able to penetrate into some surfaces in certain circumstances, yielding subsurface information

such as soil moisture content. However, this represents an added complication because, to understand the energy–matter interactions taking place, one has to understand volume interactions as well as surface interactions. A complete understanding of all these processes remains elusive, but the data provided by orbital SAR systems are proving to be very useful for global monitoring. Because they provide their own radiation, SAR systems can operate both day and night. Furthermore, because microwave radiation can pass through clouds, radars have an all-weather capability, a major advantage over passive multispectral systems.

Observing Changing Environments. Remote sensing techniques play a critical role in monitoring many aspects of the changing global environment. Some of the major applications are discussed below; numerous other applications are covered in sources listed in the bibliography.

Climate. Prior to the advent of satellite data, components of the Earth radiation balance, such as albedo and outgoing energy flux, were estimated rather than measured. Nowadays, satellites monitor a range of variables intrinsic to the global climate system: energy and radiation budgets, global moisture and temperature distributions, cloud cover, and wind flow. The main use of these data is as input into numerical climate models, and also to validate the output of these models over shorter time scales. To evaluate anthropogenic impacts on climate, it is first necessary to establish global-scale baseline regimes for climate variables. Although the time series of satellite data (three decades or so) is probably too short to yield a multiyear climatology suitable for detection of trends, satellites enable collection of global data that are more complete, uniform, frequent, and objective than data collected by conventional field-based techniques.

Several large programs have been set up to ensure that these data are put to effective use. Examples include the World Climate Research Programme (WCRP), the International Satellite Cloud Climatology Project (ISCCP), the International Satellite Land Surface Climatology Project (ISLSCP), and the Global Energy and Water Cycle Experiment (GEWEX). The WCRP aims to develop the fundamental scientific understanding of the climate system that is needed to determine the extent to which climate can be predicted, and the extent of human influence on climate. The ISCCP was established as part of the WCRP to collect and analyze satellite radiance measurements to infer the global distribution of clouds, the primary focus being the elucidation of their effects on the radiation balance. The ISLSCP was established under the United Nations Environment Programme to promote the use of satellite data for the global land surface data sets needed for climate models. A series of field experiments have been conducted to collect and validate satellite data for land surface models. The First ISLSCP Field Experiment (FIFE) was conducted over the period 1987–1989 on the Konza Prairie in Kansas, to provide satellite-derived data on land surface states such as biomass, cover type, and temperature, and on land surface processes such as transpiration and photosynthesis. This work was continued in the Boreal Ecosystem–Atmosphere Study (BOREAS) in Canada. GEWEX was initiated by the WCRP to observe and model the hydrologic cycle and energy fluxes in the atmosphere, at the land surface, and in the upper oceans. The Global Precipitation Climatology Project (GPCP) is an element of GEWEX set up to provide monthly mean precipitation data on a 2.5 × 2.5° latitude–longitude grid for the period 1986–2000, by merging infrared and microwave satellite estimates of precipitation with rain gauge data from more than thirty thousand stations.

The Global Climate Observing System (GCOS) is being developed to provide the observational data required by these programs. The U.S. National Aeronautics Space Administration's (NASA's) Upper Atmosphere Research Satellite (UARS) was launched in 1991 and carries four instruments (CLAES, ISAMS, MLS, and HALOE) that measure atmospheric composition and temperature,

two instruments (HRDI and WINDII) that observe atmospheric winds, and three other instruments (SOLSTICE, SUSIM, and PEM) that measure the energy inputs from solar radiation and charged particles. A tenth instrument (ACRIM II) continues NASA's solar constant measurements. The Earth Probe Total Ozone Mapping Spectrometer (TOMS) makes measurements of ultraviolet (UV)-absorbing aerosols in the troposphere, which play a major role in the Earth's climate. The TOMS instrument also enables detailed mapping of the Antarctic ozone hole and the springtime decrease of ozone in the Northern Hemisphere. The Tropical Rainfall Measuring Mission (TRMM), launched November 1997, is a joint mission between NASA and the National Space Development Agency (NASDA) of Japan designed to monitor and study tropical rainfall and the associated release of energy that helps to power the global atmospheric circulation. TRMM carries five instruments: the first spaceborne Precipitation Radar (PR), the TRMM Microwave Imager (TMI), a Visible and Infrared Scanner (VIRS), a Clouds and the Earth's Radiant Energy System (CERES), and a Lightning Imaging Sensor (LIS).

Oceans. The oceanic environment presents some major challenges to environmental monitoring because of its highly dynamic nature and the sparse direct observations that are available. Remote sensing enables mapping and monitoring of many oceanic variables, including sea surface temperature, ocean currents, and ocean color.

The ability to measure sea surface temperature is a vital part of global environmental monitoring, since the oceans have an enormous heat-storing capacity and thus can exchange large amounts of energy with the atmosphere. Traditionally, sea surface temperature measurements were collected from a number of sources: data buoys, weather ships, or engine room intake temperatures from shipping. Prior to the advent of satellite observations, the U.K. Meteorological Office produced charts of five-day-mean sea surface temperatures based on these data. These showed highly generalized contours, but lacked spatial detail. However, the critical role of the oceans in the Earth system means that more detailed data are required.

The use of thermal channels on multispectral instruments enables estimates of sea surface temperature to be made. This is because the oceans are very good absorbers and emitters of energy, enabling thermal infrared radiance measurements to be converted to "brightness temperature" estimates using the inverse of Planck's radiation equation. Thermal channels on the Advanced Very High Resolution Radiometer (AVHRR) carried on board the U.S. National Oceanic and Atmospheric Administration (NOAA) series of meteorological satellites can measure sea surface temperatures to an accuracy of approximately 1 K. However, climate models require accuracies of 0.2 K. More recent systems, such as the Along Track Scanning Radiometer (ATSR) carried by the European Earth Resources Satellite (ERS) missions, enable improved estimation close to this accuracy. The ATSR system yields two independent looks at each pixel, each with a different atmospheric path length, allowing better correction for the radiance of the intervening atmospheric column. Other systems attempt to correct for atmospheric path radiance using simultaneous measurements at different wavelengths, the "split-window technique."

Problems of comparing satellite-derived temperatures with *in situ* measurements arise because the satellite is measuring what is known as the skin temperature, the temperature of a surface film of water less than 1 millimeter thick, whereas *in situ* data correspond to the upper few meters of the ocean, and this is usually of more importance to the oceanographer. The skin temperatures are usually around 1 K cooler than the bulk temperatures 1 meter below the surface.

Ocean currents can often be determined from multitemporal analysis of sea surface temperature maps, but other systems monitor the changes in sea level associated with the currents. To relate changes in ocean currents to atmospheric and climate patterns, TOPEX/Poseidon, launched in 1992, measures sea level with an accuracy of less than 13 centimeters using radar altimeters. It complements a number of international oceanographic and meteorological programs, including the World Ocean Circulation Experiment (WOCE) and the Tropical Ocean and Global Atmosphere (TOGA) program, both sponsored by the WCRP.

Ocean color is another important global parameter that is monitored by remote sensing. The Coastal Zone Colour Scanner mission (1978–1986) demonstrated the potential of ocean color instruments; it is being continued by the Sea-Viewing Wide Field-of-view Sensor mission, launched in August 1997. Other systems that sense radiation in the visible part of the spectrum can also be used. Ocean color is related to productivity, since the instruments are picking up photosynthetic activity of phytoplankton. The role of phytoplankton in acting as a sink for atmospheric carbon dioxide is one of the main uncertainties of the global warming debate, and accurate and global monitoring of oceanic productivity is therefore a vital remote sensing task. The same approach can be used for monitoring cultural eutrophication in coastal and inland waters.

Ice. Snow, sea ice, and land ice exert a profound influence on local and global climatic and oceanic regimes. They cover some 10 percent of the Earth surface area, and their high albedos and thermal and radiative properties are climatically highly significant. Changes in ice cover in the polar regions and at high elevations are likely to provide early indications of global climate changes. However, detection of any such trends requires a long time series of internally consistent global data sets, which is where remote sensing can be of use. The same information is important for navigation through polar waters.

Passive microwave radiometers, a technology adopted by Russian missions but now widely employed on many missions, can be used to map sea ice extent. Because emitted radiation at these frequencies is of a low intensity, the spatial resolution of these systems is poor, typically 25–30 kilometer pixels. Problems also occur as a result of different brightness temperatures of first-year and multiyear ice. The situation is simpler in Antarctica than the Arctic, since less of the first-year ice survives over the summer. Active microwave (SAR) systems are able to resolve much smaller sea ice features. The Canadian RADARSAT mission, launched in 1995, provides a variety of beam selections that can image swaths from 35 to 500 kilometers with resolutions from 10 to 100 meters. Although used for numerous applications, one of the primary roles is monitoring of sea ice around Canada's coasts. [*See* Sea Ice.]

Vegetation. Issues of food security under changing environments demand current and accurate information on a global basis with respect to the extent and condition of the world's major food and fiber crops. Data from satellites such as Landsat and SPOT are widely used to study vegetation patterns, and have been used to collect crop inventories and other data over large areas, as in the case of the Large Area Crop Inventory Experiment (LACIE) initiated in 1974. The Landsat program is one of the longest-running remote sensing missions. The first Landsat satellite was launched in 1972. The most recent mission, Landsat 7, was launched in April 1999. The instruments on the Landsat satellites have recorded millions of images, archived in the United States and at receiving stations around the world, forming a unique resource for global change research and other applications. The main Landsat sensors are the Multispectral Scanner (MSS), with four spectral bands covering visible to near infrared wavelengths at a 79-meter spatial resolution, and the Thematic Mapper (TM), with six spectral bands covering the visible to shortwave infrared at 30-meter spatial resolution and a thermal band with 120-meter resolution.

The SPOT mission is a collaborative venture between France, Belgium, and Sweden. SPOT-1, launched in 1986, was pointable (giving it a stereo capability), and it had a higher spatial resolution than existing civilian missions; 10 meters in panchromatic mode and 20 meters in multispectral (visible green, visible red, and near infrared) mode. It was followed by SPOT-2 and SPOT-3. SPOT-4, launched in March 1998, extends the multispectral capabilities of the SPOT mission into the short-wave infrared. It also carries the Vegetation instrument, a very wide-angle (2,000-kilometer swath) instrument with a spatial resolution of around 1 kilometer and the same spectral bands used on the earlier SPOT missions.

Remote sensing has proved particularly useful for monitoring extensive land cover types such as tropical forests and savannah rangelands. The requirement for global data requires a commensurate low spatial resolution to avoid data overload problems. Most commonly used for regional vegetation mapping are the 1.1-kilometer spatial resolution AVHRR data, known as Local Area Coverage (LAC) data; for global vegetation mapping these data are resampled at a rate of four pixels out of every fifteen to a nominal resolution of about 4 kilometers, known as Global Area Coverage (GAC) data. The AVHRR Land Biosphere data set has been generated from GAC data for global change studies. Vegetation and brightness temperature maps are provided at 8 kilometers and 1° (latitude, longitude) spatial resolutions and temporal resolutions of daily, ten day, and monthly. Currently, over eleven years of data are available (1981–1992). [See Forests.]

Future Prospects. NASA's Mission to Planet Earth (MTPE) aims to put in place a system for monitoring global change well into the new century. The first major MTPE mission is the Earth Observing System (EOS) AM-1 satellite, launched December 1999. This carries several instruments of importance to environmental monitoring. The Moderate Resolution Imaging Spectrometer (MODIS) enables the compilation of a comprehensive global database of sea and land surface temperature, ocean color, vegetation, clouds and aerosols, and snow cover. The Advanced Spaceborne Thermal Emission and Reflection Radiometer (ASTER) includes a five-channel thermal radiometer with significant potential for improved lithological mapping at 90-meter spatial resolution. The Multi-Angle Imaging Spectroradiometer (MISR) improves global maps of albedo by making observations of the surface at different angles. The Measurement of Pollution in the Troposphere (MOPITT) instrument enables global measurement of carbon monoxide and methane. The Clouds and the Earth Radiation Energy System (CERES) experiment allows the compilation of long-term measurements of global radiation budget. EOS AM-1, along with the many other planned missions, will ensure a massive data stream of environmental information over the next decade, but further effort is needed to ensure that the user community has the necessary tools and trained personnel to process and incorporate these data into models of environmental change, so that we may derive maximum benefit from our investment in remote sensing.

[See also Global Monitoring; Land Use; and Water Quality.]

BIBLIOGRAPHY

Asrar, G., ed. *Theory and Applications of Optical Remote Sensing.* New York: Wiley, 1989.
Carleton, A. M. *Satellite Remote Sensing in Climatology.* London: Belhaven, 1991.
Cracknell, A. P. *The Advanced Very High Resolution Radiometer.* London: Taylor and Francis, 1997.
Drury, S. A. *Image Interpretation in Geology.* 2d ed. London: Allan and Unwin, 1993.
Engman, E. T., and R. J. Gurney. *Remote Sensing in Hydrology.* London: Chapman and Hall, 1991.
King, M. D., and D. D. Herring. "Monitoring Earth's Vital Signs." *Scientific American* (April 2000), pp. 92–97. An illustrated account of Terra, the fourth satellite in NASA's Earth Observing System. It uses five state-of-the-art sensors to diagnose the planet's health.
Kingsley, S., and S. Quegan. *Understanding Radar Systems.* London: McGraw-Hill, 1992.
Kondratyev, K. Y., et al. *Remote Sensing of the Earth from Space: Atmospheric Correction.* Berlin: Springer, 1992.
Kramer, H. J. *Earth Observation Remote Sensing.* Berlin: Springer, 1992.
Massom, R. A. *Satellite Remote Sensing of Polar Regions.* London: Belhaven, 1991.
Rees, W. G. *Physical Principles of Remote Sensing.* Cambridge: Cambridge University Press, 1990.

—KEVIN WHITE

RENEWABLE ENERGY SOURCES

Renewable energy sources are a diverse group of energy resources that share two important characteristics: First, renewable energy sources tend to be nondepletable, or natural, energy flows rather than stock resources, making them sustainable energy sources. Second, the renewables tend to have a low level of risk and environmental impact in comparison with other energy sources, such as fossil fuels and nuclear energy. The principal harnessable renewable energy sources include biomass, hydroelectric, geothermal, solar, and wind. Renewable energy resources are distributed unevenly around the globe. Nearly every place on Earth has the potential to use at least one of the renewable sources of energy successfully.

Renewable energy sources are the oldest energy resources used by humankind: biomass, water, and wind energy have been in use for hundreds or thousands of years. Renewables are also among the newest of energy sources, with many promising, innovative renewable energy technologies in precommercial stages of development. Renewable resources can be converted into virtually any energy form, including solid, liquid, and gaseous fuels, heat, and electricity. Renewables can provide for any end-use application that requires energy as an input. Many believe that renewables are poised to make an increasing contribution to the world's energy supplies.

Biomass. Resources for biomass energy include plant matter and products derived therefrom. Biomass represents solar energy that is collected and stored by the Earth's biota, and is available in the form of chemical energy. Most applications of biomass energy involve combustion processes, similar to the use of fossil fuels, although advanced, noncombustion conversion technologies, such as fuel cells, are under active development.

Most of the biomass used as an energy resource is woody material, the majority of which can be classified as waste or residue material. Most of this material is derived from forestry and forest products manufacturing operations, the remainder mainly from agricultural operations. Nonwoody biomass resources such as agricultural residues and animal wastes are also used for energy production, often in liquid or gaseous fuels applications.

There are two fundamentally different kinds of biomass energy use in the world today: residential heating and cooking applications, and commercial energy applications. Biomass fuels are used for residential heating and cooking by a large number of the world's poorest people, usually employing cheap, low-efficiency conversion devices (cooking stoves and heaters). In many cases, this type of biomass energy use is causing serious environmental damage, as increasing numbers of people lacking access to commercial fuels deplete finite local supplies of biomass resources. Commercial biomass energy applications, such as electricity, steam, and alcohol fuels production, are usually performed in conjunction with higher-valued forestry and agricultural operations, and in most cases can be operated in such a way as to enhance the environmental performance of the overall enterprise by providing a productive and environmentally superior waste disposal alternative for residues that, in the absence of energy applications, would require some other form of disposal.

Biomass fuel cycles can include a variety of processes and transformations. The following are some of the most commonly employed biomass fuel cycle steps: production; harvesting/collection; transportation; physical processing; chemical transformation; storage; end use.

Commercially proven technologies for each of these fuel cycle steps are readily available. Solid-fuel biomass power plants, for example, have been in continuous service for over fifty years. On the other hand, many of the technologies in common use today continue to benefit from progress down their learning curves, and a variety of new technologies that offer the promise of significant efficiency improvements and cost savings in the future are under development.

Biomass energy can contribute a significant, but not unlimited, amount of energy to world commercial energy supplies. Biomass energy production is an inherently expensive source of energy because of the small size typical of biomass conversion systems and the relatively high costs for fuel handling and storage, the latter relating to the fact that biomass is a solid material of low energy density. Thus economic rather than physical considerations ultimately limit the amount of biomass energy that will be used. Table 1 shows estimates of the amounts of renewable energy that might be producible at a global level, as well as current U.S. production levels.

The one economic advantage that biomass energy systems can have over fossil fuel systems is in the area of fuel cost. Residues and byproducts produced in the course of higher-valued forestry and agricultural activities in many situations can be delivered as fuels for little or no cost. More extensive use of a region's biomass energy resources will require the use of increasingly expensive fuel sources, which produces an economically self-limiting system. Table 2 shows estimates of the cost of electricity production from renewable resources.

Renewable Energy Sources. TABLE 1. Global Renewable Resource Availability

	GLOBAL FLOW (TW)*	"HARVESTABLE"[†] (TW)	UNITED STATES INSTALLED CAPACITY (GW)	UNITED STATES ENERGY PRODUCED (BILLION KWH)
Biomass	100	10	10.4	64.1
Hydroelectric	41,000	3	78.5	379.7
Geothermal	26	<1	2.8	16.9
Solar Thermal	86,000	50	0.33	0.9
Wind	1,500	1.5	1.8	3.5

*TW = terawatts = trillion watts; GW = gigawatts = billion watts; kWh = kilowatt hour.

[†]Estimates of the maximum amount of energy from each source that could be harvested, given development of all reasonable sites in the world.

SOURCE: Ehrlich et al. (1977); United States Department of Energy (1997).

Renewable Energy Sources. TABLE 2. Cost of Electricity Production from Renewable Resources

	U.S.$ PER KILOWATT HOUR	CHARACTERISTICS
Biomass	0.06–0.11	Base load generating source, size limited by resource availability
Hydroelectric	<0.01–0.06	Major global energy source, from small scale to huge
Geothermal	0.02–0.05	Base load generating source, available in limited regions
Solar thermal	0.09–0.15	Peak generating source, storage can extend to intermediate load
Photovoltaics	0.08–0.15	Peak generating source, ideal for remote applications
Wind	0.04–0.07	Intermittent source, increasingly competitive

Advocates of truly large-scale utilization of biomass as an energy resource look to energy crops as the means to provide the amounts of biomass fuels that would be required, but the unfavorable economics of such an enterprise make energy crops a very unlikely option for the foreseeable future.

Hydroelectric Power. The hydrologic cycle represents one of the major global flows of solar energy. Water that is evaporated from the world's oceans and deposited on land contains potential energy that can be collected and transformed into forms suitable for human use. Hydroelectric (hydro) power has been used for centuries in the provision of mechanical energy, and has always been a mainstay of the world's electricity supply. Some of the world's largest structures are hydroelectric dams. [See Dams.] These megaprojects are the largest electric generating units in the world. Hydroelectricity can also be generated at very small and intermediate scales, however.

The conversion of hydro energy into useful forms is accomplished by directing descending water through a turbine, which converts the energy into spinning mechanical energy and then into electricity. The amount of hydroelectricity that can be generated at a given site is a function of two factors: the amount of water flow that can be directed through the power house, and the vertical drop between the inflow and the outflow. Hydro turbines can be powered by running river water, or an impoundment can be created to provide seasonal storage and power production modulation. Hydro dams are often multipurpose projects, providing consumptive water supply, flood protection, and recreation, in addition to electricity.

There are two primary types of hydro turbine: impulse turbines, and reaction turbines. The impulse turbine is the simpler type. Impulse turbines operate at atmospheric pressure, and are able to convert only the kinetic energy in flowing water. The classic water wheel is an example of an impulse turbine. Reaction turbines and their associated penstocks are sealed systems that operate at pressures above atmospheric, and can convert both the kinetic and the hydrostatic pressure of flowing water. Most large-scale hydroelectric generating facilities have reaction-type turbines.

In the best applications, hydroelectricity can be one of the cheapest sources of electricity generation, as shown in Table 2. It is difficult to generalize about the economics of hydroelectric generation, however, because the costs are very site-specific. Usually more than half of the cost of hydroelectric generation is represented by the dam and associated facilities. The cost can also be a factor of the remoteness of the location of the generating source.

Many of the best hydro generating sites in the world have already been developed. Many of the world's countries and regions have electric grids that are heavily dependent on hydroelectric generating sources, to the extend that their grids experience supply interruptions during periods of drought. Both of these factors limit the potential expandability of hydroelectric generation in the future, although considerable potential still exists in some areas.

Geothermal Energy. The only renewable energy source that is not related to the flow of solar energy is geothermal energy. The source of geothermal energy is stored heat and nuclear decay in the Earth's core and mantle. Geothermal energy flows throughout the Earth; however, the flows are highly nonuniform, and geothermal energy production is mainly of interest in regions of high geothermal flows. Geothermal resource zones tend to be located in regions with high seismic potential, such as the Pacific Rim.

Geothermal resources provide lower temperatures and pressures for energy production than fossil fuel and biomass systems, which means that energy conversion efficiencies tend to be lower. The major categories of exploitable geothermal energy resources include dry steam sources, hot brines, and hot dry rocks. Dry steam sources are the easiest and cheapest to exploit, because the dry steam that is brought to the surface can be used directly as a working fluid for energy conversion and distribution. Hot brines require heat exchange equipment that can withstand the corrosive conditions of the resource, and hot dry rocks require the injection of water to the underground resource zone.

Geothermal energy resources can be used for direct heating applications, such as district heating and industrial process uses, and for electricity production. Geothermal energy resources are used in more than twenty countries located in all areas of the world. Worldwide installed geothermal electric generating capacity is more than 5,800 megawatts, almost half of which is in the United States (see Table 1). In addition, more than 4,000 megawatts of direct heat applications use geothermal energy.

The first stage in the development of a geothermal resource is the drilling of exploratory wells in candidate resource zones, which is an expensive, high-risk activity. When a site has been proven for development, the next step is to drill production and injection wells. The production wells are used to bring the geothermal resources to the surface. Injection wells are used to dispose of the used fluids after energy has been extracted, and to introduce a heat transfer fluid for hot dry rock sources.

For power production, geothermal energy sources are converted to electricity with the use of heat engines. High-quality geothermal resources can be used to power conventional steam turbines, either using the geothermal steam directly in the turbine, or heat exchange in a heat-recovery boiler to protect the turbine from the corrosive geothermal fluids. For poorer-quality resources, turbines using alternative working fluids are more appropriate than steam turbines. A variety of specialized turbines have been developed for the production of energy from geothermal resources.

The production of geothermal energy at good resource sites is cost competitive with conventional energy sources, as shown in Table 2. This is a characteristic that geothermal energy shares only with hydroelectric power among the renewable energy options. Geothermal energy production is pursued successfully in many areas of the world without any special subsidies or inducements. In California, geothermal systems can produce electricity for costs in the range U.S.$0.02–0.05 per kilowatt hour.

Solar Energy. The Earth–atmosphere system receives a constant input of solar radiation at a rate of approximately 1,350 watts per square meter. At any given time, exactly half of the Earth's surface is being irradiated by the Sun. A variety of technologies have been developed to collect and convert solar radiation into useful energy supplies. Solar energy can be used to provide thermal energy for heating, cooking, and a variety of process applications, or it can be converted into electricity. Electricity can be produced from collected solar heat using heat engines, or solar radiation can be converted directly into electricity via photovoltaic conversion devices.

The total insolation received at any given spot is a combination of direct radiation from the Sun, diffuse radiation from the sky, and reflected radiation from surrounding terrain. Direct radiation is the kind of light that can cast shadows. It is the only kind of solar energy that can be reflected and focused. Depending on atmospheric conditions, the proportion of available solar energy that is in the form of direct radiation can vary from almost 100 percent on a clear day to zero under full cloud cover.

One of the oldest forms of solar energy use is passive solar architecture. Buildings are fixed structures that receive solar radiation on a daily cycle that varies seasonally. Passive solar architecture uses design techniques such as angles, shadings, glazings, orientation, window placement, and insulation to allow a building to minimize solar heat gain during the summer and maximize solar heat gain during the winter. A carefully designed passive solar building can cut energy use for interior heating and cooling by 70 percent or more compared with conventional buildings.

The simplest type of active solar energy collection device is the flat-plate collector. Flat-plate collectors come in a variety of configurations, which can vary from a sheet of metal or plastic to a coil of hose. The essential elements of a flat-plate collector include the absorber surface and a circulating heat-transfer fluid, which is usually water or air. Flat-plate collectors can receive both direct and diffuse solar energy. Insulation, selective coatings, and transparent cover sheets can be used to boost the collector's performance, as can tilting of the collector to be as close as possible to perpendicular to the Sun's direct radiation.

Flat-plate collectors are limited in terms of the intensity of heat energy that they can deliver. In general, flat-plate collectors can produce heat energy of temperatures up to approximately 80°C. To produce higher working temperatures, it is necessary to concentrate the solar energy that is being collected. Solar energy can be focused through a lens or reflected by a field of mirrors on to a surface, significantly raising the temperatures of working fluids. Higher working-fluid temperatures represent higher-quality energy, which can expand the range of applications that can be powered with solar energy. However, the boost in energy quality comes at a cost, both in terms of higher capital and operating costs for the equipment, and lower energy conversion efficiencies. In general, concentration factors of up to about ten times can be accomplished with focusing collectors, while applications that require concentration ratios of more than ten times require reflector systems.

Concentrating solar collectors can only utilize direct solar insolation. Because they rely on focusing or reflecting the incident solar beam, they must usually be steered to follow the Sun's movement through the sky, which occurs on both a daily and a seasonally variable pattern. Collectors can track the Sun with either one- or two-axis tracking mechanisms. Two-axis tracking is more expensive, but provides more precise tracking of the Sun.

There are several different kinds of concentrating solar energy collector system. The major technologies that have been developed include flat and Fresnel lens focused collectors, parabolic-trough and dish collectors, and central-receiver systems that use a field of reflectors called heliostats. Central receivers are the most expensive, require the most precise tracking, and can achieve the highest concentration ratios. Working-fluid temperatures in the range of thousands of degrees range have been achieved with central-receiver configurations.

Solar thermal electric technology. In addition to providing energy for a variety of heating applications, solar collectors can be used to produce electricity using conventional heat engines. The efficiency of solar heat conversion to electricity is limited by a physical paradox: high working-fluid temperatures have a positive effect on heat engine efficiencies, but a negative effect on collector efficiencies.

A variety of technologies are in use or under development for the conversion of solar heat energy to electricity. The technology that has achieved the greatest commercial development is the Luz parabolic-trough technology, in which parabolic-trough collectors focus solar energy on tubes through which a mineral oil heat transfer fluid is circulated. The hot oil is used to generate steam in a heat exchanger, with the steam used to drive a conventional turbine. The hot-oil system includes a storage component, which allows a partial decoupling of the time of electricity generation from the peak of solar insolation. This improves the reliability of the system as a supplier of high-value peak electricity to the power grid. In the deserts of Southern California, 350 megawatts of commercial Luz solar generators are in operation.

Central-receiver solar power plants have also achieved a measure of technical if not yet commercial success. The largest solar central-receiver power plant in the world is a 10-megawatt demonstration facility, Solar 1, built in Barstow, California by a consortium of government, utility, and supplier participants. Solar 1 was judged to be a technical success, achieving all of the engineering specifications and goals for the project. The central-receiver generating configuration promises to be the most efficient low-cost solar thermal generating option in the long term; however, achieving full commercialization of the technology will be very difficult because of the very high current cost of the technology,

and the need to build very large-scale installations during the development period.

Another solar thermal generating technology that shows commercial promise, the solar dish–Sterling engine generator, is at the other end of the scale spectrum from the solar central receiver. Solar dishes are individual collectors that focus solar energy on a focal point that is suspended above the middle of the dish. Solar dishes can be operated in parallel to drive a conventional turbine generator, but a more promising option is to mount a Stirling engine generator at the focal point of each dish, creating a totally modular generating system. The Stirling engine is a piston engine that is powered by an external heat source, rather than internal combustion of a fuel. This technology is at the precommercial stage of development, and requires further development of both the dish receiver systems and the solar-coupled Stirling engines before it will be ready for commercial application.

A final design option for solar thermal power generation, the solar pond, allows complete decoupling of the generator from the solar insolation cycle. In this technology, a large saline pond is used as the collector. The heat collected in the pond can be converted into electricity using a low-temperature turbine engine, with an appropriate working fluid such as ammonia. The solar pond configuration is characterized by a low generating efficiency, which is balanced by a low-cost collection system and electricity output that can be dispatched in response to electricity demand.

Photovoltaic technology. Through this technology, solar energy can be converted directly into electricity without the use of a heat engine and without moving parts. In photovoltaic generators, the solar photons absorbed in semiconductor materials undergo a change in valence level, allowing them to jump an energy barrier and create a voltage potential. This voltage potential can be tapped to power a circuit with direct-current electricity. Photovoltaic generators are completely passive devices, although, in configurations that involve tracking, the tracking devices have moving parts. To use photovoltaic generators for conventional alternating-current applications, it is necessary to include an inverter in the configuration. For remote applications, it is usually necessary to couple the photovoltaic generator with a battery and/or backup engine generator to provide power when it is needed.

Photovoltaic generators are modular devices that can be used for a wide variety of applications. They can be manufactured from a variety of semiconductor materials, although the vast majority of existing photovoltaic devices are manufactured from silicon. Other candidate materials, such as gallium arsenide and cadmium sulfide, offer the promise of higher efficiencies for converting solar energy into electricity; however, they involve the use of toxic substances, cost more than silicon, and have received considerably less developmental effort. Conversion efficiencies in excess of 20 percent have been achieved with silicon solar cells.

The most expensive part of photovoltaic power generation is the photovoltaic cell itself. To maximize the power generated by a given solar cell, a variety of schemes have been developed for tracking the Sun and for focusing solar energy on the cells. Solar cells are capable of converting both direct and diffuse solar radiation. Tracking and focusing can increase the cells' exposure to direct radiation, but not to diffuse radiation.

All current options for electricity generation from solar energy share one important characteristic: they are expensive, as shown in Table 2. They cost two to six times as much as conventional fuel-burning power plants of comparable size, and they deliver much less annual energy per unit of capacity. These high capital costs overwhelm the operational savings of fuel-free power generation. Solar power generation has costs in the neighborhood of U.S.$0.08–0.15 per kilowatt hour. In many grid-connected applications, solar electric generators have the advantage of supplying peak-period electricity, which can receive a premium price. In remote applications, where demand is often dominated by lighting, the daily generating peak and electric demand peak are usually completely out of phase, necessitating the use of large, expensive battery systems.

Wind Power. One of the oldest energy resources used by humans, wind power contributed strongly to the early industrialization of Europe. Early applications of wind power included water pumping, grinding of grain, and sawing of wood. However, by the middle of the twentieth century, the use of wind power had disappeared almost entirely from the world. The wind power industry began its revival in the early 1970s, in response to the two oil crises that occurred during that decade. Wind power represents the greatest modern success story among the renewable energy technologies.

Wind energy, like biomass and hydro, is a secondary form of solar energy. Winds occur because of uneven solar heating of the Earth–atmosphere system. The exploitable energy in wind is provided by the kinetic energy of moving air. The power density of wind is a cubic function of the wind's speed, so that small variations in wind speed lead to large variations in its energy. This property is one of the most challenging factors in the design of wind turbines. The power density is proportional to the density of the moving air, so hot temperatures and high elevations have a negative effect on wind power availability.

The efficiency of extracting power from the wind is limited by technical as well as mechanical considerations. The theoretical maximum proportion of the wind that can be extracted, called the Betz limit, is less than

60 percent. State-of-the-art wind turbines available today can achieve conversion efficiencies as high as 45 percent. When the winds drop below design speed, the turbine's output drops off quickly. When winds blow at speeds above design speeds, most turbines have mechanisms to spill wind for purposes of modulation. Above a certain wind speed, most turbines shut down completely to protect the equipment.

There are two basic types of wind power generators: horizontal-axis turbines and vertical-axis turbines. The former, which look like propeller blades, are the most common. The design of the turbine's rotor entails the greatest engineering challenge. The rotor has to be able to stand up to tremendous forces and shears, in all weather conditions, and respond to constant changes in wind velocity. Two-, three-, and five-bladed designs are common. The horizontal-axis rotor has to be steered to face the wind, which is constantly changing in direction. The steering mechanism is called a yaw; steering is achieved via a yaw system.

Vertical-axis turbines look like egg beaters. They have several theoretical advantages over horizontal-axis machines, such as no need for steering, location of the generator and gear box at ground level, and the ability to use lightweight, inexpensive blade materials. However, for a variety of reasons, including unsolved engineering problems and the fact that these machines capture mainly ground-level wind, vertical-axis machines are falling increasingly behind horizontal-axis machines, and there is little prospect of this trend changing in the foreseeable future.

Wind power generating systems have been developed for both utility-scale use and small-scale, remote applications. Utility wind power installations usually involve "wind farm" configurations, in which a field of turbines is laid out and interconnected through a common substation. State-of-the-art utility-scale turbines are being manufactured in the 500- to 600-kilowatt range. The next generation of turbines is expected to be twice as large. Small-scale, remote power applications of wind turbines usually involve one to five turbines, of 20–150 kilowatts each. Remote applications usually involve the use of an energy storage system and/or an auxiliary generator to provide continuous, reliable power.

Wind power generation technology has made steady progress down the learning curve over the past couple of decades. Installed costs for utility-scale installations have dropped by more than a factor of two to a current level of about U.S.$1,000 per kilowatt of capacity. Operating and maintenance costs have dropped by a greater proportion, to the neighborhood of U.S.$0.010–0.015 per kilowatt hour, and reliability and availability have increased by large factors. For example, early turbines installed in California's Altamont Pass resource area achieved operating factors of approximately 9 percent, while recent installations are routinely achieving 27 percent. This has brought the cost of wind-generated power down to the range of approximately U.S.$0.04–0.07 per kilowatt hour in good resource areas for utility-scale systems, which in many cases is competitive with new sources of conventional supply (see Table 2).

Other Renewables. In addition to the major renewable energy resources discussed above (biomass, hydro, geothermal, solar, and wind), several other flows of renewable energy have been considered as exploitable energy sources. Most of the flows in this group are related to the oceans, and include tides, waves, and the difference in temperature between deep ocean water and surface water. Serious efforts during the past two decades have been devoted to developing technologies to harness each of these energy sources, although none has shown much promise to be able to lead to commercially viable machinery in the near to middle term. These flows of energy tend to be of low intensity, even for renewables, and the ocean tends to be a very difficult environment in which to work. Moreover, tidal power exploitation, which entails water impoundments in estuarine zones, has serious environmental liabilities.

[*See also* Biomass; Electrical Power Generation; Energy; Energy Policy; Hydrogen; *and* Resources.]

BIBLIOGRAPHY

Burtraw, D., J. Darmstadter, K. Palmer, and J. McVeigh. "Renewable Energy: Winner, Loser, or Innocent Victim?" *Resources (Resources for the Future)* (Spring 1999), 9–13.

Ehrlich, P., et al. *Ecoscience: Population, Resources, Environment.* San Francisco: W. H. Freeman, 1977.

Flavin, C., and S. Dunn. *Rising Sun, Gathering Winds: Policies to Stabilize the Climate and Strengthen Economies.* Worldwatch Paper No. 138, Washington, D.C., November 1997.

United States Department of Energy. *Renewable Energy Annual 1997*, vol. 1. Washington, D.C., 1997.

—GREGORY P. MORRIS

RENEWABLE RESOURCES. *See* Renewable Energy Sources; *and* Resources.

RESERVOIRS. *See* Dams.

RESOURCES

As world populations continue to grow and less developed nations become progressively more industrial, our use of resources increases rapidly, raising legitimate concerns about impacts on the environment and about the life of resources. The subject is very broad. In some applications, resources may be said to include human talent, ideas, and energy; but more often it is useful to maintain the dichotomy between humankind and the natural resources that we employ for various purposes.

The Environment and Resources. If human economic activities are seen schematically within the environment as a whole, which provides materials and absorbs waste products (Figure 1), then resources are essentially identical to the environment. Although many discussions focus on fuels, building materials, and raw materials for industrial production, in fact air and water, which absorb wastes, are even more important as resources essential to life. As we learn about newly discovered plant species that prove useful as sources of medicines and chemicals, the equivalence of natural resources and the environment becomes clear.

Resource extraction has various effects that may be regarded either as impacts on the environment or as interactions with other resources. Cutting of forests, for instance, can lead to increased runoff and erosion of soil and can affect the atmosphere by increasing the concentration of carbon dioxide. At the same time, severe air pollution can affect the health of forests. In another example, mining of potash and its subsequent use as a fertilizer can affect water quality and reduce fish resources in streams and estuaries. In each case, the threat is to what would some would call resources and others would call the environment.

Because resource use is intimately entwined with pollution of air and water and the accumulation of solid wastes, a vital issue is whether extraction and processing of certain resources can continue without due regard for environmental costs. If the price of a refined metal were to include the costs of preventing or remediating damage to land, air, and water, then higher prices for the metal would presumably reduce the amounts of raw resource being mined. High prices would, of course,

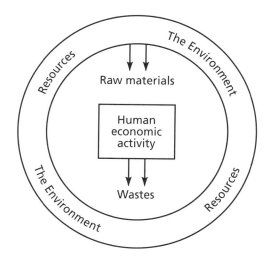

Resources. FIGURE 1. Resources (the Environment) and Human Activity.

tend to reduce standard of living. This conundrum complicates the question of how to encourage developing nations to advance while observing a more harmonious relationship with the environment than has been enjoyed by the now-industrial nations. [*See* Mass Consumption; *and* Sustainability.]

Attitudes toward Resources. The ways in which humans interact with resources is determined by social, cultural, and ideological factors, which intervene as a lens or filter, controlling how we perceive the resources and how profoundly we alter them (Figure 2). The most potent of cultural factors is the scientific or technological level of a society. An early human traveling on foot may have regarded an oil seep as only a barrier to be crossed; a person traveling by canoe would recognize the gummy material as good for patching holes in the hull; while a twentieth-century technologist regards it as a source of crude oil for numerous applications—and, furthermore, has the drilling rigs or mining machines to extract oil in immense quantities. Of course, human impact on resources depends on population numbers as well as technological level and affluence—a connection formalized by the expression

$$\text{Impact} = \text{Population} \times \text{Affluence} \times \text{Technology}$$

Equally important is the ideological factor: political or religious beliefs can make one society better stewards of the land and another more exploitive. [*See* Belief Systems; Conservation; Human Impacts, *article on* Human Impacts on Earth; *and* IPAT.]

In the absence of organization or regulation, individuals (or groups, or industries) may satisfy their own needs without regard for others who also need that same resource. Any such natural resource—and there are few

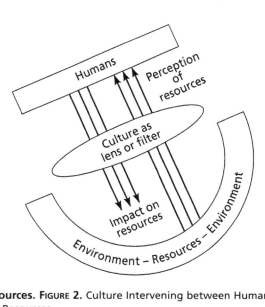

Resources. Figure 2. Culture Intervening between Humans and Resources.

that do not qualify—are considered common pool resources, or common property resources. On a global scale, the atmosphere and the oceans are such resources; more locally, grazing lands or a particular groundwater aquifer are examples. In today's global economy it could be argued that all natural endowments, including mineral deposits, forests, fishing grounds, and wildlife, should be considered common, regardless of national boundaries, because any world citizen, or the descendants of that person, may be compromised by the loss of a scarce metal or a threatened plant species. [*See* Commons; *and* Ethics.]

While some resource uses such as ocean fishing are regulated by international arrangements, usually it is national policy that influences the extraction of mineral or forest resources. In North America there are still national policies that encourage exploration for and production of these resources and perpetuate a frontier attitude toward the land: one is the depletion allowance that permits companies to deduct, from taxable income, the value of resources produced. The private company, therefore, benefits from recognizing depletion of its assets; that is, the minerals or forests whose production yields gross income. However, in the United States and most other nations, this depletion of natural resources is not considered when calculating net national product—unlike capital assets like factories and equipment, whose depreciation is charged against the value of national production. Thus, "A country could exhaust its mineral resources, cut down its forests, erode its soils, pollute its aquifers, and hunt its wildlife and fisheries to extinction, but measured income would not be affected as these assets disappeared" (Repetto, 1989).

Renewable versus Nonrenewable Resources. Generally, air, water, animals and plants, including crops, are considered renewable, while mineral resources are nonrenewable. That simple division can be enriched by recognizing a spectrum or range of renewability based on the time required for regeneration of a resource (Figure 3).

At the more robust end of the scale are constant-flow resources—solar radiation, air, wind, and surface water. Requiring only a few years for renewal are plant and animal life, such as annual crops, trees that are pruned each year for fuel, and livestock that mature to provide meat within a few years. At the next level are trees for lumber that require decades to regrow. Geothermal heat in shallow, exploitable occurrences can be quenched in three or four decades of use and may require a similar time to recover, although in some discussions this energy is called *renewable* because the ultimate source is inexhaustible. Ground water, if mined to exhaustion, will require decades or centuries to be replenished, depending on the climate and the nature of the aquifer. The replacement of half a meter of soil lost to erosion

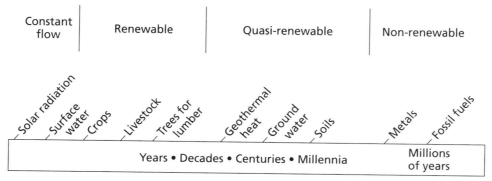

Resources. FIGURE 3. The Spectrum of Resource Renewability.

would require many thousands of years, even in a moist climate.

When economic minerals such as metals and fossil fuels are considered, the scale shifts drastically to hundreds of millions of years. These resources all are clearly in the nonrenewable category, but there is another useful distinction: whereas metals, once refined, can be reused, fossil fuels yield their energy just once.

Ironically, the most serious deterioration of resources is occurring at the renewable end of the scale. Although their volumes are renewable, rivers, lakes, and estuaries can be so degraded by pollutants that decades are required for recovery; and severe poisoning may exceed nature's ability to restore their natural state. Ground water, while less exposed to most pollutants, may require centuries to recover from pollution, because its flow rates are so low. And the atmosphere, although able to dilute vast volumes of emissions, will carry some pollutants for thousands of miles, and can be altered for decades by particularly persistent chemicals. [*See* Ozone.]

Distribution of Mineral Resources. The uneven endowment of mineral wealth across the world is a significant factor in the economic history of any nation. While uneven, the distribution of minerals on a global or continental scale is not random, but follows the patterns of the major rock families that make up every continent. Among the many and varied mineral resources, metals and fossil fuels are extremely important groups; the factors affecting their distribution within a continent are outlined here.

The core of a continent is rock that is igneous or metamorphic, that is, it was formed directly from molten rock, or has a history of high temperatures, severe deformation, or intrusion by molten rock. This environment favored the separation and concentration of many metallic ores. While buried in many parts of a continent, such rock is exposed in some mountain belts and in shield areas, which are sites of ancient mountains and form the oldest parts of a continent.

Fossil fuels do not form in rock of that kind, and would not survive the processes that led to such rock. Coal, crude oil, and natural gas depend upon the preservation and alteration of organic matter, which accumulates in water-lain sediments and appears today in sedimentary rock (sandstones or limestones, for instance) formed from those sediments. Because sedimentary rock, when present, covers and obscures the igneous and metamorphic basement rock, the areas favorable for fossil fuels and those that favor metallic ores tend to be mutually exclusive. That is not strictly true, because some metallic ores form in sedimentary rock through radically different concentration processes; but it is safe to say that any continental area lacking relatively thick sedimentary rock will lack fossil fuels. By the same token, a chain of volcanic islands such as Japan will be short of fuels. But the continental shelves of many island nations such as Indonesia are built of thick sedimentary rock and have potential for oil and gas accumulations.

The world pattern of major rock types (see, for example, Espenshade, p. 6) makes clear that nations of continental size—Russia, Canada, Australia, and the United States, for instance—have the possibility of a wide variety of mineral wealth. To understand more fully why some regions are richer in fossil fuels than others, it is necessary to consider the major chapters of Earth history and how the movement of crustal plates has favored certain continental belts. [*See* Earth History; Fossil Fuels; *and* Plate Tectonics.]

Amounts of Nonrenewable Resources Remaining. While there is reason to be concerned about environmental impacts of the mining and refining of mineral resources, there is also reason to ask how long these nonrenewable substances will last: specifically, the questions are how much remains, and how it will endure in the face of current and future rates of use.

Estimates of renewable resource amounts, such as volumes of lumber or metric tons of biomass, are not simple, but they do involve straightforward assessment of land areas that are evident and measurable. Similarly, crop production, and the potential for increased or diminished crop production, are assessed by experts on the basis of agricultural economics. The results are presented in terms that are usually simple and unambiguous. The same is not true of nonrenewable or mineral resources, first because there may be more uncertainties involved, and second because key terms are apt to be misused. Furthermore, estimates from different authorities will be different, and they will change through time.

Our mineral endowment is often said to be finite, implying that only so much is there, and it will not grow. The amounts, though, are rather indefinite because of two uncertainties. The first is due to incomplete exploration: there will always be some possibility of undiscovered deposits of metallic ores or crude-oil accumulations, and those undiscovered amounts can only be estimated. The second uncertainty is due to changing economic factors and technological advances, both of which can alter the definition of what constitutes a usable or economic deposit. The two uncertainties must be recognized whenever mineral resource amounts are tabulated.

The necessary terms and concepts can be defined by a rectangle whose boundaries enclose all the existing resources of some mineral substance in a specified region or nation, whether those resources are discovered or undiscovered (Figure 4). The horizontal dimension expresses how thoroughly defined the deposits or occurrences are: identified amounts are toward the left-hand side, while undiscovered amounts are on the right. The vertical dimension accommodates differences in

economic feasibility: rich deposits that are shallow or easily recovered and processed are placed toward the top and classed as economic, while deposits more deeply buried, less rich, or otherwise difficult to attain are toward the lower end of the scale, and classed as subeconomic. The criterion for economic amounts is that they be recoverable at current prices and with current technology. This framework can be applied to any mineral resource; but when the concepts are applied to some specific mineral, both the geologic and economic dimensions may be divided further to recognize gradations in the certainty and in the economic feasibility of extraction.

Any amounts that are both identified and economic are considered reserves (these amounts are in the ground, not in stockpiles). Other resources of the same substance do not qualify as reserves: they may be attractive economically but not yet discovered (position X in Figure 4); or they may be well defined geologically but not economic (position Y).

Although reserves are defined firmly, their magnitude changes through time. Obviously, production from a deposit will diminish reserves; but there are two processes that augment them. First is the discovery of suitable resources that allow the reserve category to expand toward the right. Equally important, though, are rising prices or new technologies, both of which can lower the economic threshold and transform known subeconomic amounts into reserves.

When estimating the life of some specific mineral resource, it is necessary to recognize the potential for expansion of reserves in the future. By estimating undiscovered amounts and the probable future yield from deposits that are known but still subeconomic (and adding these to reserves), we can arrive at total remaining amounts. To this can be applied current production (use) rates, or, instead, rates that increase according to some assumptions. The result will be a reasonable estimate of life. Any estimate of resource life that uses only current reserve figures will produce a short estimate that is not only unrealistic but will brand the author an alarmist, and will undermine the author's effort to encourage conservation.

If rates of use increase continually at a fixed percentage, the impact upon resource amounts is staggering. For instance, if production increases steadily at 3.5 percent per year (a rate consistent with world energy use in the 1990s), then the cumulative amount used will double in twenty years, implying that if the total remaining amount of some mineral resource were half gone by the year 2010, it would be all gone by 2030. Conversely, if some discovery were to double our estimate of the world endowment of some mineral resource, the reprieve is only twenty years.

[*See also* Agriculture and Agricultural Land; Land

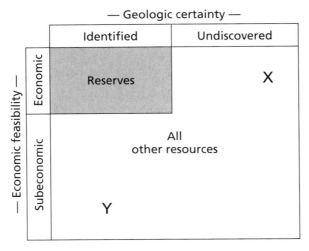

Resources. Figure 4. General Scheme for Classifying Mineral Resource Amounts. (From United States Geological Survey, 1975.)

Use, *article on* Land Use and Land Cover; Metals; Renewable Energy Sources; Soils; Water; *and* Wilderness.]

BIBLIOGRAPHY

Craig, J. R., D. J. Vaughan, and B. J. Skinner. *Resources of the Earth: Origin, Use, and Environmental Impact*. 2d ed. New York: Prentice-Hall, 1996. A textbook covering the occurrence and availability of resources and how human activities impact the environment.

Espenshade, E. B., ed. *Goode's World Atlas*. 19th ed. Skokie, Ill.: Rand McNally, 1995.

Hawken, P., A. Lovins, and L. Hunter Lovins. *Natural Capitalism: Creating the Next Industrial Revolution*. New York: Little, Brown, 1999.

Jones, G., and C. Bollier. *Resources, Society, and Environmental Management*. London: Paul Chapman Publishing, 1997.

Repetto, R., et al. *Wasting Assets: Natural Resources in the National Income Accounts*. Washington, D.C.: World Resources Institute, 1989. A monograph developing the need for improved natural-resource accounting, using Indonesia's petroleum and soil resources as examples.

Tietenberg, T. *Environmental and Natural Resource Economics*. 4th ed. New York: Harper Collins, 1996.

United States Geological Survey. "Mineral Resource Perspectives." Professional Paper No. 940. Washington, D.C.: USGS, 1975. A review of resource concepts, with fuller development of the rectangular summary diagram used in this article.

World Resources Institute. *World Resources 1998–99*. New York and Oxford: Oxford University Press, 1998. Series published annually in June. Articles follow a theme for each year and are applied to world problems and trends. Includes updated tables of economic indicators, demographic and health data, resource use, and resource inventories.

—DAVID J. CUFF

REVELLE, ROGER

Roger Randall Dougan Revelle (1909–1991), American oceanographer, population/resources advisor, and international statesman of science, was born in Seattle, Washington. He was a doctoral student at the University of California's Scripps Institution of Oceanography in La Jolla in the 1930s when his analysis of ocean sediments led to an interest in the carbon cycle. In 1934 Revelle and coauthors found that a complex buffering action was involved in the absorption of carbon dioxide in the oceans. Seawater chemistry continued to interest Revelle during his years in the navy (1941–1948), especially during Operation Crossroads, where he studied the diffusion of radioactive wastes and the environmental effects of the atomic test at Bikini Atoll.

Revelle was director of the Scripps Institution of Oceanography (1950–1961) when Hans Suess demonstrated that the amount of carbon dioxide in the atmosphere could be derived from radiocarbon measurements. Revelle's 1956 calculations proved that the oceans were not taking carbon dioxide up at a rate sufficient to absorb the increasing levels of atmospheric carbon dioxide. Suess and Revelle were coauthors of a 1957 article that found that atmospheric carbon dioxide was increasing, and strongly recommended further study and measurement. Revelle, Suess, and others suggested that this increase might adversely affect global climate through the greenhouse effect, thought previously to improve the subarctic climate and increase harvests.

In 1956, as chairman of the U.S. oceanographic panel planning the International Geophysical Year (IGY), Revelle was positioned to fund Charles David Keeling's measurements of atmospheric carbon dioxide. These measurements, known as the "Keeling Curve," demonstrated a steady rise in atmospheric carbon dioxide from preindustrial levels. Revelle's growing national and international prestige provided opportunities to discuss the issue at high government levels and publicly beginning in 1956. Revelle continued his research in climate change after he left Scripps to become head of the Center for Population Studies at Harvard (1964–1976), and in 1965 he was responsible for putting the matter before the public in an influential White House report, *Restoring the Quality of Our Environment*. Revelle chaired the National Academy of Sciences Energy and Climate Panel in 1977, which found that about 40 percent of the anthropogenic carbon dioxide has remained in the atmosphere, two-thirds of it from fossil fuel, and in 1982 he published a widely read paper on carbon dioxide and world climate in *Scientific American*. He served on the National Research Council committee that issued the 1983 report *Changing Climate*.

After his retirement from Harvard, Revelle returned to the University of California, San Diego (1976–1991), the university he had founded in 1960. He received a plethora of awards and honors for his broad contributions to oceanography, geophysics, and population/resources, including the Tyler Ecology Energy Prize and the Balzan Prize. In 1990, when a journalist asked him why he had received the National Medal of Science, Revelle replied that he got the award for being "the grandfather of the greenhouse effect."

[*See also* Atmospheric Chemistry.]

BIBLIOGRAPHY

Moberg, E. G., et al. "The Buffer Mechanism of Sea Water." *Scripps Institution of Oceanography Bulletin* 3 (1934), 231–278.

Revelle, R., and W. Munk. "The Carbon Cycle and the Biosphere." In *Energy and Climate*, pp. 140–178. Washington, D.C.: National Academy of Sciences, 1977.

Revelle, R., and H. E. Suess. "Carbon Dioxide Exchange between Atmosphere and Ocean and the Question of an Increase of Atmospheric Carbon Dioxide during the Past Decades." *Tellus* IX (1957), 19–20.

Revelle, R., et al. "Atmospheric Carbon Dioxide." In *Restoring the Quality of Our Environment: Report of the Environmental*

Pollution Panel, President's Science Advisory Committee, pp. 111–133. Washington, D.C.: The White House, 1965.

Weart, S. R. "Global Warming, Cold War, and the Evolution of Research Plans." *Historical Studies in the Physical and Biological Sciences* 27 (1997), 319–356.

—DEBORAH COZORT DAY

RIO CONFERENCE. *See* United Nations Conference on Environment and Development.

RIO DECLARATION

The Rio Declaration on Environment and Development is one of the products of the United Nations Conference on Environment and Development (UNCED), which met in Rio de Janeiro, Brazil, from 3 to 14 June 1992, to mark the twentieth anniversary of the Stockholm Conference. Like the Stockholm Declaration, it is a legally nonbinding, political instrument, but one of considerable significance for the development of international environmental policy and law. The Rio Declaration is similar in structure to its Stockholm predecessor, comprising a preamble, albeit a much shorter one, and twenty-seven principles.

As its title indicates, the Rio Declaration addresses development issues as much as environmental problems. It puts more emphasis on economic development than the Stockholm Declaration, although it should be noted that, contrary to a widespread misconception, the latter by no means disregarded the social and economic concerns of developing countries. What is new in the Rio Declaration is the international community's attempt to merge the environmental and developmental agenda under the banner of a single, integrated policy objective, that of achieving "sustainable development." Although "sustainable development" were the buzzwords of the entire UNCED process, the Rio Declaration does not explicitly define the concept.

From the outset, the Rio Declaration takes a resolutely anthropocentric approach. The very first sentence of the Declaration states unambiguously that "human beings are at the center of concerns for sustainable development" (Principle 1). In doing so, the Declaration falls far short of the ambitions of the proponents of an Earth Charter, who had hoped that UNCED would adopt a declaratory instrument recognizing the obligations of humankind toward the planet. The Rio Declaration also stops short of unequivocally recognizing the existence of a human right to a healthy environment. In contrast to the Stockholm Declaration, it only contains an oblique reference to human rights, where it states that human beings "are entitled to a healthy and productive life in harmony with nature" (Principle 1).

Other fundamental tenets of sustainable development are set out in Principle 3 of the Declaration, which provides that "the right to development must be fulfilled so as to equitably meet developmental and environmental needs of present and future generations," and in Principle 4, which proclaims that "in order to achieve sustainable development, environmental protection shall constitute an integral part of the development process and cannot be considered in isolation from it." Other provisions of the Declaration associate sustainable development with the eradication of poverty (Principle 5), with the elimination of "unsustainable patterns of production and consumption" (Principle 8), with "endogenous capacity-building" and the transfer of technology (Principle 9), and with the promotion of "a supportive and open international economic system that would lead to economic growth and sustainable development in all countries" (Principle 12). The latter provision, which implicitly equates globalization and economic growth with sustainable development and environmental protection, contrasts sharply with some provisions of the Stockholm Declaration, which echoed the call of developing countries for a "new international economic order."

Several provisions of the Rio Declaration are of special significance from the perspective of the development of international environmental law. The Declaration explicitly recognizes the principle of the "common but differentiated responsibilities" of industrialized and developing countries for the protection of the global environment (Principle 7). It also affirms, for the first time at the global level, the precautionary principle (Principle 15) and the polluter-pays principle (Principle 16) as fundamental principles of environmental policy and law. It reaffirms the responsibility of states to avoid causing transboundary environmental damage (Principle 2) and further specifies their obligations in this respect, by recognizing the existence of duties to notify and consult with potentially affected states (Principles 18 and 19) as well as the duty to undertake environmental impact assessments (Principle 17). Finally, the Declaration recognizes, albeit in rather vague and noncommittal terms, each individual's rights of access to environmental information held by public authorities, participation in decision-making processes, and access to judicial and administrative proceedings in environmental matters (Principle 10).

[*See also* Stockholm Declaration; *and* United Nations Conference on Environment and Development.]

BIBLIOGRAPHY

Pallemaerts, M. "International Environmental Law from Stockholm to Rio: Back to the Future?" *Review of European Community and International Environmental Law* 1 (1992), 254–266. A critical analysis of the Rio Declaration and the other UNCED instruments in a historical perspective.

———. "International Environmental Law in the Age of Sustainable Development: A Critical Assessment of the UNCED Process." *Journal of Law and Commerce* 15 (1996), 623–676.

Panjabi, R. K. L. "From Stockholm to Rio: A Comparison of the Declaratory Principles of International Environmental Law." *Denver Journal of International Law and Policy* 21 (1993), 215–289. A comparative analysis of the Stockholm and Rio Declarations.

Porras, I. M. "The Rio Declaration: A New Basis for International Co-operation." *Review of European Community and International Environmental Law* 1 (1992), 245–253. An analysis of the Rio Declaration and its drafting history by a member of the Costa Rican delegation to UNCED.

Wirth, D. A. "The Rio Declaration on Environment and Development: Two Steps Forward and One Back, or Vice Versa?" *Georgia Law Review* 29 (1995), 599–653.

—MARC PALLEMAERTS

RISK

Dictionaries typically define risk as "exposure to the chance of injury or loss." This definition has two key elements: at least one of the possible outcomes is undesirable, and the actual outcome is uncertain. An undesired outcome is referred to as a "hazard." The outcome of a risk can be an all-or-nothing issue (dead or alive; intact or destroyed), or it can fall within a wide range of possible results (slightly to very sick; 5 to 95 percent destroyed). A simple risk with only a binary set of outcomes can be characterized by a single probability number, while more complex risks, involving a range of outcome levels or several distinct outcomes, are best described by one probability distribution, or a set of them.

Psychologists have found that people's evaluations of risks have much more complex bases than simply the expected value of death, injury, monetary loss, or whatever other hazard is involved. Other factors—such as equity, controllability, and degree of knowledge about a risk—also affect their evaluations. Thus, risks and their associated hazards should be recognized as "multiattribute" phenomena. [*See* Natural Hazards; Nuclear Hazards; *and* Technological Hazards.]

Assessing Risks. Different methods for evaluating or assessing risks have been developed by researchers working in different fields. The differences are accounted for in part by the analytic approaches typically used in each field, in part by the nature of the information available, and in part by the purpose for which the analysis is to be used. Regardless of the approach being employed, risk assessment begins with the identification of a hazard, since that motivates the assessment.

In the field of health risks, the likelihood of a hazard's occurring is estimated through the analysis of exposure and effects processes. In assessing human health risks from an environmental pollutant, for ex-

ample, exposure studies would first investigate how the pollutant is released into the environment from one or more sources. Next, its dispersal in the environment and possible changes it undergoes during dispersal (e.g., becoming bound to soil particles or being chemically altered by exposure to ultraviolet light) would be studied. Finally, ways that it might be ingested by people would be considered (e.g., inhalation of an airborne contaminant, or ingestion of contaminated soil by children). For each of these steps, a variety of sources of information might be used, including empirical information, laboratory studies, theoretical models, and expert judgments.

Effects studies address the incidence of the hazard(s) associated with different levels of exposure. A dose–response function is used to provide a summary characterization of effects processes; it relates different levels of exposure (e.g., concentrations of a chemical in the blood, or inhalation of air contaminated with different quantities of a chemical for a given period of time) with expected effects (e.g., number of incidences of a specific disease per 100,000 persons exposed). Again, a variety of information sources could be used to support development of a model of effects.

In combination, exposure and effects studies provide a basis for estimating the probability of a hazard's occurring as a result of a given activity, and hence for developing a risk characterization for that activity. This approach has been developed in the context of assessing health risks, but there are clear parallels with exposure and effects processes in the field of climate change. For example, the emission and accumulation of greenhouse gases in the atmosphere correspond to exposure processes, and the possible changes induced in global climate—and, in turn, human communities and economies—correspond to effects processes.

A number of tools have been developed to analyze situations in which a risk involves discrete outcomes (e.g., an accident happens or does not happen). Often, such situations involve engineered systems. The two primary approaches are fault tree analysis and event tree analysis (also called failure modes and effects analysis). As implied by their names, each of these approaches involves the construction of a branching diagram, or "tree." Fault tree analysis begins with the identification of the final undesirable event or failure (e.g., release of a chemical to the atmosphere) that the analyst wishes to avoid. Then, based on a functional characterization of the system involved (e.g., a chemical plant), the combinations of events that could lead to the failure are identified at successive levels (subsystems and components of systems). Once completed, the tree provides a basis for evaluating probabilities of different combinations of bottom-level events and, by tracing them through to the top level, assessing the risk of the failure. Each branch of the tree corresponds to a different combination of lower-level events that could lead to the top-level failure.

In contrast, an event tree analysis begins with the identification of a bottom-level failure (e.g., failure of a pump). It then traces the sequences of events that could flow from this initiating event. Each branch of the tree corresponds to a different sequence of events; some of these sequences may lead to a top-level failure.

Both fault tree analysis and event tree analysis offer the advantage that they provide a "map" of the sequences of events that may lead to a failure (i.e., hazard), and hence they can be very useful for identifying ways to reduce the probability of the failure's occurring. However, both also require exhaustive information about the system under consideration. They have most often been used in the contexts of engineered systems such as chemical processing, aircraft and spacecraft, and hazardous materials handling. Although the extensiveness and complexity of global systems probably preclude the application of these methods to the overall problem of global change, they may well be useful for addressing risks in some subsystems.

These are not the only approaches that have been applied to the assessment of risks. For example, actuarial approaches that utilize data on large bodies of experience with well-defined hazards are utilized by the insurance industry to analyze risks. However, because of their reliance on extensive experience, such approaches are unlikely to be applicable to climate change, for which such a record of experience is unavailable.

The issue of uncertainty is vitally important to any assessment of risk, regardless of the method employed. Uncertainty is the hallmark of risk; if an adverse event is certain to happen it may be regarded as unfortunate or even tragic, but it is not regarded as a risk. Uncertainty may be inherent in a risk situation. For example, not every person exposed to a carcinogenic substance will develop cancer as a result; only some will, and there is no way to predict which they will be. Other situations in which risks arise may be strictly determined, but it may be impossible to obtain enough information about the situation to predict outcomes with certainty. For example, a pump may fail only if certain conditions precede the failure (e.g., materials flaws or fatigue), but there may be no feasible nondestructive method of testing for those conditions. In some instances, this distinction blurs, in that it is unclear whether enough information could be obtained, even in theory, to remove all uncertainty. In any case, a key aspect of risk assessment will always be the evaluation of probabilities that certain conditions will prevail or that certain events will occur. Statistical methods for estimating probabilities based on available data are therefore cru-

cial in the process of assessing risk, regardless of the method employed. In many instances, sufficient data to estimate probabilities are unavailable, and expert judgment has to be used. This may well be the case in assessing many risks associated with global change.

Managing Risks. Typically, risk assessment is not an end in itself. Rather, it is undertaken to support a decision about whether and how to manage a risk.

Risk management can be accomplished by intervening at any of several points in the chain of events leading to a risk. Actions can be taken to reduce the exposures that have the potential to lead to adverse outcomes. Other actions can reduce or modify effects despite the fact that exposure occurs. Even if adverse outcomes occur, opportunities for risk management are not necessarily foreclosed. Actions may be available that reduce valuations or perceptions of the severity of those outcomes, or compensation may be provided to offset losses. Each of these basic approaches is potentially applicable to some of the risks posed by global change.

Risk management actions can take many forms. One is to provide information about a risk so that individuals can decide whether and how to take steps to reduce it. This is one approach (though not the only one) used in the case of prescription drugs that, while providing valuable medical benefits, also carry a risk of undesirable side effects.

Tort law, which defines respective responsibilities among individuals in situations where someone may be harmed and provides a means of determining how any harms that occur should be corrected, provides an institutional means of managing risks. Tort law serves a valuable function by enabling the various parties involved in a risk situation to foresee how different outcomes will be dealt with legally; hence, it creates incentives for them to avoid exposing others to unacceptable risks.

Voluntary standards provide another important way to identify and manage risks, especially those arising from industrial activities. Many industries have formed their own organizations for setting standards that reduce risks, to which their members voluntary adhere. Others follow standards established by governmental or quasi-governmental organizations. In the end, it matters little whether voluntary adherence to these standards is seen as a defensive action taken to avoid imposition of mandatory governmental standards, or as altruistic; the fact remains that it is an important means for controlling many risks today.

Insurance is another vital institutional mechanism for managing risks. It enables individuals and organizations exposed to similar risks to pool their resources, through the intermediary of an underwriting organization, so that no one of them will bear the entire brunt of potential adverse consequences. Insurance can enable individuals and organizations to undertake socially beneficial activities that carry small probabilities of substantially adverse outcomes; without a means of pooling the risks, they might avoid those activities altogether. [*See* Insurance.]

Regulatory standards, by which governments require actions to reduce risks or prohibit actions that create unacceptably high risks, are another approach to risk management. Regulatory standards may be set on the basis of a maximum acceptable risk; any activity that creates higher risk is then prohibited. An acceptable level of zero is generally unrealistic, though it has been used in some instances. In the United States, an acceptable risk level of one death in one million over a lifetime is generally applied in environmental standards.

Regulatory standards may also be technology-based—i.e., they may specify the technology that must be used to control a risk. Examples of technology-based standards are "as low as reasonably achievable" and "best available technology"; each requires case-by-case determination of what technology meets the standard in a given instance. [*See* Regulation.]

Decisions about how to manage risks invariably require that risk be balanced against other considerations. This, in turn, requires valuation of outcomes, including not only the hazards that may occur but also any positive outcomes that result from a risk-creating activity. Because outcomes often have characteristics that are different from those of goods or activities that have market prices, outcome valuation can be challenging and controversial. Economists have developed a number of alternative approaches to outcome valuation, such as contingent valuation methods.

Risk-benefit analysis is one approach to analyzing risk management decisions. It is essentially similar to cost-benefit analysis, except that it values uncertain outcomes by weighting them by their probabilities. Because risk management actions may themselves create new risks, these must also be considered in the analysis and treated in the same way as the original risk being managed; analyses that include this consideration are sometimes referred to as "risk-risk analyses."

Decision analysis is an analytic approach developed specifically to address uncertainties about the outcomes of decisions, and so it is readily applied to decisions about risk management. If it is being applied to an existing risk, that risk is characterized as an outcome of the "no action" alternative, to which actions to reduce the risk are then compared. Decision analysis relies on calculations of expected values as a means of weighting the possible outcomes of decisions by their probabilities. It could thus be characterized as a probabilistic

form of benefit-cost analysis. This is clearly an appropriate approach when a decision will be made repeatedly in similar circumstances (because it accurately summarizes total value of the outcomes that can be expected to occur); however, it is debatable whether it is appropriate for making unique decisions. Decision analysis has two additional advantages. One is that it is readily combined with multi-attribute utility analysis, which provides a well-developed means for comparing outcomes that differ on multiple dimensions. Another is that it provides a method for assessing the value of information—the extent to which the expected value of the possible outcomes of a decision would increase if additional information on which to base the decision were available. In a field such as global change, where resources may be used either to take immediate action or to obtain additional information, such an assessment can be especially valuable.

Risk Perceptions. Psychologists have done extensive research on the subject of public perceptions of risks. In large part, this research was initially motivated by the observation that risk experts and the general public differ significantly in the rankings they assign to risks according to the degree of concern or attention they deserve. Experts tend to focus on the number of adverse effects expected over a given period of time as a result of different risks, and to consider risks with similar expected effects to warrant similar degrees of concern. Public risk rankings are affected by a much broader range of considerations, encompassing not only expected harm but also the nature of the harm, the nature of the activity leading to a risk, the degree of understanding of the processes underlying a risk, and the social contexts in which decisions about risks are made.

Regarding the nature of the harm, public concern typically increases if the possible harm associated with a risk is severe (e.g., death rather than injury), dreaded (e.g., cancer), inequitably distributed, catastrophic, irreversible, delayed (i.e., a relatively long interval of time between exposure and effect), or if it affects future generations or children. Regarding the nature of the activity, concern increases if it is unfamiliar, not viewed as widely beneficial, or not readily modified in order to reduce the risk. Regarding the degree of understanding of the processes underlying a risk, concern increases if that understanding is relatively poor on the part of either scientists or members of the public themselves. Finally regarding the social contexts in which decisions about risks are made, concern increases if decisions are seen as leading to inequities, as imposing involuntary risks on people, or as being made by institutions in which there is relatively little public trust. These factors are all important because they significantly affect public acceptance of activities that give rise to risks, whether these are specific actions—such as the development of individual industrial facilities—or more general actions, such as the use of carbon-emitting fossil fuels to generate electricity.

It will always be debated whether public perceptions of risks driven by the factors described above result from misguided foolishness that prevents the implementation of activities that could otherwise provide significant societal benefits, or from a sort of public wisdom that reflects a deeper understanding than that afforded by narrowly focused analytic approaches. It is clear, however, that members of the public, who generally possess little expertise regarding statistics and probability, are prone to making some systematic errors in using available information to make judgments about probabilities, and that these errors may affect their perceptions of risks to some degree. Psychological studies have revealed, for example, that people tend to be overconfident in their judgments of probabilities, and that this overconfidence can lead them to ignore contrary evidence. They also tend to overlook or give insufficient weight to the base rates at which events occur and to place too much reliance on information based on small sample sizes. The probability of events' occurring is also likely to be overestimated if examples of those events are widely reported in popular media. Taken together, the effect of these and similar biases can lead members of the public to adopt incorrect beliefs about the likelihood of some outcomes associated with some risks.

Risk Communication. Risk communication has been a subject of interest to many researchers only since about 1980, though it has been practiced by public relations experts for a longer time. Effective risk communication is clearly very important if decisions about risk are made democratically, or if the public has the de facto power to prevent activities perceived to be risky.

Risk communication can be defined as the purposeful activity of providing information about risks and the situations in which risks occur to the general public or to stakeholders with specific interests in a risk situation. Much advice given in the past about risk communication was based on conventional wisdom; unfortunately, research has since shown that some (though not all) of this advice is not well founded. Approaches to risk communication range from attempts to persuade the public that certain risks are acceptable (one-way communication) to attempts to foster informative dialogue between the public and parties with specific interests in certain risk situations (two-way communication)—for example, between proponents of industrial facilities perceived to create risks and the communities hosting them.

Risk communication, especially if poorly done, can provoke unintended reactions. For example, information about specific hazards may frighten members of the public by drawing their attention to the hazards, rather than reassuring them. Risk communication messages that appear to belittle public concerns (e.g., comparisons that are inappropriate because they juxtapose voluntary risks, like the risk of smoking tobacco, with involuntary risks) may anger members of the public. In general, attempts at risk communication that are predicated on the belief that what matters most to risk experts is also what should matter most to the public are likely to lead to unsatisfactory results.

Approaches to risk communication that are more likely to be productive begin with an attempt to investigate empirically the beliefs and concerns of interested members of the public. If specific misconceptions are identified, they can be addressed directly through communications. For example, research has shown that many people believe that global change and depletion of stratospheric ozone are very closely linked when, in fact, they are not. Gaps in public knowledge regarding information necessary to understand a risk can also be identified and corrected in communications. Alternatives can be clarified and described realistically. The risk perception factors described above can serve as a partial guide to what the public attends to in a risk situation. However, no methods have been identified (nor do they seem likely to be) for designing effective risk communication messages without empirically testing them on the audiences for which they are intended. It is also important to clarify who is responsible for making decisions about risks, and on what basis, and what the role of the public will be in making decisions. It is not surprising that the credibility of sources of messages about risk has been shown to be a crucial factor in their reception by the public.

[See also Disease; Drought; Earthquakes; Insurance; Surprise; and Volcanoes.]

BIBLIOGRAPHY

Boroush, M. *Understanding Risk Analysis: A Short Guide for Health, Safety, and Environmental Policy Making.* Washington, D.C.: American Chemical Society, 1999.

Glickman, T., and M. Gough. *Readings in Risk.* Washington, D.C.: Resources for the Future, 1990.

Kahneman, D., P. Slovic, and A. Tversky. *Judgment under Uncertainty: Heuristics and Biases.* Cambridge and New York: Cambridge University Press, 1982.

Merkhofer, M. W. *Decision Science and Social Risk Management.* Norwell, Mass.: D. Reidel, 1987.

Morgan, M. G., and M. Henrion. *Uncertainty: A Guide to Dealing with Uncertainty in Quantitative Risk and Policy Analysis.* Cambridge and New York: Cambridge University Press, 1990.

National Research Council. *Understanding Risk: Informing Decisions in a Democratic Society.* Washington, D.C.: National Academy Press, 1996.

———. *Improving Risk Communication.* Washington, D.C.: National Academy Press, 1989.

—GORDON L. HESTER

RIVERS AND STREAMS

Rivers and streams contain only a fraction of 1 percent of the world's fresh water, but they have played a fundamental role in the development of human civilizations. Early, highly structured hydraulic civilizations developed along the Tigris, Euphrates, Nile, and Indus Rivers some four thousand years ago. Since then, humans have sought to control rivers for flood control and land drainage, for domestic and industrial water supply and irrigation, and for navigation; they have used streams and rivers to remove wastes; they have exploited their stores of sand and gravel to provide building materials, and have utilized the rich biological resources of river corridors. In addition to these direct impacts, rivers have been affected by air pollution and climate change, and by widespread changes in land use. Rivers drain land areas—their catchments—and so have been changed as a result of land clearance, wetland drainage, timber harvesting, livestock grazing, intensive cultivation, and urban and industrial expansion. Increased flooding, prolonged droughts, siltation, and nutrient enrichment are typical signals of catchment disturbance in temperate regions; salinization of rivers and floodplain soils and water bodies is one legacy of catchment disturbance in more arid climates.

Rivers in Nature. River ecosystems are key components of the landscape in all ecological regions (Figure 1). At the global scale, the main drivers of the abiotic milieu of river ecosystems—hydrology, temperature, and channel form—reflect regional-scale climate (as shown, for example, by a river's flow regime, Figure 1) modified by geology. The ten largest rivers—by length—are listed in Table 1. The Zaire has the largest drainage basin, nearly 3.5 million square kilometers, with a mean flow of over 40,000 cubic meters per second. Rivers also transport sediment—the product of the weathering and erosion of the land surface. For the planet as a whole, the average sediment yield is about 125 metric tons per square kilometer per year, and this represents a lowering of the land surface by 30 millimeters every thousand years. However, sediment yields vary enormously depending upon climate, geology, topography, vegetation, and land use—maximum values in regions such as India and China exceed 2,000 metric tons per square kilometer per year, and the Jing River in China has an average sediment yield of over 8,000 metric tons per square kilometer per year.

Superimposed upon such global patterns, individual rivers show strong longitudinal gradients. In natural drainage basins, the strong unidirectional flow carries the products of physical and chemical rock weathering and soil erosion together with biological products, organic matter, and the components of dead animals and plants. The downstream spiraling—transport, storage,

and processing—of these materials together with downstream changes of temperature and hydraulic conditions produces a sequence of plant and animal communities. This longitudinal dimension of river systems has been conceptualized by Vannote et al. (1980) as the River Continuum Concept.

The classic high-gradient mountain stream with a small channel, cold temperatures, and highly oxygenated water, dominated by fast-water habitats, contrasts with low-gradient sectors rivers with large flood plains and a diversity of channel forms and flood plain water bodies (Figure 2). Coupled with this downstream pattern of hydrologic and geomorphologic changes is a characteristic zonation of flora and fauna. Classic faunal schemes for western European rivers change from trout (*Salvelinus fontinalis* and *Salmo trutta*) in headwater streams, through grayling (*Thymallus thymallus*) and barbel (*Barbus fluviatilis*) in middle reaches, to bream (*Abramus brama*), carp (*Cyprinus carpio*), and tench (*Tinca tinca*) in lowland flood plain reaches. At the smaller scale of a single reach of river, flow and channel structure again combine to produce a complex pattern of hydraulic conditions that sustain a diversity of flora and fauna.

River ecosystems comprise not only the aquatic system of the river channel but also the semiaquatic, seasonally flooded system: any islands between the channels, the riparian zones, and the alluvial plains. Natural river corridors are biologically diverse and highly productive. Flood plain forests, sustained by flooding and periodic rejuvenation by channel erosion, contain a diversity of habitat patches of different types and ages that sustain a rich diversity of biota. The vital role of the annual flood for sustaining these systems has been synthesized by Junk et al. (1989) as the Flood Pulse Concept. This stresses the importance of the lateral dimension (river–flood plain connectivity), especially within large, low-gradient rivers where flood plains contribute significantly to the productivity and diversity of the river system (Figure 2). River corridors provide temporary habitats for a wide range of species, corridors for spectacular annual migrations, and routes for the dispersal of species throughout the landscape. The Mississippi, for example, acts as a flyway for 36 percent of North American waterfowl.

Rivers Today. River corridors are vital for the conservation of biodiversity and have important functions for human societies. However, they are sensitive to any change in the quantity and quality of water, to changes in loads of sediment and organic materials reaching them from the drainage basin upstream, to disruption of the natural connections between the river channel and its adjacent flood plains, and to the loss of habitat diversity as a result of channel engineering works. The severity of human impacts upon river ecosystems increased most dramatically with advances in coordina-

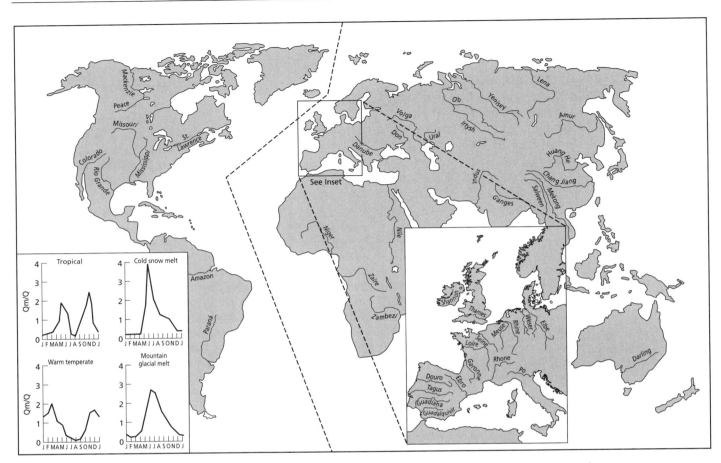

Rivers and Streams. Figure 1. Major World Rivers and Their Contrasting Flow Regimes.

tion and administration systems—not simply with technological progress. These advances have roots in Europe in the late sixteenth and early seventeenth centuries, a period characterized by commercial expansion and a change from feudal to early capitalist systems of land evaluation, as well as rapid advances in hydraulic engineering. These led to the modern era of the megaproject, which opened in the second half of the nineteenth century, popularized by the pioneering vision of humankind's struggle to tame wild rivers and led by entrepreneurs motivated by the desire for economic growth. In 1853, Charles Ellet wrote (pp. 303–304):

> The banks of the Ohio and Mississippi, now broken by the current and lined with fallen trees, . . . may yet, in the course of a very few years, be cultivated and adorned down to the water's edge . . . the grass will hereafter grow luxuriantly along the caving banks; all material fluctuations of the waters will be prevented, and the level of the river's surface will become nearly stationary. Grounds, which are now frequently inundated and valueless, will be tilled and subdued. . . . The channels will become stationary. . . . The Ohio first, and ultimately the Missouri and Mississippi, will be made to flow forever with a constant, deep, and limpid stream.

By 1965, virtually every river in Europe and North America had been "improved." On other continents, progress toward river regulation and land development is rapid, such that few rivers remain that are not affected in some way.

Rivers and Streams. Table 1. The World's Longest Rivers*

RIVER	LENGTH (KILOMETERS)
Nile	6,695
Amazon	6,280
Mississippi–Missouri	6,270
Ob'–Irtysh	5,570
Yangzi (Chiang Jiang)	4,990
Zaire (Congo)	4,670
Amur (Heilong Jiang)	4,510
Yellow (Huang He)	4,350
Lena	4,260
Mackenzie–Peace	4,240

*See Figure 1 for locations.

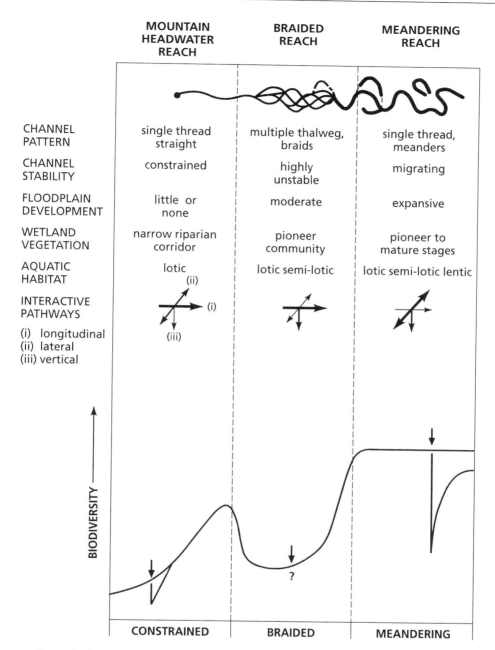

Rivers and Streams. FIGURE 2. The Model River System.

Shows the main features of the three dominant reaches, including the relative strength of interactions in three dimensions (upstream to downstream, channel and riparian zone or flood plain, surface water and ground water) and idealized downstream pattern of biodiversity, with an indication of how biodiversity is modified by regulation below a dam in the constrained reach and by embanking and channelization in the braided and meandering reaches. (Adapted from Ward and Stanford, 1995.)

The degradation of river ecosystems has been widespread (Table 2). Dams and channel works have had dramatic impacts, isolating the channel from its flood plain and converting fast-running rivers to slow-flowing impoundments: in both cases with a loss of instream habitat diversity. The hypothetical impact of dams on biodiversity is shown in Figure 2. Atlantic Salmon (*Salmo salar*) disappeared from many rivers of western Europe following river impoundment, with dams acting as barriers to migration, and habitat has been lost as a result of the changes in flow, sediment load, and water quality. Similarly, the catches of sturgeon (Acipenseridae) in

Rivers and Streams. TABLE 2. Examples of Environmental Impacts of River "Improvements" in the United States

- Twenty-five thousand kilometers of fast-flowing main river has been converted to still-flowing lakes by dam construction
- Fifty-four percent of the wetlands have been reclaimed
- Sixty-six percent of the riparian habitat has been lost
- The loss of lateral connectivity—access from the main channel to flood plain backwaters, lakes, and marshes—has severely impacted fish stocks, reducing multispecies fish yield by between 30 and 60 percent
- Along the Mississippi below the Ohio confluence, most of the 98,000 square kilometers of flood plain has been leveed and drained for agriculture
- Along the Sacramento river, the loss of riparian habitat has resulted in a dramatic decline in bird populations, with 95 percent fewer birds and 32 percent fewer species

eastern Europe and Pacific salmon (*Oncorhynchus* species) in the northwestern United States have fallen dramatically following the building of dams. Because of the strong unidirectional flow in rivers, changes are seen for long distances below a point of impact. For example, for 400 kilometers below Glen Canyon Dam on the Colorado River, the water is now too cold for most native fish, and changes in the surface salinity patterns within the southeastern Mediterranean Sea have been associated with the construction of the Aswan Dam on the Nile River about 1,000 kilometers upstream from the coast.

Pollution problems impacting the water quality of rivers have been classified by Meybeck and Helmer (1989) as follows: fecal, organic, and metal pollution; eutrophication; salinization; contamination by organic micropollutants, and acidification. [*See* Pollution.] In Europe, pollution problems began before 1850 and peaked in the 1960s and 1970s, but the legacy of contaminated sediments remains along many rivers. The flora and fauna of rivers have also been altered, both deliberately and accidentally, by the introduction of exotic species that are implicated in the decline of native flora and fauna through predation, competition, habitat destruction, and introduction of diseases. The introduction of trout (*Salmo trutta*) to all continents following the discovery of the means of transporting ova in 1852 has been one European export. Problem imports to Europe include the giant hogweed (*Heracleum mantegazzianum*), the Japanese knotweed (*Fallopia japonica*), and the Himalayan balsam (*Impatiens glandulifera*), brought to decorate gardens and parks in the nineteenth century. Today, few rivers remain that have

not been altered—degraded in ecological terms—to some degree. [*See* Exotic Species.]

Rivers in the Future. Primary aims for many countries are to achieve water and food security, to develop drylands, and to prevent desertification and drought. Four human needs will be the driving forces determining the future of rivers and streams: the need to provide clean and reliable water supplies to meet the growing demands of rapidly expanding populations, the need to maintain supplies for expanding irrigation agriculture, the need to develop hydroelectric power, and—in potential conflict with the other three—the need to protect biodiversity and to restore rivers and their corridors that have been degraded by past impacts of land and water developments. There are two important lessons for the future. First, all environmental changes will impact rivers and streams. Second, in many cases the most dramatic impacts have resulted from poor planning, ineffective administration, and bad management of development schemes. Water and land development projects with gestation periods of fifteen to twenty years in countries with high population growth will have to proceed, because the human risks of not harnessing these resources in a timely manner may be too high. The challenge is to develop land and water resources in ways that ensure that river corridor ecosystems are sustainable, that biodiversity is protected, and that the security of biological resources is achieved for the benefit of future generations.

[*See also* Dams; Irrigation; Water; *and* Water Quality.]

BIBLIOGRAPHY

Recent collections of scientific papers on key topics are found in the journal *Regulated Rivers*; examples include: Sustaining the Ecological Health of the Upper Mississippi (Volume 11, 2, 137–248, 1995), Habitat Hydraulics (Volume 12, 2–3, 127–344, 1996), and Remedial Strategies in Regulated Rivers (Volume 12, 4–5, 345–561, 1996). An issue of the journal *BioScience* (Volume 45, 3, 125–231, 1995) includes a set of key papers on the problem of applying recent scientific findings to the management of large rivers.

Brookes, A. *Channelized Rivers*. Chichester, U.K.: Wiley, 1988.
Calow, P., and G. E. Petts, eds. *The Rivers Handbook*, vols. 1 and 2. Oxford: Blackwell Scientific, 1992, 1994. A valuable reference work on all aspects of the subject, including case studies. Volume 1 focuses on the fundamental scientific principles—hydrologic, geomorphologic, and biological—and Volume 2 applies these principles to river management problems.
Cosgrove, D. E., and G. E. Petts, eds. *Water, Engineering and Landscape*. London: Belhaven, 1990.
Davies, B. R., and K. F. Walker, eds. *The Ecology of River Systems*. Dordrecht: Junk, 1986.
Degens, E. T., et al., eds. *Biogeochemistry of Major World Rivers*. Chichester, U.K.: Wiley, 1991.
de Waal, L. C., et al., eds. *Ecology and Management of Invasive Riverside Plants*. Chichester, U.K.: Wiley, 1994.

Ellet, Charles. *The Mississippi and Ohio Rivers*. Philadelphia: Lippincott, Grambo, 1853.

Junk, W. J. "The Flood-Pulse Concept in River-Floodplain Systems." *Canadian Special Publication of Fisheries and Aquatic Sciences* 106 (1989), 110–127.

Malanson, G. P. *Riparian Landscapes*. Cambridge: Cambridge University Press, 1993.

Maser, J. R., and J. R. Sedell. *From the Forest to the Sea: The Ecology of Wood in Streams, Rivers, Estuaries and Oceans*. Delray Beach, Fla.: St. Lucie Press, 1994.

Meybeck, M., and R. Helmer. *Palaeogeography, Palaeolimnology, Palaeoecology* 75 (1989), 283–309.

Petts, G. E. *Impounded Rivers*. Chichester, U.K.: Wiley, 1984 (reprinted 1992).

Petts, G. E., et al., eds. *Historical Analysis of Large Alluvial Rivers: Western Europe*. Chichester, U.K.: Wiley, 1989.

Vannote, R. L., et al. "The River Continuum Concept." *Canadian Journal of Fisheries and Aquatic Sciences* 37 (1980), 130–137.

Ward, J. V., and J. A. Stanford. "The Serial Discontinuity Concept: Extending the Model to Foodplain Rivers." *Regulated Rivers* 10 (1995), 159–168.

Welcomme, R. L. *Fisheries Ecology of Floodplain Rivers*. London: Longman, 1979.

Williams, M., ed. *Wetlands: A Threatened Landscape*. London: Institute of British Geographers, 1990.

—G. E. Petts

S

SAHEL DROUGHT. *See* Desertification; *and* Drought.

SALINIZATION

Although salinity is a normal and natural feature of soils and water, especially in areas of water deficit (Szabolcs, 1979), various human activities are increasing its extent and severity—a process called *accelerated salinization.* This has a range of undesirable consequences. For example, as irrigation water is concentrated by evapotranspiration, calcium and magnesium components tend to precipitate as carbonates, leaving sodium ions dominant in the soil solution. The sodium ions tend to be absorbed by colloidal clay particles, disaggregating them and leaving the resultant structureless soil impermeable to water and unfavorable to root development. The death of vegetation in areas of saline patches, due to both poor soil structure and toxicity, creates bare ground, which becomes a focal point for erosion by wind and water. Probably the most serious impact of salinization is on plant growth. This takes place partly through its effect on soil structure, but more significantly through its effects on osmotic pressures and through direct toxicity. When a water solution containing large quantities of dissolved salts comes into contact with a plant cell, it causes a shrinkage of the protoplasmic lining. The phenomenon is due to the osmotic movement of the water, which passes from the cell toward the more concentrated soil solution. The cell collapses and the plant succumbs. The toxicity effect varies with different plants and different salts. Sodium carbonate, by creating highly alkaline soil conditions, may damage plants by a direct caustic effect; while high nitrate may promote undesirable vegetative growth in grapes or sugarbeets at the expense of sugar content. Boron is injurious to many crop plants at solution concentrations of more than 1 or 2 parts per million.

Water salinity limits the use that can be made of drinking water for humans or their domestic stock, and this can be a major constraint on the development of river water and, more significantly, of ground water.

One consequence of increasing salinity levels is the accelerated weathering of buildings and engineering structures (Goudie and Viles, 1997). Salts crystallize, hydrate, and expand volumetrically in stone and concrete, cause mineralogical changes in cements, and corrode iron reinforcements. This has caused the decay of some of the world's great cultural treasures, including the Pharaonic temples and the Sphinx in Egypt, the baked-brick city of Mohenjo-Daro in Pakistan, and the Islamic treasures of Uzbekistan. The same applies to the fabric of some of the great new cities of the Middle East, including those of Bahrain, the United Arab Emirates, and Egypt. [*See* Building Decay.]

There are a variety of reasons why soil and water salinity is spreading. First, and most importantly, the area of irrigated land has increased from roughly 8 million hectares (20 million acres) at the end of the eighteenth century to 250 million hectares at the end of the twentieth (Thomas and Middleton, 1993). The extension of irrigation and the use of a wide range of different techniques for water abstraction and application can lead to a buildup of salt levels in the soil through the raising of ground water so that it is near enough to the ground surface for capillary rise and subsequent evaporative concentration to take place. Table 1 provides some data on the rise of ground water following the introduction of irrigation. In the case of the semiarid northern plains of Victoria in Australia, for instance, the water table has been rising at around 1.5 meters per year, so that now in many areas it is almost within 1 meter of the surface. When ground water comes within 3 meters of the surface in clay soils (less for silty and sandy soils), capillary forces bring moisture to the surface, where evaporation takes place (Currey, 1977). A survey of the problem in southeastern Australia is provided by Grieve (1987).

Second, many irrigation schemes require the addition of large quantities of water over the soil surface. This is especially true for rice cultivation. Such surface water is readily evaporated, so that salinity levels build up. Third, the construction of large dams and barrages to control water flow and to give a head of water creates large reservoirs from which further evaporation can take place.

Fourth, notably in areas of soils with high permeability, water seeps laterally and downward from irrigation canals so that further evaporation occurs. Many distribution channels in a gravity scheme are located on the elevated areas of a flood plain or riverine plain to make maximum use of gravity. The elevated landforms selected are natural levees, river-bordering dunes, and terraces, all of which are composed of silt and sand, which may be particularly prone to seepage loss.

Increases in soil and water salinity are not restricted to irrigated areas. In certain parts of the world, salin-

Salinization. TABLE 1. Increase in Level of Water Table Due to Irrigation

		Water Table (meters)	
IRRIGATION PROJECT	COUNTRY	ORIGINAL DEPTH	RISE/YEAR
Nubariya	Egypt	15–20	2.0–3.0
Beni Amir	Morocco	15–30	1.5–3.0
Murray-Darling	Australia	30–40	0.5–1.5
Amibara	Ethiopia	10–15	1.0
Xinjang Farm 29	China	5–10	0.3–0.5
Bhatinda	India	15	0.6
SCARP 1	Pakistan	40–50	0.4
SCARP 6	Pakistan	10–15	0.2–0.4

SOURCE: From Tolba et al. (1992, p. 94).

ization has resulted from vegetation clearance (Peck, 1978). The removal of native forest vegetation allows a greater penetration of rainfall into deeper soil layers, which causes groundwater levels to rise, creating seepage of saline water in low-lying areas. Through this mechanism, an estimated 200,000 hectares of land in southern Australia, which at the start of European settlement supported good crops or pasture, is now suitable only for halophytic (salt-tolerant) species. Similar problems also exist in North America, notably in Manitoba, Alberta, Montana, and North Dakota.

The clearance of the native evergreen forest (predominantly *Eucalyptus* forest) in southwestern Australia has led both to an increase in recharge rates of ground water and to an increase in the salinity of streams. Replanting can reverse the process (Bari and

Salinization. TABLE 2. Stream Salinity of Major Rivers in Western Australia

CATCHMENT	PERIOD OF RECORD	AREA CLEARED (PERCENT)	AVERAGE STREAM SALINITY OVER LAST FIVE YEARS OF RECORD (MG L^{-1})	RATE OF STREAM SALINITY INCREASE OVER PERIOD OF RECORD (MG L^{-1} YR^{-1})	RATE OF STREAM SALINITY INCREASE OVER PERIOD SINCE 1965 (MG L^{-1} YR^{-1})
Denmark R.	1960–86	17	890	25	26
Kent R.	1956–86	40	1870	52	58
Frankland R.	1940–86	35	2192	44	74
Warren R.	1940–86	36	870	12	15
Perup R.*	1961–86	19	3410	132	117
Wilgarup R.*	1961–86	33	863	20	14
Blackwood R.	1956–86	85	2192	52	58
Capel R.	1959–76	50	423	15	14
Preston R.	1955–75	50	354	8	11
Thomson R.	1957–85	45	534	18	17
Collie R.	1940–86	24	730	11	24
Murray R.	1939–86	75	2792	39	93
Williams R.†	1966–86	90	2425	95	95
Hotham R.†	1966–86	85	3711	89	89
Woorollo Bk	1965–86	50	2092	44	39
Brockman R.	1963–86	65	2040	76	72
Helena R.	1966–85	10	1257	48	48

*Tributaries of the Warren River.

†Tributaries of the Murray River.

SOURCE: Ghassemi et al., 1995 (Table 2.6). With permission of the Centre for Resource and Environmental Studies, The Australian National University, Canberra.

SEAWATER INCURSION AND THE GHYBEN–HERZBERG RELATIONSHIP

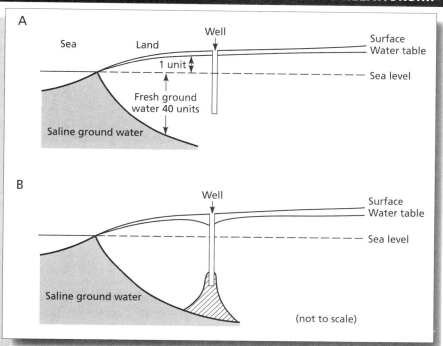

(A) The Ghyben–Herzberg relationship between fresh and saline ground water. (B) The effect of excessive pumping from the well, showing the increasing incursion of saline water. (After Goudie and Wilkinson, 1977, Figure 63. With permission of Cambridge University Press.)

In coastal areas salinity problems are created by seawater incursion brought about by overpumping of ground water. This can be explained as follows. Fresh water has a lower density than salt water, such that a column of sea water can support a column of fresh water approximately 2.5 percent higher than itself (or a ratio of about 40:41). So where a body of fresh water has accumulated in a reservoir rock that is also open to penetration from the sea, it does not simply lie flat on top of the slat water but forms a lens, whose thickness is approximately forty-one times the elevation of the piezometric surface above the sea level. This is called the Ghyben–Herzberg principle (see figure). The corollary of this rule is that if the hydrostatic pressure of the fresh water falls as a result of overpumping in a well, then the underlying salt water will rise by forty units for every unit by which the freshwater table is lowered.

This problem presents itself on the coast of Israel, in California, on the island of Bahrain, and in some of the small coastal dune aquifers of the United Arab Emirates.

The problem of seawater incursion as a result of overpumping of aquifers is not, however, restricted to arid and semiarid areas. It was noted as early as the middle of the last century in London and Liverpool, England, and there are now many records of this phenomenon in Germany, the Netherlands, Japan, and the eastern seaboard of the United States.

—Andrew S. Goudie

Schofield, 1992). Data on trends for stream salinity in western Australia are shown in Table 2.

Salinity can also be increased by translocation of saline materials from lake beds that desiccate as a consequence of interbasin water transfers. Around 30–40 million metric tons per year are blown off the shrunken Aral Sea, for example, and these add to the salt content of soils downwind. [See Aral Sea, Desiccation of the.]

In coastal areas, salinity problems are created by seawater incursion brought about by overpumping. This can be explained as follows. Fresh water has a lower density than salt water, such that a column of sea water can support a column of fresh water approximately 2.5 percent higher than itself (or a ratio of about 40:41).

So where a body of fresh water has accumulated in a reservoir rock that is also open to penetration from the sea, it does not simply lie flat on top of the salt water but forms a lens, whose thickness is approximately forty-one times the elevation of the piezometric surface above sea level. This is called the *Ghyben–Herzberg Principle.* The corollary of this rule is that if the hydrostatic pressure of the fresh water falls as a result of overpumping in a well, the underlying salt water will rise by forty units for every unit by which the freshwater table is lowered. The problem presents itself on the coastal plain of Israel, in parts of California, on the island of Bahrain, and in some of the coastal aquifers of the United Arab Emirates. A comparable situation has also

Salinization. TABLE 3. Extent of Salt-Affected Soils by Continent and Subcontinent*

REGION	MILLIONS OF HECTARES
North America	15.7
Mexico and Central America	2.0
South America	129.2
Africa	80.5
South Asia	84.8
North and Central Asia	211.7
Southeast Asia	20.0
Australia	357.3
Europe	50.8
Total	952.0

*"Salt-affected" includes both saline soils and alkaline soils.
SOURCE: After Szabolcs (1979).

arisen in the case of the Nile Delta, although here the problem is not necessarily due to groundwater over-pumping, but may be the result of changes in water levels and freshwater recharge occasioned by the construction of the Aswan High Dam.

Urbanization can also lead to changes in groundwater conditions. In some large desert cities, the importation of water and its usage, wastage, and leakage can produce the ingredients to feed this phenomenon. This has, for example, been identified as a problem in Cairo and its immediate environs. The very rapid expansion of Cairo's population has outstripped the development of an adequate municipal infrastructure. In particular, leakage losses from water pipes and sewers have led to a substantial rise in the groundwater level.

In those areas of the world with severe winter frosts, salts can build up in the environment from another source. Rock salt (sodium chloride) has been used in increasing quantities since World War II to minimize the dangers to motorists and pedestrians from icy roads and sidewalks. With the rise in the number of vehicles there has been a corresponding increase throughout Europe and North America in the use of salt for deicing purposes (see, for example, Howard and Beck, 1993). Data for the United Kingdom demonstrate that, while there is considerable interannual variability (related to weather severity), there has also been a general upward trend so that, from the mid-1970s to the late 1980s, more than 2 million metric tons of deicing salt were being purchased each year (Dobson, 1991). Data on deicing salt application in North America are given by Scott and Wylie (1980). They indicate that the total use of deicing salts in the United States increased at a nearly exponential rate between the 1940s and the 1970s, increasing from about 200,000 metric tons in 1940 to approximately 9 million metric tons in 1970. This represented a doubling time of about five years.

With regard to the future, global changes in climate and sea level could have implications for salinity conditions. For example, increasing drought risk in Mediterranean Europe could lead to a substantial increase in

Salinization. TABLE 4. Global Estimate of Secondary Salinization in the World's Irrigated Land

COUNTRY	CROPPED AREA (Mha)	IRRIGATED AREA (Mha)	SHARE OF IRRIGATED TO CROPPED AREA (PERCENT)	SALT-AFFECTED LAND IN IRRIGATED AREA (Mha)	SHARE OF SALT-AFFECTED TO IRRIGATED LAND (PERCENT)
China	96.97	44.83	46.2	6.70	15.0
India	168.99	42.10	24.9	7.00	16.6
Commonwealth of Independent States	232.57	20.48	8.8	3.70	18.1
United States	189.91	18.10	9.5	4.16	23.0
Pakistan	20.76	16.08	77.5	4.22	26.2
Iran	14.83	5.74	38.7	1.72	30.0
Thailand	20.05	4.00	19.9	0.40	10.0
Egypt	2.69	2.69	100.0	0.88	33.0
Australia	47.11	1.83	3.9	0.16	8.7
Argentina	35.75	1.72	4.8	0.58	33.7
South Africa	13.17	1.13	8.6	0.10	8.9
Subtotal	842.80	158.70	18.8	29.62	20.0
World	1473.70	227.11	15.4	45.4	20.0

SOURCE: From Ghassemi et al. (1995, Table 18). With permission of the Centre for Resource and Environmental Studies, The Australian National University, Canberra.

salt-prone areas (Imeson and Emmer, 1992; Szabolcs, 1994), while higher sea levels in susceptible geomorphologic locations (coastal deltas, the sabkhas of the Arabian Gulf) could change the position of the all-important salt/freshwater interface and the height of the water table.

At present, however, it has been estimated that the area of salt-affected and waterlogged soils amounts to 50 percent of the irrigated area in Iraq, 23 percent of all Pakistan, 50 percent in the Euphrates valley of Syria, 30 percent in Egypt, and over 15 percent in Iran (Worthington, 1977, p. 30). In Africa, on the other hand, less than 10 percent of salt-affected soils are so affected because of human action (Thomas and Middleton, 1993). Tables 3 and 4 present data on the extent of salt-affected lands by continent and subcontinent, and for individual countries.

On a global basis, the calculations of Rozanov et al. (1991) make grim reading. They estimate (p. 120) that "From 1700 to 1984, the global areas of irrigated land increased from 50,000 to 2,200,000 km^2, while at the same time some 500,000 km^2 were abandoned as a result of secondary salinization." They believe that in the last three centuries total soil loss due to irrigation is 1 million square kilometers of land destroyed, plus 1 million square kilometers of land with diminished productivity due to salinization.

Given the seriousness of the problem, a range of techniques for the eradication, conversion, or control of soil salinity have been developed. These have been reviewed by Rhoades (1990). They can be divided into three main types: eradication, conservation, and control.

Eradication predominantly involves the removal of salt, either by improved drainage or by the addition of quantities of fresh water to leach the salt out of the soil. Both solutions involve considerable expense and pose severe technological problems in areas of low relief and limited freshwater availability. Improved drainage can either be provided by open drains or by the use of tube-wells to reduce groundwater levels and associated salinity and waterlogging. A minor eradication measure that may have some potential is the biotic treatment of salinity through the harvesting of salt-accumulating plants such as Suaeda fruticosa (shrubby sea-blite).

Conversion involves the use of chemical methods to convert harmful salts into less harmful ones. For example, gypsum is frequently added to sodic soils to convert caustic alkali carbonates to soluble sodium sulfate and relatively harmless calcium carbonate:

$$Na_2CO_3 + CaSO_4 = CaCO_3 + Na_2SO_4$$
$$\downarrow \text{ leachable}$$

Some of the most effective ways of reducing the salinity hazard involve miscellaneous control measures, such as

less wasteful and lavish application of water through the use of sprinklers rather than traditional irrigation methods; the lining of canals to reduce seepage; the realignment of canals through less-permeable soil; and the use of more salt-tolerant plants. Because salinity is a particularly serious threat at the time of germination and for seedlings, various strategies can be adopted during this critical phase of plant growth: plots can be irrigated lightly each day after seeding to prevent salt buildup; major leaching can be carried out just before planting; and areas to be seeded can be bedded in such a way that salts accumulate at the ridge tops, with the seed planted on the slope between the furrow bottom and the ridge top.

To conclude, accelerated salinization created problems for Mesopotamian farmers four thousand years ago, and it remains a very real environmental problem today. Land-cover changes, the spread of irrigation, the exploitation of ground water, and the application of salts for deicing purposes are all involved in the process. Several methods are available for reducing the problem that accelerated salinization creates, but some parts of the world may suffer in the future if sea levels rise and rates of evapotranspiration increase.

[See also Desertification; Irrigation; and Soils.]

BIBLIOGRAPHY

Bari, M. A., and N. J. Schofield. "Lowering of a Shallow Saline Water Table by Extensive Eucalyptus Reforestation." *Journal of Hydrology* 133 (1992), 273–291.

Currey, D. T. "The Role of Applied Geomorphology in Irrigation and Groundwater Studies." In *Applied Geomorphology*, edited by J. R. Hails, pp. 51–83. Amsterdam: Elsevier, 1977.

Dobson, M. C. "De-Icing Salt Damage to Trees and Shrubs." *Forestry Commission Bulletin* 101 (1991).

Ghassemi, F., A. J. Jakeman, and H. A. Nix. *Salinisation of Land and Water Resources*. Wallingford, U.K.: CAB International, 1995. A very full and up-to-date analysis of the problem in a global context.

Goudie, A. S., and H. A. Viles. *Salt Weathering Hazards*. Chichester, U.K.: Wiley, 1997. An analysis of salt attack on buildings in a wide change of environments.

Goudie, A. S., and J. C. Wilkinson. *The Warm Desert Environment*. Cambridge: Cambridge University Press, 1977.

Grieve, A. M. "Salinity and Waterlogging in the Murray–Darling Basin." *Search* 18 (1987), 72–74.

Howard, K. W. F., and P. J. Beck. "Hydrogeochemical Implications of Groundwater Contamination by Road De-Icing Chemicals." *Journal of Contaminant Hydrology* 12 (1993), 245–268.

Imeson, A., and I. M. Emmer. "Implications of Climatic Change on Land Degradation in the Mediterranean." In *Climatic Change and the Mediterranean*, edited by L. Jeftic, J. D. Milliman, and G. Sestini, pp. 95–128. London: Edward Arnold, 1992.

Peck, A. J. "Salinization of Non-irrigated Soils and Associated Streams: A Review." *Australian Journal of Soil Research* 16 (1978), 157–168.

Rhoades, J. D. "Soil Salinity: Causes and Controls." In *Techniques for Desert Reclamation*, edited by A. S. Goudie, pp. 109–134. Chichester, U.K.: Wiley, 1990.

Rozanov, B. G., V. Targulian, and D. S. Orlov. "Soils." In *The Earth as Transformed by Human Action*, edited by B. Turner et al., pp. 203–214. Cambridge: Cambridge University Press, 1991.

Scott, W. S., and N. P. Wylie. "The Environmental Effects of Snow Dumping: A Literature Review." *Journal of Environmental Management* 10 (1980), 219–240.

Szabolcs, I. *Review of Research on Salt-Affected Soils.* Paris: UNESCO, 1979.

———. "State and Perspectives on Soil Salinity in Europe." *European Society for Soil Conservation Newsletter* 3 (1994), 17–24.

Thomas, D. S. G., and J. J. Middleton. "Salinization: New Perspectives on a Major Desertification Issue." *Journal of Arid Environments* 24 (1993), 95–105.

Tolba, M. K., and O. A. El-Kholy. *The World Environment 1972–1992.* London: Chapman and Hall, 1992.

Worthington, E. B. *Arid Land Irrigation in Developing Countries: Environmental Problems and Effects.* Oxford: Pergamon, 1977.

—ANDREW S. GOUDIE

SALT MARSHES. *See* Wetlands.

SANITATION

The term *sanitation* derives its meaning from the Latin *sanitas*, or health. In its broad, traditional sense, sanitation refers to measures taken to control or change the physical environment to prevent the transmission of diseases to human beings. Classically, this has involved the control of community water supplies, excreta and wastewater disposal, refuse disposal, vectors of disease, housing conditions, food supplies and handling, atmospheric conditions, and the work environment.

Although many physical, biological, and chemical substances in the environment can adversely affect human health, current usage and modern operational practices have come to focus the meaning of sanitation on the collection and disposal of human excreta and waste water. In 1986, a World Health Organization (WHO) Study Group defined sanitation as "the means of collecting and disposing of excreta and community liquid wastes in a hygienic way so as not to endanger the health of individuals and the community as a whole." These wastes include, in particular, human excreta (urine and feces) and household sullage (used water from washing, bathing, and other domestic activities).

The definition of sanitation adopted here will therefore be limited to the management of human excreta and other liquid household wastes such that the pathogenic substances they carry do not come into contact with domestic water supplies (including water for drinking, cooking, personal hygiene, and general household cleanliness), food crops, people, or animals. Of these, the most important wastes from a health standpoint are human excreta. Although the primary purpose of sanitation interventions is to prevent or limit the transmission of diseases arising from poor environmental conditions, other factors, such as convenience, social status, and cost, influence the choices that people make for sanitation systems. However, the ultimate rationale for sanitation and for sanitation interventions is that they are essential for the promotion and maintenance of health.

Sanitation System Options. In general, options for excreta and wastewater disposal can be divided into "dry" and "wet" categories.

Dry sanitation systems. Such systems are those in which the wastes are deposited directly into an area or container that safely isolates the pathogenic substances (bacteria, viruses, worms, and so forth) from contact with people, water supplies, food, and animal and insect vectors. Dry systems may range from simple pits in the earth to elaborate composting devices. All promote the basic processes of biological decomposition to convert the pathogenic substances into less hazardous materials. The main types of dry sanitation options are bucket latrines; simple pit latrines; improved latrines; and composting latrines.

Bucket latrines involve the deposition of excreta directly into a bucket or similar container that is periodically emptied, often daily, and taken away to a disposal site. In some Asian countries, fresh excreta from bucket latrines is routinely spread over agricultural fields. Bucket latrine systems can be found in traditional communities, in which a container with excreta is manually removed through a small opening in the wall of a house, as well as in modern situations, such as airplanes and ships, in which excreta is collected and held in elaborate mechanical containers for later removal. Traditional bucket latrines often pose health hazards because of the dangers involved in the manual handling and disposal of fresh excreta.

Simple pit latrines, at the most basic level, can be shallow holes scratched into the ground, each serving a single user, as well as long trenches utilized by numerous users. In both cases, the excreta should be immediately covered with earth to keep the site sanitary. A more lasting latrine involves digging a pit, covering it with a platform on which the user squats or sits over a hole, and surrounding the user with a shelter made of thatch, wood, stone, or bricks. Excreta is deposited directly into the pit by the user squatting or sitting on the platform. The volume of the pit and the number of users determines the "life," or duration, of the latrine. At an average accumulation of 0.06 cubic meters of fecal matter per person per year, a pit one meter in diameter and two meters deep will serve a family of six for about four years before becoming full.

Ventilated improved pit (VIP) latrines involve the addition of a vent pipe to remove odors and prevent flies from escaping the pit. The vent pipe rises from the pit and extends above the roof of the surrounding superstructure. A fly-proof screen at the top of the pipe allows the passage of gases from the pit but prevents the escape of flies that breed in the collected excreta. A variation on the VIP is the Reed Odorless Earth Closet (ROEC), which offsets the pit from the superstructure and connects it to the latrine by means of a chute. Both the VIP and the ROEC latrines are intended to remain partially dark so that flies in the pit are attracted to the light at the top of the vent pipe, where they are trapped by the screen and die. When latrine pits become full, a new latrine must be constructed or the pit must be emptied—a hazardous task since fresh excreta is pathogenic. It is preferable to close the pit and allow it to remain unused for at least a year, after which the decomposed excreta may be safely removed and used as a compost or soil fertilizer. The offset ROEC system allows alternative pits to be used with the same latrine superstructure by shifting the drop chute from one pit to the other.

Composting latrines consist of shallow vaults into which kitchen and other organic wastes as well as excreta are deposited. The wastes decompose and are periodically removed for use as fertilizer. There are many different designs of composting latrine. In Europe and North America, they are frequently manufactured units installed within residential or commercial buildings. Some models employ sloping pans that allow the excreta to decompose as it slowly moves down to a holding bin. Others use special organic additives to speed up the process of decomposition. In developing countries, composting latrines are similar to pit latrines but usually have two shallow vaults under the latrine floor. When one becomes full, it is closed and the second vault is used. After a year or more the first vault is opened and the compost used as an agricultural fertilizer. All composting latrines must be kept dry and must have daily additions of organic wastes or other biological nutrients. Because of the need to maintain proper biological conditions in the vaults, composting latrines are more costly to build than ordinary pit latrines and are more difficult to operate properly.

Wet sanitation systems. These systems use water to transport the wastes to the point of disposal. In some systems, the water also serves as a medium for the biological decomposition of the wastes. Wet systems range from simple pour flush latrines with a water-seal trap to modern sewerage systems leading to sewage treatment plants. The main types of wet sanitation options are pour flush latrines, aqua privies, septic tanks, conventional sewerage, and low-cost sewerage.

Pour flush latrines use a pan with a water-seal trap that prevents flies and odors from entering the superstructure from the pit. Excreta is deposited in the pan and then a small quantity of water, usually 1–2 liters, is manually poured into the pan, flushing the wastes into the pit but leaving behind a seal of water. The pit may be under the latrine superstructure or, more commonly, offset to allow periodic emptying. Two pits are sometimes constructed to allow continuous use of the latrine when the first pit is full. The liquid wastes that enter the pit are allowed to infiltrate into the ground. Pour flush latrines must have a reliable supply of water to operate or the pan will quickly become clogged.

Aqua privies contain a drop pipe leading to a watertight tank filled with water below the latrine floor. Excreta enters the tank through the drop pipe, which extends below the surface of the water to prevent the escape of odors and flies. Excreta solids accumulate in the tank, where they slowly decompose. Excess liquid wastes are carried out of the tank by an overflow pipe to a soakpit or underground disposal field. Proper operation of aqua privies requires continuous maintenance of the water level in the tank to cover the drop pipe as well as a regular desludging, perhaps every three years, of the accumulated solids in the tank.

Septic tanks are multichambered, watertight underground tanks where excreta and other household waste waters are separated into solids and scum and excess liquids. They can be used to process the larger quantities of water and wastes conveyed by household plumbing systems (flush toilets, sink and bath drains, etc.) connected to piped water supplies. Solids are retained in one of the chambers of the tank, where they undergo partial decomposition and excess liquids are discharged to soakaways and underground drainfields. Septic tanks provide a low-maintenance and hygienic system for handling both excreta and household wastewater where access to an off-site sewerage system is not available. To operate properly, however, septic tanks must be periodically emptied, approximately every three years, and the drainfields must be in permeable soils to accept the large quantities of effluent.

Conventional sewerage involves the use of underground pipes to remove excreta and household waste waters to an off-site location for treatment and eventual disposal. Because large quantities of water are required to move excreta solids through the pipes, conventional sewerage systems are appropriate only where reliable and ample supplies of water (generally 100 liters of water per person per day) are available. Sewer pipes in and near the household normally are 150 millimeters and larger, while those that collect and transport sewage to treatment facilities may range in diameter from 200 millimeters to over 2 meters. Conventional treatment of sewage normally occurs at a municipal facility, and may consist of screening, settlement of solids, biological decomposition through trickling filters, activated sludge or oxidation ponds, and, finally, sludge removal and drying. Sewage treatment is essential to prevent the discharged effluent from contaminating rivers, ground water, and other water bodies. Even with conventional treatment, sewage effluent may contain a large number of pathogenic organisms. Most sewerage systems around the world currently discharge untreated or inadequately treated effluent into their receiving water bodies. In Latin America, it is estimated that only 10 percent of the sewage collected receives adequate treatment before discharge back into the environment.

Two low-cost variations of conventional sewerage are settled sewerage and simplified sewerage. Settled sewerage systems are suitable in areas with existing septic tanks where small-diameter sewer pipes can be laid at relatively shallow slopes to carry away liquid effluents. Solids and other heavy wastes are retained in the septic tanks, but liquids flow away in the small-diameter sewers to the treatment and/or disposal site. Simplified sewerage systems, on the other hand, accept all excreta and household wastewater without prior separation in septic tanks. The wastes progress though small-diameter, shallow-slope sewers in a series of intermittent surges when households flush their wastes into the system. Simplified sewerage, also called condominial sewerage, is most appropriate in high-density, low-income areas where housing units all have individual water connections.

Sanitation System Costs. The costs of building and maintaining sanitation systems vary from nearly zero for single-use pits and basic trench latrines to thousands of dollars for conventional sewerage and sophisticated composting latrines. Even within similar sanitation systems, great cost variations can occur as a result of design differences, materials employed, and regional cost factors. Pit latrines, for example, may cost as much as U.S.$1,000 each if costly materials are used for the superstructure, floor, and pit. On the other hand, if local materials are used and the construction is carried out by the household itself, the actual out-of-pocket cost may be only U.S.$2–3 for cement and reinforcing for the latrine floor slab. In general, the simpler sanitation systems offer more opportunities for household inputs of labor and materials.

Bearing in mind these factors, rough capital cost estimates per household for different sanitation systems can be made as follows: pit latrines (both simple and improved), U.S.$5–100; composting latrines, U.S.$20–1,000; pour flush latrines, U.S.$20–150; aqua privies, U.S.$500–2,000; septic tanks, U.S.$500–3,000; conventional sewerage, U.S.$1,000–5,000; and low-cost sewerage, U.S.$200–1,000. In 1990, the United Nations Development Programme and the World Bank estimated that urban sewerage and treatment have a global average cost of U.S.$350 per person served, while United Nations Children's Fund (UNICEF) estimated that rural latrines have a global average cost of U.S.$20 per per-

son. WHO data for 1990 indicate that per capita costs of urban sanitation varied from a regional low of U.S.$95 in Latin America and Southeast Asia to a regional high of U.S.$370 in the western Pacific. Data for rural sanitation ranged from U.S.$10 per capita in Southeast Asia to U.S.$70 in the eastern Mediterranean. Projecting these data to the expected global population needing improved sanitation in the year 2025, WHO estimates that a total of U.S.$335 billion will have to be spent on new construction by that date.

Social Preferences for Sanitation Systems. In addition to cost, the choice of sanitation system is strongly influenced by cultural practices and the availability of water and other cleansing materials. Perhaps half of the world's population adopts a squatting posture during defecation, while the other half prefers to sit on some sort of seat or pedestal. Similarly, a significant minority uses water for anal cleansing, while the majority employs paper, leaves, or other traditional materials. In areas where water is scarce, dry sanitation systems predominate. In areas where water is abundant, there is greater demand for wet systems. Among high-income populations, there is usually great demand for the convenience and status of water-borne (i.e., sewerage) systems. Cultural practices and sanitation-related behaviors can be changed over time through public information and hygiene education. The key factor is the belief by the people that the adoption of change will be to their benefit.

Access to Sanitation Services. Environmental sanitation was given a major boost by the United Nations Water Conference, held at Mar del Plata, Argentina, in 1977, when the concept of a global decade-long effort to meet the water supply and sanitation needs of all the peoples of the world was initiated. At the time, only 44 percent of the population of the developing world had access to safe drinking water and 46 percent had basic sanitation. This meant that around 1.8 billion people lacked potable water and nearly as many were without sanitation (United Nations, 1990). During the resulting International Drinking Water Supply and Sanitation Decade (1981–1990), some 1.5 billion additional people were served with safe water and about 750 million with adequate excreta disposal facilities. Because of population growth in the developing countries of 800 million people over the decade, however, there remained by 1990 a total of over one billion people without safe water and 1.75 billion without adequate sanitation.

Overall progress in reaching the unserved has been poor since 1990. The most recent data (1994) indicate that more than 1.1 billion people, or one-quarter of the population of the developing countries, still lack safe water and perhaps 2.9 billion, or two-thirds, do not have adequate excreta disposal facilities. Table 1 shows the percentage of people in the developing world lacking

Sanitation. TABLE 1. Regional Sanitation Coverage: Urban and Rural Areas, 1980, 1990, 1994, and 2000*

	1980		*1990*		*1994*		*2000 (est.)*	
REGION	URBAN	RURAL	URBAN	RURAL	URBAN	RURAL	URBAN	RURAL
Africa	65	18	65	23	55	24	43	25
Latin America and the Caribbean	78	22	83	33	73	34	60	35
Asia and the Pacific	65	42	62	18	61	15	59	12
Western Asia	79	34	70	60	70	64	66	69
Global	69	37	67	20	63	18	57	16

*Units are percent served.

SOURCE: United Nations (1990, 1995).

access to adequate means of sanitation (i.e., sanitary excreta disposal) since 1980, with projections to the year 2000. Since 1990, sanitation coverage has stagnated or declined in most regions, with the decline most notable in Asia and the Pacific region, which includes both China and India. In 1994, China reported only 7 percent rural sanitation coverage, while India reported only 14 percent.

The coverage declines in Table 1 are attributable to rapid population growth, lagging rates of sanitation expansion, and stricter national definitions of adequate sanitation. Population in the developing countries, for instance, which was around 3.2 billion people in 1980, will rise to an estimated 4.9 billion by the year 2000. Unless the current rate of coverage is increased, the expansion of sanitation (and water supply) services will

Sanitation. TABLE 2. Estimates of Morbidity and Mortality of Diseases Related to Poor Environmental Sanitation

DISEASE	MORBIDITY	MORTALITY (DEATHS PER YEAR)	RELATIONSHIP OF DISEASE TO ENVIRONMENTAL SANITATION
Diarrheal diseases, including dysentery	4,002,000,000*	2,473,000	Strongly related to unsanitary excreta disposal, poor personal hygiene, unsafe drinking water
Typhoid fever	16,000,000*	600,000	Strongly related to drinking water and food contaminated by human excreta, poor personal hygiene
Dengue and dengue hemorrhagic fever	3,100,000*	138,000	Strongly related to unsanitary solid waste disposal
Amoebiasis	48,000,000*	70,000	Related to unsanitary excreta disposal, poor personal hygiene, food contaminated by human excreta
Hookworms	151,000,000[†]	65,000	Strongly related to soil contaminated by human excreta, poor personal hygiene
Ascariasis	250,000,000[†]	60,000	Related to unsanitary disposal of human feces, food contaminated by soil containing human feces, poor personal hygiene
Schistosomiasis	200,000,000[†]	20,000	Strongly related to unsanitary excreta disposal and absence of nearby sources of safe water
Trichuriasis	45,530,000[†]	10,000	Related to soil contaminated by human feces, poor personal hygiene
Cholera	120,000*	6,000	Strongly related to drinking water contaminated by human feces
Giardiasis	500,000*	—	Strongly related to drinking water contaminated by human fecal matter, poor personal hygiene
Trachoma	152,420,000[†]	—	Related to poor personal hygiene, lack of soap and water
Dracunculiasis	130,000[†]	—	Strongly related to drinking water containing infected copapods

*Episodes per year.

[†]Cases per year.

SOURCE: World Health Organization (1997a).

continue to be matched, or exceeded, by population growth into the foreseeable future.

Disease Burden of Poor Environmental Sanitation. Many infectious diseases are related to poor environmental sanitation. The burden of this suffering falls disproportionately upon the poorest members of society, especially those in isolated rural communities and periurban slums where sanitation services are often poor. Of the approximately six billion people populating our planet today, the poorest one billion suffer seven times more mortality from infectious diseases and maternal and perinatal conditions than do the richest billion. The great majority of these deaths are attributable to infectious diseases, with most caused by poor environmental sanitation. Regional health statistics can mask great variations that often exist between countries. In Latin America, for example, infant mortality and child mortality rates for the region are considerably lower than global averages. Nevertheless, national rates for infant and child mortality are six to seven times higher in some Latin American countries than in others.

Mortality statistics, however, are only one measure of overall health conditions. They provide limited information on the total disease burden and very little guidance on interventions to reduce infectious diseases. This latter function is the role of environmental sanitation interventions, which are primarily intended to prevent the transmission of diseases, not to prevent mortality directly. Proper environmental sanitation limits the occurrence of illness, and hence controls morbidity, which in turn reduces the number of sick people at risk of dying from the diseases.

Diseases resulting from poor environmental sanitation constitute a major component of the total disease burden. WHO reports that almost half of the world's population suffers from diseases associated with insufficient or contaminated water. Currently, diarrheal diseases, including dysentery, are the leading cause of global morbidity (incidence of disease), with over four billion new cases in 1996, and the sixth leading cause of mortality, with almost 2.5 million deaths in that year. WHO estimates that approximately 90 percent of the global diarrheal disease burden is related to the combination of poor sanitation and lack of access to clean water and safe food.

Other diseases related to poor sanitation conditions include those caused by contaminated water and food, such as typhoid fever, cholera, and giardiasis. When contaminated water supplies are linked to inadequate general sanitation and poor personal hygiene, the health outcomes can be devastating. For example, giardiasis and typhoid are spread by fecally contaminated water, and cholera is spread by fecally contaminated water and food. Poor sanitation also contributes to vector-borne diseases. Dengue and dengue hemorrhagic fever flour-ish in overcrowded cities with large accumulations of solid waste and poor drainage of surface water where *Aedes aegypti* mosquitoes breed. Schistosomiasis, moreover, is acquired by swimming or working in freshwater bodies containing intermediate snail hosts infected by human excreta. Improper excreta disposal also results in intestinal parasitic infections arising from worms living in fecally contaminated soil.

Table 2 summarizes some of the morbidity and mortality rates for the main diseases related to poor environmental sanitation.

The Role of Environmental Sanitation. The unsanitary disposal of human excreta is the main cause of most of the diseases in Table 2. Improper disposal of human excreta allows pathogenic organisms to contaminate the soil and water sources, and eventually to spread to drinking water, cooking utensils, food, and even people themselves. While some of the listed diseases, such as dengue fever, trachoma, and dracunculiasis, are not transmitted through human fecal matter, they tend to flourish where general cleanliness, personal hygiene, and sanitary behaviors are either poor or lacking.

There is a strong interaction between water and wastes. Water is a vehicle: for maintaining life, for aiding cleanliness, and for transporting pathogens. Wastes, especially human excreta, harbor the pathogens that contaminate the environment and result in sickness. When poorly managed, water serves as a vehicle for spreading pathogens through fecal–oral transmission routes, contamination of the household environment, and creation of vector breeding sites. Sanitation systems are intended to minimize the spread of pathogens, prevent the contamination of water sources and food stocks, and promote good hygienic practices through proper management of human excreta and household waste water.

[*See also* Disease; Human Health; Sustainable Development; *and* Water Quality.]

BIBLIOGRAPHY

Franceys, R., et al. *A Guide to the Development of On-Site Sanitation.* Geneva: World Health Organization, 1992.

Huttly, S. R. A. "The Impact of Inadequate Sanitary Conditions on Health in Developing Countries." *World Health Statistics Quarterly* 43.3 (1990), 118–126.

United Nations. "Achievements of the International Drinking Water Supply and Sanitation Decade 1981–1990." Report of the Secretary-General. General Assembly (A/45/327). New York, 1990.

———. "Progress Made in Providing Safe Water Supply and Sanitation for All during the First Half of the 1990s." Report of the Secretary-General. Economic and Social Council (E/1995/86). New York, 1995.

U.S. Agency for International Development/UNICEF. *Better Sanitation Programming: A UNICEF Handbook.* EHP Applied Study No. 5. Washington, D.C., 1997.

Warner, D. B. "Environmental Sanitation and Child Health: The

Missing Link in Child Survival." In *The Changing Status of Children in Latin America: Issues in Child Health and Children's Rights*. Notre Dame, Ind.: Kellogg Institute, 1998.

World Bank. *Appropriate Technology for Water Supply and Sanitation*. Transportation, Water and Telecommunications Department. Washington, D.C., 1980. A series of twelve comprehensive volumes reporting on World Bank investigations into appropriate technologies for water supply and waste disposal in developing countries. See especially J. M. Kalbermatten et al., *Technical and Economic Options* (vol. 1); and, by the same authors, *A Sanitation Field Manual* (vol. 11).

World Health Organization. "Evaluation of the International Drinking Water Supply and Sanitation Decade, 1981–1990." Report by the Director-General. World Health Assembly (A45/15). Geneva, 1992.

———. *Cholera and Other Epidemic Diarrhoeal Diseases Control: Fact Sheets on Environmental Sanitation*. WHO/EOS/96.4. Geneva, 1996a. A compilation of sixty-nine technical guidelines giving concise information on all aspects of sanitation, with particular reference to diarrheal disease control.

———. *The World Health Report 1996: Fighting Disease, Fostering Development*. Report of the Director-General. Geneva, 1996b.

———. *Participatory Hygiene and Sanitation Transformation: A New Approach to Working with Communities*. WHO/EOS/96.11. Geneva, 1996c.

———. *The World Health Report 1997: Conquering Suffering, Enriching Humanity*. Report of the Director-General. Geneva, 1997a.

———. *Health and Environment in Sustainable Development: Five Years after the Earth Summit*. WHO/EHG/97.8. Geneva, 1997b.

———. *Sanitation Promotion*. Geneva, 1998. A compilation of forty-four articles prepared for the purpose of promoting improved sanitation through better understanding of needs, political will, partnerships, child-centered approaches, participatory approaches, empowerment, and innovative technologies.

World Health Organization/UNICEF/WSSCC. *Water Supply and Sanitation Sector Monitoring Report 1996*. (Sector status as of 31 December 1994.) WHO/EOS/96.15. Geneva, 1996.

—DENNIS B. WARNER

SATELLITES. *See* Global Monitoring; *and* Remote Sensing.

SAUER, CARL

The long life and voluminous writing career of Carl Ortwin Sauer (1888–1975), American cultural geographer and Professor and Head of Geography at Berkeley from 1925 to 1975, is difficult to typify easily. The term *polymath* has been applied to him because of his wide knowledge in the humanities and natural sciences, especially where these impinged on his research interests in Ibero-America and early humans during the Pleistocene. He displayed an ability to link diverse evidence together and then take bold, intuitive leaps and speculative sweeps. The importance of the past in under-standing the contemporary cultural landscape was central to his thinking. "Cultural geography" became associated with his name, and his many students spread the word about the Berkeley School of cultural geography throughout universities in the United States.

Sauer developed a deep concern about "a good Earth." During the early 1920s he had worked with the Economic Land Survey in the Michigan Cutovers and became aware that not all use of the land use was beneficial or wise, and that, in the name of progress, humans could destroy as well as improve an area. Later work on the erosion of the old cotton- and tobacco-growing lands in the Piedmont of the Carolinas, Georgia, and Alabama reinforced this.

Sauer had two intellectual inspirations for his concerns: George Perkins Marsh's 1864 publication of *Man and Nature* and Ernst Friedrich's 1904 *Wesen und Geographische Verbreitung der "Raubwirtschaft"* ("destructive exploitation"). Applying this concept to Latin America, he saw that the Spanish conquest had led to the ravaging of New World societies. They were decimated by disease, warfare, and enslavement, and their land and traditional value systems were totally disrupted. An early exposition of these concerns came in 1938 with two biting critiques of the destruction caused by the diffusion of new and technologically superior societies.

Because of Sauer's scholarly reputation, he was asked to organize a major symposium of international scholars on "Man's Role in Changing the Face of the Earth." But due to his pessimism about the future world, he handed over part of the organization to Marston Bates and Louis Mumford and retreated into a consideration of "how we got to where we are."

In later life Sauer became increasingly critical of Western technology, ways of life, and intellectual trends. Americans seemed to think it a civic duty to "live beyond one's means," while communities were disintegrating under the pressures of mass production ("commodity fetishism"). Globally, he felt the "imperialism of production" was as bad as the old, colonial imperialism, and mass culture was destroying older and less robust societies. Social theory was insidious because it led to cultural hegemony and homogeneity, leading to the end of diversity and individual action and scholarship.

A deeply conservative person, Sauer was never formally an environmentalist, and, indeed, thought the movement little more than an "ecological binge." However, his ideas had a resonance with many activists and intellectuals who extolled his work as an example of cultural and ecological sensitivity and respect, tinged with deep historical insight and scholarship, and made attractive by a pithy and penetrating prose. The legacy of his intellect in geography and Earth history is far-reaching.

[*See also* Global Change, *article on* History of Global Change.]

BIBLIOGRAPHY

WORKS BY CARL O. SAUER

Sauer, C. O. "Destructive Exploitation in Modern Colonial Expansion." *Comptes Rendus du Congres International de Geographie, Amsterdam* 2 (1938a), 494–499. One of two strong indictments of the ecological consequences of colonialism and technology, the other being "Theme of Plant and Animal Destruction in Economic History."

———. "Theme of Plant and Animal Destruction in Economic History." *Journal of Farm Economics* 20 (1938b), 765–775.

———. *Agricultural Origins and Dispersals.* Bowman Memorial Lectures, Series 2. New York: American Geographical Society, 1952. An example of Sauer's speculative, interdisciplinary approach.

———. "Folkways of Social Science." In *The Social Sciences at Mid-Century: Papers Delivered at the Dedication of Ford Hall, April 19–21, 1951.* Minneapolis: University of Minnesota Press, 1952. A condemnation of social sciences and an eloquent plea for individual scholarship and enquiry.

———. "The Agency of Man on Earth." In *Man's Role in Changing the Face of the Earth,* edited by W. L. Thomas, Jr., et al., pp. 49–69. Chicago: University of Chicago Press, 1956. Sauer's scene-setting contribution to this massive, hallmark inquiry into the human use of the Earth.

———. "The End of the Ice Age and its Witnesses." *Geographical Review* 47 (1957), 29–43. Another imaginative, and essentially correct, interpretation of early Earth history.

WORKS ON CARL O. SAUER

Entrikin, J. N. "Carl Sauer: Philosopher in Spite of Himself." *Geographical Review* 74 (1984), 387–408. An excellent survey of Sauer's philosophical stance.

Kenser, M. S., ed. *Carl O. Sauer: A Tribute.* Corvallis: Oregon State University Press, 1987. A collection of essays on Sauer's intellectual legacy and thought.

Leighly, J. "Carl Ortwin Sauer, 1889–1975." In *Geographers: Biobibliographical Studies,* edited by T. W. Freeman and P. Pinchemel, pp. 99–108. London: Mancell, 1976. A comprehensive evaluation of Sauer and his work.

Spencer, J. E. "What's in a Name?: The 'Berkeley School'." In *Historical Geography Newsletter* 6 (1976), 7–11. The spread of cultural geography.

Williams, M. "The Apple of My Eye: Carl Sauer and Historical Geography." *Journal of Historical Geography* 9 (1983), 1–28. An examination of Sauer's concepts of culture and time, based largely on his private correspondence.

———. "Carl Sauer and 'Man's Role in Changing the Face of the Earth.'" *Geographical Review* 77 (1987), 218–231. How the *Man's Role* symposium evolved, and an evaluation of its impact.

OTHER WORKS

Freidreich, E. "Wesen und Geographische Verbreitung der 'Raubwirtschaft'." *Petermanns Mitteilungen* 50 (1904), 68–79, 92–95. The origin of the concept of "destructive exploitation."

Marsh, G. P. *Man and Nature: Physical Geography as Modified by Human Action.* Cambridge: Harvard University Press (Belknap Press), 1965. The first and classic work to synthesize knowledge on the human impact on the Earth; first published in 1864.

—MICHAEL WILLIAMS

SAVANNAS

Savannas (or "savannahs" in the pre-1956 spelling) comprise the most important vegetation formation of the lowland seasonal tropics and subtropics. The term is derived from the sixteenth-century Spanish *zavanna* (modern Spanish *sabana*), and was recorded in 1535 by Fernández de Oviedo, the Spanish chronicler and colonial administrator, as coming originally from Carib, a language of the southern West Indies.

Ecologically, the term is used to describe a continuum of tropical and subtropical vegetation types in which there is codominance between a fairly continuous grass cover and a range of woody plants from dwarf shrubs to trees. The tree/grass ratio, however, varies enormously between different savanna types. Certain savannas look just like parklands. By contrast, in some virtually treeless savannas, such as the Serengeti Plains of Tanzania, East Africa, the woody cover may be as low as 2 percent; in others, such as the dipterocarp savanna forests of mainland Southeast Asia and the eucalypt savanna woodlands of northern Australia, the canopy cover, when in full leaf, may be as high as 50 to 80 percent. Nevertheless, even these wooded savannas are clearly distinguishable from true forests by their continuous ground cover of grasses, sedges, and herbs (Figure 1). Paradoxically, at the opposite end of the climatic spectrum, the absence of a grass cover also separates savannas from semidesert and desert communities. Fire is a key factor in savanna ecology, partly because of this grass cover, which, when cured in the dry season, forms—along with the leaf litter from the trees—an easily ignitable fuel.

The open grassy character of the savannas is frequently associated with a distinctive and often very visible mammal fauna of predators, such as the lion (*Panthera leo*) and the cheetah (*Acinonyx jubatus*), and large herds of grazers and browsers, including wild cattle, antelope, and deer, as well as a range of highly characteristic savanna mammals, such as, in Africa, zebras (*Equus grevyi* and *E. burchelli*) and the giraffe (*Giraffa camelopardalis*). The silhouetted flat umbrella shape of many savanna trees reflects the basic browsing pattern of these herbivores. Certain savannas are also noted for their more specialized animals, including the endangered Gouldian finch (*Erythrura gouldiae*) in northern Australia, the Komodo dragon (*Varanus komodoensis*), the largest living lizard, in eastern Indonesia, and the giant anteater (*Myrmecophaga tridactyla*) in the *cerrado* of Brazil. Yet the most important faunal element of all savannas undoubtedly comprises the insects, especially the ants and the termites, which play such a vital role in both herbivory and seed dispersal. The landscapes of many savannas are punctuated by tall termite mounds and towers.

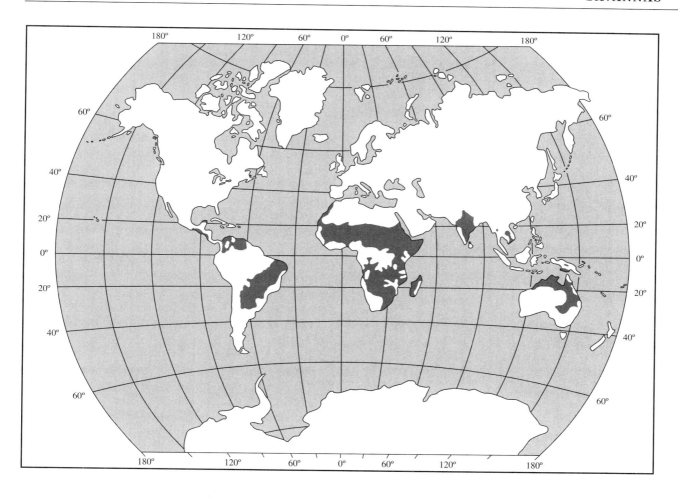

Savannas. Figure 1. Worldwide Savanna Distribution. (After Archibold, 1995, p. 60, Figure 3.1. With permission of Kluwer Academic Publishers.)

Savannas occupy a very wide area of the tropics and subtropics where there is a combination of a relatively low total annual rainfall of between 400 and 1,500 millimeters (with extremes at 200 millimeters and 2,000 millimeters) and a marked seasonality in the rainfall distribution, with a normal dry season of between four to eight months of the year (extremes at two months and ten months). Under such monsoonal climatic conditions, fire is a common annual or biennial phenomenon during the dry season, and both natural fires, through lightning strike, and human-induced fires are endemic to nearly all savanna areas—although it is important to note that fire is not in itself necessarily a determining factor. Nevertheless, in certain locations, protection from fire will trigger succession to a more wooded environment, while too frequent or intense fires may force the system into a grassless thorn scrub.

Biologically, savanna plants exhibit a wide range of adaptations to both fire and drought, including thick bark, thorns, reduced and leathery (sclerophyllous) leaves, sunken and protected stomata, subterranean stems, complex lateral roots, deep terminal roots, underground storage organs (geophytes), and specialized life cycles. Most of the perennial grasses are what are termed *hemicryptophytes*, plants that are able to resprout from the surface of the ground within a very short period after a fire. Such plants are also well adapted to heavy grazing pressures. Many of the tree species are leaf shedders, and woody plants possess various strategies for germinating fruits: some fruits and seeds requiring the scarifying (breaking open by heat) effects of fire, whereas other species disperse their fruits after the fires have gone through.

Savannas are further distinguished by the fact that their dominant grass species belong to what is known as the C4 group of photosynthetic plants. These are plants that initially fix carbon dioxide as a four-carbon compound, called oxalocetic acid, and that are especially adapted to hot and dry environments, such as the savannas, their optimum temperature for carbon dioxide fixation lying between 30° and 45°C. Savannas are therefore clearly differentiated from tropical grasslands, which tend to be dominated by grasses of the C3 group of photosynthetic plants, with their carbon dioxide fixed initially as a three-carbon compound, phosphoglyceric acid. Tropical grasslands also tend to have fewer woody species and to occur on higher, cooler plateaus and mountains, such as in the Drakensberg range in southern Africa. [*See* Carbon Cycle.]

Savanna Distribution. It is the very wide climatic tolerance of the savannas that essentially accounts for their areal dominance throughout the tropics and the subtropics. Savannas occupy no less than 45 percent of South America (including the grassy *llanos* of Venezuela and the woody *cerrado* of Brazil), 65 percent of Africa (with *Acacia* savannas, *Burkea africana* savannas, bottle-tree [*Adansonia*] savannas, and the wooded *miombo* of central southern Africa), and 60 percent of Australia (with eucalypt and *Acacia* savannas). Savannas range from Louisiana—"The Big Thicket"—and Texas, north of the Tropic of Cancer, to well south of the Tropic of Capricorn, near Port Elizabeth in South Africa. They are also widespread in the Caribbean, on the Indian subcontinent—the *sàl* (*Shorea robusta*) savanna woodlands—and in both mainland and maritime Southeast Asia, especially east of Wallace's line (the hypothetical line that separates the distinctive floras and faunas of Australia and Southeast Asia). It is often forgotten that savanna forests are the most widespread formation in Burma, Thailand, Laos, and Cambodia; interestingly, the Buddha is thought to have been born under a savanna forest tree.

The majority of people in the tropics, comprising no less than one-fifth of the world's population, live in the savannas, which form the core of the world's monsoon lands that, overall, support some 50 percent of the global population. Savannas are therefore the single most important terrestrial biome, and to gain an understanding of their role in global environmental change, both past and present, is unquestionably a vital ecological task.

Savanna Ecology: Past and Present. Until the mid-1980s, savanna studies were based on the concepts of ecology first developed in Europe and North America between 1910 and 1940. In these concepts, plant communities were essentially seen as "organisms," or ecosystems, the equilibrium state of which would be ultimately determined by one prime ecological factor such as climate or geology. However, there was marked disagreement as to the main ecological determinant of savannas. German scholars working in South West Africa (now Namibia) and South America tended to view savannas as climatically determined formations, whereas British foresters living in West Africa thought them to be anthropogenic (human-generated) communities, created from the forests by cutting and burning. French workers in Indochina (Laos, Cambodia, and Vietnam) saw savannas as essentially fire climaxes, while certain

geographers tried to interpret them as formations determined by soil or geology. There was little debate or agreement between the different interpreters, and savanna studies became somewhat nationalistic, regionally limited, and outdated.

Since 1984, by contrast, savanna research has grown increasingly interdisciplinary and international, and it is now thought that all savannas are determined by the complex interplay of at least six main ecological determinants: plant available moisture (PAM), plant available nutrients (PAN), fire, herbivory, major historical anthropogenic (human) events, and, at certain locations, special regional factors (such as frost or wind). PAM and PAN are seen as the prime determinants of savanna form, which is then modified by fire, herbivory, and any relevant special factors or historical anthropogenic events (such as the abandonment of human settlement or enhanced global warming) triggering savannas into new ecological states. The relationships between this complex of variables are analyzed multivariately by the application of ecological modeling or hierarchy theory, and the PAM/PAN plane (a two-dimensional plane in which the axes are defined by measurements of PAM and PAN) can be used to make basic international, national, and regional savanna comparisons.

Still more importantly, however, savannas are no longer regarded as representing simple equilibrium communities, but rather as formations that are always under a regime of change, with their biology driven by both constant and catastrophic variations in the six ecological determinants. Some scholars think of savannas as ever moving between what are termed *multiple equilibrium states*, such as open savanna, wooded savanna, and woodland, whereas other scholars, including the present author, are more radical and see savannas as being intrinsically nonequilibrium systems, in which every savanna organism is responding individualistically to the changes in the ecological determinants. These new approaches obviously place savannas at the very center of the discussion of global change, since the six ecological determinants link savannas directly with both world-scale and local-scale environmental fluctuations. Any ecological change, of any scale, will work through the complex of determinants to adjust the tree/grass ratios, the C3/C4 grass mixes, the species complements, and the geographic ranges of the world's savannas, which in turn will impact back on the ecological processes in question.

Savanna Change: Past and Present. Until recently, many ecologists and conservationists, particularly in the United Kingdom and North America, have tended somewhat automatically to regard large areas of savanna as representing a recent byproduct of the processes of tropical deforestation, brought about largely by cutting and burning for agricultural development.

These writers have also seen the burning of savanna plant biomass as a major issue in studying the links between gas/aerosol emissions and global atmospheric change, particularly because carbon dioxide (CO_2) is the dominant emission from biomass flame combustion, along with associated measures of nitric oxide (NO), nitrogen dioxide (NO_2), sulfur dioxide (SO_2), and water vapor; likewise, carbon monoxide (CO) is the main emission from smoldering combustion. According to one estimate, savanna fires contribute 75 percent of all the carbon dioxide emitted to the atmosphere through biomass burning in the tropics, a figure that rises to around 85 percent for sub-Saharan Africa.

On both counts, however, these arguments are fundamentally flawed. With regard to the effects of savanna fires, it is essential to remember that savannas have always burned, originally through lightning strike and other natural causes such as refraction, then with an intensification of fire use by hominids taking place as far back as 1.4 million years ago, and with a further intensification and spread by *Homo sapiens* some fifty thousand years ago. Very few scholars have bothered to build these historical patterns into their calculations.

There may even have been more emissions in the past than there are today, especially because it is now well substantiated that, despite widespread popular misconceptions, the savannas have above all retreated during the period since the end of the last ice age. Around eighteen thousand years ago, tropical climates were much drier and cooler than they are now, so that areas in both Amazonia and Southeast Asia that currently carry tropical rainforests were then savannas. There was, for example, a savanna corridor, with its own savanna fauna, running through the peninsula of Malaysia, linking the present-day disjunct savannas of mainland Southeast Asia with those of maritime Southeast Asia. In South America, there is growing evidence that savanna animals and plants once occupied areas long thought to have been rain forest refuges during the last ice age. Moreover, even in more recent times, the story is not always one of forest loss. Work in Gambia, West Africa, by foresters and anthropologists has clearly demonstrated a pattern of constant forest–savanna interchange since 1900 CE. Finally, in many parts of the tropics, subtropics, and mediterranean zones, such as in southern Africa, it is worth recalling that savannas, along with other nonforest formations, including tropical grasslands, the *fynbos*, and the Karoo, have been the dominant formations for millions of years. There has never been any significant forest cover in these areas.

Most savannas, therefore, have wide ancient cores, which have ebbed and flowed constantly at their margins, and around forest islands, in response to environmental change, the changes being mediated through the complex ecological determinants of PAM, PAN, fire, herbivory, and local factors. The process continues today. Traditionally, human populations in the savannas, particularly pastoralists like those in East Africa, have responded to these changes in an opportunistic manner, well attuned to the essential nonequilibrium character of the savanna biome. Such equilibrium concepts as overstocking, overgrazing, and carrying capacity are now seen to be problematic when applied to development in these environments. Some savanna areas are also experiencing rapid urbanization, as around the Pretoria/Johannesburg complex in South Africa and near to Brasilia in Brazil, while pasture improvement is a significant factor in places such as Queensland, Australia.

More specific environmental change problems facing savanna ecologists include the potential effects of carbon dioxide enhancement on the relative performance of C3 and C4 grasses, because C4 plants show little response to elevated concentrations of carbon dioxide. This may mean that their competitive advantage is reduced under increased atmospheric carbon dioxide, having significant effects on both the composition and the productivity of the grass stratum in tropical savannas. However, predictions are very difficult because of the complicating influence of the other ecological factors, especially temperature and PAM.

Savannas are also increasingly seen as one of the most biodiverse formations in the tropics. Like the tropical rainforests, they are known to possess, for many groups of organisms, continuously rising minimal-area curves (namely, graphs that show an increase in sample area continuously matched by an increase in the number of species encountered). This intrinsic biodiversity partly reflects the fundamental nonequilibrium of savannas, an inverse relationship having been established between stability and diversity, but also their heterogeneous patch structure, created by the codominance of grasses and trees. There are also important intercontinental and regional differences, with, for example, the *cerrado* of Brazil exhibiting noteworthy diversity in its woody element, a diversity with enormous potential for food and drug production. Insects, by contrast, appear to be biodiverse in all savanna areas.

Plant and animal introductions, both from other savannas and from different habitats, are also a significant feature of savanna environments, and, as with the Asian water buffalo (*Bubalus bubalis*) in the eucalypt savannas of northern Australia and various African grass species in the savannas of Latin America, these can greatly alter both local ecology and biodiversity. Further important debates surround the conservation of many large savanna mammals, such as the discussion over the need to make the conservation of big game, like the African elephant (*Loxodonta africana*), pay for itself through controlled commercial hunting. [*See* Elephants.]

Change is therefore at the very heart of all savanna

ecology, both past and present. During the next decades, the careful management of savannas will be vital for the future of both wildlife and the fifth of the world's population that inhabits these core environments. The ecological resilience and persistence of savannas lie above all in their biodiversity and in the opportunistic response of this biodiversity to nonequilibrium change. In linking savannas with global change, it is crucial to recall the recent words of Sîan Sullivan in the *Journal of Biogeography* (1996). She argues that dryland ecology must celebrate "variability as well as average values, process and pattern as well as structure, stasis and order, and creative as well as conservative behaviour."

[*See also* Biomes; Climate Change; Fire; *and* Grasslands.]

BIBLIOGRAPHY

Bourlière, F., ed. *Tropical Savannas*. Amsterdam: Elsevier, 1982. A good, if now slightly dated, general world survey.

Bullock, S. H., et al., eds. *Seasonally Dry Tropical Forests*. Cambridge: Cambridge University Press, 1995. Detailed studies of the more wooded and forested savannas, as well as the monsoon forests.

Cole, M. M. *The Savannas: Biogeography and Geobotany*. London: Academic Press, 1986. An idiosyncratic survey, stressing the importance of geology and soils.

Furley, P. A., et al., eds. *Nature and Dynamics of Forest–Savanna Boundaries*. London: Chapman and Hall, 1992. A series of detailed studies of savanna–forest boundary determinants, especially in Latin America.

Huntley, B. J., and B. H. Walker, eds. *Ecology of Tropical Savannas*. Berlin: Springer, 1982. A useful world survey, if now a little dated.

Leach, M., et al. *Second Nature: Building Forests in West Africa's Savannas*. Haywards Heath, U.K.: Cyrus Productions, 1997. A most important video examining the human use of forest and savanna in West Africa. Highly recommended.

Mistry, J. *World Savannas. Ecology and Human Use*. London: Prentice-Hall, 2000. The most up-to-date survey of the world's savanna ecosystems.

Sarmiento, G. *The Ecology of Neotropical Savannas*. Cambridge, Mass.: Harvard University Press, 1984. Remains one of the best detailed studies of plant life cycles in savannas; focuses on Latin America, especially Venezuela.

Scholes, R. J., and B. H. Walker. *An African Savanna: Synthesis of the Nylsvley Study*. Cambridge: Cambridge University Press, 1993. The best and most up-to-date detailed ecological study of any savanna ecosystem: South Africa. Highly recommended.

Solbrig, O., ed. "Savanna Modelling for Global Change." *Biology International* 24 (1991), 11–47. A special issue of the journal: an essential introduction to savanna ecological determinants and savanna modeling.

Stott, P. "Recent Trends in the Ecology and Management of the World's Savanna Formations." *Progress in Physical Geography* 15 (1991), 18–28. A relatively simple guide to some of the new ideas in savanna ecology.

———. "Savanna Landscapes and Global Environmental Change." In *Global Environmental Change*, edited by Neil Roberts, pp. 287–303. Cambridge, Mass.: Blackwell, 1994. A detailed analysis of savanna landscapes, particularly in relation to global climate change; also helpful on hierarchy theory and C3/C4 grasses.

Sullivan, S. "Towards a Nonequilibrium Ecology: Perspectives from an Arid Land." *Journal of Biogeography* 23 (1996), 1–5. A short but useful introduction to nonequilibrium ideas and their implications.

Tothill, J. C., and J. J. Mott, eds. *Ecology and Management of the World's Savannas*. Canberra: Australian Academy of Science, 1984. A useful general survey, focused on Australia.

Walker, B. H., and J. C. Ménaut, eds. *Research Procedure and Experimental Design for Savanna Ecology and Management*. Melbourne: CSIRO, 1988. A helpful guide to research methods in savanna ecology.

Werner, P. A., ed. *Savanna Ecology and Management: Australian Perspectives and Intercontinental Comparisons*. Oxford: Blackwell Scientific, 1991. One of the more up-to-date surveys of current problems in savanna ecology, emphasizing Australia and Latin America.

Young, M. D., and O. T. Solbrig. *Savanna Management for Ecological Sustainability, Economic Profit and Social Equity*. Paris: UNESCO, 1992. A useful introduction to the applied ecology and economics of savannas.

———, eds. *The World's Savannas: Economic Driving Forces, Ecological Constraints and Policy Options for Sustainable Land Use*. Paris and Carnforth, U.K.: UNESCO and Parthenon Press, 1993. A more advanced study of the applied ecology and economics of savannas.

—Philip Stott

SCENARIOS

If there is one thing we can all agree on, it is that the future is uncertain. Yet the pressing nature of many problems facing us makes it useful to discuss and to study the future. This can only mean that we consider at least something in the future to be predictable. A disciplined approach toward separating the predictable from the uncertain is clearly helpful for better understanding. The development of scenarios helps in this process. This approach starts from the premise that if the future is uncertain there can, in fact, be multiple equally plausible futures, called *scenarios*. A set of scenarios about the future reflects our understanding of what in the system is predetermined and predictable, and what we believe to be fundamentally indeterminate.

Why would such an approach be useful? We study the future in order to understand it better, helping us to make more confident, and hopefully better, decisions. This means both taking account of what is predictable, and allowing for what is uncertain. But deciding the boundary line between the predictable and the uncertain is not a trivial matter. When we enter a decision-making situation for the first time, our perception of uncertainty will be due more to our lack of understanding than to fundamental indeterminacy in the system. At that stage, the quality of our decision making can be improved by learning more about the system and its predictable elements.

Why would anything in the outside world be predictable at all? When we observe unfolding events we are inclined to discern trends. Once things are going up, they may continue doing so for a while. Or certain events always seem to come together. We wonder why this might be, and we try to explain it. We do this by imposing an underlying structure of cause and effect linking things together. Typical cues for causality are (Einhorn and Hogarth, 1982):

- Temporal order, such as trends over time
- Related behavior, or covariance, among variables
- Spatial or temporal closeness
- Similarity in form or pattern

The most obvious examples of such underlying structures are laws of nature. However, our understanding of structure goes much further. For example, we believe that human nature or cultural factors make people predictable. In that way we explain events that would otherwise be highly ambiguous and therefore problematic. The boundaries of ambiguity can be pushed back by discovering this type of underlying structure.

But where to begin to find such structures? Often we just dive in on impulse, for example following someone's suggestion of what the problem is. We hope that we are lucky in our choice and find something that will lead us to a useful insight. This haphazard analytical approach is inefficient and often ineffective. One reason is that in this way we remain stuck in our business-as-usual world. How can we find more visionary research questions? Experienced researchers know that the success or failure of good research depends critically on defining the right question.

Scenarios as a Tool. A proper scenario approach helps us to analyze problems or situations effectively. It does this by exploiting a group's combined intuitive knowledge of a situation for the purpose of defining appropriate research questions on which further exploratory work can be based. As first proposed by Pierre Wack (1985a and 1985b), the approach iterates between exploring with scenarios or stories and analyzing the underlying systems based on the questions raised. This iterative approach aims at increasing understanding of systems that are too complex to be understood by taking them apart. In principle it amounts to creating a perturbation in the system, and observing what happens, compared with one's expectations. If a difference arises, a research question has been raised to be answered: Why is this system behaving differently from what I expected? If this question is researched successfully, one has learned something about the system's structure that one did not know before.

In a scenario project the objective is to challenge one's own "mental model of the future," sometimes called the "business as usual" future. The first step is to

draw on one's intuition to identify the main factors driving the system, in particular those that are significantly uncertain. By stretching these variables to their limits of credibility, one tries to create a number of possible futures that, while plausible, are significantly different from "business as usual." One then tries to make sense of these future states by developing stories describing how the transition from the present to that end-state could happen. It is in the process of developing these stories in detail that gaps in one's understanding are discovered. These indicate research areas in which new knowledge about the system needs to be created.

A classic example of this process in action followed the publication of the *Limits to Growth* scenarios in 1972. These were good examples of internally consistent but challenging stories about global ecology created on the basis of stretching a number of main parameters to their limits of plausibility. Many readers were surprised by the logical outcome of the assumptions made, which they felt were at variance with their own extrapolation. This publication made a significant impact through its effect on the thinking of many readers who tried to explain why these outcomes seemed so different from their own business-as-usual worlds. As a result, a lot of analytical work and useful learning took place, leading to a better understanding of the underlying system, and ultimately to better decision making.

This perspective on the scenario methodology highlights the aim of uncovering predetermined elements in the outside world, allowing better anticipation of what could happen, and better understanding of what is fundamentally unpredictable. Improving our understanding of this context of our decision making is clearly useful. However, it is only part of what the scenario process is about.

Social Interaction. An alternative perspective— known as the *processual* view—focuses on groups of people influencing and creating their own reality in a process of social interaction, and points us toward paying attention to the group and institutional aspects of decision making.

The ongoing institutional conversation influences the direction of the attention of its participants. Sharing of the business-as-usual mental model focuses attention in the group on confirming experiences, reinforcing the mental model in the minds of the group members. In the processual perspective, the issue is whether the resulting prevailing mental models will allow the group to react skillfully to unexpected events in the outside world.

An interesting example can be found in the area of human rights. For years the human rights community has been debating whether human rights and norms have to be considered as universally valid, or culturally determined. The processualist would argue that ideas about human rights are formed continually by the ongoing conversation. And different conversations lead to different perspectives; for example, one group's terrorist is another group's freedom fighter. The conversations include powers (such as states, armies, employers, and so forth) and people (subjects, civilians in wartime, employees, and so forth) and they take place among various different cultures (Asian, Western, and so forth). The conclusion is that human rights are not only culturally determined but will also depend on power relationships and other contextual factors.

A Management Dilemma. A group of people wishing to improve the effectiveness of joint decision making will often face a fundamental dilemma. Group action requires a degree of consensus. The more the members of a group agree with each other, that is, the more they align their individual mental models, the stronger the joint action can be. And the joint experience that results from joint action is needed for the group to learn about the outside world so that new decisions can be made and new actions taken that lead to further learning, and so on.

Does this mean that with more consensus the group will be more successful? Consensus approaches will focus on the business-as-usual mental model. But if unexpected change takes place, signals need to be perceived outside this frame if the group is to adapt successfully. Signals can only be received if they can be related to something that is already present in the mental model. Without this the group will display tunnel vision and fail to acquire skills of adaptation to a new environment.

The danger of the impoverishment of mental models through too much consensus in organizations is called *group-think*. A much-quoted example is the International Business Machines (IBM) corporation, which in the late 1980s ran into severe business problems as its shared and strongly felt business-as-usual mental model, based on central mainframe computing, became increasingly disconnected from the needs of the market for distributed computing. As a result, the company had to adjust strongly and painfully when this divergence from the market began to affect its profitability.

The start of a fundamental change in the environment must already be present conceptually somewhere in the group in order to make it discernible. If it is the purpose of the group to adapt itself continuously and smoothly, the degree of variety in the mental models needs to match the variety of the environment (Ashby, 1983).

Too much integration leads to group-think, but too much differentiation leads to increasing divergence and fragmentation and to less effective strategic conversation. Eventually everyone follows his or her own agenda, and institutional functioning stops. In such circumstances, groups seem drawn to the issues likely to do them most damage. An interesting example was the state of the British Conservative Party prior to the 1997 elections. Although the British electorate is traditionally consistent in severely punishing internal strife within a party, conservative politicians found it impossible to steer away from the most divisive issues during the campaign, inexorably driving the party to its biggest defeat ever. Differentiation is necessary, but fragmentation is dangerous.

Groups and institutions have to stay away from the two extremes of fragmentation and group-think if they wish to survive. This requires constant attention, active management of the group dynamics, and effective leadership. For example, groups suffering from group-think can broaden their perspective and increase differentiation of ideas by bringing in "new blood" from the outside world, as IBM did at the top of the company. Or fragmented groups can increase integration of ideas by identifying and removing skeptics and militants and engaging in "team building."

These interventions need to be carefully designed to ensure that they work toward a balance between integration and differentiation of ideas. The leadership problem is to facilitate the conversation in the group to help steer a middle way between fragmentation and group-think.

This is where scenarios make their powerful contribution. The scenario approach creates a strategic conversation, allowing for and reflecting different perceptions of a situation, but in such a way as to create room for people to hear the arguments of others and engage in a meaningful comparison of different viewpoints. Scenarios introduce a variety of ideas, creating room for everyone, but also lead to a gradual alignment in the understanding of what a new situation means for the group and what needs to be done to respond to it.

An example of such a scenario-based conversation was the Mont Fleur project, which is reported to have made an important contribution toward breaking the apartheid logjam in South Africa in the early 1990s. The power of this project was in its demonstration of how a disparate group of individuals representing a wide variety of opinions in the country, who had been at loggerheads with each other in the recent past, could nevertheless come up with a shared coherent analysis of the situation and its inherent threats and opportunities (Kahane, 1996).

The processual perspective on scenarios is not in the first place concerned with questions of prediction or the mapping of mental models to reality. The focus is on steering a middle way between fragmentation and group-think, thus allowing a group or organization to start moving forward in a difficult situation. Once effective action has been created, this will lead to further experiences and learning about the situation and further effective action. Making this loop possible by creating the first successful step is seen as more important than trying to figure out the world in advance.

Scenarios and Global Change. The complex turbulent world of global change is impossible to understand deductively in all its aspects. Every representation offers only one of many possible perspectives, focusing on some aspects of the problem, while ignoring others. Everyone interested in exploring such complex systems in depth will need to embrace perspectives other than their own, rather than seeing these as competitive. Multiple perspectives are helpful in giving us a more complete picture of reality. The scenario approach has something to offer in terms of both an anticipatory and a processual perspective. We can either see it as a way to improve our understanding and anticipation of the future, or a way to help institutional groups to start moving forward more skillfully in uncertain times.

The vexing question of global climate change is a case in point. Climate models still need to be considered in their infancy and new relevant science is discovered daily, causing a frequent restatement of the problem. [See Climate Models.] Such a state of affairs could easily lead to a feeling of paralysis, stopping decision making in its tracks. However, some relevant scenarios will illustrate the point that there is no time to lose. Decision making will need to take place in a state of considerable uncertainty. In these circumstances, it is more important to aim for a skillful process than to attempt to get to "the right answer." This is why process is as important as analysis.

Keeping both perspectives in mind helps us to remain aware of the fact that there is no single right answer to complex problems. The dilemmas underlying these problems often cannot be resolved, but require continuous active management. Scenario planning tools can help in that process.

[See also Climate Impacts; Future Studies; Growth, Limits to; Integrated Assessment; Modeling of Natural Systems; and Surprise.]

BIBLIOGRAPHY

Ashby, W. R. "Self-Regulation and Requisite Variety." In Systems Thinking, edited by F. E. Emery. New York: Penguin, 1983.
Einhorn, H. J., and R. M. Hogarth. "Prediction, Diagnosis and Causal Thinking in Forecasting." Journal of Forecasting 1 (1982), 22–36.
Kahane, A. "Learning from Mont Fleur: Scenarios as a Tool for Discovering Common Ground." Emeryville, Calif.: GBN, 1996.
Meadows, D. The Limits to Growth: A Report to the Club of Rome Project on the Predicament of Mankind. New York: Universe Books, 1972.
van der Heijden, K. Scenarios: The Art of Strategic Conversation. Chichester, U.K.: Wiley, 1996.
Wack, P. "Scenarios, Uncharted Waters Ahead." Harvard Business Review (September–October 1985a), 73–90.
———. "Scenarios, Shooting the Rapids." Harvard Business Review (November–December 1985b), 131–142.

—Kees van der Heijden

SCHUMACHER, ERNST FRIEDRICH

Ernst Friedrich ("Fritz") Schumacher (1911–1977), German–British economist and philosopher, was born in Bonn, Germany. As a Rhodes scholar he studied economics at Oxford, and then at Columbia University. When Hitler consolidated his power, Schumacher moved to Britain. During World War II he worked on a farm and corresponded with many, including John Maynard Keynes, who was influenced by his work on international finance. In 1942 he joined the Oxford Institute of Statistics and later, as a British citizen, returned to Germany as a member of the British Control Commission. He became Economic Advisor to the National Coal Board (NCB) from 1950 to 1970 and, later, Director of Statistics and Director of Planning as well.

Schumacher continued his studies in many fields—economics, philosophy, religion (especially Buddhism and Christianity), energy, development, and agriculture—while traveling widely. In 1955, he spent three months in Burma as an economic adviser. This exposure to a Buddhist society made a lasting impression on him and he began to write about Buddhist economics, questioning the underlying assumptions and prescriptions of Western economics. He noted the extraordinary dependency of industrialized economies on nonrenewable resources and the need to reestablish economies based on renewable resources. These ideas anticipated the debate about limits to growth some fifteen years later.

During a visit to India in 1962, he began thinking about "intermediate technology": improved, small-scale technology accessible to existing producers that could increase production without creating unemployment. He became convinced that intermediate technology offered an alternative and better path to development than large-scale capital projects. In 1970 he resigned from the NCB to devote himself full-time to the Intermediate Technology Development Group Ltd, which he founded in 1966 and chaired until his death in 1977.

After leaving the NCB, he wrote his two influential books: Small is Beautiful (1973) and A Guide for the Perplexed (1977). In the former, subtitled "economics as if people mattered," he argued that economic growth could not be sustained because of resource and environmental limits. He also believed that more value should be given to work for its own sake rather than increased output. In A Guide for the Perplexed, he offered a critique of contemporary views about humanity predicated on "materialistic Scientism," and offered a decidedly religious guide to the "art of living."

Small is Beautiful brought Schumacher fame, honors (a C.B.E., numerous honorary degrees, Fellow of the Royal Society of Arts), and influence among world leaders, industrialists, and the general public. The emerging field of ecological economics is built on many of the ideas that he helped to develop. He died while on a train in Switzerland during a lecture tour. *A Guide for the Perplexed* was published posthumously. Its influence is less easy to determine. However, if Schumacher is correct that "the modern experiment to live without religion has failed," in the long run it may be the book for which he is best remembered.

[*See also* Growth, Limits to; *and* Sustainable Development.]

BIBLIOGRAPHY

Hession, C. H. "E. F. Schumacher as Heir to Keynes' Mantle." *Review of Social Economy* 44 (April 1986), 1–12. An assessment of Schumacher's work, emphasizing Keynes's high regard for him, based on Wood's biography.

Schumacher, E. F. *Small is Beautiful*. London: Blond and Briggs, 1973. A powerful critique of economics, modern society, and development for which Schumacher is famous.

———. *A Guide for the Perplexed*. London: J. Cape, 1977. A religiously based philosophical work designed to help people take action.

Wood, B. *Alias Papa*. New York: Harper and Row, 1984. An excellent biography of Schumacher written by his daughter.

—PETER A. VICTOR

SCIENTIFIC COMMITTEE ON PROBLEMS OF THE ENVIRONMENT

The Scientific Committee on Problems of the Environment, known throughout the world by its acronym SCOPE, was created by the International Council for Science in 1969 on the recommendation of geophysicists and biologists. They were concerned that exponential and asymmetrical demographic growth on finite planet Earth was generating environmental problems transcending existing scientific knowledge, political boundaries, and traditional scientific disciplines. A nonpolitical institutional mechanism operating under the aegis of the world's leading scientists was required to put in place the knowledge base necessary for sound policy decisions in the public and the private sectors. [*See* International Council for Science (ICSU).]

The two-fold mission of SCOPE is (1) to assess, integrate, and further develop knowledge concerning the impact of human activity on the environment and the effects of environmental change on the health and welfare of people, and (2) to provide the best available scientific information to stakeholders for policy decisions on these issues. SCOPE is a nongovernmental network of forty national academies and research councils and twenty-two international scientific organizations. Close liaison is maintained with intergovernmental agencies.

SCOPE has published nearly sixty book-length reports and over one hundred other monographs on specific environmental issues that are either global in nature or shared by several nations. Topics embrace the nature of changes in air, land, water, plant, and animal life, and their mutual interaction with human activity. They range from an analysis of the major biogeochemical cycles and their interactions to a global perspective on invasions of exotic species into natural ecosystems.

These reports are prepared by special groups of volunteer scholars drawn from the relevant disciplines and convened in a series of workshops and meetings to (1) assess the current state of knowledge in a specific topic, (2) identify knowledge gaps, (3) recommend research priorities to close those gaps, and (4) provide advice on policies for sound resource management and protection of the environment. The results are published after review by a separate group of scholars.

Among studies that have been particularly influential in public policy was the series of studies on biogeochemical cycles of the main elements (carbon, nitrogen, sulfur, phosphorus, and so forth) that form a major part of the environmental life-support system. Examination of the carbon cycle served as the catalyst for the worldwide explosion of interest in global warming. The emergence of "sustainability" as an issue of public policy is generating more demands for studies linking the environmental management and society.

The two-volume report on the global environmental consequences of a nuclear war provided a comprehensive assessment of the probable impacts of a nuclear conflict on the atmosphere, ecosystems, and the global food chain. It precipitated a United Nations study and contributed significantly to the movement to reduce nuclear weaponry as a vital part of military arsenals.

A continuing theme of interest and use to governments and industry has been the fate of chemicals in the environment and their effects on ecosystems and human health, including the effects of increased ultraviolet radiation resulting from the depletion of ozone in the stratosphere. During the 1990s, SCOPE turned its attention to the fundamental issues underlying the sustainability of human-dominated ecosystems, including indicators of sustainable development and the role of biological diversity in ecosystem functioning.

Adhering bodies of SCOPE meet in a general assembly every three years to review progress and prepare plans for the future. An elected executive committee of volunteer scholars directs SCOPE's activities between these assemblies. A small secretariat is located in Paris.

[*See also* International Geosphere–Biosphere Programme.]

INTERNET RESOURCE

Web site: http://www.icsu-scope.org.

BIBLIOGRAPHY

Bolin, B., B. R. Doos, J. Jaeger, and R. A. Warwick, eds. *The Greenhouse Effects, Climatic Change and Ecosystems*. Chichester, U.K.: Wiley, 1985. A seminal report summarizing and interpreting SCOPE studies beginning in 1975 on the cycles of carbon and other biogeochemicals.

Greenway, F. *Science International: A History of the International Council of Scientific Unions*. Cambridge: Cambridge University Press, 1996. The institutional framework within which SCOPE was established.

Harwell, M. A., and T. C. Hutchinson, eds. *Environmental Consequences of Nuclear War*, vol. II, *Ecological and Agricultural Effects*. Chichester, U.K.: Wiley, 1986.

Mooney, H. A., et al. *Functional Roles of Biodiversity: A Global Perspective*. Chichester, U.K.: Wiley, 1996. An issue rapidly becoming critical.

Pittock, A. B., et al. *Environmental Consequences of Nuclear War*, vol. I, *Physical and Atmospheric Effects*. Chichester, U.K.: Wiley, 1985.

Scientific Committee on Problems of the Environment. *Programme & Directory, 2000–2002*. Paris: SCOPE, 1998. A forty-eight-page brochure available from the secretariat in Paris. Excellent summary and description; updated every three years.

—THOMAS F. MALONE

SEA ICE

An unusual property of water is that its solid form, ice, floats in liquid water. This fact, crucial for life on this planet, is due to the open crystalline structure of ice: the form found under ordinary conditions has a hexagonal structure, with oxygen atoms forming parallel sheets of puckered hexagons, like a deformed beehive. The principal axis, or c-axis, of the unit cell lies perpendicular to the plane of the sheet, which forms the basal plane. When an ice crystal grows, it is energetically easier for new molecules to join an existing sheet than to begin a new sheet. Ice crystals therefore grow more readily along the a- and b-axes (axes in the basal plane) than along the c-axis. This gives a preferred direction to ice crystals growing in water. The great length of the hydrogen bonds between the atoms creates the open structure; most bonds break when ice melts, causing a disordered higher-density structure. But even in liquid water there is short-range order, with a few molecules retaining a crystal-like structure until this is destroyed by thermal motion; this accounts for another curious property of fresh water, its maximum density at 4°C.

Freezing of Sea Water. Consider a water body being cooled from above. As the surface water cools, its density increases and it sinks, to be replaced by warmer water from below, which in turn cools, creating convective cells that cool the whole water body. For a lake, when the surface temperature reaches 4°C, further cooling results in the colder water staying at the surface, so the surface layer can reach the freezing point and ice can form even though the temperature of the underlying water may still be close to 4°C. Thus a lake can freeze early while considerable heat remains at depth.

When the salinity exceeds 24.7 psu (practical salinity units, equivalent to parts per thousand), there is no temperature of maximum density, and convection continues down to the freezing point (-1.8°C for typical sea water). The whole upper water column, down to the level of a density gradient (the pycnocline), has to reach the freezing point before ice can form at the surface. A sea therefore takes longer to freeze over than a lake.

A salinity of 24.7 psu separates brackish water from true sea water. Most polar seas have surface salinities that comfortably exceed this value; even in the Arctic, where river discharge is a diluting factor, they usually exceed 30 psu. However, the Baltic Sea and Russian coastal waters such as the Kara Sea off the mouth of the Ob' River and the Laptev and East Siberian Seas off the Yenisey are brackish. This means that the Baltic freezes early in winter, with ice that resembles lake ice. Ice also forms early on the Russian shelves, and early winter ice production can increase the density of the surface water until it sinks at the shelf edge and ventilates the deep Arctic Basin.

Ice Formation and Growth. The processes of ice formation and growth vary according to whether the sea conditions are calm or turbulent.

Calm conditions. In quiet seas, freezing begins with a skim of separate stellar-shaped crystals, with c-axes vertical and long fragile arms stretching over the surface. The dendritic arms are fragile, and soon break off, leaving a mixture of disks and arm fragments. These random-shaped small crystals form a milky suspension called *frazil* or *grease ice*. The frazil crystals grow in numbers and freeze together to form a continuous sheet of young ice; in its early stages, when transparent, it is called *nilas*. As the ice grows thicker, the nilas turns gray and finally white, becoming first-year ice, which in a single season in the Arctic reaches a thickness of 1.5–2 meters and in the Antarctic 0.5–1 meter.

Once a continuous sheet has formed, individual crystals at the ice–water interface grow downward by freezing of water molecules onto the crystal face. This is easiest for crystals with horizontal c-axes, such that growth can occur along an a- or b-direction. These crystals grow at the expense of the others, and eventually crowd them out in a process of crystalline Darwinism. Thus crystals near the top of a first-year ice sheet are small and randomly oriented, or have the c-axis vertical, while, deeper down, crystals with horizontal c-axes dominate, acquiring elongated vertical shapes. The columnar structure is an identifier of congelation ice, ice that has grown by freezing onto an existing ice bottom, and is a striking feature of first-year ice when viewed by the naked eye.

Salt from sea water cannot enter the ice crystal lattice and is rejected. The ice–water interface advances in the form of parallel rows of projecting platelets, with the rejected brine accumulating in the grooves between rows. As these platelets develop lateral connections, the brine becomes trapped in the form of tiny liquid inclusions called *brine cells*, of typical diameter 0.5 millimeters. These give young ice a bulk salinity of 10–12 psu. The brine cells gradually drain out as the ice sheet grows, via a network of brine drainage channels like a vertical river system. During winter, individual brine cells also migrate down the temperature gradient; the upper part of a cell is slightly colder than the lower, causing freezing at the top and melting at the bottom. A more rapid brine loss occurs during summer, when the overlying snow melts and fresh water percolates downward, flushing out much of the remaining brine and leaving the ice fresher and hence stronger.

Turbulent conditions. In the Antarctic, at the advancing winter ice edge, the high wave energy and turbulence do not permit nilas to form. Instead the frazil congeals into small cakes called *pancake ice* through wave-induced cyclic compression of the frazil mush. Young pancakes start at a few centimeters across, and grow by accretion from frazil until they reach 3–5 meters in diameter and 50 centimeters in thickness. Frazil still grows as well because the spaces between the pancakes permit heat to be lost to the atmosphere. Collisions between cakes pump frazil onto the cake edges, the water drains away, and the ice remains to form a raised rim—like a pancake.

Deeper inside the ice edge, sheltered from waves, the pancakes freeze together in groups that finally coalesce to form a continuous ice sheet. With the open water surface cut off, the growth rate drops to a low level and the ultimate sheet thickness at winter's end may be only a few centimeters more than the thickness of the constituent pancakes.

Such ice is called *consolidated pancake ice* and has a rough, jagged bottom morphology, unlike congelation ice. Pancakes at the time of consolidation may be rafted or upended, and freeze together in this way, with the frazil acting as "glue." The rough ice bottom provides an excellent substrate for algal growth and a refuge for krill. The thin ice also permits much light to penetrate, resulting in a winter sea ice ecosystem that is more fertile than that of the Arctic. The area of antarctic pancake ice in early winter may be 6 million square kilo-

meters, making it an important yet seldom-seen feature of the Earth's surface.

The Arctic Ocean is a cold desert, and the average snow thickness on sea ice is only a few centimeters. In the Antarctic, however, snow thicknesses in winter reach about 20 centimeters over first-year ice and 60–70 centimeters over multiyear ice (Figure 1). Since the ice itself is thin, the snow can press the ice surface below sea level, leading to the infiltration of sea water into the overlying snow and the formation of either a wet slushy layer or, in the case of freezing, a snow ice layer between the unwetted snow and the original ice surface.

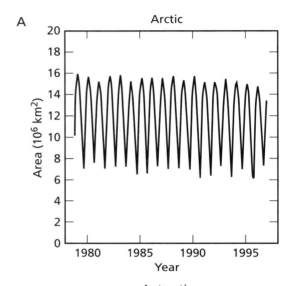

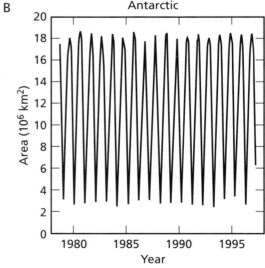

Sea Ice. FIGURE 1. Sea Ice Extents in Arctic and Antarctic, Derived from Satellite Passive Microwave Data.

In the Arctic (A), the decline since 1993 averages 3 percent per decade. In Antarctic (B), no trend is apparent, but the summer–winter changes are more profound. (After Cavalieri, et al., 1997.)

This results in a thicker ice sheet than would be expected from normal thermodynamic growth.

Summer Melt and Multiyear Ice. Summer changes the nature of an ice sheet (Figure 2). In the Arctic, the overlying snow layer melts in July, forming a network of surface meltwater pools. On smooth first-year ice the pools are initially very shallow, forming in minor depressions. Their shape becomes more fixed as they melt

their way down into the ice through preferential absorption of solar radiation by the water, which has an albedo of 0.1 compared with 0.6–0.7 for bare ice. Eventually the pools can drain off into the sea, over floe edges, through existing cracks, or by melting a thaw hole through the ice.

The drained meltwater forms a low-salinity surface layer a few meters deep that gives the water column in

A

Sea Ice. FIGURE 2A. Seasonal Change in Extent of Sea Ice in Arctic, Excluding Ice Coverage of Lesser than 12 Percent of Area. (After Central Intelligence Agency, 1978.)

B

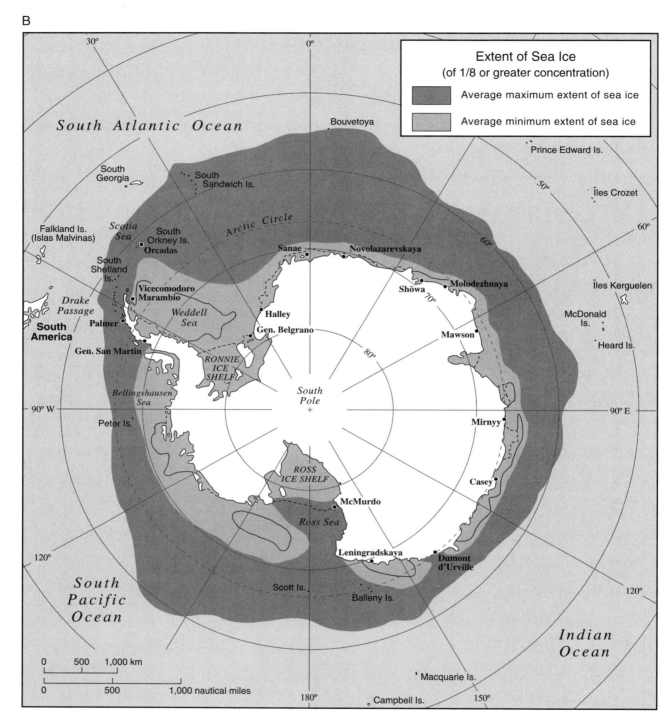

Sea Ice. FIGURE 2B. Seasonal Change in Extent of Sea Ice in Antarctic Regions, Excluding Ice Coverage of Lesser than 12 Percent of Area. (After Central Intelligence Agency, 1978.)

summer a second, shallow pycnocline. The ice underside also responds to the surface melt. Directly underneath melt pools, the ice is thinner and absorbs more incoming radiation. This causes an enhanced rate of bottom melt, so that the ice bottom develops an undulating topography to mirror the topside melt pool distribution. Some of the drained melt water may gather in underside depressions to form under-ice melt pools, which refreeze in autumn and partially smooth off the underside. In the Antarctic, melt pools are uncommon because ice floes continue to drift seaward after growth ceases, and hence tend to break up and melt completely at the retreating edge.

In the World Meteorological Organization definition, ice that has survived a single summer is called *second-year ice* and ice that is older than this is called *old ice*. In practice, partly because of the difficulty of visually discriminating between second-year and old ice, and partly because all ice older than first-year has properties such as greater strength, any ice older than first-year is usually simply classified as *multiyear ice*.

In the Arctic, sea ice takes several years to either make a circuit within the closed Beaufort Gyre (seven to ten years) or else be transported across the Arctic Basin and expelled in the East Greenland Current (three to four years). Much of the ice in the Arctic is therefore multiyear ice. Growth continues in yearly cycles until the ice thickness reaches about 3 meters, called the *equilibrium thickness*, at which point summer melt matches winter growth and overall growth ceases. Multiyear ice can be discriminated from first-year ice by satellite microwave techniques such as passive microwave or synthetic aperture radar. Its low salinity and high strength make it a formidable barrier to ice-breakers.

Ice Dynamics. Sea ice is constantly in motion, driven by wind, currents, and internal stresses. The long-term pattern is mainly determined by wind. In the Arctic this comprises a clockwise gyre in the Canadian Basin, called the Beaufort Gyre, and a current system, the Trans-Polar Drift Stream, which takes ice from north of Siberia, transports it across the North Pole, and pushes it into the East Greenland Current. In the Antarctic, the overall pattern far from land is an eastward drift, with a slight northerly component, in the Antarctic Circumpolar Current. Close to land the ice drift is westward in the Antarctic Coastal Current, driven by westward-turning katabatic winds, while the Weddell and Ross Seas have closed or semiclosed clockwise gyres.

Apart from this long-term pattern, differential drift also occurs—the ice is pulled apart by divergent wind stresses, opening up cracks that widen to form leads. Leads range in width from a few meters to hundreds of meters or even kilometers for major systems. Winter leads refreeze rapidly because of the enormous temperature difference between the atmosphere (typically −30°C) and the ocean (−1.8°C). When a subsequent wind stress field becomes convergent, the young ice in the refrozen leads forms the weakest part of the ice cover and is crushed, building up heaps of broken ice blocks above and below the water line. Such a linear deformation feature is called a *pressure ridge*, the above-water part being the sail and the more extensive below-water part the keel. Keels in the Arctic can reach 50 meters, although most are about 10–25 meters deep; the blocks composing them may only be a few tens of centimeters thick.

Ridged ice in the Arctic makes a major contribution to the overall mass of sea ice; probably about 40 percent on average and more than 60 percent in coastal regions. This yields overall mean ice thicknesses that range from 2–3 meters in the seas north of Russia to 7–8 meters north of Greenland and the Canadian Archipelago, where the wind drives ice toward the coast and creates enormous amounts of pressure ridging.

Antarctic ridging is much less intense. Individual ridges are shallower, and usually the block thickness is that of the floes on either side (for example, the ridge has formed by buckling of the floe itself, or through a collision between two floes, rather than by the crushing of young ice). This occurs because the floes themselves are quite thin. On average, antarctic sea ice diverges as it moves northward into the wider spaces of the Southern Ocean, so that ridge building events occur less frequently than in the Arctic.

Climatic Response. Ridges and leads are important to the overall heat budget. When a lead first opens in winter, the evaporative moisture flux may be sufficient to cause cloud formation, and although leads and young ice (less than 20 centimeters thick) in the winter arctic pack make up only 1–3 percent of the surface area, they are responsible for half of the heat exchange with the atmosphere. Ice dynamics, which creates leads and ridges, is therefore vital in determining the state of the ice cover. This makes prediction of ice cover response to climate change more difficult. Thermodynamically, warming should cause thinning of the ice cover, as should any increase in oceanic heat flux. An increase in snowfall expected as a consequence of the inflow of warmer, moister winds into the polar regions will also cause thinning because of the low thermal conductivity of snow, unless so much snow falls that it does not all melt in summer, in which case the ice cover thickens because of protection from the summer surface melt, which is the chief ablation mode. Such reasoning is valid for the effect of warming on fast ice; for instance, it is estimated that carbon dioxide doubling will cause fast ice thickness in the economically important Northwest Passage and Northern Sea Route to diminish by 0.4–0.8 meters and the ice-free season to increase by sixty days. However, predictions for moving pack must take account of accompanying changes in wind fields, which affect the occurrence of leads and ridges; numerical modeling is required (see, for example, Hibler, 1979), and the current state of understanding is discussed in Arctic Research Consortium of the United States (1997). The present distribution of sea ice, and the feedback effect of sea ice changes on other parameters, are discussed elsewhere in this encyclopedia.

[*See also* Albedo; Cryosphere; *and the vignette on* As of 1999 *in the article on* Global Warming.]

RECENT CHANGES IN THE ARCTIC OCEAN

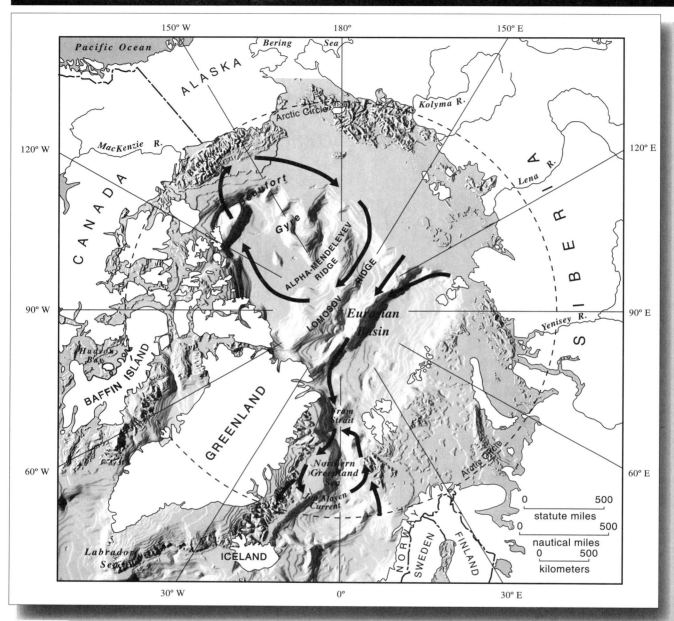

Arctic Ocean and Vicinity, Showing Selected Features and Dominant Surface Circulation. (Mountain High Maps® Copyright © 2001 www.digiwis.com)

Analysis of field measurements during the last few years have revealed some startling changes. Data have come from deep penetration of the Arctic between 1987 and 1996 by German and Swedish icebreakers, a complete Trans-Arctic section by U.S. and Canadian icebreakers in summer of 1994, and under-ice cruises by U.S. and British submarines.

The first discovery was that the *Atlantic sublayer* (derived from the North Atlantic current) has warmed substantially and encroached upon water of Pacific origin (Carmack et al., 1997; Morrison et al., 1998). The front between Atlantic and Pacific-derived waters has now shifted 300–500 miles eastward from the Lomonosov to the Alpha-Mendeleyev Ridge (see figure above). A concomitant thinning of the ice cover in the Eurasian Basin and Northern Greenland Sea has been observed (Wadhams,

1990, 1997) and is confirmed by latest observations by U.K. submarines and by U.S. data from the SCICEX project (Rothrock et al., 1999).

The next discovery was that the *polar surface layer* has changed in the Eurasian Basin. Formerly there was a cold *halocline* layer, at 100–200 meter depth, which depended upon riverine input from Siberia. The cold layer now has retreated as the river flow has been diverted eastward by changed atmospheric circulation (Steele and Boyd, 1998).

Third, in the Greenland Sea between Greenland and Norway, there have been changes in circulation and in sea ice production. Normally, the cold Jan Mayen current causes local ice growth, yielding dense salt-rich surface waters that sink to drive a deep convection flow. Tracer experiments have shown that since 1971 the convection has failed to reach the ocean bottom (Schlosser, et al., 1991) and in recent years has been greatly reduced in volume: coincidentally, the production of sea ice has been greatly reduced, and its patterns drastically altered (Wadhams, 1999).

A fourth, and striking, observation (see figure, right) is that the summertime edge of sea ice has retreated in recent years in the Beaufort Sea (Maslanik et al., 1996; McPhee et al., 1998).

The reduction of ice formation and of thermohaline convection may be symptoms of global warming, which climate simulations predict will be amplified in the Arctic through *ice-albedo feedback* in which retreat of snow and ice enhances the absorption of solar radiation, leading to more warming in the region. One general circulation model applied by the Hadley Center in Bracknell, U.K. predicts the thermohaline circulation in the Labrador Sea will collapse during the period 2000–2030 (Wood et al., 1999). [*See* Ocean Dynamics.]

A more immediate cause of some changes is the pattern of atmospheric circulation in the North Atlantic region. During the 1990s there has been an increase in the average wintertime pressure gradient between Iceland and Portugal, due to anomalous low pressures over Iceland. This has led to enhanced east winds over the Greenland Sea: as these winds are warmer, they may be responsible for reduced ice growth there. Coincidentally, the winds would reduce the gap between areas of ice growth and ice decay, altering the water density relationship and reducing convection. In addition, an enhanced wind-driven poleward flow of warm water in the North Atlantic Drift could be responsible for more warm water entering the Arctic Ocean as the *Atlantic sublayer* mentioned above.

This pattern is part of a broader wintertime oscillation of sea level pressure gradients between the entire Arctic Basin and surrounding lower latitudes, an oscillation that appears to affect the whole polar vortex, which depends upon an overall upper-air pressure gradient toward the pole. In years of high Iceland to Portugal gradient (high *North Atlantic Oscillation Index*) one effect is the reduction of the Beaufort Sea high pressure feature and its associated clockwise gyre. The weakened gyre brings less ice from the northeast to replace melted ice, explaining the progressive retreat of the summer ice edge, 1996 through 1998.

The key question is whether recent Arctic changes are primarily the result of a temporary (and cyclic?) change in pressure patterns, or are due to an inexorable warming trend. If the cause is merely an anomaly of atmospheric circulation, then we can expect a reversion to strong convection in the Greenland Sea, extended ice limits in the European Arctic and the Beaufort Sea, a colder Atlantic layer in the Arctic Ocean, and thicker ice. If an underlying warming trend is at work, we can never again

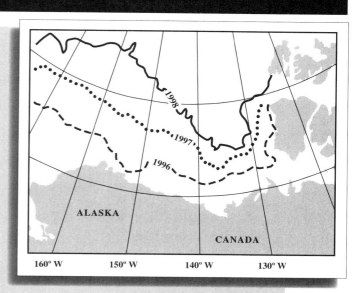

Late Summer Ice Limits in the Beaufort Sea for 1996, 1997, and 1998. (After McPhee, et al., 1999. With permission.)

(continued)

RECENT CHANGES IN THE ARCTIC OCEAN (*Continued*)

expect to see Arctic conditions like those of the 1950s and 1960s, when the Arctic and its ice cover were being intensively studied for the first time.

BIBLIOGRAPHY

Carmack, E. C., K. Aagaard, J. H. Swift, R. W. Macdonald, F. A. McLaughlin, E. P. Jones, R. G. Perkin, J. N. Smith, K. M. Ellis, and L. R. Kilius. "Changes in Temperature and Tracer Distributions within the Arctic Ocean: Results from the 1994 Arctic Ocean Section." *Deep Sea Research II* 44 (1997), 1487–1502.

Maslanik, J. A., M. C. Serreze, and R. G. Barry. "Recent Decreases in Arctic Summer Ice Cover, and Linkage to Atmospheric Circulation Anomalies." *Geophysical Research Letters* 23 (1996), 1677–1680.

McPhee, M. G., T. P. Stanton, J. H. Morison, and D. G. Martinson. "Freshening of the Upper Ocean in the Central Arctic: Is Perennial Sea Ice Disappearing?" *Geophysical Research Letters* 25 (1998), 1729–1732.

McPhee, M. G., et al. "Sea Change in the Arctic." *Science News* 155.7 (1999), 106.

Morison, J., M. Steele, and R. Andreson. "Hydrography of the Upper Arctic Ocean Measured from the Nuclear Submarine USS Pargo." *Deep Sea Research* 45 (1998), 15–18.

Rothrock, D. A., Y. Yu, and G. A. Maykut (1999). "Thinning of the Arctic Sea Ice Cover." *Geophysical Research Letters* 26 (1999), 3469–3472.

Schlosser, P., G. Bonisch. M. Rhein, and R. Bayer. "Reduction of Deepwater Formation in the Greenland Sea During the 1980s: Evidence from Tracer Data." *Science* 251 (1991), 1054–1056.

Steele, M., and T. Boyd. "Retreat of the Cold Halocline in the Arctic Ocean." *Journal of Geophysical Research* 103 (1998), 10419–10449.

Wadhams, P. "Evidence for Thinning of the Arctic Ice Cover North of Greenland." *Nature* 345 (1990), 795–797.

———. "Ice Thickness in the Arctic Ocean: The Statistical Reliability of Experimental Data." *Journal of Geophysical Research* 102 (1997), 27951–27959.

———. "The Odden Ice Tongue and Greenland Sea Convection." *Weather* 54 (3) (1999), 3–84, 91–97.

Wood, R. A., A. B. Keen, J. F. B. Mitchell, and J. M. Gregory. "Changing Spatial Structure of the Thermohaline Circulation in Response to Atmospheric CO_2 Forcing in a Climate Model." *Nature* 399 (1999), 572–575.

—PETER WADHAMS AND DAVID J. CUFF

BIBLIOGRAPHY

Arctic Research Consortium of the United States. "Modeling the Arctic System: A Workshop Report on the State of Modeling in the Arctic System Science Program." Arctic Research Consortium of the United States. Fairbanks, Alaska, 1997. A review of the current state of modeling studies of sea ice.

Carsey, F. D., ed. *Microwave Remote Sensing of Sea Ice.* Washington, D.C.: American Geophysical Union, 1992. A multiauthor monograph on how sea ice can be studied by satellites.

Cavalieri, D. J., et al. "Observed Hemispheric Asymmetry in Global Sea Ice Changes." *Science* 278 (7 November 1997), 1105.

Central Intelligence Agency. *Polar Regions Atlas*, 1978, pp. 12, 38.

Gawarkiewicz, G., et al. "Sea-Ice Processes and Water Mass Modification and Transport over Arctic Shelves." In *The Sea*, vol. 10, edited by K. H. Brink and A. R. Robinson. New York: Wiley, 1998, pp. 171–190. A useful review of the role of sea ice in modifying water masses on continental shelves.

Gloersen, P., et al., eds. *Arctic and Antarctic Sea Ice, 1978–1987: Satellite Passive-Microwave Observations and Analysis.* NASA Report SP-511. Washington, D.C., 1993. An atlas of satellite observations of the changing sea ice cover in both hemispheres.

Hibler, W. D., III. "A Dynamic Thermodynamic Sea Ice Model." *Journal of Physical Oceanography* 9 (1979), 815–846. A classic paper on sea ice modeling; almost all current modeling approaches to sea ice use this as their starting point.

Jeffries, M. D., ed. *Antarctic Sea Ice: Physical Processes, Interactions and Variability.* Washington, D.C.: American Geophysical Union, 1998. Recent research papers on the physical properties of antarctic sea ice.

Johannessen, O. M., et al., eds. *The Polar Oceans and their Role in Shaping the Global Environment: The Nansen Centennial Volume.* Washington, D.C.: American Geophysical Union, 1994. An excellent collection of recent research papers on sea-ice ocean interactions by leading researchers, the proceedings of a conference to celebrate the hundredth anniversary of the sailing of the "Fram" on her transpolar drift (1893).

Leppäranta, M., ed. *Physics of Ice-Covered Seas.* Helsinki: University of Helsinki Press, 1998. A multiauthor work on all aspects of sea ice physics, based on an Advanced Study Institute held in Savonlinna, Finland, in 1994, and intended as a successor to Untersteiner's book.

Lizotte, M. P., and K. R. Arrigo, eds. *Antarctic Sea Ice: Biological Processes, Interactions and Variability.* Washington, D.C.:

American Geophysical Union, 1998. Recent research papers on the fascinating ecosystem that is associated with antarctic sea ice.

Melnikov, I. A. *The Arctic Sea Ice Ecosystem.* Amsterdam: Gordon and Breach, 1997. An authoritative treatment of the biological role of arctic sea ice, by a leading Russian researcher.

Untersteiner, N., ed. *The Geophysics of Sea Ice.* New York: Plenum, 1986. A fundamental multiauthor treatment of every aspect of sea ice, based on a NATO Advanced Study Institute held in 1981.

Wadhams, P. "The Ice Cover." In *The Nordic Seas,* edited by B. G. Hurdle. New York: Springer, 1986, pp. 21–87. An illustrated review of the extent, variability, and properties of sea ice in the Greenland Sea.

—PETER WADHAMS

SEA LEVEL

Sea level is the dynamic surface between the atmosphere and the oceanic hydrosphere. The altitude of this surface varies over the globe at different spatial and temporal scales. On short time scales it is affected by meteorological and oceanographic phenomena such as atmospheric pressure changes, wind shear, temperature and salinity (steric) changes in surface water masses, and tides and currents. On longer time scales, the variable rate of rotation of the Earth, the addition and abstraction of water from the ocean basins during an interglacial/glacial cycle and the distribution and density of materials in the crust and mantle of the Earth affect the sea surface altitude.

The presence of submerged forests in the intertidal zones of the world, of raised gravel beaches, isolation basins, sea caves, and stacks in formerly glaciated areas, of elevated and submerged coral terraces in the tropics, of *in situ* terrestrial deposits on the continental shelves and land bridges, and of submerged buildings and structures bears witness to relative changes of sea level of many hundreds of meters (m) in some areas over the past eighteen thousand years.

Since Charles Darwin wrote in 1842 about the growth of coral atolls in response to widespread subsidence in the Pacific Ocean, and Robert Chambers concluded in 1848 that the consequence of such regional subsidence would be a worldwide fall of sea level, global average sea level changes have been accepted. Eduard Suess introduced the word *eustatic* for such global changes in 1888, and argued that there were two kinds of eustatic movement: (1) spasmodic negative movements caused by the formation of oceanic basins and the subsidence of the Earth's crust, leading to a worldwide fall of sea level of the same magnitude; and (2) slow, continuous movements caused by the accumulation of sediments in the ocean basins, leading to a worldwide rise of sea level of the same magnitude. This "eustatic" mechanism of global sea level change of the same magnitude and sign

remained largely unchallenged until the 1970s, when it was shown that there was no single globally valid curve of sea level, but rather many curves, reflecting processes in the hydrosphere and lithosphere on local, regional, hemispheric, and global scales. Relative sea level changes caused by the growth and decay of ice sheets had been considered by C. McLaren in 1842 and by T. F. Jamieson in 1865, and the concept of glacio-eustasy was advanced subsequently as an explanation. However, the known variability of the altitude of sea level spatially and temporally renders the calculation of global mean sea level of little practical value, and the search for a eustatic sea level curve is now redundant.

Evidence for Sea Level Changes. Profiles of sea level change on contrasting time scales may be derived from modern instrumental records, historical documentary, and archaeological records, and the geologic record.

Instrumental record. Tide gauges measure daily, seasonal, annual, and interannual changes in sea level and are located at ports, in estuaries, on open coasts, on islands, and in inland seas. Geodetic leveling along coasts and across continents has yielded data on the variability of altitude of the sea surface and between different oceans. Oceanographic methods rely on measures of water temperature and density to determine changes in the altitude of the ocean surface. Satellite altimetry permits high-resolution measurements of the ocean surface.

Analyses of tide gauge data show that sea level appears to have risen by 0.5–3.0 millimeters (mm) per year over the past one hundred years, with most estimates in the range 1.0–2.0 millimeters per year. The oldest tide gauges are located in northwest Europe, for example, Amsterdam (1682); Stockholm (1774); Brest, France (1807); Świnoujście, Poland (1811); and Sheerness, United Kingdom (1832). Data from these and other gauges, although discontinuous and of variable quality, have been used to show a more complex sea level pattern: a fall of sea level during 1740–1820 at a rate of 0.25 millimeters per year, and a rise during 1840–1950 of 1.1 millimeters per year, with periods of stability during 1682–1740, 1820–1840, and 1950–1970, all correlating with well-recorded climatic changes. These long-record gauges appear to show also a positive acceleration of mean sea level of 0.44 millimeters per year over the past three hundred years. Such conclusions have been contested because of the small size of the data set, which originates from a geographically restricted area in one hemisphere and is temporally uneven, and because of human interference, particularly engineering works on the coast and estuaries and in catchments. For example, reclamation of tidal flats and marshes has the effect of increasing tidal amplitudes, and a feature of tidal behavior during the last fifty years along the Dutch and German coasts has been a recorded rise of mean high-tide levels at rates faster than mean sea level. To overcome problems of geographical and temporal unevenness, the Permanent Service for Mean Sea Level was established at Bidston, United Kingdom, in 1933, and by 1998 tide gauge data from 1,750 stations worldwide had been assembled. Nevertheless, the longest runs (a run of more than sixty years is essential to calculate a reliable trend) are from gauges in the Northern Hemisphere, especially North America, northwest Europe, and Japan, all of which have been affected by tectonic and glacio-isostatic activity.

Tide gauges not only record the semidiurnal tides set up by astronomical effects, especially the mass and rotation of the moon, but also extreme water levels caused by meteorological phenomena such as pressure changes and winds. Storm surges are particularly severe in shallow seas, occurring in both the tropics and middle latitudes. Tropical storm surges are generated over the oceans between 7° and 25°–30° degrees latitude, where sea surface temperatures are at least 26°C. In the western North Pacific Ocean they are known as typhoons, in the Indian Ocean as revolving storms, and in the eastern North Pacific, Caribbean, and Atlantic Oceans as hurricanes. The disastrous Moroto Typhoon of 1934 that affected Osaka, Japan, was set up by an intense low pressure of 954 millibars and a maximum wind speed of 42 meters per second, which led to a water level three meters above predicted levels. The revolving storm or cyclone in the Bay of Bengal in 1970 has been described as the deadliest tropical cyclone in history: with a deep low pressure and onshore winds of 225 kilometers per hour, water levels were lifted to 9 meters above predicted levels, extensive flooding occurred, and half a million people perished in Bangladesh alone. The hurricane that hit Galveston, Texas, in 1900 was responsible for raising water levels by more than 4.5 meters. The North Sea and the Irish Sea are enclosed epicontinental seas and are particularly prone to storm surges. During the infamous 1953 storm surge in the North Sea, water levels rose to 3 meters above predicted levels, and in the Irish Sea in 1977 the storm surge added up to 2.5 meters, carrying the extreme water level locally at the head of estuaries to more than 7.5 meters above Ordnance Datum—the zero leveling datum for the United Kingdom. The measurement of these extreme water levels often depends on local recorders measuring water marks because tide gauges fail, as happened in February 1990: the tide gauge at Hilbre Island failed during the period of maximum water level, when sea defenses were breached at Towyn, North Wales, the sea inundated an area of ten square kilometers, and the marine limit attained an altitude of more than 5 meters above Ordnance Datum.

In Japan the dense network of tide gauges permits a

record of seismic activity: for the nine years leading up to the Niigata earthquake in 1964, sea level fell because of land uplift, but shortly before the earthquake this trend reversed and in the fortnight following the earthquake sea level rose 15 centimeters (cm). A further consequence of this submarine earthquake was that tsunamis were generated and attacked the Bay of Nezugaseki. Tsunamis are long waves set up by earthquakes, volcanic eruptions, and submarine slides. In deep water a tsunami could have a wave period of ten minutes, a wavelength of 120 kilometers, a height of one meter, and a speed of 720 kilometers per hour. Heights increase as the wave funnels up estuaries and into embayments, where the wave is confined and water depths are shallow. Wave reflection and refraction result in series of waves. The time of arrival of a tsunami can be predicted accurately, but amplitudes are difficult to predict because of local conditions. The height of the wave often overwhelms tide gauge stations, and heights and runup have to be derived from the sedimentary record. Tsunamis are frequent in the seismically active Pacific Ocean and appear in written records and the geologic record from the Indian and Atlantic Oceans and epicontinental seas such as the Mediterranean. The tsunami following the volcanic eruption of Krakatoa in 1883 had a wave height of 15 meters; when the wave inundated islands in the Sunda Strait between Java and Sumatra, an estimated thirty-six thousand coastal-dwelling people drowned. In the North Atlantic, the worst tsunami that has been recorded followed the Lisbon earthquake that destroyed the city in 1755. The height of the wave was estimated to have been thirteen meters, and progressive waves traveled up the English Channel. Associated with one of the waves, the water level at Newlyn, Cornwall, in southwest England, rose by more than three meters in ten minutes. The scale and impacts of the devastating tsunamis that overwhelmed the coast of Sundaun Province, Papua New Guinea, in 1998 have yet to be established. [See Extreme Events; and Natural Hazards.]

Geodetic leveling has shown that the altitude of the sea surface in relation to the zero leveling datum of a country varies not only along the coast but also from one ocean to another. For example, in the United Kingdom repetitive levelings have been used to show that mean sea level at Dunbar, in southeast Scotland, was 25 centimeters higher than Newlyn, in southwest England. In the United States, the mean sea level altitude in Washington State, on the West Coast, is 71 centimeters higher than in Maine, on the East Coast. The application of satellite geodesy, particularly GPS (global positioning systems), SLR (satellite laser ranging), and VLBI (very long baseline interferometry), will establish vertical accuracies for tide gauge benchmarks to the nearest centimeter and for the first time permit records of absolute sea level changes, freed from considerations of post-

VERTICAL MOTION OF CONTINENTS

Estimates of sea level rise—roughly 2 millimeters per year currently, and possibly more if the Antarctic and Greenland ice sheets shrink through global warming—are for the oceans in their entirety. At many continental shorelines, though, measurements of sea level change and predictions of future effects are complicated by the fact that continents, especially in the Northern Hemisphere, are still adjusting ponderously to the loss of the massive ice sheets that melted away roughly ten thousand years ago, at the end of the most recent continental glaciation. In areas such as Hudson Bay and central Scandinavia, where ice sheets were thickest, postglacial rebound is profound, and raised beaches are conspicuous features of the landscape. In Stockholm, for instance, sea level appears to be falling at roughly 4 millimeters per year, while along some Hudson Bay shorelines it is falling at over 10 millimeters per year.

In parts of North America and Europe, the postglacial effect is not so simple. When the ice sheets depressed northern areas, some southern areas, such as the eastern seaboard of North America, were warped upward as the continent flexed. For these areas, the gradual return to preglacial conditions entails a lowering of the shoreline at rates of 1 to 2 millimeters per year.

—DAVID J. CUFF

glacial rebound and subsidence that affects most of the tide gauge stations with the longest records in the Northern Hemisphere. Radar altimeter measurements, particularly the TOPEX-Poseidon altimetry mission from 1992 provide sea level height values to within 2 centimeters. For the period 1993–1997 a sea level rise of 1.2 ($\pm$0.15) millimeters per year globally averaged has been calculated, but there are significant regional variations ranging from +50 to −50 millimeters per year. Results of the short-lived SEASAT mission in 1978 provided for the first time a global map of geoidal relief of the Earth. The geoid is the equipotential surface set up by the resultant of the centrifugal force generated by the Earth's rotation and the gravitational attraction arising from the mass of the Earth. Variations in the distribution of density of materials in the crust and particularly the mantle of the Earth result in the geoid "topography," which has an amplitude approaching 180 meters. A geoidal low of 104 meters south of India contrasts with a geoidal high off the Papua New Guinea coast of 74 meters.

Documentary and archaeological record. Documentary records of extreme sea level events from northwest Europe, India, and Japan date back to the tenth century CE. Many record the elevation of the sea level surface associated with storm surges, cyclones, and typhoons, but others record the sea level changes associated with earthquakes, including tsunamis. In Germany, the whole coastal region was affected by well-recorded floods in the Middle Ages: the Julian flood of 1164, the first Marcellus flood of 1219, the Lucia flood of 1287, and in 1632 the worst storm surge catastrophe,

known as the second Marcellus flood. The All Saints Day floods of 1436, 1532, and 1570 were notable and catastrophic. In Holland, the water attained a level marked in Scheveningen Church and calculated to four meters above the zero leveling datum in Holland. Elsewhere water levels reached over 5 meters, the highest extreme water level ever recorded along the Dutch coast. On the south coast of England, the coastal lowland of Romney Marsh was inundated on many occasions during the thirteenth century when the shingle of Dungeness was breached and the River Rother diverted. The storms were particularly ferocious in 1250, 1252, and 1288. Throughout eastern England and the North Sea region in general, a significant increase of higher sea levels was associated with storms, from five in the twelfth century to twelve in the thirteenth century, coinciding with the Medieval Warm Period. The accounts from the monastic houses during this period show that the raised sea levels associated with the storms led to extensive flooding and destruction of their economic base.

In Japan, the documentary record during the past twelve hundred years reveals that considerable destruction has resulted along the coast from tsunamis and typhoon-induced flooding. In the Osaka area, fifty-three storm surge disasters have been recorded since 700.

The archaeological record of structures such as harbor works, fish tanks, and salt pans, constructed in relation to particular sea levels and now either submerged or elevated, or of middens on the continental shelf and on raised beaches, bear witness to relative changes of sea level. At Halieis, Greece, the foundations of the Temple of Apollo lie completely submerged in 1.5 meters of water, indicating a relative rise of sea level of at least this amount since the temple's construction. A comparison of the height of the arch of the Paglia Bridge near the Doge's Palace in Venice, Italy, above the present level compared with a sixteenth-century drawing shows that sea level has risen by 46 centimeters in the past four hundred years.

The floor of the Temple or Market of Serapis at Pozzuoli, north of Naples, Italy, is at present close to sea level, but Sir Charles Lyell had noted in 1828 that staining on the marble columns and borings of the mollusks *Modiola lithophaga* Lam. and *Mytilus lithofagus* Linn. from 3.7 to 6.4 meters in length indicated a long period of submersion in sea water during a relatively higher sea level postdating the construction of the temple. Indeed, there has been general subsidence within the gulf of Pozzuoli since Roman times of about 14 meters, but from 1969–1972 uplift of 170 centimeters was recorded, followed by a period of quiescence and renewed uplift of 160 centimeters between 1982 and 1984. Since 1969 relative sea level has fallen by 319 centimeters in this area because of tectonic activity within the Phlegraean Fields.

Archaeological remains on the continental shelves indicate that sea level has risen in the past, whereas remains such as shell middens well above present sea level indicate that there have been relative falls of level. The recovery of a Maglemosian barbed point from peat dredged from the Leman and Ower Banks in the North Sea in 1932 in 36 meters of water demonstrated the mesolithic occupation of this area some eight thousand years ago, when the North Sea was dry land and a land bridge existed between Britain and mainland Europe. In the Oresund, between Denmark and Sweden, flint artifacts have been recovered in shallower water and dated to 6400 BCE. Along the coast of Brazil between Rio de Janeiro and Rio Grande do Sul are thousands of shell middens reaching up to 25 meters in height and containing a record of changing sea levels for the past 6,000 years. In South Carolina, the oldest shell middens (4,200–3,300 years BP) occur near the mouths of estuaries, whereas the younger ones (3,300–1,000 BP) occur further landward and up estuary, implying a response by prehistoric folk to a rising sea level.

Geologic record. A depositional and erosional record of sea level changes exists for most of the last 2 million years, although the earlier record is fragmentary. The record is submerged on the continental shelves, is preserved in the sediments of the world's coastal lowlands and deltas, and has been elevated in those areas affected by glaciation and uplift following deglaciation.

The world's coastal lowlands contain a sedimentary archive of sea level changes that in many cases is continuous for the Holocene (the last 10,000 years). The sediments comprise sands, silts, and clays laid down under fully marine or brackish water conditions and interrupted by organic deposits that formed under lagoonal, marginal lake, or terrestrial conditions. In subsiding areas, inorganic sediments dominate, with thin, intercalated organic layers, whereas in coasts where vertical movements are minimal, the development, thickness, and diversity of organic deposits is greater. On rising coasts, there are interruptions and discontinuities in sedimentation, although sediments in former lagoons and lakes on elevated coral terraces and raised beaches (isolation basins) display periods of marine- and freshwater-dominated sedimentation as a manifestation of a complex interplay between land uplift, sea level change, and storm surge or tsunamis activity.

In northwest England, where land uplift following deglaciation ceased about 6,500 years ago, twelve positive tendencies of sea level movement and twelve negative tendencies have been recorded for the Holocene. The sea first crossed the Lancashire coast some 8,400 years ago at an altitude 11 meters below present mean sea level and had already penetrated Morecambe Bay a thousand years earlier, indicating a severing of the land bridge connection between England and Ireland by this time. The maximum altitude attained by the sea was about 5.5 meters above present mean sea level in southwest Lancashire, rising to 8.7 meters in the Solway Lowlands of Cumbria. The maximum landward penetration of the sea was about 6 kilometers beyond the present coast, and this occurred some 5,000 years ago.

In the tropics, similar sea level tendencies, manifest in the sediments of the coastal lowlands and deltas, have been recorded. In Rio de Janeiro State, Brazil, there are about twenty lagoons ranging in size from 1 to 200 square kilometers, with depths of 0.5 to 3.0 meters, separated from the sea and each other by barrier beaches (*restingas*) of coarse white sand, with crests in distinct populations increasing landward from 4 to 12 meters. Unconsolidated sediments beneath the lagoons between the *restingas* attain thicknesses up to 9 meters, for example, in the Lagoa de Itaipu, where the upper 3 meters of sediments are Holocene in age. These are characteristically silty clays and sandy silts of marine origin, with interleaved organic deposits of fresh- and brackish-water origin. Dates from this organic material indicate that sea level rose from −1.0 meters 7,000 years ago to +1.8 meters 5,200 years ago, with a sea level maximum of +3.0 meters at 4,000 years ago, followed by a fall to present levels.

Sedimentation in deltas is complicated by the delivery of considerable volumes of sediments from the catchments, but a similar interfingering of *in situ* organic sediments can be demonstrated. The Mississippi Delta has built seaward by way of a series of subdeltas: the

Teche, Lafourche, St. Bernard, and Plaquemines-Modern. Delta lobe switching may be associated with higher sea levels and positive tendencies of sea level movement. The St. Bernard lobe appears to be the oldest, at 3,569 years, whereas the Lafourche lobe has been dated to 1,491 years and the Plaquemines-Modern to 1,322 years. Sediments of similar thickness and complexity have been recorded from the Ganges-Meghna-Brahamputra Delta but cover a longer time period.

Dates on emerged and submerged corals have been used with great effect to establish sea level changes during the last interglacial-glacial-interglacial cycle. The lower part of the staircase of uplifted corals on the Huon Peninsula in Papua New Guinea indicates that sea level rose some 50 meters between 7,000 and 11,000 years ago. A longer record comes from Tahiti, but the most complete record is from Barbados. Here, dates largely from submerged *in situ Acropora palmata*, a reef-forming coral that is regarded as the best available sea level indicator from such environments because of its fast growth rates and considerable size, have permitted the construction of a sea level curve beginning 18,000 years ago, when sea level was 121 meters below present sea level. *Acropora* lives in water depths of up to 10 meters; hence there is an error band of this magnitude. Greater altitudinal resolution can be achieved by dating marine gastropods belonging to the Vermetidae on tropical and subtropical coasts as has been done in Brazil and in the Mediterranean. Altitudinal errors range from ±0.5 meters on near tideless coasts to ±0.5–1 meter where there are strong tides and surf. The use of coralline algae in the tropics has yielded accuracies for former sea levels of ±0.1 meter.

The elevation of raised beaches in formerly glaciated areas has been used to establish former sea levels, but their dating poses a problem unless *in situ* organic deposits such as *turfa* in isolation basins exist. The sediments in isolation basins have been used to date both the end and onset of marine conditions in Fenno-Scandinavia and Britain. In Norway, the maximum altitude of the marine limit in the Oslo area recorded by the rock bar of an isolation basin is 220 meters above present sea level, indicating this amount of uplift in the past 10,000 years. In Britain, isolation basins have been recorded along the west coast from the north shore of Morecambe Bay to northwest Scotland. One of the largest isolation basins is Loch Lomond, where the altitude of the marine limit determined by the threshold of the loch was found to be in error by 4 meters because of erosion of the threshold. Rock bars at the mouths of isolation basins forming the threshold provide the most reliable altitudes of the marine limit. Until recently with the development of cosmogenic dating, the use of wave cut platforms and notches as indices of sea level suffered from the inability to date such erosional features in the absence of *in situ* deposits associated with the end of marine conditions.

Causes of Sea Level Change. The volume of the ocean is approximately 1,322,000,000 cubic kilometers, and its total mass is about 143,000,000 metric tons. On time scales of 10 million years, the ocean volume may have fluctuated by up to 6 percent, adding or subtracting up to 80 million cubic kilometers of water, largely as a response to the growth and decay of ice sheets. The buildup of ice during glacial stages has resulted in a fall of sea level by up to 120 meters and more locally. In addition, the land has been depressed glacio-isostatically by the ice load, which may attain thicknesses of 4 kilometers. The depression has been compensated by land uplift in an aureole or peripheral forebulge around the ice limit up to 1,500 kilometers from the center of loading. During ice attenuation, withdrawal, and collapse, and for thousands of years following deglaciation, the land will rise, the forebulge will collapse and migrate toward the center of ice loading, and a succession of raised beaches will be formed, with the oldest at the highest altitudes and the youngest at the lowest altitudes. Since the final decay of the Fenno-Scandinavian Ice Cap 14,000 years ago, the area around the Gulf of Bothnia has risen by 900 meters: negative gravity anomalies indicate a contemporary deficiency of mass and a residual uplift potential of 100 meters. Geophysical models have been developed to predict relative sea level changes following deglaciation. They have shown that there was considerable variability in terms of response, but there was also some geographic coherence. Six zones have been identified in which either emerged or submerged beaches have been predicted for the past 6,000 years. Such models are valuable in providing an approximation of the likely behavior of sea levels and the response of the world's coastlines and can be constrained using empirical data. These data indicate periods of accelerated sea level rise that are not well accommodated by the models. The accelerated rates of rise are supported by calculations of meltwater discharge rates, diversions of meltwater, and the timing of these events. For example, discharge rates from Lake Agassiz, the level of which dropped rapidly by 40 meters, have been calculated to be about 30,000 cubic meters per second. The initial discharge was via the Mississippi River and into the Gulf of Mexico, but after 11,000 years ago it had switched to the St. Lawrence River as withdrawal of the Laurentide ice continued. This massive discharge of cold, fresh water disrupted biological productivity, water mass formation, and climate in the North Atlantic and caused the accelerations in the rate of rise of sea level. It has been estimated that the catastrophic discharge of meltwater from a single drumlin field in Canada could have liberated 84,000 cubic kilometers of water and raised sea level by 23 centimeters in a few weeks.

Accumulation of sediments in deltas and ocean basins adds a load to the crust (sedimento-isostasy), causing a relative fall in sea level, as does the application of a water load as sea level rises (hydro-isotasy). A sea level rise of 100 meters results in a load of 100 metric tons per square meter applied to the continental shelves and ocean basins; such a load, applied over short periods of geologic time, may trigger seismic activity along active plate margins.

At different temporal and spatial scales, sea levels are affected by atmospheric pressure, winds, waves, currents, tides, temperature, and density. An increase in atmospheric pressure of 1 millibar should result in a decrease of sea level by 1 centimeter. The annually persistent subtropical high pressure cells result in a depression of the sea level by about 10 centimeters, whereas low pressure areas around Antarctica and in the North Pacific and Atlantic Oceans result in high sea levels of 6 to 20 centimeters. The range of sea level altitudes caused by atmospheric pressure variations can amount to 32 centimeters.

Waves will elevate sea level momentarily, sometimes to considerable altitudes. A fully developed sea with wave heights of 8.5 meters probably takes about two days to set up, with an average wind speed of 20 meters per second and a fetch of 1,300 kilometers. Only about 10 percent of all waves exceed 6 meters, but freak waves 20–30 meters high have been recorded in the open ocean: for example, in the North Pacific in 1933, one wave reached a height of 34 meters, as estimated by the crew of the USS *Ramapo*.

The main tide raising forces on the Earth are the moon and the sun, and in enclosed seas and embayments, such as the Minas Basin in the Bay of Fundy, the semidiurnal mean spring tide range is further amplified to 12.09 meters. The tide-generating force is proportional to the mass of the moon and the sun and inversely proportional to the cube of the distance of the Earth from them. Because of the proximity of the moon to the Earth, its effect on tidal phenomena on the Earth is 2.17 times larger than that of the sun. Spring tides occur when the range between high and low water is at a maximum shortly after full moon and the new moon, when the Earth, moon, and sun are in line—a condition known as *syzygy*. Minimal tidal ranges, known as neap tides, occur when the moon is in the first and third quarters and the sun and moon are said to be in *quadrature*.

The sea level surface can be raised as a consequence of the geometry and water depth of enclosed seas and embayments such as the Baltic, the Mediterranean, and the Gulf of Trieste. Standing waves, or *seiches*, are generated under these conditions, and in the case of the Gulf of Trieste, sea level can be raised by up to 75 centimeters.

The density of sea water is one of its most fundamental properties, variations of which can affect sea level. Density is affected by temperature, salinity, and pressure. Seawater density will increase as salinity and pressure increase, and because dense water occupies a smaller volume, sea level will fall. Density increases as temperature increases, and this will result in a rise in sea level: an increase of temperature of 1°C in a water mass 4,000 meters thick would cause a rise in sea level of sixty centimeters. These are known as *steric* effects: they have operated in the past and at present. They will have an effect in the future as a result of global warming. During the last glaciation, when fresh water was stored on land in ice caps and glaciers, the mean salinity of the oceans was about thirty-six parts per thousand, compared with a present-day density of thirty-five parts per thousand. Hence part of the lowered sea level of about 120 meters was caused by an increase in density of the oceanic water masses and by lower temperatures.

Rates of Sea Level Change. Most sea level curves are based on the interpolation and extrapolation of lines with sea level variates plotted on age altitude graphs. Improvements in the presentation of the data have included the use of error bands and boxes and envelopes showing the general trend of sea level in an area. Changing rates of sea level have been obscured and the possibility of linking accelerated rates of change with other environmental phenomena rendered difficult.

There has been a generally accepted view that sea level changes are slow, and this has been reinforced by the tide gauge records that indicate a rise of 1.0–2.0 millimeters per year over the past century. It is clear, however, that over the past 200,000 years relative sea level change rates have varied between 1 and 75 millimeters per year. During the last interglacial in Europe (the Eemian), sea level rose during a 450-year period at rates up to 40 millimeters per year. In northwest England about 7,800 years ago, during this inter-glacial, the rate of relative sea level rise accelerated to 34–44 millimeters per year. In eastern China there appear to have been accelerations between 20 and 75 millimeters per year, with peak rates at 15,000, 12,500, 11,500, and 7,800 years ago. The sea level curve from Barbados shows accelerations of rates at 12,000 years ago of 24 millimeters per year and at 9,500 years ago some 28 millimeters per year. Higher-resolution dating from Barbados shows that from 19,000 to 14,400 years ago the rate of sea level rise was 5 millimeters per year. This increased to 37 millimeters per year from 14,400 to 13,700 years ago, then decreased to 8 millimeters per year before increasing again to 25 millimeters per year about 12,000 years ago. The consequence of these accelerations was that there were times of rapid shoreline retreat across the continental shelf and present coastline and into the present coastal lowlands. For Germany it has been calculated that the shoreline shifted landward at a rate of 160 meters per year between 8,600 and 7,100 years ago.

BEACH EROSION WITH RISING SEA LEVEL: THE BRUUN RULE

The so-called Bruun Rule, whereby a rise in sea level causes beach erosion. If the sea level(s) rise by a unit amount, so will the offshore bottom (s'). The sand necessary to raise the bottom (area b') can be supplied by waves eroding the upper part of the beach (area b). R is the amount of shoreline recession and W is the "active" portion of the profile participating in the adjustment. (After National Research Council, 1987, p. 54, Figure 5-3. With permission of National Academy Press.)

Potential sea level rise associated with possible global warming may cause inudation of low-lying environments such as deltas, lagoons, wetlands, and coral atolls. Another possible consequence, however, could be accelerated erosion of sandy shorelines as beaches adjust their form to changing conditions. In general, following the so-called Bruun Rule shown in the figure, such erosion is to be expected, but the precise amounts are difficult to quantify. However, on sandy beaches exposed to ocean waves, the coastline may erode by the order of one meter for every one centimeter rise in sea level (National Research Council, 1987).

BIBLIOGRAPHY

Bruun, P. "Sea-level Rise as a Cause of Shore Erosion." *Proceedings of Civil Engineers* 88 (1962), 117–130.
National Research Council. Committee on Engineering Implications of Changes in Relative Mean Sea Level. *Responding to Changes in Sea Level: Engineering Implications.* Washington, D.C.: National Academy Press, 1987.

—ANDREW S. GOUDIE

Response of Sea Level to Future Global Climatic Change. There have been many estimates of future sea level rise. The most recent from the United Nations Intergovernmental Panel on Climate Change for the Business-as-Usual Scenario range from 20 centimeters by the year 2050, with an error band of 7–39 centimeters, to 49 centimeters by 2100, with an error band of 20–86 centimeters, yielding average rates of rise of 4–5 millimeters per year. [*See* Intergovernmental Panel on Climate Change.] This is about ten orders less than measured rates using proxy data from the past 12,000 years and from the last interglacial (ca. 134,000 years ago), when maximum carbon dioxide concentrations have been estimated to have been approximately 296 parts per million (by volume), which is 62 parts per million lower than 1994 values. The contributions to sea level rise by 2100 are dominated by thermal expansion of surface water masses consequent upon the predicted rise of global temperatures. It is estimated that this component will contribute 28 centimeters of the rise, whereas glaciers and small ice caps will contribute 16 centimeters and the Greenland ice cap 6 centimeters. An increase of precipitation over the Antarctic ice cap will cause a fall in sea level of 1 centimeter by the end of the next century. However, considerable uncertainties arise not only from the model parameters but also from the behavior of other components of the global systems that will have an impact on sea level. On the one hand, the use and depletion of finite groundwater resources for irrigation in arid and semiarid areas from aquifers that were recharged during the last glaciation may be contributing from 0.07 to 0.38 millimeters per year in sea level rise. Deforestation and desertification may be contributing 0.15 millimeters per year, and the reclamation and loss of wetlands 0.01 millimeters per year. The withdrawal of permafrost due to global warming could add 0.1 millimeters per year to sea level. On the other hand, the construction of dams and reservoirs could result in a fall of sea level by 0.09–0.54 millimeters per year, and the cessation of groundwater withdrawal associated with deindustrialization in many western economies may also have an impact on the hydrological balance and sea level. [*See* Dams.] In fact, these positive and negative contributions to sea level driven anthropogenically may balance themselves out.

Most estimates consider only global mean sea level rise and ignore the local, regional, and hemispheric consequences of variations in density of earth materials in the crust and mantle of the Earth. In other words, how will the geoid "topography" respond to additions of water from the last remaining ice caps? The sea level rise potential based on a consideration of the volume of ice in Antarctica, Greenland, and the small ice caps is estimated to be between 72 and 77 meters. A loss of the remaining ice on the Earth is an unlikely scenario associated with a fundamental change in the Earth's energy budget. A more likely scenario, given the increasing anthropogenic contributions to the enhanced greenhouse effect, is a rise of sea level by 1 meter by the year 2500, based on a stabilization of carbon dioxide concentrations at 450 parts per million by volume (ppmv) in 2100 (compared with 358 ppmv in 1994 and rising by 1.5 ppmv annually), but with a commitment to continued rising temperatures and sea level for a further four hundred years. Although the majority of the rise of sea level for this scenario is thermal expansion, if all or part is consequential on the melting of a proportion of the remaining ice caps in Greenland and Antarctica there will be an uneven and unequal change of sea level. Modeled solutions for a partial melt of the Antarctic ice cap sufficient to cause a rise of global mean sea level by 100 centimeters showed that sea level would fall by 210 centimeters adjacent to the parts of Antarctica that had lost mass following partial deglaciation, whereas in the central Pacific the Melanesian Islands would suffer a 125-centimeter rise in sea level.

[See also Climate Change; Coastlines; Glaciation; Global Warming; Ice Sheets; and Plate Tectonics.]

BIBLIOGRAPHY

Barth, M. C., and J. G. Titus, eds. Greenhouse Effect and Sea Level Rise. New York: Van Nostrand Reinhold, 1984. This is the first book that alerted politicians, planners, managers, and decision makers to sea level rise as the consequence of the enhanced greenhouse effect.

Beets, D. J., M. M. Fischer, and W. de Gans, eds. Coastal Studies on the Holocene of the Netherlands. Special issue. Mededelingen Rijks Geologische Dienst 57 (1996). Eleven essays summarizing the results of research over the past ten years on coastal and sea level changes in one of the world's most important and vulnerable coastal lowlands.

Carter, R. W. G., and C. D. Woodroffe. Coastal Evolution: Late Quaternary Shoreline Morphodynamics. Cambridge: Cambridge University Press, 1994. An important collection of thirteen essays that considers the history of erosional and depositional coasts of the world within the context of Late Quaternary sea level changes.

Chappell, J., and N. J. Shackleton. "Oxygen Isotopes and Sea Level." Nature 324 (1986), 137–140. The key paper that links the oxygen-18 record with the sea level record from the Huon Peninsula, Papua New Guinea, for the past 260,000 years.

Clark, J. A., and J. A. Primus. "Sea Level Changes Resulting from Future Retreat of Ice Sheets: An Effect of CO_2 Warming of the Climate." In Sea-Level Changes, edited by M. J. Tooley and I. Shennan, pp. 356–370. Oxford: Blackwell, 1987. A challenging paper that models the projected change of sea level and shows that the likely effects will be unequal in magnitude and of different signs over the globe.

Devoy, R. J. N., ed. Sea Surface Studies: A Global View. London: Croom Helm, 1987. A valuable interdisciplinary text by fifteen authors on many aspects of coastal and sea level changes.

Fairbanks, R. G. "A 17,000-Year Glacio-eustatic Sea-Level Record: Influence of Glacial Melting Rates on the Younger Dryas Event and Deep Ocean Circulation." Nature 342 (1989), 637–642. A seminal contribution on sea level change including accelerated sea level rise using dated corals from a low-latitude island, Barbados.

Fairbridge, R. W. "Eustatic Changes in Sea Level." In Physics and Chemistry of the Earth, edited by L. H. Ahrens, F. Press, K. Rankama, and S. K. Runcorn, pp. 99–185. Oxford: Pergamon Press, 1961. This is the starting point for all those with an interest in the history, evidence, and interpretation of the record of sea level changes. Challenging and stimulating.

Finkl, C. W., ed. "Holocene Cycles: Climate, Sea Levels, and Sedimentation." Special issue. Journal of Coastal Research Special Issue 17 (1995). Forty-nine contributions in honor of Rhodes W. Fairbridge, of which twenty-four are a significant contribution to an understanding of sea level changes in different parts of the world.

Godwin, H. "Studies of the Post-Glacial History of British Vegetation. IV. Post-Glacial Changes of Relative Land- and Sea-Level in the English Fenland." Philosophical Transactions of the Royal Society of London, ser. B, 230 (1940), 285–303. Methodologically, this is a seminal paper for the investigation of the sea level record from unconsolidated sediments, employing stratigraphic, micropaleontological, and archaeological data.

Jelgersma, S. "Holocene Sea Level Changes in the Netherlands." Mededelingen Geologische Stichting, ser. C, 6.7 (1961), 1–100. The seminal and influential paper that expounds the techniques necessary to apply to sediments in coastal lowlands for understanding coastal and sea level changes in the Netherlands. This is a model for the investigation of the history and evolution of coastal lowlands and sets the highest standards.

Lisitzin, E. Sea-Level Changes. Amsterdam: Elsevier, 1974. An invaluable reference text that includes a chapter on the prediction of storm surges and tsunamis.

Louwe Kooijmans, L. P. The Rhine/Meuse Delta: Four Studies on Its Prehistoric Occupation and Holocene Geology. Leiden: E. J. Brill, 1974. A scholarly and skillful thesis in which prehistoric settlement patterns in the Netherlands are related to patterns of sedimentation in a deltaic coastal lowland. A model for investigations in other parts of the world.

Masters, P. M., and N. C. Flemming, eds. Quaternary Coastlines and Marine Archaeology. London: Academic Press, 1983. One of the few overviews of the evidence of human occupation on the continental shelves and land bridges of the world, with numerous examples from both the Old and New Worlds.

Morner, N. A., ed. Earth Rheology, Isostasy, and Eustasy. Chichester, U.K.: Wiley, 1980. Forty-seven chapters on crustal movements and sea level change: a benchmark collection of essays for reference.

National Academy of Science. Studies in Geophysics: Sea-Level Change. Washington, D.C.: National Academy Press, 1990. Fourteen chapters on the processes, rates, and records of past sea level changes.

Pirazzoli, P. A. Sea-Level Changes: The Last 20,000 Years. Chichester, U.K.: Wiley, 1996. An invaluable text in which the causes, evidence, and trends are reviewed critically.

Plassche, O. van de, ed. *Sea-Level Research: A Manual for the Collection and Evaluation of Data*. Norwich, U.K.: Geo Books, 1986. Twenty-two essential chapters on data acquisition, their value, interpretation, and limitations. The majority of the book is devoted to sea level indicators, but there are chapters on the age and altitude of these indicators.

Pugh, D. T. *Tides, Surges, and Mean Sea-Level*. Chichester, U.K.: Wiley, 1987. Reprinted with corrections in 1996. An updated version of the material covered by Lisitzin, but with some elaboration of engineering implications.

Schneider, D. "The Rising Seas." *Scientific American* 276.3 (1997), 96–101.

Smith, D. E., and A. G. Dawson, eds. *Shorelines and Isostasy*. London: Academic Press, 1983. Fifteen chapters by internationally recognized scientists on methodologies, shoreline development, glacio-isostasy, and hydro-isostasy, with examples from the world's coastlines, particularly middle and high latitudes in the Northern Hemisphere.

Tooley, M. J., and S. Jelgersma, eds. *Impacts of Sea-Level Rise on European Coastal Lowlands*. Oxford: Blackwell, 1992. Eleven essays on the consequences of sea level rise as the result of the enhanced greenhouse effect and a history of some of the European lowlands during the Holocene.

Tooley, M. J., A. G. Dawson, and A. J. Long. "Ocean Volume and Sea-Level Changes from Geological Evidence." In *Sea-level Change and Coastal Processes: Implications for Europe*, edited by D. E. Smith, S. Raper, S. Zerbini, and A. Anchez-Arcilla, pp. 10–24. Luxembourg: European Commission, 1999. A benchmark paper on factors affecting the volume of water in the ocean basins.

Tooley, M. J., Y. Ota, and W. W.-S. Yim, eds. *Recent Studies of Quaternary Sea-Level Changes*. Special issue. *Quaternary International* 54 (1999). Up-to-date research papers on aspects of coastal and sea level changes in many parts of the world.

Walker, R. G., and N. P. James, eds. *Facies Models: Response to Sea Level Change*. St. John's, Newfoundland: Geological Association of Canada, 1992. A geologic perspective treating all the coastal sedimentary environments affected by sea level changes.

—MICHAEL J. TOOLEY

SECRETARIATS

Global environmental treaty secretariats are the subset of international organizations that are responsible for providing executive support services to members of specific international environmental agreements, conventions, or treaties. Each secretariat services a single treaty, that is, they are treaty-specific organizations.

Organizational Profile. The organizational profile of a secretariat consists of an executive head often known as a "Secretary-General," professional personnel from a range of disciplines and areas of scientific expertise relative to the substance of the convention, and general or administrative staff including interpreters, translators, financial and public relations staff, and human resource management personnel.

Secretariat personnel are employed as international civil servants for the duration of their time with the secretariat, and most are employed on short-term contracts of one to five years. Many of the professional personnel are recruited from national government bureaucracies, environmental nongovernmental organizations, and scientific and industry organizations. General or administrative support staff are usually recruited from the host country in which the secretariat is located.

The institutional loyalty of international civil servants is to the secretariat. Internationalism rather than nationalism is supposedly the core value of an international secretariat.

Budgets and Resource Allocation. The majority of multilateral environmental treaty secretariats are resource-dependent organizations in expanding treaty systems, whose personnel and budgets are frequently inadequate to achieve their organizational objectives. Secretariat budgets are determined by the parties to the treaty, whose annual dues are typically the main source of secretariat financing. These regular contributions are usually aligned with the United Nations (UN) Scale of Assessments.

For example, in 1997, the 1973 Convention on International Trade in Endangered Species of Wild Fauna and Flora (CITES) Secretariat had 138 parties, fifteen professional and twelve support staff, and an administrative core budget of Fr 6,505,410; the Ramsar Bureau (1972 Convention on Wetlands of International Importance Especially as Waterfowl Habitat) had ninety-six parties, eight professional and nine support staff, and a total budget of Fr 2,857,839; while the FCCC (1992 United Nations Framework Convention on Climate Change) had 165 parties, twenty-six professional and seventeen support staff, and a budget of U.S.$8.5 million, not including conference costs (Fridtjof Nansen Institute, 1997).

In contrast, the UN Secretariat, with which treaty secretariats are frequently and inappropriately compared, had approximately 500,000 personnel in 1995; and a secretariat comprising several hundred personnel and a budget upward of several hundred million U.S. dollars was anticipated for the 1993 Chemical Weapons Convention (Chayes and Chayes, 1995).

Many multilateral treaty secretariats are linked either directly or indirectly to a parent organization that provides administrative support to the secretariat by way of recruitment and financial management services. The United Nations Environment Programme (UNEP) provides administrative support to the CITES Secretariat, while the International Union for the Conservation of Nature and Natural Resources (the World Conservation Union; IUCN) and the International Wildfowl Research Bureau (IWRB), as coparents of the Ramsar Bureau, assist the Bureau with administrative and database activities, respectively. However, issues of secretariat autonomy and resource allocation are frequently sources of tension in relations between secretariats and their parent organizations.

The primary responsibility of a treaty secretariat is to assist the parties in achieving the agreed treaty objectives; it is a servant of the parties. Within a specific treaty system, the secretariat is accountable to the Conference of the Parties (CoP) or its equivalent, as the key decision-making body of the convention. The secretariat also supports the Standing Committee, and any *ad hoc* committees such as scientific or financial committees.

Secretariats perform two sets of tasks, core and substantive. Core tasks, common to all secretariats, are identified in the treaty text. They include routine executive duties such as preparing and distributing documents for meetings of the CoP and acting as rapporteur for CoP meetings. The three most significant categories of substantive task performed by secretariats are overseeing national reporting and performance review; assisting developing countries with capacity building, for example by identifying technology transfer projects and organizing expert advice; and working with nonstate actors to monitor compliance (Sandford, 1996, 1997).

Secretariats are frequently undervalued as treaty system assets. A secretariat is the information hub and the institutional memory of a treaty system, and the unacknowledged significance of these organizations lies in their position as the network managers of multilateral systems. As these organizations perform their tasks, they link the formal and informal networks of the treaty system, thus substantially increasing the treaty system's chances of achieving its objectives.

[*See also* International Cooperation; *and* United Nations Environment Programme. *Many of the environmental treaty secretariats and international organizations mentioned herein are the subjects of independent entries.*]

BIBLIOGRAPHY

Chayes, A., and A. Chayes. *The New Sovereignty: Compliance with Treaties in International Regulatory Regimes.* Cambridge, Mass.: Harvard University Press, 1995.

Fridtjof Nansen Institute. *The Green Globe Yearbook of International Cooperation on Environment and Development.* New York and Oxford: Oxford University Press, 1997.

Sandford, R. "International Environmental Treaty Secretariats: A Case of Neglected Potential?" *Environmental Impact Assessment Review* 16.1 (January 1996).

———. "Secretariats as Catalysts: A Comparative Study of the Influence of Global Environmental Treaty Secretariats on Treaty Implementation." (Ph.D. diss., Department of Urban Studies and Planning, Massachusetts Institute of Technology, 1997.)

—ROSEMARY A. SANDFORD

SECURITY AND ENVIRONMENT

National security has traditionally focused on maintaining the territorial integrity and political sovereignty of nations. In turn, the security issues of the nation-state are linked to broader issues of international security. Hence threats to the security of states can also be considered threats to international security. In recent years, increased emphasis has been placed on expanding the traditional conception of security to include nonconventional threats. Such threats include resource scarcity, human-rights abuses, outbreaks of infectious disease, and environmental degradation caused by toxic contamination, ozone depletion, global warming, water pollution, soil degradation, and the loss of biodiversity.

The interest in linking environment and security emerged strongly in the mid-1980s, although discussions on the issue of environmental change and security occurred without explicit use of the term *environmental security* as early as the 1950s. The U.S. military's use of defoliants in Southeast Asia during the Vietnam War focused international attention on both the intentional and unintentional environmental damage caused by war. The Additional Protocol I to the 1949 Geneva Convention on the Protection of Victims of International Armed Conflicts (1977) was the first of two treaties with major environmental importance that stemmed from international concern over excessive environmental degradation in Vietnam.

Efforts to develop more stringent definitions for the prohibition of "widespread, long-term and severe damage to the natural environment" continued with the 1977 Convention on the Prohibition of Military or Any Other Hostile Use of Environmental Modification Techniques (the ENMOD Convention), the second of the post-Vietnam treaties.

By the early 1980s, various institutions and writers began addressing security issues beyond strictly military concerns that affect the state. The United Nations Commission on Disarmament and Security Issues made a distinction between collective security and common security. The former implied the more traditional interstate military security issues, while the latter reflected the growing array of nonmilitary threats, including economic, resource scarcity, population growth, and environmental degradation. This was followed by the new political thinking of Russian President Mikhail Gorbachev, which promoted the concept of comprehensive security as a cornerstone of international politics. Comprehensive security included various threats, including nuclear war, poverty, and global environmental issues.

At the same time, numerous writers began to address the issue of expanding the definition of security to include nonmilitary threats. The following example is from Ullman (1983):

> A threat to national security is an action or sequence of events that (1) threatens drastically and over a relatively brief span of time to degrade the quality of life for the inhabitants of a state, or (2) threatens significantly to narrow the range of policy choices available to the government of a state or to private, nongovernmental entities (person, groups, corporations) within the state.

While still circumscribing security within state boundaries, such analysts sought to expand the range of threats to security beyond the traditional military concerns.

The suggestion to broaden the definition of security to include environmental threats was by no means limited to American sources. The report of the World Commission on Environment and Development, *Our Common Future* (1987), which was best known for its definition of sustainable development, also called for recognition that security was partly a function of environmental sustainability. The Commission highlighted the causal role that environmental stress can play in contributing to conflict, while also stating that "a comprehensive" approach to international and national security must transcend the traditional emphasis on military power and armed competition. Norman Myers (1993) argued similarly for moving from security as a "freedom from" various threats to security as a "freedom to" access environmental services. Others have echoed this statement by noting that comprehensive security has two intertwined components: first, political security, with its military, economic, and humanitarian subcomponents, and second, environmental security, including protecting and utilizing the environment.

The importance of this distinction became obvious after the 1986 nuclear accident at Chernobyl placed health considerations squarely within a security framework for many people. The next year, President Gorbachev proposed "ecological security" as a top priority that de facto would serve as a forum for international confidence building.

It should be noted that discussion of the links between environment and security has extended far beyond an academic debate. Warren Christopher, former U.S. Secretary of State, has explicitly linked the two, noting that ". . . natural resource issues (are) frequently critical to achieving political and economic stability. . . ." Former Norwegian Defense Minister Johan Holst was even more explicit when he noted that "environmental degradation may be viewed as a contribution to armed conflict in the sense of exacerbating conflicts or adding new dimensions."

Whether the discussions have been among academics or in public-policy circles, there is little doubt that some confusion still exists over how environment and security are linked. This confusion persists not only within disciplines, but within government departments as well. Indeed, many researchers avoid using the term *security* altogether, preferring to focus on environmental change and social adaptation and/or armed conflict.

At least part of the confusion over identifying the links between environment and security has been the result of different institutional interpretations of the terms *environment* and *security*. At present, these interpretations include the following:

1. Security of the environment (or security of services provided by the natural environment). This has also been interpreted as nondiminishing natural capital. This includes military and defense intelligence institutions monitoring and enforcing international environmental agreements; gathering, analyzing, and disseminating scientific data on the natural environment; responding to mitigate environmental crises and disasters; implementing environmental sustainability programs; guaranteeing access to natural resources; spinning off environmental cleanup technologies; and protecting natural parks and reserves.
2. Environmental degradation or depletion stemming from military preparation for armed conflict; from the conduct of armed conflict; and from the disposal of military waste.
3. Environmental degradation and resource depletion as potential causes of violent conflict.
4. Institutional infringement on the principle of sovereignty to mitigate environmental degradation.
5. Environmental degradation and resource depletion as threats to national welfare (and, therefore, national security).
6. A broad notion of environment embedded in a range of factors that affect "human" security.

The discussions have become even more difficult because of their interdisciplinary nature; participants range from environmentalists, who may interpret a secure environment as one in which there is no further decline in the stocks of natural capital, to the military, which sees certain environmental issues as new threats, or environmental security as a "greening" of their operations. Adding to the confusion are those specialists who often interpret "security" very differently from members of the international-relations community or the defense establishment. Conversely, the introduction of new terms (such as *environmental scarcity* or *environmental refugees*) can frustrate researchers and policy makers for whom similar terms may have specific, important, and sometimes legal, meanings.

Assessments of the nature of linkages between environment and security have proven difficult. The complexity of the relationship poses tremendous empirical and methodological hurdles. The ambiguous and contested nature of the term "security" also complicates research and policy in the area of environment and security. A number of researchers have tried to circumvent this problem by ignoring the term altogether and concentrating specifically on the role of environmental change and resource depletion as potential causes of violent conflict. Such conflict, in turn, could pose a serious threat to the security of individuals, regions, and nation-states. The general discussions on the nature of security and the role of environmental degradation as a contributor to insecurity and conflict have been labeled by Marc Levy (1995) as the "first wave" of environment and conflict research. The empirical research that attempted to prove a link between environment and conflict has been labeled by Levy as the "second wave" of environment and conflict studies.

The state of environment and conflict research that defined this "second wave" is by no means complete or definitive. Yet what has emerged from the research is a set of coherent causal claims that provide a basis for debating the potential role of environmental and demographic stress as contributors to conflict. These claims also allow for a further discussion of policies that incorporate the links between environment and conflict, and provide a basis for pursuing further investigation of the complex and still poorly understood linkages, and for implementation of actions.

It appears that several types of environmental threat may have the capacity to contribute to insecurity and to produce conflict as well. Constraints on resources are a crucial factor that is often discussed in the literature. Rapid industrialization and population growth in many regions have resulted in an increased demand for both renewable and nonrenewable natural resources, and competition for resources has historically been a major cause of conflict. This simple statement seems intuitively reasonable; however, there are some who feel that it overstates the importance of resources and the environment as contributors to conflict. At first glance, the availability of water in the Middle East, the depletion of fish stocks off the eastern coast of Canada, and deforestation in Brazil, Thailand, and elsewhere have all been, or have the potential to be, sources of conflict. It has further been suggested that atmospheric change—both global warming and ozone depletion—has the potential to cause significant societal disruption. In addition, land degradation—or land use change in general—may directly affect society's ability to provide food resources for a growing population, or may indirectly affect other changes, such as global warming. Homer-Dixon (1994) provides some evidence of these relationships and concludes that "environmental scarcity" (which includes environmental change, popu-

lation growth, and an unequal distribution of resources) can cause violent conflict. While this contention remains open to debate, it is increasingly accepted that environmental degradation and resource factors are at least a contributor to conflict and insecurity.

[See also Environmental Law; International Cooperation; Migrations; Sustainable Development; and Water.]

BIBLIOGRAPHY

Canadian Global Change Program. *Environment and Security: An Overview of Issues.* Ottawa, 1996. A report that outlines the key arguments for and against linking environment and security.
Deudney, D. "Environment and Security: Muddled Thinking." *Bulletin of Atomic Scientists* (April 1991), 22–28. The second part of a debate on how environment and security are linked.
Gleick, P. "Environment and Security: The Clear Connections." *Bulletin of Atomic Scientists* (April 1991), 17–21. The first part of a debate on how environment and security are linked (see also Deudney, 1991).
Homer-Dixon, T. "On the Threshold: Environmental Changes as Causes of Acute Conflict." *International Security* 19 (1991), 76–116. A conceptual and theoretical article on how environment may affect conflict.
———. "Environmental Scarcities and Violent Conflict." *International Security* 19.1 (1994).
Levy, M. "Is the Environment a National Security Issue?" *International Security* 20.2 (1995).
Mathews, J. T. "Redefining Security." *Foreign Affairs* (1988), 163–177. One of the classic articles on expanding the definition of security.
Myers, N. "Environment and Security." *Foreign Policy* 74 (1989), 23–41. An overview article on the relationship between environment and security.
———. *Ultimate Security.* London: Norton, 1993.
Ullman, R. "Redefining Security." *International Security* 8.1 (1983), 133.
World Commission on Environment and Development. *Our Common Future.* New York and Oxford: Oxford University Press, 1987.

—STEVE LONERGAN

SEWAGE. See Ocean Disposal; Sanitation; and Water Quality.

SEXUALLY-TRANSMITTED DISEASE. See Disease.

SMOG. See Air Quality; and Atmospheric Chemistry.

SNOW COVER

Snow cover is the most spatially extensive and seasonally variable component of the global cryosphere. On average, snow covers 46 million square kilometers, or half, of the Northern Hemisphere land surface in late January, with a summer minimum of 4 million square kilometers. In addition, there is perennial snow cover over the Antarctic ice sheet (12 million square kilometers), and at the higher elevations of the Greenland Ice Sheet (about 0.6 million square kilometers).

Information on snow cover has been collected routinely at hydrometeorological stations, with records beginning in the late nineteenth century at a few stations, and more widely since the 1930–1950s. The ground is considered to be snow covered when at least half of the visible area from an observing station has snow cover. Since the 1960s, snow cover has been mapped by satellites, initially using visible-band data, which are limited by illumination and cloud cover, and since 1978 by multichannel passive microwave sensors, which are not limited by these factors. Reliable hemispheric snow cover data have been available since 1972 from the Advanced Very High Resolution Radiometer (AVHRR). The visible images are interpreted manually and snow extent is mapped over the Northern Hemisphere weekly. The charts have been digitized for grid boxes varying in size from 16,000 to 42,000 square kilometers, and these data have also been regridded to a 25 × 25 kilometer grid for 1978–1995 and combined with the extent of Arctic Sea ice mapped from passive microwave data to display the seasonal cryosphere in the Northern Hemisphere. [See Cryosphere.] There is a more limited record from AVHRR data for 1974–1986 in the Southern Hemisphere, where the snow cover extent in South America varies between about 1.2 million and 0.7 million square kilometers in July. There is a negligible cover in January in the Southern Hemisphere apart from Antarctica.

Snow cover plays an important role in the climate system. The best-known effect involves the albedo–temperature (positive) feedback, whereby an expanded snow cover increases the reflection of incoming solar radiation, reducing the temperature and thereby encouraging an expansion of the snow cover. Fresh snow has a spectrally integrated albedo of 0.8–0.9, making it the most reflective natural surface. [See Albedo.] This value decreases with age to within a range of 0.4–0.7 as the snow density increases through settling and snow metamorphism, and it is reduced more strongly by impurities within or on the snow (mineral dust, soot, aerosols, biogenic matter). The cooling effect of snow cover is illustrated by the fact that, in the upper Midwest of the United States, winter months with snow cover are about 5°–7°C colder than those without snow cover. Snow cover also insulates the soil surface, or sea ice, since it is a poor heat conductor. The storage of water in the seasonal snow cover introduces an important time delay of weeks to months into the hydrological cycle, causing a peak in the annual runoff hydrograph in spring and early summer. [See Hydrologic Cycle.]

Snowfall is reported in routine meteorological observations. The catch of solid and mixed precipitation in precipitation gauges is melted and total precipitation is usually reported. In windy environments especially, gauge totals may underestimate snowfall by 20–50 percent or more. Snow depth and the corresponding snow water equivalent (SWE) are measured at ground stations. Depth is routinely measured at fixed stakes, or by a ruler inserted into the snow pack, and this depth is reported in daily weather observations at 0900. Average maximum snow depths vary from 30 to 40 centimeters on Arctic Sea ice to several meters in maritime climates such as the mountains of western North America. The SWE along snow courses is measured from depth and density determinations made at weekly to monthly time intervals. These records are used in runoff forecasting. Such networks are currently decreasing because of cost considerations, and satellite passive microwave data are beginning to be used for SWE estimation in combination with other techniques. The basis of this approach is that microwave radiation emitted by the land surface is attenuated by snow cover. However, the effects of any liquid water due to snow melt, vegetation canopy obscuring the snow surface, microphysical changes in grain size, and terrain irregularities greatly complicate such determinations. Moreover, the typical satellite footprint is of the order of 12–25 kilometers, meaning that the signal is a complex spatial average, and hard to relate to point measurements. Nevertheless, such methods are being used for operational SWE mapping over the high plains and prairies of North America. In the western United States, SWE is determined by "pressure pillows" that record the weight of the snow packs. There are more than five hundred such stations in the western cordilleras.

Observational records from satellites indicate that, between 1972 and 1998, the annual snow-covered area in the Northern Hemisphere decreased by about 7 percent. The changes are especially marked in spring and summer, with little or no change in winter. These reductions are highly correlated with increasing air temperature. For North America, there is a sensitivity of approximately −0.6 million square kilometers of snow cover area per degree Celsius rise in temperature. Calculations also suggest that the reduced hemispheric snow cover corresponds approximately to 0.5°C of warming as a result of feedback effects on the energy balance. Global warming trends especially affect winter temperatures and in high latitudes, warmer winters, where the temperature remains below 0°C, may be snowier as a result of increased atmospheric moisture content. This effect has been observed on maritime glaciers in Norway and Alaska and is projected to occur over coastal Antarctica under future global warming.

[See also Global Warming.]

BIBLIOGRAPHY

Gray, D. M., and D. H. Hale. *Handbook of Snow Principles, Processes, Management and Use.* Toronto: Pergamon, 1981.

Groisman, P. Ya., T. R. Karl, and R. W. Knight. "Observed Impact of Snow Cover in the Heat Balance and the Rise of Continental Spring Temperatures." *Science* 263 (1994), 198–200.

Robinson, D. A., K. F. Dewey, and R. R. Heim, Jr. "Global Snow Cover Monitoring: An Update." *Bulletin of the American Meteorological Society* 74 (1993), 1689–1696.

Sevruk, B., ed. *Snow Cover Measurements and Areal Assessment of Precipitation and Soil Moisture.* Geneva: World Meteorological Organization, 1992.

—ROGER G. BARRY

SOCIAL LEARNING

Efforts to understand long-term social change have broadened over the last quarter-century to include not only traditional explanations based on interests and power but also the influence of ideas and learning. *Social learning* is a loosely defined term that has come to encompass much of the relevant literature on the adoption and spread of new concepts, skills, goals, or strategies across multiple social groups. Within the context of global change, varied conceptions of social learning share a concern with how the interactions between knowledge and action help shape humanity's response to its large-scale, long-term transformation of the environment. Social learning is not a predictive theory, a rigorous analytic framework, or even a well-structured body of empirical evidence. Rather, it is an emerging family of perspectives that strives to take seriously the simultaneously science-laden and politically charged character of society's encounter with global change, and to contribute to a more adaptive, reflective management of that encounter.

A great deal of thinking has been devoted to the determinants and processes of learning by more-or-less rationally acting individuals, organizations, and states. The most frequent use of the term *social learning* in contemporary scholarship is within the field of social psychology, where it addresses the ways in which social setting affects individual learning. Studies of social learning in the collective, politically embedded sense that concerns us here are much rarer. Most of what exists builds on the work of Karl Deutsch's *The Nerves of Government* (1963), which argued for the importance of political feedback networks as accelerators of purposive social change. Hugh Heclo's *Modern Social Politics in Britain and Sweden* (1974) developed these ideas and emphasized the especially important contributions made by networks of civil servants and other experts as agents of learning. Heclo's strong emphasis on policy outcomes (as opposed to other forms of so-

cial change) as both the motivation and the measure for learning has been retained, and his attention to the role of experts deepened, in the research program of Paul Sabatier and his colleagues on advocacy coalitions (Sabatier and Jenkins-Smith, 1999). Kai Lee's groundbreaking application of social learning perspectives to long-term, large-scale environmental problems (Lee, 1993) expands the policy domain of earlier studies to include environmental management more generally. This broadening of the domain of learning is further extended in two more recent works addressing how knowledge about, and goals for, global environmental governance have developed and spread around the world: Ronnie Lipschutz's *Global Civil Society and Global Environmental Governance* (Lipschutz, 1996) and the Social Learning Group's *Learning to Manage Global Environmental Risks* (Social Learning Group, 2001).

Contemporary perspectives on social learning in the context of global change raise, and have begun to illuminate, four questions: Who learns? What is learned? What counts as learning? How does learning occur? If these fall short of a coherent body of understanding, they nonetheless serve to suggest the directions and flavor of current research.

Who learns? At one level, the answer to this question is simple: individuals learn. Little in the body of work on social learning suggests that it is helpful to reify society as a discrete, reflective entity. That said, however, it has proven productive to identify the social groupings of individuals within which learning occurs, and the institutional forms that stabilize and transmit the resulting lessons. Early work focused on learning by national governmental elites. More recently, studies have expanded this initial focus in two directions. First, following Sabatier's studies of "advocacy coalitions," it seems clear that much of the most important learning occurs within networks or actors focused on particular issue areas (Sabatier and Jenkins-Smith, 1999). These networks often include individuals drawn from not only government but also from the scientific community, nongovernmental environmental organizations, and the private sector. Second, a body of work taking impetus from Peter Haas's studies of "epistemic communities" (Haas, 1990) suggests that such networks are often transnational in character, providing significant opportunities for global learning. The somewhat *ad hoc* character of many transnational issue networks, however, makes them uncertain repositories of the lessons that their members learn. Relatively formal international institutions may well serve a crucial stabilizing and transmittal function in social learning on global change.

What is learned? Much of the literature on learning, social or otherwise, concentrates on the incorporation of new knowledge or experience into existing models, decision processes, and practices. Thus it has been possible to trace the international spread of specific scientific findings (for example, the magnitude of the terrestrial carbon sink) or policy innovations (such as convention and protocol approaches for the management of transboundary pollutants) relevant to global change. Increasingly, however, it seems clear that some of the most important social learning involves higher-order properties such as norms, goals, and the basic framing of issues in terms of the causes and effects selected for attention. The seminal work in this latter mode is perhaps Peter Hall's work on the spread of Keynesian approaches to economic policy, *The Political Power of Economic Ideas* (Hall, 1989). In the global change arena, research has suggested that innovations in goals for management (for example, that of eliminating, rather than merely reducing, chlorofluorocarbons [CFCs]) are indeed learned across countries and thereby exert significant influence on the globalization of subsequent issue development. Interestingly, however, there are indications that, while at a general level goals and issues frames are readily learned across national borders, more specific formulations are not. Thus interactions between Germany and Sweden brought them to share a concern for the long-range transport of acidifying compounds in the mid-1980s. At the same time, however, their local framings of the acid rain problem remained divergent, one emphasizing damage to forests, the other to fish, each distinctly attuned to its own domestic conditions and politics. This raises the prospect that what is most widely learned about global change may be precisely those physical, chemical, and technical dimensions of the issues that are most general and location-independent. The feasibility and desirability of comparable cross-national learning about more localized biological, social, and political dimensions of global change still need to be assessed.

What counts as learning? Social learning is equated in much writing with the ability to utilize past experience in achieving better performance. With respect to global change issues, however, this conceptualization seems overly restrictive in at least two ways. First, the evidence from issues such as stratospheric ozone depletion is gratifyingly strong that societies do not always need to experience change before acting to manage it. More useful conceptualizations of social learning have therefore attempted to address how not only direct experience but also new scientific discoveries and monitoring results come to be incorporated in issue frames and action programs. Second, there are both conceptual and methodological difficulties in linking learning definitionally with some vague notion of progress. Often, it is simply unclear or contested what would constitute "better" performance in the global change arena. Even

when the character of "improvements" is not problematic in principle, the difficulties of defining present learning processes in terms of *post hoc* evaluations of outcome effectiveness remain substantial. Finally, it is abundantly clear that societies, like individuals, can learn the wrong lessons from history. For all these reasons, much of the most interesting work on social learning for global change has adopted a perspective that counts as learning self-consciously reflective processes that seek to utilize new information to bring about cognitive changes in the formulations of problems or options for dealing with them. As Kai Lee (1993) has pointed out, the connections between social learning and adaptive approaches to environmental management thus become very close indeed. Both are rare, requiring unusual combinations of personal and institutional commitment to error-embracing behavior.

How does learning occur? The processes through which social learning occurs may be thought of along two dimensions. The first concerns who brings new information to bear on the existing cognitive configuration of the issue. The crucial distinction here is between the "push" supply of new information by would-be teachers and the "pull" demand for new information from would-be learners. The prospect of "pushed" learning draws attention to the role of purveyors of new scientific findings, problem solutions, news stories and, more generally, advocates for particular lessons. The prospect of "pulled" learning highlights actors dissatisfied with the present state of affairs, and—returning to one of Hugh Heclo's (1974) original formulations of the issue—the importance for learning of a broadly based and pluralistic social "puzzling" over what is to be done. A second dimension of processes for social learning concerns where the new information comes from. The relatively easy case is that posed by new scientific findings, where the established mechanisms for social legitimization and dissemination include peer reviewed scholarly publications and integrated assessments. More difficult is socialization of lessons learned by particular individuals and organizations through their own direct trial-and-error experience. Much of the learning that has occurred with respect to the negotiation of international environmental accords and the conduct of international environmental assessments seems to have been of this variety. The advantages of the ease and rapidity of such learning processes are potentially offset by the weakness of quality control mechanisms to assure society at large that the personal lessons drawn through such experience are justified. Even more problematic are learning processes that seek to draw lessons from historical accounts of experience in distant issue areas or national contexts. This is the kind of social learning that is needed if long-established issues of global change such as European acid rain are to furnish useful lessons for emerging issues such as Asian acid rain or global biodiversity. As pointed out by Richard Neustadt and Ernest May in their classic *Thinking in Time* (1986), however, the pitfalls of such historical analogizing are both dense and subtle. The development of forums for the careful, critical, and continuing evaluation of historical experience across issue areas remains perhaps the central challenge facing efforts to enhance social learning for global change.

[*See also* Acid Rain and Acid Deposition; Environmental Law; Integrated Assessment; Natural Hazards; Policy Analysis; *and* Public Policy.]

BIBLIOGRAPHY

Argyris, C. *Knowledge for Action: A Guide to Overcoming Barriers to Organizational Change.* San Francisco: Jossey-Bass, 1993.

Bennett, C. J., and M. Howlett. "The Lessons of Learning: Reconciling Theories of Policy Learning and Policy Change." *Policy Sciences* 25 (1992), 275–294. A systematic review and classification of the literatures of learning.

Deutsch, K. *The Nerves of Government.* New York: Free Press, 1963.

Gunerson, L. H., et al., eds. *Barriers and Bridges to the Renewal of Ecosystems and Institutions.* New York: Columbia University Press, 1995. A collection of conceptual and case study essays on learning in ecosystem management.

Haas, P. *Saving the Mediterranean.* New York: Columbia University Press, 1990.

Hall, P. *The Political Power of Economic Ideas.* Princeton, N.J.: Princeton University Press, 1989.

Heclo, H. *Modern Social Politics in Britain and Sweden.* New Haven: Yale University Press, 1974.

Keck, M. E., and K. Sikkink. *Activists Beyond Borders: Advocacy Networks in International Politics.* Ithaca, N.Y.: Cornell University Press, 1998. An original examination of the role of nongovernmental organizations in transnational networks as agents of learning, with a chapter on environmental issues.

Lee, K. *Compass and Gyroscope.* Washington, D.C.: Island Press, 1993.

Lipschutz, R. *Global Civil Society and Global Environmental Governance.* Albany, N.Y.: State University of New York Press, 1996.

Nelson, R., and S. G. Winter. *An Evolutionary Theory of Economic Change.* Cambridge, Mass.: Harvard University Press, 1982. An early but still influential look at the development of economic institutions, from what is essentially the learning perspective set forth in this essay.

Neustadt, R., and E. May. *Thinking in Time.* New York: Free Press, 1986.

Rose, R. *Lesson-Drawing in Public Policy.* Chatham, N.J.: Chatham House Publishers, 1993. A critical collection of studies on the various kinds of lesson drawing and learning encountered in policy making.

Sabatier, P., and H. Jenkins-Smith. "The Advocacy Coalition Framework: An Assessment." In *Theories of the Policy Process*, edited by P. Sabatier, pp. 117–166. Boulder, Colo.: Westview Press, 1999.

Social Learning Group. *Learning to Manage Global Environmental Risks.* Cambridge, Mass.: MIT Press, 2001.

—WILLIAM C. CLARK

SOILS

Soils are some of the products of lithosphere breakdown created by interactions at the surface of the Earth between the lithosphere, atmosphere, hydrosphere, and biosphere. They play essential roles in supporting the terrestrial biosphere and in element cycling, and they are fundamentally important to the well-being of humans in all societies. They are increasingly used for a range of economic purposes, remain the basis of most food production, are mined and quarried, and are suffering degradation and pollution.

All soils are multicomponent systems of solids, liquids, and gases. They include organic and mineral materials, and each has its own combination of inherent properties of texture, fabric, and mineralogy, which influence strength, porosity, permeability, moisture retention, chemistry, plasticity, frost resistance, shrink/swell, and numerous other properties.

Because there are no universally agreed definitions of soil, description and understanding depends on the interests of the observer. A pedologist may take a theoretical view in an attempt to understand genesis. An agriculturalist will see soils as a natural medium for plant growth and be most concerned with chemistry and physics. An engineer will consider soil as a problem material to be built upon or as construction material and will be more interested in particle size, drainage, and mechanics. A ceramicist may be interested only in the clay fraction as a raw material for manufacturing cement, bricks, china, and high-technology engine components.

These people all describe and classify soils according to their own needs, and there is relatively little overlap in their perceptions and jargon. Such fragmented views have been a barrier to communication and understanding that needs to be broken down if we are to manage our soil resources more effectively into the next century.

Soil Formation. Mineral soils are derived from the breakdown of primary rock minerals. The processes of formation can be rationalized into five conceptual steps: (1) weathering; (2) leaching; (3) the formation of new minerals; (4) erosion, deposition, and sorting; and (5) interactions with the biosphere.

Weathering. The effects of weather may break down rock minerals into simpler entities through reaction with water. Hydrolysis is the core of this process, and different elements show an increasing resistance to it. Sodium and potassium react readily; calcium, magnesium, and ferrous iron react more slowly; ferric iron and aluminum are relatively resistant; and silicon is very resistant. Of the common rock-forming silicates, ferromagnesians (olivine, augite, etc.) break down quickly and completely; feldspars form chain silicate fragments as a precursor to clays; micas disaggregate along their cleavage planes to form new sheet-structured silicates; and quartz does not change other than to break into smaller particles.

Leaching. Taking place in aqueous solution, leaching moves the products of weathering over distances of microns to the external surface of the rock mineral, or over meters when more soluble elements such as sodium and calcium leave the soil environment as dissolved load. Leaching rates increase with water availability; the depth of calcium carbonate accumulation within a soil can be a guide to leaching intensity. This is quite shallow in an arid-zone soil and absent in a humid-zone soil. Even stronger patterns may be seen in the accumulation of common salt, but these minerals are quite ephemeral and may be indicative only of present-day processes.

On a geographical scale, leaching is the process responsible for the separation of mobile elements (sodium, potassium, calcium, and magnesium) from the relatively insoluble elements (iron, aluminum, and silicon).

New mineral formation. The entities formed and concentrated by weathering and leaching may recombine into new minerals that are stable at surface conditions. Most new minerals are clays: fine-grained silicates with sheet structures. Different clays have different chemical and physical properties that are important to soil users. The nature of the clay depends on the chemical composition of the original rock mineral and on the intensity of the weathering and leaching environment.

The end products of weathering, leaching, and new mineral formation (a set of processes that in combination is called *epimorphism*) are resistant rock silicates such as sand-sized quartz, fine-grained insoluble oxides of iron and aluminum, and clays. In most cases of simple epimorphism the end products tend to have a bimodal size distribution, with residual sands (2.0–0.2 millimeters [mm] in diameter), and fine-grained (>0.002 mm in diameter) clays or oxides being dominant. Particles of intermediate size (silt) are rare in environments subject to normal epimorphism but more common where rock minerals have been comminuted.

Particle size is an important factor in controlling soil chemistry, physics, and mechanics. Sand, for example, has a specific surface area of 0.1–0.01 square meters per gram, whereas clay can range from 10 (kaolinite) to as much as 800 (montmorillionite). The finer the soil, the greater its ability to retain nutrients, pollutants, and water. Reactive clays also have a higher shrink/swell potential. The packing of all particles is the key to porosity and most mechanical properties.

The nature of the end products of epimorphism are strongly affected by properties of the original lithospheric minerals. In other words, our understanding of soil materials must take account of inheritance from parent material. This applies both in the case of epimorphism of original igneous rock minerals and, even more importantly, in the secondary epimporphism of sedimentary rocks or sediments. Inheritance may influence soil mineralogy, texture, and fabric.

Erosion, deposition, and sorting. All epimorphism takes place on a land surface that is subject to geomorphic processes. Like the other steps in this model, the landscape is itself complex, and no one landscape is totally erosional or depositional. On any hill slope the potential movement of materials and soil water varies spatially and temporally. An appreciation of flow patterns can improve our understanding of the soil materials on that slope.

The importance of erosion processes has long been obvious to geomorphologists studying landscape evolution, but pedologists have tended to ignore them as a normal part of soil genesis. Probably the two most important erosion processes on a global scale are rainwash (raindrop-agitated surface flow) on hill slope mantles and wind erosion in moving and sorting fine materials (especially sands) in any environment with limited vegetation cover. Processes of mass movement and glaciation are often on such a scale that they disrupt soil formation to create or redistribute raw materials for a new soil cycle.

Interactions with the biosphere. The biosphere is involved in epimorphism by adjusting pH conditions through the release of organic acids and respiratory carbon dioxide. At another level, the biosphere is an essential part of leaching and the cycling of nutrients through plants and animals. Elements stored in plant biomass may be released slowly to the soil through litter decay or rapidly during a wildfire. In either event, the elements are not returned to the same point on the slope from which they were derived, and there is a net vertical movement of nutrients from weathing bedrock to the surface and a downslope concentration toward stream lines. In a more physical context, the most important biospheric process is *bioturbation*—the mixing, mounding, and overturn of soil material by treefall and burrowing organisms such as ants, worms, termites, and some vertebrates. Although the importance of such processes was recognized by Charles Darwin more than a century ago, only recently have they begun to be incorporated in soil genesis models. The combination of rapid bioturbation of a surface soil mantle and rainwash erosion creates a relatively coarse biomantle, as finer mineral particles are winnowed from the slope. Bioturbation is usually depth limited, and many soils exhibit a marked contrast in fabric and texture between the biomantle (topsoil) and underlying saprolite (subsoil) formed by *in situ* epimorphism.

Soil Identification and Classification. In the late nineteenth century, soils were recognized as independent natural bodies of earth that supported terrestrial plants. Each had a unique morphology, represented in layers or *horizons*, which were believed to be genetically determined and which reflected the integration of all the processes of soil genesis. This concept still underpins the discipline of pedology, which has become tied to horizonation and profile maturity.

By convention, soil horizons are the essential attribute of soils and are described with a range of criteria, such as texture; fabric; the presence of pans, concretions, and salts; color, and pH. Particular horizon combinations make up accepted soil types, which are the basis of most soil surveys.

The most widely used classification of soils is that of the U.S. Department of Agriculture. The text *Soil Taxonomy* (Soil Survey Staff, 1984) divides soils into mineral and organic types. Mineral soils are further classified on the presence or absence of six diagnostic surface horizons (epipedons) and seventeen diagnostic subsurface horizons.

At a lower level, *Soil Taxonomy* considers soil moisture and temperature regimes. Parameters that refer back to older concepts of the importance of climate in controlling zonal soil profiles.

The full sequence of the *Soil Taxonomy* classification is the recognition of a hierarchy: at the top are ten orders (alfisols, aridsols, entisols, histosols, inceptisols, mollisols, oxisols, spodosols, ultisols, and vertisols), fifty suborders, and about two hundred great groups; further down are descriptions of subgroups, families, series, and finally soil types with a specific geographic distribution.

Perhaps the best example of the difficulties this zonalist and hierarchical approach has created can be seen in the geography of soil with a classic podsol morphology. Most workers agree about the general nature of such a profile. It is a soil with an acid plant litter horizon and an organic sandy topsoil over a prominent bleached horizon (eluvial zone). Beneath the bleach, iron oxides or humic materials or both have accumulated as complex pans in the sandy subsoil (illuvial zone). The same workers, however, do not agree about an acceptable nomenclature for the podsol profile, or about the genesis of this soil.

In the current *Soil Taxonomy* classification, podsol profiles are recognized as spodosols; in other classifications they have been given different names, such as placosols and podosols. Very commonly they are grouped together with other superficially similar profiles as podsolized soils, inferring that the eluvial and illuvial processes are a universal set.

Early soil workers noted the close relationship between the podsol and the climate and vegetation of the regions where it was found. From these and other observations, a genesis model developed that emphasized the dominant role of the "active factors" in soil formation, namely; vegetation (or the biosphere) and climate, which acted over time on the parent material of the soil at a particular site (topography) to form zonal profiles. The podsol was accepted as such a profile.

Consideration of the recent geological history of the Earth and the patterns of Northern Hemisphere soil distribution can explain the initial success and subsequent failure of the zonal genesis model. Those parts of Northern Hemisphere high latitudes that were extensively glaciated during the Pleistocene ice ages are exactly the regions in which the first successful correlations were made between soil profiles, vegetation, and climate. Thus the podsols were identified in the cool, humid, coniferous forests, and the chernozems in the cold, semiarid, prairie grasslands or steppes. From a geological perspective these are the regions of outwash sands beyond the front of the ice sheets and the areas blanketed by windblown loess. Taking parent material into account, it is apparent that podsols are linked to deep sand bodies and chernozems to deep silts.

In Australia, ice age glaciation was very limited, but profiles identical to the classic podsol are widely distributed along the east coast from Tasmania to Cape York. Clearly, there is no obvious link to the "active factors" of soil formation at this scale, but there is a link to the parent material. In every case, the podsol profile is formed in deep quartz sands. In extreme cases, the key features of the podsol (bleaches and pans) can develop in porous, inert, quartz sandstone. Such a profile in rock would not ordinarily be recognized as a soil; this illustrates the difficulty inherent in attempting to demarcate the discipline of pedology from related disciplines of geology, geomorphology, and ecology.

Two points should be emphasized in this discussion: (1) parent material is a major factor in the nature of the soils formed at any place; and (2) the transfer of explanations from one part of the world to another, with the erection of descriptive jargon moved from its original context, has done more to confuse the science of pedology that it has to elucidate it.

Soil Geography. An alternative global model of soil genesis can be based on the distribution of rock types and megageomorphology of the plate tectonics model of the lithosphere. This model defines regions where particular combinations of the environmental factors and the balance of soil formation processes have lead to similar assemblages of soil materials.

Plate centers. Australia is a good example of a plate center province where the landscape has been subject to soil formation for a considerable period of time with a minimum of tectonic activity and landscape rejuvenation. Many of the soil genesis processes are approaching their end points. The topography is subdued, there is no active volcanism, and Quaternary glaciation affected only a limited area. Typical soils exhibit the effects of extreme epimorphism. Fabric and texture contrast profiles are common on hill slopes. Completely weathered red and yellow soils are abundant in the tropics. Extensive areas of well-sorted sandy soils have accumulated in the coastal zone and in arid deserts, and deep, harsh alluvial clay soils are found along the inland drainage lines. Similar soil assemblages caused by the same combination of factors can be recognized in India, much of Asia, Africa, South America, and smaller regions of Europe and North America.

Plate margins. A different assemblage of soil materials is associated with the fold-mountain belts that ring the Pacific and extend through Indonesia, Southeast Asia, the Himalayas, the Middle East, the Mediterranean, and the West Indies. Topographic instability is so great that erosion processes operate on a different scale. The continuous addition of primary rock minerals from andesitic volcanic eruptions makes early-stage products of epimorphism much more common.

The soils of New Zealand provide examples from this environment. All of the processes of soil formation have a different emphasis and relative balance in New Zealand than in nearby Australia, and the following points are critical to understanding the nature and distribution of soil materials.

1. Over most of the country, topographic relief is considerable and slopes are steep to very steep; therefore, mass movement processes are common.
2. Active tectonism, extensive volcanism, an abundance of metamorphic rocks, and a dominance of sedimentary graywacke containing high proportions of feldspars and partly altered mafic minerals present a complex surface geology from which the soils are derived. Mineralogic and fabric inheritance is therefore important in almost all situations. In the North Island, twenty-six Holocene tephra units blanket the landscape, ranging in composition from rhyolite to basalt. In the South Island, Pleistocene fluvioglacial and eolian sediments are widespread. Most soil profiles exhibit little epimorphism and a dominance of slope movement processes. Paleosols (buried soils) are common.
3. Rainfall is high to very high in most parts of the country. Therefore, fluvial erosion and leaching processes are very active. At altitudes above 1,300–1,500 meters, snow accumulation is sufficient to cause valley glaciation, and in the drier rainshadow regions east of the Southern Alps, freeze/thaw processes are important in rock breakdown and regolith mass movement.
4. Several features of the natural vegetation and biota have had a greater effect on soil formation processes than is usually observed elsewhere. These include an abundance of earthworms; the absence of large native herbivores; the rarity of wildfire; the high polyphenol leaching capacity of kauri forests, in which individual trees can live for many centuries; and Polynesian deforestation beginning about one thousand years ago.

Areas subject to Pleistocene glaciation. A completely different assemblage of soil materials is found in those areas of the world, particularly in the Northern Hemisphere, where the longer-term processes of soil genesis have been disturbed as a result of the Quaternary ice age, and their renewed operation on homogenized and unconsolidated material has spanned only a few thousand years. The soil materials in these regions include all the classic profiles of the peatlands, podsols, podsolics, and chernozems. The distribution of these soils reflects latitudinal patterns of glacial advance and sediment accumulation and parallels modern climates and vegetation.

Soils affected by human activity. All over the world there are areas where humans have had a major impact on natural soils, and several resulting soil profiles have been specifically identified. For example, *Soil Taxonomy* describes anthropic and plaggen epipedons, which have been strongly influenced by long periods of intensive human activity. These are most common in Northern Hemisphere regions with a long history of cultivation.

An anthropic epipedon is typically well structured and dark colored and generally has moderate to high levels of plant nutrients, having been managed by the repeated application of shells or lime and bone or fertilizers. A plaggen epipedon is a sod soil formed by frequent cultivation with the incorporation of large amounts of animal manures and straw. These additives raise the organic carbon content, increase water-holding capacity, soil biota, and plant growth.

Paddy soils are another example of soil materials extensively modified by continued human use over centuries and even millennia in the cultivation of rice. They include a wide variety of natural soil types modified by cultivation and flooding to the extent that they are puddled, saturated, almost anoxic, and have a specialized soil biota. With this treatment paddy soils typically increase in acidity, and although the availability of some nutrients can increase, the crops rely on blue-green algae and Azolla water fern to provide nitrogen. There are estimated to be more than 100 million hectares of potential paddy soil undeveloped in Asia because they are naturally too acidic or too saline. It is not beyond our ability to change these conditions if the need is great enough.

In many coastal regions of the world, shallow estuaries have been dyked and drained and the sediments converted to arable soils in polder lands. The best-known examples are in the Netherlands and Belgium, where the techniques of polder development have been proven over centuries. Within ten years of drainage, polder lands can carry productive forests and estuarine sediments begin to become soils in that they support an expanding and dynamic terrestrial biota. One of the most important steps in this conversion process is the colonization of the sediments with soil biota, especially earthworms; the process of converting sediment to soil has been described as "zoological ripening."

These environments are emerging and developing ecosystems. They provide a salutory reminder that not all human interference with the soil environment is necessarily negative.

Soils and Global Change. Given our universal dependence on soils as an agricultural medium, their value as a construction material, the importance of their related biodiversity, and their critical roles in essential element cycles, any environmental or management change that accelerates soil pollution and degradation threatens human well-being.

The threats include all forms of physical, chemical, and biological damage to the soil environment. Soil erosion at rates exceeding natural soil genes is probably the most important problem on a global scale, but unlike the greenhouse threat of increasing atmospheric carbon dioxide, this problem is localized at a multitude of sites. Degradation of the soil as a growing medium through salinization, depletion of soil fauna, increased acidification, inappropriate use of fertilizers, and physical damage to soil fabric are also major threats. Commonly, the land degradation processes involved enter negative feedback loops when a certain threshold of degradation is encountered. For example, the loss of soil organic matter by any means usually leads to a decrease in soil moisture capacity. With reduced soil moisture there is reduced growth, less input to soil organic matter, loss of soil structure, further reductions in soil moisture, and then increased soil erosion. Breaking these loops and reversing degradation depends on recognition and understanding of the processes, and remedies can be put in place only in favorable economic, social, and political climates.

Following are some of the major soil degradation topics likely to be most affected by global changes in the next century.

Desertification. This term can include all forms of land degradation but is also specifically applied to degradation in marginal arid zones in the sense of expanding desert conditions. Changes in aridity have been a problem since ancient times but accelerated in the twentieth century with increased human pressure on the soil, the advent of mechanized agriculture, and the breakdown of traditional land management. The future of the more than 1 billion people who live in these en-

vironments is at risk, both from their continued inappropriate range management and any negative climate change. [*See* Desertification.]

Soil erosion. Loss of soil by erosion occurs from all unprotected surfaces subject to the passage of water and wind. It is worst on steep slopes and in unvegetated sands, but erosion is inevitable because it is a natural part of the rock cycle. It is estimated that global soil erosion rates are twenty to one hundred times greater than average rates of soil renewal. In the long term, this relationship must be checked through appropriate soil management. In farming, this means using practices such as zero tillage, strip-cropping, intercropping, and constructing soil conservation works. In urban areas soil losses from construction sites also need to be controlled because of the impact of sediments and turbidity in urban stream systems. [*See* Erosion.]

Salinization. Increased salinity and waterlogging of soils in irrigated lands has been a problem to humans for six thousand years, but we still allow it to happen through inadequate irrigation scheme design and water management. About one-third of the world's irrigated land is presently salinized; although this loss is not enormous in terms of total land degradation, the land affected was some of the most productive and the capital costs of its development were considerable.

The problem can be avoided by providing adequate drainage, but once salinity is established it is difficult to reverse. Some sodic soils can be reclaimed by exchanging sodium ions with calcium ions through the addition of gypsum, calcium chloride, iron sulfate, aluminum sulfate, sulfuric acid, sulfur, or pyrite. Effective leaching and safe disposal of drainage water is essential if this treatment is done because the exchange process liberates salts. Most large-scale irrigation areas are in inland basins with low topographic relief, where the lack of good drainage was part of the problem in the first place. [*See* Salinization.]

Soil acidification. Increasing acidity in soils is a serious problem in both tropical and temperate regions with three different causes. In each case, the result is a decline in agricultural production, because when pH falls below 5.0, most plant nutrients become less available and the levels of soluble iron, aluminum, and manganese in the soil can become toxic.

In the tropics, the primary cause is inappropriate clearing of forests growing on extremely weathered soil mantles. These ecosystems normally operate on a rapid nutrient cycle through plants, litter, and topsoil with very small soil reserves. After removal of the forest and depletion of the litter by fire and cultivation, the system collapses with an increase in soil erosion, establishment of weedy but stable monocultures of poor grasses, and an increase in the acidity of streamflow that can impact offshore fisheries and coral reefs. Reversion of the system to forests is slow and difficult.

In temperate regions, there are two causes: (1) an excessive use of superphosphate in conjunction with nitrogen-fixing clover leys in grain crops without maintaining a neutral pH with lime products, and (2) acid rain from industrialized countries. [See Acid Rain and Acid Deposition.]

The total impact of induced soil acidity is largely unknown, because most soils have several other sources of acidity and it is difficult to rank the role of any anthropogenic cause. The impact of another source of acid will largely depend on the buffering capacity of the soil; that is, how much base material exists in the soil that is able to neutralize acids. In a limestone soil, for example, this will be considerable, but in a soil that is near neutral and only has limited amounts of calcium or organic matter, increased acidity can occur quickly.

Laterization and podsolization. Much has been written about these processes as agents of soil degradation, but their global extent and importance is difficult to evaluate. *Laterization* is a rather loose term that refers to the irreversible hardening of some soil materials that are naturally rich in oxides and hydroxides of iron and aluminum. Such profiles are the product of extreme epimorphism and are common in tropical environments. They are not confined to tropical regions, and not all iron-rich soils behave in this way, but extensive clearing of tropical forests and woodlands has often resulted in the abandonment of agricultural development allegedly because of widespread development of laterites, iron pans, or plinthites. The fact that such lands were not suitable for large-scale agriculture in the first place tends to be ignored in favor of invoking laterization as an excuse for the failure.

The process of accelerated podsolization is more subtle. Many plant species assist the leaching of iron and aluminum and increase soil acidity. The process is important in the genesis of podsol profiles; in a soil material with limited buffering capacity, a single generation of pine forest (for example) can acidify the soil and strip limited plant nutrients from it. Second-generation forests have slower growth rates. Again, the problem becomes an explanation for economic failure rather than a means of recognizing the inadequacies of those environments and management practices. Unlike the laterization problem, an increase in soil acidity can at least be addressed with the application of lime or other basic materials.

Soils and greenhouse gases. Soils are an intimate and important part of the global carbon budget. The flux of carbon through soil organic matter is both vital to ecologically sustainable development and a significant part of the problem of enhanced greenhouse climate change. [See Global Warming.]

It is uncertain how big a part soils play in the global carbon budget. Several computer models have been developed, but all lack reliable data about carbon partioning into above- and below-ground biomass and provide only a rough indication of the scale of turnover processes. Intensive agriculture contributes carbon dioxide to the atmosphere through the loss of soil organic matter, and intensive rice cultivation has been identified as one of the more important sources of methane, another greenhouse gas. Reversal of soil organic-matter loss could allow us to use soils as a sink for greenhouse gases, but this depends on achieving a good balance between biospheric processes in the soil and maintaining good soil structure. The potential for increasing soil carbon stores as a hedge against atmospheric carbon dioxide buildup is limited; it is more important in the short term, at least, to substantially increase carbon storage in growing forests. Carbon sequestration in forests is greatest in tropical regions of rapid growth, where vast areas of forests have regrettably been cleared and the soils seriously degraded. Another great challenge in the next few decades is to reverse this trend. [See Carbon Cycle.]

With global climate change, land use change will occur. But the human response will not be instantaneous, because it is individual farmers and ranchers who must respond to the pressures. Farmers, by their very nature, are optimists and will maintain traditional practices for years or even decades in the expectation that good times will return. Experience in the 1930s dust bowl of the prairie states of the United States and famine conditions in the Sahel in the 1970s has clearly shown that farmers and ranchers are slow to change when their opportunities are limited by political and social factors beyond their control.

A core project of the International Geosphere–Biosphere Programme is concerned with global change and terrestrial ecosystems. One focus of this program is to include a soil research program that sets out to determine the impacts of global change on soil organic matter dynamics, predict changes in soil erosion consequent on interactive changes in land use and climate, and review the greenhouse gas emissions from agricultural soils. [See International Geosphere–Biosphere Programme.]

Soils themselves will also change in the short term, especially where a particularly ephemeral or mobile constituent is a key element in the soil classification. For example, solonchaks may be leached and create new soil types; conversely, salts may accumulate in other profiles and create solonchaks. But this degree of change is of little consequence, because the very definition of these soil types depends on the presence or absence of salts that can be mobilized in decades, as demonstrated in polder lands, or in the vast expanses of salinized soil in the world's irrigation areas.

Soil erosion rates and other forms of physical degradation are certainly likely to change. These are largely driven by extreme climatic events (rainfall, floods, drought, frost, etc.), and global climate change will affect such events. All global climate models suggest a general increase in extreme events and an expansion of the zone of impact of many such events (tropical cyclones, for example). Wherever the soils are presently under land-use pressure, any frequency shift in large events could increase soil losses.

Positive Changes in Soils and Management. Perhaps the best examples of positive change can be seen in the way engineers have increasingly utilized soils as construction materials in the past fifty years.

Soil stabilization has become more scientific. Traditionally, it was achieved by mechanical compaction, which increased soil density and strength by rolling, ramming, vibrating, or blasting. Soil mechanical properties can also be changed by the addition of components such as cement, lime, sodium silicate, salt, synthetic resins, or bitumen, and in recent years there has been a boom in the use of geotextiles.

The concept of reinforcing soils with fibrous materials goes back to ancient times with the use of straw in sun-dried mud bricks and fascines for swamp drainage. Mechanically, the principles are the same as the natural reinforcement of soils on slopes by plant roots, but in the last twenty years the rapid development of synthetic geotextiles and geogrids has created entirely new approaches. Geosynthetics are now routinely used for the separation and isolation of different soil materials, for spreading loads on weak substrates, for filtering fine particles, for sealing and containing fluids, for enhancing drainage, and to control soil erosion.

Summary. Soils will change under the enhanced greenhouse condition of the next century. But vegetation and land use will change first, and these changes will have an immediate feedback to the soils. Pedologists can make a contribution to these studies, and humans can adjust by deliberately manipulating soils to meet our changing requirements.

Our goal must be to achieve an ecologically sustainable pattern of land use that will necessarily be based on a respect for the dynamics of the soils. At the present time we are a long way from an adequate understanding of soils. We need to make concerted international efforts to address innumerable issues such as:

- An appreciation of the role of soil biota
- An understanding of biological fertility
- Effective means of reversing soil acidification
- Adequate quantification of soil carbon dynamics
- New approaches to tillage and erosion control
- Application of intercropping and polyculture techniques

- Improved modeling of salinization and its control
- Better social and political approaches to land reform
- Changed global economics with respect to cash crops and tropical forestry
- Developing means of accelerating soil formation and regenerating degraded lands
- Tightening planning regulation to prevent the sterilization of fertile and valuable soils by other land uses.

[*See also* Agriculture and Agricultural Land; *and* Carbon Dioxide.]

BIBLIOGRAPHY

Bal, L. *The Zoological Ripening of Soils.* Wageningen, Netherlands: Centre for Agricultural Publishing and Documentation, 1982. A detailed account of the development of polder lands, with an emphasis on biological processes.

Barrow, C. J. *Land Degradation: Development and Breakdown of Terrestrial Environments.* Cambridge: Cambridge University Press, 1991. A comprehensive global review of all forms of land degradation.

Commonwealth Scientific and Industrial Research Organization (CSIRO). *Soils: An Australian Viewpoint.* Melbourne: CSIRO and Academic Press, 1983. A detailed and technical account of the soils of a plate center region written largely from theoretical and agricultural viewpoints.

Ghassemi, F., A. J. Jakeman, and H. A. Nix. *Salinisation of Land and Water Resources: Human Causes, Extent, Management, and Case Studies.* Sydney: University of New South Wales Press, 1995. A detailed global review of one of the intractable soil and land degradation problems.

Gillott, J. E. *Clay in Engineering Geology.* Developments in Technical Engineering 41. Amsterdam: Elsevier, 1987. A technical overview of clay as an engineering material.

Holtz, R. D., ed. *Geosynthetics for Soil Improvement.* Geotechnical Special Publication no. 18. New York: American Society of Civil Engineers, 1988. Summary technical document describing the different types of geotextiles and their uses.

McLaren, R. G., and K. C. Cameron. *Soil Science: Sustainable Production and Environmental Protection.* Auckland: Oxford University Press, 1996. A general agricultural text dealing with the soils of New Zealand.

Paton, T. R., G. S. Humphreys, and P. B. Mitchell. *Soils: A New Global View.* London: University College of London Press, 1995. The source of the basic soil genesis model outlined in this entry.

Rounsevell, M. D. A., and P. J. Loveland, eds. *Soil Responses to Climate Change.* NATO ASI Series, ser. 1, Global Environmental Change, vol. 23. Berlin: Springer-Verlag, 1994. Invited conference papers opening all aspects of the role of soils in global climate change.

Soil Survey Staff. *Soil Taxonomy: A Basic System of Soil Classification for Making and Interpreting Soil Surveys.* USDA Handbook no. 436. New York: Wiley, 1984. The most widely used soil classification scheme in the world today. A very technical document with an excess of jargon.

—P. B. MITCHELL

SOLAR ENERGY. *See* Electrical Power Generation; Energy; Energy Policy; Renewable Energy Sources; *and* Sun.

STABILITY

The concept of stability is central to global change. In the discussion of stability, it is important to distinguish between this concept and those of constancy, equilibrium, steady-state, persistence, resilience, resistence, control and controllability, and recurrence. It is also important to understand the concepts of positive and negative feedback.

The classic idea of stability, sometimes referred to as "classic static stability," attributes two qualities to a system: (1) a system, undisturbed, remains in a constant condition; and (2) when disturbed from this constant condition but released from the disturbing influence, a system returns to an original constant condition. The pendulum of a mechanical clock has this kind of stability. The belief that this kind of stability is a characteristic of nature has an ancient lineage, expressed in the myth of the balance of nature. [See Ecological Stability.]

One common confusion is to equate stability with equilibrium, but systems can have stable and unstable equilibria. An equilibrium is a rest point, and it can be stable or unstable. Whereas a pendulum has a point of stable equilibrium in that it returns to its vertical position after being disturbed, a pencil balanced on its point is at a location of unstable equilibrium; once deflected from that position, it will not return.

Systems can be stable locally or globally. A point of local stability is one to which the system is stable against some finite, typically small, disturbance, but not against all disturbances. A point of global stability is one to which the system is stable against all disturbances. A pinball game has points of local stability (curved surfaces where the ball can rest unless the side of the table is pushed hard enough to move the ball over the edge of the surface), and one of global stability (the bottom of the game board). A seed temporarily lodged in a swale on a mountainside where it is moved about by light winds is within a region of local stability; a storm can blow the seed outside the swale and down the mountainside to the valley, where it germinates and is then located at a point of global stability.

It is typically assumed that ecological systems that have classic static stability are most likely to persist and are most easily controlled. This is not necessarily true. An analogy with the invention of aircraft is helpful here. During the early development of airplanes, there was a concern to make them both stable and controllable. A stable airplane is one that will continue to fly straight and level in spite of small gusts of winds and changes in air density. A simple way to improve one aspect of the stability of an airplane is to design the wings in the form of an upward V, called a dihedral. This shape is intrinsically stable against forces such as gusts of wind that would push one wing down and the other up. The

wing pushed upward, more to the vertical, loses lift, while the other wing, made more horizontal, increases in lift. The lower wing, with more lift, rises; the more vertical wing, with less lift, descends. As a result, the plane automatically rights itself.

During the early development of the airplane, it was quickly discovered that the more stable the plane, the harder it was to turn, and therefore the harder it was to control. A plane whose wings were so stable that the force of the pilot's hands on the stick could not cause it to bank would be uncontrollable and would crash. This experience made it clear that there was a tradeoff between stability and controllability. The less stable an airplane, the easier it was to control, but the greater the need for rapid response and constant attention. Gradually, by trial and error, pilots and engineers worked out a compromise between stability and controllability that worked best in practice. A plane moves in three dimensions, banking, rolling, and yawing. Aircraft have different degrees of stability for each of these dimensions—there is no single answer to the tradeoff between stability and controllability. Today, this is integrated into the theory and practice of aeronautical engineering. Until the invention of computers, the reflexes of a pilot placed a limit on the instability that could be designed into an airplane. Today, some aircraft are designed to be highly unstable and therefore highly maneuverable. This is made possible by onboard computers that constantly readjust the controls, faster than a pilot could do it manually. This experience tells us that the system that is best controlled may not be the most stable in the classic sense, and that there is a tradeoff between controllability and stability.

Steady-state is a condition of a dynamic system with inputs and outputs analogous to equilibrium. A system in steady-state is one for which inputs equal outputs of some variable of interest. For instance, a lake for which the inflow of water from rain, surface, and subsurface water transport is equal to the output of water from evaporation and surface and subsurface flow losses is in steady-state in regard to water quantity.

A system with feedback is one for which there is a mechanism to detect some change in the system and a response to that change. Sometimes the change is in the quantity or rate of some input or output. Sweating by a human being is an example of negative feedback related to body temperature. When body temperature begins to rise, detecting mechanisms open pores in the skin, and the rate of water evaporation increases, cooling the body. The growth of a population of bacterial cells is an example of positive feedback: although the rate of cell division can be constant for all cells, the more cells are present, the faster is the total growth of the mass of bacteria.

Whether the Earth system is characterized by classic

stability, steady-state, control, and positive and negative feedback has long been debated. These concepts apply to systems that are deterministic, without randomness or change. Systems that are characterized by stochastic properties might have negative feedback mechanisms and therefore might be stable in the classic sense described earlier, but there are additional concepts that apply only to probabilistic systems and are therefore pertinent to the Earth system. Systems with randomness may be characterized as having a set of states that the system revisits. States that are revisited indefinitely are referred to as "recurrent." States that are visited a finite number of times and therefore have a last time are called "non-recurrent." It is also possible to speak of a system as "persistent within bounds," meaning that the system varies within some finite and definable range. It is becoming common in discussions of environmental variables to speak of the "historic range of variation," or the range that is known either from scientific monitoring of a variable over time, or from reconstruction of that variation through some means. The data sources include written records and the records left in the growth rings of trees, in trapped gases in pockets in glacial ice, or the ratios of isotopes in marine sediments. This information can be used to reconstruct the historic range of variation for factors important to global change.

[*See also* Extreme Events; Gaia Hypothesis; Human Impacts; *article on* Human Impacts on Earth; Natural Hazards; Sustainable Development; *and* System Dynamics.]

BIBLIOGRAPHY

Botkin, D. B. *Discordant Harmonies: A New Ecology for the Twenty-first Century.* New York: Oxford University Press, 1990.

—DANIEL B. BOTKIN

STEWARDSHIP. *See* Belief Systems; *and* Religion.

STOCKHOLM DECLARATION

The Stockholm Declaration is a political declaration adopted by the United Nations Conference on the Human Environment, which met in the Swedish capital from 5 to 16 June 1972. It is a relatively short text, consisting of a preamble in narrative form, followed by twenty-six concisely worded "principles" that reflect the political consensus of the international community on how to address the emerging environmental issues of the early 1970s.

The declaration's stated purpose was not to codify the international legal obligations of states, but merely to lay down "common principles to inspire and guide the peoples of the world in the preservation and enhancement of the human environment." Its provisions, reflecting commitments of a political and moral rather than a legal nature, are addressed not only to governments, but also to peoples, enterprises, communities, and even individuals. Notwithstanding its nonlegal character, the Stockholm Declaration is generally regarded as the foundation piece of modern international environmental law. Many principles and concepts that were first articulated in it were later further elaborated and transformed into binding provisions of international environmental treaties. In substance, the declaration can be described as a hybrid product of early developed-world environmentalism and the developing world's postcolonial socioeconomic agenda.

The main environmental themes in the Stockholm Declaration—those that were of most concern to governments at the time of the Stockholm Conference—are the conservation and management of natural resources and the control of pollution. The declaration provides that both the renewable and the nonrenewable resources of the Earth are to be carefully managed and safeguarded for the benefit of present and future generations (Principles 2, 3, and 5). The conservation of wildlife and natural habitats is declared a "special responsibility" of man (Principle 4). The discharge of toxic and other pollutants is to be controlled insofar as it "exceeds the capacity of the environment to render them harmless" (Principle 6). In particular, states are to "take all possible steps" to prevent marine pollution (Principle 7). Reflecting the prevailing scientific and technological optimism, the Stockholm Declaration expresses the faith of the international community in the development of science and technology as a means of identifying and solving environmental problems (Principle 18).

Contrary to a much-rehearsed cliché, the development concerns of the developing world and the relationship between environmental protection and economic development were also an important theme of the Stockholm Conference, and feature prominently in the declaration itself. In fact, the word "development" occurs more often in the Stockholm Declaration than the word "environment" in its 1992 successor, the Rio Declaration on Environment and Development. [*See* Rio Declaration.]

From the outset, the declaration recognizes the fundamental human right to "adequate conditions of life, in an environment that permits a life of dignity and well-being" (Principle 1) and also stresses that "economic and social development is essential for ensuring a favourable living and working environment for man" (Principle 8). It specifically calls for "accelerated development" and increased financial and technological assistance to developing countries (Principle 9). Although it did not yet use the term *sustainable development*, the Stockholm Declaration advocated "integrated" and "rational" planning as a means of ensuring the "compatibility" of development with environmental protection (Principles 13 and 14). [*See* Sustainable Development.]

The most often cited provision of the Stockholm Declaration is Principle 21, which stipulates that all states have "the responsibility to ensure that activities within their jurisdiction or control do not cause damage to the environment of other states or of areas beyond the limits of national jurisdiction." This basic principle has recently been confirmed to be "part of the corpus of international law relating to the environment" by the International Court of Justice (Advisory Opinion of 8 July 1996 on *The Legality of the Threat or Use of Nuclear Weapons*, paragraph 29).

[*See also* United Nations Conference on the Human Environment.]

BIBLIOGRAPHY

Sohn, L. B. "The Stockholm Declaration on the Human Environment." *Harvard International Law Journal* 14.3 (1973), 423–515. A detailed and authoritative analysis of the Stockholm Declaration and its drafting history, by a leading international law scholar.

—MARC PALLEMAERTS

STORMS. *See* Extreme Events; Insurance; *and* Natural Hazards.

STRADDLING AND MIGRATORY STOCKS AGREEMENT

The United Nations Agreement on Straddling Fish Stocks and Highly Migratory Fish Stocks (in full, the Agreement for the Implementation of the Provisions of the United Nations Convention on the Law of the Sea of 10 December 1982 Relating to the Conservation and Management of Straddling Fish Stocks and Highly Migratory Fish Stocks) was negotiated specifically to address one of the shortcomings of the United Nations Convention on the Law of the Sea (UNCLOS). [*See* Law of the Sea.] Under UNCLOS, coastal states have jurisdictional rights over stocks in their Exclusive Economic Zones (EEZs). Relative freedom of the seas prevails for stocks on the high seas. However, freedom of states to fish on the high seas is limited by their treaty obligations as well as the rights, duties, and obligations of other states. While it does recognize that some stocks straddle the high seas and the EEZs, or migrate long distances through the EEZs of several coastal states, UNCLOS only provides that the states with a stake in these stocks are to agree among themselves on the shared management of the stocks. This provision was not suf-

ficiently clear for the coastal states who sometimes saw their conservation efforts in the EEZ undermined by overfishing and other destructive practices on the high seas in the area immediately adjacent to the EEZ. Their concerns were brought up at the United Nations Conference on Environment and Development (UNCED, held in Rio de Janeiro in June 1992); no agreement could be reached but a UN negotiation conference was subsequently convened. [*See* United Nations Conference on Environment and Development.] After more than three years of negotiation, the Agreement on Straddling Fish Stocks and Highly Migratory Fish Stocks, setting up a new regime for the harvesting of those stocks, was adopted and opened for signature.

Under the Agreement, the parties are required to apply the precautionary principle to ensure the sustainable and responsible harvesting of the stocks. [*See* Precautionary Principle.] The Agreement relies heavily on the establishment and/or strengthening of regional and subregional arrangements or organizations. Both coastal states and distant-water-fishing nations are invited to participate in the work of these organizations to adopt measures that ensure long-term sustainability of the stocks and promote the objective of their optimum utilization. Concurrently, the Agreement specifies that the conservation and management measures on the high seas must be "compatible" with those adopted by the coastal states in their EEZs. The Agreement thus recognizes the principle of biological unity, according to which the stocks must be managed throughout their range. One of the most striking provisions of the Agreement stipulates that, in some very limited circumstances, jurisdiction over vessels fishing on the high seas will be transferred from the flag state to other states enforcing the measures of the Agreement to which all are parties. This provision effectively puts an end to the exclusive jurisdiction of the flag state on the high seas.

While it is a strong and carefully worded instrument, the success of the Agreement will depend on the willingness of states to adopt and implement it. Ultimately, success may well depend on the willingness of flag states to curb the practices of their vessels on the high seas and within EEZs. Nonetheless, the Agreement is yet another example of the new willingness of states to curb their national prerogatives and adopt collective approaches to address the growing threat of overfishing worldwide. The negotiations also marked a departure from the traditional stock-specific approach and revealed a broader attempt on the part of states to conserve marine biodiversity.

[*See also* Fishing.]

BIBLIOGRAPHY

Balton, D. A. "Strengthening the Law of the Sea: The New Agreement on Straddling Fish Stocks and Highly Migratory Fish

Stocks." *Ocean Development and International Law* 27 (1996), 125–151.

Burke, W. T. *The New International Law of Fisheries, UNCLOS 1982 and Beyond*. Oxford: Clarendon Press, 1994.

de Fontaubert, A. C. "The Politics of Negotiation at the United Nations Conference on Straddling Fish Stocks and Highly Migratory Fish Stocks." *Ocean and Coastal Management* 29 (1995), 79.

———. "The United Nations Conference on Straddling Fish Stocks and Highly Migratory Fish Stocks: Another Step in the Implementation of the Law of the Sea Convention." *Ocean Yearbook 12*. Chicago: Chicago University Press, 1995.

Food and Agriculture Organization. "UNCED and its Implications for Fisheries." UN Doc. No. COFI/93/INF/8, January 1993.

Freestone, D. "The Effective Conservation and Management of High Seas Living Resources: Towards a New Regime." *Canterbury Law Review* 5 (1994), 341–362.

Hayashi, M. "The 1995 Agreement on the Conservation and Management of Straddling and Highly Migratory Fish Stocks: Significance for the Law of the Sea Convention." *Ocean and Coastal Management* 29 (1995), 51–69.

———. "Enforcement by Non-Flag States on the High Seas under the 1995 Agreement on Straddling and Highly Migratory Fish Stocks." *Georgetown International Environmental Law Review* 9 (1996), 1–36.

Miles, E. L., and W. T. Burke. "Pressures on the United Nations Convention on the Law of the Sea of 1982 Arising from New Fisheries Conflicts: The Problem of Straddling Stocks." *Ocean Development and International Law* 20 (1989), 343–357.

Orrego Vicuña, F. *The Changing International Law of High Seas Fisheries*. Cambridge and New York: Cambridge University Press, 1999.

United Nations. "Protection of the Oceans, All Kinds of Seas, Including Enclosed and Semi-Enclosed Seas and Coastal Areas, and the Protection, Rational Use, and Development of their Living Resources." Conference on Environment and Development, Report Doc. A/CONF. 151/26/Rev. 1, Vol. 1, 1993, chap. 17.

—A. CHARLOTTE DE FONTAUBERT

STRATIGRAPHY. *See* Dating Methods.

STRATOSPHERE. *See* Atmosphere Structure and Evolution; *and* Chlorofluorocarbons.

SUBSIDENCE. *See* Ground Water; *and* Mining.

SULFUR CYCLE

Sulfur is abundant, essential for life, and present in many oxidation states, from sulfides to sulfates. Like many nonmetals, sulfur is highly mobile in most environments, which leads to large annual movements of sulfur in the global cycle at the Earth's surface. Metallic sulfides (e.g., iron sulfide, FeS_2) are insoluble, but unstable at high temperature, giving rise to gaseous emissions from vol-

canoes. The higher oxidation states of sulfur are encountered as oxyanions (sufates, sulfites, etc.) at the Earth's surface; apart from a few important exceptions such as barium sulfate, these are soluble in water.

Sulfur was mobilized at the very beginning of the Earth's history, and Precambrian (over 610 million years) sulfate evaporites are evidence of abundant sulfur in the Ancient Ocean. Even without oxygen in the ancient atmosphere, sulfur-oxidizing microbiota could easily oxidize sulfur, possibly in early sulfur-based photosynthetic pathways:

$$H_2S + 2CO_2 + 2H_2O \xrightarrow{h\nu} 2CH_2O + 2H^+ + SO_4^{2-}.$$

Since Phanerozoic (less than 610 million years) times, sulfur has moved between the oceans and the crust, largely because of the reduction of seawater sulfate by anaerobic sulfur-reducing bacteria. This leads to the deposition of pyrite in sedimentary rocks. Evaporation of sea water also leads to the deposition of sulfate in sedimentary rocks, known as evaporites. These processes take place on geologic time scales, and evaporite and sulfide deposition do not occur at a constant rate. Evaporite formation requires the formation of basins that are filled on short geologic time scales, so that the ocean, at any given time, could easily be out of steady state with respect to inputs and losses of sulfate.

In basins, evaporite deposition from sea water is a simple process that gives a predictable sequence of salts as sea water evaporates. Calcium carbonate precipitates first, but there is relatively little carbonate in sea water compared with the amount of sulfate, which contributes to gypsum ($CaSO_4 \cdot 2H_2O$), the next salt to deposit. Presently, there are no large isolated basins that are accumulating evaporites. The few arid tidal flats such as those on the Trucial Coast of the Arabian Gulf suggest that current evaporite deposition is several orders of magnitude less than during periods in the past.

Sulfide deposition requires reduction of seawater sulfate to sulfide. This is typically a biological process that occurs in sediments, most commonly at the continental margin where the accumulation or organic material is fastest, encouraging the activities of sulfate-reducing bacteria:

$$2CH_2O + SO_4^{2-} \longrightarrow 2HCO_3^- + HS^- + H^+.$$

The sulfide is converted to pyrite (FeS_2) in a poorly understood process that can be summarized as follows:

$$Fe^{2+} + HS^- + S_2O_3^{2-} \longrightarrow FeS_2 + HSO_3^-$$

Sulfur isotopic records indicate the relative importance of the deposition of gypsum or pyrite in marine sediments over geologic time. They suggest that the Permian period was one of pervasive oxidation of sulfide to sulfate, while a massive reduction of sulfate to sulfide characterized early Paleozoic times.

The sulfur cycle in the absence of human activities is shown in Figure 1. The atmosphere and the surface of the Earth are probably close to steady state. Each year, input and output to the atmosphere are almost in balance; however, the volcanic flux can show significant annual variations. A single explosive volcanic eruption can inject large quantities of sulfur dioxide into the stratosphere, where it remains for a few years. This sulfur is slowly transformed to sulfuric acid, which exists as small droplets (aerosols) at high altitude. These droplets can affect the radiation balance of the Earth and are responsible for the slight cooling in global temperatures that is apparent after very large eruptions. The eruption of Tambora in 1815 was perhaps the most noticeable in historical times. It caused widespread crop failure because the following summer was so cool. Stratospheric sulfate particles can also affect the ozone layer by enhancing the formation of polar stratospheric clouds, which are important in springtime ozone destruction.

Volcanoes also make important contributions to sulfur in the troposphere, mostly as sulfur dioxide. Although we frequently associate the smell of hydrogen sulfide (like rotten eggs) with volcanic regions, this becomes important only where venting gases are at relatively low temperatures.

Biological emissions of sulfur to the atmosphere from both land and sea take the form of reduced sulfur gases, dimethyl sulfide, carbon disulfide, and carbonyl sulfide.

The dominant emission from the sea is dimethyl sulfide, a product of osmoregulatory activities by marine algae. Once in the atmosphere, dimethyl sulfide is rapidly oxidized to compounds such as sulfuric and methanesulfonic acids. Terrestrial biogenic sulfur emissions are much smaller and probably dominated by carbonyl sulfide. Carbonyl sulfide is relatively stable in the lower atmosphere, so that some escapes to the stratosphere where, like volcanic sulfur dioxide, it is involved in the production of sulfuric acid aerosols. Much of the sulfur returns to the Earth's surface as sulfates dissolved in rain (wet deposition), although some sulfur dioxide sticks directly to surfaces such as plant leaves in a process called dry deposition.

The Earth's surface has always delivered sulfur to the atmosphere as part of windblown dusts. The development of grazing over the last few millennia has led to a decrease in the plant cover that normally restricts wind erosion in arid regions. Plowing and, more recently, river diversion have also increased the amount of sulfate material carried aloft as dust. The Aral Sea is now so reduced in size that its exposed sediments contribute 0.1–1.0 million metric tons of sulfur each year to the atmosphere. [See Aral Sea, Desiccation of the.]

This is just one of many human impacts on the sulfur cycle, which is illustrated in Figure 2. Large amounts of sulfur are mobilized every year in mineral and fossil fuel extraction. Many minerals are bound to sulfide ores, so that refining of the metal releases sulfur to the atmo-

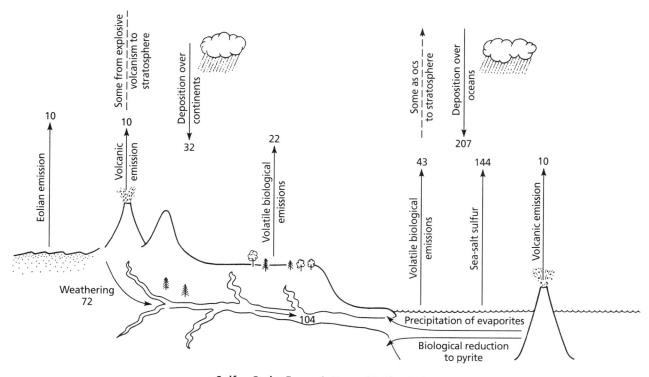

Sulfur Cycle. FIGURE 1. Natural Sulfur Cycle.

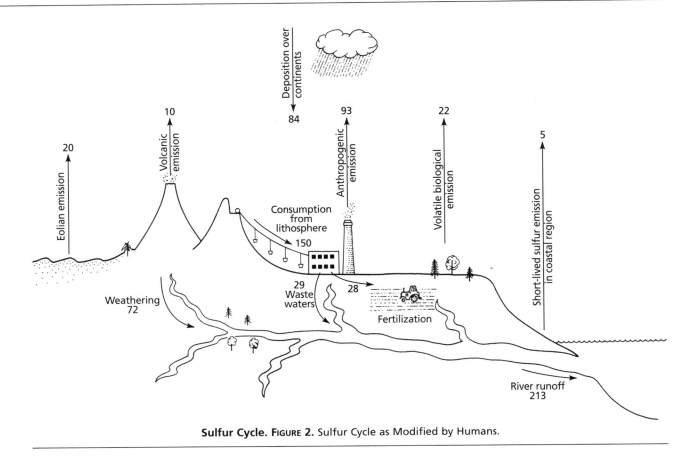

Sulfur Cycle. FIGURE 2. Sulfur Cycle as Modified by Humans.

sphere or to waste waters. Fossil fuel combustion represents the largest human emission of sulfur to the atmosphere, amounting to almost 100 million metric tons per year. Despite a reduction in emissions from North America and Europe in recent years, the growing economies of Asia are emitting increasing amounts of sulfur dioxide to the atmosphere.

Some sulfur is applied to the land as fertilizer, because it is such an important biological element. Ironically, the application of sulfates to European agricultural soils has increased in recent years because of the reduction of sulfur emissions by power stations and heavy industry. As industrial emissions have declined, the contribution that this pollutant makes to the nutrient requirement of crops has also decreased. In some areas, European soils have become sulfur deficient for plants such as cereals, so that sulfur must be added with fertilizers.

The sulfur that falls in continental rain or is applied to the land moves into drainage waters. Rivers and lakes can accumulate large amounts of sulfate. Closed basins such as the Dead Sea represent extreme examples of this. Much of the sulfur in rivers arises from the weathering of sedimentary rocks, but anthropogenic sources

such as acid mine drainage can also be an important source for rivers. Deposited sulfur also accumulates in snow packs and, when the snow melts in the spring, much of the sulfur appears highly concentrated in the early acidic meltwaters. Despite the large human impact on the sulfur content of fresh water, the sulfate concentrations of sea water are so high that human inputs to riverflow have no effect on oceanic sulfur concentrations.

In the atmosphere the human impact is more significant. Our contributions of sulfur to the atmosphere are larger than the natural emissions. This imbalance is further emphasized by the fact that human emissions are land based and largely located in the midlatitudes of the Northern Hemisphere. The emissions are further concentrated into cities or industrial regions, so that deposition is enhanced in highly industrialized areas widely spread across the globe. This generally appears as acid rain, contaminated most often with sulfuric acid.

The formation of sulfuric acid in rain takes about a day because the reactions proceed most effectively only if sulfur dioxide has first dissolved in raindrops. Naturally occurring strong oxidants (hydrogen peroxide or ozone) or oxygen in the presence of catalysts (Fe(III) or Mn(II)) convert this to sulfate. The reaction in solution can be represented as follows:

$$HSO_3^- + H_2O_2 \longrightarrow H^+ + SO_3^{2-} + H_2O$$

$$HSO_3^- + O_3 \longrightarrow H^+ + SO_3^{2-} + O_2$$

$$HSO_3^- + 0.5O_2 + catalyst \longrightarrow H^+ + SO_4^{2-}$$

Although sulfuric acid has been the most important acidifying agent in rainfall, reduced sulfur dioxide emissions in Europe and North America have meant that nitric acid makes increasing contributions to acid rain in these regions.

Sulfates in the atmosphere not only cause acid rain: they also have the potential to influence climate, because sulfate particles in the atmosphere affect the radiation balance of the Earth. Higher concentrations of sulfate particles can mean more cloud condensation nuclei and thus more clouds. This in turn would mean more clouds to reflect radiation, potentially leading to a cooler world. If a cooler Earth meant less biological emission of sulfur to the atmosphere, then biological processes could reduce the cooling and help establish a constant temperature for the Earth. Indeed, there is a possibility that this is a natural regulatory process, and it forms part of the well-known Gaia hypothesis. Although it is not yet possible to establish whether sulfur biogeochemistry controls Earth temperature, it represents an interesting postulate concerning the interconnection between biology and global processes.

[See also Acid Rain and Acid Deposition; Aerosols; Biogeochemical Cycles; Desertification; Gaia Hypothesis; and Ozone.]

BIBLIOGRAPHY

Andreae, M. O. "Ocean–Atmosphere Interactions in the Global Biogeochemical Sulfur Cycle." *Marine Chemistry* 30 (1990), 1–29.
Bates, T. S., et al. "The Biogeochemical Sulfur Cycle in the Marine Boundary Layer over the Northeast Pacific Ocean." *Journal of Atmospheric Chemistry* 10 (1990), 59–81.
Schlesinger, W. H. *Biogeochemistry: An Analysis of Global Change.* San Diego: Academic Press, 1997.
—P. Brimblecombe

SULFUR OXIDES.

SULFUR OXIDES. *See* Air Quality; *and* Electrical Power Generation.

SUN

Virtually all of the energy that drives the Earth's climate system comes from the sun. The surface temperature of the Earth is determined by the balance between incoming solar radiation (which depends on solar output and Earth–sun geometry) and outgoing terrestrial radiation (which depends mainly on atmospheric proper-

ties). Even small variations in any of these factors may result in environmental changes that could be catastrophic to the Earth's biota.

Solar Evolution. About 4.6 billion years ago, a shock wave advancing across the Milky Way initiated the contraction of interstellar gases and debris into a dense cloud that, some 30 million years later, evolved into the sun we know today. As the material in the protostar (mainly hydrogen) compressed because of gravitational attraction, its temperature rose, becoming high enough in the core for hydrogen to fuse into helium (above 1.5 million kelvins) as indicated in the following equation:

$$4_1^1H \rightarrow {}_2^4He + 2 \text{ positrons} + 2 \text{ neutrinos} + \text{energy (26.7 MeV)}$$

The conversion of about 0.7 percent of the hydrogen mass (m) into energy ($E = mc^2$, where c is the speed of light) is the source of the solar irradiance, or luminosity (at present 3.83×10^{26} W).

This reaction proceeds until most of the hydrogen in the core is converted to helium. This period, which occupies most of the lifetime of most stars, is called the "main sequence" and has a characteristic stellar luminosity and surface temperature corresponding to its mass (Figure 1). The greater the stellar mass, the faster the evolution, and the higher the resulting surface temperature. Luminosity of main-sequence stars increases with the mass raised to the power 3.5; thus a star such as Sirius that is about twice the mass of the sun is more than ten times as luminous. It is believed that the sun is approximately halfway through its lifetime; in another 4 billion years, as the hydrogen in its core becomes exhausted, it will expand into a "red giant," engulfing all of the inner planets. This should take a further billion years, by which time the core will become hot enough (over 120 million kelvins) for helium to fuse into carbon and heavier elements. As the helium is used up, the sun will start to contract, and finally collapse into a "white dwarf."

The Quiet Sun. The sun is a smaller-than-average star, with a mass of 1.99×10^{30} kilograms, a diameter of 1,392,000 kilometers, and a radiative temperature of 5,800 kelvins. Its present composition is three-quarters hydrogen and one-quarter helium by mass, with small amounts of the heavier elements. In its very dense core, fusion reactions have reduced the hydrogen content to 35 percent (65 percent helium), raising the temperature to 15 million kelvins and the pressure to 300 billion atmospheres. Temperature decreases outward from the core, through the radiative and convective envelopes, to a low of 4,000 kelvins at the outer surface of the photosphere, and then increases again to 7,000 kelvins in the chromosphere and 1–3 million kelvins in the corona. The photosphere is the main surface of the sun seen

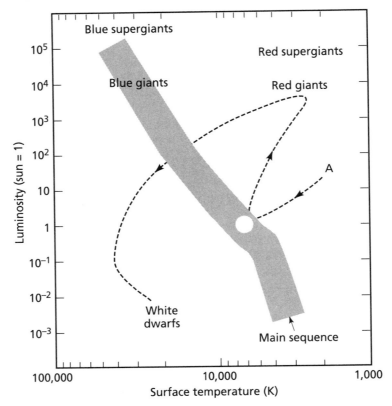

Sun. Figure 1. Hertzsprung-Russell diagram, showing the sun's evolution from interstellar matter (A) to its present position on the main sequence and its ultimate expansion to a red giant and collapse to a white dwarf.

from the Earth (the chromosphere and corona are visible only during eclipses); it rotates once in twenty-five days at the equator, and once in thirty-six days near the poles.

In the long term, solar luminosity (L) is increasing as a function of time (t):

$$\frac{L}{L_{o}} = \left[1 + 0.4\left(1 - \frac{t}{t_{o}} \right) \right]^{-1}$$

where L_{o} and t_{o} are the current luminosity and age of the sun, respectively (Figure 2). This shows a 40 percent increase in luminosity since the sun's birth, a current rate of increase of about ten microwatts per century, and predicts a further doubling in luminosity during the sun's remaining time on the main sequence.

The Active Sun. Realization that the sun's properties were not unvarying came with the discovery of sunspots: transient dark patches, typically two thousand to ten thousand kilometers in diameter, covering up to 1 percent of the solar disk. Although early reports of sunspots exist, it was not until the invention of the telescope in the seventeenth century that they were ob-

served on a regular basis; a fairly complete data set began about the year 1700 (Figure 3). An eleven-year cycle in the data was discovered by Schwabe in 1843, and since then a close relationship has been found between sunspots and other phenomena, including faculae and flares and variations in the corona and solar wind. The number of sunspots is indicative of the level of solar activity, particularly the emission of ultraviolet and extreme ultraviolet radiation.

Solar activity cycles are numbered consecutively from the start of daily observations at the Zurich Observatory in 1749; the one peaking about 2002 is cycle 23. Since the sun's magnetic field reverses every eleven years, the composite sunspot-magnetic cycle (Hale Cycle) has a period of twenty-two years. Solar activity variations are not well understood but appear to be related to distortion of the sun's magnetic field due to latitudinal variations in rotation. Short-period active-sun phenomena, such as flares, are not likely to have significant effects on the Earth's climate. However, longer-period modulations of sunspot numbers, such as the 80–90-year Gleissberg Cycle and the 180–200-year cycle, appear to be related to terrestrial climate changes. The former cycle is connected to oscillations in the solar radius, and the latter to inertial motion of the sun around the center of mass of the solar system. The best-known variations in the sunspot record are the Maunder Minimum of 1645–1715 and the weaker Dalton Minimum of 1795–1823.

Discussions of global warming and human influence on that process are put in perspective by recognizing changes in the Earth's climate through geologic time, the most relevant being profound swings in temperature during the glacial and interglacial periods of the last two million years.

A different perspective is provided by planetary scientists, who observe that the sun is shrinking slowly and heating up at roughly 1 percent per one hundred million years. This inexorable change will warm the Earth, increasing evaporation and the atmosphere's water vapor content, thus enhancing the greenhouse effect and further warming the Earth until, one billion years from now, the average temperature will be 60°C (140°F) and the Earth's oceans will slowly disappear over one hundred million years as water vapor rises up to the stratosphere and then escapes into space.

The lack of water will prevent the formation of limestone, which currently traps carbon dioxide as calcium carbonate ($CaCO_3$). The increasing concentration of carbon dioxide in the atmosphere will further raise the temperature; and, without rain to wash the atmosphere, sulfur oxides will accumulate and circulate freely, making the atmosphere acidic like that of our sister planet, Venus. This extreme summer will grip the Earth for 3.5 billion years.

Through another two billion years, the sun will expand to become a red giant, engulfing the planets Mercury, Venus, and Earth. As we look toward this event, we can look back through a comparable span of five billion years to the origin of the Earth, and realize that we now enjoy a planet whose life may be half over.

In its final stages, lasting until 7.5 billion years from now, the sun will consume its helium and flash intermittently to a brightness a thousand times that of today; then, as it consumes its heavier elements, it will glow three thousand times as brightly as today. Ultimately, the long hot summer will end, and the sun will become a dead white dwarf, all of its fuel expended, fading into perpetual winter.

BIBLIOGRAPHY

Seife, C. "Final Summer." *New Scientist* (25 July 1998), 40–41.

—DAVID J. CUFF

Direct measurement of the solar irradiance outside the Earth's atmosphere (the solar constant) has been possible only since the advent of satellite-borne sensors in the mid-1970s (Figure 4). The solar constant is the solar luminosity (L) divided by the area of the sphere of radius equal to the mean Earth-sun distance (R), that is, $L/(4\pi R^2)$. One analysis found an upward trend of about 0.036 percent in the satellite data between 1986 and 1995. Although this is not obvious in Figure 4, it is consistent with an increase of 0.5 percent per century found in data collected at the Earth's surface between 1908 and 1955. The satellite data set now spans two solar cycles and reveals a variation that is clearly in phase with the eleven-year sunspot cycle, with the solar irradiance typically about 0.1 percent higher during sunspot maxima than minima. Apparently, the lower luminosity of sunspots, the centers of which are 2,000 kelvins cooler than the quiet sun, is more than compensated for by increased irradiance from concomitant faculae, flares, and so on, elsewhere on the solar disk.

In addition to total irradiance and sunspot numbers, other aspects of solar activity observed from the Earth include the solar spectrum and magnetic field, flares, plages (bright regions surrounding sunspots), coronal mass ejections, cosmic rays, and the solar wind, 1 million metric tons per second of electrified gas (mainly hydrogen) streaming across the solar system. A solar and heliospheric observatory launched into space in December 1995 will have observed many aspects of solar activity over a complete solar cycle by the end of its mission in 2003. It has already led to an explanation for the high temperature in the solar corona, relating it to interactions between the multitude of varying magnetic fields crisscrossing the region, and provided vital information about the solar wind and other active-sun phenomena.

Sun–Earth Relationships. The distribution of solar radiation reaching the Earth's surface depends on solar luminosity and Earth–sun orbital geometry. The disposition of this energy, which affects the Earth's

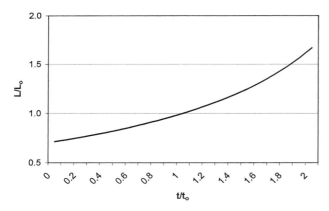

Sun. Figure 2. Variation of the solar luminosity over its lifetime on the main sequence; L_o and t_o are the current luminosity and time, respectively.

energy balance, may also be modulated by purely terrestrial factors, such as changes in atmospheric composition (the "greenhouse effect") and surface characteristics. The long-term increase in quiet-sun luminosity, shown in Figure 2, amounts to only ten microwatts per century and is negligible compared with shorter-period variations. Orbital variations, including changes in the eccentricity of the Earth's orbit (90,000–100,000-year period), the tilt of the Earth's axis (40,000–42,000 years), and the season of the Earth's closest approach to the sun (21,000–23,000 years), affect the temporal and spatial distribution of solar radiation over the Earth's surface rather than the solar constant. At present, the net effect of these orbital changes is a decrease in insolation of about 0.03 percent per century in the midlatitudes of the Northern Hemisphere. [*See* Earth Motions.]

Solar luminosity variations having periods of a decade to several centuries are related mainly to sunspot cycles (Figure 3), analysis of which is limited by the brevity of the period of reliable luminosity data (Figure 4). This has led to the use of proxy data, such as geomagnetic and auroral activity, as well as paleoclimate indicators, including evidence of glaciation and tree ring and isotopic abundance analyses. The proxy data indicate that during most of its several-billion-year history, the Earth averaged about 10°C warmer than at present, although the warmth was interspersed with periods of glaciation. Major long-term variations were presumably due to both continental drift and the orbital variations described above. [*See* Climate Change; Little Ice Age in Europe; *and* Medieval Climatic Optimum.]

Following the most recent glaciation, some ten thousand years ago, the global mean temperature rose from several degrees Celsius cooler than present until the Climatic Optimum of 5000–3000 BCE, when the Earth was 1°–2°C warmer than now. Since then, there have been several temperature fluctuations, of which the Medieval Warm Epoch of 1000–1200 CE, and the Little Ice Age of 1430–1850 CE were the most noteworthy. There were

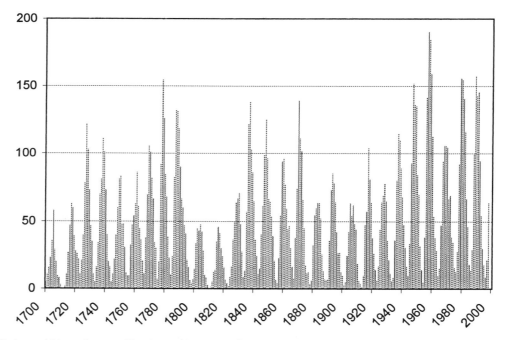

Sun. Figure 3. Annual Mean Sunspot Numbers. (Courtesy of the National Geophysical Data Center, National Oceanic and Atmospheric Administration, Washington, D.C.)

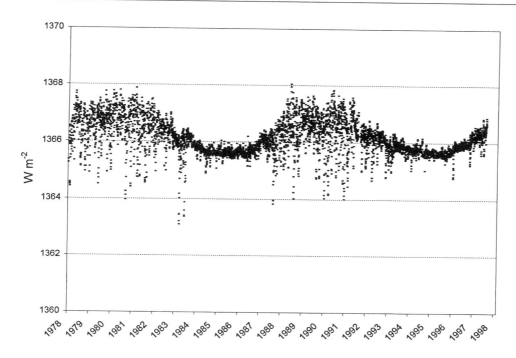

Sun. FIGURE 4. Daily Values of the Solar Constant. (Courtesy of the National Geophysical Data Center, National Oceanic and Atmospheric Administration, Washington, D.C.)

several periods of low solar activity prior to the sixteenth century, including the Oort (1010–1050), Wolf (1280–1340) and Spörer (1400–1520) Minima, and a major period of high activity called the Medieval Solar Maximum (1100–1250). Most of these solar variations coincided reasonably closely with appropriate terrestrial climatic excursions, such as the Medieval Warm Epoch and the Little Ice Age mentioned above.

Although global temperature excursions during these extreme periods were unlikely to have been greater than 1°C, it is difficult to explain them in terms of the likely solar irradiance variations; they appear to have been several times as great as changes in total irradiance warranted. For example, the decrease in solar irradiance needed to produce the Little Ice Age has been estimated to be an order of magnitude greater than the measured difference between recent solar maxima and minima shown in Figure 4. A possible explanation lies in the fact that most of the solar radiation increase during active periods is in the ultraviolet range, wavelengths that are highly absorbed in the Earth's upper atmosphere; this increases stratospheric ozone production and temperature, influencing atmospheric circulation and extratropical wind systems.

Recently, an ocean climate model was used to simulate global mean temperatures since 1617 based on an assumption that temperature during the Maunder Minimum was 1°C cooler than present. The simulation agreed well with observed data and suggested that about half of the warming between 1900 and 1955 was due to solar forcing, leaving the remainder to be explained by the greenhouse effect. Solar activity during recent sunspot maxima appears to be as high as during the Medieval Warm Epoch, following a relatively quiet 650 years. An analogy with the earlier warm period indicates that the current period, which began about 1900, will continue until 2050. The subsequent decrease is likely to be easily outstripped by greenhouse warming.

BIBLIOGRAPHY

Eddy, J. A. "The Maunder Minimum." *Science* 192 (1976), 1189–1202.

———. "The Maunder Minimum: A Reappraisal." *Solar Physics* 89 (1983), 195–207.

Hanna, E. "Have Long-Term Solar Minima, such as the Maunder Minimum, any Recognizable Climatic Effect?" *Weather* 51 (1996), 234–242, 304–312.

Hoyt, D. V., K. H. Schatten, and E. Nesmes-Ribes. "The One Hundredth Year of Rudolf Wolf's Death: Do We Have the Correct Reconstruction of Solar Activity?" *Geophysical Research Letters* 21 (1994), 2067–2070.

Jirikowic, J. L., and P. E. Damon. "The Medieval Solar Activity Maximum." *Climatic Change* 26 (1994), 309–316.

Lean, J., J. Beer, and R. Bradley. "Reconstruction of Solar Irradiance since 1610: Implications for Climate Change." *Geophysical Research Letters* 22 (1995), 3195–3198.

Pittock, A. B. "A Critical Look at Long-Term Sun-Weather Relationships." *Reviews of Geophysics and Space Physics* 16 (1978), 400–420.

Reid, G. C. "Solar Forcing of Global Climate Change since the Mid-17th Century." *Climatic Change* 37 (1997), 391–405.

Tayler, R. J. *The Sun as a Star*. Cambridge: Cambridge University Press, 1997.

White, O. R. *The Solar Output and Its Variations.* Boulder: Colorado Associated University Press, 1977.

—EARLE A. RIPLEY

SUPERFUND. *See* Hazardous Waste; *and* Land Reclamation.

SURPRISE

Surprise is the condition in which an event, process, or outcome is not known or expected. In this strict meaning, the attribution of surprise shifts toward the event, process, or outcome itself. Is it a new or wholly unexpected experience? We may expect surprises to occur, but we are surprised by the specific event, process, or outcome involved. This meaning circumvents anticipation because the very act of anticipation implies some level of knowledge or foresight. The strict definition of surprise is, therefore, not particularly interesting or useful for policy purposes. Exceptions are cases in which the conditions that might induce surprises are known. For example, rapid forcing of nonlinear systems is known to increase the likelihood of unexpected behavior (Intergovernmental Panel on Climate Change, 1996), even though the actual surprise events may not be imaginable. This exception, which Schneider et al. (1998) termed "imaginable *conditions* for surprise," could have policy meaning since actions could be proposed to mitigate the conditions in which surprise might be induced (for example, slowing down the rate of global change forcing, as suggested in Schneider, 1997a, chap. 6).

Because of the impracticality of the strict definition of surprise for policy making, various studies advocate the use of another meaning for surprise, one in which the attribution of surprise shifts more toward the expectations of the observer. Holling (1986, p. 294) recognized this meaning of surprise as a condition in which perceived reality departs qualitatively from expectations. This more interpretive or relational meaning of surprise has been labeled "imaginable surprise" by Schneider et al. (1998).

Almost every event may constitute an imaginable surprise to someone. But since global change phenomena and their environmental and societal impacts are a community-scale set of issues, little can be gained for practical purposes by focusing on whether someone, somewhere, may or may not have once predicted or hinted at some specific surprise event. More fruitful is the recognition that groups, communities, and cultures may share expectations such that a particular event is likely to qualify as a surprise for most within them. In these cases, what gets labeled as a surprise depends upon the extent to which reality departs from community expectations, and on the salience of the problems imposed.

The assumptions associated with the standard paradigm of global climate change impact assessment, for example, although recognizing a wide range of uncertainty, are essentially surprise free. One approach is to postulate low- (or uncertain-) probability cases in which little climate change, on the one hand, or catastrophic surprises, on the other hand, might occur and multiply the lower probability by the much larger potential costs or benefits. Analysts, however, customarily use a few standard general circulation model carbon-dioxide-doubling scenarios to bracket the uncertainty, rather than to postulate extremely serious or relatively negligible climatic change outcomes. A strategic approach—that is, one that considers a wide range of probabilities and outcomes—may be more appropriate for global climate change impact assessments given the high plausibility of surprises, even if we have a limited capacity to anticipate specific details right now. For example, two critical assumptions of the standard assessment paradigm are that the probabilities of climate extremes—droughts, floods, superhurricanes—either remain unchanged or will change with the mean change in climate according to unchanged variability distributions. As Mearns et al. (1984) have shown, however, changes in the daily temperature variance or the autocorrelation of daily weather extremes can either significantly reduce or dramatically enhance the vulnerability to global warming of agriculture, ecosystems, or other components of the environment that are sensitive to climate extremes. How such variability measures might change as the climatic mean changes is as yet highly uncertain, although increased evaporation with global warming is expected to increase the probability of hydrologic extremes: droughts and floods (Intergovernmental Panel on Climate Change, 1996). Karl and Knight (1998) have observed that about half of the 8 percent increase in precipitation in the United States since 1910 occurred in the top tenth percentile of rainfall intensity, that is, the most damaging heavy downpours. Nevertheless, the possibility that variability will change with climate change is not at all remote, even though it is not possible to ascertain credibly with current techniques how that might occur.

An assumption in cost-benefit calculations within the standard assessment paradigm is that nature is either constant or irrelevant. For example, ecological services (see, for example, Daily, 1997) such as pest control or waste recycling are assumed as constants or of no economic value in most assessment calculations. Yet should climatic change occur in the middle to upper range of that typically projected, it is highly likely that communities of species will be disassembled (see, for example, Root and Schneider, 1993), and significant alterations to existing patterns of pests and weeds seem virtually certain. Some argue that pests, should their patterns be altered, can simply be controlled using pesticides and herbicides or medicines. The side effects of many such controls are well known. What is not considered in the standard paradigm is a surprise scenario such as a change in public consciousness regarding the value of nature that would reject pesticide and herbicide applications as a "technology-fix" response to global changes. A related potential surprise is the suggestion that halogenated compounds are causing damage to the endocrine systems of humans and animals and could lead to a twenty-first-century human and animal health crisis (see, for example, Colborn et al., 1996).

Risk and Uncertainty. Risk is typically defined as the condition in which the event, process, or outcome, and the probability that each will occur, is known. [*See* Risk.] In reality, of course (coins and unloaded dice notwithstanding), complete or perfect knowledge of complex environmental systems that would permit the credible calculation of objective probabilities, rarely exists. Likewise, the full range of potential outcomes is usually not known. Thus, risk is almost always accompanied by varying degrees of uncertainty. Uncertainty is usually defined as the condition in which the event, process, or outcome is known (factually or hypothetically), but the probabilities that it will occur are not known, or are highly subjective estimates.

Typically, when probabilities are assigned, they are subjective (or depend upon subjective assumptions; see, for example, Moss and Schneider, 2000), and the ways to establish the reliability of different subjective probability estimates are debatable (see, for example, Morgan and Henrion, 1990; Morgan and Keith, 1995). Methods to deal explicitly and formally with uncertainty in international assessments, and further discussion and references, are contained in Hassol and Katzenberger (1997) and Moss and Schneider (2000).

From Uncertainty to Surprise. By the conventional definition, a surprise is an event that is unexpected. Potential climate change and, more broadly, global environmental change, are replete with truly unexpected events because of the enormous complexities of the processes and interrelationships involved and our insufficient understanding of them (such as the interactions among ocean, atmosphere, and terrestrial systems). For example, the Intergovernmental Panel on Climate Change (1996) summary for policymakers concludes:

> Future unexpected, large and rapid climate system changes (as have occurred in the past) are, by their nature, difficult to predict. This implies that future climate changes may also involve "surprises." In particular these arise from the nonlinear nature of the climate system. When rapidly forced, nonlinear systems are especially subject to unexpected behavior.

Much of the current work on surprise has grown out of an extensive body of research on uncertainty. Yet, although widely acknowledged and studied, uncertainty remains a difficult concept to define or codify. Different conceptualizations and approaches to uncertainty abound in the literature, crossing numerous fields of study and touching a wide range of problem types. Two basic options are usually followed in the face of uncertainty, however. The first is to reduce the uncertainties through data collection, research, modeling, simulation techniques, and so forth. Following this option, the objective is to overcome uncertainty, to make the unknown more known. But the daunting nature of uncertainties surrounding global environmental change, and the need to make decisions before the "normal science" option can provide clear resolution, force a second option—that of managing or integrating uncertainty directly into the decision-making or policy-making process. Before uncertainty can be so integrated, however, the nature and extent of the uncertainty must be clarified. This understanding may be approached in several ways (see, for example, Schneider et al., 1998). A few of these approaches are briefly mentioned here.

The fields of mathematics, statistics and, more recently, physics provide the science of uncertainty with many powerful means and techniques to conceptualize, quantify, and manage uncertainty, ranging from the frequency distributions of probability theory to the possibility and belief statements of Bayesian statistics. Addressing other aspects of uncertainty, fuzzy sets offer an alternative to classical set theory for situations in which the definitions of set membership are vague, ambiguous, or nonexclusive. In addition, researchers have proposed chaos theory and complexity theory to focus on expecting the unexpected in models and theory (see, for example, Casti, 1994).

The practical application of many of these techniques was originally pioneered by researchers in decision analysis (Raiffa, 1968). In the fields of economics and decision theory, researchers continue to study rational decision making under uncertainty and how to assess the value of collecting additional information. Methods for modeling risk attitudes, leading to the terms *risk-prone* and *risk-adverse*, attempt to capture how different people faced with making a decision react to the uncertainty surrounding the expected outcomes. Looking toward future outcomes in projecting climate change impacts and estimating marginal costs and benefits of mitigation efforts, economists such as Nordhaus (1992, 1994) explicitly address uncertainties via integrated assessment models (see, for example, Schneider, 1997b). [*See* Integrated Assessment.]

Table 1 shows the results of one such model in which the optimal carbon tax may vary from a small tax to a large tax depending on the subjective probability of climate damage per degree of global warming assigned by a group of impact assessment experts. The optimal carbon tax is one in which damages to the economy from climate change are equated with mitigation costs from

Surprise. TABLE 1. "Optimal" Carbon Taxes*

	Optimal Carbon Tax (U.S.$/ton C)		
SOURCE OF DATA	1995	2055	2105
DICE	5.24	15.04	21.73
Median	22.85	51.72	66.98
Mean	40.42	84.10	109.73
"Surprise"	193.29	383.39	517.09

*Values are calculated by applying a decision analytic survey of experts' estimates of climate damages from two global warming scenarios (Nordhaus, 1994) to the dynamic integrated climate economy (DICE) model (Nordhaus, 1992).

The table shows the comparison of Monte Carlo simulation results by Roughgarden and Schneider (1999) using the statistical distributions from the surveyed experts versus the standard DICE model. "Surprise" values are the ninety-fifth percentile results from the statistical distributions, and imply optimal taxes more than twenty times larger than for the original point value estimate of Nordhaus (1992).

carbon dioxide abatement. Optimal carbon taxes in Table 1 are calculated by applying a decision analytic survey of experts' estimates of climate damages from two global warming scenarios (Nordhaus, 1994) to the dynamic integrated climate economy (DICE) model (Nordhaus, 1992). The table shows the comparison of Monte Carlo simulation results by Roughgarden and Schneider (1998) using the statistical distributions from the surveyed experts versus the standard DICE model. The averages of the ninety-fifth percentile climate damages estimated by these experts (labeled "surprise" on the table) result from the statistical distributions and imply optimal taxes more than twenty times larger than for the original point value estimated by Nordhaus (1992). The average of the five percentile damage estimated by these experts is small and negative (that is, a subsidy to carbon dioxide emission).

This acknowledgment of uncertainty has found a prominent place in many other fields of study, each one speaking its own language of uncertainty. For example, researchers making risk assessments and setting safety standards find it most useful to distinguish between risk (the probability of a certain negative effect resulting from a hazard occurrence, given the specified level of exposure), variability (interindividual differences in vulnerability and susceptibility), and uncertainty (model parameter variability and any unexplained residual). This three-pronged distinction provides information on uncertainty tailored to the needs and research questions of the risk analyst. Researchers in other fields of study, for example computer science, may be most interested in addressing other aspects of uncertainty, such as how it affects the decision flow or logic of the computer system.

Consequently, research on uncertainty cuts across a number of different disciplines. In work related to hazards and risk, sociologists, anthropologists, psychologists, and geographers have all made important contributions to the discussions on risk perception, risk communication, and the social amplification of risk (see, for example, Kasperson et al., 1988). Similarly, work on visualizing or graphically conveying uncertainty also crosses a diverse set of disciplines, including psychology, computer science, and geographic information systems.

In the areas of environmental policy and resource management, policy makers struggle with the need to make decisions utilizing vague and ambiguous concepts (such as sustainability), with sparse and imprecise information, in decisions that have far-reaching, and often irreversible, impacts on both environment and society. Not surprisingly, efforts to incorporate uncertainty into the decision-making process quickly move to the forefront with the advent of decision-making paradigms, such as the precautionary principle, adaptive environmental management, the preventative paradigm, or stewardship (see, for example, Brown, 1997). As noted by Wynne (1992, p. 111), the shift toward prevention in environmental policy "implies an acceptance of the inherent limitations of the anticipatory knowledge on which decisions about environmental discharges [and other environmental problems] are based."

Ravetz (1986, p. 429) takes the concept of "usable knowledge in the context of incomplete science" one step further by introducing the idea of usable ignorance. To Ravetz, acknowledging the ignorance factor means becoming aware of the limits of our knowledge. Ravetz argues that ignorance cannot be entirely overcome with any amount of sophisticated measurement or calculation. Rather, coping with ignorance demands a greater awareness of how the policy process operates. He recognizes that one can only remove ignorance by gaining more knowledge, but stresses that by "being aware of our ignorance we do not encounter disastrous pitfalls in our supposedly secure knowledge or supposedly effective technique."

The emphasis on managing uncertainty rather than mastering it can be traced to work on resilience in ecology (most notably by Holling, 1986). Whereas resistance implies an ability to withstand change or impact within some measure of performance, resilience captures the ability to "give with the pressure" without disrupting the overall health of the system. In this framework, adaptation is an ecological mechanism whose aim is not to overcome or control environmental uncertainty, but to live with it.

Global change science and policy making will have to deal with uncertainty and surprise for the foreseeable future. Thus, more systematic analysis of surprise issues and more formal and consistent methods of incorporation of uncertainty into global change assessments will become increasingly necessary.

[*See also* Climate Change; *and* Ocean Dynamics.]

BIBLIOGRAPHY

Brown, P. G. "Stewardship of Climate: An Editorial Comment." *Climatic Change* 37 (1997), 329–334.

Casti, J. L. *Complexification: Explaining a Paradoxical World through the Science of Surprise.* New York: HarperCollins, 1994.

Colborn, T., et al. *Our Stolen Future: Are We Threatening Our Fertility, Intelligence, and Survival? A Scientific Detective Story.* New York: Dutton, 1996.

Daily, G. C. *Nature's Services: Societal Dependence on Natural Ecosystems.* Washington, D.C. and Covelo, Calif.: Island Press, 1997.

Hassol, S. J., and J. Katzenberger, eds. *Elements of Change.* Aspen: Aspen Global Change Institute, 1997.

Holling, C. S. "The Resilience of Terrestrial Ecosystems: Local Surprise and Global Change." In *Sustainable Development of the Biosphere*, edited by W. C. Clark and R. E. Munn. New York: Cambridge University Press, 1986.

Intergovernmental Panel on Climatic Change. *Climate Change 1995: The Science of Climate Change*, Contribution of Working Group I to the Second Assessment Report of the Intergovernmental Panel on Climate Change, edited by J. T. Houghton et al. Cambridge: Cambridge University Press, 1996.

Karl, T. R., and R. W. Knight. "Secular Trends of Precipitation Amount, Frequency, and Intensity in the U.S.A." *Bulletin of the American Meteorological Society* 79.2 (1998), 231–241.

Kasperson, R. E., et al. "The Social Amplification of Risk: A Conceptual Framework." *Risk Analysis* 8 (1988), 177–187.

Mearns, L. O., et al. "Extreme High Temperature Events: Changes in Their Probabilities and Changes in Mean Temperature." *Journal of Climate and Applied Meteorology* 23 (1984), 1601–1613.

Morgan, M. G., and M. Henrion. *Uncertainty: A Guide to Dealing with Uncertainty in Quantitative Risk and Policy Analysis.* New York: Cambridge University Press, 1990.

Morgan, M. G., and D. W. Keith. "Subjective Judgments by Climate Experts." *Environmental Science and Technology* 29 (1995), 468A–476A.

Moss, R. M., and S. H. Schneider. "Uncertainties in the IPCC TAR: Recommendations to Lead Authors for More Consistent Assessment and Reporting." *Pacific Asia Journal of Energy* (2000).

Nordhaus, W. D. "An Optimal Transition Path for Controlling Greenhouse Gases." *Science* 258 (1992), 1315–1319.

———. "Expert Opinion on Climatic Change." *American Scientist* 82 (January 1994), 45–52.

Raiffa, H. *Decision Analysis: Introductory Lectures on Choices under Uncertainty.* Reading, Mass: Addison-Wesley, 1968.

Ravetz, J. R. "Usable Knowledge, Usable Ignorance: Incomplete Science with Policy Implications." In *Sustainable Development of the Biosphere*, edited by W. C. Clark and R. E. Munn, pp. 415–432. New York: Cambridge University Press, 1986.

Root, T. L., and S. H. Schneider. "Can Large-Scale Climatic Models be Linked with Multi-Scale Ecological Studies?" *Conservation Biology* 7 (1993), 256–270.

Roughgarden, T., and S. H. Schneider. "Climate Change Policy: Quantifying Uncertainties for Damages and Optimal Carbon Taxes." *Energy Policy* 27.7 (1999), 415–429.

Schneider, S. H. *Laboratory Earth: The Planetary Gamble We Can't Afford to Lose.* New York: Basic Books, 1997a.

———. "Integrated Assessment Modeling of Global Climate Change: Transparent Rational Tool for Policy Making or Opaque Screen Hiding Value-Laden Assumptions?" *Environmental Modeling and Assessment* 2 (1997b), 229–248.

Schneider, S. H., et al. "Imaginable Surprise in Global Change Science." *Journal of Risk Research* 1 (1998), 165–185.

Wynne, B. "Uncertainty and Environmental Learning: Reconceiving Science and Policy in the Preventive Paradigm." *Global Environmental Change* (1992), 111–127.

—STEPHEN H. SCHNEIDER

SUSTAINABLE DEVELOPMENT

[*This entry consists of three articles that provide an analytical overview of the meaning of the sustainability concept and the practical implications of the adoption of such a notion as a policy objective for macroeconomic development strategies and sectoral planning and policies.*]

Principles
Practice
Commission on Sustainable Development

The first article explores the meaning and significance of the concept of sustainability and makes links to different development paths. The second article brings together the international and local actions and plans that have actually been generated via Agenda 21. The third article focuses on the roles of the United Nations Commission on Sustainable Development. For further discussion, see Agenda 21; *and* United Nations Conference on Environment and Development.]

Principles

The concept of sustainable development was popularly defined by the World Commission on Environment and

Development (WCED) as "development that meets the needs of the present without compromising the ability of future generations to meet their own needs" (World Commission on Environment and Development, 1987). In interpreting this definition, it is useful to recall that the WCED was appointed by the United Nations to address the perceived failures of development programs to (1) support robust economic growth in certain world regions, especially Latin America and sub-Saharan Africa; (2) alleviate pressing social ills such as famines, diseases caused by poor sanitation, and the widening gap between rich and poor; and (3) maintain critical natural resources such as species and ecosystems, energy resources, the stratospheric ozone layer, and climatic stability.

The WCED's emphasis on meeting the basic needs of the world's poor builds on an important literature in development economics that views the alleviation of poverty as a fundamental social objective. Although it is well known that market economies, under idealized conditions, support economic growth and the efficient allocation of productive resources, it is also recognized that the gains from trade associated with economic growth may be unevenly distributed among members of society. Economic growth, in fact, can exacerbate existing inequalities in the absence of institutional reforms that ensure that all social groups (and especially the poorest and most vulnerable) share in the benefits of development. In practical terms, the basic-needs approach employs multiple criteria in development planning so that conventional income accounts are supplemented by information on variables such as life expectancy, infant mortality, literacy, educational attainment, per capita food supply, and access to potable water. "Development" is then understood as a process that expands economic opportunity while making steady progress toward these social objectives. Although simple and appealing in principle, the basic-needs approach requires decision makers to make hard choices when trade-offs arise between alternative development indicators. In this sense, the effectiveness of this strategy is contingent on the legitimacy and competence of political institutions.

The WCED's emphasis on the sustainability of development has spawned a literature that is both more precise and, in certain respects, more contentious than the basic-needs approach. The WCED definition suggests that the aims of sustainable development are anthropocentric and fundamentally focused on the question of intergenerational fairness. The goal is to ensure that today's development programs do not diminish either the perceived utility or well-being of future generations in comparison with the present, or future generations' opportunity to enjoy the benefits of manufactured capital, technological capacity, social institutions, and natural resources and environmental quality.

Before evaluating the merits of these competing interpretations, it is important to note that the idea that present society holds moral duties toward future generations is itself controversial. A well-known philosophical argument, for example, proceeds from the premises that (1) future generations consist of hypothetical (unborn) persons whose identities and very existence are contingent on present actions and behavior; and (2) moral duties arise only with respect to actual (that is, living) persons. In this view, the concept of intergenerational fairness is logically suspect. Contributors to the sustainability literature have answered this objection by pointing out that principles of equal opportunity between contemporaries may be extended naturally to entail principles of just distribution between each generation and its living offspring. Extending this argument forward through time, a moral concern for the distant future is mediated by a sequence of well-defined moral obligations. [See Ethics.]

How such duties should be interpreted and implemented, however, is once again controversial. Authors who focus on maintaining human utility or welfare—a position that is known as *weak sustainability*—argue that the depletion of natural resources is morally acceptable provided that offsetting investments are made in manufactured capital and new technologies so that aggregate living standards are maintained over time. Natural resource economists, for example, have constructed theoretical models in which human welfare is maintained provided that a corrected measure of aggregate economic activity is constant or increasing. The relevant measure of sustainable income subtracts the monetary value of natural-resource depletion and environmental degradation from a conventional measure of net national product. This theoretical result has spawned an interesting literature on natural-resource accounting in nations where natural resources comprise a major component of economic activity.

There are, however, at least three reasons to doubt the general reliability and application of this approach. First, the relevant theoretical models typically assume that population and the state of technology are held constant over time—an unrealistic description of actual economic systems. While the approach can be generalized to adjust for changes in these variables, the resulting indicator of current sustainable income requires reliable forecasts of long-run demographic and technological trends. Questions of sustainability, in this context, cannot be resolved through appeals to mere observations of present economic data. A second difficulty concerns the task of establishing the true monetary value of natural resources and environmental services. Although progress has been made in environmental valuation, the fact remains that the valuation of

In the late 1990s, in various languages, an influential book appeared: *Factor Four: Doubling Wealth—Halving Resource Use* by Weizäcker, Lovins, and Lovins. The thesis of the book is that "If resource productivity were increased by a factor of four, the world could enjoy twice the wealth that is currently available, whilst simultaneously halving the stress placed on our natural environment." The authors aim to demonstrate that a quadrupling of resource productivity is not only technically feasible but would also produce macroeconomic gains, and make those countries engaging in the "efficiency revolution" internationally more competitive. The book provides fifty examples of means of quadrupling resource productivity in the areas of energy, materials, and transport.

BIBLIOGRAPHY

Weizäcker, E. von, A. B. Lovins, and L. H. Lovins. *Factor Four: Doubling Wealth—Halving Resource Use*. London: Earthscan, 1998.

—ANDREW S. GOUDIE

goods such as biodiversity, unique ecological systems, the ozone layer, and climatic stability involves core uncertainties over basic science, human preferences, and the relative weights attached to present and future economic benefits. Finally, the theoretical literature suggests that a constant or increasing level of "green national product" is a necessary, but not a sufficient, condition for achieving weak sustainability. Judging whether the aggregate productivity of economic systems can be sustained into the future is fundamentally a forecasting problem. Yet the behavior of long-run forecasting models depends critically on structural assumptions and empirical generalizations that are difficult to corroborate on scientific grounds.

In light of these difficulties, a number of authors have eschewed the strict focus on aggregate sustainability indicators in favor of strategies that employ multiple indicators that characterize alternative contributors to human well-being. Advocates of this approach, which is commonly known as *strong sustainability*, argue that maintaining the life opportunities or choice sets available to future generations requires the specific conservation of manufactured capital, technological capacity, social institutions, and especially what is termed *natural capital*—the constellation of natural resources and environmental systems that provides the material basis for economic activity and human welfare. This point of view, which is grounded in the long history of conservationist thought, adopts the position that future generations are ethically entitled to inherit undiminished stocks of natural resources and environmental quality. Accordingly, conservationist policies are interpreted as a matter of moral priority.

This perspective, if taken to the extreme, might serve as a major impediment to economic progress since it would lock up the resources required to foster increased economic activity. Critics point out, for example, that the expansion of agriculture and industrialization has involved the pervasive transformation of natural resources into alternative assets generating higher economic returns. Would human beings be better off, these skeptics ask, if previous generations had systematically conserved stock resources and natural ecosystems? Advocates of strong sustainability, however, have long recognized that natural-resource depletion, coupled with offsetting investments in manufactured capital and new technologies, might sometimes benefit both present and future generations in a sustainable manner. A standard example of this process is the potential transition from exhaustible fossil fuels to enhanced energy efficiency and renewable energy sources that may occur in the decades and centuries ahead, given the proper coordination of market incentives and public policies.

Proponents of strong sustainability, however, generally distrust claims that economic growth and technological innovation will necessarily relieve problems of resource depletion and environmental degradation. Instead, they place the burden of proof on those favoring resource exploitation to show that such actions in fact yield sustained economic benefits that do not involve the loss of unique—and potentially irreplaceable—natural systems. Where the costs and benefits necessary to make this case are poorly measured or undefined, as is arguably the case for biodiversity, climate stability, and other forms of "critical natural capital," then sustaining the stability and functioning of environmental systems is taken as the operational policy objective.

As the preceding paragraphs make clear, sustainable development involves the modification of traditional approaches to economic growth to (1) ensure that growth is employed instrumentally to achieve social equity and to alleviate the particular ills of poverty and destitution, (2) revise aggregate economic indicators to account for the negative impacts of economic activity on natural resources and environmental quality, and (3) maintain the stability and functioning of essential natural systems. Although controversies surround the relative importance of these modifications and their operational implications, this framework offers a synthetic approach to understanding the perceived conflicts between human development and global environmental change.

[*See also* Agriculture and Agricultural Land; Brundtland Commission; Carrying Capacity; Catastrophist–Cornucopian Debate; Commons; Economic Levels; Environmental Economics; Human Ecology; International Council for Science (ICSU); Policy Analysis; Precautionary Principle; Resources; Rio Declaration; *and the biography of Schumacher.*]

BIBLIOGRAPHY

Costanza, R. C. *Ecological Economics: The Science and Management of Sustainability.* New York: Columbia University Press, 1991. A selection of papers on sustainable development and ecological resource management.

Daly, H. E., and J. B. Cobb. *For the Common Good: Redirecting the Economy toward Community, the Environment, and a Sustainable Future.* Boston: Beacon Press, 1989. Argues for strong sustainability with a renewed focus on community.

Laslett, P., and J. S. Fishkin. *Justice between Age Groups and Generations.* New Haven: Yale University Press, 1992. An edited volume on the philosophical problem of intergenerational fairness.

Pearce, D. W., A. Markandya, and E. B. Barbier. *Blueprint for a Green Economy.* London: Earthscan, 1989. An influential text on the roles of weak and strong sustainability in project appraisal and development planning.

Pezzey, J. "Sustainability: An Interdisciplinary Guide." *Environmental Values* 1 (1992), 321–362. An excellent and comprehensive survey.

Redclift, M. *Sustainable Development: Exploring the Contradictions.* London: Methuen, 1987. Examines the social and institutional difficulties that arise in defining, and achieving, sustainable development.

Solow, R. M. "Sustainability: An Economist's Perspective." In *Economics of the Environment*, edited by R. Dorfman and N. S. Dorfman, pp. 179–187. New York: Norton, 1993. Discusses weak sustainability and its implementation through natural-resource accounting.

Streeten, P. *First Things First: Meeting Basic Human Needs in the Developing Countries.* New York: Oxford University Press, 1981. An in-depth assessment of the "basic-needs" approach to economic development.

Toman, M. A., J. Pezzey, and J. Krautkraemer. "Neoclassical Growth Theory and Sustainability." In *Handbook of Environmental Economics*, edited by D. W. Bromley, pp. 139–165. Oxford: Blackwell, 1995. Reviews the literature on economic models of sustainable development.

World Commission on Environment and Development. *Our Common Future.* Oxford: Oxford University Press, 1987.

—RICHARD B. HOWARTH

Practice

The parties to the United Nations Conference on Environment and Development (UNCED) in Rio de Janeiro in June 1992 adopted Agenda 21 as their plan for implementing sustainable development. [*See* Agenda 21.] At the same time, many parties to the conference adopted a biodiversity convention and a global climate change convention. It is also important to keep in mind that, before and since the Rio summit, the traditional vision of development as a process of transferring capital and expertise has steadily given way to a vision of development as a matter of competing effectively in the global economy. Agenda 21, the biodiversity and climate change conventions, and development as global competition entail three competing and contradictory frameworks in which the principles of sustainable development are gradually being transformed into the practice of sustainable development.

The general principles of sustainable development have translated into the following conceptual shifts that underlie new practical rules. While some see the environment as having limits beyond which we cannot push it, and others see environmental systems as complex and unpredictable, both groups agree on the "precautionary principle." [*See* Precautionary Principle.] The historical presumption has been that new technologies will arise, autonomously with the march of progress, and provide for future generations, offsetting any excessive resource consumption and environmental transformation committed by current people. The precautionary principle reverses the presumption and puts the burden on current peoples not to increase our level of resource use and environmental transformation except in cases where we are quite confident that technological solutions are in hand. The "polluter-pays" principle acknowledges that the economy can be directed more effectively toward sustainability if the producers and consumers of goods associated with pollution are given incentives not to produce and consume the good. With the increasing recognition that sustainability is a matter of assuring that future generations have adequate access to resources and environmental services, there is increasing interest both in bolstering the institutions that have historically served to assure the rights of future generations and in the design of new institutions. To a considerable extent, the practice of sustainable development has entailed increased efforts to measure the importance of resources and environmental services and to include their depletion in estimates of gross domestic product. Such information complements our ability to exercise the precautionary principle and the polluter-pays principle to assure that future generations have an equitable share of natural assets. This transition in economic thinking characterizes the new field of ecological economics (Costanza et al., 1997).

The principles of sustainable development also support other practical transitions. Agroecology, the idea that agricultural practices on the farm and agricultural planning and policy must be guided by ecological principles, is gaining adherents. Ecological engineering is the application of ecological principles to land transformation. Industrial ecology and life-cycle assessment are transforming how we think about industry and industrial products. These, along with ecological economics, are the new professions of sustainability.

The practice of sustainable development, however, has varied considerably within and between the conflicting global regimes in which development takes place. Agenda 21 was drafted through a highly participatory process with proportionate representation from developing countries. It builds on, yet transforms, the traditional understanding of development as a process of planning and transferring capital and expertise from the developed to the developing countries. It sets initial development and conservation priorities; establishes that people in the developing countries should share in the process of refining the goals; argues that all efforts need to be coordinated across governments, agencies, and economic sectors; and suggests methods for encouraging and facilitating such joint planning and coordination (United Nations, 1993). The document is wildly ambitious in that it clearly establishes a new ideal for the practice of development and conservation. The coordinated, cooperative approach acknowledges that developing countries and local peoples, even indigenous and tribal peoples, must participate in goal setting, share in the design, and assume more responsibility for the implementation of sustainable development. By addressing global problems specifically, the relative contributions of the developed and developing countries to pollution are made explicit and appropriate responsibilities are identified. Even while Agenda 21 builds on the traditional vision of development as a net transfer of capital and expertise from the developed countries to the developing countries, the processes identified in Agenda 21 stand in stark contrast to the top-down, developed-nations-know-best, technocratic approaches of the development institutions that were established following the Bretton Woods Conference in 1944.

As envisioned in Agenda 21, sustainable development entails identifying critical areas and styles of development that will benefit both the poorest among current generations and future generations overall. Win-win solutions seem to include activities such as improvement of water quality to benefit current people's health, and the maintenance of aquifer quality and biodiversity for future generations. Similarly, increasing energy efficiency can make energy more readily available to the

poor and reduce the rate of carbon dioxide emissions that threaten future generations with climate change. By using indigenous agricultural knowledge under appropriate circumstances, local peoples would become empowered and the use of costly, polluting industrial inputs in agriculture could be reduced. Since participation is identified as a critical new component of sustainable development and neither poor people nor poor nations have the political power, financial resources, or sufficient technical training, Agenda 21 invokes the need for significant transfers of power and reinvokes the traditional objectives of transferring capital and knowledge from rich to poor.

Adoption of the practice of sustainable development as outlined in Agenda 21 has been a slow process of change among established institutions; political empowerment of people in developing countries; conceptual development among academics, policy analysts, and practitioners; and technological innovation. These processes need to go on at all levels and interlock with each other. On the one hand, there is some modest evidence of a transition with respect to both North–South sharing in the process of development and the integration across disciplines of knowledge and sectors of the economy. On the other hand, the ideals set out in Agenda 21 have produced considerably more interaction than action, but perhaps fewer mistakes are being made.

The biodiversity and climate change conventions adopted at Rio have been science-driven. Scientists, initially almost entirely from the developed countries, have undertaken the research that has established that biodiversity loss and climate change are serious environmental problems that threaten development globally. The scientists organized, incorporated colleagues from developing countries, linked with the UN process, and orchestrated an effective public education program. While both the biodiversity and climate change initiatives are now actively engaged in the UN process and with governments of developing countries, it is good science that is held up as the authority in both initiatives (Lélé and Norgaard, 1996). Sustainability, in practice, has largely consisted of negotiating international rules and national responses that meet biodiversity and climate change imperatives. North–South equity, not having been built in from the beginning as in Agenda 21, has been the major difficulty in reaching agreement.

Sustainable development needs to be built into international trade. Development theorists determined in the 1980s that the developing countries that were export-oriented were doing noticeably better than others. This finding was extrapolated to a principle for all countries as a whole in conjunction with a rise in neoliberal economic thinking. The World Bank, in cooperation with the International Monetary Fund, began to provide loans on the condition that the developing country re-

ELEMENTS OF SUSTAINABLE DEVELOPMENT

The concept of sustainable development can seem rather diffuse because it is not readily translated into concrete guidelines acceptable to all constituencies. The report *World Conservation Strategy* (International Union for Conservation of Nature and Natural Resources [IUCN], 1980) did identify three clear objectives, however (see Adams, 1996, pp. 360–361):

1. Maintenance of "essential ecological processes . . . essential for food production, health and other aspects of human survival." These life support systems include agricultural land and soil, forests, and coastal and freshwater ecosystems. Threats include soil erosion, insect resistance to pesticides, deforestation and associated sedimentation, and aquatic and littoral pollution.
2. Preservation of genetic diversity in crops, livestock, and wild species—as insurance against crop diseases and as an investment for the future that will ensure the possibility of crop breeding and production of pharmaceuticals.
3. Sustainable development of species and ecosystems, particularly fisheries, forests and timber resources, and grazing land.

Our Common Future (Brundtland, 1987) augments those objectives by the need to restrict population to a sustainable level, and to reorient technology to attain certain goals. It also stipulates meeting basic needs of populations, and the necessity of building environmental factors into decision-making. Economic growth is seen as the only way to tackle poverty: it must, however, be a new kind of growth: sustainable, environmentally aware, egalitarian, and integrating economic and social development (Adams, 1996, p. 361).

At the United Nations Conference in Rio de Janeiro in 1992, industrialized countries identified global atmospheric change and tropical deforestation as key problems, while developing countries saw poverty and associated problems as pivotal. [*See* Environmental Economics.] Despite this conflict, the state of the global atmosphere—not highlighted in the two afore-mentioned documents—was added to the list of concerns.

To illustrate sustainable development, it is possible to identify a number of specific actions or strategies congruent with the goals of sustainable development in both developing and industrial nations. The following examples emerge from selected environmental and social issues that are prominent today.

- Implement the polluter-pays principle by adding to the costs of goods the value of environmental impacts. [*See* Environmental Accounting.]
- Augment national accounts, for instance, the traditional gross national product, to better reflect environmental and social impacts stimulated by the growth process.
- Continue to phase out subsidies that promote the overexploitation and inefficient use of forests and other raw materials.
- Encourage low-impact agriculture that reduces the use of chemical fertilizers, insecticides, and pesticides, and emphasizes organic fertilizers and biological pest control.

structure its economy to be more open to imports and competitively able to export. The North American Free Trade Agreement (NAFTA) expanded opportunities for capital movement, as did the Uruguay Round of the General Agreement on Tariffs and Trade (GATT). While sustainability is accepted as an objective of those advocating development through global competition, there has been much less serious discussion as to how sus-

tainability will be achieved within this vision (Runge, 1993; Andersson et al., 1995). At best, whether or not existing national environmental laws are constraints on trade will be adjudicated by the World Trade Organization established under GATT. Indeed, many sense that environmental protection even for today's people, let alone future generations, will be sacrificed in a "race to the bottom" as each nation strives to maintain its share

- Incorporate conservation tillage and no-till farming in order to reduce soil erosion.
- Plan energy growth in developing areas in terms of a balanced portfolio of energy sources, including the region's natural endowment of solar or wind potential.
- Direct international financial institutions to give more emphasis to investments in renewable energy technology and alternative fuels, rather than fossil fuel projects. [See Renewable Energy Sources.]
- Refine energy technologies that displace the combustion of fossil fuels; and assist developing nations to adopt the best available technologies as they continue to industrialize. [See Energy; and Technology.]
- As industries move to developing countries, employ the ideas of industrial ecology to reduce waste and conserve energy; continue to foster ecological efficiency in developed country industries. [See Industrial Ecology.]
- Especially in developing nations, improve the education of women so they can adopt roles as technicians, health professionals, entrepreneurs, and can choose to have smaller families.
- Undertake regional (supranational) planning of surface and groundwater resources and increase efficiency of irrigation systems.
- Help developing nations improve public transit and reduce dependence on automobiles in urban areas. [See Transportation.]
- Give priority to revitalizing villages in developing nations by installing renewable energy systems and internet connections to the global economy.

INTERNET RESOURCES

The International Institute for Sustainable Development (Canadian and Manitoba governments): http://www.iisd1.iisd.ca.
British Government Panel on Sustainable Development: http://www.open.gov.uk.
Organisation for Economic Co-operation and Development: http://www.oecd.org.
Worldwide Web Virtual Library: http://www.ulb.ac.be/ceese/meta/sustvl.

BIBLIOGRAPHY

Adams, W. M. "Sustainable Development?" In *Geographies of Global Change*, edited by R. J. Johnston, P. J. Taylor, and M. J. Watts. Oxford: Blackwell, 1996.
Brundtland, H. *Our Common Future: World Commission on Environment and Development.* Oxford: Oxford University Press, 1987.
International Union for Conservation of Nature and Natural Resources (IUCN). *World Conservation Strategy: Living Resource Conservation for Sustainable Development.* Gland: IUCN, 1980.

—DAVID J. CUFF

of global trade (Mander and Goldsmith, 1996). Thus the new development regime may be a threat to the possibility of sustainable development.

The three regimes have not replaced traditional development approaches, nor are the regimes independent of each other. The World Bank, for example, within the earlier development regime has adopted fully the goal of sustainability, has established an environment department, and has environment units within each of its operations branches. [See World Bank, The.] It cooperates with the objectives established in Agenda 21 through loans, for example, for improving the quality of drinking-water supplies, and improving energy efficiency. The Bank is also an active participant in ame-

liorating climate change and establishing reserves for biodiversity conservation. Such loans amounted to 8 percent of Bank lending between 1993 and 1996 (World Bank, 1996). In addition, the Global Environmental Facility (GEF) has been established to work in cooperation with the World Bank and United Nations agencies to fund projects whose environmental benefits extend beyond national boundaries. [See Global Environment Facility.] The World Bank, albeit only very gradually, has been employing people who can work across the fields of economics and ecology or bridge the technocratic analyses undertaken by experts in Washington, D.C. with participatory research and planning methods facilitated among the local people affected by a development project. At the same time, the Bank and similar established institutions have taken the lead in developing techniques for evaluating environmental and social options and forging integrative conceptual frameworks. Their expertise in environmental assessment and valuation, for example, once again establishes their technocratic, top-down authority, although now to promote sustainable development in an integrated manner. Equally importantly, however, as sustainability becomes a new priority, more and more of the Bank's loans are tied to whether the developing country agrees to restructure its economy so as to be more competitive in the global market. Similarly, the private capital transfers from industrial countries that once complemented the Bank's projects have switched to supporting investments in agriculture and industry directed at export markets.

[See also Agriculture and Agricultural Land; Brundtland Commission; Catastrophist–Cornucopian Debate; Carrying Capacity; Commons; Economic Levels; Environmental Economics; Ethics; Human Ecology; Policy Analysis; Resources; Rio Declaration; and the biography of Schumacher.]

BIBLIOGRAPHY

Andersson, T., C. Folke, and S. Nyström. Trading with the Environment: Ecology, Economics, Institutions and Policy. London: Earthscan, 1995.

Costanza, R., J. Cumberland, H. Daly, R. Goodland, and R. B. Norgaard. An Introduction to Ecological Economics. Boca Raton, Fla.: St. Lucie Press, 1997.

Lélé, S., and R. B. Norgaard. "Sustainability and the Scientist's Burden." Conservation Biology 10.2 (1996), 354–365.

Mander, J., and E. Goldsmith, eds. The Case Against the Global Economy. San Francisco: Sierra Club Books, 1995.

Runge, C. Ford, with F. Ortalo-Magné and P. Vande Kamp. Freer Trade, Protected Environment: Balancing Trade Liberalization and Environmental Interests. New York: Council on Foreign Relations, 1994.

United Nations. The Global Partnership for Environment and Development: A Guide to Agenda 21, Post Rio Edition. New York: United Nations, 1993.

United Nations Environment Programme. Global Environmental Outlook. New York and Oxford: Oxford University Press, 1997.

World Bank. Environment Matters at the World Bank: Annual Review. Washington, D.C.: World Bank, 1996.

—RICHARD B. NORGAARD

Commission on Sustainable Development

The United Nations Commission on Sustainable Development (CSD) was established in 1993, upon recommendation of the 1992 United Nations Conference on Environment and Development (UNCED) and UN General Assembly resolution 47/191. [See United Nations; and United Nations Conference on Environment and Development.] The role of the Commission is threefold:

to ensure effective follow-up of UNCED; to enhance international cooperation and rationalize intergovernmental decision-making capacity; and to examine progress in the implementation of Agenda 21 at the local, national, regional, and international levels. The CSD is a functional commission of the UN Economic and Social Council (ECOSOC), with 53 member states serving three-year terms. [See Agenda 21.] Other states, UN organizations, and accredited intergovernmental and nongovernmental organizations participate as observers.

The Commission meets once a year for two weeks at UN Headquarters in New York. The Commission held its first substantive session in New York from 14 to 25 June 1993, where it adopted a three-year thematic program of work to review implementation of each chapter of Agenda 21, culminating with an overall assessment in 1997.

As the CSD reviewed implementation of Agenda 21, it also created new methods to enhance the quality of its work. In 1994 the Commission initiated panel discussions on such topics as women in sustainable development and the role of the media. At its 1995 session, the Commission began holding dialogue sessions on how countries were implementing specific chapters of Agenda 21 and the establishment of National Commissions on Sustainable Development. In 1996, the CSD completed its multiyear review of Agenda 21 and began to assess its own current and future role.

In 1997, under the leadership of Egypt's Mostafa Tolba, the CSD prepared a comprehensive document to be adopted by the Nineteenth Special Session of the United Nations General Assembly to Review the Implementation of Agenda 21 in June 1997. Governments agreed that since adoption of Agenda 21 in 1992, some progress had been made in terms of institutional development, international consensus building, public participation, and private sector actions. As a result, some countries have succeeded in accelerating economic growth, reducing the incidence of poverty, curbing pollution, and slowing the rate of resource degradation. Overall, however, the CSD review concluded that the global environment continued to deteriorate and the commitments in the UNCED agreements had not been fully implemented. Among the decisions adopted at the Special Session was a new five-year CSD work program, which identified sectoral, cross-sectoral, and economic sector/major group themes for the subsequent four sessions of the CSD. Overriding issues for each year were poverty, and consumption and production patterns.

The sixth session of the CSD met from 20 April to 1 May 1998. Participants considered the economic theme of industry and the sectoral theme of strategic approaches to freshwater management. They also reviewed implementation of the Programme of Action for the Sustainable Development of Small Island Developing States and discussed the cross-sectoral themes of technology transfer, capacity building, education, science and awareness raising.

The seventh session of the CSD met during 19–30 April 1999. Participants considered the economic theme of tourism, the sectoral theme of oceans and seas, and the cross-sectoral theme of consumption and production patterns. They also prepared for the UN General Assembly's Special Session to review the Barbados Programme of Action for the Sustainable Development of Small Island Developing States. Delegates highlighted several aspects of their decision on oceans and seas, particularly a decision recommending that the General Assembly establish an open-ended informal consultative process as a means to broaden its consideration of oceans and seas issues. Other decisions addressed the need to reverse the downward trend in official development assistance (ODA), preparation for CSD-9's work on energy, and improving the integration of consumption and production policies into the CSD's work program.

The eighth session of the CSD met from 24 April to 5 May 2000. Participants considered the sectoral theme of integrated planning and management of land resources, and the cross-sectoral themes of financial resources, trade and investment, and economic growth. The session also considered the economic sector of sustainable agriculture and land management, as well as the final report of the Intergovernmental Forum on Forests.

The CSD has had several notable achievements in its first eight years. Unlike most ECOSOC commissions, the CSD has consistently generated a high level of public interest. Over fifty ministers attend the CSD each year and more than one thousand nongovernmental organizations (NGOs) are accredited to participate in the CSD's work. The CSD also keeps sustainable development issues alive within the UN system and has helped to improve the United Nations' coordination of environment and development activities. The CSD furthermore encourages governments and international organizations to host workshops and conferences on different environmental and cross-sectoral issues. The results of these expert-level meetings enhance the CSD's work and help promote sustainable development worldwide.

BIBLIOGRAPHY

Bigg, T., and F. Dodds. "The UN Commission on Sustainable Development." In *The Way Forward: Beyond Agenda 21*, edited by F. Dodd, pp. 15–36. London: Earthscan, 1997. A concise review of the history of the CSD.

Carpenter, C., et al. "Summary of the Fifth Session of the Commission on Sustainable Development: 8–25 April 1997." *Earth Negotiations Bulletin* 5.82 (28 April 1997). http://www.mbnet. mb.ca/linkages/vol05/0582000e.html/. Summarizes both the history of the CSD and the proceedings of the fifth session.

———. "Summary of the Nineteenth United Nations General Assembly Special Session to Review Implementation of Agenda 21: 23–27 June 1997." *Earth Negotiations Bulletin* 5.88 (30 June 1997). http://www.mbnet.mb.ca/linkages/vol05/0588000e.html. Contains information on the work of the CSD and its future priorities.

United Nations. *Agenda 21*. New York: United Nations, 1992. Contains Chapter 38, which sets out the recommendation for the establishment of the CSD.

United Nations Department for Policy Coordination and Sustainable Development World Wide Web Site. http://www.un.org/dpcsd. Contains background information and current information on the work of the CSD.

United Nations General Assembly. "Institutional Arrangements to Follow Up the United Nations Conference on Environment and Development (Resolution 47/191)." 22 December 1992. gopher://gopher.un.org:70/00/esc/cn17/enable/a47r191. Resolution establishing the CSD.

—Pamela S. Chasek

SWAMPS. *See* Wetlands.

SYSTEM DYNAMICS

A dynamical system is a system whose evolution from some initial state can be described by a set of rules. These rules may be conveniently expressed as mathematical equations. Such a system is best described by the so-called phase space or state space, which is a coordinate system whose coordinates are the variables that are needed to describe completely the evolution of the dynamical system. Consider a pendulum that is allowed to swing back and forth from some initial state, as shown in Figure 1. The coordinates of the corresponding phase space are x_1 and x_2, where x_1 stands for the position and x_2 stands for the velocity. The position x_1 is measured by the angle of the pendulum from the vertical. For the system there exist two equilibrium states, $\bar{x}_1 = 0, \bar{x}_2 = 0$ and $\bar{x}_1 = \pi, \bar{x}_2 = 0$. The first one is a stable equilibrium state and the second is unstable. Starting the motion of the pendulum from some initial condition $x_1(0), x_2(0)$, the mathematical possibilities are that the system may be either (1) "attracted" by the stable equilibrium state, (2) repelled by the unstable equilibrium state, or (3) engaged in a never-ending motion around the stable equilibrium state. From all those possibilities in the real world, only the first possibility is observed. We may take a system to any initial state close or far from the equilibrium state(s), but, because of friction, after some time the system settles down to the equilibrium state that is observable (in our example, the fixed point $\bar{x}_1 = 0, \bar{x}_2 = 0$). If we remove friction, the pendulum undergoes an endless periodic motion, with the period defined by the initial condition. The settling-in part of the evolution (or the transient) is modeled by

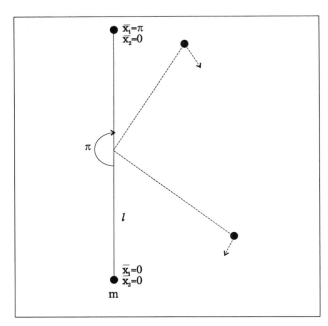

System Dynamics. Figure 1. Equilibrium States of a Pendulum of Mass *m* and Length *l*.

a trajectory in the phase space. A phase portrait is a graph depicting the evolution of the system from different initial conditions. The final state or the equilibrium state is described by the limit sets.

By definition, a limit set that collects trajectories is called an *attractor*. In our pendulum example, the attractor is the fixed point with coordinates $\bar{x}_1 = 0$, $\bar{x}_2 = 0$. It goes without saying that without friction the pendulum is simply a conservative system, whose motion is undisturbed and no energy is required to be spent. When friction is introduced, energy must be spent to overcome its opposition. Thus, the kinetic energy is gradually spent and eventually the pendulum will stop at the stable equilibrium point. The pendulum with friction is known as a *dissipative* system. The point to be made here is that conservative (nondissipative) systems never settle to an equilibrium state and, therefore, do not exhibit attractors.

Points, however, are not the only limit sets. A cycle may also be a limit set for a trajectory. An example of such an attractor can be given by the swinging pendulum of the grandfather clock, where the effect of friction is compensated via a mainspring. We may disturb the regular periodic motion of the pendulum, but soon it will assume its regular periodic motion whose frequency is dictated by the specification of the mainspring. Another familiar system that exhibits a limit cycle (periodic) final state is the human heart. The heartbeat is regular and periodic. We may disturb this cycle or we may take the "system" to various initial con-

ditions (due to panic, joy, exercise, etc.) but, soon after the "disturbance," the beat assumes its regular cycle. Such periodic motions should not be confused with periodic motions, like those of the frictionless pendulum, which are not associated with attractors.

The next simplest form of attractor is the torus. The torus looks like the surface of a doughnut. In this case, all trajectories in state space are attracted to and remain on the surface. Systems that possess a torus as an attractor are quasi-periodic. In a quasi-periodic evolution, a periodic motion is modulated by a second motion, itself periodic, but with another frequency. An example is the atmospheric temperature, with one frequency of $2\pi/24$ hours and another of $2\pi/365$ days. Geometrically, a quasi-periodic trajectory fills the surface of a torus in the appropriate state space. An important characteristic of such an attractor is that when the two frequencies have no common divisor, any two trajectories that represent the evolution of the system from different initial conditions and are close to each other when they approach the attracting surface will remain close to each other forever. This characteristic can be interpreted as follows. The two points in the state space where the trajectories enter the attractor can be two measurements (initial states), which differ by some amount. Since these trajectories remain close to each other, the states of the system at a later time are going to differ to the same extent that they differed initially. Thus, if we know the evolution of such a system from an initial condition, we can predict accurately the evolution of the system from some other initial condition. In this case (as in the case of point attractors and limit cycles), long-term predictability is guaranteed.

The above-mentioned forms of attractors are "well behaved" and usually correspond to systems whose evolution is predictable. In mathematical terms, these attractors are smooth topological submanifolds of the available state space. These attractors are therefore characterized by an integer dimension that is equal to the topological dimension of the submanifold in the state space. A very important characteristic of these attractors is that the long-term evolution of the systems they describe is not sensitive to initial conditions (resulting in long-term predictability).

When one observes the spectra of turbulent motion, one realizes that there is motion at all frequencies, with no strongly preferred frequencies. This broadband structure of the spectrum indicates that the motion is nonperiodic. Could such a nonperiodic motion be due to a simple dynamical system? Let us assume that the answer to this question is yes. In such a case the trajectory in the state space would be nonperiodic (would never repeat itself) and would never cross itself (since, once a system returns to a state it was in at some time in the past, it then has to follow the same path). Thus the trajectory should be of infinite length but confined to a finite area in the state space. This can only be the case if the attractor is not a topological manifold but rather is a fractal set (see Figure 2). Fractals are sets that are not topological. For sets that are topological, the Hausdorff–Besicovitch dimension is an integer (0 for points, 1 for any curve, 2 for any surface, etc.). For sets that are fractal, the Hausdorff–Besicovitch dimension is not an integer but a real number. Because of this, fractal sets have properties that topological manifolds do not have. The Cantor set (Figure 2A) begins with a line of length 1, then the middle third is removed, and so on. The Cantor set or Cantor "dust" is the number of points that remain. The length of all intervals removed is $1/3 + 2(1/3)^2 + 4(1/3)^3 + 8(1/3)^4 + \ldots = 1$. Thus, the length remaining must be zero. Hence in the Cantor set the number of points is obviously infinite but their total length is zero. The Hausdorff–Besicovitch dimension of this set is 0.6309. It is definitely greater than the topological dimension of a "dust" of points, which is zero. The Koch curve (Figure 2B) begins with an equilateral triangle with sides of length 1; then at the middle of each side a new equilateral triangle with sides of length one-third is added; and so on. The length of the constructed boundary is $3 \times 4/3 \times 4/3 \times 4/3 \ldots = \infty$. However, that boundary occupies no area at all and it encloses a finite area that is less than the area of a circle drawn around the original triangle. The Hausdorff–Besicovitch dimension of the Koch curve is 1.2618 (higher than the topological dimension of any curve that is equal to one). Often the Hausdorff–Besicovitch dimension is referred to as the fractal dimension. Extensions of the above to higher dimensions should be obvious. Such mathematical curiosities, abstract as they seem, have now found a place in the study of dynamical systems.

The first such system to be described was discovered in 1963 by Edward Lorenz (Lorenz, 1963). This system, described by the following differential equations, gives an approximate description of a horizontal fluid layer heated from below:

$$dx/dt = -ax + ay$$
$$dy/dt = -xz + bx - y$$
$$dz/dt = xy - cz,$$

where x is proportional to the intensity of the convective motion, y is proportional to the horizontal temperature variation, z is proportional to the vertical temperature variation, and a, b, and c are constants. The fluid at the bottom gets warmer and rises, creating convection. For a choice of the constants that correspond to sufficient heating, the convection may take place in an irregular and turbulent manner. Figure 3A depicts the path of a trajectory in the state space (x, y, z). The Lorenz attractor itself does not look like the well-

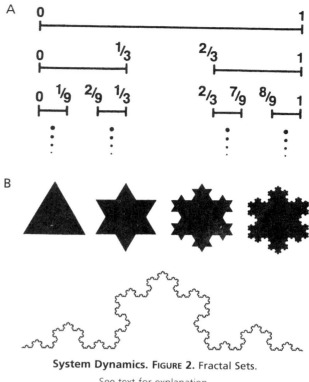

System Dynamics. FIGURE 2. Fractal Sets. See text for explanation.

behaved attractors described previously. The trajectory is deterministic (since it is the result of the solution of the above system of equations), but is strictly nonperiodic. The trajectory loops to the left and then to the right irregularly. Extensive studies have shown that the fine structure of the Lorenz attractor is made up of infinitely nested layers (infinite area) that occupy zero volume. One may think of it as a Cantor-like set in higher dimension. Its fractal (Hausdorff–Besicovitch) dimension has been estimated to be about 2.06 (see, for example, Grassberger and Procaccia, 1983a).

The fractal nature of an attractor does not only imply nonperiodic orbits. It also causes nearby trajectories to diverge. As with all attractors, trajectories that are initiated from different initial conditions soon reach the attracting submanifold, but two nearby trajectories do not stay close to each other (as was the case with the torus). They soon diverge and follow totally different paths in the attractor. This divergence is best described by the Lyapunov exponents, which are related to the average rates of convergence and/or divergence of nearby trajectories in phase space and, therefore, measure how predictable or unpredictable the system is. The idea behind Lyapunov exponents is introduced in Figure 4. In this figure we assume that the phase space is three-dimensional (however, generalization can be made for higher-dimensional phase spaces). Let us start

A.

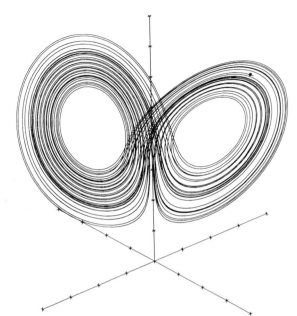

B.

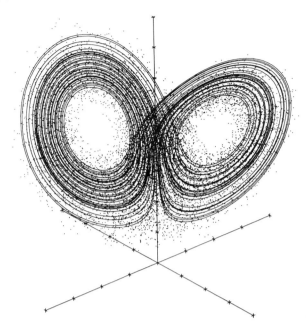

System Dynamics. FIGURE 3. (A) Example of a Strange Attractor with Implications in the Weather Forecasting Problem.

This structure in the state space represents the attractor of a fluid flow that travels over heated surfaces. (B) The effect of the divergence of initially nearby trajectories in the attractor: the dot in (A)

represents ten thousand measurements (initial conditions) that are so very close to each other that they are practically indistinguishable. If we allow each of these states to evolve according to the rules, because their trajectories diverge irregularly, after a while their states can be practically anywhere. (Figure courtesy of Dr. James Crutchfield.)

on the left column with a three-dimensional volume of initial conditions (A). If this volume, as it evolves, contracts in only one direction, we end up with a two-dimensional plane (B). Hence we say that the rate of divergence of nearby trajectories is zero along two directions and negative along the third (since the volume contracts). The spectrum of the Lyapunov exponents in this case is therefore $(0, 0, -)$. If we now move across the figure, we may construct from that plane something like a torus. Since we do not disconnect what was connected (such as making a cut or a hole), nor connect what was not (such as joining the ends of the previously unjoined string or filling in the hole), we say that the plane and the torus are topologically equivalent. Thus, systems that have a torus as their attractor exhibit the same Lyapunov exponent spectrum $(0, 0, -)$. If we now squeeze the two-dimensional plane along one direction, we end up with a one-dimensional line (C). Thus, when we go from a three-dimensional cube to a one-dimensional line, the rate of divergence of nearby trajectories is zero along only one direction, while it is negative along the other two directions. From a straight-line segment we can easily produce a circle. The circle and the straight line are topologically equivalent, so sys-

tems that exhibit a limit cycle as their attractor exhibit a $(0, -, -)$ Lyapunov exponent spectrum. If we now proceed by squeezing together the two ends of the straight-line segment, we end up with a point. During a process in which the initial cube of initial conditions contracts to a point, we have negative divergence along all directions, so systems that possess point attractors exhibit a Lyapunov exponent spectrum $(-, -, -)$.

For chaotic dynamics, the underlying attractor is not a topological manifold. Since we have divergence of nearby trajectories, in this case the Lyapunov exponent spectrum is $(+, 0, -)$. This divergence means that the evolution of the system from two slightly different initial conditions will be completely different, as may be seen in Figures 3A and 3B. The dot in Figure 3A represents ten thousand initial situations that differ only slightly from each other. If we allow these initial conditions to evolve according to the rules (equations) that describe the system, we see (Figure 3B) that after some time the ten thousand dots can be anywhere in the attractor. In other words, the state of the system after some time can be anything, despite the fact that the initial conditions were very close to each other. Apparently, the evolution of the system is very sensitive to

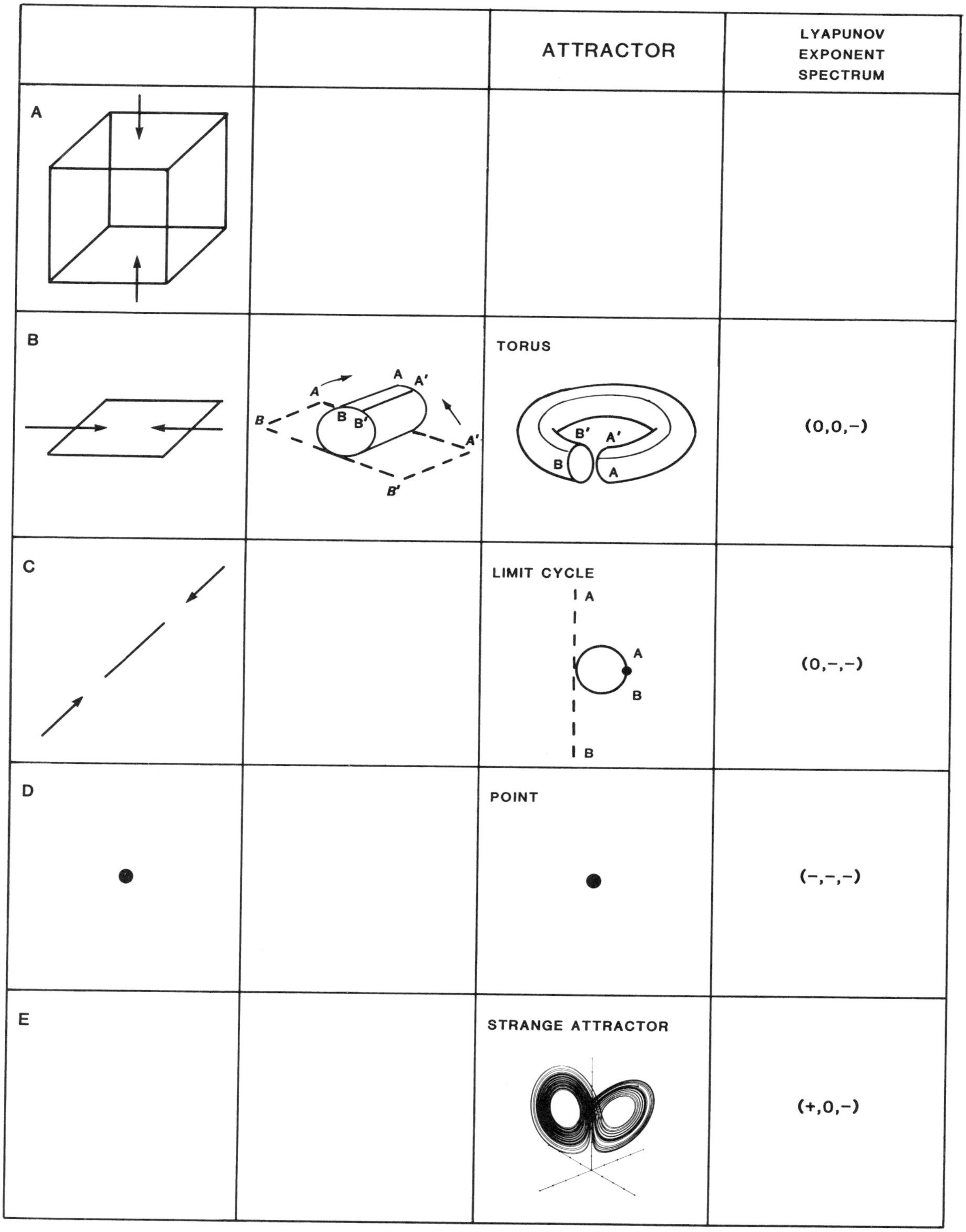

		ATTRACTOR	LYAPUNOV EXPONENT SPECTRUM
A			
B		TORUS	(0,0,−)
C		LIMIT CYCLE	(0,−,−)
D		POINT	(−,−,−)
E		STRANGE ATTRACTOR	(+,0,−)

System Dynamics. FIGURE 4. An Introduction to Lyapunov Exponents. See text for explanation.

initial conditions. In this case we say that the system has generated randomness. We can now see that there exist systems that, even though they can be described by simple deterministic rules, can generate randomness. Randomness generated in this way has been termed *chaos*. These systems are called chaotic dynamical systems, and their attractors are often called *strange* or *chaotic* attractors.

The Lorenz system discussed above is a system of ordinary differential equations. No external forcing is applied to the system. The actual climate system is, however, a forced system. The major climatic forces are external astronomical forces that dictate the amount of solar radiation reaching the planet. It is very well known that long-term climate fluctuations respond to these forces as climate oscillates between two stable states (today's climate and the ice ages). There are many mathematical systems describing nonlinear forced oscillators that exhibit chaotic dynamics. Such simple systems have been used in the past to study qualitative aspects of climate dynamics (Nicolis, 1987; Tsonis and Elsner, 1990). A simple model describing a system with two stable equilibria is the motion of a mass (m) in a (climatic) potential field exhibiting two minima. A suitable total potential energy function is

$$V = -0.5ax^2 + 0.25bx^4,$$

with a, $b > 0$. The corresponding force is

$$dV/dx = -ax + bx^3$$

with equilibria (zero force) at $x = 0$ and $x = \pm(a/b)^{1/2}$. The corresponding damped oscillator is then described by the equation

$$m\,\ddot{x} + k\,\dot{x} - ax + bx^3 = 0.$$

Extension of the above to climate may result in a model for long-term climate oscillations described by the following equation:

$$\ddot{x} + k\,\dot{x} + \alpha(x^3 - x) = f\cos\omega t$$

where x is a variable directly affected by climatic changes (for example, global temperature or ice sheet extent), k indicates the damping, f is the amplitude of the external forcing, ω is the angular frequency of the forcing, and $\alpha(x^3 - x)$ is the nonlinear restoring force. Physically, the damping is related to the tendency of the system to react to changes dictated by the restoring force and by some external force (which may be thought of in this sense as some astronomical forcing). It can easily be shown that a system like this can, for a suitable choice of the parameters, exhibit chaotic dynamics and strange attractors.

The implications of this finding are profound. If one knows the initial conditions exactly, one can follow the trajectory that corresponds to the evolution of the system from those initial conditions and basically predict the evolution forever. The problem, however, is that we cannot have perfect knowledge of initial conditions. Our instruments can only measure approximately the various parameters (temperature, pressure, etc.) that will be used as initial conditions. There will always be some deviation of the measured from the actual initial conditions. They may be very close to each other, but they will not be the same. In such a case, even if we know completely the physical laws that govern our system, because of the chaotic nature of the underlying attractor, initial errors are amplified and prediction is therefore limited.

One very important consequence of knowing the Hausdorff–Besicovitch dimensionality of an attractor, whether fractal or not, is that it indicates the minimum number of variables present in the evolution of the corresponding dynamical system (in other words, the attractor must be embedded in a state space of at least its dimension). The determination of the Hausdorff–Besicovitch dimension (or for that matter of any other generalized dimension) of an attractor therefore sets a number of constraints that should be satisfied by a model used to predict the evolution of a system. If the mathematical description of a dynamical system is given, the number of variables and thus the complete state vector $\boldsymbol{X}(t)$ is known and the generation of the state space and of the attractor is straightforward. If the mathematical formulation of a system is not available, the phase space may be produced using a single record of some observable variable $x(t)$ from that system (Packard et al., 1980; Ruelle, 1981; Takens, 1981).

According to this theory, given an observable $x(t)$, one can generate the complete state vector $\boldsymbol{X}(t)$ by using $x(t + \tau)$ as the first coordinate, $x(t + 2\tau)$ as the second coordinate, and $x(t + n\tau)$ as the last coordinate, where τ is a suitable delay. In this way we can define the coordinates of the phase space, which should approximate the dynamics of the system from which the observable $x(t)$ was sampled (or, in other words, the unknown state space). The parameter n is often referred to as the *embedding dimension*. For an n-dimensional phase space, a "cloud" or a set of points will be generated. The Hausdorff–Besicovitch dimension of this set can be estimated by covering the set with n-dimensional cubes of side length ℓ and determining the number of cubes $N(\ell)$ needed to cover the set in the limit $\ell \to 0$ (Mandelbrot, 1983). This is the so-called box-counting algorithm; if this number scales as

$$N(\ell) \propto \ell^{-d} \tag{1}$$

$$\ell \to 0$$

then the scaling exponent d is an estimate of the Hausdorff–Besicovitch dimension for the n. In a log $N(\ell)$, log

ℓ plot, the exponent d can be estimated by the slope of a straight line. Using the state vector $X(t)$, we can test equation (1) for increasing values of n. If the original time series is random, then $d = n$ for any n (a random process embedded in an n-dimensional space always fills that space). If, however, the value of d becomes independent of n (that is, reaches a saturation value D_0), this means that the system represented by the time series has some structure and should possess an attractor whose Hausdorff–Besicovitch dimensions equal D_0. The above procedure for estimating D_0 is a consequence of the fact that the actual number of variables present in the evolution of the system is not known and thus we do not know *a priori* what n should be. We must therefore vary n until we "tune" to a structure that becomes invariant in higher embedding dimensions (an indication that extra variables are not needed to explain the dynamics of the system in question).

The above numerical approach to estimating the dimension of an attractor from a time series is, however, very limited, because an enormous number of points on the attractor are required to make sure that a given area in the phase space is indeed empty and not simply visited rarely. It has been documented that a box-counting approach is not feasible for phase space dimensions greater than two. An alternative approach that is much more applicable has been developed by Grassberger and Procaccia (1983a,b). This approach again generates a cloud of points in an n-dimensional phase space. But instead of covering the set with hypercubes, it finds the number of pairs $N(r,n)$ with distances less than a distance r. In this case, if for significantly small r we find that

$$N(r,n) \propto r^{d_2}, \tag{2}$$

then we call the scaling exponent d_2 the correlation dimension of the attractor for that n. We then test equation (2) for increasing values of n and check as previously for a saturation value D_2, which will be an estimate of the correlation dimension of the attractor. It should be mentioned at this point that τ can be small, but care should be taken not to include in the sums pairs whose time separation is less than the correlation time. The correlation dimension D_2 is less than the Hausdorff–Besicovitch (or fractal) dimension D_0 and actually measures the spatial correlation of the points that lie on the attractor. For a random time series, there will be no such spatial correlation in any embedding dimension and thus no saturation will be observed in the exponent d_2.

The search for attractors in weather and climate is driven by the desire to understand the observed complexity in the atmosphere. The theory of chaos provides us with new tools to do just that. An exact mathematical formulation of atmospheric processes has not yet been fully developed; hence observable weather variables are considered in the search for attractors in weather and climate. Notable early studies include the analysis of Nicolis and Nicolis (1984), who were the first to apply the above ideas to climate studies. They used single-variable values of oxygen isotope records of deep-sea cores spanning the past million years. These data are related to global temperature fluctuations during that time interval. They reported a dimension for the climatic attractor equal to 3.1. Fraedrich (1986) applied the same analysis over a period of fifteen years using daily pressure data, and Essex et al. (1987) applied the analysis over a period of forty years using daily geopotential data. Both groups reported a dimension of the weather attractor between 6 and 7. Tsonis and Elsner (1988) extended that analysis to very short time scales. Many more studies have followed. At this point, although the existence of attractors in weather is still an open question (see Tsonis, 1992; Tsonis et al., 1993, 1994a, 1994b; Lorenz, 1991), it is significant that many empirical studies indicate that low-dimensional attractors may be present in weather and climate. The fact that the inferred dimensions seem to be different for different time scales may indicate that the attractors (and thus the predictability) are different and are a function of the space/time scale. As such we may be looking at loosely connected subsystems within a "grand" attractor (Tsonis, 1996).

Chaos theory has opened new horizons in science and is already considered by many to be the most important discovery in physics in the twentieth century after relativity and quantum mechanics. Many systems in nature are chaotic. Developments in the study of chaotic dynamical systems have suggested that nature imposes limits on prediction. At the same time, however, it has been realized that the very existence of the attractors implies that randomness is restricted to the attractors. The atmosphere may be chaotic, but its evolution is confined to a specific area in the state space that is occupied by the attractor. No states outside this area are allowed. The theory of chaotic dynamical systems has improved our understanding of the behavior of the atmosphere. At the same time, even though it has provided an excuse for the unpredictability of weather, the theory of dynamical systems is slowly shaping our methods of investigating the weather and its prediction. For example, it may very well be that generalizations based on the study of specific cases (which may never happen exactly again) can no longer be appropriate. The study of chaotic dynamical systems offers grounds both for pessimism and for optimism. We may never be able to predict the weather exactly, but improvements in weather forecasting are feasible if we improve the completeness and accuracy with which we measure the initial condition of the atmosphere, and if we understand predictability at different time scales.

[*See also* Atmosphere Dynamics; Climate Change; Ocean Dynamics; *and* Stability.]

BIBLIOGRAPHY

Essex, C., et al. "The Climate Attractor over Short Time Scales." *Nature* 326 (1987), 64–66.

Fraedrich, K. "Estimating the Dimensions of Weather and Climate Attractors." *Journal of Atmospheric Sciences* 432 (1986), 419–432.

Grassberger, P., and I. Procaccia. "Characterization of Strange Attractors." *Physical Review Letters* 50 (1983a), 346.

———. "Measuring the Strangeness of Strange Attractors." *Physica* 9D (1983b), 189–208.

Hentschel, H. G. E., and I. Procaccia. "The Infinite Number of Generalized Dimensions of Fractals and Strange Attractors." *Physica* 8D (1983), 435–444.

Lorenz, E. N. "Deterministic Nonperiodic Flow." *Journal of Atmospheric Sciences* 20 (1963), 130–141.

———. "Dimension of Weather and Climate Attractors." *Nature* 353 (1991), 241–244.

Mandelbrot, B. B. *The Fractal Geometry of Nature*. New York: Freeman, 1983.

Nicolis, C. "Long-Term Climate Variability and Chaotic Dynamics." *Tellus* 39A (1987), 1–9.

Nicolis, C., and G. Nicolis. "Is there a Climatic Attractor?" *Nature* 311 (1984), 529–532.

Packard, N. H., et al. "Geometry from a Time Series." *Physical Review Letters* 45 (1980), 712–716.

Ruelle, D. "Chemical Kinetics and Differentiable Dynamical Systems." In *Nonlinear Phenomena in Chemical Dynamics*, edited by A. Pacault and C. Vidal. Berlin: Springer, 1981.

Takens, F. *Dynamical Systems and Turbulence*. New York: Springer, 1981.

Tsonis, A. A. *Chaos: From Theory to Applications*. New York: Plenum, 1992.

———. "Dynamical Systems as Models for Physical Processes." *Complexity* 1.5 (1996), 23–33.

Tsonis, A. A., and J. B. Elsner. "The Weather Attractor over Very Short Time Scales." *Nature* 333 (1988), 545–547.

———. "Multiple Attractors, Fractal Basins and Long-Term Climate Dynamics." *Beiträge zur Physik Atmosphäre* 63 (1990), 171–176.

Tsonis, A. A., et al. "Estimating the Dimension of Weather and Climate Attractors: Important Issues about the Procedure and Interpretation." *Journal of Atmospheric Sciences* 50 (1993), 2549–2555.

———. "An Investigation on the Ability of Nonlinear Methods to Infer Dynamics from Observables." *Bulletin of the American Meteorological Society* 75 (1994a), 1623–1633.

———. "Searching for Determinism in Observed Data: A Review of the Issues Involved." *Nonlinear Processes in Geophysics* 1 (1994b), 12–25.

—A. A. TSONIS

T

TECHNOLOGICAL HAZARDS

The terms *risk* and *hazard* are often used interchangeably. Hohenemser et al. (1985, p. 67), however, make a subtle and important distinction between hazards as "threats to humans and what they value" and risks as "quantitative measures of hazard consequences expressed as conditional probabilities of experiencing harm." Ordinarily, we make a distinction between natural and technological hazards based on the primary causal agent. This is relatively straightforward for natural hazards. For example, Burton and Kates (1964, p. 415) distinguish between geophysical (i.e., meteorological/climatological versus geologic/geomorphologic) and biological (i.e., floral versus faunal) causal agents.

Technological hazards, by contrast, are threats that originate from the development and use of technologies (Zeigler et al., 1983, pp. 11–12). Identifying the technology *per se* as the primary causal agent, however, may at times be problematic, since all technological hazards involve natural processes and are set in a socioeconomic and political context. Thus, for example, oil tanker spills may be considered technological hazards, but human factors and severe weather are often contributing elements in any spill event. The number of technological hazards is enormous, ranging from aerosol cans to genetically engineered crops, and new hazards of new and old technologies are discovered daily. Many technological hazards have global significance. Some technological hazards, such as hazardous waste sites, may appear to have only relatively local impacts taken in isolation, but, taken collectively or cumulatively, they may represent truly global hazards. Other technological hazards, such as carbon dioxide, dioxin, and heavy-metals emissions, pesticide residues, and radioactive fallout, may have systemic pathways of exposure and impacts. For example, elevated levels of heavy metals and pesticides have been found in animals, plants, and soils far distant from the primary sources of emission. Together, these technological hazards form the global risk mosaic (Zeigler et al., 1983, p. 50).

Sorting these hazards into appropriate analytic categories is a daunting task. For example, we may divide technological hazards according to the primary technology involved (e.g., nuclear power plants, automobiles, pesticides), the types of consequences (e.g., human health, economic impacts, ecological damage), the type of human health effect (e.g., cancer, heart disease, birth defects), the routes of exposure (e.g., air, land, or water), and the populations exposed (e.g., workers, young, old, pregnant). The categories chosen will depend on the problem at hand, the purpose of the analysis, and what entity is conducting the analysis.

Several different taxonomies that attempt to capture some of these analytic distinctions have been proposed (e.g., Litai et al., 1983; von Winterfeldt and Edwards, 1984; Slovic, 1987). By scoring a range of ninety-three different technological hazards according to a set of hazard descriptors (Figure 1), Hohenemser et al. (1985) developed one of the most elaborate taxonomies (Table 1). Technological hazards of global significance include carbon dioxide emissions, ozone depletion, recombinant deoxyribonucleic acid (DNA), and nuclear radiation. This taxonomic analysis could be extended and adapted to include additional technological hazards of global concern. Such taxonomic analysis allows us to identify which problems are of the greatest concern as well as to identify those problems that are similar in nature and might be amenable to similar management approaches (Clark, 1990).

The analytical framework developed by Hohenemser et al. can also be used to examine the anatomy of any technological hazard and to explore options for its management. For example, Figure 2 (Hohenemser et al., 1985, p. 32) uses a five-stage causal chain to map out the range of consequences that may result from the use of coal-fired power plants to generate electricity. Ordinarily, the causal chain comprises a seven-stage sequence from human needs to consequences, but additional stages (such as primary and secondary initiating events and first- and second-order consequences) may be added as necessary and the initial stages of "human needs" and "human wants" are often omitted. The model is especially useful because it forces one to identify systematically what management interventions might be feasible for each link in the chain (Figure 3; Kasperson et al., 1985, p. 47).

While technological risk assessment is a relatively new field (Golding, 1992), considerable effort has been expended over the past twenty-five years to develop appropriate methods for the quantitative assessment of risk. Engineers have refined the methods of "probabilistic risk assessment" (PRA) that rely on the use of fault and event tree analysis to identify the likelihood of failure within some part of an engineered system. By contrast, epidemiologists and toxicologists have focused further downstream in the causal chain to examine the likely health consequences of hazardous exposures

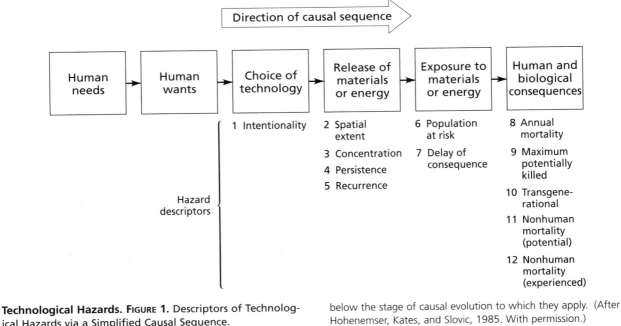

Technological Hazards. FIGURE 1. Descriptors of Technological Hazards via a Simplified Causal Sequence.

Hazard descriptors used in our classification of hazards are shown below the stage of causal evolution to which they apply. (After Hohenemser, Kates, and Slovic, 1985. With permission.)

through refined methods of "quantitative risk assessment" (QRA). There has been considerable debate within the scientific community about the validity and use of these methods, particularly in regard to the inherent problems of uncertainty and variability. Economists have extended the use of cost-benefit analysis to incorporate human health and ecological impacts through the use of techniques such as contingent valuation, willingness-to-pay surveys, and the analysis of cost per life saved (Graham and Vaupel, 1981; Mitchell and Carson, 1989; Nichols and Zeckhauser, 1986), although these approaches have been severely criticized (Kelman, 1981). More recently, ecologists have begun to adapt the methods of PRA and QRA to examine ecological impacts from technological hazards (Environmental Protection Agency, 1993).

Unfortunately, these methods are not readily adaptable for the analysis of technological risks on a global scale, in part because of the inadequacies of the data and the enormous inherent variabilities and uncertainties, but also because of the way in which risk is conceived as a function of probability times the consequences of a particular hazardous event or technology. As one moves to the global scale, the potential magnitude of the consequences becomes enormous even if the probabilities are extremely small, merely because the size of the population exposed (whether human or nonhuman) is so large. Thus, most global technological hazards fall into the realm of postnormal science, where the decision stakes and systems uncertainty are high (Figure 4; Funtowicz and Ravetz, 1992, p. 254).

Technological Hazards. TABLE 1. The Clark Taxonomy of Risk

CLASSES	EXAMPLES
1. Multiple extreme hazards (extreme in more than one factor)	Nuclear war—radiation, recombinant DNA, pesticides, nerve gas—war use, dam failure
2. Extreme hazards (extreme in one factor)	
a) Intentional biocides	Chain saws, antibiotics, vaccines
b) Persistent teratogens	Uranium mining, rubber manufacture
c) Rare catastrophes	Liquified natural gas (LNG) explosions, commercial aviation crashes
d) Common killers	Auto crashes, coal mining—black lung
e) Diffuse global threats	Fossil fuel—CO_2, supersonic transport (SST)—ozone depletion
Hazards (extreme in no factor)	Saccharin, appliances, aspirin, skateboards, power mowers, bicycles

SOURCE: Hohenemser, Kates, and Slovic (1985).

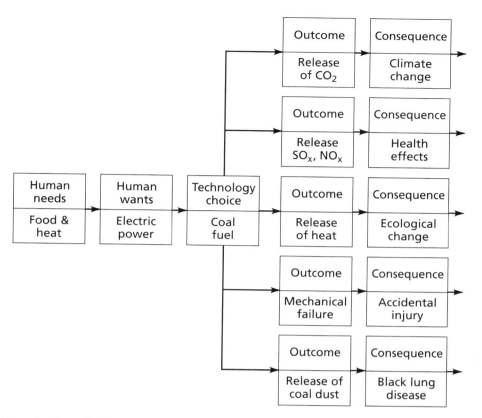

Technological Hazards. FIGURE 2. The Anatomy of a Technological Hazard.

There are at least five separate outcomes, each involving the release of a different kind of energy or material and each leading to a distinct set of consequences. (After Hohenemser, Kates, and Slovic, 1985. With permission.)

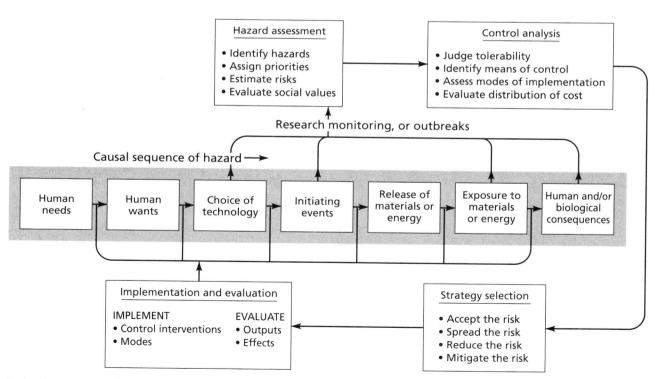

Technological Hazards. FIGURE 3. Stages in the Management of Technological Risk. (After Kasperson, Kates, and Hohenemser, 1985. With permission.)

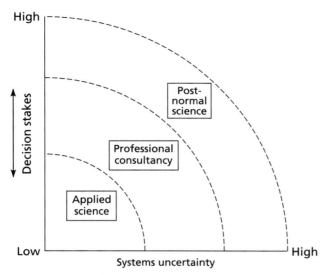

Technological Hazards. FIGURE 4. Post-Normal Science According to Ravetz and Funtowicz. (Redrawn from Funtowicz and Ravetz, 1985. Copyright 1992. Reproduced with permission of Greenwood Publishing Group.)

Nevertheless, the methods of technological hazard and risk assessment and management have much to offer in the analysis of global environmental change, including frameworks for the decomposition of problems, the identification of management options, and indicators of possible policy alternatives.

[*See also* Catastrophist–Cornucopian Debate; Hazardous Waste; Industrialization; Natural Hazards; Nuclear Hazards; Risk; Technology; *and* Vulnerability.]

BIBLIOGRAPHY

Burton, I., and R. W. Kates. "The Perception of Natural Hazards in Resource Management." *Natural Resources Journal* 3.3 (1964), 415.

Clark, W. C. "Toward a Useful Assessment of Global Environmental Risks." In *Understanding Global Environmental Change: The Contributions of Risk Analysis and Management*, edited by Roger E. Kasperson et al., pp. 5–22. ET-90–01/HDCP-RA-R001. Worcester, Mass.: Clark University, 1990.

Environmental Protection Agency (EPA). "A Review of Ecological Assessment Case Studies from a Risk Assessment Perspective." EPA/630R-92/005. USEPA: Washington, D.C., 1993.

Funtowicz, S. O., and J. R. Ravetz. "Three Types of Risk Assessment and the Emergence of Post-Normal Science." In *Social Theories of Risk*, edited by S. Krimsky and D. Golding, pp. 251–274. Westport, Conn.: Praeger, 1992.

Golding, D. 1992. "A Social and Programmatic History of Risk Research." In *Social Theories of Risk*, edited by S. Krimsky and D. Golding, pp. 23–52. Westport, Conn.: Praeger, 1992.

Graham, J. D., and J. W. Vaupel. "Value of a Life: What Difference Does It Make?" *Risk Analysis* 1.1 (1981), 89–95.

Hohenemser, C., R. W. Kates, and P. Slovic. "A Causal Taxonomy." In *Perilous Progress: Managing the Hazards of Technology*, edited by R. W. Kates et al., pp. 67–89. Boulder, Colo.: Westview Press, 1985.

Kasperson, R. E., R. W. Kates, and C. Hohenemser. "Hazard Management." In *Perilous Progress: Managing the Hazards of Technology*, edited by R. W. Kates et al., pp. 43–66. Boulder, Colo.: Westview Press, 1985.

Kates, R. W. "Natural Hazards in Ecological Perspective: Hypotheses and Models." NHRWP No. 14. Boulder, Colo.: Institute of Behavioral Science, University of Colorado, 1970.

Kelman, S. "Cost–Benefit Analysis: an Ethical Critique." *Regulation* 5.1 (1981), 33–40.

Krimsky, S., and D. Golding. "Factoring Risk into Environmental Decision Making." In *Environmental Decision Making: A Multidisciplinary Perspective*, edited by R. A. Chechile and S. Carlisle, pp. 92–119. New York: Van Nostrand Reinhold, 1991.

Litai, D., et al. "The Public Perception of Risk." In *The Analysis of Actual vs. Perceived Risks*, edited by V. T. Covello et al. New York: Plenum, 1983.

Mitchell, R. C., and R. T. Carson. *Using Surveys to Value Public Goods: The Contingent Valuation Method*. Washington, D.C.: Resources for the Future, 1989.

Nichols, A. L., and R. J. Zeckhauser. "The Perils of Prudence: How Conservative Risk Assessments Distort Regulation." *Regulation* (Nov–Dec 1986), 13.

Slovic, P. "Perception of Risk." *Science* 236 (17 April 1987), 282.

von Winterfeldt, D., and W. Edwards. "Patterns of Conflict about Risky Technologies." *Risk Analysis* 4 (March 1984), L55–68.

Zeigler, D. J., et al. *Technological Hazards*. Washington, D.C.: Association of American Geographers, 1983.

—DOMINIC GOLDING

TECHNOLOGY

Technology is the aspect of culture that, more than any other, defines how humans are limited by their physical environment, and at the same time how deeply they affect that environment. Ideological factors—such as the anthropocentric view that nature is man's to subdue—are also important, but technology always has been central to humans' relationship with the environment. [*See* Belief Systems.] Tools, the beginning of technology, defined the stages of prehistory and the growing human ability to survive and prosper as scavengers and hunter-gatherers; and, in the past few decades a decline in heavy industry caused population to decrease in the U.S. Northeast, while computer technology attracted migrants to the Silicon Valley of California.

The rate of change in technologies today is startling. Innovations like the telephone, aircraft, and the automobile suddenly altered society, then advanced slowly and predictably. The latest technologies seem to be self-accelerating: new computer chips, for instance, immediately spawn the next generation of even faster chips. Moreover, technologies interact: computers make gene sequencing possible, and simultaneously, deoxyribonucleic acid (DNA) is being considered as a medium for computation (see Brand, 2000).

This article emphasizes recent and emerging technologies—biotechnologies, computers and information science, aerospace, and energy technologies with less emphasis on the history of technology, the environmental impacts of the Industrial Revolution, the transformation of agriculture, and the emergence of the service sector in industrial nations. [*See* Agriculture and Agricultural Land; Industrialization; *and* Manufacturing.*] These themes are treated thoroughly in many publications, most relevantly in Gruebler (1998).

Although technology may be blamed for many of our environmental ills, it can also provide solutions—not just technical fixes, but profound changes in energy sources or transportation, or in the ways rural areas develop. [*See* Geoengineering.] An important example, explored in a section below, is the way information and communication technologies can benefit the environment and promote sustainable development in less-developed parts of the world. This capacity of technology to be both detrimental and beneficial is a recurrent theme in any discussion of technology and global change (Gray, 1989).

Technological advances already have greatly reduced the impact of industrial activity. One example is the reduction in materials used per unit of industrial output, a process called *dematerialization.* Another is improvements in energy efficiency, often expressed as reduction in the energy intensity of output (see Gruebler, 1998, pp. 238–242, 284–290). Without these advances, the stress on resources and the alteration of the atmosphere would be far more serious than they are now.

Further gains in this regard, especially in the reduction of wasted materials and rejected energy, can be attained through new technologies and by collaboration among industries that are complementary. [*See* Industrial Ecology.] In the past, all the economies realized through dematerialization and reduced energy intensity have been overbalanced by the rebound effect—the overall growth in production as populations and economies expand. A more optimistic view of the industrial future predicts that competition will lead to ever greater efficiency in use of materials and energy (Ausubel, 1998).

Another vital question is whether progress in technology should be autonomous or whether governments should intervene in order to accomplish certain goals, adopting the concept of appropriate technology. This question is crucial in a world that is now largely adopting a development path similar to that followed by presently industrial nations. Early in the industrial age, access to coal-fired steam power worsened some processes that were of concern before the end of the eighteenth century, including loss of forests, coal-mining disturbance, and decline in the quality of urban air. Subsequently, there have been entirely new kinds of impact caused by new substances—plastics and other petrochemicals, and various toxins that accumulate in the biosphere—and by the daily expenditure of massive amounts of energy through combustion of fossil fuels, with serious effects on the atmosphere at local, regional,

and world scales. Any vision of the future will require decisions about whether and how to intervene, especially with regard to energy technologies, and whether to encourage developing nations to embrace technologies more sustainable than those employed by the developed ones. [*See* Global Warming; Kyoto Protocol; *and* Sustainable Development.]

Technology Examined. Early in the nineteenth century, voices were raised against the advance of technology and the ways machines altered society. Organized textile workers, the Luddites, resisted the installation of machinery in textile mills in 1811; their agricultural counterparts opposed horse-drawn threshing machines in the 1830s; and in 1829, Thomas Carlyle observed how mechanization had disrupted traditions, and caused workers to lose faith in individual endeavor (Carlyle, 1957).

In the twentieth century, the social and political ramifications of technology were examined by such thinkers as Lewis Mumford (1970) and Jacques Ellul (1964). Perhaps most influential on nonspecialists was E. F. Schumacher's *Small Is Beautiful: Economics as if People Mattered* (1973), which proposed methods of economic advance in harmony with the existing conditions of traditional societies. The implicit concept, dubbed *appropriate technology*, was taken up by a number of organizations during the 1970s which applied the idea not only to traditional societies but also to industrial nations (see Winner, 1989, pp. 62–74).

More recently, the ethical and philosophical implications of technology have been explored by Mitcham (1994) and by Winner (1989). Winner's book presents a strong statement of the need to examine and steer technology toward goals that will benefit society. A similar stance is taken by Freeman Dyson (1999), whose chapter dealing with the revival of villages through solar energy, bioengineered crops, and Internet connections is titled "Technology and Social Justice."

There are a number of institutions worldwide concerned with science and technology. In the United States, the Office of Technology Assessment (OTA) was established in 1972, but eliminated in 1995 when funding was cut. Its successor, not a federal office, is the Institute for Technology Assessment (http://www.mtppi. org/ita/ita), a nonprofit organization with ties to Congress through a board of legislative advisors. Its goals include maintaining contact with industry, universities, and the public, suggesting that it may serve as a pipeline for ideas on establishing priorities. The White House Office of Science and Technology Policy was established in 1976 "to provide the President with timely policy advice and to coordinate science and technology investment" (http://www.whitehouse.gov/WH/EOP/OSTP). Since 1993, it has coordinated with the National Science and Technology Council, which establishes national goals for federal investments in science and technology (http://www.whitehouse.gov/WH/EOP/OSTP/NSTC).

This list favors events in Earth and atmospheric science, the advances of industry and the electronic age, and the recognition of human impact on the Earth.

1090	Water-driven mechanical clock.
1240	Leonardo Fibonacci promotes use of Arabic numerals.
1453	Johann Gutenberg introduces movable type in printing.
1504	Amerigo Vespucci recognizes New World is not Asia.
1510	Leonardo da Vinci proposes water-driven turbine and many other science concepts.
1521	Ferdinand Magellan's circumnavigation confirms Earth's size.
1543	Nicolas Copernicus publishes *De Revolutionibus*, heliocentric theory.
1568	Gerhart Mercator's map projection for sailors and explorers.
1600	William Gilbert explains Earth's magnetism.
1608	Galileo improves telescope, advances ideas on gravity and motion.
1609	Johann Kepler recognizes planetary motions.
1640	Coke first made from coal.
1643	Evangelista Torricelli's first measurement of atmospheric pressure.
1654	Blaise Pascal and Pierre de Fermat formulate theory of probability.
1665–1680	Isaac Newton's differential calculus, concepts of gravity and motion.
1670	Anton van Leeuwenhoek refines microscopy, observes spermatozoa, bacteria.
1690	Christian Huygens's wave theory of light.
1735	Surveys initiated by French proved polar flattening of Earth. Carolus Linnaeus's classification of flora and fauna.
1761	John Harrison perfects seagoing chronometer for determining longitude.
1770	Joseph Priestley's concepts of electricity and nature of gases.
1775	James Watt improves steam engine.
1785	Watt and Boulton install rotary steam engine in cotton factory.
1787	Antoine Laurent Lavoisier's systematic chemical terminology.
1788	James Hutton's uniformitarian view of geologic processes.
1791	Metric system begun, and meter defined.
1793	Eli Whitney invents cotton gin.
1796	Edward Jenner introduces vaccination against smallpox.
1798	Thomas Robert Malthus publishes *Essay on Population.*
1802	John Dalton develops atomic theory in chemistry, pioneers meteorology.
1814	George Stephenson invents first practical steam locomotive.
1815	W. Smith's geologic map of England and Wales.
1830	Sir Charles Lyell's *Principles of Geology* recognizes Earth's age.
1831	Michael Faraday devises the first electric generator.
1834	Charles Babbage designs analytical engine directed by punch cards. Cyrus H. McCormick invents reaping machine.
1835	Gustave Gaspard de Coriolis identifies basis for gyres in atmospheric flow.
1837	J. Louis Agassiz's *Discours de Neuchatel* on glaciation.
1839	Charles Goodyear invents vulcanization of rubber. Crawford W. Long uses ether for surgical anesthesia.
1843	I. K. Brunel designs first iron-hulled screw-propellor ship to cross Atlantic.
1844	Samuel Morse installs 40-mile telegraph line, Baltimore to Washington.
1851	Jean Bernard Leon Foucault demonstrates rotation of Earth on its axis.
1856	Sir Henry Bessemer introduces blast furnace for steel-making.

1859	First commercial oil well drilled in the United States.
	Charles Robert Darwin's *On the Origin of Species by Natural Selection*.
1862	Jean Foucault measures speed of light, using rotating mirror.
1860s	Gregor Johann Mendel specifies principles of genetics.
1863	Sir Francis Galton develops modern techniques of weather mapping.
	John Tyndall recognizes principles of greenhouse effect.
1864	G. Perkins Marsh publishes *Man and Nature*.
1865	Louis Pasteur introduces germ theory of disease, inoculations for immunity.
	Joseph Lister introduces antiseptic surgery, using carbolic acid.
	James Clerk Maxwell unifies theories on electricity, magnetism, and light.
1866	Alfred Nobel invents dynamite.
1869	E. M. Haeckel coins the term *ecology*.
	Dmitri Ivanovich Mendeleev constructs the periodic table of the elements.
1872	R. A. Smith coins the term *acid rain*.
1875	Alexander Graham Bell invents the telephone.
1876	Nikolaus August Otto invents first four-stroke internal combustion engine.
1880	Thomas A. Edison and J. W. Swan invent first practical electric light bulb.
1882	Thomas A. Edison builds first hydroelectric plant.
1883	William Thomson (Lord Kelvin) publishes *On the Size of Atoms*.
1884	World conference establishes system of meridians and time zones.
	Nikola A. Tesla, with George Westinghouse, builds electric motor.
1888	J. B. Dunlop develops the pneumatic tire.
1892	Diesel engine patented.
1895	Wilhelm Roentgen discovers X-rays.
1896	A. H. Bequerel discovers radiation.
	S. A. Arrhenius proposes greenhouse effect and role of carbon dioxide.
1897	J. J. Thomson discovers the electron.
1898	Pierre and Marie Curie discover the elements radium and polonium.
1901	Max Planck publishes *Laws of Radiation*.
	M. G. Marconi transmits radiotelegraph message across Atlantic.
1903	Orville and Wilbur Wright accomplish first controlled powered flight.
1904	Ronald Ross establishes connection between malaria and *Anopheles* mosquito.
1905	Albert Einstein's Special Theory of Relativity; equivalence of mass and energy; Brownian theory of motion; photon theory of light.
1907	B. B. Boltwood uses uranium decay as indicator of age of rocks.
1908	A. Mohorovicic recognizes boundary between Earth's crust and mantle.
1909	First manufacture of Bakelite (beginning of Plastics Age).
	A. Penck and E. Bruckner publish their view of the ice age.
1911	W. Burton invents thermal cracking for refining petroleum.
1913	Haber-Bosch process for fixing atmospheric nitrogen (fertilizers).
	Henry Ford establishes first true assembly line.
	Niels Bohr formulates theory of atomic structure.
1915	Albert Einstein publishes General Theory of Relativity.
	Alfred Wegener publishes theory of continental drift.
1919	Jacob Bjerknes theorizes air masses, fronts, and the nature of cyclonic storms.

(continued)

MILESTONES IN TECHNOLOGY (*Continued*)

1920	Ernest Rutherford achieves first artificially induced nuclear reaction.
	Milutan Milankovitch publishes astronomical theory of Pleistocene ice ages.
1921	E. M. East and G. M. Shull develop hybrid corn strain for higher yields.
1924	W. P. Köppen and A. Wegener study climates of geological past.
1926	Production of compound fertilizers (nitrogen, phosphorus, potassium).
	Robert H. Goddard launches first liquid-fuel rocket.
	J. L. Baird demonstrates first television.
1927	Charles Lindbergh flies from New York to Paris.
1928	Alexander Fleming discovers penicillin.
1929	Motonori Matuyama recognizes reversals in Earth's magnetic field.
	Robert Goddard launches first rocket carrying meteorological instruments.
1930	Acrylic plastics, polyvinyl chloride.
1932	J. D. Cockroft and E. T. S. Walton: split the atom.
1934	A. G. Tansley coins term *ecosystem*.
1939	Paul Muller synthesizes DDT.
	Invention of polyethylene.
	Igor Sikorsky builds first helicopter.
1940	First electron microscope demonstrated by RCA.
1941	Edwin McMillan and Glen T. Seaborg discover plutonium.
1942	V-2 rocket first launched.
	Enrico Fermi achieves first nuclear chain reaction in uranium.
1945	First atomic bomb detonated, Alamogordo, New Mexico.
1946	ENIAC, first automatic computer, built.
	Chester Carlton invents xerography process.
1947	W. F. Libby invents radiocarbon dating.
1948	Bell Laboratories invents the transistor.
1951	First nuclear electric plant, Arcon, Idaho.
1952	First hydrogen bomb exploded.
1953	J. D. Watson and F. H. C. Crick formulate molecular structure of DNA as basis of heredity.
1954	Bell Telephone Company produces first photoelectric cell.
1955	C. Emiliani publishes oxygen isotope studies of ocean cores.
1956	B. C. Heezen and M. Ewing note significance of Mid-Atlantic Ridge.
	Symposium, *Man's Role in Changing the Face of the Earth.*
1957	USSR launches *SPUTNIK* I and II, the first Earth satellites.
1960	Harry Hess publishes theory of sea-floor spreading.
	Jacques Piccard, in bathyscape *Trieste*, reaches 35,800 feet (10,910 meters) in Mariana Trench.
	First weather satellite, *TIROS* I, transmits images of cloud cover.
1961	Texas Instruments patents the silicon chip.
	Manned space flight by Yuri Gagarin and Alan Shepard.
1962	Rachel Carson publishes *Silent Spring.*
1963	Fred Vine and Drummond Matthews clinch theory of sea-floor

Energy and Materials. After the coal-fired steam engine propelled industrialization, the world as a whole used progressively more energy, especially after 1950. Sources of primary energy shifted from the renewables—wood, wind, and hydro—to mineral fuels: coal, oil and gas, and nuclear fuels. [*See* Energy; *and* Industrialization.] The question now is what energy sources and technologies will power the future (for selected energy scenarios, see Gruebler, 1998; McDonald, 1998). Reliance on fossil fuels will continue to yield intractable

1967	Stanford biochemists produce synthetic DNA.
1968	J. D. Watson publishes *The Double Helix*.
	First forensic use of DNA fingerprinting.
1969	U.S. *Apollo XI* lands astronauts on the moon.
	United States takes steps to ban DDT.
	J. Lovelock proposes Gaia hypothesis.
1972	Launch of *LANDSAT*, first of a series of Earth resources satellites.
1974	F. S. Rowland and M. Molina warn that chlorofluorocarbons affect ozone layer.
1977	Apple II, the first personal computer.
1978	Launch of *SEASAT* to monitor ocean temperatures and currents.
1979	Three Mile Island nuclear accident.
1980	Luis W. and Walter Alvarez propose meteor impact as cause of Cretaceous–Tertiary extinctions.
1981	IBM launches its first personal computer.
1985	AT&T–Bell Laboratories transmit 300,000 simultaneous phone messages on one fiber-optic line.
1985	Deep ocean vents and unique life found in Mid-Atlantic ridge.
	British Antarctic Survey finds hole in ozone layer over Antarctica.
1986	Chernobyl nuclear accident.
1987	Transatlantic glass fiber cable laid.
	Soviet *COSMOS*, the world's two-thousandth satellite, launched.
	Montreal Protocol on Substances That Deplete the Ozone Layer.
1989	U.S. Defense Department launches first satellite in Global Positioning System.
1990	Launch of Hubble Space Telescope.
1992	Earth Summit in Rio de Janeiro.
	Greenland Ice-Core Project (GRIP) ice core completed.
1996	Intergovernmental Panel on Climate Change endorses probability of human influence on global warming.
1997	IBM's *Deep Blue* defeats world chess champion Garry Kasparov.
	Ian Wilmut clones sheep.
	NASA lands *Mars Pathfinder*, and places *Global Surveyor* in orbit.
	British Petroleum recognzies that burning fuel warms the atmosphere.
2000	Mapping of human genome nominally completed.
	Two Japanese automobile companies market hybrid gasoline–electric automobiles.

BIBLIOGRAPHY

Asimov, I. *Asimov's Biographical Encyclopedia of Science and Technology.* 2d ed. New York: Doubleday, 1982.

Gruebler, A. *Technology and Global Change.* New York: Cambridge University Press, 1998.

Grun, B. *The Timetables of History.* 3d ed. New York: Simon and Schuster, 1991.

Williams, T. *Science: A History of Discovery in the Twentieth Century.* New York: Oxford University Press, 1990.

—DAVID J. CUFF

wastes and the well-known atmospheric results unless we make the transition to more benign fuels, and ultimately to noncombustion sources of electrical energy. [*See* Air Quality; Carbon Dioxide; Fossil Fuels; Global Warming; *and* Greenhouse Effect.] There are many promising alternative energy technologies that await further development and refinement (see Flavin, 1994 for a sample of how alternative energy technologies may be applied). [*See* Renewable Energy Sources.]

Discussions of appropriate technologies and how the

industrialized nations should provide sustainable technologies for developing nations will confront energy choices and their connection to transportation technologies. [*See* Transportation.] Wind-powered generators will function well in certain regions. High-temperature solar heat for electrical generation will suit areas with clear skies. Photovoltaic electrical generation will operate in many different climates.

The technology that may alter the world most profoundly, however, is the use of hydrogen as a fuel and as a feedstock for fuel cells generating electricity in buildings and vehicles. [*See the vignette on* Fuel Cells *in the article on* Electrical Power Generation.] If the world were able to switch from fossil fuels to a hydrogen economy, then many underdeveloped areas could become suppliers of hydrogen, using either electrolytic or biological methods according to their climatic setting, while energy users around the globe would have a fuel or feedstock that is nearly nonpolluting and would not contribute to global warming. [*See* Hydrogen.]

In the field of energy technologies, the U.S. federal government and various state governments have offered economic incentives to encourage research and development in renewable-energy technologies. This is a prime example of intervention to steer technological change.

An industrial society uses a staggering quantity and variety of materials. In one year, an average U.S. citizen is responsible for the consumption of thirty-seven tons of wood, stone, gravel, metal, fertilizers, and plastics, in addition to food and fuels; Americans alone use about one-third of all the materials that churn through the global economy (see Gardner, 1999). Today's materials draw from all ninety-two naturally occurring elements in the periodic table, compared with roughly twenty elements utilized in 1900. About 100,000 synthetic chemicals have been introduced in the twentieth century. Energy-using technology has lowered the cost of mining, facilitated the concentration and refining of metals from ores of ever-diminishing grade, and increased efficiency in cutting and processing of trees for paper and lumber. [*See* Metals.]

In the energy industries, technological advances have improved exploration and production methods and provided ways to use fossil fuels with less impact on the atmosphere. [*See* the *vignette on* Technological Change and Fossil Fuels *in the article on* Fossil Fuels.] For a thorough study of the role of technology in natural resources, see "Technological Innovation in Natural Resource Industries," chapter 1 in R. David Simpson's *Productivity in Natural Resource Industries: Improvement through Innovation.*

A rational and more sustainable use of materials will require new incentives and policies, such as eliminating subsidies that encourage the use of virgin materials. But there will also be technical solutions which create manufactured goods that are easy to remanufacture or to recycle. There is also the prospect, offered by materials science, of working at the molecular level to build desired substances, such as photonics materials, materials for information storage, biomedical materials, new polymers, and diamond for industrial uses. Whether this approach can make an impact on traditional mining and manufacturing practices remains to be seen (see Ball, 1997).

Agriculture. During the past two centuries, there have been revolutionary increases in agricultural productivity—per person and per acre—that have sustained the growth of global population and contributed to large-scale migration from rural to urban areas. [*See* Agriculture and Agricultural Land.] The technologies responsible have provided fertilizers and pesticides, biological innovations, and mechanization. Among the technological highlights are the 1913 Haber-Bosch process for nitrogen fixation and producing nitrogen fertilizers, some controversial pesticides, and many remarkable genetic advances. For a thorough account of the technologies and their influences on agriculture, see Gruebler (1998, pp. 131–194).

In the future, precision agriculture may play a greater role than it does today. By dividing a farm into grid cells, using the Global Positioning System (GPS) to track progress, and carefully monitoring all inputs and yields, a farmer can apply only the needed amounts of fertilizers, pesticides, and herbicides, which improves economic return and reduces chemical impacts on surface and ground water. An alternative is to employ continuous sampling and analysis of soil chemistry while machinery moves through a field, applying chemicals immediately in accord with the analysis (for information and links to other sites, see University of Sydney, Australian Center for Precision Agriculture at http://www.usyd.edu.au./su/agric/acpa).

Pest and Weed Control. Chemicals of some kinds have been used on crops since the fifteenth century, when inorganic compounds containing toxic metals were used to kill insects. In the seventeenth and eighteenth centuries, various natural products were derived from plants to serve as insecticides. A revolution occurred in 1939 with the formulation and production of dichlorodiphenyltrichloroethane (DDT), a chemical that earned its discoverer the Nobel Prize in Medicine because the compound was so successful against insects that transmitted diseases. Like other wonder chemicals, this compound had unanticipated effects on wildlife, publicized in 1962 by Rachel Carson's book *Silent Spring.* [*See the vignette on* The Wonder Chemicals *in the article on* Chemical Industry.] DDT and other second-generation pesticides have been used since 1945, but many have now been replaced by less persistent chemicals in developed countries.

Aside from their ability to poison humans and other creatures unintentionally, insecticides entail the same problem as antibiotics: they promote the development of resistance among their target populations, as some mutated individuals survive the chemical attack, then reproduce to create a resistant population which requires heavier applications of the chemical or the use of a new chemical insecticide. This is one reason that DDT, banned in much of the developed world, is being used again in some developing nations (Raloff, 2000).

The alternative biological approach includes using a pest's natural enemies, such as parasitic wasps or bacterial agents, or employing genetic tools to modify crops to resist predators (for journal articles and other information, see the Center for Integrated Pest Management, managed by the National Science Foundation and North Carolina State University, at http://ipmwww.ncsu.edu, and Integrated Pest Management at http://www. IPMnet.org).

Genetic Science and Agriculture. Between 1950 and 1965, genetic science made monumental changes in agriculture. Newly bred varieties of crops led to higher yields in industrial nations; then, around 1965, high-yielding varieties of wheat and rice were introduced to developing nations in what has been called the "Green Revolution." The increased yields were enough to forestall famine in some regions. The new varieties demand inorganic fertilizers, irrigation, and farm machinery, so their cultivation represents an exporting of industrial agriculture to developing nations, as well as dependence on related technologies. By 1990, some crops, such as cotton, had also been genetically modified to resist pests. Recently, work has been done on salt-tolerant plants that could yield food, livestock feed, and oils on the world's 130 million hectares (320 million acres) of unused land that is near oceans and could be irrigated with salt water (see Glenn, 1998).

A phenomenon of the late 1990s was the boom in transgenic, or genetically modified, strains of familiar crops bred with one or more of these traits: resistance to pests, tolerance of pesticides, tolerance of herbicides, drought resistance, and improved nutritional content. The new crops are controversial, praised by some as essential to feeding the world's growing population, but condemned by others as an ecological threat (see Mann, 2000a). Worldwide, the adoption of transgenic crops has been very rapid; planted areas have increased from 1.74 million hectares (4.3 million acres) in 1996 to 50 million hectares (123 million acres) in 1999. Roughly three-quarters of the total is in the United States (largely in corn and soybeans), but there has been rapid expansion of soybean acreage in Argentina. Some believe that more must be done to transfer this technology to developing nations. Improved strains of rice (rich in vitamin A), cassava, and millet would be beneficial and should be pro-

vided free from royalties paid to the companies that own the patents. A new international agency may be needed to act as a technology trust to negotiate matters of liability and intellectual property and to aid in the transfer of biotechnology to developing countries (Prakash, 2000, p. 32; also see http://www.agbioworld.org and the International Service for Acquisition of Agri-Biotech Applications at http://www.isaaa.org).

Opposition to biotech strains has been pronounced, especially in wealthy nations. Idaho farmers' use of a biotech potato resistant to aphids and the Colorado potato beetle has been shut down by protests relayed through fast-food companies. A more general apprehension is that herbicide-tolerant crops may hybridize with their wild relatives to produce superweeds immune to herbicides and impossible to control. In one example, a transgenic herbicide-resistant sorghum was developed to allow control of *Striga*, or witchweed, a parasite that attacks cereals and legumes in Kenya; in 1996, it was shown that sorghum hybridizes with Johnson grass, an undesirable weed relative that could spread and cause huge crop losses, so the development was ended (see Mann, 2000a, p. 42).

The Human Genome and Health. The sequencing of biochemical markers in human DNA, nominally completed in June 2000 (see articles in *Scientific American* Special Report, July 2000) unites engineering and biochemistry, using new machines called *sequencers* which combine "wet biology" with high-speed computers to read the markers, recognize overlaps, and assemble fragments. New disciplines have sprouted in association with the advances in molecular biology. Bioinformatics is a science–technology that provides custom analysis of the newly available sequencing data, searching for a match between the genetic material from a given tumor, for instance, and a portion of the human biomarker sequence. The match will point to a protein useful in combating the disease. Because they control processes in the body, proteins (whose production in the body is controlled by genes) are the key to treatment of disease; and knowing the shapes of protein molecules is essential in designing drugs that will either enhance or block protein function. This study of protein form and function, called *proteomics* or *structural genomics*, is an emerging science technology that adapts older technologies to a new task.

The analysis of proteins uses mass spectrometers (a technology devised in the 1920s) to sort the gaseous ions in a protein and learn its chemical composition. Deducing the shapes of protein molecules, however, relies on adaptation of X-ray crystallography, or X-ray diffraction, the technology employed first by Max Laue in 1913 to determine whether X-rays were particles or electromagnetic waves with very short wavelength. For visible light, the wave character can be demonstrated with a diffraction grating; but because no suitably fine grating could be manufactured, Laue experimented with mineral crystals. As he had predicted, the X-rays passed around the atoms in the crystal, interfered with one another, and struck a photographic plate, creating a diffraction pattern that confirmed the wave character of X-rays but also revealed the spacing of atoms in the crystal. Immediately, mineralogists and chemists had a new tool for the study of crystals and the structure of molecules. This technology was used by Francis H. C. Crick and James D. Watson to recognize the double helix structure of DNA in 1953, and in subsequent refinements that identified the ladder form with cross-members joining pairs of biomarkers on either side of the ladder.

In current proteomics work, proteins are coaxed into crystal form, then exposed to X-rays at a series of different angles. The resulting maps, showing atom locations in two dimensions, are analyzed geometrically to yield the X, Y, and Z coordinates of each atom. Graphics programs then create a three-dimensional portrait of the protein molecule whose shape suggests a drug molecule that may be directed toward that protein. As this process becomes more and more automated, there is the prospect of a full catalog of the molecular structure of all proteins essential to human biochemical processes. Armed with access to this information on proteins and the genes (sequences of biomarkers) that direct their functioning, molecular biologists now envision the design and production of new drugs that will fit the critical protein molecules and directly affect the progress of diseases whose genetic character has been identified by matching with portions of the human genome (see Garber, 2000).

This suggests a new era in which chronic diseases will be better understood and gene-based medicines will target the disease process, conceivably using drugs custom-made for a person's unique genetic makeup—though this may be very costly, in contrast to relatively inexpensive mass-marketed drugs. If genetically based medicine lives up to its promise, it could have a significant impact on world population numbers and age structure. If chronic diseases are reduced significantly, the effect could be a wave of death control among older persons, comparable to the death control among infants and children accomplished in the years following World War II. In those years, modern medical technology exported to developing nations greatly reduced the impact of infectious diseases. In the absence of birth control, the result was rapid population growth in the affected regions. In the decades ahead, reduced mortality among older groups will probably occur first in wealthy nations, accentuating the present trend to older populations in those regions.

Another aspect of the new genomic science is the ability to detect a mutation that makes an individual susceptible to a certain disease. Although this could facilitate early treatment, it raises concerns about the confidentiality of that information, and the possibility that health insurance might be withheld if a susceptibility were diagnosed. (For information on ethical, legal, and social implications of genomic science, see National Human Genomic Research Institute [NHGRI] at http://www.nhgri.nih.gov, and a site maintained by *Nature*, http://www.nature.com/genomics.)

Whatever the ultimate results, the new genetically based medicine has been made possible by a cluster of technologies: the rich genetic data bank provided by the combination of private and government-funded sequencing of the biological markers in DNA; advanced X-ray beam apparatus for diffraction patterns that reveal protein structures; and high-speed computers (and the software) needed to assemble the biological markers, conduct searches of the genetic data bank, process diffraction patterns, and create three-dimensional models of protein molecules.

Modern Medicine and Resistance to Antimicrobials. In wealthy nations, the use of over-the-counter and prescription drugs has become so prevalent that residues from pain relievers and cholesterol-lowering drugs are now found in sewage effluent and streams, and estrogen from birth-control pills has turned up in concentrations that appear to affect the mating behavior of fish (Raloff, 2000). More important, the overuse of antibiotic drugs is contributing to the evolution of microbes that are unaffected by the drugs.

In 1928, Alexander Fleming discovered the antibiotic effects of a mold, and the first miracle drug—penicillin—was born. Later discoveries included streptomycins, tetracycline, quinolones, antifungals, antiparasitics, and—more recently—antivirals. Collectively known as *antimicrobials*, these drugs, along with improvements in sanitation and nutrition, brought the world's infectious diseases under control and defined an era in which the remaining challenge was thought to be chronic diseases such as cancer and heart disease. [*See* Disease; *and* Human Health.]

At the end of the twentieth century, however, infectious diseases are again on the rise: gonorrhea, typhoid, tuberculosis (TB), and malaria are increasingly difficult to control because their agents have developed resistance to drugs. This chink in the armor that protects humans against infectious diseases is now in the forefront of public health concerns (see World Health Organization Factsheet No. 194, May 1988, at http://www.who.int/inffs/en/fact194).

Resistant strains of bacteria develop when mutant forms survive their exposure to an antibiotic as a result of either underuse or overuse of the drug. In developing nations, a patient often cannot afford a full course of treatment and stops the medication prematurely, allowing marginally resistant strains to survive and reproduce. Conversely, in wealthy nations there is excessive exposure to drugs, and each exposure is an opportunity for resistant strains to survive. Prescribing drugs unnecessarily is one avenue to overexposure; prescribing the wrong drug is another. In the home, antibacterial soaps and cleaning solutions contribute to the problem.

The use of antibiotics in foods is rampant. Of all antibiotics produced, half are used to treat sick livestock, to promote growth in livestock, or to treat produce. When resistant bacteria develop in livestock, they are sometimes able to jump to humans and cause an outbreak of disease.

Recent increases in international trade and travel provide opportunities for a resistant microbe originating in Africa or Southeast Asia to arrive in North America one day later. Resistant strains of gonorrhea originating in Asia and Africa have now spread throughout the world; and drug-resistant TB, a serious problem in eastern Europe, could soon become a threat to other regions. Resistant TB strains are now found in China, India, Iran, Mozambique, and the United States (see World Health Organization, 2000a).

In June 2000, the World Health Organization defined this problem and outlined policy changes and individual efforts needed to combat it. The report suggests that research and development must make rapid progress during the first decade of the twenty-first century (World Health Organization, 2000b).

Computers and Information Technology. One hallmark of technologies prominent at the end of the twentieth century is that they generate massive amounts of data that can be handled only with the aid of computers. [*See* Information Technology.] Satellites, scanning the Earth with a number of different sensors that resolve the viewed area into thousands of pixels, produce continual streams of digital signals that must be stored, sorted, edited, and ultimately converted into map images on screen or on paper. Furthermore, the satellites and space probes would never reach their orbits and trajectories without the combination of physics, engineering, and computation that launch and guide the vehicles. The analysis of weather data, improved storm predictions, and the modeling of atmospheric processes to better understand the impacts of natural events or human inputs all depend on high-speed computers. Sifting, sorting, and matching the patterns of biochemical markers in DNA is a task that could not be approached in the pre-computer era.

In fact, all fundamental and applied research now relies heavily on computers to capture, store, and analyze data. Tracking the explosive generation of particles in high-energy physics, or the painstaking comparison of sequential optical and radio images in astronomy, are only two examples. Laboratories of all kinds around the world rely on computers as a matter of course for storing and displaying data, computation, and statistical analysis.

Science and research aside, the modern world runs with the aid of computers so pervasive and commonplace they are invisible. The entire telecommunications industry—telephones, wireless phones, and the Internet—depends on computer-controlled sorting and switching of electronic and optical signals pulsing through wires and glass strands. Financial records and transactions are managed and recorded digitally: computers make the global economy function. Manufacturing uses computer-aided design, robots, and process controls. Both suppliers and retailers manage their resources, inventories, and accounts with computers. Shipping companies track their parcels, and airlines manage their flights. Government agencies around the world store and process data on the demographics, taxes, and pensions of billions of individuals, while mapping their territories with methods that depend on satellites and computers.

Remarkable advances in hardware have made all this management of data possible with installations that progressively are more compact and less expensive. But none of it would work without software that expresses the logic of all the calculations and manipulations required. As essential tools, crafted for special purposes, software is a key technology of our time. Even though some software seems ill-designed for the user, it is encouraging to see some projects directed toward systems that are more user-friendly (see Dertouzos, 1999).

The advances in hardware since the advent of the personal computer are now commonplace. The rapid miniaturization is described by Moore's Law: the amount of information stored on a given area of silicon has doubled every eighteen months since 1970. The law is apparently self-fulfilling: the implication is that somebody, somewhere, will build a better chip than you if you rest on your laurels.

The recent recognition that physical limitations of silicon-based technology will make it difficult to maintain Moore's Law could be met cheerfully, were it not for the belief that the economic boom of the 1990s was partly due to increased productivity linked to this very increase in computer capacity and to the lowered prices that made computers more affordable for individuals and businesses (Mann, 2000b). Searching for new approaches to supplant silicon-based machines, researchers now consider molecular computing, quantum computing, biological computing, and DNA computing (see *Technology Review*, special issue, "Beyond Silicon," May–June 2000). At the same time, to improve connections to the Internet, workers in academic institutions and in the private sector are exploring cable, optical, and wireless schemes to provide homes and businesses with broadband high-speed access to the Internet (see Clark, 1999).

More significant than tweaking Internet access for citizens in wealthy nations are the possible impacts of information and communication technologies on serious problems in our rapidly changing world. The anticipated "paperless office" has not materialized; in fact, U.S. consumption of paper has risen more than 50 percent since 1980 as computers have proliferated and printers have captured messages, documents, and materials from the Internet—fueling the papermaking industry, which uses large amounts of energy and pollutes both air and water. The manufacture of semiconductors requires a number of solvents that threaten the environment.

Computers and other information devices are becoming the largest source of growth in electrical demand in commercial buildings; coincidentally, power consumption often increases as computer and communication speeds increase. There are technical fixes that will help, including the conversion of communication systems to all-optical technology, which uses optical switches to avoid converting optical signals to electrical at Internet hubs (Fairley, 2000). In the home, too, energy use is growing because of home office systems, television and audio equipment, and portable phones. Most stereos, televisions, and videocassette recorders use power even when they apparently are turned off. These "standby losses" account for 5 to 15 percent of residential energy use in the United States (Kelly, 1999).

There are ways, however, in which computer and information technology can benefit the environment. An increase of 8 percent in the gross domestic product of the United States between 1996 and 1998 was accompanied by a growth of only 1 percent in energy use, because information technology businesses were part of the economic growth, and they do not process as large tonnages of materials as manufacturing operations do. Moreover, information technology has improved the efficiency of resource use through improved design of products, intelligent production processes, and intelligent operation of buildings, aircraft, and vehicles.

How to use the growing power of information and communication technologies to further economic growth—especially, sustainable growth—in developing nations is a problem that underlines the relative roles of government and the private sector. The subject is addressed by the United Nations Commission on Science and Technology for Development, which, in a 1966 report, points out the opportunities, the constraints, and the actions needed to realize the development potential of computer and information technologies (United Nations Educational, Scientific, and Cultural Organization, 1996). Another general overview of the complex issue is provided by the summary of a conference held at the European Commission, Brussels, in December 1995.

Those reviews are useful and lead the reader to related work and key persons, but they do not define specific strategies. One scheme that does is proposed by Allen Hammond (1999), senior scientist and director of strategic analysis at the World Resources Institute. He notes that four disturbing trends in poor nations must be arrested: continued rapid population growth; growing degradation of biological resources, including soils; persistent poverty and rising malnutrition; and new threats to security arising from conflicts over water, other resources, migrations, and acquired immune deficiency syndrome (AIDS) and other emerging diseases. His development model, called Market World, is a "bottom-up" scheme which uses public–private partnerships, satellites in low Earth orbits, and cellular phone service to take information, credit, and other self-help tools to communities and individuals in developing regions. Hammond asks leading companies in the information and communication business to collaborate in demonstration projects.

Another scheme, also dependent on information and communication technology, is offered by Freeman J. Dyson, Professor Emeritus at the Institute for Advanced Study, Princeton. He proposes to attack rural poverty and migration to megacities by reviving villages through a combination of technologies. First, villages are electrified by solar photovoltaic power. Then, genetically engineered crops are grown to produce fuels, drugs, or materials that can be exported. Finally, a network of satellites allows wireless connections that end the isolation of villages, provide information and training to the people, and connect them to the global economy (Dyson, 1999, pp. 61–74).

Aerospace. In 1969, a long series of triumphs in ballooning, heavier-than-air flight, supersonic flight, rocketry, Earth-orbit flights, and Moon-orbit flights culminated in landing humans on the Moon—the ultimate expression of how science and technology can work together toward a specific goal, spurred in this case by competition between two world powers. That feat, and subsequent unmanned excursions to the planets and their moons, have revised our view of the Earth and altered our attitudes toward it.

The photos of Earth snapped by Apollo astronauts made obvious for the first time the sphericity of our globe; blue oceans under white swirls of cloud made images irresistible to journalists and textbook publishers. These views led readers to see our planet as an extraterrestrial might see it—a moist, fertile sphere, unique in the Solar System, deserving the utmost in care. The full-sphere view of Earth from space became the centerpiece of the Earth Flag (http://earthflag.net), symbolic of allegiance to the Earth, not just to one's country of birth. The impetus given to environmental movements at the time is impossible to measure because the Moon landing coincided roughly with influential writings by the biologists Paul Erlich, Barry Commoner, and Garrett Hardin, and with events such as the conflagration of Cleveland's oil-polluted Cuyahoga River and the crude-oil leak from an offshore well near Santa Barbara, California. Nevertheless, those images were an awakening and a milestone marking our entry to a new era. Coincidentally, the first annual Earth Day was held in the United States in April 1970.

About ten years later, a more profound image was sent to Earth from a spacecraft—this time, Voyager 1, approaching the edge of the solar system. Looking back toward the Sun, it captured Earth, more than 3 billion miles away, as a tiny, pale-blue dot, apparently illuminated by a dramatic beam of light. Seeing that image, Carl Sagan was struck by how isolated and lonely is our planet—the only world that harbors life, as far as we know. This distant view of our tiny world "underscores our responsibility to deal more kindly with one another, and to preserve and cherish the pale blue dot, the only home we've ever known" (Sagan, 1997, p. 7).

Preserving the Earth has been furthered by various special-purpose satellites which, since the 1960s, have become available for monitoring Earth's vital signs. [See Global Monitoring; and Remote Sensing.] The latest in the U.S. National Aeronautics and Space Administration's (NASA's) Earth Observing System (EOS), a satellite called *Terra*, was launched in December 1999 to join three others in the EOS series. *Terra* will measure solar energy, winds, productivity of oceans, forest cutting and burning, ice and snow cover, greenhouse gases, clouds, and aerosols. Other satellites monitor storms and aid in weather prediction; still others provide underpinnings for the GPS and for the communications systems essential to the global economy.

Some scientific communities, encouraged by successful space probes, have nurtured the ideas of migrating to Mars or colonizing the asteroid belt, while possibly mining distant bodies for mineral resources exhausted on Earth. Their opponents argue that a preoccupation with colonizing other planets may engender a conscious or unconscious reduction in the sense of urgency with regard to maintaining the environment that must support Earth's burgeoning population. Sagan, after thoughtfully considering the options, concludes that since there is no life elsewhere in the Solar System to be endangered by our exploration and colonization, we should "vastly increase our knowledge of the Solar System and then begin to settle other worlds," and "If our long-term survival is at stake, we have a basic responsibility to our species [to] venture to other worlds"

(1997, p. 312). Without addressing the need for such space travel, a number of specialists have proposed ingenious technologies for propulsion in space (*Scientific American*, March 2000; http://www.sciam.com) and for cheap missions to Mars (Zubrin, 2000; also see The International Mars Society at http://www.marssociety. org). There appear to be two reasons to colonize Mars: first, to search for life there; and second, to find a refuge for *Homo sapiens*, whose existence is threatened at home by their own actions. To relieve population pressure at home, however, it would be necessary to launch nearly one-quarter million persons per day into space to match the 1999 annual growth rate of 83 million per year.

BIBLIOGRAPHY

Ausubel, J. H. "The Environment for Future Business: Efficiency Will Win." *Pollution Prevention Review* (Winter 1998), 39–52.

Ball, P. *Made to Measure: New Materials for the 21st Century.* Princeton, N.J.: Princeton University Press, 1997.

Brand, S. "Is Technology Moving Too Fast?" *Time* (19 June 2000), 108–109.

Carlyle, T. "Signs of the Times." In *Selected Works, Reminiscences and Letters*, edited by Julian Symons. Cambridge, Mass.: Harvard University Press, 1957.

Carson, R. *Silent Spring.* Boston: Houghton Mifflin, 1962.

Clark, David D. "High-Speed Data Races Home." *Scientific American* (October 1999), 94–115.

Dertouzos, M. L. "The Future of Computing." *Scientific American* (August 1999), 52–55.

Dyson, F. J. "The Next Biotech Harvest." *Technology Review* (Sept.–Oct. 1998), 34–41.

———. *The Sun, the Genome, and the Internet.* New York: Oxford University Press, 1999.

Ellul, J. *The Technological Society.* New York: Knopf, 1964.

Fairley, P. "The Microphotonics Revolution." *Technology Review* (July–August 2000), 38–44.

Flavin, C., and N. Lenssen. *Power Surge: Guide to the Coming Energy Revolution.* New York: Norton, 1994.

Garber, K. "The Next Wave of the Genomics Business." *Technology Review* (July–August 2000), 46–56.

Gardner, G., and P. Sampat. "Forging a Sustainable Materials Economy." In *State of the World 1999.* New York: Norton, 1999.

Glenn, E. P., J. Brown, and J. W. O'Leary. "Irrigating Crops with Seawater." *Scientific American* (August 1998). See http://www. sciam.com/featurearch98.

Gray, P. "The Paradox of Technological Development." In *Technology and Environment*, edited by J. H. Ausubel and H. E. Sladovich, pp. 192–204. Washington, D.C.: National Academy Press, 1989.

Gruebler, A. *Technology and Global Change.* Cambridge: Cambridge University Press, 1998.

Hammond, Allen. "A Vision: A World That Is Genuinely Better, Not Just Wealthier." *iMP Magazine* (Oct. 1999).

Kelly, H. "Information Technology and the Environment: Choices and Opportunities." *iMP Magazine* (22 October 1999). See http://www.cisp.org/imp/october99/10 99kelly.

King, M. D., and D. D. Herring. "Monitoring Earth's Vital Signs." *Scientific American* (April 2000), 92–97.

Mann, C. "Biotech Goes Wild." *Technology Review* (July–August 2000a), 36–43.

———. "The End of Moore's Law." *Technology Review* (May–June 2000b), 46.

McDonald, A. *Global Energy Perspectives.* Cambridge: Cambridge University Press, 1998.

Mitcham, C. *Thinking through Technology: The Path between Engineering and Philosophy.* Chicago: University of Chicago Press, 1994.

Mumford, L. *The Myth of the Machine: The Pentagon of Power.* New York: Harcourt Brace Jovanovich, 1970.

Prakash, C. S., "Hungry for Biotech." *Technology Review* (July–August 2000), 32.

Raloff, J. "Excreted Drugs: Something Looks Fishy." *Science News* (17 June 2000), 388.

———. "The Case for DDT." *Science News* (1 July 2000), 12–14.

Sagan, C. *Pale Blue Dot.* New York: Ballantine Books, 1997.

Schumacher, E. F. *Small is Beautiful: Economics as If People Mattered.* New York: Harper and Row, 1973.

Scientific American. "Sending Astronauts to Mars." Special report 282 (March 2000), 40–63.

Simpson, R. D. *Productivity in Natural Resource Industries: Improvement through Innovation.* Washington, D.C.: Resources for the Future, 1999.

Technology Review. "Beyond Silicon." Special issue (May–June 2000).

United Nations Educational, Scientific, and Cultural Organization (UNESCO). *Information and Communication Technologies in Development: A UNESCO Perspective.* Paris: UNESCO, 1996. See http://www.unesco.org.webworld/telematics/uncstd.

White, L. "The Historical Roots of our Ecological Crisis." *Science* (March 1967), 1203–1207.

Winner, L. *The Whale and the Reactor.* Chicago: University of Chicago Press, 1989.

World Health Organization. *Antituberculosis Drug Resistance in the World.* Report no. 2. Geneva: WHO and IUATLD, 2000a.

———. *Overcoming Antimicrobial Resistance, World Health Report on Infectious Diseases 2000.* Geneva: WHO, 2000b.

Zubrin, R. "Mars Direct." *Scientific American* (March 2000). See http://www.sciam.com.

—DAVID J. CUFF

TELECOMMUNICATION. *See* Information Technology.

THERMAL POLLUTION. *See* Pollution; *and* Water Quality.

THOREAU, HENRY DAVID

Henry David Thoreau (1817–1862), celebrated American naturalist and philosopher, was born in Concord, Massachusetts, and graduated from Harvard University in 1837. Best known for his stay at Walden Pond (July 1845–September 1847), he worked intermittently as a surveyor and as a pencil maker. Traditionally characterized as a Transcendentalist, Thoreau is now understood as a "new renaissance man" whose outlook on culture and nature was informed by a nascent evolutionary paradigm. While littérateurs emphasize his literary style, his works can be read as arguing that the good life is not lived in opposition to but in harmony with nature (thereby anticipating present-day discourse on sustainable development). [*See* Sustainable Development.] Thoreau was not only a cultural iconoclast, but skeptical of abstract (scientific or philosophical) knowledge unleavened by immediate and personal contact with and later reflection on nature.

In the context of global change, the usefulness of Thoreau's writings increases, since they represent sustained observations of the anthropogenic modification of the New England bioregion. He is widely acknowledged as originating the theory of ecological succession; he recorded the extinction of indigenous flora and fauna, the ecological consequences of agriculture and forestry, and the seasonal cycles of nature. Thoreau is a principal contributor to the wilderness idea, a concept crucial to conservation and preservation philosophy. [*See* Wilderness.] Thoreau's texts inspired the work of Frederick Law Olmstead and John Muir in the nineteenth century, and Aldo Leopold and Joseph Wood Krutch in the twentieth. [*See the biography of Leopold.*] A trenchant observer of culture, he offers penetrating insights into the psychological and sociological dimensions of the mid-nineteenth-century American political economy, and relentless criticism of narrowly economic purposes that lead to the ruin of human character and the mindless exploitation of nature. He was among the first intellectuals to grapple with the implications of evolution for humankind's self-conception, theory of culture, and historical change itself. He was also a seminal contributor to the literature of civil disobedience, influencing Mahatma Gandhi as well as the American civil rights and global environmental movements. [*See* Environmental Movements.]

While *Walden* (1854) and "Civil Disobedience" (1849), are better known texts, Thoreau's *Journal* (1906) is considered an essential text. His published works reflect the journal (often verbatim). More crucially, the *Journal* offers unparalleled mid-nineteenth-century sociological, anthropological, botanical, and climatological baselines that are invaluable in the assessment of the rate and consequences of cultural and ecological change. Other works include *A Week on the Concord and Merrimack Rivers* (1849), and the posthumously published "Walking" (1862), *The Maine Woods* (1864), and *Cape Cod* (1865).

While Thoreau was eclipsed by Ralph Waldo Emerson during his lifetime, his accomplishments were not unacknowledged by his peers. He worked with Louis Agassiz at Harvard, and was offered membership (he declined) in the (now American) Association for the Advancement of Science. [*See the biography of Agassiz.*] While Emerson was a major early influence on Thoreau, and while Emerson believed that Thoreau failed to realize his potential, new assessments of Thoreau position him as one of the greatest of nineteenth-century American intellectuals. Clearly, he was in the vanguard of evolutionary thinkers, thus underscoring the relevance of his work to the disciplines dealing with the issues of environmental change and human society.

BIBLIOGRAPHY

WORKS BY THOREAU

Thoreau, H. D. *The Writings of Henry David Thoreau*. Boston: Houghton Mifflin, 1906. The complete collection of Thoreau's writings.

———. *The Journal of Henry David Thoreau*. Salt Lake City: Peregrine Smith Books, 1984. A paperback reprint of the 1906 edition.

WORKS ON THOREAU

Harding, W. *The Days of Henry Thoreau: A Biography*. New York: Dover Publications, 1982. The standard biography of Thoreau.

Oelschlaeger, Max. "Henry David Thoreau: Philosopher of the Wilderness." In *The Idea of Wilderness: From Prehistory to the Age of Ecology*, pp. 133–171. New Haven: Yale University Press, 1991. A reinterpretation of Thoreau in the context of the idea of wilderness.

Richardson, R. *Henry Thoreau: A Life of the Mind*. Berkeley: University of California Press, 1986. The most interesting recent intellectual history of Thoreau.

—MAX OELSCHLAEGER

THREATENED SPECIES. *See* Extinction of Species.

TIME SERIES ANALYSIS

Climate varies on all time scales. The size and nature of climate variation depends on one's location on the Earth and the climate proxy measurement. The latter includes historical records of temperature, precipitation, and atmospheric pressure, or more indirect measures such as faunal abundances, tree rings, and the relative proportion of heavy and light oxygen isotopes in the shells of marine microfossils. One view of global change focuses on secular and/or catastrophic changes. It highlights irreversible events such as the closing of the seawater channel at the Isthmus of Panama that helped set up contemporary deep-water circulation patterns in the North Atlantic. Much climate change, however, whether it is caused by external forcing or by internal interactions, has a repeatable or cyclic character. On human time scales, we can perceive the yearly progression of the seasons associated with our planet's transit around the Sun, or the irregular sequence of storms in the midlatitude winter caused by the eastward drift of self-sustaining atmospheric waves. On geologic time scales, scientists have learned that the ice age of human prehistory was merely one of a series of glacial advances and retreats, whose timing follows (in part) predictable cyclic variations in the Earth's orbit around the Sun. Similarly, the detection of anthropogenic greenhouse warming is complicated by the recent discovery of several natural, but irregular, coupled oscillations of the atmosphere–ocean system, each capable of producing multiyear warming and cooling episodes on global and/or regional scales. Scientists study these cyclic phenomena in the "frequency" domain, applying time series analysis and spectrum estimation techniques.

The nature of a data set determines the appropriate analysis method. The simplest type of data series $\{x_n\} = x_1, x_2, x_3, \ldots, x_N$ is a set of measurements equally spaced in time, where one can assume that each measured value x_j does not depend on any other x_k. In this situation the data are statistically independent. If each x_j can be treated as a random variable from a time-invariant Gaussian-normal distribution, the data series is termed a *white noise series*. Most time series algorithms are designed for use on data series with white-noise characteristics, e.g., to estimate a deterministic signal immersed in a white-noise "background." Climate data series are rarely "white," however. Daily or monthly temperature anomalies T_n, defined as deviations from a climatological average, resemble "red noise," because measured T_n can be shown to have a significant correlation with T_{n-1}, the previous temperature anomaly value. This implies that temperature anomalies have some memory of past conditions (roughly twelve months in twentieth-century data), and behave similarly to a random walk. Short-term correlation in a data series can be investigated with an autoregressive (AR), or prediction filter, method. In the simplest AR model for temperature anomaly data, one assumes a relation

$$T_n = a_1 T_{n-1} + x_n,$$

where a_1 is a fixed parameter that quantifies the dependence of a temperature value on its previously recorded value, and $\{x_n\}$ is a white-noise data series that generates the observed random deviations from the predicted $T_n = a_1 T_{n-1}$. A data series with a more complex memory can be modeled with a higher-order AR model

$$T_n = \Sigma_n + 3a_m T_{n-m}$$

that assumes a prediction filter $\{a_1, a_2, a_3, \ldots a_M\}$. The coefficients of an Mth-order prediction filter can be estimated by treating the autoregressive equation as a least-squares problem. Higher-order prediction filters may not be justified by the data, however, and can lead the researcher to identify spurious or misrepresentative oscillatory behavior in a data set.

The Fourier Transform and Spectrum Estimation. A better way to estimate oscillatory signals in a data set is spectrum estimation via the Fourier transform. If the sampling interval is τ, the Fourier transform $X(f)$ of a data series $\{x_n\}$ is computed by

$$X(f) = \Sigma \; x_n \exp(i2\pi fn\tau) = \Sigma \; x_n[\cos(2\pi fn \; \tau) + i \, \sin(2\pi fn \; \tau)].$$

The frequency f has units of cycles per unit time. Note that the time series data are discrete, but the complex-valued Fourier transform $X(f)$ is a continuous function of frequency. In practice one computes $X(f)$ for discrete values of f with a variant of the fast Fourier transform (FFT). For an N-point data series, the FFT returns

$$X(0), X(f_R), X(2f_R), \dots X((N/2) f_R),$$

where $f_R = (N\tau)^{-1}$ is the Rayleigh frequency resolution and $(N/2) f_R = f_N$ is the Nyquist frequency. Signals in the data with $f > f_N$ are "aliased" to lower frequencies, because the sampling interval τ is too coarse to obtain sufficient measurements (at least two) per cycle. The Fourier transform of $\{x_n\}$ can be interpolated by "padding" the data series with zeroes to some larger value $N' > N$, obtaining a nominal

$$\Delta f = (N'\tau)^{-1} < f_R.$$

This does not add new information to the Fourier transform, but can make its graphed values easier to interpret.

Oscillatory signals in the time series should appear as peaks in the amplitude of $X(f)$, but many such peaks are generated randomly. If no zero-padding is applied before the FFT, the statistics of $X(f)$ for a white-noise data series mirror those of the series itself: the real and imaginary parts of $X(f)$ are Gaussian-normal random variables. One estimate of the spectrum $S(f)$ is the periodogram $S(f) = |X(f)|^2$. For a white-noise spectrum the expected value $\langle S(f) \rangle = S_o$ is a constant, namely, a flat spectrum, but stochastic fluctuations cause the periodogram to behave as a chi-squared random variable with two degrees of freedom. For this case a peak in $S(f)$ must exceed $3S_o$ to appear nonrandom at 95 percent confidence, that is, the signal-to-noise ratio must exceed 3 in the frequency domain. Better detection capability can be gained with a smoothed-periodogram spectrum estimate, formed by a moving average of the periodogram. If $|X(mf_R)|^2$ is averaged with just its nearest neighbors $|X((m-1)f_R)|^2$ and $|X((m+1)f_R)|^2$, the statistics follow a chi-squared distribution with six degrees of freedom, and a peak in $S(f)$ must exceed only $(2.1)S_o$ to appear nonrandom at 95 percent confidence. Improved detection capability comes at the cost of coarser frequency resolution. Still, smoothed-periodogram spectrum estimates are usually much easier to interpret than raw periodograms.

The periodogram has severe shortcomings, caused primarily by "spectral leakage." Leakage occurs when oscillatory behavior at one oscillation frequency f' con- taminates the spectral estimate $S(f)$ at a "distant" frequency f, where distant is defined by $|f-f'| >> f_R$. The primary cause of spectral leakage is that the Fourier transform assumes implicitly that the data series $x_n = 0$ for all times outside the finite duration of the data series. This is rarely true. For processes that are stationary (for example, those that persist indefinitely in time without a change in statistical properties), the true Fourier transform $Z(f)$ is related to the measured FFT by a convolution with an averaging kernel $W(f)$:

$$\int_{-fN}^{fN} W(f')Z(f - f')\mathrm{d}f' \tag{1}$$

For a simple Fourier transform, $W(f)$ is proportional to $(\sin 2\pi f\tau)/\pi f$. This function has a central peak surrounded by sidelobes that decrease in amplitude with f^{-1}. This decrease is often too weak for "red" or "colored" spectra, so that the sidelobes from large spectral peaks obscure the spectral features of low-amplitude signals. The solution is to multiply the data by a "taper" $\{w_n\}$. A taper typically resembles a smooth bell curve, peaked in the center and tending gradually to zero at the ends of the data series. The Fourier transform of the taper replaces the averaging kernel in the convolution (1), and trades off a more-rapid decrease in sidelobe amplitude with a wider central lobe. If the sidelobes are small, one can extend with confidence most spectrum estimation algorithms from "white" spectra to "locally white" spectra, that is, to all spectra that do not possess a large, essentially discontinuous drop in amplitude.

One objection to tapering a time series before the Fourier transform is that it downweights data near the series endpoints, effectively discarding information. D. J. Thomson of Bell Laboratories solved this problem in the early 1980s by computing and applying a short sequence of tapers $\{w_n^{(0)}\}, \{w_n^{(1)}\}, \dots \{w_n^{(K-1)}\}$ to data and forming "multitaper" spectrum estimates out of the resulting sequence of Fourier transforms. The tapers are derived as the eigenfunctions of a variational problem to minimize spectral leakage outside a bandwidth $[f - pf_R, f + pf_R]$ that prescribes the width of the central lobe of $W(f)$. The variational problem ensures that the tapers are mutually orthogonal, so that the sequence of tapered Fourier transforms $X^{(0)}(f), X^{(1)}(f) \dots X^{(K-1)}(f)$ can be treated as statistically independent for "locally white" spectra. This property simplifies greatly the statistics of coherence and correlation estimates, introduced below. It also underpins a technique for distinguishing phase-coherent oscillations (e.g., the yearly cycle of temperature) from quasi-periodic signals (for example, El Niño–Southern Oscillation (ENSO) variability), for which the timing of cycles is irregular. Resolving this distinction can be important in identifying the nature of a climate signal. For example, one can test whether the bedding thicknesses in layered carbonate/marl sediments are associated with Milankovitch orbital cycles, or some more random internal cycle.

Coherence and Correlation between Climate Proxy Records. Climate signals are observed simultaneously in many different locations and with different proxy variables. To determine their strength, location, and possible underlying mechanisms, one can determine the frequency-dependent coherence or cross-correlation of two or more data series. Qualitatively, two data series $\{x_n\}$ and $\{y_n\}$ are coherent at frequency f if their fluctuations on the time scale $T = 1/f$ are similar, perhaps with a time delay. Quantitatively, coherence is a normalized inner product of the Fourier transforms $Y(f)$ and $X(f)$ in the frequency neighborhood of f:

$$C(f) = \frac{[\Sigma \; Y^*(f + mf_R)X(f + mf_R)]}{[\Sigma \; X^*(f + mf_R)X(f + mf_R)]^{1/2}[\Sigma \; Y^*(f + mf_R)Y(f + mf_R)]^{1/2}} \quad (2)$$

where * indicates complex conjugation. If the sum extends over $2p + 1$ transform values ($m = -p, -p + 1, \ldots p - 1, p$), the statistics of $C(f)$ are constrained by $4p + 2$ degrees of freedom. (A similar formula applies for multitaper spectra, using K tapered spectrum estimates evaluated at f.) $C(f)$ is complex valued with modulus bounded by 0 and 1. $|C(f)|^2$ follows a standard distribution, relatable to the F distribution, that determines confidence levels for nonrandom coherence. For $K = 2$, there are ten degrees of freedom in (2), and $|C(f)|^2$ must exceed 0.53 to be nonrandom at 95 percent confidence.

A cross-correlation estimate is similar. It arises from an attempt to determine a linear relationship $Y(f) = a(f)X(f)$ between the transforms, with the implication that the process described by the data series $\{x_n\}$ has a causal influence on the process described by the data series $\{y_n\}$. The correlation coefficient $a(f)$ can be estimated with a least-squares solution in the neighborhood of f, summing over $m = -p, -p + 1, \ldots p - 1, p$:

$$a(f) = \frac{\Sigma \; Y^*(f + mf_R)X(f + mf_R)}{\Sigma \; Y^*(f + mf_R)Y(f + mf_R)}. \quad (3)$$

Coherence and cross-correlation are used to assess the likelihood that two data series have a causal relationship. The Milankovitch theory of ice ages was boosted by coherence estimates between climate proxy data from ocean sediment cores and astronomical time series of insolation variations caused by the Earth's variable tilt, precession, and eccentricity of orbit. In the case of 100,000-year variability, however, the ice volume proxy data and orbital eccentricity series show nonrandom coherence, but $|C(f)|^2$ is not sufficiently large for eccentricity to be the only causal factor. This has opened the way to nonlinear models of late-Pleistocene climate change that interpret the 100,000-year ice age cycle as a strange attractor limit cycle, influenced but not driven by eccentricity.

Coherence and cross-correlation estimates can be extended to more than two records by means of the singular-value decomposition (SVD). If one decomposes a matrix **A** of $2p + 1$ Fourier transform values from N data series:

$$A = \begin{bmatrix} X^{(1)}(f - pf_R) & X^{(1)}(f - (p - 1)f_R) \ldots & X^{(1)}(f + pf_R) \\ \vdots & \vdots & \vdots \\ X^{(N)}(f - pf_R) & X^{(N)}(f - (p - 1)f_R) \ldots & X^{(N)}(f + pf_R) \end{bmatrix} \quad (4)$$

into singular values λ_k and singular vectors V_k, one can determine linear combinations of data series with maximum mutual coherence. The confidence levels for nonrandomness for the largest singular value λ_1 can be determined from Monte Carlo simulations using computer-generated noise as input, or by bootstrap resampling of the data series themselves. This technique has been used to confirm the presence of interannual, decadal, and interdecadal climate signals in globally gridded historical temperature and pressure data. The singular vector V_1 associated with maximum mutual coherence can be used to reconstruct the spatial and timing relationships of these climate patterns, demonstrating centers of action in the North Atlantic for climate variability near seven and eleven year periods, and in the North and Equatorial Pacific for fifteen- to seventeen-year variability.

A Final Caveat: Detecting Climate Transitions. Most time series algorithms assume the data series to be stationary, that is, not to change in character over time. It is possible for the climate system to undergo an irreversible shift while a data series is recorded. In fact, the estimation of transient frequency-dependent behavior is quite important. For instance, has the time scale and/or spatial pattern of ENSO changed over recent centuries? To address such questions, one can apply evolutive spectrum estimation, in which one computes Fourier transforms on a sliding window within a larger data series. A similar approach involves wavelet analysis, in which the sines and cosines of the Fourier transform are replaced by pulse-like functions that are both transient and concentrated on a single time scale. Wavelets for shorter time scales have shorter durations, making wavelet analysis potentially more useful in estimating the character of sudden changes in the climate system. Wavelet analysis of the Southern Oscillation Index, for instance, has drawn attention to an episode of weak variability in 1920–1940 that may mark a transition in the spatial pattern of ENSO dynamics.

[*See also* Climate Change; El Niño–Southern Oscillation; *and* Natural Climate Fluctuations.]

BIBLIOGRAPHY

Berger, A., et al. *Milankovitch and Climate: Understanding the Response to Astronomical Forcing*, parts 1 and 2. Hingham, Mass.: D. Riedel, 1984. A NATO Advanced Research Workshop volume with papers on the astronomical theory of climate change, geologic evidence for cyclic climate change throughout Earth history, and the time series analysis that links theory and observation together.

Bloomfield, P. *Fourier Analysis of Time Series: An Introduction.* New York: Wiley, 1976. A good introduction to time series algorithms and the statistical concepts that underpin them, with many examples.

Gu, D., and S. G. H. Philander. "Secular Changes of Annual and Interannual Variability in the Tropics During the Last Century." *Journal of Climate* 8 (1995), 864–876. Application of wavelet analysis to the Southern Oscillation Index. Demonstrates a weakness in the sea level pressure signal associated with ENSO in 1920–1940, perhaps indicating a climate transition.

Kuo, C., et al. "Coherence Established between Atmospheric Carbon Dioxide and Global Temperature." *Nature* 343 (1990), 709–713. A careful study of the potential linkage between atmospheric carbon dioxide and global temperature records, estimating the coherence of small-amplitude oscillations with periods T greater than one year. Comes to the conclusion that cyclic changes in carbon dioxide follow changes in temperature rather than precede them, suggesting that increases in global temperature drive dissolved carbon dioxide out of the oceans and other heat-sensitive carbon reservoirs.

Mann, M. E., and J. Lees. "Robust Estimations of Background Noise and Signal Detection in Climatic Time Series." *Climate Change* 33 (1996), 409–445. Addresses the red-noise character of most climate time series using low-order autoregressive prediction filters.

Mann, M. E., and J. Park. "Joint Spatiotemporal Modes of Surface Temperature and Sea-Level Pressure Variability in the Northern Hemisphere during the Past Century." *Journal of Climate* 9 (1996), 2137–2162. Uses the SVD-coherence of historical temperature and pressure data to discover and reconstruct interannual oscillations of the ocean–atmosphere system, including a long-term (fifteen- to seventeen-year) ENSO-like oscillation.

Thomson, D. J. "Spectrum Estimation and Harmonic Analysis." *IEEE Proceedings* 70 (1982), 1055–1096. A seminal paper on multitaper spectrum analysis techniques.

—JEFFREY PARK

TOURISM

Tourism, in one form or another, has been with us since biblical times, but its emergence as a major industry with significant global impacts did not occur until after World War II. One estimate of its current size is provided by the World Travel and Tourism Council, which considers that world tourism revenues in 1995 were worth U.S.$3.5 trillion and that the industry employed one worker in nine worldwide. Such a dramatic growth rate is a manifestation of general worldwide socioeconomic and technological change that has resulted in the rise of the general tertiary or service economic sector.

Growth. Three significant contributors to the growth of tourism have been rising standards of living, increased levels of personal mobility, and the global information explosion. The principal generators of tourism have been the advanced economies of western Europe, North America, and Southeast Asia. It is now the turn of East Asia and the Pacific to lead in the growth and development of tourism. Between 1980 and 1992, tourist arrivals increased by an average growth rate of 8.9 percent per annum and receipts by 15 percent per annum (Hobson, 1994).

As individuals have secured more disposable income and leisure time, they have converted them into travel experiences. Since tourists have tended to travel in family groups, we have created a generation of young and experienced travelers who are likely to be more insatiable and demanding than in the past. Indeed, modern tourism is now a collection of niche or special-interest markets.

The growth in cars and the concomitant expansion of highways has permitted the traveler to penetrate more areas of the world than ever before. While the automobile has been the vehicle of choice for most domestic and interregional travel, it was the arrival of the jet engine that heralded the surge in long-distance international travel. Pan Am entered the jet age with the first purchase of a Boeing 707, flying from New York to Paris in half the time of previous propeller-driven planes. There were also the advantages that flights were smoother and that "real" airline prices actually fell over the next twenty years (Murphy, 1985).

Before people travel they need information, especially for more-distant trips to previously unknown destinations. The rapid diffusion of television has provided a window onto the world that has raised awareness and curiosity about other lands and cultures far beyond any previous communications mode. As people have traveled they have grown dependent on the existence of an international banking system, the availability of international reservation systems, and, not least, international air traffic controls. New technology provides an impetus to new tourism by providing the ability to handle the high volumes of complex information associated with global deregulation practices (Poon, 1994).

Impacts of Tourism. Tourism's extensive growth has had a variety of impacts on host destinations. In most cases it has brought the expected benefits of increased employment, increased revenue and taxes, a regional redistribution of income, and an increased appreciation of natural and cultural heritage. In many economies, tourism now represents 5 percent or more of the gross domestic product and has become a significant socioeconomic component of local life. However, because of its ubiquitous nature, tourism seldom receives the full economic recognition it deserves, and is more often associated with negative impacts resulting from its high visibility.

One of the key issues in tourism is its impact on fragile ecosystems and local cultures. The very size of the modern tourism market places such environments under considerable stress, and they need to be managed carefully if they are to survive as both living communities and tourist attractions. National parks, alpine areas, tropical islands, wetlands, and wilderness areas are some of the sensitive areas recording tourism-induced stress (De Kadt, 1979; Theobald, 1994; Cater and Lowman, 1996). Even the most remote areas can no longer escape. There are now eight times more tourists than researchers visiting Antarctica. Stressful situations are not in tourism's best interests and, where planning controls are lacking, industry operators are beginning to produce their own guidelines on appropriate behavior and scale.

In many cases, overloading of the physical environment can be linked to associated stress on the local inhabitants and societal norms. Communities in developing countries and rural and wilderness areas are particularly susceptible to stress and change when invaded by large numbers of tourists who have different lifestyles and expectations (Cater and Lowman, 1996, pp. 78, 81, 177). A common problem faced by all host communities, regardless of size and complexity, is the issue of how much to put on show and how it should be done (Murphy, 1985). Each community needs to decide its local balance on the "authenticity–staged event" continuum, and how much it is willing to "commoditize" its cultural heritage for the convenience of visitors (Cohen, 1979).

Ecotourism Option. One suggested tactic for easing the problems of environmental and social change related to tourism is to emphasize the concept of ecotourism. Ecotourism has been described as an "enlightening natural travel experience that contributes to conservation of the ecosystem while respecting the integrity of host communities" (Wight, 1994, p. 39). It has been promoted as an alternative form of tourism that can match the growing special-interest niches with specific small-scale travel and learning experiences that are less intrusive and stressful (Cater and Lowman, 1996, pp. 3, 32, 36).

While a true ecotourism approach avoids the pitfalls of excessive numbers and offers a more compatible linkage of tourist and destination interests, it is not a panacea. First, its intent and scope will always limit its applicability to a small segment of the tourism market. Second, the inquisitive nature of ecotourists may render them more intrusive than the usual tourist. Third, the small scale and low-key emphasis works against large income-generation opportunities in host communities.

Tourism is both a product of and a contributor to global change. It has certainly benefited from the rising living standards in economically developed nations and from the technological improvements in transportation and information flows around the world. But in facilitating the movement of millions of people and opening up every corner of the Earth to their examination, it has become a major agent of change in its own right. It is an industry that caters to the best and worst of our travel motives and thereby influences the form and function of every destination in the world, be it a small African village or a major western metropolis.

[*See also* Parks and Natural Preserves; *and* Wilderness.]

BIBLIOGRAPHY

Cater, E., and G. Lowman, eds. *Ecotourism: A Sustainable Option?* 4th ed. Chichester, U.K.: Wiley, 1996. A case-by-case study of the growing demand for an environmentally sensitive approach to tourism.

Cohen, E. "Rethinking the Sociology of Tourism." *Annals of Tourism Research* 6.1 (1979), 18–35. An examination of the sociological typologies involved in modern mass tourism.

De Kadt, E. *Tourism: Passport to Development?* New York and Oxford: Oxford University Press, 1979. A seminal study that examines the social and cultural effects of tourism in developing countries with a view to influencing policy decisions.

Hobson, P. "Growth of Tourism in East Asia and the Pacific." *Tourism Management* 15.2 (1994), 150–155. This paper examines the growing level of tourism in this part of the world and its impact on infrastructure, human resources, and environmental degradation.

Murphy, P. E. *Tourism: A Community Approach.* London: Methuen, 1985. A major work that examines the significance of tourism development from the host-community viewpoint.

Poon, A. *Tourism, Technology and Competitive Strategies.* 2d ed. Wallingford, U.K.: CAB International, 1994. An innovative examination of the relationships between information technology and tourism.

Theobald, W., ed. *Global Tourism: The Next Decade.* London: Butterworth Heinemann, 1994. A useful review of recent tourism impacts and associated policy and planning.

Wight, P. "Environmentally Responsible Marketing of Tourism." In *Ecotourism: A Sustainable Option?*, edited by E. Cater and G. Lowman, pp. 39–56. Chichester, U.K.: Wiley, 1994. This study examines the potential positive and negative impacts of ecotourism marketing on the sustainability of resources.

—PETER E. MURPHY

TOXIC WASTE. *See* Hazardous Waste; *and* Ocean Disposal.

TRADE AND ENVIRONMENT

There are numerous connections between international trade and environmental quality. Many of these connections are the same as those that link domestic trade and environmental quality. For example, opportunities for trade affect the scale and composition of production, which can have implications for pollution and resource use. Yet there are also ways in which international trade presents different challenges than internal commerce. For example, alien organisms brought in on imported products can disturb ecosystems. Problems also arise when countries with different environmental policies compete with each other in world commerce.

The recognition of connections between trade and environment is not new; some of the earliest international environmental treaties (such as the 1902 treaty on birds) contained trade provisions. In 1972, the Secretariat of the General Agreement on Tariffs and Trade (GATT) prepared a thoughtful study on pollution control and international trade. But it was not until 1990 that trade and environment became a significant focus of attention.

Three largely independent events raised the profile of the trade and environment nexus. First, several European countries, led by Austria, called attention to this issue at the 1990 ministerial conference of the Uruguay Round trade talks. Second, after U.S. President George Bush launched negotiations for a free trade agreement with Mexico, critics pointed to the poor environmental conditions along the border between the United States and Mexico as a demonstration of the spillover effects from trade. This forced negotiators to make environment an issue in the ongoing trade talks. Third, in 1991, a GATT panel issued an infamous decision in a dispute between the Mexican and U.S. governments over Mexican tuna fishing practices that were killing numerous dolphins. At issue was a U.S. law that banned imports of tuna from Mexico because of high dolphin kill rates. The GATT panel held that international trade law did not permit a government to ban imports so as to protect the environment outside its geographic borders. This decision alarmed environmentalists, who were unexpectedly confronted with an entirely new political threat to environmental law. [See Environmental Law.]

Because both trade and environmental policy are broad and expanding, the issues that come under the rubric of trade and environment are myriad. One approach for exploring these issues is to group them into four categories: (1) effects of trade on environment, (2) effects of environmental policy on trade, (3) effects of trade rules and trade agreements on the environment, and (4) the need for coordination among trade and environmental institutions.

Effects of Trade on Environment. There are several ways in which trade can affect the environment. The clearest is when a traded product causes direct physical effects. For example, toxic waste might be transferred to a country where it will be improperly handled. Services such as transportation can also cause harm. In some circumstances, a traded product can trigger a physical benefit rather than a harm. For example, a new technology can facilitate cleaner production in the country obtaining access to it.

Another way in which trade affects the environment is by engendering physical effects through the market.

This occurs when trading opportunities change the scale or composition of production in the country of export. For example, in the early twentieth century, the demand in the United Kingdom and the United States for feathers in women's fashions led to widespread killing of exotic birds in other countries. Similarly, demand for certain metals in industrial countries has led to mining in fragile ecosystems. Not all changes induced by trade are harmful to the environment. For example, green product specifications in a big market can upgrade worldwide industry standards. Transnational corporations can bring high environmental standards with them when they build new plants.

Trade can also affect the environment by engendering economic changes through the market. When it increases economic growth and national welfare, trade can enhance a country's willingness to pay for environmental cleanup. Economists have detected an inverted U-relationship between national income per capita and certain kinds of pollution. That is, pollution initially increases with income and then decreases as income grows higher. Such findings have led to the hypothesis that richer consumers will demand more environmental regulation from government. Some analysts suggest that growth-promoting trade will be beneficial for the environment. Skeptics deny that inverted U curves have predictive value and point out that, in any event, some pollutants and emissions do not exhibit this relationship to national income.

A public choice hypothesis posits environmental regulation as being influenced by producers rather than consumers. When domestic corporations compete with foreign corporations operating under lower environmental regulation, domestic corporations will use competitiveness as an argument against higher environmental standards or taxes. Seen in this way, an open economy puts pressure on national standard-setting that might not exist in a less open economy. Skeptics challenge this view by noting that less open economies do not have higher environmental standards. They also note a lack of evidence that lower environmental standards are an important factor attracting new corporate investment into polluter havens.

If governmental environment policies were perfect—that is, if government properly and successfully regulated pollution and resource overuse—then trade liberalization would enrich a country without adversely affecting the environment. In a world in which environmental policies are imperfect, however, trade liberalization can have either positive or negative effects. Trade economists do not deny this, but suggest that the proper response is to seek both open trade and correct environmental policies. But this view ignores the way in which the competition ion to export can make it harder to set correct environmental policies. This is particularly so when environmental practices have transborder or global effects. For example, large timber-export profits can hinder domestic efforts to set appropriate forest conservation policy. Domestic subsidies on energy, water, coal, agriculture, and fisheries may support inefficient production, including production for export, which causes adverse environmental effects.

Effects of Environmental Policy on Trade. Changes in environmental policy affect supply and demand, and hence affect international trade. For example, concern about global warming might decrease demand for carbon-based fuel and therefore reduce exports of coal; and policies in the International Whaling Commission have nearly eliminated trade in whale products.

The issue of greatest interest to business groups is ecoprotection. This is the use of environmental laws and standards ostensibly to safeguard the environment, but in reality to protect domestic producers from foreign competition. There is no objective way to detect ecoprotection—it is in the eyes of a frustrated exporter. For example, a tax on beer cans in a country where domestic beer is typically produced in bottles might be viewed as unwarranted ecoprotection. When analysts have tried to size up ecoprotection, they have found it to amount to only a small percentage of regular protection implemented through tariffs and quotas.

Another way in which environmental practices affect trade is through ecolabels such as "green seal," "blue angel," or "ecomark." Since labeling programs are typically national, there is a concern that criteria can be written so as to favor the products made domestically even though they may not be any more environmentally friendly than products made elsewhere. The growing tendency of labels to take a life cycle approach raises even more concerns because labeling certifiers might not be fair in evaluating environmental practices in other countries.

Effects of Trade Rules on the Environment. The General Agreement on Tariffs and Trade (GATT) was based on the principle that the imposition of tariffs would be acceptable government behavior if all GATT member nations were treated equally. In other words, Country A could impose a tariff on widgets so long as it applied to Countries B, C, and so on. Environmental policy makers can run afoul of trade rules because they care about where imports come from and how they are made. For example, if the import is fish and the fish in B are caught using a driftnet and those in C are not, environmental policy might seek to ban the fish from B but not from C.

When a member of GATT objected to a trade barrier in another member country, it was able to lodge a complaint. Panels were then appointed to consider whether the barrier violated GATT rules. In the eight environment-related complaints considered by GATT from 1982 to 1994, panels found five of these measures to be a violation of GATT rules. Several of the cases focused on Article XX of GATT, which provides exceptions for measures "necessary to protect human, animal or plant life or health" and for measures "relating to the conservation of exhaustible natural resources." The GATT panels interpreted these provisions strictly to deny their applicability to the environmental measures in dispute.

Under the World Trade Organization (WTO)—which succeeded GATT institutionally and incorporated most of its rules—trade-related environmental measures remain subject to challenge. In the first complaint to come before the WTO, the panel found that a United States Clean Air Act regulation violated trade rules. [*See* World Trade Organization.] Unlike GATT, however, where compliance with panel reports was effectively voluntary, governments are now required to comply or face possible trade sanctions from the winning party. Following its loss at the WTO, the United States Environmental Protection Agency (EPA) changed its clean air regulation in an effort to comply with trade rules. EPA said it could do so without reducing air quality. Future conflicts may force losing governments to choose between adherence to trade rules and safeguarding their environment.

The power of the new WTO dispute settlement system is worrisome because panelists consider only international trade law, not international environmental law. Moreover, the panelists are typically trade bureaucrats or lawyers with little expertise in environmental regulation. Many environmentalists fear that a complaint will be filed about a trade measure used in a multilateral environmental agreement, and the ensuing adverse decision will undermine the agreement.

Trade measures are employed in at least twenty-six multilateral environmental agreements. For example, the Convention on International Trade in Endangered Species of Wild Fauna and Flora forbids international trade for commercial purposes of species threatened with extinction. [*See* Convention on International Trade in Endangered Species.] The Montreal Protocol on Substances that Deplete the Ozone Layer prohibits imports of controlled substances (such as chlorofluorocarbons), or products containing them, from nonparties (unless the nonparty country has been determined to be in compliance with the protocol). [*See* Montreal Protocol; *and* Ozone.] The Basel Convention on the Control of Transboundary Movements of Hazardous Wastes prohibits trade in waste products with nonparties (but allows bilateral arrangements with nonparties that do not derogate from the environmentally sound management required by the convention). [*See* Basel Convention; *and* Hazardous Waste.]

Under GATT Article XX interpretations propounded by recent panels, all of these trade measures might be found to violate GATT, particularly if the complaining country were not a party to the environmental treaty. So far, no complaint has been lodged. If trade measures were deleted from environmental treaties, the resulting treaties would be less effective. For example, the trade provisions in the Montreal Protocol prevent evasion of the Protocol's regulations.

In addition to reinforcing GATT rules with tough dispute settlement, the WTO also added new discipline that constrains the ability of governments to use environmental policies to restrict trade. The Agreement on the Application of Sanitary and Phytosanitary Measures requires governments to justify food safety measures that apply to imports. The Agreement on Technical Barriers to Trade contains disciplines on product standards and labeling.

Coordination among Institutions. The most valuable feature of the trade and environment debate is that the two regimes have learned more about each other. Before 1991, environmental policy makers paid little attention to the trade effects of environmental regulation. Similarly, trade policy makers paid little attention to the tools of environmental regulators. Today, there is more mutual understanding and dialogue.

Because they were accustomed to open processes in the United Nations Environment Programme (UNEP), environmentalists were critical of the lack of transparency at GATT. In the early 1990s, many GATT documents were not publicly released. Panel decisions were not released to the public until after they were debated and approved by the GATT Council. This has now changed: the WTO is a more transparent institution than GATT was. Environmentalists and public interest groups deserve some of the credit for stimulating this reform.

The main institutional innovation for addressing trade and environment was the creation of a GATT/WTO Committee on Trade and Environment in 1994. So far the Committee has accomplished very little. The most critical defect of the committee is one that it shares with the WTO, namely, institutional insularity. Although it carries out joint activities with the United Nations Conference on Trade and Development, the WTO has made little effort to coordinate its work with other agencies such as UNEP, the International Labour Organisation, and secretariats of multilateral environmental treaties. The WTO also continues to resist giving consultative status to nongovernmental organizations such as environment, development, business, and consumer groups.

One of the most salutary suggestions that has surfaced in the trade and environment debate is that proposed trade agreements should receive environmental impact assessments, and proposed environmental agreements should receive trade impact assessments. Despite the potential impact of the Uruguay Round on the environment, no such assessments were carried out before completion of the negotiations. A few governments drafted reports after the trade round, but they were descriptive rather than analytical.

Regional Agreements. The coordination of trade and environment policy can also occur at the regional level. The increasing number of regional trade agreements offers opportunities for achieving multilateral linkage among like-minded countries. The first major effort to do this arose through negotiations for the North American Free Trade Agreement (NAFTA). Although NAFTA contains a few provisions related to the environment, the most significant development was the approval of the parallel North American Agreement on Environmental Cooperation. This Agreement set up a trinational commission to examine environmental protection throughout the region and to promote research and policy coordination. This commission's secretariat may investigate complaints from nongovernmental organizations that one of the parties is not enforcing its environmental laws. For example, several Canadian citizen groups petitioned the commission in April 1997, alleging that the Quebec government was failing to enforce agricultural pollution laws. In October 1999, the secretariat decided that the matter warranted the development of a "factual record." Canada opposes this step, however, and the three governments have withheld approval for any investigation.

The secretariat may also prepare reports on environmental problems. In 1994, about 40,000 birds died near a Mexican lake. This triggered a successful request for the secretariat to sponsor an investigation. A panel of scientists found that the deaths were largely caused by botulism and made recommendations to the Mexican government for preventing such disasters.

Building on these NAFTA precedents, many environmental groups have proposed that ongoing regional trade negotiations—such as the Free Trade Area of the Americas and the forum for Asia–Pacific Economic Cooperation Forum (APEC)—should include an environmental dimension. The proponents argue that these negotiations are already projected to be much broader than trade liberalization and therefore should not ignore the benefits of improving coordination of ecological and economic policy. The opponents of linkage worry that industrial countries will try to dictate higher environmental standards to developing countries in order to reduce their competitiveness. As in other forums of the trade and environment debate, the differing perspectives are being poorly integrated.

[*See also* Global Economy; *and* International Cooperation.]

BIBLIOGRAPHY

Anderson, K., and R. Blackhurst, eds. *The Greening of World Trade Issues.* London: Harvester Wheatsheaf, 1992. The first book on trade and the environment; contains twelve articles mainly by economists.

Andersson, T., C. Folke, and S. Nyström. *Trading with the Environment: Ecology, Economics, Institutions and Policy.* London: Earthscan, 1995. A survey of trade and environment issues by ecological economists.

Cameron, J., et al., eds. *Trade and the Environment: The Search for Balance.* London: Cameron and May, 1994. Two volumes. Volume 1 contains nineteen chapters by separate authors about different aspects of the debate. Volume 2 contains a wealth of source material.

Chang, H. F. "Carrots, Sticks, and International Enternalities." *International Review of Law and Economics* 17 (1997), 309–324. Demonstrates the difficulty of a "carrots-only" approach to trade and environment bargaining.

Charnovitz, S. "A Critical Guide to the WTO's Report on Trade and Environment." *Arizona Journal of International and Comparative Law* 14 (1997), 342–379.

Dua, A., and D. C. Esty. *Sustaining the Asia Pacific Miracle.* Washington, D.C.: Institute for International Economics, 1997. Discusses the environmental issues of Asia–Pacific economic integration.

Esty, D. C. *Greening the GATT.* Washington, D.C.: Institute for International Economics, 1994. A comprehensive review of legal and economic issues of the trade and environment debate.

International Institute for Sustainable Development. "The World Trade Organization and Sustainable Development: An Independent Assessment." Winnipeg: International Institute for Sustainable Development, 1996.

Johnson, P. M., and A. Beaulieu. *The Environment and NAFTA.* Washington, D.C.: Island Press, 1996. A comprehensive review of NAFTA and the environment.

Moltke, K. von. "International Environmental Management, Trade Regimes and Sustainability." Winnipeg: International Institute for Sustainable Development, 1996.

Organisation for Economic Co-operation and Development. *The Environmental Effects of Trade.* Paris: Organisation for Economic Co-operation and Development, 1994. A good survey chapter plus chapters on five sectors.

Petersmann, E.-U. *International and European Trade and Environmental Law after the Uruguay Round.* London: Kluwer Law International, 1995. Trade and environment from an international legal perspective.

Stone, C. D. "Too Many Fishing Boats, Too Few Fish: Can Trade Laws Trim Subsidies and Restore the Balance in Global Fisheries?" *Ecology Law Quarterly* 24 (1997), 505–544.

Tay, S., and D. C. Esty, eds. *Asian Dragons and Green Trade.* Singapore: Times Academic Press, 1996. Contains fourteen chapters by policy makers and leading analysts on trade and environment.

Vogel, D. *Trading Up: Consumer and Environmental Regulation in a Global Economy.* Cambridge, Mass.: Harvard University Press, 1995. A survey of trade and environment issues by a political scientist.

Webster, D. "The Looting and Smuggling and Fencing and Hoarding of Impossibly Precious, Feathered and Scaly Wild Things." *The New York Times Magazine* (16 February 1997), 26. A good description of the endangered species trade.

Westin, R. A. *Environmental Tax Initiatives and Multilateral Trade Agreements.* Cambridge, Mass.: Kluwer, 1997.

—STEVE CHARNOVITZ

TRAINS. *See* Transportation.

TRANSPORTATION

Transportation services are vital for the satisfaction of a wide range of fundamental human needs. They foster economic development by enabling the integration of new markets, by providing an increasing number of services, and by delivering more and more specialized inputs into the economy. Transportation also encourages social and cultural interaction, which ultimately results in a higher quality of life. While human activities were geographically concentrated before the onset of industrialization, the introduction of motorized transportation systems has dramatically increased the spatial separation of work, education, and personal business. Today, transportation provides leisure travel opportunities to most locations around the world.

At the same time, however, transportation systems have had undesirable consequences. The strong growth in transportation demand has not only caused rapidly rising levels of congestion and traffic noise, but also severe environmental impacts: the transportation sector is already the major contributor to deteriorating urban air quality and acid rain within the industrialized world and in many developing countries. [*See* Acid Rain and Acid Deposition.] Moreover, the transportation sector's leading role in contributing to such regional environmental hazards may soon shift to a global level: over the last twenty years, transportation has become the fastest-growing energy sector. Almost the entire transportation sector is fueled by oil products, and the release of carbon dioxide associated with the combustion of these fuels adds increasingly to the anthropogenic greenhouse effect. In 1990, humans released 6 billion metric tons of carbon into the atmosphere, of which the transportation sector accounted for 1.4 billion metric tons, or 23 percent (see Figure 1).

Transportation Demand. The transportation sector consists of passenger travel and freight transportation. Their particular characteristics are discussed below.

Passenger travel. People spend a fixed share of their income on transportation, averaging 3 percent if the associated households rely on public transportation services (such as is predominantly the case in the developing world) and around 10 percent if they own at least one automobile (predominantly the industrialized world). Figures from the United States, for example,

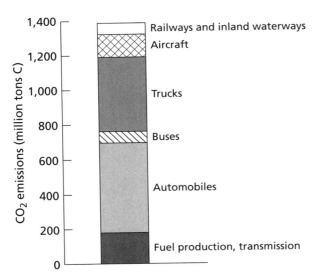

Transportation. FIGURE 1. Approximate World Transportation Sector Carbon Dioxide Emissions in 1990.

Carbon dioxide emissions in the transportation sector alone result in 1.2 billion metric tons of carbon. Taking into account the energy required for fuel processing, transmission, distribution, and storage, carbon dioxide emissions rise to 1.4 billion metric tons of carbon.

show that this travel money budget remained roughly constant even during the two oil price shocks of the 1970s; at that time, travelers compensated for higher operating costs by demanding less expensive (and more fuel-efficient) new vehicles, or by temporarily reducing demand.

Humans also dedicate a constant amount of time—on average, between one and one and a half hours per day—to their daily travel. The income stability of the travel time budget is shown in Figure 2: inhabitants of African villages spend an average of sixty-six minutes per day traveling, as do residents of Latin American metropolitan areas or highly industrialized countries.

Because of their fundamental nature, the two budgets govern the daily travel behavior of virtually every person, irrespective of cultural, geographic, and economic setting. In fact, as suggested by quantitative analyses of travel surveys, the basic relationships in travel behavior are qualitatively very similar across national boundaries. Since, however, economic and land use settings can vary substantially, so do the mean values in travel patterns. For example, in very low-income rural areas of developing countries, nearly all trips are within a trip distance of 5 kilometers—the distance that can be covered on foot within the travel time budget. With rising income, humans can afford faster modes of transportation and thus increase their range of daily interaction. In the high-income, automobile-dominated in-

dustrialized countries (notably the United States), more than 95 percent of all trips occur within a trip length of 50 kilometers—the distance that can be covered by an automobile within the travel time budget.

Projection of total world traffic volume. Since the travel money budget allocates a fixed proportion of income to travel, per capita travel demand grows approximately in proportion to income. This relationship, which is shown in Figure 3 for eleven world regions and the world as a whole, is especially tight in the industrialized world, where a doubling of income has led to an approximate doubling in per capita traffic volume (the aggregate of car, bus, train, and aircraft volume). In developing countries, the trajectories are curved (convex), in part because of the substitution of motorized transportation (for which statistics are included in the data) for nonmotorized transportation, such as walking and biking (which is excluded from the data).

Given the predictable relationship between income and transportation spending, the traffic volume should continue to rise with income, provided no major economic shocks occur. Using plausible assumptions for both the very long-term development of these trajectories and rates of future income growth (averaging a 4.3-fold growth in world economic output), world travel demand will increase from 23.2 trillion passenger-kilometers in 1990 to 105 trillion passenger-kilometers in 2050. Developing countries will contribute a rising share of global traffic volume, and ultimately account for half of it in 2050 because, although their per capita traffic volume will stay lower, both their populations and their average incomes will grow faster than those of advanced industrialized nations. Table 1 summarizes historical (1960, 1990) and projected (2020, 2050) levels of per capita and total traffic volume for the world and regional aggregations.

Future modes of passenger transportation. If people hold their time for travel constant but also become more mobile as their income rises, they must select faster modes of transportation to cover more distance within the same time. This consistent trend in modal split changes is shown in Figure 4 from 1960 to 1990 for five world regions: Central Asia, eastern Europe, western Europe, Latin America, and North America. Incorporating additional constraints on land use (the share of public transportation modes is higher in areas of high urban population densities) and path dependence of infrastructures (infrastructural changes occur only slowly because of their long lifetime and large sunk costs), the relative importance of the future modes of transportation can be estimated (continuous lines in Figure 4, which show estimates for 1990 to 2050).

In the industrialized countries, the share of traffic volume supplied by buses and automobiles will decline as high-speed transportation (aircraft and high-speed

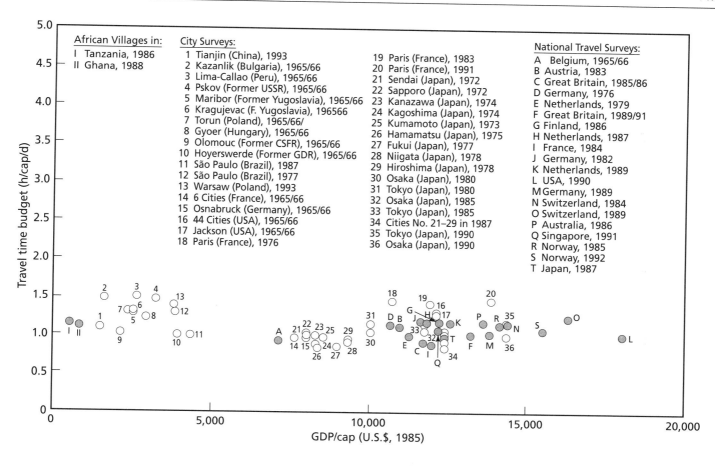

Transportation. FIGURE 2. Income Stability of the Daily Travel Time Budget in Different Parts of the World.

Numbers are derived from time use and travel surveys. (After Schafer and Victor, 2000. Reproduced with permission of Elsevier.)

trains) rises sharply; already this is evident in the sharp rise in air travel and the relative decline of the slowest modes. In developing countries, the strongest increase will be in the shares first for buses and later for automobiles. Globally, these trends in bus and automobile transportation are partially offsetting. From 1960 to 2050, the share of world traffic volume contributed by buses will remain roughly constant, and the automobile share will decline only gradually to 42 percent. High-speed transportation should account for some 36 percent of all passenger-kilometers traveled in 2050. In all regions the share of low-speed rail transportation will continue its steady and already strongly evident decline. Figure 5 shows the growth in traffic volume by mode of transportation in 1960, 1990, 2020, and 2050.

Despite the strongly rising share of air travel, other types of vehicles, especially automobiles, will remain crucial elements of the transportation system. Even in

North America, where the relative decline of automobiles will be steepest, the absolute traffic volume supplied by cars will decline only after peaking at 22,000 passenger-kilometers per person in 2010. In 2050, automobiles will still supply 16,000 passenger-kilometers per person, which means that people will still be driving roughly as much as they did in 1978.

Freight transportation. Freight transportation demand is closely related to the material intensity of the economy. While, in an agricultural economy, the ratio of freight metric tons to gross domestic product (GDP) is comparatively low, this ratio rises with the onset of industrialization. At higher income levels, when the material-intensive infrastructure (roads, railways, factories, etc.) exists and the economy becomes increasingly service-oriented, the material intensity of the economy and the ratio decrease. Similar trajectories can be observed in the energy economy (ratio of commercial energy used to GDP) and in per capita material use.

Projection of total world traffic volume. If, in addition to the roughly predictable development of the ratio of freight metric tons to GDP, transportation distances are taken into account, total freight traffic volume can be projected. World traffic volume rises in proportion to assumed income growth from 14 trillion

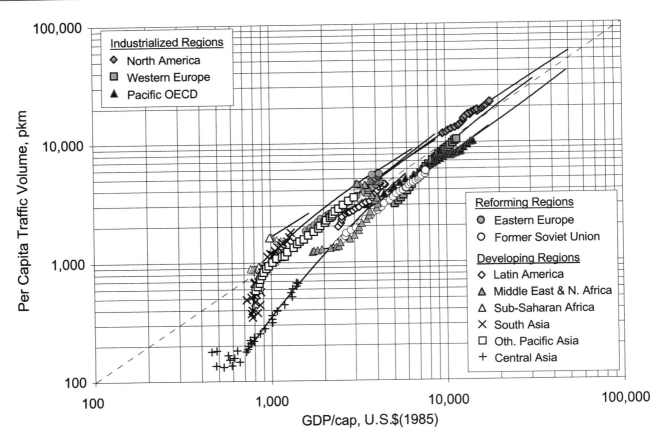

Transportation. Figure 3. Per Capita Traffic Volume versus Income.

Per capita GDP is used as an approximation for income. (After Schafer and Victor, 2000. Reproduced with permission of Elsevier.)

to about 60 trillion metric ton-kilometers in 2050 (the numbers exclude sea transportation and the traffic volume associated with the movement of energy carriers, such as vehicles carrying coal and oil). More than half of the 2050 traffic volume will be in the developing countries, where—in addition to higher rates of economic growth—the ratio of transported freight metric tons to GDP is still rising.

Future modes of freight transportation. Each type of economic structure requires the dominance of a mode that can best satisfy its transportation needs. In agricultural economies, the low demand for freight shipments is often satisfied by nonmotorized modes. With the onset of industrialization, modal requirements change drastically: the large quantities of raw materials (predominantly of low value) that often have to be transported over long distances are typically transported by vehicles with a large carrying capacity (barges and railways) and subsequently shipped from the port or railway terminal to the point of destination via flexible transportation modes, notably trucks. With develop-

ment toward a postindustrial economy, new requirements govern the increasingly frequent movement, in smaller shipments, of high-value goods: flexibility, accessibility, speed, and reliability with regard to shipment time. These needs can be best satisfied by an increasing share of trucks with smaller size classes and, for longer distances, by aircraft. As a result, trucks (of all size classes) are projected to provide between 80 and 90 percent of global total freight traffic volume in 2050 (compared with 50 percent in 1990).

Transportation Supply Characteristics. Land infrastructure, vehicles, and fuels required to run them are the important characteristics of transportation supply.

Land infrastructure. Road infrastructure density rises with population density: 0.06 kilometers of road per square kilometer of surface area in Saudi Arabia, 2 kilometers per square kilometer in Germany, 3 kilometers per square kilometer in Japan, and nearly 4.5 kilometers per square kilometer in Singapore. The infrastructure of railroads and inland waterways is typically one to two orders of magnitude less dense. Although total transportation infrastructure accounts for less than 1 percent of the Earth's land area overall (including the negligible spatial spread of airports), its share is typically 10–25 percent in urban areas. The distribution of road quality varies mainly with income: paved roads account for only a few percent of the road network in very low-income countries of the develop-

MOTOR VEHICLES STILL SCARCE IN DEVELOPING COUNTRIES

Although vehicles cause severe air pollution in some cities in the developing world, they still are relatively scarce on a per capita basis. Europe and Africa hold roughly the same populations, but Africa's fleet is one-tenth that of Europe's. If China were to attain a per capita rate comparable to Europe's, it would hold over 300 million vehicles. Considering that motor vehicles now contribute more than 15 percent of the world's fossil fuel releases of carbon dioxide, the prospect of an expanding global fleet suggests that new technologies for vehicles will be essential.

NATION	MOTOR VEHICLES (PER THOUSAND PERSONS)	1997 POPULATION (MILLIONS)	NUMBER OF VEHICLES (MILLIONS)
United States	750	271.6	203.7
Japan	519	125.6	65.2
Europe	270	729.2	196.8
Brazil	97	163.1	15.8
Hong Kong	87	6.2	0.54
Africa	22	758.4	16.7
China	8	1,243.7	9.95
India	7	960.2	6.72

SOURCE: *World Resources 1998–99*, p. 172.

BIBLIOGRAPHY

World Resources 1998–99: A Guide to the Global Environment: Environmental Change and Human Health. New York and Oxford: Oxford University Press, 1998.

—DAVID J. CUFF

ing world, but for nearly 100 percent in industrialized countries.

Vehicles and their usage. The transportation supply system incorporates a variety of modes, ranging from nonmotorized means such as walking, to highly sophisticated motorized technology such as aircraft. Here, only the most important motorized modes of transportation will be described briefly in terms of their technical and

Transportation. TABLE 1. Historical and Projected Levels of Per Capita and Total Motorized Traffic Volume*

	1960		*1990*		*2020*		*2050*	
	PASSENGER KILOMETERS PER CAPITA	TRILLION PASSENGER KILOMETERS	PASSENGER KILOMETERS PER CAPITA	TRILLION PASSENGER KILOMETERS	PASSENGER KILOMETERS PER CAPITA	TRILLION PASSENGER KILOMETERS	PASSENGER KILOMETERS PER CAPITA	TRILLION PASSENGER KILOMETERS
Industrialized world	4,400	3.8	14,280	12.4	28,200	27.8	43,590	43.8
North America	11,850	2.4	22,080	6.2	40,580	14.0	58,460	21.2
Western Europe	3,070	1.1	10,620	4.7	20,390	9.9	33,480	16.6
Reforming economies	1,550	0.5	5,670	2.3	7,920	3.8	13,220	7.1
Eastern Europe	1,820	0.2	5,390	0.7	6,820	0.9	11,140	1.6
Developing countries	580	1.2	2,130	8.6	3,420	22.0	6,341	54.0
Central Asia	150	0.1	640	0.8	1,780	3.1	5,240	10.4
Latin America	1,980	0.4	5,090	2.2	6,720	4.5	10,460	8.8
World	1,810	5.5	4,380	23.2	6,780	53.7	10,430	104.9

*The projections are based on income growth rates of the Intergovernmental Panel on Climate Control "a" and "e" scenarios (Leggett et al., 1992) and World Bank projections of population growth (Bos et al., 1992).
SOURCE: From Schafer and Victor (2000). Reprinted with permission of Elsevier.

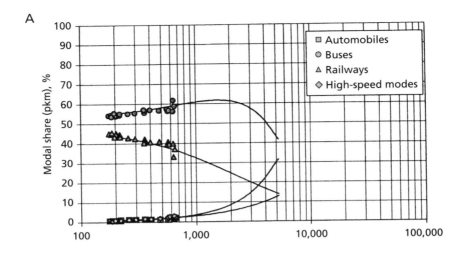

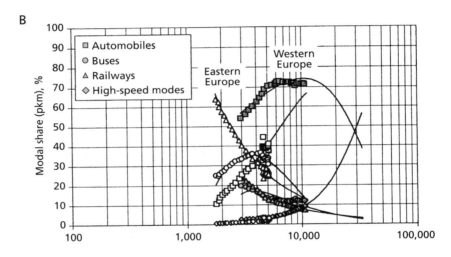

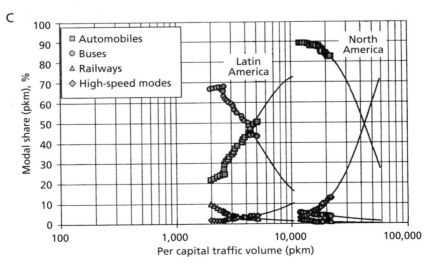

Transportation. FIGURE 4. Modal Split Changes in Five World Regions: (A) Central Asia, (B) Eastern Europe and Western Europe, and (C) Latin America and North America. (After Schafer and Victor, 2000. Reproduced with permission of Elsevier.)

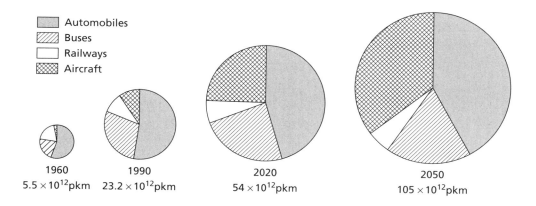

Transportation. FIGURE 5. World Passenger Traffic Volume by Mode of Transportation in 1960 and 1990, with Projections for 2020 and 2050. (After Schafer and Victor, 1997. With permission of *Scientific American*.)

usage characteristics. The wide range of intermediate modes of transportation operating in the developing world (nonmotorized modes, and intermediate motorized modes such as two- and three-wheelers) are not discussed here, although their importance in providing local transportation services should not be overlooked.

Automobiles. Of the almost 480 million automobiles registered worldwide in 1995, the industrialized world accounts for nearly 80 percent. There, automobiles that are only driven an average of 30–50 kilometers per day (a result of the fixed travel time budget) are the dominant mode of transportation for trip distances between 1 and 1,000 kilometers. Because fuel typically accounts for only 15–25 percent of the total cost of owning and operating a car, consumers in many countries have shifted toward larger, more powerful, and less fuel-efficient vehicles. In addition, declining average household size and rising motorization rates have resulted in a continuous decline in mean car occupancy to the current level of 1.5 persons per vehicle. Overall, energy intensity (energy use per passenger-kilometer) has increased in many countries (for example, from 1.7 to 2.2 megajoules per passenger-kilometer in West Germany between 1960 and 1990).

While the average age of the vehicle fleet is typically seven to eight years in industrialized countries, it is significantly higher in the developing world. Vehicle fuel consumption differ in developing countries, being typically lower in Asia (where the car fleet builds on simple technology but consists of smaller vehicles) and nearly twice as high in parts of Latin America and Africa (because of the high share of imported, large-size, and outdated vehicles from the industrialized world). In developing countries, the 50–100 percent higher mean occupancy rate is declining with ongoing economic growth, resulting in increasingly energy-inefficient vehicle use, as observed in the industrialized world.

Heavy-duty vehicles. In 1995, the world heavy-duty vehicle fleet consisted of 170 million vehicles, the industrialized world accounting for about 70 percent. In the automobile-dominated industrialized world, buses are increasingly designed for operation in niche markets by dedicated vehicle type and size. Similarly, a wide range of truck models exists for the satisfaction of each type of freight service. By contrast, in the developing world, the same type of heavy-duty vehicle generally satisfies different types of transportation service (namely, short- and long-distance movements).

Because of the operator's inherent interest in maximizing profitability, which generally goes in hand with minimizing operation costs, incentives for fuel efficiency of heavy-duty vehicles are greater than those for automobiles; at the high annual traffic volume typical for commercial vehicles (up to several hundreds of thousands of kilometers per year), small differences in kilometer-specific costs can result in a large annual total. Bus energy intensity depends strongly on the operation mode (generally higher in medium-occupancy, stop-and-go urban traffic and lower in high-occupancy, continuous intercity operation). Truck energy intensity depends critically on gross vehicle weight. In postindustrial economies such as the United States and Japan, where the average payload is typically below 2 metric tons per vehicle, mean truck energy use is 3.5–4.5 megajoules per metric ton-kilometer (the average payload is defined as total metric ton-kilometers divided by total vehicle-kilometers). In many developing countries, this number is significantly lower because of the larger mean truck size. In China, for example, where the mean carried load is close to 4 metric tons, average energy use is still low (only slightly above 2 megajoules per metric ton-kilometer). However, with ongoing economic development, the mean size class will also decline and thus energy intensity will increase. For logistical reasons, the truck load factor (metric ton-kilometers per vehicle-kilometer) is roughly 60 percent across all countries, and is stable over time (since 1960).

High-speed transportation. High-speed modes consist of nine to ten thousand commercial jet aircraft operating worldwide (accounting for nearly 96 percent of world high-speed traffic volume) and high-speed trains. Since aircraft, the dominant mode of transportation at distances greater than 1,000 kilometers, are in flight for half of their lifetime and thus cover enormous distances, small gains in fuel efficiency result in substantial fuel and thus cost savings. Thus not surprisingly, aircraft have experienced the strongest reduction in fuel consumption of all modes of transportation: since the introduction of civil jet aircraft approximately forty years ago, fuel consumption per passenger-kilometer has been reduced by 70 percent, or 3 percent per year.

High-speed trains, currently accounting for some 4 percent of world high-speed transportation traffic volume, are rapidly gaining travel share at trip distances of up to 600 kilometers—a result of their high speed and operation between city centers. Very high-speed applications aim at replacing the current wheel-on-rail systems with magnetic levitation trains, ultimately operating in low-pressure tubes. Occupancy rates of both aircraft and high-speed trains are 60–70 percent.

Table 2 summarizes energy intensity levels of different types of vehicle in the United States.

Fuels and emissions. Since the early twentieth century, almost the entire transportation sector has been driven by hydrocarbon fuels, essentially oil products (oil accounted for 97 percent of all transportation fuels consumed in 1990). Besides mechanical power, their combustion produces a range of exhaust gases, consisting primarily of water vapor (H_2O) and carbon dioxide (CO_2). Incomplete combustion further results in the production of unburned hydrocarbons (C_xH_y) and carbon monoxide (CO). The formation of nitrogen ox-

ides (NO_x) and nitrous oxide (N_2O) can be attributed to the nitrogen content in the atmosphere. Other pollutants include different classes of particulates (lead, organic particulates, and sulfates), the type and amount of which depend on the fuel composition. Some of the byproduct gases are direct greenhouse gases as well, such as methane (CH_4) and N_2O. Other exhaust gases (C_xH_y, CO, and NO_x) contribute to the greenhouse effect indirectly by for example, forming tropospheric ozone.

The exhaust concentration of these compounds depends on the fuel, engine type, various engine parameters, and type of exhaust gas cleaning. For example, methane emissions are only 0.02–0.06 grams per kilometer in gasoline-fueled automobiles equipped with three-way catalysts (TWCs), but are almost one order of magnitude higher in TWC-equipped compressed natural gas vehicles. By contrast, measurements in Jet A-fueled (typical fuel for commercial aircraft) gas turbine aircraft engines have shown only negligible exhaust gas concentrations of methane. Vehicle emission standards, first introduced in the late 1960s in parts of the industrialized world, are continuously becoming more stringent and thus continue to reduce nearly all emissions discussed above. Table 3 shows approximate levels of emissions per vehicle-kilometer for gasoline-fueled automobiles in different parts of the world.

Balancing Demand and Supply. The growing worldwide demand for transportation poses significant challenges in terms of energy use and pollution control.

Energy use and carbon dioxide emissions. Assuming that the rising energy intensity of trucks and automobiles and the demand shift toward more energy-intensive modes will be compensated by reductions in the energy intensity of aircraft, the projected increase in total passenger and freight traffic volume would cause world transportation sector final energy use to

Transportation. TABLE 2. Average Energy Intensity by Mode of Transportation in the United States in 1995*

PASSENGER MODES	MEGAJOULES PER PASSENGER-KILOMETERS	FREIGHT MODES	MEGAJOULES PER METRIC TON-KILOMETERS
Automobiles	3.7	All trucks	4.30
Personal trucks	5.7	Combination trucks	1.68
Urban railways	4.0	Railways	0.24
Commuter railways	3.0	Inland waterways	0.25
Intercity railways	2.4	Oil pipelines	0.17
Urban buses	4.9		
Intercity buses	0.9		
Aircraft	4.5		

*The comparatively high-energy intensity of urban buses results from the low average occupancy rate of only 8.6 passengers per bus. The numbers for trucks relate to 1990.

Transportation. TABLE 3. Approximate Exhaust Gas Emissions for Gasoline-Fueled Automobiles*

	GERMANY	UNITED STATES	INDIA	MEXICO CITY
Gasoline consumption, 1/100 kilometer	9.0	11.8	9.2	16.7
Emissions, grams/kilometers				
CO_2	197	242	170	334
CO	7.8	20.7	24.0	35.2
C_xH_y,	1.4	2.1	3.6	2.5
CH_4	0.02	0.02	0.06	0.06
NO_x	2.1	2.6	1.6	n.a.
N_2O	0.02	0.02	0.005	0.005
SO_2	0.1	0.1	n.a.	n.a.

*Estimates are based on a literature survey. CH_4 and N_2O emission factors are based on the assumption that all automobiles in Germany and the United States are equipped with a three-way catalyst, but that none in India and Mexico City are so equipped.

rise almost 4.4 times over the 1990 level through 2050, that is, to 260 exajoules (1 exajoule = 10^{18} joules). If oil products continue to fuel almost the entire transportation sector, direct world transportation sector carbon dioxide emissions will rise from 1.2 to 5.3 billion metric tons of carbon by 2050. Taking into account emissions associated with fuel production, transmission, and distribution, transportation-related carbon dioxide emissions in 2050 will account for roughly 6 billion metric tons of carbon, which is comparable to the total anthropogenic industrial carbon emissions in 1990. The quantity of emissions other than carbon dioxide depends critically on the type of exhaust gas treatment technology used.

Mitigation options. Transportation sector emissions can be controlled by management measures and technological modifications. Theoretically, behavioral changes offer an additional potential for reducing emissions. However, in light of the relationships discussed above, there is little prospect of, for example, voluntary increases in vehicle occupancy rates or shifts toward less energy-intensive and thus generally slower modes.

Transportation systems management. Transportation systems management aims at satisfying transportation demand through more efficient use of the existing infrastructure, rather than further increases in its density. This is achieved by reducing the number of vehicle-kilometers traveled, by changing vehicle travel in the dimensions of space and time, and by smoothing traffic flows. Table 4 provides a systematic classification of such measures.

Experience shows that transportation systems management can only be successful if it includes strictly enforced land use policies. In Portland, Oregon, land use restrictions along with investment in public transportation have increased housing densities and altered community behavior. Although the number of downtown jobs has increased by approximately 50 percent since

the 1970s, downtown traffic has not risen because 43 percent of all commuters travel by bus or rail (this number is three to four times higher than in many other U.S. cities, and only in New York City is the proportion higher). In the Brazilian metropolitan area of Curitiba, a combination of strict land use policies and prioritization of public and nonmotorized modes of transportation, along with innovative financing schemes, has resulted in a comparatively high usage of public transportation. Although the motorization rate is the second highest in Brazil (around 0.25 cars per capita), per capita fuel consumption is 25 percent lower than in comparable Brazilian cities; as a result, ambient air pollution is among the lowest in the country. In Singapore, where the most restrictive transportation policy measures in the world—consisting of regulations of ownership and usage of cars, restricted auto zones, road pricing, priority to public transportation, and land use policies—have been adopted, the free flow of road traffic has been largely maintained in the central business district.

These examples suggest that well designed transportation systems management measures are crucial for confronting traffic-related externalities such as downtown traffic congestion. However, travel demand is rising continuously even in countries with severe transportation systems management measures (a consequence of human travel behavior, as discussed above). Thus, it is highly uncertain whether such measures can reduce energy use and carbon dioxide emissions. Even in Singapore, both motorization rate and per capita gasoline consumption have doubled since 1975, despite import taxes and registration fees for new automobiles in the order of 220 percent of their import value. These measures have not even suppressed single-occupant driving: the mean automobile occupancy rate in Singapore is below 1.5 persons per car, as in the rest of the industrialized world.

The extent to which new information and telecom-

Transportation. TABLE 4. Transportation Systems Management*

DEMAND-SIDE MANAGEMENT	SUPPLY-SIDE MANAGEMENT
Land use and zoning policies	Smoothening of road traffic operation
Communication substitutes	Preferential treatment of public and nonmotorized transportation versus individual motorized transportation
Traveler information systems	
Economic measures (incentives for public transportation and pricing of individual motorized transportation)	Improving public transportation operations
	Directing freight traffic on to less-used roads
Administrative measures (e.g., flexible work schedules, auto-restricted zones, and parking management)	

*Demand-side management measures aim at influencing travel decisions before the trip occurs. By contrast, supply-side management focuses mainly on travel that is already occurring. In practice, both work together.

munication technologies can contribute in recapturing existing infrastructure capacity is still controversial. Historical analogies with mail and telephone suggest that new communication technologies have ultimately created new links between distant people and in turn caused transportation demand to rise. Far from supplanting mobility, communications give people the urge to travel. Similarly, intelligent transportation systems, which are intended to increase the capacity of the existing infrastructure through, for example, vehicle guidance and automated highway systems, could also attract additional traffic and subsequently reach their new capacity limits again.

Technological measures. Technological measures aim at reducing fuel consumption, shifting toward less carbon-intensive transportation fuels, or a combination of the two.

In the very short term (five years), opportunities for reductions in fuel consumption for all modes of transportation are limited. Low-rolling-resistance tires, improved engine inspection, and aerodynamic add-ons for medium-sized trucks can reduce vehicle fuel consumption by roughly 5 percent each. A larger reduction potential (up to 30 percent) exists for automobiles through shifting toward the most fuel-efficient passenger car within the size class: that is, state-of-the-art direct-injection diesel engine vehicles.

In the medium term (twenty years) and especially in the long term (fifty years), enormous technical fuel reduction potentials exist for most motorized modes of transportation, typically in the order of 50–70 percent over the average new vehicle (or aircraft) sold in 1990. This potential can be achieved through a combination of strongly reduced driving (flight) resistance and drastic improvements in engine efficiency. Additional measures for road vehicles are new types of transmission and, especially, alternative drivetrains: for example, hybrid and fuel cell electric vehicles with highly energy-efficient power storage systems. However, the achievement of extremely low fuel consumption levels still requires that a number of fuel-efficiency trade-offs

(reduced road vehicle occupant safety, increased emissions of other pollutants, and so forth) be addressed successfully.

In addition, the economic potential for reductions in fuel consumption is significantly smaller from today's point of view. This is especially true for automobiles, where market forces favoring the use of fuel-efficient technologies are generally too weak. As a rough estimate, the fuel consumption of a typical automobile might be reduced by only about one-third at low cost; such a passenger car might consist of a slightly more efficient internal combustion engine and transmission, adjusted (downsized) to a platform with lower rolling resistance and a lighter, more aerodynamically shaped steel body and frame. It is highly uncertain whether hybrid and fuel cell automobiles will ever be cost-effective relative to conventional vehicles without policy intervention. Only in heavy-duty vehicles, where the low production volume and the associated high costs of conventional driveline systems keep the cost increase lower, have hybrid drive trains already begun to be applied. This is especially true for urban low-floor buses, where usage is also driven by design requirements.

In light of the projected 4.4-fold rise in transportation sector energy use and carbon dioxide emissions, a hypothetical reduction of energy intensity by even 50 percent would still result in a growth of transportation sector energy use and carbon dioxide emissions by 120 percent in 2050. Also, in combination with transportation systems management measures, carbon dioxide emissions would far exceed the 1990 emission levels. This suggests the need for alternative transportation fuels if carbon dioxide emissions are to be reduced below 1990 levels.

Although alternative fuels have often been considered as oil substitutes, the low long-term price of crude oil has led only a few countries to implement large-scale programs. Besides the Proalcohol program in Brazil, the largest alternative fuel program to date, an estimated 1.1 million vehicles operate on compressed natural gas, most of them in Canada and New Zealand. Hydrogen,

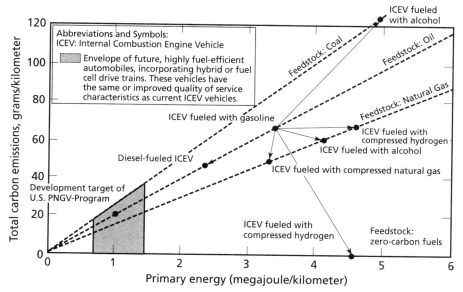

Transportation. FIGURE 6. Total Carbon Emissions versus Primary Energy Use for Selected Automobiles Using Different Transportation Fuels.

The indicated data points include energy use and carbon emissions from fuel extraction, processing, transmission, and distribution, and vehicle use. It is assumed that the energy input into any of these conversion processes is derived from one and the same fuel feedstock. Feedstocks are represented by straight lines, here: coal, oil, natural gas, and zero-carbon fuels. Efficiency improvements in any of the processes push data points toward the zero-point. Shifts from the gasoline-fueled reference car toward alternative transportation fuels correspond to a change in the feedstock line (arrows). The reference gasoline internal combustion engine vehicle has a fuel consumption of 9.3 liters of gasoline per 100 kilometers. Energy use of other vehicles and processes are typical values from the literature.

which has become the most important fuel in space propulsion, has only been applied in a few prototype road vehicles and test fleets. Aircraft have been operated successfully with liquefied natural gas and liquid hydrogen; research and development efforts for the use of liquid hydrogen in aircraft are ongoing.

Most alternative transportation fuels are secondary energy carriers—they are produced from other, primary fuels—which has two important implications. First, since a range of different feedstocks can often be used for the production of one secondary fuel, a consideration of the entire fuel cycle, consisting of fuel processing, transmission, distribution, storage, and vehicle use, is critical to any assessment of the emission mitigation potential. Figure 6 illustrates the results of such a fuel cycle analysis of primary energy use and total carbon dioxide emissions for different fuel and automobile technology strategies. Second, the production costs of alternative transportation fuels such as ethanol and compressed hydrogen from renewable electricity are typically two to four times higher than for refined oil. Although these costs can be reduced to some extent through the comparatively higher fuel efficiency of engines running on these fuels and through research and development, as well as learning curve effects of fuel production, a low- or zero-carbon transportation sector will require substantially higher transportation costs than the oil-based transportation systems in use today.

[*See also* Air Quality; Energy; Energy Policy; Fossil Fuels; Greenhouse Effect; *and* Petroleum Hydrocarbons in the Ocean.]

BIBLIOGRAPHY

Birk, M. L., and P. C. Zegras. *Moving Toward Integrated Transport Planning: Energy, Environment, and Mobility in Four Asian Cities.* Washington, D.C.: International Institute for Energy Conservation, 1990. A detailed review of transportation options in the developing world.

Bos, E., et al. *World Population Projections.* Published for the World Bank. Baltimore: Johns Hopkins University Press, 1992.

Brewer, G. D. *Hydrogen Aircraft Technology.* Boca Raton, Fla.: CRC Press, 1991. An introduction to hydrogen aircraft technology.

Davis, S. C. *Transportation Energy Data Book.* Oak Ridge, Tenn.: Oak Ridge National Laboratory, various years. A rich annually compiled data book on transportation economic variables.

Grübler, A. *The Rise and Fall of Infrastructures.* Heidelberg: Springer, 1990. A detailed analysis of the dynamics of evolution in transportation.

International Energy Agency. *Cars and Climate Change.* Paris: IEA/OECD, 1993. A good introduction to automobile greenhouse gas emissions and options for their reduction.

Leggett, J., et al. "Emissions Scenarios for IPCC: An Update." In *Climate Change 1992*, edited by J. T. Houghton, et al. Cambridge: Cambridge University Press, 1992.

Marchetti, C. "Anthropological Invariants in Travel Behavior." *Technological Forecasting and Social Change* 47 (1994), 75–88. An interesting overview of travel regularities.

Office of Technology Assessment. *Advanced Automobile Technology: Visions of a Super-Efficient Family Car.* OTA-ETI-638, September 1995. Available on the Internet at http://www.wws.princeton.edu/~ota/html2/cataA.html. One of the most comprehensive studies of tomorrow's highly fuel-efficient automobiles.

Organisation for Economic Co-operation and Development. *Congestion Control and Management.* Paris: OECD, 1994. An excellent summary of demand- and supply-side management measures.

Orski, K. *International Mobility Observatory: Window on the World of Transportation Innovation.* 2d ed. The Cooperative Mobility Program, Massachusetts Institute of Technology. Cambridge, 1997. An extensive collection and brief synthesis of transportation policy measures throughout the world (limited distribution).

Pucher, J., and C. Lefèvre. *The Urban Transport Crisis in Europe and North America.* Basingstoke: Macmillan, 1996. A comprehensive cross-country analysis of urban transportation problems and policy.

Rabinovitch, J., and J. Leitman. "Urban Planning in Curitiba." *Scientific American* (March 1996), 46–53. An excellent summary of the successful Curitiba transportation planning case.

Rennie, J., ed. "The Future of Transportation." *Scientific American* (Special Issue, October 1997). A comprehensive collection of articles on transportation demand and supply options on land, air, and water.

Salomon, I., et al., eds. *A Billion Trips a Day: Tradition and Transition in European Travel Patterns.* Dordrecht: Kluwer, 1993. A comparison of the development of transportation demand and policies in European countries.

Schafer, A. "The Global Demand for Motorized Mobility." *Transportation Research A* (August 1998), 455–477. A global analysis of the future demand for travel and various implications including carbon dioxide emissions.

Schafer, A., and D. Victor. "The Past and Future of Global Mobility." *Scientific American* (1997), 56–59.

———. "The Future Mobility of the World Population." *Transportation Research A.* (April 2000), 171–205. The only existing long-term projection of passenger travel for all major modes of transportation in all parts of the world.

Schipper, L. "Determinants of Automobile Use and Energy Consumption in OECD Countries." *Annual Review of Energy and the Environment* 20 (1995), 325–386. An overview of passenger transportation energy use in OECD countries.

Zahavi, Y. "The TT-Relationship: A Unified Approach to Transportation Planning." *Traffic Engineering and Control* (August/September 1973), 205–212. An excellent and readable introduction to travel budgets.

—ANDREAS SCHAFER

TREE RINGS. *See* Climate Reconstruction; *and* Dating Methods.

TSUNAMI. *See* Earthquakes.

TUNDRA

The word *tundra* is derived from a Finnish word describing treeless landscapes in northern latitudes. However, it has been used specifically to characterize one particular vegetation zone in the Arctic, and it has also been used very loosely during and since the International Biological Programme's Tundra Biome project to include all treeless vegetation zones resulting primarily from low temperatures. Here, tundra will be taken to mean the landscapes and vegetation north of the latitudinal treeline in the Northern Hemisphere. This includes high arctic and alpine vegetation where it is difficult to distinguish between a latitudinal and an altitudinal treeline. The southern boundary of the tundra is characterized by the taiga or forest tundra consisting of open woodland of deciduous trees in maritime areas and evergreen coniferous trees in continental areas. The northern boundary is the northernmost extent of arctic land (Figure 1).

Tundra potentially occupies those lands occurring north of the Arctic Circle (66° north latitude). However, in Fennoscandia (Norway, Sweden, Finland, and the adjacent parts of Russia), the warming influence of the North Atlantic Drift pushes the southern boundary some 3° north, while in eastern Canada, the cooling influence of the returning cold Atlantic currents displaces the southern boundary to about 55° north latitude. This southern boundary is associated with the northern limit of closed forest, the mean July isotherm for 10°C, the southern limit of permafrost, the southern limit of auroral activity, the isoline for areas with air temperatures above 0°C for less than 140 days, and marked decreases in annual absorbed and net solar radiation. Together, arctic landscapes cover some 7.57 million square kilometers, but this includes 1.97 million square kilometers of arctic icecaps and 0.85 million square kilometers of polar desert. Arctic lands are found in Eurasia (34 percent), Canada (33 percent), Greenland (28 percent), and Alaska (5 percent).

Vegetation of the Arctic. A North American classification divides the Arctic into the high Arctic and the low Arctic. The high Arctic is subdivided into polar desert, with herb-cryptogam communities (mainly lichens and mosses), and polar semidesert with herb-cryptogam, cushion plant-cryptogam, and mire communities; neither polar desert nor polar semidesert has continuous vegetation cover. In contrast, the low Arctic has a continuous vegetation cover of tundra vegetation *sensu stricto*, consisting of low shrub-sedge, tussock-dwarf shrub, and mire communities. An alternative Russian classification divides arctic vegetation into the tundra zone and the polar desert zone. The polar desert zone is characterized by cryptogam-herb communities,

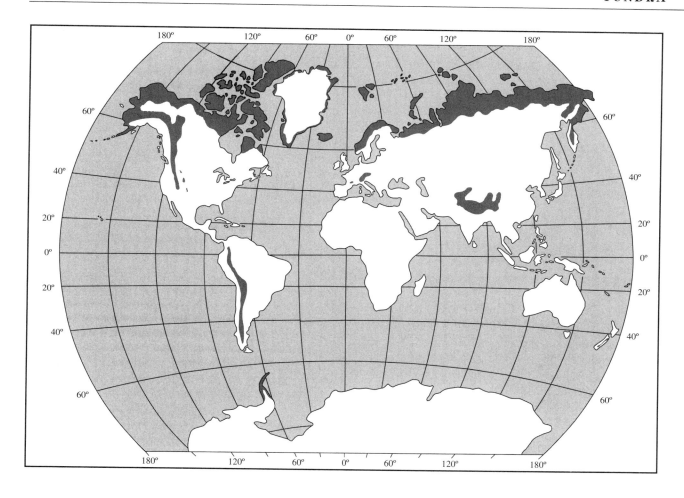

Tundra. FIGURE 1. Worldwide Tundra Distribution. (After Archibold, 1995, p. 280, Figure 9.1. With permission of Kluwer Academic Publishers.)

whereas the tundra zone is subdivided into arctic tundra, characterized by dwarf shrub-herb communities, typical tundra, characterized by sedge-dwarf shrub, polygonal mire communities, and southern tundra characterized by low shrub-sedge, tussock-dwarf shrub, and mire communities.

Arctic Environments. Low incoming radiation results in long, cold winters and short, cool, snow-free periods in late summer. Mean annual surface temperatures range from 0°C at Murmansk, Russia through −12.2°C at Point Barrow, Alaska and −16.3°C at Resolute, Canada to −28.1°C at the highest point of the Greenland Ice Sheet. January temperatures vary from less than −30°C in Siberia to only −10°C in northern Europe. July mean temperatures vary from less than 5°C in coastal areas to over 10°C in inland continental areas. Precipitation is also variable and decreases toward the north, where many arid regions occur. Small differences in mi-

crotopography (tens of centimeters) and plant shape can result in large surface temperature differentials of over 20°C.

Low air temperatures result in permafrost, defined as materials with a temperature at or below 0°C for at least two consecutive years. Permafrost covers about 21 percent of the land area of the Northern Hemisphere. The layer above the permafrost that freezes and thaws each year is called the *active layer*: this is where most biological activity takes place. In the northern part of the tundra, permafrost underlies this surface as a continuous layer, but becomes discontinuous and finally sporadic at the southern boundary of the tundra. The presence of permafrost strongly affects landform development, vegetation, soil processes, and hydrology, through changes in freeze–thaw cycles and development of ground ice. Tundra polygons are repeated patterns in the landscape, often polygonal in shape, resulting from ground ice activity that produces troughs between adjacent polygons, raised rims along borders, and centers that rise and sink. They are an important manifestation, and there is a close relationship between vegetation succession and polygon dynamics. The decay of ground ice

THERMOKARST

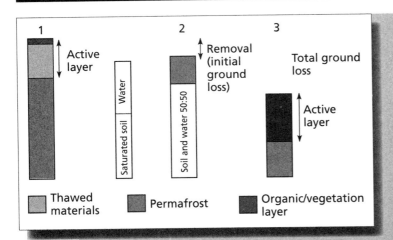

How Disturbance of High-Ice Content Terrain Can Lead to Permanent Ground Subsidence.

Numbers 1–3 indicate stages before, immediately after, and subsequent to, disturbance. (After Mackay in French, 1976, Figure 6.1.)

Around a quarter of the Earth's land surface is underlain by permafrost. If permafrost melts, ground subsidence occurs, producing irregular, hummocky terrain with hollows and disorganized drainage. The subsidence can also damage engineering structures, including pipelines, bridges, and buildings. The development of this thermokarst terrain is due primarily to the disruption of the thermal equilibrium of the permafrost and an increase in the depth of the active layer (the surface soil zone that melts in the summer). This is illustrated in the accompanying figure. Following French (1976, p. 106), consider an undisturbed tundra soil with an active layer of 45 centimeters. Assume that the soil below this depth is supersaturated permafrost and yields upon thawing, on a volume basis, 50 percent excess water and 50 percent saturated soil. If the top 15 centimeters were removed, the equilibrium thickness of the active layer, under the bare ground conditions, might increase to 60 centimeters. Since only 30 centimeters of the original layer remains, 60 centimeters of the permafrost must thaw before the active layer can thicken to 60 centimeters, since 30 centimeters of supernatant water will be released. Thus, the surface subsides 30 centimeters because of thermal melting associated with the degrading permafrost, to give an overall depression of 45 centimeters.

Therefore, the key process involved in thermokarst subsidence is the state of the active layer and its thermal relationships. When, for example, surface vegetation is cleared for agricultural or constructional purposes, the depth of the thaw will tend to increase. The movement of tracked vehicles has been particularly harmful to surface vegetation, and deep channels may soon result from permafrost degradation. Similar effects may be produced by the siting of heated buildings on permafrost, and by the laying of oil, sewerage, and water pipes in or on the active layer (Ferrians et al., 1969; Lawson, 1986).

Global warming could cause permafrost melting and degradation over extensive areas, thereby leading to a spread in thermokarst development.

BIBLIOGRAPHY

Ferrians, O. J., et al. "Permafrost and Related Engineering Problems in Alaska." *United States Geological Survey Professional Paper* 678 (1969).

French, H. M. *The Periglacial Environment*. London and New York: Longman, 1976.

Lawson, D. E. "Response of Permafrost Terrain to Disturbance: A Synthesis of Observations from Northeast Alaska, USA." *Arctic and Alpine Research* 18 (1986), 1–17.

—ANDREW S. GOUDIE

due to changing climate leads to land subsidence, formation of thermokarst terrain and, on sloping ground, to slumping and sliding of the thawed soil layer.

Climate in the Arctic has changed dramatically over time. The last ice age started about 115,000 BP: after its end, about 13,000 BP, the climate began to warm during the Bølling-Allerød period, but it suddenly became cooler during the Younger Dryas Period. [*See* Younger Dryas.] Temperatures in Greenland dropped back by about 7°C for about thirteen hundred years. After the Younger Dryas Period, the climate became warmer and wetter, but since then there has been a gradual cooling until the present, with a general retreat in altitudinal and latitudinal treelines. During the fourteenth century, climatic conditions in much of the tundra became cooler during the Little Ice Age. Since the end of this period, some 130 years ago, global temperatures have increased by about 0.6°C. During the thirty-year period 1966–1995, mean annual temperatures have risen in continental areas of North America and Siberia by as much as 4°–5°C, but Baffin Bay and southwestern Greenland have cooled by the same amount; whereas in some areas temperatures have remained more or less constant.

General circulation model scenarios of future climates vary, but all agree that warming will be greatest at high latitudes, over land, at nighttime, and in the winter. Recent simulations predict summer warming of 2°–4°C and winter warming of 1°–5°C for a doubling of atmospheric carbon dioxide. Even though precipitation is expected to increase, for example by 20–25 percent over North America, the increased temperatures are expected to extend the snow-free growing season by several weeks.

Vegetation History in the Arctic. Some high-arctic landmasses contain fossils indicating the presence of forests as late as the Tertiary period. Although this might have been a warmer period, it is also likely that these landmasses were farther south when the forests were growing. This and subsequent arctic vegetation was largely displaced by glaciations. Now, most of the vegetation—and fauna—of the Arctic is relatively modern, having been established since the end of the last full glacial maximum, some eighteen thousand years ago. The vascular flora is now somewhat smaller than what existed in the last interglacial period (about one thousand compared with fifteen hundred species), and in general has probably been formed from alpine elements and cold-night desert plants migrating along temperate mountain chains into the Arctic and from cool temperate plants of bogs and heaths. Plant endemism is low, and adaptations are relatively not far advanced.

The revegetation of the Arctic in the early Holocene probably occurred through two main processes. According to the tabula rasa theory, plants displaced to southern temperate latitudes during the glacial period colonized deglaciated land as the ice sheets retreated northward. However, even during the full glacial maximum, ice-free valleys, coastal areas, mountaintops, and larger areas existed in Beringia, mideastern Greenland, east-central Siberia, parts of central Alaska, and possibly parts of Iceland and Norway. According to the Nunatak hypothesis, these areas acted as refugia for some arctic plant species during the last ice age, and they now support relatively old floras. During the early Holocene, vegetation probably spread outward from the refugia.

During the Holocene, there have been climatic fluctuations but temperatures have decreased overall, and the recent Little Ice Age from about the fourteenth century to the mid-nineteenth century was the Holocene's coldest period. Both in Central Alaska and Siberia, steppe vegetation and parkland occurred during the early part of the Holocene. This might, to some extent, have been maintained by the grazing and browsing of large Pleistocene mammals, which became extinct during a phase of increased human activity. Over the past five to six thousand years, however, the regional floras of the wet coastal tundra on the North Slope of Alaska and the taiga forests and bogs of central Alaska have changed little. Near Fairbanks, vegetation has fluctuated between sedge meadows with low shrubs, and spruce–birch woodlands.

The Abisko area of northern Swedish Lapland was deglaciated about 8500 BP. Following this, the area has been dominated by a subalpine birch woodland tundra except for the period between 5500 and 3500 BP, when the boreal pine–birch forest zone reached the area and the treeline extended up to 100 meters above the present limit. Within the last fourteen hundred years, summer temperatures determined from pine tree rings have varied from modern norms (1951–1970) by +1.9° to −2.1°C for individual years. Cool periods have alternated with relatively warm periods. The cool period between roughly 1190 and 1360 CE seems to be associated with the onset of peat formation on ombrotrophic mires around Abisko. During the twentieth century, high temperatures existed in the 1930s, after which there was some cooling, but temperatures in the 1990s are now exceeding those in the earlier warm period. The current relatively warm period seems to be associated with a switch in the bogs from carbon sink to source, as has been documented for a north–south transect through Alaska. Spring temperatures have risen by 1.5°C since 1870, and the growing season is now one to three weeks longer (1913–1994). The birch treeline has been relatively stable since 500 CE, although there has been a recent increase in altitude of 25–50 meters in response to the warm period in the 1930s.

Arctic Animals. Arctic lakes and ponds often have a high productivity of insects, with aquatic larval stages and other invertebrates that form the food source of higher aquatic or terrestrial animals. Some trophic (food chain) levels containing predators of invertebrates, such as fish, may be absent. Thus the Arctic contains abundant food and attracts migratory birds during the short summer.

Most birds of the Arctic and some mammals are migratory species. A few species stay in the Arctic all year round and either remain active (such as reindeer) or enter diapause (invertebrates), or hibernate (such as bears).

The fertility of many birds and mammals is often cyclical. Lemming populations fluctuate in density in three- or four-year cycles. This cyclicity interacts with other trophic levels and results in similar population patterns for predators and for primary production, which is reduced by grazing. Invertebrates usually follow well determined life cycles with one generation per summer, but opportunistic life cycles can occur. The population dynamics of migrant animals, mainly birds, depends on factors in areas other than the Arctic, such as hunting laws and changes in agriculture or land use along the migration routes and in their overwintering areas. Generally this decreases the population sizes of migrant birds, but in some cases population sizes can increase to the extent that increased grazing pressure can denude ecosystems, as for example in the case of snow geese in Hudson Bay.

Impacts of Climate Change in the Tundra. Tundra ecosystems are becoming increasingly threatened by human activity. Greater accessibility and awareness of vast natural resources have resulted in increased settlement in the Arctic. The development of transport routes and oil pipelines and the establishment of extractive industries have sometimes produced large impacts on the tundra, fragmenting wilderness areas. Slow-growing, long-lived plants with low replacement rates, which often already experience the multiple stresses of severe climates and limited resources, are particularly sensitive to disturbance and, once damaged, require long periods to recover. Areas surrounding metal-smelting towns in the Kola Peninsula of Russia are extreme examples, with desertification occurring in the former subarctic forests there. Transboundary pollution could become of significance throughout the tundra: deposition of atmospheric nitrogen has great impacts on the strongly nitrogen-limited tundra vegetation, while persistent organochlorines and radionuclides accumulate in tundra animals and affect the health and livelihood of indigenous peoples.

In the context of possible future anthropogenic warming, the temperature increase is predicted to be largest toward the highest northern latitudes, and arctic ecosystems are potentially responsive because species existing close to their lower limits for physiological activity and survival tend to show great responses even to small changes in temperature. [*See* Global Warming.]

The responses of plants and their assemblages to predicted climatic change will be complex. Increases in temperature cannot be considered alone: interactions with other environmental change factors such as precipitation, atmospheric nitrogen deposition, increased ultraviolet radiation, and increased levels of atmospheric carbon dioxide can also be important. Moreover, the impacts of even one factor such as temperature are complex. Although all biological processes are responsive to temperature, indirect effects of temperature on ecosystems might be more important than direct effects. However, the impacts of temperature seem to be specific according to ecosystem type, plant community type, plant functional group, plant species, and plant process such as vegetative growth, photosynthesis, or reproduction.

Experiments simulating climate change in the tundra show that individualistic species responses will result in community disassociation. Early responses, often associated with the increased dominance of grasses and sedges over dwarf shrubs, may not be indicative of longer-term (decadal) responses. Simulation experiments show that mosses and lichens in the understory of tundra communities will probably be most disadvantaged by climatic change. Responses to increased temperatures are greatest at the coldest locations such as high arctic and alpine regions. Elsewhere, factors that increase nutrient availability, such as atmospheric nitrogen deposition and possible increased decomposition and nutrient mineralization rates in warmer soils, will have a more profound impact. While several experiments show changes in dominance of existing species and loss of some cryptogams in a simulated warmer climate, apparently only one so far has recorded the immigration of species not previously found at the site into its open, polar, semidesert community.

Comparisons of plant growth between years over decadal periods have shown that interannual summer temperature variations can be greater than the expected increases in temperature due to the greenhouse effect. Also, many arctic plant species are very widespread and, throughout most of their northern ranges, can tolerate temperature increases of the magnitude of those expected to occur by the end of the present century. It is therefore at their warmer, southern boundaries that they could be displaced. Although some species are likely to be displaced directly through temperature increases, for example by exceeding the thermal tolerance of green tissues or by generating an imbalance between photosynthesis and respiration, it is likely that competition from invading species will be the main mechanism of displacement of tundra plant species.

These processes are relatively slow, and predictions that about 20–32 percent of tundra will be displaced by the end of the next century because of the northward expansion of the boreal forest biome must be treated with caution: boreal tree migration rates are slower than predicted rates of climate shift. For example, a warming of 2°C could result in a 4°–5° northward latitude shift of the climate zone currently associated with the taiga of Eurasia; that is, a shift of 400–500 kilometers by the year 2020. If the taiga could migrate at the same rate, tundra would be totally displaced from the Eurasian mainland by 2020. However, the migration rates of taiga trees are only about 10–1,000 meters per year. Exceptions to the expected gradual change in distribution of organisms occur where corridors for migration are created by human activities. In general, however, the inequality in rates of climate and vegetation shift will subject large areas of vegetation to supraoptimal climate regimes in which damage from extreme weather, fire, and insect pests will increase.

Overall, tundra vegetation seems to be remarkably resilient to change, and sophisticated mechanisms exist in many species to overcome environmental adversity in both space and time. An exception to this resilience, however, may be related to disturbance events. In particular, thawing of permafrost is likely to change hydrology dramatically and could physically disrupt communities. Such processes that create gaps in the vegetation facilitate the establishment of invading species and accelerate vegetation change.

Climatic change can impact arctic animals both directly and indirectly, and animal responses are probably more complex than those of plants. The higher the position of an animal in a food chain, the greater the uncertainty in predicting its response to climatic change, since this is determined by the sum of the responses of all levels within the food chain and the multiplication of all the associated uncertainties of response.

The responses of herbivorous invertebrates to simulated climate change are greatest where climate is harshest, whereas the responses of soil-dwelling invertebrates are limited by buffering of soil warming. In the sub-Arctic, there is a significant negative correlation between incidence of low winter temperature and insect damage during outbreaks of *Epirritia autumnata*, a moth caterpillar that defoliates sub-Arctic birch trees. Overwintering eggs are killed in cold depressions and in cold winters when temperatures drop below −36°C. Predicted increases in winter temperature could lead to increased survival of eggs and greater destruction of birch forests, perhaps creating new tundra.

Mobile animals can probably change their distributions rapidly, and this phenomenon has been used to infer rapid changes in climate during the Holocene from changes in distributions of beetles (species and assemblages currently characterized by particular temperature regimes, when found in dated deposits, can be used to indicate past climates). Overall, a more benign future climate in the Arctic is likely to decrease mortality in most animal groups during summer, but nonmigratory animals could be severely impacted by altered winter snow conditions, which affect the availability of food and shelter and energy expenditure during foraging. If winter temperatures increase, and, in particular, if the frequency of events with temperatures above zero increases, thawing and freezing events could result in ice crust formation in the snow, thus preventing larger mammals (reindeer, musk-oxen) from reaching the vegetation below the snowpack, and small rodents living in the subnivean space from utilizing the vegetation encrusted in the ice.

Increases in primary production *per se* are uncertain, but changes in food quality (for example, plant tissue chemistry) are well documented. Increased plant growth, during which extra carbohydrates dilute the nutrient concentration in forage, particularly when plants are grown under high carbon dioxide concentrations, requires that the herbivore must increase food intake to compensate for its lower nutrient concentration. Such a temperature-dependent decline of forage quality has indeed been observed in plants during naturally occurring warm summers, while higher levels of ultraviolet (UV) B radiation can decrease plant tissue quality and adversely affect dependent organisms such as various invertebrate groups.

Climate Feedbacks from Arctic Terrestrial Ecosystems. While arctic landmasses are impacted by climate, they also modify climate. The Arctic currently cools the Earth by reflecting more incoming solar radiation than it absorbs. Ice and snow have the greatest reflectance, and tundra vegetation has higher reflectivity (albedo) than dark, coniferous boreal forests. A result of intensive warming at high latitudes will be an eventual decrease in the extent of snow and ice on land and a northward shift in the boreal forest zone. The resulting positive albedo feedback will be greater than that of the emissions of carbon from the biosphere. [*See* Albedo.]

The large stock of carbon stored in the tundra soils, estimated to be about 11 percent of that stored in soils globally, is a potentially important source of greenhouse gases (carbon dioxide and methane) to the global atmosphere. Carbon dioxide is released to the atmosphere by oxidation of organic carbon compounds in plants, animals, and microorganisms during respiration, and is reassimilated and transformed to organic carbon through plant photosynthesis. Methane (CH_4) is formed in anaerobic environments such as bogs and other wetlands by bacterial degradation of soil organic matter, and can be oxidized by other forms of soil bacteria under aerobic conditions.

In general, it is likely that the tundra has acted as a net sink for carbon throughout the Holocene by sequestration of atmospheric carbon in organic soils and peat. This process has occurred mainly through low microbial decomposer activity in soils that are cold and often waterlogged and where the input of carbon through plant litter is low and the litter is often relatively difficult to decompose. Under climatic warming, the tundra will act as an atmospheric source of carbon if belowground processes are stimulated more by changes in temperature and/or moisture than by plant productivity. On the other hand, the Arctic can continue to act as a sink for atmospheric carbon, even under climatic warming, if plant productivity is enhanced by increasing atmospheric carbon dioxide concentrations, or by increased availability of nutrients from decomposition and nutrient mineralization. The Arctic could also act as a sink for carbon if waterlogging increases as a result of permafrost thawing. [*See* Carbon Cycle.]

Sink–source relationships will probably vary both on a local basis and regionally. The open vegetation of the high Arctic will probably become a net sink for atmospheric carbon dioxide, whereas it is not known if the tundra in the middle Arctic with a closed vegetation cover will increase its sink action marginally, or act as a source of carbon dioxide as a result of increased microbial respiration but little increase in productivity. However, some workers have already reported a change of some Alaskan and Fennoscandian ecosystems from carbon-sink to carbon-source status.

The production and emission of methane occur principally in water-saturated areas of the tundra, for instance in the wet sedge tundra. Methane is, on the other hand, consumed by oxidizing bacteria in drier tundra areas, even in polygon rims as little as 1.5–20 centimeters higher than waterlogged, methane-generating depressions. Both the quantity of methane produced over the tundra area and the balance between methane production and consumption are poorly known. A particular gap in carbon flux measurements is the calculation of annual rather than summer-only budgets, and the establishment of a balance of research between potential carbon source areas in the middle Arctic and potential carbon sink areas to the north and south of this zone.

[*See also* Biomes; Cryosphere; Methane; Permafrost; *and the vignette on* Thermokarst.]

BIBLIOGRAPHY

EDITED VOLUMES CONTAINING SEVERAL RELEVANT PAPERS

Bliss, L. C., O. W. Heal, and J. J. Moore. *Tundra Ecosystems: A Comparative Analysis.* Cambridge: Cambridge University Press, 1981.
Callaghan, T. V., W. C. Oechel, T. Gilmanov, U. Molau, B. Maxwell, M. J. Tyson, B. Sveinbjörnsson, and J. I. Holten, eds. *Global Change and Arctic Terrestrial Ecosystems*, proceedings of papers contributed to the international conference, 21–26 August 1993, Oppdal, Norway. Luxembourg: European Commission, 1995.
Chapin, F. S., III, R. L. Jefferies, J. F. Reynolds, G. R. Shaver, and J. Svoboda, eds. *Arctic Ecosystems in a Changing Climate: An Ecophysiological Perspective.* London: Academic Press, 1992.
Chapin, F. S., III, and C. Körner, eds. *Arctic and Alpine Biodiversity: Patterns, Causes and Ecosystem Consequences.* Berlin: Springer, 1995, pp. 149–164.
Heal, O. W., T. V. Callaghan, J. H. C. Cornelissen, C. Körner, and S. E. Lee, eds. *Scenarios of Global Change Impacts in Europe's Cold Regions.* Luxembourg: European Commission, 1998.
Henry, G. H. R. "The International Tundra Experiment (ITEX), Short-Term Responses of Tundra Plants to Experimental Warming." *Global Change Biology* 3 (1997), 164.
Hofgaard, A., K. Danell, J. Ball, and T. V. Callaghan. "Animal Responses to Global Change in the North." *Ecological Bulletins* 47 (2000).
Nutall, M., and T. V. Callaghan. *The Arctic: Environment, People, Policy.* Reading, U.K.: Harwood Academic Publishers, 2000.

Oechel, W. C., T. V. Callaghan, T. Gilmanov, J. I. Holten, B. Maxwell, U. Molau, and B. Sveinbjörnsson, eds. *Global Change and Arctic Terrestrial Ecosystems.* New York: Springer, 1997.
Reynolds, J. F., and J. D. Tenhunen, eds. *Landscape Function and Disturbance in Arctic Tundra.* Berlin: Springer, 1996.
United Nations Environment Programme. *Environmental Effects of Ozone Depletion.* Nairobi: UNEP, 1998.
Wright, J. L., and Sheehan, eds. *Arctic Systems: Natural Environments, Human Actions, Nonlinear Processes*, proceedings of the International Conference for Arctic Research Planning, December 1995, Hanover, New Hampshire. Oslo: IASC, 1996.

INDIVIDUAL PUBLICATIONS

Alley, R. B., et al. "Climate Change, Ozone and Ultraviolet Radiation." In *Arctic Monitoring and Assessment Programme, AMAP*, edited by E. C. Weatherhead and C. M. Morseth. Oslo: AMAP, 1999.
Callaghan T. V., B. A. Carlsson, M. Sonesson, and A. Temesvary. "Between-Year Variation in Climate-Related Growth of Circumarctic Populations of the Moss *Hylocomium Splendens*." *Functional Ecology* 11 (1997), 157–165.
Chapin, F. S., III, and G. R. Shaver. "Individualistic Response of Tundra Plant Species to Environmental Manipulations in the Field." *Ecology* 66 (1985), 564–576.
Chapin, F. S., III, G. R. Shaver, A. E. Gibbling, K. J. Nadelhoffer, and J. A. Laundre. "Responses of Arctic Tundra to Experimental and Observed Changes in Climate." *Ecology* 76 (1995), 694–711.
Jonasson, S., J. A. Lee, T. V. Callaghan, M. Havstrom, and A. Parsons. "Effects of Increasing Temperature on Subarctic Ecosystems." *Ecological Bulletins* 45 (1996), 180–191.
Molau, U., and J. M. Alatalo. "Responses of Subarctic-Alpine Plant Communities to Simulated Environment Change: Biodiversity of Bryophytes, Lichens, and Vascular Plants." *Ambio* 27.4 (1998), 322–329.
Oechel, W. C., S. J. Hastings, M. Jenkins, G. Reichers, N. Grulke, and G. Vourlitis. "Recent Change of Arctic Tundra Ecosystems from a Carbon Sink to a Source." *Nature* 361 (1993), 520–526.
Press, M. C., T. V. Callaghan, and J. A. Lee. "How Will European Arctic Ecosystems Respond to Projected Global Environmental Change?" *Ambio* 27.4 (1998), 306–311.
Press, M. C., J. A. Potter, M. J. W. Burke, T. V. Callaghan, and J. A. Lee. "Response of a Sub-Arctic Dwarf Shrub Heath Community to Simulated Environmental Change." *Journal of Ecology* 86 (1998), 315–327.
Robinson, C. H., P. A. Wookey, J. A. Lee, T. V. Callaghan, and M. C. Press. "Plant Community Responses to Simulated Environmental Change at a High Arctic Polar Semi-Desert." *Ecology* 79 (1998), 856–866.
Schlesinger, W. H. "Soil Organic Matter: A Source of Atmospheric Carbon Dioxide." In *The Role of Terrestrial Vegetation in the Global Carbon Cycle, Methods of Appraising Changes*, edited by C. M. Woodwell, pp. 111–127. Chichester, U.K.: Wiley, 1984.
Strathdee, A. T., and J. S. Bale. "Life on the Edge: Insect Ecology in Arctic Environments." *Annual Review of Entomology* 43 (1998), 85–106.
Tissue, D. T., and W. C. Oechel. "Responses of *Eriophorum Vaginatum* to Elevated Carbon Dioxide and Temperature in the Alaskan Tussock Tundra." *Ecology* 68 (1987), 401–410.

—TERRY V. CALLAGHAN
AND JOHAN KLING

U

ULTRAVIOLET RADIATION. *See* Chlorofluorocarbons; *and* Ozone.

UNCERTAINTY. *See* Surprise.

UNITED NATIONS

The United Nations (UN) is the world's political organization. It was established by the UN Charter signed in 1945 as a successor to the League of Nations. Its purposes, as set out more fully in Article I of the Charter, are (1) to maintain international peace and security, (2) to develop friendly relations among nations, and (3) to achieve international cooperation in solving international problems. The United Nations currently has 185 member states; its headquarters, headed by the Secretary General, are located in New York City.

The main representative body of the United Nations is the General Assembly, in which each member has one vote. The General Assembly acts by nonbinding resolution. The main UN decision-making body is the Security Council, comprising fifteen states, five of whom (China, France, Russia, the United Kingdom, and the United States) are permanent members. The remaining ten are elected by the General Assembly for two-year terms. Decisions of the Security Council on nonprocedural issues require at least nine votes, including those of all permanent members, and are binding on all members.

The United Nations is at the center of a network of fourteen specialized agencies and over thirty other bodies, which are international technical organizations with defined mandates. These range from the World Health Organization (WHO) to the World Meteorological Organization (WMO) and the Food and Agriculture Organization (FAO), and include programmatic bodies like the United Nations Development Programme (UNDP) and the United Nations Environment Programme (UNEP). These bodies increasingly include the secretariats of various international environmental treaties established under UN auspices, such as the United Nations Framework Convention on Climate Change (FCCC). [*See* Food and Agriculture Organization; United Nations Environment Programme; United Nations Framework Convention on Climate Change; World Health Organization; *and* World Meteorological Organization.]

The first formal recognition of the importance of global environmental issues by the United Nations was the General Assembly Resolution [2398 (XXIII)] to convene the 1972 United Nations Conference on the Human Environment, which itself resulted in the creation of UNEP [by Resolution 2997 (XXVII)]. In 1988, the General Assembly first recognized the significance of possible global climate change and endorsed the establishment of the Intergovernmental Panel on Climate Change (Resolution 43/905). It convened the 1992 United Nations Conference on Environment and Development (where the Rio Declaration, Agenda 21, the Convention on Biological Diversity, the FCCC, and a Statement of Forest Principles were adopted) and set up the Commission on Sustainable Development. The United Nations has initiated and administers many legal instruments that address global environmental issues. These include the 1982 Law of the Sea Convention, the 1985 Vienna Convention on the Protection of the Ozone Layer and its 1987 Montreal Protocol on Substances that Deplete the Ozone Layer, the 1989 Basel Convention on the Control of Transboundary Movements of Hazardous Wastes and their Disposal, the 1994 United Nations Convention to Combat Desertification, and, more recently, the 1997 Kyoto Protocol to the FCCC.

[*See also* Agenda 21; Convention on Biological Diversity; Intergovernmental Panel on Climate Change; Kyoto Protocol; Law of the Sea; Rio Declaration; Sustainable Development; *and* United Nations Conference on Environment and Development.]

BIBLIOGRAPHY

Churchill, R., and D. Freestone. *International Law and Global Climate Change*. London: Graham and Trotman/Martinus Nijhoff, 1991. A collection of essays, written pre-UNCED, addressing legal aspects of global change, with extensive UN and other official documentation.

Muller, J., ed. *Reforming the United Nations: New Initiatives and Past Efforts*. The Hague: Kluwer, 1997. Assessment of the contemporary issues facing the United Nations.

United Nations. *The United Nations Charter, San Francisco*. New York: United Nations, 1945.

Werksman, J., ed. *Greening International Institutions*. London: Earthscan, 1996. Sets the United Nations and its family organizations in the context of the environmental movement.

Wolfrum, R., ed. *United Nations: Law, Policies and Practice*. Dordrecht: Martinus Nijhoff, 1995.

—DAVID FREESTONE

UNITED NATIONS CONFERENCE ON ENVIRONMENT AND DEVELOPMENT

The United Nations Conference on Environment and Development (UNCED), frequently referred to as the "Earth Summit," took place June 3–14, 1992 in Rio de Janeiro, Brazil. The conference produced two binding international agreements and several substantive declarations, contributed to the development of environmental governance in general, and provided evidence of a growing concern about the relationship between environmental protection and economic development.

The Rio conference took place on the twentieth anniversary of the United Nations Conference on the Human Environment in Stockholm, and was motivated in part by *Our Common Future*, the 1987 report of the United Nations Commission on Environment and Development. A preparatory committee for the conference held four negotiating sessions from 1990 to 1992.

One hundred seventy-eight states were represented at the conference, many by heads of state. It was considered to be the largest gathering of world leaders in history. Representatives from UN agencies and other international organizations attended as well.

Individuals associated with up to seven thousand nongovernmental organizations (NGOs) came to Rio. Nearly fifteen hundred NGOs were officially accredited to the conference itself, one third of them from developing countries. Some organizations participated in the negotiations prior to the conference, and some served on national delegations. A global forum of NGOs took place concurrently with the UN conference, and featured exchanges of information and negotiation of agreements among the groups present. Much of the press coverage of the conference focused on some of the more colorful elements of the forum. The parallel NGO activities provided an opportunity to organizations from different parts of the world and with different focuses to exchange information and build alliances.

The negotiations before and during the conference were contentious, with a split apparent between the positions of developed and developing countries. Developing countries focused on their rights to economic development and sovereignty over their natural resources. They insisted that countries in the developed world accept responsibility for the environmental problems of industrialization. Developed countries, on the other hand, wanted all countries to take action to address global environmental problems, and worked to avoid acknowledging specific responsibility for creating them.

Two treaties negotiated separately from the preparations for UNCED were concluded so as to be signed at the conference. The United Nations Convention on Bi-ological Diversity requires domestic commitments to protect biodiversity and sets up a process for cooperation to protect species and areas. The United Nations Framework Convention on Climate Change (FCCC) attempts to "prevent dangerous anthropogenic interference with the climate," by encouraging developed-country action to stabilize greenhouse gas emissions. Each of these treaties was signed by more than 150 states at the conference. The United States met with criticism over its reticence with respect to these treaties; it refused to accept any specific targets for the phasing out of greenhouse gas emissions in the FCCC, and did not sign the Convention on Biodiversity for fear that United States biotechnology firms would suffer. [*See* Convention on Biological Diversity; *and* Framework Convention on Climate Change.)

There were several other important documents negotiated as a part of the conference. The Rio Declaration on Environment and Development laid out twenty-seven principles to direct policy relating to both environment and development. Important among these are the reiteration of states' rights to development and to sovereignty over their natural resources, the emphasis on the importance of both the precautionary principle and the polluter-pays principle, and discussion of widespread participation in decisions on issues of environment and development. Agenda 21, the action plan of the conference, consists of forty chapters (covering nearly eight hundred pages) that lay out suggestions for addressing the environment and development goals of states at the conference. For each of the issues the document addresses, it suggests priorities and programs and gives an estimate of the costs involved. Although neither of these documents is legally binding, the contentiousness of the negotiating process indicates the seriousness with which the states approached these topics. The final negotiated agreement of the conference was a "non-legally binding authoritative statement of principles" on forests that was reached when a binding treaty proved too contentious. [*See* Agenda 21; *and* Rio Declaration.]

An underlying theme of the conference was the generation of additional financial resources to assist countries with environment and development needs. Although no new resources were allocated specifically to support the programs of Agenda 21, developed countries reaffirmed their goal to designate 0.7 percent of their gross national product for development assistance. UNCED also designated the Global Environmental Facility (GEF) as the main funding mechanism for international environmental issues. Another important theme at Rio was the collection of information: the two treaties require national reporting of information, and the UNCED process requires reports from participating states on their experiences with environment and development. [*See* Global Environment Facility.]

In the wake of the conference, the United Nations General Assembly created the Commission on Sustainable Development, to address implementation of issues from Agenda 21. Other issues discussed but not resolved at Rio were taken up shortly thereafter: negotiations were completed on the United Nations Convention to Combat Desertification in 1994, and a United Nations agreement on Straddling and Migratory Fish Stocks was negotiated in 1995. Negotiations on protocols to both of the UNCED treaties have taken place, requiring substantive obligations from states. The Rio+5 conference in 1997 examined states' progress in implementing the recommendations and obligations from the conference.

Some criticize UNCED, and the documents signed there, for not going far enough to address potential conflicts between environment and development. It is clear that, without new sources of funding, many of the agreements will prove impossible to implement. But although the specific results of the Rio conference may seem modest, it is likely that the conference's legacy will be large. It raised awareness about environmental issues in a way that might have a lasting impact. It contributed to the creation of new principles of international law and the generation of new information, and brought many more into the process of addressing environment and development issues than might otherwise have been involved.

[*See also* Straddling and Migratory Stocks Agreement; *and* Sustainable Development, *article on* Commission on Sustainable Development.]

BIBLIOGRAPHY

Grubb, M., M. Koch, A. Munson, F. Sullivan, and K. Thomson. *The Earth Summit Agreements: A Guide and Assessment*. London: Earthscan, 1993.

Haas, P. M., M. A. Levy, and E. A. Parson. "Appraising the Earth Summit: How Should we Judge UNCED's Success?" *Environment* 34.8 (1992), 6–11, 26–33.

Johnson, S. P., ed. *The Earth Summit: The United Nations Conference on Environment and Development*. London, Dordrecht, and Boston: Graham and Trotman/Martinus Nijhoff, 1993. This volume mixes overview and assessment of the conference with documents, presented thematically.

Middleton, N., P. O'Keefe, and S. Moyo. *Tears of the Crocodile: From Rio to Reality in the Developing World*. London and Boulder: Pluto Press, 1993. The first and last chapters of this book provide criticism of the conference's impact on developing countries; the other chapters critically examine issues taken up or ignored at Rio.

Panjabi, R. K. L. *The Earth Summit at Rio: Politics, Economics, and the Environment*. Boston: Northeastern University Press, 1997.

Parson, E., P. M. Haas, and M. A. Levy. "A Summary of the Major Documents Signed at the Earth Summit and the Global Forum." *Environment* 34.8 (1992), 12–15, 34–36.

—ELIZABETH R. DeSOMBRE

UNITED NATIONS CONFERENCE ON THE HUMAN ENVIRONMENT

The United Nations (UN) Conference on the Human Environment, held in Stockholm, Sweden June 5–16, 1972, was the first global conference to address broadly defined environmental issues. It focused on the relationship between human beings and the natural environment and on the creation of a UN framework for addressing environmental issues.

Scandinavian concern over acid rain was an important precursor to the idea of a UN-sponsored environment conference, as was the growing awareness more generally of the environmental problems of industrialized countries. Sweden first raised the issue of a UN conference to address human interactions with the environment in the Economic and Social Council (ECOSOC) of the United Nations in July 1968. After ECOSOC supported the idea, the General Assembly voted to convene a conference in 1972. The philosophy of the conference was laid out in a document entitled *Only One Earth* (Ward and Dubos, 1972), designed to provide an intellectual framework for the meeting. This document called for international responsibility for studying the relationship between humans and the environment, an internationally coordinated policy for addressing global environmental issues, and a shared "loyalty to the earth."

One hundred and thirteen states sent representatives to Stockholm. States from most parts of the globe participated, with the exception of eastern European states, most of which stayed away from the conference over the issue of the voting status of East Germany. More than four hundred international organizations and nongovernmental organizations (NGOs) were present as well, and a UN-sanctioned forum for NGOs took place outside the official negotiations. Although some complained that the separation between the NGO activity and the official meetings had the effect of diminishing the influence these groups could have on the negotiations themselves, the conference is credited with providing a new voice for NGOs in global environmental politics.

The Stockholm meeting also represented a new role for developing countries in approaching environmental issues. Preparatory meetings before the conference addressed developing-country fears that their process of development would be harmed by focusing on environmental protection. Concerns of developing countries helped to broaden the agenda of the conference to include environmental issues relating to poverty and development, as well as those relating to industrialization. Developing countries also reiterated their sovereign rights over their natural resources and their rights to determine their own environmental priorities.

The conference produced a Declaration, a List of Principles, an Action Plan, and several Resolutions. After the conference, the UN General Assembly followed up on a central recommendation from the Action Plan to create the United Nations Environment Programme (UNEP). Stockholm ushered in a new era of environmental negotiation. Negotiations on agreements to protect world heritage, to address ocean pollution, and to regulate trade in endangered species began at the conference and were concluded shortly thereafter; many other global or regional cooperative arrangements followed.

[*See also* Stockholm Declaration; *and* United Nations Environment Programme.]

BIBLIOGRAPHY

Caldwell, L. K. *International Environmental Policy: Emergence and Dimensions.* 2d ed. Durham, N.C. and London: Duke University Press, 1990. Chapter 3 on "The Stockholm Conference and its Legacy" provides a good overview; Chapter 2 indicates precursors of the conference.

McCormick, J. *Reclaiming Paradise: The Global Environmental Movement.* Bloomington and Indianapolis: Indiana University Press, 1989. See Chapter 5, "The Stockholm Conference."

United Nations. *Report of the United Nations Conference on the Human Environment.* New York: United Nations, 1973. This report gives the text of the declarations and resolutions adopted by the conference, and other information about the proceedings of the conference.

Ward, B., and R. Dubos. *Only One Earth.* New York: Norton, 1972. Document written at the request of Maurice Strong, Secretary-General of the conference.

—ELIZABETH R. DeSOMBRE

UNITED NATIONS CONVENTION ON THE LAW OF THE SEA. *See* Law of the Sea.

UNITED NATIONS ENVIRONMENT PROGRAMME

The United Nations Environment Programme (UNEP), a specialized agency of the United Nations, was created by the UN General Assembly in 1972 to be the "environmental conscience of the UN system," in response to a recommendation from the United Nations Conference on the Human Environment (Stockholm). The organization coordinates the environmental activities of UN agencies, works to increase national capacity for environmental protection in member states, assists in negotiations of, and provides support to, international agreements, oversees environmental monitoring activities and the gathering of scientific information, and in general works to increase the ability of the UN system to address environmental problems.

UNEP is overseen by a Governing Council composed of fifty-eight states, elected by the General Assembly to staggered four-year terms. Geographic balance is maintained, with sixteen representatives from African states, thirteen from western Europe, Oceania, and North America, thirteen from Asia, ten from Latin America and the Caribbean, and six from eastern Europe. The organization's secretariat is located in Nairobi, Kenya, making it the first UN agency to be headquartered in a developing country. The budget of the organization has grown from U.S.$20 million in 1973 to approximately U.S.$105 million in 1997. The four Executive Directors of UNEP (Maurice Strong of Canada, 1973–1975; Mostafa Tolba of Egypt, 1976–1992; Elizabeth Dowdswell of Canada, 1993–1998; and Klaus Töpfer, 1998 to the present) have played influential roles within and outside the organization in increasing its legitimacy and mandate.

UNEP has played an increasingly active role in negotiations of international agreements—nearly half of the multilateral environmental agreements concluded since the organization's creation have been under UNEP auspices. The organization provides secretariat services to a number of these agreements, and acts as an implementing agency for projects carried out under the Global Environmental Facility and the Montreal Protocol Multilateral Fund. It has similarly overseen international conferences on such issues as human settlements, water, desertification, and, most importantly, the United Nations Conference on Environment and Development in 1992. It has worked to draw up guidelines for addressing a variety of environmental concerns, such as the management of shared natural resources, environmental impact assessment, and disposal of toxic waste. UNEP has also been active in creating management arrangements for regional seas, under its Oceans and Coastal Areas and Regional Seas program. The first of these was the Mediterranean Action Plan in 1975, after which many subsequent programs have been modeled.

Assessment and monitoring activities have formed an important part of UNEP's mandate, under the Earthwatch program. This program includes the Global Environmental Monitoring System (GEMS), an information-referral program (INFOTERRA), and the Global Resource Information Database (GRID). Other programs monitor water quality, food contamination, chemicals, and concentrations of atmospheric pollutants.

UNEP also works toward building capacity in countries for improving environmental management. The organization trains officials within countries, sponsors demonstration projects, and provides information.

Although the organization has experienced mixed success in its programs, it has helped to increase the awareness of environmental issues globally, and the ability of the UN system to manage them effectively.

[*See also* Global Environment Facility; International

Cooperation; Mediterranean Sea; Secretariats; *and* United Nations Conference on the Human Environment.]

BIBLIOGRAPHY

Gray, M. A. "The United Nations Environment Programme: An Assessment." *Environmental Law* 20 (1990), 291–319. A critical appraisal of the organization's mandate and activities.
Haas, P. M. "Institutions: United Nations Environment Programme." *Environment* 36.7 (1994), 43–45.
McCormick, J. *Reclaiming Paradise: The Global Environmental Movement.* Bloomington and Indianapolis: Indiana University Press, 1989. See Chapter 6 for a good overview of UNEP's first ten years.

—Elizabeth R. DeSombre

UNITED NATIONS FRAMEWORK CONVENTION ON CLIMATE CHANGE. *See* Framework Convention on Climate Change.

URANIUM. *See* Nuclear Hazards; *and* Nuclear Industry.

URBAN AREAS

Urban settlements, or cities, became home for a majority of the world's people by the end of the twentieth century. In many countries, such as in Europe and North America, 70–80 percent or more of the population lives in cities, and there are very few countries left with less than 30–40 percent urban population, these being very poor nations in Africa, Asia, and Latin America. Cities are among the most dominant physical evidence of human existence on the planet, with thousands of urban centers of widely varying sizes scattered around the world. This reality is especially vivid when viewing the planet from space at night, when the urban centers stand out as bright points of light, giving real meaning to the concept of global change.

Cities around the world are alike in many ways, yet also very different. Their similarities lie in common purposes, found in the age-old need of humans to collect together at certain sites to exchange goods and services, administer peoples and territories, worship gods, develop cultures, and carry out the myriad other activities of civilization that can best be performed in concentrations of people. With the rapid spread of machine technology and mass communications, a global economy and supranationalism, modern architecture, and the automobile society, some degree of physical homogeneity also seems to be spreading among cities, especially the larger ones. Yet cities still retain their distinctiveness in many ways, reflecting the many peoples and cultures around the world and their histories, as well as the widely varying physical environments in which cities arise. Cities in many ways also represent the best and the worst elements of human civilization. At their best, cities are physically and functionally vibrant as centers of arts, human creativity, and beauty. At their worst, cities can be nearly unmanageable concentrations of appalling squalor and poverty. These latter cities' dismal character seems pervasive and has little likelihood of immediate improvement.

The growth in numbers and sizes of cities, and the striking contrast between developed and developing regions, are clearly shown by illustration (Figures 1 and 2, Table 1). Since 1950, the gap between the developed and the developing world in numbers of urban agglomerations has steadily widened, especially since the 1970s (Figure 1). Cities in developing regions are growing faster than cities ever did in developed regions, and are also becoming larger relative to those in developed regions. Only four of the sixteen largest urban agglomerations in 1996, the "megacities" of the world, were in developed regions (Table 1). The twelve megacities of the developing world are also predicted to continue growing, albeit at varying rates, with Bombay and Lagos projected to be close behind Tokyo for top spot by 2015 (Figure 2). These megacities are of particular concern, because of the huge populations found in them, their precarious environmental situations, and the problems of the cities' economies and governance systems in meeting adequately the basic human needs of so many people. Even the four megacities in the developed regions, Tokyo, Osaka, New York, and Los Angeles, are not without problems in this regard. Thus the growth of so many cities and their increasing size pose major challenges, raising questions of whether they can function effectively and be sustained as ecosystems. At what point does a city become too large in population or in area? This question becomes even more critical in those countries in which a single megacity dominates the country. These cities, known as "primate cities," are

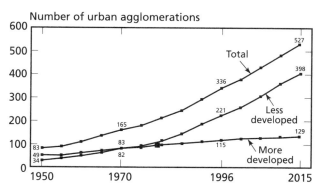

Urban Areas. Figure 1. Number of Urban Agglomerations with One Million or More Inhabitants: 1950–2015. (After United Nations, 1996.)

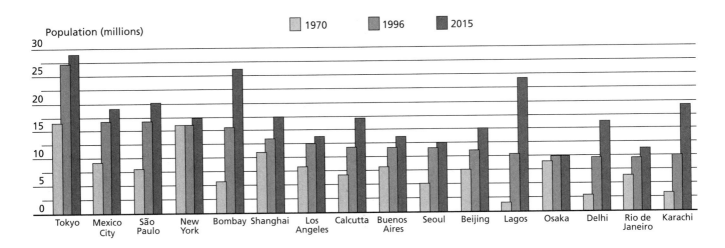

Urban Areas. FIGURE 2. World's Urban Agglomerations with Populations of Ten Million or More Inhabitants in 1996: 1970, 1996, and 2015. (After United Nations, 1996.)

found in both developed and developing countries, but are especially a problem in developing nations because the primate cities tend to be the destination for most rural migrants, the national capital, and the overwhelmingly dominant commercial, cultural, and economic center. The result is serious regional imbalances in population and standards of living, as well as uncertain human futures. These imbalances can contribute directly to social and political unrest. Many of these developing-world primate cities are the legacy of colonialism, and freedom from colonialism does not easily change urban primacy.

Historical Perspective. Cities are as old as human history, but there has never been common agreement as to what constitutes a city or urban center, and what names to attach to these centers. Village, town, city, metropolis, megalopolis, conurbation, urban center, urban place, urban agglomeration, human settlement—these are some of the more common terms that have been coined to designate a concentration of people, each usually associated with a certain relative number of people and/or size of cluster. In general, however, cities have historically been differentiated by the fact that a majority of the people living in the cluster are not involved in agricultural or other rural activities. Thus a purely farm village, regardless of its size, in most countries will not be classified as a city or urban center. Indeed, it was the transferring out of agriculture into nonagricultural activities of significant numbers of people that initiated urbanization thousands of years ago. Nonetheless, ambiguities in the terminology still abound today among scholars and governments.

Throughout most of human history, cities have been associated with the functions of government, culture, religion, defense, trade, and manufacturing. The oldest cities were found in the culture hearths of world civilization—the great river valleys of the Yellow (China), the Indus–Ganges (India and South Asia), the Tigris–Euphrates (Mesopotamia or present-day Iraq and neighbors), and the Nile (Egypt). Later centers were in the high Indian cultures of Middle and South America, and some early centers in western and southern Africa, before European colonialism. Many of these ancient civilizations developed cities to a high level of sophistication and beauty, such as the classical cities of ancient China, typified by the great Tang dynasty capital of Changan (modern Xian). The Western world had its first golden age of cities in the Greek and Roman empires, with Rome as the first known "million" city (population of more than one million) in history, but then fell into disunion and a decline in urbanization. Thus, until the European Age of Discovery and the Renaissance, out of which evolved colonialism and the Industrial Revolution of the nineteenth and twentieth centuries, the largest and best-developed cities were found in parts of Latin America, Africa, and Asia.

Nonetheless, contemporary urban processes are most closely associated with the Industrial Revolution that swept the world, starting in the early nineteenth century in Great Britain, then spreading to the continent of Europe and to North America. These processes included distinctive urban features that are still sweeping through the past colonial realms of the former imperial powers. Industrial manufacturing, replacing the small-scale cottage industry of the past, was the driving force in this process, fueled by the rivalries of extraterritorial colonial empires for raw materials and markets for their goods. Thus, existing cities assumed new faces, forms, and sizes, as people flocked to the cities to work in the rapidly expanding industrial and service economies,

Urban Areas. TABLE 1. World's Urban Agglomerations of Ten Million or More Inhabitants, Estimated 1999

CITY AND COUNTRY	INCLUDES	POPULATION
Tokyo, Japan	Yokohama, Kawasaki	34,200,000
New York, United States	Newark, Patterson	20,150,000
São Paulo, Brazil		19,750,000
Seoul, South Korea	Inchon, Songnam	19,350,000
Mexico City, Mexico	Nezahualcoyotl, Ecatepec de Morelos	18,000,000
Osaka, Japan	Kobe, Kyoto	17,700,000
Bombay, India	Kalyan, Thane, Ulhasnagar	17,200,000
Los Angeles, United States	Riverside, Anaheim	15,950,000
Cairo, Egypt	El Giza	13,950,000
Moscow, Russia		13,200,000
Buenos Aires, Argentina	San Justo, La Plata	13,100,000
Manila, Philippines	Quezon City, Caloocan	13,000,000
Calcutta, India	Haora	12,650,000
Lagos, Nigeria		12,450,000
Jakarta, Indonesia		12,100,000
Karachi, Pakistan		11,800,000
London, England		11,750,000
Shanghai, China		11,600,000
Rio de Janeiro, Brazil		11,450,000
Delhi, India		11,100,000
Tehran, Iran	Karaj	10,150,000
Paris, France		10,050,000

SOURCE: Brinkhoff (1999).

fleeing the backbreaking labor and poverty of rural life. Whole new cities also sprang into existence along coastlines and railroads. Cities increasingly became the centers of wealth, creativity, and political and economic power. London and Paris, for example, accelerated to the forefront as Europe's two largest and wealthiest cities because they were the centers of the world's two largest colonial empires.

This model of urban development, in Europe and later in North America, had distinctive features. These industrial cities had specifically designated areas for heavy and light industry, and associated transportation land uses. [*See* Transportation.] Workers for the most part lived nearby. Retailing and wholesaling land uses were found in close proximity. Central parts of the cities became known as the "Central Business District"(CBD), reflecting the concentration there of high land values and the resultant focus on critical activities that could afford the cost, such as banking, hotels, retailing, and government. As land values increased, technology improved, and competition for central locations strengthened, the profile of the CBD became ever taller, with the emergence of high-rise buildings that made maximum

effective use of limited ground space. Many scholars have studied the land use patterns of cities, especially in the developed countries, and have devised various schematic models that attempt to provide generalizations that can explain the process of urban development and the use of land in cities. However, all of these models are imperfect instruments, reflecting the complexities and differences that persist in cities, even in today's shrinking world.

One commonality that seems eventually to appear in most cities in all countries is that of urban sprawl and suburbanization. As industrialization and urbanization increase and transport improves with increased reliance on automobiles and private transportation, industry, services, and people begin to move farther and farther outward, seeking better and cheaper housing, cleaner air and physical environment, less crowding, perhaps a safer environment away from central-city crime and social problems, and better transportation access to work, shopping, and recreation. [*See* Industrialization.] This horizontal process is farthest along, of course, in the developed, highly industrialized countries of western Europe and North America. In the United States, the process is also closely associated with ethnic tensions and class divisions that persist as deeply embedded social problems; and most other European countries are not entirely free of these problems. Former colonials, guest workers (labor migrants), and people of color are the new cultural layers.

In the United States, this sprawl and suburbanization is also reflected in the administrative and political fragmentation of urban centers, sometimes referred to as the *doughnut model*, in which the central city (the hole in the doughnut) faces a declining population and tax base while the politically independent suburbs (the doughnut itself) undergo rapid population increase and a rising tax base as the economy of the metropolitan area becomes concentrated in the ring of suburban communities.

Types of City. As a result of the long evolution of urban centers around the world, cities in the contemporary world can be categorized into a number of types. Most cities have combinations of these different elements, while some fit distinctively into one category.

Preindustrial cities. These cities emerged on to the cultural landscape before industrialization, and they have been in existence for longer than all other types. They originally had very distinctive roles, as noted above, and were often characterized by city walls, narrow pedestrian streets, compact structure and high density of population, open squares, grand public buildings such as temples or churches or palaces, gardens, and other features. Many of these cities were obliterated during the colonial era, but many more survived into modern times, undergoing transformation during and after colonialism and on into industrialization; examples are Addis Ababa (Ethiopia), Samarqand (Uzbekistan), Kano (Nigeria), and Fez (Morocco). Thus, their appearance today is often eclectic, a sharp contrast between old and new, with the old city typically surrounded by a much larger modern city, usually poorly planned, with many of the problems found throughout the world's urban places. Very few preindustrial cities remain unchanged to at least some degree by the modern era, although many of them have not been highly successful in industrializing. This has contributed directly to the inability of such cities to produce jobs fast enough for the migrants flooding into them from rural areas, and is the crux of the problem for those countries and cities.

Colonial cities. Although colonialism has nearly disappeared from the Earth today, one of its most visible legacies is the former colonial city, found widely in Latin America, Africa, and Asia. Many of the largest cities in the world today owe their existence to colonialism. Typically built on a port or river site for easy transport access, the colonial city took many forms, but in general resulted from an effort by the colonial power to recreate in a foreign locale the urban setting of the

mother country, often the capital city such as Paris or London. Thus, cities such as Saigon (now Ho Chi Minh City) in Vietnam or Dakar in Senegal became imitations of Paris. Singapore, Hong Kong, Bombay, and Nairobi (Kenya) became outliers of British culture and urban design. Batavia (now Jakarta) was an attempt to transpose Dutch urban life to the tropics of the East Indies (present-day Indonesia). Rio de Janeiro and the other cities of Brazil were built with a Portuguese flavor. Mexico City, Lima, and other cities in Latin America were recreations of Spanish urban centers. The Japanese imitated European colonial powers in building their colonial capitals of Taipei (Taiwan) and Seoul (Korea). Even in China, which was never entirely controlled by a single colonial ruler, vestiges of European urban design crept into the urban development of various cities, such as the International Settlement in Shanghai. Racial segregation and extreme inequality between colonial rulers and ruled were the norm in these cities. Although the colonial rulers are for the most part now long gone (the most recent departure was the British from their colony of Hong Kong in mid-1997 and the Portuguese from Macao in 1999), the physical legacy of their rule lingers on in the architecture, street patterns, and culture of countless cities around the world. There are even careful efforts to preserve the colonial past as part of the city's historical heritage, often to support commercial tourism.

Industrial cities. These cities arose from the early 1800s onward, with the Industrial Revolution referred to above. Many of them had highly specialized economies, focused initially on heavy industry such as iron and steel, motor vehicles, aircraft, or military hardware. Others became quite diversified in their economic base, with shipbuilding, chemicals, food products, textiles, household goods, furniture, and so on. Old industrial cities seeking a smooth entry into postindustrial economies have frequently experienced serious problems, such as in the Rust Belt of the old industrial northeast of the United States (Cleveland and Detroit) and the Midlands and north of England (Birmingham, Manchester, and Liverpool).

Postindustrial cities. These are cities whose economies are built on services rather than on heavy or light industry. Service economies include finance, real estate, insurance, education, printing and publishing, research and development, telecommunications, recreation, heath care, and government. While most cities, including preindustrial and industrial cities, have portions of their labor force in these service categories, what distinguishes the postindustrial city is the high proportion of the labor force in services. Some of these cities are highly specialized in one or another service, including many that have emerged in recent decades in Europe, North America, and other regions. Many, if not most, postindustrial cities are nonetheless fairly diversified.

Cities around the world in general are increasingly dependent on the tertiary or service sector. Some cities have very little history of industry, especially not one identified with central city locations. Washington, D.C., is a particularly good example of a city that never really had a true industrial (manufacturing) base and is almost totally dominated by a highly diversified service economy. Such cities today have growth associated with highway systems and airports rather than rivers or railroads. They owe their economic strength to suburban and new town developments that benefit from government programs that build airports, interstate highways, and mass transit systems, and from national and international private corporations that invest in office and residential complexes, massive shopping centers, and leisure or amenity services. The term *edge cities* has been coined to describe the independent suburban communities that have emerged in recent decades around the periphery of older central cities in the United States. This trend is particularly striking in the post-1960s Sunbelt, the tier of states in the southern half of the United States, where cities such as Phoenix, Houston, Atlanta, Orlando, and others have seen phenomenal growth. Edge-city development is, however, found throughout the United States today.

Transportation and communications have thus played a critical role in the evolution of urban centers. The siting of cities, and their future success or failure as urban centers, have always been closely associated with one or more transportation modes. Ports, river crossings, canals, and primitive land routes played key roles in most cities throughout history. With the Industrial Revolution, improved roads and the railroad rose to critical importance. In most countries, the golden age of the railroad was from the late 1900s to World War II. Since the 1940s, the airlines and superhighways (associated with trucking and private motor vehicles) have risen to dominance as the railroad has withered, especially in the United States. Port cities, once all-dominant in the world's urban system, while still important, must share the stage with inland cities that have thrived on other transport modes. With the advent of the Information Age and the ever-increasing sophistication of service economies, linkages by telecommunications are even supplanting fixed transportation modes. Singapore, for example, has staked its future as the telecommunications and electronic center of Southeast Asia, a financial and managerial metropolis plugged directly into the world's power centers of Europe, North America, and East Asia.

Socialist cities. These cities were a phenomenon peculiar to the twentieth century, but are a dying breed today. They are closely associated first with the former Soviet Union, then Eastern Europe, China, and a few other socialist (communist) states such as North Korea and Cuba. These countries experienced rapid urban growth from the 1930s onward, under the guise of centrally planned (command) economies. Socialist cities were designed differently and had very different land uses from cities in the Western world, for the primary reason that there was no private ownership of land and all land use decisions were made by government planners. Supposedly classless societies were created that reflected egalitarian ideals, but in reality masked severe shortages of goods and services, drab and poor-quality housing, and terrible environmental pollution as central governments focused on heavy industry and military buildup. [*See* Pollution.] In short, political ideology was directly reflected in the urban landscape, and most people found the final product uninviting. Socialism of this kind is in its last waning days now, a failed experiment of the twentieth century responding to the excesses of free-market capitalism. With the end of the Cold War, even in those countries such as China or Vietnam where quasisocialist governments still nominally rule but free-market capitalism is being encouraged, former socialist cities are undergoing a transformation, getting a capitalist facelift, and acquiring many of the features found in recent industrial and postindustrial cities of Europe, North America, and Asia. Disappearing are the drabness, ugliness, and sterility of the true socialist city; appearing are such features as American fast foods and American popular culture, English-language schools, theaters showing the latest Hollywood movies, advertising, private ownership of shops and businesses, Western music and video stores, Western television programs, and other such features. For better or for worse, the people of these former socialist cities have spoken and made it clear that they prefer what they see in the Western or nonsocialist world.

Planned or "new" cities. In some respects, completely planned cities are a separate category in their own right. While planning has been employed in virtually all cities at some time or other, truly planned cities are those built from scratch according to a master plan, as opposed to those in which planning has been imposed on spontaneously developed cities, which is true of most urban centers (for example, the redesign of Paris in the nineteenth century by Hausmann, or the rebuilding of London under Christopher Wren after the Great Fire of 1666).

Many of these new cities were created as new national capitals, designed to provide politically neutral administrative centers for new nations (for example, Washington, D.C. for the United States, Canberra for Australia) or to symbolize new regional thrusts of development (for example, Brasilia for Brazil, Islamabad for Pakistan). A much larger number of these urban centers are often referred to as *new towns*, reflecting their relatively small size and distinctive purpose. The New

Town movement itself is a phenomenon largely of the twentieth century, evolving out of the Garden City movement in Britain. New towns were supposed to be small, completely planned, urban utopias that combined the best of rural and urban lifestyles without the problems of big cities. Like all utopias, the goal was never really achieved, but hundreds of new towns have been built throughout Europe, North America, and elsewhere. The former Soviet Union built many new towns as part of that country's industrialization drive from the 1930s onward, but those towns bore little resemblance to the European ideal.

World cities. With increased globalization of the world's peoples and economies, a new category of city has emerged. These world cities, as the name suggests, are those whose hinterlands (the regions served by the cities) extend far beyond the national boundaries of the country in which the city is located. Colonialism and the rise of the early industrial powers of Europe and North America were the initial factors creating this kind of city. There is no universal agreement on which are, or are not, true world cities, with economic, cultural, and political reaches that span the globe. New York, London, Paris, Tokyo, and perhaps one or two others are clearly at the top of the list, but below them are a larger group of imprecise number that also warrant the label, at least in part, and could include such cities as Washington, D.C., Beijing, Moscow, Cairo, Geneva, Los Angeles, Toronto, Rome, Hong Kong, Singapore, São Paulo, and Mexico City. Another tier might include Chicago, Houston, Miami, Frankfurt, Sydney, Buenos Aires, Rio de Janeiro, and Capetown. Size alone has little to do with world-class status; many of the world's megacities do not really qualify. For example, most cities in China and India, while very large, are not yet world cities. Among the distinguishing features of these world cities are the following: headquarters for major transnational corporations, major media and financial centers, concentrations of nongovernmental and intergovernmental organizations, major airline hubs, recognized centers of culture and education, and telecommunications or electronics centers.

Impact of Cities. The sheer size and numbers of cities, now containing at least half the world's total population of more than six billion, means that cities have an increasing impact, mostly negative, on the world's natural environment. Consider the following realities. First, cities consume vast amounts of precious farmland, often the best land located in plains and river valleys where urban development is most convenient and desirable. This problem is bad enough in relatively land-rich countries such as the United States, but in overpopulated nations in Asia, for example, the issue has reached crisis proportions, directly endangering the ability of those nations to meet their people's basic food needs.

Second, the concentration of factories, electricity-generating plants, and motor vehicles in urban areas, and the huge volumes of waste (garbage) and sewage generated, results in often-severe pollution of the air, water, and land. Many of China's major cities, such as Beijing and Shanghai, routinely have air pollution indexes above 300, with anything above 100 considered bad. Most Western cities have indexes in the range of 80–100. Living in Mexico City has been likened to smoking several packs of cigarettes a day. Water in rivers, lakes, or underground is so badly polluted, sometimes with dangerous heavy metals and chemicals, that even water-purification plants cannot effectively clean up the water for urban human consumption. Water shortages are also common in major cities, especially in developing countries, because of competing demands from residential, commercial, and industrial users for limited supplies of potable water.

Third, the high economic growth rates demanded by societies with high mass consumption leads to prodigious consumption of the world's energy and other raw materials to feed an ever-expanding economic base. The world's economic system is dependent on this pattern, and it is in the cities that the effects are concentrated. How long can the world sustain this pace of development, with so many nations clamoring to get on board?

Fourth, this urban-focused high-consumption lifestyle contributes in a major way to the global-level environmental problems that increasingly worry scientists and laypersons alike, including global warming with its potential for melting of polar ice packs, loss of biodiversity and threatened ecosystems, increasing numbers and severity of hurricanes and tropical storms, and other dangers. With a large proportion of the world's population and major cities sited in coastal and hazard-prone locations, the risk exists for catastrophic impacts in the future.

For better or worse, the destiny of humanity lies increasingly in the cities of the world and the degree to which they can meet the needs of people and nation-states in the future at the same time as solutions to the environmental impacts of cities are sought. The challenge for humanity is enormous.

[*See also* Air Quality; Human Populations; Land Use, *article on* Land Use and Land Cover; *and* Soils.]

BIBLIOGRAPHY

Brinkhoff, Th. *Principal Agglomerations and Cities of the World.* Online. http://www.citypopulation.de. 1999.

Brunn, S. D., and J. F. Williams, eds. *Cities of the World: World Regional Urban Development.* New York: Harper Collins, 1993. A survey of urban development throughout the world, with individual chapters devoted to the ten major culture realms.

Dogan, M., and J. Kasarda, eds. *The Metropolis Era*, 2 vols. Beverly Hills, Calif.: Sage Publications, 1988. Vol. 1, *A World of Giant Cities*, examines the explosive growth of giant cities in developing countries and the steady deconcentration of population in more developed countries. Vol. 2, *Megacities*, presents an in-depth analysis of ten giant cities around the world.

Hall, P. *Cities of Tomorrow*. New York: Basil Blackwell, 1988. A history of the ideology and practice of urban planning through the twentieth century. Regarded by some as the successor to Lewis Mumford's *Culture of Cities*.

King, A. D. *Urbanism, Colonialism, and the World Economy: Cultural and Spatial Foundations of the World Urban System*. New York: Routledge, 1991. The cultural and spatial links between metropolitan core and colonial periphery, and the role of colonialism in creating the spatial features and urban systems of former colonial territories.

Lowder, S. *The Geography of Third World Cities*. New York:

Barnes and Noble Books, 1986. A comprehensive examination of the urban structure of cities in developing countries.

United Nations. *Urban Agglomerations*. Department of Economic and Social Affairs, Population Division. New York, 1996.

Vance, J. E., Jr. *The Continuing City: Urban Morphology in Western Civilization*. Baltimore: Johns Hopkins University Press, 1990. Explores the morphogenesis of the city in Western civilization from earliest times to the present.

Young, M. W., ed. *Cities of the World*. Detroit: Gale, 1982. A general survey of countries and their major cities in four volumes: Africa; Western Hemisphere; Europe and Mediterranean Middle East; and Asia, Pacific, and Asiatic Middle East.

—STANLEY D. BRUNN AND JACK F. WILLIAMS

URBANIZATION. *See* Human Populations; Industrialization; *and* Urban Areas.

V

VALUATION

Human values are the fundamental reasons why global change is a concern for human societies. If human values were not significantly affected, we would be unlikely to notice or care much about global change. Valuation is the process of making judgments about the significance of global change impacts for specific human values.

Global change involves valuation issues more demanding and ethically charged than almost any other human endeavor, with complexities far beyond those of the standard resource allocation problems for which conventional valuation approaches were developed. These issues severely tax the analytic methods and abilities of those who purport to represent how significant global change impacts may be for human societies, now and in the future.

The most commonplace valuations of global change are made implicitly, as simple attitudinal responses among members of the public about what they perceive to be the impacts of global change, or what they encounter in the media about these processes. Valuation for informing policies about global change is also made explicitly, in quantitative terms, within a conceptual framework for conducting policy analysis. [See Policy Analysis.] The focus in this entry is primarily on quantitative evaluation for policy analysis purposes, stressing the conceptual frameworks underlying different approaches to valuation, and practical issues that arise in their application. Qualitative approaches to valuation are also addressed, as are some of the profound and complex analytic, ethical, and behavioral questions that arise in attempting to judge how global change may affect human values.

The valuation issues arising in decisions about global change are conceptually daunting. How should (and do) societies value potential impacts of global change on future generations? On nonhuman species? On people living in less industrialized countries? If one simplifies by considering only the values relevant for the current generation within a given society, how valuable is it to reduce the risk of species extinction? [See Extinction of Species.] The risk of depleting ecological services? Without cooperative efforts on a large scale, the chances of influencing most global change processes are slim. How then to impute the value to one organization or one government of taking policy action to address a global change concern, given the uncertainty over what other organizations or governments will do?

Despite these complexities, valuation efforts for global change are needed at many levels. Such efforts should provide one basis for informing choices about the kinds of policies a particular government should pursue in response to specific global change trends. Valuation is also needed to help select the best policies to achieve a designated policy target. To be helpful in informing these choices, valuation efforts should be explicit about what is included and what is not, the basis for the value judgments underlying the analysis, and the uncertainties in the findings. While most valuation efforts work toward meeting these criteria, their results are almost universally interpreted as more complete, defensible, and reliable than they deserve.

Judgmental Basis of Valuation. Any approach to valuation for global change relies on specific judgments. While these judgments are often made implicitly, they are fundamental to conducting formal policy evaluation, and so merit some clarification. The required judgments include: (1) What are the valued consequences of a global change policy decision that are meaningful and require attention? These judgments set the agenda for analysis by specifying the kinds of impact that matter and should receive analytical attention. (2) What are the levels of impact (or technical consequences) that are predicted for a given policy alternative? Judgments about levels of impact for global change processes are often informed by building scenarios about the future, given assumptions about behaviors, policies, technologies, and trends. [See Scenarios.] A crucial judgment task is then to decide which of many possible scenarios is more likely, and to characterize uncertainties about scenarios with probabilities. (3) How significant are these uncertain technical consequences in terms of the relevant human values? Here questions such as the identification of the groups and the choice of units of measurement are especially important.

Judgment (informed by the available scientific information, ethics, and other relevant perspectives) therefore provides the conceptual and practical basis for conducting valuation. Evaluation approaches based on economics often underplay the role of judgment in such analyses, by making implicit judgments about what is important and how to measure it, without making these explicit. Yet, informed, explicit judgment is the cornerstone of responsible valuation, not a stumbling block.

Analytic Frameworks for Valuation. The mainstream analytic framework employed for valuation efforts concerning global change is social benefit-cost

475

analysis, as practiced by economists. A second framework, gaining increased attention in global change issues, is decision analysis. A third framework, which relies more on qualitative judgments by skirting the need for quantitative benefits estimates, is the precautionary approach. Each has its own underlying view of the nature of environmental values, and thus the nature of the valuation tasks that should be employed.

Social benefit-cost analysis. A version of applied welfare economics, social benefit-cost analysis is the most widely used analytic framework. The conceptual basis is a market analogy, in which preferences are represented through purchase behavior, reflecting an individual's willingness to pay for, or accept compensation for accepting, a proposed change in status. The analyst attempts to quantify whether a policy alternative is desirable by estimating how all the important consequences would be valued in an idealized, or perfectly competitive, market, as divisible marketed outputs, measured in money terms. The crucial task facing analysts is to impute market-like prices for relevant nonmarket values (for example, safety, aesthetics, the survival of particular species) reflecting the incremental value of a specific change in a specific good to society.

The underlying ethical perspective for benefit-cost analysis is utilitarianism, which focuses attention on aggregate impacts to society as a whole, ignoring who gains and who loses. The rationale is to avoid making interpersonal comparisons of utility (for example, is change X in benefits to person 1 better from society's viewpoint than change Y in benefits to person 2?), in hopes of a more objective basis for evaluation. Thus the emphasis is on aggregating impacts that are measurable in money terms (directly or indirectly), reflecting values of individuals as consumers of marketed goods and ignoring the distribution of impacts.

Conceptually, social benefit-cost analysis can deal with all manner of impacts, including those that do not involve values well registered in dollar terms. Examples might include society's value for reducing the risk of loss of ecological services, cultural and spiritual values for certain species and ecosystems, the aesthetic value of existing landscapes, or the value to the current generation of meeting its ethical responsibilities to future generations. In practice, the willingness of current generations to pay for these goods provides an increasingly questionable basis for such valuation efforts as the items in question become further removed from market goods. Mainstream economists base their efforts at clarifying values for nonmarket goods on the assumption that humans are rational, utility-maximizing beings, with well-defined preferences. Thus, valuation is seen as a measurement task for values that are implicitly understood but not yet articulated. Aggregating across the individual willingness-to-pay estimates can thus provide a statistically imputed value reflecting societal willingness to pay.

Social benefit-cost analysis is best applied to marginal policy changes, ones for which assumptions regarding "all else being equal," reversibility of transactions, and substitution of one kind of goods for another make sense. Nonmarginal impacts, such as those associated with global change issues and policies, pose substantial challenges for social benefit-cost analysis, because many of the major assumptions about welfare economics as a basis for analysis no longer hold.

Decision analysis. Based on multiattribute utility theory, decision analysis springs from axioms for decision making under uncertainty first articulated in the 1940s. Its conceptual focus is to inform choice among alternatives for a single decision maker, based on subjective judgments about preferences and beliefs about uncertainties. In public sector applications, the focus has shifted to informing the decision-making process by providing insight into how key groups of stakeholders view important tradeoffs and thus the choice among alternatives. There is greater emphasis on diverse judgments, interaction between those providing value judgments and the analyst, and smaller samples of participants, compared with value elicitation in economic approaches. Recognizing that there is no single right answer when one accepts the lack of a single decision maker and multiple views on tradeoffs and uncertainties, the emphasis in a public-policy-oriented decision analysis is on gaining insight into what drives the choice in the decision, rather than expecting analysis to indicate what to do.

Decision analysis shares with behavioral psychology the view that people do not have well-defined preferences for unfamiliar goods, and few have the ability to process or complete complex judgment tasks on their own. Thus, valuation in this paradigm is seen as a value clarification or synthesis process, rather than a measurement process. The basic tasks in valuation involve difficult judgments such as "how much of a change in performance on dimension A is just equal to a stated change in performance on dimension B?" Both A and B could be stated in natural units, reflecting the trade-off at hand (for example, hectares of land, species loss, dollars). Participants provide judgments that reflect their advice on appropriate societal trade-offs, rather than their individual willingness to pay. Decision analysis approaches to value elicitation are far more constructive in the sense that the analyst aids those providing judgments by creating workable tasks that begin simply and build in complexity, employ multiple framing, and provide feedback to point out inconsistencies. The underlying assumption is that participants can be heuristically aided in providing value judgments in which they have more confidence.

The strengths of decision analysis in addressing issues of global change include its explicit attention to decision making under uncertainty, its flexibility in incorporating different perspectives as a basis for judging the desirability of outcomes, its explicit attention to a wide range of measures and decision criteria, and its explicit reliance on subjective judgment as a basis for both preferences and probabilities. Conceptually, decision theory provides a broad, flexible framework for societal decision making; in fact, the economic efficiency criteria underlying benefit-cost analysis could be viewed as one objective in a broader multiple-objective decision analysis. Yet the relationship between these approaches seems often to be misunderstood. For example, Chapter 3 of the 1996 Intergovernmental Panel on Climate Change (IPCC) Working Group III report casts benefit-cost comparisons as one possible decision rule in decision analysis, while Chapter 5 of the same report casts decision analysis as a version of benefit-cost analysis.

The precautionary approach. Sometimes referred to as the sustainability approach, the precautionary approach springs from the notion that, because the probabilities of specific levels of harm that could stem from global change are unknowable, the benefits of avoiding that harm are unquantifiable. Yet, it is argued, the current generation has a responsibility to avoid actions that could irreversibly damage or reduce the opportunities available to future generations. Hence, potential damage to future generations should be avoided by taking precautionary actions to avoid harm, regardless of the lack of quantified benefits and costs. Practical implementation has focused attention on the proportionality of possible benefits and costs, raising the issue of informal balancing (in qualitative terms) as one aspect of appraising precautionary investments. A variant is the modified precautionary principle, or safe minimum standard, which argues that precautionary actions should be taken unless the costs are unacceptably large to the current generation. Thus, the precautionary approach involves valuation judgments that are more qualitative, stressing political and societal feasibility, rather than quantitative willingness to pay or explicit judgment of trade-offs and probabilities. [*See* Precautionary Principle.]

Valuation studies. Many examples of valuation efforts directed at global change issues have been published within the last decade. Reference to several key valuation studies for biodiversity issues can be found in the *Global Biodiversity Assessment* (Heywood, 1995). The range of valuation studies conducted for biodiversity issues is remarkable. Many economic analyses have focused on the value of species protection in terms of market and nonmarket outputs that could be derived from the genetic information and intact ecosystems. Other studies have adopted a broader perspective, with

several examples cast in the decision analysis and precautionary frameworks. Some of the most important studies related to climate change are summarized in Chapter 6 of the 1996 IPCC Working Group III report; virtually all studies synthesized there are cast within the benefit-cost analysis framework.

Biodiversity valuation studies. One reason for broader approaches in biodiversity valuation may be the more localized context. While the benefits of biodiversity preservation clearly extend beyond a particular country or region, its costs will often be entirely localized. The costs of biodiversity protection are also more straightforward to estimate, and the needed actions far more manageable to implement, compared with climate change. Hence there has been greater emphasis on decision analytic treatments of specific biodiversity policy issues, as well as precautionary-based studies considering a safe minimum standard of protection for specific populations. A remarkable finding in several studies is that the costs of biodiversity protection are relatively low, often entailing foregone economic rents from resource extraction activities such as forestry, mining, or fishing. However, the relatively low net benefits of these activities masks their regional economic importance, which is the basis for virtually all the opposition to biodiversity protection. [*See* Forests.]

Climate change valuation studies. The following discussion draws on key findings of the 1996 IPCC Working Group III valuation efforts. Chapter 6 of that report reviews several findings regarding the economic costs of potential impacts associated with a doubling of carbon dioxide in the atmosphere. That review places the range of costs for such a scenario (which would occur somewhere in the middle of the next century given current trends) as follows:

1. World impact: 1.5–2.0 percent reduction of world gross domestic product (GDP) annually
2. Developed-country impact: 1.0–1.5 percent of GDP annually
3. Developing-country impact: 2–9 percent of GDP annually

These summary estimates have enormous policy significance, and have attracted considerable attention and criticism. These criticisms include the following.

Treatment of uncertainty. While the authors of the report took pains to explain the uncertainties associated with these estimates in the text of the report, those caveats did not show up in the summary statements. Hence these findings have been taken to be more reliable and comprehensive than is appropriate.

Reliance on U.S. studies. The analytic basis for the estimates rests almost entirely on extrapolation of studies done for the United States. Little or no primary information is available on impacts and values related to developing countries, where impacts are expected to be far greater.

Cost of early deaths. These estimates address the economic cost of early deaths due to climate change impacts based on willingness-to-pay concepts. The result is far higher costs for early deaths in developed than developing countries, because of the greater ability to pay in the developed world. This approach was by far the most controversial aspect of the whole IPCC Working Group III process, especially among those who believe there is an ethical imperative that all lives should be counted as equally important when analyzing global change policies. One study that employed an equal cost of early deaths for all countries and yielded much higher estimates of the costs of a doubling of carbon dioxide was not considered in the IPCC estimates noted above.

Value of nonmarket impacts. In the original studies on which these estimates are based, it is often difficult to determine what kinds of nonmarket impacts are included in the analysis, and the basis for value estimates. Yet it is certain that issues, such as risk of impairment of any of a vast array of ecological services, risk of species loss, risk of major change in ecosystem type and function, risk of aesthetic changes, risk of health and comfort changes, and many other nonmarket impacts are not meaningfully addressed in these studies, in part because the probabilities of many of these impacts are not quantified in an informed manner. Moreover, economic theory shows that, for nonmarket changes involving perceived losses, willingness to accept compensation, rather than willingness to pay, is the appropriate valuation concept. Many economists argue that there should be little difference between these two measures but, in practice, the difference between them is large and consistent. Were compensation-based measures used to estimate the costs of climate change impacts, the magnitude of the estimates would be vastly increased. Hence, nonmarket impacts are at best poorly represented in the estimates above, in concept and in practice. These omissions could be important enough to raise the potential impacts of a carbon dioxide doubling by many times, particularly if a major unexpected change in ecosystem function occurs.

Adjustment impacts. Simply put, these estimates are built by beginning with the present world economy, superimposing a doubling of carbon dioxide and the resulting impacts on that economy, and estimating the value of resulting aggregate output in GDP terms. The estimates pay no attention to transition costs, which are the impacts associated with the transition from one climate state to another. Yet these impacts may involve massive costs, particularly since the rate of change and ultimate extent of impacts from climate change are unknown. It is clear, though, that doubling of carbon dioxide by somewhere near the middle of the next century could involve transition impacts that extend over

decades and perhaps into the subsequent century. Without major policy changes, the doubling carbon dioxide milestone would come and go, trends would continue, and impacts would continue to increase in severity. Some economists argue that these transition costs would be minimal as the economy adjusts to climate change over time. Others argue that the costs could be enormous because the pace and extent of climate change is not predictable.

The economics framework. A fundamental but rarely considered issue is whether the standard welfare economics framework, with all the assumptions and value judgments that it entails, is an appropriate basis for valuing the consequences of climate change. This framework was initially developed to consider incremental changes in social well-being for a specific referent group due to marginal changes in resource allocation, for goods whose impacts fall primarily within a market context. It is based on a particular ethical perspective, utilitarianism in a welfare economics framework, with no consideration of broader deontological values. When we contemplate massive environmental changes on a worldwide scale, with nothing resembling a market context for some of the most important impacts, enormous uncertainties regarding the scale of impacts, and no basis for generalizing market values from one region to impacts throughout the world, some people ask whether this framework is appropriate. The controversy over values for early death in the IPCC analysis reflects these concerns. Many critics would go further. They would argue that the estimated willingness of citizens in one generation to pay for avoiding large-scale environmental impacts that could extend for centuries, involve irreversible losses, and are unknowable in terms of extent and severity, is simply not a responsible and just basis for making collective policy choices of this nature.

[*See also* Ethics; *and* Wilderness.]

BIBLIOGRAPHY

BIODIVERSITY AND WILDERNESS
VALUATION STUDIES

Bishop, R. "Endangered Species and Uncertainty: The Economics of a Safe Minimum Standard." *American Journal of Agricultural Economics* 60 (1978), 10–18. The key reference on the safe minimum standard and the precautionary principle in biodiversity valuation.

Costanza, R., et al. "The Value of the World's Ecosystem Services and Natural Capital." *Nature* 387 (1997), 253–260. An important and controversial macroanalysis of the total economic value of the world's ecological services.

Heywood, V. H. *Global Biodiversity Assessment.* Cambridge: Cambridge University Press, 1995.

McDaniels, T., L., and C. Roessler. "Multiattribute Elicitation of Wilderness Preservation Benefits: A Constructive Approach." *Ecological Economics* 27 (1998), 299–312. A multiattribute approach to value elicitation for biodiversity and wilderness.

Norton, B. G. *Why Preserve Natural Variety?* Princeton: Princeton University Press, 1987. An insightful review of the broader values and ethical concerns associated with biodiversity issues.

Pearce, D., and D. Moran. *The Economic Value of Biodiversity.* London: Earthscan, 1994. Published in association with the Biodiversity Program of the World Conservation Union (IUCN). A textbook-like introduction to economic valuation for biodiversity.

Perrings, C., et al. "The Economic Value of Biodiversity." In *Global Biodiversity Assessment*, edited by V. H. Heywood. Cambridge: Cambridge University Press, 1995. A thorough compendium of economic valuation studies for biodiversity.

CLIMATE CHANGE VALUATION STUDIES

Cline, W. R. *The Economics of Global Warming.* Washington, D.C.: Institute for International Economics, 1992.

Demeritt, D., and D. Rothman. "Figuring the Costs of Climate Change: An Assessment and Critique." *Environment and Planning A* 31 (1999), 389–408. A penetrating critique of mainstream economic valuation studies of climate change impacts. It discusses difficulties with other references noted in this section.

Nordhaus, W. D. *Managing the Global Commons: The Economics of Climate Change.* Cambridge, Mass.: MIT Press, 1994. A controversial analysis showing that the market-based costs of climate change are low, while the costs of control efforts are high.

Pearce, D. W., et al. "The Social Costs of Climate Change: Greenhouse Damage and the Benefits of Control." In *Climate Change 1995: Economic and Social Dimensions of Climate Change*, edited by J. P. Bruce et al. Cambridge: Cambridge University Press, 1996. A thorough compendium of mainstream economic valuation concepts and estimates for climate change. Other chapters also have important and useful treatments of valuation issues, particularly in discussing decision making, equity, and discounting issues.

Schelling, T. C. *Costs and Benefits of Greenhouse Gas Reduction.* Washington, D.C.: AEI Press, 1998. A slim but insightful volume about the broader political economy of greenhouse gas policies.

VALUATION APPROACHES

Fischhoff, B. "Value Elicitation: Is there Anything in There?" *American Psychologist* 46 (1991), 835–847. A critique of the contingent valuation approach, arguing that value elicitation is a synthesis or "constructive" task rather than a measurement task.

Johansson, P.-O. *The Economic Theory and Measurement of Environmental Benefits.* Cambridge: Cambridge University Press, 1987. An introduction to mainstream economic valuation for environmental resources.

Keeney, R. L. *Value-Focused Thinking.* Cambridge, Mass.: Harvard University Press, 1992. A creative guide to multiattribute valuation, with an emphasis on problem structuring.

O'Riordan, T., and J. Cameron, eds. *Interpreting the Precautionary Principle.* London: Earthscan, 1994. Despite many typographical and editorial difficulties, the best treatment of how the precautionary principle is addressed in practice.

—TIMOTHY L. MCDANIELS

VOLCANOES

Volcanoes and volcanic eruptions occur in three different settings dictated by plate tectonics and by active molten rock (magma) production zones, or mantle plumes, within the Earth. While the greatest amount of volcanic activity and the most numerous volcanoes are situated under the oceans, this article concentrates mainly on activity on land. The location and variety of active volcanism on our planet controls the two issues that most impact humankind—the impact of eruptions on the global atmosphere and environment, and volcanic hazards. In the subaerial environment, volcanism is either effusive, that is, lava-producing, or explosive, forming volcanic ash (more correctly called *pyroclastic ejecta*). Activity is thought to be entirely effusive under the deep oceans because hydrostatic pressure inhibits explosive activity.

Sites of Volcanism. Volcanic activity occurring at spreading centers (divergent plate boundaries), where new oceanic crust is created at the midocean ridges, is dominantly submarine. Little of this activity is seen above the ocean surface but occasional ocean island volcanoes, such as the Azores in the Atlantic Ocean, are a reminder of this hidden and little-known volcanic realm. Continental rift zones such as the East African Rift Valley are also sites of volcanism controlled by the same process.

Magma generation and rise at spreading plate boundaries is controlled by decompression melting of the upper mantle, caused by divergence of the tectonic plates. Magma may rise from the generation zone (more than 50 kilometers deep) to the surface with little, or only brief, pause for storage in the crust. The magma generated is dominated by the type known as *basalt* and the style of volcanism is usually effusive to mildly explosive, forming lava flows and shield volcanoes on land. Effusive venting dominates in the submarine environment, forming pillow lavas. Other magma types that can build large cone-like volcanoes and erupt explosively are produced under the continental rift zones.

Subduction zones, or collisional (destructive) plate boundaries, are host to a wide variety of volcanism including some of the largest and most explosive eruptions. From our land-based perspective, these long-arc-shaped volcanic zones, whether island volcanoes, such as the Aleutian chain or mainly on land such as in Japan or the Andes, are the most active volcanic regions on Earth. Melting is caused in the mantle wedge between the overriding and the downgoing plate by the thermal energy released by subduction. Little of this magma, however, makes it to the surface in its original state. The rising molten material, charged with volatile elements derived from the top of the subducting plate, melts the base of the plate above, giving rise to a bewildering variety of magma types at the surface. Magma generation processes are complex, but most situations demand time for storage in crustal reservoirs, and thus mixing of magmas with different compositions is possible. The most familiar magma type is andesite, which is a mixture of mantle-derived basalt and crustal-melt-derived magmas such as dacite or rhyolite. [*See* Plate Tectonics.]

A third setting for volcanoes is "hot spots," which can apparently occur anywhere on Earth, either in midplate locations (subaerial and submarine) or at spreading plate boundaries. The Hawaiian volcanoes are an example of the former, and Iceland of the latter. Hot spots are caused by the rise of mantle plumes, thermal perturbations originating at depths within the Earth anywhere from midmantle (650–1,000 kilometers) to the core–mantle boundary (around 2,900 kilometers). New mantle plumes cause huge flood basalt lava eruptions when they first impact the crust. Flood basalt episodes have happened at intervals of several tens of millions of years throughout most of Earth history, and thus the flood basalt provinces of various geologic ages provide a record of mantle plume activity within our planet. None are occurring presently. After initiation, a mantle plume remains somewhat stationary and may continue to produce basaltic magma at a hot spot for over 100 million years (the Hawaiian one is at least seventy million years old). The long-term magma production rate is much lower than at the start, and some old hot spots yield just a trickle of lava. As the melting begins deep down in the mantle, the plates slide over the rising plume of melt and leave a "hot-spot track," such as the Hawaiian Island Emperor seamount (underwater, extinct volcano) chain.

As well as recognized hot spots, volcanoes pop up in hard-to-explain places under both continental and oceanic parts of plates, sometimes in short-lived flareups most probably related to mountain building. Thus there are volcanoes scattered throughout China, and in North America in places like Colorado and New Mexico. Magma generation under hot spots and in these other settings is due either to excess heat or to decompression in the mantle (or both). It is largely basaltic in composition, with other types generated if the magma is stored for a long time in a crustal reservoir or if parts of the crust are melted. Activity is again largely effusive, but with some large explosive events.

Distribution, Eruption Frequency, and Magnitude. The global distribution of active volcanoes imparted by the present configuration of plate margins gives three main latitudinal belts of volcanism. The first is a tropical–equatorial belt, including volcanoes in Indonesia, New Guinea, the Philippines, Central America, northern South America, and Africa. This zone contains more active volcanoes than any other zone. Ash and gas clouds from explosive eruptions of these volcanoes can attain global atmospheric distribution, depending upon the latitude and season of the activity. Another belt is in the middle to high latitudes of the Northern Hemisphere, consisting of volcanoes in Japan, China, the Kurile–Aleutian island chains, North America, and southern Europe. The third belt contains volcanoes in the southern Andes and New Zealand, as well as some ocean islands. Eruption clouds from both these volcanic zones will most likely be limited to the one hemisphere.

The bulk of the world's population lives in the most northerly volcano zone, so this is where volcanic risk is perhaps the greatest, although any population center near an active or potentially active volcano is at risk. Also, more passenger and transport aircraft fly across this same northern hemisphere zone than other regions, and thus the risk of aircraft encountering ash and gas clouds is also greatest. Although there has not been a disaster from an aircraft–ash encounter, there have been some near misses in the past fifteen years.

There are forty to sixty volcanoes active globally in any given year. This number includes several consistently active ones such as Kilauea in Hawaii and Yasur in Vanuatu (a group of islands in the southwestern Pacific). In terms of newly awakened volcanoes per year, the number is about half, or twenty to thirty. Most eruptions are small affairs producing lava and/or low eruption clouds of gas and pyroclastic ejecta, but larger events take place on average a few times per decade. The most rigorous way to estimate the size of an eruption is by the mass of magma yielded (magnitude) or the mass eruption rate (intensity), although volumes of magma are more often given; these are a little easier to gauge. In either unit, mass or volume, magnitudes and intensities, even in recent decades, have spanned many orders of magnitude. The range is from tiny lava outpourings of less than 0.01 cubic kilometers that take years to dribble out (for example, at Oldinyo Lengai, Africa) to huge explosive events expelling about 10 cubic kilometers of magma in a matter of a few hours, such as Mount Pinatubo (Philippines) in 1991 or Katmai-Novarupta (Alaska) in 1912. [See Mount Pinatubo.] Katmai, at 13–15 cubic kilometers, was the largest eruption of the twentieth century.

It should come as no surprise that the larger the eruption, the fewer there are, and really big events such as Tambora (Indonesia) in 1815, which produced 50 cubic kilometers of magma in about one day, occur every few hundred years. Lava-forming events on this scale are not known in the recent geologic past, the largest being in the 15–20 cubic kilometer range from Iceland; these occur once per thousand years or so. How big can eruptions get? In the geologic past, lava flows of up to 2–3,000 cubic kilometers were produced during flood basalt episodes, and explosive eruptions of similar size, forming huge sheets of welded ash deposits and a type of collapsed volcano called a caldera, are known from as recently as 75,000 BP. Such extreme events may have an average global frequency of one every few hundred thousand years or so. The size of an eruption does not necessarily correlate directly with its violence, or its destructive potential if humans live nearby.

Eruption Mechanisms. Volcanic eruptions are driven by magma—a three-phase mixture of silicate melt, crystals, and volcanic gases (mainly CO_2, H_2O, SO_2, H_2S, HCl, HF, H_2, and assorted trace gases). Magma rising under a volcano usually forms a magma chamber. Eruptions occur when the pressure within a part of the magma chamber exceeds the strength of the overlying magma and rock. Pressure builds when the rate at which gases are supplied to the top few kilometers of a magma plumbing system exceeds the rate at which they leak out of that system, when confining pressure decreases (because of magma ascent or fracturing or removal of overlying rock), or when crystallization of magma concentrates gas in a diminishing fraction of melt. The volume of an eruption depends on the amount of gas-charged magma that can be tapped. The explosivity of an eruption depends on the gas content of the magma and how quickly the gas is released once magma reaches the surface. The largest, most explosive, and most dangerous eruptions are those involving large volumes of magma in which gas accumulates to high concentrations until the magma and the gases suddenly break through to the Earth's surface.

Eruption Types and Hazards. Nonexplosive or weakly explosive volcanic activity produces lava flows, as during most Hawaiian eruptions. Usually, people can escape from lava flows but structures are destroyed. The volcanic activity known as *Hawaiian* forms widespread, thin, black flows of basalt lava and small cones around the vents. Liquid basalt lava is of low viscosity, at one end of the spectrum of physical properties of magma types. Stacks of basaltic lava flows build up shield volcanoes. Explosive eruptions fragment the magma into sand- or silt-sized "ash," pebble-sized "lapilli," and even larger "volcanic bombs." The more explosive an eruption, the greater the fragmentation and the smaller the pyroclasts. *Strombolian* activity is akin to Hawaiian in that it forms both lava flows and pyroclastic deposits, and is characterized by basaltic to andesitic magmas. Magmas forming Strombolian eruptions are slightly more viscous and gas-rich, causing a higher proportion to fragment into pyroclasts. Bigger cones, called *scoria cones*, therefore form around Strombolian vents. Strombolian eruptions also display pulsating fire fountains, higher eruption columns, and a wider dispersal of scoria and ash fallout, but they are still not very hazardous unless a town is immediately nearby, as in Heimaey (Iceland) in 1973.

Vulcanian is a catch-all term covering a range of explosive behavior, often accompanied by effusive activity forming lava domes of andesite or dacite magma. Closely related is *Pelean* activity, named for the notorious Mount Pelée. An eruption from this volcano caused the instantaneous death of thirty thousand people in the town of Saint Pierre on Martinique (Lesser Antilles) on 8 May 1902. Vulcanian eruptions involve moderately viscous and gas-rich magma that may shatter with great force, fragmenting the magma into tiny pieces of hot ash. The force with which the pent-up gases blow the fragments out of the vent leads to towering eruption columns that rise by convection and commonly reach 12–20 kilometers (65,000 feet) in altitude. The pyroclastic material rises high in the column, promoting wide dispersal of fallout as it is blown downwind. However, ash falls are rarely fatal unless roofs collapse under the weight. Sometimes a volcanic explosion can be directed sideways because of a plug of lava over the vent, or for other reasons. A directed blast is formed, as at Mount Saint Helens in 1980. This phenomenon, and the ground-hugging, hot flows of pyroclastic material that it spawns, caused the utter devastation at Saint Pierre.

Plinian activity occurs when more silica-rich, highly viscous, gas-rich magma such as dacite or rhyolite erupts, causing huge columns of ash and gas that convect up to heights of 40 kilometers (130,000 feet) into the atmosphere. Great eruptions such as Pinatubo (Philippines, 1991), Krakatau (Indonesia, 1883), and Tambora (Indonesia, 1815) are most often of this type. Widespread fall deposits of pumice and fine ash form downwind of the vent. The lowermost parts of the eruption columns may collapse to form flows of pyroclastic material along the ground, depositing the volcanic rock type ignimbrite (also called ash-flow tuff). Within areas swept by pyroclastic flows, nearly all life is killed and nearly all structures are demolished. When mixed with water from crater lakes, snowpack, or heavy rain, loose pyroclastic deposits also form lahars, which are fast-moving, often lethal volcanic mudflows. [*See* Natural Hazards.]

Detecting Volcanic Eruptions. The principal precursors of volcanic eruptions are small, often imperceptible earthquakes, deformation of the ground by the expanding magma or heated pore water in the overlying rock, and emission of magmatic gases. [*See* Earthquakes.] Flux rates of gases, especially sulfur dioxide (SO_2), are a clue to how much unerupted magma is present and degassing beneath the surface; changes in the ratios of various species can suggest the depth and degree of degassing. Gas fluxes and types released can be used to assess the amount of remaining gas and its potential for escape. Less frequently, changes are observed in temperatures of gas vents and hot springs, in the local magnetic, gravitational, and electric fields, or in the water table. Seismicity is traditionally measured with seismometers that are designed to measure seismic waves at 1–10 hertz, but volcanic seismicity is increasingly tracked over a wider frequency spectrum with broadband seismometers. Ground deformation is measured with high-precision surveying tools, including precise levels, laser rangefinders, tiltmeters, borehole strainmeters, Global Positioning Systems (GPS), and, most recently, with radar interferometry.

Gas emissions were once measured by direct sampling of fumaroles, but such measurements are too infrequent and risky to serve for forecasting. Sampling of volcanic plumes from manned aircraft is possible but more expensive than most volcano observatory budgets allow. Remote spectroscopic measurement of sulfur dioxide has been possible for over two decades, but remote measurements of CO_2, HCl, H_2S, CO, and SiF_4 are only now becoming possible—principally through lidar and infrared spectroscopic techniques.

Atmospheric Effects of Volcanic Eruptions. The emission of gases from the Earth, manifested as volcanic activity, created a significant portion of the atmosphere and continues to modify it. Volcanic aerosol clouds are a short-lived, natural atmospheric perturbation that can influence the radiation budget, surface temperatures, and circulation patterns. [See Aerosols.] Considerable observational evidence now exists for the connection between explosive volcanism, the generation of volcanic aerosols, and climatic cooling. Other atmospheric effects, such as ozone depletion, are also associated with periods of enhanced atmospheric aerosols. Volcanic aerosols also affect stratosphere stability and tropospheric dynamics, and may provide nuclei for upper tropospheric cirrus clouds.

Scientists first recognized and observed volcanic atmospheric dust veils in the year after Krakatau erupted in 1883, but it was then thought that fine-grained silicate dust was the cause. Since the discovery of the stratospheric sulfate aerosol, it has become evident that this layer in the atmosphere, which plays an important role in modulating the net incoming solar radiation, is mostly generated by sulfur dioxide released from erupting magma and injected to stratospheric heights by explosive eruption columns.

Sulfur is released into the atmosphere during eruptions mainly as SO_2 gas, which is converted by photochemical oxidation to sulfuric acid (H_2SO_4) via OH. H_2SO_4 and H_2O are the dominant components (H_2SO_4 and H_2O are in the approximate ratio of 70:30 percent). Stratospheric residence time ranges from days through weeks, months, and years for regional, zonal, hemispheric, and global distribution, respectively. The injection of other volatiles such as HCl and H_2O may alter atmospheric composition, but evidence for long-term residence of Cl compounds from volcanic HCl emission is lacking. Aerosol composition is further altered by heterogeneous reactions on sulfate aerosol surfaces. Depletion of stratospheric ozone in temperate latitudes occurs after volcanic aerosol events; processes involving sulfate aerosols as sites of heterogeneous chemical reactions are implicated, but this phenomenon may only have existed since the time when atmospheric chlorofluorocarbons (CFCs) have been present in our atmosphere. [See Ozone.] Recent studies have established a strong correlation between certain types of eruption and climate change, and some workers have suggested that there may be a simple relationship between the sulfur yield of a volcanic eruption and decrease in surface temperature. [See Climate Change.] This may be true for smaller sulfur yields, but may not apply to large eruptions. It is known that enhanced levels of aerosols after volcanic eruptions coincide with periods of a few years' duration with lowered incident solar radiation, lower surface and tropospheric temperatures, and stratospheric warming.

Benjamin Franklin is usually credited with first making the association between a volcanic eruption and climate or weather. While he was U.S. Ambassador in Paris in 1783, he theorized that the awful haze or dry fog, presumably sulfuric acid aerosols, that hung over the city in the latter part of 1783 was caused by an eruption in Iceland. In fact, one of the world's greatest historic lava-producing eruptions occurred at Laki, Iceland from June 1783 to February 1784. In this event, most of the aerosols generated may have been limited to the troposphere; this is a good example of an eruption of long duration maintaining tropospheric aerosols. Under this haze, as with other aerosol veils, the Sun's rays were dimmed, and anomalously hot or cold weather occurred, including bitter cold in August and the coldest winter on record in New England. Crop failures were commonplace the next year and were also experienced after the next large eruption, which occurred in 1815.

The year 1816, "the Year without a Summer," is probably the best known example of a volcanically induced climate cooling event. It was largely caused by the eruption of Tambora, which yielded 100 metric megatons (10^{14} grams) of sulfuric acid aerosols in one of the largest known eruptions of the past few millennia. The aerosol veil caused cooling of up to 1°C regionally and probably more locally, with effects lasting until the end of 1816 and extending to both hemispheres. It snowed in New England in June, and abnormally cool temperatures in Europe led to widespread famine and misery, although the connection to volcanic aerosols was not recognized at the time.

The aftermath of Krakatau's climactic eruption in August 1883 was probably the first time that scientists widely took notice of a volcanically induced atmospheric event, because the developed world rapidly learned of the eruption by telegraphic communication. Observers could ascribe to the eruption the colorful sunsets and other optical phenomena that spread over the Northern Hemisphere in the months following. The Royal Society of London in 1888 published a volume that documented the eruption and the ensuing dust veil. After Krakatau, scientists measured and reported decreases in incoming radiation following volcanic eruptions in 1902 and 1912.

Several recent eruptions have proven invaluable in improving our understanding of the connection between volcanism, aerosols, and climate change. Two eruptions of very sulfur-rich magma at El Chichón, Mexico, in 1982 and Mount Pinatubo, in Luzon, Philippines in 1991 have been thoroughly documented in terms of the stratospheric aerosols produced, their spread and atmospheric residence time, and their climatic effects. El Chichón was a small-volume eruption of unusually sulfur-enriched magma that produced the first large aerosol veil to be tracked by instruments on satellites. Its impact on surface temperatures has, however, been difficult to assess. Pinatubo was the second-largest eruption in the twentieth century (the largest was in Alaska in 1912), and its aerosol veil hung over the Earth for more than eighteen months, causing spectacular sunsets and sunrises worldwide. During this period there was more material in the aerosol layer than at any time since Krakatau erupted. General circulation models of temperature changes expected under this aerosol cloud predicted Northern Hemisphere surface cooling of as much as 0.5°C, and these appear to have been verified by the meteorological data.

Simple models suggest that eruptions on the scale of large prehistoric events have the potential to alter climate to a much greater degree than has been observed following historical events. How large an impact on climate can volcanic eruptions have in terms of affecting surface temperature, precipitation, and weather patterns—either short-term effects from individual events, or longer-term changes controlled by periods of enhanced volcanism? Although large eruptions are less frequent than smaller ones, they are nevertheless a certainty in the future. We have an imperfect record of past eruptions and of changes in temperature and weather; future events will provide natural experiments in which we can study the impact of volcanic aerosols, an effort that has already begun.

Perhaps the most important challenge to the research effort on global change for the purposes of making policy decisions will be the early detection of the effects of global warming caused by human activities. It will be essential to recognize and remove effects resulting from natural phenomena, among which volcanic aerosols are significant. Nevertheless, we are still a long way from understanding fully the effects of volcanic eruptions on atmospheric composition, climate, and weather.

[*See also* Natural Climate Fluctuations.]

BIBLIOGRAPHY

Chester, D. *Volcanoes and Society*. London: Edward Arnold, 1993.
Decker, R., and B. Decker. *Volcanoes*. 3d ed. San Francisco: Freeman, 1998.
Francis, P. *Volcanoes: A Planetary Perspective*. New York and Oxford: Oxford University Press, 1993.
Harington, C. R., ed. *The Year without a Summer? World Climate in 1816*. Ottawa: Canadian Museum, 1992.
Kelly, P. M., et al. "The Spatial Response of the Climate System to Explosive Volcanic Eruptions." *International Journal of Climate* 16 (1996), 537–550.
Rampino, M. R., et al. "Volcanic Winters." *Annual Review of Earth and Planetary Science* 16 (1988), 73–99.
Scarpa, R., and R. I. Tilling. *Monitoring and Mitigation of Volcanic Hazards*. Berlin: Springer, 1996.
Sigurdsson, H., B. F. Houghton, S. McNutt, H. Rymer, J. Stix, eds. *Encyclopedia of Volcanoes*. San Diego: Academic Press, 2000.
Sparks, R. S. J., et al. *Volcanic Plumes*. New York: Wiley, 1997.
Stothers, R. B. "The Great Eruption of Tambora and Its Aftermath." *Science* 224 (1984), 1191–1198.
Toon, O. B., and J. B. Pollack. "Atmospheric Aerosols and Climate." *American Scientist* 68 (1980), 268–278.

—STEPHEN SELF

VULNERABILITY

Vulnerability is an intuitively simple notion that is surprisingly difficult to define, conceptualize, and measure. Commonly, vulnerability means being prone to or susceptible to damage or injury. Given the variety and complexity of global environmental changes, it is not feasible to study vulnerability to global change per se. Rather, researchers have begun to study vulnerability to discrete sets of changes or environmental hazards, such as sea level rise (for example, see Barth and Titus, 1984) and famine (for example, see Bohle, 1993).

While models of global environmental change remain rudimentary, we do know that the nature and magnitude of environmental changes vary considerably over time and space (Houghton et al., 1992). Some regions, places, groups, and individuals may benefit from these changes, while others may suffer biophysical, socioeconomic, psychological, and cultural harms. Those that are most likely to be harmed are considered to be the most vulnerable. In part, this reflects differences in exposure, but it also reflects differences in the abilities of some nations, groups, and individuals to resist the hazard event and recover afterwards. It is relatively straightforward to identify those most severely affected after a hazardous event (such as flood, drought, or famine). The goal for any analysis of vulnerability in a policy context, however, is to identify in advance who is most likely to be harmed, where, and why, and what to do to prevent or limit such harm. Unfortunately, models of physical and social processes are currently unable to identify in advance precisely those who are most vulnerable.

In the absence of more refined measures, vulnerability is often equated with the extent of exposure and poverty (for example, see Chambers, 1989). In these terms, the global outlook is bleak, since the number of people living in poverty continues to rise (United Nations Development Programme, 1990) and an increasing proportion of the world's population is becoming increasingly exposed (Dow, 1992, p. 418). Poverty and exposure to environmental changes are only rough sur-

Vulnerability. TABLE 1. A Synthetic Model of the Vulnerability of Food Systems

CRISIS CONCEPT	CONCEPTION OF FOOD CRISIS	CAUSAL FACTORS	SCOPE OF EXPLANATION	MECHANISMS	CONCEPTS OF VULNERABILITY	THEORETICAL PERSPECTIVE
CONJUNCTURAL (sporadic/short-term)	Food exchange crisis	Declining economic command over food	Proximate causes (triggers, external to the food system)	• Deteriorating exchange relations • Market volatility • War, geopolitics • Natural hazards	• Loss of assets/endowments • Inadequate capability	ENTITLEMENT
	Food consumption crisis	Powerlessness/poverty		• Poverty/lack of social welfare • Demographic growth • Demise of moral economy • Denial of political rights	• Disenfranchisement • Marginalization	EMPOWERMENT
STRUCTURAL (processual/long-term)	Food production and reproduction crisis	Social relations of production	Ultimate causes (structural, internal to the food system)	• Patterns of accumulation • Surplus appropriation • Exploitation • Ecological degradation	• Crisis-proneness • Conflicts/contradictions	POLITICAL ECONOMY/ECOLOGY

SOURCE: From Bohle (1993). With permission of Verlag für Entwicklungspolitik Saarbrücken GmbH.

rogates for vulnerability, however, and the most vulnerable groups and individuals are not necessarily the most exposed or the most impoverished. Many other factors contribute to vulnerability (for example, see Liverman, 1990), and a profusion of definitions, terms, and concepts has developed, but consensus remains elusive (Cutter, 1996).

Vulnerability is a function of both exposure and coping abilities. Early natural-hazards researchers recognized this ecological relationship and viewed natural hazards as "extreme events of nature that exceed the capabilities of the system to reflect, absorb, or buffer them" (Kates, 1970). This perspective introduced three important concepts (Burton et al., 1978). First, natural hazards cannot be viewed as purely physical events. Second, human systems are dynamic and constantly adapt and adjust to the vagaries of the natural environment. Third, harm occurs when various thresholds are crossed. The notion of vulnerability is essential but remains implicit.

Burton et al. were severely criticized (for example, Torry, 1979) for their emphasis on extreme events (such as exposure) and on individual perception and behavior (such as choice of coping responses). The critics argued that social marginalization (for example, poverty) pushes people into hazard-prone areas and disrupts indigenous coping mechanisms so that vulnerability increases as the ability to resist and recover from hazard events is reduced. From this political economic perspective, vulnerability is conceived as the "degree to which different classes in society are differentially at risk" (Susman et al., 1983). Blaikie et al. (1994) build on this perspective in the development of their disaster "pressure and release" model in which root causes (such as limited access to power and resources) generate dynamic pressures (for example, rapid population growth and urbanization) that create unsafe conditions. Natural-hazard events act as triggers that create disasters. Thus vulnerability is the "capacity to anticipate, cope with, resist, and recover from the impact of a natural hazard" (Blaikie et al., 1994, p. 9).

Bohle (1993) integrates entitlement theory (Sen, 1981), empowerment theory (Beck, 1989), and political ecological perspectives (Blaikie, 1985) to develop a synthetic model of the vulnerability of food systems (Table 1). Long-term structural processes, such as marginalization and disenfranchisement, generate a baseline vulnerability (Downing, 1991) and tendency to crisis (Figure 1). Events external to the food system (such as drought, war, and economic crisis) act as triggers that may lead to escalating vulnerability and ultimately famine disaster unless internal coping strategies and external interventions are sufficient to counteract the crises. The level of resilience and completeness of recovery will determine the new baseline of vulnerability.

Perhaps the most elaborated conception of vulnerability is as "a multi-layered and multidimensional social space defined by the determinate political, economic

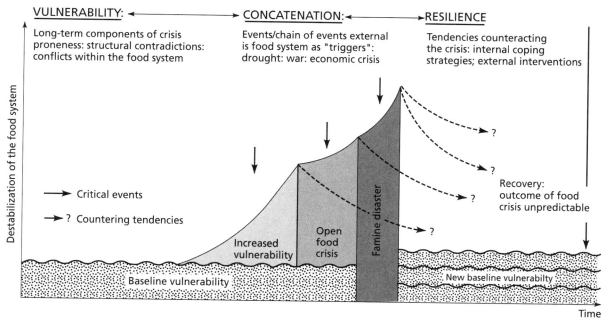

Vulnerability. FIGURE 1. Bohle's Model of Food Crisis. (After Bohle, 1993. With permission of Verlag für Entwicklungspolitik Saarbrücken GmbH.)

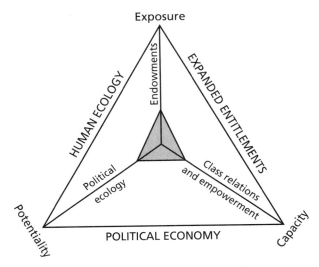

Vulnerability. FIGURE 2. The Causal Structure of Vulnerability. (Reprinted from Bohle, Downing, and Watts, 1994. With permission from Elsevier Science.)

and institutional capabilities of people in specific places at specific times" (Bohle, Downing, and Watts, 1994, p. 39). Bohle, Downing, and Watts suggest that the most vulnerable individuals, groups, classes, and regions are those most exposed to perturbation, who possess the most limited coping capacity, who suffer the most from the "impact of a crisis or environmental perturbations (such as climate change), and who are endowed with circumscribed potential for recovery." In other words, vulnerability can be defined in terms of exposure, capacity, and potentiality (see Figure 2; Bohle, Downing, and Watts, 1994, p. 38).

Researchers have developed more comprehensive and complex models of vulnerability that are better able to explain and predict social responses to natural hazards and global environmental changes. Nevertheless, the models operate best at regional and local scales and require considerable local knowledge and data to implement in any meaningful fashion. Future research is, therefore, likely to generate a set of hazard- and location-specific analyses of vulnerability rather than generic, global measures. Gross measures, such as poverty and exposure, are likely to remain the best large-scale surrogate measures of vulnerability to most global environmental changes.

[*See also* Global Change, *article on* Human Dimensions of Global Change; Natural Hazards; Nuclear Hazards; Risk; *and* Technological Hazards.]

BIBLIOGRAPHY

Barth, M. C., and J. G. Titus, eds. *Greenhouse Effect and Sea Level Rise*. New York: Van Nostrand Reinhold, 1984.

Beck, J. "Survival Strategies and Power Among the Poorest in a West Bengal Village." *IDS Bulletin* 20.2 (1989), 23–32.

Blaikie, P. *The Political Economy of Soil Erosion in Developing Countries*. London: Longman, 1985.

Blaikie, P., T. Cannon, I. Davis, and B. Wisner. *At Risk: Natural Hazards, People's Vulnerability, and Disasters*. London: Routledge, 1994.

Bohle, H. G. "The Geography of Vulnerable Food Systems." In *Coping With Vulnerability and Criticality*, edited by H. G. Bohle et al., pp. 15–29. Saarbrucken: Verlag Breitenbach, 1993.

Bohle, H. G., T. Downing, and M. Watts. "Climate Change and Social Vulnerability: Toward a Sociology and Geography of Food Insecurity." Global Environmental Change (1994), 37–48.

Browder, J. O., ed. *Fragile Lands of Latin America: Strategies for Sustainable Development*. Boulder, Colo.: Westview Press, 1989.

Burton, I., R. W. Kates, and G. F. White. *The Environment as Hazard*. New York: Oxford University Press, 1978.

Chambers, R. "Vulnerability, Coping and Policy." *IDS Bulletin* 21 (1989), 1–7.

Cutter, S. L. "Vulnerability to Environmental Hazards." *Progress in Human Geography* 20.4 (1996), 529–539.

Dow, K. "Exploring Differences in Our Common Future(s): The Meanings of Vulnerability to Global Environmental Change." *Geoforum* 23.3 (1992), 417–436.

Downing, T. "Vulnerability to Hunger in Africa: A Climate Change Perspective." *Global Environmental Change* 1.5 (1991), 365–380.

Hewitt, K. "The Idea of Calamity in a Technocratic Age." In *Interpretations of Calamity*, edited by K. Hewitt, pp. 3–32. Boston: Allen and Unwin, 1983.

Houghton, J. T., B. A. Callander, and S. K. Varney, eds. *Climate Change 1992: The Supplementary Report to the IPCC Scientific Assessment*. Cambridge: Cambridge University Press, 1992.

Kates, R. W. "Natural Hazard in Human Ecological Perspective: Hypotheses and Models." *Economic Geography* 47.3 (1970), 438–451.

Liverman, D. M. "Vulnerability to Global Environmental Change." In *Understanding Global Environmental Change*, edited by R. E. Kaspuson, K. Dow, D. Golding, and J. X. Kaspuson, pp. 27–44. Worcester, Mass.: The Earth Transformed (ET) Program, Clark University, 1990.

Sen, A. *Poverty and Famines: An Essay on Entitlement and Deprivation*. New York and Oxford: Oxford University Press, 1981.

Susman, P., P. O'Keefe, and B. Wisner. "Global Disasters, a Radical Interpretation." In *Interpretations of Calamity*, edited by K. Hewitt, pp. 263–283. Boston: Allen and Unwin, 1983.

Torry, W. I. "Hazards, Hazes and Holes: A Critique of *The Environment as Hazard* and General Reflections on Disaster Research." *Canadian Geographer* 23.4 (1979), 368–383.

United Nations Development Programme. *Human Development Report 1990*. New York: Oxford University Press, 1990.

—DOMINIC GOLDING

W

WALKER, GILBERT

Sir Gilbert Thomas Walker (1868–1958) was one of the greatest British climatologists of the twentieth century and made fundamental and innovative contributions to the study of climatic oscillations and of global climate variability. His academic career started with a Fellowship at Trinity College, Cambridge (where he read mathematics as an undergraduate) in 1891. For his work on various dynamical problems, he was elected a fellow of the Royal Society in 1904. In the same year he went to India to become the second Director-General of Observatories and remained in this post, employing his great organizational and administrative skills, until he reached retirement age in 1924. He was awarded a knighthood in that year. He then became Professor of Meteorology at Imperial College, London, and held that post until 1934. In retirement he edited the *Quarterly Journal of the Royal Meteorological Society*. He was a man of unbounded but highly disciplined interests who, in addition to his climatological researches, was an expert, *inter alia*, on the dynamics and design of the boomerang and an authority on the theory and evolution of the flute.

The significance of Walker in the context of global change is that during the 1920s and 1930s, he statistically defined and named the concept of the Southern Oscillation and described a distinctive circulation pattern in the equatorial Pacific Ocean, which is now generally called the Walker Circulation. He recognized a general principle that, when pressure is high in the Pacific Ocean, it tends to be low in the Indian Ocean from Africa to Australia. His original definition of the Southern Oscillation was based on the difference in pressure observations at Santiago, Honolulu, and Manila and those at Jakarta, Darwin, and Cairo, together with the temperatures in Madras, rainfall in India and Chile, and the Nile flood record.

The Southern Oscillation has subsequently come to be regarded as one of the most striking examples of interannual climate variability on a global scale. It has been seen to be associated with considerable fluctuations in rainfall, sea surface temperatures, the intensity of trade wind activity, and some extreme weather events. The Southern Oscillation has also become closely identified with El Niño events in the tropical Pacific, and the combined El Niño–Southern Oscillation event has now become widely known as ENSO. [*See* El Niño–Southern Oscillation.]

Walker was especially interested in forecasting monsoonal rainfall (Kutzbach, 1995) by developing regression equations from the pattern of correlations found between Indian rainfall and remote surface observations. In an effort to extend and improve his forecast formulae, he accumulated as many meteorological and hydrological series as he could, and looked for statistically significant relationships among the variables. In addition to the Southern Oscillation, he identified two other oscillations: the North Atlantic Oscillation, involving out-of-phase atmospheric pressure conditions between the regions of the Azores and Iceland, and the North Pacific Oscillation, involving out-of-phase pressure conditions between Alaska and the Hawaiian Islands. It became apparent, however, that it was the Southern Oscillation that provided the greatest potential in terms of long-term forecasting. [*See the vignette on* The North Atlantic Oscillation *in the article on* Natural Climate Fluctuations.]

BIBLIOGRAPHY

Allan, R., J. Lindesay, and D. Parker. *El Niño Southern Oscillation and Climatic Variability.* Victoria: CSIRO, 1996. See especially Chapter 1.

Kutzbach, G. 1995. "Concepts of Monsoon Physics in Historical Perspective: The Indian Monsoon (Seventeenth to early Twentieth Century)." In *Monsoons*, edited by J. S. Fein and P. L. Stephens, pp.159–209. Chichester, U.K.: Wiley, 1995.

P.A.S. Obituary notice. "Sir Gilbert Walker, C.S.I., F.R.S." *Quarterly Journal of the Royal Meteorological Society* 85 (1959), 186.

Taylor, G. I. "Gilbert Thomas Walker 1868–1958." *Biographical Memoirs of Fellows of the Royal Society* 8 (1962), 167–174. A good summary of Walker's life; includes a full bibliography of Walker's published works.

—ANDREW S. GOUDIE

WAR. *See* Nuclear Winter; *and* Security and Environment.

WASTE MANAGEMENT

The three basic processes of the global economy, extraction, processing and consumption, all involve the generation of waste products that eventually find their way back into the environment. Too much waste in the wrong place at the wrong time can cause changes in the environment and harm to animals, plants, and ecosystems. The careful management of waste can limit the damage done to the environment and can conserve scarce resources. To this end, the 1992 Earth Summit in Rio de Janeiro produced several Agenda 21 objectives for the sustainable management of waste, including minimizing wastes, maximizing waste reuse and recycling, promoting environmentally sound waste disposal and treatment, and extending waste services to more people. These areas were seen to be interrelated, and an integrated plan was therefore sought for the environmentally sound management of wastes. [*See* Agenda 21.]

Waste can be defined as a material that has been "left over after use," or that "no longer serves a purpose." It is usually its lack of value that makes it a waste product rather than a useful resource. This lack of value may stem from its mixed state, as in mixed household waste, its potential for pollution, as in hazardous waste, or its location, as in the case of low-value materials that are expensive to transport, such as demolition waste.

Waste Generation. There are many different types of waste that arise in different forms: solid, liquid, and gaseous. They are often categorized according to their source; for example, household waste, industrial waste, sewage sludge, hazardous waste. Waste composition can vary considerably, particularly between developed and developing countries. For example, municipal waste in developing countries tends to contain greater quantities of biodegradable kitchen waste, since food is generally purchased unprocessed. In developed countries, greater quantities of processed food are purchased, so that food waste comes from the food industry rather than individual householders. In developing countries there may be low levels of industry and thus less industrial waste. However, where there is a tendency for industries to use old technology, the waste may be more hazardous (Tables 1 and 2).

Waste Collection. It is estimated that half of the urban population in developing countries is now without adequate solid waste disposal services. One of the objectives of Agenda 21 is the provision of a safe waste collection and disposal service to all people. In particular, priority should be given to the extension of waste management services to the urban poor, especially those in "illegal" settlements. At present it is thought that, globally, approximately 5.2 million people die each year from waste-related diseases, including four million children under five years of age.

Some of the problems with waste collection in poor urban areas are due to inadequate infrastructure combined with the difficulty of access in overcrowded conditions. The problems are exacerbated by the need, in many hot countries, for a daily collection because of the rapid deterioration of the waste, which often has a high biodegradable content. In some areas, low-technology solutions such as hand- and animal-drawn carts are used for the initial collection. The wastes are then transferred to open trucks or refuse vehicles for transport to a transfer station or a waste disposal facility.

In developed countries the waste is usually collected on a weekly basis from the roadside (sometimes from the back door), either in plastic sacks or large bins on wheels. Waste collection sometimes includes the collection of separated recyclable materials, or this may be carried out independently. Industrial and commercial premises make their own arrangements with waste disposal companies for waste to be collected, usually in

Waste Management. TABLE 1. Quantities of Different Types of Waste for Selected Countries*

	YEAR	CONSTRUCTION/ DEMOLITION	SEWAGE SLUDGE	SCRAPPED MOTOR VEHICLES	PACKAGING	MUNICIPAL WASTE (1992)
Canada	1992	11,000	7,450	1,000	10,500	18,800
United States	1986	34,692	11,454	N.A.[†]	64,000	187,790
Japan	1991	58,431	169,693	N.A.	N.A.	50,767
Australia	1992	1,568	60,000	271	914	12,000
Denmark	1993	2,374	192	N.A.	N.A.	2,377
France	1992	25,000	865	N.A.	6,900	27,000
W. Germany	1992	121,892	2,630	N.A.	8,000	21,615[‡]
Italy	1991	34,374	3,428	1,400	N.A.	20,033
Spain	1990	22,000	10,000	N.A.	N.A.	14,256
Czech Rep.	1987	2,677	2,750	N.A.	N.A.	N.A.
Hungary	1992	N.A.	30,000	N.A.	500	4,000

*In units of 1,000 metric tons.

[†]N.A. = not available.

[‡]1990.

SOURCE: OECD/OCDE (1995).

Waste Management. TABLE 2. Generation and Composition of Municipal Waste for Selected Countries

	MUNICIPAL WASTE (KG/CAPITA)	PAPER AND PAPERBOARD (PERCENT)	FOOD AND GARDEN WASTE (PERCENT)	PLASTICS (PERCENT)	GLASS (PERCENT)	METALS (PERCENT)	TEXTILES (PERCENT)
United States	730	38	23	9	7	8	16
Canada	660	28	34	11	7	8	13
France	470	30	25	10	12	6	17
Denmark	460	30	37	7	6	3	17
Japan	410	46	26	9	7	8	12
Turkey	390	6	64	3	2	1	24
Spain	360	21	44	11	7	4	13
Poland	340	10	38	10	12	8	23
Iran	324	8	74	5	3	1	2
Greece	310	20	49	9	5	5	13
Mexico	310	14	52	4	6	3	20
China	285*	3	60	4	1	0	2
Year	1992	1993	1993	1993	1993	1993	1993

*Henderson et al. (1997); + 30 percent inorganics.
SOURCE: OECD/OCDE (1995).

skips or large wheeled bins. Hazardous wastes need special arrangements for collection and disposal.

Waste Disposal. There are many different methods of disposing of waste. Many countries have a hierarchy of waste management, which generally favors waste minimization, reuse, and recycling. The least favored methods are landfill and incineration without energy recovery (Table 3).

In some countries it is now recognized that the waste management hierarchy should be applied with some flexibility to take into consideration environmental, economic, and social costs. It is understood that the best practicable environmental option (BPEO) will vary for individual waste streams and local circumstances. However, the European Commission does consider that waste prevention should remain the first priority. In some countries, integrated waste management is promoted, accepting that there can be several complementary management options for one waste stream: for example, the recycling of noncombustible components of household waste followed by the incineration with energy recovery of the remaining waste stream.

Prevention. Methods of reducing waste at source vary considerably, from encouraging householders to compost their kitchen and garden waste at home to improving process efficiency in an industrial unit so that the amount of waste is reduced. Some industries have found that they can reduce their waste quite cheaply, and sometimes profitably, through good housekeeping methods such as better levels of maintenance, reduction of leaks, and recycling nonproducts within the plant rather than disposing of them: for example, the cleaning and reuse of solvents. Waste minimization can also be achieved by installing less-polluting technology. Another aspect to be taken into consideration is the harmfulness of the waste. It may be possible for an industry

Waste Management. TABLE 3. European Commission Waste Management Hierarchy

Prevention	Promotion of clean technologies and products
	Reduction of the hazardousness of wastes
	Establishment of technical standards
	Promotion of re-use and recycling
Recovery	Preference should be given to materials recycling over energy recovery operations
Final disposal	Care should be taken to avoid incineration without energy recovery and uncontrolled landfill sites

SOURCES: Adapted from European Commission Waste Management Strategy (1996), and European Commission (1996).

to change its raw materials or processes so that the waste produced is less damaging to the environment, for example the reduction of chlorofluorocarbon (CFC) refrigerants. The design of products is also important, and can be manipulated to reduce harmfulness (for example, the replacement of aerosols by pump sprays), to improve recyclability (for example, so that cars can be dismantled rather than scrapped); and to encourage overall waste prevention (for example, the reduction of excess packaging).

Recovery. Following the prevention of waste in the hierarchy, recovery includes the reuse and recycling of materials and the recovery of energy. There has been considerable debate as to the relative values of materials and energy recovery from waste. The recovery of materials often saves large quantities of energy, but for some materials there are reprocessing and marketing problems.

Composting. Composting is "aerobic digestion," the biological decomposition of biodegradable waste in the presence of oxygen. It can take the form of a garden compost heap, which reduces household waste and produces a useful garden compost. On a larger scale, biodegradable kitchen and garden waste can be collected separately and used to produce compost via a centralized biological treatment plant. Many industrial and agricultural wastes can also be treated in this way. Some mixed wastes need treatment to remove the majority of the nonorganic fractions prior to composting, and the remainder may still only produce a low-grade product suitable for landfill cover. Separately collected organic material and purely organic waste streams can, however, produce a high-quality product. To obtain a good rate of decomposition, it is important that oxygen be constantly available. This is achieved either by the use of forced air or by a "windrow" system, where the piles of material are regularly turned to expose them to the air. Further information on composting can be found in White et al. (1995).

Energy Recovery from Waste. The energy value of waste varies with its composition. A large proportion of paper and plastics will give a high energy value. In many developing countries, municipal waste has a substantial proportion of biodegradable kitchen waste, making it more suitable for composting than for energy recovery.

There are four main methods of recovering energy from waste: (1) the combustion of unsorted waste in a large purpose-built incinerator that has energy recovery (mass burn incineration), (2) the burning of partially sorted waste in a purpose-built incinerator (flock fuel or coarse refuse-derived fuel [RDF]), (3) the processing of waste to separate the combustible components to produce an RDF that can be burned on specially adapted

boilers, and (4) the recovery of methane and carbon dioxide from landfill sites (landfill gas).

The main difference between the first three methods is the degree of processing that the waste receives prior to combustion. Waste entering a mass incinerator generally receives no pretreatment, although ferrous metal is often recovered from the ashes. A flock fuel system involves the separation and removal of most of the noncombustibles for recycling, leaving a more uniform waste stream with a higher energy value than raw waste. RDF plants have the same or a higher level of sorting, but the fuel is then usually compacted and pelletized so that it can be stored. Other advantages of flock fuel and RDF are that they have a lower heavy metal content than municipal waste, requiring less stringent air cleaning systems, and that, with less noncombustible components, they produce less ash.

Despite these advantages, the predominant method of recovering energy from waste is mass incineration. This is mostly because the technology is reliable and relatively straightforward. It achieves maximum volume reduction of the waste without having to use less-reliable waste separation techniques, and does not incur any marketing problems with respect to the recovered recyclable materials. An alternative method of combustion is a fluidized-bed design in which the waste is burned on a bed of inert material such as sand, which is fluidized by currents of air. This method is popular in Japan, but less so in Europe where moving-grate incinerators are well established.

The main benefit of recovering energy from waste is that the recovered energy displaces energy generated by other fuels. In countries where the displaced energy is from fossil fuels, large quantities of carbon dioxide emissions are also displaced. Energy can be recovered as heat, electricity, or combined heat and power (CHP). Heat recovery requires customers that are located close to the waste facility, since the cost of installing pipelines to transport hot water is high. Although the generation of electricity is less efficient than heat recovery (20 percent rather than 60–70 percent), it is easier to sell since it can be exported directly into the national electricity supply. CHP improves the efficiency (80 percent) but again requires a pipe network. A mass burn incinerator will recover 8–10 gigajoules per metric ton of municipal waste.

Gas cleaning systems are used to control various emissions, including particulate matter, acid gas, dioxins, and NO_x. In Europe, incineration plants must now meet high pollution control standards, as required by national and European Union legislation.

Landfill. Although the disposal of waste as landfill is the least favored method in the waste hierarchy, it remains the main disposal method in many countries. In the United Kingdom, for example, an estimated 85 percent of controlled waste is disposed to landfill, while in the United States, 70 percent of municipal waste is thought to follow the same route. Even in countries where alternative methods of disposal predominate, there is a need for landfill sites to dispose of residues such as incinerator ash. The underlying reason for the popularity of landfill is its relative cheapness, particularly in countries where unregulated landfill is permitted. In recent years, however, there has been increasing awareness of the pollution problems that can arise from these waste "dumps," and stringent regulations have been introduced in some countries, resulting in sophisticated landfill sites with leachate collection systems and landfill gas recovery. There has been a subsequent increase in cost, but landfill generally remains cheaper than other disposal options.

When organic waste decomposes anaerobically (without oxygen) in a landfill site, it produces a liquid, known as *leachate*, and landfill gas. Both emissions can be polluting if they escape into the environment. Landfill gas is composed of carbon dioxide and methane, both major greenhouse gases, plus water vapor and trace organic compounds. The decomposition of waste in landfill sites is considered to be one of the main sources of methane. The U.S. Environmental Protection Agency's global change program (Thorneloe, 1991) has estimated that, globally, methane from the decomposition of municipal waste could account for 7–20 percent of all anthropogenic methane emissions. Migrating landfill gas can also become a local fire or explosion hazard, either at the landfill or in adjacent properties. Landfill gas can also be an asphyxiation risk in an inadequately ventilated enclosed space. The smell from raw landfill gas is another potential nuisance to people living near the landfill.

To mitigate these problems, landfill gas can be collected though a system of perforated pipes and either flared off or used as an energy source. Estimates of the efficiency of gas collection systems range from 40 to 85 percent, with the remaining gas escaping into the environment. Flaring is an effective method for controlling methane emissions, which are converted into carbon dioxide during combustion. However, a valuable energy source with its environmental and financial benefits is lost. The amount of energy recovered depends on the methane content of the recovered gas, which varies with the waste composition and the environmental conditions of the site. On average, 4 gigajoules of electricity is generated per metric ton of municipal waste in developed countries.

In the past it was not considered necessary to control leachate, and a system of "dilute and disperse" was and still is operated in many countries. As a conse-

quence, leachate can pose a serious risk to groundwater supplies. For example, the U.S. Environmental Protection Agency has estimated that approximately forty thousand landfill sites in the United States may be contaminating ground water (Uehling, 1993). In some developed countries, new landfill sites are now operated on a dry containment basis, with multiple liners and leachate collection and treatment systems. This results in a reduction in waste decomposition, so that the landfill sites are regarded as a method for the long-term storage of waste rather than a form of waste treatment.

There is an alternative view that landfill sites should be regarded as bioreactors and the decomposition accelerated by recirculation of the leachate. The argument is that the majority of the gas and leachate production should take place in the beginning of a landfill site's life, when the gas and leachate collection systems are operating effectively (White et al., 1993). However, in Europe this idea may be thwarted by the European Commission's Draft Directive on the Landfill of Waste, which aims at reducing the amount of biodegradable waste disposed in landfills. The proposal also recommends the pretreatment of all waste prior to landfill and the banning of "codisposal," which is a method of disposing of liquid hazardous waste into trenches cut into landfill sites containing household waste.

NIMBY. Many waste facilities suffer from the "NIMBY" ("not in my backyard") syndrome, with the main concern being health risks. In particular there are concerns about dioxin emissions from waste incinerators, which has led to several large studies, some with conflicting results. Experts tend to use the relative-risk approach, comparing the risk posed by the chemical exposure from a waste site with risks such as traffic accidents, smoking, and alcoholism. On this basis, the waste site can be shown to be a relatively low risk. However, individuals see the risk from a waste facility as being involuntary—it is being imposed on them—and there are also problems of misinformation and misperception. Petts (1992) provides further discussion of the risk perception of waste facilities.

Economic Instruments. Waste management policy has traditionally been secured by the use of regulatory standards, with the threat of some penalty if these are not met. [*See* Regulation.] This has resulted in some waste disposal options being priced at levels that do not take environmental costs and benefits into consideration. These costs and benefits are borne by society in general, and are not accounted for in the decisions made about waste. For example, the cost of disposal to landfill does not include the external costs associated with the global warming potential of methane emissions. Social costs and benefits are known as "externalities," and can include air emissions, water pollution and health impacts, and benefits from the displacement of emissions from energy generated from fossil fuels.

If all waste management options reflected their true social cost, then market forces could achieve the optimal mix of waste management options. However, because of market and information failure, this is not the case. The overall result is that levels of waste minimization and recycling are too low and the level of disposal is too high. Several countries have recognized the limitations of the regulatory approach and have introduced market-based instruments to influence behavior in the direction of sustainable waste management.

There are a range of economic instruments, including raw material and product charges, deposit–refund systems, waste collection and disposal charges, tradable recycling targets, taxes, and subsidies.

Variable charging of household waste. Householders generally pay an average amount for the collection and disposal of their waste, which is unrelated to the quantity of waste that they dispose of. The fee is often included in a general local tax and not separately identified. Variable charging relates the amount paid to the amount of waste produced, excluding materials separated for recycling. This is also known as "pay by the bag," "volume-based fees," or "unit pricing." A variety of methods are used, the most common being the purchase of distinctive refuse bags by the householder, the cost of which includes the full cost of collection and disposal. Alternatively, stickers can be purchased for placement on ordinary refuse bags. It is now also possible for waste in wheeled bins to be weighed as it is being tipped into a refuse vehicle and for the householder to be charged automatically for the disposal of that quantity of waste.

The countries (approximately fifteen) that have already introduced this system have experienced increased recycling and decreases in disposal by up to 50 percent, which offsets landfill demand, rewards recyclers, and fosters long-term changes in consumer be-

havior. The disadvantages are an increase in fly-tipping and waste burning and the extensive education program that is required. It can also be considered unfair for low-income families and those with children. The system does not work so well in larger apartment buildings and rural areas and is expensive to administer.

Deposit–Refund Systems. This approach is essentially a combination of a tax and a subsidy, which may be market-generated or imposed by law. A deposit is added to the price of a product such as a can or bottle of drink, which is refunded to the consumer if they return the waste packaging. The container can either be refilled or recycled, depending on the material and the contents. This system has been introduced in several U.S. states and in some northern European countries (Table 4). Experience has shown that the management of deposit–refund schemes is best carried out by beverage producers, and the containers returned by the customers to the retailers. United States beverage container systems have had return rates of 72–98 percent, but overall they tend to have led to relatively small reductions in the volume and cost of waste disposal, and are expensive to operate. [See Recycling.]

The benefits of deposit–refund systems are a reduction in the cost of waste collection and disposal, reduced litter, and reduced energy and material resources used in container production. The disadvantages are an increase in storage and handling costs and possible inconvenience to the householder. Evidence suggests that return rates are not very sensitive to the size of deposit, more important being the number and convenience of return points, although a greater number of return points means higher system costs for handling, storage, and transportation. In the United Kingdom, where there is no monetary reward, about 20 percent of glass bottles are returned to bottle banks, but 95 percent of milk bottles are returned. These are collected from the doorstep by the person delivering the milk, the key factor here being convenience. De-

Waste Management. TABLE 4. Examples of Deposit–Refund Schemes

COUNTRY	INITIATOR	TARGET	DEPOSIT SIZE ($U.S.)	RETURN RATE (PERCENT)
Germany	Beverage producer	PET*	0.27	96
Netherlands	Beverage producer	PET	0.05–0.51	50–90
Norway	Beverage producer	Glass	0.16–0.32	98
Sweden	Beverage producer	Glass	0.08–0.37	80–98
United Kingdom	Beverage producer	Glass	0.08–0.19	90
United States (California)	Beverage producer	All types	0.02–0.03	69

*PET = polyethylene terephthlate.
SOURCE: Environmental Resources Ltd (1991).

Waste Management. TABLE 5. Landfill Taxes in Europe

COUNTRY	WASTE TYPE	COST ($U.S./ METRIC TON)
Denmark	All	33.07
France	Municipal	4.00
	Industrial, hazardous	8–12.80
Germany	Industrial, hazardous	16–65.60
Belgium (Flanders)	Municipal	1.6–4.8
	Industrial, hazardous	0.96–11.20
The Netherlands	All	16.80

SOURCE: U.K. Waste Ltd (1995).

posit–refund systems can also be used to target the safe disposal of hazardous household waste such as batteries.

Recycling credits. Recycling credits are not a subsidy, but they do correct a market failure of the waste management system. Recycling of household waste obviously removes waste from the disposal stream, saving a proportion of the cost of waste collection and disposal. The aim of recycling credits is to pass on these financial savings to local authorities and third parties who operate the recycling schemes. In the United Kingdom, the Recycling Credits Scheme was introduced under the Environmental Protection Act (1992) to transfer the financial savings to the organizations who collect and sort the waste for recycling. The payments are made by Waste Collection and Disposal Authorities to the recycling operators such as local authorities, private organizations, and community groups.

Landfill tax. A landfill tax is a disposal charge that internalizes the externalities of landfill, raises revenue, and reduces the amount of waste going to landfill through increased recycling and/or waste minimization. Six European Union countries have landfill taxes: Denmark, France, Germany, Belgium, the United Kingdom, and the Netherlands. The cost per metric ton varies between U.S.$1.6 and U.S.$33.07 (Table 5). In some countries, the tax is hypothecated—the tax revenue is used for a specific purpose. In France, for example, it is used to finance the Modernization Fund for Waste Management.

[*See also* Environmental Economics; Greening of Industry; Growth, Limits to; Hazardous Waste; Human Health; Industrialization; Industrial Metabolism; Land Use, *article on* Land Use Planning; Manufacturing; Ocean Disposal; *and* Sustainable Development.]

BIBLIOGRAPHY

Abduli, M. A. "Solid Waste Management in Tehran." *Waste Management and Research* 13.6 (1995), 519–531. A good description of waste management in a developing country.

British Medical Association. *Hazardous Waste and Human Health*. London, 1991. This book is a useful guide to methods of treatment and disposal of hazardous wastes and links exposure to ill health. Starting to get dated but still useful.

Environmental Resources Ltd. *Economic Instruments and Recovery of Resources from Waste: A Study*. London: HMSO, 1992.

European Commission. *European Union Strategy for Waste Management*. Brussels: European Commission, 1990.

European Commission. "Review of Community Waste Management Strategy." COM (96) 399, September 10, 1996. Contains full details of the European Community Waste Management Policy.

Henderson, J. P., et al. "Solid Waste Practices in China." *International Solid Waste Association Times* 3 (1997), 16–20. An interesting description of waste management in China.

Her Majesty's Stationery Office. *Making Waste Work: A Sustainable Waste Strategy*. Discusses the aims and objectives of the U.K. waste strategy. London, 1995.

Hickling. *Options for Managing Emissions from Solid Waste Landfills*. Toronto, 1994. Prepared by Hickling (Toronto, Ontario) for Environment Canada (Ottawa, Ontario). An in-depth study of the control and utilization of methane emissions from landfills in Canada.

Intergovernmental Panel on Climate Change. *Technologies, Policies, and Measures for Mitigating Climate Change*. Geneva: IPCC, 1996.

Organisation for Economic Co-operation and Development. *Environmental Data Compendium*. Paris: OECD, 1995.

Petts, J. "Incineration Risk Perceptions and Public Concern, Experience in the UK Improving Risk Communication." *Waste Management and Research* 10 (1992), 169–182.

Powell, J., and A. Craighill. "The UK Landfill Tax." In *Ecotaxation*, edited by T. O'Riordan, pp. 304–320. London: Earthscan, 1997. Describes in detail the introduction and operation of the landfill tax in the United Kingdom.

Turner, R. K., and J. C. Powell. "Solid and Hazardous Waste." In *Blueprint 3, Measuring Sustainable Development*, edited by D. Pearce, pp. 78–97. London: Earthscan, 1993. This chapter looks at the sustainable management of U.K. waste from an economics perspective.

Turner, R. K., et al. *Green Taxes, Waste Management and Political Economy*. CSERGE Working Paper WM 96–03, Centre for Social and Economic Research on the Global Environment, University of East Anglia and University College London, 1996. This paper surveys recent developments in the context of waste management policy and the emergence of resources such as recycling credits and the landfill tax.

Uehling, M. "Keeping Rubbish Rotten to the Core." *New Scientist* 139 (28 August 1993), 12–13.

U.K. Waste Ltd. *Response to the U.K. Government Consultation on Landfill Tax*. High Wycombe, U.K.: Waste Management Ltd., 1995.

White, P. R., et al. *Integrated Solid Waste Management: A Lifecycle Inventory*. London: Blackie, 1995. A very useful and detailed guide to all methods of solid waste management. Included in the book is a computer disc containing lifecycle assessment spreadsheet models (Lotus and Excel) to calculate the environmental impacts from any waste management scenario.

—JANE C. POWELL

WASTE WATER. *See* Sanitation.

WATER

The planet Earth could just as easily have been named Water—approximately three-fifths of the surface area of the planet is covered with water, and water is vital for nearly all aspects of human and ecosystem well-being and health. Water is the most widespread substance in the natural environment. It exists in three different forms: solid (as ice), liquid, and gaseous (as water vapor), and it constantly changes form as it moves through the hydrologic cycle. [See Cryosphere; and Hydrologic Cycle.] For this reason, water plays a critical role in almost every geophysical process.

Problems associated with access to or the quality of fresh water have become an increasingly important focus of concern by the world's scientific community and by the public and policy makers. This concern has manifested itself in a growing number of conferences, studies, analyses, policy meetings, and publications about all aspects of the world's water resources. Scientists, policy makers, and the public are beginning to perceive the intricate connections between water and human well-being, water quality and health, water availability and ecosystem function, and water pricing and equity issues, as well as the role that economics and politics play in determining water policies around the world.

The World's Supply and Flows of Fresh Water. During the twentieth century, the focus of water policy makers and managers was on constructing infrastructure to provide reliable water supplies. In the past few years, however, this emphasis has begun to shift toward a better understanding of water needs and policies to try to improve how humans manage and use water (Gleick, 1998). At the same time, great uncertainties remain about water availability, the natural variations over time in the hydrologic cycle, and our freshwater stocks and flows. Despite our increasingly accurate remote-sensing technology, mapping capabilities, and modeling abilities, even the total amount of water on the planet is not known to a high degree of accuracy. Water is found in many places and takes many forms, and it is in continuous and rapid transformation from one form and stock to another.

The basic hydrologic cycle. Fresh water is a renewable resource made available on a continuous basis by the flow of solar energy reaching the Earth from the sun. This energy evaporates fresh water into the atmosphere from the oceans and land surfaces and redistributes it around the world in the *hydrologic cycle.* Atmospheric water is constantly being diminished by precipitation and replenished by evaporation. Less water falls on the oceans as precipitation than is lost through evaporation: thus there is a continuous transfer of water to the land, which runs off in rivers and streams or goes into long-term storage in lakes, soils, and groundwater aquifers.

Because of the heterogeneity of our atmosphere, land surfaces, and energy fluxes, the distribution of fresh water around the world is also heterogeneous. In fact, one of the most important characteristics of fresh water is its uneven distribution in both space and time. Some places receive enormous quantities of water regularly; others are extremely arid. At one extreme, regions in India and the rainforests on the island of Kauai can receive more than ten meters of rainfall in a given year, while the dry deserts of South America may receive no measurable rainfall for long periods of time.

Most regions also experience great variability in when that water comes. Seasonal cycles of rainfall and evaporation are the rule, not the exception, and variability from one period to another can be large. Water planners and managers must take all of these characteristics into account when designing and operating water systems. A sophisticated science of hydrology and water management has developed over the past millennia to deal with precisely these characteristics.

Stocks and flows of water. A clear understanding of the natural hydrological cycle requires reliable estimates of the stocks and flows of freshwater resources. Despite vast improvements in monitoring technology, data storage, and modeling, information on the amount of fresh water on Earth is still not reliable or accurate. Estimates of water stocks and flows remain approximations. This is partly the result of inadequate efforts to actually monitor water stocks and partly the result of the impossibility of accurately measuring—and integrating multiple measurements of—things like soil moisture, water in wetlands and groundwater aquifers, and vastly complex and chaotic flows of water vapor and liquids. Even the volume of water in lakes, glaciers, polar ice, and other well-defined stocks can be only approximated.

Many assessments have been made over the years, giving a rough idea of how much water there is and in what forms. Table 1 shows one estimate of the major stocks of water in the hydrologic cycle. Current estimates are that the Earth contains around 1.4 billion cubic kilometers of water. Approximately 97.5 percent of this water is salt water, held in the world's oceans and saline lakes. The other 2.5 percent—about 35 million cubic kilometers—is fresh water in ice sheets, glaciers, groundwater aquifers, rivers, lakes, the atmosphere, soils, and the biota. Table 2 presents estimates of major freshwater stocks. The principal sources of water for human use are lakes, rivers, soil moisture, and relatively shallow groundwater basins. These stocks hold, on average, only about 200,000 cubic kilometers of water—less than 1 percent of all freshwater on Earth.

In addition to stocks of water, the hydrologic cycle consists of continuous flows of water into and out of every stock under the influence of inputs of solar

Water. TABLE 1. Water Reserves on the Earth

LOCATION	VOLUME (CUBIC KILOMETERS)
World oceans	1,338,000,000
Ground water	23,400,000
Glaciers/permanent snow cover	24,064,000
Antarctic	(21,600,000)
Greenland	(2,340,000)
Other	(124,000)
Ground water/permafrost	300,000
Water in lakes and swamps	176,400
River flows	2,120
Biological water	1,120
Atmospheric water	12,900
Total water reserves*	1,385,984,000
Total freshwater reserves*	35,029,000

*Totals may not add because of rounding; significant figures as in original.

SOURCE: Shiklomanov (1993).

energy, the dynamics of the atmosphere, gravity, and human activities. The rates of flux of water vary enormously: the average time a molecule of water stays in the atmosphere between evaporation and precipitation is approximately eight days; the residence time of water in glaciers or deep ground water may be hundreds or thousands of years. These cycling rates are of great importance when evaluating the possible use of water for human activities and the impacts of those uses on natural systems.

The major flows of fresh water are evaporation and

Water. TABLE 2. Major Freshwater Stocks

	VOLUME (1,000 KM³)	PERCENT OF TOTAL FRESH WATER
Ground water (fresh)	10,530	30.1
Soil moisture	16.5	0.05
Glaciers and permanent snow cover	24,064	68.7
Ground ice/permafrost	300	0.86
Freshwater lakes	91	0.26
Wetlands	11.5	0.03
Rivers	2.1	0.006
Biota	1.1	0.003
Atmospheric water vapor	12.9	0.04
Total*	35,029	100

*Totals may not add because of rounding; significant figures as in original.

SOURCE: Shiklomanov (1993).

precipitation. Water both evaporates off of and precipitates onto land and ocean surfaces. Approximately 505,000 cubic kilometers evaporates annually from the oceans. Another 72,000 cubic kilometers evaporates each year from land surfaces. Approximately 90 percent of all precipitation, or about 458,000 cubic kilometers, returns to the oceans as precipitation; the remaining 119,000 cubic kilometers of precipitation falls over land (Shiklomanov, 1993). The difference between precipitation and evaporation on land is runoff and groundwater recharge—approximately 47,000 cubic kilometers per year.

These global averages hide considerable variation in both the spatial and temporal distribution of water. Yet these variations are of vital importance to understanding the dynamics of water on Earth and in assessing the consequences of various forms of development. Precipitation and evaporation vary on every time scale, ranging from interannual variations to sharp differences in the intensity of storm events. Nearly 80 percent of all runoff in Asia occurs between May and October; three-quarters of runoff in Africa occurs between January and June; in Australia as much as 30 percent of runoff may occur in the single month of March. Another way to think about these variations over time is to realize that nearly seven thousand cubic kilometers more water is stored on land in snow, soil moisture, and lakes in March than in September, and that six hundred cubic kilometers more water is stored in the atmosphere in September than in March (Van Hylckama, 1970).

Similar variability is evident in the regional and annual distribution of runoff. Table 3 shows one estimate of the average annual water balance of major continental areas, including precipitation, evaporation, and runoff. Table 4 shows a more recent data set from the same author that shows average runoff by continent together with maximum and minimum flows, excluding nonrenewable runoff and Antarctica ice flows. Global runoff is unevenly distributed, even accounting for differences in area. More than half of all runoff occurs in Asia and South America; in fact, an unusually large fraction of all runoff occurs in just a single river—the Amazon, which carries more than six thousand cubic kilometers of water a year. Brazilian rivers all together account for nearly 20 percent of all global renewable freshwater resources—35 percent more than Russia, and about twice as much as both Canada and China, which have the third and fourth largest average annual runoff volumes (Gleick, 1998).

Table 4 also presents water availability per square kilometer of land area and per person. South America and Asia have the largest volumes of runoff annually; because South America, however, is considerably smaller in size and population, it has a much larger amount of water available on a per capita or areal ba-

Water. TABLE 3. Surface Water Balances

CONTINENT	PRECIPITATION (CUBIC KILOMETERS/YEAR)	EVAPORATION (CUBIC KILOMETERS/YEAR)	RUNOFF* (CUBIC KILOMETERS/YEAR)
Europe	8,290	5,320	2,970
Asia	32,200	18,100	14,100
Africa	22,300	17,700	4,600
North America	18,300	10,100	8,180
South America	28,400	16,200	12,200
Australia/Oceania	7,080	4,570	2,510
Antarctica	2,310	0	2,310
Total land area	118,880	71,990	46,870

*Runoff includes flows to ground water, inland basins, and ice flows of Antarctica. These data can be compared with Table 4, which excludes nonrenewable water flows and Antarctica ice flows.
SOURCE: Shiklomanov (1993).

sis. Australia and Oceania, which includes New Zealand and most of the Pacific island nations, receive the least amount of water overall, but have the highest per capita availability because of their low populations. Figure 1 shows total average annual runoff by continent. Figure 2 shows runoff by continent on a per capita basis. While total runoff volumes are greatest in Asia, the greatest per capita availability is in South America. Indeed, using per capita measures, Asia has the lowest availability of a continental area.

To report on the quantitative characteristics of water resources, many different measures or indicators are used. Among the most common are *absolute* indicators, which measure total volumes of water, and *relative* or *specific* indicators, which normalize water volumes to some other standard such as population, area, or economic values.

The most common absolute measure for a stock of water is a volume; for a flow of water, a volume per unit time. Thus, a stock of water in a lake or groundwater aquifer might be measured in millions of cubic meters or in cubic kilometers. River flow might be measured in cubic meters per second or cubic kilometers per year (km^3/yr). When flows are described, it is critical to know the period over which the flow is presented. Typical river flows are described as averages or mean flows, meaning an average of a number of individual measurements. The most common relative measures for water resources are per capita water availability or use (such as cubic meters per person).

Efforts to evaluate total water availability are hindered by data gaps and a lack of information from many parts of the world. Many national and international organizations, such as the U.S. Geological Survey in the

Water. TABLE 4. Renewable Water Resources and Water Availability by Continents*

CONTINENT	AREA (MILLION KM^2)	POPULATION (MILLIONS, 1995)	Water Resources (km^3/year) AVERAGE	MAX	MIN	Specific Water Availability (km^3/year) PER KM^2	PER CAPITA
Europe	10.46	685	2,900	3,410	2,254	277	4.23
Asia	43.5	3,445	13,510	15,008	11,800	311	3.92
Africa	30.1	708	4,050	5,082	3,073	134	5.72
North America	24.3	453	7,890	8,917	6,895	324	17.4
South America	17.9	315	12,030	14,350	10,320	672	38.2
Australia and Oceania	8.95	28.7	2,360	2,843	1,850	264	82.2
The world	135	5,633	42,740	44,712	39,742	317	7.60

*Excluding nonrenewable water flows and Antarctic ice flows.
SOURCE: Shiklomanov (1998).

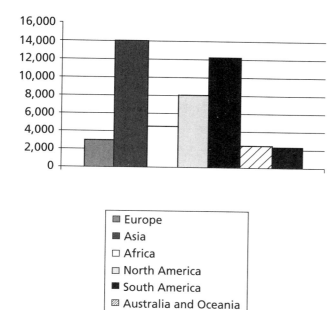

Water. FIGURE 1. Continental Average Runoff.

United States and the World Meteorological Organization of the United Nations, maintain stations to measure water availability, but these stations are unevenly distributed, maintained, and monitored. Given these limitations, care should be taken in using any particular estimates.

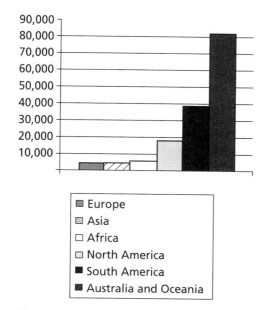

Water. FIGURE 2. Per Capita Water Availability by Continent Using 1995 Populations.

Water Use. Many of the world's water concerns are related to how much water is available for use in different qualities and at different times of the year. But many of the most serious problems also relate to how, when, and where humans use water. Water-resources development around the world has taken many different forms and directions. Huge economic expenditures have been made to modify the natural hydrologic cycle to make water more available for particular uses. Humans move, store, and redirect natural waters to make them more reliable and useful. [See e.g., Dams.] Because many humans live in cities or in arid and semiarid regions, water supplies have to be brought from distant sources. As early as five thousand years ago humans were building irrigation canals and ditches to move water from rivers to fields; designers in ancient cities were building aqueducts to permit dense urban populations to survive.

Human needs for water helped lead to advances in civil engineering and the hydrologic sciences. The Industrial Revolution and population growth of the nineteenth and twentieth centuries led to dramatic and extensive modifications of the hydrologic cycle and the construction of massive engineering projects for flood control, water supply, hydropower, and irrigation. There have been three major drivers to the enormous expansion of water-resources infrastructure in the past century: (1) population growth, (2) industrial development, and (3) expansion of irrigated agriculture. All three factors have increased dramatically. Between 1900 and 2000 the population of the world grew from 1.6 billion to over 6 billion people. Land under irrigation increased from around 50 million hectares at the turn of the century to over 260 million hectares in 2000. These and other factors have led to a nearly sevenfold increase in freshwater withdrawals (Figure 3). [See Irrigation.]

The difference in meaning among the terms *use*, *withdrawal*, and *consumption* is important here. The term *water use* encompasses many different ideas, including the withdrawal of water, gross water use, and the consumptive use of water. The term *withdrawal* refers to the act of taking water from a source for storage or use. Not all water withdrawn is necessarily consumed. For many processes, water is often withdrawn and then returned directly to the original source after use, such as water used for cooling thermoelectric power plants. *Gross water use* is distinguished from water withdrawal by the inclusion of recirculated or reused water. For many industrial processes, water requirements may exceed actual water withdrawn for use because that water is reused several times. *Water consumption* or *consumptive use* refers to the use of water in a manner that prevents its immediate reuse, such as through evaporation, plant transpiration, contamination, or incorporation into a finished product. Water withdrawn for agriculture may have both consumptive

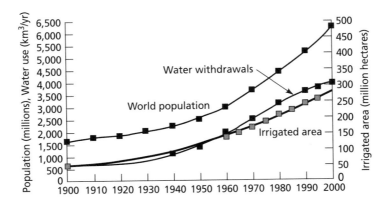

Water. Figure 3. World Population, Water Withdrawals, and Irrigated Area, 1900–2000. (Excerpted from Gleick, 1998. Copyright 1998 by Island Press. Reprinted by permission of Island Press.)

and nonconsumptive uses, as part of the water is transpired into the atmosphere or incorporated into plant material, while the remainder may return to ground water or the surface source from where it originated.

Freshwater withdrawals worldwide increased from an estimated 580 km³/yr in 1900 to 3,800 km³/yr in 1995, a sixfold increase (Table 5). In the industrialized world, the increases in withdrawals were even more dramatic. In the United States, 56 cubic kilometers were with-

drawn for all purposes in 1900. In twenty years, this had doubled to over 120 km³/yr. By 1950 total water withdrawals were 250 km³/yr and by 1970 had doubled a third time, to over 500 km³/yr. Water use in the United States peaked in 1980 at over 610 km³/yr (Solley et al., 1998)—a tenfold increase in water withdrawals during a period when population increased by a factor of four (Gleick, 1998). Globally, it is estimated that humans already appropriate 54 percent of accessible runoff on Earth and that future population growth and economic development could lead humans to use more than 70 percent of accessible runoff by 2025 (Postel et al., 1996).

Although water needs in many regions continue to grow, long-term projections of future water needs have been steadily declining. Several of these projections are shown in Figure 3. This figure also shows actual water

Water. Table 5. Dynamics of Water Use (Withdrawal and Consumption) in the World by Continents (km³/year)*

CONTINENT	1900	1940	1950	1960	1970	1980	1990	1995
Europe	37.5 / 17.6	71 / 29.8	93.8 / 38.4	185 / 53.9	294 / 81.8	445 / 158	491 / 183	511 / 187
North America	70 / 29.2	221 / 83.8	286 / 104	410 / 138	555 / 181	677 / 221	652 / 221	685 / 238
Africa	41.0 / 34.0	49.0 / 39.0	56.0 / 44.0	86.0 / 66.0	116 / 88.0	168 / 129	199 / 151	215 / 160
Asia	414 / 322	689 / 528	860 / 654	1,222 / 932	1,499 / 1,116	1,784 / 1,324	2,067 / 1,529	2,157 / 1,565
South America	15.2 / 11.3	27.7 / 20.6	59.4 / 41.7	68.5 / 44.4	85.2 / 57.8	1 11 / 71.0	152 / 91.4	166 / 97.7
Australia & Oceania	1.6 / 0.6	6.8 / 3.4	10.3 / 5.1	17.4 / 9.0	23.3 / 11.9	29.4 / 14.6	28.5 / 16.4	30.5 / 17.6
Total (rounded)	579 / 415	1,065 / 704	1,366 / 887	1,989 / 1,243	2,573 / 1,536	3,214 / 1,918	3,590 / 2,192	3,765 / 2,265

*Nominator = water withdrawal; denominator = water consumption. These numbers exclude water used directly as precipitation by crops.

SOURCE: Shiklomanov (1998).

withdrawals over time. As these data show, the earlier projections greatly overestimated future water demands by assuming that use would continue to grow at the historical rate (the dotted lines). Actual global withdrawals for 2000 turned out to be about half of what they were expected to be thirty years earlier.

Beginning in the mid-1980s and early 1990s, the historical rapid increases in demand for water slowed in many industrialized nations despite continued increases in population and economic wealth—a radical departure from the expectations and experience of water planners. Industrial water use in the United States, for example, has dropped nearly 40 percent from its peak in 1970 as industrial water-use efficiency has improved and as the mix of U.S. industries has changed. Yet industrial output and productivity have continued to soar, clearly demonstrating the possibility of breaking the link between increased water use and industrial production. New technologies for water use and new approaches to improving water-use efficiency are key to the changing nature of water planning.

In a constantly growing society with untapped and underutilized water resources, planning for growth requires planning new physical infrastructure. As a result, water agencies have always focused on engineering solutions and planned for more and more supply, just as energy planners in electric utilities did during the 1950s, 1960s, and 1970s. And just as energy planners did, water planners are suddenly coming up against physical resource constraints, economic limitations, and the accumulated environmental consequences of their prior actions. Traditional approaches to water planning are beginning to change. Among the factors driving these changes are high construction costs, tight budgets, environmental concerns, technological advances, and the development of alternative approaches to water management. The search for new solutions is also being pushed along in some places by the changing nature of demand for water. Without constantly increasing demand of 3–4 percent per year, the pressure to build new water infrastructure has diminished, because existing supplies can be reallocated to other users. But the changing philosophy away from new development has also been driven by two other important factors: the increasing concern about the environmental impacts of water projects and their increasing economic costs. More people now place a high value on maintaining the integrity of water resources and the flora, fauna, and human societies that have developed around them. There are growing calls for the costs and benefits of water management and development to be distributed in a more fair and prudent manner and for unmet basic human needs to be addressed. And more efforts are being made to understand and meet the diverse interests and needs of all affected stakeholders. If the next genera-

tion of water planners continues to try to integrate these principles, a new era of innovative water management will ensue.

Twenty-first-Century Water Issues. Problems of scarcity and quality dominated the water agenda in the twentieth century. Many of these problems are still with us and must be addressed in the coming decades. Now, however, there is a new set of issues that must also be factored into water planning, management, and policy. These include the need to meet basic human and ecosystem needs for water, the impacts of climate change for water and water systems, the risks of conflict over scarce water resources, and the use of new technology and management strategies to address water problems.

Meeting basic human and ecosystem water needs. Much of the world's population, particularly in developing countries, remains without access to clean drinking water or adequate methods to dispose of human wastes. The lack of clean drinking water and sanitation services leads to many hundreds of millions of cases of water-related diseases and between 5 million and 10 million deaths annually, primarily of small children. A concerted decade-long effort to meet these needs began in 1980 with the International Drinking Water Supply and Sanitation Decade, coordinated by the United Nations and international aid organizations. Despite the substantial progress made by 1990, rapid population growth and serious economic problems in Asia and Africa limited the overall gains. According to UN estimates, in the mid-1990s nearly 3 billion people lacked access to adequate sanitation services, while over 1.2 billion people lacked adequate clean drinking water. While most water policy makers agree that the failure to meet basic needs is the most pressing water problem facing nations, there is still little agreement about the most effective ways of meeting those needs.

In addition to the minimum water needs of humans, the water needs of the natural environment are rarely considered or guaranteed. In the United States and Europe, some minimum flow requirements have been set for rivers and some minimum quality or temperature standards have been promulgated to protect environmental assets. In the United States, legislation has protected stretches of certain pristine rivers from development, and some water has been reallocated from major water projects and users to the environment. In California, for example, a combination of federal and state laws have set aside nearly 30 billion cubic meters of annual runoff for environmental purposes, including the protection of wild and scenic rivers, the Sacramento–San Joaquin Delta, and instream and wetlands flow protections for fish and waterfowl. Similar legal efforts are underway internationally. Despite these efforts, aquatic ecosystems throughout the world are under severe stress and threat of destruction. Globally, over one thousand species of fish, amphibians, and aquatic plants are considered threatened with extinction. [*See* Extinction of Species.] Basic water requirements to protect these species and, more broadly, whole ecosystems, must be identified and provided.

Water and climate change. The world's leading climate scientists believe that we are now on the verge of changing our climate through human activities that produce trace gases, including the burning of fossil fuels, the destruction of forests, and a wide range of industrial and agricultural activities. [*See* Climate Change; Global Warming; Greenhouse Effect; Intergovernmental Panel on Climate Change; *and* Lakes.] Indeed, a growing number of scientists believe that some human-induced climatic changes are already beginning to occur or are unavoidable even if we act now to reduce our emissions of these gases. These climatic changes—the so-called greenhouse effect—will have widespread consequences for water resources and water management. The climate determines where and when it rains, the kinds of crops we grow and the water needed for their success, the location, size, and operation of dams and reservoirs, the kinds of structures we build along our coastlines, and how much water we need to drink. Among the most important consequences of the greenhouse effect will be impacts on water resources, including both the natural hydrologic system and the complex water-management schemes we have built to alter and control that system. Changes may be necessary in the design of projects being planned. Modifications may be required to existing facilities to permit them to continue to meet their design objectives. New projects may need to be built or old projects removed, and new institutions may need to be created or old ones revamped, in order to cope with possible changes.

There is little doubt that climatic change will alter the hydrologic cycle in a variety of ways, but there is little certainty about the form these changes will take or when they will be unambiguously detected. The hydrologic system—an integrated component of the Earth's geophysical system—both affects and is affected by climatic conditions. Changes in temperature affect evapotranspiration rates, cloud characteristics, soil moisture, storm intensity, and snowfall and snowmelt regimes. Changes in precipitation affect the timing and magnitude of floods and droughts, shift runoff regimes, and alter groundwater recharge characteristics. Synergistic effects will alter cloud formation and extent, vegetation patterns and growth rates, and the behavior of soil moisture.

Among the expected impacts of climatic changes on water resources are increases in global average precipitation and evaporation; changes in the regional patterns of rainfall, snowfall, and snowmelt; changes in the intensity, severity, and timing of major storms; rising sea level and saltwater intrusion into coastal aquifers; and a wide range of other geophysical effects. These changes will also have many secondary impacts on freshwater resources, altering both the demand and supply of water and changing its quality.

The impacts of climate change on water-resources supply and availability will lead to direct and indirect effects on a wide range of institutional, economic, and social factors. The nature of these effects is not well understood, nor is the ability of society to adapt to them. If water managers and planners can easily and cheaply adapt to any climatic disruptions that may occur, actions to prevent climate change will be less urgent. If we overestimate our ability to adapt, we may ignore inexpensive and successful actions that can reduce the impacts of climate change early.

Adaptation and innovative management will certainly be a useful and necessary response to climatic changes. Several factors, however, suggest that relying solely or even principally on adaptation may prove a dangerous policy. First, the impacts of climate change on the water sector will be very complicated and at least partly unpredictable. Second, many impacts may be nonlinear and chaotic, characterized by surprises and unusual events. Third, climatic changes will be imposed on water systems that will be increasingly stressed by other factors, including population growth, competition for financial resources from other sectors, and disputes over water allocations and priorities. Finally, some adaptive strategies may help mitigate some adverse consequences of climate change while simultaneously worsening others.

Many difficulties hinder clear assessments of the impacts of climate changes on global or regional hydrology. [*See* Intergovernmental Panel on Climate Change.] Important hydrologic processes occur at fairly small spatial scales that are not yet capable of being accurately modeled. Limitations in data availability and quality affect our ability to validate models or verify results accurately. And the complex human modifications of watersheds must be incorporated into any detailed analysis of impacts and adaptation.

Conflicts over shared water resources. There is a long history of conflicts over water shared by two or more political entities (see the chronology of water-related conflicts at http://www.worldwater.org). Fresh water is integral to all ecological and societal activities, including the production of food and energy, transportation, waste disposal, industrial development, and human health. Yet the uneven and irregular distribution of water leads to local and international frictions and tensions, particularly in regions short of water. Not all water-resources disputes will lead to violent conflict; indeed, most lead to negotiations, discussions, and non-violent resolutions. But in certain regions of the world, water is a scarce resource that is becoming increasingly important for economic and agricultural production and increasingly scarce owing to growing population and resource degradation. In these regions, shared water is evolving into an issue of high politics, and the probability of water-related disputes is increasing. As we move into the twenty-first century, water and water-supply systems are increasingly likely to be both instruments of political conflict and the objectives of military action as human populations grow, standards of living improve, and global climatic changes make water supply and demand more problematic and uncertain.

There are four major links between water and conflict. Water has been used as a military and political goal. Water has been used as a weapon of war. Water-resources systems have been targets of war. And inequities in the distribution, use, and consequences of water resources management and use can be a source of tension and dispute (Gleick, 1998). These links can occur at local, national, and international levels.

Policy makers must be alert to the likelihood of disagreements over water resources and to possible changes in international water law, regional political arrangements, and patterns of use that could minimize the risk of conflict. Various regional and international approaches exist for reducing water-related tensions. Among the approaches are legal agreements, the application of proper technology, institutions for dispute resolution, and innovative water management. Unfortunately, these mechanisms have never received the international support or attention necessary to resolve many conflicts over water. Efforts by the United Nations, international aid agencies, and local communities to ensure access to clean drinking water and adequate sanitation can reduce the competition for limited water supplies and the economic and social impacts of widespread waterborne diseases. Improving the efficiency of water use in agriculture can extend limited resources, increase water supplies for other users, strengthen food self-sufficiency, reduce hunger, and lower expenditures for imported food. In regions with shared water supplies, third-party participation in resolving water disputes can also help end conflicts.

Improving the productivity of water use. A key component of nonstructural approaches to water-resources management is the growing focus on using water more productively. In the late 1980s and early 1990s, arguments against developing new supplies of water began to gain favor, driven in part by concerns over the high costs of new large dams and irrigation systems and over the accumulating environmental consequences of past actions. During this period, it was argued that the need to develop new sources of water

supply could largely be avoided by implementing intelligent water conservation and demand management programs, installing new efficient equipment, and applying appropriate economic and institutional incentives to shift water among users.

Vast improvements in water-use efficiency appear possible in almost all sectors in both developed and developing countries. While many developing countries could benefit from increases in overall water availability, existing systems often waste much of the available supply through poor distribution systems, faulty or old equipment, and inappropriately designed or maintained irrigation systems. In Jordan, for example, at least 30 percent of all domestic water supplies never reach users because of flaws and inadequacies in the water-supply network, and the losses reach 50 percent in Jordan's capital, Amman (Salameh and Bannayan, 1993). It has been estimated that the amount of water lost in Mexico City's supply system is equal to the amount needed to supply a city the size of Rome (Falkenmark and Lindh, 1993). Gupta et al. (1989) describe how increased water prices and government restrictions on wastewater discharges encouraged the Zuari Agro-Chemical fertilizer plant in Goa, India, to reduce total daily water use 50 percent between 1982 and 1988. Similar efforts in Tianjin, China, reduced industrial water use per unit of industrial output there by about 60 percent, and economic incentives led to improvements in industrial water-use efficiency by between 42 and 62 percent in three industrial plants in São Paulo, Brazil, in the early 1980s (Bhatia and Falkenmark, 1992).

Great improvements are possible in the industrialized world as well. Industrial output in Japan has steadily risen since the 1970s, while total industrial water use there has dropped more than 25 percent. In 1965 Japan used nearly 48,000 cubic meters of water to produce a million dollars of industrial output; by 1989 this had dropped to 13,000 cubic meters of water per million dollars of output (in real terms)—a tripling of industrial water productivity (Postel, 1997). In California, where water use has been subject to close scrutiny for years, great potential still exists for reducing water use without sacrificing economic productivity or personal welfare. Total industrial water use in California dropped 30 percent between 1980 and 1990 without any formal or intentional efforts, because of natural economic and technological changes that occurred during the decade. Over the same period, total gross industrial production rose 30 percent in real terms (Gleick et al., 1995; Gleick, 1998).

In all economic activities, water demands depend on two factors—what is being produced and the efficiency with which it is produced. Total water use thus depends on the mix of goods and services demanded by society and on the processes chosen to generate those goods and services. Making a ton of steel in the 1930s consumed sixty to one hundred tons of water. Today that same steel can be produced with less than six tons of water. Yet producing a ton of aluminum today requires only one and a half tons of water (Gleick, 1993). Replacing old steel-making technology with new can reduce water needs. Replacing steel with aluminum, as has been happening for many years in the automobile industry for other reasons, can also reduce water needs.

Water-use efficiency can also be improved in outdoor gardens, municipal lawns, golf courses, and other urban landscapes. In some parts of the United States, as much as half of all residential or institutional water demand goes to watering gardens and lawns. Improvements in watering efficiency could reduce that demand substantially, as could changes in the composition of these gardens. "Xeriscaping"—the use of drought-resistant plants—is being pursued in many major western U.S. cities. Innovative garden designs, combined with new technology, can reduce outdoor water use in homes by 25 to 50 percent or more depending on homeowner's preferences, the price of water, and the cost of alternatives (Gleick et al., 1995). In some regions, outdoor municipal and institutional landscape irrigation is being done with reclaimed water, completely eliminating the use of potable water for this purpose.

Agriculture is the largest single user of water, and this water use is largely inefficient—water is lost as it moves through leaky pipes and unlined aqueducts, as it is distributed to farmers, and as it is applied to grow crops. Some analysts estimate that the overall efficiency of agricultural water use worldwide is only 40 percent (Postel, 1997), meaning that more than half of all water diverted for agriculture never produces food. Even modest improvements in irrigation efficiency can free up vast quantities of water for growing more food or for meeting other needs. New sprinkler designs, such as low-energy precision application (LEPA), can increase sprinkler efficiencies from 60 to 70 percent to as high as 95 percent. Drip irrigation, invented in Israel to deal with both water scarcity and salinity problems, has expanded worldwide. Over half of Israel's irrigated land is served by drip irrigation. In California, more than 400,000 hectares of crops are watered using drip systems, and more and more crops are being covered by such methods. Where high-valued crops are grown in relatively permanent settings such as orchards and vineyards, drip irrigation is now the dominant irrigation method, and it is being used increasingly even for row crops such as strawberries, asparagus, peppers, melons, tomatoes, cotton, and sugar cane.

[See also Aral Sea, Dessication of the; Conservation; Desalination; Energy; Environmental Law; Erosion; Ground Water; Resources; Rivers and Streams; Salinization; Sanitation; Water Quality; and Water Resources Management.]

BIBLIOGRAPHY

Bhatia, R., and M. Falkenmark. "Water Resource Policies and the Urban Poor: Innovative Approaches and Policy Imperatives." Background paper for the Working Group on Water and Sustainable Urban Development, delivered at International Conference on Water and the Environment, Dublin, Ireland, 26–31 January 1992.

Falkenmark, M., and G. Lindh. "Water and Economic Development." In *Water in Crisis: A Guide to the World's Fresh Water Resources*, edited by P. H. Gleick, pp. 80–91. New York: Oxford University Press, 1993.

Gleick, P. H. *The World's Water, 1998–1999.* Washington, D.C.: Island Press, 1998.

———. *The World's Water, 2000–2001.* Washington, D.C.: Island Press, 2000.

———, ed. *Water in Crisis: A Guide to the World's Fresh Water Resources.* New York: Oxford University Press, 1993.

Gleick, P. H., P. Loh, S. Gomez, and J. Morrison. *California Water, 2020: A Sustainable Vision.* Oakland, Calif.: Pacific Institute for Studies in Development, Environment, and Security, 1995.

Gupta, D. B., M. N. Murty, and R. Pandey. *Water Conservation and Pollution Abatement in Indian Industry.* New Delhi, India: National Institute of Public Finance and Policy, 1989.

Intergovernmental Panel on Climate Change. "Hydrology and Freshwater Ecology." In *Climate Change, 1995: Impacts, Adaptations, and Mitigation of Climate Change.* Contribution of Working Group II to the Second Assessment Report of the Intergovernmental Panel on Climate Change. Cambridge: Cambridge University Press, 1996.

Postel, S. *Last Oasis: Facing Water Scarcity.* 2d ed. New York: Worldwatch Institute, Norton, 1997.

Postel, S. L., G. C. Daily, and P. R. Ehrlich. 1996. "Human Appropriation of Renewable Fresh Water." *Science* 271 (9 February 1996), 785–788.

Salameh, E., and H. Bannayan. *Water Resources of Jordan: Present Status and Future Potentials.* Amman, Jordan: Friedrich Ebert Stiftung, 1993.

Shiklomanov, I. "World Fresh Water Resources." In *Water in Crisis: A Guide to the World's Fresh Water Resources*, edited by P. H. Gleick, 13–24. New York: Oxford University Press, 1993.

———. "World Water Resources and World Water Use." Data archive from the State Hydrological Institute, St. Petersburg, Russia, 1998.

Solley, W. B., R. R. Pierce, and H. A. Perlman. *Estimated Use of Water in the United States in 1995.* U.S. Geological Survey Circular 1200. Denver: U.S. Department of the Interior, 1998.

Van Hylckama, T. E. A. "Water Balance and Earth Unbalance." In *Symposium on World Water Balance* 2: 434–444. International Association of Scientific Hydrology Publication No. 93. Paris: UNESCO, 1970.

—PETER H. GLEICK

WATER QUALITY

Water quality has many definitions. For geochemists the term refers simply to the chemical composition of a water sample: a set of concentrations, chemical speciations (such as NO_3^-, NH_4^+, NO_2^-, organic nitrogen) and physical partitions (such as dissolved, colloidal, fine particulate, or coarse particulate matter; Chapman, 1996). For most ecologists it refers to the physicochemical conditions of an aquatic system that may sustain a healthy aquatic biota community in equilibrium with the local natural conditions. For sanitary engineers, water quality is considered at a given location mostly with regard to human health, including concerns over water-borne and water-related diseases. Finally, water management engineers define the water quality depending on its potential uses by humans, such as drinking water, irrigation, industrial use, transportation, or power generation. [*See* Energy; *and* Irrigation.]

Descriptors of water quality include: physical (color, transparency, pH, temperature, and total suspended solids or TSS), chemical (for water and particulates), bacteriological (total coliforms and fecal coliforms), and ecological (chlorophyll, biotic indices) characteristics. An extension of water quality is now made to include the overall quality of the aquatic ecosystem, based on the water, the particulate matter, the health of the biological communities and organisms, and the nature of the riverbed. Such broader definitions also take into account the time variability of the physicochemical conditions, including water level and water velocity (Chapman, 1996).

In many regions of the world, the most critical health issue is still water-borne and water-related diseases such as malaria, bacterial diarrhea, and onchocerciasis and schistosomiasis (bilharzia), related to parasites. These issues still affect a much greater population than that exposed to severe chemical pollution. Water-related diseases require the treatment of both wetlands (for malaria) and fast-flowing waters (for onchocerciasis) by appropriate pesticides, particularly in densely populated tropical regions, by filtration, or by chemical processes. Such issues will not be treated here as for the radioactivity issue. [*See* Disease; *and* Human Health.]

Pollution is here considered as a broad generic term for the impacts on natural or artificial aquatic systems caused by anthropogenic activities that may adversely affect aquatic biota, reduce actual and potential water uses, impair human health, or reduce water-related amenities. [*See* Pollution.] The water quality descriptors, or variables, have greatly increased in number (Figure 1), and sometimes evolved in nature, since the first regular monitoring began a hundred years ago at some cities' water intakes (e.g., Paris), or downstream from major sources of pollution (e.g., London). At that time only few descriptors were considered, including NH_4^+, temperature, dissolved oxygen (DO or O_2), and total coliforms. The development of analytical chemistry and the increasing use of water for irrigation led to the monitoring of major ions (Ca^{++}, Mg^{++}, Na^+, K^+, Cl^-, $SO_4^=$, HCO_3^-) and of dissolved silica (SiO_2). These are sometimes measured as total dissolved solids (TDS), which are proportional to electrical conductivity (expressed in $\mu S.cm^{-1}$). When properly analyzed, the cations sum (TZ^+ in eq/L) should be equal to the anions sum (TZ^-).

Since the 1930s the biological oxygen demand, measured at five days (BOD_5), and the chemical oxygen demand (COD) have been used to assess changes in dissolved oxygen in rivers receiving untreated waste waters. Nutrient elements (N, P, Si) that are taken up by phytoplankton and macrophytes during photosynthesis have not been routinely monitored before the 1950s or 1960s, when eutrophication—the overdevelopment of algae (autochthonous organic matter)—was first considered as a serious issue. Chlorophyll a, the photosynthesis pigment expressed in $\mu g/L$, and phaeopigments, its decaying form, are now widely surveyed in lakes, reservoirs, and more recently rivers exposed to eutrophication.

In the 1960s and 1970s, developments in analytical equipment permitted the regular monitoring of toxic metals (Cd, Cu, Hg, Pb, Zn) and metalloids (As, Se, Sn). In the 1980s, other sets of parameters were considered, such as dissolved (DOC), particulate (POC), and total organic carbon (TOC), which replaced the former permanganate or dichromate oxidation values.

Specific organic substances that may occur naturally in some waters, such as hydrocarbons and phenols, as well as substances that are purely the result of human

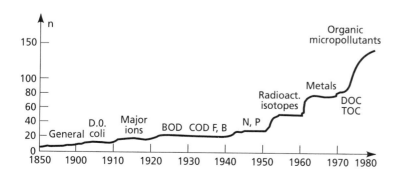

Water Quality. FIGURE 1. Evolution of the Total Number of Chemical Descriptors of Water Quality Used in Monitoring Programs. (After Meybeck and Helmer, 1989).

activities—xenobiotic substances—are now analyzed in waters or particulates through a great variety of techniques, such as high pressure liquid chromatography (HPLC). Following these technical developments and the exponential use of the new organic molecules produced, the list of water quality parameters regularly monitored in some locations jumped from thirty in the 1960s to more than one hundred now (Chapman, 1996), including such highly toxic substances as polychlorinated biphenyls (PCBs), other chlorinated hydrocarbons such as dichlorodiphenyltrichloroethane (DDT) and lindane, polyaromatic hydrocarbons such as anthracene (PAHs), perchloroethylene (PCE), and trichloroethylene (TCE).

There is a continuum of river-borne material, from sand to true dissolved substances. The conventional filtration on 0.45 or 0.5 μm pore filters still differentiate the "dissolved" from the particulate states, although colloids are arbitrarily split between these classes.

Natural Water Quality. The major natural origins of river-borne material include atmospheric inputs of oceanic and terrestrial origins (Figure 2, flux A), chemical weathering of minerals, mechanical erosion of rock and soil particles, and soil leaching (Drever, 1988; Hem, 1989), which transits through the surface and subsurface (flux B) or through ground waters (flux C). Bio-

geochemical processes within water bodies (flux E), such as algal uptake, and at their interfaces or ecotones (flux D), such as denitrification, may modify the dissolved concentrations, as may evaporation (flux F).

In pristine conditions, only natural sources and pathways are present in aquatic systems, thus defining the natural background quality. Because of the global transport of atmospheric contaminants, near-pristine conditions now occur only in some subarctic regions (e.g., Siberia, Northern America) and in parts of the humid tropics (e.g., central Amazon and Congo River basins).

The most salient feature of atmospheric inputs is the general exponential decrease from the coast to inland of Cl^- and related elements derived from oceanic aerosols (Na^+, Mg^{++}, and $SO_4^=$ with a ratio to Cl^- similar to that of sea water). As a result, small coastal streams located in poorly weathered basins (granite, sandstone, etc.) are often dominated by oceanic Na^+ and Cl^-, the typical "rain-dominated" type (Gibbs, 1970). If atmospheric inputs are important or contaminated, these waters may even be of the $Ca^{++}-SO_4^=$ or $Na^+-SO_4^=$ types.

At the streams scale (10 square kilometers [km^2]), the resulting rock-weathering water chemistry can be quite variable depending on local lithology. Different ionic assemblages such as $Ca^{++}-HCO_3^-$, $Mg^{++}-HCO_3^-$, $Na^+-SO_4^=$, $Ca^{++}-SO_4^=$, and Na^+-Cl^- can be found (Mey-

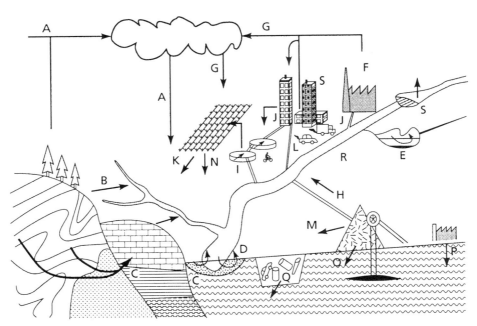

Water Quality. FIGURE 2. Major Natural and Anthropogenic Sources and Pathways of Water-Borne Material.

Natural sources and pathways: A. Oceanic and salt fallout; B. Soil leaching and erosion; C. Mineral dissolution by ground water; D. Biogeochemical processes at ecotones; E. Processes within water bodies; F. Evaporation. Anthropogenic sources and pathways: G. Atmospheric pollution; H. Direct release of mine water;

I. Release of urban waste waters; J. Release of industrial waste waters; K. Runoff from agricultural land; L. Runoff from urban areas; M. Runoff from mine tailing; N. Leaching of contaminated soils to ground waters; O. Leaching of mine tailing to ground waters; P. Pollutant dumps leaks; Q. Waste release to ground waters. R. River channelization; S. Damming.

beck, 1986; Hem, 1989). The sum of major cations (TZ^+) varies from 60 to 30,000 μeq/L, and the dissolved silica from 1.2 to 36 mg/L. Therefore, the well-used Gibb's assumption (1970) of rock-weathering dominance characterized only by the Ca^{++}–HCO_3^- type does not apply at the stream scale (Meybeck, 1986). In river basins with areas greater than 100,000 km^2, however, the Ca^{++}–HCO_3^- type largely dominates, owing to the greater lithological homogeneity and to the general occurrence of calcite at such a scale. Examples of lithological control on tropical rivers and streams are given in Table 1.

Under arid and semiarid conditions, surface waters gradually evaporate, leading to a gradual precipitation of carbonates and to salinization. These "evaporated" waters are common in arid regions in Central Asia, the Middle East, the southwestern United States, Mexico, and Argentina, and in most endorheic basins (i.e., not flowing to oceans). A full gradient of surface water salinization resulting from climatic conditions has been described by Russian scientists (Tsirkunov, chapter 6 in Kimstach et al., 1998). Such rivers are usually non-perennial and highly mineralized ($TZ^+ > 8$ μeq/L, TDS $> 1g/L$); an example is Oued Sahoura, 45,000 km^2, in southeastern Morocco (Table 2).

In closed or endorheic lakes there is a full spectrum of total dissolved solids, from a few g/L up to 400g/L; most common are combinations of Ca^{++}, Mg^{++}, and Na^+ and of Cl^-, $SO_4^=$, and HCO_3^-. Such environments may accumulate precious minerals such as natron (Na_2CO_3), bromide, and lithium salts, which are mined in Lake Natron (Kenya), the Dead Sea, and Kara Bogaz (Kazakhstan).

In most exorheic lakes (with an outlet), water chemistry reflects inputs from river systems and the atmosphere. A great variety of chemical types can be found, similar to those of Table 1, with a major dominance of the Ca^{++}–HCO_3^- type, at global scale, as for major rivers.

Groundwater chemistry depends on the depth of aquifers. For alluvial and other surficial aquifers, as for surficial waters, elemental concentrations depend mostly on the dominant minerals, and their ranges are very close to those found in Table 1. Such aquifers are also very sensitive to climate conditions: in Russia the main factor regulating groundwater chemistry is the water deficiency (or deficit; Polkanov, in Kimstach et al., 1998). In deeper waters the temperature increase and the long residence time modify the water-rock interaction: Ca^{++}, $SO_4^=$, or Na^+–Cl^- types gradually replace the common Ca^{++}–HCO_3^- type found in surficial aquifers. Deep ground waters, when anoxic, are much enriched in reduced species, such as H_2S and highly soluble Fe^{++} and Mn^{++}.

The leaching of soil organic matter during rainfall or snowmelt, releases allochtonous dissolved and particulate organic matter, usually analyzed as DOC and POC, with small amounts of NO_3^- and NH_4^+. Those carbon and nitrogen compounds originate from the atmosphere through CO_2 uptake and nitrogen fixation during the photosynthesis of terrestrial vegetation. In rivers and lakes the natural DOC commonly varies between 1 and 10 mg/L. NO_3^- and NH_4^+ in pristine rivers are less than 0.3 mgN/L and 0.05 mgN/L, respectively. The other key nutrient, orthophosphate ($H_2PO_4^-$ mostly, generally reported as P–PO_4^{-3}) also originates from soil leaching, but its primary source is the weathering of parent rock. Natural levels of P–PO_4^{-3} are generally well below 30 μgP/L and can be buffered by phosphorus circulation between soils and terrestrial vegetation. When the weathering rate is low, many elemental cycles (K, N, P, S, Si) may be controlled by the internal cycle within the forest stand from root uptake to fallen leaves decay. After logging, these cycles are broken, and a general release of elements is noted in surficial waters.

Water Quality Issues in Natural Conditions. Depending on local or regional conditions, the water qual-

Water Quality. TABLE 1. Lithological Influences on Perennial and Nonperennial Tropical Rivers (milligrams per liter)

LITHOLOGY*	SiO_2	Ca^{+2}	Mg^{+2}	Na^+	K^+	Cl^-	SO_4^{-2}	NCO_3^-	$TZ^{+\dagger}$
1. Quartz sands	7.6	0.76	0.25	0.57	0.73	0.20	0.16	3.8	105
2. Noncarbonated sandstone	13.2	2.2	0.70	2.0	1.2	2.7	—	12.1	285
3. Plutonic/metamorphic	11.7	3.2	1.0	2.9	0.95	1.05	2.8	18.1	394
4. Misc. volcanic	22.4	6.1	5.8	9.1	3.1	3.2	1.6	68.7	1,260
5. Basaltic	75	27.3	14.1	10.8	3.9	8.15	—	165	3,095
6. Carbonate rocks	18.6	38.5	17.6	10.2	0.8	10.3	18.1	198	3,845
7. Evaporites	12.5	111	21.5	131	7.0	200	214	181	13,200
8. Evaporated	—	122	53.2	356	7.2	582	348	152	26,150

*Analyses include a limited influence of ocean aerosols in all basins. (1) to (7) perennial rivers: (1) Tefe (Brazil), (2) Siem Reap (Cambodia), (3) Mahakam (Borneo), (4) Rivière de l'Est (Réunion), (5) Kompong Sar (Cambodia), (6) Lufira (Zaire), (7) Urubamba (Peru). (8) Nonperennial river: Oued Sahoura (Morocco) after a flood. Full references in Meybeck, 1996.

†$TZ^+ = Ca^{+2} + Na^+ + K^+$ expressed in microequivalents per liter (μeq/l).

SOURCE: From Meybeck (1996).

Water Quality. TABLE 2. Range of Natural Concentrations in Pristine Major Rivers, Drinking Water Standards, and Extreme Concentrations Found in Unpolluted Streams

SUB-STANCE*	Major Rivers		Drinking Water	Rare Unpolluted River Waters			
	RANGE (MG L^{-1})	MCNC† (MG L^{-1})	STANDARD (MG L^{-1})	EXTREME LEVEL (MG L^{-1})	EXTREME NORMAL	EXTREME DRINKING STD.	TYPE
Ca^{+2}	2–50	8.0	/	210	26		
Mg^{+2}	0.85–12	2.4	/	80	33		
Na^+	1.3–25	3.7	150	6,300	1,700	42	Salted
Cl^-	0.6–25	3.9	200	9,400	2,400	47	
SO_4^{-2}	2.2–48	4.8	250	1,300	270	5.2	
pH	6.0–8.5	7.0	—	3.2	—	—	Acidic
DOC	1.0–20	4.2		43.4	10		Humic
K^+	0.5–3.9	1.0	12	160	160	13	Geothermal
SiO_2	2.4–20	10.8		280	26		
TSS	10–1700	150‡		400,000	2,600		Turbid
TOC	3–20	7.2		2,000	280		

*DOC = dissolved organic carbon; TOC = total organic carbon; TSS = total suspended solids.

†Most common natural concentration (Meybeck and Helmer, 1989).

‡Discharge weighted means.

SOURCE: Meybeck (1996).

ity of rivers may differ by two or three orders of magnitude from the "most common natural concentration" of chemicals as defined on major pristine rivers (Meybeck and Helmer, 1989). Such rare unpolluted water can still be unsuitable for some human uses, just as sea water is not fit for drinking (Table 2).

In addition to the "evaporated" type, five different types of such extreme river waters have been defined (Meybeck, 1996). (1) *Salted rivers* result from the dissolution of dominant evaporitic minerals (gypsum, halite). They can be found in any continent and under any climatic conditions. Salted rivers are characterized by highly mineralized Ca^{++}–$SO_4^=$ or Na^+–Cl^- or a combination of both (with $TZ^+ > 6$ μeq/L; see the Urubamba river in Peru, Table 1). About 1 percent of the continental area is underlain by evaporitic deposits. (2) *Acidic streams* or reaches are caused by inputs from acidic springs or lakes linked to active volcanism (Indonesia, Japan). Their pH is commonly below five and their mineralization is high ($TZ^+ > 6$ μeq/L). (3) *Geothermal rivers* are also linked to volcanism and can be characterized by very high SiO_2, K^+, F^-, or As concentrations. They are found in East Africa, Japan, New Zealand, and the United States. (4) *Humic rivers*, with very high DOC levels ($10 < DOC < 40$ mg/L, pH < 5.5), are found downstream of peat bogs or in poorly drained terrains. These waters are generally very poor in cations ($TZ^+ < 0.1$ μeq/L) and can be common in such regions as the central Amazon and Congo River basins and tun-

dra rivers. (5) *Turbid rivers* are characterized by high TSS ($>> 1$ g/L) and are found in some specific regions such as northeastern China (Huang He basin).

For some ground waters, and in the deep layers of nonmixed (meromictic) lakes as Tanganyika, Kivu, and Malavi, the natural concentrations of minerals may also render the water unfit for drinking and other human uses. Such ground waters are widely found in all continents, for example in northern Chile (arsenic), Senegal and Tanzania (fluoride), and Radjasthan (fluoride, TDS). In Bengal the very high arsenic illness of local farmers may have been enhanced by local geochemical changes due to groundwater uses. In all the instances, the natural water quality exceeds one or several guidelines for drinking water quality (see Table 2). Yet many of these water sources are used every day by local populations.

Common and Frequent Water Quality. The variability of water quality in time and space is important. The following definitions for spatial distribution over a given territory have been proposed (Meybeck, 1996): concentrations are considered "common" between deciles C_{10} and C_{90}, "uncommon" from C_1 to C_{10} and from C_{90} to C_{99}, "rare" from $C_{0.1}$ to C_1 and from C_{99} to $C_{99.9}$, and "very rare" outside $C_{0.1}$ and $C_{99.9}$. These definitions can be applied to both natural and actual chemical compositions. Many natural distributions are log-normal ones, which correspond to a straight line on a log-probability diagram (Figure 3). In natural conditions the upper decile (C_{90}) of the spatial distribution

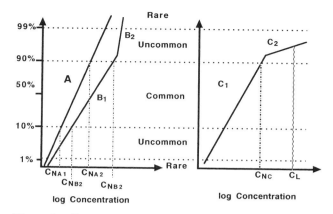

Water Quality. FIGURE 3. Cumulative Statistical Distributions of Natural Chemical Concentration over a Given Territory (Based on Averages at Each Station).

A = Nonreactive element of single natural origin (e.g., K^+).
B = Element reaching a saturation limit (e.g., Ca^{++} and HCO_3^-).
C = Element of more than one origin (e.g., Na^+). C_{N1-2} = Range of common natural levels. C_L = Example of regulatory concentration for a specific human use.

can be considered to define the upper value of the "natural" range (C_{N2} on Figure 3). For example, the natural variability of SO_4^- concentration in the Lower Amazon, the Mackenzie River basin, and unpolluted French streams can be compared. In the Lower Amazon, SO_4^- levels are among the world's lowest ($C_1 = 0.75$mg/L; $C_{99} = 2.5$ mg/L); they mostly originate from atmospheric sulfur recycling over the rainforest (see Tefe River, Table 1). In the Mackenzie River (Canada), the range is wider ($C_1 = 1.3$mg/L, $C_{99} = 300$mg/L), while in French streams it is from 1.1 to 800 mg/L.

When the monitoring activity is regular, temporal distribution of concentrations can be set up at each station for a given period and various quantiles can be determined (C_1, C_{10}, C_{50}, C_{90}, C_{99}, and sometimes C_{99} for the longest records). It is here proposed to describe as "frequent" the concentration interval between the lower and upper deciles C_{10} to C_{90}, "infrequent" from C_1 to C_{10} and from C_{90} to $C_{99.9}$, "occasional" from $C_{0.1}$ to C_1, and from C_{99} to $C_{99.9}$, and "exceptional" for the rest of the distribution.

Contaminants Origins and Pathways, Modifications of Aquatic Systems. Most pathways of contaminants to surface and ground waters are similar to those of natural compounds: as atmospheric pollution (Figure 2, flux G); direct release of treated or untreated waste waters from mines (H), cities (I), and industries (J); runoff from agricultural land (K), urbanized areas (L), and mine tailings (M); and leaching of contaminated soil waters to ground waters from agriculture (N), mines (O), industries (P), and dump leaks (Q). When contaminant inputs can be collected and treated they are re-

ferred to as *point sources*, while sources that cannot be collected, typically atmospheric fallout and agricultural runoff, are called *diffuse sources*. Intermediate types of sources such as cars and scattered housing, that can be collected or treated individually, may be termed *dispersed sources*.

River channelization (Figure 2, flux R), wetland filling, river damming (S) associated with reservoir construction, and sand extraction in floodplains correspond to another category of important impacts on aquatic systems. They all modify the river/ground water interface that regulates the concentrations of such key compounds as NO_3^- and O_2. Most reservoirs store from 70 to 99 percent of incoming particulates, with attached toxins and nutrients, which in turn may be released from the sediments to the bottom layers if anoxic conditions are established, a common feature of deep reservoirs. These modifications have a global impact on aquatic communities, particularly for the thousands of major reservoirs exceeding fifteen meters in height.

Water Quality Regime. Time scales of chemical variations range from the minute to secular trends. If water quality regimes can be described, they are even more complex than water discharge regimes: each water quality descriptor has its peculiar variability, most of the time station-specific. Unlike water discharge, only a few descriptors can be continuously monitored *in situ* (pH, conductivity, dissolved oxygen, turbidity, chlorophyll), or through online measurements, as for some total metals and total organic micropollutants at sophisticated automatic alert stations. Therefore the great majority of chemical information still comes from discrete samples taken in the field and analyzed in the laboratory: there is generally no access to the real-time variability of water quality.

In rivers, sample frequency is typically around twelve per year; that is, it is implicitly assumed that the seasonal variability is far greater than those found at shorter periods, such as day/night variability, and during flood events. This assumption is generally not valid in small and medium basins ($<100,000$ km²). The principal cause of variations in concentration (Ci) is the change in water discharge (Q) linked to mixing of waters (e.g., soil water and ground water, different tributaries, sewage effluent diluted in receiving waters). The Ci versus Q relations are multiple (Figure 4) and present dilution patterns (type 4), leaching patterns (type 2), simple (type 1) and complex (type 3) erosion/deposition patterns of particulates, and complex dilution/leaching pattern (type 5). The very few concentrations that are stable with Q (type 6) are mostly linked to atmospheric inputs. Such variations linked with discharge are much shorter for streams and small river basins (a few hours to a few days) than for major rivers (up to a few weeks).

Pollution maxima generally occur during low flows,

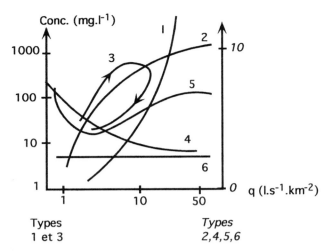

Types
1 et 3

Types
2,4,5,6

Water Quality. FIGURE 4. Typical Concentrations versus Discharge Relationships in Rivers (q in $l.s^{-1}.km^{-2}$).

1. Simple erosion/deposition of particulates. 2. Leaching.
3. Complex erosion/deposition of particulates. 4. Dilution.
5. Complex dilution/leaching. 6. Stable.

but other peaks of contaminants, lasting from a few days to a few weeks depending on river size, are related to the first flushing of agricultural soils by rainfall after pesticide application (Figure 4, types 2 and 3). In many cases these peaks exceed the water quality standards but are generally missed by routine monitoring with fixed sampling days and monthly frequency. The daily, weekly, or seasonal release of waste waters in rivers may also result in specific variations.

Multiple time scales of water quality variation can be observed at a given station. In the regulated alpine Rhone, upstream from Lake Geneva, which is continuously monitored for electrical conductivity, pH, O_2, and temperature, the following processes are observed: (1) daily quality variations linked to water discharge cycles resulting from snow and ice melt in spring and summer and from the daily operations of large alpine valley reservoirs in autumn and winter; (2) the impact of rainstorm flood events, typically lasting some days; (3) very regular weekly cycles throughout the year due to reservoir operation; (4) seasonal variations marked by low winter flow and summer glacier melt, resulting in more turbid and more dilute waters, respectively; (5) moderate year-to-year variations (humid/dry and cold/warm), with higher maximum discharges during hotter summers; and (6) general trends over twenty years, such as an increase in Cl^- and Na^+ due to deicing salts and an increase then decrease of PO_4^{-3}.

Time Lags of Water Quality Issues. Water quality issues are characterized by multiple time scales: contamination length, pollution remediation length, recovery duration, and the time variability of chemical concentrations (e.g., daily variations and trends). The duration of contamination depends on the water residence time: a few days or months for rivers, a few months to decades for surficial aquifers and most lakes. The largest aquatic systems generally have the longest residence times (Baikal, 350 years; Tanganyika, 500 years; Superior, 180 years), but much smaller water bodies can also be renewed very slowly, such as Lake Tahoe (250 years) or Crater Lake (150 years). When the pollution source has stopped, the period of recovery is generally two or three times longer than the contamination period. This environmental inertia is linked to contaminant storage in sediments and soils, to the nonpiston flow renewal of water and to the slow recovery of aquatic biota.

Added to these natural time lags are multiple social, political, and technical time lags. Time is needed to detect a water quality issue in the first place, and more time is needed to develop the social and administrative awareness of the issue, to formulate a sociopolitical response leading to appropriate actions, and to marshal the financial and technical resources necessary to implement these actions. In most documented cases, these cumulative lags take decades: the trend detection can be delayed for lack of appropriate monitoring, the sociopolitical reaction may be postponed by lack of concern or by lobbying, and financial or administrative constraints may slow down the technical solutions, particularly when water bodies are shared by several countries. Meanwhile, the environmental degradation continues. The sociopolitical reaction is longer for major or shared water bodies and for slow, chronic, and diffuse types of pollution, and is shorter for acute, point-source pollutions, which are easier to detect, collect, and treat.

In western Europe, for instance, nitrate contamination started in the 1950s, but the cause-effect relationship between nitrogen fertilizer and NO_3^- increase was proven by isotopic analyses only in the early 1970s. In France, it took another fifteen years before agriculture was officially recognized as responsible for this issue. Yet the drastic changes needed in agricultural practices have not been realized or enforced for economic and political reasons. Moreover, the natural inertia of the soil and water system is great. The nitrate accumulated in the nonsaturated soil layer is likely to contaminate ground waters for more than a decade after fertilizer application. Nitrate pollution will probably be a multidecade issue. [*See* Nitrogen Cycle.]

Lake Geneva (Léman) eutrophication is another well-documented example. The first indices of algal changes were published by limnologists in the 1950s. In 1962 the official International Léman Commission was established when the lake was still oligo-mesotrophic. In the 1970s environmental measures to curb the phosphate inputs, such as generalized sewage collection and tertiary treatment were taken. The maximum phosphorus level in Léman, nine times the original 10 μg/L level, was reached in 1976 and then started to decrease very slowly. A model projection showed that this trend was too slow to save the lake, and in 1986 a complete ban of phosphorus detergents in Switzerland led to a marked acceleration of phosphorus decrease, with levels close to 40 μg/L in 1996—still above the target. Yet the excess phosphorus load stored in the lake will continue to be released from anoxic sediments for a long time. Even though the sociopolitical response to this environmental issue was extremely rapid in this case, the lake response (water residence time is twelve years) is very long. It will take another decade or two before the chlorophyll and dissolved oxygen levels return to those recorded in the 1950s.

Global Trends in Water Quality. On a multiyear scale, changes in land and water use, urbanization, industrialization, deforestation, and pollution control activities (regulation, prevention, waste collection and treatment, water reuse, landscape engineering) gradually change the quality of water bodies. General trends of water quality are difficult to describe because both deterioration and improvements are found (United Nations Environment Programme [UNEP], 1994, 1995, 1996). Yet a broad picture can be drawn on the basis of a few water chemistry records for forty to one hundred years, environmental archives of particulate pollution (registered in sediment cores from river flood plains, deltas, lakes, and estuaries), and expanding water quality monitoring since the 1970s.

Fecal contamination has now improved in most western countries (Europe, North America). Maximum counts between 10,000 or 100,000 total coli per 100 ml were frequently observed in the 1960s and 1970s. They have decreased as the result of domestic sewage collection and treatment. In such heavily populated and fast-developing countries as China, India, Brazil, Mexico, Indonesia, and Nigeria, fecal contamination may still be the number one water quality issue. Yet, where wastewater treatment increases faster than population, an improvement can be observed: over the last ten years the peak contamination of total coli of the Lower Ganges at Rajmahal dropped from more than 100,000/100 ml to few 1,000/100 ml, according to the Central Pollution Control Board in Delhi.

In many western Europe rivers (Rhine, Thames, Seine, Scheldt) where the population density is high ($>$250 people/km^{-2}), the dissolved oxygen levels were once below the 2 mg/L limit for cyprinidae fish survival and even near zero downstream of major sources of pollutants. For instance, the Rhine River (220,000 km^2) with O_2 below 3 mg/L between 1955 and 1975 and BOD_5 up to 10 mg/L, saw a spectacular increase in the mid-1970s.

Major O_2 problems can still be found during the low flow season for many rivers exposed to untreated domestic sewage.

The ammonia issue, which concerns both fishes and human health, is somewhat parallel to the fecal issue and to the oxygen demand issue. For instance, in the Rhine, NH_4^+ peaked in the early 1970s then dropped dramatically in ten years.

A global increase of nitrate originating from nitrogen fertilizers is noted in all river basins affected by agricultural activities: in western Europe (Rhine, Seine, Po, Danube), in North America (Mississippi), and China (Huang He, Chang Jiang). This trend is also noted in ground waters for the same regions. In some cases the nitrate level may now exceed the World Health Organization (WHO) drinking water standard (50 mg NO_3^-/L).

Phosphate, not a toxic substance per se but the key nutrient responsible for excess algal growth, is increasing in most populated river basins as the result of domestic sewage collection without tertiary phosphorus removal and of phosphorus detergent use since the 1950s. When environmental regulations are very strict, as for the North American Great Lakes and the Rhine basin, the PO_4^{-3} level in river and lakes has dropped considerably. These regulations combine a complete ban on phosphorus detergents, a removal of remaining phosphorus from domestic and industrial waste waters at treatment plants, and a control of total phosphorus leaching from agricultural soils. Where the phosphorus control is only starting, as in the Seine basin, the present levels may have reached fifty times the preanthropogenic values (700 μgP/L, compared to 10 to 20 μgP/L). In this river the resulting algal biomass is responsible for a marked hypoxia in the turbid estuarine zone, where bacterial respiration dominates the primary production (P/R $\ll$ 1). In lakes and reservoirs the excess algal production is responsible for the hypoxia and anoxia of bottom waters with subsequent release of NH_4^+, metals, and PO_4^{-3}, a common feature of eutrophied water bodies in western Europe, North America, and now Asia (UNEP, 1994). [See Phosphorus Cycle.]

The inputs of nitrogen and phosphorus to the oceans have been globally increased by a factor of three and by factors of ten to fifty at some regional and local scales. Dissolved silica, used by diatoms, is not released to aquatic systems by man's activities; on the contrary, its uptake by diatoms as a result from eutrophication results in a long-term SiO_2 decrease in eutrophied rivers. The N:P:Si ratio in rivers is one of the fastest and most remarkable global changes and will ultimately affect coastal ecosystems, such as in Louisiana and Romania.

Many major ions, such as Na$^+$, Cl$^-$, and SO$_4^=$, steadily increase in many rivers and lakes. On exceptional occasions they exceed WHO recommendations, as in dry environments such as Colorado, Amu Dar'ya, and Syr

Dar'ya, when much water is withdrawn and then returned after irrigation and subsequent evaporation. For the Lower Amu Dar'ya $SO_4^=$ increased from a natural range of 200 to 300 mg/L in the 1950s. Now the range is between 600 to 750 mg/L, well above WHO guideline of 250 mg/L (Tsirkunov, in Kimstach et al, 1998).

Trends in heavy metals are much more difficult to assess owing to a lack of reliable data. In few cases, long-term trends have been derived from sediment cores or by past suspended sediments analyses (Table 3). The highest increase of metals (tens to hundreds of times larger than the natural background) are observed in small and medium-sized basins (Seine, Rhine), where the additional metal inputs are not much diluted by particulates such as clays and quartz. In bigger basins the contamination is much less obvious, as for the major Chinese rivers or the Mississippi, which carry 100 millions tons of TSS. A slight (10 μg/g) decrease in particulate lead in the Mississippi sediments from 1970 to the early 1980s implies an enormous change in lead transport of the order of two thousand tons per year, which has been attributed mostly to atmospheric lead control. In a few industrialized regions, waste collection and recycling have been successful. In the Rhine the marked decrease in the 1970s of most toxic inorganic products—arsenic, cadmium, mercury, lead—is still going on now (Table 3). In the River Seine, levels up to 10 μg/g of mercury and 50 μg/g of cadmium—that is, more than one hundred times the natural background levels—were measured downstream of local industrial sources of pollutions in the 1980s. These extreme peaks are no longer found, but the present metal contents in the particulates

downstream of Paris are still more than ten times the natural background values for cadmium and mercury, and well exceed many national standards for copper, zinc, and lead in sediments (Table 3). [*See* Metals.]

Trends of organic micropollutants are even less well documented except in sedimentary archives. Their monitoring is very recent, still expensive, and requires careful and sometimes frequent sampling. Where DDT has been banned there is a marked drop in river and lakes particulates after 1970 but traces of DDT in soil particles carried by rivers are still detectable. The manufacture of PCBs, but not their use, has now been stopped in North America and Europe, and these contaminants are always found in riverine particulates, though concentrations are beginning to decline.

New xenobiotic products appear on the global market every year. Atrazine, a widely used herbicide, started to be detected in the 1980s and is now present in many rivers where its short-term peaks may exceed WHO standard. The new generation of pesticides is less harmful than previous ones, but there is still much debate between the manufacturers of new chemicals and environmental engineers. It takes more than ten years to detect a new product in environmental samples, control its impacts, and develop the low-cost analysis procedure that permits its routine monitoring. By the time the appropriate monitoring is set up, a new chemical is put on the market.

Economic Losses Due to Poor Water Quality. Many water quality problems have multiple causes. For example, eutrophication can originate from a variety of sources, including nutrient inputs from cities, industries,

Water Quality. TABLE 3. Examples of Heavy Metal Content (micrograms per gram) in the Suspended Matter of World Rivers

	YEARS	CADMIUM	MERCURY	LEAD	ZINC
European rivers					
Seine	1976–1982	24	3.5	195	1,100
Seine	1990/1995	3.3	0.87	147	510
Rhine	1972	52	8	580	2,900
Rhine	1990	3.0	1	123	574
Po	1988/90	1.7	1.54	75	342
Other rivers					
Mississippi	1980s	1.0		39	193
Ob	>1990	0.2	0.05	15.8	50
Yenissey	>1990		0.05	30	110
Lena	>1990	0.26	0.23	23	28
Huang He	1983–1986	0.18		16	70
Chang Jiang	1984–1986	0.32		50	120
Reference values					
USSR	"background"*	0.39	0.15	6.3	31
Seine	background	0.35	0.05	19	60
Canada	"low effect limit"*	0.6	0.2	31	120
Canada	"severe effect limit"*	10	2.0	250	820

*Bottom sediments.

SOURCE: From Meybeck (1998).

Water Quality. TABLE 4. Effects of Contaminants and Some Aquatic Organisms on Water Use

	Most Demanding Uses				Least Demanding Uses		
CONTAMINANTS	DRINKING WATER	AQUATIC WILDLIFE, FISHERIES	RECREATION	INDUSTRIAL USES	IRRIGATION	POWER AND COOLING	TRANSPORT
Pathogens	xx	0	xx	0 to xx^1	x	na	na
Suspended solids	xx	xx	xx	x	x	x^2	xx^3
Organic matter[14]	xx	x	xx	x to xx^4	$+$	x^5	na
Nitrate	xx	x	na	0 to xx^1	$+$	na	na
Salts[9] (major ions)	xx	xx	na	x to xx^{10}	xx	na	na
Inorganic toxics [11]	xx	xx	x	x	x	na	na
Organic toxics	xx	xx	x	x to xx^1	x	na	na
Protons (acidification)	x	xx	x	x	na	x	na
Aquatic biota	$x^{5, 6, 15}$	x^7	$xx^{12, 15}$	x to xx^4	$+$	$x^{5, 13}$	x^8

xx: Marked impairment causing major treatment or excluding the desired use

x: Minor impairment

0: No impairment

na: Not applicable

$+$: Degraded water quality may be beneficial for this specific use

1: Food industries

2: Abrasion

3: Sediment settling in channels

4: E.g., electronic industries require low DOC

5: Filter clogging by phytoplankton

6: Odor, taste from bacteria activity

7: In fish ponds, higher algal biomass can be accepted

8: Development of water hyacinth

9: Also includes boron, fluoride, etc.

10: Ca, Fe, Mn in textile industries, etc.

11: As, Cd, Cu, Hg, Pb, Se, Sb, Sn, Zn, etc.

12: Loss of transparency from algal development

13: Development of zebra mussels in pipes

14: Both allochtonous and autochthonous

15: Algal toxins

SOURCE: Meybeck (1998). Modified from Meybeck and Helmer (1992).

agriculture, and changes in the hydrological regime of surface waters. In turn, the degradation in quality can greatly limit the water's specific uses. Drinking water, aquatic biota, and fisheries are the most demanding uses; transports, power, and cooling are among the least (Table 4).

In recent decades, new global issues related to specific aquatic organisms have also developed. The zebra mussel (*Dreissena polymorpha*) is spreading in Europe, from the Caspian Sea to the North Sea, and in North America. It is severely clogging water intakes, including the cooling pipes of nuclear power plants, and has even resulted in stopping their operation. The water hyacinth (*Eichhornia crassipes*) is now found in all tropical waters, where its algal mats may completely stop fluvial transport. Such invasions are related to the extraordinary capacities for reproduction and adaptation of both species, which have spread without much connection to water chemistry changes.

Global Pollution Hot Spots. Some single pollution sources may affect wide areas because of the amount, density, or nature of their pollutant loads. These "hot spots" include megacities, major mining and smelting areas, some industrial regions, and nuclear facilities. With respect to the last, the catastrophic Chernobyl accident has reminded the world about the possible global contamination of water from only one facility through the long-range atmospheric transport of radionuclides.

Major mining or smelting can occur anywhere, in densely populated regions (e.g., Sudbury, Ontario) or in such remote places as the sub-Arctic (e.g., Severonikel in the Kola peninsula, Norilsk in the Pyasina basin), South America, Central Africa, or New Guinea. In many of these places, environmental regulations either do not exist or are inadequately enforced. The result is that high concentrations and enormous pollution loads can be discharged to the atmosphere and surface waters, some being equivalent to natural loads originating from areas 1,000 or 100,000 times larger.

Many megacities, such as Delhi, Moscow, Paris, Chicago, and Cairo are located on rivers and have an enormous impact. The impact of Paris (10 million people) on the River Seine (65,000 km^2) can be taken as an example. About four-fifths of Paris waste water is collected and treated at a single plant. This treated sewage corresponds to a small "river" of 25 m^3/s (i.e., from 25 to 35 percent of the Seine's discharge during droughts), with still very high levels of BOD_5 (38 mg/L), NH_4^+ (24.7

mgN/L), and PO_4^{-3} (3.6 mgP/L). Before the waste water was properly treated in the 1960s, the Seine was sometimes completely anoxic in the summer season. The Seine's nitrogen and phosphorus inputs to the ocean are presently equivalent to 2 million km^2 of natural land.

Global Freshwater Issues. Table 5 presents a schematic list of mid-1990s water quality issues for various water bodies found in the well-monitored regions of the temperate Northern Hemisphere (Japan, North America, Europe, and the asiatic part of Russia; a detailed assessment can be found in Meybeck et al., 1989 and UNEP, 1994, 1995, and 1996). In the fast-developing and densely populated countries that are typical of tropical regions, this picture can be aggravated, whereas in countries with a sparse population or in very humid environments (surface runoff exceeding 500 mm/y), most issues are less critical. These issues can be grouped into a first set of chemicals-related problems and a second set of physical, biological, and health issues. Acidification is mostly related to the combination of sensitive local soils and acid atmospheric fallout.

Global climate change is presently not the most critical issue for water quality. It is much slower than most other global changes, such as water diversion and reservoir building, the global increase of inputs of nutrients, metals, and toxic organic chemicals to oceans and regional seas, and wetland filling. However, global climate change will affect semi-arid areas that are most sensitive to the modification of their water balance, where

severe salinization problems are likely in the future. In coastal zones, seawater intrusion in coastal aquifers resulting from sea level rise will be also a major issue.

Monitoring Water Quality. Monitoring water quality requires long-term, standardized measurements and observations of the aquatic environment in order to define status and trends (Meybeck et al., in Chapman, 1996). It is generally performed on a network of stations on rivers, ground waters, lakes, reservoirs, and sometimes wetlands. Since the quality varies over the three spatial dimensions as well as time, and because the analytical work can be quite expensive, some dimensions should be privileged: lateral dimensions for aquifers, longitudinal and time variations for rivers, vertical variations for lakes, and a combination of the three for reservoirs.

When they were first established twenty to forty years ago, monitoring objectives were multiple, with a long list of water quality variables, typically sampled once per month. Now more specific monitoring methods are developing (Meybeck et al., in Chapman, 1996), such as:

1. Basic surveys: identification and spatial distribution of major issues
2. Operational surveillance: water quality for specific uses or issues (e.g., metal contamination, eutrophication)
3. Trend monitoring: long-term (>10 years) repetitive

Water Quality. TABLE 5. Major Freshwater Quality Issues at the Global Scale, for Populated Regions of the Temperate Northern Hemisphere*

ISSUE	RIVERS	RESERVOIRS	LAKES	GROUND WATERS
Organic pollution	X (XX)	X (?)	X (?)	X
Eutrophication	X (X)	XX (X)[†]	X (X)	NA
Nitrate pollution	XX (X)	X (?)	O (?)	XXX (XX)
Salinization	X (XX)	O (X?)	O (?)	O (X to XX)
Metal contaminants	XX (XX)	X (?)	X (X)	XX (XX?)
Toxic organic substances	XXX (XX)	X (?)	X (X)	XX (XX?)
Acidification	X (X)	X (?)	XX (X)	O
Microbial pathogens	X (XXX)	X (X?)	X (X?)	X (XX?)
Hydrological changes	XXX (XXX)	NA	X (X)	X
Water related diseases	O (XXX)	O (XX)	O (XXX)	(XX)
Biological invasion[‡]	X (XX)		X (X)	NA
Relative recovery period[§]	Years to decades	Years	Years to centuries	Decades to centuries

Note: X = Limited issue; XX = Important issue; XXX = Critical issue; O = Very limited or local; NA = Not applicable.

*Items in parentheses represent issues for the densely populated tropical zone.

[†]In some cultures eutrophication can be regarded as beneficial.

[‡]Dreissena in temperate waters, Eichhornia in tropical waters.

[§]Higher figure for larger water bodies or high water residence time.

measurements, which may be focused on specific periods (e.g., droughts, high fluxes, summer period for lakes)

4. Emergency surveys: rapid inventory of potential pollutants and of space and time distribution for a limited period
5. Early warning surveillance: continuous, at sensitive water use locations such as water intakes at major cities (alert stations)
6. Early change detection: detection of new contaminants and new issues (e.g., screening of micropollutants at low frequency)

The original multipurpose monitorings were a combination of types 1–3. Other approaches to water quality include background surveys, mostly realized in near-pristine areas, preliminary surveys (to check space and time variability before routine monitoring), and modeling surveys (focused on processes within the water body).

Each monitoring category is defined by its station density and location, the sampling and observation frequency, the type of descriptors considered, its duration, and the interpretation lag after the field operation. For example, lake surveys are characterized by multidepths profiles, particularly where strong vertical chemical gradients are expected, and during the algal growth period; emergency surveys should provide results in twenty-four hours; and river flux monitoring is focused on flood events. Full details on monitoring activities can be found in Chapman (1996) and Adriansee et al. (1995).

All monitoring activities should include at least the following steps: definition of objectives; monitoring design; field sampling and observations, including necessary hydrological measurements (e.g., water discharge, water table level); laboratory analyses, including data quality control, data storage, treatment, and reporting; and water quality assessment with respect to water use criteria, background references, and aquatic biota conservation. After one cycle of operation, water management recommendations should be set up and the monitoring design should be questioned, optimized (dropping duplicate data), and complemented: this constitutes the monitoring spiral (Adriansee, 1995), whose operations can be regarded as a chain. Any weaker link greatly limits the chain solidity: wrong station location, wrong sampling period, poor sample preservation, lack of analytical insurance, loss of data after some time of storage, and, too often, lack of interpretation or diffusion of results.

Scales of Water Quality. Water chemistry is here regarded from three regulatory viewpoints, which require as much qualification (use of specific water quality attributes) as quantification (Figure 5). The qualification is here limited to four grades. Three sets of scales are presented (users scale, aquatic scale, and integrated scale), each divided into four categories. They are together with the temporal and spatial variation scales, which are simply descriptive.

In these scales the qualifying terms are neutral and have no negative connotation (such as "polluted"). They can be applied to any water body (surface and ground

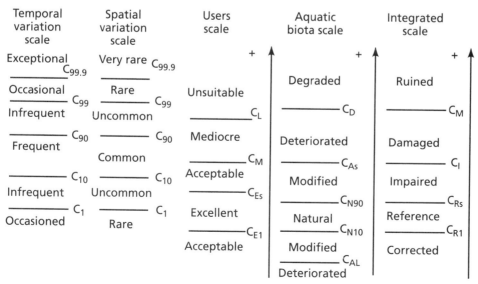

Water Quality. FIGURE 5. Attributes of Chemical Water Quality through Five Approaches.

C_1, C_{10}, C_{90}, C_{99}, $C_{99.9}$ = percentiles of statistical distributions.

C_{Ei}, C_{Es}, C_M, C_L; C_{AL}, C_{As}, C_D; C_{Ri}, C_{Rs}, C_I, C_M = regulatory threshold values. C_{N10}–C_{N90} = regional range of natural values.

waters), either in a pristine state (see extreme aquatic environments in Table 2) or affected by human activities. Each user category may have its own set of regulatory values. Although there is a continuous evolution of water quality adequacy for a given use, the need for regulatory constraint, also met in other water quality scales, implies threshold values limited by strict boundaries. These boundaries may vary from one country to another and may evolve in time.

Use of the term "natural pollution" is highly confusing and should be here discouraged: for example, natural brackish waters (TDS 1 to 3 mg/L), or anoxic waters (found in such deep lakes as Kivu, Tanganyika, and Malawi) should be regarded as "mediocre" or "unsuitable" for many uses.

The first scales are the *user scales*. The best-known one concerns drinking water, but other scales have been established for irrigation, various industries, and fish farming (Chapman and Kimstach, in Chapman, 1996). The latter generally focus on fewer descriptors than for drinking water, such as Na^+, Ca^{++}, Cl^-, boron for irrigation, DOC for electronics, and fecal indicators for canning. Depending on the chemical concentration found, those categories of waters have been defined as "excellent" if water can be used directly without any treatment, "acceptable" if a minor treatment—such as filtration—is needed, "mediocre" for an important treatment as a chemical one, and "unsuitable" if the water treatment is much too complex and expensive (e.g., sea water for drinking water). Each of these grades can be defined by threshold values C_{Ei}, C_{ES}, C_M, C_L (see Figure 5).

The second set of scales is related to *aquatic biota*. Water quality guidelines for aquatic biota exist in many countries, including the United States, Canada, and Russia (see Chapman and Kimstach, in Chapman, 1996). Local conditions may be quite variable, and natural concentrations may exceed the national guidelines in some places or at some periods. Wherever possible, it is advisable to consider first the natural background quality to which the biota is well adapted, which is defined here within the lower and upper deciles of the regional distribution (C_{N10} and C_{N90}). As for the user scale, the aquatic biota of water quality is proposed with four grades (Figure 5). Because a slight change from these "natural" ranges may not always lead to any impact on the biotic communities (e.g., a K^+ or Cl^- change from 1 to 10 mg/L), this state is here referred to with the neutral term "modified." Above a certain threshold (C_A), an impact on biota may be observed, defining a "deterioration" state. Another threshold (C_D) defines the "degradation" state, marked by major biological changes. Such scales are not universal for most water quality descriptors and should be set up for homogeneous ecological regions.

The third set of water quality scales, the *integrated*

scale, is related to the estimated overall value generally regarded in economic terms of the aquatic environment, with regard to actual or potential uses. The bases of such scales are the "reference" water quality set up for a river reach, a lake, or an aquifer as an achievable goal. This target generally takes into account the actual pressures and demands on the aquatic system, maximizes its potential uses (including those of the aquatic fauna), minimizes the use restriction (minimum water treatment for most users), and optimizes the restoration cost of the aquatic environment. If beyond the reference level (C_R) some economic value of the aquatic system is lost, the system is termed "impaired," although it may still have some capacity for self-recovery. Above a second critical level (C_I) the system is "damaged," that is, unfit for many human uses, with an important loss of biotic integrity and corresponding restoration cost and a very limited capacity for self-recovery. Above the ultimate threshold (C_M) the system is "ruined," implying not only a total loss of economic and biotic value but also a threat to humans requiring treatment and a very high cost of restoration. A "corrected" grade is added in this integrated scale: it refers to changes from a mediocre natural state made in order to permit some water uses. A decrease of a high TDS level resulting from the diversion of surface waters may be termed "corrected." It must be noted that the "reference" levels chosen are generally not the pristine state, which may be impossible or too costly to achieve; rather, they correspond to "modified" or "acceptable" states, or even to "deteriorated" or "mediocre" states.

Integrated scales are not always perceived as a compromise by their users and are sometimes presented as absolute scales. Actually, these scales measure only the sheer concentration of chemicals and their variations in time and space. Such integrated scales are relative and may vary from one basin to another according to the local biogeochemical conditions and human perception of the aquatic environment. They are therefore closely linked to local economic and cultural conditions. For instance, the perception of eutrophication in Southeast Asia is quite different from the perception in Canada or northern Europe. The drinking water scale is probably the most universal one, but it may also vary from one country to another, modified as a result of ecotoxicological studies. The aquatic biota and the integrated scales are related to the difference between a target state, or a pristine state, and observed states.

In some countries a continuous grade between chemical concentrations and water quality has been established. Their combination results in continuous scales of water quality (e.g., from zero to one hundred). Such continuous scales permit a full quantification, and therefore a better comparison, of the water quality for a station or a territory. Although the system looks simple, it is actually very complex and is based on weighting rules for each water descriptor quality (e.g., comparing dissolved O_2, Cl^-, chlorophyll, particulate lead, and total herbicides), rules for time integration (e.g., governing excesses observed less than 10 percent of the time), and rules for space integration (e.g., determining how to compare a stream station to the station controlling the whole basin). Other problems are also arising: What to do with organic micropollutants that are generally not detected? How to compare the biological indices, with continuous records of O_2, discrete monthly analyses of dissolved chemicals, and once-a-year analyses of sediments? The study of water quality is still expanding quickly; as in other fields, the difference between the few well-monitored waters, as in North America and few European countries, and the rest of the world is growing greater every day.

[*See also* Desalination; Environmental Law; Erosion; Global Environment Facility; Hydrologic Cycle; International Cooperation; Salinization; Sanitation; Water; Water Resources Management; *and the biography of Carson.*]

BIBLIOGRAPHY

Adriansee, M., H. A. G. Niederlander, and P. B. M. Stortelder. *Monitoring Water Quality in the Future.* Zoetermeer, Netherlands: Ministry of Environment, 1995. Water monitoring.

Chapman, D., ed. *Assessment of the Quality of the Aquatic Environment through Water, Biota, and Sediment.* 2d ed. London: E & FN Spon, 1996. A general presentation of the various approaches to water quality.

Drever, J. I. *The Geochemistry of Natural Waters.* 2d ed. Englewood Cliffs, N.J.: Prentice-Hall, 1988. Water quality as seen by a geochemist.

Gibbs, R. J. "Mechanisms Controlling World Water Chemistry." *Science* 170 (1970), 1088–1090. A seminal paper on the spatial distribution of major ions.

Hem, J. D. *Study and Interpretation of the Chemical Characteristics of Natural Waters.* 3d ed. Reston, Va.: U.S. Geological Survey, 1989. A very handy book with many case studies.

Horowitz, A. J. *The Use of Suspended Sediment and Associated Trace Elements in Water Quality Studies.* International Association of Hydrological Sciences Special Publication 4. Reading, U.K., 1995. A complete presentation of heavy metal surveys in water and sediments.

Kimstach, V., M. Meybeck, and E. Baroudy, eds. *From Dniepr to Baïkal: Water Quality in the Former Soviet Union.* London: E & FN Spon, 1998. An example of the multiple aspects of water quality issues over 20 million square kilometer territory.

Meybeck, M. "River Water Quality, Global Ranges, Time and Space Variabilities." *Verhandlungen International Vereingung Limnologie* 26 (1996), 81–96. From the natural variability of river water quality to human impacts.

———. "Surface Water Quality: Global Assessment and Perspectives." In *Water: A Looming Crisis.* Paris: Unesco Press, 173–185, 1998. Discusses water quality issue scaling.

Meybeck, M., D. Chapman, and R. Helmer, eds. *Global Freshwater Quality. A First Assessment.* London: Blackwell, 1989. The first global overview of water quality issues in rivers, lakes, reservoirs, and ground waters.

Meybeck, M., and R. Helmer. "The Quality of Rivers: From Pristine Stage to Global Pollution." *Global Planetary Change* 1 (1989), 283–309. Discusses pristine river quality and human impacts.

Meybeck, M., and A. Ragu. *Rivers Discharges to the Oceans: An Assessment of Suspended Solids, Major Ions, and Nutrients.* Nairobi: United National Environmental Programme, 1996. The first water quality register of world rivers discharging to oceans, with more than two hundred rivers documented.

Salomons, W., and U. Forstner. *Metals in the Hydrological Cycle.* New York: Springer, 1984. A seminal book on the origins and fate of metals in aquatic systems.

United Nations Environment Programme (UNEP). *The Pollution of Lakes and Reservoirs.* UNEP Environment Library, no. 12. Nairobi: UNEP, 1994. *Water Quality of World River Basins.* UNEP Environment Library, no. 14. Nairobi: UNEP, 1995. *Ground Water: A Threatened Resource.* UNEP Environment Library, no. 15. Nairobi: UNEP, 1996. Three specific booklets on water quality issues.

—Michel H. Meybeck

WATER RESOURCES MANAGEMENT

Unlike other mineral resources, water, because of its fundamental nature as a fugitive resource that is essential for life, has many social dimensions that have to be managed along with the physical resource base itself. The current emphasis of national and international institutions is that water management should be integrated into the social, economic, and institutional web of society. Hence *integrated water resources management*, IWRM, is the preferred term. The use of water by humans can cause many external effects that impact others than the user. These effects, usually called *externalities*, can be both positive and negative. Positive externalities can include stabilization of downstream low flows and flood peak reduction due to upstream storage. Most emphasis, however, is usually placed upon the negative externalities: reduction of flow downstream due to upstream diversions, deterioration of water quality from upstream to downstream, and flood damages downstream due to upstream flood protection levees are just a few of the most obvious examples. It is the existence of externalities that makes it imperative to manage water resources in an integrated way so as to be able to internalize the externalities. Water and water services can also take on the attributes of public goods (for example, it is impossible to exclude nonpurchasers from benefiting from the provision of the service), such as flood control, or they can be purely private goods, such as municipal water supply, often within the same multipurpose water plan. These conflicting attributes make planning for water use extremely complex and outside the range of normal economic planning.

Water is an amazing resource in that it can exist in many different states (rain water, ice, snow, and water vapor; fresh, saline, or polluted surface water in lakes and streams; and both shallow and deep ground water) that, at a cost, can be substituted for one another. [*See* Ground Water.] Hydrologists, the scientists who study water, have developed accounting tools (the water balance or hydrologic cycle) to keep track of the stocks and flows entering and leaving these various states over a time period of interest. [*See* Hydrologic Cycle.] These myriad waters are accessed by many different users with many different and competing claims. An important distinction in water use is between consumptive uses and nonconsumptive uses. Consumptive uses either evaporate the water, making it unavailable for other nearby users (as in irrigated agriculture), embody it in products, some of which are returned quickly to the hydrologic cycle (as in soft drinks and beer), and some of which may be embedded in the product for a long time (as in the hydrolization of cement for concrete), or contaminate it in a way that makes it unfit for reuse. The largest user, worldwide, is irrigated agriculture, which typically accounts for as much as 85 percent of the total consumptive use of water. The remaining 15 percent is split between industry, commerce, households, and maintaining the aquatic environment. In terms of non-consumptive uses, electric power generation cooling is by far the largest in most countries. Most of the cooling water is returned quickly to the streams, lakes, or oceans at slightly elevated temperatures.

From the social point of view the most remarkable thing about water is that in most countries users do not have simple property rights but depend upon a variety of government regulations that can be changed arbitrarily to reassign rights. The lack of clear title to water distinguishes it from most other resources and makes it hard for private industry to develop markets and investment strategies. Property rights for water in the United States are based upon three doctrines. The Western states generally follow the doctrine of prior appropriation, whereby the assignment of property rights for water use dates back to the first persons to appropriate the water for use. The remainder of the country is governed either by the riparian rights doctrine, whereby the riparian landowners own the access to the water in the stream subject to not causing damage to downstream property owners, or by the correlative rights doctrine, which is a loose combination of the other two doctrines. As can be expected, there is substantial legal wrangling about property rights, particularly in the definitions of substantial harm being caused to other users (valuing the externalities). In the United States, only the Western states have well-developed water markets based upon the clear titles established under the prior appropriation doctrine.

The lack of clear title leads inexorably to the need for government regulation and management of the resource. This has led to integrated water resources management becoming one of the most studied areas of government regulation of resource use, both in the United States and elsewhere. It also demands that politics, economics, environment, and engineering be among the disciplines involved in devising water management plans and implementing developments. As early as the Flood Control Act of 1936 the implementing agencies were exhorted to use economics as well as engineering in ensuring that "the benefits to whomsoever they accrue shall exceed the costs"; the first application of benefit-cost analysis in the federal government. Early interdisciplinary attempts were made to develop such an integrated methodology, both at the University of Chicago (Hirshliefer et al., 1960) and at Harvard University (Maass et al., 1962). These studies were supported and followed up by major U.S. federal water agencies such as the Corps of Engineers, the Bureau of Reclamation, the Soil Conservation Service, and the Tennessee Valley Authority with limited success in the 1970s and 1980s (Rogers, 1993).

Recent Developments. The concept of sustainable development espoused by Agenda 21 of the United Nations Conference on Environment and Development held in Rio de Janeiro, Brazil, in 1992 has been a heavy influence on recent developments in water management. [*See* Agenda 21.] This concept has forced water planners, for the first time, to take a step back and examine the entire resource base from the point of view of sustainability, given the present and expected future demands placed upon the resource. This has led many to conclude that there will be a major crisis in meeting these demands and, hence, a large water crisis literature has developed (see Gleick, 1993). The response of the United Nations, the World Bank, and other international and bilateral agencies has been to sponsor new international institutions (the Global Water Partnership and the World Water Council) focusing on water and water policy. The ostensible goal of these institutions is to ensure that the best polices for water management are followed, and both are heavily committed to the concepts involved in IWRM as a way to economize on water use and, hence, to avoid the predicted resource shortfall. These developments have put water management on top of the international resource management agenda.

This emphasis on sustainability has come at a time when, in the United States and elsewhere in the developed world, there is great opposition to building new supply infrastructure for water, and concern for water quality and ecosystem protection is being promoted. The major old-line water agencies such as the Corps of Engineers, the Bureau of Reclamation, and the Tennessee Valley Authority are all changing their water management approaches, with an emphasis on demand-side management instead of supply management. There

One indication of vulnerability is the extent to which a country depends upon surface water that flows from a neighboring nation. Here are some examples.

COUNTRY	PERCENTAGE OF SURFACE FLOWS ORIGINATING BEYOND COUNTRY BORDERS	COUNTRY	PERCENTAGE OF SURFACE FLOWS ORIGINATING BEYOND COUNTRY BORDERS
Egypt	97	Niger	68
Hungary	95	Iraq	66
Mauritania	95	Albania	53
Botswana	94	Uruguay	52
Bulgaria	91	Germany	51
Netherlands	89	Portugal	48
Gambia	86	Bangladesh	42
Cambodia	82	Thailand	39
Romania	82	Austria	38
Luxembourg	80	Pakistan	36
Syria	79	Venezuela	35
Congo	77	Senegal	34
Sudan	77	Belgium	33
Paraguay	70		

SOURCE: From Gleick (1993).

BIBLIOGRAPHY

Frederick, K. D. "Water as a Source of International Conflict." *Resources* 123 (1996), 9–12.
Gleick, P. *Water in Crisis: A Guide to the World's Fresh Water Resources*. New York and Oxford: Oxford University Press, 1993.

—DAVID J. CUFF

is also growing concern for the maintenance of aquatic ecosystems. This has manifested itself in a new concern for reducing withdrawals from streams, and even using water stored for other purposes in reservoirs to augment low instream flows during critical seasons for the ecosystem.

Demand-Side versus Supply-Side Management. Of all of the recent developments, demand-side management has the largest potential to help resolve the water crisis. Traditionally, engineers estimated the future needs of the population based upon population size and norms for per capita water use. In doing so there is a great risk in either underestimating or overestimating the demands and making self-fulfilling forecasts. In most cases, because of the natural conservatism of engineers, the future human needs were greatly exaggerated, while the needs of the aquatic ecosystem were overlooked. This has led to large overinvestment in water supply infrastructure. To avoid the worst features of this, the em-

phasis is now on sending signals to consumers via pricing, regulatory, and educational mechanisms, and allowing them to set their own appropriate consumption levels. In its simplest form, demand-side management entails correct pricing of the water to allow for market adjustment of demand and supply at that price. In most cases, however, demand-side management requires other significant management inputs in addition to pricing. First, without adequate metering and monitoring, pricing will not have the desired effect. Second, customers need a fair amount of education to understand their potential responses to increased prices. Third, institutions providing the water services need to have appropriate financial skills and competencies. They must have the ability and the authority to collect revenue and build forward-looking investment strategies for dealing with future demands. Fourth, despite expectations to the contrary, there will in many cases be a need for increased government regulation. Because of the nature of water, it is not a simple economic good such as soap, and the market for all sorts of water services exhibits some form of market failure. For example, as mentioned earlier, there are major external effects due to water use; some water services such as flood control exhibit public good attributes; and others such as privately owned municipal water supplies that appear much more like regular economic goods are, nevertheless, natural monopolies because of the economies of scale inherent in the distribution and water treatment systems. These forms of market failure can only be addressed by regulatory action on the part of governments. Finally, even if there were no market failures, markets would fail to look out for the legitimate needs of the nonhuman aquatic ecosystem.

Global Change. The concern over global warming has increasingly settled upon water resources as one of the sectors most likely to be heavily impacted. The Intergovernmental Panel on Climate Change (1996), however, while outlining potentially disastrous effects, was unable to ascribe a high level of certainty to them. The predictions for a wetter global climate are supported by most model studies, but the specific regional impacts are extremely difficult to predict—with different models giving different predictions for the same hydrologic regions on the surface of the Earth. Even within the United States, Lettenmaier et al. (1996) show that, depending upon which model one chooses to characterize the future, radically different conclusions can be reached. They concluded that we are currently unable to make strong predictions about global climate effects upon water supplies and supply variations in various basins. The potential global warming effects need to be monitored closely and adaptive water management strategies developed.

International River Basin Conflicts. One of the most noticeable aspects of water resources management is the recent discovery that, when the resources become scarcer as a result of increasing demands upon them, nations that previously had good relations with their downstream or other co-riparian neighbors are now faced with rancorous disputes over water use. Over 50 percent of the world's population now lives within internationally shared river basins. Unfortunately, the supranational institutions needed to effectuate integrated water resources management in these basins do not exist, and the international community is hard pressed to determine how such institutions should be set up. International river basin commissions exist in a few parts of the world, but they have not been particularly successful in resolving disputes between countries. The current dispute that appears to be the most pressing is between Israel, Jordan, and Palestine over the waters of the Jordan and the aquifers of the West Bank, but there are also conflicts surrounding most of the other Middle Eastern rivers, from the Nile to the Euphrates. New water management mechanisms will have to be developed soon to deal with this class of problem before the conflicts get out of hand.

The Special Role of Irrigated Agriculture. Given the magnitude of the water resources devoted entirely to irrigated agriculture, it is apparent that this sector is the one most in need of serious reevaluation. A 10 percent reduction in diversions to agriculture would lead to a 50 percent increase in the water available for all other uses. Water used in agriculture is worth only a fraction of water used in other activities, hence simple economic logic would indicate that water be diverted from agriculture to the other higher-valued uses. Seckler et al. (1997), however, claim that in the long run the amount of water allocated to irrigation will have to be increased just to provide an adequate diet for the large increase in population expected by the year 2020. [*See* Irrigation.*] How can this contradiction be resolved? In many parts of the world, more attention needs to be paid to rain-fed agriculture or to supplemental irrigation to rain-fed crops. This may help reduce the demand for water. In other situations, water may be imported already embedded in food crops. This "virtual" water already plays a large role in augmenting the water balances in arid countries such as Egypt, and could be further utilized to reduce pressure on supplies in other water-scarce regions.

[*See also* Climate Impacts; Dams; Desalination; Drought; Security and Environment; *and* Water.]

BIBLIOGRAPHY

Gleick, P. H. *Water in Crisis: A Guide to the World's Fresh Water Resources.* New York and Oxford: Oxford University Press, 1993.
Hirschleifer, J., et al. *Water Supply: Economics, Technology, and Policy.* Chicago: University of Chicago Press, 1960.
Intergovernmental Panel on Climate Change. *Climate Change 1995.* Cambridge: Cambridge University Press, 1996.
Lettenmaier, D., et al. "Global Climate Change: Effect on Hydrologic Cycle." In *Water Resources Handbook,* edited by L. Mays, chap. 29. New York: McGraw-Hill, 1996.
Maass, A., et al. *Design of Water Resources Systems.* Cambridge, Mass.: Harvard University Press, 1962.
Rogers, P. *America's Waters.* A Twentieth Century Fund Book. Cambridge, Mass.: MIT Press, 1993.
Seckler, D., et al. "Demand for Irrigation Water." International Irrigation Management Institute Research Report No. 7. Colombo, Sri Lanka, 1997.

—PETER P. ROGERS

WATER VAPOR

Water vapor is the gaseous form of water (H_2O) and is one of the constituents of the Earth's atmosphere. [*See* Atmosphere Dynamics.] It plays a central and varied role in the determination of the Earth's climate. Many of the uncertainties in prediction of climate changes—whether they be due to solar variability or increase in carbon dioxide (CO_2)—stem from uncertainties in the modeling of various aspects of the way water vapor affects climate.

The first class of water vapor effects stems from the energy involved in the phase change between liquid (or solid) water and the vapor state. It takes about 2.5×10^6 joules of energy to change one kilogram of liquid water into a vapor at the same temperature; conversely, when one kilogram of water vapor condenses into a liquid, the same amount of energy is released to the surroundings. Stored energy of this sort is known as *latent heat*. The latent heat of one kilogram of water vapor is equivalent to the energy released by burning seventy-two milliliters of gasoline. Put another way, if the tropical sun on a clear day beats down on the ocean surface with an intensity of three hundred watts per square meter (W/m^2), the solar energy absorbed in the course of a day could be compensated by the evaporation of a layer of water only one centimeter deep. In fact, this is the primary means by which solar energy is communicated to the atmosphere. Only about 20 percent of the incident solar energy is absorbed directly by the atmosphere. The balance is absorbed at the surface, where it is largely employed in the evaporation of water. The resulting water vapor enters the atmosphere, and the stored solar energy is released where the water vapor condenses back to a liquid. [*See* Hydrologic Cycle.] This could be thousands of kilometers (km) distant from the site where the solar energy was absorbed. Water vapor is important to energy transport in the atmosphere because it allows the atmosphere to store large amounts of energy without actually heating up.

Latent heat is released in the ascending branches of large-scale midlatitude storms and in deep convective towers occurring in both the tropics and midlatitudes. The release of latent heat affects the *lapse rate*, which is the rate at which atmospheric temperature declines with height. An ascending parcel cools as it expands, but part of this cooling is offset by the latent heat released through condensation. Dry ascent would yield a lapse rate of about 10 kelvins (K) per kilometer (the *dry adiabat*), whereas the observed lapse rate is more like 6.5 K/km. The physics determining the lapse rate is not simple, and the lapse rate is affected by many dynamic phenomena as well as by condensation. The lapse rate is important to the greenhouse effect, with higher lapse rates favoring a stronger greenhouse effect, all other things being equal. A higher lapse rate means that for fixed surface temperature, the upper atmosphere is colder. In this circumstance, the atmosphere radiates to space at a temperature much colder than the surface temperature, yielding a large greenhouse effect. In the extreme opposite limit of an isothermal atmosphere

held at the same temperature as the surface, there would be no greenhouse effect, regardless of the CO_2 concentration. Thus the way lapse rate changes with changing climate affects the response of the system to perturbations. [*See* Atmosphere Structure and Evolution.]

The maximum amount of water vapor that can be stably held at a fixed volume without condensation occurring is measured by the *saturation vapor pressure*. The saturation vapor pressure is governed by the *Clausius Clapeyron* relation, which implies that the water-holding capacity of the air increases roughly exponentially with temperature. Specifically, at saturation the water vapor concentration is 2.06 parts per thousand (volume) at 260 K and 1,000 millibars (mb) pressure, but rises to 6.14 parts per thousand at 273 K and 35.9 parts per thousand at 300 K. For this reason, water vapor is generally much more important in warm regions than in cold regions, with an important exception to be noted below. The ratio of the actual water content of an air parcel to the water content at saturation is known as the *relative humidity*, generally expressed as a percentage. Air at 100 percent relative humidity is saturated.

The second way water vapor affects climate is through its influence as a greenhouse gas. [*See* Greenhouse Effect.] A no-atmosphere planet with a surface temperature of 300 K (typical of the Earth's tropics) would radiate infrared energy to space at a rate of 459 W/m^2. Using a typical tropical temperature profile, adding an atmosphere whose only greenhouse gas is CO_2 at 300 parts per million (volume) brings the radiated energy down to 409 W/m^2. However, if water vapor is added to the atmosphere to achieve 50 percent relative humidity, the radiated energy drops to 303 W/m^2. For 40 percent relative humidity the value is 309 W/m^2, whereas for 60 percent it is 297 W/m^2. Because so much of the greenhouse effect is directly due to the presence of water vapor in the atmosphere, climate predictions are sensitive to the way water vapor content changes as the climate is altered.

This does not mean that the greenhouse effect of CO_2 and other trace gases is negligible compared to that of water vapor. Water vapor has a short lifetime in the atmosphere and therefore responds as a feedback as long-term variables such as CO_2 concentration, orbital parameters, and solar output are changed. In the simplest picture, water vapor amplifies climate sensitivity. As an atmosphere warms, it can hold more water vapor (and therefore presumably does). Thus a small warming due directly to, say, doubling CO_2 is boosted to a much larger value by the greenhouse effect of the water vapor added to the atmosphere. In extreme cases, such as presumably happened to Venus in its early history, the destabilizing effect of water vapor can be so great that the process ends only when all the oceans have evaporated into the atmosphere. Even short of a *runaway greenhouse* of this type, water vapor greatly enhances climate sensitivity. The importance of water vapor feedback in anthropogenic global warming was first made clear in one-dimensional climate models by the pioneering work of Manabe and Strickler in the late 1960s. Were it not for the water vapor feedback, the temperature increase due to doubling of CO_2 would not be a cause for concern.

Atmospheric temperature declines with height, and therefore most of the water vapor in any given atmospheric column is generally contained in its lowest few kilometers. However, the small amount of water vapor aloft—the upper tropospheric humidity, or UTH—is disproportionately important for the greenhouse effect. The first part of the reason for this is that one obtains a greenhouse effect by making the atmosphere radiate infrared at a temperature colder than the surface; this is achieved by making the atmosphere optically thick in the infrared, at a place where it is cold. Water vapor aloft achieves this, whereas water vapor near the ground does not. The second part of the reason is that even a small quantity of a greenhouse gas induces considerable infrared absorption near the center of the absorption lines, before the radiation at those wavelengths has been depleted.

UTH is a challenging quantity to model accurately, because it represents only a small portion of the water in the climate system and therefore is highly sensitive to moisture sources. The pattern of UTH is complex and is strongly influenced by the disposition of convective moisture source regions and by the wind patterns that transport water into dry regions far from the source.

With regard to climate modeling uncertainties, most of the problems posed by water vapor stem from the fact that the most crucial aspects of water-related physics cannot be directly represented by first-principals computation within a model, but instead must be represented indirectly as *parameterizations*. [*See* Climate Models.] The water vapor physics enters climate models most directly through the *moist convection parameterization*, although there are also important unresolved issues revolving around the representation of evaporation and the numerical methods used to advect water vapor. A model's moist convection parameterization in large measure determines the way the model's lapse rate and relative humidity change in response to climate forcings such as the doubling of CO_2. An important means of checking the fidelity of a model's water vapor representation is to compare modeled water vapor fluctuations in the course of natural variability (such as the seasonal cycle or El Niño cycle) against observed water vapor fluctuations. The increasing availability of high-quality satellite measurements of UTH has made this endeavor feasible. Results to date show an encouraging degree of similarity between modeled and observed humidity fluctuations, but much remains to be done in this area.

Correction of any remaining inadequacies in the current simulation of water vapor could either increase or decrease estimates of the sensitivity of climate to doubling of CO_2 (or indeed to other radiative forcings, such as fluctuation in the sun's brightness). If, in a warming climate, convective regions pick up additional moisture less rapidly than current models predict, or dry nonconvective regions lose much of their remaining moisture, then estimates of climate sensitivity would be revised downward. Conversely, if, for example, the vast dry regions of the subtropics substantially contract in area or if they become notably moister than currently anticipated, estimates of climate sensitivity would be revised upward.

Water vapor further affects climate through its control of the formation of clouds. [*See* Clouds.]

[*See also* Climate Change; Global Warming; *and* Ocean–Atmosphere Coupling.]

BIBLIOGRAPHY

Held, I. M., and B. J. Soden. "Water Vapor Feedback and Global Warming." *Annual Review of Energy and the Environment*, in press. A modern review emphasizing implications of water vapor feedback for global change.

Manabe, S., and R. T. Wetherald. "Thermal Equilibrium of the Atmosphere with a Given Distribution of Relative Humidity." *Journal of Atmospheric Sciences* 24 (1967), 241–259. The classic paper that introduced the idea of simple models of water vapor feedback.

Pierrehumbert, R. T. "Subtropical Water Vapor as a Mediator of Rapid Climate Change." In: *Mechanisms of Global Climate Change at Millennial Time Scales*, Geophysical Monograph 112, edited by P. U. Clark, R. S. Webb, and L. D. Keigwin, pp. 339–361. Washington, D.C.: American Geophysical Union, 1999. Another review, emphasizing paleoclimate problems as well as global change. Also available at http://geosci.uchicago.edu/~rtp1.

Spencer, R. W., and W. D. Braswell. "How Dry is the Tropical Free Troposphere? Implications for Global Warming Theory." *Bulletin of the American Meteorological Society* 78 (1997), 1097–1106. Contains satellite images illustrating the role of dynamics in modulating the water vapor field. More images of this type can be viewed at http://geosci.uchicago.edu/~rtp1/research/water.

—RAYMOND T. PIERREHUMBERT

WEATHER FORECASTING

The word *forecast* was first associated with the weather by Admiral Robert Fitzroy, Chief Meteorologist to the Board of Trade in Great Britain in the 1850s. Fitzroy formulated several popular forecasting "remarks" for predicting the weather. For instance, he related the rise and fall (the tendency) of the mercury in a barometer, an instrument for measuring atmospheric pressure, with weather events: "A fall of half a tenth of an inch or more in half an hour is a sure sign of a storm."

Fitzroy started a weather forecast and gale warning service for the public in 1861, which was made available to the press. Unfortunately, however, he committed suicide in 1865 after an incorrect forecast for the Navy led to several ships being lost in a storm in the English Channel. The weather forecasts were stopped on the recommendation of the Royal Society, who thought the existing state of scientific knowledge was insufficient. They were resumed in 1876 and have continued up to the present day.

In 1895 in the United States a postcard forecast service was initiated whereby the forecast issued by the Weather Bureau was stamped onto the back of a card and mailed to subscribers. At its peak, ninety thousand cards were sent out each day, but the service declined with the growth of radio in the 1920s.

Of course people had been attempting to predict the weather for centuries before Fitzroy, and many weather sayings and rhymes have survived to this day. That most famous forecast:

> Red sky at night,
> Shepherd's delight,
> Red sky in morning,
> Shepherd's warning.

appears in both the old and new testaments of the Bible, for example:

> When it is evening, ye say It will be fair weather; for the sky is red. And in the morning, It will be foul weather today; for the sky is red and lowring. (Matthew 16:2–3)

The weather was of great importance to farmers and sailors alike, and any sensible prediction was of great value. Weather forecasting was very much an art rather than a science right up until the middle of the twentieth century.

After the invention and development of reliable instruments to measure the weather, it became fashionable to keep a weather diary that would record the air temperature, wind direction, atmospheric pressure, amount of rainfall, and a few notes on the day's weather in terms of sunshine, cloud, and so on. These were isolated observations and, although they were exchanged between observers to determine differences in climate (see, for example, Gilbert White, 1789), it was not until 1816 that the first weather map was drawn by the German physicist Heinrich Brandes, based on observations made in 1783.

In 1803, Luke Howard, a London chemist, published his Linnean classification of clouds, which included the three basic types: cirrus, cumulus, and stratus. There was little knowledge at this time about why these differing cloud types developed, but they were used with experience as an indicator of the state of the atmosphere.

The foundation of modern weather forecasting was made with the invention of the electric telegraph by Samuel Morse in about 1836. This enabled simultaneous weather observations from several different locations to be collated, and by 1851 the first published weather maps were being sold to the public for one penny at the Great Exhibition in London by the Electric Telegraph Company. By 1857 the *Washington Evening Star* was publishing weather information collected by the American telegraph companies.

Buys Ballot's Law, stated in 1857 by the Dutch meteorologist C. H. D. Buys Ballot, showed how wind speed and direction are related to high and low pressure, and synoptic charts of wind and pressure were developed from simultaneous hourly observations, using Greenwich Mean Time. Weather forecasts were based on the experience of the forecaster.

During World War I (1914–1918), Vilhelm Bjerknes and his son Jakob made extensive observations from a network of weather stations in Norway. They put forward the theory of weather "fronts" that exist between air masses of different origin. This allowed much better estimates of the timing of weather events since frontal movements could be predicted.

As an understanding gradually developed of how the atmosphere behaved, it was speculated that the future state of the atmosphere might be predicted by using a set of equations, just as astronomers determined a future eclipse of the moon. The first serious attempt to model the atmospheric in this way was made by the Englishman, Lewis Fry Richardson. In his book, *Weather Prediction by Numerical Process*, published in 1922, he set out the fundamental equations (known as *primitive equations*) and the required calculus. He attempted to make a six-hour forecast of the likely change in pressure over part of Germany. His answer, which took several months to calculate, was completely wrong, but his methods laid the foundation for what is now called *numerical weather prediction* (NWP). He recognized that the main reason for the failure of his forecast was the inadequacy of the initial observational database, and he was confident enough to speculate that it might be possible to keep up with the weather by employing an army of sixty-four thousand "computers" (human mathematicians) with slide rules, who would be housed in a circular building like the Albert Hall in London, and whose calculations would be directed by a series of "conductors" to produce weather forecasts. (More recent estimates have shown that, to get ahead of the weather, at least one million people would be needed!)

The Russian meteorologist I'lya Kibel produced a simplified set of equations in 1940 to yield one- to two-day forecasts, but it was the advent of electronic computers in the early 1950s that enabled Richardson's dream to come true. John von Neumann, the Hungarian-American mathematician, led a group at Princeton University who developed a simplified atmospheric model on a simple computer called MANIAC (Mathematical Analyzer, Numerical Integrator and Computer). The results were good enough to encourage others around the world to develop other weather forecasting models. The first operational model to produce regular weather forecasts in real time was operated by the Swedish Military Weather Service in 1954. Since then there has been a rapid growth in the number and the sophistication of models. By the late 1960s, multilevel models had been developed to take into account the upper atmosphere and to predict precipitation as well as pressure and wind. The 1970s and 1980s saw an increase in the accuracy of forecasts as more and more powerful computers became available and global observations were fed into the models. Gradually, the computer-based forecasts became as good as those produced by experienced human forecasters. The 1990s has seen the introduction of global forecast models and the use of "ensemble" forecasts because computers are now powerful enough to run the models many times for slightly changing initial conditions, giving a probability of different, developing weather events. The models are also coupled to ocean models to give a more representative forecast.

Weather forecasting now takes place on a variety of temporal and spatial scales, described in Table 1. Weather satellites and weather radar have now been introduced, and are particularly useful for "nowcasting" and for short-period forecasts. They give a snapshot of what is happening to the weather over large spatial areas and are useful both to verify model predictions over areas where there are few observations, such as over the oceans, and to fill in the gaps between model forecasts.

Weather forecasting is a continuous process that today requires a sophisticated and reliable global communications and computer network. Weather observations are made at fixed times around the globe and then sent to national weather centers who use the data to initialize their models and verify previous forecasts.

For the purposes of model simulation, the atmosphere is divided up into a number of grid boxes covering the globe. The temperature, pressure, and other weather elements for each grid box are initialized from global observations, and a set of equations is then used to predict how these elements will change with time. The number of vertical levels has been increased progressively and the grid size has been reduced, but reduction in grid box size is no longer the main priority of increased computer power: present practice is to use increased computer capacity primarily to improve the physical modeling and data analysis rather than reduce the grid size.

The models are now global, and probably the most sophisticated one is the spectral model that is run by the European Centre for Medium-Range Weather Forecasting (in Reading, U.K), which forecasts the wind, air temperature, and humidity at more than four million points throughout the atmosphere. Smaller-scale models with a much higher resolution, such as the mesoscale model currently being used by the U.K. Meteorological Office, which has thirty-one layers with a 17-kilometer grid, are being developed in an attempt to bridge the gap between global models and the commercial requirements for local site-specific weather forecasts.

To produce a forecast of anticipated weather at a specific point and at a specific time, a weather forecaster has to interpret the inputs and outputs (namely, data and pressure patterns, respectively) of numerical weather prediction models. The models are not yet capable of predicting all the weather elements by themselves, but some outputs, such as wind velocity for aircraft, can be inferred directly.

The weather that is observed at a point in space and time is an aggregate of temperature, cloud, wind, precipitation, sunshine, visibility, and humidity. The person receiving a weather forecast is only interested in the weather parameters that affect his or her personal comfort, leisure interest, or commercial activity. Eventually it may be possible to produce numerical forecasts on a small enough scale to provide all these elements to a client at a given location—on perhaps a 1- or 2-kilometer grid.

Most standard observations are land based, but satellites, aircraft, ships, radiosondes, and radar are increasingly relied upon to give a reasonable coverage over the oceans and in the upper atmosphere. The acquisition of observations of the weather around the world to initialize the forecast models is of great importance. Altogether there are about 100,000 sets of weather observations made every day around the globe,

Weather Forecasting. TABLE 1. Temporal and Spatial Scales of Weather Forecasting

Approximate Temporal Scales
Nowcasting: zero to six hours
Short-period forecasts: six to forty-eight hours
Medium-range forecasts: two to ten days
Long-range forecasts: ten days–month–season–year
Climate forecasts: year–centuries

Approximate Spatial Scales
Site specific: 1–20 meters
Microscale: 20 meters to 2 kilometers
Mesoscale: 2–200 kilometers
Synoptic-Scale: 200–2,000 kilometers
Global scale: greater than 2,000 kilometers

but perhaps only about one-third of these are fed into a typical NWP forecast. Improved data assimilation techniques are constantly being developed to check the data and to allow more data to be used.

The phenomenal growth in new technology for data observation and collection should result in better assessments of weather forecast quality. Data that previously had to be estimated, such as road surface temperatures, are now being measured. The exact locations of thunderstorms and bands of rain are now being obtained. It should therefore be easier to determine if a weather forecast for rain or for thunderstorms was correct.

The principal outputs from NWP models include projected pressure levels, clouds, and winds from which the forecast weather charts are produced. The forecaster has to interpret the likely weather for a particular place or region in terms of expected winds, air temperature, likely precipitation, and cloud/sunshine.

Weather forecasts are largely based upon NWP model output; the human forecaster has the role of fine-tuning and adding value. There are two main reasons why such models do not yield perfect forecasts: First, there is the limitation of the modeling itself (for example, simulation of the complex processes of transferring heat, momentum, and moisture through the atmospheric boundary layer); second, the starting conditions, from which the complex equations are integrated forward in time, are imperfectly specified. Ideally, NWP models need about one million data points for initialization. But even if all observations from around the world could be used, the number of points would be at least an order of magnitude less.

If the model output is incorrect, the forecaster may pass on these errors in the weather forecast. However, there is a skill in interpreting the model output, and in some situations the forecaster may use experience to overcome the model deficiencies. Today the human forecaster cannot compete with the computer forecasts beyond about twenty-four hours.

The prediction of severe weather is of vital importance so that, if possible, mitigating steps can be taken to reduce potential damage and threat to life. Forecasts of hurricanes, tornadoes, severe snow, fog, high winds, floods, heat waves, and so on are now being issued with probability indicators to give customers and the general public an idea of their likelihood.

Weather forecasting can give useful information up to about six days ahead, extending to ten days at most. Chaos theory suggests that the behavior of the atmosphere cannot be predicted beyond that range. Long-range forecasting of weather up to three or six months ahead has had limited success, and usually only predicts whether temperature and precipitation will be above, at, or below average levels for the time of year.

Climate prediction uses similar computer models to those used for weather forecasting, but they are run for decades rather than hours. These models are called general circulation models (GCMs), and are coupled to models of the oceans. To produce a climate forecast, the GCM is run for a number of past and future decades; the results for the predicted present climate are compared with our current knowledge of global climate. Once the GCM is tuned to model the present climate, it can be used to predict future climates—for example, providing estimates of global warming due to the increase in greenhouse gases.

A weather forecast can easily be verified by comparing the predicted weather with that actually observed. It is impossible to verify the prediction from a climate model in the same way.

[*See also* Climate Models; Geographic Information Systems; Information Management; International Cooperation; Modeling of Natural Systems; Remote Sensing; Time Series Analysis; *and* World Meteorological Organization.]

BIBLIOGRAPHY

Browning, K. A., and G. Szejwach. "Developments in Observational Systems for Weather Forecasting." *Meteorological Applications* 1.1 (1994), 3–21.

Burroughs, W. J. *Watching the World's Weather.* Cambridge: Cambridge University Press, 1991.

Gaster, F. "Weather Forecasts and Storm Warnings." *Quarterly Journal of the Royal Meteorological Society* 22 (1896), 212–228.

Murphy, A. H. "Weather Forecast Assessment: Accuracy or Quality?" *Weather* 46 (1991), 180.

Richardson, L. F. *Weather Prediction by Numerical Process.* Cambridge: Cambridge University Press, 1922. Reprint, London: Dover, 1965.

White, G. *The Natural History of Selborne.* New York: Penguin, 1997.

—JOHN E. THORNES

WEATHER MODIFICATION

Deliberate efforts to modify the weather are likely to be one of the responses to global climate changes that may occur over the next few decades. Possible responses may include large-scale weather modification efforts to modify surface albedo or atmospheric constituents, but substantial advances would be necessary before these could become realistic alternatives. At present, and for the immediate future, weather modification related to clouds and precipitation presents a more realistic option.

Weather modification on a local or regional scale can be a useful, although limited, technology to reduce some of the most undesirable consequences of global climate change. This has been demonstrated by weather modification research and operations already carried out that encompass the range of climatic variations that could reasonably be expected with any projected climate changes. The difference may be a change in frequency the modification efforts employed. Weather changes that have been studied include fog clearance, cloud-cover modifications, orographic (mountain) precipitation augmentation, modification of rain, hail, and severe weather from convective clouds, and modification of hurricanes and extratropical storms (Hess, 1974).

In the western United States over the past fifty years, research into and implementation of weather modification has been cyclic: very extensive and intense during drought cycles, particularly in the mid-1950s and mid-1970s, and very limited during wet periods. In some areas, specifically in California and Utah, programs have continued throughout the period since the early 1950s. These are areas in which augmentation of normal levels of precipitation is desirable, or where reservoirs are available to store water from wet years to be used in drier ones. Projects such as these would probably expand if climate change were to produce drier regional climates. Some areas in the western United States already have sufficient mountain precipitation in most years and thus have only occasionally resorted to weather modification during drought periods. At the other extreme, there are areas in which, even during normal or dry years, there would be no significant benefit from slightly increased precipitation, and thus weather modification has not been seriously employed. Other areas fall into an intermediate category that can benefit from increased precipitation in most years, and especially in drought years. In California, as many as twenty programs have been active in a single year. Most of these have been designed to increase snow in the mountain watersheds of the Sierra for enhanced hydro-electric power generation. Others have focused on Californian agriculture or supplemental water for municipalities. Fifteen programs were active in California during the 1994–1995 season. Two of these programs have operated almost every year for more than forty years, and one has an unbroken record of forty-five years of continuous operation (Henderson, 1997). These programs operate in a marginal area where, in most years, there is a need for more water. Wetter areas that have more frequent droughts in a future climate-change scenario are likely to resort to weather modification, which is a technology that can be employed or discontinued with almost no time lag.

Advances in Science and Technology. The technology of cloud modification, precipitation enhancement, and some types of severe-weather abatement is gradually becoming more soundly based as vastly improved tools for research and for operational programs become available. During a discovery period in the late 1940s and 1950s, it was established that some induced changes in clouds were feasible. Statistical experiments during the 1960s and 1970s, supported by physical studies with the tools available at that time, indicated that economically and socially beneficial effects could be achieved. However, the complex nature of the cloud systems and the treatment processes limited the researchers' physical understanding of the cloud-process changes and the treatment technology and, consequently, their confidence in the statistical results. The understanding of the physical processes and the treatment technology has been greatly enhanced during the past twenty years. The increased investigative capabilities have included (1) laboratory capabilities for describing nucleation modes and specific requirements applicable to different cloud regimes (DeMott, 1995), (2) computer capabilities for studying cloud and treatment models (Farley et al., 1997, Heimbach et al., 1997), (3) multiwavelength and polarized remote-sensing capabilities for continuous observation of cloud and treatment processes, (4) instrumentation for direct in-cloud observations of cloud particles and processes, and (5) enhanced particulate-tracing capabilities for improved cloud-treatment systems. In addition, long-term programs have provided a continuously increasing sample size for statistical analysis. The physical studies and new statistical results are generally supportive of the findings from the earlier statistical studies.

Current Capabilities. A number of experiments have shown that artificial treatments can increase mountain precipitation by 10–15 percent. Many researchers and water users have concluded that this is the type of weather modification most ready for practical, beneficial application.

The results of experiments for the seeding of convective clouds to augment precipitation or decrease hail have been less consistent in supporting a beneficial result. Continuing research is providing knowledge as to which convective clouds are suitable for beneficial treatment and which are not. With the research tools now available, it is likely that more consistent beneficial treatment results will be possible for convective cloud systems within the next few years. Hail suppression is even more complex than precipitation augmentation for convective clouds. While some types of hailstorm are treatable with present technology, some of the more intense supercell storms are not, and may remain unsuitable for treatment for hail reduction. However, the indications from both the physical and the statistical studies of hailstorms increasingly support the feasibility of beneficial treatment of many of the hail-producing cloud systems.

The possibility of beneficial modification of tropical and extratropical systems must be relegated to the more distant future. Perhaps the most likely option for altering these large-scale systems will be in cirrus cloud

HAIL SUPPRESSION IN ALBERTA

In an average year, around forty major hailstorms advance from the Rocky Mountain foothills to the west, and pummel an area in southern Alberta known as Hail Alley, which includes extensive grain fields, and the cities of Calgary and Red Deer. This is one of North America's most violent hail zones, where crops, automobiles, roofs, and windows suffer significant damage from hailstones.

For nearly three decades until 1986, the Alberta government funded a cloud-seeding program, using silver iodide generators mounted on the ground. The theory is that supercooled water droplets will freeze around particles of silver iodide, forming rain or small hailstones and preventing growth of large dangerous hailstones.

On 7 September 1991, insurance companies were hit hard by a massive storm that pounded Calgary with hailstones as big as tennis balls. Claims totaled U.S.$342 million, the second-largest storm-related claim in Canadian history (second only to the ice storm in eastern Canada in the winter of 1997–1998). In response, the industry formed the Alberta Severe Weather Management Society in 1995 and hired an American company to attack storm clouds from the air. Now, when radar indicates hail-forming conditions, pilots fly low into small thunderstorms that feed a major storm and release silver iodide from flares in wing racks or fly above these feeder storms and drop flares into them.

Similar efforts in North Dakota and in Russia apparently have reduced hail by half; but for any single storm the hail that would have occurred without cloud-seeding can never be known. In the Alberta project, insurance claims will be the criterion: if they decrease during five years of effort, the project will be considered a success.

Hail-Suppression Project Area in Southern Alberta. (After Sheremata, 1998. With permission of *Canadian Geographic*.)

BIBLIOGRAPHY

Sheremata, D. "Shooting for the Clouds." *Canadian Geographic* (July–August 1998), 66–70.

—DAVID J. CUFF

cover, which could change the balance of incoming and outgoing radiation. It has been observed that there are sometimes large upper-atmospheric layers that are supersaturated with respect to ice, and in which cirrus cloud systems can be created.

In summary, it appears likely that weather modification as one response to climate change can and will be used to augment water supplies from mountainous areas. It seems probable that, with further advances in our understanding of the dynamic and microphysical processes of convective systems, artificial treatment of these clouds for economically beneficial result will become increasingly feasible. It is unlikely that modification of large-scale weather systems will be a feasible response to climate change in the near future.

[*See also* Drought; *and* Geoengineering.]

BIBLIOGRAPHY

DeMott, P. J. "Quantitative Description of Ice Formation Mechanism of Silver Iodide-Type Aerosols." *Atmospheric Research* 38 (1995), 63–99.
Farley, R. D., D. L. Hjmerstad, and H. D. Orville. "Numerical Simulation of Cloud Seeding Effects during a Four-Day Storm Period." *Journal of Weather Modification* 29 (1997), 49–55.
Heimback, J. A., Jr., W. D. Hall, and A. B. Super. "Modeling and Observations of Valley-Released Silver Iodide during a Stable Winter Storm over the Wasatch Plateau of Utah." *Journal of Weather Modification* 29 (1997), 33–41.
Henderson, T. J. "New Assessment of the Economic Impacts from Ten Winter Snowpack Augmentation Projects." *Journal of Weather Modification* 29 (1997), 42–48.
Hess, W. N., ed. "Weather and Climate Modification." New York: Wiley, 1974.

—LEWIS O. GRANT

WEEDS. *See* Exotic Species.

WEGENER, ALFRED

The German geophysicist Alfred Wegener (1880–1930) is irrevocably associated with the notion of continental drift because he was the first to put forward substantial evidence for a coherent and logically argued hypothesis that took account of a wide variety of natural phenomena.

Wegener was an outsider to the geologic profession. Born in Berlin, the son of an evangelical minister, Wegener studied at the universities of Heidelberg, Innsbruck, and Berlin and took his doctorate in astronomy. From his early days as a student he had cherished an ambition to explore in Greenland, and he had also become fascinated by the comparatively new science of meteorology. In preparation for expeditions to the Arctic he undertook a program of arduous exercise. He also mastered the use of kites and balloons for making weather observations and was so successful as a balloonist that, in 1906, with his brother Kurt, he established a world record with an uninterrupted flight of fifty-two hours. Wegener was rewarded in his assiduous preparations by being chosen as a meteorologist to a Danish expedition to northeastern Greenland. On returning to Germany he accepted a junior teaching position in meteorology at the University of Marburg and, within a few years, had written a textbook on the thermodynamics of the atmosphere. A second expedition to Greenland, with the Danish expeditioner J. P. Koch, took place in 1912; it was notable for the longest crossing by foot of the icecap ever undertaken.

In 1913 Wegener married Else Köppen, the daughter of the meteorologist W. P. Köppen. After World War I he succeeded his father-in-law as director of the Meteorological Research Department of the Marine Observatory at Hamburg. In 1926 he was finally offered and accepted a chair of meteorology and geophysics at the University of Graz in Austria; it had taken a long time to obtain adequate recognition for his wide-ranging contributions to science. Wegener died while leading a third expedition to Greenland in 1930, probably as a result of a heart attack. His laudatory obituaries concentrated on his great achievements as an arctic explorer and pioneer meteorologist, for which he received several medals, whereas today, of course, he is best known as the most notable proponent of continental drift, although this was, by his own admission, little more than a peripheral interest for much of his professional lifetime.

Some of the key evidence that provoked Wegener to propose his radical hypothesis in 1915 came from the continents bordering the South Atlantic. Apart from the suggestive "jigsaw fit" of these continents, there was pa-leontological evidence for a former direct connection between them, but the widely accepted alternative of the subsequent sinking of a land bridge beneath the ocean was deemed implausible because of the principle of isostasy. This principle requires that the higher topography of the Earth is compensated by the presence of continental crustal rocks, which cannot be made to magically disappear. There were also a number of geologic links between the continents that were more plausibly explained by former contiguity. Wegener later added some interesting paleoclimatological arguments suggestive of both polar wandering and continental drift. Unfortunately he failed to come up with a plausible mechanism for continental drift and, for this and other reasons, his views were generally dismissed until his posthumous vindication via the plate tectonics revolution of the late 1960s.

[*See also* Earth Structure and Development; *and* Plate Tectonics.]

BIBLIOGRAPHY

Hallam, A. "Alfred Wegener and the Hypothesis of Continental Drift." *Scientific American* 203 (February 1975), 88–97. An outline of the principal arguments deployed by Wegener and the critical response to them.

Schwarzbach, M. *Alfred Wegener: The Father of Continental Drift.* Madison, Wis.: Science Tech, 1986. This translation is the only full English-language biography.

Wegener, A. *The Origin of Continents and Oceans.* London: Methuen, 1966. Translated from the fourth revised German edition.

Wegener, E. *Alfred Wegener.* Wiesbaden: Brockhaus, 1960. The fullest biographical account by his widow.

—ANTHONY HALLAM

WETLANDS

Wetlands is the collective name increasingly given to all those types of terrain in which there is an interplay between land and water, and that shares the characteristics of both. Swamps, bogs, fens, mires, peatlands, marshes, sloughs, wet meadows, prairie, river bottom lands, and even pothole country and pocosin (the commonly accepted Indian name for evergreen shrub bogs), are all subsumed under the one name.

Wetlands were formerly considered wastelands, neither sound land nor good water, and fit only to be filled in for urban or industrial purposes, dredged out for harbors or marinas, reclaimed for agricultural land, or used as waste disposal dumps. Consequently, they have been disappearing at an ever-increasing rate. But, while economic pressures have intensified, wetlands have become a more valued environment as their hydrologic/physical, chemical, biological, and socioeconomic benefits have been investigated and acknowledged, and their basic Earth-sustaining qualities and biodiversity recognized.

Perhaps above all, wetlands are perceived increasingly as an environment in which air, land, and water, and their fauna and flora, meet in an attractive and delicate environment that has caught the scientific and popular imagination. Demands for their conservation and nonuse are therefore widespread. Their common qualities are emphasized rather than their individual, unique ones, and a pride in achievement at their transformation has given way to a concern at their loss.

The Nature of Wetlands. Wetlands are estimated to cover some 7.8 million square kilometers, or 6 percent of the world's surface (a little less than, for example, tropical rainforests), but they are highly fragmented and diverse. They rarely cover large contiguous stretches of land, except in, for example, the Everglades, the Fenland of eastern England, the Dutch polders, and the deltas of major rivers. Most wetlands were formed during the Holocene, about 10,000 years BP, and many were formed from the deposition, immature drainage, and fluctuating sea levels that followed the retreat of the ice. Others have been formed by human action in the historical era. They are ubiquitous, and are found in every climatic zone from the tundra mires of the Arctic to the tropical mangroves of the equator, and in every continent except Antarctica. [*See* Mangroves.] Their diversity has been simplified by Cowardin et al. (1979) into the marine and estuarine wetlands of the coast, and the riverine, lacustrine (of or near lakes), and palustrine (of or near marshes, usually topographic lows and areas underlain by impermeable strata) wetlands of the interior, a classification that emphasizes their commonalities.

Hydrology is the key to the formation of wetlands, and they have a distinctive botanical composition that arises from being at the junction between dry terrestrial ecosystems and permanently wet aquatic ecosystems. They are formed and conditioned by water and waterlogging, and are adapted to anoxic biochemical processes. Vegetation is adapted to wet (hydrophytic) conditions because it is water-covered for part of the year and is deficient in oxygen. It decomposes slowly and contributes to the formation of the wetland by trapping silt and forming, in time, actual soil (for example, peat). Much of the fauna is adapted to either deep water (fish and shellfish) or dry land (waterfowl, amphibians), moving seasonally into the wetland.

The physical volatility and constant flux from flooding, nutrient flows, and vegetation growth means that wetlands are highly diverse ecosystems, the productivity of which is exceeded only by tropical rainforests. Consequently they have been a constant lure to humankind for settlement and use.

Attitudes to Wetlands. The neglect and denigration of wetlands changed after the early 1960s with greater scientific understanding of their common physical processes and attributes and with a shift in attitude toward them as a unique and valued environment. Interest emanated from the United States, where recreational, hunting, and wildlife enthusiasts, with the active support of the Fish and Wildlife Service (FWS), promoted wetland preservation during the 1930s, as did the private duck hunting lobby, Ducks Unlimited. In total, 1.7 million hectares (4.2 million acres) were purchased, created, or otherwise preserved. In addition, the integrated ecosystems approach stimulated curiosity about wetlands, and research centers focusing on wetland issues were set up at Baton Rouge (Louisiana), Sapelo Island (Georgia), and Miami (Florida). These trends came together as public and administrators alike became concerned at losses through marina dredging, prairie pothole filling, and flood control measures. By 1972, many U.S. coastal states had enacted legislation to protect their shores.

The importance of wetlands for water quality control and wastewater treatment, and a growing appreciation of their aesthetic qualities, led to a raft of U.S. government legislation. Permits became necessary for dredge-and-fill activities, and were only granted after scrutiny by the Environmental Protection Agency (EPA) and the FWS, the objectives and actions of the Corps of Engineers were redefined, and, in 1977, presidential Executive Orders 11988 and 11990 on Flood Plain Management and Wetlands Protection made wetlands a matter of national policy. By 1986, the Emergency Wetlands Resources Act directed the FWS to acquire wetlands with socioeconomic value, and a national wetlands survey was begun.

There was no equivalent wetlands lobby in Europe; in the postwar drive to maximize food production, wetland drainage was underwritten with generous grants from the Common Agricultural Policy of the European Community. Not until the mid-1970s were protests voiced about losses.

Value of Wetlands. The natural processes and functions of wetlands have a value to humans and are used as a counterargument to their destruction. For example, the physical/hydrologic benefits include flood mitigation, coastal protection, recharging of aquifers, sediment trapping, and possibly effects on atmospheric and climatic fluctuations through trapping of carbon dioxide. Chemical functions include pollution trapping, removal of toxic residues, and waste recycling, while biological functions include biomass production and wildlife habitats. The socioeconomic consumptive benefits include food production, fuel from organic soils, fiber from hardwood forests, mangroves, and reed swamps, and fish, fowl, and other fauna.

Compared with the above, the nonconsumptive benefits are much more difficult to define, prove, and value in a monetary sense. These include scenic, recreational, educational, aesthetic, archaeological, scientific, heritage, and historical benefits. These are largely subjective. Recreation values can often be quantified by, for example, payment for fishing and hunting licenses, but there is an imperceptible transition between active involvement in the natural environment and passive enjoyment of a scene that can never be valued. A vast literature has been generated on attempts to quantify nonconsumptive values (5,600 abstracts in the FWS Value Data Base by 1988 alone), and there is still no consensus.

Two nonconsumptive aspects have caught the public imagination, namely, wildlife habitats and archaeology. The intensely moving sight of migrating wildfowl was probably the first, and has remained the most powerful, cause for positive action for preservation. [See Ramsar Convention.] And in Europe in particular, a spate of archaeological finds in wetlands has given tangible evidence of their heritage value. Organic matter is preserved in the waterlogged environment and found in identifiable stratified deposits. The Neolithic villages around Swiss lakes, Romano-British settlements in the Fenland, the complex of late Mesolithic and early Neolithic trackways across the Somerset Levels in southwestern England, and, in the United States, the excavations at Key Marco (Florida) have put wetlands high on the historical/heritage agenda, although their precise monetary value is still undetermined.

The Human Impact. Nearly every human activity can have an actual or potential effect on wetlands. In the upland portions of watersheds, vegetation change, the surfacing of roads, and soil compaction will accelerate runoff and possibly reduce the recharge of water. Agricultural drainage enhances these processes. Mineral extraction, cultivation, and construction of all kinds increases erosion and downstream transport of sediment. A variety of chemical and thermal discharges come from industry, agriculture, and sewage, such as acid runoff from old coal mining areas or heated cooling water from power stations. Downstream, wetlands are affected directly by dredging, filling, construction of dams and pipelines, coastal protection works, piers and quays, and the excavation of ditches and canals. Less directly, offshore drilling, gas, water, and mineral extraction, and offshore "island" construction can all have an effect.

The only quantitative evidence of change is in the United States between 1955 and 1975, when a net loss of 4.625 million hectares was calculated. Of the 5.939 million hectares of freshwater wetlands lost, 79.9 percent succumbed to agricultural conversion, followed by urban infilling (6.3 percent), and impounding for reservoirs and lakes (4.2 percent). In the 0.195 million hectares of saltwater wetlands lost, dredging for canals, ports, and marinas accounted for 55.6 percent of the total. However, the volatility of the wetlands is highlighted by the fact that there was a gain of 1.465 million hectares

of freshwater wetlands and 0.044 million hectares of saltwater wetlands, the former largely through active succession around the margins of new farm ponds, or through the neglect of existing land drainage, and the latter through the formation of new salt marshes and mud flats. How far these figures can be transferred to other parts of the world is open to question, but it would be fair to suggest that agricultural conversion accounts for a good four-fifths of losses, and urban–industrial impacts for another one-tenth.

The Agricultural Impact. Draining for agriculture and grazing intensification is one of the major processes of global change. It accounts for the bulk of the 1.606 million square kilometers of wetlands lost by 1985, although some of that may be connected with the draining of irrigated lands. Nearly three-quarters of the agricultural reclamation has been in the temperate world. The inherent biological wealth of the wetlands bordering the North Sea was important in the transformation of the late medieval economy, and they became some of the most prosperous lands in Europe. In the Netherlands and the English Fenlands, the shrinkage of organic soils upset drainage patterns, a process exacerbated by fuel stripping, which went so far as actually to create the lakes of northern Holland and the Norfolk Broads in eastern England. Progressively, new draining techniques of polders, sea walls, and windmills, eventually superseded by steam and then electric pumps, overcame the problem of land below sea level. The creation of the bulk of the Netherlands is a monument to this activity.

In the United States, the reduction of wetlands has been enormous, although the exact extent of this loss is open to question. Three main types of land are affected: the extensive swamps of the Atlantic coast, which merge with the mangroves of the Gulf and the Everglades of Florida; the alluvial, riverine bottom lands of the Mississippi and its tributaries; and the glacially derived heavy clay soils, with low relief and immature drainage, that stretch across the Midwest from Ohio to Iowa and southern Minnesota, with scattered areas of peat in the three "Lake" states of Wisconsin, Michigan, and Minnesota. Whatever the exact amount, the magnitude of the loss is clear (see Table 1). Drainage in the Midwest took place mainly from 1880 to 1930, with clay pipe underdrainings, but the accelerating deficit is now in the Mississippi and tributary river bottom lands that are being cleared of hardwoods, ditched, walled, pumped, and planted to soybean and other crops. Recent losses in the South between 1937 and 1978 may be as much as 2.67×10^6 hectares, with no end in sight.

For millennia, some of the greatest losses have been in the tropical wetlands of southern and eastern Asia. Guesses can only be made as to their magnitude because these transformations are now an integral part of the "normal" landscape of wet rice or paddy. But the re-

Wetlands. TABLE 1. Estimates of U.S. Wetlands: Original, circa 1955, circa 1975, and Intervening Losses*

	Area (×10⁶ hectares)			*Loss (×10⁶ hectares)*		
	ORIGINAL	C. 1955	C. 1975	ORIGINAL, 1955	1955–1975	APPROX. ANNUAL RATE, 1955–1975 (HECTARES)
CEQ (1978)	51.40	33.18	28.33	18.22	4.85	242,500
Tiner (1984)	87.01	43.70	40.07	43.31	3.63	181,500
OTA (1984)	74.87	40.47	36.08	34.40	4.39	219,500

*Units are millions of hectares; acres are converted to the nearest metric equivalent.

SOURCE: Council for Environmental Quality (1978); Tiner (1984); Office of Technology Assessment (1984). Based on Williams (1990, Table 6.1, p. 200).

duction of the Sundarabans of the Ganges–Brahmaputra, and the deltaic plains of the Irrawaddy, Chao Phraya, Zhu (Pearl), and other Chinese rivers cannot be less than 100,000 square kilometers.

Currently, some of the greatest pressures on wetlands are in Africa, where more than 120 dam and/or irrigation schemes will reduce the magnitude of wet-season floods and the seasonal agriculture and fisheries that they support. Particularly noteworthy are the Jonglie Canal, Sudan, planned to cut off a bend in the White Nile and reclaim the flood plain of the Sudd, and the Bakolori dam in northern Nigeria, with detrimental effects on indigenous smallholders.

Urban and Industrial Impacts. Urban and industrial impacts are greatest in coastal locations. The extension of deep-sea port facilities and the development of port-related industries such as petroleum refining, steel making, and bulk handling of various sorts all contribute to the losses. The sediment dredged from channels to keep them open is often dumped on adjacent wetlands to consolidate them for further urban/industrial uses. Classic cases of urban and industrial expansion in wetlands are Rotterdam, Bombay, Tunis, Sydney, Boston, New York, Miami, Saint Petersburg (Florida), Hong Kong, Singapore, and the urban accretions around Tokyo Bay, where over 250 square kilometers have been infilled or new land created. The dumping in San Francisco Bay became a *cause célèbre* of the environmental movement in California during the 1970s.

Recreational Impacts. The management of recreational impacts is difficult because they are neither uniform nor homogeneous. Canal-based residential dredge and fill, or pollution and bank damage from speedboats, is of a different order than birdwatching, fishing, or ecological study, and most recreational impacts are multiple and their deleterious effect may be synergistic. Moreover, the mix and intensity of impacts varies with population density, affluence, mobility, and even fad: for example, the advent of dune buggies and windsurfing. What does seem to be happening, however, is that values in Western societies are moving more from the active/consumptive to the passive/appreciative, which makes the outright banning of traditional activities highly contentious.

The Future of Wetlands. The threat to the future of wetlands comes broadly from two sources, internal and external, although they are intimately connected.

Internally, rising global population numbers mean a greater need for food, and hence potentially productive wetland will continue to be drained and utilized for agriculture. Expanding urbanization and industrialization (which has so often begun near coastal and estuarine locations) will put greater pressure on prime lowland sites, so that the apparent wasteland of the wetland is the obvious place to expand.

Externally, global warming will almost inevitably lead to rising sea levels and the drowning of coastal marshes and estuaries, with untold effects on fisheries, storm protection, and recreational facilities. The expense of remedial measures such as the heightening of protective walls in the Netherlands, the Fens, and around major urban conurbations may be exorbitant, but within the grasp of affluent societies (for example, the Thames flood barrier for London). The similar heightening of sea walls around Bangladesh, at costs that are variously estimated at between U.S.$20 billion and U.S.$50 billion, is prohibitively expensive and might never happen, with catastrophic consequences. Similarly, the Nile delta may disappear. Similar dilemmas face smaller delta areas around the world. [*See* Sea Level.]

There is another dimension: the fact that wetlands may account for 24 percent of the primary productivity of the world means that any loss of their biomass, either through human activity or as a consequence of global warming and sea level rise, could have long-range implications for carbon budgets, which may feed back into the global circulatory system and engender further global warming. Against all this gloom, however, is the knowledge that sea level and water table shifts can also create new wetlands, thereby increasing primary productivity. As ever, the future of wetlands is uncertain.

BIBLIOGRAPHY

WETLAND CHARACTERISTICS, USE, AND MISUSE

Hook, D. D., et al., eds. *The Ecology and Management of Wetlands.* 2 vols. London: Croom Helm, 1988. A heterogeneous, but informative, collection of papers about wetland ecology and its management.

Mitsch, W. J., and J. G. Gosselink. *Wetlands.* New York: Van Nostrand Reinhold, 1986. A good general survey of the physical properties and management problems of wetlands.

Williams, M., ed. *Wetlands: A Threatened Landscape.* Oxford: Basil Blackwell, 1990. A comprehensive review of knowledge of all physical and human/historical aspects of wetlands.

DISTRIBUTION, NATURE, AND
PHYSICAL CHARACTERISTICS

Chapman, V. J., ed. *Wet Coastal Ecosystems.* Ecosystems of the World, vol. 1. Amsterdam: Elsevier, 1977. The definitive survey of the formation and character of coastal wetlands.

Cowardin, L. M., et al. *Classification of Wetlands and Deepwater Habitats in the United States.* United States Department of the Interior, Fish and Wildlife Service, FWS/OBS-79/31. Washington, D.C., 1979. Probably the most widely used classification for wetland management.

Gore, A. J. P., ed. *Mires: Swamp, Bog, Fen and Moor.* Ecosystems of the World, vol. 4A. Amsterdam: Elsevier, 1983a. Together with its companion volume (below) the definitive survey on the formation and character of inland wetlands.

———. *Mires: Swamp, Bog, Fen and Moor. Regional Studies.* Ecosystems of the World, vol. 4B. Amsterdam: Elsevier, 1983b.

Kivinen, E., and P. Pakarinen. "Geographical Distribution of Peat Resources and Major Peatland Complex Types in the World." *Annals of the Academy Sciencia Fennia, Series A, Geology-Geography* 132 (1981), 1–28. A thorough survey of peat wetlands.

ATTITUDES, VALUES, AND AESTHETICS

Gosselink, J. G., et al. *The Value of the Tidal Marsh.* LSU-SG-74-03. Baton Rouge: Louisiana State University, Center for Wetland Resources, 1974. The classic, integrated ecological study that attempts to assess the functions and values of a wetland.

Greeson, P. E., et al., eds. *Wetlands Functions and Values: The State of our Understanding.* Proceedings of the National Symposium on Wetlands, Lake Buena Vista, Florida. Water Resources Association, Technical Publication TPS 79–2. Minneapolis, 1979. An excellent survey of opinion on this topic.

ARCHAEOLOGY

Coles, J. *The Archaeology of Wetlands.* Edinburgh: Edinburgh University Press, 1984. A preliminary survey of a new topic.

Coles, J. M., and B. J. Coles. *People of the Wetlands.* London: Thames and Hudson, 1989. A well-illustrated review of the human occupants of the wetlands in the past.

HUMAN IMPACTS

Baldock, D. *Wetland Draining in Europe: The Effects of Agricultural Policy in Four EEC Countries.* London: Institute for European Environmental Policy/International Institute for Environment and Development, 1984. An analysis of the detrimental effects of agricultural policies.

Clark, J. R., and J. Benforado, eds. *Wetlands of Bottomland Hardwood Forests.* New York: Elsevier, 1981. Investigates current bottomland losses in the United States.

Council for Environmental Quality. *Environmental Quality: 1978.* The Ninth Annual Report of the Council on Environmental Quality. Washington, D.C.: U.S. Government Printing Office, 1978.

Darby, H. C. *The Changing Fenland.* Cambridge: Cambridge University Press, 1983. The classic historical geography of the draining and management of the fenland.

Lambert, A. M. *The Making of the Dutch Landscape: An Historical Geography of the Netherlands.* London: Academic Press, 1985. A nontechnical, well illustrated, historical geography of the creation of the Netherlands.

Office of Technology Assessment. *Wetlands, their Use and Regulation.* U.S. Congress OTA-0-206. Washington, D.C., 1984. Concerned with wetland loss in general and the United States in particular.

Ruddle, K. "The Impact of Wetland Reclamation." In *Land Transformation in Agriculture,* edited by M. G. Wolman and F. G. A. Fournier. Chichester, U.K.: Wiley, 1987, pp. 171–202. The human impact in Asian wetlands.

Tiner, R. W. *Wetlands of the United States: Current Status and Recent Trends.* Washington, D.C.: United States Fish and Wildlife Service, Department of the Interior, 1984. The definitive survey of U.S. wetlands

RECREATIONAL IMPACTS

Fish and Wildlife Service. *The 1980 National Survey of Hunting and Wildlife Associated Recreation.* Portland, Oreg.: Fish and Wildlife Service, 1980. An overview of U.S. wetland recreational uses.

Leitch, J. A., and D. F. Scott. *A Selected Annotated Bibliography of Economic Values of Fish and Wildlife and their Habitats.* Fargo: Department of Agricultural Economics, North Dakota State University, 1977. An indispensable aid to understanding the importance and valuation of consumptive and nonconsumptive values of wildlife.

FUTURE OF WETLANDS

Armentano, T. V., and J. T. A. Verhoven. "The Contribution of Freshwater Wetlands to the Global Biogeochemical Cycles of Carbon, Nitrogen and Sulfur." In *Wetland and Shallow Continental Water Bodies,* edited by B. Patten. The Hague: SPB Academic Publishers, 1989. The relationship between wetlands and climate.

Hoffman, J. S., et al. *Projecting Future Sea-Level Rise: Methodology, Estimates to the Year 2100, and Research Needs.* U.S. Environmental Protection Agency, EPA 230-09-007. Washington, D.C., 1983.

Zelazny, J., and J. S. Feieraband, eds. *Increasing our Wetland Resources.* Washington, D.C.: National Wildlife Federation, 1987. A review of how more wetland might be created.

—MICHAEL WILLIAMS

WHALING. *See* Fishing; *and* Greenpeace.

WHALING CONVENTION

The International Whaling Commission (IWC), created by the International Convention for the Regulation of Whaling (ICRW) in 1946, is the world's principal institution for the management of whales and whaling. Its preamble describes its purpose as the sustainable use of whales, to "provide for proper conservation of whale stocks and thus make possible the orderly development of the whaling industry." Members make decisions on important questions by a three-quarters majority vote. Principal decisions are embodied in amendments to a Schedule that specifies its regulatory rules. Special but regulated status for indigenous peoples is also granted in the Schedule. Decisions should be "based on scientific findings" and "optimal utilization of the whale resources." A Scientific Committee is therefore one of its key internal organs. Member states that disagree with an IWC decision may opt out by filing an objection. States may also issue permits to take whales for scientific research. The Commission organizes studies, collects data, and may make recommendations to contracting governments. As is the case for most of international law, IWC's decisions are enforced by member states upon themselves. A small secretariat provides coordination and continuity.

For much of its early history, the IWC was ineffective in halting the decimation of the great whales. It used inappropriate catch criteria (the notorious Blue Whale Units—the total catch quota was measured in "blue whale" equivalents; that is, one blue whale equaled 2 fin or 2.5 humpbacks, or 6 sei whales), and set quotas too high. Decisions were dominated by industry managers. Moreover, there was significant underreporting of whales caught by the Soviet Union in the 1950s and 1960s. Reform efforts began in 1961 to put whaling management on a more scientific basis with the appointment of a population dynamics committee, which recommended drastic catch reductions. They were resisted. Reform was bolstered by the report of the 1972 United Nations Conference on the Human Environment (held in Stockholm), which called for a whaling moratorium. The IWC responded in 1974 with a New Management Procedure based on the notion of maximum sustainable yield (MSY). Unfortunately, the scheme proved to be unworkable and, in 1982, a worldwide moratorium was declared, to be imposed in the 1985–1986 season. The ostensible purpose of the moratorium was to allow stocks to revive and to give the Scientific Committee enough time to develop a replacement for MSY. The moratorium was to be reviewed by 1990.

A new majority of IWC members, some believing whales are special creatures, ignored the review deadline and seemed to prefer a permanent moratorium. IWC politics had changed drastically, with a new three-quarters majority of member states who were no longer, or never were, whalers, and direct participation of nongovernmental organizations permitted in almost all phases of IWC activities. As a result, IWC meetings became more confrontational, democratic, and chaotic. The IWC was transformed from a conservation to a

"preservation" regime, even though it is questionable whether its delegates had the legal authority to make this change. The Scientific Committee had developed a Revised Management Procedure (RMP), a sophisticated algorithm for determining safe catch levels, and the plenary session accepted it but refused to put it into practice. This forced the Chair of the Scientific Committee to resign. The new majority insisted that a Revised Management Scheme (RMS), with inspection and other management tools, be developed, but made no effort to submit provisions to implement it. In 1995, a Southern Ocean Sanctuary—prohibiting all whaling in rich antarctic waters—was created. The current regime is enforced by unilateral threats by the United States, under the Pelly Amendment, to impose trade sanctions on states that "diminish the effectiveness" of environmental treaties. While Canada, Norway, Japan, and Iceland have been cited, only limited punishments have been imposed.

At this writing, the majority still refuses to develop regulations needed to promulgate the RMS, and declines to submit conflict issues to third-party mediation, conciliation, or settlement. Japan engages in limited whaling in both the North Pacific and the Southern Ocean (under an objection). Norway has resumed commercial whaling, defying the Commission but imposing upon itself limitations built into the RMP. There is no quota for smallholders who are not indigenous (for example, Japanese whaling from small coastal ports) and, although indigenous people retain quotas, they complain of the majority's cultural imperialism. A potentially rival organization—the North Atlantic Marine Mammal Commission—has been formed, but as yet makes no decisions concerning the regulation of whaling. Seemingly, the IWC is in perpetual crisis.

[*See also* Fishing; *and* Greenpeace.]

BIBLIOGRAPHY

Birnie, P. *International Regulation of Whaling.* Dobbs Ferry, N.Y.: Oceana Publications, 1985.

Friedham, R. L., ed. *Toward a Sustainable Whaling Regime.* Seattle: University of Washington Press, 2000.

Tonnessen, J. N., and A. O. Johnson. *The History of Modern Whaling.* Berkeley: University of California Press, 1982.

—Robert L. Friedheim

WILDERNESS

[*This entry consists of two articles to explain the idea of wilderness areas and their importance in global systems. The first article outlines the U.S. legal definition of a wilderness area and discusses the idea of wilderness in human belief systems, the major controversies about wilderness areas, and management strategies, such as zoning for differ- ent uses. The second article focuses on the impor- tance of wilderness areas to biological diversity and to other aspects of Earth systems and reviews the species that can be preserved now only in wilder- ness areas.]*

The Idea

In contrast to cultures that retain aboriginal ways, the idea of wilderness has a long history in Western culture. As farming and herding supplanted hunting and gather- ing during the Neolithic, an inchoate awareness of dis- tinctions between the artifice of human society and the natural community of life appeared. Refined notions distinguishing the domestic and the wild evolved over subsequent millennia and were reflected in biblical, philosophical, and other ancient texts. Today the wilder- ness idea is a mélange of competing beliefs, ranging from anthropocentric perspectives, such as resource conser- vation, to ecocentric perspectives such as conservation biology. Wild nature, on the former account, is valued in instrumental, economic ways; the watchwords of envi- ronmental policy are efficiency and utility. On the latter account, wild nature (land, flora, fauna, evolution itself) possesses intrinsic value apart from economic schemes; ecological integrity and the conservation of biodiversity are the watchwords of environmental policy. Viewed prospectively, the idea of wilderness occupies a contin- uum: at one end, it is a romantic anachronism; at the other, a category associated with perspectives that value biological and ecological diversity as well as evolution- ary processes.

As the humanization of the planet continues, driven by population growth and economic development, the wilderness idea paradoxically assumes new importance. Considered inclusively, the idea represents the abun- dance of life, the diversity of land forms, the biospheric processes upon which life depends, and the processes of evolution. Advocates such as preservationists, deep ecologists, and conservation biologists contend that wilderness conservation is fundamental to the mainte- nance of life and civilization. In contrast, the culturally dominant ideology (variously termed "anthropocen- trism," "industrialism," or "resourcism") makes wilder- ness "other," that is, antithetical to civilization. So viewed, nature's wildness is evident not only in such phenomena as hurricanes and earthquakes, but in envi- ronmental dysfunctions such as the depletion of strato- spheric ozone and the collapse of oceanic fisheries; the problems of global change thus reinforce the notion that wild nature must be controlled and bent to human pur- poses through engineering. In contrast, wilderness pro- ponents contend that there are no technological fixes for the problems of global change, which are largely the consequence of economically misguided technology and the assumption that natural processes are simple and linear rather than complex and nonlinear. Thus, contin- uing global industrialization, driven by the global mar- ket, threatens biodiversity and impairs biospheric processes upon which civilization depends.

Disputes between those who hold an inclusive idea of wilderness and the supporters of so-called sustain- able development are conceptually and politically com- plicated. Scientists and others who believe that wild nature is a self-sustaining, nonequilibrium process ar- gue that globalist visions for sustainable development are fundamentally self-contradictory, since humans lack the scientific knowledge and the technological means to replace naturally evolved biophysical processes with artificial life support systems. They also argue that an- thropocentrism remains institutionalized in Agenda 21 (United Nations Program of Action for Sustainable De- velopment), and that the political economy of the new world order responds neither to the genuine needs of impoverished people nor to the conservation of biodi- versity; rather, Agenda 21 and other development plans are driven by the imperatives of nationalism, capitalism, and materialism. Advocates of sustainable development believe that environmental dysfunctions and poverty can be ameliorated within the dominant conceptual and institutional framework, that human survival depends on refining the processes of economic development (in- dustrialization) and the technological control of nature, and that proponents for wilderness preservation and the conservation of biodiversity are misguided icono- clasts who ignore the causes of and remedies for eco- nomic destitution. [*See* Agenda 21; *and* Sustainable Development.]

Beyond these contested notions involving the role of wilderness in the next century are issues concerning the importance of wilderness experience. Some human ecologists, psychologists, and others believe that isola- tion from wild nature jeopardizes essential processes of cognitive and psychological development, arguing that dynamic interactions with animals, plants, and natural habitats shaped human intelligence, that the human species has been and remains embedded in the web of life, and that wilderness experience rekindles aware- ness of living connections between humans and their environments. Thus encounters with land forms and flo- ral and faunal domains outside the bounds of the built environment are critical to the development and con- tinuing nurture of humans. Critics argue that, in the con- text of urban, industrial society, wilderness experience is at best atavistic, and at worst an evasion of respon- sibilities of economically privileged individuals to deal with the problems of global change.

The first officially protected wilderness in the United States was proposed by Aldo Leopold in 1922. Now known as the Aldo Leopold Wilderness, it was established in 1924 under the aegis of the Forest Service and comprises 82,000 hectares (202,000 acres). Today the United States is an international exemplar in preserving wilderness, partly because of the Wilderness Act (1964), which established the National Wilderness Preservation System, and because large areas of relatively unhumanized land existed in the United States long after their disappearance in Europe. The Wilderness Act defines wilderness as a place untrammeled by humans, where humans are visitors, where natural ecological processes operate freely, where the primeval character of the land and natural influences are retained, and where opportunities for solitude and primitive recreation experiences abound.

The federal government controls 29 percent of the land in the United States. Almost 55 percent of all designated wilderness is in Alaska, nearly 19 percent of the state; less than 4 percent of the 48 contiguous states has been designated as or recommended for wilderness, and 95 percent of these areas are west of the Mississippi River (Table 1). The Forest Service (FS), the National Park Service (NPS), the Fish and Wildlife Service (FWS), and the Bureau of Land Management (BLM) are the agencies responsible for preparing and implementing wilderness management plans, and recommending to Congress additional lands for wilderness designation; nearly 40 million hectares (100 million acres) have been added to the original 3.6 million hectares. There are presently more than 630 areas, ranging in size from more than 3 million hectares to less than 1 hectare.

The United Nations Man and the Biosphere (MAB) program (1990), which focuses on ecological research with a conservation policy, resource use, and management orientation, is analogous to the U.S. preservation system in creating more than three hundred protected areas in approximately eighty participating countries. However, MAB is unlike the U.S. wilderness system in that biosphere reserves include not only core wilderness areas, but buffer zones and zones of transition subject to human development.

Disputes over the protection and management of wilderness habitats range over three categories. The first concerns disagreements between nations, especially governments and environmental nongovernmental organizations in the Northern Hemisphere and the governments of developing nations in the Southern Hemisphere. Northern Hemisphere conservation groups, for example, favor a preservationist stance on policies affecting tropical rainforests, such as Amazonia, primarily lying within Brazil. Brazilian interests favor a development stance, arguing that it is unfair for developed nations, who have

Wilderness: The Idea. TABLE **1.** Twenty Large Designated U.S. Wilderness Areas

NAME (AND AGENCY*)	LOCATION	TOTAL SIZE (HECTARES)
Wrangell–St. Elias (NPS)	Alaska	3,675,577
Arctic (FWS)	Alaska	3,238,866
Gates of the Arctic (NPS)	Alaska	2,901,697
Noatak (NPS)	Alaska	2,334,181
Frank Church–River of No Return (FS)	Idaho, Montana	957,305
Togiak (FWS)	Alaska	919,028
Misty Fiords (FS)	Alaska	867,305
Denali (FS)	Alaska	860,236
Selway–Bitterroot (FS)	Idaho, Montana	542,696
Everglades (NPS)	Florida	524,899
Bob Marshall (FS)	Montana	408,646
Admiralty (FS)	Alaska	379,538
Boundary Waters Canoe Area (FS)	Minnesota	323,594
Washakie (FS)	Wyoming	285,131
Teton (FS)	Wyoming	236,938
John Muir (FS)	California	234,949
Glacier Peak (FS)	Washington	231,716
Trinity Alps (FS)	California	201,677
Weminuche (FS)	Colorado	186,075
High Uintas (FS)	Utah	184,901

*FS = Forest Service; FWS = Fish and Wildlife Service; NPS = National Park Service.

historically and continue presently to exploit their forests economically, to demand that they preserve theirs. Developing nations also argue that the Northern Hemisphere fueled its own economic advance by exploiting the natural resources of developing countries, and that global capitalism continues to exert environmentally destructive pressures; thus, the Northern Hemisphere is ethically obligated to pay for the conservation of biodiversity and wildlands in the Southern Hemisphere. Another issue concerns land management; the Southern Hemisphere argues that indigenous people, including subsistence hunters and gatherers, and traditional agriculturists, are good stewards of natural habitats who should not be excluded from wildlands because of conservation agendas of the Northern Hemisphere.

Disagreements also exist between interest groups within nations, as for example between American preservationists and the wise-use movement or "localists," or between environmentalists and industrialists. Localists argue that urban interests in wilderness preservation reflect selfish desires for recreational playgrounds while denying the rights of people who have traditionally mined, logged, grazed, and ranched the land. Preservationists argue that the Wilderness Act allows mining and grazing for preexisting operations, that the amenity value of wilderness far exceeds traditional economic uses, and that the wise-use movement itself is a very small but highly visible group funded by corporate logging and mining interests. Another issue arises over rights of access between owners of wildlands and groups of people who have traditionally hunted, fished, and gathered on them. Finally, controversies have arisen over the rights of private property holders to develop wildlands, since various agencies have acted to prevent development under the mandate of the Endangered Species Act.

A third area of debate involves the policies and procedures used by federal agencies for designating and managing wilderness. For example, critics argue that wilderness areas are abundant in rock and ice, with scant biodiversity, leaving old-growth ecosystems rich in biodiversity vulnerable to logging; that the zoning of wilderness areas too often designates lands that are too small and too isolated to allow the continuation of evolutionary processes; that fire suppression is rooted in the failure to understand its role in natural ecosystems; that fees for access to wilderness and the granting of licenses to concessionaires (so-called private–public ventures) mark the final chapter in commodifying wilderness; that too many people visit wilderness areas, thereby destroying any possibility of wilderness experience; that the very notion of wilderness management is oxymoronic; and that ecosystem management is more a bureaucratic buzzword than a scientifically grounded procedure.

[*See also* Biomes; Global Change, *article on* Human Dimensions of Global Change; Parks and Natural Preserves; Stability; World Heritage Sites; *and the biography of* Thoreau.]

BIBLIOGRAPHY

Burks, D. C., ed. *Place of the Wild: A Wildlands Anthology.* Washington, D.C.: Island Press, 1994. A collection of essays concerning wilderness and the protection of biodiversity.

Foreman, D., and H. Wolke. *The Big Outside: A Descriptive Inventory of the Big Wilderness Areas of the United States.* rev. ed. New York: Harmony Books, 1992. A description of large primitive areas and their biological importance.

Forestra, R. A. *Amazon Conservation in the Age of Development: The Limits of Providence.* Gainesville: University of Florida Press, 1991. Analyzes the hypothesis that long-term preservation of Amazonia is more likely to succeed outside development initiatives.

Glacken, C. *Traces on the Rhodian Shore: Nature and Culture in Western Thought from Ancient Times to the End of the Eighteenth Century.* Berkeley: University of California Press, 1968. A magisterial study of changing conceptions of the land.

Grumbine, R. E., ed. *Environmental Policy and Biodiversity.* Washington, D.C.: Island Press, 1994. Multifaceted discussions of the role of wilderness in the conservation of biodiversity.

Hendee, J. C., et al. *Wilderness Management.* 2d ed. Golden, Colo.: Fulcrum Publishing, 1990. A comprehensive account of the theory and practice of wilderness management.

Knight, R. L., and K. J. Gutzwiller, eds. *Wildlife and Recreationists: Coexistence through Management and Research.* Washington, D.C.: Island Press, 1995. A scientific analysis of the consequences of wilderness recreation on habitat, flora, and fauna in the United States.

Leopold, A. *A Sand County Almanac.* New York: Oxford University Press, 1949. An original statement of the scientific and ethical underpinnings for wilderness preservation.

Nash, R. *Wilderness and the American Mind.* 2d ed. New Haven and London: Yale University Press, 1973. A study of the role of the wilderness idea in U.S. public lands policy.

Oelschlaeger, M. *The Idea of Wilderness: From Prehistory to the Age of Ecology.* New Haven and London: Yale University Press, 1991. A comprehensive study of the evolution of the wilderness idea in Western culture.

Rudzitis, G. *Wilderness and the Changing American West.* New York: Wiley, 1996. A study of the changing ideas of public lands management in the American West.

Shepard, P. *The Others: How Animals Made Us Human.* Washington, D.C.: Island Press, 1996. An inquiry into the historical and contemporary importance of interactions between wild animals and humans.

Snyder, G. *The Practice of the Wild.* San Francisco: North Point Press, 1990. Essays that deny the cogency of the wilderness–civilization dichotomy and affirm a place for humans in wild nature.

Wright, W. *Wild Knowledge: Science, Language, and Social Life in a Fragile Environment.* Minneapolis: University of Minnesota Press, 1992. An extension of the wilderness idea to the question of what counts as knowledge in the context of environmental crisis.

—MAX OELSCHLAEGER

Ecological Character

Land use changes have eradicated many wildlife habitats and reduced others to disconnected remnants that may have lost much of their ecological integrity. Although the functional aspects of ecosystems have long been recognized, only recently has this issue become of fundamental concern in conservation. The principal objective of conservation efforts is to maintain or increase a species population. In the past, this was attempted in a rather isolated fashion, often relying on zoos or botanic gardens to maintain the species outside its natural habitat. Such efforts mainly focused on large mammals and birds and vascular plants. Today the roles of all species in an ecosystem forms the basis of conservation efforts that aim to preserve the entire biotic complex. Such an approach requires that ecological, behavioral, and evolutionary processes be able to operate at various spatial and temporal scales. Wilderness areas that still retain their primitive characteristics are essential to this method. In wilderness areas, all life forms are considered important and contribute to the area's biodiversity. However, keystone or system-directing species that have a great influence on overall diversity are usually given highest priority in conservation efforts. Successful wilderness conservation must therefore preserve genetic diversity within a taxon, species diversity within an area, and community diversity within different habitats. For this reason, the design of wilderness areas is critical to their success. [See Conservation.]

Natural area theory was initially based on ideas formulated from island biogeography and assumed that large reserves would contain more species and have lower extinction rates than small ones. In addition, a single large reserve was expected to favor more species than several smaller ones with the same total area. Groups of reserves were considered to be more efficient if they were in close proximity and preferably equidistant and connected by corridors that facilitated population exchange. Because the shape of the reserve is critical for obligate interior species, a circular boundary with minimal edge effect was preferred. Some of these assumptions have not been upheld in conservation studies. Species diversity is typically higher in several small reserves if they provide more varied habitats than in a single larger area. Similarly, smaller reserves may lessen the risk of extinction, especially for rare species with limited distributions. Conversely, larger areas are needed to conserve viable wild populations of species, such as caribou and bison, that move seasonally to different parts of their range. [See Parks and Natural Preserves.]

Ideally, wilderness areas should include substantial populations of endemic species, but it is rarely possible to select sites that provide all of the natural features needed for successful conservation. Frequently, the locations are chosen in an opportunistic manner driven by land availability and political strategies and traditionally focus on preserving the breeding areas of high-profile species. Consequently, reserves created in the past to protect a species often were poorly designed because of limited emphasis on dispersal and behavior. The long-term survival of a species is threatened when its range becomes limited to a single area or when the population becomes isolated with no effective means of dispersal. Population viability analysis provides a means of assessing the risk of extinction over a specified time period; it is a way of determining how many individuals, dispersed in what pattern, over which habitats and throughout what region are needed to prevent extinction due to environmental uncertainty and chance demographic and genetic events (Wilcox, 1990). For mammalian herbivores, 95 percent population persistence for one hundred years requires a minimum viable population (MVP) of one thousand individuals, while ten times that number are needed for small herbivores (Belovski, 1987). This is far greater than estimates based solely on genetic data (Lande, 1988). MVP requirements are now available for many species, but they assume that the ecosystem in which they are found will be maintained; this obviously requires persistence of all of its components. Minimum area-requirements for ecosystems can be estimated by assessing the MVPs of area-sensitive species, which will then provide a protective umbrella for others. Species with low population densities are ideal for this type of analysis. Candidate species might include those with large body size, those at the top of the food chain, and those dependent on unpredictable habitats. Keystone mutualists figure prominently in this work because their demise would have repercussions for many other species. Similarly, birds and bats, which disperse pollen and seeds, act as mobile links between plants that function as hosts for other species (Gilbert, 1980).

Because the majority of the world's species exist only in the wild, *in situ* preservation is the most effective way of maintaining biodiversity. An ecosystem approach to conservation can ensure that representative examples of important plant and animal habitats will be protected. The advantage of this approach is that it offers an opportunity to protect species for which there is limited knowledge. In Britain, over 75 percent of nationally threatened plant species are represented in nature reserves; about 50 percent of the 3,635 threatened plant species in Australia are in conservation reserves; in southern Africa, practically all of the endangered fynbos species occur in protected areas (Groombridge, 1992). Animals are similarly protected in some parts of the world; in southern Africa 92 percent of amphibian and reptilian, 97 percent of avian, and 93 percent of mammalian species native to the region are represented in breeding populations in protected areas (Siegfried, 1989). High percentages of native bird species are reported in protected areas in many other parts of Africa (Sayer and Stuart, 1988), but elsewhere, especially in Oceania, the protected area network is inadequate (Groombridge, 1992). The occurrence of a species in a protected area does not guarantee its survival. Many of these areas are too small to maintain viable populations, and habitat degradation outside of protected areas continues to erode long-term success, as many species must migrate across park boundaries.

Wilderness areas were selected in the past mainly on the basis of aesthetics or simply because they were not suitable for development. Consequently, there is a disproportionately large amount of rugged and ice-covered terrain. Only recently have scientific principles been used in the selection and management of wilderness areas and other landscape-size reserves in order to enhance their role in preserving biodiversity. Efforts to retain tracts of wildland of all ecosystems are increasing worldwide. As well as establishing isolated reserves, there is growing interest in problems of connectivity and the benefits of wilderness recovery networks. These comprise a system of strictly protected areas (core reserves) surrounded by lands used in a manner that is compatible with conservation (buffer zones) and linked in a way that provides functional interconnectivity (Noss, 1992). Visionary plans of this type have been prepared for several regions in North America. The Wildlands Project in Florida proposes to link ecologically sensitive areas including the Everglades, Okefenokee Swamp, and upper Gulf Coast by way of the major river systems. Long-distance dispersal of grizzly bears is a principal objective of the proposed Y2Y project that will link Yellowstone National Park with the Yukon Territories in Canada. The general strategy in these schemes is to build on existing wilderness by expansion and linkages with other areas of high biodiversity.

[See also Biomes; Global Change, article on Human Dimensions of Global Change; Stability; Sustainable Development; World Heritage Sites; and the biography of Thoreau.]

BIBLIOGRAPHY

Belovski, G. E. "Extinction Models and Mammalian Persistence." In Viable Populations for Conservation, edited by M. E. Soulé, pp. 35–57. Cambridge: Cambridge University Press, 1987.

Gilbert, L. E. "Food Web Organization and the Conservation of Neotropical Diversity." In Conservation Biology: An Evolutionary-Ecological Perspective, edited by M. E. Soulé and R. A. Wilcox, pp. 11–33. Sunderland, Mass.: Sinaur, 1980.

Groombridge, B., ed. Global Biodiversity: Status of the Earth's Living Resources. London: Chapman and Hall, 1992.

Lande, R. "Genetics and Demography in Biological Conservation." Science 241 (1988), 1455–1460.

Noss, R. F. "The Wildlands Project: Land Conservation Strategy." Wild Earth, special issue (1992), 10–25.

Sayer, J. A., and S. Stuart. "Biological Diversity and Tropical Forests." Environmental Conservation 15 (1988), 193–194.

Siegfried, W. R. "Preservation of Species in Southern African Nature Reserves." In Biotic Diversity in Southern Africa, edited by B. J. Huntley, pp. 186–201. Cape Town: Oxford University Press, 1989.

Wilcox, B. A. "In situ Conservation of Genetic Resources." In The Preservation and Valuation of Biological Resources, edited by G. H. Orians, G. M. Brown, W. E. Kunin, and J. E. Swierzbinski, pp. 45–77. Seattle: University of Washington Press, 1990.

—O. W. ARCHIBOLD

WILDLIFE MANAGEMENT

Wildlife management is the act, discipline, and profession of managing wildlife populations. The term wildlife sometimes refers to all wild animals, including fishes and plants. However, in the context of the discipline of wildlife management, it refers to free-ranging birds and mammals. Wildlife management is stewardship of the wildlife resource. As such, it seeks to achieve human goals for wildlife resources by working with wildlife populations, their habitats, and people.

Management Options. A wildlife manager has four basic options for managing a wildlife population. First, make the population increase. This option usually applies to small, depleted, or decreasing populations. Second, make the population decrease. This usually applies to populations that are judged to be too high or those that are increasing too rapidly. Third, exploit the population by harvesting it for a sustained, continuing yield. Fourth, monitor it but do not seek to manipulate it. The first three options imply manipulative management, which involves changing the population level of the species involved, either through direct methods, such as hunting, or indirectly by changing the habitat, for example through provision of water or reduction of predators or disease. The fourth option represents custodial management: for example, in the management of a national park or reserve where the objective is to "let nature take its course."

Three decisions must be made in the management of a wildlife population. The first is to decide on the goal of the management process. This decision represents a value judgment and is the responsibility of the political system or other decision makers, not that of the wildlife manager. The second decision is to determine which management option is appropriate to achieve the goal, and the third is how to implement that management approach. The second and third decisions are technical judgments, and they are the responsibility of the wildlife manager.

Management Goals. When wildlife management was developed as a discipline in the early 1930s, the goal was to provide wildlife resources for sport hunting. Aldo Leopold, who is regarded as the father of wildlife management, defined wildlife management as the art of making land produce sustained annual crops of wild game for recreational use. With the exception of predator control, support of sport hunting remained the principal and often the sole goal of wildlife management for nearly forty years. However, by the 1960s, because of, or as part of, a growing environmental awareness and concern among the public, the attention of the wildlife management profession began slowly to broaden its focus to include nongame wildlife and nonconsumptive uses of wildlife. Gradually the goals were broadened. Today, in addition to providing sport hunting, the goals involve managing wildlife in support of a number of human interests and concerns, including the following: (1) maintenance of the ecosystems of which they are a component and the ecological services that they and their ecosystems provide, (2) protection and restoration of populations of endangered species, (3) maintenance of healthy wildlife populations in national parks and reserves, and (4) encouragement of suitable wildlife species in urban situations. In countries other than the United States, the provision of a sustainable yield of wildlife for commercial and subsistence purposes is another current goal of wildlife management.

Reduction or elimination of species that are considered undesirable is an important goal of wildlife management in some countries. Examples range from reduction of kangaroo populations that compete with sheep in Australia to control of predators that prey on livestock or even humans in Africa and Asia. In the United States, predator control long predated the establishment of wildlife management as a discipline and profession, and it has continued as an increasingly controversial component of management. Federal and state programs to control predators and other "pest species" existed long before modern wildlife management was developed. In the 1970s, these programs were curtailed somewhat because of public objections to their excesses, but predator control still remains an active, if somewhat minor and increasingly controversial goal of wildlife management.

Evolution of the Profession. Historically, wildlife in the United States has been the property of the state and has usually been treated as a common property resource. It was an important resource of food and other animal products in the early pioneering days, but some forms were also perceived as competitors or threats. Laws that provided bounty payment for killing of predators date from the original colonies. Settlers sought to remove grazing species such as deer, elk, and bison that competed with livestock, and predators such as wolves, bears, and cougars, and by 1900 most such animals were greatly reduced. Several species were exterminated, in-

cluding the eastern and Oregon bisons, the eastern wapiti, and several forms of grizzly bear. Until about 1870, predators were eliminated to assist livestock raisers. After that time such "control" was also promoted as a way to increase game animals. Commercial take of wildlife began early: the fur trade, for example, played a major role in explorations of the American West, and market hunters were a major user of the wildlife resource from the earliest days. The resultant slaughter of the bison and passenger pigeon provided dramatic evidence of the devastating impact of uncontrolled hunting and raised public consciousness of the need for conservation.

Even by the mid-1800s, many forms of wildlife were so decimated that some members of the public sought to bring in conservation measures. Sportsmen's organizations sought laws to ban the hunting and sale of game when the animals were breeding and raising young, and seasonal closure of hunting was the principal form of wildlife management until the late 1800s, when these laws were augmented by the establishment of protected areas (led by the establishment of Yellowstone National Park in 1872). Some of the private sportsmen's clubs developed into the first official state fish and wildlife agencies.

Concern with depletion of wild birds led to the establishment of several bird conservation organizations, notably the American Ornithologists' Union (AOU) in 1883, and the Audubon Society in 1886, both of which became effective instruments for channeling public conservation concern into government action. In 1885 the AOU was instrumental in convincing Congress to establish what became the Bureau of Biological Survey, much later renamed the U.S. Fish and Wildlife Service. The AOU and Audubon later persuaded President Theodore Roosevelt to create a system of Federal Bird Reservations that became the National Wildlife Refuge System.

In the late 1800s, restocking of depleted game and introduction of exotic species were added to the list of principal methods of wildlife management. Local sportsmen or sportsmen's groups began restocking whitetail deer, which had been virtually eliminated from the eastern United States by overhunting and habitat loss, and, starting with ring-necked pheasants in 1881, foreign game birds were introduced in many parts of the country.

Until the early 1930s, actions undertaken to achieve wildlife management were focused primarily on the species itself. The actions were aimed at reducing mortality by reducing natural enemies (predator control), protecting the populations from hunting (closed seasons and provision of refuges), and increasing game populations by restocking with artificially raised native birds and animals and with exotic species. More recently, it has been recognized that predator control has a negative rather than a positive effect on wildlife; that refuges have limited value, except to protect endangered species; that bounty payments for predators simply do not work; that restocking of depleted species has generally been a failure unless the habitat condition has improved; that, except in a few cases (for example, the ring-neck pheasant), introduced exotics cause more harm than good; and that protection from hunting is often essential, but insufficient to restore depleted wildlife populations unless there is parallel habitat improvement. The whole approach to wildlife management was changed by Aldo Leopold, who put it on an ecological basis.

In 1933, Leopold, a forest scientist, retired from the U.S. Forest Service to join the faculty at the University of Wisconsin. He took the chair in wildlife management, which was the first such academic chair in the country. Leopold taught a theory he was developing, which combined population dynamics of wildlife species with a broad ecological approach, emphasizing the importance of habitat suitability and condition as the basis for supporting wildlife populations. Leopold's work laid the foundations for wildlife management as a discipline and profession.

The following year, Congress authorized the Cooperative Wildlife Research Unit Program, initially with units at ten colleges around the country supported jointly by the state wildlife agency and the college. The program was intended to provide training in the new discipline of wildlife management and to conduct research on key wildlife conservation problems. This program has since been expanded to twenty-two additional colleges and, in recent years, curricula in wildlife management have been established in colleges and universities throughout the country and abroad.

In 1935 the American Wildlife Institute, since renamed the Wildlife Management Institute, was established as a nongovernmental organization funded largely by sporting arms and ammunition companies. Its objective was to promote wildlife management for sport hunting through support to the wildlife units at colleges, and through research and public education. The following year, the General Wildlife Federation, now the National Wildlife Federation, was established as a federation of local sportsmen's groups throughout the country. And, in 1937, the Wildlife Society was established as the professional society for the new discipline of wildlife management, with a high-quality professional journal.

That year also saw the passage of the federal Aid in Wildlife Restoration Act, which dedicated a 10 percent excise tax on sporting arms and ammunition for use by states in approved wildlife research, land acquisition, and management. The act required that the states receiving federal funding pass enabling legislation and apply all revenues from hunting licenses to wildlife conservation. This act was a major milestone in advancing wildlife management.

By World War II, wildlife management was established as a discipline and a profession, with a body of wildlife law, government institutions at federal and state levels, university departments to provide trained staff and to conduct research, a professional society and journal, and a constituency represented by several active nongovernmental supporting organizations. It was also firmly anchored to its original goals of supporting sport hunting, which in turn, provided virtually all the funds to support wildlife management. However, as discussed above, the focus of the profession is broadening to encompass the whole realm of wildlife and of human interests in it. Until recently, most consumptive use of wildlife was based on the concept of maximum sustainable yield, the maximum production per unit time that can be sustained, estimated from the theoretical logistic (S-shaped) growth curve of the target species, calculated without reference to the rest of its ecosystem. But no species exists in isolation from its environment, so this approach does not work, and wildlife management is now moving away from it.

Wildlife management today has become a largely scientific discipline. Research is a particularly important component, including sophisticated experimental design and treatment of data, advanced field and laboratory techniques, and population and habitat analysis. Management includes research, census, monitoring, law enforcement, habitat acquisition and improvement, protection of species as necessary, and regulated taking. It also must involve public education and interactions with the public and with decision makers. It has shown itself sufficiently flexible that, although it started in the United States, it is now practiced throughout the world. Like other resource management professions, it was slow to recognize and adopt the changing goals of the broader public wildlife constituency, but to a large degree it has now done so.

The greatest challenge for the future for wildlife management will be to recognize and adapt to global changes in both biophysical and socioeconomic conditions.

[See also Animal Husbandry; Biological Diversity; Carrying Capacity; Convention on Biological Diversity; Fishing; Wilderness; and the biography of Leopold.]

BIBLIOGRAPHY

Bookhout, T. A., ed. Research and Management Techniques for Wildlife and Habitats. Bethesda, Md.: The Wildlife Society, 1996.

Caughley, G., and A. R. E. Sinclair. Wildlife Ecology and Management. Boston: Blackwell, 1994.

Leopold, A. Game Management. New York: Scribner, 1933.

—LEE M. TALBOT

WIND POWER. *See* Energy Policy; *and* Renewable Energy Sources.

WORLD BANK, THE

The World Bank is an international institution established by treaty and governed by public international law. Its formal title is the International Bank for Reconstruction and Development (IBRD). The IBRD was established in 1944 by the Bretton Woods Agreement and is based in Washington, D.C. After the establishment of the United Nations (UN) in 1945, the IBRD became a UN specialized agency. [*See* United Nations.] The World Bank Group now includes the International Finance Corporation (IFC), the International Development Association (IDA), and the Multilateral Investment Guarantee Agency (MIGA), as well as the International Centre for Settlement of Investment Disputes (ICSID).

The World Bank is the only global multilateral development bank. It has an annual disbursement portfolio of some U.S.$30 billion, with a total portfolio of environment-related projects of some U.S.$12 billion. It is owned by its shareholders, that is, those states that are parties to its Articles of Agreement. In January 2000, these numbered 181. Its governing body is a Board of twenty-four Executive Directors, with voting weights reflecting the shareholdings. The Board is chaired by the president, currently James D. Wolfensohn. The regular and fixed-term professional staff of more than 5,000 are organized within twenty-eight vice presidencies, six of which represent the regions of the developing world within which the Bank operates (Africa, East Asia and the Pacific, South Asia, Latin America and the Caribbean, eastern Europe and Central Asia, and the Middle East and North Africa).

Over the last decade The World Bank has developed a series of Operational Policies and Directives, binding on its staff to ensure that, *inter alia*, its projects are subject to appropriate environmental and social assessment and that they comply with relevant national and international environmental laws and standards. Since 1994, these internal rules have been subject to review by an inspection panel—a group of three independent experts led by a full-time chairman—with the power to receive and investigate complaints from a number of eligible persons, including those claiming to have been affected by their breach. (The Bank has also published, with the United Nations Environment Programme (UNEP), the United Nations Industrial Development Organization (UNIDO), and the World Health Organization (WHO), its environmental requirements for industrial infrastructure projects, which have been widely used by other bodies and the private sector.) [*See* United Nations Environment Programme.]

The World Bank has played a major role in the development of a number of initiatives aimed at providing funding for global environmental problems. In March 1991, the Bank's Board first approved the establishment of a Global Environment Facility (GEF) for a three-year pilot phase, subsequently replenished and restructured in 1994, with a second replenishment in 1998. [*See* Global Environment Facility.] The Bank is the GEF Trustee and, with UNEP and the United Nations Development Programme (UNDP), is an Implementing Agency for projects. The Ozone Projects Trust Fund finances investment projects with resources transferred from the Multilateral Fund that was established in 1990 by the parties to the 1987 Montreal Protocol on Substances that Deplete the Ozone Layer. [*See* Montreal Protocol; *and* Multilateral Fund.] The Rainforest Trust Fund was established in 1992 to fund a program to conserve the Brazilian rainforests. The World Bank has also assisted with the design and establishment of national environmental funds in a number of countries including Bhutan, Uganda, Peru, and Mexico. In light of the 1997 Kyoto Protocol to the Framework Convention on Climate Change, the World Bank established a prototype Carbon Fund in July 1999 to facilitate joint implementation of projects leading to greenhouse gas offsets that are permitted under the Protocol and to cooperate with the "clean development mechanism" envisaged by Article 12. [*See* Kyoto Protocol.]

BIBLIOGRAPHY

Sand, P. H. "Trusts for the Earth: New Financial Mechanisms for International Environmental Protection." 1994 Josephine Onoh Memorial Lecture. In *Sustainable Development and International Law*, edited by W. Lang, pp. 167 ff. London, Dordrecht, Boston: Graham and Trotman/Martinus Nijhjoff, 1995. A lively, well-informed, and readable introduction to the subject.

Shihata, I. A. F. I. *The World Bank in a Changing World*, vols. 1 and 2. Dordrecht: Martinus Nijhoff, 1991, 1995. A series of essays by the General Counsel of the World Bank, providing an exhaustive treatment of the legal aspects of its work, including the environment.

———. *The World Bank Inspection Panel: In Practice.* 2d ed. New York and Oxford: Oxford University Press, 2000. An authoritative treatment of this new body.

The World Bank. *Pollution Prevention and Abatement Handbook*. Washington, D.C.: The World Bank, 1998. A definitive guide to environmental requirements for World Bank funded projects.

—David Freestone

WORLD COMMISSION ON ENVIRONMENT AND DEVELOPMENT. *See* Brundtland Commission.

WORLD CONSERVATION UNION, THE

The International Union for the Conservation of Nature and Natural Resources (IUCN, also known as The World Conservation Union) played a critical role in the global conservation movement of the second half of the twentieth century.

In October 1948, governments, public services, organizations, institutions, and associations concerned with the conservation of nature and natural resources met in the Château of Fontainebleau, on the invitation of United Nations Educational, Scientific, and Cultural Organization (UNESCO), the French government, and the Swiss League for the Protection of Nature. That group's agenda gave organizational form to an ambitious set of ideas. In a postwar context in which numerous intergovernmental fora were created, and in a period when many colonial territories became independent nations, the men and women at Fontainebleau created the world's first "GONGO"—both a governmental and nongovernmental organization. It was a creative leap, bringing together scientists and policy makers.

The formal act constituting the International Union for the Protection of Nature (IUPN) was signed on 5 October 1948 by delegates representing eighteen governments, seven international organizations, and 107 national organizations. The secretariat was based in Brussels under a Belgian secretary general, Jean-Paul Harroy. The new union's objectives included fostering cooperation between all those concerned with the protection of nature and promoting national and international action to preserve wildlife and the natural environment. The IUPN was renamed International Union for the Conservation of Nature and Natural Resources in 1956, a name shortened to The World Conservation Union in 1990 (although the longer version remains the union's official title).

One of the union's early innovations was the inception of technical commissions made up of volunteer experts. The commissions advise the union on species survival; protected areas; environmental law; education and communication; environmental, economic, and social policy; and ecosystem management.

The 1950s and 1960s were a period of consolidation. Working with limited resources, IUCN moved its headquarters to Switzerland in 1961, and leading figures active within the union created the World Wildlife Fund for Nature (formerly World Wildlife Fund; WWF), with a view to gathering more financial support for conservation.

During the 1980s and early 1990s, the union contributed to setting the global environmental agenda by publishing the *World Conservation Strategy* (1980) and *Caring for the Earth* (1991) both in cooperation with WWF and the United Nations Environment Programme. *World Conservation Strategy* launched the concept of sustainable development and *Caring for the Earth* emphasized the human dimension of conservation and development and the imperative of sustainability. In this, its approach paralleled that of many development assistance agencies which, since the late 1980s, have been the Union's strongest financial supporters.

The World Conservation Union today is the world's largest conservation-related organization, with over nine hundred governmental and nongovernmental members from 138 countries. It has contributed to drafting major global conventions on biological diversity, wetlands, world heritage, and trade in endangered species of flora and fauna. It is also a global network of networks, with over nine thousand scientists and field practitioners from government and nongovernmental organizations working voluntarily, and has forty-six offices around the world employing over eight hundred permanent staff with an annual budget (1998) of over fifty million U.S. dollars. The World Conservation Union works with and through its members and strategic partners—grassroots, governmental, intergovernmental, academic, research, and corporate organizations—and prides itself on "sound science, socially delivered."

The union's mission is to influence, encourage, and assist societies throughout the world to conserve the integrity and diversity of nature and to ensure that any use of natural resources is equitable and ecologically sustainable.

[*See also* Convention on International Trade in Endangered Species; *and* Nongovernmental Organizations.]

BIBLIOGRAPHY

International Union for the Conservation of Nature and Natural Resources (IUCN). United Nations Environment Programme (UNEP). World Wide Fund for Nature (WWF). *Caring for the Earth: A Strategy for Sustainable Living.* Gland, Switzerland: IUCN/UNEP/WWF, 1991.

———. *World Conservation Strategy: Living Resource Conservation for Sustainable Development.* Gland, Switzerland: IUCN/UNEP/WWF, 1980.

—JAVED AHMAD

WORLD HEALTH ORGANIZATION

The World Health Organization (WHO), founded in 1948 as a specialized agency of the United Nations, has as its objective "the attainment by all peoples of the highest possible level of health." WHO's responsibility to direct and coordinate international health work has led to smallpox eradication (perhaps its major achievement), efforts to reform health systems to increase the availability and quality of primary health care, and important programs including those on childhood immunization, prevention of diarrheal disease and respiratory disease mortality, tropical disease and reproductive health research and, more recently, prevention and control of the human immunodeficiency virus/acquired immune deficiency syndrome (HIV/AIDS) pandemic.

In the past decade, WHO's traditional practice of providing technical advice and setting biomedical standards while avoiding political controversies has been challenged by two major issues: globalization and health inequity.

Globalization of health involves both recognition that disease crosses borders and awareness of the transnational nature of conditions (economic, political, environmental) that strongly influence population health status. The HIV/AIDS pandemic, outbreaks of Ebola virus, and the discovery of antibiotic-resistant strains of pathogenic bacteria, among other recent events, have stimulated considerable interest in the subject of emerging and reemerging diseases. In response, WHO has proposed to create a global capacity for surveillance and response. The Organization is also concerned with the health impacts of large-scale environmental issues such as global climate changes, implicated for example in recent cholera epidemics in the Western Hemisphere. However, WHO has been less successful in developing a framework for understanding the influence of transnational economic forces, such as movements of capital and labor, on health status.

The WHO Constitution states that "unequal development in different countries in the promotion of health control of disease . . . is a common danger." Nevertheless, WHO has experienced great difficulty in conceptualizing or implementing substantive efforts to address fundamental global inequities in health status. A recent, dramatic example of inequity involves new agents for treatment of HIV/AIDS, both highly effective and extremely expensive (in excess of U.S.$10,000 per person per annum), yet essentially unavailable for over 90 percent of HIV-infected people: those living in the developing world.

Looking to the future, WHO must learn to engage effectively with the broad range of global issues affecting health. However, as an organization of member states, each of which is concerned about its sovereignty and prerogatives in the health domain, WHO remains timid with respect to the societal dimensions of health. This difficulty has been exacerbated in the past decade by inadequate leadership, so that a framework for global cooperation for health remains to be elaborated. The election of a new Director-General in May 1998 offers hope and opportunity for renewal of the only organization within the United Nations family with a clear mandate to promote and protect global health.

[See also Disease; and Human Health.]

BIBLIOGRAPHY

Godlee, F. British Medical Journal 309: 1424–1428, 1491–1495, 1566–1570, 1636–1639; 310: 110–112, 178–182, 389–393, and 583–586.

The Lancet. "WHO: Where There is No Vision, the People Perish; A Vital Opportunity for Global Health." The Lancet 350 (1997), 749–751. Open letter to the Executive Board of WHO.

Wilson, M. "Anticipating New Diseases." Current Issues in Public Health 1 (1995), 90–95.

World Health Organization. Basic Documents. 39th ed. Geneva: WHO, 1992.

—JONATHAN M. MANN

WORLD HERITAGE SITES

World Heritage Sites, known collectively as the "World Heritage List," are a select group of natural areas and cultural sites that are formally designated, recognized, and protected for their universal significance by the sovereign governments of the world, acting together through the World Heritage Committee. As of 2000, 630 World Heritage Sites in 118 countries were inscribed on the World Heritage List. The Statue of Liberty, the Taj Mahal, Vatican City, Machu Picchu, and the Great Wall of China are examples of cultural sites on the List. Natural World Heritage Sites include parks and protected areas such as Sagarmatha National Park, including Mount Everest (Nepal), the Serengeti Plain (Tanzania), and Yellowstone National Park (United States). (Natural sites may also simultaneously bear other international designations, such as Biosphere Reserve or Ramsar Site.) [See Parks and Natural Preserves.]

The World Heritage List is the contemporary successor to the ancients' list of the wonders of the world. It was established by the World Heritage Convention (formally known as the Convention Concerning the Protection of the World Cultural and Natural Heritage), a multilateral treaty adopted at the General Conference of the United Nations Educational, Scientific, and Cultural Organization (UNESCO) in 1972. The Convention's goals may be summarized as the establishment of a system of international cooperation through which the world's heritage can be protected and enhanced in an orderly way throughout the world.

The United States, which was the first nation to propose the concept of linking nature and culture in a single World Heritage List, was also the first to ratify the World Heritage Convention, in 1973. After a quarter century, the Convention is, with 160 signatories (technically known as "States Parties") participating, the most widely accepted international conservation treaty in human history.

Under the Convention, nations voluntarily nominate their most important natural wonders and cultural treasures for inscription on the World Heritage List and pledge to preserve and protect those sites in perpetuity by taking appropriate legal, scientific, technical, administrative, and financial measures. The Convention also calls on the signatories to work together to preserve all World Heritage Sites as the common heritage of humanity. It is important to note, however, that, under the Convention, each nation explicitly retains sovereignty over and complete ownership, legal authority, and management responsibility for its World Heritage Sites.

The governing body established by the Convention is the World Heritage Committee, the popular designation for the Intergovernmental Committee for the Protection of the World Cultural and Natural Heritage. Its twenty-one members are elected for six-year terms on a rotating basis by all signatories at biennial General Assemblies. The Committee has no permanent members; all principal regions of the world are represented. Between meetings, its business is supervised by an elected chair, and conducted by a permanent staff, known as the "World Heritage Centre." The work of the Committee is also assisted by three nongovernmental expert advisory bodies—the International Union for the Conservation of Nature and Natural Resources (the World Conservation Union; IUCN), the International Council on Monuments and Sites (ICOMOS), and the International Centre for the Study of the Preservation and Restoration of Cultural Property (ICCROM); the first two provide evaluations of proposed World Heritage Sites.

World Heritage Sites are selected by the committee. A nomination for the list must meet extraordinarily stringent criteria of international significance and document the nominating nation's measures to protect the site. Natural areas may be selected if they outstandingly illustrate stages of the Earth's history, represent ecological or biological processes exceptionally well, possess exceptional beauty and aesthetic importance, or contain very important habitats for conservation of biological diversity. [See Biological Diversity.] The criteria for selection of cultural sites permit recognition of outstanding traditional human settlements, exceptionally important architectural or engineering works, sites that exceptionally represent cultural traditions, masterpieces of human creative genius, and, under exceptional circumstances, sites associated with events, living traditions, and ideas and beliefs of universal significance.

The committee also reviews voluntary monitoring reports on sites and may name sites to the List of World Heritage in Danger, a nonpunitive listing aimed at mobilizing support and assistance to threatened sites. Technical assistance and professional training are also provided for World Heritage Sites from the World Heritage Fund.

The World Heritage Program and process have been criticized as being too selective and as lacking universality because the sites identified to date have been disproportionately from Europe and North America and far more cultural than natural sites have been selected. World Heritage funding is also small (currently slightly over U.S.$4 million a year) relative to the formidable conservation and preservation needs of the sites. World Heritage designation, however, has had manifold positive effects. It has led to measures to improve conditions at World Heritage Sites and has helped mobilize financial resources to assist them; a provision for emergency assistance under the Convention's auspices has proved very useful. Projects to assist sites such as Garamba National Park (Zaire), the Galápagos Islands (Ecuador), Delphi (Greece), and Angkor Wat (Cambodia), among others, have been carried out. More generally, recognition under the Convention has encouraged tourism, particularly to lesser-known sites, serving as an economic stimulus for those sites and their surrounding communities. The World Heritage List provides a framework that the international donor community can use in considering assistance to sites.

A major virtue of the World Heritage Convention is its linkage of nature and culture, which serves as a permanent reminder of the relationship between humans and their environment and the necessity for maintaining harmony and equilibrium between them. This is the fundamental vision that inspired the Convention and continues to guide work under it.

INTERNET RESOURCE

World Heritage Centre. http://www.unesco.org/whc/archive/index. htm/. The World Heritage Committee has been active for over two decades, first meeting in 1977 and first listing sites in 1978. The extensive records of its statutory and other meetings are deposited, along with related materials, in the UNESCO Archives in Paris, France. Many key documents from this collection, including the minutes and many of the reports of Committee meetings, may be consulted in full at this Web site. These documents are typically found in English and French, the working languages of the World Heritage Committee. Records of participation in the work of the Committee by national government delegations have not been studied or cataloged and remain in the hands of the national authorities. Little of this material is of sufficient age to have found its way into archival depositories. Some may not be available for public release.

BIBLIOGRAPHY

BOOKS AND ENCYCLOPEDIAS
Harper-MacRae and Associates, Inc./IUCN. *Masterworks of Man and Nature.* Sydney, 1994. A finely illustrated one-volume encyclopedia of the World Heritage List, which also includes numerous brief essays and reflections by scholars, prominent individuals, and persons active in the Convention's work.
———. *Paradise on Earth: The Natural World Heritage List.* Sydney, Australia: 1995. A handsome one-volume compendium of the natural World Heritage Sites, including several issue-oriented essays and summaries of information on the sites deriving from the collections of the World Conservation Monitoring Centre in Cambridge, United Kingdom.
———. *Our North American World Heritage.* Sydney, 1997. This volume lavishly showcases the World Heritage Sites of Canada, Mexico, and the United States.
INCAFO/UNESCO. *Patrimonio de la Humanidad.* Madrid, 1995. Encyclopedia of World Heritage Sites in twelve volumes (in Spanish).
Kodansha/UNESCO. *The World Heritage.* Tokyo, 1996–1997. A second twelve-volume encyclopedia describing World Heritage Sites (in Japanese).

Pressouyre, L. *The World Heritage Convention, Twenty Years On.* Paris: UNESCO, 1993. A brief history of the application of the World Heritage Convention to cultural sites by the distinguished Vice President of the University of Paris, a scholar who formerly oversaw the professional reviews of cultural site nominations (in English and French).

Thorsell, J. *World Heritage Twenty Years Later.* Gland, Switzerland: IUCN, 1992. As Senior Advisor on Natural Heritage to the World Conservation Union, the author has superintended the review of the natural site nominations for the World Heritage Committee; this essay offers his observations and reflections on that important work.

Verlagshaus Stuttgart/Plaza y Janes/UNESCO. *World Heritage.* Stuttgart, Germany, 1996–1997. A twelve-volume encyclopedia describing World Heritage Sites (in German.)

von Droste, B., et al. *Cultural Landscapes of Universal Value.* Jena, Germany: Fischer Verlag, 1995. Bernd von Droste, the then Director of the World Heritage Centre, and Mechtild Rossler, the natural sites specialist for the Centre, joined with Harald Plachter, a German scholar and sometime member of German delegations to meetings of the World Heritage Committee, in this important discussion of "mixed" World Heritage Sites, that is, those that combine cultural and natural attributes.

PERIODICALS

United Nations Educational, Scientific, and Cultural Organization (UNESCO). *The UNESCO Courier.* Generally contains one or two articles on World Heritage Sites. (Published monthly in English, French, and Spanish.)

————. *The World Heritage Review.* Publishes feature articles and updates on World Heritage Sites. (Issued quarterly in English, French, and Spanish.)

—SHARON J. CLEARY

WORLD METEOROLOGICAL ORGANIZATION

The World Meteorological Organization (WMO) is a specialized agency of the United Nations established in 1951 as a successor to the nongovernmental International Meteorological Organization, which had coordinated the collection and dissemination of weather data since 1873. Based in Geneva, the WMO has been instrumental in establishing and maintaining networks of meteorological observing stations throughout the world, in standardizing the gathering and publishing of weather and hydrologic information, and in facilitating the rapid exchange of these data and their application to aviation, shipping, agriculture, and other human activities.

The World Weather Watch (WWW) is WMO's principal program for the gathering, compiling, and distribution of meteorological data. WWW's member-operated worldwide network of ten thousand weather stations on land, seven thousand stations on ships, and three hundred automated stations on moored and drifting buoys gathers a continuous supply of weather and hydrologic data. These data are transmitted by four satellites in polar orbits and five in geostationary orbits to thirty-five regional and 183 national centers for preparation of weather forecasts.

The WMO has been a partner in several international research projects on climate and the atmosphere. It cosponsored, with the International Council for Science (ICSU), the Global Atmospheric Research Programme of 1968–1981, which gathered immense quantities of scientific data on the dynamics of climate and the atmosphere. [*See* International Council for Science (ICSU).] Growing concerns about climate changes, both naturally occurring and human-induced, led the WMO to become the lead sponsor of the World Climate Programme (WCP). Inaugurated in 1979, the WCP is a cluster of programs that monitor climate, warn governments of impending climate changes and impacts, analyze response strategies, and facilitate continuing research on the world's climate. The WMO participates in the Global Climate Observing System, which was launched in 1992 to support the WCP by coordinating the monitoring of the principal components of the climate system, including the atmosphere, biosphere, cryosphere, and oceans.

The WMO has also informed policy makers of scientists' concerns about climate change and the general state of the atmosphere. In 1979, it convened the landmark First World Climate Conference, a meeting that drew worldwide attention to the threat of climate change and led to the creation of the WCP. In 1988, the WMO collaborated with the United Nations Environment Programme (UNEP) in creating the Intergovernmental Panel on Climate Change (IPCC). [*See* Intergovernmental Panel on Climate Change; *and* United Nations Environment Programme.] The IPCC has produced a series of authoritative assessments of the state of scientific knowledge on climate change, which were reported to the Second World Climate Conference in 1990 and informed negotiations on the 1992 Framework Convention on Climate Change and follow-up agreements.

The WMO is widely looked upon as a highly effective UN agency and a prototype for promoting international scientific cooperation. Its broad array of programs has not only notably enhanced the accuracy and duration of weather forecasts, but has also significantly enhanced knowledge of the determinants of weather and climate and the dynamics of the atmosphere. The WMO's accomplishments have been attributed by some to the focus of its directors on the organization's technical and scientific missions, while leaving it to other bodies, such as UNEP and the UN General Assembly, to address politically sensitive policy issues.

BIBLIOGRAPHY

Davies, A., ed. *Forty Years of Progress and Achievement: A Historical Review of WMO.* Geneva: World Meteorological Association, 1990. A comprehensive history of the WMO and a detailed description of its programs, commissioned by the WMO for its fortieth anniversary.

Soroos, M. S., and E. Nikitina. "The World Meteorological Organization as a Purveyor of Global Public Goods." In *International Organizations and Environmental Policy*, edited by R. V. Bartlett, et al. Westport, Conn.: Greenwood Press, 1995, pp. 69–82. An overview and critical review of the history and programs of the WMO.

—MARVIN S. SOROOS

WORLD TRADE ORGANIZATION

The World Trade Organization (WTO), established in 1995, is an intergovernmental organization that oversees national policies relating to trade. The WTO is considered to be a relatively powerful multilateral agency. It administers several different agreements covering issues such as agriculture, services, subsidies, product standards, food safety, and intellectual property. The WTO also contains a robust dispute settlement mechanism that can authorize trade sanctions to enforce a judgment.

The need for an intergovernmental organization covering trade first dawned in the postwar planning of 1919. No such organization was established, however. In succeeding decades, it became clearer that national tariff and trade policies were often protectionist—designed to stifle trade and externalize costs on other economies. In 1946, the United Nations Economic and Social Council convened a series of preparatory meetings to culminate in the United Nations Conference on Trade and Employment of 1947–1948. That conference approved a forward-looking treaty for an International Trade Organization. Unfortunately, this treaty was never put into force.

In the absence of an official trade organization, government trade officials improvised by building on the General Agreement on Tariffs and Trade (GATT) of 1947. GATT was a set of rules about how contracting governments would treat each other. The core rule was nondiscrimination. Over the next four decades, several rounds of negotiations lowered tariffs and helped promote greater trade. In 1986–94, the Uruguay Round succeeded in lowering tariffs, erecting better disciplines against nontariff barriers, and establishing the WTO.

The WTO differs in several key respects from many other international organizations. It is not part of the UN system. It has a large governmental membership (now 136), yet it remains exclusionary. For example, China and Russia have not been permitted to join. (China may join soon.) The WTO is also selective in choosing agencies to coordinate with. Although it maintains programmatic links to the International Monetary Fund and the United Nations Conference on Trade and Development, the WTO has resisted establishing similar links to the United Nations Environment Programme.

The WTO plays no role in determining the composition or flows of cross-border trade. Moreover, the WTO does not get involved in private international trade law. The WTO is only concerned with government policies that contradict its rules. Trade restrictions per se are not a WTO violation. For example, the WTO would allow a government to impose special tariffs on shrimp imports that are priced too low (in other words, "dumped"). But the WTO has directed the U.S. government to stop banning shrimp caught in ways that kill sea turtles.

In a globalizing economy, the WTO will remain an important institution and will probably gain an enhanced role. For example, in 1997 the WTO began considering how it might supervise national investment policies. Although the multilateral trading system has always been attentive to the way in which trade policies affect global economic change, the WTO continues to be inattentive to how international trade and investment affect natural resource use and environmental quality. While trade officials are correct in pointing out that these ecological problems were never legally assigned to the WTO, optimal policies to address global change may require a greater coordination among intergovernmental agencies.

Located in Geneva, the WTO (in 2000) has a staff of 500 and an annual budget of U.S.$73 million.

[*See also* Global Economy; *and* Trade and Environment.]

BIBLIOGRAPHY

Charnovitz, S. "New WTO Adjudication and its Implications for the Environment." *International Environment Reporter* 19 (18 September 1996), 851–856.

Dam, K. W. *The GATT: Law and the International Economic Organization.* Chicago: University of Chicago Press, 1970. A classic in trade policy; though somewhat dated, it remains very useful for understanding the evolution of the GATT.

Hudec, R. E. *The GATT Legal System and World Trade Diplomacy,* 2d ed. Salem: Butterworth Legal, 1990. A good historical summary and analytical review of GATT dispute settlement.

Jackson, J. *The World Trading System.* Cambridge, Mass.: MIT Press, 1989. An informative discussion of old and new trade policy issues.

Raworth, P., and L. C. Reif, eds. *The Law of the WTO: Final Text of the GATT Uruguay Round Agreements.* New York: Oceana, 1995. Contains the text of the GATT and the Uruguay Round agreements.

Schott, J. J., ed. *The World Trading System: Challenges Ahead.* Washington, D.C.: Institute for International Economics, 1996. Contains fifteen chapters by international experts on key issues in the trading system.

—STEVE CHARNOVITZ

WORLD WIDE WEB. *See* Information Technology.

Y

YOUNGER DRYAS

The Younger Dryas (YD) is a cold climatic interval that took place between approximately 12,900 and 11,600 BP (Alley et al., 1993). This pronounced and rapid cooling, identified almost a century ago from Scandinavian macrofossil records, is named for the arctic-alpine herb *Dryas octopetala*, whose preserved leaves and fruits were discovered in terrestrial records overlying sediments that contained indicators of a previously warmer climate. This climate change was the third and most extensive reversal to colder climate conditions in Europe following the general climate warming that occurred after maximum ice age cold conditions. Hence it followed the Oldest Dryas and the Older Dryas. Its definition as a *chronozone* (Mangerud et al., 1974) permits the search for its correlatives throughout the world. Unfortunately, however, a plateau exists in the carbon-14 chronology at about 11,600 BP, along with some possible reversals during the YD, which limit precise correlations.

By 12,900 BP, retreat from maximum glacial conditions resulted in an ice-free British Isles, substantial recession of Scandinavian glaciers, and retreat of the Laurentide Ice Sheet well back into Canada. The global sea level curve from Barbados suggests that ice extent had diminished to less than half of ice age conditions (Fairbanks, 1989). However, as the YD occurred, glaciers actually reformed in the Scottish highlands, and prominent YD glacial moraines are characteristic of the entire Scandinavian coastline. More recently, montane glacial advances in the western Rocky Mountains of North America have also been correlated with the YD (Osborne and Gerloff, 1997).

The discovery of the Younger Dryas in Scandinavia was followed in the 1930s by a large number of pollen investigations into lake and bog sediments throughout Europe (Watts, 1980). Tundra pollen was diagnostic of the YD, since it followed the establishment of forest pollen that indicated the late-glacial warming. Dramatic changes in vegetation characterized both coastal and inland areas all the way from northern Norway to the Mediterranean (Walker, 1994). In the British Isles, birch forest was replaced by shrubs and herbs, and over sixty late-glacial pollen records are found in Scotland alone. Many continental European records show relatively small changes in pollen percentages, but a marked lithologic change from organic to inorganic deposition, and a rise in *Artemisia* pollen, indicating a more open, disturbed landscape. However, as far south as northern

Spain, estimates from botanical data suggest that mean July temperatures may have been as much as 8°C below modern values.

Within the YD chronozone itself, there are indications of an ameliorating climate during the latter part. While in some areas of Europe, such as Britain and Ireland, the increase in steppe and halophytic taxa may indicate a drier climate, in other areas it appears to have been slightly wetter. Geomorphologic and lithologic changes as well as faunal (for example, beetles) and isotopic shifts provide additional evidence for the climatic fluctuation at numerous European sites.

At the eastern margin of the Laurentide Ice Sheet, numerous late-glacial buried sequences found more than fifty years ago reveal a sudden oscillation in climate. For many years, problems with conventional carbon-14 dating precluded their correlation with the YD event, but the advent of accelerator mass spectrometry (AMS) dating combined with very detailed macrofossil analysis has resulted in very strong correlation of the changes in North America with Europe (Mayle et al., 1993). In northern Nova Scotia, herb tundra replaced shrub tundra as the climate cooled. In southern New Brunswick and central Nova Scotia, shrub tundra replaced spruce forest. The lake sediment itself is characterized by higher levels of silts and sands due to the erosion of the landscape. Surface water temperature reconstructions derived from modern midge fly larvae indicate temperature declines of 6°–7°C (Walker et al., 1991).

Southern New England also shows a strong regional pattern of late-glacial palynological change (Peteet et al., 1993). Fluctuations in a mixed coniferous–deciduous forest (spruce, fir larch, white pine, oak, ash) are marked at the onset of the YD by a rapid disappearance of the warmth-loving trees and a marked increase in the boreal trees (spruce, fir, larch, paper birch, alder) as the climate cooled. The abundance of the boreal macrofossils indicates their local dominance on the landscape, and their AMS carbon-14 dating agrees with the European chronology, confirming the climatic correlation. The summer cooling inferred for the YD is 3°–4°C, based upon the type of vegetational changes and their modern analogues in the Adirondack Mountains. The sharp return to warmer conditions at 11,600 BP is marked by the dominance of white pine and loss of the boreal trees.

In the midwestern United States, a pollen shift in the Till Plains area has been correlated with the YD, showing a rapid recurrence of spruce just prior to the Holocene warming (Shane and Anderson, 1993). Future attention to AMS dating is needed to refine the chronology. The coastline of the Pacific Northwest shows changes that are also correlative with the YD. Mountain hemlock is indicative of cooling in British Columbia, while, further north, in southeastern Alaska near Glacier Bay, tundra elements dominate (Mathewes, 1993). On Kodiak Island, Alaska, a dominance of crowberry and loss of ferns along with marked increases in inorganic lake sediments is characteristic of coastal stratigraphy (Peteet and Mann, 1994).

The YD event is extremely well defined in Greenland ice cores, as evidenced by the coring records at Camp Century, Dye 3, and Renland, confirmed in the GRIP and GISP2 deep cores retrieved in the last decade (Dansgaard et al., 1993). [See the vignette on GRIP and GISP2 in the article on Climate Reconstruction.] The signal is observed as a several parts per million shift in oxygen isotope ratios, corresponding to temperatures about 15°C colder than today (Cuffey et al., 1995). The event is also marked by significantly higher dust levels and chemical concentrations compared to adjacent intervals. The onset of the YD in the ice cores is gradual, and the termination abrupt, occurring in as little as one to three years in some indicators. The snow accumulation rate in the YD was about half that of the Preboreal, and about one third of modern. The changes at the end of the YD were completed in three five-year steps spread over about forty years (Taylor et al., 1993), and snow accumulation changed by about 90 percent in one year (Alley et al., 1993). The discovery of a YD methane signal in antarctic ice cores (Chappellaz et al., 1990) first showed the global imprint of the changes that were characteristic of this time interval.

In the 1980s, the discovery of North Atlantic faunal changes concurrent with the terrestrial European signal led to the conclusion that the North Atlantic polar front readvanced to its glacial position at that time (Ruddiman and McIntyre, 1981). Subsequent geochemical analyses indicate that the production of North Atlantic Deep Water (NADW), which today is responsible for bringing heat to Europe, was greatly reduced at this time, as it was during the ice age. The cause for the presence of this deep-water cessation is still in dispute. Recent evidence from the Cariaco Basin indicates an increase in wind-induced upwelling during the YD off coastal Venezuela (Hughen et al., 1996). North Pacific investigations now show that the YD was expressed in the Japan Sea as well as off coastal California (Behl and Kennett, 1996).

The geographic distribution of the YD event is a topic under close scrutiny. While the research of the last two decades has showed that its distribution is not limited to Europe but instead is expanded to North America and Greenland, the question of its occurrence in the Southern Hemisphere is highly disputed. Figure 1 shows a global map of the distribution of palynological evidence for the YD cooling generated by an International Geological Correlation Project Working Group (Peteet, 1995). The most convincing evidence outside North America is from Colombia, South America, where many sites show an oscillation but await precise AMS carbon-14 dating. Controversial regions where some sites seem to have an oscillation and others do not are Central America, southern South America, and the eastern Mediterranean region. A clear absence of a YD signal is not yet confirmed in any area, because very high-resolution AMS-dated sites are rare, and none has been cited to prove that an oscillation is lacking during this interval. Regions where existing data suggest that no palynological oscillation took place include Ecuador and Peru, South Africa, and New Zealand, but in some of these same areas (New Zealand, possibly Peru) glacial advances do indicate a YD correlative.

Today, the most accepted hypothesis for the cause of the YD oscillation is the slowdown of NADW production (Broecker et al., 1985). A colder, fresher North Atlantic would have stopped the sinking of dense, saline water that today is responsible for releasing heat to the atmosphere. Sources for this colder water that would have formed a freshwater "lid" may have been the retreating Laurentide and Scandinavian ice sheets. However, the echo of a YD-type signal throughout the Holocene in marine and ice core records suggests that the signal may be a complicated recurring climate oscillation that was magnified during the YD by meltwater from receding ice sheets.

Other causal possibilities include major changes in the hydrologic cycle leading to a freshwater North Atlantic buildup. These may or may not include explanations that involve ice advances and retreats. Harvey (1989) used an energy balance model to test various causal hypotheses, including lowered carbon dioxide, and found that a low salinity lid from meltwater led to warming (not cooling) in summer, that lowered carbon dioxide levels caused an annual global cooling of about 1°C, and that North Atlantic iceberg floods caused significant summer cooling in the Northern Hemisphere but much smaller temperature declines in the Southern Hemisphere.

Several atmospheric groups have investigated the YD climate using a global climate model (GCM). The first of these experiments used the hypothesis that a colder North Atlantic would have caused the YD through an atmospheric response (Rind et al., 1986). However, the results of the experiment indicated that the cooling was produced only in the vicinity of the North Atlantic, and do not explain a cooling elsewhere around the world. Subsequent experiments with the same Goddard Institute for Space Studies GCM included a 2°C cooling of the North Pacific, which resulted in a widespread North-

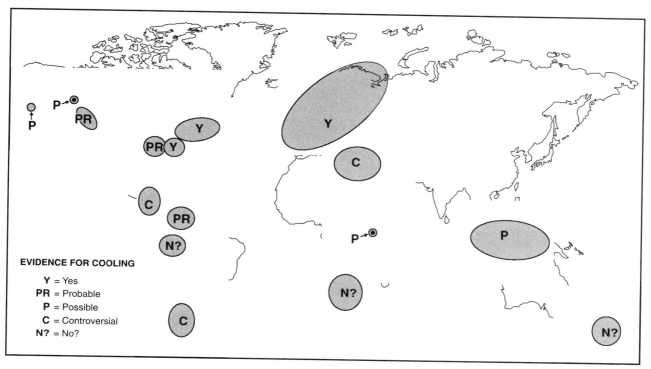

Younger Dryas. FIGURE 1. Global Map of Distribution of Palynological Evidence for the Younger Dryas Cooling, 12,900–11,600 BP.

Where clear palynological evidence exists for a climate oscillation in three or more sites, with AMS carbon-14 dating, Y denotes a "Yes YD" (e.g., maritime Canada). For regions where three or more sites show a palynological oscillation, but it is not yet AMS-dated, a PR is designated for "Probable YD" (e.g., Colombia). For sites where one or two oscillations exist, a P denotes "Possible YD" (e.g., southern Alaska). For areas where some sites show an oscillation and others do not, a C denotes "Controversial YD." Finally, where evidence for a YD is lacking, an N? is given for "No? YD," unless three or more sites have been investigated, in which case the designation would be N for "No YD." (After Peteet, 1995. With permission of Elsevier.)

ern Hemisphere cooling and snow expansion along the North Pacific coastline (Peteet et al., 1997). Renssen (1997) obtained similar results using the Hamburg model. Using a coupled ocean–atmosphere model, Mikolajewicz et al. (1997) found a primary atmospheric forcing due to a shutdown of the thermohaline circulation in the North Atlantic, suggesting that teleconnections may have taken place.

One possible impact of the YD on human populations is the possibility that it contributed to the beginnings of agriculture around the fertile crescent (Moore and Hillman, 1992). On the North Slope of Alaska, the disappearance of humans at the Mesa site argues for the impetus that the severe climate gave for migration (Kunz and Reanier, 1996). The YD occurred between times when Greenland was nearly as warm as today. Similar climate changes, although not as large as the YD and much briefer, are evident in ice cores, the North Atlantic records, and even on land during the last ten thousand years. Because we do not understand the causes of such climatic reversals, it is difficult to predict their occurrence in future climates. One emerging hypothesis,

however, suggests that our anthropogenic greenhouse warming could produce another YD-type effect as a result of increased precipitation around the North Atlantic basin, leading to weaker NADW production (Manabe and Stouffer, 1997).

[*See also* Climate Change; Climate Models; Earth History; Glaciation; Hydrologic Cycle; Ocean–Atmosphere Coupling; *and* Ocean Dynamics.]

BIBLIOGRAPHY

Alley, R. B., et al. "Abrupt Increase in Greenland Snow Accumulation at the End of the Younger Dryas Event." *Nature* 362 (1993), 527–529.

Behl, R. J., and J. P. Kennett. "Brief Interstadial Events in the Santa Barbara Basin, NE Pacific, during the Past 60 Kyr." *Nature* 379 (1996), 243–246.

Broecker, W., et al. "Does the Ocean–Atmosphere Have More Than One Stable Mode of Operation?" *Nature* 315 (1985), 21–26.

Chappellaz, J., et al. "Atmospheric CH$_4$ Record over the Last Climatic Cycle Revealed by the Vostok Ice Core." *Nature* 345 (1990), 127–131.

Cuffey, K. M., et al. "Large Arctic Temperature Change at the Wisconsin-Holocene Glacial Transition." *Science* 270 (1995), 455–458.

Fairbanks, R. G. "A 17,000-Yr Glacio-Eustatic Sea Level Record: Influence of Glacial Melting Rates on the Younger Dryas Event and Deep-Ocean Circulation." *Nature* 342 (1989), 637–642.

Harvey, L. D. D. "Modelling the Younger Dryas." *Quaternary Science Reviews* 8 (1989), 137–149.

Hughen, K., et al. "Rapid Climate Changes in the Tropical Atlantic Region during the Deglaciation." *Nature* 380 (1996), 51–54.

Kunz, M., and R. Reanier. "Paleoindians in Beringia." *Science* 263 (1996), 660–662.

Manabe, S., and R. J. Stouffer. "Coupled Ocean–Atmosphere Model Response to Freshwater Input: Comparison to the Younger Dryas Event." *Paleoceanography* 12 (1997), 321–336.

Mathewes, R. W. "Evidence for Younger Dryas Age Cooling on the North Pacific Coast of America." *Quaternary Science Reviews* 12 (1993), 321–332.

Mikolajewicz, U., et al. "Modelling Teleconnections between North Atlantic and North Pacific during the Younger Dryas." *Nature* 387 (1997), 384–387.

Moore, A. M. T., and G. C. Hillman. "The Pleistocene to Holocene Transition and Human Economy in Southwest Asia: The Impact of the Younger Dryas." *American Antiquity* 57.3 (1992), 482–494.

Osborne, G., and L. Gerloff. "Latest Pleistocene and Early Holocene Fluctuations of Glaciers in the Canadian and Northern American Rockies." *Quaternary International* 38/39 (1997), 7–19.

Peteet, D. "Global Younger Dryas?" *Quaternary International* 28 (1995), 93–104.

Peteet, D., et al. "Sensitivity of Northern Hemisphere Air Temperatures and Snow Expansion to North Pacific Sea Surface Temperatures in the GISS General Circulation Model." *Journal of Geophysical Research* 102D.20 (1997), 23781–23791.

Renssen, H. "The Global Response to Younger Dryas Boundary Conditions in an AGCM Simulation." *Climate Dynamics* 13 (1997), 587–599.

Ruddiman, W. F., and A. McIntyre. "The North Atlantic Ocean During the Last Deglaciation." *Paleogeography, Paleoclimatology, Paleoecology* 35 (1981), 145–214.

Taylor, K. C., et al. "The 'Flickering Switch' of Late Pleistocene Climatic Change." *Nature* 361 (1993), 432–436.

—DOROTHY M. PETEET

Directory of Contributors

Abdalati, Waleed

Research Scientist, Laboratory for Hydrospheric Processes, NASA Goddard Space Flight Center, Greenbelt, Maryland
Ice Sheets

Agnew, C. T.

Professor of Geography, University of Manchester, United Kingdom
Drought, *overview article*

Ahmad, Javed

Director of Communications, IUCN, The World Conservation Union, Gland, Switzerland
World Conservation Union, The

Allen, Myles R.

Head of the Climate Dynamics Group, Space Science and Technology Department, Rutherford Appleton Laboratory, Didcot; and NERC Advanced Research Fellow, Department of Physics, University of Oxford, United Kingdom
Climate Change, *article on* Climate Change Detection; *and* Natural Climate Fluctuations

Anderson, Ewan W.

Professor of Geopolitics, Centre for Middle Eastern and Islamic Studies, University of Durham, United Kingdom
Middle East

Angel, David P.

Associate Professor of Geography, Clark University, Worcester, Massachusetts
Greening of Industry

Archer, David

Associate Professor of Geophysical Sciences, University of Chicago, Illinois
Ocean Structure and Development

Archibold, O. W.

Professor of Geography, University of Saskatchewan, Saskatoon, Canada
Biological Realms; Grasslands; Human Impacts, *article on* Human Impacts on Biota; *and* Wilderness, *article on* Ecological Character

Arrigo, Kevin R.

Oceanographer, NASA Godard Space Flight Center, Greenbelt, Maryland
Ocean Life

Ayoub, Josef J.

Renewable Energy Consultant, Anschau International, Montreal, Quebec, Canada
Desalination

Ayres, R. U.

Sandoz Professor of Management and the Environment, INSEAD, The European Institute of Business Administration, Fontainebleau, France
Industrial Ecology; Industrial Metabolism; *and* Manufacturing

Barendregt, Rene W.

Professor of Geography and Geology, University of Lethbridge; and Adjunct Professor of Geography, University of Calgary, Alberta, Canada
Dating Methods

Barker, Randolph

Senior Advisor to the Director General, International Irrigation Management Institute, Battaramulla, Sri Lanka
Irrigation

Barkin, J. Samuel

Assistant Professor of Political Science, University of Florida, Gainesville
Global Economy

Barry, Roger G.

Professor of Geography, University of Colorado, Boulder
Snow Cover

Becker, Miles B.

Research Associate, Global Business Network, Emeryville, California
Future Studies

Beinat, Euro

Senior Environmental Management Researcher, Free University, Amsterdam, The Netherlands
Land Use, *article on* Land Use Planning

Berger, A.

Professor of Climatology, Université Catholique de Louvain, Institut d'Astronomie et de Géophysique Georges Lemaître, Belgium
Earth Motions; *and* Milankovitch, Milutin

Bird, Eric C. F.

Principal Fellow, Department of Geography, University of Melbourne, Parkville, Victoria, Australia
Mangroves

Bodansky, Daniel M.
Professor of Law, University of Washington School of Law, Seattle
Framework Convention on Climate Change; *and* Precautionary Principle

Boisson de Chazournes, Laurence
Professor and Director of the Department of International Law and International Organization, Faculty of Law, University of Geneva, Switzerland
Environmental Law

Botkin, Daniel B.
Research Professor, Department of Ecology, Evolution, and Marine Biology, University of California, Santa Barbara
Biomass; Biosphere, *definition article;* Ecological Stability; *and* Stability

Bowman, David
Principal Research Fellow, Key Centre for Tropical Wildlife Management, Northern Territory University, Darwin, Australia
Australia

Boydak, Melih
Professor of Silviculture, University of Istanbul, Turkey
Deforestation

Breitmeier, Helmut
Research Scholar, Department of Political Science, Darmstadt University of Technology, Germany
Desertification, *article on* Desertification Convention

Bridgman, Howard A.
Associate Professor of Geography and Environmental Science, University of Newcastle, Callagnan, New South Wales, Australia
Methane; *and* Pollution

Briggs, Shirley A.
Executive Director Emeritus, Rachel Carson Council, Bethesda, Maryland
Carson, Rachel

Brimblecombe, P.
Professor of Atmospheric Chemistry, University of East Anglia, Norwich, United Kingdom
Sulfur Cycle

Brooks, Elizabeth A.
Independent Scholar, Washington, D.C.
Ogallala Aquifer, Depletion and Restoration of the

Brown, Nick
Lecturer in Forestry and Fellow of Linacre College, Department of Plant Sciences, University of Oxford, United Kingdom
Fire, *article on* Indonesian Fires

Brückner, Helmut
Professor of Physical Geography, University of Marburg, Germany
Mediterranean Sea

Brunn, Stanley D.
Professor, Department of Geography, University of Kentucky, Lexington
Urban Areas

Callaghan, Terry V.
Professor of Arctic Ecology, Abisko Scientific Research Station, Royal Swedish Academy of Sciences
Tundra

Canney, Susan
Professor, Department of Zoology, University of Oxford, United Kingdom
Biological Feedback

Carpenter, Chad W.
Project Officer, International Institute for Sustainable Development (IISD), New York
Kyoto Protocol, *vignette on* After Kyoto

Challinor, David
Senior Scientist Emeritus, Smithsonian Institution, National Zoo, Washington, D.C.
Extinction of Species; *and* Hunting and Poaching

Chao, Hung-po
Area Manager, Policy and Risk Analysis, Electric Power Research Institute, Palo Alto, California; and Consulting Professor, Management Science and Engineering, Stanford University
Electrical Power Generation

Charnovitz, Steve
Director of the Global Environment and Trade Study, Yale Center for Environment Law and Policy, Yale University, New Haven, Connecticut; and Attorney at Wilmer, Cutler & Pickering, Washington, D.C.
Trade and Environment; *and* World Trade Organization

Chasek, Pamela S.
Doctor of Philosophy, and Editor, Earth Negotiations Bulletin, International Institute for Sustainable Development, New York
Intergovernmental Panel on Forests; *and* Sustainable Development, *article on* Commission on Sustainable Development

Chen, Jen-Ping
Professor, Department of Atmospheric Sciences, National Taiwan University, Taipei
Clouds, *article on* Clouds and Atmospheric Chemistry

Clark, Robert B.
Professor Emeritus, Department of Marine Sciences, University of Newcastle upon Tyne, United Kingdom
North Sea

Clark, William C.
Harvey Brooks Professor of International Science, Public Policy and Human Development, John F. Kennedy School of Government, Harvard University, Cambridge, Massachusetts
Social Learning

Cleary, Sharon J.
Chief of the Office of International Affairs, National Parks Service, Department of the Interior, Washington, D.C.
World Heritage Sites

Coates, Peter
Reader in American and Environmental History, University of Bristol, United Kingdom
Parks and Natural Preserves, *historical overview article*

Craig, James R.
Professor of Geology, Virginia Polytechnic Institute and State University, Blacksburg
Metals

Crawford, Elisabeth
Senior Research Fellow, Centre National de la Recherche Scientific (CNRS), Paris, France
Arrhenius, Svante

Cuff, David J.
Professor Emeritus of Geography, Temple University, New Hope, Pennsylvania
Economic Levels; Forests; Fossil Fuels; Resources; Technology; *and numerous vignettes*

Cushing, D. H.
Doctor, Retired, Suffolk, United Kingdom
Fishing

Dando, William A.
Professor and Chairperson, Department of Geography, Geology, and Anthropology, Indiana State University, Terre Haute
Famine; *and* Food

Day, Deborah Cozort
Archivist, Scripps Institution of Oceanography, University of California, San Diego
Revelle, Roger

de Fontaubert, A. Charlotte
Marine Program Officer, IUCN, The World Conservation Union, Washington, D.C.
Driftnet Convention; *and* Straddling and Migratory Stocks Agreement

De Silva, Sena S.
Professor of Aquaculture, Deakin University, Warrnambool, Victoria, Australia
Fish Farming

DeSombre, Elizabeth R.
Assistant Professor of Environmental Studies and Government, Colby College, Waterville, Maine
Convention on International Trade in Endangered Species; Multilateral Fund; United Nations Conference on Environment and Development; United Nations Conference on the Human Environment; *and* United Nations Environment Programme

Dietz, Thomas
Chair, U.S. National Research Council Committee on Human Dimensions of Global Change; and College of Arts and Sciences Distinguished Professor of Sociology and Environmental Science and Public Policy, George Mason University, Fairfax, Virginia
Policy Analysis

Dixon, Robert K.
Director of the U.S. Country Studies Program, Washington, D.C.
Climate Impacts

Donahue, Neil M.
Research Associate, Department of Chemistry, Harvard University, Cambridge, Massachusetts
Atmospheric Chemistry

Dowlatabadi, Hadi
Director of the Center for Integrated Study of the Human Dimensions of Global Change, Carnegie Mellon University, Pittsburgh, Pennsylvania
Integrated Assessment

Ehrenfeld, John R.
Senior Lecturer in Technology and Policy, Massachusetts Institute of Technology, Cambridge
Chemical Industry

Emanuel, Kerry A.
Professor of Meteorology, Massachusetts Institute of Technology, Cambridge
Extreme Events; *and* Greenhouse Effect

Engelman, Robert
Vice President for Research, Population Action International, Washington, D.C.
Population Policy

Epstein, Paul R.
Associate Director, Center for Health and the Global Environment, Harvard Medical School, Boston, Massachusetts
Human Health

Fairman, David M.
Senior Associate, Consensus Building Institute, Cambridge, Massachusetts
Global Environment Facility

Fearnside, Philip M.
Research Professor, Department of Ecology, National Institute for Research in the Amazon (INPA), Manaus-Amazonas, Brazil
Amazonia, Deforestation of

Flenley, John
Head of the Department of Geography, Massey University, Palmerston North, New Zealand
Easter Island

Foster, Stephen
Assistant Director, British Geological Survey, Nottingham, United Kingdom; and Visiting Professor of Hydrogeology, University of London, United Kingdom
Ground Water

Frakes, Lawrence A.
Professor Emeritus of Geology, University of Adelaide, Australia
Glaciation

Freestone, David
Chief Counsel, Environment and International Law, Legal Department, The World Bank, Washington, D.C.
Environmental Law; United Nations; *and* World Bank, The

Friedheim, Robert L.
Professor of International Relations, University of Southern California, Los Angeles
Law of the Sea; *and* Whaling Convention

Friedland, Andrew J.
Professor of Environmental Science, Dartmouth College, Hanover, New Hampshire
Acid Rain and Acid Deposition

Furlong, Kevin P.
Professor of Geosciences, Pennsylvania State University, University Park
Earthquakes

Geyer, L. Leon
Professor of Environmental and Agricultural Law and Economics, Virginia Polytechnic Institute and State University, Blacksburg
Ecotaxation

Gilbert, Geoffrey
Professor of Economics, Hobart and William Smith Colleges, Geneva, New York
Malthus, Thomas Robert

Gimingham, Charles H.
Professor Emeritus of Botany, University of Aberdeen, Scotland
Heathlands

Gleick, Peter H.
President of the Pacific Institute for Studies in Development, Environment, and Security, Oakland, California
Dams; *and* Water

Golding, Dominic
Research Assistant Professor, George Perkins Marsh Institute, Clark University, Worcester, Massachusetts
Technological Hazards; *and* Vulnerability

Goodchild, Michael F.
Professor of Geography, University of California, Santa Barbara
Geographic Information Systems; *and* Global Monitoring

Goodman, Daniel
Professor of Biology, Montana State University, Bozeman
Population Dynamics

Goudie, Andrew S.
Professor of Geography, University of Oxford, United Kingdom
Anthropogeomorphology; Bennett, Hugh Hammond; Biomes; Climate Change, *article on* Abrupt Climate Change; Convention on Long-Range Transboundary Air Pollution; Dust Storms; Forests; Lakes; Land Surface Processes; Medieval Climatic Optimum; Paleoclimate; Salinization; Walker, Gilbert; *and numerous vignettes*

Gould, W. T. S.
Head of the Department of Geography, University of Liverpool, United Kingdom
Human Populations

Grant, Lewis O.
Professor Emeritus of Atmospheric Science, Colorado State University, Fort Collins
Weather Modification

Grieve, Richard A. F.
Chief Geoscientist, Geological Survey of Canada, Ottawa, Ontario
Impacts by Extraterrestrial Bodies

Grove, Jean M. (deceased)
Life Fellow, Girton College, Cambridge, United Kingdom
Little Ice Age in Europe

Hahn, Robert W.
Director of the American Enterprise Institute—Brookings Joint Center for Regulatory Studies, Washington, D.C.; Resident Scholar, American Enterprise Institute, Washington, D.C.; and Research Associate, Harvard University, Cambridge, Massachusetts
Market Mechanisms; *and* Regulation

Hallam, Anthony
Lapworth Professor of Geology, University of Birmingham, United Kingdom
Wegener, Alfred

Hambler, Clive
Hertford College Lecturer in Biological and Human Sciences, University of Oxford, United Kingdom
Biological Feedback

Harrison, Christopher G. A.
Professor of Geophysics, University of Miami, Florida
Plate Tectonics

Harvey, L. D. Danny
Assistant Professor of Geography, University of Toronto, Ontario, Canada
Global Warming, *article on* Global Warming Potential; *and* Impulse Response

Havstad, Kris M.
Supervisory Scientist, U.S. Department of Agriculture, Agricultural Research Service, Jornada Experimental Range, Las Cruces, New Mexico
Animal Husbandry

Heerdegen, Richard G.
Senior Lecturer in Geography, School of Global Studies, Massey University, Palmerston North, New Zealand
Parks and Natural Preserves, *article on* Ecological Value

Henderson-Sellers, A.
Director of Environment, Australian Nuclear Science and Technology Organisation, Menai, New South Wales
Climate Models; *and* Modeling of Natural Systems

Hester, Gordon L.
Research Manager, Electric Power Research Institute, Palo Alto, California
Risk

Hobbs, Richard J.
Professor of Environmental Science, Murdoch University, Western Australia
Heathlands

Howarth, Richard B.
Associate Professor of Environmental Studies, Dartmouth College, Hanover, New Hampshire
Sustainable Development, *article on* Principles

Hughes, Jennifer B.
Research Scientist in the Center for Conservation Biology, Stanford University, California
Growth, Limits to

Humayun, Munir
Assistant Professor of Geophysical Sciences, University of Chicago, Illinois
Ocean Structure and Development

James, I. N.
Senior Lecturer in Geophysical Fluid Dynamics, University of Reading, United Kingdom
Atmosphere Dynamics; *and* Planetary Atmospheres

Jepma, Catrinus J.
Professor of International (Environmental) Economics, University of Amsterdam, Open University, University of Groningen, The Netherlands
Joint Implementation

Kagbo, Robert B.
Independent Scholar, ARDI, Annandale, Virginia
Consultative Group on International Agricultural Research; *and* Pest Management

Kalm, Volli
Professor of Applied Geology and Vice Rector, University of Tartu, Estonia
Dating Methods

Karplus, Valerie
Undergraduate Student, Yale University, New Haven, Connecticut; and Intern, Council for Foreign Relations, New York
Cartagena Protocol

Kasting, James F.
Professor of Geosciences, Pennsylvania State University, University Park
Planets

Keith, David W.
Assistant Professor, Department of Engineering and Public Policy, Carnegie Mellon University, Pittsburgh, Pennsylvania
Geoengineering

Kelly, Henry
President of the Federation of American Scientists, Washington, D.C.
Energy and Human Activity

Kemp, David D.
Professor of Geography, Lakehead University, Thunder Bay, Ontario, Canada
Global Warming, *overview article*

Kemp, Tom S.
Curator of the Zoological Collection, Oxford University Museum of Natural History, United Kingdom
Evolution of Life

Keohane, Robert O.
James B. Duke Professor of Political Science, Duke University, Durham, North Carolina
International Cooperation

Keys, Eric G.
Doctoral Candidate, Graduate School of Geography and George Perkins Marsh Institute, Clark University, Worcester, Massachusetts
Agriculture and Agricultural Land; Carrying Capacity; Land Use, *article on* Lane Use and Land Cover

Kimmins, J. P. (Hamish)
Professor of Forest Ecology, University of British Columbia, Vancouver, Canada
Forestation

Klein, Emily M.
Associate Professor of Geography, Duke University, Durham, North Carolina
Earth Structure and Development

Kling, Johan
Researcher, Swedish Society for Nature Protection, Göteborg, Sweden
Tundra

Knight, C. Gregory
Professor of Geography, Pennsylvania State University, University Park
Regional Assessment

Kohler, Larry R.
Executive Director of the International Human Dimensions Programme on Global Environmental Change (IHDP), Bonn, Germany
International Human Dimensions Programme on Global Environmental Change

Koppen, Ida J.
Director of the Sustainability Challenge Foundation, Siena, Italy; and Visiting Lecturer of European Community Law, University of Siena, Italy
European Community

Kummer, Katharina
Consultant on Environmental Law and Policy; and Lecturer on Environmental Law, Faculty of Law and Economics, University of Berne, Switzerland
Basel Convention

Lachenbruch, Arthur H.
Research Geophysicist, U.S. Geological Survey, Menlo Park, California
Permafrost

Lanchbery, John
Climate Change Policy Officer, Royal Society for the Protection of Birds, Bedfordshire, United Kingdom
Ramsar Convention

Large, W. G.
Deputy Head o the Oceanography Section, National Center for Atmospheric Research, Boulder, Colorado
Ocean—Atmosphere Coupling

Leggett, Jeremy
Chief Executive Officer and Managing Director of The Solar Century Ltd., Oxford, United Kingdom
Insurance

Lemons, John
Professor of Biology and Environmental Science, Department of Life Sciences, University of New England, Biddeford, Maine
Ecological Integrity

Lenton, Tim
Centre for Ecology and Hydrology—Edinburgh, Midlothian, United Kingdom
Gaia Hypothesis

Lewis, Chris H.
American Studies Instructor, University of Colorado, Boulder
Elton, Charles

Lindzen, Richard S.
Alfred P. Sloan Professor of Meteorology, Massachusetts Institute of Technology, Cambridge
Greenhouse Effect

Linville, Charles D.
Assistant Professor of Computer Science and Information Systems, American University, Washington, D.C.; and Doctoral Candidate in Engineering and Public Policy, Carnegie Mellon University, Pittsburgh, Pennsylvania
Information Technology

Loeb, Norman G.
Research Professor of Atmospheric Sciences, Hampton University/NASA Langley Research Center, Virginia
Albedo

Lonergan, Steve
Professor of Geography, University of Victoria, British Columbia, Canada
Security and Environment

Louis, Garrick E.
Assistant Professor, Department of Systems Engineering, University of Virginia, Charlottesville
Recycling

Lowenthal, David
Professor Emeritus of Geography, University College London, United Kingdom
Marsh, George Perkins

Lozier, M. Susan
Associate Professor of Earth and Ocean Sciences, Duke University; Durham, North Carolina
Ocean Dynamics

MacDonald, Ian R.
Associate Research Scientist, Geochemical and Environmental Research Group, Texas A&M University, College Station
Petroleum Hydrocarbons in the Ocean

Maguire, Lynn A.
Associate Professor of Environmental Management; and Director of Professional Studies, Duke University, Durham, North Carolina
Biological Diversity

Mahaney, William C.
Professor and Director of the Geomorphology and Pedology Laboratory, York University, Ontario, Canada
Dating Methods

Malone, Thomas F.
University Distinguished Scholar Emeritus, North Carolina State University, Raleigh
International Council for Science; International Geosphere-Biosphere Programme; *and* Scientific Committee on Problems of the Environment

Mann, Jonathan M. (*deceased*)
Francois-Xavier Bagnoud Professor of Health and Human Rights, Harvard School of Public Health, Boston, Massachusetts
World Health Organization

Marty, Martin E.

Fairfax M. Cone Distinguished Service Professor Emeritus,
University of Chicago Divinity School, Illinois
Religion

Mason, Robert J.

Associate Professor of Geography, Temple University,
Philadelphia, Pennsylvania
Friends of the Earth

McCartney, Michael S.

Senior Scientist, Department of Physical Oceanography,
Woods Hole Oceanographic Institution, Massachusetts
Ocean Dynamics

McDaniels, Timothy L.

Professor of Resource Management and Public Policy,
University of British Columbia, Vancouver, Canada
Valuation

McDonald, Alan

Program Officer, Environmentally Compatible Energy
Systems Project, International Institute for Applied Systems
Analysis, Laxenburg, Austria
International Institute for Applied Systems Analysis

McIntyre, A. D.

Professor Emeritus of Fisheries and Oceanography,
University of Aberdeen, Scotland
Marginal Seas

McManus, Phil

Lecturer in Geoscience, University of Sydney, Australia
Environmental Impact Assessment

McSpadden, Lettie

Professor of Political Science, Northern Illinois University,
DeKalb
Pinchot, Gifford; *and* Public Policy

Meadows, Michael E.

Associate Professor of Biogeography, University of Cape
Town, Rondebosch, South Africa
Mediterranean Environments

Mégie, Gérard J.

Professor of Atmospheric Physics and Chemistry, Institut
Pierre Simon Laplace, Paris, France
Ozone

Meine, Curt D.

Research Associate, International Crane Foundation,
Baraboo, Wisconsin
Leopold, Aldo

Meybeck, Michel H.

Research Geochemist (Director de Recherche), Centre
National de la Recherche Scientifique, Geologie Appliquee,
Universite de Paris VI, France
Water Quality

Meyer, William B.

Independent Scholar, Bradford, Massachusetts
Catastrophist—Cornucopian Debate; Global Change, *article on*
History of Global Change; Human Ecology; Human Impacts,
article on Human Impacts on Earth; *and* Land Reclamation

Michener, William K.

Senior Research Scientist, LTER Network Office, University
of New Mexico, Department of Biology, Albuquerque
Information Management

Micklin, Philip

Professor Emeritus of Geography, Western Michigan
University, Kalamazoo
Aral Sea, Desiccation of the

Mitchell, P. B.

Honorary Senior Research Associate, Division of
Environmental and Life Sciences, Department of
Physical Geography, Macquarie University,
New South Wales, Australia
Soils

Mitchell, Ronald B.

Assistant Professor of Political Science, University of Oregon,
Eugene; and Visiting Associate Professor, Stanford
University, Palo Alto, California
Marine Pollution Convention

Morgan, R. P. C.

Professor of Soil Erosion Control, Cranfield University,
Bedford, United Kingdom
Erosion

Morris, Gregory P.

Principle, Future Resources Associates, Inc., Berkeley, California
Renewable Energy Sources

Morris, S. C.

Energy and Environmental Consultant, Port Jefferson,
New York
Energy Policy

Moses, Julianne I.

Staff Scientist, Lunar and Planetary Institute,
Houston, Texas
Atmosphere Structure and Evolution

Moss, Richard H.

Head of IPCC Working Group II Technical Support Unit,
Washington, D.C.
Intergovernmental Panel on Climate Change

Mounfield, Peter R.

Senior Lecturer in Geography, University of Leicester,
United Kingdom
Nuclear Industry

Murck, Barbara

Director of Environmental Programs, University of Toronto
at Mississauga, Ontario, Canada
Earth History

Murphy, Peter E.
Professor of Tourism and Hospitality, La Trobe University, Bundoora, Victoria, Australia
Tourism

Nakicenovic, Nebojsa
Leader of Environmentally Compatible Energy Strategies Project, International Institute of Applied Systems Analysis, Laxenburg, Austria
Decarbonization

Nicholson, Sharon E.
Professor of Meteorology, Florida State University, Tallahassee
Drought, *article on* Sahel Drought in West Africa

Nijkamp, Peter
Professor of Regional and Environmental Economics, Free University, Amsterdam, The Netherlands
Land use, *article on* Land Use Planning

Nordstrom, Karl F.
Professor of Marine and Coastal Sciences, Rutgers University, New Brunswick, New Jersey
Estuaries

Norgaard, Richard B.
Professor of Energy and Resources, University of California, Berkeley
Sustainable Development, *article on* Practice

Nunn, Patrick D.
Professor of Oceanic Geoscience, University of the South Pacific, Suva, Fiji
Reefs

Oechel, Walter C.
Director of the Global Change Research Group, and Professor of Biology, San Diego State University, California
Biological Productivity

Oelschlaeger, Max
McAllister Chair of Community, Culture, and Environment, Northern Arizona University, Flagstaff
Thoreau, Henry David; *and* Wilderness, *article on* The Idea

Ogden, Joan M.
Research Scientist, Center for Energy and Environmental Studies, Princeton University, New Jersey
Hydrogen

Ogilvie, A. E. J.
Associate Director of the Institute of Arctic and Alpine Research, University of Colorado, Boulder
Lamb, Hubert Horace

Oliver, Chadwick D.
Professor of Silviculture and Forest Ecology, University of Washington, Seattle
Deforestation

O'Neill, Brian C.
Scientist, Environmental Defense Fund, New York
IPAT

O'Neill, John
Reader in Philosophy, Lancaster University, United Kingdom
Ethics, *overview article*

Openshaw, Stan
Professor of Geography, University of Leeds, United Kingdom
Nuclear Hazards

O'Riordan, Timothy
Professor, School of Environmental Sciences, University of East Anglia, Norwich, United Kingdom; and Fellow of the British Academy
Conservation; *and* Industrialization

Ostrom, Elinor
Arthur F. Bentley Professor of Political Science; Co-Director of the Workshop in Political Theory and Policy Analysis; and Co-Director of the Center for the Study of Institutions, Population, and Environmental Change, Indiana University, Bloomington
Commons

Pallemaerts, Marc
Lecturer in International Environmental Law, Vrije Universiteit Brussel, Belgium
Rio Declaration; *and* Stockholm Declaration

Palmer, Karen
Senior Fellow, Quality of the Environment Division, Resources for the Future, Washington, D.C.
Recycling

Park, Jeffrey
Associate Professor of Geology and Geophysics, Yale University, New Haven, Connecticut
Time Series Analysis

Parkinson, Claire L.
Senior Scientist, Oceans and Ice Branch, NASA Goddard Space Flight Center, Greenbelt, Maryland
Agassiz, Louis

Patten, Duncan T.
Professor Emeritus of Plant Biology, Arizona State University, Tempe
Colorado River, Transformation of the

Penner, Joyce E.
Professor of Atmospheric, Oceanic, and Space Sciences, University of Michigan, Ann Arbor
Aerosols

Perrins, Christopher
Director of the Edward Grey Institute of Field Ornithology, University of Oxford, United Kingdom
Nicholson, Max

Peteet, Dorothy M.
Research Scientist, NASA Goddard Institute for Space Studies, New York; and Adjunct Research Scientist, Lamont Doherty Earth Observatory, Palisades, New York
Younger Dryas

Peterson, Larry
Associate Professor of Marine Geology and Geophysics, University of Miami, Florida
Climate Reconstruction

Petit-Maire, Nicole
Director of Research, Centre National de la Recherche Scientifique (CNRS), France
Holocene in the Sahara

Petts, G. E.
Professor of Physical Geography, University of Birmingham, United Kingdom
Rivers and Streams

Pierrehumbert, Raymond
Professor of Geophysical Sciences, University of Chicago, Illinois
Water Vapor

Plucknett, Donald L.
President and Principal Scientist, ARDI, Annandale, Virginia
Consultative Group on International Agricultural Research; *and* Pest Management

Posey, Darrell Addison
Director of the Program for Traditional Resource Rights, Mansfield College, Oxford, United Kingdom
Ethnobiology

Post, Wilfred M.
Senior Research Scientist, Oak Ridge National Laboratory, Tennessee
Carbon Cycle

Powell, Jane C.
Senior Research Fellow, Centre for Social and Economic Research on the Global Environment (CSERGE), University of East Anglia, Norfolk, United Kingdom
Waste Management

Price, Martin F.
Director, Centre for Mountain Studies, Perth College, University of the Highlands and Islands, United Kingdom
Mountains

Pryde, Philip R.
Professor of Geography, San Diego State University, California
Chernobyl

Ramani, Raja V.
Professor and Holder of the Deike Chair in Mining Engineering, and Head of the Department of Mineral Engineering, Pennsylvania State University, University Park
Mining

Reynolds, Vernon
Professor of Biological Anthropology, Oxford University, United Kingdom
Budongo Forest Project

Ripley, Earle A.
Professor Emeritus of Plant Sciences, University of Saskatchewan, Saskatoon, Canada
Chlorofluorocarbons; Ocean Chemistry; *and* Sun

Rogers, Peter P.
Professor of Environmental Engineering, Harvard University, Cambridge, Massachusetts
Water Resources Management

Rolston, Holmes, III
Professor of Philosophy and University Distinguished Professor, Colorado State University, Fort Collins
Ethics, *article on* Environmental Bioethics

Rosier, Johanna
Senior Lecturer, Resource and Environmental Planning, Massey University, Palmerston North, New Zealand
Parks and Natural Preserves, *article on* Ecological Value

Ruttenberg, K. C.
Assistant Scientist, Department of Marine Chemistry and Geochemistry, Woods Hole Oceanographic Institution, Massachusetts
Phosphorus Cycle

Sale, John B.
International Consultant on Biodiversity, Oswestry, United Kingdom; and Former Chief Technical Adviser of the United Nations Food and Agricultural Organization
Elephants

Sandford, Rosemary A.
Lecturer, Antarctic and Southern Ocean Law and Policy, Institute of Antarctic and Southern Ocean Studies, University of Tasmania, Australia
Secretariats

Sands, Philippe J.
Reader in International Law, University of London, United Kingdom
Antarctica, *article on* Antarctic Treaty System; *and* Nuclear Accident and Notification Conventions

Sarachik, Edward S.
Professor of Atmospheric Sciences, University of Washington, Seattle
El Niño–Southern Oscillation

Schafer, Andreas
Research Associate, Center for Technology, Policy and Industrial Development and the Massachusetts Institute of Technology Joint Program on the Science and Policy of Global Change, Cambridge
Transportation

Schally, Hugo-Maria
Head of Unit, Development Policy and Multilateral Issues, and Directorate General for Development, European Commission, Brussels, Belgium
Food and Agriculture Organization; *and* Montreal Protocol

Schlesinger, William H.
James B. Duke Professor of Biology, Duke University, Durham, North Carolina
Biogeochemical Cycles; Biosphere, *article on* Structure and Development; Desertification, *overview article; and* Nitrogen Cycle

Schneider, Stephen H.
Professor of Biological Sciences, and Senior Fellow, Institute for International Studies, Stanford University, California
Surprise

Schwartz, Peter
Chairman of Global Business Network, Emeryville, California
Future Studies

Seckler, David
Director General of the International Irrigation Management Institute, Battaramulla, Sri Lanka
Irrigation

Sedjo, Roger A.
Senior Fellow, Resources for the Future, Washington, D.C.
Deforestation

Self, Stephen
Professor of Volcanology; University of Hawaii at Manoa, Honolulu
Mount Pinatubo; *and* Volcanoes

Sherratt, Andrew
Reader in European History, Ashmolean Museum, Oxford, United Kingdom
Civilization and Environment

Shih, Jhih-Shyang
Fellow, Quality of the Environment Division, Resources for the Future, Washington, D.C.
Recycling

Sirocko, Frank
Professor of Sedimentology, Institut für Geowissenschaften, Johannes Gutenberg-Universität Mainz, Germany
Emiliani, Cesare

Skeldon, Ronald
Professorial Fellow, University of Sussex, United Kingdom
Migrations

Skolnikoff, Eugene B.
Professor of Political Science, Massachusetts Institute of Technology, Cambridge
International Atomic Energy Agency

Smith, Keith
Professor of Environmental Science, University of Stirling, Scotland
Natural Hazards

Soroos, Marvin S.
Professor of Political Science and Public Administration, North Carolina State University, Raleigh
Agenda 21; Brundtland Commission; *and* World Meteorological Organization

Sowers, Joseph K.
Associate Economist, The WEFA Group, International Agriculture Service, Eddystone, Pennsylvania
Ecotaxation

Stephens, Graeme L.
Professor of Atmospheric Science, Colorado State University, Fort Collins
Clouds, *article on* Clouds in the Climate System

Stern, Paul C.
Principal Staff Officer, Commission on Behavioral and Social Sciences and Education, National Research Council, Washington, D.C.
Mass Consumption

Stokes, Stephen
Director of the Luminescence Dating Laboratory, University of Oxford, United Kingdom
Climate Change, *overview article*

Stokke, Olav Schram
Research Director, Fridtjof Nansen Institute, Lysaker, Norway
London Convention of 1972

Stott, Philip
Professor of Biogeography, School of Oriental and African Studies, University of London, United Kingdom
Savannas

Swanson, Robert Lawrence
Director of the New York State Waste Reduction and Management Institute, State University of New York, Stony Brook
Ocean Disposal

Talbot, Lee M.
Professor of Environmental Science and Public Policy, George Mason University, Fairfax, Virginia
Exotic Species; *and* Wildlife Management

Thiele, Leslie Paul
Professor of Political Science, University of Florida, Gainesville
Environmental Accounting; *and* Environmental Movements

Thomas, David S. G.
Professor of Geography, and Director of the Sheffield Centre for International Drylands Research, University of Sheffield, United Kingdom
Deserts

Thornes, John E.
Director of the Atmospheric Impacts Research Group, School of Geography and Environmental Sciences, University of Birmingham, United Kingdom
Weather Forecasting

Tooley, Michael J.
Head of the School of Geography and Geology, University of St. Andrews, Fife, Scotland
Sea Level

Tsonis, A. A.
Professor of Atmospheric Sciences, University of Wisconsin, Milwaukee
System Dynamics

Turco, Richard P.
Professor of Atmospheric Sciences, University of California, Los Angeles
Nuclear Winter

Turner, B. L., II
Milton P. and Alice C. Higgins Professor of Environment and Society, Graduate School of Geography and George Perkins Marsh Institute, Clark University, Worcester, Massachusetts
Agriculture and Agricultural Land; Carrying Capacity; *and* Land Use, *article on* Land Use and Land Cover

Turner, R. Kerry
Professor of Environmental Science, School of Environmental Sciences, University of East Anglia, Norfolk, United Kingdom
Environmental Economics; *and* Ethics, *article on* Intergenerational Equity

Turnock, David
Reader in Geography, Department of Geography, University of Leicester, United Kingdom
Eastern Europe

Van Cappellen, Philippe
Associate Professor of Geochemistry, Georgia Institute of Technology, Atlanta
Oxygen Cycle

van der Heijden, Kees
Professor of Business Administration, Strathclyde University, Glasgow, Scotland
Scenarios

Vernon, Raymond (*deceased*)
Clarence Dillon Professor of International Affairs Emeritus, Harvard University, Cambridge, Massachusetts
Multinational Enterprises

Victor, David G.
Robert W. Johnson, Jr., Senior Fellow for Science and Technology, Council on Foreign Relations, New York
Cartagena Protocol; convention on Biological Diversity; Kyoto Protocol; Nongovernmental Organizations; *and* Prior Informed Consent for Trade in Hazardous Chemicals and Pesticides

Victor, Peter A.
Dean and Professor of the Faculty of Environmental Studies, York University, North York, Ontario, Canada
Schumacher, Ernst Friedrich

Viles, Heather A.
Reader In Geomorphology, University of Oxford, United Kingdom
Building Decay; Coastal Protection and Management; *and* Coastlines

Wadhams, Peter
Reader in Polar Studies, Scott Polar Research Institute, University of Cambridge, United Kingdom
Cryosphere; *and* Sea Ice

Walbridge, Mark R.
Associate Professor of Biology, George Mason University, Fairfax, Virginia
Ecosystems

Wallach, Bret
Professor and Chair of Geography, University of Oklahoma, Norman
Belief Systems

Walton, D. W. H.
Head of the Terrestrial and Freshwater Life Sciences Division, British Antarctic Survey, Cambridge, United Kingdom
Antarctica, *article on* Threats and Responses

Wapner, Paul Kevin
Associate Professor of International Politics, American University, Washington, D.C.
Greenpeace

Ward, Roy C.
Professor Emeritus of Geography, University of Hull, United Kingdom
Hydrologic Cycle

Warner, Dennis B.
Chief of Water, Sanitation, and Health (Retired), World Health Organization, Peron, France
Sanitation

Weiss, Ray F.
Professor of Geochemistry, Scripps Institution of Oceanography, University of California, San Diego
Nitrous Oxide

Whelan, Robert J.
Professor of Biological Sciences, Australian Flora and Fauna Research Centre, University of Wollongong
Fire, *overview article*

White, Kevin
Lecturer in Geography, University of Reading, United Kingdom
Remote Sensing

Willcocks, Ann D.
The Monitoring and Assessment Research Centre (MARC), King's College London, United Kingdom
Air Quality; Carbon Dioxide; *and* Hazardous Waste

Willett, James D.
Professor, Institute for Biosciences, Bioinformatics and Biotechnology, George Mason University, Manassas, Virginia
Biotechnology

Williams, Jack F.
Professor of Geography, Michigan State University, East Lansing
Urban Areas

Williams, Michael
Fellow of the British Academy, Professor of Geography, and Director of the Masters Program in Environmental Change and Management, University of Oxford, United Kingdom
Glacken, Clarence J.; Sauer, Carl; *and* Wetlands

Wills, Peter R.
Associate Professor of Physics, University of Auckland, New Zealand
Origin of Life

Wilson, Mary Elizabeth
Chief of Infectious Diseases, Mount Auburn Hospital; Associate Professor of Population and International Health, Harvard School of Public Health; and Associate Professor of Medicine, Harvard Medical School, Cambridge, Massachusetts
Disease

Wood, Denis
Independent Scholar, Raleigh, North Carolina
Popular Culture

Yokota, Fumie
Research Assistant, American Enterprise Institute, Washington, D.C.; and Doctoral Candidate, Harvard University, Cambridge, Massachusetts
Market Mechanisms; *and* Regulation

Yung, Yuk L.
Professor of Planetary Science, California Institute of Technology, Pasadena
Atmosphere Structure and Evolution

Zelinsky, Wilbur
Professor Emeritus of Geography, Pennsylvania State University, University Park
Global Change, *article on* Human Dimensions of Global Change

Zwally, H. Jay
ICESat Project Scientist, Laboratory for Hydrospheric Processes, NASA Goddard Space Flight Center, Greenbelt, Maryland
Ice Sheets

Synoptic Outline of Contents

The entries in the *Encyclopedia of Global Change* pertain to the general conceptual categories listed on this page. The following pages in this section provide a detailed synoptic outline of the contents, organized by conceptual category. Some entries are listed more than once in the synoptic outline because the conceptual categories are not mutually exclusive. Entries in the encyclopedia proper are organized alphabetically.

FRONT MATTER

CONCEPTS OF GLOBAL CHANGE

EARTH AND EARTH SYSTEMS
Principal Articles
Geological Processes
Atmosphere
Ocean
Biosphere

HUMAN FACTORS
Human Populations
Agriculture and Fishing
Industrial Activity
Social, Cultural, and Ideological Factors
Hazards and Human Health

RESOURCES
Principal Article
Water and Air
Land and Land Use
Mineral and Energy Resources

RESPONSES TO GLOBAL CHANGE
Scientific and Technological Tools
Economic and Social Policies

AGREEMENTS, ASSOCIATIONS, AND INSTITUTIONS
Agreements
Associations and Institutions

BIOGRAPHIES

CASE STUDIES

BIOGRAPHIES

CASE STUDIES

Index

coastlines and, 1:207, 1:208
disease and, 1:183, 1:600
and drought conditions in Brazil, Southeast Asia,
    Africa, and Australasia, 1:259, 1:442–43
droughts and floods in Australia, 1:84
dune systems, 1:260
effects of warm and cold phases of, 1:343
effects on food, fuel, and fiber, 1:182
effects on world food crop production, 1:460
and fire in Amazonia, 1:36
global effects, 1:344f
impacts on reefs, 2:301, 2:302, 2:302t
increased frequency, 1:170
monsoonal rainfalls and, 1:276
ocean circulation and, 2:110, 2:161
predicting and using predictions, 1:343–45
and redistribution of heat energy in atmosphere, 1:639
schematic illustration, 1:67f
Southern Ocean and, 1:44
time series analysis and, 2:439
Elsner, J. B., 2:419
Elton, Charles, **1:345–46,** 1:412, 2:34. *See also* Exotic
    species
Emanuel, Kerry A., 1:421, 1:565, 1:566
    as contributor, 1:421–24, 1:562–66
Embedding dimension, 2:418
Embleton, C., 2:22
EM-DAT, 2:133
Emden, R., 1:564
Emerged reefs, 2:300
Emergency Wetlands Resources Act, 2:527
Emergent properties, 1:101
Emerson, Ralph Waldo, 1:388, 2:285, 2:436–37
Emigration, 2:92
Emiliani, Cesare, 1:163, **1:346–47.** *See also* Climate
    change; Earth motions; *and the biography of Lamb*
    Planet Earth, 1:346
    "Pleistocene Temperatures," 1:346
Emission, defined, 2:264
Emission and discharge standards, 1:79, 1:380
Emissions. *See* Air quality; Market mechanisms; *and*
    Pollution
Emissions tax, 1:360, 2:310
Emissions trading, 2:1, 2:2, 2:6, 2:7–9
Emissions Trading Program, 2:58–59
Emissivity, 1:563
Emmanuel, W. R., 1:115
Emmer, 1:602
Emo, Giovanni, 1:87
Empowerment theory, 2:485
Emu, 1:83
Enclosure, 2:34
Endangered species
    biotechnology and, 1:120
    hunting of, 1:625–26
    protection and restoration of, 2:537
    smuggling, 1:99
Endangered Species Act, 1:93, 1:98, 1:419, 1:633, 2:308, 2:534
Endangered Species Convention. *See* Convention on
    International Trade in Endangered Species (CITES)

Endemism, 1:35, 1:53, 1:99, 1:106, 2:66, 2:459
End moraines, 1:506
End-of-pipe technologies, 1:582
Endogenous polycyclic aromatic hydrocarbons, 2:194
Endolithic (inside-rock environments), 1:117
Endorheic basins, 2:505
Endosymbiosis, 1:408
Energy and human activity, **1:347–57,** 2:237. *See also*
    Carbon dioxide; Electrical power generation; Energy
    policy; Fossil fuels; Global warming; Greenhouse
    effect; Growth, limits to; Hydrogen; Industrialization;
    Nuclear industry; Pollution; Renewable energy
    sources; *and* Resources
    energy audits, 1:362
    energy conservation, 1:27, 1:28
    energy demands, 1:347–48
    energy supplies, 1:350–55
    energy use, 1:242, 1:348, 1:348f, 1:351f
    issues of scale, 1:355
    material flows and, 1:664–65
    nonanimate sources of energy, 1:658
    policy issues, 1:355–56
    potential for efficiency improvements, 1:348–50
    regulations and pricing, 1:356
    research and development, 1:356
    technology and, 2:428–30
Energy balance models (EBMs), 1:189, 1:190
Energy crops, 2:321
Energy policy, **1:357–64.** *See also* Air quality; Carbon
    dioxide; Economic levels; Electrical power
    generation; Energy; Environmental economics;
    Fossil fuels; Greenhouse effect; *and* Renewable
    energy sources
    climate policy and, 1:358
    deregulation, 1:361
    in developing countries, 1:363
    difficulties in implementing, 1:362–63
    efficiency standards, 1:362
    in energy-producing countries, 1:363–64
    goals, 1:358–59
    history, 1:357–58
    information, 1:361
    market mechanisms, 1:359–60
    privatization, 1:360–61
    regulation, 1:359
    research and development, 1:361
    strategies for intervention, 1:359–62
    targets, 1:361–62
    tax policy and, 1:359
    technology transfer and, 1:363–64
    transportation, 1:362
    voluntary action, 1:361
Energy Star program, 1:361, 1:362
Energy taxes, 1:328, 1:329
Engelman, Robert, as contributor, 2:276–82
Engels, Friedrich: *Dialectics of Nature*, 1:91
Engineering, soil conservation, 1:394
England. *See* United Kingdom
English, as the world language, 1:524
English Alkali Act of 1863, 1:144

French Guiana, 1:31
Frenzel, B., 2:40
Freons, 1:151, 2:186
Fresh water
  acidification of in Scandinavia, 1:604
  ammonia in, 2:509
  arsenic in, 2:510
  budget and cycle, 2:181–83
  contamination of, 1:604
  flux, and evaporation, 2:162, 2:495
  human impacts on, 1:610
  issues, 2:512
  major stocks, 2:495t
Fresnel lens focused collectors, 2:323
Friction, 1:58
  in ocean dynamics, 2:171
  surface, gas giant planets, 2:248
Friction-free capitalism, 1:678
Friedheim, Robert L., as contributor, 2:33–34, 2:530–31
Friedland, Andrew J., as contributor, 1:1–6
Friedrich, Ernst, 1:518, 2:351
Friends of the Earth, 1:365, **1:487–88**. *See also*
  Environmental movements; *and* Nongovernmental
  organizations
Friends of the Earth and the National Taxpayers Union,
  1:365
Fringing reefs, 2:299
From the Earth to the Moon (Verne), 2:269
FRONTIERS (Forecasting Rain Optimised using New
  Techniques of Interactively Enhanced Radar and
  Satellite), 1:636
Frost wedges, 1:506
Fruit flies, 1:81
Frye, J. C., 1:235
Fuel Administration, 1:357
Fuel cells, 1:333, 1:334f, 1:335, 1:352, 1:473, 1:628–29,
  1:629f, 2:320, 2:430, 2:454
Fuel consumption, reductions in, 2:454
Fuel-efficient vehicles, 1:362
Fuel production, climate change impacts, 1:181–82
Fuelwood, 1:247–48
  desertification and, 1:254
  relation of use and population density to deforestation
    by region, 1:248t
Fugger, Jacob, 1:87
Full-cost pricing, 1:365–66, 2:294
Fulmar, 2:145
Fumaroles, 2:481
Functional theory of natural resources, 1:592–93
FUND, 2:305
Fung, I., 1:7
Fungi, 1:272, 1:420, 1:438
Furans, 1:581
Furlong, Kevin P., as contributor, 1:301–5
Furrowing, 1:706
Fur trade, 2:537
Future, 1:488
The Futures Group, 1:488
Future studies, **1:488–89**. *See also* Modeling of natural
  systems; *and* Scenarios

Future Studies, 1:488
Futuribles, 1:488
Fynbos, 1:584, 1:585, 1:586, 2:65, 2:66, 2:68, 2:355, 2:535

G

G-7 countries, 1:36
Gabbro, 2:254
Gabcikovo-Nagymaros, 1:385
Gadoid outburst, 1:453, 1:454f
Gaia hypothesis, 1:92, 1:102–3, 1:103, **1:491–95,** 2:196,
  2:397. *See also* Atmospheric chemistry;
    Biogeochemical cycles; Global warming; Sulfur
    cycle; *and* System dynamics
Galah, 1:82
Galápagos Islands
  Darwin's finches, 1:405, 1:410
  feral pigs, 1:101
  goats, 1:411
  protection of, 1:419
  World Heritage Site project, 2:542
Galileo, 1:87
Gallium arsenide, 2:323–24
Gambia, 1:266
  forest-savanna interchange, 2:355
Game birds, 1:411, 2:537
Game Management (Leopold), 2:34
Game preserves, 2:218–19
Gandar, M. V., 1:437
Gandhi, Indira, 2:280
Gandhi, Mahatma, 2:436
Ganges-Brahmaputra Delta, 1:208, 2:373, 2:529
Ganges River
  basin, 1:20, 1:182, 1:184
  Lower, 2:509
Ganymede, 1:70
Gap analysis, 1:99
Garamba National Park, 2:542
Garcia, S. M., 1:448
Garden City movement, 2:472
Gardens
  design, 1:90
  Renaissance, 1:88
Garfield, James, 2:246
Gas giant planets, 2:246, 2:249
  planetary circulation type, 2:248
  rotation rates, 2:248
Gas hydrates, 1:477, 2:241
Gasoline
  lead additives, 1:612, 2:58, 2:59, 2:78
  taxes, 1:359, 1:362, 1:366
Gas-phase chemistry, clouds and, 1:200
Gas phase sources, of aerosols, 1:7
Gas transfer coefficient, 1:127
Gastric *(helicobacter pylori)* cancer, 1:264
Gates, Bill, 1:678
Gates, D. M., 1:113
Gaussian-normal distribution, 2:437, 2:438
Gaye, Marvin, 2:270
Gazprom, 1:360